MEDIA STUDIES

A READER
THIRD EDITION

Edited by
Sue Thornham, Caroline Bassett
and Paul Marris

EDINBURGH UNIVERSITY PRESS

© editorial matter and organisation Sue Thornham,
Caroline Bassett and Paul Marris, 1996, 1999,
2009

Second edition published by Edinburgh University
Press in 1999.

Edinburgh University Press Ltd
22 George Square, Edinburgh

www.euppublishing.com

Typeset in Sabon and Gill
by Servis Filmsetting Ltd, Stockport, Cheshire, and
printed and bound in Great Britain by
Athenaeum Press Ltd, Gateshead

A CIP record for this book is available from the
British Library

ISBN 978 0 7486 3783 6 (hardback)
ISBN 978 0 7486 3784 3 (paperback)

Media Studies
Third Edition

Media Studies
Third Edition

CONTENTS

GENERAL INTRODUCTION

The second edition of this reader was published in 1999: before the 9/11 attacks on the World Trade Center and the 'war on terror' that followed them. It was also published before a man of mixed race, with family in Kenya and Hussein for a middle name, had been elected President of the United States of America, after running a media campaign designed to reach out to grassroots supporters that even his opponents described as highly media savvy.

Obama's election, an event of obvious global significance, was undeniably also a global media event. It was also a *new* media event. The election coverage/campaign bloomed like algae, reaching out across that series of connected platforms – some new, some old, some remediated, some networked, some relatively discrete – that currently constitute the new media ecology. It included moments of public spectacle designed for television, although some of these – notably Obama's victory speech in Chicago – referred in their mode of address back to a form of oratory popular in an earlier age. Alongside this, the Obama campaign in particular successfully utilised social networks of all kinds to address different social demographics – from Facebook teenagers to Linked-In professionals. It understood that networks could operate virally and with some autonomy – many supporters took it upon themselves to propagate the Obama message in unofficial ways. These included innovative forms of culture jamming, for instance the mashed-up and personalised injunctions to vote that circulated around e-mail lists. But Obama's campaign was also typical of the contemporary public media landscape in that, alongside the bloom and buzz of social media, was a highly orchestrated and controlled campaign that set out to take no chances in getting its message across – and that included constructing a particular *kind* of message, one short on complexity and high on image.

The election was formally an American affair but information about it, in the form of campaign news, satire, comment and statistics, was more immediately accessible to those beyond the States than in any previous election. Digital access to US news feeds and US stations, global TV and in some underdeveloped countries improved basic access to media through satellite and mobile technology ensured this was so. In commentary surrounding his win

Obama himself was repeatedly taken both to embody a history of segregation and its overcoming, and to inaugurate a new era in which race and ethnicity might be a less significant marker of identity, or at least a different one. While the first of these relates very particularly to American history, the second is a comment on globalisation and the prospects for a more cosmopolitan form of culture – it comes interestingly enough *both* from America (as a superpower) and from Black America (historically a dominated group).

These are the new grounds within which media studies operates. This is the environment, these are the media forms and technologies and practices that are ripe for investigation. What then about media studies itself – should it mould its approaches to new environments, cleave to earlier models, reject or adapt them? Let us turn back for a moment to the US election campaign and ask a 'media technology' question about the relation between media technology and society that it provokes. The question is whether the Obama camp were able to use new social networking tools so effectively because their fundamental approach, the *content* of their political philosophy, suited the bias of this media? To accept this argument would be tantamount to suggesting that such technology is inherently progressive (the contrast might be with a technology such as nuclear power which Langdon Winner famously claimed was inherently totalitarian in its tendencies). Many theorists of the social construction of media technologies would suggest that this gives technology too much power, arguing instead that innovation occurs at the intersection between socially produced needs and desires and technological possibilities and trajectories. Others would suggest the specific attributes of a technology have no connection with culture but simply 'carry it'. The point being made here is that crucial elements conditioning the outcome of any investigation of the interaction between media, technology and culture are the general theoretical models and approaches taken by the theorists concerned.

Media studies is the site of many debates and dispute about theory, theoretical models, critical approaches and methodologies. Its history can be traced through some of these debates and disputes. There are two caveats here. The first is that this is not only a linear history – many approaches are revived in response to new conditions. It is perhaps in this sense that media studies is always in *process* rather than being a finished discipline. The second is that media studies is something more than a neutral site, a place that may be retooled completely in response to each new media wave: this is why so many of the contributions made early on remain useful and important today.

Beginning to identify what makes media studies distinctive we might turn to the work of Stuart Hall and others at the Birmingham Centre for Cultural Studies, which constituted a crucial break for media studies in Britain in the 1970s, providing a clear approach to the study of media power which divided the UK approach from that of mass communications theory and the psychology of individual effects. One key characteristic of this approach was that even as it suggested ways in which the media system exerted forms of power, it also suggested ways in which this (symbolic) power is limited and can be contested by groups or individuals in certain situations.

Developing these ideas, Hall drew directly on Gramsci and the concept of hegemony (the uneven battle of ideas that tends to mean the ideas of the powerful come to be accepted as right) to develop an understanding of how different moments (articulations) of the media system operate. His vision is of a hegemonic media system. This signals other allegiances. In so far as it mounts a critique of social power and domination and the ways that it operated in mass culture, Hall's approach can be included within a body of writing and thinking that is critical not only of the role and function of the media in mass society but of modern capitalist society more generally. The Frankfurt School's reading of culture as mass deception, its attack on technocratic rationality, is part of this tradition, for instance, though the two approaches, Birmingham and Frankfurt, are often understood to be antithetical to one another. Finally, Hall and others, in developing parallel approaches, also drew on the American mass communications tradition even as they interrogated its failures, and they were clearly influenced by both 1970s film theory and a particular tradition of literary work in the UK (for instance that of Richard Hoggart and Raymond Williams).

Hall's contribution then, marks not an absolute beginning or a final word, but it does signal a general approach – one that is tested: the intervening decades have contained many critiques of the Hall model, which was attacked, among other things, for its structural absolutism (it remained a model that insisted on the integrated nature of the social world rather than its fragmentation) *and* for its stress on the (relative) autonomy of the articulations it described. In particular, the 'free reading' it seemed to some to promote, was said to disregard structural constraints and inequalities, especially the realities of the global political economy of the media with its Western bias. Our sense, however, is that Hall and the general approach of the work his contribution emblematises, remains important in an age of new media – and new media studies.

At some level theory is always made in the world. Hall himself, for instance, was writing in response to particular social conditions (one of the articles reproduced here is written in response to race, racism and policing in the UK in the years after Enoch Powell made the 1968 Rivers of Blood speech – also in Birmingham). It is also the case, and in a similarly qualified way, that we are justified in suggesting that the world *makes* theory. In this decade the break in the study of the media, the demand for forms of rethinking and forms of reconfiguration, comes not primarily from inside theory, but from the two connected developments already mentioned in the discussion of the US election: the rise of pervasive information networks on the one hand and globalisation as process involving the accelerated flows of material and immaterial goods, people and capital around the world on the other.

These developments demand a reappraisal of the object of study – the question of what constitutes the media is a real one in an age of biotech, embedded controllers, GPS, for instance. It also provokes a reconsideration of *how* to study this newly constituted object of study. Once again, there are critical-theoretical as well as real-world choices: it is possible to explore the developing semantic ('intelligent') web, for instance, in terms that are purely market driven, or to measure technological developments through categories such as 'efficiency gains'. Work coming out of the critical media studies tradition, however, would want to examine the categories being used. This allows some inconvenient questions to be asked: 'efficiency' – 'for whom? for which groups? where? 'gains' – 'at whose expense?' Media studies' methodologies, designed to connect symbolic forms, technical processes and materials, forms of communication and the developing economy of the culture industries to questions of social power and to governance are highly relevant here.

This emphasis on continuity isn't to negate the need for new probes, to use the old McLuhan term. There is less media studies work on sense perception and affect than there needs to be. There is a need to reconfigure the relationship between medium theory and media studies, perhaps to redress the relative neglect of material culture in favour of representation in future work. Challenges for the study of contemporary global media ecologies include: how to find new distinctions between forms of programming that were previously discrete, so they may be meaningfully investigated; how to find ways to grapple with structures that are not amenable to traditional forms of inquiry; how to understand the forms of control exercised by a low-level protocol; how to understand the forms of labour involved in social networking; how to conduct ethnographies when media use is increasingly mobile and fragmented; how to locate and understand new and ephemeral forms of public space; how to consider questions of accountability. A key question, and one we have spent much time on in this book, is how to conceptualise issues of citizenship, the public sphere and the media in relation to global media organisations, flows and peoples.

It also requires redefining forms of thinking in traditional arenas. Film, for instance, was traditionally studied somewhat separately from other media forms. That distinction is increasingly difficult to sustain as the cinematic apparatus is replaced with digital equipment. Some argue this might represent the termination of the project of 'cinema' (or rather its transformation into a historical project), but this of course raises the question of how to explore *emerging* forms of spectatorship within newly combined or forged platforms (on low-status terrestrial TV, via large-screen entertainment venues or via web services such as YouTube, for instance). In sum, the evolving landscape of the media requires the development of distinctive theoretical positions, the reappraisal and refashioning of older ones, returns to neglected threads from earlier traditions which may now seem more important and new blends and melds of earlier approaches previously thought incompatible.

Writing a revised edition of a media studies Reader designed for new and established media scholars, the question of continuity or innovation is stark.

It comes down to this: should we ignore the old theory and old theorists and bring on the 'all new' in sympathy with our subject? As is already clear there is a great deal that is new in this Reader. There are articles on new media forms and formats, updated critiques, new case studies. You will also find much that will give you a sense of media's history, a sense of how various critical questions and empirical issues have been approached over many decades, in different historical conditions and from different perspectives. This is essential, we feel, in order to avoid a blindness to context and history. It also signals a degree of unease with the absolute prioritisation of the new. This is partly because even *within* the category of 'new media' itself, there is a history of theory, a social history of use and a political economy that has boomed and bust spectacularly; at over fifty the internet is hardly young – it is, for instance older than America's new president. It is also because, in the media as a whole, moments of innovation are counterbalanced by the weight of reme-diation – of original content (via endless repeats) or form (genre, format), of audience responses (through their repurposing and recirculation, potentially or in reality, on various digital or older media technologies and platforms), even perhaps of media technologies – 'cinema' is imported onto DVD, for instance. Finally there is an ideological objection. The media's own focus on innovation, its voracious demand for the new, for more to consume, exempli-fied in 24-hour news, flash fame via reality shows and constant hardware/software and platform innovation, needs to be explored, put into context and questioned. It does not need to be adopted as a *credo* for media studies itself. On the contrary, media studies needs to explore many aspects of the contem-porary media ecology and its users that are hidden or neglected because of the unrelenting focus on the moment of the new – and on those population groups who best exemplify it.

Stressing continuity as well as transformation in this book we organise a series of readings around overlapping subject areas that seem important to us. We are not neutral. While we have included a wide range of different flavours and approaches and covered a lot of ground, we do not claim to be comprehensive, which would be impossible, and nor do we claim to be entirely 'objective', which would also be impossible and arguably undesirable. The Reader includes a balance of classic articles, important interventions written during the past ten years or so which have shaped a particular area, and new work – some of this explicitly addresses questions of innovation, much of it, however, gets on with the investigation at hand. Around two-thirds of these are new, the rest are retained from earlier editions. These readings are organ-ised into thematic sections, each displaying internally the kind of meta-balance outlined above. The first half of the book provides frameworks for studying the media, the second offers various kinds of case studies. The division is useful but has in fact been difficult to maintain. The expansion of the remit of media studies and the diversification in the forms and approaches being adopted to investigate the media mean that a traditional division between theory and its application is untenable. Perhaps it always was. The collection in the end is a wager about what matters, what still matters and what will come to matter about information and the media in the twenty-first century.

PART ONE
STUDYING THE MEDIA

SECTION I
FOUNDATIONS

INTRODUCTION: FOUNDATIONS

Foundations: the term implies that certain theorists and certain texts began Media Studies and that their founder status and position within the discipline is understood and is secured permanently. This is not the reality. While there is history to be traced, the interrelation between texts and their relative influence is commonly reassessed with the benefit of hindsight. Media studies continually disturbs, revisits, re-evaluates and sometimes rejects what have previously been held as key texts. It performs the same act of revision upon the discipline itself, so that shared understandings of what media studies is, what groups of media scholars feel it ought to be, what it ought to study, is always under review. At times this process is evolutionary, at others it produces calls for full-scale revisions.

The reasons for this instability are multiple, but chief among them are changes in the intellectual climate which favour particular critical positions at certain times and deselect them at others, interventions which introduce new perspectives (for instance the rise of media archaeology), shifts in the political and economic conditions within which academic research is carried out (for instance globalisation) and changes in the media itself, whether these concern the political economy of ownership, regulation and media geographies, technological innovation, altered use or viewing practices, or new forms of production. By the way, it is easy to see *that* these spheres are intimately connected: the interesting questions concern *how* they intersect and what is at stake in that intersection.

A reasonable place to locate the beginnings of modern media would be in the early the twentieth century. In these decades the mass media develops within and is an integral element of the rise of mass consumption and the mass society. There are other possibilities: some media historians argue the real break came with the telegraph, labelled the first modern communications technology because it divorced the message content from the materiality of the carrier for the first time (see Carey, 1989).

Others trace the history of the media far further back. Archaeologists of the media from the German school, for instance Oliver Grau (2007) and Siegfried Zielinksi (2006) have traced a pathway between contemporary imaging systems and fabulous imaging machines of the early Catholic Church, for instance. Others have made connections between early automata and contemporary information machines. In a different register, historians and theorists of writing technology have written contemporary media systems into the *longue durée* of writing cultures (see Derrida, Ong and others). Finally, many would argue that the interpretive form of media sociology that Stuart Hall helped to initiate through the Birmingham School of Cultural Studies in the 1970s provides a proximate starting place for modern media studies.

So, finding absolute points of origin is not the issue. What are gathered together here are some texts that have launched distinctive forms of thinking around key problems and issues in media studies. Each deals with issues that tend to return with each new generation. Many of the readings included in this section are not strictly 'about' the media. Rather, they are part of a theoretical web that *informs* many more tightly media-focused accounts, providing a world-view within which debates are conducted, informing debates around the relationships between media and power, technology and culture, the symbolic and the real. To some extent these texts, mapping developments in the field over time, need to be understood within their historical contexts. However, the debates they launch or contribute to also cross and re-cross the years, representing forms of thought that are knotted together, that have been fought over, rejected and re-adopted, in many different ways.

ADORNO AND THE CRITIQUE OF MASS CULTURE

In New York in 1947, only a year or so after the ending of the Second World War, two refugees from the Frankfurt School, a critical research establishment in Germany, arrived at the Institute for Social Research in New York. There they wrote a famous indictment of the society of mass culture and mass entertainment they saw arising around them. Their case was that the culture industries hollowed out old categories of culture (including high art or authentic popular culture) and produced nothing to take their place except fake promises, shallow gratifications, pseudo-novelty and an increasingly constrained form of 'free' selection masquerading as free choice or even democracy. There was nothing to be found except various forms of what was memorably called 'mass deception' (21), the deceit inhering in part in the sense that, in the final analysis, the logic of the system of consumer capitalism is the reduction of all forms of value to profit.

In the *Culture Industry Reconsidered*, written in the early 1960s, Theodor Adorno, the better known of the two writers (the other was Max Horkheimer), recapitulates and clarifies some of the key arguments of the early work and reaffirms his sense of the depredations of mass culture and mass media. In this piece Adorno explains that the term culture industry replaced that of mass culture (which was originally used) because both authors wished to stress that their critique was of a particular mode of cultural production, which they claimed had nothing to do with anything popular.

Despite this clarification, many theorists since then have critiqued the work of the Frankfurt School for the perceived elitism of at least some of its aesthetic judgements. The work has also been critiqued for its presumed pessimism, perhaps with less justification, since it retains at heart a work that finds strength to the sense that another world is needed, even if it is not in the least clear how one might be possible. In this way it retains a sense of ambition missing in later more straightforwardly reformist work – which might unkindly be said to wallow in fragments of resistance found around the edges of the culture machine. Either way it remains important, firstly as one of the first sustained analyses of many aspects of mass culture – for instance, it draws attention to the undoubted tendencies towards standardisation, commoditisation and conformity of mass media systems. Secondly, it makes a distinctive contribution in that it raises the question of popular culture – in Adorno's terms, it takes it seriously. Thirdly, it makes an important contribution to a set of debates around the media technologies, aesthetics and politics.

McLuhan and Medium Theory

In the *Culture Industry Reconsidered* the technologies of mass communication are viewed as intrinsic to the development of a mass society characterised by growing constraint on freedom and deception or alienation. This is explicitly contrasted with Walter Benjamin's argument that 'mechanical reproduction' (cinema) can have a positively democratic potential, not only showing us new worlds, but also providing an explosive new perspective through which to judge the old one more clearly (Benjamin, 1973).

A later but also very well known intervention into early debates around the relationship between (media) technology, cultural form and political transformation comes in the shape of Marshall McLuhan's media-centric explorations of the technologies of emerging global media systems. In a markedly technologically deterministic argument McLuhan argued that new media systems would re-organise the human sensorium and with it the scale, pace and interconnectedness of human affairs, producing the 'global village'. The tone of McLuhan's work (he was known as a media prophet in his time) makes it easy to set aside, but the questions he raises, about the informing force of media technology on the temporality and spatiality of everyday life and about the relationship between humans and their media extensions or prostheses, are complex, and have arisen repeatedly in relation to later developments in media technology (notably around mobile/intimate technologies). In addition, the tradition from which McLuhan comes, that of Canadian medium theory, has been successful in finding ways to explore the many aspects of media that escape the narrowly defined limits of representation. These theorists, sharing a sense of the importance of media technologies (the medium not the message perhaps), have had an endearing influence on media theorists trying to understand the role of the media in the transformation and organisation of everyday life and its rhythms and rituals (see, for instance, Silverstone, 1994) and on accounts exploring questions of mediation and sense perception.

MASS PUBLICS: HABERMAS AND BAUDRILLARD

The question of the degree to which and the ways in which the media constitute a sphere for rational debate, or for debate of any kind, is one that is central to media studies. One critical question asked today (but of course it was also asked in Horkheimer and Adorno's time) is why the media so obviously fall short of their idealised role as important guarantors of free speech and informed debate within these societies. Two theorists included here chart very different routes through these issues, Jürgen Habermas' hugely influential historical work on the rise and fall of the public sphere, the latter defined as a realm where rational debate free from private interests can be held so that issues of common interest can be resolved in meaningful ways, sparked fierce debates within media studies and political science. Habermas found in the coffee house gatherings of eighteenth-century London a glimpse of the kind of rational public debate that might, despite its exclusions, constitute a normative model for the development of a universal public sphere. His argument, and here the lineage in the Frankfurt School Habermas claims is clearly visible, was that technocratic rationality – the mass media, mass culture, the culture industries – had extinguished these early possibilities. Forms of mass spectacle replace the potential for transparent and honest communication (deliberation) between equal citizens.

Habermas' work, clearly ground-breaking, has been criticised by a number of critics within the media and beyond. Some have criticised the historical accuracy of the picture given of eighteenth-century London; others have argued, more fundamentally, that the simple extension of the communicative regime it embodies (for instance, the inclusion of women and others excluded from public life at the time) would not be enough to correct the model. Nancy Fraser, for instance, has convincingly argued that it may be more productive to cultivate (or recognise) multiple forms and forums for discussion than to cultivate a single universal public sphere based on the assumption that the goal of perfect communication across a unified sphere would be possible or desirable. The cultivation of multiple spheres might help construct a communicational regime capable of enabling and respecting difference rather than one relying on the cultivation of 'universal' norms (Fraser 1990).

A very different approach comes from Baudrillard, a French critical theorist best known for his exploration of the rise of postmodern cultural forms where value and reality are increasingly located *at* face value. At the extreme limit of this, as a famous figure had it, there is no territory accessible under the 'life size' map that overlays it but only the map itself; the reality it seems to point to, the claim it makes to *map*, is an illusion. In the *Implosion* Baudrillard looks at the dynamics of this obsession with surface as it pertains to questions of mass media, making a beautiful case for the revenge of the mass on the media, a revenge he discerns in the relative failure of those who seek to pre-configure public opinion (the pollsters) in the face of a mass. His point is that the mass refuses to play the prescribed game. In Baudrillard there is a fascination not only with the visual (the simulacra), the flattening, but also with forms of engagement that slip beneath representation/signification. The silent refusals that Baudrillard sees in those who play with, rather than playing along with, opinion polls, for instance, brings to mind contemporary debates around viewer participation – and the degree to which interactive media delivers (or fails to deliver) user/consumer intelligence to producers (see Section 9 on new media).

FEMINISM, KNOWLEDGE AND POWER

Feminist scholarship, itself often categorised into successive waves, has played an important part in the ongoing development of media studies, influencing the objects of its study, its methodologies and critical theorisation. Feminism's critical theoretical viewpoints, particularly those demanding recognition of the situated position of the researcher, have been important, particularly in the media studies tradition in the UK, Australia and the Nordic countries.

The piece from Annette Kuhn included here is only one of a series of influential texts that signal a particular intervention (among the others are Laura Mulvey's work on visual pleasure and narrative cinema, De Lauretis' work on film and desire and Donna Haraway's writings on technology and feminism, which gave us a powerful methodology for the study of science and knowledge, and work from series of academics exploring gender, media and domesticity, often through media histories – see for instance Ann Gray's work in this volume). Kuhn's question in this article concerns the future for feminism within the university system, a question that has not been answered – the fate of women's studies departments remains uncertain in many institutions. Her demand that the intersection of power and knowledge be recognised as it pertains to questions of gender and representation is powerfully made and is as relevant to today's 'post-feminist' times as it was in her own.

The more general case Kuhn makes in this reading is for the power and force of representation to be recognised so that activity on this terrain is in turn recognised as an aspect of feminist political critique and struggle. At the time she was intervening in dialogue where the relative importance of base and superstructure (economism versus cultural Marxism) was in dispute: many feminists felt the real issues were to be found in the workplace or were to be fought for through the courts. Today this might once again have to be argued out, but this time not in relation to debates among the left, but in relation to a widespread (post-feminist) sense that gender issues *in general* are irrelevant to questions of political freedom, and with them many issues concerning representation. In some areas of media studies the issue of femininity and its representations has often dislocated itself from questions of feminist *critique* almost entirely – as a series of studies of video game content might suggest.

HALL AND THE CIRCUIT OF CULTURE

Stuart Hall's intervention into debates around the circuit of communication came in 'Encoding/Decoding', the article abstracted here. In this article, which specifically is about television, Hall argued that communications-theoretical models of the media were inadequate because their information theory-based transmission model (based on the idea of the closed message transmitted between sender and receiver) could not grapple with questions of social power and its operation across the 'relatively autonomous' spheres of production, text and consumption. Hall's model gave us a circuit of culture so that for the first time iterative media circuits, where, for instance, audience response might shape the future media output or where the consequences of the political economy of production could be traced through the text and its reception, were open to investigation. Hall's account both affirms and undermines the media text as the central point of media analysis. It is an account that gives much weight to semiosis as the central moment in the media circuit. At the same time, the attention given to other moments in the circuit, those of production and consumption, open up new routes for media studies, particularly those based on audience research and everyday lives and practices.

'Encoding/Decoding' was also a broadside against crude behaviourist models of media effects. Hall understood the force and impact of television (and more broadly the media) to be a consequence of social relations rather than individual psychology and so set out to understand how the power and force of particular ideas might be formulated, encapsulated and decoded in circumstances that are at once specific and individual *and* part of a shared social horizon in which particular sets of ideas (those of the powerful) tend to dominate. Hall's suggestion was that readers tend to decode media productions along the ideological lines cued up in the text (and often also found in their lives), but that they may also produce negotiated readings or absolutely oppositional or anti-hegemonic readings of various kinds. This helped to launch audience and reception studies of a new kind, later developed by a series of media studies scholars. Hall's message was that the power and force of the text was bound up less with absolute values or formal constructions, but more with the conditions in which it was made and – above all – the conditions within which it was read.

Hall's project in 'Encoding/Decoding' was specifically with the media, but work from the Centre for Cultural Studies was marked by its insistence on taking many kinds of popular, street and minority culture seriously. This concern with the popular, with understanding the ways in which everyday life operates, is one shared by the French sociologist Pierre Bourdieu.

POPULAR CULTURE: BOURDIEU: TASTE, CLASS AND CULTURAL CAPITAL

The sociologist Pierre Bourdieu wrote very little directly on the media, and yet his work on the social construction of taste, on the alignments between various forms of embodied, material, symbolic and economic capital and on the sociology of value has been much taken up in media studies. Bourdieu's work offers a way in to think through questions of the *relationship* between cultural, economic and social capital – to ask how questions of taste and judgement are socially formed and maintained. A central paradox for Bourdieu concerns the contradiction between individuals who believe themselves to act as free agents, but who are constrained in their judgements, activities, tastes and choices by the structures within which they live and by their social positioning within these structures. Questions of structure and agency are thus at the heart of his writing. Bourdieu's most famous work, *Distinction*, was a report on an investigation of the forms and practices of French everyday life. This showed that different taste formations (valorising a more immediate and 'earthy' versus a more aestheticised taste) operated in a connected way across a series of cultural forms and practices (e.g. eating, cooking, art) characterised as working-class and upper-class culture respectively, confirming those who exhibited them or practised them as members of a particular social strata. As Bourdieu himself put it, the research showed that 'taste classifies and it classifiers the classifier'.

The work reproduced here is bound into this central argument and introduces some key terms from Bourdieu's work. Its central focus is the way in which various forms of social and cultural capital are produced, held and transferred. The reading thus looks at the relationship between the habitus, defined as 'a system of dispositions acquired by implicit or explicit learning which functions as a system of generative choices', and fields which are defined as semi-discrete but connected areas of cultural activity within which individuals operate. Bourdieu's contention is that cultural capitals or systems of values are fought over in discrete fields but also map across to other fields. Cultural capitals thus have a transfer value, and in the end map also onto social and economic capital.

A criticism of Bourdieu's work is that it refuses individuals any agency, and certainly he forcibly points out that active participation does not automatically represent freedom – indeed, since 'those who take part . . . help to reproduce the game . . .' (95), the opposite might be true. Bourdieu, however, has argued that this account of cultural transmission is not brutally reductive because fields and bodies are not terminally formed but in a state of continuous motion so that 'the structure of the field is a *state* of power relations among the agents or institutions engaged in the struggle' (95).

DE CERTEAU

Where Bourdieu stresses the degree to which individual activities are bound to produce structures of domination, his fellow Frenchman, De Certeau, focused on the forms of micro-resistance available to those who live in an increasingly rationalised society in which forms of control are very finely grained. De Certeau's work on various forms of everyday consumption has been widely taken up in media analysis to explore the actions of audiences of all kinds. In *The Practice of Everyday Life*, his most famous work and the one from which we have abstracted here, De Certeau sets out to explore and celebrate the forms of tactical resistance by the 'dominated elements' in society – those 'whose status . . . is concealed by the euphemistic term "consumers"' (76). This is understood in temporal terms as a seizing of the time, a temporary re-appropriation of space, a way not of overturning but writing against the established order. Against an increasingly clamorous form of 'rationalised' production which is symbolised in much of his work by the visual, de Certeau thus sets *another* production 'called consumption' which operates by filching time and remaking meaning. In his words 'everyday life invents itself by poaching in countless ways on the property of others' (76). For De Certeau this poaching is a way in which those caught in Foucault's 'nets of discipline' evade them by throwing up 'a network of anti-discipline'.

De Certeau says consumers are 'unrecognized producers, poets of their own acts', and he extends this poetic, creative sense, to include forms of reception: 'the viewer reads the landscape of his childhood in the evening news . . . a different world (the reader's) slips into the author's place . . . this mutation makes the text habitable, like a rented apartment' (84). Despite the romanticism of his writings, De Certeau shares with Michel Foucault, to whom we will now turn, a sense of the intensification of forms of social control which emerges alongside the rise of mass media and mass consumption, although for De Certeau it is an object of faith that the object of control evades its subject. As he puts it, the consumer is a sphinx.

FOUCAULT AND DELEUZE

The interview with Foucault in *Truth and Power* abstracted here gives a glimpse into the sinuous thinking of a French critical theorist whose work has been immensely influential in media studies. Foucault's thought, only gestured at here since his writings are wide and extensive, has percolated through the discipline in all kinds of ways. At its heart is a concern with the ways in which systems of knowledge are formed and reformed and the ways in which these systems or discourses intersect (govern each other) and are powerful or productive, tending to produce regimes of truth. Foucault himself often explored these questions historically, researching the genealogies of particular institutions (e.g. the clinic, the madhouse, the prison) and sexualities (homosexuality), and also producing, in the *Order of Things*, an archaeological account of knowledge itself.

Foucault's work is invoked particularly in relation to explorations of the role of visual and other media in systems of discipline, surveillance and control, in relation to subject formation and identity, and in relation to questions of knowledge formation: it is after all easy to understand why media systems – from broadcasting to the Internet and beyond – play a key role in the articulation, dissemination and circulation of the various discourses that constitute social truths or 'norms' – including constituting the norms of what counts as legitimate or illegitimate forms of identity.

Finally, Foucault's claim for the central role of discourse in constituting particular regimes of truth or framing understandings of particular issues has been widely adopted to help constitute a particular research methodology. Foucauldian versions of discourse analysis seek to explore how particular discourses are cited and developed to confirm (or undermine) specific forms of public knowledge and general 'truths'. We should perhaps here distinguish between discourse analysis and the science of signs (semiotics) that appears in, for instance, the Hall article reproduced in this section. Foucault is clear that what he is analysing is *more* than language, in that it concerns relations of force and conflict: 'I believe one's point of reference should not be to the great model of language and signs, but to that of war and battle . . . relations of power, not relations of meaning' (65).

Foucault's work has sometimes been adopted by those who have sought to depoliticise media and cultural studies. However, Foucault's work, in particular his discussion of power as dispersed through the meshwork of discursively articulated practices and actions that constitute the social world and that constitute knowledge, is intrinsically concerned with questions of discipline and domination, although this is not viewed in terms of repression but of production. Moreover, his sense of truth as intimately engaged with power certainly produces a '*political* economy of truth' (my italics) (131).

DELEUZE

Gilles Deleuze' response to Foucault's analysis of power, made as a postscript to one of Foucault's own works, has been important to thinking around the forms of subjectivity, action and practice possible in an information society. The *PostScript to the Societies of Control* is probably, despite its rather obscure name and occasional gnomic aphorisms, one of the most readable and accessible of Deleuze's writings. In it Deleuze underscores the historical specificity of the disciplinary society illuminated in Foucault's writings. After the Second World War, he says, 'a disciplinary society was what we already no longer were, what we had ceased to be' (89). In the place of discipline – and its institutions – ands its visual mechanics, Deleuze follows up on Foucault's vision and announces the 'societies of control' (90) whose mechanisms operate 'like a sieve whose mesh will transmute from point to point' (90), and adds that in this new regime control is no longer a case of singling out individuals from the mass but of modulating the behaviour of 'dividuals' who can't be divided out as they were previously, this time through the operations of code (for instance, the password, the ID check). Even this brief reference to the language Deleuze is using here indicates the degree to which Deleuze is exploring what he views as a technologically influenced change in the operations of power – and the move he is making is from machines involving energy (which powered the disciplinary societies of which Foucault wrote) to computers or information machines. Its hard to say if this is causal for Deleuze: he observes that 'types of machines are easily matched with each type of society', but adds that this is 'not that machines are determining, but because they express those social forms capable of generating and using them' (6). What is clear is the centrality accorded to information within the world order that Deleuze describes, which is elsewhere – and in a wide variety of registers – described as the information society.

REFERENCES

Benjamin, W., *Illuminations* (London: Collins, [1935] 1973) pp. 219–54.

Carey, J., 'Technology and ideology: the case of the telegraph', in *Communication as Culture* (London: Routledge, 1989).

Derrida, J., *Archive Fever* (London: University of Chicago Press, 1995).

Fraser, N., 'Rethinking the public sphere: a contribution to the critique of actually existing democracy', *Social Text* 8:9 (1990) pp. 56–80.

Ong, W., *Orality and Literacy: The Technologizing of the Word* (London: Routledge, 1998).

Silverstone, R., *Television and Everyday Life* (London: Routledge, 1994).

Zielinski, S., *Deep Time of the Media* (Boston: MIT, 2006).

I

CULTURE INDUSTRY RECONSIDERED

Theodor W. Adorno

The term culture industry was perhaps used for the first time in the book *Dialectic of Enlightenment*, which Horkheimer and I published in Amsterdam in 1947. In our drafts we spoke of 'mass culture'. We replaced that expression with 'culture industry' in order to exclude from the outset the interpretation agreeable to its advocates: that it is a matter of something like a culture that arises spontaneously from the masses themselves, the contemporary form of popular art. From the latter the culture industry must be distinguished in the extreme. The culture industry fuses the old and familiar into a new quality. In all its branches, products which are tailored for consumption by masses, and which to a great extent determine the nature of that consumption, are manufactured more or less according to plan. The individual branches are similar in structure or at least fit into each other, ordering themselves into a system almost without a gap. This is made possible by contemporary technical capabilities as well as by economic and administrative concentration. The culture industry intentionally integrates its consumers from above. To the detriment of both it forces together the spheres of high and low art, separated for thousands of years. The seriousness of high art is destroyed in speculation about its efficacy; the seriousness of the lower perishes with the civilizational constraints imposed on the rebellious resistance inherent within it as long as social control was not yet total. Thus, although the culture industry undeniably speculates

Originally a broadcast talk given on the Hessian Broadcasting System, Federal Republic of Germany in spring 1963, this piece was published in this translation by Anson G. Rabinbach, *New German Critique* no. 6 (Fall 1975) pp. 12–19; repr. as ch. 3 of Theodor W. Adorno, *The Culture Industry: Selected Essays on Mass Culture*, ed. with an introduction by J. M. Bernstein (London: Routledge, 1991) pp. 85–92.

on the conscious and unconscious state of the millions towards which it is directed, the masses are not primary, but secondary, they are an object of calculation; an appendage of the machinery. The customer is not king, as the culture industry would have us believe, not its subject but its object. The very word mass-media, specially honed for the culture industry, already shifts the accents onto harmless terrain. Neither is it a question of primary concern for the masses, nor of the techniques of communication as such, but of the spirit which sufflates them, their master's voice. The culture industry misuses its concern for the masses in order to duplicate, reinforce and strengthen their mentality, which it presumes is given and unchangeable. How this mentality might be changed is excluded throughout. The masses are not the measure but the ideology of the culture industry, even though the culture industry itself could scarcely exist without adapting to the masses.

The cultural commodities of the industry are governed, as Brecht and Suhrkamp expressed it thirty years ago, by the principle of their realization as value, and not by their own specific content and harmonious formation. The entire practice of the culture industry transfers the profit motive naked onto cultural forms. Ever since these cultural forms first began to earn a living for their creators as commodities in the market-place they had already possessed something of this quality. But then they sought after profit only indirectly, over and above their autonomous essence. New on the part of the culture industry is the direct and undisguised primacy of a precisely and thoroughly calculated efficacy in its most typical products. The autonomy of works of art, which of course rarely ever predominated in an entirely pure form, and was always permeated by a constellation of effects, is tendentially eliminated by the culture industry, with or without the conscious will of those in control. The latter include both those who carry out directives as well as those who hold the power. In economic terms they are or were in search of new opportunities for the realization of capital in the most economically developed countries. The old opportunities became increasingly more precarious as a result of the same concentration process which alone makes the culture industry possible as an omnipresent phenomenon. Culture, in the true sense, did not simply accommodate itself to human beings; but it always simultaneously raised a protest against the petrified relations under which they lived, thereby honouring them. In so far as culture becomes wholly assimilated to and integrated in those petrified relations, human beings are once more debased. Cultural entities typical of the culture industry are no longer *also* commodities, they are commodities through and through. This quantitative shift is so great that it calls forth entirely new phenomena. Ultimately, the culture industry no longer even needs to directly pursue everywhere the profit interests from which it originated. These interests have become objectified in its ideology and have even made themselves independent of the compulsion to sell the cultural commodities which must be swallowed anyway. The culture industry turns into public relations, the manufacturing of 'goodwill' *per se*, without regard for particular firms or saleable objects. Brought to bear is a general uncritical consensus, advertisements produced for the world, so that each product of the culture industry becomes its own advertisement.

Nevertheless, those characteristics which originally stamped the transformation of literature into a commodity are maintained in this process. More than anything in the world, the culture industry has its ontology, a scaffolding of rigidly conservative basic categories which can be gleaned, for example, from the commercial English novels of the late seventeenth and early eighteenth centuries. What parades as progress in the culture industry, as the incessantly new which it offers up, remains the disguise for an eternal sameness; everywhere the changes mask a skeleton which has changed just as little as the profit motive itself since the time it first gained its predominance over culture.

Thus, the expression 'industry' is not to be taken too literally. It refers to the standardization of the thing itself – such as that of the Western, familiar to every movie-goer – and to the rationalization of distribution techniques, but not strictly to the production process. Although in film, the central sector of the culture industry, the production process resembles technical modes of operation in the extensive division of labour, the employment of machines and the separation of the labourers from the means of production – expressed in the perennial conflict between artists active in the culture industry and those who control it – individual forms of production are nevertheless maintained. Each product affects an individual air; individuality itself serves to reinforce ideology, in so far as the illusion is conjured up that the completely reified and mediated is a sanctuary from immediacy and life. Now, as ever, the culture industry exists in the 'service' of third persons, maintaining its affinity to the declining circulation process of capital, to the commerce from which it came into being. Its ideology above all makes use of the star system, borrowed from individualistic art and its commercial exploitation. The more dehumanized its methods of operation and content, the more diligently and successfully the culture industry propagates supposedly great personalities and operates with heart-throbs. It is industrial more in a sociological sense, in the incorporation of industrial forms of organization even when nothing is manufactured – as in the rationalization of office work – rather than in the sense of anything really and actually produced by technological rationality. Accordingly, the misinvestments of the culture industry are considerable, throwing those branches rendered obsolete by new techniques into crises, which seldom lead to changes for the better.

The concept of technique in the culture industry is only in name identical with technique in works of art. In the latter, technique is concerned with the internal organization of the object itself, with its inner logic. In contrast, the technique of the culture industry is, from the beginning, one of distribution and mechanical reproduction, and therefore always remains external to its object. The culture industry finds ideological support precisely in so far as it carefully shields itself from the full potential of the techniques contained in its products. It lives parasitically from the extra-artistic technique of the material production of goods, without regard for the obligation to the internal artistic whole implied by its functionality (*Sachlichkeit*), but also without concern for the laws of form demanded by aesthetic autonomy. The result for the physiognomy of the culture industry is essentially a mixture of streamlining, photographic hardness and precision on the one hand, and individualistic residues, sentimentality and an already rationally disposed and adapted rom anticism on the other. Adopting Benjamin's designation of the traditional work of art by the concept of aura, the presence of that which is not present, the culture industry is defined by the fact that it does not strictly counterpose another principle to that of aura, but rather by the fact that it conserves the decaying aura as a foggy mist. By this means the culture industry betrays its own ideological abuses.

It has recently become customary among cultural officials as well as sociologists to warn against underestimating the culture industry while pointing to its great importance for the development of the consciousness of its consumers. It is to be taken seriously, without cultured snobbism. In actuality the culture industry is important as a moment of the spirit which dominates today. Whoever ignores its influence out of scepticism for what it stuffs into people would be naive. Yet there is a deceptive glitter about the admonition to take it seriously. Because of its social role, disturbing questions about its quality, about truth or untruth, and about the aesthetic niveau of the culture industry's emissions are repressed, or at least excluded from the so-called sociology of communications. The critic is accused of taking refuge in arrogant esoterica. It would be advisable first to indicate the double meaning of importance that slowly worms its way in unnoticed. Even if it touches the lives of innumerable people, the function of something is no guarantee of its particular quality. The blending of aesthetics with its residual communicative aspects leads art, as a social phenomenon, not to its rightful position in opposition to alleged artistic snobbism, but rather in a variety of ways to the defence of its baneful social consequences. The importance of the culture industry in the spiritual constitution of the masses is no dispensation for reflection on its objective legitimation, its essential being, least of all by a science which thinks itself pragmatic. On the contrary: such reflection becomes necessary precisely for this reason. To take the culture industry as seriously as its unquestioned role demands, means to take it seriously critically, and not to cower in the face of its monopolistic character.

Among those intellectuals anxious to reconcile themselves with the phenomenon and eager to find a common formula to express both their reservations against it and their respect for its power, a tone of ironic toleration prevails unless they have already created a new mythos of the twentieth century from the imposed regression. After all, those intellectuals maintain, everyone knows what pocket novels, films off the rack, family television shows rolled out into serials and hit parades, advice to the lovelorn and horoscope columns are all about. All of this, however, is harmless and, according to them, even democratic since it responds to a demand, albeit a stimulated one. It also bestows all kinds of blessings, they point out, for example, through the dissemination of information, advice and stress reducing patterns of behaviour. Of course, as every sociological study measuring something as elementary as how politically informed the public is has proven, the information is meagre or indifferent. Moreover, the advice to be gained from manifestations of the culture industry is vacuous, banal or worse, and the behaviour patterns are shamelessly conformist.

The two-faced irony in the relationship of servile intellectuals to the culture industry is not restricted to them alone. It may also be supposed that the consciousness of the consumers themselves is split between the prescribed fun which is supplied to them by the culture industry and a not particularly well-hidden doubt about its blessings. The phrase, the world wants to be deceived, has become truer than had ever been intended. People are not only, as the saying goes, falling for the swindle; if it guarantees them even the most fleeting gratification they desire a deception which is nonetheless transparent to them. They force their eyes shut and voice approval, in a kind of self-loathing, for what is meted out to them, knowing fully the purpose for which it is manufactured. Without admitting it they sense that their lives would be completely intolerable as soon as they no longer clung to satisfactions which are none at all.

The most ambitious defence of the culture industry today celebrates its spirit, which might be safely called ideology, as an ordering factor. In a supposedly chaotic world it provides human beings with something like standards for orientation, and that alone seems worthy of approval. However, what its defenders imagine is preserved by the culture industry is in fact all the more thoroughly destroyed by it. The colour film demolishes the genial old tavern to a greater extent than bombs ever could: the film exterminates its imago. No homeland can survive being processed by the films which celebrate it, and which thereby turn the unique character on which it thrives into an interchangeable sameness.

That which legitimately could be called culture attempted, as an expression of suffering and contradiction, to maintain a grasp on the idea of the good life. Culture cannot represent either that which merely exists or the conventional and no longer binding categories of order which the culture industry drapes over the idea of the good life as if existing reality were the good life, and as if those categories were its true measure. If the response of the culture industry's representatives is that it does not deliver art at all, this is itself the ideology with which they evade responsibility for that from which the business lives. No misdeed is ever righted by explaining it as such.

The appeal to order alone, without concrete specificity, is futile; the appeal to the dissemination of norms, without these ever proving themselves in reality or before consciousness, is equally futile. The idea of an objectively binding order, huckstered to people because it is so lacking for them, has no claims if it does not prove itself internally and in confrontation with human beings. But this is precisely what no product of the culture industry would engage in. The concepts of order which it hammers into human beings are always those of the status quo. They remain unquestioned, unanalysed and undialectically presupposed, even if they no longer have any substance for those who accept them. In contrast to the Kantian, the categorical imperative of the culture industry no longer has anything in common with freedom. It proclaims: you shall conform, without instruction as to what; conform to that which exists anyway, and to that which everyone thinks anyway as a reflex of this power and omnipresence. The power of the culture industry's ideology is such that conformity has replaced consciousness. The order that springs from it is never confronted with what it claims to be or with the real interests of human beings. Order, however, is not good in itself. It would be so only as a good order. The fact that the culture industry is oblivious to this and extols order *in abstracto*, bears witness to the impotence and untruth of the messages it conveys. While it claims to lead the perplexed, it deludes them with false conflicts which they are to exchange for their own. It solves conflicts for them only in appearance, in a way that they can hardly be solved in their real lives. In the products of the culture industry human beings get into trouble only so that they can be rescued unharmed, usually by representatives of a benevolent collective; and then in empty harmony, they are reconciled with the general, whose demands they had experienced at the outset as irreconcileable with their interests. For this purpose the culture industry has developed formulas which even reach into such non-conceptual areas as light musical entertainment. Here too one gets into a 'jam', into rhythmic problems, which can be instantly disentangled by the triumph of the basic beat.

Even its defenders, however, would hardly contradict Plato openly who maintained that what is objectively and intrinsically untrue cannot also be subjectively good and true for human beings. The concoctions of the culture industry are neither guides for a blissful life, nor a new art of moral responsibility, but rather exhortations to toe the line, behind which stand the most powerful interests. The consensus which it propagates strengthens blind, opaque authority. If the culture industry is measured not by its own substance and logic, but by its efficacy, by its position in reality and its explicit pretensions; if the focus of serious concern is with the efficacy to which it always appeals, the potential of its effect becomes twice as weighty. This potential, however, lies in the promotion and exploitation of the ego-weakness to which the powerless members of contemporary society, with its concentration of power, are condemned. Their consciousness is further developed retrogressively. It is no coincidence that cynical American film producers are heard to say that their pictures must take into consideration the level of eleven-year-olds. In doing so they would very much like to make adults into eleven-year-olds.

It is true that thorough research has not, for the time being, produced an airtight case proving the regressive effects of particular products of the culture industry. No doubt an imaginatively designed experiment could achieve this more successfully than the powerful financial interests concerned would find comfortable. In any case, it can be assumed without hesitation that steady drops hollow the stone, especially since the system of the culture industry that surrounds the masses tolerates hardly any deviation and incessantly drills the same formulas on behaviour. Only their deep unconscious mistrust, the last residue of the difference between art and empirical reality in the spiritual makeup of the masses, explains why they have not, to a person, long since perceived and accepted the world as it is constructed for them by the culture industry. Even if its messages were as harmless as they are made out to be – on countless occasions they are obviously not harmless, like the movies which chime in with currently popular hate campaigns against intellectuals by portraying them with the usual stereotypes – the attitudes which the culture industry calls forth are anything but harmless. If an astrologer urges his readers to drive carefully on a particular day, that certainly hurts no one; they will, however, be harmed indeed by the stupefication which lies in the claim that advice which is valid every day and which is therefore idiotic, needs the approval of the stars.

Human dependence and servitude, the vanishing point of the culture industry, could scarcely be more faithfully described than by the American interviewee who was of the opinion that the dilemmas of the contemporary epoch would end if people would simply follow the lead of prominent personalities. In so far as the culture industry arouses a feeling of well-being that the world is precisely in that order suggested by the culture industry, the substitute gratification which it prepares for human beings cheats them out of the same happiness which it deceitfully projects. The total effect of the culture industry is one of anti-enlightenment, in which, as Horkheimer and I have noted, enlightenment, that is the progressive technical domination of nature, becomes mass deception and is turned into a means for fettering consciousness. It impedes the development of autonomous, independent individuals who judge and decide consciously for themselves. These, however, would be the precondition for a democratic society which needs adults who have come of age in order to sustain itself and develop. If the masses have been unjustly reviled from above as masses, the culture industry is not among the least responsible for making them into masses and then despising them, while obstructing the emancipation for which human beings are as ripe as the productive forces of the epoch permit.

2

THE MEDIUM IS THE MESSAGE

Marshall McLuhan

In a culture like ours, long accustomed to splitting and dividing all things as a means of control, it is sometimes a bit of a shock to be reminded that, in operational practical fact, the medium is the message. This is merely to say that the personal and social consequences of any medium – that is, of any extension of ourselves – result from the new scale that is introduced into our affairs by each extension of ourselves, or by any new technology. Thus, with automation,[1] for example, the new patterns of human association tend to eliminate jobs, it is true. That is the negative result. Positively, automation creates roles for people, which is to say depth of involvement in their work and human association that our preceding mechanical technology had destroyed. Many people would be disposed to say that it was not the machine, but what one did with the machine, that was its meaning or message. In terms of the ways in which the machine altered our relations to one another and to ourselves, it mattered not in the least whether it turned out cornflakes or Cadillacs. The restructuring of human work and association was shaped by the technique of fragmentation that is the essence of machine technology. The essence of automation technology is the opposite. It is integral and decentralist in depth, just as the machine was fragmentary, centralist, and superficial in its patterning of human relationships.

The instance of the electric light may prove illuminating in this connection. The electric light is pure information. It is a medium without a message, as it were, unless it is used to spell out some verbal ad or name. This fact,

From Marshall McLuhan, *Understanding Media: the Extensions of Man* (London: Routledge & Kegan Paul, 1964) pp. 11, 15–21, 31–3, 68–9.

characteristic of all media, means that the 'content' of any medium is always another medium. The content of writing is speech, just as the written word is the content of print, and print is the content of the telegraph. If it is asked, 'What is the content of speech?' it is necessary to say, 'It is an actual process of thought, which is in itself nonverbal.' An abstract painting represents direct manifestation of creative thought processes as they might appear in computer designs. What we are considering here, however, are the psychic and social consequences of the designs or patterns as they amplify or accelerate existing processes. For the 'message' of any medium or technology is the change of scale or pace or pattern that it introduces into human affairs. The railway did not introduce movement or transportation or wheel or road into human society, but it accelerated and enlarged the scale of previous human functions, creating totally new kinds of cities and new kinds of work and leisure. This happened whether the railway functioned in a tropical or a northern environment, and is quite independent of the freight or content of the railway medium. The airplane, on the other hand, by accelerating the rate of transportation, tends to dissolve the railway form of city, politics, and association, quite independently of what the airplane is used for.

Let us return to the electric light. Whether the light is being used for brain surgery or night baseball is a matter of indifference. It could be argued that these activities are in some way the 'content' of the electric light, since they could not exist without the electric light. This fact merely underlines the point that 'the medium is the message' because it is the medium that shapes and controls the scale and form of human association and action. The content or uses of such media are as diverse as they are ineffectual in shaping the form of human association. Indeed, it is only too typical that the 'content' of any medium blinds us to the character of the medium. It is only today that industries have become aware of the various kinds of business in which they are engaged. When IBM discovered that it was not in the business of making office equipment or business machines, but that it was in the business of processing information, then it began to navigate with clear vision. The General Electric Company makes a considerable portion of its profits from electric light bulbs and lighting systems. It has not yet discovered that, quite as much as A.T. & T., it is in the business of moving information.

The electric light escapes attention as a communication medium just because it has no 'content.' And this makes it an invaluable instance of how people fail to study media at all. For it is not till the electric light is used to spell out some brand name that it is noticed as a medium. Then it is not the light but the 'content' (or what is really another medium) that is noticed. The message of the electric light is like the message of electric power in industry, totally radical, pervasive, and decentralized. For electric light and power are separate from their uses, yet they eliminate time and space factors in human association exactly as do radio, telegraph, telephone, and TV, creating involvement in depth.

[. . .]

In accepting an honorary degree from the University of Notre Dame a few years ago, General David Sarnoff[2] made this statement: 'We are too prone to make technological instruments the scapegoats for the sins of those who wield them. The products of modern science are not in themselves good or bad; it is the way they are used that determines their value.' That is the voice of the current somnambulism. Suppose we were to say, 'Apple pie is in itself neither good nor bad; it is the way it is used that determines its value.' Or, 'The small-pox virus is in itself neither good nor bad; it is the way it is used that determines its value.' Again. 'Firearms are in themselves neither good nor bad; it is the way they are used that determines their value.' That is, if the slugs reach the right people firearms are good. If the TV tube fires the right ammunition at the right people it is good. I am not being perverse. There is simply nothing in the Sarnoff statement that will bear scrutiny, for it ignores the nature of the medium, of any and all media, in the true Narcissus style of one hypnotized by the amputation and extension of his own being in a new technical form. General Sarnoff went on to explain his attitude to the technology of print, saying that it was true that print caused much trash to circulate, but it had also disseminated the Bible and the thoughts of seers and philosophers. It has never occurred to General Sarnoff that any technology could do anything but *add* itself on to what we already are.

[. . .]

[M]echanization is achieved by fragmentation of any process and by putting the fragmented parts in a series. Yet, as David Hume showed in the eighteenth century, there is no principle of causality in a mere sequence. That one thing follows another accounts for nothing. Nothing follows from following, except change. So the greatest of all reversals occurred with electricity, that ended sequence by making things instant. With instant speed the causes of things began to emerge to awareness again, as they had not done with things in sequence and in concatenation accordingly. Instead of asking which came first, the chicken or the egg, it suddenly seemed that a chicken was an egg's idea for getting more eggs.

Just before an airplane breaks the sound barrier, sound waves become visible on the wings of the plane. The sudden visibility of sound just as sound ends is an apt instance of that great pattern of being that reveals new and opposite forms just as the earlier forms reach their peak performance. Mechanization was never so vividly fragmented or sequential as in the birth of the movies, the moment that translated us beyond mechanism into the world of growth and organic interrelation. The movie, by sheer speeding up of the mechanical, carried us from the world of sequence and connections into the world of creative configuration and structure. The message of the movie medium is that of transition from lineal connections to configurations. It is the transition that produced the now quite correct observation: 'If it works, it's obsolete.' When electric speed further takes over from mechanical movie sequences, then the lines of force in structures and in media become loud and clear. We return to the inclusive form of the icon.

To a highly literate and mechanized culture the movie appeared as a world of triumphant illusions and dreams that money could buy. It was at this moment of the movie that cubism occurred, and it has been described by E. H. Gombrich (*Art and Illusion*) as 'the most radical attempt to stamp out ambiguity and to enforce one reading of the picture – that of a man-made construction, a colored canvas.' For cubism substitutes all facets of an object simultaneously for the 'point of view' or facet of perspective illusion. Instead of the specialized illusion of the third dimension on canvas, cubism sets up an interplay of planes and contradiction or dramatic conflict of patterns, lights, textures that 'drives home the message' by involvement. This is held by many to be an exercise in painting, not in illusion.

In other words, cubism, by giving the inside and outside, the top, bottom, back, and front and the rest, in two dimensions, drops the illusion of perspective in favor of instant sensory awareness of the whole. Cubism, by seizing on instant total awareness, suddenly announced that *the medium is the message*. Is it not evident that the moment that sequence yields to the simultaneous, one is in the world of the structure and of configuration? Is that not what has happened in physics as in painting, poetry, and in communication? Specialized segments of attention have shifted to total field, and we can now say, 'The medium is the message' quite naturally. Before the electric speed and total field, it was not obvious that the medium is the message. The message, it seemed, was the 'content,' as people used to ask what a painting was *about*. Yet they never thought to ask what a melody was about, nor what a house or a dress was about. In such matters, people retained some sense of the whole pattern, of form and function as a unity. But in the electric age this integral idea of structure and configuration has become [. . .] prevalent [. . .].

[. . .]

HOT AND COLD

[. . .]

There is a basic principle that distinguishes a hot medium like radio from a cool one like the telephone, or a hot medium like the movie from a cool one like TV. A hot medium is one that extends one single sense in 'high definition.' High definition is the state of being well filled with data. A photograph is, visually, 'high definition.' A cartoon is 'low definition,' simply because very little visual information is provided. Telephone is a cool medium, or one of low definition, because the ear is given a meager amount of information. And speech is a cool medium of low definition, because so little is given and so much has to be filled in by the listener. On the other hand, hot media do not leave so much to be filled in or completed by the audience. Hot media are, therefore, low in participation, and cool media are high in participation or completion by the audience. Naturally, therefore, a hot medium like radio has very different effects on the user from a cool medium like the telephone.

A cool medium like hieroglyphic or ideogrammic written characters has very different effects from the hot and explosive medium of the phonetic alphabet. The alphabet, when pushed to a high degree of abstract visual intensity, became typography. The printed word with its specialist intensity burst the bonds of medieval corporate guilds and monasteries, creating extreme individualist patterns of enterprise and monopoly. But the typical reversal occurred when extremes of monopoly brought back the corporation, with its impersonal empire over many lives. The hotting-up of the medium of writing to repeatable print intensity led to nationalism and the religious wars of the sixteenth century. The heavy and unwieldy media, such as stone, are time binders. Used for writing, they are very cool indeed, and serve to unify the ages; whereas paper is a hot medium that serves to unify spaces horizontally, both in political and entertainment empires.

Any hot medium allows of less participation than a cool one, as a lecture makes for less participation than a seminar, and a book for less than dialogue. With print many earlier forms were excluded from life and art, and many were given strange new intensity.

[. . .]

A tribal and feudal hierarchy of traditional kind collapses quickly when it meets any hot medium of the mechanical, uniform, and repetitive kind. The medium of money or wheel or writing, or any other form of specialist speed-up of exchange and information, will serve to fragment a tribal structure. Similarly, a very much greater speed-up, such as occurs with electricity, may serve to restore a tribal pattern of intense involvement such as took place with the introduction of radio in Europe, and is now tending to happen as a result of TV in America. Specialist technologies detribalize. The non-specialist electric technology retribalizes.

[. . .]

By putting our physical bodies inside our extended nervous systems, by means of electric media, we set up a dynamic by which all previous technologies that are mere extensions of hands and feet and teeth and bodily heat-controls – all such extensions of our bodies, including cities – will be translated into information systems. Electromagnetic technology requires utter human docility and quiescence of meditation such as benefits an organism that now wears its brain outside its skull and its nerves outside its hide. Man must serve his electric technology with the same servomechanistic fidelity with which he served his coracle, his canoe, his typography, and all other extensions of his physical organs. But there is this difference, that previous technologies were partial and fragmentary, and the electric is total and inclusive. An external consensus or conscience is now as necessary as private consciousness. With the new media, however, it is also possible to store and to translate everything; and, as for speed, that is no problem. No further acceleration is possible this side of the light barrier.

Just as when information levels rise in physics and chemistry, it is possible to use anything for fuel or fabric or building material, so with electric technology all solid goods can be summoned to appear as solid commodities by means of information circuits set up in the organic patterns that we call 'automation' and information retrieval. Under electric technology the entire business of man becomes learning and knowing.

[. . .]

After three thousand years of explosion, by means of fragmentary and mechanical technologies, the Western world is imploding. During the mechanical ages we had extended our bodies in space. Today, after more than a century of electric technology, we have extended our central nervous system itself in a global embrace, abolishing both space and time as far as our planet is concerned. Rapidly, we approach the final phase of the extensions of man – the technological simulation of consciousness, when the creative process of knowing will be collectively and corporately extended to the whole of human society, much as we have already extended our senses and our nerves by the various media.

Editors' Notes

1. Automation: the 1960s term for the introduction of new information technologies; computerisation.
2. David Sarnoff (1891–1971). As a young employee of the Marconi radio company, Sarnoff is often credited with having 'invented' broadcasting as an application of the new wireless technology. He founded the first American broadcasting network, NBC, in 1926, and was head of the Radio Corporation of America from 1930 to 1966.

3

ENCODING/DECODING

Stuart Hall

Traditionally, mass-communications research has conceptualized the process of communication in terms of a circulation circuit or loop. This model has been criticized for its linearity – sender/message/receiver – for its concentration on the level of message exchange and for the absence of a structured conception of the different moments as a complex structure of relations. But it is also possible (and useful) to think of this process in terms of a structure produced and sustained through the articulation of linked but distinctive moments – production, circulation, distribution/consumption, reproduction. This would be to think of the process as a 'complex structure in dominance', sustained through the articulation of connected practices, each of which, however, retains its distinctiveness and has its own specific modality, its own forms and conditions of existence. This second approach, homologous to that which forms the skeleton of commodity production offered in Marx's *Grundrisse* and in *Capital*, has the added advantage of bringing out more sharply how a continuous circuit – production–distribution–production – can be sustained through a 'passage of forms'.[1] It also highlights the specificity of the forms in which the product of the process 'appears' in each moment, and thus what distinguishes discursive 'production' from other types of production in our society and in modern media systems.

The 'object' of these practices is meanings and messages in the form of sign-vehicles of a specific kind organized, like any form of communication or

From Stuart Hall, Dorothy Hobson, Andrew Lowe and Paul Willis (eds), *Culture, Media, Language* (London: Hutchinson, 1980), pp. 128–38; an edited extract from S. Hall, 'Encoding and Decoding in the Television Discourse', CCCS stencilled paper no. 7 (Birmingham: Centre for Contemporary Cultural Studies, 1973).

language, through the operation of codes within the syntagmatic chain of a discourse. The apparatuses, relations and practices of production thus issue, at a certain moment (the moment of 'production/circulation') in the form of symbolic vehicles constituted within the rules of 'language'. It is in this discursive form that the circulation of the 'product' takes place. The process thus requires, at the production end, its material instruments – its 'means' – as well as its own sets of social (production) relations – the organization and combination of practices within media apparatuses. But it is in the *discursive* form that the circulation of the product takes place, as well as its distribution to different audiences. Once accomplished, the discourse must then be trans-lated – transformed, again – into social practices if the circuit is to be both completed and effective. If no 'meaning' is taken, there can be no 'consump-tion'. If the meaning is not articulated in practice, it has no effect. The value of this approach is that while each of the moments, in articulation, is necessary to the circuit as a whole, no one moment can fully guarantee the next moment with which it is articulated. Since each has its specific modality and condi-tions of existence, each can constitute its own break or interruption of the 'passage of forms' on whose continuity the flow of effective production (that is, 'reproduction') depends.

Thus while in no way wanting to limit research to 'following only those leads which emerge from content analysis'[2] we must recognize that the discursive form of the message has a privileged position in the communicative exchange (from the viewpoint of circulation), and that the moments of 'encoding' and 'decoding', though only 'relatively autonomous' in relation to the communi-cative process as a whole, are *determinate* moments. A 'raw' historical event cannot, *in that form*, be transmitted by, say, a television newscast. Events can only be signified within the aural–visual forms of the televisual discourse. In the moment when a historical event passes under the sign of discourse, it is subject to all the complex formal 'rules' by which language signifies. To put it paradoxically, the event must become a 'story' before it can become a *commu-nicative event*. In that moment the formal sub-rules of discourse are 'in domi-nance', without, of course, subordinating out of existence the historical event so signified, the social relations in which the rules are set to work or the social and political consequences of the event having been signified in this way. The 'message form' is the necessary 'form of appearance' of the event in its passage from source to receiver. Thus the transposition into and out of the 'message form' (or the mode of symbolic exchange) is not a random 'moment', which we can take up or ignore at our convenience. The 'message form' is a determinate moment; though, at another level, it comprises the surface movements of the communications system only and requires, at another stage, to be integrated into the social relations of the communication process as a whole, of which it forms only a part.

From this general perspective, we may crudely characterize the tel-evision communicative process as follows. The institutional structures of broadcasting, with their practices and networks of production, their organized relations and technical infrastructures, are required to produce a programme. Using the analogy of *Capital*, this is the 'labour process' in the discursive mode. Production, here, constructs the message. In one sense, then, the circuit begins here. Of course, the production process is not without its 'discursive' aspect: it, too, is framed throughout by meanings and ideas: knowledge-in-use concerning the routines of production, historically defined technical skills, professional ideologies, institutional knowledge, definitions and assumptions, assumptions about the audience and so on frame the constitution of the programme through this production structure. Further, though the production structures of television originate the television discourse, they do not constitute a closed system. They draw topics, treatments, agendas, events, personnel, images of the audience, 'definitions of the situation' from other sources and other discursive formations within the wider socio-cultural and political structure of which they are a differentiated part. Philip Elliott has expressed this point succinctly, within a more traditional framework, in his discussion of the way in which the audience is both the 'source' and the 'receiver' of the television message. Thus – to borrow Marx's terms – circulation and reception are, indeed, 'moments' of the production process in television and are reincorporated, via a number of skewed and structured 'feedbacks', into the production process itself. The consumption or reception of the television message is thus also itself a 'moment' of the production process in its larger sense, though the latter is 'predominant' because it is the 'point of departure for the realization' of the message. Production and reception of the television message are not, therefore, identical, but they are related: they are differentiated moments within the totality formed by the social relations of the communicative process as a whole.

At a certain point, however, the broadcasting structures must yield encoded messages in the form of a meaningful discourse. The institution-societal relations of production must pass under the discursive rules of language for its product to be 'realized'. This initiates a further differentiated moment, in which the formal rules of discourse and language are in dominance. Before this message can have an 'effect' (however defined), satisfy a 'need' or be put to a 'use', it must first be appropriated as a meaningful discourse and be meaningfully decoded. It is this set of decoded meanings which 'have an effect', influence, entertain, instruct or persuade, with very complex perceptual, cognitive, emotional, ideological or behavioural consequences. In a 'determinate' moment the structure employs a code and yields a 'message': at another determinate moment the 'message', via its decodings, issues into the structure of social practices. We are now fully aware that this re-entry into the practices of audience reception and 'use' cannot be understood in simple behavioural terms. The typical processes identified in positivistic research on isolated elements – effects, uses, 'gratifications' – are themselves framed by structures of understanding, as well as being produced by social and economic relations,

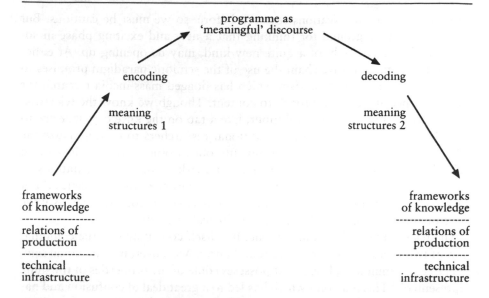

which shape their 'realization' at the reception end of the chain and which permit the meanings signified in the discourse to be transposed into practice or consciousness (to acquire social use value or political effectivity).

Clearly, what we have labelled in the diagram 'meaning structures 1' and 'meaning structures 2' may not be the same. They do not constitute an 'immediate identity'. The codes of encoding and decoding may not be perfectly symmetrical. The degrees of symmetry – that is, the degrees of 'understanding' and 'misunderstanding' in the communicative exchange – depend on the degrees of symmetry/asymmetry (relations of equivalence) established between the positions of the 'personifications', encoder–producer and decoder–receiver. But this in turn depends on the degrees of identity/non-identity between the codes which perfectly or imperfectly transmit, interrupt or systematically distort what has been transmitted. The lack of fit between the codes has a great deal to do with the structural differences of relation and position between broadcasters and audiences, but it also has something to do with the asymmetry between the codes of 'source' and 'receiver' at the moment of transformation into and out of the discursive form. What are called 'distortions' or 'misunderstandings' arise precisely from the *lack of equivalence* between the two sides in the communicative exchange. Once again, this defines the 'relative autonomy', but 'determinateness', of the entry and exit of the message in its discursive moments.

The application of this rudimentary paradigm has already begun to transform our understanding of the older term, television 'content'. We are just beginning to see how it might also transform our understanding of audience reception, 'reading' and response as well. Beginnings and endings have been announced in communications research before, so we must be cautious. But there seems some ground for thinking that a new and exciting phase in so-called audience research, of a quite new kind, may be opening up. At either end of the communicative chain the use of the semiotic paradigm promises to dispel the lingering behaviourism which has dogged mass-media research for so long, especially in its approach to content. Though we know the television programme is not a behavioural input, like a tap on the knee cap, it seems to have been almost impossible for traditional researchers to conceptualize the communicative process without lapsing into one or other variant of low-flying behaviourism. We know, as Gerbner has remarked, that representations of violence on the TV screen 'are not violence but messages about violence':[3] but we have continued to research the question of violence, for example, as if we were unable to comprehend this epistemological distinction.

The television sign is a complex one. It is itself constituted by the combination of two types of discourse, visual and aural. Moreover, it is an iconic sign, in Peirce's terminology, because 'it posseses some of the properties of the thing represented'.[4] This is a point which has led to a great deal of confusion and has provided the site of intense controversy in the study of visual language. Since the visual discourse translates a three-dimensional world into two-dimensional planes, it cannot, of course, *be* the referent or concept it signifies. The dog in the film can bark but it cannot bite! Reality exists outside language, but it is constantly mediated by and through language: and what we can know and say has to be produced in and through discourse. Discursive 'knowledge' is the product not of the transparent representation of the 'real' in language but of the articulation of language on real relations and conditions. Thus there is no intelligible discourse without the operation of a code. Iconic signs are therefore coded signs too – even if the codes here work differently from those of other signs. There is no degree zero in language. Naturalism and 'realism' – the apparent fidelity of the representation to the thing or concept represented – is the result, the effect, of a certain specific articulation of language on the 'real'. It is the result of a discursive practice.

Certain codes may, of course, be so widely distributed in a specific language community or culture, and be learned at so early an age, that they appear not to be constructed – the effect of an articulation between sign and referent – but to be 'naturally' given. Simple visual signs appear to have achieved a 'near-universality' in this sense: though evidence remains that even apparently 'natural' visual codes are culture-specific. However, this does not mean that no codes have intervened; rather, that the codes have been profoundly *naturalized*. The operation of naturalized codes reveals not the transparency and 'naturalness' of language but the depth, the habituation and the near-universality of the codes in use. They produce apparently 'natural' recognitions. This has the (ideological) effect of concealing the practices of coding which are present. But we must not be fooled by appearances. Actually, what naturalized codes demonstrate is the degree of habituation produced when there is a fundamental alignment and reciprocity – an achieved equivalence – between the encoding and decoding sides of an exchange of meanings. The functioning of the codes on the decoding side will frequently assume the status of naturalized perceptions. This leads us to think that the visual sign for 'cow' actually is (rather than *represents*) the animal, cow. But if we think of the visual representation of a cow in a manual on animal husbandry – and, even more, of the linguistic sign 'cow' – we can see that both, in different degrees, are *arbitrary* with respect to the concept of the animal they represent. The articulation of an arbitrary sign – whether visual or verbal – with the concept of a referent is the product not of nature but of convention, and the conventionalism of discourses requires the intervention, the support, of codes. Thus Eco has argued that iconic signs 'look like objects in the real world because they reproduce the conditions (that is, the codes) of perception in the viewer'.[5] These 'conditions of perception' are, however, the result of a highly coded, even if virtually unconscious, set of operations – decodings. This is as true of the photographic or televisual image as it is of any other sign. Iconic signs are, however, particularly vulnerable to being 'read' as natural because visual codes of perception are very widely distributed and because this type of sign is less arbitrary than a linguistic sign: the linguistic sign 'cow' possesses *none* of the properties of the thing represented, whereas the visual sign appears to possess *some* of those properties.

[...]

The level of connotation of the visual sign, of its contextual reference and positioning in different discursive fields of meaning and association, is the point where *already coded* signs intersect with the deep semantic codes of a culture and take on additional, more active ideological dimensions. We might take an example from advertising discourse. Here, too, there is no 'purely denotative', and certainly no 'natural', representation. Every visual sign in advertising connotes a quality, situation, value or inference, which is present as an implication or implied meaning, depending on the connotational positioning. In Barthes's example, the sweater always signifies a 'warm garment' (denotation) and thus the activity/value of 'keeping warm'. But it is also possible, at its more connotative levels, to signify 'the coming of winter' or 'a cold day'. And, in the specialized sub-codes of fashion, sweater may also connote a fashionable style of *haute couture* or, alternatively, an informal style of dress. But set against the right visual background and positioned by the romantic sub-code, it may connote 'long autumn walk in the woods'.[6] Codes of this order clearly contract relations for the sign with the wider universe of ideologies in a society. These codes are the means by which power and ideology are made to signify in particular discourses. They refer signs to the 'maps of meaning' into which any culture is classified; and those 'maps of social reality' have the whole range of social meanings, practices, and usages, power and interest 'written in' to them. The connotative levels of signifiers, Barthes remarked, 'have a close communication with culture, knowledge, history, and it is through them, so to speak, that the environmental world invades the linguistic and semantic system. They are, if you like, the fragments of ideology'.[7]

The so-called denotative *level* of the televisual sign is fixed by certain, very complex (but limited or 'closed') codes. But its connotative *level*, though also bounded, is more open, subject to more active *transformations*, which exploit its polysemic values. Any such already constituted sign is potentially transformable into more than one connotative configuration. Polysemy must not, however, be confused with pluralism. Connotative codes are *not* equal among themselves. Any society/culture tends, with varying degrees of closure, to impose its classifications of the social and cultural and political world. These constitute a *dominant cultural order*, though it is neither univocal nor uncontested. This question of the 'structure of discourses in dominance' is a crucial point. The different areas of social life appear to be mapped out into discursive domains, hierarchically organized into *dominant or preferred meanings*. New, problematic or troubling events, which breach our expectancies and run counter to our 'common-sense constructs', to our 'taken-for-granted' knowledge of social structures, must be assigned to their discursive domains before they can be said to 'make sense'. The most common way of 'mapping' them is to assign the new to some domain or other of the existing 'maps of problematic social reality'. We say *dominant*, not 'determined', because it is always possible to order, classify, assign and decode an event within more than one 'mapping'. But we say 'dominant' because there exists a pattern of 'preferred readings'; and these both have the institutional/political/ideological order imprinted in them and have themselves become institutionalized.[8] The domains of 'preferred meanings' have the whole social order embedded in them as a set of meanings, practices and beliefs: the everyday knowledge of social structures, of 'how things work for all practical purposes in this culture', the rank order of power and interest and the structure of legitimations, limits and sanctions. Thus to clarify a 'misunderstanding' at the connotative level, we must refer, *through* the codes, to the orders of social life, of economic and political power and of ideology. Further, since these mappings are 'structured in dominance' but not closed, the communicative process consists not in the unproblematic assignment of every visual item to its given position within a set of prearranged codes, but of *performative rules* – rules of competence and use, of logics-in-use – which seek actively to *enforce* or *pre-fer* one semantic domain over another and rule items into and out of their appropriate meaning-sets. Formal semiology has too often neglected this practice of *interpretative work*, though this constitutes, in fact, the real relations of broadcast practices in television.

In speaking of *dominant meanings*, then, we are not talking about a one-sided process which governs how all events will be signified. It consists of the 'work' required to enforce, win plausibility for and command as legitimate a *decoding* of the event within the limit of dominant definitions in which it has been connotatively signified. Terni has remarked:

> By the word *reading* we mean not only the capacity to identify and
> decode a certain number of signs, but also the subjective capacity to put
> them into a creative relation between themselves and with other signs:
> a capacity which is, by itself, the condition for a complete awareness of
> one's total environment.[9]

Our quarrel here is with the notion of 'subjective capacity', as if the referent of
a televisional discourse were an objective fact but the interpretative level were
an individualized and private matter. Quite the opposite seems to be the case.
The televisual practice takes 'objective' (that is, systemic) responsibility precisely for the relations which disparate signs contract with one another in any
discursive instance, and thus continually rearranges, delimits and prescribes
into what 'awareness of one's total environment' these items are arranged.

This brings us to the question of misunderstandings. Television producers who find their message 'failing to get across' are frequently concerned
to straighten out the kinks in the communication chain, thus facilitating
the 'effectiveness' of their communication. Much research which claims the
objectivity of 'policy-oriented analysis' reproduces this administrative goal
by attempting to discover how much of a message the audience recalls and to
improve the extent of understanding. No doubt misunderstandings of a literal
kind do exist. The viewer does not know the terms employed, cannot follow
the complex logic of argument or exposition, is unfamiliar with the language,
finds the concepts too alien or difficult or is foxed by the expository narrative.
But more often broadcasters are concerned that the audience has failed to take
the meaning as they – the broadcasters – intended. What they really mean to
say is that viewers are not operating within the 'dominant' or 'preferred' code.
Their ideal is 'perfectly transparent communication'. Instead, what they have
to confront is 'systematically distorted communication'.[10]

In recent years discrepancies of this kind have usually been explained
by reference to 'selective perception'. This is the door via which a residual
pluralism evades the compulsions of a highly structured, asymmetrical and
non-equivalent process. Of course, there will always be private, individual,
variant readings. But 'selective perception' is almost never as selective, random
or privatized as the concept suggests. The patterns exhibit, across individual
variants, significant clusterings. Any new approach to audience studies will
therefore have to begin with a critique of 'selective perception' theory.

It was argued earlier that since there is no necessary correspondence
between encoding and decoding, the former can attempt to 'pre-fer' but
cannot prescribe or guarantee the latter, which has its own conditions of
existence. Unless they are wildly aberrant, encoding will have the effect of
constructing some of the limits and parameters within which decodings will
operate. If there were no limits, audiences could simply read whatever they
liked into any message. No doubt some total misunderstandings of this kind
do exist. But the vast range must contain *some* degree of reciprocity between

encoding and decoding moments, otherwise we could not speak of an effective communicative exchange at all. Nevertheless, this 'correspondence' is not given but constructed. It is not 'natural' but the product of an articulation between two distinct moments. And the former cannot determine or guarantee, in a simple sense, which decoding codes will be employed. Otherwise communication would be a perfectly equivalent circuit, and every message would be an instance of 'perfectly transparent communication'. We must think, then, of the variant articulations in which encoding/decoding can be combined. To elaborate on this, we offer a hypothetical analysis of some possible decoding positions, in order to reinforce the point of 'no necessary correspondence'.[11]

We identify *three* hypothetical positions from which decodings of a televisual discourse may be constructed. These need to be empirically tested and refined. But the argument that decodings do not follow inevitably from encodings, that they are not identical, reinforces the argument of 'no necessary correspondence'. It also helps to deconstruct the commonsense meaning of 'misunderstanding' in terms of a theory of 'systematically distorted communication'.

The first hypothetical position is that of the *dominant-hegemonic position*. When the viewer takes the connoted meaning from, say, a television newscast or current affairs programme full and straight, and decodes the message in terms of the reference code in which it has been encoded, we might say that the viewer *is operating inside the dominant code*. This is the ideal-typical case of 'perfectly transparent communication' – or as close as we are likely to come to it 'for all practical purposes'. Within this we can distinguish the positions produced by the *professional code*. This is the position (produced by what we perhaps ought to identify as the operation of a 'metacode') which the professional broadcasters assume when encoding a message which has *already* been signified in a hegemonic manner. The professional code is 'relatively independent' of the dominant code, in that it applies criteria and transformational operations of its own, especially those of a technico-practical nature. The professional code, however, operates *within* the 'hegemony' of the dominant code. Indeed, it serves to reproduce the dominant definitions precisely by bracketing their hegemonic quality and operating instead with displaced professional codings which foreground such apparently neutral-technical questions as visual quality, news and presentational values, televisual quality, 'professionalism' and so on. The hegemonic interpretations of, say, the politics of Northern Ireland, or the Chilean *coup* or the Industrial Relations Bill are principally generated by political and military elites: the particular choice of presentational occasions and formats, the selection of personnel, the choice of images, the staging of debates are selected and combined through the operation of the professional code. How the broadcasting professionals are able *both* to operate with 'relatively autonomous' codes of their own *and* to act in such a way as to reproduce (not without contradiction) the hegemonic signification of events is a complex matter which cannot be further spelled out here.

It must suffice to say that the professionals are linked with the defining elites not only by the institutional position of broadcasting itself as an 'ideological apparatus',[12] but also by the structure of *access* (that is, the systematic 'over-accessing' of selective elite personnel and their 'definition of the situation' in television). It may even be said that the professional codes serve to reproduce hegemonic definitions specifically by *not overtly* biasing their operations in a dominant direction: ideological reproduction therefore takes place here inadvertently, unconsciously, 'behind men's backs'.[13] Of course, conflicts, contradictions and even misunderstandings regularly arise between the dominant and the professional significations and their signifying agencies.

The second position we would identify is that of the *negotiated code* or position. Majority audiences probably understand quite adequately what has been dominantly defined and professionally signified. The dominant definitions, however, are hegemonic precisely because they represent definitions of situations and events which are 'in dominance' (*global*). Dominant definitions connect events, implicitly or explicitly, to grand totalizations, to the great syntagmatic views-of-the-world: they take 'large views' of issues: they relate events to the 'national interest' or to the level of geo-politics, even if they make these connections in truncated, inverted or mystified ways. The definition of a hegemonic viewpoint is (a) that it defines within its terms the mental horizon, the universe, of possible meanings, of a whole sector of relations in a society or culture; and (b) that it carries with it the stamp of legitimacy – it appears coterminous with what is 'natural', 'inevitable', 'taken for granted' about the social order. Decoding within the *negotiated version* contains a mixture of adaptive and oppositional elements: it acknowledges the legitimacy of the hegemonic definitions to make the grand significations (abstract), while, at a more restricted, situational (situated) level, it makes its own ground rules – it operates with exceptions to the rule. It accords the privileged position to the dominant definitions of events while reserving the right to make a more negotiated application to 'local conditions', to its own more *corporate* positions. This negotiated version of the dominant ideology is thus shot through with contradictions, though these are only on certain occasions brought to full visibility. Negotiated codes operate through what we might call particular or situated logics: and these logics are sustained by their differential and unequal relation to the discourses and logics of power. The simplest example of a negotiated code is that which governs the response of a worker to the notion of an Industrial Relations Bill limiting the right to strike or to arguments for a wages freeze. At the level of the 'national interest' economic debate the decoder may adopt the hegemonic definition, agreeing that 'we must all pay ourselves less in order to combat inflation'. This, however, may have little or no relation to his/her willingness to go on strike for better pay and conditions or to oppose the Industrial Relations Bill at the level of shopfloor or union organization. We suspect that the great majority of so-called 'misunderstandings' arise from the contradictions and disjunctures between hegemonic–dominant encodings and negotiated–corporate decodings. It is just these mismatches in the levels which most provoke defining elites and professionals to identify a 'failure in communications'.

Finally, it is possible for a viewer perfectly to understand both the literal and the connotative inflection given by a discourse but to decode the message in a *globally* contrary way. He/she detotalizes the message in the preferred code in order to retotalize the message within some alternative framework of reference. This is the case of the viewer who listens to a debate on the need to limit wages but 'reads' every mention of the 'national interest' as 'class interest'. He/she is operating with what we must call an *oppositional code*. One of the most significant political moments (they also coincide with crisis points within the broadcasting organizations themselves, for obvious reasons) is the point when events which are normally signified and decoded in a negotiated way begin to be given an oppositional reading. Here the 'politics of signification' – the struggle in discourse – is joined.

NOTES

1. For an explication and commentary on the methodological implications of Marx's argument, see S. Hall, 'A reading of Marx's 1857 *Introduction to the Grundrisse*', in WPCS 6 (1974).
2. J. D. Halloran, 'Understanding television', Paper for the Council of Europe Colloquy on 'Understanding Television' (University of Leicester 1973).
3. G. Gerbner *et al.*, *Violence in TV Drama: A Study of Trends and Symbolic Functions* (The Annenberg School, University of Pennsylvania 1970).
4. Charles Peirce, *Speculative Grammar*, in *Collected Papers* (Cambridge, Mass.: Harvard University Press 1931–58).
5. Umberto Eco, 'Articulations of the cinematic code', in *Cinemantics*, no. 1.
6. Roland Barthes, 'Rhetoric of the image', in WPCS 1 (1971).
7. Roland Barthes, *Elements of Semiology* (Cape 1967).
8. For an extended critique of 'preferred reading', see Alan O'Shea, 'Preferred reading' (unpublished paper, CCCS, University of Birmingham).
9. P. Terni, 'Memorandum', Council of Europe Colloquy on 'Understanding Television' (University of Leicester 1973).
10. The phrase is Habermas's, in 'Systematically distorted communications', in P. Dretzel (ed.), *Recent Sociology* 2 (Collier-Macmillan 1970). It is used here, however, in a different way.
11. For a sociological formulation which is close, in some ways, to the positions outlined here but which does not parallel the argument about the theory of discourse, see Frank Parkin, *Class Inequality and Political Order* (Macgibbon and Kee 1971).
12. See Louis Althusser, 'Ideology and ideological state apparatuses', in *Lenin and Philosophy and Other Essays* (New Left Books 1971).
13. For an expansion of this argument, see Stuart Hall, 'The external/internal dialectic in broadcasting', *4th Symposium on Broadcasting* (University of Manchester 1972), and 'Broadcasting and the state: the independence/impartiality couplet', AMCR Symposium, University of Leicester 1976 (CCCS unpublished paper).

4

THE POWER OF THE IMAGE

Annette Kuhn

The twentieth century's second wave of Western feminism has distinguished itself from other social and political movements in several important respects. Its espousal of non-hierarchical approaches to organisation and action have lent themselves particularly well to issue-oriented politics – campaigns around abortion legislation and direct action on peace and disarmament, for example. The movement's insistence on bringing to centre stage areas of life hitherto considered secondary, even irrelevant, to 'serious' politics – the division of labour in the household, relations between men and women at home and in the workplace, emotions, sexuality, even the Unconscious – also sets it apart, giving ground to a conviction that the women's movement is opening up and beginning to explore a whole new country. In this process, new maps have had to be drawn, concepts constructed, systems of thought developed, in the effort to order the apparent chaos of a neglected other side of patriarchal culture. To take just one example of the effects of all this: trade union campaigns to combat sexual harassment at work would have been inconceivable before the middle or late 1970s, if only because the phenomenon simply did not have a name before that time. One can scarcely organise around a non-existent concept.

In other words, politics and knowledge are interdependent. In the ordinary way, the link between them will often go unnoticed or be taken for granted: where feminism is concerned, however, this is impossible, precisely because knowledge has had to be self-consciously produced alongside political activity. Each has regenerated the other. This is not to imply that the relationship

From A. Kuhn, *The Power of the Image* (London: Routledge & Kegan Paul, 1985.

is always a harmonious and uncontradictory one: mutual dependency always involves difficulty and struggle. Feminists may disagree, for example, on the extent to which producing knowledge is in itself a political activity. Are theory and practice in the final instance separate categories? Or is it acceptable to posit (to use a currently rather unfashionable term) a 'theoretical practice' of feminism?

Knowledge of the kind likely to be useful to the women's movement – knowledge, that is, which increases our understanding of women's lives and the institutions and structures of power which impinge on those lives in varying degrees and in different ways, structures which construct woman as 'other' in a patriarchal society – much of this knowledge is being produced under the banner of women's studies. The fact that women's studies has come to assume an existence in the Academy, apparently independent of the women's movement, may present some problems for the relationship between a body of knowledge and the movement which was its initial *raison d'être*. However, precisely because it so evidently eschews the 'neutrality' demanded by the Academy, the status of women's studies as a subject, researched and taught in universities, polytechnics and colleges, is marginal and precarious and its future uncertain: women's studies, therefore, needs the women's movement as much as *vice versa*. Women's studies also needs an institutional space to develop, and it needs, as well, the opportunity to draw on other areas of intellectual endeavour where these promise to be useful and relevant to its project. The saying that knowledge does not come from nowhere has more than one meaning.

[. . .]

From its beginnings, feminism has regarded ideas, language and images as crucial in shaping women's (and men's) lives. In the USA in 1968, feminists staged a demonstration against the Miss America contest, protesting the event on grounds that it promoted an impossible image of ideal womanhood, and was complicit in the widespread idea that all women – not only participants in beauty contests – are reducible to a set of bodily attributes. From this beginning there followed critiques of stereotypical representations of women in advertisements and in films, and studies of the ways in which language – both vocabulary and linguistic usage – defines and confines women. From the point of view of its politics, then, the women's movement has always been interested in images, meanings, representations – and especially in challenging representations which, while questionable or offensive from a feminist standpoint, are from other points of view – if they are noticed at all – perfectly acceptable.

This interest is in part responsible for the chapters in the present book [*The Power of the Image*]. I say responsible, because without the women's movement a desire to question representation in this way could not be articulated, nor would the public or even the private space to do so exist. I say in part, however, because since the early days feminist interest in images and representations has taken a variety of forms and directions. These have been determined largely by different ways in which representation has been thought about and analysed – that is, by the theories and methods brought to bear on the question. The question, I would argue, is a feminist one: the theories and methods not exclusively so. These come, at least to begin with, from elsewhere, and are appropriated and adapted to the feminist project. Knowledge does not come from nowhere, then: just as in this instance new knowledge is generated through the desire of feminist politics, so existing knowledge is both used and transformed in the service of this desire. The use and transformation of existing knowledge also partly motivates this book, then. It does not pretend to offer a comprehensive account of feminist thought on representation, however, but rather limits itself to an in-depth exploration of certain theoretical and methodological paths, hopefully opening up one or two new byways in the process. Which paths, though, and why?

The emergence of a new feminist movement in the late 1960s coincided with a renewed interest in marxist thought on 'the superstructure' – ideas, culture, ideology – and the place and effectivity of the superstructure within the social formation.[2] The different terms used here to describe the contents of the super-structure reflect a range of tendencies within marxist theory. Certain developments around the concept of ideology, for instance, were embodied in the work of the French philosopher Louis Althusser, work which – alongside that of other intellectuals, Roland Barthes and Claude Lévi-Strauss, for instance – was associated with structuralism. Barthes had written an introduction to semiotics – the study of signification, or meaning production, in society – and his book *Mythologies* comprised a series of short semiotically informed essays on specific images and representations, and on signification in general: which elements in images produce meaning, how the process operates, and so on.[3]

In the early 1970s, art historian John Berger made a series of programmes for BBC Television called *Ways of Seeing*. In these, Berger also considered how images make meaning, though in this instance without explicit recourse to semiotic concepts. Into this effectively semiotic project Berger injected a more orthodoxly marxist concern with the status of images as commodities – artifacts which are bought and sold, which have exchange value. One particularly influential programme dealt with the female nude, both in the European high art tradition and in mass-produced pinup photographs. Analysis dealt not only with the formal qualities of these images *per se*, but also with the relationship between images and their consumers – who as well as being spectators are often buyers/owners of images too.

Althusserian thought had a certain relevance to feminism because it contained a notion that human beings are constructed by ideology, that our ways of thinking about the world, of representing it to ourselves, become so 'naturalised' that we take our conception of that world for granted. If ideology effaces itself, the process by which this takes place could, for instance, explain (though Althusser did not in fact attempt to do so) the taken-for-granted nature of social constructs of femininity. Barthes's work on images suggested, moreover, that meanings are produced through the codes at work in representations, and that while meanings might appear to be natural, obvious, immanent, they are in fact produced: they are constructed through identifiable processes of signification at work in all representations. Finally, *Ways of Seeing* showed that meaning production takes place within social and historical contexts, and that in a capitalist society representations are no more exempt than any other products from considerations of the marketplace.

It is not difficult to see a potential for crossfertilisation between these ideas and feminist concerns with representation: indeed, the work I have described forms a backcloth to the chapters in this book [*The Power of the Image*]. It is really no more than a backcloth, though. Since the early 1970s, the study of images, particularly of cinematic images, as signifying systems has taken up and developed these 'prefeminist' concerns, bringing to the fore the issue of the spectator as subject addressed, positioned, even formed, by representations. To semiotic and structuralist approaches to representation has been added psychoanalysis, whose object is precisely the processes by which human subjectivity is formed.[4] In work on the image, the cinematic image particularly, an emphasis on subjectivity has foregrounded the question of spectatorship in new ways. This, too, informs the writing in this book.

But again, that is by no means the whole story: for feminist thought has long since entered the field of representation in its own right. These chapters may be read as inhabiting a tradition of feminist work on representation which draws strategically on the strands of non-feminist or prefeminist thinking I have described, if only because their objects (images, meanings, ideologies) and their objectives (analysis, deconstruction) have something in common with feminist concerns. At the same time, though, the very process of appropriation has exposed crucial weaknesses in these systems of thought – notably gender-blindness, formalism, and certain methodological shortcomings.[5] Not only, though, has the appropriation of pre-existing theory necessarily – fruitfully – produced criticisms of it: the particular concerns of feminism, when mapped onto that theory, have been instrumental in generating qualitatively new knowledge, in constructing a new field.

Inevitably, the[se] questions [. . .] traverse both feminist concerns and knowledge-in-process. What relation, for instance, does spectatorship have to representations of women? What sort of activity is looking? What does looking have to do with sexuality? With masculinity and femininity? With power? With knowledge? How do images, of women in particular, 'speak to' the spectator? Is the spectator addressed as male/female, masculine/feminine? Is femininity constructed in specific ways through representation? Why are images of women's bodies so prevalent in our society? Such questions may sometimes be answered by looking at and analysing actual images. But although such analysis must be regarded as necessary to an understanding of the relationship between representation and sexuality, it is not always sufficient. For, in practice, images are always seen in context: they always have a specific use value in the particular time and place of their consumption. This together with their formal characteristics, conditions and limits the meanings available from them at any one moment. But if representations always have use value, then more often than not they also have exchange value: they circulate as commodities in a social/economic system. This further conditions, or over-determines, the meanings available from representations.

Meanings do not reside in images, then: they are circulated between representation, spectator and social formation. All of the chapters in this book [*The Power of the Image*] are concerned in one way or another with images – with films as well as still photographs of various kinds. Each chapter places a slightly different emphasis on each of the terms defining the representation– spectator– social formation triangle: though, given the central place accorded the instance of looking, the spectator undoubtedly sits at the apex. Nevertheless, each chapter marks a move further away from the model of the image/text as an isolated object of analysis, and closer to a conception of the image as inhabiting various contexts: cultural contexts of spectatorship, institutional and social/ historical contexts of production and consumption. At the same time, conceptualising texts as embedded within a series of contextual layers, and trying to do this without losing sight of texts as productive of meaning in their own right, does produce certain theoretical and methodological difficulties.

[. . .]

All of the texts/images discussed [. . .] may, in a broad sense, be regarded as 'culturally dominant'. Most of them – Hollywood films and softcore pornography, for example – are produced commercially for mass audiences. Where this is not the case they strive to slot into hegemonic 'high art' institutions. Hegemony is never without contradiction, however, which is one reason why analysing culturally dominant representations can be very productive. Contextual overdetermination notwithstanding, meaning can never be finally guaranteed. In practice, the operations of texts and various levels of context are rarely in harmony, and there is always some space for 'aberrant' reception of dominant representations.

[. . .]

More generally, the very existence of a book like this one is testimony t the fact that readings 'against the grain' are not only available, but often compelling. The activity of deconstruction sets loose an array of 'unintended' meanings, by their nature subversive of the apparently transparent meanings which texts offer us.

But why spend time and effort analysing images of a kind often considered questionable, even objectionable, by feminists? Why not try instead to create alternatives to culturally dominant representations? As I have argued, politics and knowledge are interdependent: the women's movement is not, I believe, faced here with a choice between two mutually exclusive alternatives, though individual feminists – if only because one person's life is too short to encompass everything – often experience their own politics in such a way. Theory and practice inform one another. At one level, analysing and deconstructing dominant representations may be regarded as a strategic practice. It produces understanding, and understanding is necessary to action.

It may also be considered an act of resistance in itself. Politics is often thought of as one of life's more serious undertakings, allowing little room for pleasure. At the same time, feminists may feel secretly guilty about their enjoyment of images they are convinced ought to be rejected as politically unsound. In analysing such images, though, it is possible, indeed necessary, to acknowledge their pleasurable qualities, precisely because pleasure is an area of analysis in its own right. 'Naive' pleasure, then, becomes admissible. And the acts of analysis, of deconstruction and of reading 'against the grain' offer an additional pleasure – the pleasure of resistance, of saying 'no': not to 'unsophisticated' enjoyment, by ourselves and others, of culturally dominant images, but to the structures of power which ask us to consume them uncritically and in highly circumscribed ways.

NOTES

1. See, for example, Robin Blackburn (ed.), *Ideology in Social Science*, London, Fontana, 1972; Raymond Williams, 'Base and superstructure in marxist cultural theory', *New Left Review*, no. 32, 1973, pp. 3–16; Louis Althusser, 'Ideology and ideological state apparatuses', *Lenin and Philosophy and Other Essays*, London, New Left Books, 1971, pp. 121–73.
2. *Elements of Semiology*, London, Jonathan Cape, 1967; *Mythologies*, London, Paladin, 1973.
3. These developments are traced in Rosalind Coward and John Ellis, *Language and Materialism*, London, Routledge & Kegan Paul, 1978.
4. See, for example, Mary Ann Doane et al., 'Feminist film criticism: an introduction', *Re-Vision: Essays in Feminist Film Criticism*, Los Angeles, American Film Institute, 1984, pp. 1–17; Annette Kuhn, 'Women's genres', *Screen*, vol. 25, no. 1, 1984, pp. 18–28.

5

THE PUBLIC SPHERE

Jürgen Habermas

CONCEPT

By 'public sphere' we mean first of all a domain of our social life in which such a thing as public opinion can be formed. Access to the public sphere is open in principle to all citizens. A portion of the public sphere is constituted in every conversation in which private persons come together to form a public. They are then acting neither as business or professional people conducting their private affairs, nor as legal consociates subject to the legal regulations of a state bureaucracy and obligated to obedience. Citizens act as a public when they deal with matters of general interest without being subject to coercion; thus with the guarantee that they may assemble and unite freely, and express and publicize their opinions freely. When the public is large, this kind of communication requires certain means of dissemination and influence; today, newspapers and periodicals, radio and television are the media of the public sphere. We speak of a political public sphere (as distinguished from a literary one, for instance) when the public discussions concern objects connected with the practice of the state. The coercive power of the state is the counterpart, as it were, of the political public sphere, but it is not a part of it. State power is, to be sure, considered 'public' power, but it owes the attribute of publicness to its task of caring for the public, that is, providing for the common good of all legal consociates. Only when the exercise of public authority has actually

From S. Seidman (ed.), *Jürgen Habermas on Society and Politics: A Reader*, trans. S. W. Nicholson (Boston: Beacon Press, 1989); originally published as 'Offentlichkeit', in J. Habermas, *Kultur und Kritik* (Frankfurt am Main: Suhrkamp Verlag, 1973).

been subordinated to the requirement of democratic publicness does the political public sphere acquire an institutionalized influence on the government, by the way of the legislative body. The term 'public opinion' refers to the functions of criticism and control of organized state authority that the public exercises informally, as well as formally during periodic elections. Regulations concerning the publicness (or publicity [*Publizität*] in its original meaning) of state-related activities, as, for instance, the public accessibility required of legal proceedings, are also connected with this function of public opinion. To the public sphere as a sphere mediating between state and society, a sphere in which the public as the vehicle of public opinion is formed, there corresponds the principle of publicness – the publicness that once had to win out against the secret politics of monarchs and that since then has permitted democratic control of state activity.

It is no accident that these concepts of the public sphere and public opinion were not formed until the eighteenth century. They derive their specific meaning from a concrete historical situation. It was then that one learned to distinguish between opinion and public opinion, or *opinion publique*. Whereas mere opinions (things taken for granted as part of a culture, normative convictions, collective prejudices and judgements) seem to persist unchanged in their quasi-natural structure as a kind of sediment of history, public opinion, in terms of its very idea, can be formed only if a public that engages in rational discussion exists. Public discussions that are institutionally protected and that take, with critical intent, the exercise of political authority as their theme have not existed since time immemorial – they developed only in a specific phase of bourgeois society, and only by virtue of a specific constellation of interests could they be incorporated into the order of the bourgeois constitutional state.

HISTORY

It is not possible to demonstrate the existence of a public sphere in its own right, separate from the private sphere, in the European society of the High Middle Ages. At the same time, however, it is not a coincidence that the attributes of authority at that time were called 'public'. For a public representation of authority existed at that time. At all levels of the pyramid established by feudal law, the status of the feudal lord is neutral with respect to the categories 'public' and 'private'; but the person possessing that status represents it publicly; he displays himself, represents himself as the embodiment of a 'higher' power, in whatever degree. This concept of representation has survived into recent constitutional history. Even today the power of political authority on its highest level, however much it has become detached from its former basis, requires representation through the head of state. But such elements derive from a pre-bourgeois social structure. Representation in the sense of the bourgeois public sphere, as in 'representing' the nation or specific clients, has nothing to do with *representative publicness*, which inheres in the concrete existence of a lord. As long as the prince and the estates of his realm 'are' the land, rather than merely 'representing' it, they are capable of this kind of representation; they represent their authority 'before' the people rather than for the people.

The feudal powers (the church, the prince, and the nobility) to which this representative publicness adheres disintegrated in the course of a long process of polarization; by the end of the eighteenth century they had decomposed into private elements on the one side and public on the other. The position of the church changed in connection with the Reformation; the tie to divine authority that the church represented, that is, religion, became a private matter. Historically, what is called the freedom of religion safeguarded the first domain of private autonomy; the church itself continued its existence as one corporate body under public law among others. The corresponding polarization of princely power acquired visible form in the separation of the public budget from the private household property of the feudal lord. In the bureaucracy and the military (and in part also in the administration of justice), institutions of public power became autonomous vis-à-vis the privatized sphere of the princely court. In terms of the estates, finally, elements from the ruling groups developed into organs of public power, into parliament (and in part also into judicial organs); elements from the occupational status groups, insofar as they had become established in urban corporations and in certain differentiations within the estates of the land, developed into the sphere of bourgeois society, which would confront the state as a genuine domain of private autonomy.

Representative publicness gave way to the new sphere of 'public power' that came into being with the national and territorial states. Ongoing state activity (permanent administration, a standing army) had its counterpart in the permanence of relationships that had developed in the meantime with the stock market and the press, through traffic in goods and news. Public power became consolidated as something tangible confronting those who were subject to it and who at first found themselves only negatively defined by it. These are the 'private persons' who are excluded from public power because they hold no office. 'Public' no longer refers to the representative court of a person vested with authority; instead, it now refers to the competence-regulated activity of an apparatus furnished with a monopoly on the legitimate use of force. As those to whom this public power is addressed, private persons subsumed under the state form the public.

As a private domain, society, which has come to confront the state, as it were, is on the one hand clearly differentiated from public power; on the other hand, society becomes a matter of public interest insofar as with the rise of a market economy the reproduction of life extends beyond the confines of private domestic power. The *bourgeois public sphere* can be understood as the sphere of private persons assembled to form a public. They soon began to make use of the public sphere of informational newspapers, which was officially regulated, against the public power itself, using those papers, along with the morally and

critically oriented weeklies, to engage in debate about the general rules governing relations in their own essentially privatized but publicly relevant sphere of
commodity exchange and labor.

THE LIBERAL MODEL OF THE PUBLIC SPHERE

The medium in which this debate takes place – public discussion – is unique
and without historical prototype. Previously the estates had negotiated contracts with their princes in which claims to power were defined on a case-
by-case basis. As we know, this development followed a different course in
England, where princely power was relativized through parliament, than on
the Continent, where the estates were mediatized by the monarch. The 'third
estate' then broke with this mode of equalizing power, for it could no longer
establish itself as a ruling estate. Given a commercial economy, a division of
authority accomplished through differentiation of the rights of those possessing feudal authority (liberties belonging to the estates) was no longer possible
– the power under private law of disposition of capitalist property is non-
political. The bourgeois are private persons; as such, they do not 'rule.' Thus
their claims to power in opposition to public power are directed not against a
concentration of authority that should be 'divided' but rather against the principle of established authority. The principle of control, namely publicness, that
the bourgeois public opposes to the principle of established authority aims at
a transformation of authority as such, not merely the exchange of one basis of
legitimation for another.

In the first modern constitutions the sections listing basic rights provide an
image of the liberal model of the public sphere: they guarantee society as a
sphere of private autonomy; opposite it stands a public power limited to a few
functions; between the two spheres, as it were, stands the domain of private
persons who have come together to form a public and who, as citizens of the
state, mediate the state with the needs of bourgeois society, in order, as the idea
goes, to thus convert political authority to 'rational' authority in the medium
of this public sphere. Under the presuppositions of a society based on the free
exchange of commodities, it seemed that the general interest, which served as
the criterion by which this kind of rationality was to be evaluated, would be
assured if the dealings of private persons in the marketplace were emancipated
from social forces and their dealings in the public sphere were emancipated
from political coercion.

The political daily press came to have an important role during this same
period. In the second half of the eighteenth century, serious competition to
the older form of news writing as the compiling of items of information arose
in the form of literary journalism. Karl Bücher describes the main outlines of
this development: 'From mere institutions for the publication of news, newspapers became the vehicles and guides of public opinion as well, weapons of
party politics. The consequence of this for the internal organization of the

newspaper enterprise was the insertion of a new function between the gathering of news and its publication: the editorial function. For the newspaper publisher, however, the significance of this development was that from a seller of new information he became a dealer in public opinion.' Publishers provided the commercial basis for the newspaper without, however, commercializing it as such. The press remained an institution of the public itself, operating to provide and intensify public discussion, no longer a mere organ for the conveyance of information, but not yet a medium of consumer culture.

This type of press can be observed especially in revolutionary periods, when papers associated with the tiniest political coalitions and groups spring up, as in Paris in 1789. In the Paris of 1848 every halfway prominent politician still formed his own club, and every other one founded his own *journal*: over 450 clubs and more than 200 papers came into being there between February and May alone. Until the permanent legalization of a public sphere that functioned politically, the appearance of a political newspaper was equivalent to engagement in the struggle for a zone of freedom for public opinion, for publicness as a principle. Not until the establishment of the bourgeois constitutional state was a press engaged in the public use of reason relieved of the pressure of ideological viewpoints. Since then it has been able to abandon its polemical stance and take advantage of the earning potential of commercial activity. The ground was cleared for this development from a press of viewpoints to a commercial press at about the same time in England, France, and the United States, during the 1830s. In the course of this transformation from the journalism of writers who were private persons to the consumer services of the mass media, the sphere of publicness was changed by an influx of private interests that achieved privileged representation within it.

THE PUBLIC SPHERE IN MASS WELFARE-STATE DEMOCRACIES

The liberal model of the public sphere remains instructive in regard to the normative claim embodied in institutionalized requirements of publicness; but it is not applicable to actual relationships within a mass democracy that is industrially advanced and constituted as a social-welfare state. In part, the liberal model had always contained ideological aspects; in part, the social presuppositions to which those aspects were linked have undergone fundamental changes. Even the forms in which the public sphere was manifested, forms which made its idea seem to a certain extent obvious, began to change with the Chartist movement in England and the February Revolution in France. With the spread of the press and propaganda, the public expanded beyond the confines of the bourgeoisie. Along with its social exclusivity the public lost the cohesion given it by institutions of convivial social intercourse and by a relatively high standard of education. Accordingly, conflicts which in the past were pushed off into the private sphere now enter the public sphere.

Group needs, which cannot expect satisfaction from a self-regulating market, tend toward state regulation. The public sphere, which must now mediate these demands, becomes a field for competition among interests in the cruder form of forcible confrontation. Laws that have obviously originated under the 'pressure of the streets' can scarcely continue to be understood in terms of a consensus achieved by private persons in public discussion; they correspond, in more or less undisguised form, to compromises between conflicting private interests. Today it is social organizations that act in relation to the state in the political public sphere, whether through the mediation of political parties or directly, in interplay with public administration. With the interlocking of the public and private domains, not only do political agencies take over certain functions in the sphere of commodity exchange and social labor; societal powers also take over political functions. This leads to a kind of 'refeudalization' of the public sphere. Large-scale organizations strive for political compromises with the state and with one another, behind closed doors if possible; but at the same time they have to secure at least plebiscitarian approval from the mass of the population through the deployment of a staged form of publicity.

The political public sphere in the welfare state is characterized by a singular weakening of its critical functions. Whereas at one time publicness was intended to subject persons or things to the public use of reason and to make political decisions susceptible to revision before the tribunal of public opinion, today it has often enough already been enlisted in the aid of the secret policies of interest groups; in the form of 'publicity' it now acquires public prestige for persons or things and renders them capable of acclamation in a climate of nonpublic opinion. The term 'public relations' itself indicates how a public sphere that formerly emerged from the structure of society must now be produced circumstantially on a case-by-case basis. The central relationship of the public, political parties, and parliament is also affected by this change in function.

This existing trend toward the weakening of the public sphere, as a principle, is opposed, however, by a welfare state transformation of the functioning of basic rights: the requirement of publicness is extended by state organs to all organizations acting in relation to the state. To the extent to which this becomes a reality, a no longer intact public of private persons acting as individuals would be replaced by a public of organized private persons. Under current circumstances, only the latter could participate effectively in a process of public communication using the channels of intra-party and intra-organizational public spheres, on the basis of a publicness enforced for the dealings of organizations with the state. It is in this process of public communication that the formation of political compromises would have to achieve legitimation. The idea of the public sphere itself, which signified a rationalization of authority in the medium of public discussions among private persons, and which has been preserved in mass welfare-state democracy, threatens to disintegrate with the structural transformation of the public sphere. Today it could be realized only on a different basis, as a rationalization of the exercise of social and political power under the mutual control of rival organizations committed to publicness in their internal structure as well as in their dealings with the state and with one another.

6

THE MASSES: THE IMPLOSION OF THE SOCIAL IN THE MEDIA

Jean Baudrillard

Up to now there have been two great versions of the analysis of the media (as indeed that of the masses), one optimistic and one pessimistic. The optimistic one has assumed two major tonalities, very different from one another. There is the technological optimism of Marshall McLuhan: for him the electronic media inaugurate a generalized planetary communication and should conduct us, by the mental effect alone of new technologies, beyond the atomizing rationality of the Gutenberg galaxy to the global village, to the new electronic tribalism – an achieved transparency of information and communication. The other version, more traditional, is that of dialectical optimism inspired by pro-gressivist and Marxist thought: the media constitute a new, gigantic produc-tive force and obey the dialectic of productive forces. Momentarily alienated and submitted to the law of capitalism, their intensive development can only eventually explode this monopoly. 'For the first time in history,' writes Hans Enzensberger, 'the media make possible a mass participation in a productive process at once social and socialized, a participation whose practical means are in the hands of the masses themselves.'[1] These two positions more or less, the one technological, the other ideological, inspire the whole analysis and the present practice of the media.[2]

It is more particularly to the optimism of Enzensberger that I formerly opposed a resolutely pessimist vision in 'Requiem for the Media.' In that I described the mass media as a 'speech without response.' What characterizes

A lecture delivered at the University of Melbourne; trans. Marie MacLean, *New Literary History*, 16:3 (Spring 1985) pp. 577–89; reprinted as Ch. 9 in Jean Baudrillard, *Selected Writings*, ed. Mark Poster (Cambridge: Polity Press, 1988) pp. 207–19.

the mass media is that they are opposed to mediation, intransitive, that they fabricate noncommunication – if one accepts the definition of communication as an exchange, as the reciprocal space of speech and response, and thus of *responsibility*. In other words, if one defines it as anything other than the simple emission/reception of information. Now the whole present architecture of the media is founded on this last definition: they are what finally forbids response, what renders impossible any process of exchange (except in the shape of a simulation of a response which is itself integrated into the process of emission, and this changes nothing in the unilaterality of communication). That is their true abstraction. And it is in this abstraction that is founded the system of social control and power. To understand properly the term *response*, one must appreciate it in a meaning at once strong, symbolic, and primitive: power belongs to him who gives and to whom no return can be made. To give, and to do it in such a way that no return can be made, is to break exchange to one's own profit and to institute a monopoly: the social process is out of balance. To make a return, on the contrary, is to break this power relationship and to restore on the basis of an antagonistic reciprocity the circuit of symbolic exchange. The same applies in the sphere of the media: there speech occurs in such a way that there is no possibility of a return. The restitution of this possibility of response entails upsetting the whole present structure; even better (as started to occur in 1968 and the '70s), it entails an 'antimedia' struggle.

In reality, even if I did not share the technological optimism of McLuhan, I always recognized and considered as a gain the true revolution which he brought about in media analysis (this has been mostly ignored in France). On the other hand, though I also did not share the dialectical hopes of Enzensberger, I was not truly pessimistic, since I believed in a possible subversion of the code of the media and in the possibility of an alternate speech and a radical reciprocity of symbolic exchange.

Today all that has changed. I would no longer interpret in the same way the forced silence of the masses in the mass media. I would no longer see in it a sign of passivity and of alienation, but to the contrary an original strategy, an original response in the form of a challenge; and on the basis of this reversal I suggest to you a vision of things which is no longer optimistic or pessimistic, but ironic and antagonistic.

I will take the example of opinion polls, which are themselves a mass medium. It is said that opinion polls constitute a manipulation of democracy. This is certainly no more the case than that publicity is a manipulation of need and of consumption. It too produces demand (or so it claims) and invokes needs just as opinion polls produce answers and induce future behavior. All this would be serious if there were an objective truth of needs, an objective truth of public opinion. It is obvious that here we need to exercise extreme care. The influence of publicity, of opinion polls, of all the media, and of information in general would be dramatic if we were certain that there exists in opposition to it an authentic human nature, an authentic essence of the social, with its needs, its own will, its own values, its finalities. For this would set up the problem of its radical alienation. And indeed it is in this form that traditional critiques are expressed.

Now the matter is at once less serious and more serious than this. The uncertainty which surrounds the social and political effect of opinion polls (do they or do they not manipulate opinion?), like that which surrounds the real economic efficacy of publicity, will never be completely relieved – and it is just as well! This results from the fact that there is a compound, a mixture of two heterogeneous systems whose data cannot be transferred from one to the other. An operational system which is statistical, information-based, and simulational is projected onto a traditional values system, onto a system of representation, will, and opinion. This collage, this collusion between the two, gives rise to an indefinite and useless polemic. We should agree neither with those who praise the beneficial use of the media, nor with those who scream about manipulation, for the simple reason that there is no relationship between a system of meaning and a system of simulation. Publicity and opinion polls would be incapable, even if they wished and claimed to do so, of alienating the will or the opinion of anybody at all, for the reason that they do not act in the time–space of will and of representation where judgement is formed. For the same reason, though reversed, it is quite impossible for them to throw any light at all on public opinion or individual will, since they do not act in a public space, on the stage of a public space. They are strangers to it, and indeed they wish to dismantle it. Publicity and opinion polls and the media in general can only be imagined; they only exist on the basis of a disappearance, the disappearance from the public space, from the scene of politics, of public opinion in a form at once theatrical and representative as it was enacted in earlier epochs. Thus we can be reassured: they cannot destroy it. But we should not have any illusions: they cannot restore it either.

It is this lack of relationship between the two systems which today plunges us into a state of stupor. That is what I said: stupor. To be more objective one would have to say: a radical uncertainty as to our own desire, our own choice, our own opinion, our own will. This is the clearest result of the whole media environment, of the information which makes demands on us from all sides and which is as good as blackmail.

We will never know if an advertisement or opinion poll has had a real influence on individual or collective wills, but we will never know either what would have happened if there had been no opinion poll or advertisement.

The situation no longer permits us to isolate reality or human nature as a fundamental variable. The result is therefore not to provide any additional information or to shed any light on reality, but on the contrary, because we will never in future be able to separate reality from its statistical, simulative projection in the media, a state of suspense and of definitive uncertainty about reality. And I repeat: it is a question here of a completely new species of uncertainty, which results not from the *lack* of information but from information itself and even from an *excess* of information. It is information itself which produces uncertainty, and so this uncertainty, unlike the traditional uncertainty which could always be resolved, is irreparable.

This is our destiny: subject to opinion polls, information, publicity, statistics; constantly confronted with the anticipated statistical verification of our behavior, and absorbed by this permanent refraction of our least movements, we are no longer confronted with our own will. We are no longer even alienated, because for that it is necessary for the subject to be divided in itself, confronted with the other, to be contradictory. Now, where there is no other, the scene of the other, like that of politics and of society, has disappeared. Each individual is forced despite himself or herself in. he undivided coherency of statistics. There is in this a positive absorption into the transparency of computers, which is something worse than alienation.

There is an obscenity in the functioning and the omnipresence of opinion polls as in that of publicity. Not because they might betray the secret of an opinion, the intimacy of a will, or because they might violate some unwritten law of the private being, but because they exhibit this redundancy of the social, this sort of continual voyeurism of the group in relation to itself: it must at all times know what it wants, know what it thinks, be told about its least needs, its least quivers, *see* itself continually on the videoscreen of statistics, constantly watch its own temperature chart, in a sort of hypochondriacal madness. The social becomes obsessed with itself; through this auto-information, this permanent autointoxication, it becomes its own vice, its own perversion. This is the real obscenity. Through this feedback, this incessant anticipated accounting, the social loses its own scene. It no longer enacts itself; it has no more time to enact itself; it no longer occupies a particular space, public or political; it becomes confused with its own control screen. Overinformed, it develops ingrowing obesity. For everything which loses its *scene* (like the obese body) becomes for that very reason *ob-scene*.

The silence of the masses is also in a sense obscene. For the masses are also made of this useless hyperinformation which claims to enlighten them, when all it does is clutter up the space of the representable and annul itself in a silent equivalence. And we cannot do much against this obscene circularity of the masses and of information. The two phenomena fit one another: the masses have no opinion and information does not inform them. Both of them, lacking a scene where the meaning of the social can be enacted, continue to feed one another monstrously – as the speed with which information revolves increases continually the weight of the masses as such, and not their self-awareness.

So if one takes opinion polls, and the uncertainty which they induce about the principle of social reality, and the type of obscenity, of statistical pornography to which they attract us – if we take all that seriously, if we confront all that with the claimed finalities of information and of the social itself, then it all seems very dramatic. But there is another way of taking things. It does not shed much more credit on opinion polls, but it restores a sort of status to them, in terms of derision and of play. In effect we can consider the indecisiveness of their results, the uncertainty of their effects, and their unconscious humor, which is rather similar to that of meteorology (for example, the possibility of verifying at the same time contradictory facts or tendencies); or again the casual way in which everybody uses them, disagreeing with them privately and especially if they verify exactly one's own behavior (no one accepts a perfect statistical evaluation of his chances). That is the real problem of the credibility accorded to them.

Statistics, as an objective computation of probabilities, obviously eliminate any elective chance and any personal destiny. That is why, deep down, none of us believes in them, any more than the gambler believes in chance, but only in Luck (with a capital, the equivalent of Grace, not with lower case, which is the equivalent of probability). An amusing example of this obstinate denial of statistical chance is given by this news item: 'If this will reassure you, we have calculated that, of every 50 people who catch the metro twice a day for 60 years, only one is in danger of being attacked. Now there is no reason why it should be *you*!' The beauty of statistics is never in their objectivity but in their involuntary humor.

So if one takes opinion polls in this way, one can conceive that they could work for the masses themselves as a game, as a spectacle, as a means of deriding both the social and the political. The fact that opinion polls do their best to destroy the political as will and representation, the political as meaning, precisely through the effect of simulation and uncertainty – this fact can only give pleasure to the ironic unconscious of the masses (and to our individual political unconscious, if I may use this expression), whose deepest drive remains the symbolic murder of the political class, the symbolic murder of political *reality*, and this murder is produced by opinion polls in their own way. That is why I wrote in *Silent Majorities* that the masses, which have always provided an alibi for political representation, take their revenge by allowing themselves the theatrical representation of the political scene.[3] The people have become *public*. They even allow themselves the luxury of enjoying day by day, as in a home cinema, the fluctuations of their own opinion in the daily reading of the opinion polls.

It is only to this extent that they believe in them, that we all believe in them, as we believe in a game of malicious foretelling, a double or quits on the green baize of the political scene. It is, paradoxically, as a game that the opinion polls recover a sort of legitimacy. A game of the undecidable; a game of chance; a game of the undecidability of the political scene, of the equifinality of all tendencies; a game of truth effects in the circularity of questions and answers. Perhaps we can see here the apparition of one of these collective forms of game which Caillois called *aléa*[4] – an irruption into the polls themselves of a ludic, aleatory process, an ironic mirror for the use of the masses (and we all belong to the masses) of a political scene which is caught in its own trap (for the politicians are the only ones to believe in the polls, along with the pollsters obviously, as the only ones to believe in publicity are the publicity agents).

In this regard, one may restore to them a sort of positive meaning: they would be part of a contemporary cultural mutation, part of the era of simulation.

In view of this type of consequence, we are forced to congratulate ourselves on the very failure of polls, and on the distortions which make them undecidable and chancy. Far from regretting this, we must consider that there is a sort of fate or evil genius (the evil genius of the social itself?) which throws this too beautiful machine out of gear and prevents it from achieving the objectives which it claims. We must also ask if these distortions, far from being the consequence of a bad angle of refraction of information onto an inert and opaque matter, are not rather the consequence of an offensive resistance of the social itself to its investigation, the shape taken by an occult duel between the pollsters and the object polled, between information and the people who receive it?

This is fundamental: people are always supposed to be willing partners in the game of truth, in the game of information. It is agreed that the object can always be persuaded of its truth; it is inconceivable that the object of the investigation, the object of the poll, should not adopt, generally speaking, the strategy of the subject of the analysis, of the pollster. There may certainly be some difficulties (for instance, the object does not understand the question; it's not its business; it's undecided; it replies in terms of the interviewer and not of the question, and so on), but it is admitted that the poll analyst is capable of rectifying what is basically only a lack of adaptation to the analytic apparatus. The hypothesis is never suggested that all this, far from being a marginal, archaic residue, is the effect of an offensive (not defensive) counterstrategy by the object; that, all in all, there exists somewhere an original, positive, possibly victorious strategy of the object opposed to the strategy of the subject (in this case, the pollster or any other producer of messages).

This is what one could call the evil genius of the object, the evil genius of the masses, the evil genius of the social itself, constantly producing failure in the truth of the social and in its analysis, and for that reason unacceptable, and even unimaginable, to the tenants of this analysis.

To reflect the other's desire, to reflect its demand like a mirror, even to anticipate it: it is hard to imagine what powers of deception, of absorption, of deviation – in a word, of subtle revenge – there is in this type of response. This is the way the masses escape as reality, in this very mirror, in those simulative devices which are designed to capture them. Or again, the way in which events themselves disappear behind the television screen, or the more general screen of information (for it is true that events have no probable existence except on this deflective screen, which is no longer a mirror). While the mirror and screen of alienation was a mode of production (the imaginary subject), this new screen is simply its mode of disappearance. But disappearance is a very complex mode: the object, the individual, is not only condemned to disappearance, but *disappearance is also its strategy*; it is its way of response to this device for capture, for networking, and for forced identification. To this *cathodic* surface of recording, the individual or the mass reply by a *parodic* behavior of disappearance. What are they; what do they do; what do they become behind this screen? They turn themselves into an impenetrable and meaningless surface, which is a method of disappearing. They eclipse themselves; they melt into the superficial screen in such a way that their reality and that of their movement, just like that of particles of matter, may be radically questioned without making any fundamental change to the probabilistic analysis of their behavior. In fact, behind this 'objective' fortification of networks and models which believe they can capture them, and where the whole population of analysts and expert observers believe that they capture them, there passes a wave of derision, of reversal, and of parody which is the active exploitation, the parodic enactment by the object itself of its mode of disappearance.

There is and there always will be major difficulties in analyzing the media and the whole sphere of information through the traditional categories of the philosophy of the subject: will, representation, choice, liberty, deliberation, knowledge, and desire. For it is quite obvious that they are absolutely contradicted by the media; that the subject is absolutely alienated in its sovereignty. There is a distortion of principle between the sphere of information, and the moral law which still dominates us and whose decree is: you shall know yourself, you shall know what is your will and your desire. In this respect the media and even technics and science teach us nothing at all; they have rather restricted the limits of will and representation; they have muddled the cards and deprived any subject of the disposal of his or her own body, desire, choice, and liberty.

But this idea of alienation has probably never been anything but a philosopher's ideal perspective for the use of hypothetical masses. It has probably never expressed anything but the alienation of the philosopher himself; in other words, the one who *thinks himself or herself other*. On this subject Hegel is very clear in his judgement of the *Aufklärer*, of the *philosophe* of the Enlightenment, the one who denounces the 'empire of error' and despises it.

Reason wants to enlighten the superstitious mass by revealing trickery. It seeks to make it understand that it is *itself*, the mass, which enables the despot to live and not the despot which makes it live, as it believes when it obeys him. For the demystifier, credulous consciousness is mistaken *about itself*.

> The Enlightenment speaks as if juggling priests had, by sleight of hand, spirited away the being of consciousness for which they substituted something absolutely *foreign* and *other*; and, at the same time, the Enlightenment says that this foreign thing is a being of consciousness, which believes in consciousness, which trusts it, which seeks to please it.[5]

There is obviously a contradiction, says Hegel: one cannot confide oneself to an other than oneself and be mistaken about oneself, since when one confides in another, one demonstrates the certainty that one is safe with the other; in consequence, consciousness, which is said to be mystified, knows very well where it is safe and where it is not. Thus there is no need to correct a mistake which only exists in the *Aufklärer* himself. It is not *consciousness*, concludes Hegel, which takes itself for another, but it is the *Aufklärer* who takes himself for another, another than this common man whom he endeavors to make aware of his own stupidity. 'When the question is asked if it is allowable to deceive a people, one must reply that the question is worthless, because it is impossible to deceive a people about itself.'[6]

So it is enough to reverse the idea of a mass alienated by the media to evaluate how much the whole universe of the media, and perhaps the whole technical universe, is the result of a secret strategy of this mass which is claimed to be alienated, of *a secret form of the refusal of will*, of an in-voluntary challenge to everything which was demanded of the subject by philosophy – that is to say, to all rationality of choice and to all exercise of will, of knowledge, and of liberty.

In one way it would be no longer a question of revolution but of massive *devolution*, of a massive delegation of the power of desire, of choice, of responsibility, a delegation to apparatuses either political or intellectual, either technical or operational, to whom has devolved the duty of taking care of all of these things. A massive de-volition, a massive desisting from will, but not through alienation or voluntary servitude (whose mystery, which is the modern enigma of politics, is unchanged since La Boétie because the problem is put in terms of the consent of the subject to his own slavery, which fact no philosophy will ever be able to explain). We might argue that there exists another philosophy of lack of will, a sort of radical antimetaphysics whose secret is that the masses are deeply aware that they do not have to make a decision about themselves and the world; that they do not have to wish; that they do not have to know; that they do not have to desire.

The deepest desire is perhaps to give the responsibility for one's desire to someone else. A strategy of ironic investment in the other, in the others; a strategy toward others not of appropriation but, on the contrary, of expulsion, of philosophers and people in power, an expulsion of the obligation of being responsible, of enduring philosophical, moral, and political categories. Clerks are there for that, so are professionals, the representative holders of concept and desire. Publicity, information, technics, the whole intellectual and political class are there to tell us what we want, to tell the masses what they want – and basically we thoroughly enjoy this massive transfer of responsibility because perhaps, very simply, it is not easy to want what we want; because perhaps, very simply, it is not very interesting to know what we want to decide, to desire. Who has imposed all this on us, even the need to desire, unless it be the philosophers?

Choice is a strange imperative. Any philosophy which assigns man to the exercise of his will can only plunge him in despair. For if nothing is more flattering to consciousness than to know what it wants, on the contrary nothing is more seductive to the other consciousness (the unconscious?) – the obscure and vital one which makes happiness depend on the despair of will – than not to know what it wants, to be relieved of choice and diverted from its own objective will. It is much better to rely on some insignificant or powerful instance than to be dependent on one's own will or the necessity of choice. Beau Brummel had a servant for that purpose. Before a splendid landscape dotted with beautiful lakes, he turns toward his valet to ask him: 'Which lake do I prefer?'

Even publicity would find an advantage in discarding the weak hypothesis of personal will and desire. Not only do people certainly not want to be *told* what they wish, but they certainly do not want to *know* it, and it is not even sure that they want to *wish* at all. Faced with such inducements, it is their evil genius who tells them not to want anything and to rely finally on the apparatus of publicity or of information to 'persuade' them, to construct a choice for them (or to rely on the political class to order things) – just as Brummel did with his servant.

Whom does this trap close on? The mass knows that it knows nothing, and it does not want to know. The mass knows that it can do nothing, and it does not want to achieve anything. It is violently reproached with this mark of stupidity and passivity. But not at all: the mass is very snobbish; it acts as Brummel did and delegates in a sovereign manner the faculty of choice to someone else by a sort of game of irresponsibility, of ironic challenge, of sovereign lack of will, of secret ruse. All the mediators (people of the media, politicians, intellectuals, all the heirs of the *philosophes* of the Enlightenment in contempt for the masses) are really only adapted to this purpose: to manage by delegation, by procuration, this tedious matter of power and of will, to unburden the masses of this transcendence for their greater pleasure and to turn it into a show for their benefit. *Vicarious*: this would be, to repeat Thorstein Veblen's concept, the status of these so-called privileged classes, whose will would be, in a way, diverted against themselves, toward the secret ends of the very masses whom they despise.

We live all that, subjectively, in the most paradoxical mode, since in us, in everyone, this mass coexists with the intelligent and voluntary being who condemns it and despises it. Nobody knows what is truly opposed to consciousness, unless it may be the repressive unconscious which psychoanalysis has imposed on us. But our true unconscious is perhaps in this ironic power of nonparticipation of nondesire, of nonknowledge, of silence, of absorption of all powers, of *expulsion* of all powers, of all wills, of all knowledge, of all meaning onto representatives surrounded by a halo of derision. Our unconscious would not then consist of drives, of *pulsions*, whose destiny is sad repression; it would not be repressed at all; it would be made of this joyful *expulsion* of all the encumbering superstructures of being and of will.

We have always had a sad vision of the masses (alienated), a sad vision of the unconscious (repressed). On all our philosophy weighs this sad correlation.

Even if only for a change, it would be interesting to conceive the mass, the object-mass, as the repository of a finally delusive, illusive, and allusive strategy, the correlative of an ironic, joyful, and seductive unconscious.

About the media you can sustain two opposing hypotheses: they are the strategy of power, which finds in them the means of mystifying the masses and of imposing its own truth. Or else they are the strategic territory of the ruse of the masses, who exercise in them their concrete power of the refusal of truth, of the denial of reality. Now the media are nothing else than a marvellous instrument for destabilizing the real and the true, all historical or political truth (there is thus no possible political strategy of the media: it is a contradiction in terms). And the addiction that we have for the media, the impossibility of doing without them, is a deep result of this phenomenon: it is not a result of a desire for culture, communication, and information, but of this perversion of truth and falsehood, of this destruction of meaning in the operation of the medium. The desire for a show, the desire for simulation, which is at the same time a desire for dissimulation. This is a vital reaction. It is a spontaneous, total resistance to the ultimatum of historical and political reason.

It is essential today to evaluate this double challenge: the challenge to meaning by the masses and their silence (which is not at all a passive resistance), and the challenge to meaning which comes from the media and their fascination. All the marginal alternative endeavors to resuscitate meaning are secondary to this.

Obviously there is a paradox in the inextricable entanglement of the masses and the media: is it the media that neutralize meaning and that produce the 'formless' (or informed) mass; or is it the mass which victoriously resists the media by diverting or by absorbing without reply all the messages which they produce? Are the mass media on the side of power in the manipulation of the masses, or are they on the side of the masses in the liquidation of meaning, in the violence done to meaning? Is it the media that fascinate the masses, or is it the masses who divert the media into showmanship? The media toss around sense and nonsense; they manipulate in every sense at once. No one can control this process: the media are the vehicle for the simulation which belongs to the system and for the simulation which destroys the system, according to a circular logic, exactly like a Möbius strip – and it is just as well. There is no alternative to this, no logical resolution. Only a logical *exacerbation* and a catastrophic resolution. That is to say, this process has no return.

In conclusion, however, I must make one reservation. Our relationship to this system is an insoluble 'double bind' – exactly that of children in their relationship to the demands of the adult world. They are at the same time told to constitute themselves as autonomous subjects, responsible, free, and conscious, and to constitute themselves as submissive objects, inert, obedient, and conformist. The child resists on all levels, and to these contradictory demands he or she replies by a double strategy. When we ask the child to be object, he or she opposes all the practices of disobedience, of revolt, of emancipation; in short, the strategy of a subject. When we ask the child to be subject, he or she opposes just as obstinately and successfully resistance as object; that is to say, exactly the opposite: infantilism, hyperconformity, total dependance, passivity, idiocy. Neither of the two strategies has more objective value than the other. Subject resistance is today given a unilateral value and considered to be positive – in the same way as in the political sphere only the practices of liberation, of emancipation, of expression, of self-constitution as a political subject are considered worthwhile and subversive. This is to take no account of the equal and probably superior impact of all the practices of the object, the renunciation of the position of subject and of meaning – exactly the practices of the mass – which we bury with the disdainful terms *alienation* and *passivity*. The liberating practices correspond to *one* of the aspects of the system, to the constant ultimatum we are given to constitute ourselves as pure objects; but they do not correspond at all to the other demand to constitute ourselves as subjects, to liberate, to express ourselves at any price, to vote, to produce, to decide, to speak, to participate, to play the game: blackmail and ultimatum just as serious as the other, probably more serious today. To a system whose argument is oppression and repression, the strategic resistance is to demand the liberating rights of the subject. But this seems rather to reflect an earlier phase of the system; and even if we are still confronted with it, it is no longer a strategic territory: the present argument of the system is to maximize speech, to maximize the production of meaning, of participation. And so the strategic resistance is that of the refusal of meaning and the refusal of speech; or of the hyperconformist simulation of the very mechanisms of the system, which is another form of refusal by overacceptance. It is the actual strategy of the masses. This strategy does not exclude the other, but it is the winning one today, because it is the most adapted to the present phase of the system.

NOTES

1. Hans Magnus Enzensberger, 'Constituents of a Theory of the Media,' *New Left Review* 64 (1970) 13–36.
2. Armand Mattelart, *De l'usage des média en temps de crise* (Paris, 1979).
3. Jean Baudrillard, *A l'ombre des majorites silencietises* (Paris, 1978).
4. Roger Caillois, *Man, Play and Games*, trans. Meyer Barash (London, 1962), ch. 8.
5. Georg Wilhelm Friedrich Hegel, *Phänomenologie des Geistes*, ed. Johannes Hoffmeister (Hamburg, 1952) pp. 391–2.
6. Hegel, ibid., p. 392.

7

TRUTH AND POWER

Michel Foucault

Q.   Could you briefly outline the route which led you from your work on
madness in the classical age to the study of criminality and delinquency?

M.F.   When I was studying during the early 1950s, one of the great problems that arose was that of the political status of science and the ideological
functions which it could serve. It wasn't exactly the Lysenko business which
dominated everything, but I believe that around that sordid affair – which had
long remained buried and carefully hidden – a whole number of interesting
questions were provoked. These can all be summed up in two words: power
and knowledge. I believe I wrote *Madness and Civilization* to some extent
within the horizon of these questions. For me, it was a matter of saying this:
if, concerning a science like theoretical physics or organic chemistry, one
poses the problem of its relations with the political and economic structures of
society, isn't one posing an excessively complicated question? Doesn't this set
the threshold of possible explanations impossibly high? But on the other hand,
if one takes a form of knowledge (*savoir*) like psychiatry, won't the question
be much easier to resolve, since the epistemological profile of psychiatry is a
low one and psychiatric practice is linked with a whole range of institutions,
economic requirements, and political issues of social regulation? Couldn't
the interweaving of effects of power and knowledge be grasped with greater
certainty in the case of a science as 'dubious' as psychiatry? It was this same

From Michel Foucault, *Power/Knowledge*, ed. Colin Gordon (Brighton: Harvester Press, 190) pp.
51–75. This interview was conducted by Alessandro Fontana and Pasquale Pasquino. Foucault's
response to the last question was given in writing.

question which I wanted to pose concerning medicine in *The Birth of the Clinic*: medicine certainly has a much more solid scientific armature than psychiatry, but it, too, is profoundly enmeshed in social structures. What rather threw me at the time was the fact that the question I was posing totally failed to interest those to whom I addressed it. They regarded it as a problem which was politically unimportant and epistemologically vulgar. [. . .]

I think there were three reasons for this. The first is that Marxism sought to win acceptance as a renewal of the liberal university tradition – just as, more broadly, during the same period the Communists presented themselves as the only people capable of taking over and reinvigorating the nationalist tradition. [. . .]

The second reason is that post-Stalinist Stalinism, by excluding from Marxist discourse everything that wasn't a frightened repetition of the already said, would not permit the broaching of uncharted domains. [. . .]

Finally, there is perhaps a third reason, but I can't be absolutely sure that it played a part. I wonder, nevertheless, whether among intellectuals in or close to the PCF there wasn't a refusal to pose the problem of internment, of the political use of psychiatry, and, in a more general sense, of the disciplinary grid of society. No doubt little was then known in 1955–60 of the real extent of the Gulag, but I believe that many sensed it; in any case, many had a feeling that it was better not to talk about those things: it was a danger zone, marked by warning signs. [. . .]

What I myself tried to do in this domain was met with a great silence among the French intellectual left. And it was only around 1968, and in spite of the Marxist tradition and the PCF, that all these questions came to assume their political significance, with a sharpness that I had never envisaged, showing how timid and hesitant those early books of mine had still been. Without the political opening created during those years, I would surely never have had the courage to take up these problems again and pursue my research in the direction of penal theory, prisons, and disciplines.

Q. So there is a certain 'discontinuity' in your theoretical trajectory. Incidentally, what do you think today about this concept of discontinuity, on the basis of which you have been all too rapidly and readily labeled a 'structuralist' historian?

M.F. This business about discontinuity has always rather bewildered me. In the new edition of the *Petit Larousse* it says: 'Foucault: a philosopher who founds his theory of history on discontinuity.' That leaves me flabbergasted. No doubt I didn't make myself sufficiently clear in *The Order of Things*, though I said a good deal there about this question. It seemed to me that in certain empirical forms of knowledge, like biology, political economy, psychiatry, medicine, etc., the rhythm of transformation doesn't follow the smooth, continuist schemas of development which are normally accepted. The great biological image of a progressive maturation of science still underpins a good many historical analyses; it does not seem to me to be pertinent to history. In a science like medicine, for example, up to the end of the eighteenth century one has a certain type of discourse whose gradual transformation, within a period of twenty-five or thirty years, broke not only with the 'true' propositions which it had hitherto been possible to formulate, but also, more profoundly, with the ways of speaking and seeing, the whole ensemble of practices which served as supports for medical knowledge. These are not simply new discoveries; there is a whole new 'regime' in discourse and forms of knowledge. And all this happens in the space of a few years. This is something which is undeniable, once one has looked at the texts with sufficient attention. My problem was not at all to say, '*Voilà*, long live discontinuity, we are in the discontinuous and a good thing too,' but to pose the question, 'How is it that at certain moments and in certain orders of knowledge, there are these sudden take-offs, these hastenings of evolution, these transformations which fail to correspond to the calm, continuist image that is normally accredited?' But the important thing here is not that such changes can be rapid and extensive, or rather it is that this extent and rapidity are only the sign of something else: a modification in the rules of formation of statements which are accepted as scientifically true. Thus it is not a change of content (refutation of old errors, recovery of old truths), nor is it a change of theoretical form (renewal of paradigm, modification of systematic ensembles). It is a question of what *governs* statements, and the way in which they *govern* each other so as to constitute a set of propositions which are scientifically acceptable, and hence capable of being verified or falsified by scientific procedures. In short, there is a problem of the regime, the politics of the scientific statement. At this level it's not so much a matter of knowing what external power imposes itself on science, as of what effects of power circulate among scientific statements, what constitutes, as it were, their internal regime of power, and how and why at certain moments that regime undergoes a global modification.

It was these different regimes that I tried to identify and describe in *The Order of Things*, all the while making it clear that I wasn't trying for the moment to explain them, and that it would be necessary to try and do this in a subsequent work. But what was lacking here was this problem of the 'discursive regime,' of the effects of power peculiar to the play of statements. I confused this too much with systematicity, theoretical form, or something like a paradigm. This same central problem of power, which at that time I had not yet properly isolated, emerges in two very different aspects at the point of junction of *Madness and Civilization* and *The Order of Things*.

Q.   We need, then, to locate the notion of discontinuity in its proper context. And perhaps there is another concept which is both more difficult and more central to your thought – the concept of an event. For, in relation to the event, a whole generation was long trapped in an *impasse*, in that following the works of ethnologists, some of them great ethnologists, a dichotomy was established between structures (the *thinkable*) and the event considered as the site of the irrational, the unthinkable, that which doesn't and cannot enter into the mechanism and play of analysis, at least in the form which this took in structuralism. In a recent discussion published in the journal *L'Homme*, three eminent anthropologists posed this question once again about the concept of event, and said: the event is what always escapes our rational grasp, the domain of 'absolute contingency'; we are thinkers who analyze structures, history is no concern of ours, what could we be expected to have to say about it, and so forth. This opposition, then, between event and structure is the site and the product of a certain anthropology. I would say this has had devastating effects among historians who have finally reached the point of trying to dismiss the event and the *évènementiel* as an inferior order of history dealing with trivial facts, chance occurrences, and so on. Whereas it is a fact that there are nodal problems in history which are neither a matter of trivial circumstances nor of those beautiful structures that are so orderly, intelligible, and transparent to analysis. For instance, the 'great internment' which you described in *Madness and Civilization* perhaps represents one of these nodes which elude the dichotomy of structure and event. Could you elaborate from our present standpoint on this renewal and reformulation of the concept of event?

M.F.   One can agree that structuralism formed the most systematic effort to evacuate the concept of the event, not only from ethnology but from a whole series of other sciences and in the extreme case from history. In that sense, I don't see who could be more of an anti-structuralist than myself. But the important thing is to avoid trying to do for the event what was previously done with the concept of structure. It's not a matter of locating everything on one level, that of the event, but of realizing that there is actually a whole order of levels of different types of events, differing in amplitude, chronological breadth, and capacity to produce effects.

The problem is at once to distinguish among events, to differentiate the networks and levels to which they belong, and to reconstitute the lines along which they are connected and engender one another. From this follows a refusal of analyses couched in terms of the symbolic field or the domain of signifying structures, and a recourse to analyses in terms of the genealogy of relations of force, strategic developments, and tactics. Here I believe one's point of reference should not be to the great model of language (*langue*) and signs, but to that of war and battle. The history which bears and determines us has the form of a war rather than that of a language: relations of power, not relations of meaning. History has no 'meaning,' though this is not to say that it is absurd or incoherent. On the contrary, it is intelligible and should be susceptible to analysis down to the smallest detail – but this in accordance with the intelligibility of struggles, of strategies and tactics. Neither the dialectic, as logic of contradictions, nor semiotics, as the structure of communication, can account for the intrinsic intelligibility of conflicts. 'Dialectic' is a way of evading the always open and hazardous reality of conflict by reducing it to a Hegelian skeleton, and 'semiology' is a way of avoiding its violent, bloody, and lethal character by reducing it to the calm Platonic form of language and dialogue.

Q.   In the context of this problem of discursivity, I think one can be confident in saying that you were the first person to pose the question of power regarding discourse, and that at a time when analyses in terms of the concept or object of the 'text,' along with the accompanying methodology of semiology, structuralism, etc., were the prevailing fashion. Posing for discourse the question of power means basically to ask whom does discourse serve? It isn't so much a matter of analyzing discourse into its unsaid, its implicit meaning, because (as you have often repeated) discourses are transparent, they need no interpretation, no one to assign them a meaning. If one reads 'texts' in a certain way, one perceives that they speak clearly to us and require no further supplementary sense or interpretation. This question of power that you have addressed to discourse naturally has particular effects and implications in relation to methodology and contemporary historical researches. Could you briefly situate within your work this question you have posed – if indeed it's true that you have posed it?

M.F.   I don't think I was the first to pose the question. On the contrary, I'm struck by the difficulty I had in formulating it. When I think back now, I ask myself what else it was that I was talking about, in *Madness and Civilization* or *The Birth of the Clinic*, but power? Yet I'm perfectly aware that I scarcely ever used the word and never had such a field of analyses at my disposal. I can say that this was an incapacity linked undoubtedly with the political situation we found ourselves in. It is hard to see where, either on the right or the left, this problem of power could then have been posed. On the right, it was posed only in terms of constitution, sovereignty, etc., that is, in juridical terms; on the Marxist side, it was posed only in terms of the state apparatus. The way power was exercised – concretely and in detail – with its specificity, its techniques and tactics, was something that no one attempted to ascertain; they contented themselves with denouncing it in a polemical and global fashion as it existed among the 'others,' in the adversary camp. Where Soviet socialist power was in question, its opponents called it totalitarianism; power in Western capitalism was denounced by the Marxists as class domination; but the mechanics of power in themselves were never analyzed. This task could only begin after 1968, that is to say, on the basis of daily struggles at the grass-roots level, among those whose fight was located in the fine meshes of the web of power. This was where the concrete nature of power became visible, along with the prospect that these analyses of power would prove fruitful in accounting for all that had hitherto remained outside the field of political analysis. To put it very simply, psychiatric internment, the mental normalization of individuals, and penal institutions have no doubt a fairly limited importance if one is only looking for their economic significance. On the other hand, they are undoubtedly essential to the general functioning of the wheels of power. So long as the posing of the question of power was kept subordinate to the economic instance and the system of interests which this served, there was a tendency to regard these problems as of small importance.

Q.   So a certain kind of Marxism and a certain kind of phenomenology constituted an objective obstacle to the formulation of this problematic?

M.F.   Yes, if you like, to the extent that it's true that, in our student days, people of my generation were brought up on these two forms of analysis – one in terms of the constituent subject, the other in terms of the economic, in the last instance, ideology and the play of superstructures and infrastructures.

Q.   Still, within this methodological context, how would you situate the genealogical approach? As a questioning of the conditions of possibility, modalities, and constitution of the 'objects' and domains you have successively analyzed, what makes it necessary?

M.F.   I wanted to see how these problems of constitution could be resolved within a historical framework, instead of referring them back to a constituent object (madness, criminality, or whatever). But this historical contextualization needed to be something more than the simple relativization of the phenomenological subject. I don't believe the problem can be solved by historicizing the subject as posited by the phenomenologists, fabricating a subject that evolves through the course of history. One has to dispense with the constituent subject, to get rid of the subject itself, that's to say, to arrive at an analysis which can account for the constitution of the subject within a historical framework. And this is what I would call genealogy, that is, a form of history which can account for the constitution of knowledges, discourses, domains of objects, etc., without having to make reference to a subject which is either transcendental in relation to the field of events or runs in its empty sameness throughout the course of history.

Q.   Marxist phenomenology and a certain kind of Marxism have clearly acted as a screen and an obstacle; there are two further concepts which continue today to act as a screen and an obstacle: ideology, on the one hand, and repression, on the other.
All history comes to be thought of within these categories which serve to assign a meaning to such diverse phenomena as normalization, sexuality, and power. And regardless of whether these two concepts are explicitly utilized, in the end one always comes back, on the one hand to ideology – where it is easy to make the reference back to Marx – and on the other to repression, which is

a concept often and readily employed by Freud throughout the course of his career. Hence I would like to put forward the following suggestion. Behind these concepts and among those who (properly or improperly) employ them, there is a kind of nostalgia; behind the concept of ideology, the nostalgia for a quasi-transparent form of knowledge, free from all error and illusion, and behind the concept of repression, the longing for a form of power innocent of all coercion, discipline, and normalization. On the one hand, a power without a bludgeon and, on the other hand, knowledge without deception. You have called these two concepts, ideology and repression, negative, 'psychological,' insufficiently analytical. This is particularly the case in *Discipline and Punish*, where, even if there isn't an extended discussion of these concepts, there is nevertheless a kind of analysis that allows one to go beyond the traditional forms of explanation and intelligibility which, in the last (and not only the last) instance, rest on the concepts of ideology and repression. Could you perhaps use this occasion to specify more explicitly your thoughts on these matters? With *Discipline and Punish*, a kind of positive history seems to be emerging, which is free of all the negativity and psychologism implicit in those two universal skeleton-keys.

M.F. The notion of ideology appears to me to be difficult to make use of, for three reasons. The first is that, like it or not, it always stands in virtual opposition to something else which is supposed to count as truth. Now I believe that the problem does not consist in drawing the line between that in a discourse which falls under the category of scientificity or truth, and that which comes under some other category, but in seeing historically how effects of truth are produced within discourses which in themselves are neither true nor false. The second drawback is that the concept of ideology refers, I think necessarily, to something of the order of a subject. Third, ideology stands in a secondary position relative to something which functions as its infrastructure, as its material, economic determinant, etc. For these three reasons, I think that this is a notion that cannot be used without circumspection.

The notion of repression is a more insidious one, or at all events I myself have had much more trouble in freeing myself of it, insofar as it does indeed appear to correspond so well with a whole range of phenomena which belong among the effects of power. When I wrote *Madness and Civilization*, I made at least an implicit use of this notion of repression. I think, indeed, that I was positing the existence of a sort of living, voluble, and anxious madness which the mechanisms of power and psychiatry were supposed to have come to repress and reduce to silence. But it seems to me now that the notion of repression is quite inadequate for capturing what is precisely the productive aspect of power. In defining the effects of power as repression, one adopts a purely juridical conception of such power; one identifies power with a law which says no; power is taken above all as carrying the force of a prohibition. Now I believe that this is a wholly negative, narrow, skeletal conception of power, one which has been curiously widespread. If power were never anything but repressive, if it never did anything but to say no, do you really think one would be brought to obey it? What makes power hold good, what makes it accepted, is simply the fact that it doesn't only weigh on us as a force that says no, but that it traverses and produces things, it induces pleasure, forms knowledge, produces discourse. It needs to be considered as a productive network which runs through the whole social body, much more than as a negative instance whose function is repression. In *Discipline and Punish*, what I wanted to show was how, from the seventeenth and eighteenth centuries onward, there was a veritable technological take-off in the productivity of power. Not only did the monarchies of the classical period develop great state apparatuses (the army, the police and fiscal administration), but above all there was established in this period what one might call a new 'economy' of power, that is to say, procedures which allowed the effects of power to circulate in a manner at once continuous, uninterrupted, adapted, and 'individualized' throughout the entire social body. These new techniques are both much more efficient and much less wasteful (less costly economically, less risky in their results, less open to loopholes and resistances) than the techniques previously employed, which were based on a mixture of more or less forced tolerances (from recognized privileges to endemic criminality) and costly ostentation (spectacular and discontinuous interventions of power, the most violent form of which was the 'exemplary,' because exceptional, punishment).

Q.   Repression is a concept used above all in relation to sexuality. It was held that bourgeois society represses sexuality, stifles sexual desire, and so forth. And when one considers, for example, the campaign launched against masturbation in the eighteenth century, or the medical discourse on homosexuality in the second half of the nineteenth century, or discourse on sexuality in general, one does seem to be faced with a discourse of repression. In reality, however, this discourse serves to make possible a whole series of interventions, tactical and positive interventions of surveillance, circulation, control, and so forth, which seem to have been intimately linked with techniques that give the appearance of repression, or are at least liable to be interpreted as such. I believe the crusade against masturbation is a typical example of this.

M.F.   Certainly. It is customary to say that bourgeois society repressed infantile sexuality to the point where it refused even to speak of it or acknowledge its existence. It was necessary to wait until Freud for the discovery at last to be made that children have a sexuality. Now if you read all the books on pedagogy and child medicine – all the manuals for parents that were published in the eighteenth century – you find that children's sex is spoken of constantly and in every possible context. One might argue that the purpose of these discourses was precisely to prevent children from having a sexuality. But their *effect* was to din it into parents' heads that their children's sex constituted a fundamental problem in terms of their parental educational responsibilities, and to din it into children's heads that their relationship with their own bodies and their own sex was to be a fundamental problem as far as *they* were concerned; and this had the consequence of sexually exciting the bodies of children while at the same time fixing the parental gaze and vigilance on the peril of infantile sexuality. The result was a sexualizing of the infantile body, a sexualizing of the bodily relationship between parent and child, a sexualizing of the familial domain. 'Sexuality' is far more of a positive product of power than power was ever repression of sexuality. I believe that it is precisely these positive mechanisms that need to be investigated, and here one must free oneself of the juridical schematism of all previous characterizations of the nature of power. Hence a historical problem arises, namely, that of discovering why the West has insisted for so long on seeing the power it exercises as juridical and negative rather than as technical and positive.

Q. Perhaps this is because it has always been thought that power is mediated through the forms prescribed in the great juridical and philosophical theories, and that there is a fundamental, immutable gulf between those who exercise power and those who undergo it.

M.F. I wonder if this isn't bound up with the institution of monarchy. This developed during the Middle Ages against the backdrop of the previously endemic struggles between feudal power agencies. The monarchy presented itself as a referee, a power capable of putting an end to war, violence, and pillage and saying no to these struggles and private feuds. It made itself acceptable by allocating itself a juridical and negative function, albeit one whose limits it naturally began at once to overstep. Sovereign, law, and prohibition formed a system of representation of power which was extended during the subsequent era by the theories of right: political theory has never ceased to be obsessed with the person of the sovereign. Such theories still continue today to busy themselves with the problem of sovereignty. What we need, however, is a political philosophy that isn't erected around the problem of sovereignty, nor therefore around the problems of law and prohibition. We need to cut off the king's head: in political theory that has still to be done.

Q. The king's head still hasn't been cut off, yet already people are trying to replace it by discipline, that vast system instituted in the seventeenth century, comprising the functions of surveillance, normalization and control, and, a little later, those of punishment, correction, education, and so on. One wonders where this system comes from, why it emerges, and what its use is. And today there is rather a tendency to attribute a subject to it, a great, molar, totalitarian subject, namely, the modern state, constituted in the sixteenth and seventeenth centuries and bringing with it (according to the classical theories) the professional army, the police, and the administrative bureaucracy.

M.F. To pose the problem in terms of the state means to continue posing it in terms of sovereign and sovereignty, that is to say, in terms of law. If one describes all these phenomena of power as dependent on the state apparatus, this means grasping them as essentially repressive: the army as a power of death, police and justice as punitive instances, etc. I don't want to say that the state isn't important; what I want to say is that relations of power, and hence the analysis that must be made of them, necessarily extend beyond the limits of the state. In two senses: first of all because the state, for all the omnipotence of its apparatuses, is far from being able to occupy the whole field of actual power relations, and further because the state can only operate on the basis of other, already existing power relations. The state is superstructural in relation to a whole series of power networks that invest the body, sexuality, the family, kinship, knowledge, technology, and so forth. True, these networks stand in a conditioning-conditioned relationship to a kind of 'metapower' which is structured essentially around a certain number of great prohibition functions; but this metapower with its prohibitions can only take hold and secure its footing where it is rooted in a whole series of multiple and indefinite power relations that supply the necessary basis for the great negative forms of power. That is just what I was trying to make apparent in my book.

[. . .]

Q. You have said about power as an object of research that one has to invert Clausewitz's formula so as to arrive at the idea that politics is the continuation of war by other means. Does the military model seem to you, on the basis of your most recent researches, to be the best one for describing power; is war here simply a metaphorical model, or is it the literal, regular, everyday mode of operation of power?

M.F. This is the problem I now find myself confronting. As soon as one endeavors to detach power with its techniques and procedures from the form of law within which it has been theoretically confined up until now, one is driven to ask this basic question: Isn't power simply a form of warlike domination? Shouldn't one therefore conceive all problems of power in terms of relations of war? Isn't power a sort of generalized war which assumes at particular moments the forms of peace and the state? Peace would then be a form of war, and the state a means of waging it.

A whole range of problems emerges here. Who wages war against whom? Is it between two classes, or more? Is it a war of all against all? What is the role of the army and military institutions in this civil society where permanent war is waged? What is the relevance of concepts of tactics and strategy for analyzing structures and political processes? What is the essence and mode of transformation of power relations? All these questions need to be explored. In any case it's astonishing to see how easily and self-evidently people talk of warlike relations of power or of class struggle without ever making it clear whether some form of war is meant, and if so what form.

Q. We have already talked about this disciplinary power whose effects, rules, and mode of constitution you describe in *Discipline and Punish*. One might ask here: Why surveillance? What is the use of surveillance? Now there is a phenomenon that emerges during the eighteenth century, namely, the discovery of population as an object of scientific investigation; people begin to inquire into birth rates, death rates, and changes in population and to say for the first time that it is impossible to govern a state without knowing its population. Moheau, for example, who was one of the first to organize this kind of research on an administrative basis, seems to see its goal as lying in the problems of political control of a population. Does this disciplinary power then act alone and of itself, or doesn't it, rather, draw support from something more general, namely, this fixed conception of a population that reproduces itself in the proper way, composed of people who marry in the proper way and behave in the proper way, according to precisely determined norms? One would then have, on the one hand, a sort of global, molar body, the body of the population, together with a whole series of discourses concerning it, and then, on the other hand and down below, the small bodies, the docile, individual bodies, the microbodies of discipline. Even if you are only perhaps at the beginning of your researches here, could you say how you see the nature of the relationships (if any) which are engendered between these different bodies: the molar body of the population and the microbodies of individuals?

M.F. Your question is exactly on target. I find it difficult to reply because I am working on this problem right now. I believe one must keep in view the fact that along with all the fundamental technical inventions and discoveries of the seventeenth and eighteenth centuries, a new technology of the exercise of power also emerged, which was probably even more important than the constitutional reforms and new forms of government established at the end of the eighteenth century. In the camp of the left, one often hears people saying that power is that which abstracts, which negates the body, represses, suppresses, and so forth. I would say instead that what I find most striking about these new technologies of power introduced since the seventeenth and eighteenth centuries is their concrete and precise character, their grasp of a multiple and differentiated reality. In feudal societies, power functioned essentially through signs and levies. Signs of loyalty to the feudal lords, rituals, ceremonies, and so forth, and levies in the form of taxes, pillage, hunting, war, etc. In the seventeenth and eighteenth centuries, a form of power comes into being that begins to exercise itself through social production and social service. It becomes a matter of obtaining productive service from individuals in their concrete lives. And, in consequence, a real and effective 'incorporation' of power was necessary, in the sense that power had to be able to gain access to the bodies of individuals, to their acts, attitudes, and modes of everyday behavior. Hence the significance of methods like school discipline, which succeeded in making children's bodies the object of highly complex systems of manipulation and conditioning. But, at the same time, these new techniques of power needed to grapple with the phenomena of population, in short, to undertake the administration, control, and direction of the accumulation of men (the economic system that promotes the accumulation of capital and the system of power that ordains the accumulation of men are, from the seventeenth century on, correlated and inseparable phenomena): hence there arise the problems of demography, public health, hygiene, housing conditions, longevity, and fertility. And I believe that the political significance of the problem of sex is due to the fact that sex is located at the point of intersection of the discipline of the body and the control of the population.

[. . .]

The important thing here, I believe, is that truth isn't outside power, or lacking in power: contrary to a myth whose history and functions would repay further study, truth isn't the reward of free spirits, the child of protracted solitude, nor the privilege of those who have succeeded in liberating themselves. Truth is a thing of this world: it is produced only by virtue of multiple forms of constraint. And it induces regular effects of power. Each society has its regime of truth, its 'general politics' of truth: that is, the types of discourse which it accepts and makes function as true; the mechanisms and instances which enable one to distinguish true and false statements, the means by which each is sanctioned; the techniques and procedures accorded value in the acquisition of truth; the status of those who are charged with saying what counts as true.

[. . .]

All this must seem very confused and uncertain. Uncertain indeed, and what I am saying here is above all to be taken as a hypothesis. In order for it to be a little less confused, however, I would like to put forward a few 'propositions' – not firm assertions, but simply suggestions to be further tested and evaluated.

'Truth' is to be understood as a system of ordered procedures for the production, regulation, distribution, circulation, and operation of statements.

'Truth' is linked in a circular relation with systems of power which produce and sustain it, and to effects of power which it induces and which extends it. A 'regime' of truth.

This regime is not merely ideological or superstructural; it was a condition of the formation and development of capitalism. And it's this same regime which, subject to certain modifications, operates in the socialist countries (I leave open here the question of China, about which I know little).

The essential political problem for the intellectual is not to criticize the ideological contents supposedly linked to science, or to ensure that his own scientific practice is accompanied by a correct ideology, but that of ascertaining the possibility of constituting a new politics of truth. The problem is not changing people's consciousnesses – or what's in their heads – but the political, economic, institutional regime of the production of truth.

It's not a matter of emancipating truth from every system of power (which would be a chimera, for truth is already power), but of detaching the power of truth from the forms of hegemony, social, economic, and cultural, within which it operates at the present time

The political question, to sum up, is not error, illusion, alienated consciousness, or ideology; it is truth itself. Hence the importance of Nietzsche.

8

THE PRACTICE OF EVERYDAY LIFE

Michel de Certeau

General Introduction

This essay is part of a continuing investigation of the ways in which users – commonly assumed to be passive and guided by established rules – operate. The point is not so much to discuss this elusive yet fundamental subject as to make such a discussion possible; that is, by means of inquiries and hypotheses, to indicate pathways for further research. This goal will be achieved if everyday practices, 'ways of operating' or doing things, no longer appear as merely the obscure background of social activity, and if a body of theoretical questions, methods, categories, and perspectives, by penetrating this obscurity, make it possible to articulate them.

The examination of such practices does not imply a return to individuality. The social atomism which over the past three centuries has served as the historical axiom of social analysis posits an elementary unit – the individual – on the basis of which groups are supposed to be formed and to which they are supposed to be always reducible. This axiom, which has been challenged by more than a century of sociological, economic, anthropological, and psychoanalytic research, (although in history that is perhaps no argument) plays no part in this study. Analysis shows that a relation (always social) determines its terms, and not the reverse, and that each individual is a locus in which an incoherent (and often contradictory) plurality of such relational determinations interact. Moreover, the question at hand concerns modes of operation

From Michel de Certeau, 'General Introduction' in *The Practice of Everyday Life* ([Place]: University of California Press, 2002) pp. xi–xxiv.

or schemata of action, and not directly the subjects (or persons) who are their authors or vehicles. It concerns an operational logic whose models may go as far back as the age-old ruses of fishes and insects that disguise or transform themselves in order to survive, and which has in any case been concealed by the form of rationality currently dominant in Western culture. The purpose of this work is to make explicit the systems of operational combination (*les combinatoires d'opérations*) which also compose a 'culture,' and to bring to light the models of action characteristic of users whose status as the dominated element in society (a status that does not mean that they are either passive or docile) is concealed by the euphemistic term 'consumers.' Everyday life invents itself by *poaching* in countless ways on the property of others.

1. Consumer Production

Since this work grew out of studies of 'popular culture' or marginal groups,[1] the investigation of everyday practices was first delimited negatively by the necessity of not locating cultural *difference* in groups associated with the 'counter-culture' – groups that were already singled out, often privileged, and already partly absorbed into folklore – and that were no more than symptoms or indexes. Three further, positive determinations were particularly important in articulating our research.

Usage, or consumption

Many, often remarkable, works have sought to study the representations of a society, on the one hand, and its modes of behavior, on the other. Building on our knowledge of these social phenomena, it seems both possible and necessary to determine the *use* to which they are put by groups or individuals. For example, the analysis of the images broadcast by television (representation) and of the time spent watching television (behavior) should be complemented by a study of what the cultural consumer 'makes' or 'does' during this time and with these images. The same goes for the use of urban space, the products purchased in the super-market, the stories and legends distributed by the newspapers, and so on.

The 'making' in question is a production, a *poiēsis*[2] – but a hidden one, because it is scattered over areas defined and occupied by systems of 'production' (television, urban development, commerce, etc.), and because the steadily increasing expansion of these systems no longer leaves 'consumers' any *place* in which they can indicate what they *make* or *do* with the products of these systems. To a rationalized, expansionist and at the same time centralized, clamorous, and spectacular production corresponds *another* production, called 'consumption.' The latter is devious, it is dispersed, but it insinuates itself everywhere, silently and almost invisibly, because it does not manifest itself through its own products, but rather through its *ways of using* the products imposed by a dominant economic order.

For instance, the ambiguity that subverted from within the Spanish colonizers' 'success' in imposing their own culture on the indigenous Indians is well known. Submissive, and even consenting to their subjection, the Indians nevertheless often *made of* the rituals, representations, and laws imposed on them something quite different from what their conquerors had in mind; they subverted them not by rejecting or altering them, but by using them with respect to ends and references foreign to the system they had no choice but to accept. They were *other* within the very colonization that outwardly assimilated them; their use of the dominant social order deflected its power, which they lacked the means to challenge; they escaped it without leaving it. The strength of their difference lay in procedures of 'consumption.' To a lesser degree, a similar ambiguity creeps into our societies through the use made by the 'common people' of the culture disseminated and imposed by the 'elites' producing the language. [. . .]

The procedures of everyday creativity

A second orientation of our investigation can be explained by reference to Michel Foucault's *Discipline and Punish*. In this work, instead of analyzing the apparatus exercising power (i.e., the localizable, expansionist, repressive, and legal institutions), Foucault analyzes the mechanisms (*dispositifs*) that have sapped the strength of these institutions and surreptitiously reorganized the functioning of power: 'miniscule' technical procedures acting on and with details, redistributing a discursive space in order to make it the means of a generalized 'discipline' (*surveillance*).[3] This approach raises a new and different set of problems to be investigated. Once again, however, this 'microphysics of power' privileges the productive apparatus (which produces the 'discipline'), even though it discerns in 'education' a system of 'repression' and shows how, from the wings as it were, silent technologies determine or short-circuit institutional stage directions. If it is true that the grid of 'discipline' is everywhere becoming clearer and more extensive, it is all the more urgent to discover how an entire society resists being reduced to it, what popular procedures (also 'miniscule' and quotidian) manipulate the mechanisms of discipline and conform to them only in order to evade them, and finally, what 'ways of operating' form the counterpart, on the consumer's (or 'dominee's'?) side, of the mute processes that organize the establishment of socioeconomic order.

These 'ways of operating' constitute the innumerable practices by means of which users reappropriate the space organized by techniques of sociocultural production. They pose questions at once analogous and contrary to those dealt with in Foucault's book: analogous, in that the goal is to perceive and analyze the microbe-like operations proliferating within technocratic structures and deflecting their functioning by means of a multitude of 'tactics' articulated in the details of everyday life; contrary, in that the goal is not to make clearer how the violence of order is transmuted into a disciplinary technology, but rather to bring to light the clandestine forms taken by the dispersed, tactical, and makeshift creativity of groups or individuals already caught in the nets of 'discipline.' Pushed to their ideal limits, these procedures and ruses of consumers compose the network of an antidiscipline[4] which is the subject of this book [*The Practice of Everyday Life*].

The formal structure of practice

It may be supposed that these operations – multiform and fragmentary, relative to situations and details, insinuated into and concealed within devices whose mode of usage they constitute, and thus lacking their own ideologies or institutions – conform to certain rules. In other words, there must be a logic of these practices. We are thus confronted once again by the ancient problem: What is an *art* or 'way of making'? From the Greeks to Durkheim, a long tradition has sought to describe with precision the complex (and not at all simple or 'impoverished') rules that could account for these operations.[5] From this point of view, 'popular culture,' as well as a whole literature called 'popular,'[6] take on a different aspect: they present themselves essentially as 'arts of making' this or that, i.e., as combinatory or utilizing modes of consumption. These practices bring into play a 'popular' *ratio*, a way of thinking invested in a way of acting, an art of combination which cannot be dissociated from an art of using.

In order to grasp the formal structure of these practices, I have carried out two sorts of investigations. The first, more descriptive in nature, has concerned certain ways of making that were selected according to their value for the strategy of the analysis, and with a view to obtaining fairly differentiated variants: readers' practices, practices related to urban spaces, utilizations of everyday rituals, re-uses and functions of the memory through the 'authorities' that make possible (or permit) everyday practices, etc. In addition, two related investigations have tried to trace the intricate forms of the operations proper to the recompositon of a space (the Croix-Rousse quarter in Lyons) by familial practices, on the one hand, and on the other, to the tactics of the art of cooking, which simultaneously organizes a network of relations, poetic ways of 'making do'.[7]

The second series of investigations has concerned the scientific literature that might furnish hypotheses allowing the logic of unselfconscious thought to be taken seriously. Three areas are of special interest. First, sociologists, anthropologists, and indeed historians (from E. Goffman to P. Bourdieu, from Mauss to M. Détienne, from J. Boissevain to E. O. Laumann) have elaborated a theory of such practices, mixtures of rituals and makeshifts (*bricolages*), manipulations of spaces, operators of networks.[8] Second, in the wake of J. Fishman's work, the ethnomethodological and sociolinguistic investigations of H. Garfinkel, W. Labov, H. Sachs, E. A. Schegloff, and others have described the procedures of everyday interactions relative to structures of expectation, negotiation, and improvisation proper to ordinary language.[9]

Finally, in addition to the semiotics and philosophies of 'convention' (from O. Ducrot to D. Lewis),[10] we must look into the ponderous formal logics and their extension, in the field of analytical philosophy, into the domains of action (G. H. von Wright, A. C. Danto, R. J. Bernstein),[11] time (A. N. Prior, N. Rescher and J. Urquhart),[12] and modalisation (G. E. Hughes and M. J. Cresswell, A. R. White).[13]

> These extensions yield a weighty apparatus seeking to grasp the delicate layering and plasticity of ordinary language, with its almost orchestral combinations of logical elements (temporalization, modalization, injunctions, predicates of action, etc.) whose dominants are determined in turn by circumstances and conjunctural demands. An investigation analogous to Chomsky's study of the oral uses of language must seek to restore to everyday practices their logical and cultural legitimacy, at least in the sectors – still very limited – in which we have at our disposal the instruments necessary to account for them.[14] This kind of research is complicated by the fact that these practices themselves alternately exacerbate and disrupt our logics. Its regrets are like those of the poet, and like him, it struggles against oblivion: 'And I forgot the element of chance introduced by circumstances, calm or haste, sun or cold, dawn or dusk, the taste of strawberries or abandonment, the half-understood message, the front page of newspapers, the voice on the telephone, the most anodyne conversation, the most anonymous man or woman, everything that speaks, makes noise, passes by, touches us lightly, meets us head on.'[15]

The marginality of a majority

These three determinations make possible an exploration of the cultural field, an exploration defined by an investigative problematics and punctuated by more detailed inquiries located by reference to hypotheses that remain to be verified. Such an exploration will seek to situate the types of *operations* characterizing consumption in the framework of an economy, and to discern in these practices of appropriation indexes of the creativity that flourishes at the very point where practice ceases to have its own language.

Marginality is today no longer limited to minority groups, but is rather massive and pervasive; this cultural activity of the non-producers of culture, an activity that is unsigned, unreadable, and unsymbolized, remains the only one possible for all those who nevertheless buy and pay for the showy products through which a productivist economy articulates itself. Marginality is becoming universal. A marginal group has now become a silent majority.

That does not mean the group is homogeneous. The procedures allowing the re-use of products are linked together in a kind of obligatory language, and their functioning is related to social situations and power relationships. Confronted by images on television, the immigrant worker does not have the same critical or creative elbow-room as the average citizen. On the same terrain, his inferior access to information, financial means, and compensations of all kinds elicits an increased deviousness, fantasy, or laughter. Similar strategic deployments, when acting on different relationships of force, do not produce identical effects. Hence the necessity of differentiating both the 'actions' or 'engagements' (in the military sense) that the system of products effects within the consumer grid, *and* the various kinds of room to maneuver left for consumers by the situations in which they exercise their 'art.'

The relation of procedures to the fields of force in which they act must therefore lead to a *polemological* analysis of culture. Like law (one of its models), culture articulates conflicts and alternately legitimizes, displaces, or controls the superior force. It develops in an atmosphere of tensions, and often of violence, for which it provides symbolic balances, contracts of compatibility and compromises, all more or less temporary. The tactics of consumption, the ingenious ways in which the weak make use of the strong, thus lend a political dimension to everyday practices.

2. THE TACTICS OF PRACTICE

In the course of our research, the scheme, rather too neatly dichotomized, of the relations between consumers and the mechanisms of production has been diversified in relation to three kinds of concerns: the search for a problematics that could articulate the material collected; the description of a limited number of practices (reading, talking, walking, dwelling, cooking, etc.) considered to be particularly significant; and the extension of the analysis of these everyday operations to scientific fields apparently governed by another kind of logic. Through the presentation of our investigation along these three lines, the overly schematic character of the general statement can be somewhat nuanced.

Trajectories, tactics, and rhetorics

As unrecognized producers, poets of their own acts, silent discoverers of their own paths in the jungle of functionalist rationality, consumers produce through their signifying practices something that might be considered similar to the 'wandering lines' (*'lignes d'erre'*) drawn by the autistic children studied by F. Deligny:[16] 'indirect' or 'errant' trajectories obeying their own logic. In the technocratically constructed, written, and functionalized space in which the consumers move about, their trajectories form unforeseeable sentences, partly unreadable paths across a space. Although they are composed with the vocabularies of established languages (those of television, newspapers, supermarkets, or museum sequences) and although they remain subordinated to the prescribed syntactical forms (temporal modes of schedules, paradigmatic orders of spaces, etc.), the trajectories trace out the ruses of other interests and desires that are neither determined nor captured by the systems in which they develop.[17]

Even statistical investigation remains virtually ignorant of these trajectories, since it is satisfied with classifying, calculating, and putting into tables the 'lexical' units which compose them but to which they cannot be reduced, and with doing this in reference to its own categories and taxonomies. Statistical investigation grasps the material of these practices, but not their *form*; it determines the elements used, but not the 'phrasing' produced by the *bricolage* (the artisan-like inventiveness) and the discursiveness that combine these elements, which are all in general circulation and rather drab. Statistical inquiry, in breaking down these 'efficacious meanderings' into units that it defines itself, in reorganizing the results of its analyses according to its own codes, 'finds' only the homogenous. The power of its calculations lies in its ability to divide, but it is precisely through this ana-lytic fragmentation that it loses sight of what it claims to seek and to represent.[18]

'Trajectory' suggests a movement, but it also involves a plane projection, a flattening out. It is a transcription. A graph (which the eye can master) is substituted for an operation; a line which can be reversed (i.e., read in both directions) does duty for an irreversible temporal series, a tracing for acts. To avoid this reduction, I resort to a distinction between *tactics* and *strategies*.

I call a 'strategy' the calculus of force-relationships which becomes possible when a subject of will and power (a proprietor, an enterprise, a city, a scientific institution) can be isolated from an 'environment.' A strategy assumes a place that can be circumscribed as *proper* (*propre*) and thus serve as the basis for generating relations with an exterior distinct from it (competitors, adversaries, 'clientèles,' 'targets,' or 'objects' of research). Political, economic, and scientific rationality has been constructed on this strategic model.

I call a 'tactic,' on the other hand, a calculus which cannot count on a 'proper' (a spatial or institutional localization), nor thus on a borderline distinguishing the other as a visible totality. The place of a tactic belongs to the other.[19] A tactic insinuates itself into the other's place, fragmentarily, without taking it over in its entirety, without being able to keep it at a distance. It has at its disposal no base where it can capitalize on its advantages, prepare its expansions, and secure independence with respect to circumstances. The 'proper' is a victory of space over time. On the contrary, because it does not have a place, a tactic depends on time – it is always on the watch for opportunities that must be seized 'on the wing.' Whatever it wins, it does not keep. It must constantly manipulate events in order to turn them into 'opportunities.' The weak must continually turn to their own ends forces alien to them. This is achieved in the propitious moments when they are able to combine heterogeneous elements (thus, in the supermarket, the housewife confronts heterogeneous and mobile data – what she has in the refrigerator, the tastes, appetites, and moods of her guests, the best buys and their possible combinations with what she already has on hand at home, etc.); the intellectual synthesis of these given elements takes the form, however, not of a discourse, but of the decision itself, the act and manner in which the opportunity is 'seized.'

Many everyday practices (talking, reading, moving about, shopping, cooking, etc.) are tactical in character. And so are, more generally, many 'ways of operating': victories of the 'weak' over the 'strong' (whether the strength be that of powerful people or the violence of things or of an imposed order, etc.), clever tricks, knowing how to get away with things, 'hunter's cunning,' maneuvers, polymorphic simulations, joyful discoveries, poetic as well as warlike. The Greeks called these 'ways of operating' *mētis*.[20] But they go much further back, to the immemorial intelligence displayed in the tricks and imitations of plants and fishes. From the depths of the ocean to the streets of modern megalopolises, there is a continuity and permanence in these tactics.

In our societies, as local stabilities break down, it is as if, no longer fixed by a circumscribed community, tactics wander out of orbit, making consumers into immigrants in a system too vast to be their own, too tightly woven for them to escape from it. But these tactics introduce a Brownian movement into the system. They also show the extent to which intelligence is inseparable from the everyday struggles and pleasures that it articulates. Strategies, in contrast, conceal beneath objective calculations their connection with the power that sustains them from within the stronghold of its own 'proper' place or institution.

The discipline of rhetoric offers models for differentiating among the types of tactics. This is not surprising, since, on the one hand, it describes the 'turns' or tropes of which language can be both the site and the object, and, on the other hand, these manipulations are related to the ways of changing (seducing, persuading, making use of) the will of another (the audience).[21] For these two reasons, rhetoric, the science of the 'ways of speaking,' offers an array of figure-types for the analysis of everyday ways of acting even though such analysis is in theory excluded from scientific discourse. Two logics of action (the one tactical, the other strategic) arise from these two facets of practicing language. In the space of a language (as in that of games), a society makes more explicit the formal rules of action and the operations that differentiate them.

In the enormous rhetorical corpus devoted to the art of speaking or operating, the Sophists have a privileged place, from the point of view of tactics. Their principle was, according to the Greek rhetorician Corax, to make the weaker position seem the stronger, and they claimed to have the power of turning the tables on the powerful by the way in which they made use of the opportunities offered by the particular situation.[22] Moreover, their theories inscribe tactics in a long tradition of reflection on the relationships between reason and particular actions and situations. Passing by way of *The Art of War* by the Chinese author Sun Tzu[23] or the Arabic anthology, *The Book of Tricks*,[24] this tradition of a logic articulated on situations and the will of others continues into contemporary sociolinguistics.

Reading, talking, dwelling, cooking, etc.

To describe these everyday practices that produce without capitalizing, that is, without taking control over time, one starting point seemed inevitable because it is the 'exorbitant' focus of contemporary culture and its consumption: *reading*. From TV to newspapers, from advertising to all sorts of mercantile epiphanies, our society is characterized by a cancerous growth of vision, measuring everything by its ability to show or be shown and transmuting communication into a visual journey. It is a sort of *epic* of the eye and of the impulse to read. The economy itself, transformed into a 'semeiocracy',[25] encourages a hypertrophic development of reading. Thus, for the binary set production-consumption, one would substitute its more general equivalent: writing-reading. Reading (an image or a text), moreover, seems to constitute the maximal development of the passivity assumed to characterize the consumer, who is conceived of as a voyeur (whether troglodytic or itinerant) in a 'show biz society.'[26]

In reality, the activity of reading has on the contrary all the characteristics of a silent production: the drift across the page, the metamorphosis of the text effected by the wandering eyes of the reader, the improvisation and expectation of meanings inferred from a few words, leaps over written spaces in an ephemeral dance. But since he is incapable of stockpiling (unless he writes or records), the reader cannot protect himself against the erosion of time (while reading, he forgets himself and he forgets what he has read) unless he buys the object (book, image) which is no more than a substitute (the spoor or promise) of moments 'lost' in reading. He insinuates into another person's text the ruses of pleasure and appropriation: he poaches on it, is transported into it, pluralizes himself in it like the internal rumblings of one's body. Ruse, metaphor, arrangement, this production is also an 'invention' of the memory. Words become the outlet or product of silent histories. The readable transforms itself into the memorable: Barthes reads Proust in Stendhal's text;[27] the viewer reads the landscape of his childhood in the evening news. The thin film of writing becomes a movement of strata, a play of spaces. A different world (the reader's) slips into the author's place.

This mutation makes the text habitable, like a rented apartment. It transforms another person's property into a space borrowed for a moment by a transient. Renters make comparable changes in an apartment they furnish with their acts and memories; as do speakers, in the language into which they insert both the messages of their native tongue and, through their accent, through their own 'turns of phrase,' etc., their own history; as do pedestrians, in the streets they fill with the forests of their desires and goals. In the same way the users of social codes turn them into metaphors and ellipses of their own quests. The ruling order serves as a support for innumerable productive activities, while at the same time blinding its proprietors to this creativity (like those 'bosses' who simply *can't* see what is being created within their own enterprises).[28] Carried to its limit, this order would be the equivalent of the rules of meter and rhyme for poets of earlier times: a body of constraints stimulating new discoveries, a set of rules with which improvisation plays.

Reading thus introduces an 'art' which is anything but passive. It resembles rather that art whose theory was developed by medieval poets and romancers:

an innovation infiltrated into the text and even into the terms of a tradition. Imbricated within the strategies of modernity (which identify creation with the invention of a personal language, whether cultural or scientific), the procedures of contemporary consumption appear to constitute a subtle art of 'renters' who know how to insinuate their countless differences into the dominant text. In the Middle Ages, the text was framed by the four, or seven, interpretations of which it was held to be susceptible. And it was a book. Today, this text no longer comes from a tradition. It is imposed by the generation of a productivist technocracy. It is no longer a referential book, but a whole society made into a book, into the writing of the anonymous law of production.

It is useful to compare other arts with this art of readers. For example, the art of conversationalists: the rhetoric of ordinary conversation consists of practices which transform 'speech situations,' verbal productions in which the interlacing of speaking positions weaves an oral fabric without individual owners, creations of a communication that belongs to no one. Conversation is a provisional and collective effect of competence in the art of manipulating 'commonplaces' and the inevitability of events in such a way as to make them 'habitable.'[29]

But our research has concentrated above all on the uses of space,[30] on the ways of frequenting or dwelling in a place, on the complex processes of the art of cooking, and on the many ways of establishing a kind of reliability within the situations imposed on an individual, that is, of making it possible to live in them by reintroducing into them the plural mobility of goals and desires – an art of manipulating and enjoying.[31]

Extensions: prospects and politics

The analysis of these tactics was extended to two areas marked out for study, although our approach to them changed as the research proceeded: the first concerns prospects, or futurology, and the second, the individual subject in political life.

[. . .]

The question bears on more than the procedures of production: in a different form, it concerns as well the *status of the individual* in technical systems, since the involvement of the subject diminishes in proportion to the technocratic expansion of these systems. Increasingly constrained, yet less and less concerned with these vast frameworks, the individual detaches himself from them without being able to escape them and can henceforth only try to outwit them, to pull tricks on them, to rediscover, within an electronicized and computerized megalopolis, the 'art' of the hunters and rural folk of earlier days. The fragmentation of the social fabric today lends a *political* dimension to the problem of the subject. In support of this claim can be adduced the symptoms represented by individual conflicts and local operations, and even by ecological organizations, though these are preoccupied primarily with the effort to control relations with the environment collectively. These ways of reappropriating the product-system, ways created by consumers, have as their goal a *therapeutics for deteriorating social relations* and make use of techniques of re-employment in which we can recognize the procedures of everyday practices. A politics of such ploys should be developed. In the perspective opened up by Freud's *Civilization and Its Discontents*, such a politics should also inquire into the public ('democratic') image of the microscopic, multiform, and innumerable connections between *manipulating* and *enjoying*, the fleeting and massive reality of a social activity at play with the order that contains it.

Witold Gombrowicz, an acute visionary, gave this politics its hero – the anti-hero who haunts our research – when he gave a voice to the small-time official (Musil's 'man without qualities' or that ordinary man to whom Freud dedicated *Civilization and Its Discontents*) whose refrain is 'When one does not have what one wants, one must want what one has': 'I have had, you see, to resort more and more to very small, almost invisible pleasures, little extras. . . . You've no idea how great one becomes with these little details, it's incredible how one grows.'[32]

NOTES

'Introduction'

1. See M. de Certeau, *La Prise de parole* (Paris: DDB, 1968); *La Possession de Loudun* (Paris: Julliard-Gallimard, 1970); *L'Absent de l'histoire* (Paris: Mame, 1973); *La Culture au pluriel* (Paris: UGE 10/18, 1974); *Une Politique de la langue* (with D. Julia and J. Revel) (Paris: Gallimard, 1975); etc.
2. From the Greek *poiein* 'to create, invent, generate.'
3. Michel Foucault, *Surveiller et punir* (Paris: Gallimard, 1975); *Discipline and Punish*, trans. A. Sheridan (New York: Pantheon, 1977).
4. From this point of view as well, the works of Henri Lefebvre on everyday life constitute a fundamental source.
5. On art, from the *Encyclopédie* to Durkheim, see below pp. 66–68.
6. For this literature, see the booklets mentioned in *Le Livre dans la vie quotidienne* (Paris: Bibliothèque Nationale, 1975) and in Geneviève Bollème, *La Bible bleue, Anthologie d'une littérature 'populaire'* (Paris: Flammarion, 1975), 141–379.
7. The first of these two monographs was written by Pierre Mayol, the second by Luce Giard (on the basis of interviews made by Marie Ferrier). See *L'Invention du quotidien*, II, Luce Giard and Pierre Mayol, *Habiter, cuisiner* (Paris: UGE 10/18, 1980).
8. By Erving Goffman, see especially *Interaction Rituals* (Garden City, N.Y.: Anchor Books, 1976); *The Presentation of Self in Everyday Life* (Woodstock, N.Y.: The Overlook Press, 1973); *Frame Analysis* (New York: Harper & Row, 1974). By Pierre Bourdieu, see *Esquisse d'une théorie de la pratique. Précédée de trois études d'ethnologie kabyle* (Genève: Droz, 1972); 'Les Stratégies matrimoniales,' *Annales: économies, sociétés, civilisations* 27 (1972), 1105–1127; 'Le Langage autorisé,' *Actes de la recherche en sciences sociales*, No. 5–6 (November 1975), 184–190; 'Le Sens pratique,' *Actes de la recherche en sciences sociales*, No. 1 (February 1976), 43–86. By Marcel Mauss, see especially 'Techniques du corps,' in *Sociologie et*

anthropologie (Paris: PUF, 1950). By Marcel Détienne and Jean-Pierre Vernant, *Les Ruses de l'intelligence. La mètis des Grecs* (Paris: Flammarion, 1974). By Jeremy Boissevain, *Friends of Friends. Networks, Manipulators and Coalitions* (Oxford: Blackwell, 1974). By Edward O. Laumann, *Bonds of Pluralism. The Form and Substance of Urban Social Networks* (New York: John Wiley, 1973).

9. Joshua A. Fishman, *The Sociology of Language* (Rowley, Mass.: Newbury, 1972). See also the essays in *Studies in Social Interaction*, ed. David Sudnow (New York: The Free Press, 1972); William Labov, *Sociolinguistic Patterns* (Philadelphia: University of Pennsylvania Press, 1973); etc.

10. Oswald Ducrot, *Dire et ne pas dire* (Paris: Hermann, 1972); and David K. Lewis, *Convention: a Philosophical Study* (Cambridge, Mass.: Harvard University Press, 1974), and *Counterfactuals* (Cambridge, Mass.: Harvard University Press, 1973).

11. Georg H. von Wright, *Norm and Action* (London: Routledge & Kegan Paul, 1963); *Essay in Deontic Logic and the General Theory of Action* (Amsterdam: North Holland, 1968); *Explanation and Understanding* (Ithaca, N.Y.: Cornell University Press, 1971). And A. C. Danto, *Analytical Philosophy of Action* (Cambridge: Cambridge University Press, 1973); Richard J. Bernstein, *Praxis and Action* (London: Duckworth, 1972); and *La Sémantique de l'action*, ed. Paul Ricoeur and Doriane Tiffeneau (Paris: CNRS, 1977).

12. A. N. Prior, *Past, Present and Future: a Study of 'Tense Logic'* (Oxford: Oxford University Press, 1967) and *Papers on Tense and Time* (Oxford: Oxford University Press, 1968). N. Rescher and A. Urquhart, *Temporal Logic* (Oxford: Oxford University Press, 1975).

13. Alan R. White, *Modal Thinking* (Ithaca, N.Y.: Cornell University Press, 1975); G. E. Hughes and M. J. Cresswell, *An Introduction to Modal Logic* (Oxford: Oxford University Press, 1973); I. R. Zeeman, *Modal Logic* (Oxford: Oxford University Press, 1975); S. Haacker, *Deviant Logic* (Cambridge: Cambridge University Press, 1976); *Discussing Language with Chomsky, Halliday, etc.*, ed. H. Parret (The Hague: Mouton, 1975).

14. As it is more technical, the study concerning the logics of action and time, as well as modalization, will be published elsewhere.

15. Jacques Sojcher, *La Démarche poétique* (Paris: UGE 10/18, 1976), 145.

16. See Fernand Deligny, *Les Vagabonds efficaces* (Paris: Maspero, 1970); *Nous et l'innocent* (Paris: Maspero, 1977); etc.

17. See M. de Certeau, *La Culture au pluriel*, 283–308; and 'Actions culturelles et stratégies politiques,' *La Revue nouvelle*, April 1974, 351–360.

18. The analysis of the principles of isolation allows us to make this criticism both more nuanced and more precise. See *Pour une histoire de la statistique* (Paris: INSEE, 1978), I, in particular Alain Desrosières, 'Eléments pour l'histoire des nomenclatures socio-professionnelles,' 155–231.

19. The works of P. Bourdieu and those of M. Détienne and J.-P. Vernant make possible the notion of 'tactic' more precise, but the socio-linguistic investigations of H. Garfinkel, H. Sacks, et al. also contribute to this clarification. See notes 8 and 9.

20. M. Détienne and J.-P. Vernant, *Les Ruses de l'intelligence*.

21. See S. Toulmin, *The Uses of Argument* (Cambridge: Cambridge University Press, 1958); Ch. Perelman and L. Ollbrechts-Tyteca, *Traité de l'argumentation* (Bruxelles: Université libre, 1970); J. Dubois, et al., *Rhétorique générale* (Paris: Larousse, 1970); etc.

22. The works of Corax, said to be the author of the earliest Greek text on rhetoric, are lost; on this point, see Aristotle, *Rhetoric*, II, 24, 1402a. See W. K. C. Guthrie, *The Sophists* (Cambridge: Cambridge University Press, 1971), 178–179.

23. Sun Tzu, *The Art of War*, trans. S. B. Griffith (Oxford: The Clarendon Press, 1963). Sun Tzu (Sun Zi) should not be confused with the later military theorist Hsün Tzu (Xun Zi).

24. *Le Livre des ruses. La Stratégie politique des Arabes*, ed. R. K. Khawam (Paris: Phébus, 1976).
25. See Jean Baudrillard, *Le Système des objets* (Paris: Gallimard, 1968); *La Société de consommation* (Paris: Denoël, 1970); *Pour une critique de l'économie politique du signe* (Paris: Gallimard, 1972).
26. Guy Debord, *La Société du spectacle* (Paris: Buchet-Chastel, 1967).
27. Roland Barthes, *Le Plaisir du texte* (Paris: Seuil, 1973), 58; *The Pleasure of the Text*, trans. R. Miller (New York: Hill and Wang, 1975).
28. See Gérard Mordillat and Nicolas Philibert, *Ces Patrons éclairés qui craignent la lumière* (Paris: Albatros, 1979).
29. See the essays of H. Sacks, E. A. Schegloff, etc., quoted above. This analysis, entitled *Arts de dire*, will be published separately.
30. See below, Part III, Chapters VII to IX.
31. We have devoted monographs to these practices in which the proliferating and disseminated bibliography on the subject will be found (see *L'Invention du quotidien*, II, *Habiter, cuisiner*, by Luce Giard and Pierre Mayol).
32. W. Gombrowicz, *Cosmos* (Paris: Gallimard Folio, 1971), 165–168; originally *Kosmos* (1965); *Cosmos*, trans. E. Mosbacker (London: MacGibbon and Kee, 1967).

9

POSTSCRIPT ON THE SOCIETIES OF CONTROL

Gilles Deleuze

I. HISTORICAL

Foucault located the *disciplinary societies* in the eighteenth and nineteenth centuries; they reach their height at the outset of the twentieth. They initiate the organization of vast spaces of enclosure. The individual never ceases passing from one closed environment to another, each having its own laws: first the family; then the school ('you are no longer in your family'); then the barracks ('you are no longer at school'); then the factory; from time to time the hospital; possibly the prison, the preeminent instance of the enclosed environment. It's the prison that serves as the analogical model: at the sight of some laborers, the heroine of Rossellini's *Europa '51* could exclaim, 'I thought I was seeing convicts.'

Foucault has brilliantly analyzed the ideal project of these environments of enclosure, particularly visible within the factor: to concentrate; to distribute in space; to order in time; to compose a productive force within the dimension of space-time whose effect will be greater than the sum of its component forces. But what Foucault recognized as well was the transience of this model: it succeeded that of the *societies of sovereignty*, the goal and functions of which were something quite different (to tax rather than to organize production, to rule on death rather than to administer life); the transition took place over time, and Napoleon seemed to effect the large-scale conversion from one society to the other. But in their turn the disciplines underwent a crisis to the benefit of new forces that were gradually instituted and which accelerated after

From *October* 59 (Winter 1992) pp. 3–7. Originally appeared in *L'Autre* journal 1 (May 1990).

World War II: a disciplinary society was what we already no longer were, what we had ceased to be.

We are in a generalized crisis in relation to all the environments of enclosure – prison, hospital, factory, school, family. The family is an 'interior,' in crisis like all other interiors – scholarly, professional, etc. The administrations in charge never cease announcing supposedly necessary reforms: to reform schools, to reform industries, hospitals, the armed forces, prisons. But everyone knows that these institutions are finished, whatever the length of their expiration periods. It's only a matter of administering their last rites and of keeping people employed until the installation of the new forces knocking at the door. These are the *societies of control*, which are in the process of replacing disciplinary societies. 'Control' is the name Burroughs proposes as a term for the new monster, one that Foucault recognizes as our immediate future. Paul Virilio also is continually analyzing the ultrarapid forms of free-floating control that replaced the old disciplines operating in the time frame of a closed system. There is no need to invoke the extraordinary pharmaceutical productions, the molecular engineering, the genetic manipulations, although these are slated to enter the new process. There is no need to ask which is the toughest regime, for it's within each of them that liberating and enslaving forces confront one another. For example, in the crisis of the hospital as environment of enclosure, neighborhood clinics, hospices, and day care could at first express new freedom, but they could participate as well in mechanisms of control that are equal to the harshest of confinements. There is no need to fear or hope, but only to look for new weapons.

2. LOGIC

The different internments of spaces of enclosure through which the individual passes are independent variables: each time one is supposed to start from zero, and although a common language for all these places exists, it is *analogical*. On the other hand, the different control mechanisms are inseparable variations, forming a system of variable geometry the language of which is numerical (which doesn't necessarily mean binary). Enclosures are *molds*, distinct castings, but controls are a *modulation*, like a self-deforming cast that will continuously change from one moment to the other, or like a sieve whose mesh will transmute from point to point.

This is obvious in the matter of salaries: the factory was a body that contained its internal forces at the level of equilibrium, the highest possible in terms of production, the lowest possible in terms of wages; but in a society of control, the corporation has replaced the factory, and the corporation is a spirit, a gas. Of course the factory was already familiar with the system of bonuses, but the corporation works more deeply to impose a modulation of each salary, in states of perpetual metastability that operate through challenges, contests, and highly comic group sessions. If the most idiotic television game shows are so successful, it's because they express the corporate situation with great precision. The factory constituted individuals as a single body to the double advantage of the boss who surveyed each element within the mass and the unions who mobilized a mass resistance; but the corporation constantly presents the brashest rivalry as a healthy form of emulation, an excellent motivational force that opposes individuals against one another and runs through each, dividing each within. The modulating principle of 'salary according to merit' has not failed to tempt national education itself. Indeed, just as the corporation replaces the factory, *perpetual training* tends to replace the *school*, and continuous control to replace the examination. Which is the surest way of delivering the school over to the corporation.

In the disciplinary societies one was always starting again (from school to the barracks, from the barracks to the factory), while in the societies of control one is never finished with anything – the corporation, the educational system, the armed services being metastable states coexisting in one and the same modulation, like a universal system of deformation. In *The Trial*, Kafka, who had already placed himself at the pivotal point between two types of social formation, described the most fearsome of judicial forms. The *apparent acquittal* of the disciplinary societies (between two incarcerations); and the *limitless postponements* of the societies of control (in continuous variation) are two very different modes of juridicial life, and if our law is hesitant, itself in crisis, it's because we are leaving one in order to enter the other. The disciplinary societies have two poles: the signature that designates the *individual*, and the number or administrative numeration that indicates his or her position within a *mass*. This is because the disciplines never saw any incompatibility between these two, and because at the same time power individualizes and masses together, that is, constitutes those over whom it exercises power into a body and molds the individuality of each member of that body. (Foucault saw the origin of this double charge in the pastoral power of the priest – the flock and each of its animals – but civil power moves in turn and by other means to make itself lay 'priest.') In the societies of control, on the other hand, what is important is no longer either a signature or a number, but a code: the code is a *password*, while on the other hand disciplinary societies are regulated by *watchwords* (as much from the point of view of integration as from that of resistance). The numerical language of control is made of codes that mark access to information, or reject it. We no longer find ourselves dealing with the mass/individual pair. Individuals have become *'dividuals,'* and masses, samples, data, markets, or *'banks.'* Perhaps it is money that expresses the distinction between the two societies best, since discipline always referred back to minted money that locks gold as numerical standard, while control relates to floating rates of exchange, modulated according to a rate established by a set of standard currencies. The old monetary mole is the animal of the space of enclosure, but the serpent is that of the societies of control. We have passed from one animal to the other, from the mole to the serpent, in the system under which we live, but also in our manner of living and in our relations with others. The disciplinary man was a discontinuous producer of energy, but the man of control is undulatory, in orbit, in a continuous network. Everywhere *surfing* has already replaced the older *sports*.

Types of machines are easily matched with each type of society – not that machines are determining, but because they express those social forms capable of generating them and using them. The old societies of sovereignty made use of simple machines – levers, pulleys, clocks; but the recent disciplinary societies equipped themselves with machines involving energy, with the passive danger of entropy and the active danger of sabotage; the societies of control operate with machines of a third type, computers, whose passive danger is jamming and whose active one is piracy or the introduction of viruses. This technological evolution must be, even more profoundly, a mutation of capitalism, an already well-known or familiar mutation that can be summed up as follows: nineteenth-century capitalism is a capitalism of concentration, for production, and for property. It therefore erects a factory as a space of enclosure, the capitalist being the owner of the means of production but also, progressively, the owner of other spaces conceived through analogy (the worker's familial house, the school). As for markets, they are conquered sometimes by specialization, sometimes by colonization, sometimes by lowering the costs of production. But in the present situation, capitalism is no longer involved in production, which it often relegates to the Third World, even for the complex forms of textiles, metallurgy, or oil production. It's a capitalism of higher-order production. It no longer buys raw materials and no longer sells the finished products: it buys the finished products or assembles parts. What it wants to sell is services but what it wants to buy is stocks. This is no longer a capitalism for production but for the product, which is to say, for being sold or marketed. Thus it is essentially dispersive, and the factory has given way to the corporation. The family, the school, the army, the factory are no longer the distinct analogical spaces that converge towards an owner – state or private power – but coded figures – deformable and transformable – of a single corporation that now has only stockholders. Even art has left the spaces of enclosure in order to enter into the open circuits of the bank. The conquests of the market are made by grabbing control and no longer by disciplinary training, by fixing the exchange rate much more than by lowering costs, by transformation of the product more than by specialization of production. Corruption thereby gains a new power. Marketing has become the center or the 'soul' of the corporation. We are taught that corporations have a soul, which is the most terrifying news in the world. The operation of markets is now the instrument of social control and forms the impudent breed of our masters. Control is short-term and of rapid rates of turnover, but also continuous and without limit, while discipline was of long duration, infinite and discontinuous. Man is no longer man enclosed, but man in debt. It is true that capitalism has retained as a constant the extreme poverty of three-quarters of humanity, too poor for debt, too numerous for confinement: control will not only have to deal with erosions of frontiers but with the explosions within shanty towns or ghettos.

3. PROGRAM

The conception of a control mechanism, giving the position of any element within an open environment at any given instant (whether animal in a reserve or human in a corporation, as with an electronic collar), is not necessarily one of science fiction. Félix Guattari has imagined a city where one would be able to leave one's apartment, one's street, one's neighborhood, thanks to one's (dividual) electronic card that raises a given barrier; but the card could just as easily be rejected on a given day or between certain hours; what counts is not the barrier but the computer that tracks each person's position – licit or illicit – and effects a universal modulation.

The socio-technological study of the mechanisms of control, grasped at their inception, would have to be categorical and to describe what is already in the process of substitution for the disciplinary sites of enclosure, whose crisis is everywhere proclaimed. It may be that older methods, borrowed from the former societies of sovereignty, will return to the fore, but with the necessary modifications. What counts is that we are at the beginning of something. In the *prison system*: the attempt to find penalties of 'substitution,' at least for petty crimes, and the use of electronic collars that force the convicted person to stay at home during certain hours. For the *school system*: continuous forms of control, and the effect on the school of perpetual training, the corresponding abandonment of all university research, the introduction of the 'corporation' at all levels of schooling. For the *hospital system*: the new medicine 'without doctor or patient' that singles out potential sick people and subjects at risk, which in no way attests to individuation – as they say – but substitutes for the individual or numerical body the code of a 'dividual' material to be controlled. In the *corporate system*: new ways of handling money, profits, and humans that no longer pass through the old factory form. These are very small examples, but ones that will allow for better understanding of what is meant by the crisis of the institutions, which is to say, the progressive and dispersed installation of a new system of domination. One of the most important questions will concern the ineptitude of the unions: tied to the whole of their history of struggle against the disciplines or within the spaces of enclosure, will they be able to adapt themselves or will they give way to new forms of resistance against the societies of control? Can we already grasp the rough outlines of the coming forms, capable of threatening the joys of marketing? Many young people strangely boast of being 'motivated'; they re-request apprenticeships and permanent training. It's up to them to discover what they're being made to serve, just as their elders discovered, not without difficulty, the telos of the disciplines. The coils of a serpent are even more complex that the burrows of a molehill.

10

SOME PROPERTIES OF FIELDS

Pierre Bourdieu

Fields present themselves synchronically as structured spaces of positions (or posts) whose properties depend on their position within these spaces and which can be analysed independently of the characteristics of their occupants (which are partly determined by them). There are *general laws of fields*: fields as different as the field of politics, the field of philosophy or the field of religion have invariant laws of functioning. (That is why the project of a general theory is not unreasonable and why, even now, we can use what we learn about the functioning of each particular field to question and interpret other fields, so moving beyond the deadly antinomy of monographic idiography and formal, empty theory.) Whenever one studies a new field, whether it be the field of philology in the nineteenth century, contemporary fashion, or religion in the Middle Ages, one discovers specific properties that are peculiar to that field, at the same time as one pushes forward our knowledge of the universal mechanisms of fields, which are specified in terms of secondary variables. For example, national variables mean that generic mechanisms such as the struggle between the challengers and the established dominant actors take different forms. But we know that in every field we shall find a struggle, the specific forms of which have to be looked for each time, between the newcomer who tries to break through the entry barrier and the dominant agent who will try to defend the monopoly and keep out competition.

A field – even the scientific field – defines itself by (among other things) defining specific stakes and interests, which are irreducible to the stakes and

From Pierre Bourdieu, *Sociology in Question* (London: Sage, 1993) pp. 72–7. From a talk given at the Ècole Supérieure, Paris, in November 1976, to a group of philologists and literary historians.

interests specific to other fields (you can't make a philosopher compete for the prizes that interest a geographer) and which are not perceived by someone who has not been shaped to enter that field (every category of interests implies indifference to other interests, other investments, which are therefore bound to be perceived as absurd, irrational, or sublime and disinterested). In order for a field to function, there have to be stakes and people prepared to play the game, endowed with the *habitus* that implies knowledge and recognition of the immanent laws of the field, the stakes, and so on.

The *habitus* of a philologist is all at once a 'craft', a collection of techniques, references, and a set of 'beliefs', such as the propensity to give as much importance to the notes as to the text. These are properties that derive from the history (national and international) of the discipline and its (intermediate) position in the hierarchy of disciplines, and which are both the condition of the functioning of the field and the product of its functioning (but not entirely: a field may simply receive and consecrate a particular type of *habitus* that is more or less fully constituted).

The structure of the field is a *state* of the power relations among the agents or institutions engaged in the struggle, or, to put it another way, a state of the distribution of the specific capital which has been accumulated in the course of previous struggles and which orients subsequent strategies. This structure, which governs the strategies aimed at transforming it, is itself always at stake. The struggles which take place within the field are about the monopoly of the legitimate violence (specific authority) which is characteristic of the field in question, which means, ultimately, the conservation or subversion of the structure of the distribution of the specific capital. (When one speaks of specific capital, this means to say that this capital is effective *in relation to* a particular field, and therefore within the limits of that field, and that it is only convertible into another kind of capital on certain conditions. You only have to think, for example, of the failure of Pierre Cardin when he tried to transfer capital accumulated in *haute couture* into high culture. Every last art critic felt called upon to assert his structural superiority as a member of a structurally more legitimate field by saying that everything Cardin did in legitimate art was contemptible, thus imposing the most unfavourable conversion rate on Cardin's capital.)

Those who, in a determinate state of the power relations, more or less completely monopolize the specific capital, the basis of the specific power or authority characteristic of a field, are inclined to conservation strategies – those which, in the fields of production of cultural goods, tend to defend *orthodoxy* – whereas those least endowed with capital (who are often also the newcomers, and therefore generally the youngest) are inclined towards subversion strategies, the strategies of *heresy*. Heresy, heterodoxy, functioning as a critical break with doxa (and often associated with a crisis), is what brings the dominant agents out of their silence and forces them to produce the defensive discourse of orthodoxy, the right-thinking, right-wing thought that is aimed at restoring the equivalent of silent assent to doxa.

Another property of fields, a less visible one, is that all the agents that are involved in a field share a certain number of fundamental interests, namely everything that is linked to the very existence of the field. This leads to an objective complicity which underlies all the antagonisms. It tends to be forgotten that a fight presupposes agreement between the antagonists about what it is that is worth fighting about; those points of agreement are held at the level of what 'goes without saying', they are left in the state of doxa, in other words everything that makes the field itself, the game, the stakes, all the presuppositions that one tacitly and even unwittingly accepts by the mere fact of playing, of entering into the game. Those who take part in the struggle help to reproduce the game by helping – more or less completely, depending on the field – to produce belief in the value of the stakes. The new players have to pay an entry fee which consists in recognition of the value of the game (selection and co-option always pay great attention to the indices of commitment to the game, investment in it) and in (practical) knowledge of the principles of the functioning of the game. They are condemned to use the strategies of subversion, but, if they are not to incur exclusion from the game, these strategies have to remain within certain limits. The *partial revolutions* which constantly occur in fields do not call into question the very foundations of the game, its fundamental axioms, the bedrock of ultimate beliefs on which the whole game is based. On the contrary, in the fields of production of cultural goods – religion, literature or art – heretical subversion claims to be returning to the sources, the origin, the spirit, the authentic essence of the game, in opposition to the banalization and degradation which it has suffered. (One of the factors protecting the various games from total revolutions, which could destroy not only the dominant agents and their domination, but the game itself, is the very size of the investment, in time, effort and so on, presupposed by entry into the game. Like the ordeals in rites of passage, this investment helps to make the pure and simple destruction of the game *unthinkable* in practical terms. Thus whole sectors of culture – with an audience of philologists, I can't help thinking of philology – are saved by the cost entailed in acquiring the knowledge needed even to destroy them with due form.)

Through the practical knowledge of the principles of the game that is tacitly required of new entrants, the whole history of the game, the whole past of the game, is present in each act of the game. It is no accident that, together with the presence in each work of traces of the objective (and sometimes even conscious) relationship to other works, one of the surest indices of the constitution of a field is the appearance of a corps of conservators of lives – the biographers – and of works – the philologists, the historians of art and literature, who start to archive the sketches, the drafts, the manuscripts, to 'correct' them (the right to 'correct' is the legitimate violence of the philologist), to decipher them, etc. These agents' interests lie in conserving what is produced in the field, and in so doing to conserve themselves. And another index that an area has started to function as a field is the trace of the history of the field in the individual work (and even in the life of the producer). For a proof of this, *a contrario*, one could analyse the history of the relations between a so-called 'naïve' painter (one who almost stumbles into the field, without paying the entry fee, the toll) such as Douanier Rousseau, and the contemporary artists, like Jarry, Apollinaire or Picasso, who play (in the literal sense, with all kinds of more or less charitable hoaxes) with someone who does not know how to play the game, who wants to paint like Bouguereau or Bonnat in the age of futurism and cubism, and who breaks the game, but unwittingly, in contrast to people like Duchamp, or even Satie, who understand the logic of the game well enough to defy it and exploit it at the same time. And then one would also have to analyse the history of the subsequent interpretation of the *œuvre*, which, through over-interpretation, pushes it back into the ranks, into the history, and endeavours to turn this weekend painter (the aesthetic principles of his painting, such as the uncompromising frontality of his portraits, are those which working-class people put into their photography) into a conscious, inspired revolutionary.

There is a field effect when it is no longer possible to understand a work (and the *value*, i.e. the belief, that it is granted) without knowing the history of the field of production of the work. That is how the exegetes, commentators, interpreters, historians, semiologists and philologists, come to be justified in existing, as the only people capable of accounting for the work and the recognition of value that it enjoys. The sociology of art or literature that *directly* relates works of art to the producers' or clients' position in social space (their social class) without considering their position in the field of production (a 'reduction' which is, strictly, only valid for 'naïve' artists) sweeps aside everything that the work owes to the field and its history – that is to say, precisely that which makes it a work of art, or science, or philosophy. A philosophical (or scientific, etc.) problem is a problem that philosophers (or scientists) recognize (in both senses) as such (because it is inscribed in the logic of the history of the field and in their dispositions, which are historically constituted by and for membership of the field) and which, by virtue of the specific authority they are recognized as having, has every chance of being very widely recognized as legitimate. Here too, the example of 'naïve' producers is very enlightening. They are people who have had the status of painters or writers (revolutionary ones, to boot) thrust upon them in the name of a problematic of which they were quite unaware. The verbal associations of Jean-Pierre Brisset, his long sequences of word equations, alliterations and incongruities, which he intended for learned societies and academic conferences, making a 'field mistake' which testifies to his innocence, would have remained the ramblings of a madman for which they were first taken, if Jarry's 'pataphysics', Apollinaire's and Duchamp's puns, or the automatic writing of the surrealists had not created the problematic in relation to which they could take on a meaning. These object-poets and object-painters, these 'objective revolutionaries', enable us to observe, in isolation, the transmuting power of the field. This power equally operates, albeit in a less striking and better grounded way, on the works of the professionals who know the game and the problematic, who know what they are doing (which does not in the least mean that they are cynical), so that the *necessity* that a consecrating reading finds in them does not appear so obviously as the product of an objective accident (which it also is, inasmuch as it presupposes a miraculous harmony between a philosophical disposition and a state of the expectations inscribed in the field). Heidegger is often Spengler or Jünger transposed into the philosophical field. He has some very simple things to say: 'technique' is the decline of the West; everything has gone downhill since Descartes, and so on.

The field, or, more precisely, the *habitus* of a professional, adjusted in advance to the demands of the field (for example, to the prevailing definition of the legitimate problematic), will function as a translating machine: being a 'revolutionary conservative' in philosophy means revolutionizing the image of Kantian philosophy by showing that at the root of this philosophy which presents itself as the critique of metaphysics, there is more metaphysics. This systematic transformation of problems and themes is not the product of a conscious (and cynically calculated) endeavour, but an automatic effect of belonging to the field and the mastery of the specific history of the field that it implies. Being a philosopher means knowing what one needs to know of the history of philosophy in order to be able to behave as a philosopher within a philosophical field.

I want to re-emphasize that the principle of philosophical (or literary) strategies is not cynical calculation, the conscious pursuit of maximum specific profit, but an unconscious relationship between a *habitus* and a field.

The strategies I am talking about are actions objectively oriented towards goals that may not be the goals subjectively pursued. And the theory of the *habitus* is aimed at establishing the possibility of a science of practices that escapes the forced choice between finalism and mechanism. (The word *interest*, which I have used several times, is also very dangerous, because it is liable to suggest a utilitarianism that is the degree zero of sociology. That said, sociology cannot dispense with the axiom of interest, understood as the *specific investment* in the stakes, which is both the condition and the product of membership of a field.) The *habitus*, a system of dispositions acquired by implicit or explicit learning which functions as a system of generative schemes, generates strategies which can be objectively consistent with the objective interests of their authors without having been expressly designed to that end. We have to learn to escape from the forced choice between naïve teleology (according to which, for example, the 'revolution' which led Apollinaire to the audacities of *Lundi rue Christine* and other poetic 'ready-mades' was motivated by the aim of placing himself at the head of the movement pioneered by Cendrars, the futurists or Delaunay) and mechanistic explanation (which would see this transformation as a direct and simple effect of social determinations). When people only have to let their *habitus* follow its natural bent in order to comply with the immanent necessity of the field and satisfy the demands contained within in it (which, in every field, is the very definition of excellence), they are not at all aware of fulfilling a duty, still less of seeking to maximize their (specific) profit. So they enjoy the additional profit of seeing themselves and being seen as totally disinterested.

FURTHER READING

For further discussion, see Bourdieu, P. (1975) 'Le couturier et sa griffe: contribution à une théorie de la magie', *Actes de la recherche en sciences sociales*, I: 7–36; (1988) *L'Ontologie politique de Martin Heidegger*, Paris: Éditions de Minuit; (1988) *The Logic of Practice*, Oxford: Polity Press.

FURTHER READING

Abbas, A. and Nguyet, E. (eds) *Internationalizing Cultural Studies: An Anthology* (London: Blackwell, 2005).

Barker, C., *Making Sense of Cultural Studies: Central Problems and Critical Debates* (London: Sage, 2002).

Benjamin, W., *Illuminations* (London: Collins, [1935] 1973) pp. 219–54.

Bourdieu, P., *The Logic of Practice* (Cambridge: Polity Press, [1980] 1992).

Bourdieu, P., 'Some Properties of Fields', in *Sociology in Question* (London: Sage, 1993) pp. 72–7.

Bourdieu, P., *In Other Words: Essays Towards a Reflexive Sociology* (Cambridge: Polity Press, [1990] 2000).

Butler, Judith, *Gender Trouble: Feminism and the Subversion of Identity* (London: Routledge, 1990).

Butler, J., *Undoing Gender* (London: Routledge, 2004).

Carey, J., 'Technology and Ideology: The Case of the Telegraph', in *Communication as Culture* (London: Routledge, 1989).

Couldry, N., *Inside Culture: Re-imagining the Method of Cultural Studies* (London: Sage, 2000).

Couldry, N., *Media and Symbolic Power: Extending the Range of Bourdieu's Field Theory,* Media@lse Electronic Working Papers No. 2. LSE, Department of Media and Communications, 2003. Online at: http://www.lse.ac.uk/collections/media@lse/Default.htm.

De Certeau, M., *The Practice of Everyday Life* (Berkeley, CA: University of California Press, 1984) pp. xi–xxiv.

De Lauretis, T., *Alice Doesn't* (London: Macmillan, 1984).

Deleuze, G., 'Postscript on the Societies of Control', *October*, 59 (Winter 1992) pp. 3–7.

Derrida, J., *Archive Fever* (London: University of Chicago Press, 1995).

Durham, M. G. and Kellner, D. (eds), *Media and Cultural Studies: Keyworks* (London: Sage, 2001) pp. ix–xxxviii.

Foucault, M., 'Subject and Power', Afterword to H. Dreyfus and P. Rabinow (eds), *Beyond Structuralism and Hermeneutics* (Brighton: Harvester, 1982).

Hall, G. and Birchall, C. (eds) *New Cultural Studies: Adventures in Theory* (Edinburgh: Edinburgh University Press, 2006).

Haraway, D., 'The Promise of Monsters', in L. Grosberg, C. Nelson and P. Treichler (eds), *Cultural Studies* (New York: Routledge 1992) pp. 295–338.

Haraway, D., *Simians, Cyborgs and Women* (London: Routledge, 1991).

Garnham, N. and Williams, R. 'Pierre Bourdieu and the Sociology of Culture: An Introduction', in Garnham, N., *Capitalism and Communication* (London: Sage, 1990).

Jenkins, H., *Convergence Culture: Where Old and New Media Collide* (New York: New York University Press, 2006).

Katz, E., Durham Peters, J., Liebes, T. and Orloff, A. (eds), *Canonic Texts in Media Research* (London: Polity, 2003).

Leslie, E., *Walter Benjamin, Overpowering Conformism* (London: Pluto Press, 2000).

Lyotard, J.-F., *The Post Modern Condition: A Report on Knowledge* (Manchester: Manchester University Press, 1984).

McLuhan, M., 'The Medium is the Message' and 'Media Hot and Cold', in *Understanding Media: The Extensions of Man* (London: MIT Press, [1964] 1994) pp. 7–21, 297.

McNay, L., *Gender and Agency: Reconfiguring the Subject in Feminist and Social Theory* (Cambridge: Polity Press, 2000).

Mattelart, A. and Mattelart, M., *Theories of Communication* (London: Sage, 1998).

Mellencamp, P. (ed.), *Logics of Television: Essays in Cultural Criticism* (Bloomington/London: Indiana University Press/BFI, 1990).

Merrin, W., *Baudrillard and the Media: A Critical Introduction* (Cambridge: Polity, 2005).

Morley, D. 'So-called Cultural Studies: Dead Ends and Reinvented Wheels', in *Media, Modernity and Technology: The Geography of the New* (London: Routledge, 2006).

Rajchman, J., *The Deleuze Connections* (Cambridge, MA: MIT Press, 2001).

Redhead, S., *The Jean Baudrillard Reader* (Edinburgh: Edinburgh University Press, 2008).

Rose, G., *Visual Methodologies: An Introduction to the Interpretation of Visual Materials*, 2nd edn (London: Sage, 2006).

Sarikakis, K., *British Media in a Global Era* (London: Hodder, 2005).

Scannell, P., *Media and Communication* (London: Sage, 2007).

Seigworth, G. J.,'Culture Studies and Gilles Deleuze', in G. Hall and C. Birchall (eds), *New Cultural Studies, Adventures of Theory* (Edinburgh: Edinburgh University Press, 2006) pp. 107–28.

Spivak, G. C., 'Can The Subaltern Speak?', in *Colonial Discourse and Postcolonial Theory: A Reader* (London: Harvester Wheatsheaf, 1993).

Taylor, P. A. and Harris, J. L., *Critical Theories of Mass Culture* (Buckingham: Open University Press, 2008).

Van Loon, J., *Media Technology, Critical Perspectives* (Buckingham: Open University Press, 2007)

Wood, D., 'Foucault and Panopticism Revisited', *Surveillance and Society* 1:3 (2003) pp. 234–9.

Yar, M., 'Panoptic Power and the Pathologisation of Vision: Critical Reflections on the Foucauldian Thesis', *Surveillance and Society* 1:3 (2003) pp. 254–71.

Zielinski, S., *Deep Time of the Media* (Boston: MIT, 2006).

Zylinksa, J., *The Ethics of Cultural Studies* (London: Continuum Books, 2005).

SECTION 2
THE MEDIA AND THE PUBLIC SPHERE

INTRODUCTION: THE MEDIA AND THE PUBLIC SPHERE

What role do the media play in public debate, in forming public opinion, in making governments accountable to their electors, in forming a consensus around the ethics of particular issues or particular forms of scientific knowledge, business practice or behaviour? All of these elements are germane to the public sphere as it is narrowly defined. A less restrictive definition introduces a broader politics of access and participation, concerns itself with mediated public spheres of many kinds and explores cultural as well as political citizenship.

The role of the media within the public sphere might be explored through the optic of mediation, representation or communication. To inquire into the functioning of the public sphere is to ask whose voices (which groups) can speak or are heard and whose are silenced. It is to ask what kind of conversation or discussion or programming (for instance, what subjects, what tone, what form of argumentation) produces forms of public talk that contribute to the constitution of a public sphere within a democracy. Is it enough that a particular form of publicity (a particular public sphere) allows those who act within it to air issues and bring matters into the public arena, or must these public debates produce consensus or be capable of contributing to the production of change? Are the judgements we make about this formal (does communication happen?), ethical (are the terms of encounter moral?) or political, that is, are there structural inequalities, questions of recognition, or a politics of listening or viewing that temper the way in which we assess the operations of specific forms of mediation?

The writings in this section begin with Edward Said's influential account of Orientalism as a discourse in which the West speaks for the East and in doing so speaks it as the Other. Said's history of Orientalism argues vehemently against understandings of communication based on 'veridic discourse' – or the attempt to transmit the truth. Truth and power, he suggests, following Foucault, are bound up, so that at issue in exploring the West's relations with what it named the Orient and with those who come from there isn't whether what is said is true or false but the effects of what is said and done by those who speak and are heard. The apparently cosmopolitan encounter may not be an encounter at all.

This is followed by Andreas Huyssen's exploration of the formation of the mass public as an element of mass culture and his consideration of its fragmentation as an element of postmodern aesthetics – a development Huyssen does not entirely regret. These two pieces, along with Jürgen Habermas' account of the modern constitution of the mediated public sphere and its decline (see Section 1) indicate some of the contexts within which contemporary reformations both of publics and of theorisations of the public sphere are being conducted. The latter are traced in the register of critical writing around globalisation and modernity/postmodernity through Thompson, in Castells' exploration of the spaces and times of information and in Sreberny's ethnographic account of mixedness and media in the UK.

Mass Publics

The media are central to the processes through which individuals and groups communicate with each other. The rise of mass media systems are integral to the rise of mass culture and are also integral to the creation of the mass as the *subjects* of mass culture. The mass constitutes a new form of public, forged as a product of consumer society (mass society) and a product of mass communications systems. At once a symptom of a technocratic rationality and the bearer of a particular form of deprivation (responsibility, choice, authenticity) the mass is often viewed ambiguously: as both impotent (controlled or deceived in their choices) and violent (the mass as irrational mob).

In his account of modernism and mass culture which explores these questions through the optic of aesthetics, Andreas Huyssen gets at this ambiguity when he considers the degree to which the mass audience, as modernism's other, has tended to be feminised (128), which might imply it has been subjected to various forms of pacification. The ambiguity comes when we consider that the mass is also demanding. Mass culture and its subject (which is the mass itself) has provided the enabling grounds for new forms of public participation, and for new kinds of previously disenfranchised publics: as he puts it, the masses 'knocking at the gate' were also women (127). In the new aesthetic climate arising out of these contradictions in the early years of the 1950s/1960s, says Huyssen, a new aesthetic, the political aesthetic of feminism, which was also a postmodern aesthetic, could thrive (135). Huyssen's claim is that this could deliver, even if in a conflicted way, a critique of forms of publicity arranged around the male gaze and a particular form of spectatorship.

The importance of Huyssen's account is that it questions a monolithic view of the 'mass' as the subject of 'mass culture', and in doing so forces us to reconsider the constitution of 'the public'. Finally, it questions the unexamined idea of progress (modernism) as the central project, the ideal outcome, in a sense the proper 'matter' of all forms of public debate. Huyssen's account provides important contexts for a series of considerations of the public sphere that focus on its spatial and temporal organisation and the battles for its expansion. Debates reappraising the nation as the natural horizon of the public sphere have come back to many of these arguments.

THE NATION AND THE PUBLIC SPHERE

The role and nature of the mediated public sphere, defined as a layer located within civil society that sits between government and the people, has been explored extensively by socials scientists of all kinds as well as media scholars. However, in the postwar decades of the twentieth century the role the mass media should play in Western democratic society seemed clear to many commentators. The national media predominated. And this national media should, it was argued, operate as a forum across which knowledge could be disseminated, issues of public interest advertised and debates around areas of shared concern conducted, so that public opinion could be formed. The result – in theory – would be that burgeoning mass media systems would contribute to the development of an informed electorate, who would in turn make politicians accountable. These dynamics would contribute to the creation of the healthy public sphere regarded as necessary for a vigorous democracy to function. The early BBC's sense of the role of the public service broadcaster, encapsulated in the famous mission to inform and entertain, clearly reflects this general position. It also underscores the degree to which the public sphere can be understood at least as much in terms of a shared culture (expressed in terms of cultural identity or cultural citizenship) as in terms of 'political communication' (Morley, cited in Couldry, 2006: 203–4), democratic deliberation or open debate.

The importance of the nation – and the nation as the locus for political power – in this account of the mediated public sphere is clear. Less obvious perhaps are the 'universal' values it promotes in its insistence that rational debate can lead to consensus among 'right thinking' people. The catch is that this assertion of universality is made even as the concept and operation of nationhood and the associated understanding of citizenship (defined as those who belong to a nation) restrict those who are able to debate, those who are allowed into the debating chamber and those who are counted as 'people' rather than 'other people' at all. Much writing about the public sphere has taken its inspiration from the classical Greek concept of the *agora*, or the marketplace (which was also a marketplace of ideas). The agora traditionally was where citizens could come together to debate and decide matters of importance, without reference to their private circumstances. But the Greek citizen was a very rare individual within the Greek city states. In such a city state 4,000 citizens might be supported by up to 40,000 others – among them women and slaves, who by their private toil supported the citizen in his forays into the public space from which they were barred. As this famous example shows, the workings of the public sphere are thus bound up, not only with questions of citizenship, where this refers to national borders, but also with 'internal' questions of inclusion and exclusion. These exclusions might cohere both around categories of individuals (those who are deemed fit to speak) and particular kinds of subject matter (since this division also defines and divides material deemed to be of public interest from material deemed to be of private concern).

Habermas' account of the structural transformation of the public sphere works through some of these issues. In this work a key moment in the origins of the modern public sphere emerges in the coffee houses of eighteenth-century London where the first genuinely free news publications circulated. For Habermas this moment is normative, not perfect in and of itself, since the forms of democratic engagement were highly restricted, but suggestive of an ideal form of open and honestly orientated communication to work towards. It stands in contrast to the later deterioration of the public sphere at the hands of mass culture and its adoption of the principle of entertainment and popularity rather than communication. In response to what he characterised as a decline of the functioning of the public sphere, Habermas' call was for the development of new forms of communication capable of supporting the kinds of rational debate and deliberative democracy which he saw glimpses of in the coffee houses. Others doubted any such return was possible and also questioned whether it would be desirable. In the 1990s, feminist theorists such as Nancy Fraser challenged the Habermasian ideal of the unified public sphere and the idea of rational debate leading to deliberative judgement at its core. Fraser pointed out that processes of inclusion of previously excluded groups (those disestablished by tradition, culture or law, as for instance most women were until the middle of the twentieth century) couldn't be completed simply by allowing these Others into a pre-defined space in which particular interests or positions had already been declared as acceptable, rational, neutral or universal. A more radical rethinking involving a redefinition of the roles and gendering of public and private spaces was required.

Fraser's call was for the establishment of multiple public spheres across which debates might flow and through which difference could be recognised and respected rather than being resolved through the invocation of culturally constructed 'universal' values. Others also working with the fracture line of modernity also want to reappraise and explore new forms of mediated citizenship – challenging Habermas' sense that the decline of this particular type of modernist rationality is (all) bad. Cultural studies theorists, working with Bakhtin's idea of carnival, for instance, discerned mocking and self-aware laughter within the supposedly inert mass as it turned increasingly emotional and sensationalist mass media coverage to its own account.

Globalisation/Digital Media

The growth of digital media systems and globalisation processes also provoked a rethinking of how the relationship between the media and public life might be theorised and understood. The advent of digital information and communications technologies (ICTs), the convergence of these new networks with older media systems and the rise of satellite, all combined to mark the end of spectrum scarcity which had produced the largely national broadcasting ecologies of the late twentieth century. Simultaneously it enabled the opening up of new spaces and forums, fragmenting any sense of the media as a single space, but potentially at least exploding the number and variety of spaces for public engagement and interaction. Many of these spaces are – of course – not nationally based. In a second influential article Nancy Fraser summed up the thinking of many when she argued that globalisation had broken the links between the mediated public sphere and nationally based democratic processes (Fraser, 2000).

Globalisation and the Public Sphere

We tend to think about globalisation as something that acts on the media industries. As Edward Thompson points out in the article abstracted in Chapter 13, the relationship is more complex. The communications industry played an early role in the history of globalisation both in terms of infrastructure and in terms of political economy: satellite technology in particular disrupted the isomorphic correspondence between national boundaries and broadcast 'footprints' (139). Thompson's account of globalisation and the media goes on to stress the structural inequalities of globalisation and the unequal flows of symbolic goods – as well as finance, people and materials – it produces. The article operates as a critique of the cultural imperialism thesis, which seeks to understand this uneven flow in terms of the symbolic violence involved when one culture's voice speaks louder and claims priority over others. Thompson's view (widely shared) is that this analysis was useful in pointing to structural features but overplayed structural dominance at the expense of agency, neglecting the importance of embedded, local experience.

The call to respect and understand the local in the global that emerges in the Thompson reading is in a sense a comment about 'where' we might locate mediated public spheres within a global system. This also concerns Castells although it is taken up in his writing in relation to a theory of space itself rather than in the register of experience or reception. The case Castells makes is for a newly reorganised geography of inclusion/exclusion, produced through the rise of global ICTs that now traverse the world. These write some groups into, not a public sphere precisely, but 'the space of flows', a fast track of globalising capital and culture. Those outside these flows, who may be found in Tower Hamlets or other European zones as well as in countries in Sub-Saharan Africa, are left to flounder, having little representation and no voice.

Large-scale investigations mapping media exclusion or access can of course be investigated in other registers, including those dealing with the culture industries or the digital economy. In '"Not Only, But Also": *Mixedness and the Media*' (Chapter 16) Annabelle Sreberny recaps forms of thinking about migration and multiculturalism (one aspect of globalisation) before relating questions raised in these areas to questions of media policy. She also takes forward and complicates the sense of interaction and intersection globalisation has produced and the forms of public culture that it might produce or encourage. Her work is in this sense typical of new waves of research exploring globalisation beyond glocal or hybrid models. At the heart of Sreberny's writing is a sense that the media are central to forms of public citizenship (this is the import of the kinds of politics of representation the media operate) and central also to the institutional policies that operate around questions of inclusion. In her article Sreberny draws on Bauman to demand a politics of recognition in the place of an identity politics based on trading distinctiveness which 're-inscribes borders and fixes them' (Bauman, cited in Sreberny, 166). She concludes by calling for the development of new forms of programming to assist in the development of a public sphere(s) based neither on consensus nor national boundaries, but on thick cosmopolitanism based on a mix of grounded and virtual interaction and on new forms of dialogism operating between distinctive voices: doubly a mixed economy.

REFERENCES

Couldry, N., 'The Productive "Consumer" and the Dispersed "Citizen"', *International Journal of Cultural Studies* 7:1 (2004) pp. 21–32.

Couldry, N., 'Culture and Citizenship: The Missing Link?', *European Journal of Cultural Studies*, 9:3 (2006) pp. 321–39.

Fraser, N., 'Rethinking the Public Sphere: A Contribution to the Critique of Actually Existing Democracy', *Social Text* 8:9 (1990) pp. 56–80.

Fraser, N., 'Rethinking Recognition', *New Left Review* 3 (May–June 2000) pp. 107–20.

11

INTRODUCTION TO *ORIENTALISM*

Edward Said

I

On a visit to Beirut during the terrible civil war of 1975–1976 a French journalist wrote regretfully of the gutted downtown area that 'it had once seemed
to belong to . . . the Orient of Chateaubriand and Nerval.'[1] He was right about
the place, of course, especially so far as a European was concerned. The Orient
was almost a European invention, and had been since antiquity a place of
romance, exotic beings, haunting memories and landscapes, remarkable experiences. Now it was disappearing; in a sense it had happened, its time was over.
Perhaps it seemed irrelevant that Orientals themselves had something at stake
in the process, that even in the time of Chateaubriand and Nerval Orientals
had lived there, and that now it was they who were suffering; the main thing
for the European visitor was a European representation of the Orient and its
contemporary fate, both of which had a privileged communal significance for
the journalist and his French readers.

Americans will not feel quite the same about the Orient, which for them is
much more likely to be associated very differently with the Far East (China
and Japan, mainly). Unlike the Americans, the French and the British – less so
the Germans, Russians, Spanish, Portuguese, Italians, and Swiss – have had a
long tradition of what I shall be calling *Orientalism*, a way of coming to terms
with the Orient that is based on the Orient's special place in European Western
experience. The Orient is not only adjacent to Europe; it is also the place of
Europe's greatest and richest and oldest colonies, the source of its civilizations

From Edward Said, *Orientalism* (New York: Pantheon, 1978) pp.1–15.

and languages, its cultural contestant, and one of its deepest and most recurring images of the Other. In addition, the Orient has helped to define Europe (or the West) as its contrasting image, idea, personality, experience. Yet none of this Orient is merely imaginative. The Orient is an integral part of European *material* civilization and culture. Orientalism expresses and represents that part culturally and even ideologically as a mode of discourse with supporting institutions, vocabulary, scholarship, imagery, doctrines, even colonial bureaucracies and colonial styles. In contrast, the American understanding of the Orient will seem considerably less dense, although our recent Japanese, Korean, and Indochinese adventures ought now to be creating a more sober, more realistic 'Oriental' awareness. Moreover, the vastly expanded American political and economic role in the Near East (the Middle East) makes great claims on our understanding of that Orient.

It will be clear to the reader (and will become clearer still throughout the many pages that follow) that by Orientalism I mean several things, all of them, in my opinion, interdependent. The most readily accepted designation for Orientalism is an academic one, and indeed the label still serves in a number of academic institutions. Anyone who teaches, writes about, or researches the Orient – and this applies whether the person is an anthropologist, sociologist, historian, or philologist – either in its specific or its general aspects, is an Orientalist, and what he or she does is Orientalism. Compared with *Oriental studies* or *area studies*, it is true that the term *Orientalism* is less preferred by specialists today, both because it is too vague and general and because it connotes the high-handed executive attitude of nineteenth-century and early-twentieth-century European colonialism. Nevertheless books are written and congresses held with 'the Orient' as their main focus, with the Orientalist in his new or old guise as their main authority. The point is that even if it does not survive as it once did, Orientalism lives on academically through its doctrines and theses about the Orient and the Oriental.

Related to this academic tradition, whose fortunes, transmigrations, specializations, and transmissions are in part the subject of this study, is a more general meaning for Orientalism. Orientalism is a style of thought based upon an ontological and epistemological distinction made between 'the Orient' and (most of the time) 'the Occident.' Thus a very large mass of writers, among whom are poets, novelists, philosophers, political theorists, economists, and imperial administrators, have accepted the basic distinction between East and West as the starting point for elaborate theories, epics, novels, social descriptions, and political accounts concerning the Orient, its people, customs, 'mind,' destiny, and so on. *This* Orientalism can accommodate Aeschylus, say, and Victor Hugo, Dante and Karl Marx. A little later in this introduction I shall deal with the methodological problems one encounters in so broadly construed a 'field' as this.

The interchange between the academic and the more or less imaginative meanings of Orientalism is a constant one, and since the late eighteenth century there has been a considerable, quite disciplined – perhaps even regulated – traffic between the two. Here I come to the third meaning of Orientalism, which is something more historically and materially defined than either of the other two. Taking the late eighteenth century as a very roughly defined starting point Orientalism can be discussed and analyzed as the corporate institution for dealing with the Orient – dealing with it by making statements about it, authorizing views of it, describing it, by teaching it, settling it, ruling over it: in short, Orientalism as a Western style for dominating, restructuring, and having authority over the Orient. I have found it useful here to employ Michel Foucault's notion of a discourse, as described by him in *The Archaeology of Knowledge* and in *Discipline and Punish*, to identify Orientalism. My contention is that without examining Orientalism as a discourse one cannot possibly understand the enormously systematic discipline by which European culture was able to manage – and even produce – the Orient politically, sociologically, militarily, ideologically, scientifically, and imaginatively during the post-Enlightenment period. Moreover, so authoritative a position did Orientalism have that I believe no one writing, thinking, or acting on the Orient could do so without taking account of the limitations on thought and action imposed by Orientalism. In brief, because of Orientalism the Orient was not (and is not) a free subject of thought or action. This is not to say that Orientalism unilaterally determines what can be said about the Orient, but that it is the whole network of interests inevitably brought to bear on (and therefore always involved in) any occasion when that peculiar entity 'the Orient' is in question. How this happens is what this book tries to demonstrate. It also tries to show that European culture gained in strength and identity by setting itself off against the Orient as a sort of surrogate and even underground self.

Historically and culturally there is a quantitative as well as a qualitative difference between the Franco-British involvement in the Orient and – until the period of American ascendancy after World War II – the involvement of every other European and Atlantic power. To speak of Orientalism therefore is to speak mainly, although not exclusively, of a British and French cultural enterprise, a project whose dimensions take in such disparate realms as the imagination itself, the whole of India and the Levant, the Biblical texts and the Biblical lands, the spice trade, colonial armies and a long tradition of colonial administrators, a formidable scholarly corpus, innumerable Oriental 'experts' and 'hands,' an Oriental professorate, a complex array of 'Oriental' ideas (Oriental despotism, Oriental splendor, cruelty, sensuality), many Eastern sects, philosophies, and wisdoms domesticated for local European use – the list can be extended more or less indefinitely. My point is that Orientalism derives from a particular closeness experienced between Britain and France and the Orient, which until the early nineteenth century had really meant only India and the Bible lands. From the beginning of the nineteenth century until the end of World War II France and Britain dominated the Orient and Orientalism; since World War II America has dominated the Orient, and approaches it as

France and Britain once did. Out of that closeness, whose dynamic is enormously productive even if it always demonstrates the comparatively greater strength of the Occident (British, French, or American), comes the large body of texts I call Orientalist.

It should be said at once that even with the generous number of books and authors that I examine, there is a much larger number that I simply have had to leave out. My argument, however, depends neither upon an exhaustive catalogue of texts dealing with the Orient nor upon a clearly delimited set of texts, authors, and ideas that together make up the Orientalist canon. I have depended instead upon a different methodological alternative – whose backbone in a sense is the set of historical generalizations I have so far been making in this Introduction – and it is these I want now to discuss in more analytical detail.

II

I have begun with the assumption that the Orient is not an inert fact of nature. It is not merely *there*, just as the Occident itself is not just *there* either. We must take seriously Vico's great observation that men make their own history, that what they can know is what they have made, and extend it to geography: as both geographical and cultural entities – to say nothing of historical entities – such locales, regions, geographical sectors as 'Orient' and 'Occident' are man-made. Therefore as much as the West itself, the Orient is an idea that has a history and a tradition of thought, imagery, and vocabulary that have given it reality and presence in and for the West. The two geographical entities thus support and to an extent reflect each other.

Having said that, one must go on to state a number of reasonable qualifications. In the first place, it would be wrong to conclude that the Orient was *essentially* an idea, or a creation with no corresponding reality. When Disraeli said in his novel *Tancred* that the East was a career, he meant that to be interested in the East was something bright young Westerners would find to be an all-consuming passion; he should not be interpreted as saying that the East was *only* a career for Westerners. There were – and are – cultures and nations whose location is in the East, and their lives, histories, and customs have a brute reality obviously greater than anything that could be said about them in the West. About that fact this study of Orientalism has very little to contribute, except to acknowledge it tacitly. But the phenomenon of Orientalism as I study it here deals principally, not with a correspondence between Orientalism and Orient, but with the internal consistency of Orientalism and its ideas about the Orient (the East as career) despite or beyond any correspondence, or lack thereof, with a 'real' Orient. My point is that Disraeli's statement about the East refers mainly to that created consistency, that regular constellation of ideas as the pre-eminent thing about the Orient, and not to its mere being, as Wallace Stevens's phrase has it.

A second qualification is that ideas, cultures, and histories cannot seriously be understood or studied without their force, or more precisely their configurations of power, also being studied. To believe that the Orient was created – or, as I call it, 'Orientalized' – and to believe that such things happen simply as a necessity of the imagination, is to be disingenuous. The relationship between Occident and Orient is a relationship of power, of domination, of varying degrees of a complex hegemony, and is quite accurately indicated in the title of K. M. Panikkar's classic *Asia and Western Dominance*.[2] The Orient was Orientalized not only because it was discovered to be 'Oriental' in all those ways considered commonplace by an average nineteenth-century European, but also because it *could be* – that is, submitted to being – *made* Oriental. There is very little consent to be found, for example, in the fact that Flaubert's encounter with an Egyptian courtesan produced a widely influential model of the Oriental woman; she never spoke of herself, she never represented her emotions, presence, or history. *He* spoke for and represented her. He was foreign, comparatively wealthy, male, and these were historical facts of domination that allowed him not only to possess Kuchuk Hanem physically but to speak for her and tell his readers in what way she was 'typically Oriental.' My argument is that Flaubert's situation of strength in relation to Kuchuk Hanem was not an isolated instance. It fairly stands for the pattern of relative strength between East and West, and the discourse about the Orient that it enabled.

This brings us to a third qualification. One ought never to assume that the structure of Orientalism is nothing more than a structure of lies or of myths which, were the truth about them to be told, would simply blow away. I myself believe that Orientalism is more particularly valuable as a sign of European-Atlantic power over the Orient than it is as a veridic discourse about the Orient (which is what, in its academic or scholarly form, it claims to be). Nevertheless, what we must respect and try to grasp is the sheer knitted-together strength of Orientalist discourse, its very close ties to the enabling socio-economic and political institutions, and its redoubtable durability. After all, any system of ideas that can remain unchanged as teachable wisdom (in academies, books, congresses, universities, foreign-service institutes) from the period of Ernest Renan in the late 1840s until the present in the United States must be something more formidable than a mere collection of lies. Orientalism, therefore, is not an airy European fantasy about the Orient, but a created body of theory and practice in which, for many generations, there has been a considerable material investment. Continued investment made Orientalism, as a system of knowledge about the Orient, an accepted grid for filtering through the Orient into Western consciousness, just as that same investment multiplied – indeed, made truly productive – the statements proliferating out from Orientalism into the general culture.

Gramsci has made the useful analytic distinction between civil and political society in which the former is made up of voluntary (or at least rational and noncoercive) affiliations like schools, families, and unions, the latter of state institutions (the army, the police, the central bureaucracy) whose role in the polity is direct domination. Culture, of course, is to be found operating within civil society, where the influence of ideas, of institutions, and of other persons works not through domination but by what Gramsci calls consent. In any society not totalitarian, then, certain cultural forms predominate over others, just as certain ideas are more influential than others; the form of this cultural leadership is what Gramsci has identified as *hegemony*, an indispensable concept for any understanding of cultural life in the industrial West. It is hegemony, or rather the result of cultural hegemony at work, that gives Orientalism the durability and the strength I have been speaking about so far. Orientalism is never far from what Denys Hay has called the idea of Europe,[3] a collective notion identifying 'us' Europeans as against all 'those' non-Europeans, and indeed it can be argued that the major component in European culture is precisely what made that culture hegemonic both in and outside Europe: the idea of European identity as a superior one in comparison with all the non-European peoples and cultures. There is in addition the hegemony of European ideas about the Orient, themselves reiterating European superiority over Oriental backwardness, usually overriding the possibility that a more independent, or more skeptical, thinker might have had different views on the matter.

In a quite constant way, Orientalism depends for its strategy on this flexible *positional* superiority, which puts the Westerner in a whole series of possible relationships with the Orient without ever losing him the relative upper hand. And why should it have been otherwise, especially during the period of extraordinary European ascendancy from the late Renaissance to the present? The scientist, the scholar, the missionary, the trader, or the soldier was in, or thought about, the Orient because he *could be there*, or could think about it, with very little resistance on the Orient's part. Under the general heading of knowledge of the Orient, and within the umbrella of Western hegemony over the Orient during the period from the end of the eighteenth century, there emerged a complex Orient suitable for study in the academy, for display in the museum, for reconstruction in the colonial office, for theoretical illustration in anthropological, biological, linguistic, racial, and historical theses about mankind and the universe, for instances of economic and sociological theories of development, revolution, cultural personality, national or religious character. Additionally, the imaginative examination of things Oriental was based more or less exclusively upon a sovereign Western consciousness out of whose unchallenged centrality an Oriental world emerged, first according to general ideas about who or what was an Oriental, then according to a detailed logic governed not simply by empirical reality but by a battery of desires, repressions, investments, and projections. If we can point to great Orientalist works of genuine scholarship like Silvestre de Sacy's *Chrestomathie arabe* or Edward William Lane's *Account of the Manners and Customs of the Modern Egyptians*, we need also to note that Renan's and Gobineau's racial ideas came out of the same impulse, as did a great many Victorian pornographic novels (see the analysis by Steven Marcus of 'The Lustful Turk'[4]).

And yet, one must repeatedly ask oneself whether what matters in Orientalism is the general group of ideas overriding the mass of material – about which who could deny that they were shot through with doctrines of European superiority, various kinds of racism, imperialism, and the like, dogmatic views of 'the Oriental' as a kind of ideal and unchanging abstraction? – or the much more varied work produced by almost uncountable individual writers, whom one would take up as individual instances of authors dealing with the Orient. In a sense the two alternatives, general and particular, are really two perspectives on the same material: in both instances one would have to deal with pioneers in the field like William Jones, with great artists like Nerval or Flaubert. And why would it not be possible to employ both perspectives together, or one after the other? Isn't there an obvious danger of distortion (of precisely the kind that academic Orientalism has always been prone to) if either too general or too specific a level of description is maintained systematically?

My two fears are distortion and inaccuracy, or rather the kind of inaccuracy produced by too dogmatic a generality and too positivistic a localized focus. In trying to deal with these problems I have tried to deal with three main aspects of my own contemporary reality that seem to me to point the way out of the methodological or perspectival difficulties I have been discussing, difficulties that might force one, in the first instance, into writing a coarse polemic on so unacceptably general a level of description as not to be worth the effort, or in the second instance, into writing so detailed and atomistic a series of analyses as to lose all track of the general lines of force informing the field, giving it its special cogency. How then to recognize individuality and to reconcile it with its intelligent, and by no means passive or merely dictatorial, general and hegemonic context?

III

I mentioned three aspects of my contemporary reality: I must explain and briefly discuss them now, so that it can be seen how I was led to a particular course of research and writing.

1. *The distinction between pure and political knowledge.* It is very easy to argue that knowledge about Shakespeare or Wordsworth is not political whereas knowledge about contemporary China or the Soviet Union is. My own formal and professional designation is that of 'humanist,' a title which indicates the humanities as my field and therefore the unlikely eventuality that there might be anything political about what I do in that field. Of course, all these labels and terms are quite unnuanced as I use them here, but the general truth of what I am pointing to is, I think, widely held. One reason for saying that a humanist who writes about Wordsworth, or an editor whose specialty is Keats, is not involved in anything political is that what he does seems to

have no direct political effect upon reality in the everyday sense. A scholar whose field is Soviet economics works in a highly charged area where there is much government interest, and what he might produce in the way of studies or proposals will be taken up by policymakers, government officials, institutional economists, intelligence experts. The distinction between 'humanists' and persons whose work has policy implications, or political significance, can be broadened further by saying that the former's ideological color is a matter of incidental importance to politics (although possibly of great moment to his colleagues in the field, who may object to his Stalinism or fascism or too easy liberalism), whereas the ideology of the latter is woven directly into his material – indeed, economics, politics, and sociology in the modern academy are ideological sciences – and therefore taken for granted as being 'political.'

Nevertheless the determining impingement on most knowledge produced in the contemporary West (and here I speak mainly about the United States) is that it be nonpolitical, that is, scholarly, academic, impartial, above partisan or small-minded doctrinal belief. One can have no quarrel with such an ambition in theory, perhaps, but in practice the reality is much more problematic. No one has ever devised a method for detaching the scholar from the circumstances of life, from the fact of his involvement (conscious or unconscious) with a class, a set of beliefs, a social position, or from the mere activity of being a member of a society. These continue to bear on what he does professionally, even though naturally enough his research and its fruits do attempt to reach a level of relative freedom from the inhibitions and the restrictions of brute, everyday reality. For there is such a thing as knowledge that is less, rather than more, partial than the individual (with his entangling and distracting life circumstances) who produces it. Yet this knowledge is not therefore automatically nonpolitical.

Whether discussions of literature or of classical philology are fraught with – or have unmediated – political significance is a very large question that I have tried to treat in some detail elsewhere.[5] What I am interested in doing now is suggesting how the general liberal consensus that 'true' knowledge is fundamentally non-political (and conversely, that overtly political knowledge is not 'true' knowledge) obscures the highly if obscurely organized political circumstances obtaining when knowledge is produced. No one is helped in understanding this today when the adjective 'political' is used as a label to discredit any work for daring to violate the protocol of pretended suprapolitical objectivity. We may say, first, that civil society recognizes a gradation of political importance in the various fields of knowledge. To some extent the political importance given a field comes from the possibility of its direct translation into economic terms; but to a greater extent political importance comes from the closeness of a field to ascertainable sources of power in political society. Thus an economic study of long-term Soviet energy potential and its effect on military capability is likely to be commissioned by the Defense Department, and thereafter to acquire a kind of political status impossible for a study of

Tolstoi's early fiction financed in part by a foundation. Yet both works belong in what civil society acknowledges to be a similar field, Russian studies, even though one work may be done by a very conservative economist, the other by a radical literary historian. My point here is that 'Russia' as a general subject matter has political priority over nicer distinctions such as 'economics' and 'literary history,' because political society in Gramsci's sense reaches into such realms of civil society as the academy and saturates them with significance of direct concern to it.

I do not want to press all this any further on general theoretical grounds: it seems to me that the value and credibility of my case can be demonstrated by being much more specific, in the way, for example, Noam Chomsky has studied the instrumental connection between the Vietnam War and the notion of objective scholarship as it was applied to cover state-sponsored military research.[6] Now because Britain, France, and recently the United States are imperial powers, their political societies impart to their civil societies a sense of urgency, a direct political infusion as it were, where and whenever matters pertaining to their imperial interests abroad are concerned. I doubt that it is controversial, for example, to say that an Englishman in India or Egypt in the later nineteenth century took an interest in those countries that was never far from their status in his mind as British colonies. To say this may seem quite different from saying that all academic knowledge about India and Egypt is somehow tinged and impressed with, violated by, the gross political fact – and yet *that is what I am saying* in this study of Orientalism. For if it is true that no production of knowledge in the human sciences can ever ignore or disclaim its author's involvement as a human subject in his own circumstances, then it must also be true that for a European or American studying the Orient there can be no disclaiming the main circumstances of *his* actuality: that he comes up against the Orient as a European or American first, as an individual second. And to be a European or an American in such a situation is by no means an inert fact. It meant and means being aware, however dimly, that one belongs to a power with definite interests in the Orient, and more important, that one belongs to a part of the earth with a definite history of involvement in the Orient almost since the time of Homer.

Put in this way, these political actualities are still too undefined and general to be really interesting. Anyone would agree to them without necessarily agree-ing also that they mattered very much, for instance, to Flaubert as he wrote *Salammbô*, or to H. A. R. Gibb as he wrote *Modern Trends in Islam*. The trouble is that there is too great a distance between the big dominating fact, as I have described it, and the details of everyday life that govern the minute discipline of a novel or a scholarly text as each is being written. Yet if we elimi-nate from the start any notion that 'big' facts like imperial domination can be applied mechanically and deterministically to such complex matters as culture and ideas, then we will begin to approach an interesting kind of study. My idea is that European and then American interest in the Orient was political according to some of the obvious historical accounts of it that I have given here, but that it was the culture that created that interest, that acted dynamically along with brute political, economic, and military rationales to make the Orient the varied and complicated place that it obviously was in the field I call Orientalism.

Therefore, Orientalism is not a mere political subject matter or field that is reflected passively by culture, scholarship, or institutions; nor is it a large and diffuse collection of texts about the Orient; nor is it representative and expressive of some nefarious 'Western' imperialist plot to hold down the 'Oriental' world. It is rather a *distribution* of geopolitical awareness into aesthetic, scholarly, economic, sociological, historical, and philological texts; it is an *elaboration* not only of a basic geographical distinction (the world is made up of two unequal halves, Orient and Occident) but also of a whole series of 'interests' which, by such means as scholarly discovery, philological reconstruction, psychological analysis, landscape and sociological description, it not only creates but also maintains; it *is*, rather than expresses, a certain *will* or *intention* to understand, in some cases to control, manipulate, even to incorporate, what is a manifestly different (or alternative and novel) world; it is, above all, a discourse that is by no means in direct, corresponding relationship with political power in the raw, but rather is produced and exists in an uneven exchange with various kinds of power, shaped to a degree by the exchange with power political (as with a colonial or imperial establishment), power intellectual (as with reigning sciences like comparative linguistics or anatomy, or any of the modern policy sciences), power cultural (as with orthodoxies and canons of taste, texts, values), power moral (as with ideas about what 'we' do and what 'they' cannot do or understand as 'we' do). Indeed, my real argument is that Orientalism is – and does not simply represent – a considerable dimension of modern political-intellectual culture, and as such has less to do with the Orient than it does with 'our' world.

Because Orientalism is a cultural and a political fact, then, it does not exist in some archival vacuum; quite the contrary, I think it can be shown that what is thought, said, or even done about the Orient follows (perhaps occurs within) certain distinct and intellectually knowable lines. Here too a considerable degree of nuance and elaboration can be seen working as between the broad superstructural pressures and the details of composition, the facts of textuality. Most humanistic scholars are, I think, perfectly happy with the notion that texts exist in contexts, that there is such a thing as intertextuality, that the pressures of conventions, predecessors, and rhetorical styles limit what Walter Benjamin once called the 'overtaxing of the productive person in the name of . . . the principle of "creativity,"' in which the poet is believed on his own, and out of his pure mind, to have brought forth his work.[7] Yet there is a reluctance to allow that political, institutional, and ideological constraints act in the same manner on the individual author. A humanist will believe it to be an interesting fact to any interpreter of Balzac that he was influenced in the

Comédie humaine by the conflict between Geoffroy Saint-Hilaire and Cuvier, but the same sort of pressure on Balzac of deeply reactionary monarchism is felt in some vague way to demean his literary 'genius' and therefore to be less worth serious study. Similarly – as Harry Bracken has been tirelessly showing – philosophers will conduct their discussions of Locke, Hume, and empiricism without ever taking into account that there is an explicit connection in these classic writers between their 'philosophic' doctrines and racial theory, justifications of slavery, or arguments for colonial exploitation.[8] These are common enough ways by which contemporary scholarship keeps itself pure.

Perhaps it is true that most attempts to rub culture's nose in the mud of politics have been crudely iconoclastic; perhaps also the social interpretation of literature in my own field has simply not kept up with the enormous technical advances in detailed textual analysis. But there is no getting away from the fact that literary studies in general, and American Marxist theorists in particular, have avoided the effort of seriously bridging the gap between the superstructural and the base levels in textual, historical scholarship; on another occasion I have gone so far as to say that the literary-cultural establishment as a whole has declared the serious study of imperialism and culture off limits.[9] For Orientalism brings one up directly against that question – that is, to realizing that political imperialism governs an entire field of study, imagination, and scholarly institutions – in such a way as to make its avoidance an intellectual and historical impossibility. Yet there will always remain the perennial escape mechanism of saying that a literary scholar and a philosopher, for example, are trained in literature and philosophy respectively, not in politics or ideological analysis. In other words, the specialist argument can work quite effectively to block the larger and, in my opinion, the more intellectually serious perspective.

Here it seems to me there is a simple two-part answer to be given, at least so far as the study of imperialism and culture (or Orientalism) is concerned. In the first place, nearly every nineteenth-century writer (and the same is true enough of writers in earlier periods) was extraordinarily well aware of the fact of empire: this is a subject not very well studied, but it will not take a modern Victorian specialist long to admit that liberal cultural heroes like John Stuart Mill, Arnold, Carlyle, Newman, Macaulay, Ruskin, George Eliot, and even Dickens had definite views on race and imperialism, which are quite easily to be found at work in their writing. So even a specialist must deal with the knowledge that Mill, for example, made it clear in *On Liberty* and *Representative Government* that his views there could not be applied to India (he was an India Office functionary for a good deal of his life, after all) because the Indians were civilizationally, if not racially, inferior. The same kind of paradox is to be found in Marx, as I try to show in this book. In the second place, to believe that politics in the form of imperialism bears upon the production of literature, scholarship, social theory, and history writing is by no means equivalent to saying that culture is therefore a demeaned or denigrated thing.

Quite the contrary: my whole point is to say that we can better understand the persistence and the durability of saturating hegemonic systems like culture when we realize that their internal constraints upon writers and thinkers were *productive*, not unilaterally inhibiting. It is this idea that Gramsci, certainly, and Foucault and Raymond Williams in their very different ways have been trying to illustrate. Even one or two pages by Williams on 'the uses of the Empire' in *The Long Revolution* tell us more about nineteenth-century cultural richness than many volumes of hermetic textual analyses.[10]

Therefore I study Orientalism as a dynamic exchange between individual authors and the large political concerns shaped by the three great empires – British, French, American – in whose intellectual and imaginative territory the writing was produced. What interests me most as a scholar is not the gross political verity but the detail, as indeed what interests us in someone like Lane or Flaubert or Renan is not the (to him) indisputable truth that Occidentals are superior to Orientals, but the profoundly worked over and modulated evidence of his detailed work within the very wide space opened up by that truth. One need only remember that Lane's *Manners and Customs of the Modern Egyptians* is a classic of historical and anthropological observation because of its style, its enormously intelligent and brilliant details, not because of its simple reflection of racial superiority, to understand what I am saying here.

The kind of political questions raised by Orientalism, then, are as follows: What other sorts of intellectual, aesthetic, scholarly, and cultural energies went into the making of an imperialist tradition like the Orientalist one? How did philology, lexicography, history, biology, political and economic theory, novel-writing, and lyric poetry come to the service of Orientalism's broadly imperialist view of the world? What changes, modulations, refinements, even revolutions take place within Orientalism? What is the meaning of originality, of continuity, of individuality, in this context? How does Orientalism transmit or reproduce itself from one epoch to another? In fine, how can we treat the cultural, historical phenomenon of Orientalism as a kind of *willed human work* – not of mere unconditioned ratiocination – in all its historical complexity, detail, and worth without at the same time losing sight of the alliance between cultural work, political tendencies, the state, and the specific realities of domination? Governed by such concerns a humanistic study can responsibly address itself to politics *and* culture. But this is not to say that such a study establishes a hard-and-fast rule about the relationship between knowledge and politics. My argument is that each humanistic investigation must formulate the nature of that connection in the specific context of the study, the subject matter, and its historical circumstances.

[. . .]

Notes

1. Thierry Desjardins, *Le Martyre du Liban* (Paris: Plon, 1976), p.14.
2. K. M. Panikkar, *Asia and Western Dominance* (London: George Allen & Unwin, 1959).
3. Denys Hay, Europe: *The Emergence of an Idea*, 2nd ed. (Edinburgh: Edinburgh University Press, 1968).
4. Steven Marcus, *The Other Victorians: A Study of Sexuality and Pornography in Mid-Nineteenth Century England* (1966; reprint ed., New York: Bantam Books, 1967), pp. 200–19.
5. See my Criticism *Between Culture and System* (Cambridge, Mass.: Harvard University Press, forthcoming).
6. Principally in his *American Power and the New Mandarins: Historical and Political Essays* (New York: Pantheon Books, 1969) and *For Reasons of State* (New York: Pantheon Books, 1973).
7. Walter Benjamin, *Charles Baudelarie: A Lyric Poet in the Era of High Capitalism*, trans. Harry Zohn (London: New Left Books, 1973), p.71.
8. Harry Bracken, "Essence Accident and Race," *Hermanthena* 116 (Winter 1973): 81–96.
9. In an interview published in *Diacritics* 6, no. 3 (Fall 1976): 38.
10. Raymond Williams, *The Long Revolution* (London: Chatto & Windus, 1961), pp. 66–7.

12

MASS CULTURE AS WOMAN:
MODERNISM'S OTHER

Andreas Huyssen

I

One of the founding texts of modernism, if there ever was one, is Flaubert's
Madame Bovary. Emma Bovary, whose temperament was, in the narrator's words, 'more sentimental than artistic,' loved to read romances.[1] In his
detached, ironic style, Flaubert describes Emma's reading matter: 'They [the
novels] were full of love and lovers, persecuted damsels swooning in deserted
pavilions, postillions slaughtered at every turn, horses ridden to death on
every page, gloomy forests, romantic intrigue, vows, sobs, embraces and tears,
moonlit crossings, nightingales in woodland groves, noblemen brave as lions,
gentle as lambs, impossibly virtuous, always well dressed, and who wept like
fountains on all occasions.'[2] Of course, it is well known that Flaubert himself
was caught by the craze for romantic novels during his student days in the
Collège at Rouen, and Emma Bovary's readings at the convent have to be read
against this backdrop of Flaubert's life history – a point which critics rarely
fail to make. However, there is ample reason to wonder if the adolescent
Flaubert read these novels in the same way Emma Bovary would have, had
she actually lived – or, for that matter, as real women at the time read them.
Perhaps the answer to such a query will have to remain speculative. What is
beyond speculation, however, is the fact that Emma Bovary became known,
among other things, as the female reader caught between the delusions of the

From Andreas Huyssen, *After the Great Divide* (Basingstoke: Palgrave Macmillan, 1986). The
essay originally appeared in Tania Modleski (ed.), *Studies in Entertainment: Critical Approaches
to Mass Culture* (Bloomington: Indiana University Press, 1986).

trivial romantic narrative and the realities of French provincial life during the July monarchy, a woman who tried to live the illusions of aristocratic sensual romance and was shipwrecked on the banality of bourgeois everyday life. Flaubert, on the other hand, came to be known as one of the fathers of modernism, one of the paradigmatic master voices of an aesthetic based on the uncompromising repudiation of what Emma Bovary loved to read.

As to Flaubert's famous claim: 'Madame Bovary, c'est moi,' we can assume that he knew what he was saying, and critics have gone to great lengths to show what Flaubert had in common with Emma Bovary – mostly in order to show how he transcended aesthetically the dilemma on which she foundered in 'real life.' In such arguments the question of gender usually remains submerged, thereby asserting itself all the more powerfully. Sartre, however, in his monumental *L'Idiot de la Famille*, has analyzed the social and familial conditions of Flaubert's 'objective neurosis' underlying his fantasy of himself as woman. Sartre has indeed succeeded in showing how Flaubert fetishized his own imaginary femininity while simultaneously sharing his period's hostility toward real women, participating in a pattern of the imagination and of behavior all too common in the history of modernism.[3]

That such masculine identification with woman, such imaginary femininity in the male writer, is itself historically determined is clear enough. Apart from the subjective conditions of neurosis in Flaubert's case, the phenomenon has a lot to do with the increasingly marginal position of literature and the arts in a society in which masculinity is identified with action, enterprise, and progress – with the realms of business, industry, science, and law. At the same time, it has also become clear that the imaginary femininity of male authors, which often grounds their oppositional stance vis-à-vis bourgeois society, can easily go hand in hand with the exclusion of real women from the literary enterprise and with the misogyny of bourgeois patriarchy itself. Against the paradigmatic 'Madame Bovary, c'est moi,' we therefore have to insist that there is a difference. Christa Wolf, in her critical and fictional reflections on the question 'who was Cassandra before anyone wrote about her?,' put it this way:

> 'We have admired this remark [Flaubert's "Madame Bovary, c'est moi"] for more than a hundred years. We also admire the tears Flaubert shed when he had to let Madame Bovary die, and the crystal-clear calculation of his wonderful novel, which he was able to write despite his tears; and we should not and will not stop admiring him. But Flaubert was *not* Madame Bovary; we cannot completely ignore that fact in the end, despite all our good will and what we know of the secret relationship between an author and a figure created by art.'[4]

One aspect of the difference that is important to my argument about the gender inscriptions in the mass culture debate is that woman (Madame Bovary) is positioned as reader of inferior literature – subjective, emotional and passive – while man (Flaubert) emerges as writer of genuine authentic literature – objective, ironic, and in control of his aesthetic means. Of course, such positioning of woman as avid consumer of pulp, which I take to be paradigmatic, also affects the woman writer who has the same kind of ambition as the 'great (male) modernist.' [. . .]

II

What especially interests me here is the notion which gained ground during the 19th century that mass culture is somehow associated with woman while real, authentic culture remains the prerogative of men. The tradition of women's exclusion from the realm of 'high art' does not of course originate in the 19th century, but it does take on new connotations in the age of the industrial revolution and cultural modernization. Stuart Hall is perfectly right to point out that the hidden subject of the mass culture debate is precisely 'the masses' – their political and cultural aspirations, their struggles and their pacification via cultural institutions.[5] But when the 19th and early 20th centuries conjured up the threat of the masses 'rattling at the gate,' to quote Hall, and lamented the concomitant decline of culture and civilization (which mass culture was invariably accused of causing), there was yet another hidden subject. In the age of nascent socialism *and* the first major women's movement in Europe, the masses knocking at the gate were also women, knocking at the gate of a male-dominated culture. It is indeed striking to observe how the political, psychological, and aesthetic discourse around the turn of the century consistently and obsessively genders mass culture and the masses as feminine, while high culture, whether traditional or modern, clearly remains the privileged realm of male activities.

To be sure, a number of critics have since abandoned the notion of *mass* culture in order to 'exclude from the outset the interpretation agreeable to its advocates: that it is a matter of something like a culture that arises spontaneously from the masses themselves, the contemporary form of popular art.'[6] Thus Adorno and Horkheimer coined the term culture industry; Enzensberger gave it another twist by calling it the consciousness industry; in the United States, Herbert Schiller speaks of mind managers, and Michael Real uses the term mass-mediated culture. The critical intention behind these changes in terminology is clear: they all mean to suggest that modern mass culture is administered and imposed from above and that the threat it represents resides not in the masses but in those who run the industry. While such an interpretation may serve as a welcome corrective to the naive notion that mass culture is identical with traditional forms of popular art, rising spontaneously from the masses, it nevertheless erases a whole web of gender connotations which, as I shall show, the older terminology 'mass culture' carried with it – i.e., connotations of mass culture as essentially feminine which were clearly also 'imposed from above,' in a gender-specific sense, and which remain central to understanding the historical and rhetorical determinations of the modernism/ mass culture dichotomy.

It might be argued that the terminological shift away from the term 'mass culture' actually reflects changes in critical thinking about 'the masses.' Indeed, mass culture theories since the 1920s – for instance, those of the Frankfurt School – have by and large abandoned the explicit gendering of mass culture as feminine. Instead they emphasize features of mass culture such as stream-lining, technological reproduction, administration, and Sachlichkeit – features which popular psychology would ascribe to the realm of masculinity rather than femininity. Yet the older mode of thinking surfaces time and again in the language, if not in the argument. Thus Adorno and Horkheimer argue that mass culture 'cannot renounce the threat of castration,'[7] and they feminize it explicitly, as the evil queen of the fairy tale when they claim that 'mass culture, in her mirror, is always the most beautiful in the land.'[8] Similarly, Siegfried Kracauer, in his seminal essay on the mass ornament, begins his discussion by bringing the legs of the Tiller Girls into the reader's view, even though the argument then focuses primarily on aspects of rationalization and standardization.[9] Examples such as these show that the inscription of the feminine on the notion of mass culture, which seems to have its primary place in the late 19th century, did not relinquish its hold, even among those critics who did much to overcome the 19th century mystification of mass culture as woman.

The recovery of such gender stereotypes in the theorizing of mass culture may also have some bearing on the current debate about the alleged feminin-ity of modernist/avant-gardist writing. Thus the observation that, in some basic register, the traditional mass culture/modernism dichotomy has been gendered since the mid-19th century as female/male would seem to make recent attempts by French critics to claim the space of modernist and avant-garde writing as predominantly feminine highly questionable. Of course this approach, which is perhaps best embodied in Kristeva's work, focuses on the Mallarmé-Lautréamont-Joyce axis of modernism rather than, say, on the Flaubert-Thomas Mann-Eliot axis which I emphasize in my argument here. Nevertheless, its claims remain problematic even there. Apart from the fact that such a view would threaten to render invisible a whole tradition of women's writing, its main theoretical assumption – 'that "the feminine" is what cannot be inscribed in common language'[10] – remains problematically close to that whole history of an imaginary male femininity which has become prominent in literature since the late 18th century.[11] This view becomes possible only if Madame Bovary's 'natural' association with pulp – i.e., the discourse that persistently associated women with mass culture – is simply ignored, and if a paragon of male misogyny like Nietzsche is said to be speaking from the position of woman. Teresa de Lauretis has recently criticized this Derridean appropriation of the feminine by arguing that the position of woman from which Nietzsche and Derrida speak is vacant in the first place, and cannot be claimed by women.[12] Indeed, more than a hundred years after Flaubert and Nietzsche, we are facing yet another version of an imaginary male femininity, and it is no coincidence that the advocates of such theories (who also include major women theoreticians) take great pains to distance themselves from any form of political feminism. [. . .]

Here, then, some remarks about the history of the perception of mass culture as feminine. Time and again documents from the late 19th century ascribe pejorative feminine characteristics to mass culture – and by mass culture here I mean serialized feuilleton novels, popular and family magazines, the stuff of lending libraries, fictional bestsellers and the like – not, however, working-class culture or residual forms of older popular or folk cultures. A few examples will have to suffice. In the preface to their novel *Germinie Lacerteux* (1865), which is usually regarded as the first naturalist manifesto, the GO NL-court brothers attack what they call the false novel. They describe it as those 'spicy little works, memoirs of street-walkers, bedroom confessions, erotic smuttiness, scandals that hitch up their skirts in pictures in bookshop windows.' The true novel (*le roman vrai*) by contrast is called 'severe and pure.' It is said to be characterized by its scientificity, and rather than sentiment it offers what the authors call 'a clinical picture of love' (*une clinique de l'amour*).[13] Twenty years later, in the editorial of the first issue of Michael Georg Conrad's journal *Die Gesellschaft* (1885), which marks the beginning of 'die Moderne' in Germany, the editor states his intention to emancipate literature and criticism from the 'tyranny of well-bred debutantes and old wives of both sexes,' and from the empty and pompous rhetoric of 'old wives criticism.' [. . .]

It is easy to see how such statements rely on the traditional notion that women's aesthetic and artistic abilities are inferior to those of men. Women as providers of inspiration for the artist, yes, but otherwise *Berufsverbot* for the muses,[14] unless of course they content themselves with the lower genres (painting flowers and animals) and the decorative arts. At any rate, the gendering of an inferior mass culture as feminine goes hand in hand with the emergence of a male mystique in modernism (especially in painting), which has been documented thoroughly by feminist scholarship.[15] What is interesting in the second half of the 19th century, however, is a certain chain effect of signification: from the obsessively argued inferiority of woman as artist (classically argued by Karl Scheffler in *Die Frau und die Kunst*, 1908) to the association of woman with mass culture (witness Hawthorne's 'the damned mob of scribbling women') to the identification of woman with the masses as political threat.

This line of argument invariably leads back to Nietzsche. Significantly, Nietzsche's ascription of feminine characteristics to the masses is always tied to his aesthetic vision of the artist-philosopher-hero, the suffering loner who stands in irreconcilable opposition to modern democracy and its inauthentic culture. Fairly typical examples of this nexus can be found in Nietzsche's polemic against Wagner, who becomes for him the paradigm of the decline of genuine culture in the dawning age of the masses and the feminization of culture: 'The danger for artists, for geniuses . . . is woman: adoring women confront them with corruption. Hardly any of them have character enough not to be corrupted – or "redeemed" – when they find themselves treated like gods: soon they condescend to the level of the women.'[16] Wagner, it is implied, has succumbed to the adoring women by transforming music into mere spectacle, theater, delusion:

> 'I have explained where Wagner belongs – *not* in the history of music. What does he signify nevertheless in that history? *The emergence of the actor in music.* . . . One can grasp it with one's very hands: great success, success with the masses no longer sides with those who are authentic – one has to be an actor to achieve that. Victor Hugo and Richard Wagner – they signify the same thing: in declining cultures, wherever the decision comes to rest with the masses, authenticity becomes superfluous, disadvantageous, a liability. Only the actor still arouses *great* enthusiasm.'[17]

And then Wagner, the theater, the mass, woman – all become a web of signification outside of, and in opposition to, true art: 'No one brings along the finest senses of his art to the theater, least of all the artist who works for the theater – solitude is lacking; whatever is perfect suffers no witnesses. In the theater one becomes people, herd, female, pharisee, voting cattle, patron, idiot – *Wagnerian*.'[18] What Nietzsche articulates here is of course not an attack on the drama or the tragedy, which to him remain some of the highest manifestations of culture. When Nietzsche calls theater a 'revolt of the masses,'[19] he anticipates what the situationists would later elaborate as the society of the spectacle, and what Baudrillard chastises as the simulacrum. At the same time, it is no coincidence that the philosopher blames theatricality for the decline of culture. After all, the theater in bourgeois society was one of the few spaces which allowed women a prime place in the arts, precisely because acting was seen as imitative and reproductive, rather than original and productive. Thus, in Nietzsche's attack on what he perceives as Wagner's feminization of music, his 'infinite melody' – 'one walks into the sea, gradually loses one's secure footing, and finally surrenders oneself to the elements without reservation'[20] – an extremely perceptive critique of the mechanisms of bourgeois culture goes hand in hand with an exhibition of that culture's sexist biases and prejudices.

III

The fact that the identification of woman with mass has major political implications is easily recognized. Thus Mallarmé's quip about '*reportage universel*' (i.e., mass culture), with its not so subtle allusion to '*suffrage universel*,' is more than just a clever pun. The problem goes far beyond questions of art and literature. In the late 19th century, a specific traditional male image of woman served as a receptacle for all kinds of projections, displaced fears, and anxieties (both personal and political), which were brought about by modernization and the new social conflicts, as well as by specific historical events such as the 1848 revolution, the 1870 Commune, and the rise of reactionary mass movements which, as in Austria, threatened the liberal order.[21] [. . .]

This kind of thinking is exemplified by Gustave Le Bon's enormously influential *The Crowd* (*La Psychologie des foules*, 1895), which as Freud observed in his own *Mass Psychology and Ego Analysis* (1921) merely summarizes arguments pervasive in Europe at the time. In Le Bon's study, the male fear of woman and the bourgeois fear of the masses become indistinguishable: 'Crowds are everywhere distinguished by feminine characteristics.'[22] And: 'The simplicity and exaggeration of the sentiments of crowds have for result that a throng knows neither doubt nor uncertainty. Like women, it goes at once to extremes. . . . A commencement of antipathy or disapprobation, which in the case of an isolated individual would not gain strength, becomes at once furious hatred in the case of an individual in a crowd.'[23] And then he summarizes his fears with a reference to that icon which perhaps more than any other in the 19th century – more even than the Judiths and Salomés so often portrayed on symbolist canvases – stood for the feminine threat to civilization: 'Crowds are somewhat like the sphinx of ancient fable: it is necessary to arrive at a solution of the problems offered by their psychology or to resign ourselves to being devoured by them.'[24] Male fears of an engulfing femininity are here projected onto the metropolitan masses, who did indeed represent a threat to the rational bourgeois order. The haunting specter of a loss of power combines with fear of losing one's fortified and stable ego boundaries, which represent the *sine qua non* of male psychology in that bourgeois order. We may want to relate Le Bon's social psychology of the masses back to modernism's own fears of being sphinxed. Thus the nightmare of being devoured by mass culture through co-option, commodification, and the 'wrong' kind of success is the constant fear of the modernist artist, who tries to stake out his territory by fortifying the boundaries between genuine art and inauthentic mass culture. Again, the problem is not the desire to differentiate between forms of high art and depraved forms of mass culture and its co-options. The problem is rather the persistent gendering as feminine of that which is devalued.

IV

Seen in relation to this kind of paranoid view of mass culture and the masses, the modernist aesthetic itself – at least in one of its basic registers – begins to look more and more like a reaction formation, rather than like the heroic feat steeled in the fires of the modern experience. At the risk of oversimplifying, I would suggest that one can identify something like a core of the modernist aesthetic which has held sway over many decades, which manifests itself (with variations due to respective media) in literature, music, architecture, and the visual arts, and which has had an enormous impact on the history of criticism and cultural ideology. If we were to construct an ideal type notion of what the modernist art work has become as a result of successive canonizations – and I will exclude here the poststructuralist archeology of modernism which has shifted the grounds of the debate – it would probably look somewhat like this:

- The work is autonomous and totally separate from the realms of mass culture and everyday life.
- It is self-referential, self-conscious, frequently ironic, ambiguous, and rigorously experimental.
- It is the expression of a purely individual consciousness rather than of a Zeitgeist or a collective state of mind.
- Its experimental nature makes it analogous to science, and like science it produces and carries knowledge.
- Modernist literature since Flaubert is a persistent exploration of and encounter with language. Modernist painting since Manet is an equally persistent elaboration of the medium itself: the flatness of the canvas, the structuring of notation, paint and brushwork, the problem of the frame.
- The major premise of the modernist art work is the rejection of all classical systems of representation, the effacement of 'content,' the erasure of subjectivity and authorial voice, the repudiation of likeness and verisimilitude, the exorcism of any demand for realism of whatever kind.
- Only by fortifying its boundaries, by maintaining its purity and autonomy, and by avoiding any contamination with mass culture and with the signifying systems of everyday life can the art work maintain its adversary stance: adversary to the bourgeois culture of everyday life as well as adversary to mass culture and entertainment which are seen as the primary forms of bourgeois cultural articulation.

[...]

V

The deeper problem at stake here pertains to the relationship of modernism to the matrix of modernization which gave birth to it and nurtured it through its various stages. In less suggestive terms, the question is why, despite the obvious heterogeneity of the modernist project, a certain universalizing account of the modern has been able to hold sway for so long in literary and art criticism, and why even today it is far from having been decisively displaced from its position of hegemony in cultural institutions. What has to be put in question is the presumably adversary relationship of the modernist aesthetic to the myth and ideology of modernization and progress, which it ostensibly rejects in its fixation upon the eternal and timeless power of the poetic word. From the vantage point of our postmodern age, which has begun in a variety of discourses to question seriously the belief in unhampered progress and in the blessings of modernity, it becomes clear how modernism, even in its most adversary, anti-bourgeois manifestations, is deeply implicated in the processes and pressures of the same mundane modernization it so ostensibly repudiates. It is especially in light of the ecological and environmental critique of industrial and post-industrial capitalism, and of the different yet concomitant feminist critique of bourgeois patriarchy, that the subterranean collusion of modernism with the myth of modernization becomes visible.

I want to show this briefly for two of the most influential and by now classical accounts of the historical trajectory of modernism – the accounts of Clement Greenberg in painting and of Theodor W. Adorno in music and literature. For both critics, mass culture remains the other of modernism, the specter that haunts it, the threat against which high art has to shore up its terrain. And even though mass culture is no longer imagined as primarily feminine, both critics remain under the sway of the old paradigm in their conceptualization of modernism.

Indeed, both Greenberg and Adorno are often taken to be the last ditch defenders of the purity of the modernist aesthetic, and they have become known since the late 1930s as uncompromising enemies of modern mass culture. (Mass culture had by then of course become an effective tool of totalitarian domination in a number of countries, which all banished modernism as degenerate or decadent.) While there are major differences between the two men, both in temperament and in the scope of their analyses, they both share a notion of the inevitability of the evolution of modern art. To put it bluntly, they believe in progress – if not in society, then certainly in art. The metaphors of linear evolution and of a teleology of art are conspicuous in their work. I quote Greenberg: 'It has been in search of the absolute that the avant-garde has arrived at "abstract" or "nonobjective" art – and poetry, too.'[25] It is well known how Greenberg constructs the story of modernist painting as a single-minded trajectory, from the first French modernist avant-garde of the 1860s to the New York School of abstract expressionism – his moment of truth.

Similarly, Adorno sees a historical logic at work in the move from late romantic music to Wagner and ultimately to Schönberg and the second school of Vienna, which represent *his* moment of truth. To be sure, both critics acknowledge retarding elements in these trajectories – Stravinsky in Adorno's account, surrealism in Greenberg's – but the logic of history, or rather the logic of aesthetic evolution, prevails, giving a certain rigidity to Greenberg's and Adorno's theorizing. Obstacles and detours, it seems, only highlight the dramatic and inevitable path of modernism toward its telos, whether this telos is described as triumph as in Greenberg or as pure negativity as in Adorno. In the work of both critics, the theory of modernism appears as a theory of modernization displaced to the aesthetic realm; this is precisely its historical strength, and what makes it different from the mere academic formalism of which it is so often accused. Adorno and Greenberg further share a notion of decline that they see as following on the climax of development in high modernism. Adorno wrote about 'Das Altern der Neuen Musik,' and Greenberg unleashed his wrath on the reappearance of representation in painting since the advent of Pop Art.

At the same time, both Adorno and Greenberg were quite aware of the costs of modernization, and they both understood that it was the ever increasing pace of commodification and colonization of cultural space which actually propelled modernism forward, or, better, pushed it toward the outer margins of the cultural terrain. Adorno especially never lost sight of the fact that, ever since their simultaneous emergence in the mid-19th century, modernism and mass culture have been engaged in a compulsive *pas de deux*. To him, autonomy was a relational phenomenon, not a mechanism to justify formalist amnesia. His analysis of the transition in music from Wagner to Schönberg makes it clear that Adorno never saw modernism as anything other than a reaction formation to mass culture and commodification, a reaction formation which operated on the level of form and artistic material. The same awareness that mass culture, on some basic level, determined the shape and course of modernism is pervasive in Clement Greenberg's essays of the late 1930s. To a large extent, it is by the distance we have traveled from this 'great divide' between mass culture and modernism that we can measure our own cultural postmodernity. And yet, I still know of no better aphorism about the imaginary adversaries, modernism and mass culture, than that which Adorno articulated in a letter to Walter Benjamin: 'Both [modernist art and mass culture] bear the scars of capitalism, both contain elements of change. Both are torn halves of freedom to which, however, they do not add up.'[26]

But the discussion cannot end here. The postmodern crisis of high modernism and its classical accounts has to be seen as a crisis both of capitalist modernization itself and of the deeply patriarchal structures that support it. The traditional dichotomy, in which mass culture appears as monolithic, engulfing, totalitarian, and on the side of regression and the feminine ('Totalitarianism appeals to the desire to return to the womb,' said T. S. Eliot[27]) and modernism appears as progressive, dynamic, and indicative of male superiority in culture, has been challenged empirically and theoretically in a variety of ways in the past twenty years or so. New versions of the history of modern culture, the nature of language, and artistic autonomy have been elaborated, and new theoretical questions have been brought to bear on mass culture and modernism; most of us would probably share the sense that the ideology of modernism, as I have sketched it here, is a thing of the past, even if it still occupies major bastions in cultural institutions such as the museum or the academy. The attacks on high modernism, waged in the name of the postmodern since the late 1950s, have left their mark on our culture, and we are still trying to figure out the gains and the losses which this shift has brought about.

VI

What then of the relationship of postmodernism to mass culture, and what of its gender inscriptions? What of postmodernism's relationship to the myth of modernization? After all, if the masculinist inscriptions in the modernist aesthetic are somehow subliminally linked to the history of modernization, with its insistence on instrumental rationality, teleological progress, fortified ego boundaries, discipline, and self-control; if, furthermore, both modernism and modernization are ever more emphatically subjected to critique in the name of the postmodern – then we must ask to what extent postmodernism offers possibilities for genuine cultural change, or to what extent the postmodern raiders of a lost past produce only simulacra, a fast-image culture that makes the latest thrust of modernization more palatable by covering up its economic and social dislocations. I think that postmodernism does both, but I will focus here only on some of the signs of promising cultural change. [. . .]

I do not intend here to add yet another definition of what the postmodern *really* is, but it seems clear to me that both mass culture and women's (feminist) art are emphatically implicated in any attempt to map the specificity of contemporary culture and thus to gauge this culture's distance from high modernism. Whether one uses the term 'postmodernism' or not, there cannot be any question about the fact that the position of women in contemporary culture and society, and their effect on that culture, is fundamentally different from what it used to be in the period of high modernism and the historical avant-garde. It also seems clear that the uses high art makes of certain forms of mass culture (and vice versa) have increasingly blurred the boundaries between the two; where modernism's great wall once kept the barbarians out and safe-guarded the culture within, there is now only slippery ground which may prove fertile for some and treacherous for others.

At stake in this debate about the postmodern is the great divide between modern art and mass culture, which the art movements of the 1960s intentionally began to dismantle in their practical critique of the high modernist canon and which the cultural neo-conservatives are trying to re-erect today.[28] One of the few widely agreed upon features of postmodernism is its attempt to negotiate forms of high art with certain forms and genres of mass culture and the culture of everyday life.[29] I suspect that it is probably no coincidence that such merger attempts occurred more or less simultaneously with the emergence of feminism and women as major forces in the arts, and with the concomitant reevaluation of formerly devalued forms and genres of cultural expression (e.g., the decorative arts, autobiographic texts, letters, etc.). However, the original impetus to merge high art and popular culture – for example, say in Pop Art in the early 1960s – did not yet have anything to do with the later feminist critique of modernism. It was, rather, indebted to the historical avantgarde – art movements such as Dada, constructivism, and surrealism – which had aimed, unsuccessfully, at freeing art from its aestheticist ghetto and reintegrating art and life.[30] Indeed, the early American postmodernists' attempts to open up the realm of high art to the imagery of everyday life and American mass culture are in some ways reminiscent of the historical avantgarde's attempt to work in the interstices of high art and mass culture. In retrospect, it thus seems quite significant that major artists of the 1920s used precisely the then widespread 'Americanism' (associated with jazz, sports, cars, technology, movies, and photography) in order to overcome bourgeois aestheticism and its separateness from 'life.' Brecht is the paradigmatic example here, and he was in turn strongly influenced by the post-revolutionary Russian avantgarde and its daydream of creating a revolutionary avantgarde culture for the masses. [. . .]

In relation to gender and sexuality, though, the historical avantgarde was by and large as patriarchal, misogynist, and masculinist as the major trends of modernism. One needs only to look at the metaphors in Marinetti's 'Futurist Manifesto,' or to read Marie Luise Fleisser's trenchant description of her relationship to Bertolt Brecht in a prose text entitled 'Avantgarde' – in which the gullible, literarily ambitious young woman from the Bavarian province becomes a guinea pig in the machinations of the notorious metropolitan author. Or, again, one may think of how the Russian avantgarde fetishized production, machines, and science, and of how the writings and paintings of the French surrealists treated women primarily as objects of male phantasy and desire.

There is not much evidence that things were very different with the American postmodernists of the late 1950s and early 1960s. However, the avantgarde's attack on the autonomy aesthetic, its politically motivated critique of the highness of high art, and its urge to validate other, formerly neglected or ostracized forms of cultural expression created an aesthetic climate in which the political aesthetic of feminism could thrive and develop its critique of patriarchal gazing and penmanship. [. . .] The road from the avantgarde's experiments to contemporary women's art seems to have been shorter, less tortuous, and ultimately more productive than the less frequently traveled road from high modernism. Looking at the contemporary art scene, one may well want to ask the hypothetical question whether performance and 'body art' would have remained so dominant during the 1970s had it not been for the vitality of feminism in the arts and the ways in which women artists articulated experiences of the body and of performance in gender-specific terms. [. . .]

In conclusion, then, it seems clear that the gendering of mass culture as feminine and inferior has its primary historical place in the late 19th century, even though the underlying dichotomy did not lose its power until quite recently. It also seems evident that the decline of this pattern of thought coincides historically with the decline of modernism itself. But I would submit that it is primarily the visible and public presence of women artists in *high* art, as well as the emergence of new kinds of women performers and producers in mass culture, which make the old gendering device obsolete. The universalizing ascription of femininity to mass culture always depended on the very real exclusion of women from high culture and its institutions. Such exclusions are, for the time being, a thing of the past. Thus, the old rhetoric has lost its persuasive power because the realities have changed.

NOTES

1. Gustave Flaubert, *Madame Bovary*, trans. Merloyd Lawrence (Boston: Houghton Mifflin, 1969), p. 29.
2. Flaubert, p. 30.
3. Cf. Gertrud Koch, 'Zwitter-Schwestern: Weiblichkeitswahn und Frauenhass – Jean-Paul Sartres Thesen von der androgynen Kunst,' in *Sartres Flaubert lesen: Essays zu Der Idiot der Familie*, ed. Traugott König (Rowohlt: Reinbek, 1980), pp. 44–59.
4. Christa Wolf, *Cassandra: A Novel and Four Essays* (New York: Farrar, Straus, Giroux, 1984), p. 300f.
5. Stuart Hall, paper given at the conference on mass culture at the Center for Twentieth Century Studies, Spring 1984.
6. Theodor W. Adorno, 'Culture Industry Reconsidered,' *New German Critique*, 6 (Fall 1975), 12.
7. [Copy to follow].
8. Max Horkheimer and Theodor W. Adorno, 'Das Schema der Massenkultur,' in Adorno, *Gesammelte Schriften*, 3 (Frankfurt am Main: Suhrkamp, 1981), p. 305.
9. Siegfried Kracauer, 'The Mass Ornament,' *New German Critique*, 5 (Spring 1975), pp. 67–76.
10. Sandra M. Gilbert and Susan Gubar, 'Sexual Linguistics: Gender, Language, Sexuality,' *New Literary History*, 16, no. 3 (Spring 1985), 516.
11. For an excellent study of male images of femininity since the 18th century see Silvia Bovenschen, *Die imaginierte Weiblichkeit* (Frankfurt am Main: Suhrkamp, 1979).
12. Teresa de Lauretis, 'The Violence of Rhetoric: Considerations on Representation and Gender,' *Semiotica* (Spring 1985), special issue on the Rhetoric of Violence.
13. Edmond and Jules de Goncourt, *Germinie Lacerteux*, trans. Leonard Tancock (Harmondsworth: Penguin, 1984), p. 15.
14. Cf. Cäcilia Rentmeister, 'Berufsverbot für Musen,' *Ästhetik und Kommunikation*, 25 (September 1976), 92–113.
15. Cf., for instance, the essays by Carol Duncan and Norma Broude in *Feminism and Art History*, ed. Norma Broude and Mary D. Garrard (New York: Harper & Row, 1982) or the documentation of relevant quotes by Valerie Jaudon and Joyce Kozloff, '"Art Hysterical Notions" of Progress and Culture,' *Heresies*, 1, no. 4 (Winter 1978), 38–42.
16. Friedrich Nietzsche, *The Case of Wagner*, in *The Birth of Tragedy and the Case of Wagner*, trans. Walter Kaufmann (New York: Random House, 1967), p. 161.
17. Nietzsche, *The Case of Wagner*, p. 179.
18. Friedrich Nietzsche, *Nietzsche Contra Wagner*, in *The Portable Nietzsche*, ed. and trans. Walter Kaufmann (Harmondworth and New York: Penguin, 1976), pp. 665f.
19. Nietzsche, *The Case of Wagner*, p. 183.
20. Nietzsche, *Nietzsche Contra Wagner*, p. 666.
21. For a recent discussion of semantic shifts in the political and sociological discourse of masses, elites, and leaders from the late 19th century to fascism see Helmuth Berking, 'Mythos und Politik: Zur historischen Semantik des Massenbegriffs,' *Ästhetik und Kommunikation*, 56 (November 1984), 35–42.
22. Gustave Le Bon, *The Crowd* (Harmondworth and New York: Penguin, 1981), p. 39.
23. Le Bon, p. 50.

24. Le Bon, p. 102.
25. Clement Greenberg, 'Avant-Garde and Kitsch,' in *Art and Culture: Critical Essays* (Boston: Beacon Press, 1961), p. 5f.
26. Letter of March 18, 1936, in Walter Benjamin, *Gesammelte Schriften*, 1, 3 (Frankfurt am Main: Suhrkamp, 1974), p. 1003.
27. T. S. Eliot, 'Notes Towards a Definition of Culture', published with *The Idea of a Christian Society as Christianity and Culture* (New York: Harcourt, Brace, (1968), p. 140.
28. For a discussion of the neo-conservatives' hostility toward postmodernism see the essay 'Mapping the Postmodern.'
29. While critics seem to agree on this point in theory, there is a dearth of specific readings of texts or art works in which such a merger has been attempted. Much more concrete analysis has to be done to assess the results of this new constellation. There is no doubt in my mind that there are as many failures as there are successful attempts by artists, and sometimes success and failure reside side by side in the work of one and the same artist.
30. On this distinction between late 19th-century modernism and the historical avant-garde see Peter Bürger, *Theory of the Avant-Garde* (Minneapolis: University of Minnesota Press, 1984).

13

THE GLOBALIZATION OF COMMUNICATION

John B. Thompson

PATTERNS OF GLOBAL COMMUNICATION TODAY: AN OVERVIEW

While the origins of the globalization of communication can be traced back to the mid-nineteenth century, this process is primarily a phenomenon of the twentieth. For it is during the twentieth century that the flow of information and communication on a global scale has become a regularized and pervasive feature of social life. There are, of course, many dimensions to this process; the twentieth century has witnessed an unparalleled proliferation of the channels of communication and information diffusion. The rapid development of systems of radio and television broadcasting throughout the world has been an important but by no means the only aspect of this process. The globalization of communication has also been a structured and uneven process which has benefited some more than others, and which has drawn some parts of the world into networks of global communication more quickly than other parts. Since the late 1960s, the characteristics of global communication flows have been studied in some detail by researchers in international communication – well before the term 'globalization' gained currency in the social sciences.[1] In this section I shall draw on this literature for the purpose of analysing some of the main patterns of global communication today. I shall not attempt to analyse these patterns in a detailed and comprehensive fashion, but merely to identify some of the main dimensions of globalized communication processes; and I shall be concerned above all to highlight their structured and uneven character. While the range of relevant issues is potentially very wide, I shall restrict

From John B. Thompson, *The Media and Modernity* (Cambridge: Polity Press, 1984).

my attention to four themes: (1) the emergence of transnational communication conglomerates as key players in the global system of communication and information diffusion; (2) the social impact of new technologies, especially those associated with satellite communication; (3) the asymmetrical flow of information and communication products within the global system; and (4) the variations and inequalities in terms of access to the global networks of communication.

(1) The globalization of communication in the twentieth century is a process that has been driven primarily by the activities of large-scale communication conglomerates. The origins of these conglomerates can be traced back to the transformation of the press in the nineteenth century [. . .]. The change in the economic basis of newspapers, precipitated and promoted by the introduction of new methods of production, set in motion a long-term process of accumulation and concentration in the media industries. In the course of the twentieth century, this process has increasingly assumed a transnational character. Communication conglomerates have expanded their operations in regions other than their countries of origin; and some of the large industrial and financial concerns have, as part of explicit policies of global expansion and diversification, acquired substantial interests in the information and communication sector. Through mergers, acquisitions and other forms of corporate growth, the large conglomerates have assumed an ever-greater presence in the global arena of the information and communication trade.

The names of some of the largest communication conglomerates are well known: Time Warner, formed by the merger of Time, Inc., and Warner Communications in 1989 and now the largest media enterprise in the world, has subsidiaries in Australia, Asia, Europe and Latin America. The German-based Bertelsmann group, with strong interests in publishing, television, music and high-tech information systems, has operations in Europe, the United States and Latin America. Rupert Murdoch's News Corporation, which has substantial interests in publishing, television and film, probably has the most extensive reach, with subsidiaries in Europe, the United States, Australia and Asia. These and other large communication conglomerates operate increasingly in a worldwide market and organize their activities on the basis of strategies which are effectively global in design. But nearly all of the large conglomerates are based in North America, Western Europe, Australia or Japan; very few are based in Third World countries, although the latter provide important markets for their goods and services.[2] Hence the development of communication conglomerates has led to the formation of large concentrations of economic and symbolic power which are privately controlled and unevenly distributed, and which can deploy massive resources to pursue corporate objectives in a global arena. It has also led to the formation of extensive, privately controlled networks of communication through which information and symbolic content can flow.

The nature and activities of some of the large communication conglomerates have been documented in the literature and I shall not examine them further here.[3] There is a need, however, for more up-to-date comparative research on the activities of these conglomerates, on the ways in which they are adapting to the changing economic and political circumstances of the 1990s, and on their exploitation of new technological developments.

(2) The development of new technologies has played an important role in the globalization of communication in the late twentieth century, both in conjunction with the activities of communication conglomerates and independently of them. Three interrelated developments have been particularly important. One is the deployment of more extensive and sophisticated cable systems which provide much greater capacity for the transmission of electronically encoded information. A second development is the increasing use of satellites for the purposes of long-distance communication, often in conjunction with land-based cable systems. The third development – in many ways the most fundamental – is the increasing use of digital methods of information processing, storage and retrieval. The digitalization of information, combined with the development of related electronic technologies (microprocessors, etc.), has greatly increased the capacity to store and transmit information and has created the basis for a convergence of information and communication technologies, so that information can be converted relatively easily between different communication media.

All three of these technological developments have contributed in fundamental ways to the globalization of communication. Most obviously, the use of telecommunications satellites, positioned in geosynchronous orbits and interlinked, has created a system of global communication which is virtually instantaneous and which dispenses with the need for terrestrial relays and transmission wires. Since their development in the early 1960s, telecommunications satellites have been used for a variety of purposes.[4] The needs of the military and of large commercial organizations have always played an important role, and many multinational corporations make extensive use of satellite communication. Satellites have also been increasingly integrated into the normal telecommunications networks, carrying a growing proportion of the international traffic in telephone, telex, fax, electronic mail and related communication services.

From the outset, telecommunications satellites were also used as relay stations and distribution points for television broadcasting. They formed an integral part of national network systems in the USA, the former USSR and elsewhere, and they were used as distribution points to supply cable systems on a national and international basis. In recent years, however, the development of more sophisticated satellites, capable of transmitting stronger, well-targeted signals, has made possible the introduction of direct broadcasting by satellite (or DBS). The first DBS systems began transmitting programmes in the USA in 1975, and the first European systems began operating in 1986; by the early

1990s, a variety of DBS systems were operating or planned in other parts of the world. Part of the significance of DBS is that it creates new distribution systems outside of the established terrestrially based networks of broadcasting – systems which are often privately owned and controlled and in which the large communication conglomerates may have a substantial stake. Moreover, these new distribution systems are inherently transnational since, from a technical point of view, there is no reason why the reception area (or 'footprint') of a DBS satellite should correspond even roughly to the territorial boundaries of a particular nation-state.

In addition to creating new transnational distribution networks, the development of DBS and other technologies (including cable and video cassette recorders) has expanded the global market for media products. The international flow of films, TV programmes and other materials has increased as producers and distributors seek to exploit the lucrative markets created by satellite and cable channels and by videocassette rentals and sales. This expansion of the global market should be viewed against the blackcloth of earlier trends in the international flow of media products.

(3) A central feature of the globalization of communication is the fact that media products circulate in an international arena. Material produced in one country is distributed not only in the domestic market but also – and increasingly – in a global market. It has long been recognized, however, that the international flow of media products is a structured process in which certain organizations have a dominant role, and in which some regions of the world are heavily dependent on others for the supply of symbolic goods. Studies carried out in the early 1970s by Nordenstreng and Varis showed a clear asymmetry in the international flow of television programmes: there was, to a large extent, a one-way traffic in news and entertainment programmes from the major exporting countries to the rest of the world.[5] The United States was (and remains) the leading exporter in television programming, selling far more material to other countries (especially to Latin America, Europe, Canada, Australia and Japan) than it imports from abroad. Some European countries, such as Britain and France, were also major exporters (and remain so); but, unlike the United States, they also imported a significant quantity of programming from abroad (mainly from the US). Subsequent studies by Varis and others have tended to confirm the unevenness of flow, although they have also produced a more complex picture and have highlighted the growing importance of intraregional trade (for instance, countries like Mexico and Brazil have emerged as major producers and exporters of programming material to other parts of Latin America).[6]

The structured character of the international flow of symbolic goods is the outcome of various historical and economic factors. In the domain of news, the patterns of dependence reflect the legacy of the international news agencies established in London, Paris and New York (although the precise significance of Western-based news agencies remains a matter of some dispute[7]). In the sphere of entertainment, the economic power of Hollywood continues to exert a major influence on the international flow of films and TV programmes. Many television stations in less developed countries do not have the resources to produce extensive programming of their own. The import of American serials, at prices negotiated on a country-by-country basis, is a relatively inexpensive (and financially very attractive) way to fill broadcasting schedules.

While some of the broad patterns of international flow have been documented over the years, the research remains fragmentary. There are many sectors of the information and communication industries which have yet to be studied in detail from this point of view. And the ways in which existing patterns of international flow will be affected by new technological developments – such as those associated with satellite and cable systems, or those linked more generally to the digitalization of information – is a question which demands a good deal more research. Given the complexity of global networks of transmission and trade and the huge volume of material which passes through them, it is unlikely that our understanding of patterns of international flow will ever be more than partial. But further research could help to shed light on some of the more significant trends.

(4) In addition to analysing the patterns of international flow, it is essential to consider the patterns of access to and uptake of material transmitted through global networks. Much of the research on patterns of international flow has been based on the content analysis of television broadcasting schedules in different countries. But in some parts of the world, access to television broadcasting services was restricted for many years to the relatively small proportion of the population which lived in the major urban areas. For the rural population, which comprises 70–90 per cent of the population in many Third World countries, radio has probably been a more important medium of communication than television.[8] Of course, this situation is changing continuously as more resources are devoted to the development of television services and as more individuals and families are able to gain access to them. But significant inequalities remain in terms of the capacity of individuals in different parts of the world, and in different parts and social strata of the same country, to gain access to the materials which are diffused through global networks.

Quite apart from these inequalities of access, globalized symbolic materials are subjected to different patterns of uptake. Taken on its own, the content analysis of programming schedules tells us relatively little about who watches which programmes, how long they watch them for, etc., and hence tells us relatively little about the extent of uptake of globally distributed material.[9] Moreover, if we wish to explore the impact of the globalization of communication, we must consider not only the patterns of uptake but also the *uses* of globalized symbolic materials – that is, what recipients do with them, how they understand them, and how they incorporate them into

the routines and practices of their everyday lives. These are issues to which
we shall return.

THE THEORY OF CULTURAL IMPERIALISM: A REASSESSMENT

So far I have been concerned to retrace the development of the globalization
of communication and to examine some of the patterns of global communication in the world today. But what kind of theoretical account can be offered
which would help to explain the structured patterns of global communication
and which would shed light on their likely consequences? Various theoretical
accounts can be found in the literature on international communications.[10]
During the last few decades, however, there is one account which has occupied a particularly prominent role: this is the view that the globalization of
communication has been driven by the pursuit of the commercial interests of
large US-based transnational corporations, often acting in collaboration with
Western (predominantly American) political and military interests; and that
this process has resulted in a new form of dependency in which traditional
cultures are destroyed through the intrusion of Western values. This view was
articulated with particular acuity by Herbert Schiller in *Mass Communications
and American Empire*, first published in 1969, and the argument has been
updated and extended in various publications since then.[11] The argument
developed by Schiller and others is generally described as the 'cultural imperialism thesis'.[12] It has been enormously influential: much of the research in
international communications in the 1970s and early 1980s (including some
of the material drawn on in the previous section) was influenced directly or
indirectly by it. But Schiller's work has also been subjected to a great deal of
criticism and there are few scholars today who would accept his analysis unreservedly.[13] Nevertheless, it is useful to reconsider briefly Schiller's argument.
By identifying some of its main strengths and weaknesses, we can gain a clearer
sense of the processes which must be taken into account, and the pitfalls which
must be avoided, by a theory of the globalization of communication.

Schiller argues, very broadly, that the period since the Second World War
has been characterized by the growing dominance of the United States in
the international arena.[14] As the traditional colonial empires of the nineteenth century – the British, French, Dutch, Spanish and Portuguese empires
– declined in significance, they were replaced by a new emergent American
empire. This new imperial regime is based on two key factors: economic
strength, stemming primarily from the activities of US-based transnational
corporations; and communications know-how, which has enabled American
business and military organizations to take the leading roles in the development and control of new systems of electronically based communication in
the modern world. Schiller argues that the American system of broadcasting
– essentially a commercial system dominated by the large networks and funded
primarily by advertising revenue – exemplifies the way in which some of the

most important communication systems have been thoroughly permeated by commercial interests. Moreover, the American system of broadcasting has served as a model for the development of broadcasting systems elsewhere in the world, especially in Third World countries. The dependence on American communications technology and investment, coupled with the new demand for TV programmes and the sheer cost of domestic production, have created enormous pressures for the development of commercial broadcasting systems in many Third World countries and for the large-scale importation of foreign – mainly American – programmes. The result is an 'electronic invasion' which threatens to destroy local traditions and to submerge the cultural heritage of less developed countries beneath a flood of TV programmes and other media products emanating from a few power centres in the West. These programmes are infused with the values of consumerism, since they are geared above all to the needs of the manufacturers who sponsor television through advertising. Hence, when developing countries adopt a commercial system of broadcasting, they are also, argues Schiller, implicated in a process of cultural transformation and dependency in which the values of consumerism override traditional motivations and alternative patterns of value formation, and through which individuals are harnessed increasingly to a global system of communication and commodity production based largely in the US.

Schiller's argument, sketched here only briefly, has the considerable merit of highlighting the global character of electronically based communication systems, of emphasizing their structured character and of underscoring the fact that communication systems are interwoven in fundamental ways with the exercise of economic, military and political power. Moreover, Schiller's argument brings sharply into focus the enormous financial constraints faced by Third World countries seeking to develop their own communication systems, constraints which make the importation of foreign-produced programmes very attractive. However, even if one sympathizes with Schiller's broad theoretical approach and his critical perspective, there are many respects in which his argument is deeply unsatisfactory. I shall not attempt to address all of the difficulties here. Rather, I want to focus on three main problems, all closely linked to the themes I am pursuing in this chapter and elsewhere.

First, let us consider a little further Schiller's portrayal of global structures of power in the post-Second World War period. Schiller's argument was originally developed at a time when American hegemony in the global system seemed – at least to some observers – to be self-evident and secure. The United States, as the major industrial power and the home of many of the largest transnational corporations, appeared to be the military-industrial heartland of the postwar global system; the thesis of cultural imperialism was effectively an argument about the extension and consolidation at the level of communications and information of a power that was fundamentally economic in character. However, this argument provides at best a very partial account of the complex and shifting relations of economic, political, military and symbolic power which characterized the immediate postwar period. It takes relatively little account, for instance, of the fundamental political and symbolic conflicts of the Cold War era, and of the significance of communism and nationalism as mobilizing systems of belief. Moreover, whatever the shortcomings of Schiller's argument with regard to the immediate postwar period, it seems very doubtful indeed whether it could be applied with any degree of conviction to the changing global context of the late twentieth century. In the economic domain alone, the last few decades have witnessed a profound process of global restructuring which has eroded the position of the United States as the preeminent industrial power. The global economy has become increasingly multipolar; Europe (especially Germany), Japan and the newly industrializing countries of South-East Asia have assumed an increasingly important role.[15] Relations of political, coercive and symbolic power have also changed shape in complex ways. The collapse of the communist regimes in Eastern Europe and the dissolution of the Soviet Union have created an altogether new geopolitical situation – not only in Europe but throughout the world. Supranational bodies such as the United Nations and the European Commission are playing an increasing – although as yet relatively limited – role in international affairs. New forms of symbolic power, in some cases linked to the resurgence of nationalism and fundamentalist religious beliefs, have emerged in different parts of the world.

This process of global restructuring has also affected the various industries concerned with information and communication. In terms of the production of electronic components (semiconductors and microprocessors, etc.), the postwar dominance of the United States has been dramatically eroded as production has increasingly shifted to Western Europe, Japan and the Pacific rim. The United States has similarly lost its position of dominance in the manufacture of electronic consumer goods; in television manufacture, for example, Asia is the leading region in the world today and China is the largest single producer, manufacturing 19 per cent of total world output in 1987.[16] The global shift in economic power is also reflected in the growing role of foreign capital in the American market. While Hollywood remains an important producer of films and television entertainment, a growing number of Hollywood studios are owned by foreign-based corporations. In November 1989, Columbia Pictures and Tristar Pictures were bought by the Sony Corporation for $3.4 billion – higher than any price previously paid by a Japanese concern for a US company.[17] Sony had previously acquired CBS Records, so the purchase of Columbia and Tristar represented a further move into the entertainment sector by a company which had established a strong base in the manufacture of audio and video hardware. Shortly after the Sony takeover, another Japanese-based multinational, Matsushita, acquired MCA for $6.9 billion. MCA operates Universal Studios and has a range of other interests in entertainment, retailing, publishing and leisure activities; Matsushita is the largest manufacturer of consumer electronic goods in Japan and one of the largest in the world. Moreover, despite the continued importance of Hollywood, non-North American industries are becoming increasingly important as regional producers and exporters of films and television programmes. This includes industries based in Western Europe and Australia; but it also includes industries based in other parts of the world, such as Mexico, Brazil and India. It would be quite implausible to suggest that this complex and shifting field of global power relations could be analysed in terms of the thesis of cultural imperialism. The thesis is simply too rigid and one-dimensional to do justice to a global situation which is in considerable flux.

Reflecting on his work 25 years later, Schiller recognizes that the cultural imperialism thesis can no longer be sustained in its original form.[18] He acknowledges that since the late 1960s global relations of power have changed in significant ways, and that as a result the thesis would have to be recast today. The global dominance of American culture and media products has not appreciably declined – if anything, argues Schiller, it has become more pronounced, with the collapse of state-socialist regimes in the former Soviet Union and Eastern Europe and with the demise of UNESCO-based attempts to create a new information order. But the economic basis of this dominance has changed. Transnational corporations have assumed an increasingly important role in the global communications industry, and investment capital has been drawn from an increasingly diverse range of sources. So while cultural domination remains American in terms of the form and content of media products, the economic basis of the domination has been internationalized. American cultural imperialism has become, in Schiller's words, 'transnational corporate cultural domination'.[19]

While this revision of the thesis goes some way to address the changes that have taken place in recent decades, it does not go far enough. Schiller still presents too uniform a view of American media culture (albeit a culture which is no longer exclusively at the disposal of American capital) and of its global dominance. He still maintains that American media culture is defined by the overriding objective of promoting consumerism, and that it is this objective which renders it so useful for the global capitalist system. But the composition, the global flow and the uses of media products are far more complex than this characterization would suggest. Schiller's revision of the cultural imperialism thesis is, in effect, a way of acknowledging the globalization of economic activity while still insisting on the continued dominance of American media culture. It would be better to accept that, in the sphere of information and communication as well as in the domain of economic activity, the global patterns and relations of power do not fit neatly into the framework of unrivalled American dominance.

A second problem with Schiller's argument is that it tends to assume that before the electronic invasion led by the United States most Third World countries had indigenous, authentic traditions and cultural heritages which were largely untainted by values imposed from outside. What is at stake in the electronic invasion, explains Schiller, 'is the cultural integrity of weak societies whose national, regional, local or tribal heritages are beginning to be menaced with extinction by the expansion of modern electronic communications'.[20] But this vision of the cultural integrity of Third World countries is a somewhat romantic view which, in many cases, does not stand up to careful scrutiny.[21] The traditions and cultural heritages of many so-called Third World countries were shaped by a long and often brutal process of cultural conflict, a process through which many traditional practices were destroyed and some of the values and beliefs of external powers were imposed on indigenous populations.[22] But the imposition of values and beliefs was rarely a straightforward matter. It generally involved a complex process of adaptation and incorporation whereby extraneous values and beliefs were adapted to new conditions, selectively appropriated by indigenous populations and gradually interwoven with pre-existing traditions and practices. The Spanish conquest of Mexico and the colonization of other parts of Central and South America offer many vivid examples of this process.[23]

The issues addressed by Schiller should be placed, therefore, in a much broader historical perspective. Rather than assuming that prior to the importation of Western TV programmes etc. many Third World countries had indigenous traditions and cultural heritages which were largely unaffected by external pressures, we should see instead that the globalization of communication through electronic media is only the most recent of a series of cultural encounters, in some cases stretching back many centuries, through which the values, beliefs and symbolic forms of different groups have been superimposed on one another, often in conjunction with the use of coercive, political and economic power. Most forms of culture in the world today are, to varying extents, *hybrid cultures* in which different values, beliefs and practices have become deeply entwined. This does not imply, of course, that the globalization of communication through the electronic media may not give rise to new forms of cultural domination and dependency. But it does imply that we cannot understand these new forms, nor can we gain a clear view of their consequences, if we proceed on the assumption that previous cultures were largely untainted by values imposed from outside.

A third problem with Schiller's argument concerns the ways in which imported media products are thought to affect their recipients in the Third World and elsewhere. Schiller argues, in essence, that TV programmes which are made for a commercial television system will unavoidably express consumerist values, both in the programmes themselves and in the advertising which constitutes the financial basis of the system; and that these representations will in turn create wants and foster consumerist motivations in their recipients, in such a way that these recipients become harnessed to a Western-based system of commodity production and exchange. No doubt this rather hasty argument, in its concern to highlight the connection between broadcasting media and a capitalist system of commodity production and exchange, has placed too much emphasis on the role of consumerist values and has neglected the enormous diversity of themes, images and representations which characterize the output of the media industries. But there is another weakness in this argument which is of particular relevance to the issues that concern us here: the argument presupposes a much too simplified account of what is involved in the reception and appropriation of media products.[24] Like many arguments influenced by Marxism, Schiller's argument commits a version of what I have described elsewhere as the 'fallacy of internalism':[25] Schiller tries to infer, from an analysis of the social organization of the media industries, what the consequences of media messages are likely to be for the individuals who receive them. But inferences of this kind must be treated with scepticism. Not only are they very speculative but, more importantly, they disregard the complex, varied and contextually specific ways in which messages are interpreted by individuals and incorporated into their day-to-day lives. In short, Schiller's argument ignores the hermeneutic process of appropriation which is an essential part of the circulation of symbolic forms (including media products).

In recent years a number of researchers have shown – through ethnographic studies in contexts that are particularly suitable for assessing the plausibility of the cultural imperialism thesis – that the processes of reception, interpretation and appropriation of media messages are much more complicated than Schiller's argument assumes. Thus Liebes and Katz, in a well-known study, examined the reception of *Dallas* among different ethnic groups in Israel, comparing their responses with groups in the United States and Japan.[26] They show that different groups found different ways of making sense of the programme, different ways of 'negotiating' its symbolic content. The process of reception was not a one-way transmission of sense but rather a creative encounter between, on the one hand, a complex and structured symbolic form and, on the other, individuals who belong to particular groups and who bring certain resources and assumptions to bear on the activity of interpretation. So Liebes and Katz found, for instance, that there were systematic differences in the ways that groups recounted the programmes they had seen. The groups of Israeli Arabs and Moroccan Jews emphasized kinship relations, interpreting the motivation of characters primarily in terms of the hierarchical order of the family and the continuity of the dynasty. The groups of Russian émigrés, by contrast, paid relatively little attention to kinship relations and were more inclined to take a critical view, seeing the characters as manipulated by the writers and producers of the programme. The groups of kibbutz members and of Americans were also inclined to take a critical view but they interpreted the programme in more psychological terms, as an ongoing saga of interpersonal relations and intrigue.

Studies such as this have shown convincingly that the reception and appropriation of media products are complex social processes in which individuals – interacting with others as well as with the characters portrayed in the programmes they receive – actively make sense of messages, adopt various attitudes towards them and use them in differing ways in the course of their day-to-day lives. It is simply not possible to infer the varied features of reception processes from the characteristics of media messages considered by themselves, or from the commercial constraints operating on the producers of TV programmes. In this respect, Schiller's argument involves a theoretical and methodological short-circuit. The electronic invasion of American films and TV programmes would serve to extend and consolidate a new imperial regime only if it could be reliably assumed that the recipients of these programmes would internalize the consumerist values allegedly expressed in them; but it is precisely this assumption that must be placed in doubt.

This line of criticism presses to the heart of the cultural imperialism thesis. It shows that this thesis is unsatisfactory not only because it is outdated and empirically doubtful, but also because it is based on a conception of cultural phenomena which is fundamentally flawed. It fails to take account of the fact that the reception and appropriation of cultural phenomena are fundamentally hermeneutical processes in which individuals draw on the material and symbolic resources available to them, as well as on the interpretative assistance offered by those with whom they interact in their day-to-day lives, in order to make sense of the messages they receive and to find some way of relating to them. For the cultural imperialism thesis, the process of reception is essentially a 'black box' into which media products infused with consumerist values are poured, and from which individuals oriented towards personal consumption supposedly emerge. But this clearly will not do.

While Schiller's argument is ultimately unsatisfactory, it is nevertheless important as an attempt – indeed, probably the only systematic and moderately plausible theoretical attempt – to think about the globalization of communication and its impact on the modern world. But if Schiller's argument and the cultural imperialism thesis more generally do not provide a satisfactory theoretical framework, what alternatives are there? In the remainder of this chapter I shall try to develop an alternative framework which takes account both of the structured character of global communication and of the contextualized, hermeneutical character of the reception process.

Notes

1. Among the most important and influential of the early studies were the UNESCO-sponsored surveys carried out by Nordenstreng and Varis in 1971–3 and by Varis in 1983. See Kaarle Nordenstreng and Tapio Varis, *Television Traffic – A One-Way Street? A Survey and Analysis of the International Flow of Television Programme Material*, Reports and Papers on Mass Communication, no. 70 (Paris: UNESCO, 1974); Tapio Varis, *International Flow of Television Programmes*, Reports and Papers on Mass Communication, no. 100 (Paris: UNESCO, 1986). Numerous other studies have been carried out. For useful discussions of the relevant literature, see Jeremy Tunstall, *The Media are American: Anglo-American Media in the World* (London: Constable, 1977); Ehihu Katz and George Wedell, *Broadcasting in the Third World: Promise and Performance* (Cambridge, Mass.: Harvard University Press, 1977); Smith, *The Geopolitics of Information*; Ralph Negrine and S. Papathanassopoulos, *The Internationalization of Television* (London: Pinter, 1990); Preben Sepstrup, *Transnationalization of Television in Europe* (London:

John Libbey, 1990); Annabelle Sreberny-Mohammadi, 'The Global and the Local in International Communications', in James Curran and Michael Gurevitch (eds), *Mass Media and Society* (London: Edward Arnold, 1991); Geoffrey Reeves, *Communications and the 'Third World'* (London: Routledge, 1993).

2. A recent UNESCO report on world communications showed that, of the 78 largest communication conglomerates ranked according to total media turnover, 39 were based in the United States, 25 in Western Europe, 8 in Japan, 5 in Canada and 1 in Australia; none were based in the Third World. (See *World Communication Report* (Paris: UNESCO, 1989), pp. 104–5.)

3. See, for example, Ben H. Bagdikian, *The Media Monopoly*, 4th edn (Boston: Beacon Press, 1992); Anthony Smith, *The Age of Behemoths: The Globalization of Mass Media Firms* (New York: Priority Press, 1991); Tunstall and Palmer, *Media Moguls*.

4. For further discussion of historical and technical aspects of satellite communications, see Abram Chayes, James Fawcett, Masami Ito, Alexandre-Charles Kiss et al., *Satellite Broadcasting* (London: Oxford University Press, 1973); Jonathan F. Galloway, *The Politics and Technology of Satellite Communications* (Lexington, Mass.: D. C. Heath, 1972).

5. Nordenstreng and Varis, *Television Traffic – A One Way Street?*; see also Tapio Varis, 'Global Traffic in Television', *Journal of Communication*, 24 (1974), pp. 102–9.

6. See Varis, *International Flow of Television Programmes*; Annabelle Sreberny-Mohammadi, 'The "World of the News" Study: Results of International Cooperation', *Journal of Communications*, 34 (1984), pp. 121–34; Sepstrup, *Transnationalization of Television in Europe*.

7. Some commentators have argued that the influence of Western-based news agencies has been exaggerated. See, for example, Robert L. Stevenson, 'The "World of the News" Study: Pseudo Debate', *Journal of Communications*, 34 (1984), pp. 134–8; Michael Tracey, 'The Poisoned Chalice? International Television and the Idea of Dominance', *Daedalus*, 114 (1985), pp. 17–55.

8. See Katz and Wedell, *Broadcasting in the Third World*, ch. 1.

9. For a discussion of some of the issues involved in studying patterns of consumption in relation to the globalization of communication, see Sepstrup, *Transnationalization of Television in Western Europe*, ch. 4.

10. For a concise overview of the theoretical debates, see Sreberny-Mohammadi, 'The Global and the Local in International Communications', pp. 119–22.

11. See especially Herbert. Schiller, *Mass Communications and American Empire* (New York: Augustus M. Kelley, 1969). A second edition of this book appeared in 1992 with a substantial new chapter by Schiller in which he reflects on the relevance of the work in the changing global conditions of the late twentieth century; see Schiller, 'A Quarter-Century Retrospective', in *Mass Communications and American Empire*, 2nd edn (Boulder, Colo.: Westview Press, 1992), pp. 1–43. For work in a similar vein see, for example, A. F. Wells, *Picture Tube Imperialism? The Impact of US Television on Latin America* (New York: Orbis, 1972); A. Dorfman and A. Mattelart, *How to Read Donald Duck: Imperialist Ideology in the Disney Comic* (New York: International General Editions, 1975); Herbert I. Schiller, *Communication and Cultural Domination* (White Plains, N.Y.: International Arts and Sciences Press, 1976); Kaarle Nordenstreng and Herbert I. Schiller (eds), *National Sovereignty and International Communication* (Norwood, N.J.: Ablex, 1979); Cees J. Hamelink, *Cultural Autonomy in Global Communications: Planning National Information Policy* (London: Centre for the Study of Communication and Culture, 1988).

12. A distinction is sometimes drawn between 'cultural imperialism' and 'media imperialism', but I shall not pursue this distinction here. (See, for example, Oliver

Boyd-Barrett, 'Media Imperialism: Towards an International Framework for the Analysis of Media Systems', in James Curran, Michael Gurevitch and Janet Woollacott (eds), *Mass Communication and Society* (London: Edward Arnold, 1977), pp. 116–35.)

13. The critical literature is extensive. For helpful commentaries, see Tunstall, *The Media are American*, ch. 2; John Tomlinson, *Cultural Imperialism: A Critical Introduction* (London: Pinter, 1991); Reeves, *Communications and the 'Third World'*, ch. 3.

14. This reconstruction of Schiller's argument is based on the original 1969 edition of *Mass Communications and American Empire*.

15. See Dicken, *Global Shift*, especially ch. 2.

16. Ibid., p. 316.

17. See Janet Wasko, *Hollywood in the Information Age: Beyond the Silver Screen* (Cambridge: Polity Press, 1994), ch. 4.

18. See Schiller, 'A Quarter-Century Retrospective'.

19. Ibid., p. 39.

20. Schiller, *Mass Communications and American Empire* (1969 edn), p. 109.

21. See Tunstall, *The Media are American*, pp. 57–9.

22. For a perceptive account of the different forms of cultural encounter and conflict associated with European expansion, see Urs Bitterli, *Cultures in Conflict: Encounters Between European and Non-European Cultures, 1492–1800*, trans. Ritchie Robertson (Cambridge: Polity Press, 1989).

23. See, for example, Nathan Wachtel's classic study of the Spanish conquest of Peru, *The Vision of the Vanquished: The Spanish Conquest of Peru Through Indian Eyes, 1530–1570*, trans. Ben and Sian Reynolds (Hassocks, Sussex: Harvester Press, 1977); see also Serge Gruzinski, *The Conquest of Mexico: The Westernization of Indian Societies from the Sixteenth to the Eighteenth Century*, trans. Eileen Corrigan (Cambridge: Polity Press, 1993).

24. For further discussion of this point, see Tomlinson, *Cultural Imperialism*, pp. 45–64; Sreberny-Mohammadi, 'The Global and the Local in International Communications', pp. 130–4.

25. See Thompson, *Ideology and Modern Culture*, especially pp. 24–5, 105, 291.

26. See Tamar Liebes and Elihu Katz, *The Export of Meaning: Cross-Cultural Readings of 'Dallas'*, 2nd edn (Cambridge: Polity Press, 1993). See also Daniel Miller's discussion of the significance of soap operas in Trinidad in his *Modernity – An Ethnographic Approach: Dualism and Mass Consumption in Trinidad* (Oxford: Berg, 1994), pp. 247–53.

14

AN INTRODUCTION TO THE INFORMATION AGE

Manuel Castells

In the last decade I was struck, as many have been, by a series of major historical events that have transformed our world/our lives. Just to mention the most important: the diffusion and deepening of the information technology revolution, including genetic engineering; the collapse of the Soviet Union, with the consequent demise of the international Communist movement, and the end of the Cold War that had marked everything for the last half a century; the restructuring of capitalism; the process of globalization; emergence of the Pacific as the most dynamic area of the global economy; the paradoxical combination of a surge in nationalism and the crisis of the sovereign nation-state; the crisis of democratic politics, shaken by periodic scandals and a crisis of legitimacy; the rise of feminism and the crisis of patriarchalism; the widespread diffusion of ecological consciousness; the rise of communalism as sources of resistance to globalization, taking in many contexts the form of religious fundamentalism; last, but not least, the development of a global criminal economy that is having significant impacts in international economy, national politics, and local everyday life.

I grew increasingly dissatisfied with the interpretations and theories, certainly including my own, that the social sciences were using to make sense of this new world. But I did not give up the rationalist project of understanding all this, in a coherent manner, that could be somewhat empirically grounded and as much as possible theoretically oriented. Thus, for the last 12 years I

From *City: Analysis of Urban Trends, Culture, Theory, Policy, Action* 2:7 (1997) pp. 6–16. Originally an address to the conference on 'Information and the City' held at Oxford University, March 1996.

undertook the task of researching and understanding this wide array of social trends, working in and on the United States, Western Europe, Russia, Asian Pacific, and Latin America. Along the way, I found plenty of company, as researchers from all horizons are converging in this collective endeavour.

My personal contribution to this understanding is the book in three volumes that I have now completed, *The Information Age*. [. . .] The first volume analyses the new social structure, the network society. The second volume studies social movements and political processes, in the framework of and in interaction with the network society. The third volume attempts an interpretation of macro-social processes, as a result of the interaction between the power of networks and the power of identity, focusing on themes such as the collapse of the Soviet Union, the emergence of the Pacific, or the ongoing process of global social exclusion and polarization. It also proposes a general theoretical synthesis.

I will take this opportunity to share with you the main lines of my argument, hoping that this will help a debate that I see emerging from all directions in the whole world.

[. . .]

[. . .] I will follow a schematic format. I will focus on identifying the main features of what I consider to be the emerging, dominant social structure, the network society, that I find characteristic of informational capitalism, as constituted throughout the world. I will not indulge in futurology: everything I say is based on what I have perceived, rightly or wrongly, already at work in our societies. I will organize my lecture in one disclaimer, nine hypotheses, and one conclusion.

DISCLAIMER

I shall focus on the structure/dynamics of the network society, not on its historical genesis, that is how and why it came about, although in my book I propose a few hints about it. For the record: in my view, it resulted from the historical convergence of three *independent* processes, from whose interaction emerged the network society:

- The Information Technology Revolution, constituted as a paradigm in the 1970s.
- The restructuring of capitalism and of statism in the 1980s, aimed at superseding their contradictions, with sharply different outcomes.
- The cultural social movements of the 1960s, and their 1970s aftermath (particularly feminism and ecologism).

The Information Technology Revolution *did not* create the network society. But without Information Technology, the Network Society would not exist.

Rather than providing an abstract categorization of what this Network Society is, let me summarize its main features and processes, before attempting a synthesis of its embedded logic in the diversity of its cultural/institutional variations. There is no implicit hierarchy in the sequence of presentation of these features. They all interact in, guess what, a network.

1 AN INFORMATIONAL ECONOMY

It is an economy in which sources of productivity and competitiveness for firms, regions, countries, depend, more than ever, on knowledge, information, and the technology of their processing including the technology of management, and the management of technology. This is not the same as a service economy. There is informational agriculture, informational manufacturing, and different types of informational services, while a large number of service activities, e.g. in the developing world, are not informational at all.

The informational economy opens up an extraordinary potential for solving our problems, but, because of its dynamism and creativity, it is potentially more exclusionary than the industrial economy if social controls do not check the forces of unfettered market logic.

2 GLOBAL ECONOMY

This is not the same as a world economy. That has existed, in the West, at least since the sixteenth century. The global economy is a new reality: it is an economy whose core, strategically dominant activities have the potential of working as a unit in real time on a planetary scale. This is so for financial and currency markets, advanced business services, technological innovation, high technology manufacturing, media communication.

Most economic activity in the world, and most employment are not only national but regional or local. But, except for subsistence economies, the fate of these activities, and of their jobs, depends ultimately on the dynamics of the global economy, to which they are connected through networks and markets. Indeed, if labour tends to be local, capital is by and large globalized – not a small detail in a capitalist economy. This globalization has developed as a fully fledged system only in the last two decades, on the basis of information/communication technologies that were previously not available.

The global economy reaches out to the whole planet, but it is not planetary, it does not include the whole planet. In fact, it excludes probably a majority of the population. It is characterized by an extremely uneven geography. It scans the whole world, and links up valuable inputs, markets, and individuals, while switching off unskilled labour and poor markets. For a significant part of people around the world, there is a shift, from the point of view of dominant systemic interests, from exploitation to structural irrelevance.

This is different from the traditional First World/Third World opposition, because the Third World has become increasingly diversified, internally, and the First World has generated social exclusion, albeit in lesser proportion, within its own boundaries. Thus, I propose the notion of the emergence of a Fourth World of exclusion, made up not only of most of Africa, and rural Asia, and of Latin American shanties, but also of the South Bronx, La Courneuve, Kamagasaki, or Tower Hamlets of this world. A fourth world that, as I document extensively in volume three, is predominantly populated by women and children.

3 THE NETWORK ENTERPRISE

At the heart of the connectivity of the global economy and of the flexibility of informational capitalism, there is a new form of organization, characteristic of economic activity, but gradually extending its logic to other domains and organizations: the *network enterprise*. This is not the same as a network of enterprises. It is a network made either from firms or segments of firms, or from internal segmentation of firms. Multinational corporations, with their internal decentralization, and their links with a web of subsidiaries and suppliers throughout the world, are but one of the forms of this network enterprise. But others include strategic alliances between corporations, networks of small and medium businesses (such as in Northern Italy or Hong Kong), and link-ups between corporations and networks of small businesses through subcontracting and outsourcing.

[. . .]

4 THE TRANSFORMATION OF WORK AND EMPLOYMENT: THE FLEXI-WORKERS

Work is at the heart of all historical transformations. And there is no exception to this. But the coming of the Information Age is full of myths about the fate of work and employment.

With the exception, and an important one, of Western Europe, there is no major surge of unemployment in the world after two decades of diffusion in information technology. Indeed, there is much higher unemployment in technologically laggard countries, regions, and sectors.

All evidence and analysis points to the variable impact of technology on jobs depending on a much broader set of factors, mainly firms' strategies and governments' policies. Indeed, the two most technologically advanced economies, the US and Japan, both display a low rate of unemployment. In the US in the last four years there is a net balance of 10 million new jobs, and the educational content for these new jobs is significantly higher than that of the pre-existing social structure: many more information-intensive jobs than hamburger flippers jobs have been created. Even manufacturing jobs are at an all time high on a global perspective: between 1970 and 1989, manufacturing jobs in the world increased by 72 per cent, even if OECD countries, particularly the US and the UK, have indeed deindustrialized.

[. . .]

There is indeed a serious unemployment problem in the inner cities of America, England, or France, among the uneducated and switched off populations, or in low technology countries around the world, particularly in the rural areas.

For the majority of people in America, for instance, unemployment is not a problem. And yet, there is tremendous anxiety and discontent about work. There is a real base for this concern:

(a) There is the transformation of power relationships between capital and labour in favour of capital, through the process of socio-economic restructuring that took place in the 1980s, both in a conservative environment (Reagan, Thatcher), and, to a lesser but real extent, in a less conservative environment (Spain, France). In this sense, new technologies allowed business to either automate or shift production offshore or outsource supplies or to subcontract to smaller firms or to obtain concessions from labour or all the above.

(b) The development of the network enterprise translates into downsizing, subcontracting, and networking of labour, inducing flexibility of both business and labour, and individualization of contractual arrangements between management and labour. So, instead of layoffs what we often have are layoffs followed by subcontracting of services on an *ad hoc*, consulting basis, for the time and task to be performed, without job tenure and without social benefits provided by the firm.

This is indeed the general trend, exemplified by the rapid growth in all countries of self-employment, temporary work, and part-time, particularly for women. In England, between 40 and 45 per cent of the labour force seems to be already in these categories, as opposed to full-time, regularly salaried employment, and is growing. Some studies in Germany project that in 2015, about 50 per cent of the labour force would be out of stable employment. And in the most dynamic region in the world, Silicon Valley, a study we have just completed shows that, in the midst of a job creation explosion, in the last ten years, between 50 per cent and 90 per cent of new jobs, most of them highly paid, are of this kind of nonstandard labour arrangements.

The most significant change in work in the information age is the reversal of the socialization/salarization of labour that characterized the industrial age. The 'organization man' is out, the 'flexible woman' is in. The individualization of work, and therefore of labour's bargaining power, is the major feature characterizing employment in the network society.

5 SOCIAL POLARIZATION AND SOCIAL EXCLUSION

The processes of globalization, business networking, and individualization of labour weaken social organizations and institutions that represented/protected workers in the information age, particularly labour unions and the welfare state. Accordingly, workers are increasingly left to themselves in their differential relationship to management, and to the market place.

Skills and education, in a constant redefinition of these skills, become critical in valorizing or devaluing people in their work. But even valuable workers may fall down for reasons of health, age, gender discrimination, or lack of capacity to adapt to a given task or position.

As a result of these trends, most societies in the world, and certainly OECD countries, with the US and the UK at the top of the scale, present powerful trends towards increasing inequality, social polarization and social exclusion. There is increasing accumulation of wealth at the top, and of poverty at the bottom.

[. . .]

The Information Age does not have to be the age of stepped-up inequality, polarization and social exclusion. But for the moment it is.

6 THE CULTURE OF REAL VIRTUALITY

Shifting to the cultural realm, we see the emergence of a similar pattern of networking, flexibility, and ephemeral symbolic communication, in a culture organized around electronic media, including in this communication system the computer-mediated communication networks. Cultural expressions of all kinds are increasingly enclosed in or shaped by this world of electronic media. But the new media system is not characterized by the one-way, undifferentiated messages through a limited number of channels that constituted the world of mass media. And it is not a global village.

Media are extraordinarily diverse, and send targeted messages to specific segments of audiences and to specific moods of the audiences. They are increasingly inclusive, bridging from one to another, from network TV to cable or satellite TV, radio, VCR, musical video, walkman type of devices, connected throughout the globe, and yet diversified by cultures, constituting a hypertext with extraordinary inclusive capacity. Furthermore, slowly but surely, this new media system is moving towards interactivity, particularly if we include CMC networks, and their access to text, images, sounds, and will eventually link up with the current media system.

Instead of a global village we are moving towards mass production of customized cottages. While there is oligopolistic concentration of multimedia groups around the world, there is at the same time, market segmentation, and increasing interaction by and among the individuals that break up the uniformity of a mass audience. These processes induce the formation of what I call *the culture of real virtuality*. It is so, and not virtual reality, because when our symbolic environment is, by and large, structured in this inclusive, flexible, diversified hypertext, in which we navigate every day, the virtuality of this text is in fact our reality, the symbols from which we live and communicate.

7 Politics

This enclosure of communication in the space of flexible media does not only concern culture. It has a fundamental effect on *politics*. In all countries, the media have become the essential space of politics. Not all politics takes place through the media, and image making still needs to relate to real issues and real conflicts. But without significant presence in the space of media, actors and ideas are reduced to political marginality. This presence does not concern only, or even primarily, the moments of political campaigns, but the day-to-day messages that people receive by and from the media.

I propose the following analysis:

- To an overwhelming extent people receive their information, on the basis of which they form their political opinion, and structure their behaviour, through the media, particularly television and radio.
- Media politics needs to simplify the message/proposals.
- The simplest message is an image. The simplest image is a person. Political competition revolves around personalization of politics.
- The most effective political weapons are negative messages. The most effective negative message is character assassination of opponents' personalities. The politics of scandal, in the US, in Europe, in Japan, in Latin America etc. is the predominant form of political struggle.
- Political marketing is the essential means to win political competition in democratic politics. In the information age it involves media advertising, telephone banks, targeted mailing, image making, image unmaking, image control, presence in the media, staging of public appearances etc. This makes it an excessively expensive business, way beyond that of traditional party politics, so that mechanisms of political financing are obsolete, and parties use access to power as a way to generate resources to stay in power or to prepare to return to it. This is the fundamental source of political corruption, to which intermediaries add a little personal twist. This is also at the source of systemic corruption, that feeds scandal politics. The use of scandal as a weapon leads to increased expense and activity in intelligence, damage control, and access to the media. Once a market is created, intermediaries appear to retrieve, obtain, or fabricate information, offering it to the highest bidder. Politics becomes a horse race, and a soap opera motivated by greed, backstage manoeuvres, betrayals, and, often, sex and violence, becoming hardly distinguishable from TV scripts.
- Those who survive in this world become politically successful, for a while. But what certainly does not survive, after a few rounds of these tricks, is political legitimacy, not to speak of citizens' hope.

8 Timeless Time

As with all historical transformations, the emergence of a new social structure is necessarily linked to the redefinition of the material foundations of life, *time and space*. Time and space are related, in society as in nature. Their meaning, and manifestations in social practice, evolve throughout histories and across cultures, as Giddens, Thrift, Harvey, Adams, Lash, and Urry, among others, have shown.

I propose the hypothesis that the network society, as the dominant social structure emerging in the Information Age, is organized around new forms of time and space: timeless time, the space of flows. These are the dominant forms, and not the forms in which most people live, but through their domination, they affect everybody. Let me explain, starting with time, then with some greater detail on space, given the specific interests of many in this conference.

In contrast to the rhythm of biological time of most of human existence, and to the clock time characterizing the industrial age, a new form of time characterizes the dominant logic of the network society: *timeless time*. It is defined by the use of new information/communication technologies in a relentless effort to annihilate time, to compress years in seconds, seconds in split seconds. Furthermore, the most fundamental aim is *to eliminate sequencing of time*, including past, present and future in the same hypertext, thus eliminating the 'succession of things' that, according to Leibniz, characterizes time, so that without things and their sequential ordering there is no longer time in society. We live, as in the recurrent circuits of the computer networks in the encyclopedia of historical experience, all our tenses at the same time, being able to reorder them in a composite created by our fantasy or our interests.

David Harvey has shown the relentless tendency of capitalism to eliminate barriers of time. But I think in the network society, that is indeed a capitalist society, but something else at the same time, all dominant processes tend to be constructed around timeless time. I find such a tendency in the whole realm of human activity. I find it certainly in the split second financial transactions of global financial markets, but I also find it, for instance, in instant wars, built around the notion of a surgical strike that devastates the enemy in a few hours, or minutes, to avoid politically unpopular, costly wars. Or in the blurring of the life cycle by new reproductive techniques, allowing people a wide range of options in the age and conditions of parenting, even storing their embryos to eventually produce babies later either by themselves, or through surrogate mothers, even after their procreators are dead. I find it in the twisting of working life by the variable chronology of labour trajectories and time schedules in increasingly diverse labour markets. And I find it in the vigorous effort to use medical technology, including genetic engineering, and computer-based medical care to exile death from life, to bring a substantial proportion of the population to a high level of life-expectancy, and to diffuse the belief that, after all, we are eternal, at least for some time.

As with space, timeless time characterizes dominant functions and social groups, while most people in the world are still submitted to biological time and to clock time. Thus, while instant wars characterize the technological powers, atrocious, lingering wars go on and on for years, around the planet, in a slow-motion destruction process, quasi-ignored by the world until they are discovered by some television programme.

I propose the notion that a fundamental struggle in our society is around the redefinition of time, between its annihilation or desequencing by networks, on one hand, and, on the other hand, the consciousness of glacial time, the slow-motion, inter-generational evolution of our species in our cosmological environment, a concept suggested by Lash and Urry, and a battle undertaken, in my view, by the environmental movement.

9 THE SPACE OF FLOWS

Many years ago (or at least it seems to me as many) I proposed the concept of Space of Flows to make sense of a body of empirical observation: dominant functions were increasingly operating on the basis of exchanges between electronic circuits linking up information systems in distant locations. Financial markets, global media, advanced business services, technology, information. In addition, electronically based, fast transportation systems reinforced this pattern of distant interaction by following up with movements of people and goods. Furthermore, new location patterns for most activities follow a simultaneous logic of territorial concentration/decentralization, reinstating the unity of their operation by electronic links, e.g. the analysis proposed in the 1980s on location patterns of high tech manufacturing; or the networked articulation of advanced services throughout the world, under the system labelled as 'global city'.

Why keep the term of space under these conditions? Reasons: (1) These electronic circuits do not operate in the territorial vacuum. They link up territorially based complexes of production, management and information, even though the meaning and functions of these complexes depend on their connection in these networks of flows. (2) These technological linkages are material, e.g. depend on specific telecommunication/transportation facilities, and on the existence and quality of information systems, in a highly uneven geography. (3) The meaning of space evolves – as the meaning of time. Thus, instead of indulging in futurological statements such as the vanishing of space, and the end of cities, we should be able to reconceptualize new forms of spatial arrangements under the new technological paradigm.

To proceed with this conceptualization I build on a long intellectual tradition, from Leibniz to Harold Innis, connecting space and time, around the notion of space as coexistence of time. Thus, my definition: space is the material support of time-sharing social practices.[1]

What happens when the time-sharing of practices (be it synchronous or asynchronous) does not imply contiguity? 'Things' still exist together, they share time, but the material arrangements that allow this coexistence are inter-territorial or transterritorial: *the space of flows is the material organization of time-sharing social practices that work through flows.* What concretely this material organization is depends on the goals and characteristics of the networks of flows, for instance I can tell you what it is in the case of high technology manufacturing or in the case of global networks of drug traffic. However, I did propose in my analysis some elements that appear to characterize the space of flows in all kinds of networks: electronic circuits connection information systems; territorial nodes and hubs; locales of support and social cohesion for dominant social actors in the network (e.g. the system of VIP spaces throughout the world).

Dominant functions tend to articulate themselves around the space of flows. But this is not the only space. *The space of places continues to be the predominant space of experience*, of everyday life, and of social and political control. Places root culture and transmit history. (A place is a locale whose form, function, and meaning, from the point of view of the social actor, are contained within the boundaries of physical contiguity.)

In the network society, a fundamental form of social domination is *the prevalence of the logic of the space of flows over the space of places.* The space of flows structures and shapes the space of places, as when the differential fortunes of capital accumulation in global financial markets reward or punish specific regions, or when telecom systems link up CBDs to outlying suburbs in new office development, bypassing/marginalizing poor urban neighbourhoods. The domination of the space of flows over the space of places induces intra-*metropolitan dualism* as a most important form of social-territorial exclusion, that has become as significant as regional uneven development. The simultaneous growth and decline of economies and societies within the same metropolitan area is a most fundamental trend of territorial organization, and a key challenge to urban management nowadays.

But there is still something else in the new spatial dynamics. Beyond the opposition between the space of flows and the space of places. As information/communication networks diffuse in society, and as technology is appropriated by a variety of social actors, segments of the space of flows are penetrated by forces of resistance to domination, and by expressions of personal experience. Examples:

(a) Social movements. *Zapatistas* and the Internet (but from the Lacandona forest). But also American Militia.
(b) Local governments, key agents of citizen representation in our society, linking up through electronic networks, particularly in Europe (see research by Stephen Graham).
(c) Expressions of experience in the space of flows.

Thus, we do witness an increasing penetration, and subversion, of the space flows, originally set up for the functions of power, by the power of experience, inducing a set of contradictory power relationships. Yes, it is still an elitist means of communication, but it is changing rapidly. The problem is to integrate these observations in some theory, but for this we still lack research, in spite of some insightful elaborations, such as the one by Sherry Turkle at MIT.

The new frontier of spatial research is in examining the interaction between the space of flows, the space of places, function, meaning, domination, and challenge to domination, in increasingly complex and contradictory patterns. Homesteading in this frontier is already taking place, as shown in the pioneering research by Graham and Marvin, or in the reflections of Bill Mitchell, but we are clearly at the beginning of a new field of study that should help us to understand *and to change* the currently prevailing logic in the space of flows.

CONCLUSION: THE NETWORK SOCIETY

So, what is the Network Society? It is a society that is structured in its dominant functions and processes around networks. In its current manifestation it is a capitalist society. Indeed, we live more man ever in a capitalist world, and thus an analysis in terms of capitalism is necessary and complementary to the theory of the network society. But this particular form of capitalism is very different from industrial capitalism, as I have tried to show.

The Network Society is not produced by information technology. But without the information technology revolution it could not be such a comprehensive, pervasive social form, able to link up, or de-link, the entire realm of human activity.

So, is that all? Just a morphological transformation? Well, historically, transformation of social forms has always been fundamental, both as expressions and sources of major social processes, e.g. standardized mass production in the large factory as characteristic of the so-called Fordism, as a major form of capitalist social organization; or the rational bureaucracy as the foundation of modern society, in the Weberian conception.

But this morphological transformation is even more significant because the network architecture is particularly dynamic, open-ended, flexible, potentially able to expand endlessly, without rupture, bypassing/disconnecting undesirable components following instructions of the networks' dominant nodes. Indeed, the February 1997 Davos meeting titled the general programme of its annual meeting 'Building the Network Society'.

This networking logic is at the roots of major effects in our societies. Using it:

- capital flows can bypass controls
- workers are individualized, outsourced, subcontracted
- communication becomes at the same time global and customized
- valuable people and territories are switched on, devalued ones are switched off.

The dynamics of networks push society towards an endless escape from its own constraints and controls, towards an endless supersession and reconstruction of its values and institutions, towards a meta-social, constant rearrangement of human institutions and organizations.

Networks transform power relationships. Power in the traditional sense still exists: capitalists over workers, men over women, state apparatuses still torture bodies and silence minds around the world.

Yet, there is a higher order of power: the power of flows in the networks prevails over the flows of power. Capitalists are dependent upon uncontrollable financial flows; many workers are at the same time investors (often unwillingly through their pension funds) in this whirlwind of capital; networkers are interrelated in the logic of the network enterprise, so that their jobs and income depend on their positioning rather than on their work. States are bypassed by global flows of wealth, information, and crime. Thus, to survive, they band together in multilateral ventures, such as the European Union. It follows the creation of a web of political institutions – national, supranational, international, regional, and local – that becomes the new operating unit of the information age: the network state.

In this complexity, the communication between networks and social actors depends increasingly on shared *cultural codes*. If we accept certain values, certain categories that frame the meaning of experience, then the networks will process them efficiently, and will return to each one of us the outcome of their processing, according to the rules of domination and distribution inscripted in the network.

Thus, the challenges to social domination in the network society revolve around the redefinition of cultural codes, proposing alternative meaning and changing the rules of the game. This is why the affirmation of *identity* is so essential, because it fixes meaning autonomously *vis-à-vis* the abstract, instrumental logic of networks. I am, thus I exist. In my empirical investigation I have found identity-based social movements aimed at changing the cultural foundations of society to be the essential sources of social change in the information age, albeit often in forms and with goals that we do not usually associate with positive social change. Some movements, that appear to be the most fruitful and positive, are proactive, such as feminism and environmentalism. Some are reactive, as in the communal resistances to globalization built around religion, nation, territory, or ethnicity. But in all cases they affirm the preeminence of experience over instrumentality, of meaning over function, and, I would dare to say, of use value of life over exchange value in the networks.

The implicit logic of the Network Society appears to end history, by enclosing it into the circularity of recurrent patterns of flows. Yet, as with any other social form, in fact it opens up a new realm of contradiction and conflict, as people around the world refuse to become shadows of global flows and project their dreams, and sometimes their nightmares, into the light of new history making.

1. Leibniz: 'Space is something purely relative, like time; space being an order of coexistences as time is an order of successions. For space denotes in terms of possibility and order of things that exist at the same time, in so far as they exist together ... When we see several things together we perceive this order of things among themselves.'

15

'NOT ONLY, BUT ALSO': MIXEDNESS AND MEDIA

Annabelle Sreberny

[. . .]

One of the biggest conundrums of multicultural policy, in which media practices are deeply implicated, is how to recognise and support cultural difference
without reification and fixity. A danger is that multicultural media policies and
practices concerned to foster excluded voices actually work to fix monological
minority subcultures without developing channels and genres that cross over
ethnic divisions and foster dialogic understanding.

In the multiculturalist model of equal worth as proposed by Taylor, amongst
others, different and excluded voices deserve respect and recognition, especially
since we 'live together' more and more, both 'on a world scale and commingled
in each individual society' (Taylor 1994: 72).

The problem is the assumption of 'culture' as an exclusive club with sealed
boundaries within which only some people are full members, rather than as
fluid and pliable depending on people's choices and lived contexts. As Appiah
(1994: 156) has argued, much multicultural talk 'presupposes conceptions
of collective identity that are remarkably unsubtle in their understandings
of the processes by which identities, both individual and collective, develop'.
Baumann takes up that notion of 'develop' and talks about identities being
'postulated, asserted, and then filled with prescriptive norms by people with
interests' (1999: 115). He critiques much work on multiculturalism and recognition as treating culture as simple and one-dimensional, whereas 'the very
essence of any cultural identity lies in its dialogical character with others'

From *Journal of Ethnic and Migration Studies*, 31:3 (2005) pp. 443–59.

(1999: 116). Thus culture is 'not an imposition of fixed and normed identities, but a dialogical process of making sense with and through others' (1999: 117) so that 'different cultural identifications can and will, in a multicultural society, cut across each other's reified boundaries' (1999: 119). For him, much of actual multicultural policy-making is based on a position that he calls 'difference multiculturalism', which 'parades the distinctiveness of each so-called cultural group and remains in thrall to each reified understanding of culture'. This stance, instead of breaking down cultural boundaries, actually reinscribes the borders and fixes them.

With an action frame of culture as live and moving, reifying discourses of absolute differences should give way to more processual discourses of relational differentiations (Baumann 1999: 132). The shifting terrain of identities, on global, national and local levels, summons up new 'we–they balances' (Elias 1991) at the collective level and at the individual level, situating everyone in multiple, complex skeins of identity-formations. Such a mode of thinking demands, first, a recognition of interconnectedness; a multirelational thinking that accepts that 'the so-called "others" form a necessary part of what "we" think we are and want' (Baumann 1999: 125). Second, it requires a better understanding of individual complexity which, as Hall describes (1991: 57), 'is the politics of recognizing that all of us are composed of multiple social identities, not one. That we are all complexly constructed through different categories, of different antagonisms, and these may have the effect of locating us socially in multiple positions of marginality and subordination, but which do not operate on us in exactly the same way'. The processual mode of thinking accepts that 'nothing in social life is based on an absolute, not even the idea of what counts as a majority or even a cultural group' (Baumann 1999: 141). Nor indeed is it any longer clear who counts as a 'minority' – an odd and shifting term, as Alibhai-Brown has acknowledged (2000). Beyond notions of hybridity, younger scholars are suggesting that we pay more attention to the notion, and experience of, 'mixedness' as a powerful mode of being in the world (Sreberny-Mohammadi 2003).

THE COMPLICATIONS OF ADDING 'MEDIA'

My concern, [. . .] in [. . .] this paper [. . .], is what happens when 'media' is added to this debate. More specifically, does adding media to the multicultural conundrum actually work to reify difference rather than support complexity?

A considerable amount of recent research on the media has focused on the development of minority ethnic and diasporic media channels. Work on 'diasporic media' has grown out of the comparatively recent reproblematisation of movements of people as part of the processes of globalisation. The emergence of 'transnational communities' that use various forms of media and communications technologies to keep in touch with erstwhile homes and members of their 'community' spread around the world is increasingly well-documented (see, for example, Cunningham and Sinclair 2000; Dayan 1998; Sreberny 2002). Yet often such developments are heralded as radically new, rather than more intensive development of trends evident for some time. A different and older literature exists about ethnic minority media (for example, Husband 1994; Riggins 1992) that has long posed the tension between the need for recognition of minority voices (Honneth 2001) and the tendency toward fragmentation of the public sphere. [...]

Such media channels clearly provide some possibility of collective self-representation, challenge the often debilitatingly narrow and stereotypic representations of the mainstream, and are often independently owned and not part of large media conglomerates. They offer representations of (parts of) themselves to minority audiences (Millwood Hargrave 2002), although they are usually watched within a complex selection of programming content that includes mainstream channels also (Sreberny 2001). Indeed, an analysis of the media habits of Iranians living in London revealed a pattern of media use determined as much by gender and age as by diasporic experience (Sreberny 2002). So the development of such channels is broadly seen as positive; indeed, how could that not be so, since such media appear to give a voice to the previously unvoiced, and better representation to those who were poorly represented in mainstream media content.

But there is an interesting tension between finding a voice as a minority group and being forced, or allowed, to only speak as a member of that minority group to similar others. [...] There is a still-operating assumption that people 'belong' to a single minority ethnic group and that that group exists within a single, national public sphere. [...] Yet work around ethnicity and diaspora challenges that frame. Such work sets up both a more intensive gaze inward toward the fragments of the nation and a more extensive gaze outward to the original points of departure of minority groups, earlier erstwhile homes that may or may not still exert some claims of attachment. Indeed, I have argued in earlier work (Sreberny 2002) that it makes better sense to think of ethnicity, diaspora and exile not in absolute terms of some existential state of 'being' but in more fluid terms of 'gazing' – back toward the old home, in toward the new home, and around about the world of new diasporas. The complex variety of media channels constructed by minorities helps develop and maintain such gazes, with different media helping to direct the gaze backwards, inwards and all around.

[...] [H]istorically, media systems have been deeply embedded within the nation-state system, most obviously through the structures of state and public service broadcasting but also with privately-owned systems (Ekecrantz 2001). But slowly we have come to understand that being hailed by one 'national consciousness' does not rule out an invitation by another; indeed, many groups delight in competition for multiple citizenships and their entitlements (although clearly mere passport-holding is an indicator of neither political nor cultural attachment).

The increased movements of people have produced multiple media niche channels – print, broadcast and net-based – catering to a wide menu of possible identities. Such media channels can maintain, even re-invoke, attachments to old homes, they can encourage involvements with new homes and can support more 'transnational' or diasporic consciousness of multi-sited ethno-cultural attachments. These are not either/or possibilities, because different media amongst the same group can invoke different 'gazes' (Sreberny 2002). A new sense of belonging does need to erase any 'earlier' involvements with other groups, more physically remote and distinct.

Empirical research and theoretical understanding about minority groups and the media has grown in significance over the past decade. Work has burgeoned on multicultural audiences, representations of ethnic groups, the development of minority media forms and the use of media by transnational communities. Cunningham (2001) has offered the felicitous neologism of 'multiple public sphericules' for the variety of spaces into which minority voices and perspectives can be inserted. And these developments are broadly taken as positive, giving voice to the unvoiced, and better representations to those who were poorly represented. Such media provide some possibility of self-representation, creating voices of a 'difference multiculturalism'.

[. . .] [I]nvolvement in a variety of socio-political spaces may encourage a richer and more varied set of identifications that go beyond simple and single minority positions. What is needed is a 'not only, but also' approach to the analysis of minority media that recognises multiple cross-cutting affiliations and equally complex media use.

Importantly, such an argument is developing not only amongst academics in media studies, trying to theorise and explore contemporary cultural configurations, but also amongst the very audiences, the multiple publics, who are living these configurations.

The Pitfalls of Minority Media

On the one hand, the challenge is to combat racism and make all areas of British life as accessible to different people as possible. The development of ethnic and diasporic media that provide spaces for different voices is significant here. On the other hand, the challenge is to avoid the hypostatisations and reductionism of racial and ethnic classifications – and that includes thinking that a minority media channel alone [. . .] satisfies the expressive needs of a minority group.

In Britain, there is mounting evidence from a variety of sources about dissatisfaction in regard to minority representations. From empirical studies about minority ethnic media production and minority ethnic audiences (Millwood Hargrave 2002; Sreberny 2001) the following lines of argument have emerged:

- that there is a need not only for minority media channels, but also adequate minority representation within mainstream media;
- that minorities should not only be required to 'represent' their skin/ethnicity but also to 'play' others in colour-blind casting;
- that minority producers should not only be expected to produce their skin/ethnicity but also to be creative across the gamut of cultural expression;
- that mainstream media should not only show ethnic enclaves, but also the more complex multicultural relationships of British society; and
- that not only do the media need to improve minority representations but they also need to improve the employment and training opportunities, and break the racialised 'glass ceiling' of the commissioning process.

There is mounting evidence, from a variety of sources, about dissatisfaction in regard to minority representations, and also about proposed solutions. For example, non-white actors do not want to *act* their skin colour, and especially not in negative representations. The soul singer Beverley Knight in a recent interview talked of wanting to see an episode of *Casualty* where the black doctor

> doesn't turn out to be part of some evil immigration storyline. It winds me up so much that as soon as you introduce a character of colour, it's like that scriptwriters think automatically, 'Ooh, yes, we must involve the arranged marriage thing, clearly there's going to be some drugs issue, maybe some Yardies'. Sorry, but not in my household (cited in Hoggard 2003).

The implication that minority programming is simply about some crude markers of visible difference has annoyed many people, both as audience members and as media producers.[1]

> [...] I think multicultural is a polite euphemism for showing different races here on screen. And I think that's a shame because I think it's something more. One genuinely multicultural programme that no-one could ever argue with was a film that Sonali Fernando made, about Pakistanis who had gone to live on one of the islands right in the North of Scotland and it was about how the two communities came to become neighbours. . . . So bad multiculturalism is where it is skin deep I think, where it is just about the skin and nothing more (programme director, Channel 4).

Sometimes people were hard put to even talk about 'minority ethnic programming':

> I don't know (laughs). How to define an ethnic minority? I don't even know what it is. It's such a large thing. [. . .] I don't often see any Chinese stuff on TV, or Greek, there's not many of them in production, I don't know any Greek production company. . . . I don't see a programme about them. So what is it, a minority? Ethnic minority programming is really about Black and Asian people and that's it (independent producer).

For audience members, the concern is to keep the minority group in focus across the range of broadcast programming, not just at special moments of recognition:

> You know what really pisses me off though is like when Channel 2 or Channel 4 will do 'A week in the eyes of a Black person' and they will be showing all Black films and Black interviews. What's that about? It should be like that 24–7. And the same for Turkish people, not like just once in a while, oh the Turkish film festival, you know what I mean? (male, London focus group).

Similarly, minority media professionals do not want to *produce* their skin/ethnicity. Playwright Tanika Gupta has said 'I'm so fed up with being called an "Asian playwright". They would never describe Tom Stoppard as a "white playwright", or say "with an all-white cast", like they say "with an all-Asian cast"' (cited in Hoggard 2003). This position is echoed by freelance producer Syeda Irtizaali, who said that

> [. . .] I happen to be Asian, but as far as I'm concerned that is neither here nor there. My skills are not to do with my colour. I come from a light entertainment background, I can write and I can do comedy.

Black writers talk about the difficulty of writing white characters and getting the response that 'you've got to write from your own experience'. Given that it has long been accepted that male writers can write women's roles and vice versa, and indeed that the logic of 'across-the-board multiculturalism' is that white teams can make multicultural programming, 'We should be able to accept that a black writer can write white roles, yet it's still a thing that's thrown up' (PACT – Producers' Alliance for Cinema and Television[2]).

Indeed, for many of the media professionals interviewed, there is no such thing as a 'minority ethnic producer'. Most people consider themselves to be independent television producers whose first concern is to make good programmes:

> Obviously I'm Black and everything I do is going to be tinged with Black culture. But I grew up in a White culture so I'm in a really privileged position where I can mix, I understand both one hundred per cent.

Black culture is kind of the most vibrant within European culture and
... in American culture because it's an organic thing that's constantly
growing and constantly reproduced because it's been suppressed for
so long, through slavery and apartheid. And Black peoples' opportunities, now they find they are becoming a little more equal, Black culture
is finally being freed and released, and it is really vibrant and a lot of
things happen. I see myself as a Black film-maker in that sense. As an
independent I do different things. I don't necessarily do something that's
Black, might be the idea that I come up with is Black-scented, but as a
film-maker I would do anything (independent producer).

[. . .]

In the rapidly changing political economy of minority media, part of the
driving force away from 'ghetto slots' is that it is now impossible to sustain a
business by only producing for multicultural slots. The majority of Black and
Asian producers do not want to be seen as companies who only make minority programmes, partly because there are very few opportunities for that, but
partly because many are second- and third-generation British who feel more
integrated and see themselves first of all as producers who 'happen' to be Black
or Asian. While audience fragmentation was once the cutting edge of the media
business, now it appears that commerce pushes toward larger audiences, away
from the interests of specific audience fractions:

In this new commercialised environment, everyone wants majorities.
Going for the minority is suicide (independent television producer).

[. . .]

THE CHANGING NOMENCLATURE OF MEDIATED DIFFERENCE

Channel 4's changing rhetoric once proposed a tripartite division of
programming:

[. . .] What we've actually done as a channel is split up the notion of
multicultural into three sub-genres. Mono-cultural, cross-cultural and
multicultural (Channel 4 professional).

Such a strategy does seem to be governed partly by the need to maximise
audience size:

We've got no mono-cultural programmes in our schedules this year
because we're trying to move away from that. I mean, the nearest thing
we've got to mono-cultural is *Flava*, and *Asian-Flava*. But I would argue
they're not mono-cultural in that sense because, if you look at where
we're doing most of our programmes, cross-cultural programmes, we're

taking programmes which come from an ethnic perspective, but which draw larger audiences (Channel 4 professional).

However, at the same time, Channel 4 is pressing that every programme proposal must explain how it makes a contribution to multiculturalism:

> Now there are two ways in which you can make multicultural programmes. One way is you throw in a Black character here there and everywhere, you sort of brown it up a bit. But what people always say about those characters is they're not authentic. The other way, which we're trying to do, is to have Black people writing these characters, and who are on the film crew so you get more authentic characters. [. . .] [I]n future, all production companies will be asked to state on their proposals how in an appropriate way, or if appropriate, their programme intends to reflect multicultural Britain. So we put the onus on them to start doing the thinking (Channel 4 professional).

When Michael Jackson headed Channel 4, he reinvented its multicultural remit – which had focused on distinct cultural minorities – toward a hybrid, 'less homogenous, more pick-and-mix culture' and argued that the channel was at its best when it was 'open-minded, uninhibited, forward-looking and cosmopolitan' (Jackson 1999). This spoke rather more to the development of a post-modern youthful channel than to one which continued to acknowledge the ethnic and cultural differentiation of Britain and which sought to address diverse minority cultural needs. One danger is that the policy of mainstreaming on Channel 4 might actually lead to safe programming, or populism based on fictional fun, sexy youth TV and political correctness. Quite the contrary, more programming should allow a diversity of genres to develop including both niche and mainstream programming which should free Black programmers from the 'burden of responsibility'. The exemplar here would be *Queer as Folk*, which started as a gay drama but became simply a contemporary drama. The trajectory of *Goodness Gracious Me* was also out of the minority ghetto and into the mainstream where its Asian provenance was tempered by its widespread popularity. New drama written for television such as *Second Generation*, as well as contemporary fiction reworked for the small screen like *White Teeth*, focused on contemporary British Asian experience in ways that made good television, not 'Asian programming'.

Amongst independent television producers, the changing rhetoric has a mixed reception. The new attitude toward multiculturalism was described as

> aggressively populist and anti-anti racist. It's like whingeing is old hat, we've all got to be positive, it's part of the Blairite conjuring trick (independent producer).

Some minority media producers feel that the shift in the position of the terrestrial channels was not matched by adequate development in the private sector:

> It's like they think that we've gone beyond the point of a need for a ghettoised sector, that we now have a pluralistic society and that protectionism is reactionary, it actually puts Blacks down. But I'm not so sure, is there a sufficient mass for a Black middle-class production sector? (independent producer).

The broadcasting commissioning process has received the most negative criticism. Commissioning editors were seen as conservative, insufficiently sensitive to this range of issues and of minority background themselves.

The first thing would be to kick out the commissioning editors who commission the programmes, they've got no backbone ... it's such a shame. They commission the major white companies to do this (programmes with minority themes) (independent producer).

[. . .]

The sense from independents was that it is getting to be harder, not easier, to put an idea before a commissioning editor.

[. . .]

This is because the vast bulk of programming is actively sought out by commissioning editors.

> They are becoming much more proactive. In a sense, the process is reversed. They have a clearer idea of what they want and who they want to work with (independent producer).

There are some schemes in place to try to address the concerns about training, commissioning and general access to mainstream channels. The Cultural Diversity Network (CDN) was launched in October 2000, with members signing up to targets for increasing ethnic minority representation on and off screen. [. . .]

'MIXEDNESS' AND MULTICULTURALISM

For all the theoretical discussion about cosmopolitanism, it has not often addressed the experiential issue on the ground, namely that in Britain (as perhaps elsewhere) many of the real cosmopolitans are members of minorities who live amongst other minorities and move seamlessly in and out of relationships, languages and cultural settings with a fine attunement to them all.

Tanika Gupta has produced an Asian adaptation of *Hobson's Choice*, where the Asian daughters marry white guys, one Jewish, and one a local northern lad, because 'I thought, that's the world I live in, that's what happens'. He comments that white critics of an earlier work, *Fragile Land*, which also includes a very ethnically mixed group of people, suggested that it seemed unreal that all those people would hang out together, and I thought, 'Well, maybe not in your world' (cited in Hoggard 2003).

Ekow Eshun[3] echoes the positive mixedness of contemporary British life, arguing that the problem is

> Blacks and Asians are imagined to be members of hermetic communities with their own strange customs and beliefs. . . . Watch how teenagers of all percentages behave and you'll notice them borrowing clothes, accent and language from each other with gleeful promiscuity. Britain is no longer an island of fixed racial positions. We're living in Technicolor, not black and white. TV programme makers re-tune your sets. You have nothing to lose but your prejudices.

Britain's population is increasingly not just 'mixed' but 'mixed-up'. Already, in 1997, a Policy Studies Institute report identified that half of all Black men born here are in a relationship with a white partner, as are one third of Black women, one fifth of Asian men and one tenth of Asian women. It has been estimated that 1 in 20 pre-school children is 'mixed-race'. Recent changes were made in the census categories to include the estimated 240,000 mixed-race Britons who were previously officially invisible. [. . .]

In research about minority ethnic representations, the issue of mixedness was often volunteered by audience respondents, who mainly bemoaned the absence of visual representations of people with mixed heritage:

> I don't feel represented. I don't feel it's right, y'know 'cause there's loads of mixed-race people out there. It's not just half Black and half White. There's like half-Asian, half-White, or whatever, there's just so many 'mixed-races' out there now. If they're gonna represent people on television, they should represent everybody, not like just Black and White, like there's no in-between (Leicester female).

> You don't see any mixed-heritage people on TV; that's why I identify with, like, Afro-Caribbean people. 'Cause when you look at me, the first thing you see is that I'm Black anyway, you don't see like I'm half-White. Then you look deeper and you'll know that I'm half-White or whatever (Leicester female).

[. . .]

MULTIPLE IDENTIFICATIONS, INCLUDING BRITAIN?

Some of the complexity of multiple identifications is reflected in the manner in which people describe themselves. The British Standards Council project produced a long list of categories in response to the open question 'What is your ethnicity?' But what is perhaps most significant about this list is not the number but that almost half the labels include two elements (e.g. 'British Asian'). What comes through very strongly from this material is that any collective naming in the way that 'Black' functioned in the 1970s has disappeared, and there appears to be a search for complex definitions that adequately capture the sense of multiple cultural allegiances.

Many Britons are living with and enacting a complex set of multiple identifications:

> I'd class myself as an African Caribbean British person because obviously African, that's where, y'know, my ancestors are; and Caribbean because my mum and dad were born there. And British, 'cause of where I was born. But 'cause I'm always around my African Caribbean parents so I can relate to that, so I would say that I am half and half. But if someone was to say to me 'what is your race, what is your ethnic background?' I would say African Caribbean British (Leicester male).

Some found little point of connection to Britain, expressing alienation and a sense of non-fit:

> I don't feel British because it goes back into the history, slave trade and all that. It goes back into all of that. And that's why I don't feel British because at the end of the day, none of us, if you go back, you're not from Britain, so you're not British, if you see what I mean. You're not really a British person, okay, and I don't feel British at all (Leicester male).

[. . .]

THE DANGERS OF MINORITY CHANNELS

The dangers inherent in developing a multiplicity of minority channels were acknowledged, not least for the possibility of walls of ignorance being built up between groups:

> I think in America how it works, there's more channels, more channels on more networks but what that's also done is isolate the groups; there you have for every ethnic minority you have a channel for them and that would change it but that would just put up barriers against other people. I think its wrong [dedicated channels for different minorities] but then I

can think this is the only way they are gonna get it, you know, if they can have their equal media (London male).

[...]

I still feel that instead of separate channels, some of the programmes should be included in the national channel broadcasting. That's the problem of identity; we want to be included with everybody, not isolated (Leicester female).

The overwhelming preference repeated across the groups was for 'mixed-up' programming:

They need to have different groups communicating together . . . because everyone watches the TV and if they see it on TV then they might start doing it normally (London female).

They need to have different groups communicating together (London female).

I think every programme on television should have mixed-race, every race in it. It shouldn't be more White people, less Black people; more Black people, less White people. It should be mixed because the more we work together the more we learn to respect ourselves, we begin to know what each and everyone is capable of (London male).

Many respondents consider Britain to be multicultural and want the kind of representation that fully reflects that reality. This was most powerfully expressed by a Bristol Asian adult:

I don't think that anybody should water down the culture, um, because I think it's a very strong cultural heritage that you've got, hold on to it. And mixing that. Western culture is a strong culture, Eastern culture is. Blend it in! There's nothing wrong with that, you can live side by side, parallel, in harmony, respecting each other's culture, and moving it forward. That's what makes life much more interesting and positive . . . the multicultural, that people can truly live together, that's no problem. If I'm praying to Krishna, and you want to pray to Allah and he wants to pray to Jesus, three of us should be able to do that quite nicely, joining hands, and doing it, why not? What's stopping it? . . . I think that respect word is so important, that each other must respect the other's culture. You integrate, but you don't disintegrate. . . . I should not totally become a white man. I should not pretend to become a totally English man and say, hold on, yes, I'm ashamed to say I love my curry . . . people should be able to mix together. So an Indian child and an English child can sit together one day and eat fish and chips quite happily, and chicken tikka the next . . . that's the sort of culture, that's the sort of programme I want to see . . . I want to see programmes here which contribute and say what my daughter's generation feels like . . . and then a true representation and true views are represented. . . . Because we are British Asians. Why should I be either or? I've been in this country the longest in my life, from the age of 16, and I'm 54 now. I've spent the most time in this country. I've gone out to the discos. I like my beer. But I still like to sit with a friend and sometimes listen to the Bhangra group playing. What's wrong with it? I enjoy it (Bristol male).

Audience demand is moving in the direction of 'mixed-up' programming that reflects the ethnic jumble of urban life:

I think that the BBC spends so much money on period dramas, they spend a fortune on things like Pride and Prejudice and Sense and Sensibility and then export them abroad as comments on English life. If they spent more money on programmes that reflect inner-city multicultural life I think more people would be happy. Not just Black people, the White working-class as well, the Irish, other groups that feel they are invisible on television, like the Welsh (Bristol female).

To me, it's not enough to say we are multicultural, or we are equal ops, I don't think. To become truly multicultural, you really have to go a lot deeper into, and make resources available, change some of your set patterns that has been set into stone, to say, 'well, no, hold on, they have to think like that, they have to change' because we are truly looking at multicultural. . . . I want to see Black, people, White people, Chinese people into normal dramas, into normal movies; if you're a good actor, go forward (Bristol male).

Minority audiences want to see mixed-up programmes with mixed-up relationships:

A wider range of interracial relationships, White people, Black people, Asian people, Turkish people, all that related together, working together. Not just about Turkish people or Black people on their own (London female).

Audience members recognise that change needs to come from within media organisations:

I say that it would be better for us to have more Black actors, directors and scriptwriters. I am sure it's going to increase but it's just like the TV companies giving them a chance (London male).

> I think they should have more Black people, you know, writing, produc-
> ing and directing the script, and these kind of things as well. Or look to
> Black people and say, 'You know how does a Black person do this, that
> or the other thing'. And have somebody there to say, 'Well, actually,
> that's not right' (Leicester female).

Some raised the question of institutionalised racism, and the glass ceiling that
minorities often encounter in media organisations:

> Corporations, broadcasting corporations and all that, they need to take
> on the right people, on their boards, on their selection. Not somebody
> who makes the tea, so they say we have got three Black people working
> for us, one cleans the front door, one is the receptionist and one helps us
> out delivering in the programme. At the right level, where they can influ-
> ence making the programmes, and give them a true sense of direction, as
> to how they should go (Bristol male).

CONCLUSION

Much of this argument traces the twin tracks of representation, of politics
and of mediated constructions (Spivak 1988). Mediated representations are
increasingly niche-specific, but when it comes to political representation, the
need to participate in a 'national conversation' remains as important as ever.
The challenge for mainstream broadcasters is to reflect the lived and complex
multiculturalism of contemporary Britain, and partly that has to be done by
confronting the institutionalised racism in mainstream media organisations.

But this paper has also tried to explore the hidden dangers of uncritically
celebrating minority media channels as cultures supposedly sealed off from one
another forever by ethnic lines, with all the attendant essentialist assumptions
about totality, identity and exclusion (Hall 1991). Using their voices, it has
shown that minority ethnic respondents are well aware of such issues, and do
not want to be limited to or by such channels. The paper has tried to go further
and explore the increasing mixedness in Britain's population which suggests
a need for a far more complex multiculturalism. This would better recognise
the mixed-race Britons who were previously officially invisible and the mixed
relationships and multicultural lives that many Britons actually lead. We seem
to be approaching a moment of multicultural convergence that is not about
adjustment, acculturation or integration, and need not be simply defined by a
hegemonic majority (Baumann 1999: 127). Minorities finding and developing
their voices is thus central to the redefinition of Britishness and who 'we' are
(Parekh 2000).

But if multiculturalism requires 'challenging, revising, and relativising basic
notions and principles common to dominant and minority cultures alike, so
as to construct a more vital, open and democratic *common* culture' (Turner

1993: 416), then a highly differentiated public sphere, with minorities only talking to and amongst themselves and a deaf majoritarian culture, does not help to promote that shared space. Baumann's (1999: 141) suggestions for a 'multiculti future' include trying 'to unreify all accepted reifications by finding cross-cutting cleavages', which seems to me to be a more creative solution than reifying majoritarian and minority cultures and their respective media channels.

Thus I have suggested that we need a 'not only, but also' approach to the analysis of minority media, that recognises multiple cross-cutting affiliations and equally complex media use. On the one hand, minority media channels and minority representations give voice to diversity, a kind of 'strategic essentialism' (Spivak 1988). On the other, they divide us off from each other and foster fragmentation. A truly multiculti media environment has yet to be devised, although there are programmes and schedules that hint at its possibility – one example is Channel Multikulti in Berlin (Vertovec 2000).

Social theory is slowly recognising these dilemmas. Mixedness augurs a more cosmopolitan, even post-ethnic, environment (Hollinger 1995) and the recognition of multiple situatedness. The evidence suggests the experience and the practices of the audience are already well-developed.

Notes

1. The following quotations are from respondents in a research project, funded by the Broadcasting Standards Council and the Independent Television Commission, which focused on minority ethnic audiences and producers in Britain. The original research included focusgroup work with audience members in Bristol, Leicester and London and in-depth interviews with minority ethnic producers and media executives. The designation after each quotation provides information about the location and gender of the respondent. For a full account of the project and findings see Sreberny (1999) and, for follow-up research, Millwood Hargrave (2002).
2. The UK trade association which represents and promotes the commercial interests of independent feature-film, television, animation and interactive-media companies; online at www.pact.co.uk
3. 'Do Not Adjust Your Set: Race in Britain', *The Observer*, 25 November 2001.

References

Alibhai-Brown, Y. (2000) *Who Do We Think We Are? Imagining the New Britain*. London: Allen Lane.
Appiah, A. (1994) 'Identity, authenticity, survival: multicultural societies and social reproduction', in Gutman, A. and Taylor, C. (eds) *Multiculturalism*. Princeton: Princeton University Press, 149–64.
Baumann, G. (1999) *The Multicultural Riddle*. London: Routledge.
Cunningham, S. (2001) 'Popular media as public "sphericules" for diasporic communities', *International Journal of Cultural Studies*, 4(2): 131–47.
Cunningham, S. and Sinclair, J. (eds) (2000) *Floating Lives: The Media and Asian Diaspora*. Brisbane: University of Queensland Press.
Dayan, D. (1998) 'Particularistic media and diasporic communications', in Liebes, T. and Curren, J. (eds) *Media, Ritual and Identity*. London: Routledge, 103–13.

Ekecrantz, J. (2001) 'Public spaces, historical times and media modernities: media and historical spaces', in Kivikuru, U. (ed.) *Contesting the Frontiers: Media and Dimensions of Identity*. Gotheburg: Nordicom, 15–34.

Elias, N. (1991) *The Society of Individuals*. Oxford: Basil Blackwell.

Hall, S. (1991) 'Old and new identities, old and new ethnicities', in King, A. (ed.) *Culture, Globalization and the World System*. London: Macmillan, 41–68.

Hoggard, L. (2003) Different Strokes. *The Observer Review*, 6 April 2003: 5.

Hollinger, D. (1995) *PostEthnic America*. New York: Basic Books.

Honneth, A. (2001) 'Recognition or redistribution? Changing perspectives on the moral order of society', *Theory Culture and Society, 18*(2–3): 43–57.

Husband, C. (ed.) (1994) *A Richer Vision: The Development of Ethnic Minority Media in Western Democracies*. London: John Libbey.

Jackson, M. (1999) Four the Record. *The Guardian*, 5 July 1999.

Millwood Hargrave, A. (2002) *Multicultural Broadcasting: Concept and Reality*. London: Broadcasting Standards Commission.

Parekh, B. (2000) *The Future of Multi-Ethnic Britain*. London: Profile Books.

Riggins, S.H. (1992) *Ethnic Minority Media*. California: Sage.

Spivak, G. (1988) 'Can the subaltern speak?', in Nelson, C. and Grossberg, L. (eds) *Marxism and the Interpretation of Culture*. London: Macmillan Education, 271–313.

Sreberny, A. (1999) *Include Me In. Rethinking Ethnicity on Television: Audience and Producer Perspectives*. London: Broadcasting Standards Commission.

Sreberny, A. (2001) 'The role of the media in the cultural practices of diasporic communities', in Bennett, A. (ed.) *Differing Diversities*. Strasbourg: Council of Europe, 155–69.

Sreberny, A. (2002) 'Collectivity and connectivity: diaspora and mediated identities', in Stald, G. and Tufte, T. (eds) *Global Encounters: Media and Cultural Transformation*. Luton: University of Luton Press, 217–34.

Sreberny-Mohammadi, L. (2003) 'Mixed Ethnicity: Tick One Box Only': The One-Box Rule of Ethnic Identity. Manchester: University of Manchester, Department of Social Anthropology, unpublished BSc dissertation.

Taylor, C. (1994) 'The politics of recognition', in Gutman, A. and Taylor, C. (eds) *Multiculturalism*. Princeton: Princeton University Press, 25–74.

Turner, T. (1993) 'Anthropology and multiculturalism: what is anthropology that multiculturalists should be mindful of it?', *Cultural Anthropology, 8*(4): 411–29.

Vertovec, S. (2000) *Fostering Cosmopolitanisms: A Conceptual Survey and a Media Experiment in Berlin*. Oxford: University of Oxford, Faculty of Anthropology and Geography, Transnational Communities Programme, Working Paper WPTC-2K-06.

FURTHER READING

Askoy, A. and Robins, K., 'New Complexities of Transnational Media Cultures', in O. Hemer and T. Tufte (eds), *Media and Glocal Change* (Göteburg: Clacso, 2005) pp. 41–58.

Bauman, Z., *Wasted Lives* (Polity: Cambridge, 2004).

Couldry, N., 'Mediated Self-Disclosure: Before and After the Internet', in *Media Rituals: A Critical Approach* (London and New York: Routledge, 2003) pp. 115–33.

Couldry, N., 'The Productive "Consumer" and the Dispersed "Citizen"', *International Journal of Cultural Studies* 7:1 (2004) pp. 21–32.

Downing, J., 'Audiences and Readers of Alternative Media: The Absent Lure of the Virtually Unknown', *Media, Culture and Society* 25:5 (2003) pp. 625–46.

Fraser, N., 'Rethinking Recognition', *New Left Review* 3, May–June (2000) pp. 107–20.

Gilroy, P., 'Cosmopolitanism Contested', in *After Empire* (London: Routledge, 2006).

Guins, R. and Omayra, Z. C., *Popular Culture: A Reader* (London: Sage, 2005).

Hardt, H., *Myths for the Masses: An Essay on Mass Communication* (London: Sage, 2004).

Mumford, L., *Technics and Civilization* (London: Routledge, 1946).

Murdock, G. and Golding, P., 'Culture, Communications and Political Economy', in J. Curran and M. Gurevitch (eds), *Mass Media and Society*, 4th edn (London: Edward Arnold, 2005) pp. 60–83.

Negt, O. and Kluge, A. *Public Sphere and Experience* (Minneapolis: University of Minnesota Press, 1993) pp. 96–129.

Peters, J. D., *Speaking into the Air: A History of the Idea of Communication* (Chicago: University of Chicago Press, 1999).

Peters, J. D., 'The Subtlety of Horkheimer and Adorno: Reading "The Culture Industry"', in E. Katz et al. (eds), *Canonic Texts in Media Research* (Cambridge: Polity, 2003) pp. 58–73.

Scannell, P., 'Public Service Broadcasting and Modern Public Life', *Media, Culture and Society* 11 (1989).

Splichal, S., 'In Search of a Strong European Public Sphere: Some Critical Observations on Conceptualizations of Publicness and the (European) Public Sphere', *Media, Culture and Society* 28 (2006) pp. 695–714.

Williams, K., *European Media Studies* (London: Hodder, 2005).
Zoonen, L. Van, 'Distinctions', in *Entertaining the Citizen: When Politics and Popular Culture Converge* (Lanham, MD: Rowman & Littlefield, 2004) pp. 1–18.

SECTION 3
REPRESENTATION

3.1
TEXTUAL STRUCTURES

INTRODUCTION: TEXTUAL STRUCTURES

If one strand of academic work on the mass media has been rooted in the social sciences and been concerned with large-scale systems of public communication and their economic, political and cultural power, another very different strand develops from work in the humanities, and literary study in particular. In Britain, the work of F. R. Leavis and his followers from the 1930s onwards emphasised the centrality of language and the literary text in expressing society's deepest values. The literary critic, in this view, became a crucial figure in developing both detailed analytical skills ('practical criticism') and an understanding of the text's relationship to the broader history and society of which it forms part. Leavis himself saw the mass media as a threat to the 'great tradition' of English literary culture, arguing that cinema trades in the 'cheapest emotional appeals' and that films, broadcasting, advertising and commercial fiction all constitute a 'levelling down' of culture (Leavis 1930, in Storey 1994). Nevertheless, three elements in the Leavisite position – close attention to the (literary) text, an interest in its connections with wider social processes, and the notion that the nature of the media's output is indicative of the general state of civilisation – were available for a reconfiguration that would treat the media with seriousness and without automatic hostility. Richard Hoggart, Raymond Williams and Stuart Hall all took up this challenge in the 1960s in the development of what became the 'cultural studies' strand of media studies. In an important conceptual shift, the mass media's 'messages' became seen as 'texts' – as bearers of complex meanings – and detailed attention to the forms, structures and meanings of newspapers or broadcast programmes assumed an important place in the study of the media.

In this, a developing media studies both drew on and challenged the insights and analytical methods of 1960s and 1970s film studies. Film studies in this period drew on the ideas of semiology, or semiotics, to examine the work of meaning-making in films (see Lapsley and Westlake 1992), and the study of other media began to follow suit in the 1970s. Semiotics – the study of signs and their processes of generating meaning – had originated in a suggestion by the Swiss linguist, Ferdinand de Saussure (1857–1913), that 'a science that studies the life of signs within society is . . . conceivable' (1974: 16). For Saussure, the production of meaning depends on language, and language is a representational system: a system of signs governed by cultural and linguistic codes. In his collection of essays, *Mythologies* (1973), the French critic Roland Barthes extended this approach, applying it to a range of readings of popular culture, from soap powders to 'the world of wrestling' and 'the face of Greta Garbo'. These activities and objects, which seemed so self-evident or 'transparent', could be analysed as structures of signs – or as texts to be read. In a similar way, film critics analysed the film text as equivalent to a linguistic structure: as a signifying system which constructs, rather than merely reflecting or transmitting, meaning. Cinema, they argued, transforms the world into narrative, through a complex structure of shots and segments organised via codes of editing, lighting, framing, costume and so on.

In media studies, Stuart Hall's hugely influential 'Encoding/Decoding' model (see Chapter 3), although it is more often seen as a model for understanding audience responses, also drew on these ideas. In opposition to the then dominant tradition of 'mass communications' research which saw media 'content' as 'a preformed and fixed meaning or message' that was then simply transmitted from sender to receiver (Hall 1994: 253), Hall argued that 'the television sign' is a complex text to be read. But in opposition to traditions in film studies, he insisted that to understand its meanings we need to look at more than simply the text itself. What Hall in 'Encoding/Decoding' called 'the communicative process' and was later to term 'the circuit of culture' (see in particular Hall 1997) is a process, a set of practices, through which textual meanings are socially produced via specific technologies and specific institutional structures.

It is this process, and the formal properties of the media texts thus produced, which is the focus of the first two chapters in this section. Both concern television, and both are concerned to distinguish the formal properties of a mass medium characterised by continuous programming from those of earlier media forms like the novel, play or film, all of which are discrete texts able to be viewed as a single sequential whole. Chapter 16 is an extract from Raymond Williams' 1972 book *Television, Technology and Cultural Form*. Williams suggests here that the technical character of broadcasting as the continuous emission of a signal for domestic reception, combined with its institutionalisation within a fundamentally commercial system that aims above all to retain audiences' attention, makes for an output whose 'characteristic organisation . . . is one of sequence or flow'. The continuous availability of television, the

heterogeneity of programme types, the intermixing of commercials and programme chunks, the constant station announcements, promotions and trailers,
the ceaseless flux, the remorseless onward drive through time: taken together,
these features mean that 'both internally, in its immediate organisation, and as
a generally available experience, this characteristic of flow seems central'.

Chapter 17 by John Ellis picks up and develops these insights. In a study
which argues the *difference* of television from film – a medium with which
it so clearly shares many formal properties – Ellis, like Williams, argues that
the best definition of the broadcast text is not the individual programme. Like
Williams, Ellis points to the 'open-ended' and repetitive nature of television
programming. He also points to two further key characteristics of the television text. First, there is the reliance of television on the narrative 'segment' to
organise and present its material. In the domestic setting of its reception, television cannot be sure of unbroken attention, so whether the programme format
is drama, news or advertisement, it proceeds by relatively self-contained segments, often with loose connections between them and a reliance on the soundtrack to provide continuity. Second, there are the connections which are made
across time within serials, series and long-running news or magazine shows,
all of which rely on patterns of repetition, innovation and constant updating.
Thus the television text is both smaller and at the same time larger and more
dispersed than the cinematic.

Chapters 18 and 19 point to two further organising features of media
texts: stereotypes and genres. Stereotypes are 'shortcut' representations which
reduce people to a few, recognisable characteristics which are identified with
the social group of which they are a member and which are seen as fixed. This
social group might be defined by age, gender, nationality, ethnicity, class,
sexual orientation, religious affiliation and so on. In semiotic terms, the collection of signs that make up the stereotype mobilise a social mythology, or ideological evaluation, of the group. These characteristics are frequently negative
and 'stereotyping' is usually seen as prejudiced. In Chapter 18 Richard Dyer
argues that stereotypes are essentially ways of ordering the world: a means of
drawing boundaries between an imagined 'us' and an illegitimate and unacceptable 'them'. To the extent that societies need ordering concepts in order to
make sense of the world, such representational shortcuts are perhaps necessary
and inevitable. What makes them hugely problematic, however, is their relationship to social power. Media representations tend to emanate from socially
powerful groups, disparaging less powerful groups by defining or constructing
them as *essentially* 'other' to the legitimate group: 'us'. Thus for Dyer, 'it is not
stereotypes, as an aspect of human thought and representation, that are wrong,
but who controls and defines them, what interests they serve'.

In a development borrowed from the study of painting and literature, film
studies adopted a method of classifying texts according to 'genre' – literally
'type'. This has been extended more generally into media analysis; thus we
can speak of the television game show or sitcom, or the lifestyle or women's

magazine. In the case of television, genres form part of the process of repetition and innovation which John Ellis sees as one of its defining features. In Chapter 19, Christine Gledhill provides an analysis of how genre works in relation to one of the most popular television genres, the soap opera. Popular genres, she writes, are ways of standardising production through the repetition of established formats. They are ways of stabilising audiences, by offering familiar appeals and pleasures. Finally, as texts they are ways of organising representations of the world. This is the case not only in the sense that genres create recognisable fictional worlds and narrative patterns, so that what is credible within the science fiction series, for example, would be unacceptable in a soap opera. It is also true in the sense that, in the same way as stereotypes, they are a way of organising social *values*, through their choice of heroes and villains, those with whom we are invited to identify and those who are constructed as 'other'. Finally, however, Gledhill argues that because of the constant pressure on popular genres to innovate, they can never fix boundaries of meaning and value. Instead, through their constant search for new material popular genres like the soap opera 'become key sites for the emerging articulation of and contest over [social] change'.

The final two chapters in this section move us away from more familiar forms of textual analysis and categorisation. What concerns Roger Silverstone in Chapter 20 is the way in which television addresses its audience and thus constructs a 'discursive space' inhabited by both text and audience. He identifies three such spaces. The first is that of rhetoric: the television text appeals to and seeks to persuade its audience, making claims on their understanding which must be negotiated or resisted. The second such space is that of play: particular texts construct sites of fantasy with shared sets of rules, in which reality is simultaneously tested and suspended. Silverstone's final 'discursive space' is that of performance. The 'performative' television text, he writes, produces a discursive space which invites activity and identification from its audience, and may extend beyond the spaces of television as in the case of fan culture. Silverstone's chapter thus insists on the active nature of the media audience at the same time as it reaffirms the power of the text to invite and produce modes of audience response.

Finally, Chapter 21 takes us beyond the medium of television to consider the textual characteristics of 'new media'. Unlike previous media, argues Lev Manovich, the characteristic organisation of new media is not via narrative but via the database, in which meaning is not linearly expressed but structured as a list. In semiotic terms, the database is organised not via syntagmatic structures, in which signs or words are arranged in sequence to construct meaning, but via paradigmatic structures, in which words or signs are selected from other possible choices. As opposing ways of ordering meanings, both forms, he argues, existed long before modern media, in the shape of the story and the encyclopaedia. The computer, with its ability to store, classify and retrieve vast amounts of information, has rendered the database dominant over its rival, yet the constant creation of 'interactive narratives' demonstrates our continuing need for narrative. Finally, then, Manovich asks what new kinds of narrative might be constructed in a culture in which the database has become the dominant symbolic form.

References

Barthes, R., *Mythologies* (London: Paladin, 1973).
Hall, S., 'Reflections upon the Encoding/Decoding Model: An Interview with Stuart Hall', in J. Cruz and J. Lewis (eds), *Viewing, Reading, Listening: Audiences and Cultural Studies* (Boulder, CO: Westview Press, 1994) pp. 253–74.
Hall, S. (ed.), *Representation: Cultural Representations and Signifying Practices* (London: Sage, 1997).
Lapsley, R. and Westlake, M., *Film Theory: An Introduction* (Manchester: Manchester University Press, 1992) pp. 32–66.
Leavis, F. R., 'Mass Civilisation and Minority Culture' [1930], in J. Storey (ed.), *Cultural Theory and Popular Culture: A Reader* (London: Harvester Wheatsheaff, 1994) pp. 12–20.
Saussure, F. de, *Course in General Linguistics* (London: Fontana, [1916] 1974).

16

PROGRAMMING AS SEQUENCE OR FLOW

Raymond Williams

[. . .]

In all developed broadcasting systems the characteristic organisation, and therefore the characteristic experience, is one of sequence or flow. This phenomenon, of planned flow, is then perhaps the defining characteristic of broadcasting, simultaneously as a technology and as a cultural form.

In all communications systems before broadcasting the essential items were discrete. A book or a pamphlet was taken and read as a specific item. A meeting occurred at a particular date and place. A play was performed in a particular theatre at a set hour. The difference in broadcasting is not only that these events, or events resembling them, are available inside the home, by the operation of a switch. It is that the real programme that is offered is a *sequence* or set of alternative sequences of these and other similar events, which are then available in a single dimension and in a single operation.

Yet we have become so used to this that in a way we do not see it. Most of our habitual vocabulary of response and description has been shaped by the experience of discrete events. We have developed ways of responding to a particular book or a particular play, drawing on our experience of other books and plays. When we go out to a meeting or a concert or a game we take other experience with us and we return to other experience, but the specific event is ordinarily an occasion, setting up its own internal conditions and responses. Our most general modes of comprehension and judgement are

From Raymond Williams, *Television: Technology and Cultural Form* (London: Fontana, 1974) pp. 86–96.

then closely linked to these kinds of specific and isolated, temporary, forms of attention.

Some earlier kinds of communication contained, it is true, internal variation and at times miscellaneity. Dramatic performances included musical interludes, or the main play was preceded by a curtain-raiser. In print there are such characteristic forms as the almanac and the chapbook, which include items relating to very different kinds of interest and involving quite different kinds of response. The magazine, invented as a specific form in the early eighteenth century, was designed as a miscellany, mainly for a new and expanding and culturally inexperienced middle-class audience. The modern newspaper, from the eighteenth century but very much more markedly from the nineteenth century, became a miscellany, not only of news items that were often essentially unrelated, but of features, anecdotes, drawings, photographs and advertisements. From the late nineteenth century this came to be reflected in formal layout, culminating in the characteristic jigsaw effect of the modern newspaper page. Meanwhile, sporting events, especially football matches, as they became increasingly important public occasions, included entertainment such as music or marching in their intervals.

This general trend, towards an increasing variability and miscellaneity of public communications, is evidently part of a whole social experience. It has profound connections with the growth and development of greater physical and social mobility, in conditions both of cultural expansion and of consumer rather than community cultural organisation. Yet until the coming of broadcasting the normal expectation was still of a discrete event or of a succession of discrete events. People took a book or a pamphlet or a newspaper, went out to a play or a concert or a meeting or a match, with a single predominant expectation and attitude. The social relationships set up in these various cultural events were specific and in some degree temporary.

Broadcasting, in its earliest stages, inherited this tradition and worked mainly within it. Broadcasters discovered the kinds of thing they could do or, as some of them would still normally say, transmit. The musical concert could be broadcast or arranged for broadcasting. The public address – the lecture or the sermon, the speech at a meeting – could be broadcast as a talk. The sports match could be described and shown. The play could be performed, in this new theatre of the air. Then as the service extended, these items, still considered as discrete units, were assembled into programmes. The word 'programme' is characteristic, with its traditional bases in theatre and music-hall. With increasing organisation, as the service extended, this 'programme' became a series of timed units. Each unit could be thought of discretely, and the work of programming was a serial assembly of these units. Problems of mix and proportion became predominant in broadcasting policy. Characteristically, as most clearly in the development of British sound broadcasting, there was a steady evolution from a general service, with its internal criteria of mix and proportion and what was called 'balance', to contrasting types of service, alternative programmes. 'Home', 'Light' and 'Third', in British radio, were the eventual names for what were privately described and indeed generally understood as 'general', 'popular' and 'educated' broadcasting. Problems of mix and proportion, formerly considered within a single service, were then basically transferred to a range of alternative programmes, corresponding to assumed social and educational levels. This tendency was taken further in later forms of reorganisation, as in the present specialised British radio services One to Four. In an American radio programme listing, which is before me as I write, there is a further specialisation: the predominantly musical programmes are briefly characterised, by wavelength, as 'rock', 'country', 'classical', 'nostalgic' and so on. In one sense this can be traced as a development of programming: extensions of the service have brought further degrees of rationalisation and specialisation.

But the development can also be seen, and in my view needs to be seen, in quite other ways. There has been a significant shift from the concept of sequence as *programming* to the concept of sequence as *flow*. Yet this is difficult to see because the older concept of programming – the temporal sequence within which mix and proportion and balance operate – is still active and still to some extent real.

What is it then that has been decisively altered? A broadcasting programme, on sound or television, is still formally a series of timed units. What is published as information about the broadcasting services is still of this kind: we can look up the time of a particular 'show' or 'programme'; we can turn on for that item; we can select and respond to it discretely.

Yet for all the familiarity of this model, the normal experience of broadcasting, when we really consider it, is different. And indeed this is recognised in the ways we speak of 'watching television', 'listening to the radio', picking on the general rather than the specific experience. This has been true of all broadcasting, but some significant internal developments have greatly reinforced it. These developments can be indicated in one simple way. In earlier phases of the broadcasting service, both in sound and television, there were *intervals* between programme units: true intervals, usually marked by some conventional sound or picture to show that the general service was still active. There was the sound of bells or the sight of waves breaking, and these marked the intervals between discrete programme units. There is still a residual example of this type in the turning globe which functions as an interval signal in BBC television.

But in most television services, as they are currently operated, the concept of the interval – though still, for certain purposes, retained as a concept – has been fundamentally revalued. This change came about in two ways, which are still unevenly represented in different services. The decisive innovation was in services financed by commercial television. There was a specific and formal undertaking that 'programmes' should not be interrupted by advertising; this could take place only in 'natural breaks': between the movements of a symphony, or between the acts in *Hamlet*, as the Government spokesman said in the House of Lords! In practice, of course, this was never complied with, nor was it ever intended that it should be. A 'natural break' became any moment of convenient insertion. News programmes, plays, even films that had been shown in cinemas as specific whole performances, began to be interrupted for commercials. On American television this development was different; the sponsored programmes incorporated the advertising from the outset, from the initial conception, as part of the whole package. But it is now obvious, in both British and American commercial television, that the notion of 'interruption', while it has still some residual force from an older model, has become inadequate. What is being offered is not, in older terms, a programme of discrete units with particular insertions, but a planned flow, in which the true series is not the published sequence of programme items but this sequence transformed by the inclusion of another kind of sequence, so that these sequences together compose the real flow, the real 'broadcasting'. Increasingly, in both commercial and public-service television, a further sequence was added: trailers of programmes to be shown at some later time or on some later day, or more itemised programme news. This was intensified in conditions of competition, when it became important to broadcasting planners to retain viewers – or as they put it, to 'capture' them – for a whole evening's sequence. And with the eventual unification of these two or three sequences, a new kind of communication phenomenon has to be recognised.

Of course many people who watch television still register some of these items as 'interruptions'. I remember first noticing the problem while watching films on British commercial television. For even in an institution as wholeheartedly commercial in production and distribution as the cinema, it had been possible, and indeed remains normal, to watch a film as a whole, in an undisturbed sequence. All films were originally made and distributed in this way, though the inclusion of supporting 'B' films and short features in a package, with appropriate intervals for advertising and for the planned selling of refreshments, began to develop the cinema towards the new kind of planned flow. Watching the same films on commercial television made the new situation quite evident. We are normally given some twenty or twenty-five minutes of the film, to get us interested in it; then four minutes of commercials, then about fifteen more minutes of the film; some commercials again; and so on to steadily decreasing lengths of the film, with commercials between them, or them between the commercials, since by this time it is assumed that we are interested and will watch the film to the end. Yet even this had not prepared me for the characteristic American sequence. One night in Miami, still dazed from a week on an Atlantic liner, I began watching a film and at first had some difficulty in adjusting to a much greater frequency of commercial 'breaks'. Yet this was a minor problem compared to what eventually happened. Two other films, which were due to be shown on the same channel on other nights, began to be inserted as trailers. A crime in San Francisco (the subject of the original

film) began to operate in an extraordinary counterpoint not only with the deo-
dorant and cereal commercials but with a romance in Paris and the eruption of
a prehistoric monster who laid waste New York. Moreover, this was sequence
in a new sense. Even in commercial British television there is a visual signal –
the residual sign of an interval – before and after the commercial sequences,
and 'programme' trailers only occur between 'programmes'. Here there was
something quite different, since the transitions from film to commercial and
from film A to films B and C were in effect unmarked. There is in any case
enough similarity between certain kinds of films, and between several kinds of
film and the 'situation' commercials which often consciously imitate them, to
make a sequence of this kind a very difficult experience to interpret. I can still
not be sure what I took from that whole flow. I believe I registered some incidents as happening in the wrong film, and some characters in the commercials
as involved in the film episodes, in what came to seem – for all the occasional
bizarre disparities – a single irresponsible flow of images and feelings.

Of course the films were not made to be 'interrupted' in this way. But this
flow is planned: not only in itself, but at an early stage in all original television
production for commercial systems. Indeed most commercial television 'programmes' are made, from the planning stage, with this real sequence in mind.
In quite short plays there is a rationalised division into 'acts'. In features there
is a similar rationalised division into 'parts'. But the effect goes deeper. There
is a characteristic kind of opening sequence, meant to excite interest, which is
in effect a kind of trailer for itself. In American television, after two or three
minutes, this is succeeded by commericals. The technique has an early precedent in the dumbshows which preceded plays or scenes in early Elizabethan
theatre. But there what followed dumbshow was the play or the scene. Here
what follows is apparently quite unconnected material. It is then not surprising that so many of these opening moments are violent or bizarre: the interest
aroused must be strong enough to initiate the expectation of (interrupted but
sustainable) sequence. Thus a quality of the external sequence becomes a mode
of definition of an internal method.

At whatever stage of development this process has reached – and it is still
highly variable between different broadcasting systems – it can still be residu-
ally seen as 'interruption' of a 'programme'. Indeed it is often important to see
it as this, both for one's own true sense of place and event, and as a matter of
reasonable concern in broadcasting policy. Yet it may be even more important to see the true process as flow: the replacement of a programme series of
timed sequential units by a flow series of differently related units in which the
timing, though real, is undeclared, and in which the real internal organisation
is something other than the declared organisation.

For the 'interruptions' are in one way only the most visible characteristic of a
process which at some levels has come to define the television experience. Even
when, as on the BBC, there are no interruptions of specific 'programme units',
there is a quality of flow which our received vocabulary of discrete response

and description cannot easily acknowledge. It is evident that what is now called 'an evening's viewing' is in some ways planned, by providers and then by viewers, *as a whole*; that it is in any event planned in discernible sequences which in this sense override particular programme units. Whenever there is competition between television channels, this becomes a matter of conscious concern: to get viewers in at the beginning of a flow. Thus in Britain there is intense competition between BBC and IBA in the early evening programmes, in the belief – which some statistics support – that viewers will stay with whatever channel they begin watching. There are of course many cases in which this does not happen: people can consciously select another channel or another programme, or switch off altogether. But the flow effect is sufficiently widespread to be a major element in programming policy. And this is the immediate reason for the increasing frequency of programming trailers: to sustain that evening flow. In conditions of more intense competition, as between the American channels, there is even more frequent trailing, and the process is specifically referred to as 'moving along', to sustain what is thought of as a kind of brand-loyalty to the channel being watched. Some part of the flow offered is then directly traceable to conditions of controlled competition, just as some of its specific original elements are traceable to the financing of television by commercial advertising.

Yet this is clearly not the whole explanation. The flow offered can also, and perhaps more fundamentally, be related to the television experience itself. Two common observations bear on this. As has already been noted, most of us say, in describing the experience, that we have been 'watching television', rather than that we have watched 'the news' or 'a play' or 'the football' 'on television'. Certainly we sometimes say both, but the fact that we say the former at all is already significant. Then again it is a widely if often ruefully admitted experience that many of us find television very difficult to switch off; that again and again, even when we have switched on for a particular 'programme', we find ourselves watching the one after it and the one after that. The way in which the flow is now organised, without definite intervals, in any case encourages this. We can be 'into' something else before we have summoned the energy to get out of the chair, and many programmes are made with this situation in mind: the grabbing of attention in the early moments; the reiterated promise of exciting things to come, if we stay.

But the impulse to go on watching seems more widespread than this kind of organisation would alone explain. It is significant that there has been steady pressure, not only from the television providers but from many viewers, for an extension of viewing hours. In Britain, until recently, television was basically an evening experience, with some brief offerings in the middle of the day, and with morning and afternoon hours, except at weekends, used for schools and similar broadcasting. There is now a rapid development of morning and afternoon 'programmes' of a general kind. In the United States it is already possible to begin watching at six o'clock in the morning, see one's first movie at eight-thirty, and so on in a continuous flow, with the screen never blank, until the late movie begins at one o'clock the following morning. It is scarcely possible that many people watch a flow of that length, over more than twenty hours of the day. But the flow is always accessible, in several alternative sequences, at the flick of a switch. Thus, both internally, in its immediate organisation, and as a generally available experience, this characteristic of flow seems central.

Yet it is a characteristic for which hardly any of our received modes of observation and description prepare us. The reviewing of television programmes is of course of uneven quality, but in most even of the best reviews there is a conventional persistence from earlier models. Reviewers pick out this play or that feature, this discussion programme or that documentary. I reviewed television once a month over four years, and I know how much more settling, more straightforward, it is to do that. For most of the items there are some received procedures, and the method, the vocabulary, for a specific kind of description and response exists or can be adapted. Yet while that kind of reviewing can be useful, it is always at some distance from what seems to me the central television experience: the fact of flow. It is not only that many particular items – given our ordinary organisation of response, memory and persistence of attitude and mood – are affected by those preceding and those following them, unless we watch in an artificially timed way which seems to be quite rare (though it exists in the special viewings put on for regular Reviewers). It is also that though useful things may be said about all the separable items (though often with conscious exclusion of the commercials which 'interrupt' at least half of them) hardly anything is ever said about the characteristic experience of the flow sequence itself. It is indeed very difficult to say anything about this. It would be like trying to describe having read two plays, three newspapers, three or four magazines, on the same day that one has been to a variety show and a lecture and a football match. And yet in another way it is not like that at all, for though the items may be various the television experience has in some important ways unified them. To break this experience back into units, and to write about the units for which there are readily available procedures, is understandable but often misleading, even when we defend it by the gesture that we are discriminating and experienced viewers and don't just sit there hour after hour goggling at the box.

For the fact is that many of us do sit there, and much of the critical significance of television must be related to this fact. I know that whenever I tried, in reviewing, to describe the experience of flow, on a particular evening or more generally, what I could say was unfinished and tentative, yet I learned from correspondence that I was engaging with an experience which many viewers were aware of and were trying to understand. There can be 'classical' kinds of response, at many different levels, to some though not all of the discrete units. But we are only just beginning to recognise, let alone solve, the problems of description and response to the facts of flow.

BROADCAST TV NARRATION

John Ellis

Commercial entertainment cinema is overwhelmingly a narrative fiction medium. Non-fiction films have always had a precarious place in the commercial cinema, and nowadays they are practically non-existent. Broadcast TV on the other hand carries large amounts of non-fiction: news, documentaries, announcements, weather forecasts, various kinds of segments that are purely televisual in their characteristic forms. It could be argued, therefore, that any model of televisual narration would have to give pride of place to this division of TV products between fiction and non-fiction. Whereas the classical narrative model, basically a fiction model, still underlies our assumptions about the entertainment film, it would seem that no such generalised conception of TV narration would be possible. In fact, this does not seem to be the case. Quite the reverse, the non-fiction and fiction modes of exposition of meanings seem to have converged within TV, under the impulsion of the characteristic broadcast TV forms of the segment and the series, and the pervasive sense of the TV image as live. This has produced a distinctive regime of fictional narration on TV which owes much to its non-fictional modes. After all, the first true use of the open-ended series format would seem to be the news bulletin, endlessly updating events and never synthesising them.

The mode of narration on TV does not have to be divided into two distinct models, one appropriate to fiction, the other to non-fiction. Instead, one model seems to be enough, a model that is capable of inflection by fictional or non-fictional concerns. This explains the ease that TV has long since had of

From John Ellis, *Visible Fictions: Cinema, Television, Video* (London: Routledge & Kegan Paul, 1982) Ch. 9.

producing programmes that are ambiguous in their status: the documentary-drama, or the drama-documentary, forms that seem to have existed in the late 1950s at least on the BBC. The divisions between fiction and non-fiction exist at another level to that of narration; they are chiefly concerned with the origin of material used in the programme.

Any model of narration on broadcast TV therefore has to be based on the particular institutional and material nature of that TV as we now know it. It depends on the conception of the broadcast output as that of segment following segment, segments which by no means always have any connection between them. It depends on the counterpart to this segmental process, the programme series with its distinctive forms of repetition and favoured forms of problematic. It depends on the conception of TV as a casual, domestic form, watched without great intensity or continuity of attention. It assumes the ideology of TV as a medium which transmits events as they happen, even though (especially in Britain) this is virtually never the case. It is worth repeating in this connection that, although the overwhelming mass of TV output is recorded, it still carries a different sense of immediacy from the cinematic image. Broadcast TV is capable of adopting a filmic mode of narration as a kind of borrowing from an already established medium. This will almost always be announced as such: by the form of the TV movie (often a 'pilot' for a series), or by the designation of a programme as a prestigious cultural event. This tends to mean that the programme will not so much have been made on film as made within a cinematic mode of narration. In this sense, TV acknowledges a certain inferiority to cinema. Cinema, for TV, means the culturally respectable, the artistic text. The designation 'film' for a TV transmission indicates that this transmission is to be viewed despite TV; it is not to be segmented, interruptions in terms of advertisements breaks or viewer attention 'at home' are to be kept to a minimum. The 'film' transmission on TV will then proceed to construct a more cinematic narration. The vast majority of such events, indeed, are cinema films which have already been exhibited in a cinematic context. Cinema is currently not capable of a similar borrowing of broadcast TV forms, however: the collective exhibition of TV material is still a novelty or an aberration.

Cinema narration has a strong internal dynamic, a movement from an initial equilibrium that is disrupted towards a new harmony that is the end of the fiction. Broadcast TV narration has a more dispersed narrational form: it is extensive rather than sequential. Its characteristic mode is not one of final closure or totalising vision; rather, it offers a continuous refiguration of events. Like the news bulletin series, the broadcast TV narrative (fiction and non-fiction) is open-ended, providing a continuous update, a perpetual return to the present. Since closure and finality is not a central feature of TV narration (though it does occur in specific major ways), it follows that the hermetic nature of the cinema narrative, with its patterns of repetition and novelty, is also absent. Repetition in the TV narrative occurs at the level of the series: formats are repeated, situations return week after week. Each time there is novelty. The characters of the situation comedy encounter a new dilemma; the documentary reveals a new problem; the news gives us a fresh strike, a new government, another earthquake, the first panda born in captivity. This form of repetition is different from that offered by the classic cinema narrative, as it provides a kind of groundbase, a constant basis for events, rather than an economy of reuse directed towards a final totalisation.

The series is composed of segments. The recognition of the series format tends to hold segments together and to provide them with an element of continuity and narrative progression from one to the next. The segment form itself has a strong internal coherence. Certain forms of segments are free-standing: the spot advertisement and the item in the news bulletin are both examples. They occur alongside similar segments which have no connection with them except a similarity of class. Other segments, those in a documentary exposition of a particular situation, or a fictional depiction of characters, will have definite connections of a narrative kind. But again, the movement from event to event is not as concentrated and causal as it tends to be in classic cinema narration. Broadcast TV's fictional segments tend to explore states and incidents in real time, avoiding the abbreviation that is characteristic of cinema. Hence a certain sense of intimacy in TV drama, a different pace and attention from entertainment cinema.

The segment is self-contained in TV production partly because of the fragmentary nature of much broadcast TV (especially if it carries spot advertising), but also because of the attention span that TV assumes of its audience, and the fact that memory of the particular series in all its detail cannot be assumed. People switch on in the middle and get hooked; they miss an episode or two; someone phones up in the middle. The TV production cannot be hermetic in the way that the film text is, otherwise the audience for a long-running soap opera like *Coronation Street* would now consist of half a dozen ageing addicts. The segment and the series are the repository of memory, and thus of the possibility of repetition and coherence.

The segment is a relatively self-contained scene which conveys an incident, a mood or a particular meaning. Coherence is provided by a continuity of character through the segment, or, more occasionally, a continuity of place. Hence many fictional segments consist of conversations between two or three characters, an encounter which produces a particular mood (embarrassment, relief, anger, love-at-first-sight, insults, anxiety) and tends to deliver a particular meaning which is often encapsulated in a final line. The segment ends and, in conventional TV fiction, is succeeded by another which deals with a different set of (related) characters in a different place, or the same characters at a different time. There is a marked break between segments. The aspect of break, of end and beginning, tends to outweigh the aspect of continuity and consequence. The non-fiction segment tends to operate in the same way, though in the expository or investigatory documentary it is a series of fragments (interviews, stills, captions, studio presenters, reporter-to-camera in locations) which are held together as a segment by the fact that they all combine to deliver a particular message. Each segment then represents a 'move' in the argument of the overall programme. In both drama and investigatory documentary, the segment is relatively self-contained and usually does not last longer than five minutes.

Being self-contained, the segment tends to exhaust its material, providing its own climax which is the culmination of the material of the segment. It is a characteristic of soap operas that they withhold the climactic revelation or action to the end of the segment and the end of the episode. [. . .] This process of climaxing directly followed by a break to other forms of segments (title sequences, advertisements, programme announcements, etc.) generates a series of segments in the next episode which effectively chart the repercussions of the climactic event. A series of conversations and actions exhaustively explores and, in the process, recapitulates the climactic action or revelation. The discovery of a husband's affair is followed by a rush of disconnected segments, adverts and so on; a week's wait produces a series of conversations: wife to friend, children, neighbours; husband to lover, colleague; and perhaps even The Couple themselves. Each depicts a certain attitude and mood, produces subsidiary revelations and mulls over the situation. These segments are self-exhausting: enough is said, done and shown to convey a particular meaning. This completion and internal coherence means that movement from one segment to the next is a matter of succession rather than consequence.

This effect of the self-containedness of the segment is intensified, especially in fiction and observational documentary work, by the use of real time. Where cinema elides actions within a scene by cutting out 'dead time' (a character's movement across a room that has no directly narrative function, for example), TV tends to leave this 'dead time' in. This stems directly from the studio multiple camera technique, where events are staged in temporal sequence and picked up by a number of cameras one of whose images is selected at any one moment by the director. Where cinema stages events in a very fragmentary way (sometimes just a gesture, a look), TV will stage much more like a theatrical scene. The result is that events unroll in real time for the audience, in the time that they took. A segment will tend to hold to temporal unity, especially if it is a conversation. This produces a sense of intimacy within the segment, and a sharp break between segments.

[. . .]

The narrative movement between segments does not follow the cinematic pattern of a relatively rapid transition from event to event in causal sequence. The movement from event to event is more circumspect. This circumspection shows itself in two ways. The first is the multiplication of incidents whose consequences and conclusion are suspended. This is a characteristic of the TV action series like the cop saga *Starsky and Hutch*. Our heroes perpetually encounter fresh incidents, and equally often find themselves suspended in an ambiguous position at the end of a segment (cue for commercial break). The second form of circumspect movement from event to event is that characterised by the soap opera and the drama alike. Events are at a premium: when they occur they generate tidal waves of verbiage, of gossip, discussion, speculation, recrimination. Guilt, jealousy, worry and an immense curiosity about people is generated by this form. The action series tends to generate car journeys, car chases, interrogations and the segment that reveals the furtive goings-on that the action-heroes will head off.

In each form, the events that take place are anticipated. For the soap opera/ drama, the deliciousness of the anticipation is worth in many instances more than the event itself. Speculation abounds; the event is perfunctory; the mulling over of the repercussions is extended. But it is a characteristic of the action series too that it carries few surprises. Its form of suspense is more incidental. Rather than proposing a central 'whodunnit' problem, it is more characteristic to find the central mystery revealed fairly early in the programme. Suspense then becomes a serial affair: the heroes and villains become entangled in a series of different situations, each of which involves escape, chase, shoot-out, etc. Narration in the cinematic sense is relatively perfunctory. Little play is made with the fact that the solution to the 'whodunnit' has been revealed to the audience before it has to the heroes. This differential knowledge and ana-lytic attitude to the actions of the heroes, characteristic of a cinema director like Fritz Lang (who usually reveals the narrative enigma to the audience), is relatively absent.

[. . .]

The unifying principle behind TV programmes is not as it is in cinema (sig-nificant patterns of repetition and innovation of meanings; narrative sequence; central problematic); it is the series which provides coherence between seg-ments. The series provides the unity of a particular programme, pulling together segments into a sense of connection which enables a level of narrative progression to take place between them. The series is the major point of repeti-tion in TV, matching the innovation that takes place within each segment. This pattern of repetition and innovation is very different from the cinematic model. Where the cinematic form is a closed system which aims to reuse as much material as possible and to balance kinds of repetition and innovation against each other, the TV form is more open-ended. It is a pattern of repetition that is far more centred on the narrative problematic than in cinema. Cinema's single texts tend to inaugurate a novel problematic, a new story subject, for each film. The TV series repeats a problematic. It therefore provides no resolution of the problematic at the end of each episode, nor, often, even at the end of the run of a series. Hence again the reduction of onward narrative progres-sion. The TV series proposes a problematic that is not resolved; narrative resolution takes place at a less fundamental level, at the level of the particular incidents (clinches, confrontations, conversations) that are offered each week (in the case of situation comedies) or between one week and the next (with the cliff-hanger serial ending). Fundamentally, the series implies the form of the dilemma rather than that of resolution and closure. This perhaps is the central contribution that broadcast TV has made to the long history of narrative forms and narrativised perception of the world.

The series is based on the repetition of a problematic. It repeats a situation, a situation which can be fictional or non-fictional. Hence the news series and the current affairs series both present a certain inquiring, fact-finding vision: the situation of reporters observing and collating information, then organising it for presentation to an uninformed public. This is as much a situation as a father and son running a scrap business with a totter's horse and cart and a crowded London yard (*Steptoe and Son*). The news and current affairs series present a problematic of vision and of explanation. Specific characters encounter a specific set of circumstances every week. But across the specificity of the week's circumstances runs the generality of the same problematic: that of how to see, how to understand. The terms of the understanding are always specified by the programme format. It will be 'we go behind the scenes' (*Panorama*), 'we ask the awkward questions' (*World in Action*), 'we update and see how this affects London' (*The London Programme*), 'we glance around' (*Nationwide*). In addition to these specific forms of understanding, there are the terms in which these understandings are cast: 'moderate/extremist', 'the housewife', 'But surely you don't think that . . . ?' The role of presenter is fundamental to these operations. The characters who investigate and explain for us are a loose group remarkably similar to the cast of a soap opera: some are central, long-running figures (presenters, anchor-persons); others come and go (reporters). In some areas of current affairs, the soap opera aspect becomes more or less explicit. *Nationwide* and *That's Life* are specific examples. The series format constitutes a stable basis of repetition in the programme format, its cast of characters, and its particular kind of reporting attention. Novelty in each edition is provided by the specific circumstances that these characters and their vision run up against. It is often explicit that the particular focus of attention for the characters is provided by outside forces over which they have no control, the world of current events. This world tends to be constituted as a place where problems occur. The political actions that the current events series is constituted to explain thus become a particular modality of action: they are problems, troubles, disturbances. The current events series provides a security against these disturbances. The result is that the political arena tends to be given the same status as the emotional problems encountered by soap opera characters. This is one effect of the series format, and one aspect of it.

The fictional series, too, repeats a basic problematic or situation week after week. Like the news and current affairs series, the situation comedy, the crime drama and the hospital series all return to the stability of the basic dilemma at the end of the week's episode. There is no development at all across the series. The serial marks a long slow narrative movement towards a conclusion, but often that conclusion is tentative (allowing a second series) or incidental (the dispersion of the characters). The situation that provides the steady core is a state of permanent or semi-permanent relationships between a stable but antagonistic group of characters. This is most fully developed in the situation comedy. *Steptoe and Son* may well hate each other, but they also love each other, and Harold's repeated threats to leave his father were never serious. This is exactly the dilemma that situation comedy deals with: it presents conflicting forces or emotions that can never be resolved. Hence the series situation is highly suited to present a particular static vision of the family and of work relations. What is particularly marked about the situation series is that the characters lose all memory of the previous week's incidents. They never learn.

[. . .]

Repetition across the series is one of problematic, of both characters and the situation (or dilemma) in which they find themselves. These situations provide a steady state to which audience and fiction return each week. Specific incidents are fed into this steady state, to provide fresh ammunition for our embattled family to fire at each other and the world, or for our reporters to look into and arrange for our inspection and concern. The incidental problems are solved, but the series format provides no real place for its own resolution. There is no final closure to the series' own recurring problematic. The run of a series ends without resolving its basic dilemma. This marks a basic difference between the cinema narrative and the TV series narrative. The film text aims for a final coherent totalising vision, which sets everything back into order. The series does not share this movement from stable state to stable state. The basic problematic of the series, with all its conflicts, is itself a stable state.

[. . .]

18

THE ROLE OF STEREOTYPES

Richard Dyer

The word 'stereotype' is today almost always a term of abuse. This stems from the wholly justified objections of various groups – in recent years, blacks, women and gays, in particular – to the ways in which they find themselves stereotyped in the mass media and in everyday speech. Yet when Walter Lippmann coined the term, he did not intend it to have a wholly and necessarily pejorative connotation. Taking a certain ironic distance on his subject, Lippmann none the less lays out very clearly both the absolute necessity for, and the usefulness of, stereotypes, as well as their limitations and ideological implications:

> A pattern of stereotypes is not neutral. It is not merely a way of substituting order for the great blooming, buzzing confusion of reality. It is not merely a short cut. It is all these things and something more. It is the guarantee of our self-respect; it is the projection upon the world of our own sense of our own value, our own position and our own rights. The stereotypes are, therefore, highly charged with the feelings that are attached to them. They are the fortress of our tradition, and behind its defenses we can continue to feel ourselves safe in the position we occupy. (1956: 96)

We can begin to understand something of how stereotypes work by following up the ideas raised by Lippmann – in particular his stress on stereotypes

From Jim Cook and Mike Lewington (eds), *Images of Alcoholism* (London: British Film Institute, 1979). Reprinted as Ch. 3 of Richard Dyer, *The Matter of Images: Essays on Representations* (London: Routledge, 1993).

as (i) an ordering process, (ii) a 'short cut', (iii) referring to 'the world', and (iv) expressing 'our' values and beliefs. The rest of this essay is structured around these topics, concluding with some tentative remarks on the relevance of what has gone before [in Dyer, 1993] to the representation of alcoholism. Throughout, I move between the more sociological concern of Lippmann (how stereotypes function in social thought) and the specific aesthetic concerns (how stereotypes function in fictions) that must also be introduced into any consideration of media representations. The position behind all these considerations is that it is not stereotypes, as an aspect of human thought and representation, that are wrong, but who controls and defines them, what interests they serve.

An Ordering Process

Stereotypes as a form of 'ordering' the mass of complex and inchoate data that we receive from the world are only a particular form – to do with the representation and categorization of persons[1] – of the wider process by which any human society, and individuals within it, make sense of that society through generalities, patternings and 'typifications'. Unless one believes that there is some definitively 'true' order in the world which is transparently revealed to human beings and unproblematically expressed in their culture – a belief that the variety of orders proposed by different societies, as analysed by anthropology and history, makes difficult to sustain – this activity of ordering, including the use of stereotypes, has to be acknowledged as a necessary, indeed inescapable, part of the way societies make sense of themselves, and hence actually make and reproduce themselves. (The fact that all such orderings are, by definition, partial and limited does not mean that they are untrue – partial knowledge is not false knowledge, it is simply not absolute knowledge.)

There are, however, two problems about stereotypes within this perspective. Firstly, the need to order 'the great blooming, buzzing confusion of reality' is liable to be accompanied by a belief in the absoluteness and certainty of any particular order, a refusal to recognize its limitations and partiality, its relativity and changeability, and a corresponding incapacity to deal with the fact and experience of blooming and buzzing.

Secondly, as the work of Peter Berger and Thomas Luckmann, amongst others, on the 'social construction of reality' stresses, not only is any given society's ordering of reality an historical product but it is also necessarily implicated in the power relations in that society – as Berger and Luckmann put it, 'he who has the bigger stick has the better chance of imposing his definitions of reality' (1967: 127). I shall return below to these two problems of Lippmann's formulation – order (stereotypes) perceived as absolute and rigid, order (stereotypes) as grounded in social power.

A Short Cut

Lippmann's notion of stereotypes as a short cut points to the manner in which stereotypes are a very simple, striking, easily-grasped form of representation but are none the less capable of condensing a great deal of complex information and a host of connotations. As T. E. Perkins notes in her key article 'Rethinking Stereotypes', the often observed 'simplicity' of stereotypes is deceptive:

> to refer 'correctly' to someone as a 'dumb blonde', and to understand what is meant by that, implies a great deal more than hair colour and intelligence. It refers immediately to *her* sex, which refers to her status in society, her relationship to men, her inability to behave or think rationally, and so on. In short, it implies knowledge of a complex social structure. (1979: 139)

The same point emerges from Arnold S. Linsky's analysis (1970–1) of the representation of the alcoholic in popular magazines between 1900 and 1966, where changing depictions of alcoholics are shown to express complex and contradictory social theories not merely of alcoholism but of free will and determinism.

Reference

Lippmann refers to stereotypes as a projection on to the 'world'. Although he is not concerned primarily to distinguish stereotypes from modes of representation whose principal concern is not the world, it is important for us to do so, especially as our focus is representations in media *fictions*, which are aesthetic as well as social constructs. In this perspective, stereotypes are a particular subcategory of a broader category of fictional characters, the type. Whereas stereotypes are essentially defined, as in Lippmann, by their social function, types, at this level of generality, are primarily defined by their aesthetic function, namely, as a mode of characterization in fiction. The type is any character constructed through the use of a few immediately recognizable and defining traits, which do not change or 'develop' through the course of the narrative and which point to general, recurrent features of the human world (whether these features are conceptualized as universal and eternal, the 'archetype', or historically and culturally specific, 'social types' and 'stereotypes' – a distinction discussed below).[2] The opposite of the type is the novelistic character, defined by a multiplicity of traits that are only gradually revealed to us through the course of the narrative, a narrative which is hinged on the growth or development of the character and is thus centred upon the latter in her or his unique individuality, rather than pointing outwards to a world.

In our society, it is the novelistic character that is privileged over the type, for the obvious reason that our society privileges – at any rate, at the level of social rhetoric – the individual over the collective or the mass. For this reason, the majority of fictions that address themselves to general social issues tend nevertheless to end up telling the story of a particular individual, hence returning social issues to purely personal and psychological ones. Once we address ourselves to the representation and definition of social categories – e.g. alcoholics – we have to consider what is at stake in one mode of characterization rather than another. Where do we want the emphasis of the representation to lie – on the psychological (alcoholism as a personal problem), on the social (alcoholism as an aspect of society) or in some articulation of the two? The choice or advocacy of a more novelistic or a more typical representation implicitly expresses one or other of these emphases.

THE EXPRESSION OF VALUES

It is Lippmann's reference to *our* tradition, and indeed his use of 'our' and 'we' throughout the passage quoted, that takes us into the most important, and most problematic, issue in stereotyping. For we have to ask, who exactly are the 'we' and 'us' invoked by Lippmann? – is it necessarily you and me?

The effectiveness of stereotypes resides in the way they invoke a consensus. Stereotypes proclaim, 'This is what everyone – you, me and us – thinks members of such-and-such a social group are like', as if these concepts of these social groups were spontaneously arrived at by all members of society independently and in isolation. The stereotype is taken to express a general agreement about a social group, as if that agreement arose before, and independently of, the stereotype. Yet for the most part it is *from* stereotypes that we get our ideas about social groups. The consensus invoked by stereotypes is more apparent than real; rather, stereotypes express particular definitions of reality, with concomitant evaluations, which in turn relate to the disposition of power within society. Who proposes the stereotype, who has the power to enforce it, is the crux of the matter – *whose* tradition is Lippmann's 'our tradition'?

Here Orrin E. Klapp's distinction between stereotypes and social types is helpful. In his book *Heroes, Villains and Fools* (1962) Klapp defines social types as representations of those who 'belong' to society. They are the kinds of people that one expects, and is led to expect, to find in one's society, whereas stereotypes are those who do not belong, who are outside of one's society. In Klapp, this distinction is principally geographic – i.e. social types of Americans, stereotypes of non-Americans. We can, however, rework his distinction in terms of the types produced by different social groups according to their sense of who belongs and who doesn't, who is 'in' and who is not. Who does or does not belong to a given society as a whole is then a function of the relative power of groups in that society to define themselves as central and the rest as 'other', peripheral or outcast.

In fictions, social types and stereotypes can be recognized as distinct by the different ways in which they can be used. Although constructed iconographically similarly to the way stereotypes are constructed (i.e. a few verbal and visual traits are used to signal the character), social types can be used in a much more open and flexible way than can stereotypes. This is most clearly seen in relation to plot. Social types can figure in almost any kind of plot and can have a wide range of roles in that plot (e.g. as hero, as villain, as helper, as light relief, etc.), whereas stereotypes always carry within their very representation an implicit narrative. Jo Spence has argued in the context of the representation of women that, despite the superficial variety of images, they all carry within them an implicit narrative pattern:

> visual representations which may appear to deal with diverse ideas but which are all aimed at women tend to act as part of an implicit narrative. This has a 'beginning' and a 'middle' (birth, childhood, marriage, family life) but there is only minimal representation of its 'end', of growing old and dying. (1980: 29–45)

In an article dealing with the stereotyping of gays in films, I tried to show how the use of images of lesbians in a group of French films, no matter what kind of film or of what 'artistic quality', always involved an identical plot function (1977: 33–5). Similarly, we surely only have to be told that we are going to see a film about an alcoholic to know that it will be a tale either of sordid decline or of inspiring redemption. (This suggests a particularly interesting potential use of stereotypes, in which the character is constructed, at the level of dress, performance, etc., as a stereotype but is deliberately given a narrative function that is not implicit in the stereotype, thus throwing into question the assumptions signalled by the stereotypical iconography.)

The social type/stereotype distinction is essentially one of degree. It is after all very hard to draw a line between those who are just within and those definitely beyond the pale. This is partly because different social categories overlap – e.g. men 'belong', blacks do not, but what of black men? It is also because some of the categories that the social type/stereotype distinction keeps apart cannot logically be kept apart in this way. The obvious examples here are men and women, and it is this that causes T. E. Perkins to reject the distinction (1979: 140–1). As applied to men and women, the social type/ stereotype distinction implies that men have no direct experience of women and that there could be a society composed entirely of men: both of these are virtually impossible. Yet it seems to me that what the distinction points to, as applied to women and men, is a tendency of patriarchal thought[3] to attempt to maintain the impossible, by insisting on the 'otherness' of women and men (or rather the 'otherness' of women, men being in patriarchy the human norm to which women are 'other') in the face of their necessary collaboration in history and society. (The distinction does also refer in part to a real separation in social arrangements, i.e. the fact of male and female 'preserves': the pub, the beauty salon, the study, the kitchen, etc.) What the distinction also maintains is the *absolute* difference between men and women, in the face of their actual relative similarity.

This is the most important function of the stereotype: to maintain sharp boundary definitions, to define clearly where the pale ends and thus who is clearly within and who clearly beyond it. Stereotypes do not only, in concert with social types, map out the boundaries of acceptable and legitimate behaviour, they also insist on boundaries exactly at those points where in reality there are none. Nowhere is this more clear than with stereotypes dealing with social categories that are invisible and/or fluid. Such categories are *invisible*, because you cannot tell just from looking at a person that she or he belongs to the category in question. Unless the person chooses to dress or act in a clearly and culturally defined manner (e.g. the working-class man's cloth cap, the male homosexual's limp wrist) or unless one has a trained eye (as those dealing with alcoholics have?), it is impossible to place the person before one, whereas many social groups – women and men, different races, young and old – are visibly different, and this difference can be eradicated only by disguise. Social categories can be *fluid*, in the sense that it is not possible in reality to draw a line between them and adjacent categories. We make a fuss about – and produce stereotypes about – the difference between women and men, yet biologically this is negligible compared to their similarity. Again, we are led to treat heterosexuality and homosexuality as sharply opposed categories of persons when in reality both heterosexual and homosexual responses and behaviour are to some extent experienced by everybody in their life. Alcohol use is clearly in this category – it is notoriously difficult to draw the line between harm-free and harmful drinking. But stereotypes can.

The role of stereotypes is to make visible the invisible, so that there is no danger of it creeping up on us unawares; and to make fast, firm what is in reality fluid and much closer to the system cares to admit.

In the widest sense, these functi nected to Lippmann's insistence o the tendency towards rigidity that to have relatively stable boundarie achieved within a context that rec concepts. Such a stability is, howeve opposed to imposed, consensus. The otype indicates the degree to which it to a reality whose invisibility and/or f of society promoted by those with th so very different from men, why are t so easily distinguished from social drin acceptance of the latter and condemnati

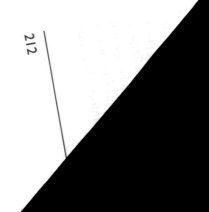

212

[...]

NOTES

1. I confine myself here to the discussion of stereotypes as a form of representing persons, although the word itself (especially in adjectival form) is also used to refer to ideas, behaviour, settings, etc.
2. It is important to stress the role of conceptualization in the distinction between, on the one hand, archetypes, and, on the other, social and stereotypes, since what may be attributed to a type as a universal and eternal trait, hence making it archetypal, may only be a historically and culturally specific trait misunderstood as a universal and eternal trait – it is, after all, the tendency of dominant value systems in societies to pass their values off as universally and eternally valid.
3. By patriarchy I mean the thought system that legitimates the power of men and the subordination of women in society; I do not mean that it is necessarily and simply how all men think of women, although it is an overwhelming determinant on that.

REFERENCES

Berger, Peter and Luckmann, Thomas (1967) *The Social Construction of Reality*, London: Allen Lane/Penguin Press.

Dyer, Richard (1977) 'Stereotyping', in Richard Dyer (ed.) *Gays and Film*, London: British Film Institute.

Klapp, Orrin E. (1962) *Heroes, Villains and Fools*, Englewood Cliffs: Prentice-Hall.

Linsky, Arnold S. (1970–1) 'Theories of Behaviour and the Image of the Alcoholic in Popular Magazines 1900–1960', *Public Opinion Quarterly* 34: 573–81.

Lippmann, Walter (1956) *Public Opinion*, New York: Macmillan. (First published 1922.)

Perkins, T. E. (1979) 'Rethinking Stereotypes', in Michèle Barrett, Philip Corrigan, Annette Kuhn and Janet Wolff (eds) *Ideology and Cultural Production*, London: Croom Helm, 135–59.

Spence, Jo (1980) 'What Do People Do All Day? Class and Gender in Images of Women', *Screen Education* 29.

19

GENRE, REPRESENTATION AND SOAP OPERA

Christine Gledhill

[. . .]

As one of a range of popular fictional types or genres, soap opera belongs to the overarching *genre system* which governs the division of mass-produced print and audio-visual fictions into distinct kinds: romantic novels, detective stories, westerns, thrillers, sitcoms, as well as soap operas. I shall, therefore, be turning to *genre theory* – especially as it has been applied to film and television fiction – for a number of concepts which together offer a productive approach to the work of soap opera within the context of the media industries. For it is within the working of the genre system that economic and production mechanisms, particular textual forms, and audiences or readers interconnect and struggles for hegemony takes place.

The genre product

First, what does the term 'genre' imply about the product to which it is applied? A particular genre category refers to the way the individual fictions which belong to it can be grouped together in terms of similar plots, stereotypes, settings, themes, style, emotional affects and so on. Just naming these different popular genres – the detective story, soap opera, etc. – will probably invoke for you certain expectations about the kind of stories and affects they offer, even if you rarely read or watch them. Indeed such categories function as important guides to our viewing choices and practices.

From S. Hall (ed.), *Representation* (London: Sage, 1997).

[. . .] Such expectations arise from our familiarity with the *conventions* of each genre – the police series, the soap opera, the western or science fiction. These conventions represent a body of rules or codes, signifiers and signs, and the potential combinations of, and relations between, signs which together constitute the genre.

[. . .]

One aspect of the genre product, then, is that it is recognizable by its *similarity* to other products of its kind. It is this that leads to the frequent complaint of predictability. Given an initial clue, we can fill in the rest. Within the ideology of mass culture this use of 'convention' is often associated with industrial mass production as a source of plot formulae, stereotypes and clichés. In this respect, *convention* takes on an inherently conservative connotation, its main function being to reinforce normative meanings and values. Genre theory was developed as a means of countering this deterministic conception by seeking to understand the productive work of convention in the context of three interconnected but distinct 'moments' or 'stages' in the cultural work of the media industries:

1. *Production and distribution*: financiers, studios, TV companies, producers and controllers, censors, script-writers, directors, stars, festivals and awards, advertising and publicity, trade press, etc.
2. *The product or text*: genres and programme formats, conventions, narrative structures, styles, iconography, performances, stars, etc.
3. *Reception*: going to the cinema, the TV schedule, 'girls' night out', the family audience, the kitchen TV, the gaze at the cinema screen, the glance at the TV screen, pin-ups, reviews and reviewers, etc.

[. . .]

The [. . .] approach, developed by genre theory, is useful because it enables us to define the relationship between these three stages, not as the imposition of 'media domination' but rather as a struggle over which meanings, which definitions of reality, will win the consent of the audience and thus establish themselves as the privileged reading of an episode (hegemony). Hegemony is established *and* contested in the interaction and negotiation between: (1) industrial production, (2) the semiotic work of the text, and (3) audience reception. Moreover, each stage contains within itself potential tensions and contradictions between the different economic, professional, aesthetic and personal practices and cultural traditions involved.

GENRE AS STANDARDIZATION AND DIFFERENTIATION

First let us examine the genre system at the level of production, focusing on the *repeatability* of genre conventions as a key to the *mass production* of fictions.

The economic rationale for genre production is, perhaps, most vividly illustrated by the Hollywood studio system. As is frequently asserted, film-making is a hugely costly affair requiring capital investment both in plant – studio buildings, technological hardware, laboratories, cinemas – and in individual productions. Economies of scale require *standardization of production* and the emergence of popular genres – which began with the growth of nineteenth-century mass fiction and syndicated theatrical entertainments – served this need. The elaborate sets, costume designs, and props of one genre film can be re-utilized with a modicum of alteration in the next production; writers familiar with the conventions of plotting and dialogue appropriate to a particular genre can move from script to script in assembly-line fashion; bit-part actors and stars can be groomed to produce the gestural mannerisms, style of delivery and overall 'image' appropriate to the protagonists of a particular genre; studio technicians, cameramen (rarely women), editors and directors become increasingly efficient in the design, lighting and cinematography required to produce the particular visual world and mode of narration of the given genre. *Genre becomes a means of standardizing production.*

[. . .]

In looking at soap opera from this perspective you may have noted that the form offers production companies the advantage of extended use of sets and properties over time. This made it economically worthwhile, for example, for Granada to build a permanent set for *Coronation Street* [. . .]. The longevity of soap opera, however, plays havoc with continuity of personnel and story-line. For example, changes of writers can produce terrible mistakes out of ignorance of past relationships or events, to the point that *Coronation Street* employs a serial historian in order to avoid embarrassing slips! This demonstrates an important tension between the pressures for economy at the production stage through standardization and the 'rules' which govern a fictional world, which once brought into being, take on a certain life of their own, not least in the memories of listeners and viewers who ring studios to tell producers when they get things wrong.

This example also shows that genre not only standardizes the production process, it serves *to stabilize an audience.* What we buy with our cinema ticket, television licence or cable subscription is the promise of a certain type of experience – entry to a fictional world as a means of being entertained., This, however, is a state of being, the conditions for which are notoriously difficult to predict or control! By offering familiar tried and tested worlds with familiar appeals and pleasures, genres serve not only to standardize production but to predict markets and stabilize audiences. For the film studio or television company, genres become a means of reaching an audience and hopefully of developing a bond with that audience – inducing a kind of 'brand loyalty'.

[. . .]

Genre production, however, is not just about standardization – about fixing conventions and audiences. If all soap operas were exactly like one another, they would soon lose their audiences because they would become too predictable and repetitive. So genre production is equally about *differentiation* – managing product differentiation to maximize, and appeal to, different audiences and to keep tabs on changing audiences. This manifests itself in two ways: the production of a *variety of genres* for different audiences, and *variation within genres* between one example and the next. Thus, for example, one western will in some respects be much like another, but it will differ in well-known ways from a gangster film or a family melodrama. Similarly, the soap opera is defined partly in its difference from the police series, for example. Equally, a new western will differ from past westerns, and a new soap opera will try to open up different territory from its rivals [. . .].

Such differentiation is vital, ensuring both the pleasure of recognition, along with the frisson of the new. For while we may stick to our favourite brands of soap or washing powder, we don't on the whole want to see the same film or television programme over and over again. On the other hand we may have a particular liking for some genres over others and experience pleasure in revisiting that 'world' again and again. Thus the genre system offers the possibility of variety, enabling film studios and TV companies to offer choice and acknowledge differences among audiences, while retaining the advantage of standardized production procedures with its attendant rewards. For audiences, then, the question that brings us back to our favourite genre is less *what* is going to happen, which as detractors point out we can probably predict, but *how*. The popular audience, far from being the *passive consumers* constructed within the ideology of mass culture, are required to be *expert readers* in order to appreciate the twists and innovations within the familiar which are the pleasures of the genre system.

THE GENRE PRODUCT AS TEXT

I want now to consider more precisely the work of the genre text as a semiotic site for the production and negotiation of representations, meanings and identities.

What does it mean to define a popular genre as a 'signifying practice'? [. . .] I have suggested that any given genre provides [. . .] a system of underlying rules and codes by which films or TV programmes are produced and understood. At its most basic level the genre system orchestrates signifiers which determine the attributes of different fictional worlds: for example, *settings* (e.g. the American West, an East End community); *locations* (e.g. a saloon bar, a launderette); *character types* (e.g. the outlaw, the manageress of the motel); *iconography* (e.g. a smoking Winchester 73, three flying ducks on a living-room wall), *plots* (e.g. a new sheriff arrives to establish law and order by driving out corrupt business interests, the community social worker finds out that her underage daughter is pregnant by her ex-lover). At first sight, generic codes consist of rules of inclusion and exclusion governing what can and cannot appear or happen within particular generic worlds. [. . .] These settings, character types and images become *signs* for a particular kind of fictional world.

However, it is unwise to assert too confidently that particular attributes *cannot* appear or happen in a particular genre, because sooner or later you will be proved wrong. The rules or codes establish limits but they are not eternally fixed. In the early days of analysis of soap opera, it was said, first, that you would never see inside a factory in a soap opera and, later, when Mike Baldwin opened up his clothing factory in *Coronation Street*, that you'd never have a strike in a soap opera. Within a year the Baldwin factory was closed down while the female workforce came out on strike. This is because the semiotic principles of signification determine that generic signs produce meanings through relationships of similarity *and difference*. Of course, repetition and similarity are necessary to establish familiarity with the codes which bind signifier to signified, but meaning is produced only in the difference between signs. For example, the code that matches the iconography of a white hat and horse/black hat and horse with the upright Westerner and the outlaw, plays on a binary colour coding to mark the difference, and it is that which produces the meaning of the character types. But there are several different combinations that can be made with even these few elements. Switch hats and character types and the new combination produces new meanings through the difference – about, for instance, the moral complexity of the law, or the ambivalent position of the outsider. In other words, rather than inert counters with already assigned, fixed and predictable meanings – white hat and horse means upright westerner, black hat and horse means outlaw – generic conventions *produce* meanings through a process of constantly shifting combination and differentiation.

Genres and binary differences

This has led some critics to analyse genres in terms of a shifting series of binary differences or oppositions. For example, Jim Kitzes (1969) explores the western in terms of a series of structuring differences or 'antimonies' which he traces back to the core opposition, Wilderness versus Civilization. Together these represent a 'philosophical dialectic, an ambiguous cluster of meanings and attitudes that provide the traditional/thematic structure of the genre'. Within this flexible set of shifting antinomies the opposition masculinity/femininity constitutes one of the ideological tensions played out. Typically in the western, masculinity is identified with the Wilderness/the Individual/Freedom and femininity with Civilization/Community/Restriction [. . .]. [A]ny given genre film produces its meanings from a shifting pattern of visual, thematic and ideological differences and gender is a key signifying difference in this orchestration.

[. . .]

Drawing up such lists of oppositions can illuminate what is at stake in the conflicts orchestrated by a particular genre. However, the point of the exercise is not to fix signifiers in permanent opposition, but to uncover a pattern, the terms of which can be shifted to produce a different meaning. It is the shifting of ideological and cultural values across the terms of the oppositions that enables us to pursue the processes of and struggles over meaning.

Genre boundaries

So far I have argued that it is not possible to fix the meaning of particular generic signifiers. Neither is it possible to define genres through a fixed set of attributes unique to themselves. So, for example, guns are key to both the western and the gangster film, and weddings are important to both romantic comedies and soap operas. What defines the genre is not the specific convention itself but its placing in a particular relationship with other elements – a relationship which generates different meanings and narrative possibilities according to the genre: for example, the gun wielded against the wilderness in the western, or against society in the gangster film; the wedding as a concluding integration of warring parties in the romantic comedy or the wedding as the start of marriage problems in soap opera.

Given such overlaps, the boundaries between genres are not fixed either: rather we find a sliding of conventions from one genre to another according to changes in production and audiences. This sliding of conventions is a prime source of generic evolution. So, for example, when soap opera left the daytime women's television audience for primetime, with the appearance of *Dallas*, echoes of the western evoked by the Southfork ranch, its landscape and its menfolk extended soap opera's domestic terrain as part of an attempt to produce a more inclusive gendered address for the evening audience. This has led to arguments as to whether, given these western elements, strong male roles, and business intrigues, it is correct to identify *Dallas* as a soap opera. But this effort to fix genre boundaries ignores the dynamic and interdependent processes of signification and media production, where new meanings and generic innovation are produced by breaking rules, pushing at boundaries and redefining difference. The point is less whether *Dallas* is a soap opera or not, but rather what meanings are produced when signifiers from different genres intersect, and in this case when differently gendered genres are involved. [The] sliding of meaning as signifiers shift across the boundaries that demarcate one genre from another produces negotiations around gender difference which are highly significant for our study of the media and representation.

[. . .]

To sum up so far: despite a grounding in repetition and similarity, difference is key to the work of genre. Our knowledge of any generic system can only be provisional. Genre is a system or framework of conventions, expectations and possibilities, or, to put it in [. . .] semiotic terms [. . .], the *genre* conventions function as the deep-structure or *langue*, whilst individual programmes, which realize these underlying rules, function as *paroles*. Moreover, as the French literary structuralist Tzvetan Todorov argues (1976), each new manifestation of a genre work changes the possibilities of future works, extending the genre's horizon of expectations and changing what can and cannot be said within the framework of a particular generic world. Steve Neale (1981) insists that generic production, like any system for producing meaning, must be considered not as a fixed and static body of conventions but as a *process*.

SIGNIFICATION AND REFERENCE

To this point we have considered the work of genre convention as internal to the genre system. Now I want to turn to the question of the relation between the production of genre fictions and social reference, which is central to our consideration of genre's work of cultural negotiation. [. . .] [T]he signs and signifiers of the genre code take signs from our social and cultural world not simply to represent that world but to produce another, fictional, one. In this case we are considering highly specialized signs, produced within and for the genre system. But what exactly is the relation between the signifiers of the generic world and the social? How does genre production engage in reference to the social world while in the process of constructing a fictional one?

[. . .]

Steve Neale, in his article on genre (1981), makes two useful distinctions which are helpful in understanding the work of the referent in genre films. First he distinguishes between *verisimilitude* and *realism*. These terms refer in significantly different ways to the work of the referent. *Realism* is today the more familiar term through which we judge whether a fiction constructs a world we recognize as like our own; but [. . .], realism is a highly problematic category. Steve Neale, therefore, revives a concept from literary history, to underline the fact that, in fiction, 'reality' is always constructed. *Verisimilitude*, he argues, refers not to what may or may not *actually* be the case but rather to what the dominant culture *believes* to be the case, to what is generally accepted as credible, suitable, proper. Neale then distinguishes between *cultural verisimilitude* and *generic verisimilitude*. In order to be recognized as a film belonging to a particular genre – a western, a musical, a horror film – it must comply with the rules of that genre: in other words, genre conventions produce a second order verisimilitude – what ought to happen in a western or soap opera – by which the credibility or truth of the fictional world we associate with a particular genre is guaranteed. Whereas generic verisimilitude allows for considerable play with fantasy *inside* the bounds of generic credibility (e.g. singing about your problems in the musical; the power of garlic in gothic horror movies), cultural verisimilitude refers us to the norms, mores, and common sense of the social world *outside* the fiction.

Different genres produce different relationships between generic and cultural verisimilitude. For example, the generic verisimilitude of the gangster film in the 1930s drew heavily on cultural verisimilitude – what audiences then knew about actual bootlegging and gang warfare in the streets, if not from first-hand experience, then from other cultural sources such as the press – whereas the horror film has greater licence to transgress cultural verisimilitude in the construction of a generic world full of supernatural or impossible beings and events.

[...]

We can now return to the distinction between *verisimilitude* and *realism*. Although these two concepts cannot in practice be cleanly separated, the distinction is useful because it suggests how and why *realism* is always a matter of contest. For the demand for realism won't go away, however problematic the notion. And while the concept of verisimilitude refers to normative perceptions of reality – what is generally accepted to be so – the demand for a 'new' realism from oppositional or emerging groups opens up the contest over the definition of the real and forces changes in the codes of verisimilitude. For conventions of cultural verisimilitude get in the way of pressures for social change – newly emerging social groups or practices demand changes in the conventions of representation. Thus *realism* becomes a polemic in an assault on *cultural verisimilitude*: it demands representation of what has not been seen before, what has been unthinkable because unrepresentable. But the new signifiers of the real in their turn solidify into the established codes of cultural verisimilitude and become open to further challenge. The Women's Movement saw this happen in the 1970s, when the dress codes and body language which signified 'women's liberation' circulated into the pages of fashion magazines and advertising – for example, the frequently attacked Virginia Slims adverts which tried to identify liberation with smoking. However, what this demonstrates is that 'cultural verisimilitude' is not monolithic, but fractured by the different signifying practices and discourses through which different social groups stake out their identities and claims on the real.

[...]

Media Production and Struggles for Hegemony

The tension between *realism* and *cultural* and *generic verisimilitude* enables us to link the industrial production of genre fiction to conceptions of hegemony and cultural struggle [...], suggesting how and why the media industries participate in contests over the construction of the real.

We have seen that both the competition for markets and the semiotic conditions of genre production entail a search for difference, for innovation. A genre such as soap opera – a daily 'story of everyday life', itself incorporated into the daily routines of listeners and viewers – is heavily invested in *cultural verisimilitude*. Since, as I have argued, the conventions of cultural verisimilitude are constantly mutating under pressure from shifting cultural discourses and newly emerging social groups, soap operas are driven to engage in some way with social change, if they are not to fall by the wayside as 'old fashioned'. The need to maintain the recognition of existing audiences and attract newly emerging ones, together with the constant need for new story material and the need for an edge over competitors, makes topicality, being up-to-date, controversy, all vital factors in the form's continuance. [. . .]

These multiple pressures towards innovation and renewal mean that popular genres not only engage with social change but become key sites for the emerging articulation of and contest over change. So the discourses and imagery of new social movements – for example, the women's, gay, or black liberation movements – which circulate into public consciousness through campaign groups, parliamentary and social policy debates, new and popular journalism, and other media representations, provide popular genres with material for new story lines and the pleasures of dramatic enactment. It is important, though, not to let this suggest a linear model of representation – social change followed by its representation in the media. Rather, what we seek to locate is the circulation of images, representations, and discourses from one area of social practice to another.

How, exactly, does this process take place within the production process? Christine Geraghty [(1991)] reminds us of the variety of vested and conflicting interests caught up in the process of media production. Company executives, advertisers, producers, writers, directors and actors, also have different professional and personal stakes in the process of generic innovation and social change.

While such struggles can be viewed on the ground as conflicts between business executives and creative personnel, or between men and women, the acts and decisions of these 'agents' of conflict take place within the movement of cultural discourses [. . .]. Julie D'Acci (1994), for example, in her study of the American television police series, *Cagney and Lacey*, beloved by female audiences for its substitution of a female for a male police partnership, suggests that the series would not have originated without the public spread of ideas circulated by the Women's Movement. For the writing/producing trio (two women friends and a husband) were inspired by the feminist journalist, Molly Haskell's critique of the buddy movie, centring on the bonding of two male heroes, for its displacement of good women's roles in the late 1960s and 1970s. For the executives and advertisers at CBS the constant search for new and contemporary ideas meant that the innovation of a female buddy pairing in a cop show seemed like a good idea – at the time, that is. Despite successful ratings and an Emmy award, the series came under frequent threat of cancellation from CBS, who were fearful for their advertising revenue, in large part, D'Acci argues, because of the problematic definitions of 'woman' and female sexuality that it invokes. Particularly problematic was the unmarried Christine Cagney, whose fierce independence and intense friendship with Mary Beth Lacey led to two changes of actress in an effort to bring the series under control and reduce the implication of lesbianism – something such strategies singularly failed to do. The fact that the show survived for three series was in part to do with a concerted campaign by an audience of white, middle-class women who used the networks of the Women's Movement to counter-threaten CBS's advertisers with supermarket boycotts and so on. While the arguments were not mounted specifically around lesbianism, and the British female fan club refuses the identification 'feminist', nevertheless contradictory discourses of sexuality and gender can be seen at work mobilizing and shaping the conflict.

If, for the executives at CBS, gender reversal seemed like a commercially good prospect, for the writers putting a female buddy pairing in *Cagney and Lacey* was an assault on the cultural verisimilitude of the police series in the name of the reality of changing gender roles in society. But the attempt to adapt to changing codes of recognition – women are in fact on career routes within the police force; they do try to juggle the demands of paid work and homemaking – had an inevitable impact on the codes of generic recognition: on what until then had been the norm for the police series. The production of a female partnership had to draw on a different set of generic codes and stereotypes, for example the woman's film, soap opera, the independent or liberated woman.

Moreover, such a partnership could be convincingly constructed only by drawing on the subcultural codes of women's social discourse and culture. Inside a soap opera those codes are taken for granted as part of its cultural as well as generic verisimilitude. Inside a police series, however, they have a range of consequences for both genre and ideology. When female protagonists, for example, have to function as law enforcers and confront criminal behaviour – both associated with male authority and action – gendered conflict inevitably follows. In the search for credibility with the American female middle-class professional audiences which the series sought, this meant drawing on discourses about sexism put into public circulation by the Women's Movement. Such discourses become in their turn a new source of drama and ideological explanation. The plotting of *Cagney and Lacey*, then, is itself made out of a series of negotiations around definitions of gender roles and sexuality, definitions of heterosexual relations and female friendships, as well as around the nature of law and policing.

SUMMARY

To sum up [. . .]: popular genres represent patterns of repetition and difference, in which difference is crucial to the continuing industrial and semiotic existence of the genre. Far from endless mechanical repetition, the media industries are constantly on the look-out for a new angle, making genre categories remark-ably flexible. Genres produce fictional worlds which function according to a structuring set of rules or conventions, thereby ensuring recognition through their conformity to generic verisimilitude. However, they also draw on events and discourses in the social world both as a source of topical story material and as a means of commanding the recognition of audiences through conformity to cultural verisimilitude. The conventions of cultural verisimilitude are under constant pressure for change as social practices and mores change and newly emerging social groups (and potential audiences) put pressure on representa-tion. This highlights the need to consider the changing historical circumstances of fictional production and consumption. These changing circumstances deter-mine that genres cannot exist by mere repetition and recycling past models, but have to engage with difference and change, in a process of negotiation and contest over representation, meaning and pleasure.

[. . .]

REFERENCES

D'Acci, J. (1994) *Defining Women: television and the case of Cagney and Lacey*, London and Chapel Hill, NC, University of North Carolina Press.
Geraghty, C. (1991) *Women and Soap Opera: a study of prime time soaps*, Cambridge, Polity Press.
Kitzes, J. (1969) *Horizons West*, London, Thames and Hudson/BFI.
Neale, S. (1981) *Genre*, London, BFI.
Todorov, T. (1976) 'The origin of genres', *New Literary History*, Vol. 8, No. 1 (Autumn).

20

RHETORIC, PLAY, PERFORMANCE

Roger Silverstone

[. . .] This chapter has [. . .] as its aim a modest sketch of an epistemology. Television documentary will be the focus of an effort to address the ways in which television itself is an address. The aim is to question how television grounds its appeal and how it can be seen to construct its own common ground.

[. . .]

DISCURSIVE SPACES

[. . .]

What I am interested in here is the *discursive* spaces that contain both text and audience. The metaphor refers both to a literal space (the places and times of everyday life) and to a symbolic space (the place where meanings are negotiated and made). At issue are the conditions for the possibility of meaning in any given communicative interaction, an interaction in television which demands attention to the interrelationship of technology, text and audience. And I am interested in the nature of the activity that takes place in these spaces. This interest is in a strict sense a phenomenological interest, occupying its own discursive space between epistemology and ontology, and subject to increasingly sophisticated enquiry [. . .].

I am therefore searching for a way of thinking about, and seeking the specificities and variations of, not just the *modes of address* within documentary science

From Jostein Gripsrud (ed.), *Television and Common Knowledge* (London: Routledge, 1999).

and other forms of television, but possible frameworks for understanding the *discursive spaces* within which those modes of address are presented and negotiated, the spaces in which viewers and listeners or readers participate in the construction of meaning – and the different ways in which they may do so. Given my starting point, my aim is to enquire into this construction not from the point of view of the viewer – the individual inside or outside an interpretative community – but from the point of view of the claimed authority of the text itself, rejecting the currently dominant epistemology of audience–text relationships.

[. . .]

What I am going to propose is this: that we can identify different, non-discrete – I have already called them – *discursive spaces* from within which different relationships of text and reader are claimed and constructed. I shall describe three – minimally and inadequately – in order to argue that they provide a way of identifying distinct *textual claims*, inviting and legitimating different relationships both to knowledge and to reader response. Each articulates too – as a result, of course – a different textual politics.

I will call these discursive spaces the spaces of *rhetoric, play and performance*. I think it is possible to argue that any two of these can be seen to be subcategories of the third (that is, that play and performance can be considered versions of rhetoric; or rhetoric and play as versions of performance, and so on). But I actually think it is worth trying to distinguish them for what they can reveal about the different textual strategies that television's texts can adopt, and, even more importantly, to see them as offering a different way of engaging an audience in a text-dependent discourse, exercising power through their inscription on the screen [. . .] and, of course, offering a legitimation of their own authority and truth claims, and in so doing laying claim to a particular kind of audience engagement. So, for example, I believe that it is possible to distinguish (though, as I have just indicated, by no unambiguous divide):

- *rhetoric* as the domain of cognitive truth and language to stimulate action;
- *play* as the domain of emotional truth and language conjoined with action;
- *performance* as the domain of experiential truth and language as action.

I am going to try and argue for an understanding of the relationship between text and audience as being dependent (in some degree) on the presence or absence of such discursive spaces. While each of these can be seen in literary manifestations, they have their origins in, and are sustained by, visual and oral (non-literary) culture. While each of these can be identified analytically as discrete, as one might expect in the empirical world, they are likely to overlap and sometimes compete or contradict each other within a given viewing experience. Likewise, it is possible to suggest that each of the three depends to different degrees on the dominance of text or technology, message or medium in the viewing experience.

While clearly not approximating to anything approaching interactivity with the specific sense of active participation in a common project by two or more participants, the sense of discursive space that I wish to convey can be profitably compared to Brenda Laurel's (1993) discussion of the creation of a 'common ground'. Her discussion of computer-mediated interaction stresses the need to go beyond a model of interaction as turn-taking 'conversation'. Following Clark and Brennan (1990), she argues that the common ground, both precondition and consequence of any interactive communication, is

> a jointly inhabited 'space' where meaning takes shape through the collaboration and successive approximations of the participants. . . .The notion of common ground not only provides a superior representation of the conversational process but also supports the idea that an interface is not simply the means whereby a person and a computer represent themselves to one another; rather it is a shared context for action in which both are agents. (Laurel 1993: 4)

This is not the place to engage in any discussion of 'conventional' television viewing as interactive, but it is nevertheless important to point out that there is a version of activity which is required in understanding audiences' relations to mediated texts – elsewhere I have called this 'engagement' (Silverstone 1994). And it is crucial to understand the importance of this 'common ground' as a mutual participation of (motivated) texts and readers, as well as a precondition of readers' participation in meaning-construction. It is also important to point out that the presence of common ground does not preclude failures of communication, surprise or other deviations from a supposed matching of intention and response. Indeed, it is my contention within this paper that we need to understand better than we appear now to do what elements make up the complex common ground, or indeed common grounds, which, in turn, make up the television experience.

RHETORIC

[. . .]

Documentary is perhaps, above all, the form of television that is most consistently persuasive, embodying, in a sense ideal-typically, the Lasswellian (1948) model of media communication. As Michael Renov suggests, 'The documentary "truth claim" (which says, at the very least, "Believe me, I'm of the world") is the baseline of persuasion for all non-fiction, from propaganda to rock doc' (Renov 1993: 30).

Rhetoric, in its Aristotelian or Ciceronian guise, is the science of persuasion. It involves both an aesthetic and a pragmatic agenda. We are encouraged to speak well and to some purpose.

Television, it could be argued, can be seen through the filter of rhetorical theory as a medium, and not just in documentary, of persuasion – persuading its viewers to believe or to suspend disbelief, to accept the claims for verisimilitude as well as the claims, literally, to be heard, understood and accepted. Different contemporary approaches to rhetoric stress its different functions: as persuasion (Burke 1962), as argument (Billig 1987) and as the structuring of knowledge (McKeon 1987).

Rhetoric has its divisions (invention, arrangement, expression, memory and delivery), its forms of argumentation (its figures and its tropes) and its mechanisms of engagement in its commonplaces (the short cuts in argumentation, the places of recognition). Rhetoric has been divined in the patterns, 'the perambulatory rhetorics', of everyday life (de Certeau 1984), in the homological narratives that link the literary and personal and structure time (Ricoeur 1980, 1983), and in the metaphors (Lakoff and Johnson 1980) of everyday life. Rhetoric involves appeals which are both cognitive and critical, intellectual and emotional – for attention, for assent; and, in the sharing of communication and understanding, for both common sense and community (see, especially, Billig 1987: 200ff.).

A focus on the rhetoric of television and of its texts therefore involves the consideration not just of persuasion and appeal, but also of the mutual involvement by producer and consumer, addresser and addressee in the structuring of meaning and experience (Morley and Silverstone 1990). It also involves the rehabilitation of a notion of intention, as well as invention (*inventio*) and argument in the analysis of television's communication. We are required to see behind and within the text the agents and activities – individuals, groups acting both coherently and contradictorily – whose creative work in the construction of narratives and the mobilization of genre results in a series of textual calls and claims which on their own, or in the context of the wider (the widest) viewing experience, require response. To see this as a process of encoding and decoding is to see it too mechanically. What is missing from this formulation is a sense of the complex to-ing and fro-ing of meanings being defined in and through a common ground, a common ground of commonplaces (of received wisdoms, and the familiar metaphors and tropes of contemporary culture). And what is involved is simultaneously a process of cognition and recognition, as viewers engage with (or resist) television's rhetorical appeal.

[...]

The rhetorical address, then, offers a distinct discursive space – both claiming and inviting – in which viewers of documentary, prototypically, as well as other television genres, negotiate their meanings: a space to think, a space to persuade and be persuaded, a space to affect and be affected. This discursive space is the one we in turn think of when we discuss effects on attitudes and influences on behaviour. It is the space in which things are learnt and where we may (or may not) be persuaded to change our minds. It is a space of attention, of primary viewing. But it is not the only discursive space released by television in general or documentary in particular.

PLAY

I want now to change focus slightly. I have already observed that textual claims are not simply the product of a text and that context too, in this case the context of the televisual, has to be understood as dynamic. The rhetorical appeal of a specific documentary, and the discursive space that it claims and enables, has therefore to be understood alongside or against another set of claims which derive as much from the medium as from the message. It is this other set of claims which I now want to consider. The claims concern play.

Play, it has been argued, is a central component of what is to be human. Jan Huizinga, in his seminal (but much criticized) essay on play in human society, defines it in the following way:

> [P]lay is a voluntary activity. Play to order is no longer play . . . A second characteristic is closely connected with this, namely, that play is not 'ordinary' or 'real' life. It is rather a stepping out of 'real' life into a temporary sphere of activity with a disposition all of its own . . . As regards its formal characteristics, all students lay stress on the *disinterestedness* of play. Not being 'ordinary' life it stands outside the immediate satisfaction of wants and appetites . . . Play is distinct from 'ordinary' life both as to locality and duration. This is the third main characteristic of play: its secludedness, its limitedness . . . [play] creates order, is order . . . All play has its rules. They determine what 'holds' in the temporary world circumscribed by play. (Huizinga 1970: 26–30)

For Huizinga, play involves, both literally and metaphorically, a bounded space. Play is the general category of which games are the specific embodiment, so the notion of play both exceeds and contains the game. Play is associated with ritual, and ritual with performance. Play involves the suspension of dis belief, not 'complete illusion' (*ibid.*: 41). Play lies outside morals. It is neither good nor bad. Huizinga's pursuit of play and games leads him, as other commentators have noted, into a less than satisfactory terrain of elitist and pessimistic judgements. His arguments also tend to misread the social significance of play and especially games, placing both play and games unreasonably outside the material world and excluding material interest. He also fails to develop any significant psychology of play, ignoring especially, as George Steiner (1970) points out, the contribution that psychoanalysis had already made at the time of his writing to an understanding of play.

I have argued elsewhere (Silverstone 1981) for a conceptualization of television which takes its relation to play seriously. In this conceptualization television's mediation is seen as being dependent on its capacity to engage an audience within spaces and times that are distinguished – marked off – from the otherwise relentless confusions of everyday life. This can be seen to be expressed in the physical presence of the television set and in the presence or co-presence of viewers within its range. It can also be found within the frame of the screen, and within the bounded security of the schedule and of narrative forms. It can be identified within the rules of behaviour and precedence that individuals and families insist upon, the more or less ritualized, taken-for-granted patterns of behaviour that mark the viewing experience (the control of the remote, the favourite chair, the rules of inclusion or exclusion; for example adults excluding children on the basis of judgements of suitability of programming, children excluding adults – especially in watching videos – for similar reasons). In each of these broad dimensions of television a distinct discursive space emerges, structured through textual claims and social practices quite different from those already identified as emerging from television's rhetoric.

Roger Caillois (1958) both develops and offers a critique of Huizinga. Play involves freedom within rule-governed limits. He, too, describes play as essentially free, circumscribed within limits of time and space, uncertain, unproductive, governed by rules under conventions that suspend ordinary laws, and involving make-believe. It is 'accompanied by a special awareness of a second reality or of a free unreality, as against real life' (*ibid.*: 10). Play is therefore simultaneously both inside and outside everyday life, contained within the holding structures of the ordinary, but released from and legitimated by that ordinary as distinct and, arguably, in their containment, as a consequence, relatively unthreatening.

[. . .]

[. . .] I want to follow Huizinga and Caillois in stressing the centrality of play to television, a centrality that can be explored both through the specificities of genre and programming and through the character of the viewing experience. Play involves, as does rhetoric, mutual participation; players and audiences, and audiences who become, even at one remove, players, together are involved in a specific discursive space that television claims and constructs. It is important to note here, as Caillois does particularly, the tensions identified in play and games between 'contained freedom', 'secure creativity', 'active passivity', 'voluntary dependence' – both of the TV experience as a whole (if such a thing exists), but mobilized and reinforced by particular kinds of texts, and by the continuities and consistencies of the textualities of the interruptible flow of television. There is a precariousness in television play, the product of this constant tension between the two sides of the oxymora of the medium. It is a precariousness recognized by the psychoanalyst D. W. Winnicott in his discussion of the relationship between playing and reality:

> Play is immensely exciting. It is exciting not because the instincts are involved, *be it understood*! The thing about playing is always the precariousness of the interplay of personal psychic reality and the experience of control of actual objects. This is the precariousness of magic itself, magic that arises in intimacy, in a relationship that is being found to be reliable. (Winnicott 1971: 55)

Winnicott places play at the centre of his psychology of childhood. He sees play as being at the heart of culture in a psychodynamic sense. His approach is based on the analysis of the pre-linguistic child and his or her object-relations, principally and initially with the mother, and then in a process of separation and individuation with transitional objects which become the site of fantasy, and the negotiation of illusion and disillusion. Here, too, play occupies a space, both literally and metaphorically, in which the trusting child explores the world through the manipulation of objects and the construction of fantasy. Through play, and within an environment which offers trust and security, and in which play can be both stimulated and contained, a child pleasurably constructs for herself or himself a place in culture. Play occupies and depends on a transitional space, transitional between the inner world and external reality in which, as it were, both can be tested against one another in a creative way. This is what the child does, argues Winnicott, in the manipulation of objects; playing is doing. External reality is tested; internal reality is defined, gradually, through such testing and through the near-hallucination that play requires.

Here is a possible approach to the psychology of play which links closely with the broader culturalist theories so far discussed but which provides an element that neither of the earlier theories adequately provides. Together they find play to be a central component of culture, and in each case there is a tension between a view of play as both, or either, progressive and regressive. Despite the clinical approach in the psychoanalyst and the moral-political approach in the two cultural critics, play as such is not seen as essentially either negative or positive. What they share also is a sense of the specialness of play, its location in distinct spaces and times, protected and trusted spaces and times, and spaces and times in which all participants (all of whom might be considered as players) engage in a distinct if often extremely limited creative work.

Whereas it could be argued that it is the *commonplace* that provides the ground for a meeting of speaker and listener, a condition for the possibility of the participation of receivers in the discursive space created by *rhetoric* (a cognitive security), in *play* that role is taken by the trust of a shared or shareable set of rules and the consequent emotional security that this offers; and in *performance*, as I shall go on to argue, such participation is predicated on a shared or shareable *identification* – though, as I shall suggest, not in any singular or straightforward way.

I suggest that the textual claims of television involve both a rhetorical and a ludic appeal. In *Television and Everyday Life* (Silverstone 1994) I argued for an ontological security/transitional object model for television as a whole. This general and perhaps overly reductive approach requires some modification, confronted as it is now is with the complexity and specificity of the textual address. [. . .] The discursive spaces offered by television in and to which we as audiences contribute are clearly more complex than a singular model will allow. The claims that television makes are dependent on its status as a specific medium, until now an essentially broadcast medium, and one which is located and consumed principally in the home; but they also depend on the more specific textual claims. This is obvious and challenging, a challenge that is increased once it is recognized that such claims require a response and that they are indeed negotiated on the common ground that familiarity with the medium and with generic conventions both requires and constructs.

[. . .]

PERFORMANCE

In a recent essay Bill Nichols (1994) draws attention to what he takes to be a new mode of documentary address, the 'performative documentary'. The performative documentary involves a suspension of the realist impulse which underpins, in one way or another, all documentary claims:

> Performative documentary puts the referential aspect of the message in brackets, under suspension. Realism finds itself deferred, dispersed, interrupted and postponed. These films make the proposition that it is possible to know difference differently. . . . Performative documentary clearly embodies a paradox: it generates a distinct tension between performance and document, between the personal and the typical, the embodied and disembodied, between, in short, history and science. (Nichols 1994: 96–7)

Performative documentary, in Nichols's view of it, involves a figurative aesthetic, claiming evocative rather than literal truth, iconic rather than indexical, and a dialectic between the particular and the general, the local and the global. Reality is embodied (the body is a social text). Priority is given to affect and to a politics of identity. Nichols suggests that performative documentary is the creation of its time, and in particular of the postmodern turning away from grand narratives and towards the fragmented, dispersed, diasporic cultures of the late twentieth century.

I want to say both more and less than Nichols. Less, because I do not wish to construct specific documentaries as 'performative' necessarily, or even to argue a periodic classification of documentary form as he does. More, because I do want to identify the performative (and performance) as a distinct textual claim and the basis for describing an analytically distinct discursive space.

Performance is the thing done: memory, identity, desire, claimed or fixed, for the moment, in the act, the word, the image. In a sense, and from a certain point of view, the notion of performance is redundant, since the social in its entirety can be (must be) considered as performed in linguistic and symbolic as well as material work. Yet the consideration of the social as performative dislocates action from any ontological grounding, from a security or fixity in time passing, or the mapping of social or physical space. Performance is of the moment, drawing on and in memory, both of performers and audiences, who become – and not even at one remove – performers too. Consideration of the social as performed, and of culture as performative, requires an acceptance that there is no prior reality on which the performance is based or on which it can call. Performance is based on an 'epistemology grounded not on the distinction between truthful models and fictional representations but on different ways of knowing and doing that are constitutionally heterogeneous, contingent and risky' (Diamond 1996: 1). What is fixed, as Judith Butler (1990) argues, is only what is repeated. Performance, then, is both pastiche and parody, yet in both the claims are for originality, for reinscription, redefinition, refiguration.

One thing that postmodernism insists on is the denial of the modernist separation between play and seriousness (Ehrmann 1968; cited in Benamou 1977). This, together with Raymond Williams's (1974) observation that we live in a society dramatized by television, offers a starting point for consideration of how television's mediation within and across its various genres can claim another kind of discursive space, both integrative and transcendent of those offered by rhetoric and play. On the one hand, we can identify the specificity of particular genres and modes of representation and address as Nichols (1994) does in his discussion of documentary. On the other hand, we can see in the fragmentation of television's new forms of textuality, as well as in the behaviour of audiences, in the displaced textuality that presupposes, and to a degree relies on, the mutual fragmentation of narratives and everyday life, the requirement to make and to perform choice and choices, as attention wanders, and as the culture of display becomes ever more insistent and, it might be said, ever more hysterical. At performativity's root is, perhaps, as Benamou (1977: 4) acknowledges an indeterminacy, a denial of the authority of the text, and the (re)assertion of the authority of reader and audience that present theory encourages us to accept. Intertextuality, citation, gossip and the traces of memory and experience are performed in collusion, but also against each other's grain, by texts and audiences together. The performative television text facilitates a discursive space in which its own authority is masked (but never entirely denied) by the liberating freedoms granted to audiences to be and to behave, singularly and collectively, as active participants both with and against the textual grain. Ludic boundaries are breached as games expand into everyday life, as they do perhaps most exceptionally in various manifestations of fan culture. Fans, it could be suggested, are involved in television (and other) texts as, perhaps above all, performers.

As technologies invite more interactivity, as choices, which are perhaps not quite choices, are increasingly being required but at the same time constrained, the discursive spaces that television now creates are increasingly synthetic, both rhetorical and ludic, offering a common ground which is common only for the moment, and whose commonness is claimed as much by the reader as by the text. It is a claim that depends above all on the momentary (but profound) identification of situation and person, image and word, repeated, played back (both literally and metaphorically), structured and restructured in the incessant orality and the continuous interchange of performance.

Identification is a key component of audiences' relationship with what they see and hear on television, and the performative cannot lay claim exclusively to identification as the basis for the common ground which underpins the discursive space that audiences enter. Yet it could be argued that the performative privileges identification, offering experiential truth claims to audiences, truth claims that are grounded in the endlessly iterative figuration of character and situation. Of course, audiences participate in this discursive space, as in others, as social beings. There is no compulsion, no determination. Yet here, as elsewhere, there is a deal, a contract, implicitly made, not necessarily consciously made, among audiences, texts and media, a deal which involves both public and private identities, and public and private communications.

Indeed, within this performativity critics detect a new political space, for critique, for mobilization, and for the construction of both individual and communal identity. Such are the hopes. Yet this televisual performativity has to be understood not just in the relationships between texts and audiences, and in the discursive spaces that are constructed on the common ground between them, but in the compromising contexts of changing media environments. In this sense the naked promise of performance and performativity, as it is articulated in treatises on aesthetics and sexuality – that uniqueness and authenticity can be composed in the event and in its iteration – must be qualified. The new performativity, while distinct in its address from that of rhetoric and play, and inviting quite different modes of engagement, is a performativity mobilized by and on behalf of the same forces that have found in rhetoric and play a way of claiming attention and response. The differences are significant and, although one might be forgiven for supposing that the shift towards performativity is [. . .] symptomatic and even evolutionary, it is possible also to argue *both* that the baseline relationships of a political economy of media still hold and that the discursive spaces released by television are becoming more open, more variable and more contested.

Conclusion

A number of concluding observations can be made.

No single televisual text will create or intend to, or indeed can, create a unitary discursive space, any more than those who watch television operate within one. These spaces conjoin and confront each other, offering distinct, sometimes reinforcing, sometimes contradictory, frameworks for textual engagement or participation.

Scientists, and others, when complaining about the ways in which television treats their profession or their product, tend to base their complaints – principally that science is seen by the media as a singular and uniform activity, and that it is constructed through a very limited repertoire of frameworks – on two presuppositions: first, that television is itself a singular and uniform medium; and, second, that it is essentially passive. An approach which grounds our understanding of neither the medium as singular nor its audiences as passive needs to be based, I would argue, on a more thoroughgoing epistemology of the medium, one which is based on an understanding of what I have described here as the discursive spaces in which television creates and recreates itself each time it is switched on (and also in the secondary discourses and forms of talk that sustain it when it is not being watched – it is, of course, always on).

[. . .]

This [. . .] raises the question of the different terms under and within which viewers or receivers of communication are invited to participate in television's mediation. This is a question of the different epistemologies of viewing that draw together intentions and responses, in both of which agency is involved. Clearly, a sense of these non-discrete but identifiably distinct discursive spaces would force a re-evaluation of the encoding or decoding model of text-audience relationships. It would also challenge the equally reductive notion that audiences come to their viewing with class and gender positions fixed and determining. Finally, it would recover, and necessarily so in my view, a concern with both text and textuality (textuality that includes consideration of technology) as a precondition for any understanding of electronic mediation and for assessing the social and cultural production of knowledge in the late twentieth century.

REFERENCES

Benamou, Michael (1977) 'Presence and play', in Michael Benamou and Charles Caramello (eds) *Performance in Modern Culture*, Madison, WI: Coda Press.

Billig, Michael (1987) *Arguing and Thinking: A Rhetorical Approach to Social Psychology*, Cambridge: Cambridge University Press.

Burke, Kenneth (1962) *A Rhetoric of Motives*, New York: George Brazillier.

Butler, Judith (1990) *Gender Trouble: Feminism and the Subversion of Identity*, London: Routledge.

Caillois, Roger (1958) *Man, Play, and Games*, New York: Free Press.

Clark, Herbert H. and Brennan, Susan E. (1990) 'Grounding in communication', in L. B. Resnick, J. Levine and S. D. Behrend (eds) *Socially Shared Cognition*, American Psychological Association.

de Certeau, Michel (1984) *The Practice of Every Day Life*, Berkeley, CA: University of California Press.

Diamond, Elin (ed.) (1996) *Performance and Cultural Politics*, London: Routledge.

Ehrmann, Jacques (ed.) (1968) *Game, Play, Literature*, Boston, MA: Beacon Press.

Huizinga, Jan ([1949] 1970) *Homo Ludens*, London: Maurice Temple Smith.

Lakoff, George and Johnson, Mark (1980) *Metaphors We Live By*, Chicago, IL: Chicago University Press.

Lasswell, Harold (1948) 'The structure and function of communication in society', in L. Bryson (ed.) *The Communication of Ideas: A Series of Addresses*, New York: Harper & Brothers.

Laurel, Brenda (1991/1993) *Computers as Theatre*, Reading, MA: Addison-Wesley.

McKeon, Richard (1987) *Rhetoric: Essays in Invention and Discovery*, Woodbridge: Ox Bow Press.

Morley, David and Silverstone, Roger (1990) 'Domestic communication: technologies and meanings', *Media, Culture and Society* 12(1): 31–56.

Nichols, Bill (1994) *Blurred Boundaries: Questions of Meaning in Contemporary Culture*, Bloomington, IN: Indiana University Press.

Renov, Michael (1993) 'Towards a poetics of documentary', in M. Renov (ed.) *Theorizing Documentary*, New York: Routledge.

Ricoeur, Paul (1980) 'Narrative time', *Critical Inquiry* 7(1): 169–90.

—— (1983) *Time and Narrative*, vol. 1, Chicago, IL: University of Chicago Press.

Silverstone, Roger (1981) *The Message of Television: Myth and Narrative in Contemporary Culture*, London: Heinemann Educational Books.

—— (1994) *Television and Everyday Life*, London: Routledge.

Steiner, George (1970) 'Introduction', in Jan Huizinga ([1949] 1970) *Homo Ludens*, London: Maurice Temple Smith.

Williams, Raymond (1974) *Television: Technology and Cultural Form*, London: Fontana.

Winnicott, D. W. (1971) *Playing and Reality*, Harmondsworth: Penguin.

21

DATABASE AS A SYMBOLIC FORM

Lev Manovich

THE DATABASE LOGIC

After the novel, and subsequently cinema, privileged narrative as the key form of cultural expression of the modern age, the computer age introduces its correlate – database. Many new media objects do not tell stories; they don't have beginning or end; in fact, they don't have any development, thematically, formally or otherwise which would organize their elements into a sequence. Instead, they are collections of individual items, where every item has the same significance as any other.

Why does new media favor database form over others? Can we explain its popularity by analyzing the specificity of the digital medium and of computer programming? What is the relationship between database and another form, which has traditionally dominated human culture – narrative? These are the questions I will address in this article.

Before proceeding I need to comment on my use of the word database. In computer science database is defined as a structured collection of data. The data stored in a database is organized for fast search and retrieval by a computer and therefore it is anything but a simple collection of items. [. . .] New media objects may or may not employ these highly structured database models; however, from the point of view of user's experience a large proportion of them are databases in a more basic sense. They appear as a collection of items on which the user can perform various operations: view, navigate, search. The user experience of such computerized collections is therefore

From Lev Manovich, 'Database as Symbolic Form' (1998).

quite distinct from reading a narrative or watching a film or navigating an architectural site. Similarly, literary or cinematic narrative, an architectural plan and database each present a different model of what a world is like. It is this sense of database as a cultural form of its own which I want to address here. Following art historian Ervin Panofsky's analysis of linear perspective as a 'symbolic form' of the modern age, we may even call database a new symbolic form of a computer age (or, as philosopher Jean-François Lyotard called it in his famous 1979 book. [*The*] *Postmodern Condition*, 'computer-ized society'),[1] a new way to structure our experience of ourselves and of the world. Indeed, if after the death of God (Nietzche), the end of grand Narratives of Enlightenment (Lyotard) and the arrival of the Web (Tim Berners-Lee) the world appears to us as an endless and unstructured collection of images, texts, and other data records, it is only appropriate that we will be moved to model it as a database. But it is also appropriate that we would want to develop poetics, aesthetics, and ethics of this database.

Let us begin by documenting the dominance of database form in new media. The most obvious examples of this are popular multimedia encyclopedias, which are collections by their very definition; as well as other commercial CD-ROM titles which are collections as well – of recipes, quotations, photo-graphs, and so on. The identity of a CD-ROM as a storage media is projected onto another plane, becoming a cultural form of its own. Multimedia works which have 'cultural' content appear to particularly favor the database form. Consider, for instance, the 'virtual museums' genre – CD-ROMs which take the user on a 'tour' through a museum collection. A museum becomes a database of images representing its holdings, which can be accessed in different ways: chronologically, by country, or by artist. Although such CD-ROMs often simulate the traditional museum experience of moving from room to room in a continuous trajectory, this 'narrative' method of access does not have any special status in comparison to other access methods offered by a CD-ROM. Thus the narrative becomes just one method of accessing data among others. Another example of a database form is a multimedia genre which does not [have] an equivalent in traditional media – CD-ROMs devoted to a single cultural figure such as a famous architect, film director or writer. Instead of a narrative biography we are presented with a database of images, sound record-ings, video clips and/or texts which can be navigated in a variety of ways.

CD-ROMs and other digital storage media (floppies, and DVD-ROMs) proved to be particularly receptive to traditional genres which already had a database-like structure, such as a photo-album; they also inspired new database genres, like a database biography. Where the database form really flourished, however, is on the Internet. As defined by original HTML, a Web page is a sequential list of separate elements: text blocks, images, digital video clips, and links to other pages. It is always possible to add a new element to the list – all you have to do is to open a file and add a new line. As a result, most Web pages are collections of separate elements: texts, images, links to other pages or sites. A home page is a collection of personal photographs. A site of a major search engine is a collection of numerous links to other sites (along with a search function, of course). A site of a Web-based TV or radio station offers a collection of video or audio programs along with the option to listen to the current broadcast; but this current program is just one choice among many other programs stored on the site. Thus the traditional broadcasting experience, which consisted solely of a real-time transmission, becomes just one element in a collection of options. Similar to the CD-ROM medium, the Web offered fertile ground to already existing database genres (for instance, bibliography) and also inspired the creation of new ones such as the sites devoted to a person or a phenomenon (Madonna, Civil War, new media theory, etc.) which, even if they contain original material, inevitably center around the list of links to other Web pages on the same person or phenomenon.

The open nature of the Web as medium (Web pages are computer files which can always be edited) means that the Web sites never have to be complete; and they rarely are. The sites always grow. New links are being added to what is already there. It is as easy to add new elements to the end of [a] list as it is to insert them anywhere in it. All this further contributes to the anti-narrative logic of the Web. If new elements are being added over time, the result is a collection, not a story. Indeed, how can one keep a coherent narrative or any other development trajectory through the material if it keeps changing?

DATA AND ALGORITHM

Of course not all new media objects are explicitly databases. Computer games, for instance, are experienced by their players as narratives. In a game, the player is given a well-defined task – winning the match, being first in a race, reaching the last level, or reaching the highest score. It is this task which makes the player experience the game as a narrative. Everything which happens to her in a game, all the characters and objects she encounters either take her closer to achieving the goal or further away from it. Thus, in contrast to the CD-ROM and Web databases, which always appear arbitrary since the user knows that additional material could have been added without in any way modifying the logic of the database, in a game, from a user's point of view, all the elements are motivated (i.e., their presence is justified).

Often the narrative shell of a game ('you are the specially trained commando who has just landed on a Lunar base; your task is to make your way to the headquarters occupied by the mutant base personnel . . .') masks a simple algorithm well-familiar to the player: kill all the enemies on the current level, while collecting all [the] treasures it contains; go to the next level and so on until you reach the last level. [. . .] While computer games do not follow database logic, they appear to be ruled by another logic – that of an algorithm. They demand that a player executes an algorithm in order to win.

An algorithm is the key to the game experience in a different sense as well. As the player proceeds through the game, she gradually discovers the rules which operate in the universe constructed by this game. She learns its hidden logic, in short its algorithm. Therefore, in games where the game play departs from following an algorithm, the player is still engaged with an algorithm, albeit in another way: she is discovering the algorithm of the game itself. I mean this both metaphorically and literally: for instance, in a first person shooter, such as 'Quake,' the player may eventually notice that under such and such condition the enemies will appear from the left, i.e. she will literally reconstruct a part of the algorithm responsible for the game play. [. . .]

What we encountered here is an example of the general principle of new media: the projection of the ontology of a computer onto culture itself. If in physics the world is made of atoms and in genetics it is made of genes, computer programming encapsulates the world according to its own logic. The world is reduced to two kinds of software objects which are complementary to each other: data structures and algorithms. Any process or task is reduced to an algorithm, a final sequence of simple operations which a computer can execute to accomplish a given task. And any object in the world – be it the population of a city, or the weather over the course of a century, a chair, a human brain – is modeled as a data structure, i.e. data organized in a particular way for efficient search and retrieval. Examples of data structures are arrays, linked lists and graphs. Algorithms and data structures have a symbiotic relationship. The more complex the data structure of a computer program, the simpler the algorithm needs to be, and vice versa. Together, data structures and algorithms are two halves of the ontology of the world according to a computer.

The computerization of culture involves the projection of these two fundamental parts of computer software – and of the computer's unique ontology – onto the cultural sphere. If CD-ROMs and Web databases are cultural manifestations of one half of this ontology – data structures, then computer games are manifestations of the second half – algorithms. Games (sports, chess, cards, etc.) are one cultural form which required algorithm-like behavior from the players; consequently, many traditional games were quickly simulated on computers. In parallel, new genres of computer games came into existence such as a first person shooter ('Doom,' 'Quake'). Thus, as was the case with database genres, computer games both mimic already existing games and create new game genres.

It may appear at first sight that data is passive and algorithm is active – another example of passive-active binary categories so loved by human cultures. A program reads in data, executes an algorithm, and writes out new data. [. . .] However, the passive/active distinction is not quite accurate since data does not just exist – it has to be generated. Data creators have to collect data and organize it, or create it from scratch. Texts need to written, photographs need to be taken, video and audio need to be recorded. Or they need to be digitized from already existing media. [. . .] Once it is digitized, the data has to be cleaned up, organized, indexed. The computer age brought with it a new cultural algorithm: reality→media→data→database. The rise of the Web, this gigantic and always changing data corpus, gave millions of people a new hobby or profession: data indexing. There is hardly a Web site which does not feature at least a dozen links to other sites, therefore every site is a type of database. [. . .]

DATABASE AND NARRATIVE

As a cultural form, a database represents the world as a list of items and refuses to order this list. In contrast, a narrative creates a cause-and-effect trajectory of seemingly unordered items (events). Therefore, a database and a narrative are natural enemies. Competing for the same territory of human culture, each claims an exclusive right to make meaning out of the world.

[. . .]

Database becomes the center of the creative process in the computer age. Historically, the artist made a unique work within a particular medium. Therefore the interface and the work were the same; in other words, the level of an interface did not exist. With new media, the content of the work and the interface become separate. It is therefore possible to create different interfaces to the same material. These interfaces may present different versions of the same work, as in David Blair's *WaxWeb*.[2] Or they may be radically different from each other, as in Moscow WWWArt Centre.[3] This is one of the ways in which the already discussed principle of *variability* of new media manifests itself. But now we can give this principle a new formulation. *The new media object consists of one or more interfaces to a database of multimedia material.* If only one interface is constructed, the result will be similar to a traditional art object; but this is an exception rather than the norm.

This formulation places the opposition between database and narrative in a new light, thus redefining our concept of narrative. The 'user' of a narrative is traversing a database, following links between its records as established by the database's creator. An interactive narrative (which can be also called 'hyper-narrative' in an analogy with hypertext) can then be understood as the sum of multiple trajectories through a database. A traditional linear narrative is one, among many other possible trajectories; i.e. a particular choice made within a hyper-narrative. Just as a traditional cultural object can now be seen as a particular case of a new media object (i.e., a new media object which only has one interface), traditional linear narrative can be seen as a particular case of a hyper-narrative.

This 'technical,' or 'material' change in the definition of narrative does not mean that an arbitrary sequence of database records is a narrative. To qualify as a narrative, a cultural object has to satisfy a number of criteria, which literary scholar Mieke Bal defines as follows: it should contain both an actor and a narrator; it also should contain three distinct levels consisting of the text, the story, and the fabula; and its 'contents' should be 'a series of connected events caused or experienced by actors.'[4] Obviously, not all cultural objects are narratives. However, in the world of new media, the word 'narrative' is often used as all-inclusive term, to cover up the fact that we have not yet developed a language to describe these new strange objects. It is usually paired with another over-used word – interactive. Thus, a number of database records linked together so that more than one trajectory is possible, is assumed to constitute 'interactive narrative.' But to just create these trajectories is of course not sufficient; the author also has to control the semantics of the elements and the logic of their connection so that the resulting object will meet the criteria of narrative as outlined above. Another erroneous assumption frequently made is that by creating her own path (i.e., choosing the records from a database in a particular order) the user constructs her own unique narrative. However, if the user simply accesses different elements, one after another, in a usually random order, there is no reason to assume that these elements will form a narrative at all. Indeed, why should an arbitrary sequence of database records, constructed by the user, result in 'a series of connected events caused or experienced by actors'?

In summary, database and narrative do not have the same status in computer culture. In the database/narrative pair, database is the unmarked term.[5] Regardless of whether new media objects present themselves as linear narratives, interactive narratives, databases, or something else, underneath, on the level of material organization, they are all databases. In new media, the database supports a range of cultural forms which range from direct translation (i.e., a database stays a database) to a form whose logic is the opposite of the logic of the material form itself – a narrative. More precisely, a database can support narrative, but there is nothing in the logic of the medium itself which would foster its generation. It is not surprising, then, that databases occupy a significant, if not the largest, territory of the new media landscape. What is more surprising is why the other end of the spectrum – narratives – still exist in new media.

The Semiotics of Database

The dynamics which exist between database and narrative are not unique in new media. The relation between the structure of a digital image and the languages of contemporary visual culture is characterized by the same dynamics. As defined by all computer software, a digital image consists of a number of separate layers, each layer containing particular visual elements. Throughout the production process, artists and designers manipulate each layer separately; they also delete layers and add new ones. Keeping each element as a separate layer allows the content and the composition of an image to be changed at any point: deleting a background, substituting one person for another, moving two people closer together, blurring an object, and so on. What would a typical image look like if the layers were merged together? The elements contained on different layers will become juxtaposed resulting in a montage look. Montage is the default visual language of composite organization of an image. However, just as database supports both the database form and its opposite – narrative – a composite organization of an image on the material level supports two opposing visual languages. One is modernist-MTV montage – [the] two-dimensional juxtaposition of visual elements designed to shock due to its impossibility in reality. The other is the representation of familiar reality as seen by a photo of a film camera (or its computer simulation, in the case of 3-D graphics). During the 1980s and 1990s all image-making technologies became computer-based thus turning all images into composites. In parallel, a renaissance of montage took place in visual culture, in print, broadcast design and new media. This is not unexpected – after all, this is the visual language dictated by the composite organization. What needs to be explained is why photorealist images continue to occupy such a significant space in our computer-based visual culture.

It would be surprising, of course, if photorealist images suddenly disappeared completely. The history of culture does not contain such sudden breaks. Similarly, we should not expect that new media would completely substitute narrative by database. New media does not radically break with the past; rather, it distributes weight differently between the categories which hold culture together, foregrounding what was in the background, and vice versa. As Frederick Jameson writes in his analysis of another shift, in this case from modernism to post-modernism: 'Radical breaks between periods do not generally involve complete changes but rather the restructuration of a certain number of elements already given: features that in an earlier period of system were subordinate become dominant, and features that had been dominant again become secondary.'[6]

Database–narrative opposition is the case in point. To further understand how computer culture redistributes weight between the two terms of opposition in computer culture I will bring in a semiological theory of syntagm and paradigm. According to this model, originally formulated by Ferdinand de Saussure to describe natural languages such as English and later expanded by Roland Barthes and others to apply to other sign systems (narrative, fashion, food, etc.), the elements of a system can be related on two dimensions: syntagmatic and paradigmatic.[7] As defined by Barthes, 'the syntagm is a combination of signs, which has space as a support.' To use the example of natural language, the speaker produces an utterance by stringing together the elements, one after another, in a linear sequence. This is the syntagmatic dimension. Now, let's look at the paradigm. To continue with an example of a language user, each new element is chosen from a set of other related elements. For instance, all nouns form a set; all synonyms of a particular word form another set. In the original formulation of Saussure, 'the units which have something in common are associated in theory and thus form groups within which various relationships can be found.'[8] This is the paradigmatic dimension.

The elements on a syntagmatic dimension are related *in praesentia*, while the elements on a paradigmatic dimension are related *in absentia*. For instance, in the case of a written sentence, the words which comprise it materially exist on a piece of paper, while the paradigmatic sets to which these words belong only exist in the writer's and reader's minds. Similarly, in the case of a fashion outfit, the elements which make it, such as a skirt, a blouse, and a jacket, are present in reality, while pieces of clothing which could have been present instead – different skirt, different blouse, different jacket – only exist in the viewer's imagination. Thus, syntagm is explicit and paradigm is implicit; one is real and the other is imagined.

Literary and cinematic narratives work in the same way. Particular words, sentences, shots, scenes which make up a narrative have a material existence; other elements which form an imaginary world of an author or a particular literary or cinematic style and which could have appeared instead exist only virtually. Put differently, the database of choices from which narrative is constructed (the paradigm) is implicit, while the actual narrative (the syntagm) is explicit.

New media reverses this relationship. Database (the paradigm) is given material existence, while narrative (the syntagm) is de-materialized. Paradigm is privileged, syntagm is downplayed. Paradigm is real, syntagm is virtual. To see this, consider the new media design process. The design of any new media object begins with assembling a database of possible elements to be used. [. . .] This database is the center of the design process. It typically consists [of] a combination of original and stock material distributed such as buttons, images, video and audio sequences, 3-D objects, behaviors and so on. Throughout the design process new elements are added to the database; existing elements are modified. The narrative is constructed by linking elements of this database in a particular order, i.e. designing a trajectory leading from one element to another. On the material level, a narrative is just a set of links; the elements themselves remain stored in the database. Thus the narrative is more virtual than the database itself. (Since all data is stored as electronic signals, the word 'material' seems to be no longer appropriate. Instead we should talk about different degrees of virtuality.)

The paradigm is privileged over syntagm in yet another way in interactive objects presenting the user with a number of choices at the same time – which is what typical interactive interfaces do. For instance, a screen may contain a few icons; clicking on each icon leads the user to a different screen. On the level of an individual screen, these choices form a paradigm of their own which is explicitly presented to the user. On the level of the whole object, the user is made aware that she is following one possible trajectory among many others. In other words, she is selecting one trajectory from the paradigm of all trajectories which are defined.

[. . .]

Interactive interfaces foreground the paradigmatic dimension and often make explicit paradigmatic sets. Yet, they are still organized along the syntagmatic dimension. Although the user is making choices at each new screen, the end result is a linear sequence of screens which she follows. This is the classical syntagmatic experience. In fact, it can be compared to constructing a sentence in a natural language. Just as a language user constructs a sentence by choosing each successive word from a paradigm of other possible words, a new media user creates a sequence of screens by clicking on this or that icon at each screen. Obviously, there are many important differences between these two situations. For instance, in the case of a typical interactive interface, there is no grammar and paradigms are much smaller. Yet, the similarity of basic experience in both cases is quite interesting; in both cases, it unfolds along a syntagmatic dimension.

Why does new media insist on this language-like sequencing? My hypothesis is that it follows the dominant semiological order of the twentieth century – that of cinema. Cinema replaced all other modes of narration with a sequential narrative, an assembly line of shots which appear on the screen one at a time. For centuries, a spatialized narrative where all images appear simultaneously dominated European visual culture; then it was delegated to 'minor' cultural forms as comics or technical illustrations. 'Real' culture of the twentieth century came to speak in linear chains, aligning itself with the assembly line of an industrial society and the Turing machine of a post-industrial era. New media continues this mode, giving the user information one screen at a time. At least, this is the case when it tries to become 'real' culture (interactive narratives, games); when it simply functions as an interface to information, it is not ashamed to present much more information on the screen at once, be it in the form of tables, normal or pull-down menus, or lists. In particular, the experience of a user filling in an online form can be compared to pre-cinematic spatialized narrative: in both cases, the user is following a sequence of elements which are presented simultaneously.

A Database Complex

To what extent is the database form intrinsic to modern storage media? For instance, a typical music CD is a collection of individual tracks grouped together. The database impulse also drives much of photography throughout its history, from William Henry Fox Talbot's 'Pencil of Nature' to August Sander's monumental typology of modern German society 'Face of Our Time,' to the Bernd and Hilla Becher's equally obsessive cataloging of water towers. Yet, the connection between storage media and database forms is not universal. The prime exception is cinema. Here the storage media supports the narrative imagination. We may quote once again Christian Metz who wrote in the 1970s, 'Most films shot today, good or bad, original or not, "commercial" or not, have as a common characteristic that they tell a story; in this measure they all belong to one and the same genre, which is, rather, a sort of "super-genre" ["sur-genre"].'[9] Why then, in the case of photography storage media, does technology sustain database, while in the case of cinema it gives rise to a modern narrative form par excellence? Does this have to do with the method of media access? Shall we conclude that random access media, such as computer storage formats (hard drives, removable disks, CD-ROMs), favor database, while sequential access media, such as film, favor narrative? This does not hold either. For instance, a book, this perfect random-access medium, supports database forms such as photo-albums and narrative forms such as novels.

Rather than trying to correlate database and narrative forms with modern media and information technologies, or deduce them from these technologies, I prefer to think of them as two competing imaginations, two basic creative impulses, two essential responses to the world. Both have existed long before modern media. The ancient Greeks produced long narratives, such as Homer's epic poems *The Iliad* and *The Odyssey*; they also produced encyclopedias. The first fragments of a Greek encyclopedia to have survived were the work of Speusippus, a nephew of Plato. Diderot wrote novels – and also was in charge of [the] monumental *Encyclopédie*, the largest publishing project of the 18th century. Competing to make meaning out of the world, database and narrative produce endless hybrids. It is hard to find a pure encyclopedia without any traces of a narrative in it and vice versa. For instance, until alphabetical organization became popular a few centuries ago, most encyclopedias were organized thematically, with topics covered in a particular order (typically, corresponding to [the] seven liberal arts). At the same time, many narratives, such as the novels by Cervantes and Swift, and even Homer's epic poems – the founding narratives of the Western tradition – traverse an imaginary encyclopedia.

Modern media are the new battlefield for the competition between database and narrative. It is tempting to read the history of this competition in dramatic terms. First the medium of visual recording – photography – privileges catalogs, taxonomies and lists. While the modern novel blossoms, and academicians continue to produce historical narrative paintings all through the nineteenth century, in the realm of the new techno-image of photography, database rules. The next visual recording medium – film – privileges narrative. Almost all fictional films are narratives, with few exceptions. [The] magnetic tape used in video does not bring any substantial changes. Next storage media – computer-controlled digital storage devices (hard drives, removable drives, CD-ROMs, DVD-ROMs) privilege database once again. Multimedia encyclopedias, virtual museums, pornography, artists' CD-ROMs, library databases, Web indexes, and, of course, the Web itself: database is more popular than ever before.

Digital computer turns out to be the perfect medium for the database form. Like a virus, databases infect CD-ROMs and hard drives, servers and Web sites. Can we say that database is the cultural form most characteristic of a computer? In her 1978 article 'Video: The Aesthetics of Narcissism,' probably the single most well-known article on video art, art historian Rosalind Krauss argued that video is not a physical medium but a psychological one. In her analysis, 'video's real medium is a psychological situation, the very terms of which are to withdraw attention from an external object – an Other – and invest it in the Self.'[10] In short, video art is a support for the psychological condition of narcissism. Do new media similarly function to play out a particular psychological condition, something which can be called a database complex? In this respect, it is interesting that database imagination has accompanied computer art from its very beginning. In the 1960s, artists working with computers wrote programs to systematically explore the combinations of different visual elements. In part they were following art world trends such as minimalism. Minimalist artists executed works of art according to pre-existent plans; they also created series of images or objects by systematically varying a single parameter. So, when minimalist artist Sol LeWitt spoke of an artist's idea as 'the machine which makes the work,' it was only logical to substitute the human executing the idea by a computer.[11] At the same time, since the only way to make pictures with a computer was by writing a computer program, the logic of computer programming itself pushed computer artists in the same directions. Thus, for artist Frieder Nake a computer was a 'Universal Picture Generator,' capable of producing every possible picture out of a combination of available picture elements and colors.[12] In 1967 he published a portfolio of 12 drawings which were obtained by successfully multiplying a square matrix by itself. Another early computer artist Manfred Mohr produced numerous images which recorded various transformations of a basic cube.

[. . .] Today all software for media creation arrives with endless 'plug-ins' – the banks of effects which with a press of a button generate interesting images from any input whatsoever. In parallel, much of the aesthetics of computerised visual culture is effects driven, especially when a new techno-genre (computer animation, multimedia, Web sites) is just getting established. For instance, countless music videos are variations of Witney's 'Catalog' – the only difference is that the effects are applied to the images of human performers. This is yet another example of how the logic of a computer – in this case, the ability of a computer to produce endless variations of elements and to act as a filter, transforming its input to yield a new output – becomes the logic of culture at large.

NOTES

1. Jean-François Lyotard, *The Postmodern Condition: A Report on Knowledge*, trans. Geoff Bennington and Brian Massumi (Minneapolis: University of Minnesota Press, 1984), 3.
2. http://jefferson.village.virginia.edu/wax/, accessed September 12, 1998.
3. http://www.cs.msu.su/wwwart/, accessed October 22, 1998.
4. Mieke Bal, *Narratology: Introduction to the Theory of Narrative* (Toronto: University of Toronto Press, 1985), 8.

5. The theory of markedness was first developed by linguists of the Prague School in relation to phonology but subsequently applied to all levels of linguistic analysis. For example, 'bitch' is the marked term and 'dog' the unmarked term. Whereas 'bitch' is used only in relation to females, 'dog' is applicable to both males and females.

6. Fredric Jameson, 'Postmodernism and Consumer Society,' in *The Anti-Aesthetic. Essays on Postmodern Culture*, ed. Hal Foster (Seattle: Bay Press, 1983), 123.

7. Roland Barthes, *The Elements of Semiology* (New York: Hill and Wang, 1968), 58.

8. Ibid.

9. Christian Metz, 'The Fiction Film and its Spectator: A Metapsychological Study,' in *Apparatus*, edited by Theresa Hak Kyung Cha (New York: Tanam Press, 1980), p. 402.

10. Rosalind Krauss, 'Video: The Aesthetics of Narcissism,' in *Video Culture*, edited by John Hanhardt (Rochester: Visual Studies Workshop, 1987), 184.

11. Qtd. in Sam Hunter and John Jacobus, *Modern Art: Painting, Sculpture and Architecture*, 3rd ed. (New York: Abrams, 1992), 326.

12. Frank Dietrich, 'Visual Intelligence: The First Decade of Computer Art (1965–1975),' *IEEE Computer Graphics and Applications* (July 1985), 39.

FURTHER READING

Barthes, R., *Mythologies* (London: Paladin, 1973).
Barthes, R., *Image-Music-Text*, trans. S. Heath (Glasgow: Fontana, 1977).
Bignell, J., *Media Semiotics* (Manchester: Manchester University Press, 2002).
Cohan, S. and Shires, L. M., *Telling Stories: Theoretical Analysis of Narrative Fiction* (London: Routledge, 1988).
Dyer, R., *The Matter of Images* (London: Routledge, 1993).
Ellis, J., *Visible Fictions* (London: Routledge, 1982).
Gripsrud, J. (ed.), *Television and Common Knowledge* (London: Routledge, 1999).
Hall, S. (ed.), *Representation* (London: Sage, 1997).
Hawkes, T., *Structuralism and Semiotics*, 2nd edn (London: Routledge, 2003).
Manovich, L., *The Language of New Media* (Cambridge, MA and London: MIT Press, 2002).
Neale, S., *Genre* (London: BFI, 1981).
Neale, S., 'Questions of Genre', *Screen* 31:1 (1990) pp. 45–66.
Perkins, T. E., 'Rethinking Stereotypes', in M. Barrett, P. Corrigan, A. Kuhn and J. Wolff (eds), *Ideology and Cultural Production* (London: Croom Helm, 1979) pp. 135–59.
Pickering, M., *Stereotyping: The Politics of Representation* (London: Palgrave Macmillan, 2001).
Rose, G., *Visual Methodologies: An Introduction to the Interpretation of Visual Methods* (London: Sage, 2006).
Silverstone, R., *The Message of Television: Myth and Narrative in Contemporary Culture* (London: Heinemann, 1981).
Williams, R., *Raymond Williams on Television*, ed. A. O'Connor (London: Routledge, 1989).
Williams, R., *Television, Technology and Cultural Form* (London: Routledge, 1990).

3.2
THE POLITICS OF REPRESENTATION

INTRODUCTION: THE POLITICS OF REPRESENTATION

The previous section introduced the notion that the textual structures which comprise representations can never be separated from questions of social power. As we saw in the case of stereotypes, it is always necessary to ask in whose interests representations have been produced and whose definitions of reality we are seeing. This link between social and representational or symbolic power has been theorised via a number of key concepts. The first is the Marxist concept of *ideology*. Marx argued that those groups who have economic dominance in a society also control the production and circulation of that society's 'ruling ideas'. In this view, particularly as it was further developed by French philosopher Louis Althusser (see Althusser, 1971), media representations function to make structures of social dominance appear natural and inevitable, and thus determine not only the frameworks through which we understand our lives, but also – and in consequence – the way we live them. A second key concept is that introduced by the Italian Marxist, Antonio Gramsci, who substituted for the idea of ideological determination that of *hegemony*. In Gramsci's view (see Gramsci, 1998, 2000; Jones, 2006), ideological power can never be secured once and for all; dominant groups must operate through persuasion and negotiation. Hegemonic power is power which is gained through winning the consent of subordinated groups. In this view, media representations are key sites of this struggle over meaning, with popular genres acting – through their patterns of repetition and innovation[1] – to articulate and work through points of ideological tension.

In her chapter on the situation comedy (Chapter 22), Janet Woollacott discusses the distinctive nature of the sitcom narrative, with its 'circularity' and lack of narrative progression. This, together with the use of stereotyping, leads to the question of whether sitcom humour is inevitably ideologically reactionary. Does it serve to reconcile people to their social conditions, or can it function as a vehicle of ideological resistance? Woollacott's response, which draws on Gramsci's concept of hegemony, is that the answer cannot be found in an examination of the text alone, but must consider the ways in which it, and popular fictional genres in general, intersect with the more general 'ideological formations' of the time, serving either to reinforce or to subvert them.

Chapters 23 and 24 shift our attention to questions of race and ethnicity, and in doing so also indicate a shift in theoretical framework. The Marxist framework on which the concepts of ideology and hegemony were based relied on class as its 'master category'. The move to simultaneously retain the concept of power as central to the understanding of representations while also broadening the social categories through which power could be seen to operate led to the use of a new organising theoretical concept, that of *discourse*. In Michel Foucault's formulation of this concept (Foucault, 1970, 1977, 1995), discourses are ways of constructing knowledge about specific topics or practices. Through their construction of 'regimes of truth' they determine those meanings and definitions which are deemed 'legitimate'. They are thus connected both to social institutions and practices – we can think of medical or legal discourse, for example – and to social power. For Foucault, then, 'There is no power relation without the correlative constitution of a field of knowledge, nor any knowledge that does not presuppose and constitute at the same time, power relations' (1977: 27). In adopting this framework, accounts of media representations could broaden their account of the field of power relations, or a society's dominant 'discursive formations'.

Stuart Hall's ground-breaking 'New Ethnicities' (Chapter 23) introduces the concept of a 'politics of representation' in his account of what he describes as a new phase of black cultural politics. The 'black subject', he argues, does not exist prior to representation, but is constructed within representation or discourse. These representations are thus both complex – manifesting, for example, both fear and desire on the part of dominant white discourses – and crossed also by other relations of power such as 'class, gender, sexuality and ethnicity'. They can also be contested, through representations which seek to construct 'a more diverse conception of ethnicity, to set against the embattled, hegemonic conception of "Englishness" which . . . stabilizes so much of the dominant political and cultural discourse'.

Chapter 24, by Linda Williams, continues some of these themes, this time in relation to pornography. Probing difficult questions of 'power and pleasure in interracial lust', Williams argues that an examination of pornography can reveal the mechanisms of a 'racialized sexuality', underpinned by white–black power relations, which have been concealed within more mainstream Hollywood representations. Arguing that representations of 'interracial lust' are grounded in racialised differences in power which have 'covertly permitted the white man's sexual access to black women and violently forbidden the black man's access to white women', she goes on to ask what functions these stereotyped representations serve today. Her answer is that such representations – which still 'pivot on the white man's power' – continue to depend for their appeal on a mixture of fear and desire. Their availability today to an audience which can include white and black women and men, however, renders this appeal far more ambivalent. The visual pleasures produced by such stereotypes can never be uncoupled from their history in unequal power relations, but neither do they remain wholly fixed by them.

Paul Gilroy's 'Between the Blues and the Blues Dance' (Chapter 25) also deals with questions of race, ethnicity, cultural power and desire, but this time in relation to the pleasures of sound. Gilroy takes Jimi Hendrix's notion of the 'electric church' as a way of exploring the kinds of 'cultural work' undertaken by black British diasporic communities in producing a distinctive 'black Atlantic' popular music which would both challenge and change British popular culture. The communal spaces in which such music was made and enjoyed, argues Gilroy, 'hosted a complex process of intercultural and transcultural syncretism'. Incorporating elements from Africa, the Caribbean and America, this 'world of sound' could be used to work through memories of slavery and colonialism and at the same time assert the promise of what Gilroy calls 'an alternative moral, artistic and political order' of the future.

The final chapter of this section returns us to television, although it is the contemporary genre of lifestyle and 'reality' programming in which the television text is further dispersed into accompanying websites and web diaries. In Chapter 26 Andrew Gorman-Murray addresses these examples of what Mike Featherstone has called 'the aesthetization of everyday life' (1991: 25), and the increasing presence within them of images of 'gay domesticity'. Examining two particular examples of Australian 'homemaking' programmes which featured the presence of gay male couples, he suggests that these images of the 'domestic' gay man present 'a *paradox*'. While they may serve to destabilise heteronormative discourses of domesticity and the home, by 'queering' images of Australian domestic life, they may equally work to 'sanitise' representations of gay men by linking gay masculinity with ideals of domestic family life acceptable to the mainstream. Using a rather different theoretical framework, then, Gorman-Murray, like Janet Woollacott, suggests that the meaning of representations cannot be read simply through attention to the representation itself. Instead, its positioning within wider discursive, or ideological, formations is crucial. Representations are always the product of specific historical conjunctures and specific relations of power, and remain an arena of contestation over meaning.

NOTE

1. For further discussion of this, see Chapter 19.

REFERENCES

Althusser, L., 'Ideology and Ideological State Apparatuses', *Lenin and Philosophy and Other Essays*, trans. Ben Brewster (London: New Left Books, 1971).

Featherstone, M., *Consumer Culture and Postmodernism* (London: Sage, 1991).

Foucault, M., *The Order of Discourse: An Archaeology of the Human Sciences* (London: Tavistock, 1970).

Foucault, M., *Discipline and Punish* (London: Tavistock, 1977).

Foucault, M., *Power/Knowledge* (London: Longman, 1995).

Gramsci, A., *Prison Notebooks: Selections*, eds G. Nowell-Smith and Q. Hoare (London: Lawrence & Wishart, 1998).

Gramsci, A., *The Antonio Gramsci Reader*, ed. D. Fourgacs (London: Lawrence & Wishart, 2000).

Jones, S., *Gramsci* (London: Routledge, 2006).

22

FICTIONS AND IDEOLOGIES: THE CASE OF SITUATION COMEDY

Janet Woollacott

Escapist fiction, that which purportedly allows its viewers or readers to 'escape' from the problems of the real world, was the category within which situation comedies found their home in terms of television criticism. Whereas some popular genres show obvious connections with the more general ideological formations in play at the time of their popularity (the spy thriller during the 1960s, for example, or the television crime series during the seventies), situation comedies could be held to have a more general grip on their audience. Over a longer period of time, at least for the last three decades, they have been a consistent part of the flow of the evening's television entertainment, a necessary and vital ingredient in the television controller's strategy for keeping the audience 'tuned in'. Moreover, the popularity of situation comedies has remained, throughout major shifts in more general ideological configurations in the period, and through the rise and decline of other popular genres such as the crime series. It is the aim of this article to outline some of the general characteristics of situation comedies, their narrative and comic strategies, use of character and performance; to consider some of the 'pleasures' of situation comedies and to suggest some of the issues raised by the role of situation comedies in considering the relations betweeen fictions and other ideologies.

Despite the very wide range of targets for joking and humour in situation comedies, the programmes do conform to relatively strict conventions. Clearly some aspects of their formal organisation are related to institutional constraints; the weekly half-hour slot, the limited number of characters and

From T. Bennett, C. Mercer and J. Woollacott (eds), *Popular Culture and Social Relations* (Milton Keynes: Open University Press, 1986) pp. 196–218.

the cheap sets. In this respect and others they can be considered as a television genre. Ryall suggests in relation to film genres that 'genres may be defined as patterns/forms/styles/structures which transcend individual films and which supervise both their construction by the film-maker and their reading by an audience'.[1] In the mutual expectations of television producers and audiences, genre conventions are constantly varied but rarely totally exceeded or broken. Generally situation comedies are pre-eminently texts which are linked to a comfortable practice of reading. As Stephen Neale remarks of all popular genres, 'the existence of genres means that the spectator, precisely, will always know that everything will be made right in the end, that everything will cohere, that any threat or danger in the narrative process itself will always be contained.'[2]

[. . .]

In Eaton's attempt to outline a typology of situation comedy, he suggests that the two basic 'situations' of situation comedy are those of home and work. [. . .] Within these parameters, he argues that the narrative form of situation comedies is organised around an 'inside/outside' dichotomy. Moreover, the dichotomy 'affects every aspect of production down to its finest budgetary details'.[3] In plot terms, this means that events or characters from the outside can be allowed to enter the situation but only in such a way that the outsiders don't affect the situation which can be maintained for future weekly episodes. [. . .] In Eaton's typology, the inscription of the viewer within situation comedies is made manifest rather than being rendered invisible as in so many forms of novelistic fiction. However, this particular form of inscription is not typical of [. . .] many [. . .] situation comedies. Moreover, as Eaton acknowledges, he pays little attention to the pleasures of situation comedy, suggesting only that an analysis of such pleasures would not be incompatible with his typology. One of the problems of Eaton's analysis is the extent to which it relies on simply listing the typical characteristics of situation comedies. For example, the circumstances which Eaton perceptively categorises as 'typical', the small number of characters 'stuck with one another' at work or at home, or in some other boundaried setting, may occur in other genres. The situation of *Blake's Seven*, for example, in which the characters are confined to their spaceship, with fleeting teleported trips to other worlds, is not markedly dissimilar to that described by Eaton as a feature of situation comedies, and for rather similar institutional reasons. Even jokes or comic situations are not limited to situation comedies. Soap operas usually have their comic characters and situations. Regan's wit, in a crime series like *The Sweeney*, is one much quoted reason for his popularity, while part of the format of a James Bond film is to follow an exciting 'action' sequence with a one-line joke from the hero. Indeed, the generic specificity of situation comedy is not really a question of certain exclusive elements ('situation', jokes, etc.) but of particular combinations of elements. In Neale's terms, it's a matter of 'the exclusive and particular weight given in any one genre to elements which in fact it shares with other genres'.[4]

NARRATIVE AND SITUATION COMEDY

Most forms of popular fiction involve a narrative which is initiated through the signification of a disruption, a disturbance, which the narrative proceeds to resolve. The narrative offers to the readers or the viewers a transformation of the initial equilibrium through a disruption and then a reordering of its components. Hence, it could be argued that one of the pleasures of reading a Bond novel rests on the simultaneous existence within the Bond novels of a disturbance both in a discourse of sexuality and in a discourse of imperialism and a progression towards the resolution of those disturbances through the activities of the hero. It is possible to suggest that all genres play with a disturbance, process and closure within the narrative, although in different ways. In so doing, genres construct particular temporal sequences. In the detective story, for example, the enigma with which the narrative begins structures suspense not simply by organising the narrative as a puzzle, but also by setting up a particular temporal sequence. The enigma or disturbance involves separate times; the time of the story behind the crime and the time of its reconstruction in the narrative. Closure is effected through the bringing together of the two times. Thus detective films construct a memory from instances of the story of the crime, from the story of its investigation and from the process of the text itself so that the 'memory constructed within the film duplicates the memory constructed by the film'. The temporal tension produced is the main characteristic of the suspense of a detective story.

The suspense of the thriller form is achieved slightly differently, but one common structure is that of the playing of the protagonist against a grouping of apparently disparate threats. In the Bond novels, the symbolic phallic threat takes a number of forms, that of Bond's substitute father M, that of the villains and that of the heroine. In a crime series programme such as *The Sweeney*, Jack Regan is threatened by criminals and by bureaucratic elements in the law and on occasion by problems with his family or private life. This doubling and occasionally trebling of threats to the hero not only increases the danger to him, but also sets up a temporal sequence involving both the number and complexity of the tasks which have to be performed for an effective and coherent closure to the narrative, for the story to 'end satisfactorily'. Suspense resides in the tension between the viewer's desire for the narrative to progress, although this involves a degree of risk for the hero, and the viewer's desire for the narrative to end, although this requires the full working out of the complex interconnections of the threats to the hero or heroine.[5]

Situation comedies also order the narrative and effect a particular closure, setting up a temporal sequence and positioning the subject, not in suspense but amusement and laughter. Eaton's argument suggests one aspect of the narrative of situation comedies, the lack of 'progression' involved in many situation comedies. In a sense, this lack of progression can only be identified in comparison with other genres, in which the progressive aspect of the narrative, that is the impetus towards the resolution of the initial disturbance, is more strongly weighted. In the opening episode of *Steptoe and Son*, the disturbance from the 'outside', the 'offer', does not lead to an obvious resolution in which either Harold takes the offer and leaves or rejects the offer and stays, but to Harold's inability to take the offer and his remaining without acceptance. In situation comedies, the viewer's pleasure does not lie in the suspense of puzzle-solving nor in the suspense surrounding the hero's ability to cope through action with various tasks and threats. Rather the tension of the narrative to which the viewer responds revolves around the economy or wit with which two or more discourses are brought together in the narrative. The pleasure of situation comedy is linked to the release of that tension through laughter.

Eaton's account of the 'inside/outside' dichotomy in situation comedies indicates the narrative structuring of many situation comedies around an intersection of two discourses. The resolution of the disturbance, the contradictions and resistances of the bringing together of the two discourses, has to be accomplished with economy and wit, with conscious and overt fictional manipulation. The 'circularity' of many situation comedy plots is precisely an indication of that formally articulated wit. In Tony Hancock's 'The Blood Donor', you may remember the narrative follows this type of economic circularity. The episode begins with Hancock's entry into the Blood Donor Department of a hospital.

[. . .]

The two discourses are present from the beginning. On the one hand there is Hancock's discourse, in which the hero constantly and ineffectively seeks higher status, from his name ('Anthony Aloysius St John Hancock' rather than Tony Hancock), his conviction that he has aristocratic connections, to his desire to be given a badge for giving blood. [. . .] On the other hand, there is the discourse of the hospital and the older blood donors, the resisting world against which Hancock's delusions normally clash. The intersection of the two discourses is finally marked in the text of 'The Blood Donor', by Hancock's return to the hospital to be given the pint of blood he had donated earlier. He has cut himself with a kitchen knife.

[. . .]

The pleasure and coherence of this ending is partly one of Hancock's triumph over the hospital and blood donorship. Hancock overcomes the resistance of the hospital and subordinates it to his personal demands, thus reordering the discourses in another relationship to that of the beginning, from one of altruism to one of self-interest. But our amusement is also linked to the way in which Hancock's mixture of self-interest and would-be altruism comes full circle.

The narratives of most popular situation comedies within each episode tend to follow this pattern, although over a whole series the narrative sometimes develops beyond a constant return to square one. *Whatever Happened to the Likely Lads?* sees Terry's return from the army, the re-establishment of his friendship with Bob and the events leading up to Bob's wedding to Thelma and his removal to the Elm Lodge housing estate. The three series of *Agony* see the breakup of agony aunt Jane Luca's marriage to Laurence, her living alone, her affair with Vincent Fish and with Laurence, her pregnancy, return to Laurence and the birth of her child.[6] At the same time, although events happen, the discursive relationships often remain the same. In *Whatever Happened to the Likely Lads?* the clash between Bob and Terry's long-established friendship and common interests and Bob's new relationship with Thelma remains at the centre of the narrative of each episode. Similarly, in *Agony*, the contradiction between Jane's public image of helping others and her private difficulties in helping herself, her husband and friends, continues to provide the mainspring for the comic strategies of each episode.

In one sense, it is quite clear that while watching situation comedies we already know the likely outcome, just as we know the likely outcome of a detective story or a thriller. This does not, however, eradicate a sense of narrative tension. The tension and suspense of situation comedy is produced through a particular organisation of narrative time. A simple internal example of this is the use in situation comedies of the 'anticipation of the inevitable'. The joke is telegraphed in advance and the pleasurable effects are achieved through the viewer's foreknowledge of it. The comedy stems from the timing and economy with which a scene or a series of scenes are treated.

[. . .]

IDEOLOGY AND [STEREOTYPES]

One of the recurring interests in the study of comedy is the issue of its 'subversive' nature. In the British Film Institute's Dossier on situation comedy, the question of whether situation comedy is ideologically incorporative or ideologically subversive is broached time and again and with conclusions varying from seeing situation comedy as essentially conservative despite its reputation for subversion to seeing it as a fictional form which is capable of both inflections.[7]

[. . .]

In the case of situation comedies, one characteristic mode of identifying ideological 'bias' has been that concerned with the use of stereotypes. Stereotypes are forms of characterisation which are simple, memorable, widely recognised and frequently repeated. 'Dumb blondes', for example, are a recognisable type through a range of texts from Judy Holliday in *Born Yesterday*, to Marilyn Monroe in *Some Like It Hot*, to Lucy in the *I Love Lucy* show, to Wendy Craig in situation comedies such as *And Mother Makes Five*. The notion of stereotype assumes, not altogether unjustifiably, that there are important consequences stemming from the repetition of character types.

Stereotyping is not simply a 'neutral' exercise. Forms of stereotyping in the media have been identified as part of the way in which the media define and reinforce the deviant status of particular groups. Pearce sums up news coverage of homosexuality as 'How to be immoral, and ill, pathetic and dangerous, all at the same time'.[8] In a monograph on *Gays and Films*, Sheldon suggests the difficulties for homosexuals of responding to films with negative stereotypes: 'I remember being depressed for days after seeing *Sister George*, feeling "Sure, such a relationship may exist, but what a miserable one, and what's it doing on film to pervert young minds about lesbians"'.[9] Particular stereotypes are often attacked for their failure adequately to convey the 'real', either in terms of the complexity of any one individual or in terms of the range of real concrete individuals, homosexuals, blacks or women, who make up the membership of any particular stereotyped group. Criticism of the characterisation offered in stereotypes often explicitly demands more 'realism', in the sense of being truer to the real individuals outside the text, but it may also, of course, implicitly endorse some forms of signification at the expense of others. The typical characterisation of the nineteenth-century bourgeois novel, for example, is normally seen to be more adequate than that of a popular, contemporary situation comedy. Stereotypes are also attacked, however, for their failure to offer an ideal, a positive rather than a negative image.

Richard Dyer attempts to theorise the positive and negative aspects of stereotypes, by taking up Klapp's distinction between social types and stereotypes:

> stereotypes refer to things outside one's social world, whereas social types refer to things with which one is familiar; stereotypes tend to be conceived of as functionless or dysfunctional (or, if functional, serving prejudice and conflict mainly), whereas social types serve the structure of society at many points.[10]

As Dyer makes clear, most social types turn out to be white, middle class, heterosexual and male, and the distinction between social type and stereotype refers to those characters or types who are to be seen within and outside the boundaries of normal acceptability. Stereotypes in this formulation are inevitably negative. Indeed, Dyer suggests that they form part of a wider strategy of social control.

> The establishment of normalcy through social and stereotypes is one aspect of the habit of ruling groups – a habit of such enormous political consequences that we tend to think of it as far more premeditated than it actually is – to attempt to fashion the whole of society according to their own world-view, value system, sensibility and ideology. So right is the worldview for the ruling groups that they make it appear (as it does

to them) as 'natural' and 'inevitable' – and for everyone – and insofar as they succeed, they establish their hegemony.[11]

There are one or two problems with this outline of the ideological functions of social types and stereotypes. One problem is simply the extent to which a focus on stereotypes and on their repetition leads to the neglect of differences between characters in situation comedies. Wendy Craig's Ria in the BBC2 series *Butterflies*, for example, undoubtedly plays upon certain aspects of the 'dumb blonde' stereotype, but it also differs substantially from the earlier version. Moreover, any analysis which works on the assumption of relatively unambiguous identification between the viewer or reader and the stereotype ignores the way in which identification works through textual and inter-textual formations. Identification with a character in a situation comedy follows both from the articulation of a character within a text and from the spectator's position within a particular reading formation. Neale suggests in relation to film that identification with character depends upon identification with the text itself. 'It is this primary identification that provides the basis of the spectator's relationship to the text and its characters and so requires initial attention and analysis.'[12] In one sense, this simply appears as understanding the function of the character in the text. Hence, the appearance of homosexual characters in *Whatever Happened to the Likely Lads?* appears to function simply to reinforce the 'healthy' heterosexuality of Bob and Terry, despite their intimate friendship. In 'Strangers on a Train' after Bob and Terry have re-established their friendship, they quarrel in the train buffet over Bob's marriage to Thelma. As Bob leaves, full of affronted dignity, Terry orders a Scotch and remarks to the barman that he gave the best years of his life for that man (an implicit reference to his stint in the army). The barman, however, who has been listening sympathetically, puts a comforting hand over Terry's and remarks, 'Never mind, sailor, lots of other pebbles on the beach'. The camera focuses on Terry's aghast reaction to this. The typical and dominant response of the viewer is with Bob and Terry and the camera ensures that it remains with Terry in this case rather than with the barman.

Yet to a large extent, the 'reading' relationships or 'viewing' relationships have to be conceived of in terms of an interrelationship between the reading formations of the viewers and the internal characteristics of the situation comedy. Questions about the subversive or incorporative qualities of stereotypes in situation comedy are fraught with problems, but particularly so when dependent simply on a textual analysis of a situation comedy. Medhurst and Tuck, for example, argue that situation comedies such as *Butterflies* or *Solo* lie outside the main pattern of situation comedy, moving towards melodrama because they involve themes untypical of situation comedy, that the woman rather than the male is seen as the victim of marriage and domesticity. To a certain extent this is seen as an explanation of differing views of these two series.

They are controversial series, liable to cause radical disagreements (not least between the two writers of this essay). Does *Butterflies*, for example, represent any kind of breakthrough in representations of women in comedy, or does it stand as the most insidious example of the method of inoculation? Ria is shown to be unable to cook; do we read this as a positive rejection of the housewifely role or a tired revival of the old jokes about female incompetence? Similarly, in the last episode of the first series of *Solo*, Gemma remarks of her relationship with Danny, 'If only the world hadn't changed and shown me things I really didn't want to see.' This can be taken as a positive acknowledgement of the impact of contemporary feminism, or as a glibly inoculatory gesture towards such an acknowledgement.[13]

But many 'non-controversial' situation comedies allow for different strategies of identification. In *Whatever Happened to the Likely Lads?*, the dominant critical reading undoubtedly involved identification with the 'lads'. Clive James summarises this 'male' view.

> Back from forces, Terry has spent the last couple of months trying to pull the birds. Bob, however, is on the verge of the ultimate step with the dreaded Thelma, and last week felt obliged to get rid of his boyhood encumbrances. Out of the old tea chest came the golden stuff: Dinky toys, Rupert and Picturegoer Annuals, all the frisson inducing junk that Thelma would never let weigh down the shelf units. 'I need those for reference', whined Bob with his arms full of cardboard covered books. There were Buddy Holly 78s – never called singles in those days, as Terry observed with the fantastic pedantry typical of the show. Obviously Bob will have a terrible time with Thelma.[14]

But discussions with Open University Summer School students showed a substantial proportion of them, predominantly women, who identified with Thelma as a strong maternal figure, similar to those in soap operas such as *Coronation Street*, against which the activities of Bob and Terry are simply the amusing antics of children. Clearly, this does not show that *Whatever Happened to the Likely Lads?* is a subversive text, but it does indicate that there can be very different readings of a situation comedy depending upon the operations of gendered reading formations and it itself suggests that any judgement about ideological subversion or incorporation can only be made in relation to the analysis of reading formations or viewing formations over time.

Of course, stereotypes are one attempt to bridge the gap between individual readings and more general ideological formations, but they tend to work in terms of a view in which ruling class ideas are handed down to the masses. Dyer, for example, suggests that stereotypes are one way through which ruling class groups project their own worldview. If, however, the sphere of popular fiction is viewed as occupying an area of exchange and negotiation between ruling groups and subordinate classes, it could still be said to be the case that stereotypes play a particular role in establishing elements of the ideologies of dominant groups. Homosexuals, blacks and women could all be said to have negative images in contrast with white heterosexual males but it can also be argued that there is considerable negotiation around the use of stereotypes, indicated by the shifts and differences in one stereotype across a range of texts and by the way in which social subjects established in different reading formations negotiate identification with a stereotyped character. Thus, the use of stereotypes in popular fictional forms such as situation comedies may be rather less unambiguously a reflection of dominant group views than Dyer suggests.

POPULAR FICTION AND CONSENT

Mick Eaton in a recent article quotes a Tony Allen routine in which the comic is approached by the Anti-Nazi League to perform at one of their benefits. He is questioned over the phone by the organiser over whether his humour is 'anti-black' and replies that it isn't. He is then asked whether his humour is 'anti-women' – he thinks that it isn't. Allen then warns the organiser that his humour has a broader span, 'it's anti-life'. 'That's all right', says the organiser, 'that's not an area of current concern'. Eaton uses the joke to argue that discussions of comedy cannot be separated from the ideological/political positions available in a class society. One way of conceiving the relationships between ideologies and situation comedies is to focus rather less on the 'progressive' or 'non-progressive', 'subversive' or 'non-subversive' polarities of situation comedies and more on the way in which situation comedies perform alongside and in relation to other ideologies.

Traditionally, Marxist theories of ideology were centrally concerned with determination. Indeed, the preoccupation with questions of determination, with the determining relationship between economic base and ideological superstructures, led to the problems of reductionism referred to earlier. Changes in Marxist theories of ideology, initiated largely through the work of Althusser, involved some crucial reformulations in this area. Althusser's 'structuralist' reworking of Marxist theory stressed not the view of ideology as distortion, involving false consciousness, but the notion that ideology constituted the forms and representations through which men and women 'live' in an imaginary relation, their relationship to their real conditions of existence. Althusser's work generally, with its conceptualisation of ideology as determined only 'in the last instance' by the economic base, and in conjunction with developments in semiology, refocused attention on the autonomy and materiality of the ideological and on the notion of articulation, on the relationships between parts within a structure rather than solely on determination. Theories of hegemony make use of the idea of articulation in a particular way to suggest that within a given mode of hegemony, popular consent is won and secured around an articulating principle, which ensures the establishment and reproduction of the interests of ruling groups while at the same time winning popular consent. The success of hegemonic ideological dominance can then be judged by the degree to which the articulating principle secures an ordering of different and potentially oppositional ideological discourses.

The area of popular fiction and popular culture generally works to shift and secure subject positions with the active consent of its readers and viewers. It constitutes a crucial area of negotiation of consent. When forms of popular fiction such as situation comedy rework the subject positions available to viewers they move their viewers on into different ideological frameworks. For example, regardless of whether a series like *Butterflies* truly 'subverts' or really 'incorporates', it does move its viewers on to a different set of ideological coordinates in relation to extramarital sex on the woman's part in terms of past handlings of this theme in situation comedies. In a reading framework of feminist criticism, of course, this move to a new set of ideological coordinates may not appear to be an improvement but it does occur. The popularity of a particular situation comedy or other fictional forms is an indicator of the success of that securing or shifting of subject positions.

In *Policing the Crisis*,[15] the authors outline a number of changes which have taken place in the ideological configurations of post-war Britain. *Policing the Crisis* takes as its starting point the orchestration by the media of mugging as a 'moral panic' and seeks to establish that this represents a movement from a 'consensual' to a more 'coercive' management of the class struggle, which in itself stems from the declining international competitiveness of the British economy following the post-war period, the erosion of which led to attempts to secure 'consent' by more coercive although legitimate means. The immediate post-war period saw the construction of a consensus based on the politics of affluence. Economic decline triggered the disintegration of the 'miracle of spontaneous consent' based on these politics and there was an attempt to put forward a Labourist variant of consent to replace it. The exhaustion of this form of consent, however, combined with the rise of social and political conflict, the deepening of the economic crisis and the resumption of more explicit class struggle, culminated in the 'exceptional' form of class domination through the state in the 1970s, in which the ideological articulating principle was a discourse of 'law and order'.

The media play a central part in this analysis. They are described as a 'key terrain where "consent" is won or lost', as 'a field of ideological struggle'.[16] The key to the media's involvement in the construction of consent lies in the authors' analysis of news as performing a crucial transformative but secondary role in defining social events. The primary definers are those to whom the media turn, their accredited sources in government and other institutions. Although *Policing the Crisis* emphasises the transformative nature of media news reporting, in the selection and structuring of themes and topics, the conception of the media role is one of 'structured subordination' to the primary definers. Further, the creative media role serves to reinforce a consensual view-point, by using public idioms and by claiming to voice public opinion. Thus, in the 'crisis' described, the media have endorsed and enforced primary defini-tions of industrial militancy, troublesome youth cultures, mugging, student protest movements, as part of a 'law and order' problem.

Policing the Crisis confines its account of the media largely to the area of news coverage and only touches upon the area of popular culture tangen-tially. Yet clearly the idea of the dominant articulating principle of ideologi-cal hegemony, a principle which structures ideological discourses and which involves the media in the construction of that articulation, could and should be extended beyond the confines of news coverage. One obvious area for devel-opment is in establishing the relationship between the dominant articulating principle and particular popular fictional genres. Given that genres themselves constitute specific articulations of ideological and formal elements, it would seem to follow that shifts in the dominant articulating principle would be reg-istered in the area of popular fiction by the increased popularity of appropriate genre articulations. The police crime series, for example, became popular at a time when there were major shifts in the dominant articulating principle, from the terrain of ideologies of 'affluence' to that of 'law and order'. The television crime series was a form in which both arguments for and reservations about current 'law and order' issues could be put into play in terms of the subject positions produced by the genre.

Similarly the thriller format developed around notions of Britain's inter-nal and external security in programmes such as *The Professionals* and *Sandbaggers*. *The Professionals* stands at one end of a range of programmes which focus directly on themes of 'law and order' and which extend the notion of policing quite radically. Where programmes such as *The Sweeney* suggested the dissatisfactions of a working policeman in the Flying Squad in terms of the barriers placed by bureaucratic police procedures on the arrest of criminals, *The Professionals* begins from the premise that the ordinary police cannot handle certain problems. One of the books derived from the pro-grammes describes the heroes as the 'hard men'. 'They're the hard men. The Professionals. Doing society's dirty work in the ever more bloody war against violence and destruction . . .'[17]

The process of articulation with a hegemonic principle may help explain one of the continuing problems of the study of genre – why particular genres are popular at any one historical moment and why they may increase or decrease in popularity over time. Works of fiction and specific genres are popular precisely because they articulate, work upon and attempt in different ways to resolve contemporary ideological tensions. The case of situation comedies raises two important issues in relation to this, however. In the first place any comparison of situation comedies and television crime series will indicate something of the complexities of the process whereby popular genres both organise ideological themes differently and interpellate their subjects differently. Thus the episode of *Till Death Us Do Part*, 'If we want a proper democracy we've got to start shooting a few people' (transmission October 1972), constructs one version of the 'law and order' discourse with Garnett 'pulling in' a range of problems into the same problem of law and order.

Alf	. . . Enoch's wrong, having a go at the coons.
Mike and Rita	(astonished) Oh!!!
Alf	Yes! He ain't seen the real danger. It's not the coons. We don't want 'em over here stinking the country out with their curries and making a row on their dustbin lids. But they're bloody harmless – not like yer bloody Russian Unions and yer Chinese *Take-Aways* . . . Hot beds of bloody fifth column they are. But we're on to 'em, don't worry. You'll see the next time one of them commy shop stewards goes in the nick he'll rot there. All they organise them bloody strikes for is so they can get on the bleedin' telly. I blame the BBC for encouraging 'em. They'll put anyone on the bloody telly, they will. Rock an' roll vicars . . . and sex maniacs, an' bloody Irish gunmen. Admit they put stockings over their heads first, but still. They only let the Queen go on for one show at Christmas – I don't know what they've got against that woman. She should have her own series, 'cos she's better'n Lulu. (*Rita giggles*.) Blimey, she's the best thing on at Christmas.

Garnett's mad logic takes the argument on to cover both prison conditions and the unions and the solution to it all.

Alf	And why shouldn't they get bloody slops? Prisons supposed to be a bloody deterrent annit? They ain't supposed to sit about all day scoffing and shagging! (*Else is shocked*.) I mean, blimey, they'll be putting yer Billy Butlin in charge of the prisons soon, and have bloody red-coats for warders! I mean in the old days, they used to put 'em in bloody chains and ship 'em out to the Colonies. But we can't do that now, 'cos your bloody Labour Party gave all the Colonies away. So we have to keep 'em here and feed 'em out of our taxes. And what if five of their ring leaders [of the prison officer's union] defy the law, eh? They can't bung them in prison, 'cos they're already in there.
Else	They'll have to fine their union.

Alf	Don't be so bloody daft. What are they gonna fine them? Eighty gallons of porridge? A hundredweight of hardtack? And another thing what would yer Russians have done, eh? They wouldn't have put them in prison, would they, eh? And your Chinese, eh? If five of their dockers had defied their laws, eh? They wouldn't have put them in prison, would they? Eh? No. They'd have bloody shot 'em.
Mike	And I suppose you'd like to see 'em shoot our dockers, eh?
Alf	We wouldn't! That's the trouble with this country. That's our weakness! If we want a proper democracy here, we've got to start shooting a few people . . . like yer Russians do.[18]

Till Death Us Do Part quite clearly registers a political concern with the ideological themes which were the focal point of other popular genres, notably the television crime series. At the same time, it could be argued that *Till Death Us Do Part* handles those themes rather differently. Garnett's suggestion that 'we've got to start shooting a few people' may sound more than reminiscent of the solution that is found in most episodes of *The Professionals*, but it is also a conclusion that we are supposed to laugh at rather than applaud. Moreover, while *Till Death Us Do Part* was relatively unusual amongst the popular situation comedies of its period in its direct concern with political issues, it was also organised like many other situation comedies to pull the right-wing views of the inimitable Alf Garnett into a family narrative, playing off his position outside a liberal consensus against his position within the family. Later situation comedies such as *Shelley*, *Citizen Smith* or *Agony* dealt with characters and problems relevant to 'law and order' issues (unemployment in *Shelley*, political radicalism in *Citizen Smith* and sexual permissiveness in *Agony*) in a manner which also tended to pull 'deviance' into a familiar sitcom world of 'universal' problems of family, sexuality and class. The crime series, however, tended to place those same problems and characters as threatening to and outside the parameters of the family, class and 'normal' sexuality. In important ways then situation comedies and the crime series in the 1970s work against one another rendering their themes and subjectivities in opposed directions and in so doing indicating something of the complexity of the relationship between a hegemonic principle and the fictional field.

In the second place, popular and controversial situation comedies such as *Till Death Us Do Part* raise certain questions about the relationship between specific fictional forms and more general ideological formations. It is clearly the case that some fictions are not simply popular but also play a particular part in relation to the ordering of other ideologies. Such fictions have a place in the public arena above and beyond their immediate textual base. The public outcry which surrounded *Till Death Us Do Part* and the way in which Alf Garnett became a figure in the popular imagination even for people who didn't watch television indicates this process at work. At specific historical moments, some fictions, rather than working alongside and in relation to other ideologies, come to provide a nexus through which ideologies may be actively reorganised, shifting the subjectivities at their core, while other fictions work precisely to stabilise existing subjectivities. It is in this area that it is possible to establish in historical rather than formal terms the subversive or incorporative qualities of situation comedies. Without work of this order, the discussion of situation comedies in terms of their potentially subversive effects is simply an exercise in criticism, an attempt to organise situation comedies to mean some things and not others, to establish the protocols of viewing: a perfectly legitimate but rather different exercise.

NOTES

1. T. Ryall, 'Teaching through Genre', *Screen Education*, 1976, p. 27.
2. S. Neale, *Genre*, British Film Institute, London, 1980, p. 28.
3. M. Eaton, 'Laughter in the Dark', *Screen Education*, 1981, p. 33.
4. Neale, *Genre*, p. 9.
5. Ibid., p. 27.
6. G. Hickman, *Agony*, Arrow Books, London, 1980.
7. *Television Sitcom*, BFI Dossier no. 17, British Film Institute, London, 1982.
8. F. Pearce, 'How to be immoral and ill, pathetic and dangerous, all at the same time: mass media and the homosexual', in S. Cohen and J. Young (eds), *The Manufacture of News*, Constable, London, 1973, p. 284.
9. Sheldon, quoted in R. Dyer (ed.), *Gays and Films*, British Film Institute, London, 1977, p. 16.
10. Klapp, quoted in Dyer (1977), p. 29.
11. Ibid., p. 30.
12. S. Neale, 'Stereotypes', *Screen Education*, 1979, p. 35.
13. A. Medhurst and L. Tuck, 'The Gender Game', in *British Film Institute Dossier, Television Sitcom*, p. 52.
14. C. James, *The Observer*, 11 March 1972.
15. S. Hall, C. Critcher, T. Jefferson, J. Clarke and B. Roberts, *Policing the Crisis: Mugging, the State and Law and Order*, Macmillan, London, 1978.
16. Ibid., p. 220.
17. K. Blake, *The Professionals 4: Hunter Hunted*, Sphere, London, 1978.
18. J. Speight, *Till Death Us Do Part*, The Woburn Press, London, 1973, pp. 136–7.

23

NEW ETHNICITIES

Stuart Hall

I have centred my remarks on an attempt to identify and characterize a significant shift that has been going on (and is still going on) in black cultural politics. This shift is not definitive, in the sense that there are two clearly discernible phases – one in the past which is now over and the new one which is beginning – which we can neatly counterpose to one another. Rather, they are two phases of the same movement, which constantly overlap and interweave. Both are framed by the same historical conjuncture and both are rooted in the politics of antiracism and the post-war black experience in Britain. Nevertheless I think we can identify two different 'moments' and that the difference between them is significant.

It is difficult to characterize these precisely, but I would say that the first moment was grounded in a particular political and cultural analysis. Politically, this is the moment when the term 'black' was coined as a way of referencing the common experience of racism and marginalization in Britain and came to provide the organizing category of a new politics of resistance, amongst groups and communities with, in fact, very different histories, traditions and ethnic identities. In this moment, politically speaking, 'The Black experience', as a singular and unifying framework based on the building up of identity across ethnic and cultural difference between the different communities, became 'hegemonic' over other ethnic/racial identities – though the latter did not, of course, disappear. Culturally, this analysis formulated itself in terms of a critique of the way blacks were positioned as the unspoken and invisible 'other' of predominantly white aesthetic and cultural discourses.

From James Donald and Ali Rattansi (eds), *'Race', Culture and Difference* (London: Sage, 1992).

This analysis was predicated on the marginalization of the black experience in British culture; not fortuitously occurring at the margins, but placed, positioned at the margins, as the consequence of a set of quite specific political and cultural practices which regulated, governed and 'normalized' the representational and discursive spaces of English society. These formed the conditions of existence of a cultural politics designed to challenge, resist and, where possible, to transform the dominant regimes of representation – first in music and style, later in literary, visual and cinematic forms. In these spaces blacks have typically been the objects, but rarely the subjects, of the practices of representation. The struggle to come into representation was predicated on a critique of the degree of fetishization, objectification and negative figuration which are so much a feature of the representation of the black subject. There was a concern not simply with the absence or marginality of the black experience but with its simplification and its stereotypical character.

The cultural politics and strategies which developed around this critique had many facets, but its two principal objects were: first the question of access to the rights to representation by black artists and black cultural workers themselves. Secondly, the *contestation* of the marginality, the stereotypical quality and the fetishized nature of images of blacks, by the counter-position of a 'positive' black imagery. These strategies were principally addressed to changing what I would call the 'relations of representation'.

I have a distinct sense that in the recent period we are entering a new phase. But we need to be absolutely clear what we mean by a 'new' phase because, as soon as you talk of a new phase, people instantly imagine that what is entailed is the *substitution* of one kind of politics for another. I am quite distinctly *not* talking about a shift in those terms. Politics does not necessarily proceed by way of a set of oppositions and reversals of this kind, though some groups and individuals are anxious to 'stage' the question in this way. The original critique of the predominant relations of race and representation and the politics which developed around it have not and cannot possibly disappear while the conditions which gave rise to it – cultural racism [. . .] – not only persist but positively flourish [. . .]. There is no sense in which a new phase in black cultural politics could replace the earlier one. Nevertheless it is true that as the struggle moves forward and assumes new forms, it does to some degree *displace*, reorganize and reposition the different cultural strategies in relation to one another. If this can be conceived in terms of the 'burden of representation', I would put the point in this form: that black artists and cultural workers now have to struggle, not on one, but on two fronts. The problem is, how to characterize this shift – if indeed, we agree that such a shift has taken or is taking place – and if the language of binary oppositions and substitutions will no longer suffice. The characterization that I would offer is tentative, proposed in the context of this conference mainly to try and clarify some of the issues involved, rather than to pre-empt them.

The shift is best thought of in terms of a change from a struggle over the relations of representation to a politics of representation itself. It would be useful to separate out such a 'politics of representation' into its different elements. We all now use the word representation, but, as we know, it is an extremely slippery customer. It can be used, on the one hand, simply as another way of talking about how one images a reality that exists 'outside' the means by which things are represented: a conception grounded in a mimetic theory of representation. On the other hand the term can also stand for a very radical displacement of that unproblematic notion of the concept of representation. My own view is that events, relations, structures do have conditions of existence and real effects, outside the sphere of the discursive; but that only within the discursive, and subject to its specific conditions, limits and modalities, do they have or can they be constructed within meaning. Thus, while not wanting to expand the territorial claims of the discursive infinitely, how things are represented and the 'machineries' and regimes of representation in a culture do play a *constitutive*, and not merely a reflexive, after-the-event, role. This gives questions of culture and ideology, and the scenarios of representation – subjectivity, identity, politics – a formative, not merely an expressive, place in the constitution of social and political life. I think it is the move towards this second sense of representation which is taking place and which is transforming the politics of representation in black culture.

This is a complex issue. First, it is the effect of a theoretical encounter between black cultural politics and the discourses of a Eurocentric, largely white, critical cultural theory which in recent years has focused so much analysis on the politics of representation. This is always an extremely difficult, if not dangerous, encounter. (I think particularly of black people encountering the discourses of poststructuralism, postmodernism, psycho-analysis and feminism.) Secondly, it marks what I can only call 'the end of innocence', or the end of the innocent notion of the essential black subject. Here again, the end of the essential black subject is something which people are increasingly debating, but they may not have fully reckoned with its political consequences. What is at issue here is the recognition of the extraordinary diversity of subjective positions, social experiences and cultural identities which compose the category 'black'; that is, the recognition that 'black' is essentially a politically and culturally *constructed* category, which cannot be grounded in a set of fixed transcultural or transcendental racial categories and which therefore has no guarantees in Nature. What this brings into play is the recognition of the immense diversity and differentiation of the historical and cultural experiences of black subjects. This inevitably entails a weakening or fading of the notion that 'race' or some composite notion of race around the term black will either guarantee the effectivity of any cultural practice or determine in any final sense its aesthetic value.

We should put this as plainly as possible. Films are not necessarily good because black people make them. They are not necessarily 'right-on' by virtue of the fact that they deal with the black experience. Once you enter the politics of the end of the essential black subject you are plunged headlong into the maelstrom of a continuously contingent, unguaranteed, political argument and debate: a critical politics, a politics of criticism. You can no longer conduct black politics through the strategy of a simple set of reversals, putting in the place of the bad old essential white subject, the new essentially good black subject. Now, that formulation may seem to threaten the collapse of an entire political world. Alternatively, it may be greeted with extraordinary relief at the passing away of what at one time seemed to be a necessary fiction. Namely, either that all black people are good or indeed that all black people are *the same*. After all, it is one of the predicates of racism that 'you can't tell the difference because they all look the same'. This does not make it any easier to conceive of how a politics can be constructed which works with and through difference, which is able to build those forms of solidarity and identification which make common struggle and resistance possible but without suppressing the real heterogeneity of interests and identities, and which can effectively draw the political boundary lines without which political contestation is impossible, without fixing those boundaries for eternity. It entails the movement in black politics, from what Gramsci called the 'war of manoeuvre' to the 'war of position' – the struggle around positionalities. But the difficulty of conceptualizing such a politics (and the temptation to slip into a sort of endlessly sliding discursive liberal-pluralism) does not absolve us of the task of developing such a politics.

The end of the essential black subject also entails a recognition that the central issues of race always appear historically in articulation, in a formation, with other categories and divisions and are constantly crossed and recrossed by the categories of class, of gender and ethnicity. (I make a distinction here between race and ethnicity to which I shall return.) To me, films like *Territories, Passion of Remembrance, My Beautiful Laundrette* and *Sammy and Rosie Get Laid*, for example, make it perfectly clear that this shift has been engaged; and that the question of the black subject cannot be represented without reference to the dimensions of class, gender, sexuality and ethnicity.

DIFFERENCE AND CONTESTATION

A further consequence of this politics of representation is the slow recognition of the deep ambivalence of identification and desire. We think about identification usually as a simple process, structured around fixed 'selves' which we either are or are not. The play of identity and difference which constructs racism is powered not only by the positioning of blacks as the inferior species but also, and at the same time, by an inexpressible envy and desire; and this is something the recognition of which fundamentally *displaces* many of our hitherto stable political categories, since it implies a process of identification and otherness which is more complex than we had hitherto imagined.

Racism, of course, operates by constructing impassable symbolic boundaries between racially constituted categories, and its typically binary system of representation constantly marks and attempts to fix and naturalize the difference between belongingness and otherness. Along this frontier there arises what Gayatri Spivak calls the 'epistemic violence' of the discourses of the Other – of imperialism, the colonized, orientalism, the exotic, the primitive, the anthropological and the folkloric.[1] Consequently the discourse of antiracism had often been founded on a strategy of reversal and inversion, turning the 'Manichean aesthetic' of colonial discourse upside down. However, as Fanon constantly reminded us the epistemic violence is both outside and inside, and operates by a process of splitting on both sides of the division – in here as well as out here. That is why it is a question, not only of 'black-skin, white-skin' but of *'Black-skin, white masks'* – the internalization of the self-as-other. Just as masculinity always constructs femininity as double – simultaneously Madonna and Whore – so racism constructs the black subject: noble savage and violent avenger. And in the doubling, fear and desire double for one another and play across the structures of otherness, complicating its politics.

Recently I've read several articles about the photographic texts of Robert Mapplethorpe – especially his inscription of the nude, black male – all written by black critics or cultural practitioners.[2] These essays properly begin by identifying in Mapplethorpe's work the tropes of fetishization, the fragmentation of the black image and its objectification, as the forms of their appropriation within the white, gay gaze. But, as I read, I know that something else is going on as well in both the production and the reading of those texts. The continuous circling around Mapplethorpe's work is not exhausted by being able to place him as the white fetishistic gay photographer; and this is because it is also marked by the surreptitious return of desire – that deep ambivalence of identification which makes the categories in which we have previously thought and argued about black cultural politics and the black cultural text extremely problematic. This brings to the surface the unwelcome fact that a great deal of black politics, constructed, addressed and developed directly in relation to questions of race and ethnicity, has been predicated on the assumption that the categories of gender and sexuality would stay the same and remain fixed and secured. What the new politics of representation does is to put that into question, crossing the questions of racism irrevocably with questions of sexuality. [. . .] This double fracturing entails a different kind of politics because, as we know, black radical politics has frequently been stabilized around particular conceptions of black masculinity, which are only now being put into question by black women and black gay men. At certain points, black politics has also been underpinned by a deep absence or more typically an evasive silence with reference to class.

Another element inscribed in the new politics of representation has to do with the question of ethnicity. I am familiar with all the dangers of 'ethnicity' as a concept and have written myself about the fact that ethnicity, in the form of a culturally constructed sense of Englishness and a particularly closed, exclusive and regressive form of English national identity, is one of the core characteristics of British racism today.[3] I am also well aware that the politics of antiracism has often constructed itself in terms of a contestation of 'multi-ethnicity' or 'multi-culturalism'. On the other hand, as the politics of representation around the black subject shifts, I think we will begin to see a renewed contestation over the meaning of the term 'ethnicity' itself.

If the black subject and black experience are not stabilized by Nature or by some other essential guarantee, then it must be the case that they are constructed historically, culturally, politically – and the concept which refers to this is 'ethnicity'. The term ethnicity acknowledges the place of history, language and culture in the construction of subjectivity and identity, as well as the fact that all discourse is placed, positioned, situated, and all knowledge is contextual. Representation is possible only because enunciation is always produced within codes which have a history, a position within the discursive formations of a particular space and time. The displacement of the 'centred' discourses of the West entails putting in question its universalist character and its transcendental claims to speak for everyone, while being itself every-where and nowhere. The fact that this grounding of ethnicity in difference was deployed, in the discourse of racism, as a means of disavowing the reali-ties of racism and repression does not mean that we can permit the term to be permanently colonized. That appropriation will have to be contested, the term disarticulated from its position in the discourse of 'multiculturalism' and transcoded, just as we previously had to recuperate the term 'black', from its place in a system of negative equivalences. The new politics of representation therefore also sets in motion an ideological contestation around the term, 'ethnicity'. But in order to pursue that movement further, we will have to retheorize the concept of *difference*.

It seems to me that, in the various practices and discourses of black cultural production, we are beginning to see constructions of just such a new concep-tion of ethnicity: a new cultural politics which engages rather than suppresses *difference* and which depends, in part, on the cultural construction of new ethnic identities. Difference, like representation, is also a slippery, and there-fore, contested concept. There is the 'difference' which makes a radical and unbridgeable separation: and there is a 'difference' which is positional, condi-tional and conjunctural, closer to Derrida's notion of *différance*, though if we are concerned to maintain a politics it cannot be defined exclusively in terms of an infinite sliding of the signifier. We still have a great deal of work to do to *decouple* ethnicity, as it functions in the dominant discourse, from its equiva-lence with nationalism, imperialism, racism and the state, which are the points of attachment around which a distinctive British or, more accurately, English ethnicity have been constructed. Nevertheless, I think such a project is not only possible but necessary. Indeed, this decoupling of ethnicity from the violence of the state is implicit in some of the new forms of cultural practice that are going on in films like *Passion* and *Handsworth Songs*. We are beginning to think about how to represent a non-coercive and a more diverse conception of ethnicity, to set against the embattled, hegemonic conception of 'Englishness' which, under Thatcherism, stabilizes so much of the dominant political and cultural discourses, and which, because it is hegemonic, does not represent itself as an ethnicity at all.

This marks a real shift in the point of contestation, since it is no longer only between antiracism and multiculturalism but inside the notion of ethnicity itself. What is involved is the splitting of the notion of ethnicity between, on the one hand the dominant notion which connects it to nation and 'race' and on the other hand what I think is the beginning of a positive conception of the ethnicity of the margins, of the periphery. That is to say, a recognition that we all speak from a particular place, out of a particular history, out of a particular experience, a particular culture, without being contained by that position as 'ethnic artists' or film-makers. We are all, in that sense, *ethnically* located and our ethnic identities are crucial to our subjective sense of who we are. But this is also a recognition that this is not an ethnicity which is doomed to survive, as Englishness was, only by marginalizing, dispossessing, displacing and forgetting other ethnicities. This precisely is the politics of ethnicity predicated on difference and diversity.

The final point which I think is entailed in this new politics of representation has to do with an awareness of the black experience as a *diaspora* experience, and the consequences which this carries for the process of unsettling, recombination, hybridization and 'cut-and-mix' – in short, the process of cultural *diaspora-ization* (to coin an ugly term) which it implies. In the case of the young black British films and film-makers under discussion, the diaspora experience is certainly profoundly fed and nourished by, for example, the emergence of Third World cinema; by the African experience; the connection with Afro-Caribbean experience; and the deep inheritance of complex systems of representation and aesthetic traditions from Asian and African culture. But, in spite of these rich cultural 'roots', the new cultural politics is operating on new and quite distinct ground – specifically, contestation over what it means to be 'British'. The relation of this cultural politics to the past; to its different 'roots' is profound, but complex. It cannot be simple or unmediated. It is [. . .] complexly mediated and transformed by memory, fantasy and desire. Or, as even an explicitly political film like *Handsworth Songs* clearly suggests, the relation is intertextual – mediated, through a variety of other 'texts'. There can, therefore, be no simple 'return' or 'recovery' of the ancestral past which is not re-experienced through the categories of the present: no base for creative enunciation in a simple reproduction of traditional forms which are not transformed by the technologies and the identities of the present. This is something that was signalled as early as a film like *Blacks Britannica* and as recently as Paul Gilroy's important book, *There Ain't No Black in the Union Jack*.[4] Fifteen years ago we didn't care, or at least I didn't care, whether there was any black in the Union Jack. Now not only do we care, we must: [. . .]

Notes

1. Gayatri C. Spivak, *In Other Worlds: essays in cultural politics*, London, Methuen, 1987.
2. Kobena Mercer, 'Imaging the black man's sex' in Patricia Holland *et al.* (eds) *Photography/Politics: Two*. Comedia/Methuen, 1987 and various articles in *Ten.8*, 22, 1986, an issue on 'Black experiences' edited by David A. Bailey.
3. Stuart Hall, 'Racism and reaction' in *Five Views on Multi-Racial Britain*, London, Commission for Racial Equality, 1978.
4. Paul Gilroy, *There Ain't No Black in the Union Jack: the cultural politics of race and nation*, London, Hutchinson, 1987.

24

SKIN FLICKS ON THE RACIAL BORDER: PORNOGRAPHY, EXPLOITATION, AND INTERRACIAL LUST

Linda Williams

The question of interracial sexual relations remains virtually untouched.
—Jane Gaines

* It has been argued that the so-called classical cinema is regulated by a semiotics of race relations posited on a single prohibition: 'No nonwhite man can have sanctioned sexual relations with a white woman' (Browne 1992, 8). Yet this prohibition is now regularly flouted, if not in today's Hollywood, then in that parallel universe in the San Fernando Valley where a line of contemporary pornography labeled 'interracial' aims specifically at violating precisely the taboos that once reigned supreme in Hollywood. Videos with titles like *Black Taboo, Black and White in Living Color, Black Meat, White Cream, White Dicks/Black Chicks, White Trash, Black Splash, Color Blind*, and *South Central Hookers* speak about racial differences in sex in ways that elsewhere in the culture have often remained unspeakable. The loudest thing they say is that *Crossing the Color Line* (to invoke yet another title) can be sexually exciting, especially the line between black and white that had been most firmly erected by America's history of chattel slavery. If Hollywood has been lacking in 'honest and open explorations of the complexities of interracial sexual attraction' (Gates 1991, 163), pornography and sexploitation cinema have at least been willing to explore what more polite forms do not.

Abdul JanMohamed has coined the term *racialized sexuality* to designate the field in which Michel Foucault's familiar 'deployment of sexuality' joins with a less familiar 'deployment of race' (JanMohamed 1992, 94) Racialized

From Linda Williams (ed.), *Porn Studies* (Durham, NC: Duke University Press, 2004).

sexuality is constructed around and through the policing of an (unequally permeable) racial border. Unlike 'bourgeois sexuality,' which emerged through a compulsive discursive articulation, 'racialized sexuality' has been characterized by a 'peculiar silence' (94). While Foucault teaches that bourgeois sexuality was articulated through the intersection of techniques of confession and scientific discursivity, racialized sexuality in the United States was more occulted, grounded as it was in the 'open secret' of the white master's sexual desire for, and sexual use of, the female slave (104). JanMohamed argues that this sexual relation, which implicitly acknowledged the slave's humanity, threatened the maintenance of the racial other in a subservient position. 'Unable or unwilling to repress desire, the master silences the violation of the border and refuses to recognize, through any form of analytic discursivity, the results of the infraction. This peculiar silence prevents the development of the kind of confessional and "scientific" discursivity central to the deployment of sexuality as Foucault defines it' (104). The hypersexualization of the black body (male and female) in some ways parallels the 'hysterization' of the white woman's body: both are represented as excessively saturated with sexuality. However, the discursive exploration of the female body ultimately integrates that body into the social body, while the discursive silence and lack of confession about sexual relations with the racialized other has aimed at segregating it from the social body. JanMohamed thus argues that racialized sexuality constitutes an inversion of bourgeois sexuality; where bourgeois sexuality is driven by an analytic will to knowledge, as well as an empiricist discursivity, racialized sexuality is driven by a will to conceal its mechanisms and a reliance on unempirical stereotypes (105).

The situation JanMohamed describes may be true enough for the era he describes (his essay centers on a reading of Richard Wright's *Native Son*). What happens, however, when the racialized body becomes the subject of pornography's unique brand of confession? If, as I have argued (1989), pornography seeks to confess the discursive 'truths' of sex itself, what happens when racialized bodies are asked to reveal their 'truths'? In this case, the 'peculiar silence' that JanMohamed so aptly describes can turn into a noisy confession. In contemporary video pornography, the pleasures of sexual-racial difference once the province of white masters have become commodified, mediated, and available to all.[1] Not unexpectedly, the power differentials of that original relation inform them.

Consider a contemporary porn video, marketed under the rubric 'interracial': *Crossing the Color Line* (dir. Gino Colbert, 1999). Like most examples of hard-core pornography, it presumes to confess the so-called truths of sexual pleasure. But, unique to the subgenre of interracial pornography, it speaks the once-silenced, taboo truths of racialized sexuality. The video consists of a series of interviews followed by sexual performances between African American and white performers who 'frankly' discuss their feelings and observations about race in the porn industry. The interview sections are earnest and

full of liberal sentiments of equality and the unimportance of race; the sex sections are intensely erotic, often 'nasty,' and contradict the preceding liberalism
by a fascination with racial difference. [. . .]

What does it mean to watch such comminglings of raced bodies? In a genre
that tends to suspend narrative in order to scrutinize the sights and sounds
of interpenetrating bodies – tongue in mouth, mouth around penis, penis in
vagina or anus, hand on pubis, and so on – what does it mean when these
bodies are not only differently gendered but also differently raced? And if it is
possible to say that the pleasures of heterosexual pornography have something
to do with the differences of gendered bodies, is it possible to say that pleasure
can also be taken from the sight of differently raced bodies interpenetrating?
Why is this once-forbidden commingling, as Lake puts it, 'very exciting, very
erotic'? Finally, is it possible to articulate the formal pleasures of the color
contrast without sounding like or becoming a racist?

Pornography, because it has so long existed in determined opposition to
all other forms of mainstream culture, has often become the place where
sex happens instantaneously. Pornotopia is the land, as Steven Marcus once
wrote, where it is 'always bedtime' (Marcus 1974, 269) and where the usual
taboos limiting sex are very easily overcome. Couples fall into bed at the drop
of a hat, and nothing impedes the immediate gratification of myriad forms of
sexual pleasure; the taboos that circumscribe and inform sex acts in the real
world just melt away. Because it is always bedtime in pornography, the genre
can often seem determinedly opposed to the generation of erotic excitement.
Erotica is a term frequently opposed to pornography, often by antipornogra-
phy feminists to contrast a tame and tasteful female pleasure to a more gross
and violent porn. However, this contrast belies the fact that both forms of
representation ultimately aim at sexual arousal. What may more usefully distinguish the two terms, then, is the way taboo functions in each. Pornography
as a whole defies the taboos against graphic representations of sex acts, but it
often chooses not to inscribe these taboos into the truncated narratives of its
fantasy scenarios. Erotica, in contrast, inscribes the taboo more deeply into its
fantasy. Thus erotica is not necessarily more tasteful or tame than pornography (witness the grossly transgressive literary erotica of Georges Bataille, also
the great theorist of transgression), nor is it without explicit imagery (witness
the explicit but tasteful film and video erotica of Candida Royalle), but it does
inscribe the tension of the forbidden into its fantasy.

If pornography is the realm where nothing impedes the immediate enactment of easily achieved and multiple forms of sexual pleasure, then erotic
forms of pornography are those in which the taboos and prohibitions limiting
pleasure are, at least vestigially, in force often in order to enhance the desire
that overpowers them. Eroticism in pornography thus depends on the continued awareness of the taboo. This is one reason why interracial pornographies
can sometimes have an erotic charge that other forms of pornography do not.

To transgress a taboo is certainly not to defeat it. Georges Bataille argues that transgression is the flouting of a taboo that fully recognizes the authority and power of the prohibiting law: 'Unless the taboo is observed with fear it lacks the counterpoise of desire which gives it its deepest significance' (1957, 37). Prohibitions thus often provide an element of fear that enhances desire. In much of what follows, I will be arguing that it is fear – the fear once generated by white masters to keep white women and black men apart – that gives erotic tension to interracial sex acts which in 'ordinary,' nonracialized pornography often become rote.

[. . .]

RACIAL FEAR AND DESIRE

Frantz Fanon has famously written about the experience of being interpellated as a raced being when a white boy points to him on the street to say, 'Look, a Negro. . . . I'm frightened' (1967, 112). In this classic description of the power of the white gaze to reduce the black man to an epidermalized phobic essence, Fanon sees negrophobia as a form of white sexual anxiety. The white gaze sees the organ of black skin and immediately feels fear. According to Fanon, the deepest cause of this fear lies in the reduction of the black man to a penis, which ultimately constitutes a pathological projection on the part of the white man of his own repressed homosexuality (170). The white man's fear is thus, to Fanon, also his desire. Yet, as Mary Ann Doane (1991, 221) has shown, the specific instances of negrophobia analyzed by Fanon tend to ground the pathology of this projection especially in the white woman. The white woman's fear of rape by a Negro is viewed as an 'inner wish' to be raped: 'It is the woman who rapes herself' (Fanon 1967, 179). Pathology thus marks the white woman's desire for the black man. Fanon similarly pathologizes the black woman's desire for the white man. Yet, as Doane shows, Fanon does not equally pathologize the black man's desire for the white woman. Indeed, he does not find anything in his behavior that is motivated by race. This man is simply a typical 'neurotic who by coincidence is black' (Fanon 1967, 79).

Fanon's (unequal) condemnation of the epidermalization of racial fear and desire is understandable given his quest for revenge on the system that so fixes him. But his protestation that the man of color's desire is not itself racially influenced remains unconvincing. It is as if Fanon's response to the negative stereotype of the oversexed black man can only be to create another set of negative stereotypes: the oversexed white woman and the undersexed white man (a repressed homosexual to Fanon). Originally writing in 1952, Fanon, for good reason, cannot conceive of a world in which epidermal difference would become a commodity fetish grounded in the very fear expressed by the child who once hailed him. Nor can he admit that this fear-desire might exist (unequally but powerfully) on both sides of the racial border. He thus cannot imagine a black man's desire for a white woman as grounded in a fear that enhances desire.

[. . .]

If we are willing to acknowledge that interracial lust evolves out of the taboos initially imposed by the white master, but which now serve to eroticize a field of sexuality that is no longer his sole province, then we begin to recognize the validity of varieties of commodification in contemporary visual culture, and not only in much-discussed, high art incarnations. But what if we now turn to a decidedly 'low' example of interracial lust, which no one could call high art and which [. . .] seems vigorously to embrace its crudest stereotypes?

Let Me Tell Ya 'bout White Chicks (dir. Dark Brothers, 1984) is a porn video that became notorious, and popular, for its articulation of all the stereotypes and clichés of racial difference. Since its release in 1984, when it won the XRCO Best Picture award, it has acquired something of a cult status and has, unlike many other porn titles, been subsequently reissued as a 'classic.' The video box proclaims it 'The Original Interracial Classic.' Its director, Gregory Dark, is a white man who also pioneered hip, politically incorrect 'New Wave' straight porn and then briefly turned his hand to interracial pornography in the mid-1980s. Dark proudly proclaims that 'you will not find one sensitive moment in any of my work' (Bright n.d., n.p.). Like Spike Lee's *Jungle Fever* (1991), it unearths the most regressive sexual stereotypes of taboo desire. Unlike Lee, who chooses to tell his version of the story from the perspective of an upwardly mobile black man who momentarily succumbs to 'jungle fever' and then learns better, Dark revels in the black male enthusiasm for the ever more outlandish conquest of 'white chicks.'[. . .]

Let Me Tell Ya 'bout White Chicks thus [. . .] does not function, as did Reconstruction and Progressive Era racial fantasies, to keep black men in 'their place.' Rather, it represents a new kind of racial pornographic fantasy come into being due to America's history of racial oppression but not a simple repetition of these past racist stereotypes. [. . .] The video reworks the phobic white fear of the black man's sex, and the related fear of the white woman's animalistic preference for that sex, into a pornographic fantasy that may have originated from but is no longer 'owned' by the white man. Is it then a positive or negative stereotype? Perhaps the conventional language of stereotypes fails us in the attempt to analyze the refunctioning that has occurred around this phobia. For the phobia's original purpose was to prevent precisely the kind of black male–white female couplings celebrated in these videos.

The problem in thinking about stereotypes, as Mireille Rosello has pointed out, is our stereotypes about them (1998, 32) [. . .]. Rosello argues that stereotypes are important objects of study not because we can better learn to eliminate them from our thinking, but rather because they cannot be eliminated. Stereotypes persist, and perhaps even thrive on, the protestations against them; the louder the protest, the more they thrive. Instead of protest, Rosello offers a nuanced study of the changing historical contexts of stereotypes. Something like this seems to be what we need in our understanding of stereotypes of interracial lust as well. To forbid all utterance or depiction of the stereotype of the originally phobic image of the large black penis is to grant it a timelessness and immortality that it does not really possess. Once uttered, however, a stereotype does have an enormous power to endure. Racial stereotypes especially, as Homi Bhabha has noted, take on a fetishistic nature as a 'form of knowledge and identification that vacillates between what is always "in place" as already known, and something that must be anxiously repeated . . . as if the essential duplicity of the Asiatic or the bestial sexual license of the African that needs no proof, can never really, in discourse be proved' (1994, 66). In the perpetual absence of proof (say a random sampling of penis size and actual sexual behavior of black men), there is no truth to the stereotype. But precisely because there is no truth the claim must be repeated. Rosello, however, argues that the refunctioned repetition of stereotype shows what happens when what the culture thinks it knows comes in contact with the stereotyped person's reaction to that supposed knowledge. In this case, the 'iteration' of the refunctioned stereotype does not deny it, but uses it in historically new ways that are more erotic than phobic. In other words, the racial stereotype of the big black 'buck' that right-thinking Americans have now come to label as unjustly 'negative' (but have in no way eliminated as a vacillating form of knowledge and belief) has ceased to function in the same way it did when the Klan was riding. It has ceased to so function precisely because it has, in the intervening years, been refunctioned to different ends by black men who have willingly occupied the fantasy position of the hypersexed black man in order to instill fear in the white man and to counter the older stereotype of the passive Uncle Tom.[2]

The typical argument against stereotypes is to say that 'real' people do not resemble them. But as Steve Neale (1979–80, 35) and Jane Gaines (1992, 27) point out, it is almost never actually 'real people' who are asked to offer the antidote to harmful stereotypes, but an imaginary ideal that can serve as a 'positive image' for stigmatized minorities. Harmful, negative stereotypes are not measured against the real but against the culturally dominant ideal. Jane Gaines quotes Isaac Julian and Kobena Mercer on this point: 'It's not as if we could strip away the negative stereotypes of black men . . . and discover some "natural" black masculinity which is good, pure and wholesome' (Gaines 1992, 27; Mercer and Julien 1986, 6). Historically, then, the negative stereotype of the oversexed black buck was countered in the late 1950s and early 1960s by the positive stereotype of the supercivilized (handsome but never overtly sexual) Sydney Poitier. But this desexed image of the black man was in turn countered by more explicitly sexualized – 'bad' – images of black men produced in reaction to the perceived passivity of the Tom figure. Thus the reappearance of the stereotype of the black buck in the post-civil rights era does not represent a return to a *Birth of a Nation*-style stereotype. Stereotypes, if we follow Rosello, do not simply repeat. The very emergence of this figure, in a newly aboveground, post-civil rights era pornography, would seem to provide evidence that the older function of what Foucault calls the deployment of power through 'systems of alliance' and a 'symbolics of blood' (1978, 147) indeed does give way to a newer deployment and analytics of sexuality. But like so much else in Foucault, these two modes of power are intertwined.

A stereotype that once functioned to frighten white women and to keep black men in their place (as in JanMohamed's stereotyping allegory), now functions to solicit sexual desire in the form of a transgressive, pornographic tale. However, this arousal remains propped on the original phobic stereotype aimed precisely at prohibiting the very sexual commerce depicted. Are black men and white women kept any less 'in their place' by this sexual fantasy whose point of origin is the power of the white man? I would argue that the white man's power remains the pivotal point around which these permutations of power and pleasure turn. The sexual fantasies depicted primarily constitute rivalries between white and black men. The agency of white women, and black women even more, is difficult to discern. Nevertheless, there is a big difference, as Tessa Perkins has observed, between 'knowing' racist stereotypes and 'believing' them (qtd. in Gaines 1992, 27). I suggest that pornographic and erotic fantasies of interracial lust rely on all viewers, male and female, black and white, *knowing* these stereotypes. Although nothing necessarily rules out their also *believing* them – that is, they can certainly be interpreted in a racist manner – the pleasure taken in pornographic depictions of interracial lust does not depend on believing them. It would seem that what is involved instead is a complex flirtation with the now historically proscribed stereotype operating on both sides of the color line. Thus the very taboos that once effectively policed the racial border now work in the service of eroticizing its transgression.

'FEAR OF [AND DESIRE FOR] A MANDINGO SEXUAL ENCOUNTER'

We have seen that a mix of fear and desire lies at the heart of interracial pornography's erotic tension. The resister figure in *White Chicks* who admitted his fear of white women was also, inadvertently, admitting his fear of white men. White men, for their part, have historically feared black male prowess, even while (and as a means of) exercising sexual sovereignty over black women. White male fear of the black man's sexual threat to white women has been the ostensible reason, as JanMohamed notes, for countless acts of violence against black men. What we see in the above examples of interracial pornography is that this fear has now been iterated in a new way. Where it once operated in a more exclusively phobic mode to keep the black man and the white woman apart, now its reversal in pornographic fantasy shows how the stereotype informs the erotic tension of representations of interracial lust. I do not mean to suggest, however, that a racialized mix of fear and desire informing contemporary pornography now renders it totally innocuous. Quite the contrary. One of the worst riots of recent American history was precipitated by the phantasmatic projection of one white man's racial-sexual fear, envy, and resentment grounded in just such a scenario of interracial lust.

When the white Los Angeles police sergeant Stacey Koon saw a power-fully built black man holding his butt and gyrating his hips at a white female highway patrol officer, he claimed to see a lurid scenario of interracial sex that then triggered the beating of Rodney King. Koon's reading of King's pornographic gestures is described in his book, *Presumed Guilty*.

> Melanie Singer . . . shouted at King to show her his hands. Recognizing the voice as female, King grinned and turned his back to Melanie Singer. Then he grabbed his butt with both hands and began to gyrate his hips in a sexually suggestive fashion. Actually, it was more explicit than suggestive. Melanie wasn't so much fearful as offended. She was being mocked in front of her peers. . . . Control and common sense were cast aside. Melanie's Jane Wayne and Dirty Harriet hormones kicked in. She drew her pistol, and advanced to within five feet of the suspect. (Koon 1992, 33–34)

In the original manuscript of this book, however, Koon had offered a slightly different version of his reason for intervening, stressing this time not Singer's 'offense' but what he called her 'fear of a Mandingo sexual encounter' (Fiske 1996, 145). In a May 16, 1992, interview with the *Los Angeles Times* after his acquittal in the first (state) trial, Koon tried to explain what he meant by these words, which were eventually eliminated from the book: 'In society there's this sexual prowess of blacks on the old plantations of the South and intercourse between blacks and whites on the plantation. And that's where the fear comes in, because he's black.'[. . .]

[. . .] Koon's use of the phrase *sexual prowess of blacks* intimates something of white sexual envy of black men; it is hardly a phrase old-fashioned racists like Thomas Dixon or D. W. Griffith would have invoked. This envy, I suggest, is inherited from a much more recent legacy of pornography and exploitation cinema that has culminated in the fantasy depictions of interracial lust cited above. While Stacey Koon would like us to believe that Singer's 'fear of a Mandingo sexual encounter,' caused him to initiate Rodney King's beating, his motives differed from Dixon and Griffith's brand of racism. Like them, he wants to keep black men and white women in their place. But unlike them, he seems aware of the various ways in which the fantasy of the black male sexual threat to the white woman has also become material for overtly titillating scenarios.

One clue to his different deployment of the figure of the 'black beast' may lie in Koon's peculiar use of the word *Mandingo* – which designates, along with the variant *Mandinka*, a tribe of African warriors – instead of *black* or *African* or any of the other available animalistic epithets apparently used by police before and during King's beating. This word signals Koon's own semi-conscious acknowledgment that the scenario he invokes has since the 1970s become something more than the white patriarch's fear of the pollution of his own racial line by a hypersexual African slave and the subsequent loss of control over 'his' women. *Mandingo* does not mean to Stacey Koon's generation what *African* meant to Dixon and Griffith's. One reason may be that in 1975, a popular sexploitation film with the very title *Mandingo*, which Stacey Koon is old enough to have seen as a teenager, had already refunctioned the older scenario of white female fear in the face of black male lust. Stacy Koon's over-reaction to King's grabbed butt and gyrated hips may have unleashed the same kind of overkill as the ride of the Klan, but the raced and gendered fear that Koon attempted to project onto Melanie Singer was no longer a historically believable emotion. This is one reason for its excision from the manuscript of his book and its replacement with the word *offense*. But in saying 'fear of a Mandingo sexual encounter,' Koon also invoked a white female *desire for* that encounter as depicted in the film of the same name. For Richard Fleischer's 1975 film is most famous for its depiction of a white mistress's taboo-breaking seduction of her husband's Mandingo slave.

[. . .]

Mandingo

Mandingo is not a pornographic film, but for many viewers who did not yet venture into the porn theaters of the era, it came close. Reviewers unanimously viewed it as an exploitative potboiler and a work of lurid 'trash.' Directed by Richard Fleischer in 1975, and a big hit at the box office, *Mandingo* has only recently begun to receive its critical due. Nor does this rather expensively pro-duced film directly belong to the category of blaxploitation films. However, it is best understood, as Ed Guerrero (1993) argues, in relation to them. *Blaxploitation* was Hollywood's word for an exploitation of both race and sex that became popular, and economically important, to the very survival of Hollywood in the early and mid 1970s. Often breakthroughs for black direc-tors, Blaxploitation films typically offered contemporary reworkings of outlaw and detective genres set in the inner city with contemporary jazz scores and tough, sexually desirable black heroes who displayed sexual prowess toward both black and white women [. . .]. *Mandingo*, in contrast, is set on a planta-tion of the Old South, was directed by a white man, and has a primary white hero. But like the blaxploitation cycle, it portrays black struggle against racism while also celebrating black male sexual prowess. Also like blaxploitation, it became popular with the same black urban audiences who played such a major role in Hollywood's recovery from economic slump in the early seventies. The film represents a new post-civil rights, post-Black Power view of the coercive sexual relations of slavery, but one which also takes a frankly lurid interest in those relations. Finally, *Mandingo* presents interracial sexual relations not only as compellingly erotic but also systematically in relation to the different economic situations of white masters and mistresses and black male and female slaves. It thus represented a revision of the most recent incarnation of the plantation genre – a type of pulp fiction already predicated, sans Black Power message, on a certain lurid fascination with black/white sexual relations.

[. . .]

Mandingo's black male revenge on the white master marks the film as post-civil rights era expression of black power. The film systematically revises happy black servility with equal parts of black rage and illicit sexual desire. There are two major interracial sex scenes. They are not the first interracial sex scenes offered up for prurient, as opposed to phobic, interest in mainstream American cinema, but they are the most sustained and the most provocative in their challenge to plantation genre precursors. Both entail transgressive erotic recognitions across racial difference.

[. . .]

[. . .] In a film in which sex acts have functioned in the economic interests of the master, these transgressive, interracial sex acts do not [. . .] overcome difference. Rather, they offer a perversely exciting form of sexual-racial recognition-in-difference.

This negativity of a destructive difference offers an important qualification for understanding erotic forms of recognition whose very eros is grounded in racialized differences of power. Consider, for example, the second big moment of interracial lust depicted in this film, that between the aptly named Blanche (Susan George), the sexually frustrated plantation mistress, and Mede, the Mandingo wrestler (the boxer Ken Norton). Blanche had disappointed Hammond by proving – due to sexual abuse by her older brother – not to be a virgin on marriage. When Ham purchases Ellen and then turns to her for love, elevating her to quasi-mistress status, Blanche seeks revenge by seducing her husband's slave. [. . .]

What kind of Hegelian recognition can we see in this scene? First of all, it is literally one that runs the 'risk of destruction' by keeping in play a negativity – a possibility of obliteration that is the very source of its erotic tension. Indeed, both mistress and slave will die as a consequence of this sexual-racial recognition. The very death at the master's hand with which Blanche threatens Mede, will be delivered to them both. The intense eroticism of the scene derives not merely from the explicit (relative to previous, nonexploitation Hollywood films) details of their sexual relations – reference to Mede's off-screen erection, nudity, shuddering orgasm – but from the way his body itself becomes a battleground between fear and desire. Here is another permutation of the fear of, and desire for, the racial other. But where Ellen risked destruction in refusing to satisfy her master, Mede risks destruction both ways – in refusing to satisfy his mistress *and* in satisfying her.

[. . .]

In the various scenarios of interracial lust we have discussed thus far, both in pornography and here in a film thought to 'exploit' (soft-core) sex in pornographic ways, the different interracial permutations of lust – those of the white woman and the black man and those of the white man and the black woman – contain a nonpresent third term that haunts the scene. This is the putatively 'proper,' same-race partner whom the spectacle of interracial lust can be said to betray. When the black woman and the white man recognize and desire one another across their differences, this recognition is nevertheless haunted and erotically animated by the missing figure of the black man, who finds his very masculinity and virility jeopardized by his exclusion. It is also haunted by the missing figure of the white woman deprived of a partner because of the white male's interest in the 'othered' woman. Similarly in the sexual-racial recognition of the white woman and the black man, it is the jealous white man who represents the absent third term and who has his masculinity (and mastery) put in jeopardy by his exclusion. To a lesser degree, the second scenario is also haunted by the black woman who loses a potential partner to the myth of superior white womanhood.

These exclusions are not equal, however. The white man has much more power in his absence to structure the scene in which he does not act than does the black man, the white woman, or the black woman. And for this reason we might say that the transgression inherent in the sex scene between the white woman and the black man is greater and therefore more erotic. The point, however, is that the interracial recognition taking place never occurs only between the two figures present in the scene and that this mutual but unequal recognition is animated, in different ways, by the desire and jealousy of an absent third person. [. . .] The lame white master who looms so large in the Blanche/Mede recognition, the sex-starved white mistress who looms so large in the Ham/Ellen recognition, are what give these erotic recognitions their sexual charge. They are the (unequally) powerful, white, transgressed-against figures whose very absence structures the erotic tension of the scenes. The black woman who would be the 'appropriately raced' partner for Mede, and the black man who would be the 'appropriately raced' partner for Ellen, do not have the same power to constitute a force in the scene as their white counterparts. The transgression, in other words, is perceived as against the dominant white power: the large power of the white master and the much smaller power of the white mistress. The 'hotter' the sex, the greater the transgressed-against power.

[. . .]

The sex scenes in *Mandingo* need to be understood not only for their ambivalent political celebration of black male and white female sexual power and pleasure but as a new kind of mainstream visual pleasure – a pleasure explicitly and knowingly derived from flirting with taboo. In 1975, amid the tumult of a mainstream film industry seeking to appeal to younger and more racially and ethnically diverse audiences, interracial lust became a new commodity, acknowledged not for the first time, but in a way that explicitly foregrounded the context of the master/slave dynamic of power as an erotic pleasure grounded in the taboos it transgresses. *Mandingo*, a film that ranked sixteenth at the box office, helps us recognize the emergence of the peculiar conjunction of Black Power, cinematic sexual explicitness, and self-conscious revisions of white myths of the Old South into a quasi-mainstream popular culture.

BEHIND THE GREEN DOOR

But, of course, not only *Mandingo* ventured into this taboo territory. I would like to conclude this essay by returning to a 'classic' work of film pornography that has already been much discussed as pornography but very little as inter-racial sex. It is the early *Behind the Green Door* (dir. Mitchell Brothers, 1972), and the scene in question is the film's first heterosexual sex act. As far as I can determine, this is the first American feature-length hard-core film to include a major interracial sex scene; yet, as far as I can also determine, this sex scene has gone unnoticed by critics.[3] [. . .]

Earlier hard-core pornography in the form of stag films had occasionally played on stereotypes of African animality. But no feature-length theatrical film shown to sexually and racially mixed audiences in 'legitimate' theaters had ever displayed these kinds of sexual-racial stereotypes for the primary purpose of producing sexual pleasure in viewers. This certainly does not mean to say that these films do not traffic in stereotypical depictions of African animality (or, indeed, white female purity [. . .]) suddenly transformed into insatiable lust. However, it is to say that the effect of the portrayal of animality differs quite markedly in a generic world that celebrates lust and the fetishes enhancing it.

It is certainly true that white men can still deploy the quasi-taboo relation of the stereotypically hypersexual African man and the white man's stereotypically pure white woman as cautionary tools to maintain the sexual-racial hierarchy of white man over black man and white woman. Nevertheless, as we have seen, the fact that the hypersexual black man no longer features as a purely phobic object in the shared cultural imaginary deeply complicates such deployments. He has become, rather, a familiar element in erotic sexual fantasy producing visual pleasure for an audience that can now include – and does include in the case of the diegetic audience in *Behind the Green Door* – white men, black men, white women, and black women, and a wide range of other sexualized and racialized beings. In 1972, this black man is thus very different from what he had been. A fear that had kept black men and white women 'in their place' now began to fuel an eroticism bringing them together, not in a happy mutual overcoming of difference, but running the risk of destruction by tempting the outrage (however vestigial) of the excluded third term.

CONCLUSION: 'IN THE BLINK OF AN EYE'

This essay has worked backward from a 1999 example of the fully commodi-fied category of interracial porn, marketed as such, to a 1972 classic of pornog-raphy that preexists the emergence of interracial porn as a marketed category, but that appears to be the first example of the pornographic commodification of interracial sex acts in aboveground feature film. The 1975 film *Mandingo*, while not an example of interracial pornography proper, has nevertheless permitted us to probe some of the deeper questions of power and pleasure in depictions of interracial lust. What conclusions can we now draw from these examples?

All depictions of interracial lust develop out of the relations of inequality that have prevailed between the races. They grow out of a history that has covertly permitted the white man's sexual access to black women and violently forbidden the black man's access to white women. The racist and sexist assumptions that underlie such unequal access to sex have generated forms of pornographic sexual fantasy with an important purchase on the American sexual imagination. To recognize the racism that has generated these fantasies does not suggest that the function they fulfill today is racist in the same way. Nor is it to say that it does not participate in aspects of an increasingly outmoded racial stereotyping. This, indeed, is the lesson of the historicity of the stereotype. Distasteful as some of the stereotypes that feed these fantasies are, I hope to have shown that the simple charge of racism is increasingly imprecise when we talk about visual pleasures generated by depictions of interracial lust. Tessa Perkins's distinction between knowing and believing racist stereotypes seems worth remembering: the excitement of interracial lust – for both blacks and whites – depends on a basic knowledge of the white racist scenario of white virgin/black beast. But the pleasure generated by the scenario does not necessarily need to *believe* in the scenario. Rather, we might say that there is a kind of knowing flirtation with the archaic beliefs of racial stereotypes.

It would seem, then, that the racialized sexuality described by Abdul JanMohamed is not always as silent as he claimed, at least not recently and at least not within the realm of pornographic and exploitation discourse. The pleasures of sexual-racial difference once available to white masters alone are now more available to all, though not equally to all. Black female viewing pleasure, it would seem, is the least well served by these newly racialized, noisy confessions of pleasure. Kobena Mercer writes, 'Blacks are looked down upon and despised as worthless, ugly and ultimately unhuman. But in the blink of an eye, whites look up to and revere black bodies, lost in awe and envy as the black subject is idolized as the embodiment of its aesthetic ideal' (1994, 210). As I have been trying to argue, aesthetic ideals are deeply imbricated in the sexual desirability of this 'black subject.' And the change to which Mercer refers may not have exactly occurred within 'the blink of an eye.' Rather, as we have seen, it has occurred through a somewhat slower, three-decade-long process of re-aestheticization and positive sexualization, in which low forms of exploitation and pornography have played an important part.

NOTES

1. They are not, of course, *equally* available to all. Jane Juffer, writing about women's consumption of pornography in the home, notes that access to pornography is radically different for women when compared to that of men (1998, 5, 107).

2. For a further discussion of this issue from the point of view of white supremacist mainstream American culture, see Williams 2001.
3. I include my own, racially unmarked discussion in *Hard Core* (1989, 157).

WORKS CITED

Bataille, Georges. 1957. *Erotism: Death and Sensuality*. Trans. Mary Dalwood. San Francisco: City Lights Books.

Bhabha, Homi K. 1994. *The Location of Culture*. New York: Routledge.

Bright, Susie. N.d. 'Inter-racial and Black Videos.' Unpublished manuscript. Courtesy of author.

Brown, Nick. 1992. 'Race: The Political Unconscious in American Film.' *East-West Film Journal* 6, 1.

Doane, Mary Ann. 1991. 'Dark Continents: Epistemologies and Racial and Sexual Difference in Psychoanalysis and the Cinema.' In *Femmes Fatales: Feminism, Film Theory, Psychoanalysis*. New York: Routledge.

Fanon, Frantz. 1967. *Black Skin, White Masks*. Trans. Charles Lam Markmann. New York: Grove.

Fiske, John. 1995. *Media Matters: Race and Gender in U.S. Politics*. Minneapolis: University of Minnesota Press.

Foucault, Michel. 1978. *The History of Sexuality. Vol. 1: An Introduction*. New York: Pantheon Books.

Gaines, Jane. 1992. 'Competing Glances: Who Is Reading Robert Mapplethorpe's *Black Book*?' *New Formations* 16 (summer): 24–39.

Gates, Henry Louis, Jr. 1991. 'Jungle Fever; or, Guess Who's Not Coming to Dinner.' In *Five for Five: The Films of Spike Lee*. New York: Workman Publications. 163–69.

Guerrero, Ed. 1993. *Framing Blackness: The African American Image in Film*. Philadelphia: Temple University Press.

JanMohamed, Abdul. 1992. 'Sexuality on/of the Racial Border: Foucault, Wright, and the Articulation of Racialized Sexuality.' In *Discourses of Sexuality*, ed. Donna Stanton. Ann Arbor: University of Michigan Press.

Juffer, Jane. 1998. *At Home with Pornography: Women, Sex, and Everyday Life*. New York: New York University Press.

Julian, Isaac, and Kobena Mercer. 1986. 'True Confessions.' *Ten* 8, 22.

Koon, Stacey. 1992. *Presumed Innocent*. New York: Regency Publishing.

Marcus, Steven. 1974. *The Other Victorians: A Study of Sexuality and Pornography in mid-Nineteenth-Century England*. New York: Basic Books.

Mercer, Kobena. 1994. *Welcome to the Jungle*. New York: Routledge.

Neale, Steve. 1979–80. 'The Same Old Story: Stereotypes and Difference.' *Screen Education*: 32–35.

Perkins, Tessa. 1979. 'Rethinking Stereotypes.' In *Ideology and Cultural Production*, ed. Michele Barrett et al. London: Croom Helm.

Rosello, Mireille. 1998. *Declining the Stereotype: Ethnicity and Representation in French Cultures*. Hanover, N.H.: University Press of New England.

Williams, Linda. 1989. *Hard Core: Power, Pleasure, and the 'Frenzy of the Visible.'* Berkeley: University of California Press.

——. 2001. *Playing the Race Card: Melodramas of Black and White from Uncle Tom to O.J. Simpson*. Princeton, N.J.: Princeton University Press.

25

BETWEEN THE BLUES AND THE BLUES DANCE

Some Soundscapes of the Black Atlantic

Paul Gilroy

A note of music comes with us and is 'we'; unlike the visual arts, which seemed previously to point so far above us, out into the realm of the rigorous, objective and cosmic, but which in fact stop at our graves, it emulates good works by accompanying us beyond the grave. (Ernst Bloch)

> . . . the single factor that drove me to practice was that sound I had heard from the Hawaiian or country-and-western steel peddle guitar. That cry sounded human to me. I wanted to sustain a note like a singer. I wanted to phrase a note, like a sax player. By bending the strings by trilling my hand – and I have big fat hands – I could achieve something that approximated a vocal vibrato; I could sustain a note. I wanted to connect my guitar to human emotions: by fooling with the feedback between amplifier and instrument, I started experimenting with sounds that expressed my feelings, whether happy or sad, bouncy or bluesy. I was looking for ways to let my guitar sing. (B. B. King)

My obsessions with music and sound predated the happy day in early 1969 when my father gave me an electric guitar. A cheap white, sub-Fender Vox, impossible to intonate accurately, I played it through a succession of borrowed amplifiers until, after four years, I had eventually saved enough to buy a real instrument made in London in the long-forgotten workshop of Emile Grimshaw and Sons, sometime banjo-manufacturers of Golden Square.

From Michael Bull and Les Back (eds), *The Auditory Culture Reader* (Oxford: Berg, 2003).

[...]

At school I was laughed at for playing what was not yet named 'air guitar'. The rhythmic signature of Stovall's Plantation and the sublime ruminations of Son House and Lightnin' Hopkins would be approximated but never duplicated. Aspiring to possess the blues from the leafy edges of North London was in any case, riddled with contradictions. But Hendrix's anglophile afro-modernism resolved many of them. It certainly freed me prematurely from any mimetic obligations and pointed our generation of players and thinkers, via 'Red House' back in the direction of Albert King and the ur text of black self-making, with a voice and an electric guitar. That characteristic double address bespoke a public dialogue that drew upon different elements of self-hood. I thought I recognized it from Du Bois' helpful, pointed observations on the slaves' articulate message to the world but these were not only songs of sorrow, they were songs of triumph, obscene repudiation and transcendent dissent from the sour world that racism made.

[...]

I got into a fight at a party with somebody who took the 'Clapton is God' line then beloved of all the racist little Englanders and terrified suburbanites. Once I found more productive outlets for my evangelical fervour, I discovered that Hendrix helped yet again, not only by being the best but by being prepared creatively to damage the superficial integrity of the traditions in which he positioned himself. The modernist desire to transgress creatively was pivotal. After all, gypsy that he was, he had also wanted to be buried in England, his adopted homeland. His greatest moment as a live performer was that systematic assault upon the patriotic musical heart of the imperial nation in whose paratroops he had served with pride. It was then hell-bent upon destroying the Vietcong with the same fervour that currently guides its impossible and interminable war on terror.

In explaining artistic choices that felt eccentric then but no longer do so, Hendrix spoke from time to time about what he called 'the electric church'. It was a collective social body of musical celebrants that gathered periodically to engage the amplified modernist offshoots of the Mississippi delta and harness them in the causes of human creativity and liberation. Its ritual events had become loud, he told Dick Cavett in July 1969, not only because the appalling state of the world meant that many people were in need of being woken up by the shock that elevated volume could supply, but also because, if the wake-up-call could only be delivered on the correct frequency it could, in turn, promote a direct encounter with the souls of the people involved. Here, too, Du Bois' sense of where music augmented the power of words and writing supplied an active presence, although Hendrix's comment suggests a departure from his more conventional, and by then rather outdated, understanding of the workings of the black public sphere. Music would now produce its own public world: a social corona that could nourish or host an alternative sensibility a structure of feeling that might function to make wrongs and injustices more bearable in the short term but could also promote a sense of different possibilities, providing healing glimpses of an alternative moral, artistic and political order.

The electric church was all around us then; it was inseparable from the revolutionary upsurge of that moment. The traditional celebrations of Afro-Baptism had been profaned and adapted to the task of community defence. Under the banners of black power and anti-colonial solidarity its irregular services began to alter the political mentality of black Britons and to transform understanding of our emergent place in the post-colonial world. This could be done without a recognizably political word being spoken aloud. The church's fundamentally oppositional character was disguised by its intimate relationship with the innocent and playful music and dance with which 'negroes' re-affirmed their infra-human nature.

I argued with my Brixtonian cousins about Jimi. He had been frustratingly far from the centre of their south London world, but he and his talk about the

electric church as a source of meaning in a world from which meaning had been drained by the politicians' 'ego scene' came to mind while looking at this striking photograph of the crowd taken at a community reggae festival in south London's Brockwell Park during the summer of 1974. Taken by Chris Steele-Perkins, it has been brought back to life by Steve Barrow and Mark Ainley who have used it as the cover art for their worthwhile anthology of African American Rhythm and Blues tunes adapted into the Jamaican idiom. The idea that we could be slipping into darkness was something that then made sense at every point on the rim of the north Atlantic.

The faces of a large section of the assembled multitude have been captured as they listen raptly. They are not dancing. Movement appears to have been minimal even though the way that people danced to reggae in those days is a complex question that deserves detailed discussion beyond the scope of this brief piece. The power of this image derives largely from the way that their active listening has been en-framed. They seem to have become a community of listeners. We cannot, of course, know exactly what they were listening to. It is certainly tempting to imagine that the camera has caught them transfixed by the dread message of hope and resilience in the face of suffering that was so common to the insurgent musical culture of that moment long ago.

The image registers what must have been a routine occurrence at that time. This was a period in which, thanks to the reach and trans-local potency of phonographic technology, remote listening had acquired both social and political significance in the black Atlantic world animated by the chance to connect liberation struggles in the West with movements in what we now call the global South. Communication and analysis were conducted through the subaltern channels of a distinctive sonic and musical culture, transmitted unwittingly through the inhospitable infrastructure of greedy industries that had been colonized and had their dismal commodities bent to unorthodox purposes. It is abundantly clear from the musical forms and styles that were then popular right across this black world that hearing together had become connected to the possibility of thinking and acting together as well as to the larger processes of solidarity that were in the process of networking different black communities from Johannesburg to South Carolina via London and Kingston.

To a twenty-first century eye, this striking image shows something of what happened when the ethical and political language of human rights was articulated in the distinctive forms of the black Atlantic vernacular and transmitted into the everyday rhythm of post-colonial life in the metropole.

The mostly youthful faces caught by the camera are both male and female. They convey a mixture of deep concentration with what looks like a profound, ineffable sadness. That sorrowful mood defies being interpreted over-simply as either resignation or resistance and has seldom been captured as powerfully. Something like it can be glimpsed on page 137 of *Twelve Million Black Voices*, Richard Wright's famous exploration of the accelerated urban modernity of inter-war black life on Chicago's south side where a similarly disturbing photograph was given the caption: 'strange moods fill our children'. In Brixton forty years later, this concentrated sorrow was not the blues of the north Atlantic or the saudade of its southern counterpart though a comparable trans-coding of the history of racial terror means that it was kin to both. During that moment, with black Britain's emergent self-understanding still infused in the political language of Ethiopianist desires for flight and healing liberation, the image reveals an apprehension of the existential peril and ontological jeopardy in which racial hierarchy placed its victims. Marley, who had fled the US when his call-up papers for Vietnam had arrived in his mother's mailbox, had already delivered that message straight to black Britain's head, as the idiom of the time had it.

This portrait of community in the form of a crowd bound together by its collective mood of shock and stress as well as its shared emotion is all the more disturbing because, although the picture suggests that audience members were connected by a unanimity of feeling, they cannot actually see each others' faces. They are not in a circle and this is not a ring shout. Instead this crowd is confronted only by the backs of the heads of the people in front of them. They look forward, without staring in a strange unison, directing their synchronized rhythm of being in the world past the point where the photographer stood – between the audience and the stage that commands their attention.

They are a young and in many cases a stylish group. Today they provide us with a frozen example of what UK Blak's first poet laureate, Linton Kwesi Johnson, had identified at that very moment as 'a bran new breed of blacks'. We might add that this new formation had been, of necessity, developing a novel culture tempered by life in Britain with its distinctive mixture of feelings: promises combined with racist exclusion, violence and thwarted opportunity. Those routine post-colonial injuries were being compounded by the condescension dished out by too many supposed allies, helpers and friends. That view of black British life still bears upon interpretation of this photograph and the sonics that it silently captures. An empty benevolence mired in the assumption that the lives of black settlers could be defined by their cultural pathology, still echoes through historical reflections on the plight and destiny of this transitional generation composed mostly of young people who had not migrated as their parents had done but acceded to the dubious entitlements of British subjecthood conferred by birth alone. That view shaped almost all attempts to interpret their predicament, and its residue survives even today in a common sense view which makes the generation between the citizen migrants of the 1950s and the more assertively British-born group that succeeded them, into the custodians of a special crisis of identity, deeper and more disturbing than anything experienced by others before or since. Against that mistaken supposition, I submit this photographic evidence that suggests other more affirmative possibilities that derive from a sense of what that culture of sound and music brought into the lives of the transitional group to which I belong. We were not so much lost as lucky. An unusually eloquent, militant and musically rich culture oriented us and gave us the welcome right to employ it in order to defend ourselves, identify our interests and change our circumstances. We were buoyed up by a worldwide movement for democratic change and energized by the intensity of a very special period in the cultural life of our diaspora. Artistic innovations like Dub had, for example, taught us the value of what, in Adorno's words, could be 'communicated in the shock of the unintelligible'. The history of Punk without which post-war British life makes no sense, cannot be grasped without appreciating the force of the insights transmitted into what Dick Hebdige called its 'white ethnicity' from these dread sources.

More significant than the crowd's hip headgear, unstraightened 'Afro' hair and palpably soulful stance is that intense concentration common to their sorrowful, resilient expression. Many of them seem, understandably, to be trying to evade the camera's intrusion and surveillance. More practical issues aside, it is as though they do not want to be caught in a moment that reveals them to be as vulnerable as they are unified. They are united in the vulnerability they share as a racialized and marginalized group, in the wound they seem to carry as a collective cultural burden on their journeys towards and also away from Englishness and against the exclusionary force of its downpressive political and cultural codes. They seem to be and to belong together but that imperilled togetherness, that apparently elemental collectivity, is an untidy and asymmetrical affair marked by the way that racism intervened to block and to channel individuality into the patterns demanded by functional race hierarchy.

The photograph is also haunting because its subjects have been caught in what is wrongly understood as the inert or passive act of listening. The limitations of that view are repudiated by the common mood etched on their faces. Their concentration suggests not pleasure but a demanding variety of work. Whenever it was visible in daylight, that kind of cultural work proceeded deceptively, masquerading under the banner of play. It was mostly an orphic, underground phenomenon that did not seek overground recognition largely because it feared for its own survival in the cold light of colder northern days. The hidden public spaces in which it made its new metropolitan home and through which it found its own way hosted a complex process of intercultural and transcultural syncretism that is still poorly understood and only partially mapped. This was cultural work that incorporated defensive and affirmative elements: working over and working through the memories of slavery and colonialism, past sufferings and contemporary resistances so that they could provide resources for interpreting the present and imagining a better future for blacks and for the whole world.

The most enduring, although not perhaps its most significant result of this elaborate exercise, was the ability of many to assert their belonging to Britain with an authority and legitimacy that could not be denied and, in the process, to have changed what Britain was, largely by forcing acceptance of the fact that they were here to stay. These possibilities were celebrated and enacted in the musical cultures to which the photograph alludes. They were evident from distinctively local styles of toasting and dubbing, in the category of 'Lovers' Rock' and in the very different relationship to African American cultural and political traditions that was the conceptual premise of so much black British musicking. Dennis Matumbi was the high priest of our electric church. Shaka and Neil Fraser would eventually be its missionaries.

The late-night cultural work involved was not, of course, Labour, though in some circumstances it became Labour's active, desperate negation. Claimed back from the harsh, split world that immigrant labour made and held in place, the super-exploited social body composed of immigrants and their per-secuted children required spaces of healing and autonomy. Musical culture and the elaborate social relations that eddied around it, at least until the digital revolution changed the game, created that locus and invested it with a pre-cious democratic energy in which audiences and performers could interact and collaborate. The soundscape of that struggle and transition interests me again now as a historian. The representation of that interpretative community as an audience is especially apposite given that the ability to listen in this intense, collective way seems lately to have dropped out of black popular culture. Here were community and solidarity, momentarily constituted in the very process, in the act of interpretation itself. First pirate radio then the anti-social cultures of mobile privatization replaced the ancient authority of the electric church with something shallower and more consumer-friendly.

The Steele-Perkins photograph has another useful attribute. It directs atten-tion towards the independent power of a world of sound that was never reducible to the potency and oppositional lyricism of even the best and most compelling songs from that special period: revolutionary or compensatory. That world of sound celebrated here was specified hesitantly but repeatedly in the same vernacular code as something like a 'bass culture'. It was shaped by a fundamental awareness that as far as understanding the predicament of these sufferers was concerned, vision was not the master sense and words alone could not be a stable or trustworthy medium of expression and commu-nication. This difficult lesson had been administered by a cumulative training in tactical communication conveyed to us by the dub cuts that had begun to damage the semiotic integrity of even the most forgettable version sides.

It is worth recalling that, at this precise historical point, the black commu-nity in that part of South London found itself at the forefront of a deep and bitter conflict between its young people and the police and media, which had articulated the problem of Britain's black settlement through the diabolical figure of the mugger-deviant, predator and vanguard of black urban insur-gency. A few months earlier, a public display of fireworks for 5 November in the same park had been transformed into a large-scale disturbance. The young men roughly arrested at that event had been tried and received lengthy sen-tences for offences deriving from their refusal to accept the authority of what they saw as unjust and partial law; its universal aspirations compromised by perverse attachments to the ideas of racial difference and black inferiority.

In finely-detailed black-and-white tones, the photograph offers a striking image of black Britain emerging from the confluence of its Caribbean antecedents with novel north American aspirations buoyed up by the transnational vision of Black Power. The dissenters' goal of equal rights and justice had already been specified explicitly as alternative to peace by a whole host of artists. Again, it is impossible to know whether the crowd has been caught up in the music of a live band or, as is far more likely, just transfixed by music and/or toasting coming from one of the sound systems whose speaker boxes we can see piled up in the background. The preference for recorded rather than live performance was an interesting and disturbing feature of the soundscape of the period, which did not reveal an absolute enthusiasm for music made and heard in real time. The aesthetic and anti-aesthetic codes that governed this economy of pleasure, escape, transcendence and desire specified instead that the highest value was to be placed on and invested in art that spoke to the immediate circumstances in which it appeared but relied upon processes of intermixture and combination that made elsewhere audible. Remote black communities became present to each other by these means. When local DJs rode a Jamaican rhythm or sung over the radically unfinished version sides that had been dispatched northwards in anticipation of precisely that additional input, Britain or more accurately London and other metropolitan nodes of cosmopolitan settlement could be experienced as continuous with the increasingly distant but more easily accessible Caribbean. The sonic coming together of these divergent elements, expressions of geographically separated but genealogically related cultures, contributed to the appealing manifestation of a third, utopian space, sometimes labelled Africa, in which the wrongs and hurt of babylonian existence could be systematically undone and white supremacy overthrown in the name of higher human freedoms.

[. . .]

The physical transformation of the body in its encounters with musical sound has not been much discussed by critics and historians of the black Atlantic soundscape. It may not matter in the grand scheme of things, but that impact or rather interaction between body and sound provides a second stimulus for this argument, which is directed now against the limited idea that we encounter sound only, or even mainly through our capacity to hear and to make interpretative sense of it. For me, remembering the physical inscription of sound in matter provides a useful warning against the over-aestheticization of music and all mistaken if well intentioned attempts to approach organized sound as an exclusively cognitive problem. In the services of the electric church, the body is present as an object as well as an agent and it is not clear at all how musical sounds act upon it at various volumes particularly when drugs also become part of the experience in which music becomes organized and meaningful sound.

The idea of a bass culture raised by Ralph Ellison at the end of his epic

Invisible Man is helpful here. At the end of the novel, so concerned with the relationship of human senses to the perception of racial difference, Ellison's character aspires to speak on the lower frequencies in the name of a new and emphatically disembodied humanity. Somewhere towards the other end of the chain of cold-war humanism that encompassed black British life, Linton Kwesi Johnson articulated what we can now read as an urgent and notable response to Ellison's tentative, questioning call in his second book of poems, *Dread, Beat and Blood.*

Repeated references to the cultural world that the phonograph created, tie both texts together more tightly than the disarming actions of their 'mugger' protagonists. For Johnson, 'bass history is a moving is a hurting black story' while Ellison's picaresque hero, as is well known, falls inside the recording of Louis Armstrong singing 'What did I do to be so black and so blue?' while under the influence of a reefer. Once inside that holy space – not yet the province of the *electric* church because this is, after all, a wind-up gramophone – he discovers not only a different sense of time but 'a new analytical way of listening to music . . . that night I found myself not only hearing in time but hearing in space as well. I not only entered the music but descended, like Dante, into its depths'.[1] Johnson's complex poem 'Bass Culture' constructs a similar journey and can be read as an echoed reply. His activist choices diverge sharply from the 'cowardly' pathway taken by Ellison's retreating invisible man. His is another rebel music. This time it is heard socially in the collective communal setting of the blues dance that presents most of the same existential and political choices that bounded Ellison's Harlem but, perhaps, because Jah herb is stronger than Ellison's reefer they are embraced rather than refused:

> hotta dan de hites of fire
> livin heat doun volcano core!
> is de cultural wave a dread people deal[2]

This passionate popular rage, 'bitta cause a blues, cause a maggot suffering, cause a blood klaat pressure' is a revolutionary and utopian spirit that identifies emancipation with a change of rhythm. Shaped by the sonic innovations of dub and their novel acoustic architecture in the vernacular setting of a different underground than the over-illuminated urban cave Ellison had in mind, Johnson invests the power to act politically in the experience of hearing that damaged, beautiful beat. His words counterpoint it and associate the resulting tides of feeling with a cultural rupture that is also a musical event for which the power of the horns of Jericho provide the most appropriate Ethiopianist motif. This a musical cue that ties Rico Rodriguez's eventful contribution to the apocalyptic dub of 'Ghost Town' to the more recent offering by The Streets. While this sonic happening cannot itself abolish oppression, it can certainly [be] powerful enough to disperse and fragment it, winning important time for healing and recovery in the process and making an eventual triumph more likely:

> an the beat jus lash
> when the wall mus smash,
> an the beat will shiff
> as the culture allta
> when oppression scatta[3]

Something like that awareness of the power of sound would flow from these invigorating, disreputable sources into the mainstream of British culture through the conduits of Punk and its political adjunct, Rock Against Racism. Yet another version of it was forced upon me more recently. Last summer my ears rang for a week after standing too close to Robben Ford, soaking up his Californian Buddhist mutations of the blues. The high point of that smoky north-London encounter was his brave, delicate reading of Willie Dixon's Vietnam era tune 'It Don't Make Sense (You Can't Make Peace)'. It was heard this time in the context of an emergent global movement against American imperial power. Ford, whose elegant blues-be-bop playing I had first enjoyed twenty-seven years ago when he was a youthful member of the LA Express, had revived Dixon's wise lament during the summer of 2002. Originally directed at Nixon, Westmoreland, Kissinger and company, the song's observation that American might was sufficient to 'crush any country in a matter of weeks' had seemed apposite once more as the reinvigorated US war machine re-organized itself in Kuwait and Qatar under the direction of Bush II. The song makes no explicit mention of the war in Indo-China but, galvanized by its intertexts: the more casual references in Freddie King's 'Yonder Wall' or the more explicit fare served up by J. B. Lenoir and one or two other brave souls, it loses nothing by its calculated indirectness.

Listening to Robben raise the spirits of Albert Collins, Otis Rush and, of course, Albert King, while taking in the surprisingly large number of black people in the room, I felt obliged to ask how we should articulate the evident connections between the sculpted soundscape of tone, volume, voice and rhythm and the emotional and psychological effects that it both solicits and creates. There should be nothing automatic or overly mystical in this of course, but we do need to leave room for it in analyses of the way music is heard and made useful as an image of the will: individual and collective.

These questions point firstly to more than a refined understanding of the technological capacities of sound reproduction. And secondly to what might be called a phenomenology of sonic pleasures. On another occasion, after rushing over to Hammersmith to enjoy Anita Baker's first British appearance, I remember being disappointed by her live shows because I had only shivered once during the entire performance. It had seemed antiseptic and overly rehearsed. The physical effects on the body are not the same where pre-recorded music is played and modified even in the odd acoustic space of the sound-system environment that nurtured Linton Kwesi Johnson's radical phenomenology of liberation. The frequencies of address are different and the patterns of sociality vary where a different balance is being struck between hearing and movement and there is a bigger space for theatricality, grace and dance. I got that telltale shiver when Robben tore into his solo on 'It don't Make Sense'. There were swirling torrents of sound: cascading mutant be-bop pentatonics, Milesified probings, angry sounds in sheets of smouldering melancholy. Chorus after swelling chorus, wave after wave of crisp wailing notes breaking on the beach of our wounded subjectivity. There was the electric church all right and Willie Dixon was absolutely right, none of the absurd world against which that musical attack was directed made any sort of sense.

Here, I begin to run out of words and must face the fact that sound becomes an esoteric subject very quickly when we shift away from thinking about its reception and reproduction and consider, instead, the immediate intricacies of its musical production. Historically and analytically, there are difficulties involved in integrating or braiding together the resulting strands of thought into a single overarching diasporic soundscape that reveals the localization as well as the globalization of the world. The shared obligation to convene the public space of the electric church helps but it does not solve these difficulties. It is telling and perplexing that the 'auratic' properties of real time music were never the favoured vehicle for the patterns of play and memory that grew up around music in the Caribbean and subsequently set the template for black Britain's musical cultures.

Tonight that enigma bothers me while I peer into the grille of my amplifier assessing the subtle sonic properties of different types of EL34 and the infinitely variable characteristics of the various custom pick ups and string gauges I employ with the different instruments I play obsessively. Making that music, that sound, in real time has gone out of style. If it meets at all, the electric church has to operate under the disabling weight of computerized dance music that is easily commodified and privatized so that it can afford the simplest of routes into simulated ecstasy of togetherness.

[. . .]

NOTES

1. Ellison, R., *Invisible Man*, Penguin, p. 11.
2. Kwesi Johnson, L., *Dread, Beat and Blood*, p. 58.
3. Ibid., p. 59.

26

QUEERING HOME OR DOMESTICATING DEVIANCE?

Interrogating Gay Domesticity Through Lifestyle Television

Andrew Gorman-Murray

LIFESTYLE TELEVISION AND GAY DOMESTICITY

Across the Anglophonic west there is increasing mainstream interest in gay men's domestic sensibilities. This is evident in the growing visibility of gay men on lifestyle television in the US, the UK and Australia, particularly those programmes concerned with homemaking and the care of self through home. *Queer Eye for the Straight Guy* [US] is perhaps the most obvious case, built on the premise that gay men are arbiters of good taste, with inherent concern and flair for domestic styling. But this is not the only example. Attwood (2005: 92) contends that home makeover shows 'favour the depiction of gay or camp men, both as designers and contestants'. Dandy (if not gay-identified) designers feature in a number of home improvement shows, including *Home Front: Inside Out* [UK] (Attwood, 2005), *Groundforce* [Australia] and *The HotHouse* [Australia]. Moreover, gay men have appeared as participants and contestants in several home makeover programmes, including *Home Front* [UK] (Brunsdon, 2003), both series of *The Block* [Australia] and *The HotHouse* [Australia]. Despite the growing literature on lifestyle television, there is no sustained interrogation of the increasing presence of gay men on homemaking shows. I address this gap here, contributing not only to this literature, but also to the wider range of work on sexuality and home.

Specifically, I seek to examine 'gay domesticity' through the lens of lifestyle television, focusing on two Australian programmes which included gay male couples as participants: *The Block* (2003) and *The HotHouse* (2004). By gay

From *International Journal of Cultural Studies* 9:2 (2006) pp. 227–47.

domesticity I refer to the diverse ways in which gay men design, create and use domestic spaces, and how these constructions articulate, or challenge, the dominant understanding of home in the Anglophonic west as a hetero-sexualized family space (Johnson, 2000). In doing this I consider the intertwining of the material and the discursive in perceptions of home, and how this emerges through the presence and homemaking practices of the gay couples featured in the shows. For instance, just as the heterosexual family-based ideology of home shapes the material form of domestic spaces, this normalized discourse is also challenged through designs not intended to accommodate nuclear families. The Australian context is useful here because a fruitful comparison is enabled by the two programmes: the attitude to home, interior design and homemaking practices of each couple reflects a different reaction to the prevailing image of the nuclear family home. These divergent responses exemplify a paradox of gay domesticity. While the couple featured in The Block challenged the heteronormalization of home, the couple in The HotHouse reinforced this dominant image.

[. . .]

In this context, the widespread appeal of gay domesticity takes on new meaning, purpose and power. Of all the images of gay masculinity circulated in Australian society, these domestically inclined gay men present a type of gay masculinity which most neatly aligns with the core values of 'the great Australian dream', such as pride in the home, upward mobility and a sober domestic life. My argument, then, is that the image of the 'domestic' gay man presents a *paradox*. While gay domesticity challenges and subverts the normative heterosexuality of the home, this association also provides a way to regulate and sanitize a dissident sexuality, linking gay masculinity with ideals of domestic family life acceptable to mainstream Australia. The image of the domestic gay man both *queers* ideas of home and *domesticates* a 'deviant' sexuality. I contend that the divergent images of gay domesticity represented in and through The Block and The HotHouse exemplify this paradox.

ANALYSING LIFESTYLE TELEVISION

The Block and *The HotHouse* were produced and televised in 2003–2004 at the height of an unprecedented housing boom, with record property prices across Australia (Buchanan, 2004). But the obsession with 'domestopia' did not stop with home-buying. Australians were simultaneously spending more money than ever before on home renovation – over AU$5 billion per annum (Buchanan, 2004). Each year around 70,000 households spent over AU$70,000 each on home improvements (Dowling, 2003). Similarly, a significant growth in consumer spending since 2000 was largely underpinned by increased expenditure on furniture, white goods and home entertainment (Dowling, 2003). This willingness to spend on home improvement and domestic lifestyling fuelled a proliferation of successful Australian homemaking programmes during the period (Dolgopolov, 2003).

In this context, *The Block* was created by two Nine Network executives, Julian Cress and David Barbour, to capitalize on the triumph of renovation shows, while also drawing on the equally successful 'reality' format. The result was the highest rating series of 2003, with around 3 million viewers per episode and 4.4 million viewers for the final episode (Dolgopolov, 2003). The premise was simple: Nine Network purchased a run-down block of four two-bedroom units in Bondi, a Sydney beachside suburb, and selected four couples, one for each apartment. The couples represented a range of Sydney's social groups: 'yuppies' from Sydney's north; 'battlers' (working-class) from Sydney's south; experienced renovators from Sydney's west; and an inner-city gay couple, Warren and Gavin. Each couple was given 12 weeks and AU$40,000 to renovate their apartment and had to live in the unit during this time, where 'reality renovation' was filmed. At the end, all four units were auctioned: the couples kept any money above the set reserve price, and the pair whose unit achieved the highest price won an extra AU$100,000.

The premise of *The HotHouse* was somewhat different, and it must be noted that the show did not rate as well. Fourteen couples were chosen to help build from scratch a AU$2 million home in Bribie Island, south-east Queensland, providing manual labour and making high-level design decisions. The home itself was the prize – and only one couple could win. Here *The HotHouse* incorporated greater audience participation than *The Block*. Each week one couple had to leave the programme, and the audience ultimately decided who; the contestants nominated who should leave *The HotHouse* and the viewing public voted for who should be saved from elimination, with the 'least favoured' couple 'laid off'. This continued for 14 weeks until the house was complete and one couple remained. The original 14 couples comprised 12 heterosexual partnerships, one gay male couple, Brett and Jeff, and one pair of sisters. Brett and Jeff were ultimately the second runners-up, remaining till week 13. Consequently, debates about sexuality, family and home were a mainstay of *The HotHouse*.

The Block and *The HotHouse* differ from the British programmes previously considered in the literature. Rather than an education-by-entertainment format with expert presenters, these shows blended reality television with lifestyle programming. *The Block* and *The HotHouse* turned home improvement into a competition. Several 'real-life' couples pitted their homemaking skills against one another, 'attempt[ing] to out-design, out-decorate, out-renovate and out-pose each other' to win the ultimate prize (Dolgopolov, 2003: 143). The tears, tantrums and triumphs of renovation – the interactions between and amongst contestants, tradespeople and neighbours – were filmed and televised to the viewing audience in weekly episodes. There was no 'design expert' on *The Block*, while his presence was marginal on *The HotHouse*. Consequently, these shows allow us to examine the domestic sensibilities of 'ordinary' gay men, and how these articulate with or differ from 'everyday' heterosexual couples, in a largely unmediated manner. What did affect the relationship between gay domesticity and the heteronormalization of home, however, was external arbitration, especially in *The HotHouse*, where the progressive elimination of couples by a public vote influenced their behaviour.

[. . .]

QUEERING HOME: THE BLOCK

Since only four couples were required, and given the mainstream appeal of the show, it may appear surprising that a gay couple was included in *The Block*. Cress' explanation, taken from a 2004 interview about the casting process, is illuminating:

> We set out very much not to discriminate against anyone, and not to avoid reaching anyone in the casting process. We expected to get applications from gay couples because of the nature of the program. (Hunter, 2004)

This is revealing; applications were *expected* from gay couples *because* the show was concerned with home renovation. The taken-for-granted quality of Cress' statement reflects mainstream acceptance of the association of gay men with gentrification and homemaking, suggesting that gay domesticity sits alongside the nuclear family home in the Australian domestic imaginary. In the end, Cress and Barbour cast Warren and Gavin, and Nine Network were completely supportive of the decision, 'treat[ing] them like any other couple coming into the program' (Hunter, 2004).

Yet, Cress and Barbour knew that gay domesticity was not unquestioningly accepted across the Australian population. Controversy about the casting was expected, says Cress:

> It lit a fuse on a debate that was due to be had, where it went from right-wing radio to the tabloid press within 24 hours, and then immediately jumped the firebreak into the broadsheets, and became quite an interesting debate. (Hunter, 2004)

The debate, flamed by right-wing 'shock-jocks', concerned the inclusion of a gay couple in a homemaking show televised in the 'family-friendly' timeslot of 6.30pm Sunday evening. The morning after the first episode, Sydney radio broadcaster Steve Price ignited the issue:

> I just have a query about why Channel Nine needed to include a gay couple in the mix. Two blokes. Nice enough I guess . . . [but] I can tell

you that *The Block* will attract lots of kids, a lot of viewers under the age of 10. . . . Do I really need that conversation late on a Sunday at the end of a great weekend of relaxation? (Sutton, 2003: 46)

For these broadcasters, *The Block* was inappropriately promoting homosexual lifestyles in a family viewing zone by showing two men being affectionate towards each other (Enker, 2003; Sutton, 2003).

As Price intimates, their objections were underpinned by a taken-for-granted synonymity between home and family which, for them, excluded gay sexuality. In this way, the presence of Warren and Gavin in a family-friendly home-making show presented a multi-layered challenge to the heteronormalization of the Australian home. At one level, they believed that Nine Network was deliberately seeking to profit from a popular assumption of gay men's 'inherent' domestic sensibilities, using the presence of the first 'real-life' gay couple on television to garner ratings (Hunter, 2004). At the same time, they seemed to take offence that Warren and Gavin were easily labelled by Nine Network as a 'couple', with their relationship given the same level of respect as the three heterosexual couples. Nine Network's apparent acceptance of Warren and Gavin subverted normative understandings of coupling and, by extension, family. Finally, Price, for one, heatedly objected to the way *The Block* insinuated images of a gay couple into 'family' homes all over the county, sparking conversations about gay sexuality *amongst* families, *within* the homes of viewers (Probyn, 2003). These televised images destabilized the normative heterosexuality underpinning Australian family homes, encouraging parents to address the issue of same-sex relationships with their children.

Perhaps the basis of the broadcasters' objections was the way Warren and Gavin related easily in the domestic setting, challenging the taken-for-granted presumption of the home as a privatized *heterosexual* family space by establishing parallels between gay relationships and heterosexual marriage. Warren and Gavin themselves believe that their presence on *The Block* contested the preconceptions of conservative Australians and raised the ire of right-wing shock-jocks because 'we're just a real couple who hold hands and are comfortable with ourselves [rather than] over-the-top *Priscilla, Queen of the Desert* characters' (Sutton, 2003: 46). Indeed, Hunter (2004) argues that the public exposure of Warren and Gavin's domestic lives has contributed to the normalization of the gay men and lesbians in Australia by 'demonstrat[ing] that gay men live in loving, domestic relationships' just as heterosexual couples (ideally) do. *The Block* brought attention to their domestic bliss by juxtaposing Warren and Gavin's easy interaction with the tension-filled relationship of their neighbours, Adam and Fiona. While the prospect of winning invoked aggressive competitiveness within Adam, leading him to treat Fiona like an apprentice, and placing tangible stress on their relationship, Warren and Gavin stayed calm and emotionally mature (Browne, 2003; Dolgopolov, 2003). Even their few disagreements were painfully mundane; according to Gavin,

'We didn't argue that much. . . . We had a fight over a dustpan. I thought I could dust better than he could.' (Browne, 2003: 3)

It seems, then, that Warren and Gavin's domestic lives were interesting *only* because they were a gay couple. But the very banality of their interaction helps to normalize – and extend – notions of gay domesticity. Gay men are not only trendy gentrifiers, but also mutually loving domestic partners. Hence, the presence of Warren and Gavin on *The Block* encourages a broader understanding of the Australian family home that includes gay couples as constitutive of 'normal' familial domesticity.

But in other sequences from *The Block*, they begin to specifically *queer* the notion of the Australian family home through their attitude towards homemaking. For Warren and Gavin, as for the shock-jocks, home and family are synonymous, but this imbrication is even more intimate in their approach to domestic life. For them, home is not simply the site for privatized family life to take place – the home *is* the family. This attitude was made apparent in the opening episode when the cameras recorded the following discussion about what home means to them:

Gavin: Our home is really like our baby. We just love creating an incredible place to be in. We love seeing the untapped potential in a place. We love renovating.

Warren: I think why we say our baby is because so much of us goes into it.

[. . .]

This type of attitude to homemaking tellingly reshapes the imbrication of 'home' and 'family', subverting conventional ideas of the family home as a mere site of privatized family life. Instead, the home itself is the project of family life. This is not to say that homemaking practices in actual family homes cannot be like this. Blunt and Dowling (2006) similarly argue that family homes are not static sites, but actively practised, continuously (re)generated through flexible homemaking practices which accommodate the shifting relationships between parents and children. But Warren and Gavin perhaps take this a step further, suggesting that the dwelling *itself* constitutes family. This destabilizes the taken-for-granted link between *hetero*sexuality and the family home. Instead, the home-*as*-family is available *across* the spectrum of sexual identities, equally open to heterosexual *and* gay couples. Warren and Gavin not only challenge the heteronormalization of the Australian home by asserting a counter-claim of gay domesticity, but find a versatile way to bring together notions of home, family and sexuality in the process queering images of Australian domestic life.

Moreover, some of their renovation efforts militated against family occupancy. To be certain, Warren and Gavin, like the other three couples, renovated and designed a two-bedroom apartment. This form of housing, unlike the suburban free-standing house, is not typically associated with family life in the Australian domestic imaginary (Fincher, 2004; Mason, 2005). Beach-side apartments are imagined as holiday flats, not permanent family homes. Indeed, the three heterosexual couples also paid little attention to family needs, largely converting the second bedrooms into studies for childless working couples. Even so, the final design of Warren and Gavin's apartment precluded family living even more clearly than their neighbours' efforts. This was most palpably manifested in the removal of the permanent wall separating the living area and the second bedroom, and its replacement with a roller-screen. While ostensibly this allowed more flexible usage of the room (it could be used to enlarge the living area, or closed off for private use), it effectively created a one-bedroom apartment. Since one-bedroom apartments are not considered suitable for families with children, this move made family occupancy largely untenable. Against the popular discourse which links home and family, Warren and Gavin created a residence unaccommodating of nuclear families, instead fashioning a 'queer' home for other household types.

DOMESTICATING DEVIANCE: *THE HOTHOUSE*

The HotHouse provides a contrast to *The Block*. Whereas the presence and homemaking practices of Warren and Gavin followed a tradition of 'trendy' gay gentrification, contesting and queering the dominant notion of the Australian home as a nuclear family home, a family-based ideology firmly underpinned *The HotHouse* project. In this context, Brett and Jeff presented themselves and their design rationale as *congruent with* the emphasis on family values. Rather than playing the role of stylish gay gentrifiers, they demonstrated normative familial attitudes and qualities. Consequently, rather than queering home, Brett and Jeff's homemaking ideas and practices demonstrate how the association of gay men with domestic sensibility can sanitize gay masculinity, circumscribing publicly acceptable representations of gay men. This is especially pertinent given some of Brett's more sexualized and risqué activities – like nude modelling – mention of which was absent from *The HotHouse*.

Family values did not underwrite the initial premise of *The HotHouse*, but they emerged in the first fortnight through two particular incidents and came to dominate discussions amongst contestants and commentaries about the show. The first incident occurred within the first few days, and is significant for showing how the values of the family home regulated Brett and Jeff's later behaviour. One of the first high-level design tasks on which the couples had to decide was the orientation of the home's common areas. Two plans were presented: the 'party house', with a socialite's kitchen integrated into living spaces intended for entertaining guests; and the 'family house' with a less integrated and more work-oriented kitchen. The debate between the couples was heated, and Brett spear-headed the push for the 'party house', aligning himself early on against the idea of a family home. In the end, a majority of eight couples favoured the 'family house' plan. This early shift to a family-based ideology set the agenda for later discussions about the design and use of the house – and fuelled arguments about who should eventually live there. The outcome also precipitated a change in Brett and Jeff's stance on the home's design features, and they soon sided with the dominant family rhetoric, distancing themselves from their early support for a 'party house'.

The growing support for a family home by the couples was soon manifested in the second incident. The sisters, Jacinta and Siobhan, received many votes from the other couples in the first elimination round, and were soon voted out in the second week (in this early stage elimination was decided by the couples' votes rather than a public vote). The overwhelming reason given for eliminating Jacinta and Siobhan – offered by Brett and Jeff, too – was that they were *not* a 'couple'. With the project taking on a 'family house' design, it was argued that a family should eventually occupy the house. And 'family' was not understood simply as consanguinity, but as a nuclear family unit involving parents and their children. Being a couple was seen as a pre-requisite for starting a nuclear family. In this context, the sisters were not 'family', and not worthy of eventually living in *The HotHouse*.

I suggest that family values became a key player also partly because of the dwelling type involved. In contrast to *The Block*, *The HotHouse* project concerned the creation of a housing form continuously associated with privatized family life in Australia: a free-standing house with ample yard. This helped to shape the imagined future use of *The Hothouse*, and informed perceptions of who should eventually occupy the house. Moreover, the format of the show facilitated the insinuation of family values into the contestants' design rationales. The weekly elimination of couples from *The HotHouse* by a public vote rendered the show a popularity contest as well as an exercise in homebuilding. Each couple had to appeal to wide public support to ensure 'survival'. In this situation, to have a chance at success, Brett and Jeff, like the other couples, had to align themselves closely with the core family values of Australian society.

In this context, then, the elimination of Jacinta and Siobhan effectively cemented the emerging idea that *The HotHouse* would be a nuclear family home, and sparked further realignment and self-regulation on the part of Brett and Jeff. As a gay couple, legally unable to marry or adopt children, it seemed they were also unworthy of living in *The HotHouse*. At this point, then, they began to talk of the importance of family, and of one day having their own family, in both the episodes and their web-diaries. [. . .]

Brett and Jeff also palpably shifted the principles which underpinned how they designed their parts of the house (each couple was responsible for designing particular rooms). After initially pushing for a 'party house', they now asserted that their desire to have their own family informed their approach:

> Brett and Jeff are actually designing The HotHouse with their future family in mind. 'Everything that we do at the child's areas of the home, we look at what we're going to put in there for our children', said Brett. (HotHouse News, 2004)

Supporting a family-based ideology of home, they actively militated against ostentatious and flamboyant design elements. *The HotHouse* featured a professional design consultant, Jean Pierre, who offered advice to couples on how to approach the task of interior design. For Brett and Jeff, 'Jean Pierre [was] a man with taste centred around extremes, glamour and the Versace look', and they often disagreed with his suggestions, seeking instead to create a subtle, sober and family-friendly environment (Brett and Jeff's Diary 2, 17 March 2004). For instance, in regard to the kitchen, for which they were responsible:

> Jean Pierre . . . recommended that we change our white cupboards to a chocolate colour. We politely told him that we will go with rather a subtle change and not one of extravagance. (Brett and Jeff's Diary 2, 17 March 2004)

To affirm their family-centred focus, the viewing public was also constantly reminded of Brett and Jeff's extensive experience working with children through repeated reference to the fact that they operated a 'family fitness centre' in Port Kennedy, Western Australia, specializing in children's gymnastics coaching. Their web-diaries constantly reinforced their love for children and family values, referring on many occasions to the support shown to them by the Bribie community's local children; for instance:

> Over the weekends we have been overwhelmed with the amount of people who have come to the fence to cheer us on, especially the local kids. Some of the kids even spent hours on decorating some tennis balls and teddy bears to give to us. (Brett and Jeff's Diary 3, 7 April 2004)

[. . .]

Thanks to this adherence to, and emphasis of, normative family values, Brett and Jeff came close to winning *The HotHouse*. While the heterosexual couples were voted off in turn, Brett and Jeff remained, becoming the second runners-up. I suggest that [they] were accepted by the other contestants and the public because of their perceived normalcy. Given the centrality of home-and-family-life in the 'great Australian dream', the process of building and designing the Australian 'dream home' was the perfect opportunity to demonstrate allegiance to core social values like domestic family life. Indeed, it seems that Brett and Jeff wanted acceptance on the basis of their similarity to the Australian mainstream:

'We just wanted people to see us for being just guys or blokes – and that's been really accepted here. . . . It's a really nice thing to be around, and be accepted to the level that we have been,' Brett said. (Hothouse News, 2004)

But acceptance based on normative values works against the recognition and embracing of sexual difference. Instead, Brett and Jeff's sexuality was downplayed, and their family values emphasized. This, then, is an acceptance of gay masculinity which does not require a questioning and realignment of mainstream values. In this way, the homemaking practices of Brett and Jeff provide an example of how gay domesticity does *not* always challenge the heteronormalization of the Australian home. Just as depictions of gay domesticity can queer the home, such images also domesticate gay masculinity, providing a way to sanitize representations of gay men for mainstream Australian society.

THE PARADOX OF GAY DOMESTICITY

The Block and *The HotHouse* exaggerated homemaking practices, but they also responded to wider ideas of domestic lifestyle. By analysing the episodes and related media commentaries we can uncover shifting and competing attitudes to home in Australia. What emerges from this analysis is a complex interplay between perceptions of gay masculinity and heterosexual family-based ideologies in shaping ideas of home and domestic life. Analysed and compared, *The Block* and *The HotHouse* exemplify the paradox of gay domesticity. Through an enduring connection between gay men and the gentrification of inner-city houses, gay domesticity presents a long-standing challenge to the heterosexual nuclear family home [in] the Australian domestic imaginary. The homemaking practices of Warren and Gavin challenged the idea of the home as simply a site of privatized family life, queering notions of domesticity. But simultaneously, the association of gay masculinity with homely aesthetics can domesticate, regulate and sanitize public perceptions of gay men, circumscribing the limits of acceptable gay masculinity in Australian culture. Only those types of gay men that 'fit' the normative ideals of domestic family life are 'proper'. Brett and Jeff adhered as best they could [to] these normative ideals, playing down their sexuality, emphasizing their concern for children and family values, and underpinning their design practices with familial ideals.

This paradox, however, may be somewhat resolved through further consideration and application of the notion of 'queer'. Queer advocates the fundamental indeterminacy of identity itself, suspending identity as fixed and coherent (Phelan, 1997). Applying this logic to gay identity politics, queer challenges and unpacks the homogeneity connoted by the category 'gay', expanding and blurring the boundaries of gay identity in two ways. First, rather than denoting a single 'gay' subject position, queer emphasizes the multiplicity, diversity and fluidity of sexual identities subsumed beneath the interpellation

(Fortier, 2001; Reynolds, 1994). This can partially explain the divergent representations of domestic gay masculinity represented through *The Block* and *The HotHouse*: Warren and Gavin and Brett and Jeff can be seen to perform different manifestations of gay male coupling, one more 'anti-normative' and one more 'normative'. But here another queer blurring of sexual identities becomes highly relevant.

Queer also disrupts the heterosexual/homosexual binary, demonstrating the leakage between these identities (Fortier, 2001; Jagose, 1996). This is not just in terms of (bi)sexual desire, but also denotes the interpenetration of attitudes, values and styles (see Butler, 1990). Hennessy (in Jagose, 1996), for instance, argues that in unpacking monolithic gay identity, queer elicits how 'gay' subjects can be inflected by heterosexuality. In this sense, Brett and Jeff demonstrate the fluidity of 'gay' and 'straight' cultural politics, where their domestic values are shaped by heterosexual norms. While some analysts would define their attitudes as assimilationist, their embracing of some (hetero)normative ideals while being a palpably anti-normative couple exhibits a queering of discrete heterosexual and homosexual categories. Likewise, while Warren and Gavin's renovation practices might challenge the heteronormalization of the Australian home, they are a cohabiting, monogamous couple of the type Dowsett says is readily accommodated into ideals of heteronormative domesticity and family values. Thus, they too straddle the heterosexual/homosexual binary.

Ultimately, however, this is only a partial resolution because heterosexual norms continue to have the power to circumscribe what is acceptable in Australian society, while 'gay' cultural forms, including gay domesticity, can only inflect the (hetero)normative to the extent by which they are accepted by the (still heterosexual) mainstream. [. . .]

REFERENCES

Attwood, Feona (2005) 'Inside Out: Men on the "Home Front"', *Journal of Consumer Culture* 5(1): 87–107.

Blunt, Alison and Robyn Dowling (2006) *Home*. London: Routledge.

Brett and Jeff's Diary 2, 17 March 2004, URL: www.thehothouse.tv.

Brett and Jeff's Diary 3, 7 April 2004, URL: www.thehothouse.tv.

Browne, Rachel (2003) 'Truth Is, Reality's Harsh', *Sun Herald*, 6 July: 3.

Brunsdon, Charlotte (2003) 'Lifestyling Britain: The 8–9 Slot on British Television', *International Journal of Cultural Studies* 6(1): 5–23.

Buchanan, Ian (2004) 'Renovating Reality TV', *Australian Humanities Review* 31–32. URL: http://www.lib.latrobe.edu.au/AHR/archive/Issue-April-2004/buchanan.html

Butler, Judith (1990) *Gender Trouble: Feminism and the Subversion of Identity*. New York: Routledge.

Dolgopolov, Grisha (2003) 'Doing Your Block: TV's Guide to Lifestyle Renovation', *Metro Magazine* 138: 140–4.

Dowling, Robyn (2003) 'Renovator's Delight', *Built Environment Newsletter* 12: 6–7.

Enker, Debi (2003) 'The Block Nails It', *The Age*, 31 July: 14.

Fincher, Ruth (2004) 'Gender and Life Course in the Narratives of Melbourne's High-rise Housing Developers', *Australian Geographical Studies* 42(3): 325–38.

Fortier, Anne-Marie (2001) 'Coming Home: Queer Migrations and Multiple Evocations of Home', *European Journal of Cultural Studies* 4(4): 405–24.

HotHouse News (2004) 'Brett and Jeff Want Babies', 19 March, URL: www.thehot-house.tv.

Hunter, Tim (2004) 'Chasing Rainbows', *The Age*, 12 March. URL: www.theage.com.au/articles/2004/03/11/1078594493300.html.

Jagose, Annamarie (1996) *Queer Theory*. Carlton: Melbourne University Press.

Johnson, Louise (2000) *Placebound: Australian Feminist Geographies*. South Melbourne: Oxford University Press.

Mason, Megan (2005) 'Fairy Storeys', *Sydney Morning Herald Spectrum*, 6 August: 10.

Phelan, Shane, ed. (1997) 'Introduction', in *Playing With Fire: Queer Politics, Queer Theories*. New York: Routledge.

Reynolds, Robert (1994) 'Postmodernism and Gay/Queer identities', in Robert Aldrich (ed.) *Gay Perspectives II: More Essays in Australian Gay Culture*, pp. 243–74. Sydney: University of Sydney.

Sutton, Candice (2003) 'Gay TV Tut-tutting Straight from the Past', *Sun Herald*, 8 June: 46.

FURTHER READING

Bad Object-Choices (ed.), *How Do I Look: Queer Film and Video* (Seattle: Bay Press, 1991).

Bennett, T., Mercer, C. and Woollacott, J. (eds), *Popular Culture and Social Relations* (Milton Keynes: Open University Press, 1986).

Bennett, T., Boyd-Bowman, S., Mercer, C. and Woollacott, J. (eds), *Popular Television and Film* (London: BFI, 1981).

Bhabha, H., 'The Other Question', in *Literature, Politics and Theory* (London: Methuen, 1986).

Bhabha, H., *The Location of Culture* (London: Routledge, 1994).

Butler, J., *Gender Trouble: Feminism and the Subversion of Identity* (New York: Routledge, 1990).

Church Gibson, P. and Gibson, R. (eds), *Dirty Looks: Women, Pornography, Power* (London: BFI, 1993).

Donald, J. and Rattansi, A. (eds), *'Race', Culture and Difference* (London: Sage, 1992).

Dyer, R., *The Matter of Images* (London: Routledge, 1993).

Dyer, R., *White* (London: Routledge, 1997).

Fanon, F., *Black Skin, White Masks* (London: Pluto, 1986).

Gilman, S., *Difference and Pathology* (Ithaca, NY: Cornell University Press, 1985).

Gilroy, P., *There Ain't No Black in the Union Jack* (London: Hutchinson, 1987).

Gilroy, P., *The Black Atlantic* (London: Verso, 1993).

Hall, S., 'The Work of Representation', in S. Hall (ed.), *Representation* (London: Sage, 1997) pp. 13–64.

Hall, S., 'The Spectacle of the '"Other"', in S. Hall (ed.), *Representation* (London: Sage, 1997), pp. 225–79.

hooks, b., *Black Looks: Race and Representation* (Boston: South End Press, 1992).

Modleski, T., *Feminism Without Women: Culture and Criticism in a 'Postfeminist' Age* (London: Routledge, 1991).

Said, E., *Orientalism* (Harmondsworth: Penguin, 1978).

Williams, L., *Hard Core* (London: Pandora, 1990).

Williams, L. (ed.), *Porn Studies* (Durham, NC and London: Duke University Press, 2004).

Wilton, T. (ed.), *Immortal, Invisible: Lesbians and the Moving Image* (London: Routledge, 1995).

3.3
FEMINIST READINGS

INTRODUCTION: FEMINIST READINGS

Feminist readings of media texts, as Annette Kuhn (Chapter 4) indicates, have been central to an understanding of the power of media representations and, at the same time, have posed a fundamental challenge to both the content and the methods of older forms of media studies. Stuart Hall, in 1992, could write of feminism 'crapp[ing] on the table' of cultural and media studies, 'reorganiz[ing] the field in quite concrete ways' (1992: 282). Whatever their differences, feminist approaches share an insistence on gender or sexual difference as a structuring principle of both our material and our symbolic worlds (see van Zoonen, 1994). They have therefore insisted that media power operates not only in the public domain, to define and/or legitimate particular social groups, but also in the private world of the self, through processes of identification and desire. Finally, it operates in the construction of the very division between public and private, and the gendering of the first as masculine, the second as feminine.

Feminist readings of media texts have drawn on the insights gained from feminist film theory and criticism, where work on the visual construction of women as object of spectacle for the male gaze, and on the gendering of visual pleasure, was developed in relation both to mainstream Hollywood film and to melodrama and 'the woman's film'. In their insistence on *taking seriously* popular media forms aimed at women, they also extended and radically challenged earlier definitions within media studies of what could constitute an object of 'political' analysis. Much feminist research, then, has focused on what Charlotte Brunsdon calls 'mass cultural fictions of femininity' (1991: 365), popular forms for women such as soap opera, the television 'magazine' or 'makeover' programme, romantic fiction, and girls' and women's magazines, and on the (often contradictory) pleasures and ideological positionings which they offer. This research has in turn raised issues around the theorising of pleasure, the relationship of gender to genre, to narrative modes and patterns of address, and the relationship of the 'ideal' spectator addressed by the text to the real social subject who responds to that address.

These are the concerns of Chapter 27, taken from Janice Winship's *Inside Women's Magazines* (1987). Winship begins by addressing the public/private split described above. 'As TV soap opera is to news and current affairs,' she writes, 'so women's magazines are the soaps of journalism', disparaged within both critical and popular discourse. The 'Woman's World' which they claim to offer us is both an affirmation of women's interests and identity, and an indication of women's marginality: 'Men do not have or need magazines for "A Man's World"; it *is* their world, out there, beyond the shelves.' This ambiguity characterises the magazines: on the one hand, woman is placed 'centre stage and powerful' here, affirming the importance of 'women's territory'; on the other, the complicitous gaze invited between model and reader reasserts the power of 'the absent man' to define both. The magazines, then, offer us 'survival skills' to deal with the real dilemmas of femininity in our culture, and 'daydreams' that these survival strategies might actually work.

Chapters 28 and 29 develop these themes. Susan Bordo's 'Reading the Slender Body' (1990), which draws on the work of Michel Foucault (see particularly Foucault, 1991), focuses on the ways in which women's bodies are regulated and disciplined within contemporary consumer culture. For Bordo, 'the body that we experience and conceptualize is always *mediated* by constructs, associations, images of a cultural nature' (1993: 35). Her analysis therefore moves between a consideration of images of the 'ideal' female body to be found in advertisements, women's magazines and television talk shows and the bodily practices through which these cultural norms are lived out. Bordo argues that at cultural moments when traditional gender norms are being challenged, male anxieties about the 'uncontrollable' nature of women's bodies and women's desires are compounded, and female body ideals become correspondingly extreme. Nevertheless, she concludes that women's – often excessive – conformity to these norms is not a simple matter of the repression of female desire. The disciplined 'slender' body, whether anorectic or lean and muscled, is also the embodiment of a desire for self-control and self-mastery, for freedom from a domestic femininity and empowerment in the 'masculine' public sphere. Such bodily self-regulation is therefore both a manifestation of the cultural conditions of femininity and an embodied protest against them.

Charlotte Brunsdon's chapter (Chapter 29) asks: 'What is at stake in the relationship between feminists and soap opera?' Her answers trace a number of histories: of feminist media research; of the relationship of a developing academic feminism to its 'others' – 'femininity' and 'the housewife'; and of the way in which changes in focus within feminist research have been played out through studies of the soap opera and its female audiences. The soap opera was important to feminism, she argues, because, as a genre which focused on and was aimed at women, its study by feminist scholars was crucial to their insistence that media power does not operate only through the reporting of the public world, just as 'the political' is not simply a matter of class and national conflict. Soap opera's confinement to the domestic and the personal, its 'bracketing out' of the public world of action and institutions, operates politically to construct and maintain gendered power relations. At the same time, media representations of the everyday life of women become sites of struggle over the changing meanings of femininity, as well as sources of pleasure and identification for their female audiences. Finally, Brunsdon argues that in their interaction with soap opera and its audiences, feminist scholars have been forced to reconsider their own troubled relationship to conventional femininities.

The final two chapters in this section extend these arguments to newer media forms. Like Brunsdon, Angela McRobbie (Chapter 30) argues that 'relations of power are . . . made and re-made within texts of enjoyment', but the texts she analyses are recent popular genres and advertisements aimed at young women, in which a focus on 'lifestyle' and 'choice' mask what are in fact, argues McRobbie, new forms of regulation and constraint. Forms of popular culture such as these, she argues, are products of a 'post-feminism' which on the one hand appears to take feminism 'into account' by acknowledging its arguments and the gains it has produced, while on the other declaring it to be a thing of the past – outmoded and no longer necessary. In this way, feminism as a political and intellectual movement is 'undone', and new forms of sexism and gendered power relations can flourish. In an era in which 'female individualism' is celebrated, she argues, 'freedom' is equated with 'personal choice', and feminism is repudiated. The price of such 'freedom', however, is silencing, since it affords no position from which to mount a critique of continuing gender inequalities or newer forms of gender regulation.

Chapter 31 by Valerie Walkerdine addresses the performance of masculinity and femininity in video game play by children. Arguing that many video games are a site for the production of masculinity through their emphasis on heroism, action, competition and technology, she asks what consequences this has for girl players who must both engage with these qualities and simultaneously maintain a femininity which is defined in opposition to them. Her analysis examines the different ways in which the subjects of her research manage these contradictions. Girls, she argues, can play video games 'with relish'. However, such aggression is seen as problematic and dangerous to norms of femininity, both by the girls themselves and by more powerful adults, so that it is constantly either diverted and 'tamed' or displaced outwards, onto others. Finally she asks why it is that for boys 'the fantasy of masculine aggressivity', with its repression of more 'feminine' qualities, can be seen as unproblematic while both femininity and female performances of masculinity continue, in these new media forms, to be pathologised.

References

Bordo, S., 'Reading the Slender Body', in M. Jacobus et al. (eds), *Body/Politics* (London: Routledge, 1990).

Bordo, S., *Unbearable Weight: Feminism, Western Culture, and the Body* (London: University of California Press, 1993).

Brundson, C., 'Pedagogies of the Feminine: Feminist Teaching and Women's Genres', *Screen* 32:4 (1991) pp. 364–81.

Foucault, M., *Discipline and Punish* (London: Penguin, 1991).

Hall, S. (1992) 'Cultural Studies and its Theoretical Legacies', in L. Grossberg, C. Nelson and P. Treichler (eds), *Cultural Studies* (New York and London: Routledge, 1992) pp. 277–94.

van Zoonen, L., *Feminist Media Studies* (London: Sage, 1994).

Winship, J., *Inside Women's Magazines* (London: Pandora Press, 1987).

27

SURVIVAL SKILLS AND DAYDREAMS

Janice Winship

[. . .]

'. . . A Story about Men; and Women'

Women's magazines, perhaps especially *Woman* and *Woman's Own*, have become as well known nationally in Britain as any of the daily or Sunday newspapers. Yet though a million of *Woman*'s 5 to 6 million readers and around one-third of *Cosmopolitan*'s, for example, are men, magazines are very specifically associated with femininity and *women's* culture. Indeed, it is impossible to think about femininity and women without considering, among other things, motherhood and family life, beauty and fashion, love and romance, cooking and knitting – and therefore romantic novels, cookery books and women's magazines. It is difficult to envisage a masculine culture without contemplating work and careers, brawls in the boxing ring or on the 'real' battlefields of war, train spotting and messing around with cars, the pub and pulling girls – and therefore newspapers, hobby journals and 'girlie' magazines. No matter that not all women are mothers or read women's magazines, and that many men loathe boxing and have rarely glanced at a 'girlie' magazine; no matter either that feminism has chipped away at the stereotypes of femininity and masculinity, those versions of two genders are still profoundly influential in our experiences of growing up. Our lives as women and men continue to be culturally defined in markedly different ways,

From J. Winship, *Inside Women's Magazines* (London: Pandora Press, 1987) pp. 5–14.

and both what we read and how it is presented to us reflects, and is part of, that difference.

The cultural image of father-reading-newspaper-at-breakfast, mother-busy-on-the-domestic-front may have been starkly present in my family thirty years ago. But it has not yet disappeared, either literally or symbolically.

The same cultural gap can be seen at any local newsstand. There on the rack marked 'Woman's World' are the women's magazines which women are glancing through and buying. A short distance away is another stand marked 'Leisure' or 'Hobbies'. There are all the 'girlie' magazines, the photography, computing and do-it-yourself magazines (crochet, cooking and sewing magazines are, of course, with the women's magazines), and *their* voyeurs and purchasers are almost exclusively men. All this we take for granted as we amble or scurry through the shop for our own purchase. Yet those labels and that separation between a 'woman's world' and 'leisure' or 'hobbies' reveal much about our gendered culture. Men do not have or need magazines for 'A Man's World'; it *is* their world, out there, beyond the shelves: the culture of the workplace, of politics and public life, the world of business, property and technology, there they are all 'boys' together. Women have no culture and world out there other than the one which is controlled and mediated by men. The 'girls' are drawn in to support the masculine quest: 'boys will be boys' whatever the game being played.

Women tend to be isolated from one another, gathering together briefly and in small huddles, stealing their pleasures in the interstices of masculine culture so graciously allowed them: family gatherings, rushed coffee mornings or the children's events, and the occasional night out with the 'girls'. The tasks they immerse themselves in, the priorities they believe in, constantly take second place to the concerns of men. In men's presence women are continually silenced, or they are ridiculed, scolded or humiliatingly ignored. Thus the 'woman's world' which women's magazines represent is created precisely because it does not exist outside their pages. In their isolation on the margins of the men's world, in their uneasiness about their feminine accomplishments, women need support – desperately. As Jane Reed, long-time editor of *Woman's Own* and then editor-in-chief of *Woman*, put it, 'a magazine is like a club. Its first function is to provide readers with a comfortable sense of community and pride in their identity' (Hughes-Hallett, 1982: 21).

Yet such is the power of masculine wisdom that women's magazines and their millions of readers are perennially belittled – by many women no less than by most men. As TV soap opera is to news and current affairs, so women's magazines are the soaps of journalism, sadly maligned and grossly misunderstood. Over the years critics have disparagingly opined that women's magazines are 'a journalism for squaws . . . you find yourself in a cosy twilit world' (1965); it is a world of 'the happy ever after trail' (1976); 'cooking and sewing – the woman's world' (1977); 'kitchen think' (1982). They lament that women's magazines do not present a true and real picture of women's lives:

'Why . . . does the image deny the world?' (1965). Worse, magazines are 'completely schizophrenic' (1958); 'experience and make-believe merge in a manner conducive to the reader's utter bewilderment' (1971).

But if the focus of women's magazines *is* predominantly home and hearth, if the world they present *is* a happy-ever-after one, if they *do* refuse the reality of most women's lives, if they *do* offer a schizophrenic mix – and none of these characteristics is quite accurate – then there are pertinent cultural reasons why this is so. I want [. . .] to delve beneath this simple and dismissive description in order both to explain the appeal of the magazine formula and to critically consider its limitations and potential for change.

Hidden Cover Lines: Talking to 'You'

If the profile of women's magazines is partly determined by the state of play between women and men, it is also (as indeed is the 'game' between women and men) shaped by a consumer culture geared to selling and making a profit from commodities, and whose sales are boosted (it's firmly believed) through the medium of advertising. As commodities, women's magazines sell their weekly or monthly wares not only by advertising proper but also by the 'advertisement' of their own covers.

On any magazine stand each women's magazine attempts to differentiate itself from others also vying for attention. Each does so by a variety of means: the title and its print type, size and texture of paper, design and lay-out of image and sell-lines (the term the magazine trade aptly uses for the cover captions), and the style of model image – but without paying much attention to *how* a regular reader will quickly be able to pick out her favourite from others nestling competitively by it. Cover images and sell-lines, however, also reveal a wealth of knowledge about the cultural place of women's magazines. The woman's face which is their hallmark is usually white, usually young, usually smoothly attractive and immaculately groomed, and usually smiling or seductive. The various magazines inflect the image to convey their respective styles – domestic or girl-about-town, cheeky or staid, upmarket or downmarket – by subtle changes of hairstyle, neckline and facial pose. They waver from it occasionally rather than regularly with royals and male celebrities, mothers-and-babies and couples. Only magazines on the fringes of women's magazines, like *Ideal Home* (concentratedly home-oriented and with a high male readership) never use the female model. It is no profundity to say that as the sign of 'woman' this cover image affirms and sells those qualities of white skin, youth, beauty, charm and sexuality as valuable attributes of femininity. In marked contrast *Spare Rib* covers break sharply with the stereotyped plasticity of the model face, and communicate immediately how far that magazine distances itself from such an evaluation of femininity.

There is one other important and defining characteristic of this cover image: the woman's gaze. It intimately holds the attention of 'you', the reader and viewer. Such an image and gaze also has a wide currency in ads directed at women and men, has a daily venue on page 3 of the *Sun* and *Star*, and appears on the cover of 'girlie' magazines like *Mayfair* and *Fiesta*. The woman's image in these latter is obviously caught up in a provocatively sexual significance. Her partially revealed body speaks the sexuality about which the facial expression often equivocates. Her gaze holds that of the male voyeur; but it is he who has the controlling look: to look or not to bother, to choose to be sexually aroused or to turn over the page. She is the object and toy for his sexual play. It would be pushing it to suggest that the covers of women's magazines work in quite this way. For one thing many completely play down the 'come-on' look, for another the covers are primarily addressed to women. Nevertheless, what I would argue is that the gaze between cover model and women readers marks the complicity between women that we see ourselves in the image which a masculine culture has defined. It indicates symbolically, too, the extent to which we relate to each other as women through absent men: it is 'the man' who, in a manner of speaking, occupies the space between model image and woman reader.

In fact few women readers will make an immediate identification with these cover images: they are too polished and perfect, so *un*like us. Paradoxically, though, we do respond to them. Selling us an image to aspire to, they persuade us that we, like the model, can succeed. For the image is a carefully constructed one, albeit that it sometimes apes a 'natural look'. The model is only the cipher, the (often) anonymous face for others' skills and a range of commodities to fill. As *Company* puts it: 'Cover photograph of Joanne Russell by Tony McGee. Vest dress by Sheridan Barnett; necklace by Pellini. Hair by Harry Cole at Trevor Sorbie. Make-up by Philippe at Sessions' (April 1983). Easy then, 'you' too can create the look – given the ready cash. *Company* continues, 'Our cover girl look can be achieved by using Charles of the Ritz signature Collection for spring: complexion, Amboise Ritz Mat Hydro-Protective Make-up; cheeks, Cinnamon Glow Revenescence Cheekglow; eyes, Country Plums Perfect Finish Powder, Eyecolour Trio, Black, Ritz Eye Pencil, Black Perfect Lash Mascara; lips, Pink Carnation Perfect Finish Lip Colour; nails, Champagne Rose Superior Nail Lacquer.' Phew! Etched though the final image is here by the combined talents of men and the myriad make-up offerings of consumer culture, it also offers 'you' hope – of sorts: she is 'successful'; why not 'you'? It is a seductive appeal.

There is, however, a counterthread to this image which perhaps provides the stonger attraction for women. Woman is placed first here; she is centre stage and powerful. The gaze is not simply a *sexual* look between woman and man, it is the steady, self-contained, calm look of unruffled temper. She is the woman who can manage her emotions and her life. She is the woman whom 'you' as reader can trust as friend; she looks as one woman to another speaking about what women share: the intimate knowledge of being a woman. Thus the focus on the face and the eyes – aspects which most obviously characterise the person, the woman – suggests that inside the magazine is a world of personal life, of emotions and relationships, clearly involving men and heterosexuality, but a world largely shunned by men. This is all women's territory.

More than that, the careful construction of the model's appearance not only points to the purchase of certain commodities but also covertly acknowledges the *creative work* involved in producing it, a work executed in everyday life not by the 'experts' but by women themselves.

The cover image shouts that this woman's world of personal life and feminine expressivity is one worth bothering about, engendering a feel for the reader that such pursuits are successful, and moreover bring happiness: the model smiles. Idealistic as all this is (some would say oppressive), it is less a denial of the 'real world' than an affirmation of how much women and feminine concerns are neglected in that 'real world'.

With the model's gaze on 'you', the magazine invites 'you' into its world. It may address you directly: 'Self-esteem: a little more will take you a long way' declares *Company*; or (You) 'Win a speed boat worth £4000' urges *Options*, the magazine 'For your way of living'. Like the language of advertising, these sell-lines for that issue's inside delights ambiguously address 'you' as an individual. There is the suggestion that the relationship being struck up is the intimate one between the magazine and 'you' – just one reader. The same is implied in the title *My Weekly*. This address to the individual [. . .] heightens the sense of, on the one hand, the magazine speaking to the 'lonely woman', and, on the other, the strength of the support the magazine provides for its readers.

What 'you' are also offered on the cover is a careful balance between practical items linked to daily life and those which draw you, dreamily, into another world. Regarded by some critics as 'conducive to the readers' utter bewilderment', this mixture of entertainment and advice has been consciously promoted by editors since the inception of women's magazines. For example, *The Lady's Magazine* of 1770 aimed to combine 'amusement with instruction'; *The Englishwoman's Domestic Magazine*, published in 1852 by Samuel Beeton (husband of that doyenne of cookery Mrs Isabella Beeton) and one of the forerunners of modern middle-class home magazines, combined 'practical utility, instruction and amusement'. More contemporarily, in 1976 Beatrix Miller, then editor of *Vogue*, remarked, 'We are 60% selling a dream and 40% offering practical advice.' And in the launch issue of *Options* in April 1982 its editor Penny Radford hopefully declared, 'We want *Options* to be a lot of information, a lot of help and a lot of fun. So enjoy it.'

Why should women's magazines offer this mix? Men's magazines seem to settle for one or the other: 'entertainment' ('girlie' magazines) or 'information' (all the hobby journals). But then men's lives tend to be more clearly compartmentalised and – often thanks to women's hidden labour – men are singular about their activities: they are at work *or* at leisure; they are watching TV *or* engaged in their hobby. Many of the activities women carry out – often several at once – cut across categories: at work they can find themselves 'being mother', entertaining visitors or giving the feminine (sensitive) ear to others' work problems; lunch breaks are devoted to the 'work' or 'pleasure' of shopping; running a home can be both 'work' and a 'hobby' – cooking and sewing are tasks which can eat up leisure time, while ironing can be done in front of the TV.

After my father had glanced through the newspaper at breakfast he would go out to work and my brother and I would rush off to school, but my mother would stay put. Working mainly in the house, she often had to take 'time off' there too. When we all came home she had to cater to our needs, switching hats according to our various moods, and moving from one thing to another as we each in turn wanted this – a clean collar (my father rushing out to a meeting) – or that – a hem of a dress pinned up (me) – even as she was baking, tidying up or doing her own sewing.

At odd moments in this many-faceted and disrupted routine she would snatch the time to escape into her *Woman's Weekly*. At other times *Woman's Weekly* would deliver 'the recipe' or the answer to a stubborn stain. Women's magazines provide for these rhythms and routines of women's lives in which private time and space are precious, work and leisure merge, activities overlap, and dreams and escape often feed on a modest vocabulary of everyday possibilities: modest partly because the horizons of women's lives are still limited and partly because women's desires are constantly forestalled. The predominantly masculine world neither welcomes women nor women's ways of doing things. Notwithstanding its (often empty) tributes to mothers and wives and page 3 pin-ups, it will do its damnedest to exclude them from certain domains, frighten them on the streets, hassle them in the pub, or stamp on their hopes and ambitions.

No wonder that women need the 'refuge' of women's magazines.

For their part most women tolerate these harassments because, whatever the costs of being a woman, there are also compensations. The balance sheet of feminine qualities far outweighs that of masculinity. Women do not want to be the kind of people men are and it is difficult to envisage *other* ways of being women (and men). Women's magazines provide a combination of (sometimes wholly inadequate) survival skills to cope with the dilemmas of femininity, and daydreams which offer glimpses that these survival strategies *do* work. They are dreams of a better and different life, but one that remains well within a spectrum of familiar possibilities.

The survival skills offered by feminist magazines like *Spare Rib* and *Every-woman* may be more political, aimed at getting women off the 'desert island' of femininity and encouraging their daydreams of a radical future. Yet the formula is similar. They offer help and, above all, hope. They present a catalogue, both sad and heartening, of women's ability to survive in a world where the odds are stacked against them.

[. . .]

REFERENCES

Adams, Carol and Laurikietis, Rae (1980), *The Gender Trap 3: Messages and Images*, Virago, London.

Adamson, Lesley (1977), 'Cooking and sewing – the woman's world', *Guardian*, 3 November.

Berger, John (1972), *Ways of Seeing*, Penguin, Harmondsworth.

Braithwaite, Brian and Barrel, Joan (1979), *The Business of Women's Magazines*, Associated Business Press, London.

Connell, Myra (1981), 'Reading Romance', MA thesis, University of Birmingham.

Coward, Rosalind (1983), *Female Desire*, Paladin, London.

Curran, Charles (1965), 'Journalism for squaws', *Spectator*, 19 November.

Ferguson, Marjorie (1978), 'Imagery and ideology: the cover photographs of traditional women's magazines', in Gay Tuchman, Arlene Kaplan Daniels and James Benet (eds), *Hearth and Home*, Oxford University Press, New York.

Ferguson, Marjorie (1983), 'Learning to be a woman's woman', *New Society*, 21 April.

Greer, Germaine (1972), *The Female Eunuch*, Paladin, London.

Hall, Stuart, Hobson, Dorothy, Lowe, Andy and Willis, Paul (eds) (1980), *Culture, Media, Language*, Hutchinson, London.

Hughes-Hallett, Lucy (1982) 'The cosy secret of a jolly good Reed', *The Standard*, 8 February.

King, Josephine and Stott, Mary (1977), *Is This Your Life?*, Virago, London.

Lefebvre, Henri (1971), *Everyday Life in the Modern World*, Allen Lane, London.

McRobbie, Angela (1977), '*Jackie*', stencilled paper, Centre for Contemporary Cultural Studies, University of Birmingham.

McRobbie, Angela and McCabe, Trisha (1982) *Feminism is Fun: An Adventure Story for Girls*, Routledge & Kegan Paul, London.

Reed, Jane (1982), 'The story so far', *Guardian*, 20 October.

Root, Jane (1983), *Pictures of Women: Sexuality*, Pandora, London.

Sharpe, Sue (1976), *Just Like a Girl*, Penguin, Harmondsworth.

Tolson, Andrew (1977), *The Limits of Masculinity*, Tavistock, London.

Toynbee, Polly (1977), 'At the end of the happy ever after trail', *Guardian*, 21 June.

White, Cynthia (1977), *Royal Commission on the Press, the Women's Periodical Press in Britain 1946–76*, Working Paper 4, HMSO, London.

28

READING THE SLENDER BODY

Susan Bordo

[. . .]

Decoding cultural images is a complex business – particularly when one considers the wide variety of ethnic, racial, and class differences that intersect with, resist, and give distinctive meaning to dominant, normalizing imagery. Even on the level of homogenizing imagery (my focus in this paper), contemporary slenderness admits of many variants and has multiple and often mutually 'deconstructing' meanings. To give just one example, an examination of the photographs and copy of current fashion advertisements suggests that today's boyish body ideals, as in the 1920s, symbolize a new freedom, a casting off of the encumbrance of domestic, reproductive femininity. But when the same slender body is depicted in poses that set it off against the resurgent muscularity and bulk of the current male body-ideal, other meanings emerge. In these gender/oppositional poses, the degree to which slenderness carries connotations of fragility, defenselessness, and lack of power over against a decisive male occupation of social space is dramatically represented.

Since it is impossible for any cultural analyst to do a full reading of the text of slenderness in the space of a single article, I will instead attempt to construct an argument about some elements of the cultural context that has conditioned the flourishing of eating disorders – anorexia, bulimia, and obesity – in our time. The first step in that argument is a decoding of the contemporary slenderness ideal so as to reveal the psychic anxieties and moral valuations contained within it – valuations concerning the correct and incorrect management of impulse

From Mary Jacobus et al. (eds), *Body/Politics* (New York and London: Routledge, 1990).

and desire. In the process, I will be describing a key contrast between two different symbolic functions of body shape and size: (1) the designation of social position, e.g., marking class status or gender role; and (2) the outer indication of the state of the 'soul.' Next, [. . .] I will turn to the 'macro-body' of consumer culture, in order to demonstrate how the 'correct' management of desire in that culture, requiring as it does a contradictory 'double-bind' construction of personality, inevitably produces an unstable bulimic personality-type as its norm, along with the contrasting extremes of obesity and self-starvation.[1] These symbolize, I will argue, the contradictions of the 'social body' – contradictions that make self-management a continual and virtually impossible task in our culture. Finally, I will introduce gender into this symbolic frame-work, showing how additional resonances (concerning the cultural management of female desire, on the one hand, and female flight from a purely reproductive destiny on the other) have overdetermined slenderness as the current ideal for women.

SLENDERNESS AND CONTEMPORARY ANXIETY

In a recent edition of the magazine show *20/20*, several ten-year-old boys were shown some photos of fashion models. The models were pencil thin. Yet the pose was such that a small bulge of hip was forced, through the action of the body, into protuberance – as is natural, unavoidable on any but the most skeletal or the most tautly developed bodies. We bend over, we sit down, and the flesh coalesces in spots. These young boys, pointing to the hips, disgustedly pronounced the models to be 'fat.' Watching the show, I was appalled at the boys' reaction. Yet I couldn't deny that I had also been surprised at my own current perceptions while re-viewing female bodies in movies from the 1970s; what once appeared slender and fit now seemed loose and flabby. *Weight* was not the key element in these changed perceptions – my standards had not come to favor *thinner* bodies – but rather, I had come to expect a tighter, smoother, more 'contained' body profile.

The self-criticisms of the anorectic, too, are usually focused on particular soft, protuberant areas of the body (most often the stomach) rather than on the body as a whole. [. . .]

Much has been made of such descriptions, from both psychoanalytic and feminist perspectives. But for now, I wish to pursue these images of unwanted bulges and erupting stomachs in another direction than that of gender symbolism. I want to consider them as a metaphor for anxiety about internal processes out of control – uncontained desire, unrestrained hunger, uncontrolled impulse. Images of bodily eruption frequently function symbolically in this way in contemporary horror movies [. . .]. While it is possible to view these new images as technically inspired by special-effects possibilities, I suggest that deeper psycho-cultural anxieties are being given form.

[. . .] In advertisements, the construction of the body as an alien attacker, threatening to erupt in an unsightly display of bulging flesh, is a ubiquitous cultural image. Until the last decade, excess weight was the target of most ads for diet products; today, one is much more likely to find the enemy constructed as bulge, fat, or 'flab.' 'Now' (a typical ad runs), 'get rid of those embarrassing bumps, bulges, large stomach, flabby breasts and buttocks. Feel younger, and help prevent cellulite build-up. . . . Have a nice shape with no tummy.' To achieve such results (often envisoned as the absolute eradication of body: e.g., 'no tummy') a violent assault on the enemy is usually required; bulges must be 'attacked' and 'destroyed,' fat 'burned,' and stomachs (or, more disgustedly, 'guts') must be 'busted' and 'eliminated.' The increasing popularity of liposuction, a far from totally safe technique developed specifically to suck out the unwanted bulges of people of normal weight (it is not recommended for the obese), suggests how far our disgust with bodily bulges has gone. The ideal here is of a body that is absolutely tight, contained, 'bolted down,' firm (in other words, body that is protected against eruption from within, whose internal processes are under control). Areas that are soft, loose, or 'wiggly' are unacceptable, even on extremely thin bodies. Cellulite management, like liposuction, has nothing to do with weight loss, and everything to do with the quest for firm bodily margins.

This perspective helps illuminate an important continuity of meaning between compulsive dieting and bodybuilding in our culture, and reveals why it has been so easy for contemporary images of female attractiveness to oscillate back and forth between a spare 'minimalist' look and a solid, muscular, athletic look. The coexistence of these seemingly disparate images does not indicate that a postmodern universe of empty, endlessly differentiating images now reigns. Rather, the two ideals, though superficially very different, are united in battle against a common platoon of enemies: the soft, the loose, unsolid, excess flesh. It is pefectly permissable in our culture (even for women) to have substantial weight and bulk – so long as it is tightly managed. On the other hand, to be slim is simply not enough – so long as the flesh jiggles. Here, we arrive at one source of insight into why it is that the image of ideal slenderness has grown thinner and thinner over the last decade, and why women with extremely slender bodies often still see themselves as 'fat.' Unless one goes the route of muscle building, it is virtually impossible to achieve a flab-less, excess-less body unless one trims very near to the bone.

SLENDERNESS AND THE STATE OF THE SOUL

This 'moral' (and, as we shall see, economic) coding of the fat/slender body in terms of its capacities for self-containment and the control of impulse and desire represents the culimination of a developing historical change in the social symbolism of body weight and size. Until the late nineteenth century, the central discriminations marked were those of class, race, and gender; the body indicated one's social identity and 'place.' So, for example, the bulging stomachs of successful mid-nineteenth-century businessmen and politicians were a symbol of bourgeois success, an outward manifestation of their accumulated wealth.[2] By contrast, the gracefully slender body announced aristocratic status; disdainful of the bourgeois need to display wealth and power ostentatiously, it commanded social space invisibly rather than aggressively, seemingly above the commerce in appetite or the need to eat. Subsequently, this ideal began to be appropriated by the status-seeking middle class, as slender wives became the showpieces of their husbands' success,[3] I will return to the gender symbolism of slenderness later.

Corpulence went out of middle-class vogue at the end of the century [. . .]; social power had come to be less dependent on the sheer accumulation of material wealth and more connected to the ability to control and manage the labor and resources of others. At the same time, excess body weight came to be seen as reflecting moral or personal inadequacy, or lack of will.[4] These associations are only possible in a culture of 'overabundance' (that is, in a society in which those who control the production of 'culture' have more than enough to eat). The moral requirement to diet depends upon the material preconditions that make the *choice* to 'diet' an option and the possibility of personal 'excess' a reality. Although slenderness has hitherto retained some of its traditional class-associations ('a woman can never be too rich or too thin'), the importance of this equation has eroded considerably over the last decade. Increasingly, the size and shape of the body has come to operate as a marker of personal, internal order (or disorder) – as a symbol for the state of the soul.

Consider one particularly clear example, that of changes in the meaning of the muscled body. Muscularity has had a variety of cultural meanings (until recently largely reserved for male bodies) which have prevented the well-developed body from playing too great a role in middle-class conceptions of attractiveness. Of course, muscles have symbolized masculine power. But at the same time, they have been associated with manual labor and chain gangs (and thus with lower-class and even criminal status), and suffused with racial meaning (via numerous film representations of sweating, glistening bodies belonging to black slaves and prizefighters). Given the racial and class biases of our culture, they were associated with the body as material, unconscious, or animalistic. Today, however, the well-muscled body has become a cultural icon; 'working out' is a glamorized and sexualized yuppie activity. No longer signifying lower-class status (except when developed to extremes, at which point the old association of muscles with brute, unconscious materiality surfaces once more), the firm, developed body has become a symbol of correct *attitude*; it means that one 'cares' about oneself and how one appears to others, suggesting willpower, energy, control over infantile impulse, the ability to 'make something' of oneself. 'You exercise, you diet,' says Heather Locklear, promoting Bally Matrix Fitness Centre on television, 'and you can do anything you want.' Muscles express sexuality, but controlled, managed sexuality that is not about to erupt in unwanted and embarrassing display.

To the degree that the question of class still operates in all this, it relates to the category of social mobility (or lack of it) rather than class *location*. So, for example, when associations of fat and lower-class status exist, they are usually mediated by qualities of attitude or 'soul' – fat being perceived as indicative of laziness, lack of discipline, unwillinginess to conform, and absence of all those 'managerial' abilities that, according to the dominant ideology, confer upward mobility. [. . .]

SLENDERNESS AND THE SOCIAL BODY

Mary Douglas, looking on the body as a system of 'natural symbols' that reproduce social categories and concerns, has argued that anxiety about the maintenance of rigid bodily boundaries (manifested, for example, in rituals and prohibitions concerning excreta, saliva, and the strict delineation of 'inside' and 'outside') is most evident and intense in societies whose external boundaries are under attack.[5] Let me hypothesize, similarly, that preoccupation with the 'internal' management of the body (i.e., management of its desires) is produced by instabilities in the 'macro-regulation' of desire within the system of the social body.

In advanced consumer capitalism, as Robert Crawford has elegantly argued, an unstable, agonistic construction of personality is produced by the contradictory structure of economic life.[6] On the one hand, as 'producer-selves,' we must be capable of sublimating, delaying, repressing desires for immediate gratification; we must cultivate the work ethic. On the other hand, as 'consumer-selves' we serve the system through a boundless capacity to capitulate to desire and indulge in impulse; we must become creatures who hunger for constant and immediate satisfaction. The regulation of desire thus becomes an ongoing problem, as we find ourselves continually besieged by temptation, while socially condemned for overindulgence. (It goes without saying that those who cannot afford to indulge, teased and frustrated by the culture, face different problems.)

Food and diet are central arenas for the expression of these contradictions. On television and in popular magazines with a flip of the page or barely a pause between commercials, images of luscious foods and the rhetoric of craving and desire are replaced by advertisements for grapefruit diets, low-calorie recipes, and exercise equipment. Even more disquieting than these manifest oppositions, however, are the constant attempts by advertisers to mystify them, suggesting that the contradiction doesn't really exist – that one *can* 'have it all.' Diets and exercise programs accordingly present themselves via the imagery of instant gratification ('From Fat to Fabulous in 21 Days,' 'Size 22 to Size 10 in No Time Flat,' 'Six Minutes to an Olympic-Class Stomach') and effortlessness ('3,000 Sit-Ups Without Moving an Inch . . . Ten Miles of Jogging Lying Flat on Your Back,' '85 pounds Without Dieting,' and even, shamelessly, 'Exercise Without Exercise'). In reality, however, the opposition is not so easily reconciled. Rather, it presents a classic 'double-bind,' in which the self is torn in two mutually incompatible directions. The contradiction is not an abstract one but stems from the specific historical construction of a 'consuming passion' from which all inclinations toward balance, moderation, rationality, and foresight have been excluded.

Conditioned to lose control at the very sight of desirable products, we can only master our desires through rigid defenses against them. The slender body codes the tantalizing ideal of a well-managed self in which all is 'in order' despite the contradictions of consumer culture. Thus, whether or not the struggle is played out in terms of food and diet, many of us may find our lives vacillating between a daytime rigidly ruled by the 'performance principle' while our nights and weekends capitulate to unconscious 'letting go' (food, shopping, liquor, television, and other addictive drugs). In this way, the central contradiction of the system inscribes itself on our bodies, and bulimia emerges as a characteristic modern personality construction, precisely and explicitly expressing the extreme development of the hunger for unrestrained consumption (exhibited in the bulimic's uncontrollable food-binges) existing in unstable tension alongside the requirement that we sober up, 'clean up our act,' get back in firm control on Monday morning (the necessity for purge – exhibited in the bulimic's vomiting, compulsive exercising, and laxative purges).

The same structural contradiction is also inscribed in what has been termed (incorrectly) the 'paradox' that we have an 'epidemic' of anorexia nervosa in this country 'despite the fact that we have an overweight majority.'[7] Far from paradoxical, the coexistence of anorexia and obesity reveals the instability of the contemporary personality construction, the difficulty of finding homeostasis between the 'producer' and 'consumer' aspects of the self. While bulimia embodies the unstable 'double-bind' of consumer capitalism, anorexia and obesity embody an attempted 'resolution' of that double-bind. Anorexia could therefore be seen as an extreme development of the capacity for self-denial and repression of desire (the work ethic in absolute 'control'); obesity similarly points to an extreme capacity to capitulate to desire (consumerism in control). Both are rooted in the same consumer-culture construction of desire as overwhelming and overtaking the self. Given that construction, total submission or rigid defense become the only possible postures.

Neither anorexia nor obesity is accepted by the culture as an appropriate response. The absolute conquest of hunger and desire (even in symbolic form) could never be tolerated by a consumer system – even if the Christian dualism of our culture also predisposes us to be dazzled by the anorectic's ability seemingly to transcend the flesh. Anorectics are proud of this ability; but, as the disorder progresses, they usually feel the need to hide their skeletal bodies from those around them. If cultural attitudes toward the anorectic are ambivalent, however, reactions to the obese are not. As Marcia Millman documents in *Such a Pretty Face*, the obese elicit blinding rage and disgust in our culture, and are often viewed in terms that suggest an infant sucking hungrily, unconsciously at its mother's breasts – greedy, self-absorbed, lazy, without self-control or willpower.[8] People avoid sitting near the obese; comics feel no need to restrain their cruelty; socially, they are unacceptable at public functions [. . .]. Significantly, the part of the obese anatomy most often targeted for vicious attack, and most despised by the obese themselves, is the stomach – symbol of consumption (in the case of the obese, unrestrained consumption taking over the organism [. . .]).

SLENDERNESS, SELF-MANAGEMENT AND NORMALIZATION

Self-management in consumer culture, I have been arguing, becomes more elusive as it becomes more pressing. The attainment of an acceptable body is extremely difficult for those who do not come by it 'naturally' (whether aided by genetics, metabolism, or high activity-level) and as the ideal becomes firmer and tauter it begins to exclude most people. Constant watchfulness over appetite and strenuous work on the body itself are required to conform to this ideal, while the most popular means of 'correction' – dieting – often ensures its own failure, as the experience of deprivation leads to compensatory binging, with its attendant feelings of defeat, worthlessness, and loss of hope. Between the media images of self-containment and self-mastery and the reality of constant, everyday stress and anxiety about one's appearance lies the chasm which produces bodies habituated to self-monitoring and self-normalization.

Ultimately, the body (besides being evaluated for its success or failure at getting itself in order) is seen as demonstrating correct or incorrect attitudes toward the demands of normalization themselves. The obese and anorectic are therefore disturbing partly because they embody resistance to cultural norms. Bulimics, by contrast, typically strive for the conventionally attractive body shape dictated by their more 'normative' pattern of managing desire. In the case of the obese, in particular, what is perceived as their defiant rebellion against normalization appears to be a source of the hostility they inspire. The anorectic at least pays homage to dominant cultural values, outdoing them in their own terms [. . .]. The anorectic thus strives to stand above the crowd by excelling at its own rules; in so doing, however, she exposes the hidden penalties. But the obese – particularly those who claim to be happy although overweight – are perceived as not playing by the rules at all. While the rest of us struggle to be acceptable and 'normal,' they must not be allowed to get away with it; they must be put in their place, humiliated, and defeated.

A number of recent talk shows make this abundantly clear. On one, much of the audience reaction was given over to disbelief, and the attempt to prove to one obese woman that she was *not* happy: 'I can't believe you don't want to be slim and beautiful, I just can't believe it,' 'I heard you talk a lot about how you feel good about yourself and you like yourself, but I really think you're kidding yourself,' 'It's hard for me to believe that Mary Jane is really happy . . . you don't fit into chairs, it's hard to get through the doorway. My God, on the subway, forget it.' When Mary Jane persisted in her assertion that she was happy, she was warned, in a viciously self-righteous tone, that it wouldn't last: 'Mary Jane, to be the way you are today, you had better start going on a diet soon, because if you don't you're going to get bigger and bigger and bigger. It's true.'[9] [. . .]

SLENDERNESS AND GENDER

It has been amply documented that women in our culture are more tyrannized by the contemporary slenderness ideal than men, as they typically have been by beauty ideals in general. It is far more important to men than to women that their partners be slim. Women are much more prone than men to perceive themselves as 'too fat.' And, as is by now well known, girls and women are more likely to engage in crash dieting, laxative abuse, and compulsive exercising, and are far more vulnerable to eating disorders than males. But eating disorders are not only 'about' slenderness, any more than (as I have been arguing) *slenderness* is only – or even chiefly – about slenderness. My aim in this section, therefore, is not to 'explain' facts about which so much has now been written from historical, psychological, and sociological points of view. Rather, I want to remain with the image of the slender body, confronting it now both as a gendered body (the slender body as female body – the usual form in which the image is displayed) and as a body whose gender meaning is never neutral. This 'layer' of gender-coded signification, suffusing other meanings, overdetermines slenderness as a contemporary ideal of specifically *female* attractiveness.

The exploration of contemporary slenderness as a metaphor for the correct management of desire becomes more adequate when we confront the fact that hunger has always been a potent cultural metaphor for female sexuality, power, and desire [. . .]. This is a message, too [. . .], that eating-disordered women have often internalized when they experience their battle with hunger in the gendered terms of a struggle between male and female sides of the self (the former described as 'spiritual' and disciplined, the latter as appetitive and dangerous). In the anorectic's lexicon, and throughout dominant Western religious and philosophical traditions, the 'virile' capacity for self-management is decisively coded as male. By contrast, all those 'bodily' spontaneities – hunger, sexuality, the emotions – seen as needful of containment and control have been culturally constructed and coded as female.[10]

The management of female desire becomes a particular problem in phallocentric cultures. Women's desires are 'other,' mysterious, threatening to erupt and challenge the patriarchal order. Some writers have argued that female hunger (as a code for female desire) is especially problematized during periods of disruption and change in established gender-relations and in the position of women. In such periods (of which our own is arguably one), nightmare images of what Bram Djikstra has called 'the consuming woman' theme proliferate in art and literature (images representing female desire unleashed), while dominant constructions of the female body become more sylphlike – unlike the body of a fully developed woman, more like that of an adolescent or boy (images that might be called female desire unborn)[11] [. . .].

The fact that our own era has witnessed a comparable shift (from the hourglass figure of the fifties to the lanky, 'androgynous,' increasingly elongated slender look that has developed over the past decade) cries out for interpretation. This shift, however, needs to be interpreted not only from the standpoint of male anxiety over women's desires (Djikstra's analysis, while crucial, is only half the story), but also from the standpoint of the women who embrace the 'new look.' For them, it may have a very different meaning; it may symbolize, not so much the containment of female desire, as its liberation from a domestic, reproductive destiny. The fact that the slender female body can carry both these (seemingly contradictory) meanings is one reason, I would suggest, for its compelling attraction in periods of gender-change.

[. . .] The characteristic anorexic revulsion toward hips, stomach, and breasts (often accompanied by a disgust at menstruation, and relief at amenorrhoea) might be viewed as expressing rebellion against maternal, domestic femininity – a femininity that represents both the suffocating control the anorectic experiences her own mother as having had over her, *and* the mother's actual lack of position and authority outside the domestic arena. Here we encounter another reason for anxiety over soft, protuberant body-parts. They evoke helpless infancy and symbolize maternal femininity as it has been constructed over the last hundred years in the West. That femininity, as Dorothy Dinnerstein has argued, is perceived as both frighteningly powerful and, as the child comes increasingly to recognize the hierarchical nature of the sexual division-of-labor, as utterly powerless.[12]

[. . .]

From this perspective, one might speculate that the boys who reacted with disgust or anxiety to fleshy female parts were reacting to evocations of maternal power, newly threatening in an age when women can bring their desires out of the confinements of the home and into the public, traditionally male arena. The buxom Sophia Loren was a sex goddess in an era when women were trained to channel their energy and desire into home, husband, and family. Today, it is required of that energy, loose in the public world, to be stripped of its psychic resonances with maternal power, and normalized according to the professional 'male' standards of the public arena. From the standpoint of male anxiety, the lean body of the professional businesswoman today may symbolize such a neutralization. With her body and her dress, she declares symbolic allegiance to the professional, white, male world, along with her lack of intention to subvert that arena with alternative 'female values.' At the same time, insofar as she is clearly 'dressing up,' *playing* 'male' (almost always with a 'softening' fashion touch to establish traditional feminine decorativeness), she represents no serious competition (symbolically, that is) to the 'real men' of the workplace.

The cultural association of slenderness with reduced power and contracted social space is strikingly revealed, as I mentioned earlier, in fashion poses that juxtapose the slender female body against the currently quite solid and powerful male body ideal. But for many women, this 'androgynous' ideal, far from symbolizing reduced power, may symbolize freedom (as it did in the 1890s and 1920s) from a reproductive destiny and a construction of femininity seen as constraining and suffocating. Correspondingly, taking on the accoutrements of the white, male world may be experienced as empowerment by women themselves, and as their chance to embody qualities – detachment, self-containment, self-mastery, control – that are highly valued in our culture. The slender body, as I have argued earlier, symbolizes such qualities. 'It was about power,' says Kim Morgan, speaking of her obsession with slenderness, 'that was the big thing . . . something I could throw in people's faces, and they would look at me and I'd only weigh this much, but I was strong and in control, and hey *you're* sloppy . . .'[13] The taking on of 'male' power-as-self-mastery is another locus where shedding pounds and developing muscles, for all their surface dissimilarities, intersect. [. . .]

In the intersection of these gender-issues and more general cultural dilemmas concerning the management of desire, we see how the tightly managed body – whether demonstrated through sleek, minimalist lines or firmly developed muscles – has been overdetermined as a contemporary ideal of specifically female attractiveness. The axis of consumption/production is gender-overlaid, as I have argued, by the hierarchical dualism which constructs a dangerous, appetitive, bodily 'female principle' in opposition to a masterful 'male' will. We would thus expect that when the regulation of desire becomes especially problematic (as it is in advanced consumer cultures), women and their bodies will pay the greatest symbolic and material toll. When such a situation is compounded by anxiety about *women*'s desires in periods when traditional forms of gender-organization are being challenged, this toll is multiplied. It would be wrong to suppose, however, that it is exacted through the simple *repression* of female hunger. Rather, here as elsewhere, power works also 'from below,' as women associate slenderness and self-management via the experience of new-found freedom (from a domestic destiny) and empowerment in the public arena. In this connection, we might note the difference between contemporary ideals of slenderness, coded in terms of self-mastery and expressed through traditionally 'male' body symbolism, and mid-Victorian ideals of female slenderness, which symbolically emphasized reproductive femininity corseted under tight 'external' constraints. But whether externally bound or internally managed, no body can escape either the imprint of culture or its gendered meanings.

NOTES

1. See Robert Crawford, 'A Cultural Account of "Health" – Self-Control, Release, and the Social Body,' *Issues in the Political Economy of Health Care*, ed. John McKinlay (New York: Methuen, 1985), 60–103.

2. See Lois Banner, *American Beauty* (Chicago: University of Chicago Press, 1983), 232.
3. Ibid., 53–55.
4. See Walden, *Historical Reflections* 12:3, 334–35, 353.
5. See Mary Douglas, *Purity and Danger* (London: Routledge and Kegan Paul, 1966), 114–28.
6. See Robert Crawford, 'A Cultural Account of "Health".'
7. John Farquhar, Stanford University Medical Center, quoted in 'Dieting: The Losing Game,' *Time*, 20 February 1986, 57.
8. See Marcia Millman, *Such a Pretty Face: Being Fat in America* (New York: Norton, 1980), esp. 65–79.
9. These quotations are taken from transcripts of the Phil Donahue show, provided by Multimedia Entertainment, Cincinnati, Ohio.
10. See Bordo, 'Anorexia Nervosa: Psychopathology as the Crystallization of Culture,' *The Philosophical Forum* 17:2 (Winter 1985).
11. Bram Djikstra, *Idols of Perversity* (New York: Oxford University Press, 1986), 29.
12. See Dinnerstein, *The Mermaid and the Minotaur* (New York: Harper and Row, 1977).
13. 'The Waist Land: Eating Disorders in America,' 1985, Gannett Corporation, *MTI* Teleprograms.

29

THE ROLE OF SOAP OPERA IN THE DEVELOPMENT OF FEMINIST TELEVISION SCHOLARSHIP

Charlotte Brunsdon

In recent years I have more than once set an examination question for third-year undergraduates along the lines of, 'Why have feminist critics been so interested in soap opera?' To my recurring disappointment, no student has yet attempted this question, which I think is probably a tribute to their much underrated ability to identify their teachers' research agendas, and the way in which these tend to frame unanswerable questions. There is also a way in which the answer can seem very obvious – because soap operas are women's programs – which may make it very unattractive in the competitive context of an examination. This essay is my attempt at an answer to this question, but I should make clear that I think this bald and simple answer, in the west, in the key period of feminist interest, is fundamentally correct, and that all that I shall do is to make things a little more complicated. This I shall do in two main ways. Initially, by sketching a rather broader semi-historical context for feminist analyses of soap opera – a 'when' of this interest – and then by tracing the different modalities of this interest – a 'how.' In this process, I hope to provide an account of the role of soap opera in feminist television scholarship. Before I start though, I want to spend a moment on establishing why I think the question is itself interesting.

First, despite what I am going to say later in the essay, I think there is still a piquancy in the juxtaposition of 'feminists' and 'soap opera.' Each noun connotes a different engagement with femininity. The common-sense understanding of 'feminist,' a much more problematic term within common sense than 'soap opera,' is partly constructed through the negation of more familiar

From Robert C. Allen (ed.), *To be continued...: Soap Operas Around the World* (London: Routledge, 1995).

modes of femininity. In the popular imaginary, feminists are still women who don't shave their legs, don't approve of page three girls, and don't like soap opera. Given the extent of feminist scholarship on soap opera in the 1980s, this residual piquancy is intriguing. What is at stake in the relationship between feminists and soap opera?

Second, the very extent of recent scholarship on soap opera, much of it within, or influenced by feminist paradigms, provokes reflection. Ann Kaplan, in her 1987 review of feminist television criticism points to the centrality of feminist work on soap opera to the increased attention to the genre from the mid-1970s.[1] Robert Allen traces the contours of research on soap opera in his 1985 book, *Speaking of Soap Operas*, outlining the growth in social science research on the genre between 1972 and 1982.[2] It is toward the middle of this period that the feminist work starts being published [. . .]. The status of soap opera, as an object of academic study, has changed radically in the last twenty years. At its simplest, this is to say that soap opera is at present studied within the academy in a wide range of disciplines – something that would have been quite inconceivable in 1970. [. . .] Soap opera has been peculiarly significant for the development of feminist television criticism, and I think it is arguable that it is for the study of soap opera that this criticism is most visible in the wider arena.

So underlying my question about why feminists have been interested in soap opera is the paradox that, on the one hand, there is a perceived incompatibility between feminism and soap opera, but, on the other, it is arguably feminist interest that has transformed soap opera into a very fashionable field for academic inquiry.

THE GENERAL CONTEXT OF FEMINIST TELEVISION SCHOLARSHIP

Many commentators have pointed out the significance of what are usually called 'the media' to post-1960s feminism. Key texts of second-wave western feminism such as Betty Friedan's *The Feminine Mystique*, Germaine Greer's *The Female Eunuch*, or Sheila Rowbotham's *Woman's Consciousness, Man's World* all have central concerns with the available repertoire of images of femininity, with the way in which women are represented.[3] This feminist movement was, from its inception, a believer in the reality and importance of images. The twenty years or so since these founding texts were written have seen enormous changes in the analysis of images of women. For our purposes, perhaps the most significant is that this type of analysis has shifted from being primarily a political, extra-academic project to having a substantial academic existence. Many courses, in subjects such as English, history of art, communications and media studies, offer units on 'the representation of women' or 'images of women.' With the percolation of feminist ideas into the academy, which has happened differentially across disciplines, there have been several key debates which have taken place in rather different forms across different disciplines. At a general level, one of the most significant of these can be seen as the debate about realist paradigms.

Early feminist approaches to the media were usually within a realist paradigm, comparing real women, or the reality of women's lives, with the available images thereof. Real women were found to be imperfectly formed, hard-working, multi-ethnic, and extremely various in contrast to the dominant ways in which they were represented.[4] This important strand of criticism, which still has relevance today, was challenged theoretically by feminists who wanted to break with the realist paradigm, and what they saw as the false distinction between 'real women' and 'images of women.' These feminists wanted to argue that what we understand as real women, indeed, how we experience ourselves as such, is inextricably bound up with these images of femininity. That is, they argued that it is not clear what 'a woman' is, except through representation.[5]

These theoretical arguments, and the related debate about 'essentialism,' structure feminist academic endeavor in a range of fields. Indeed, Michèle Barrett and Anne Phillips have [. . .] argued that we can make a periodizing distinction between 'modernist' 1970s feminism, with its optimism about discovering the cause of women's oppression, and postmodern 1990s feminism, with its sense of the fragmentation of the category 'woman,' and its stress on the significance of difference.[6] In relation to the study of the media, we can mark a move away from the study of images of women to the study of the construction of femininity, or the inscription of sexual difference. So if the general theoretical terrain involves the move from the affirmation of the presence of 'woman' in the 1970s to doubt about the validity of this category in the 1980s, there are also marked changes in attitudes to conventional/traditional femininities. The recognition that women were perhaps rather more engaged with, and constituted by, available discourses of femininity than second-wave feminism had first insisted, fundamentally shifts the objects and purposes of feminist media analysis. This we can see most clearly in the changing attitudes to the mass produced genres of femininity: romance fiction, film melodrama and 'weepies,' women's magazines, and television soap opera. Key feminist books of the early 1980s, such as Rosalind Coward's *Female Desire* and Janice Radway's *Reading the Romance*, articulate a much more sympathetic engagement with mass media femininities, even as writers such as bell hooks challenge the racism of these femininities and feminisms.[7] It is these changes which are most relevant to the construction of soap opera as an object of study central to feminist television scholarship, and which are most interesting in the answer to my question, why were feminists so interested in soap opera? Before proceeding to this issue, it is necessary to outline some distinctions in the expanding field of feminist television research.

FEMINIST RESEARCH ON TELEVISION

Feminist scholarship on television can be found in a series of academic disciplines: film studies, communication studies, mass communications, cultural studies, sociology, English, women's studies. These different disciplinary contexts govern the construction of the object of study and the methodologies employed. What researchers are interested in, and how they proceed to explore it has to be understood partly within each disciplinary context. Thus, for example, work within sociology is more likely to be concerned with the pattern of women's work within the television industries than work within English, which may be more concerned with narrative structure of particular programs. However, many of the disciplines that have proved most permeable to feminist concerns, such as cultural or media studies are themselves only semi-institutionalized – only intermittently recognized as proper subjects. This fact, in combination with the relative youth of feminist scholarship on television, and the common political origins of much of the research, means that there is also a high degree of interdisciplinarity, and a determined tendency to breach disciplinary boundaries. Widely cited work like that of Ien Ang, Ann Kaplan, Tania Modleski, or Michele Wallace which is to varying degrees directly concerned with television, cannot be contained by just one discipline.[8]

[. . .]

WHY AND HOW WERE FEMINISTS INTERESTED IN SOAP OPERA?

Having established [. . .] that feminists have indeed been interested in the genre – and that some of the best-known feminist television criticism [. . .] is on this topic, I want finally to move toward an answer to my motivating question. So – why were feminists interested in soap opera?

Because soap opera is a woman's genre

From their origins in the US radio serials directly sponsored by detergent manufacturers, soap operas have been specifically aimed at female audiences. This is less true now than at any earlier point, but the connotational femininity of the genre remains overwhelming. The early research on radio soap opera conducted by Herta Herzog, Rudolf Arnheim, and Helen Kauffman, under the aegis of the Radio Research bureau only investigated female audiences.[9] Thelma McCormack has analyzed the assumptions about the female audience in other US research literature on the genre.[10] Ellen Seiter has revealed the commitment of Irna Phillips to educating women, as well as exhorting them to buy.[11] Christine Gledhill has examined the gendering of soap opera in the context of a discussion of the melodramatic mode in general.[12] In short, women have been targeted by the makers of soap opera, women have been investigated as the viewers of soap opera, and the genre is widely and popularly believed to be feminine, despite stubborn evidence that it is not only women who watch.[13]

Early feminist writing on the media, which was strongly dependent on the idea of 'stereotyping,' characterized the representation of women as dominated by two figures, the sex-object and the housewife. If the former was found in beauty competitions and ads for cars, the latter lived in soap operas and ads for washing-powder. So one of the early feminist responses to soap opera was simply hostile. The programs were one instance of the brainwashing project of the mass media, the project to keep women thinking that all they could do was be housewives. The women who watched soap opera, in this type of analysis, needed consciousness-raising, while the women portrayed were without interest. Feminists were interested in soap opera only to the extent that they purveyed ideologies of femininity and family against which feminism was defining itself. It was a combative interest, a commitment to knowing thine enemy.

But it was also more complicated than that.

Because 'the personal is political'

'The personal is political' is the most resonant and evocative claim of 1970s western feminism. This slogan reminds us of the particular flavor of the anglophone feminist movement that emerged from the political and social upheavals of the 1960s with its fierce belief in the significance of individual experience, but its absolute determination to understand this experience socially. This slogan, while evoking a specific political movement also has a certain familiarity which is not specific, and which indicates to us something of the influence of this movement. The radical redefinition of the personal and the political associated with 1970s feminism affected a wide range of fields, among them, media research. I want to suggest here that it is partly the direct political challenge of 'the personal is political' which contributes to the changing emphasis of media research in the 1970s and 1980s away from hard news/current affairs to softer programs. Further, I want to suggest that soap opera, and the feminist influenced analysis of soap opera, is pivotal to an understanding of this structural shift in the field. Thus we cannot understand the impact of a book such as John Fiske's *Television Culture*, with its radical shift away from 'hard' programming, without noting the attention paid therein to a feminist agenda.[14] For it is feminist criticism which has insisted that the home and personal life are in and of themselves significant, and not some mystified 'effect' of an economic determination elsewhere.

In arguing for the historical significance of the assertion that 'the personal is political' for an understanding of certain patterns in media research I don't dispute the deconstruction of the personal/political opposition as specific to white middle-class women that has been offered by scholars such as Aida Hurtado.[15] Jacqueline Bobo and Ellen Seiter map out some of the implications of this argument for media research, and particularly for domestic ethnographies, in their article on *The Women of Brewster Place*.[16] The point here, though, is that it was precisely those women not subject to state surveillance and harassment in their homes and personal lives who argued not only that the personal was political, but who also turned their attention to the media representation of women's lives. It is the same moment, the same movement, which declared that the personal was political, and which saw that this might change the significance of soap opera to radical analysts of the media.

If the personal is political – if it is in the home, in relationships, in families, that women's intimate oppression – or the oppression of women as women – is most consensually secured, then the media construction and representation of personal life becomes fascinating and an urgent object of study. If the traditional leftist critique of the media, with its structuring sense of class conflict, was drawn to the reporting of the public world – to industrial disputes, to the interactions of state and broadcasting institutions, to international patterns of ownership and control – emerging feminist scholarship had quite another focus. The theoretical impulse of feminism pushed scholars not to the exceptional but to the everyday. There was, as discussed above, research into patterns of employment for women in the media, but textually the concern to look at the representation of women of necessity led away from hard news and current affairs. So the theoretical conviction that there was a politics to everyday life and that women's hidden labor in the home was essential to capitalism coincides with the actual generic distribution of (white) women on television. If the project was to analyze the representation of women on television, there was of necessity a focus on genres other than the traditional objects of critical analysis because, in the main, women neither read nor featured in hard news and current affairs.

Because 'soap opera' has a metaphoric meaning

It is evident that in the late 1970s and the 1980s the term 'soap opera' was used about programs that are in fact rather distinct: South American telenovelas, US daytime serials, British social realist serials, US prime-time shows. What do they have in common that attracts feminist scholars to all of them? Here the answer is again the perceived femininity of the programs, but here in a rather more metaphorical sense – the feminine as contemptible, as banal, as beneath serious critical attention. Thus the unity of these different programs – the reason why, in a certain sense, it was correct to call them all 'soap' in a particular period – lies in their shared place at the bottom of the aesthetic hierarchy. It was to this gendering of aesthetic judgment that feminist critics were partly addressing themselves, as we see in this comment from 1981 by Terry Lovell: 'Yet *within this almost universal denigration*, soap opera does provide the pleasures of validation, and of self-assertion, which must surely go some way to accounting for its lasting popularity with women.'[17]

Because they shouldn't be: feminist ambivalence

Early feminist work on soap opera is marked by a profound ambivalence. On the one hand, there is the repudiation of the genre that I have discussed. On the other, this sense that these programs are something that 'other women'

– non-feminists – watch, offers a political rationale for an engagement with the genre. The drive here is to make a political analysis of pleasure – pleasure that is seen to be politically regressive. However, sometimes, underneath this explicitly feminist repudiation/re-engagement structure, there is a more elusive presence, a ghost of past femininities. For many feminists, writing about soap opera – and, I would argue, comparable genres and media such as romance fiction and women's magazines – entailed an investigation of femininities from which they felt, or were made to feel, a very contradictory distance.

Ien Ang discussed this directly in her *Dallas* project where she inscribed a sense of generally condemnatory attitudes toward soap watching in her original advertisement: 'I like watching the tv serial *Dallas* but I often get odd reactions to it.'[18] She is, in the first instance, concerned to investigate what she names the 'ideology of mass culture,' but later in the book explicitly criticizes a tendency toward 'the overpoliticizing of pleasure' present in much feminist work on popular fiction. [. . .]

[. . .] The first feminists doing academic studies of these popular forms really did face opposition not from just the academy, but also from within feminism. Some parts of 1970s feminism were very keen to construct a distance between feminist identity and more conventional forms of femininity. We see this tension [. . .] when [. . .] Terry Lovell defends both the watching and the study of the British soap opera, *Coronation Street*, in these terms:

> *Coronation Street* offers its women viewers certain 'structures of feeling' which are prevalent in our society, and which are only partially recognised in the normative patriarchal order. It offers women a validation and celebration of those interests and concerns which are seen as properly theirs within the social world they inhabit. Soap opera may be the opium of masses of women, but, like religion, it may also be, if not 'the sign of the oppressed', yet a context in which women can ambiguously express *both* good humoured acceptance of their oppression *and* recognition of that oppression, and some equally good humoured protest against it . . . .[19]

This mild defense of soap opera comes after nine pages of closely argued theoretical writing about why the genre is worthy of notice.

It is this final reason 'why' that brings me back to my starting-point, that of the perceived piquancy in the relationship between feminism and soap opera. Because of the sedimented gendering of the genre, there was no way in which a political movement which was challenging gender definition could ignore soap opera. But neither could it, finally, repudiate these pleasures and identification, nor simply celebrate them. Feminists were interested in soap operas because they were women's programs, but each of these terms proves unstable on closer inspection. What was referred to as 'soap opera' often had little more than seriality and lack of prestige in common. 'Women,' as I have repeatedly found while tracing this history, has proved a very tricky category for feminism, both necessary and impossible, often excluding more people than it includes. And finally, feminist interest in these programs has had rather different forms and motivations at different moments. And in this intricate dance of attitudes and categories a little subfield of academic study has been created.

CONCLUSION

Through tracing a set of interwoven histories I have tried to suggest what was most significant about the feminist encounter with soap opera. The tense is important, for I think we can date the key period of this encounter between 1976 and 1984, and it is in these years that we see both feminism and soap opera first becoming established in their much disputed and often ridiculed academic identities. In crisis in the political arena, feminism began to establish some toe-holds in the academy, sometimes in 'its own' discipline, women's studies, sometimes in the newer disciplines such as cultural or media studies, and occasionally in more established fields. The study of television, too, changed, and the interest in popular genres, perhaps partly focused by the international success of *Dallas*, was enriched and explicitly feminized through the attention to soap opera.

Second, the study of soap opera provided a particular generic site in a new medium for the investigation of the female viewer. The question of the female reader/viewer/spectator/audience has been a recurring topic to occupy feminist scholars in a range of disciplines at both a theoretical and an empirical level. Soap opera, perceived as so evidently gendered, while also very popular inter-nationally, provided an excellent site for the analysis of this figure, whether she was theorized as a textual construct or investigated as a sociological fact.

Finally, I think we could say that feminist media scholarship explores and defines itself a little in this encounter. Taking soap opera seriously – and perhaps, most significantly, taking soap opera fans seriously – as this early feminist work began to do, also involved taking the skills, competencies, and pleasures of conventional femininities rather more seriously. Doing research with 'real people' raises complex and difficult ethical issues. It has been partly through the exploration of this 'woman's genre' and its audiences that some of the simplicities and blindnesses of second-wave feminism have been chal-lenged. So if feminism has been important in producing a context in which soap opera can be taken seriously, soap opera has been significant as a site in which feminism can learn to address its others with respect.

NOTES

1. E Ann Kaplan, 'Feminist Criticism and Television,' in Robert C. Allen (ed.), *Channels of Discourse* (Chapel Hill, NC: University of North Carolina Press, 1987), pp. 211–253.

2. Robert C. Allen, *Speaking of Soap Operas* (Chapel Hill, NC: University of North Carolina Press, 1985).

3. Betty Friedan, *The Feminine Mystique* (New York: Dell, 1963); Germaine Greer, *The Female Eunuch* (London: Paladin, 1971); Sheila Rowbotham, *Woman's Consciousness, Man's World* (Harmondsworth: Penguin, 1973).

4. For example, Josephine King and Mary Stott (eds), *Is This Your Life? Images of Women in the Media* (London: Virago, 1977).

5. An early contribution to this argument can be found in Elizabeth Cowie, Claire Johnston, Cora Kaplan, Mary Kelly, Jacqueline Rose, and Marie Yates, 'Representation vs. Communication,' in Feminist Anthology Collective (ed.), *No Turning Back* (London: The Women's Press, 1981), pp. 238–245.

6. Michèle Barrett and Anne Phillips, 'Introduction,' in Michèle Barrett and Anne Phillips (eds), *Destabilizing Theory* (Cambridge: Polity, 1992).

7. Rosalind Coward, *Female Desire* (London: Paladin, 1984); Janice Radway, *Reading the Romance* (Chapel Hill, NC: University of North Carolina Press, 1984); bell hooks, *Ain't I a Woman?: Black Women and Feminism* (Boston, Mass.: South End Press, 1981).

8. Ien Ang, *Watching 'Dallas'* (London: Methuen, 1985); E. Ann Kaplan (ed.), *Regarding Television* (Los Angeles, Calif.: American Film Institute, 1983); Tania Modleski, *Loving With a Vengeance* (Hamden, Conn.: Archon, 1982); Michèle Wallace, *Invisibility Blues* (London: Verso, 1990).

9. Herta Herzog, 'What Do We Really Know About Daytime Serial Listeners?,' in Paul Lazarsfeld and Frank Stanton (eds), *Radio Research 1942–3* (New York: Duell Sloane and Pearce, 1944), pp. 3–33; Rudolf Arnheim, 'The World of the Daytime Serial,' in ibid., pp. 34–85; Helen Kaufman, 'The Appeal of Specific Daytime Serials,' in ibid., pp. 86–107.

10. McCormack, 'Male Conceptions of Female Audiences;' Allen, *Speaking of Soap Operas*.

11. Ellen Seiter, '"To Teach and To Sell": Irna Phillips and Her Sponsors, 1930–54,' *Journal of Film and Video* 40 (1), 2 (1989), pp. 223–247.

12. Christine Gledhill, 'Speculations on the Relationship Between Soap Opera and Melodrama,' *Quarterly Review of Film and Video* 14 (1–2) (July 1992), pp. 103–124.

13. For example, essays in Suzanne Frentz (ed.), *Staying Tuned: Contemporary Soap Opera Criticism* (Bowling Green, OH: Bowling Green State University Press, 1992) use data about male and female audiences although this is not the object of investigation in most cases.

14. John Fiske, *Television Culture* (New York: Routledge, 1987).

15. Aida Hurtado, 'Relating to Privilege: Seduction and Rejection in the Subordination of White Women and Women of Color,' *Signs* 14 (4) (1989), pp. 833–855.

16. Jacqueline Bobo and Ellen Seiter, 'Black Feminism and Media Criticism: *The Women of Brewster Place*,' *Screen* 32 (3) (1991), pp. 286–302.

17. Terry Lovell, 'Ideology and *Coronation Street*,' in R. Dyer, Christine Geraghty, Marion Jordan, Terry Lovell, Richard Paterson, and John Stewart, *Coronation Street* (London: British Film Institute, 1981), p. 51 (emphasis added).

18. Ang, *Watching 'Dallas*,' p. 10.

19. Lovell, 'Ideology and *Coronation Street*,' p. 51.

30

POST-FEMINISM AND POPULAR CULTURE

Angela McRobbie

INTRODUCTION: COMPLEXIFICATION OF BACKLASH?

This article presents a series of possible conceptual frames for engaging with what has come to be known as post-feminism. It understands post-feminism to refer to an active process by which feminist gains of the 1970s and 80s come to be undermined. It proposes that through an array of machinations, elements of contemporary popular culture are perniciously effective in regard to this undoing of feminism, while simultaneously appearing to be engaging in a well-informed and even well-intended response to feminism. It then proposes that this undoing which can be perceived in the broad cultural field is compounded by some dynamics in sociological theory (including the work of Giddens and Beck) which appear to be most relevant to aspects of gender and social change. Finally it suggests that by means of the tropes of freedom and choice which are now inextricably connected with the category of 'young women,' feminism is decisively aged and made to seem redundant. Feminism is cast into the shadows, where at best it can expect to have some afterlife, where it might be regarded ambivalently by those young women who must in more public venues stake a distance from it, for the sake of social and sexual recognition. I propose a complexification then of the backlash thesis which gained currency within forms of journalism associated with popular feminism (Susan Faludi 1992).

The backlash for Faludi was a concerted, conservative response to the achievements of feminism. My argument is that post-feminism positively draws on and invokes feminism as that which can be taken into account, to suggest

From *Feminist Media Studies* 4:3 (2004) pp. 255–64.

that equality is achieved, in order to install a whole repertoire of new meanings which emphasise that it is no longer needed, it is a spent force. This was most vivid in *The Independent* (UK) newspaper column *Bridget Jones's Diary*, then in the enormously successful book and film which followed.[1] For my purposes here, post-feminism permits the close examination of a number of intersecting but also conflicting currents. It allows us to examine shifts of direction in the feminist academy, while also taking into account the seeming repudiation of feminism within this very same academic context by those young women who are its unruly (student) subjects. Broadly I am arguing that for feminism to be 'taken into account' it has to be understood as having already passed away. This is a movement detectable across popular culture, a site where 'power . . . is remade at various junctures within everyday life, (constituting) our tenuous sense of common sense' (Judith Butler, Ernesto Laclau & Slavoj Zizek 2000, p. 14). Some fleeting comments in Judith Butler's short book *Antigone's Claim* (2000) suggests to me that post-feminism can be explored through what I would describe as a 'double entanglement'. This comprises the co-existence of neo-conservative values in relation to gender, sexuality and family life (for example, George Bush supporting the campaign to encourage chastity among young people, and in March 2004 declaring that civilisation itself depends on traditional marriage), with processes of liberalisation in regard to choice and diversity in domestic, sexual and kinship relations (for example, gay couples now able to adopt, foster or have their own children by whatever means, and in the UK at least, full rights to civil partnerships). It also encompasses the co-existence of feminism as at some level transformed into a form of Gramscian common sense, while also fiercely repudiated, indeed almost hated (Angela McRobbie 2003). The taken into accountness permits all the more thorough dismantling of feminist politics and the discrediting of the occasionally voiced need for its renewal.

Feminism Dismantling Itself

The impact of this 'double entanglement' which is manifest in popular and political culture coincides, however, with feminism in the academy finding it necessary to dismantle itself. For the sake of periodisation, we could say that 1990 (or thereabouts) marks a turning point, the moment of definitive self-critique in feminist theory. At this time the representational claims of second-wave feminism come to be fully interrogated by post-colonialist feminists like Spivak, Trinh, and Mohanty among others, and by feminist theorists like Butler and Haraway who inaugurate the radical de-naturalising of the post-feminist body (Judith Butler 1990; Donna Haraway 1991; Chandra T. Mohanty 1995; Gayatri Spivak 1988; T. Minha Trinh 1989). Under the prevailing influence of Foucault, there is a shift away from feminist interest in centralised power blocks – e.g., the State, patriarchy, law – to more dispersed sites, events and instances of power conceptualised as flows and specific convergences and consolidations of talk, discourse, and attentions. The body and also the subject come to represent a focal point for feminist interest, nowhere more so than in the work of Butler. The concept of subjectivity and the means by which cultural forms and interpellations (or dominant social processes) call women into being, produce them as subjects whilst ostensibly merely describing them as such, inevitably means that it is a problematically 'she,' rather than an unproblematically 'we,' which is indicative of a turn to what we might describe as the emerging politics of post-feminist inquiry (Butler 1990, 1993).

In feminist cultural studies the early 1990s also marks a moment of feminist reflexivity. In her article 'Pedagogies of the Feminine' Brunsdon queried the hitherto assumed use value to feminist media scholarship of the binary opposition between femininity and feminism, or as she put it the extent to which the 'housewife' or 'ordinary woman' was conceived of as the assumed subject of attention for feminism (Charlotte Brunsdon [1991] 1997). Looking back we can see how heavily utilised this dualism was, and also how particular it was to gender arrangements for largely white and relatively affluent (i.e. housewifely) women. The year 1990 also marked the moment at which the concept of popular feminism found expression. Andrea Stuart (1990) considered the wider circulation of feminist values across the landscape of popular culture, in particular magazines, where quite suddenly issues which had been central to the formation of the women's movement like domestic violence, equal pay, and workplace harassment, were now addressed to a vast readership. The wider dissemination of feminist issues was also a key concern in my own writing at this time, in particular the intersection of these new representations with the daily lives of young women who as subjects ('called into being') of popular feminism, might then be expected to embody more emboldened (though also of course 'failed') identities. This gave rise to the idea of feminist success. Of course no sooner is the word 'success' written than it is queried. How could this be gauged? What might be the criteria for judging degrees of feminist success?

FEMALE SUCCESS

Admittedly there is some extravagance in my claim for feminist success. It might be more accurate to remark on the keen interest across the quality and popular media (themselves wishing to increase their female readers and audiences), in ideas of female success. As feminist values are indeed taken on board within a range of institutions, including law, education, to an extent medicine, likewise employment, and the media, high profile or newsworthy achievement of women and girls in these sectors shows the institutions to be modern and abreast with social change. This is the context then within which feminism is acknowledged and this is what I mean by feminism taken into account. Feminist success has, so far, only been described sporadically (for accounts of girls' achievement in education see Madeleine Arnot, Miriam David & Gaby

Weiner 1999; and also Anita Harris 2003). Within media and cultural studies both Brunsdon and myself have each considered how with feminism as part of the academic curriculum, i.e. 'canonised,' then it is not surprising that it might also be countered, that is feminism must face up to the consequences of its own claims to representation and power, and not be so surprised when young women students decline the invitation to identify as a 'we' with their feminist teachers and scholars (Charlotte Brunsdon [1991] 1997; Angela McRobbie 1999a). This interface between the feminist academy and the student body has also been discussed in US feminist journals particularly in regard to the decline of women's studies (Wendy Brown 1997). Back in the early 1990s and following Butler, I saw this sense of contestation on the part of young women, and what I would call their 'distance from feminism' as one of potential, where a lively dialogue about how feminism might develop would commence (Judith Butler 1992; Angela McRobbie 1994). Indeed it seemed in the very nature of feminism that it gave rise to dis-identification as a kind of requirement for its existence. But still, it seems now, over a decade later, that this space of 'distance from feminism' and those utterances of forceful non-identity with feminism have consolidated into something closer to repudiation rather than ambivalence, and it is this vehemently denunciatory stance which is manifest across the field of popular gender debate. This is the cultural space of post-feminism.

In this context it requires both imagination and hopefulness to argue that the active, sustained, and repetitive repudiation or repression of feminism also marks its (still fearful) presence or even longevity (as afterlife). What I mean by this is that there are different kinds of repudiation and different investments in such a stance. The more gentle denunciations of feminism (as in the film *Bridget Jones's Diary*) co-exists however with the shrill championing of young women as a 'metaphor for social change' on the pages of the right wing press in the UK, in particular the *Daily Mail*. This anti-feminist endorsement of female individualisation is embodied in the figure of the ambitious 'TV blonde' (Angela McRobbie 1999b).[2] These so-called 'A1' girls are glamorous high-achievers destined for Oxford or Cambridge and are usually pictured clutching A-level certificates. We might say these are ideal girls, subjects *par excellence*, and also subjects of excellence. Nor are these notions of female success exclusive to the changing representations of young women in the countries of the affluent west. As Gayatri Spivak (1999) has argued in the impoverished zones of the world, governments and NGOs also look to the minds and bodies of young women for whom education comes to promise enormous economic and demographic rewards. Young women are a good investment, they can be trusted with micro-credit, they are the privileged subjects of social change. But the terms of these great expectations on the part of governments are that young women must do without more autonomous feminist politics. What is consistent is the over-shadowing indeed displacement of feminism as a political movement. It is this displacement which reflects Butler's sorrowful account of

Antigone's life after death. Her shadowy, lonely existence, suggests a modality of feminist effectivity as spectral, she has to be cast out, indeed entombed for social organisation to once again become intelligible.

UNPOPULAR FEMINISM

The media has become the key site for defining codes of sexual conduct. It casts judgement and establishes the rules of play. Across these many channels of communication feminism is routinely disparaged. This is another Butler point, why is feminism so hated? Why do young women recoil in horror at the very idea of the feminist? To count as a girl today appears to require this kind of ritualistic denunciation, which in turn suggests that one strategy in the disempowering of feminism includes it being historicised and generationalised and thus easily rendered out of date. It would be far too simplistic to trace a pattern in media from popular feminism (or 'prime time feminism' including TV programmes like *L.A. Law*) in the early 1990s, to niche feminism (BBC Radio 4, Women's Hour, and the Women's Page of *The Guardian* newspaper), in the mid-1990s, and then to overtly unpopular feminism (new century), as though these charted a chronological 'great moving right show' as Stuart Hall might put it (1989). We would need a more developed conceptual schema to account for the simultaneous feminisation of popular media with this accumulation of ambivalent, fearful responses. We would certainly need to signal the full enfranchisement of women in the west, of all ages as audiences, active consumers of media and the many products it promotes, and by virtue of education, earning power, and consumer identity a sizeable block of target market. We would also need to be able to theorise female achievement predicated not on feminism, but on 'female individualism,' on success which seems to be based on the invitation to young women by various governments that they might now consider themselves free to compete in education and in work as privileged subjects of the new meritocracy. Is this then the new deal for, in the UK, New Labour's 'modern' young women, female individualisation and the new meritocracy at the expense of feminist politics?

There are various sites within popular culture where this work of undoing feminism with some subtlety becomes visible (see also Charlotte Brunsdon 2004). The Wonderbra advert showing the model Eva Herzigova looking down admiringly at her substantial cleavage enhanced by the lacy pyrotechnics of the Wonderbra, was through the mid-1990s positioned in major high street locations in the UK on full size billboards. The composition of the image had such a textbook 'sexist ad' dimension that one could be forgiven for supposing some familiarity with both cultural studies and with feminist critiques of advertising (Judith Williamson 1987). It was, in a sense, taking feminism into account by showing it to be a thing of the past, by provocatively 'enacting sexism' while at the same time playing with those debates in film theory about women as the object of the gaze (Laura Mulvey 1975) and even with female desire (Rosalind Coward 1984; Teresa de Lauretis 1988). The picture is in noirish black and white and refers explicitly through its captions (from 'Hello Boys' to 'Or Are You Just Pleased To See Me?') to Hollywood and the famous lines of the actress Mae West. Here is an advertisement which plays back to its viewers, well known aspects of feminist media studies, film theory and semiotics, indeed it almost offers (albeit crudely) the viewer or passing driver Laura Mulvey's theory of women as object of the gaze projected as cityscape within the frame of the billboard. Also mobilised in this ad is the familiarity of the term 'political correctness,' the efficacy of which resides in its warranting and unleashing such energetic reactions against the seemingly tyrannical regime of feminist puritanism. Everyone and especially young people can give a sigh of relief. Thank goodness it is permissible, once again, to enjoy looking at the bodies of beautiful women. At the same time the advertisement expects to provoke feminist condemnation as a means of generating publicity. Thus generational differences are also generated, the younger female viewer, along with her male counterparts, educated in irony and visually literate, is not made angry by such a repertoire. She appreciates its layers of meaning; she gets the joke.

When in a TV advertisement (1998/9) another supermodel, Claudia Schiffer, took off her clothes as she descended a flight of stairs in a luxury mansion on her way out of the door towards her new Citreon car, a similar rhetoric is at work. This advert appears to suggest that yes, this is a self-consciously 'sexist ad,' feminist critiques of it are deliberately evoked. Feminism is 'taken into account,' but only to be shown to be no longer necessary. Why? Because there is no exploitation here, there is nothing remotely naïve about this strip-tease. She seems to be doing it out of choice, and for her own enjoyment; the advert works on the basis of its audience knowing Claudia to be one of the world's most famous and highly paid supermodels. Once again, the shadow of disapproval is introduced (the striptease as site of female exploitation), only instantly to be dismissed as belonging to the past, to a time when feminists used to object to such imagery. To make such an objection nowadays would run the risk of ridicule. Objection is pre-empted with irony. In each of these cases a spectre of feminism is invoked so that it might be undone; for male viewers tradition is restored or as Beck puts it there is 'constructed certitude,' while for the girls what is proposed is a movement beyond feminism, to a more comfortable zone where women are now free to choose for themselves (Ulrich Beck 1992).

Feminism Undone?

If we turn attention to some of the participatory dynamics in leisure and every-day life which see young women endorse (or else refuse to condemn) the ironic normalisation of pornography, where they indicate their approval of and desire to be pin up girls for the centrefolds of the soft porn 'lad mags,' where it is not at all unusual to pass young women in the street wearing T-shirts bearing phrases such as 'Porn Queen' or 'Pay To Touch' across the breasts, and where in the UK at least young women quite happily attend lap dancing clubs (perhaps as a test of their sophistication and 'cool'), we are witness to a hyper-culture of commercial sexuality, one aspect of which is the repudiation of a feminism invoked only to be summarily dismissed (see also Rosalind Gill 2003). As a mark of a post-feminist identity young women journalists refuse to condemn the enormous growth of lap dancing clubs despite the opportunities available for them to do so across the media. They know of the existence of the feminist critiques and debates (or at least this is my claim) through their education, as Shelley Budgeon (2001) has described the girls in her study, they are gender aware. Thus the new female subject is, despite her freedom, called upon to be silent, to withhold critique, to count as a modern sophisticated girl, or indeed this withholding of critique is a condition of her freedom. There is quietude and complicity in the manners of generationally specific notions of cool, and more precisely an uncritical relation to dominant commercially produced sexual representations which actively invoke hostility to assumed feminist positions from the past in order to endorse a new regime of sexual meanings based on female consent, equality, participation and pleasure, free of politics.[3]

FEMALE INDIVIDUALISATION

By using the term 'female individualisation' I am explicitly drawing on the concept of individualisation which is discussed at length by sociologists including Anthony Giddens (1991), Ulrich Beck and Elisabeth Beck-Gernsheim (2002) as well as Zygmunt Bauman (2000, 2001). This work is to be distinguished from the more directly Foucauldian version found in the work of Nikolas Rose (2000). Although there is some shared ground between these authors, insofar as they all reflect on the expectations that individuals now avidly self-monitor and that there appears to be greater capacity on the part of individuals to plan 'a life of one's own,' there are also divergences. Beck and Giddens are less concerned with the effectivity of power in this new friendly guise as personal advisor, and instead emphasise the enlargement of freedom and choice, while in contrast Rose sees these modes of self government as marking out 'the shaping of being,' and thus the 'inculcation of a form of life' (Rose 2000). Bauman bewails the sheer unviability of naked individualisation as the resources of sociality (and welfare) are stripped away, leaving the individual to self-blame when success eludes him or her. (It is also possible to draw a political line between these authors with Bauman and Rose to the left, and Giddens and Beck in the centre.[4]) My emphasis here is on the work of Giddens and Beck, for the very reason that it appears to speak directly to the post-feminist generation. In their writing there are only distant echoes (if that) of the feminist struggles that were required to produce the new-found freedoms of young women in the west.

There is little trace of the battles fought, of the power struggles embarked upon, or of the enduring inequities which still mark out the relations between men and women. All of this is airbrushed out of existence on the basis that, as they claim, 'emancipatory politics' has given way instead to life politics (or in Beck's terms the sub-politics of single interest groups).

Both of these authors provide a sociological account of the dynamics of social change understood as 'reflexive modernisation' (Ulrich Beck, Anthony Giddens & Scott Lash 1994). The earlier period of modernisation ('first modernity') created a welfare state and a set of institutions (e.g. education) which allowed people in the 'second modernity' to become more independent and able, for example, to earn their own living. Young women are, as a result, now 'dis-embedded' from communities where gender roles were fixed. And, as the old structures of social class fade away, and lose their grip in the context of 'late or second modernity,' individuals are increasingly called upon to invent their own structures. They must do this internally and individualistically, so that self-monitoring practices (the diary, the life plan, the career pathway) replace reliance on set ways and structured pathways. Self-help guides, personal advisors, lifestyle coaches and gurus, and all sorts of self-improvement TV programmes provide the cultural means by which individualisation operates as a social process. As the overwhelming force of structure fades so also does the capacity for agency increase.

Individuals must now choose the kind of life they want to live. Girls must have a lifeplan. They must become more reflexive in regard to every aspect of their lives, from making the right choice in marriage, to taking responsibility for their own working lives, and not being dependent on a job for life or on the stable and reliable operations of a large-scale bureaucracy which in the past would have allocated its employees specific, and possibly unchanging, roles. Beck and Giddens each place a different inflection on their accounts of reflexive modernisation, and these arguments appear to fit very directly with the kinds of scenarios and dilemmas facing the young women characters in the narratives of contemporary popular culture (especially so-called chick lit). There is also a real evasion in this writing of the ongoing existence of deep and pernicious gender inequities (most manifest for older women of all social backgrounds but also for young black or Asian women, and also for working-class young women), but so also are Beck and Giddens inattentive to the regulative dimensions of the popular discourses of personal choice and self-improvement. Choice is surely, within lifestyle culture, a modality of constraint. The individual is compelled to be the kind of subject who can make the right choices. By these means new lines and demarcations are drawn between those subjects who are judged responsive to the regime of personal responsibility, and those who fail miserably. Neither Giddens nor Beck mount a substantial critique of these power relations which work so effectively at the level of embodiment. They have no grasp that these are productive of new realms of injury and injustice.

BRIDGET JONES

The film *Bridget Jones's Diary* (an international box office success) draws together so many of these sociological themes it could almost have been scripted by Anthony Giddens himself. Aged 30, living and working in London, Bridget is a free agent, single and childless and able to enjoy herself in pubs, bars and restaurants; she is the product of modernity in that she has benefited from those institutions (education) which have loosened the ties of tradition and community for women, making it possible for them to be disembedded and re-located to the city to earn an independent living without shame or danger. However, this also gives rise to new anxieties. There is the fear of loneliness, for example, the stigma of remaining single, and the risks and uncertainties of not finding the right partner to be a father to children as well as a husband. In the film the opening sequence shows Bridget in her pyjamas worrying about being alone and on the shelf. The soundtrack is *All By Myself* by Jamie McNeal and the audience laughs along with her, in this moment of self-doubt. We immediately know that what she is thinking is 'what will it be like if I never find the right man, if I never get married?' Bridget portrays the whole spectrum of attributes associated with the self-monitoring subject; she confides in her friends, she keeps a diary, she endlessly reflects on her fluctuating weight, noting her calorie intake, she plans, plots and has projects. She is also deeply uncertain as to what the future holds for her. Despite the choices she has, there are also any number of risks of which she is regularly reminded; the risk that she might let the right man slip from under her nose (hence she must always be on the lookout), the risk that not catching a man at the right time might mean she misses the chance of having children (her biological clock is counting). There is also the risk that partnerless she will be isolated, marginalised from the world of happy couples. Now there is only the self to blame if the right partner is not found.

With the burden of self-management so apparent, Bridget fantasies tradition. After a flirtatious encounter with her boss (played by Hugh Grant) she imagines herself in a white wedding dress surrounded by bridesmaids, and the audience laughs loudly because they, like Bridget, know that this is not how young women these days are meant to think. Feminism has intervened to constrain these kinds of conventional desires. It is, then, a relief to escape this censorious politics and freely enjoy that which has been disapproved of. Thus feminism is invoked in order that it is relegated to the past. But this is not simply a return to the past, there are, of course, quite dramatic differences between the various female characters of current popular culture from Bridget Jones to the girls in *Sex and the City* and to Ally McBeal, and those found in girls' and women's magazines from a pre-feminist era. The new young women are confident enough to declare their anxieties about possible failure in regard to finding a husband, they avoid any aggressive or overtly traditional men, and they brazenly enjoy their sexuality, without fear of the sexual double standard. In addition, they are more than capable of earning their own living, and the degree of suffering or shame they anticipate in the absence of finding a husband is countered by sexual self-confidence. Being without a husband does not mean they will go without men.

With such light entertainment as this, suffused with irony and dedicated to re-inventing highly successful women's genres of film and TV, a bold and serious argument about feminism being so repudiated might seem heavy handed. These are hardly rabid anti-feminist tracts. But relations of power are indeed made and re-made within texts of enjoyment and rituals of relaxation and abandonment. These young women's genres are vital to the construction of a new 'gender regime,' based on the double entanglement which I have described; they endorse wholeheartedly what Rose calls 'this ethic of freedom,' and young women have come to the fore as the pre-eminent subjects of this new ethic. These popular texts normalise post-feminist gender anxieties so as to re-regulate young women by means of the language of personal choice. But even 'well regulated liberty' can backfire (the source of comic effect), and this in turn gives rise to demarcated pathologies (leaving it too late to have a baby, failing to find a good catch, etc.) which carefully define the parameters of what constitutes liveable lives for young women without the occasion of re-invented feminism.

Notes

1. *Bridget Jones's Diary* appeared first as a weekly column in *The Independent* UK newspaper in 1996; its author Helen Fielding then published the diaries in book form, and the film, *Bridget Jones's Diary* directed by Sharon McGuire, opened in 2001.
2. The *Daily Mail* has the highest volume of female readers of all daily newspapers in the UK. Its most frequent efforts in regard to promoting a post-feminist sensibility involve commissioning well known former feminists to recant, and blame feminism for contemporary ills among women; for example, Saturday August 23, 2003 has Fay Weldon on 'Look What We've Done.' The caption then reads, 'For years feminists campaigned for sexual liberation. But here, one of their leaders admits all they have created is a new generation of women for whom sex is utterly joyless and hollow' (pp. 12–13).
3. By the normalisation of porn, or 'ironic pornography' I am referring to the new popular mainstreaming of what in the past would have been soft core pornography out of reach of the young on the 'top shelf.' In a post AIDS era, with sexual frankness as an imperative for prevention, the commercial UK youth media now produce vast quantities of explicit sexual material for the teenage audience; in recent years and as a strategy for being ahead of the competition this has been incorporated into the language of 'cool.' With irony as a trademark of knowingness, sexual cool entails 'being up for it' (i.e. lap dancing clubs) without revealing any misgivings, never mind criticism, on the basis of the distance entailed in the ironic experience.
4. Anthony Giddens is architect of the Third Way politics which were embraced by New Labour in its first term of office; this polemic in turn drew on his earlier work titled *Beyond Left and Right* (Anthony Giddens 1995, 1998). Likewise Ulrich Beck was connected with the *Neue Mitte* in Germany, though the German Third Way had rather less success than its UK counterpart.

REFERENCES

Arnot, Madeleine, David, Miriam & Weiner, Gaby (1999) *Closing the Gender Gap*, Polity Press, Cambridge.

Bauman, Zygmunt (2000) *Liquid Modernity*, Polity Press, Cambridge.

Bauman, Zygmunt (2001) *The Individualised Society*, Polity Press, Cambridge.

Beck, Ulrich (1992) *Risk Society*, Sage, London.

Beck, Ulrich & Beck-Gernsheim, Elisabeth (2002) *Individualisation: Institutionalized Individualism and Its Social and Political Consequences*, Polity Press, Cambridge.

Beck, Ulrich, Giddens, Anthony & Lash, Scott (1994) *Reflexive Modernization*, Polity Press, Cambridge.

Brown, Wendy (1997) 'The impossibility of women's studies', *Differences: A Journal of Feminist Cultural Studies*, vol. 9, pp. 79–102.

Brunsdon, Charlotte [1991] (1997) *Screen Tastes: Soap Opera to Satellite Dishes*, Routledge, London.

Brunsdon, Charlotte (forthcoming, 2004) 'Feminism, post-feminism: Martha, Martha, and Nigella', *Cinema Journal*.

Budgeon, Shelley (2001) 'Emergent feminist identities', *European Journal of Women's Studies*, vol. 8, no. 1, pp. 7–28, Sage, London.

Butler, Judith (1990) *Gender Trouble*, Routledge, New York.

Butler, Judith (1992) 'Contingent foundations: feminism and the question of postmodernism', in *Feminists Theorise the Political*, eds J. Butler & J. W. Scott, Routledge, New York.

Butler, Judith (1993) *Bodies That Matter*, Routledge, New York.

Butler, Judith (2000) *Antigone's Claim: Kinship Between Life and Death*, Columbia University Press, New York.

Butler, Judith, Laclau, Ernesto & Zizek, Slavoj (eds) (2000) *Contingency, Hegemony and Universality*, Verso, London.

Coward, Rosalind (1984) *Female Desire*, Paladin, London.

De Lauretis, Teresa (1988) *Technologies of Gender: Essays on Theory Film and Fiction*, Indiana University Press, Bloomington, IN.

Faludi, Susan (1992) *Backlash: The Undeclared War Against Women*, Vintage, London.

Giddens, Anthony (1991) *Modernity and Self Identity*, Polity Press, Cambridge.

Giddens, Anthony (1995) *Beyond Left and Right*, Polity Press, Cambridge.

Giddens, Anthony (1998) *The Third Way*, Polity Press, Cambridge.

Gill, Rosalind (2003) 'From sexual objectification to sexual subjectification: the resexualisation of women's bodies in the media', *Feminist Media Studies*, vol. 3, no. 1, pp. 100–106.

Hall, Stuart (1989) *The Hard Road to Renewal*, Verso, London.

Haraway, Donna (1991) *Simians Cyborgs and Women*, Free Association Books, London.

Harris, Anita (2003) *Future Girl*, Routledge, New York.

McRobbie, Angela (1994) *Postmodernism and Popular Culture*, Routledge, London.

McRobbie, Angela (1999a) *In the Culture Society*, Routledge, London.

McRobbie, Angela (1999b) 'Feminism v the TV Blondes', Inaugural lecture Goldsmiths College, University of London.

McRobbie, Angela (2003) 'Mothers and fathers who needs them? A review essay of Butler's Antigone', *Feminist Review*, vol. 73, Autumn, Palgrave, London.

Mohanty, Chandra T. (1995) 'Under western eyes', in *The Postcolonial Studies reader*, eds B. Ashcroft, G. Griffiths & H. Tiffin, Routledge, London.

Mulvey, Laura (1975) 'Visual pleasure and narrative cinema', *Screen*, vol. 16, no. 3, pp. 6–18.

Rose, Nikolas (2000) *Powers of Freedom*, Cambridge University Press, Cambridge.

Spivak, Gayatri (1988) 'Can the subaltern speak?', in *Marxism and the Interpretation of Culture*, eds C. Nelson & L. Grossberg, University of Illinois Press, Chicago, IL, pp. 271–317.

Spivak, Gayatri (1999) *A Critique of Postcolonial Reason*, Harvard University Press, Cambridge, MA.

Stuart, Andrea (1990) 'Feminism dead or alive?', in *Identity*, ed. J. Rutherford, Lawrence and Wishart, London.

Trinh, T. Minha (1989) *Woman Native Other*, Indiana University Press, Bloomington, IN.

Williamson, Judith (1987) *Decoding Advertisements*, Marion Boyars, London.

31

PLAYING THE GAME

Young Girls Performing Femininity in Video Game Play

Valerie Walkerdine

Introduction

[. . .]

While there is growing address to gender and video game play (e.g., Fromme 2003; Kennedy 2002), most of it involves analyses of the games themselves and hardly any engages with what happens when playing and even then little is about young children's play. While there is plenty of interest to be said about the construction of the games themselves, it is in playing the games that subjectivity is constituted and this means that analysis of the games alone will of necessity be a relatively poor guide to what happens when playing. The central argument that I am making here is that many video games are one site for the production of contemporary masculinity [. . .].

In making this argument, I am assuming that masculinity can be understood as produced relationally through affective, performative, and discursive relations and that masculinity is an aspiration rather than a given and involves a great deal of work to maintain it. Contemporary masculinity then becomes those sets of affective relations, performances, and discursive practices through which masculinity is known and accomplished. This does not map masculinity onto male bodies but sets up a gender difference which is constantly marked and therefore is differently lived in relation to girlhood and boyhood as differentiated. However, along with a long tradition of feminist psychoanalytic work, I argue that the cultural 'work' of masculinity and femininity is also

From *Feminist Media Studies* 6:4 (2006) pp. 519–37.

psychic work because the achievement of masculinity and femininity is always out of reach (e.g. Rose 1983).

This idea can be related to recent work on the assemblage, which understands affect as psychic, social, and cultural (Deleuze & Guattari 1987). This means that performativity always has to be judged in relation to work to shore up anxieties about not being masculine or feminine enough or indeed being too masculine or too feminine. In the book, I examine how this brings with it a number of self-management practices for boys which we could understand as working to produce the possibility of masculine performance on the one hand and a conscious abating of anxiety on the other. I have asserted here that many games are the site for the production of contemporary masculinity because they both demand and appear to ensure performances such as heroism, killing, winning, competition, action, combined with technological skill and rationality. In this sense I am attempting to produce an anti-essentialist argument while also recognising that the games produce possibilities for bodies, affectivities, discursivity and practice. My central claim is that in relation to girls, this constitutes a problem because contemporary femininity demands practices and performances which bring together heroics, rationality, etc. with the need to maintain a femininity which displays care, co-operation, concern, and sensitivity to others. This means that girls have complex sets of positions to negotiate while playing – how do you win while caring for others who may lose, for example? So, I aim to explore how the demands of contemporary femininity are lived out in the ways that girls actually play games. In what follows I discuss the management and regulation of contemporary femininity in relation to issues in my observations of game play. [. . .]

In the game playing in this research, it is the consistent engagement with both competition and co-operation that is striking, together with what look like attempts to hide the desire to win. Of course, were we to look at boys' playing we could equally find anxieties, but it is my argument that the cultural practices marshalled for masculinity offer a different kind of resolution – for example, a heroic competition that downplays sensitivity, caring, or co-operation (though there are examples of these latter within the data). This does not mean, however, that the complexities of operating in a predominantly masculine space while attempting to keep alive a femininity which can in fantasy ensure the possibility of 'womanliness' (Riviere [1929] 1986), is not a constant issue for all girls. In this paper therefore, I want to pursue the argument that many games are one site for the production of contemporary masculinity in order to think about *what this means for femininity*.

If many games are one site for the production of contemporary masculinity it follows that the task for masculinity and femininity is different. To think about this, I will combine a Foucauldian emphasis on self-management techniques as Michel Foucault elaborated in his later work (e.g. Foucault 1986), together with a sense of the complex psychic work (Walkerdine 1997) involved in trying to inhabit the fantasies of the performance of masculinity. If many games offer one site for the production and regulation of action heroic masculinity, which requires the psychic work of fantasy to do so, then this might be a difficult task for boys, but the performance of contemporary femininity may demand something in fact even more convoluted and complicated – that is, the management of co-operation *and* competition, caring *and* winning. If the performance of masculinity is what is produced in relation to game play, then isn't the self-management task for the girl that much more complex? Don't girls also at the same time have to perform femininity, attempting to keep going the oppositions and contradictions that are all too present? That is, they have to pursue the demands of contemporary femininity which blend together traditional masculinity and femininity. It is my argument that trying to do both these things while playing games is a very complex and difficult task. I am suggesting that it is possible to explain the complex performance displayed by girls if we take this as a theoretical framework.

It is with this in mind that I want to think about how the young girls in the Sydney project played games, interpreting their play through a framework which assumes that they are managing contradictory positions of masculinity and femininity. Wanting to be the action hero of video games requires work, constant hard work, the work of practice, practice, practice, as many of the children make clear. And of course, as many girls say, they are not very interested in that kind of work because its end point, action-heroic masculinity, is not the work they have to achieve – the work of femininity is different, but does involve managing the competing positions.

MANAGING FEMININITY

I want to begin by thinking about an observation made early on in the Sydney project by one of the researchers. She felt very disappointed when she was watching the girls play – she felt that they played in a different way from the boys, that is more sociably, with. game playing as an accompaniment to other activities, such as chatting, and that they didn't play to win or with the competitive edge of the boys. She was upset by this because she had been a girl at school who was good at mathematics, which had singled her out, and she felt disappointed that the girls were not displaying the technological enthusiasm she would have liked them to display. Subsequently, we analysed the way that the girls played very carefully and felt that there was no basis for suggesting in any simple terms that the girls played differently from the boys – in the sense that they wanted to win any the less or did not show interest in trying to play well. However, the researcher was not deluded – she was picking something up – a difference in *orientation* to games. This difference has been the subject of a growing body of literature (see Cassell & Jenkins 1998 for a review) about girls and video and computer games. Much of this literature looks at a number of factors to explain girls' lower participation in games, such as lack of female avatars or girl-oriented game topics or styles of game.

In my own work on girls and mathematics in the 1980s (Walkerdine 1989, 1998) it wasn't a simple matter of girls behaving more like boys – breaking rules etc. – to be understood as mathematical thinkers. Far from it. Indeed, performance which was praised by teachers in boys met with pejorative comments when displayed by girls. I am suggesting therefore that it is not simply a case of making video games 'girl friendly', nor that in any straightforward sense that girls don't like or are no good at video games. Rather, I want to raise the difficulties of *the management of femininity in the present.*

I want to explore the complex ways in which some girls who were videotaped while playing games, usually in pairs, but sometimes in larger groups, managed the contradictory positionings outlined above. It should be said at the outset that there were girls who were very keen on winning – it was very far from the case that girls didn't want to win – but it was the case that no girl was as competent or indeed interested a player as the top boys. In their interviews all boys talk about the kudos of being a good player in terms of relations with other boys and so the necessity to 'practice, practice, practice' until they are good enough to win. Boys have to try to win but girls wanting to win risk losing their designation as feminine by coming too far onto the side of masculinity. No wonder then that many girls find this task too difficult, despite the contemporary injunctions for them to be empowered, and that most of them are not as good at games as the boys or, perhaps better, as the boys would like to be.

[. . .]

PLAYING A FOUR-PLAYER GAME

Rosie and Bella are playing a four person game of Super Smash with Jo and Gaby. This is a game in which avatars attack each other with a variety of weapons. They each have a separate control and are playing separate avatars. They stay in the game as long as their avatar lives/survives. At the end of the game they engage in a perfunctory discussion of who has won and who came second, third, and fourth. This position of winning is constructed for them, as the information is displayed on screen at the end of the game. In saying that their discussion is perfunctory I'm not suggesting that they don't want or like to win – though they take quite different positions to winning. Rather, winning does not visibly confer any status on the winner. Status seems already established along other lines and is not affected in any major way by incidences of winning. Rosie for example, positions herself as a 'dumb' 'loser.' Even though she sometimes wins, often through default or cautious play, she still positions herself as the loser. Clearly, the position she takes in the group is not contingent on her winning, but on her losing or positioning herself as the loser. Jo does not always win, but she has most authority in the group. All negotiations are conducted through her and she sits most centrally and acts most centrally to the play. Winning or losing does not alter the position of control/authority that Jo assumes. The positions the girls take up are reasonably stable across the duration of the video of them playing. The girls sit right to left: Bella, Rosie, Jo, and Gaby. Jo and Rosie are central in terms of physical position and dominance. They dominate the conversation and the activity. Bella, on the outer right, is relatively silent and intensely focused on the play. The bulk of her comments are play-related self-talk directed at the on-screen characters. Gaby on the outside left says almost nothing and is most animated when she identifies her place at the end of the game. Jo and Rosie are friends and their relationship, and Jo's status as the leader, is firmly established. Thus, though Jo and Rosie dominate the talk, Jo's position as the one with most authority is unchallenged. All the girls are engaged in/by the play.

What struck me on first viewing was the position Jo takes up as a game-player. She dominates the group, the space, the game, and the noise level. She does the majority of the work in managing the group in terms of the selection of games and avatars etc. ('Alright, you ready?,' 'Everyone ready? Are they sure?'). She is loud, bossy, takes a lot of physical space, does air-punch type moves of victory, says 'whoo hoo' and other similar calls that seem to connote power and control. Jo typically says such things as 'Ar.Ar.Ar. Wait for a second . . . Fire, fire, fire. Come back, come back, come back. Yes. Oh bugger.' Rosie on the other hand typically says 'Don't hurt me. I'm innocent,' often in an affected whisper or an exaggeratedly 'girly' 'loser' voice. Gaby, though mostly silent, is more likely to make observations about her play and herself as player: 'That's me,' 'I'm flying' etc. Bella, like Jo, is intensely focused on the game and on the action of the game: 'Kick. Kick, kick, kick. Kick him up. Oh. Come on. Yer jump. Jump.' Unlike Jo, Bella engages in little social talk directed at the other players or any audience other than herself. Even Bella and Jo's laughter may be read as different from Rosie's – the former is more robust and the latter would be understood as giggling.

I am attempting to argue that the successful game playing subject is 'masculine' (both in terms of the technology and the action of fighting/killing/winning) and that those girls who are most engaged with the games, who are most successful, or have the most power in the group, take up what might generally be identified as what we would read as traditionally more masculine positions. Gaby is silent. Rosie is, in her own words, 'dumb,' 'a loser,' 'an idiot,' 'scared,' and is prone to giggling and squeamishness, 'Don't try and hurt me,' and turning away when killing takes place. Jo is in control, loud, authoritative, skilled, knowledgeable, and enjoys winning and killing; 'Weeee. Boom. [makes noises and then laughs],' 'I'm just bashing up everything.' Bella, though less engaged in the social activity/talk of the group, is very focused on the killing activity of the game and her comments are therefore more focused on the specific activity of killing: 'I'll kill you, no matter if it's the last thing I do,' 'Well I'm just killing everybody. Whoa. Cool, I'm just killing everybody,' 'I love killing people' (accompanied by a sniggering laugh), 'I want to kill someone. No offence to everyone.' What I'm attempting to suggest here is that the successful game player, in terms of being perceived as a successful and competent player, is required to take up a visibly masculine subject position in terms of stereotypical inscriptions/performances of gender. (Bella : 'I can do whatever I want. I'm a grown man now mama' followed by 'I'm talking to me mama' in an affected/exaggerated masculine voice.

Each of these girls differently manages the contradictions of femininity and masculinity and thus appears to achieve what we could recognise through a psychologised discourse as different 'personalities.' But could we understand them instead as embodied, affective, and performative engagements with these contradictions over a long period? We could understand this as unconscious social and cultural relationalities or the continuous creation of assemblages. The configurations change according to game and players (in a way that there is not space here to analyse) so we should be wary of treating these positions as too fixed, but more as an indication of how contradictions are resolved from moment to moment in the spatial and temporal flow of the game and across the many practices and relations which form embodied practices for coping. Bella does not compete with Jo's social position (of power) within the group, but makes her avatar compete with her avatar *within the game*. This allows for some power play that is legitimised by the activity of the game, but not obvious or confrontational within the social group. Again, the group looks cohesive, democratic and friendly. The negotiations about who will play which avatars is not tense or a cause of argument, though negotiations do seem to be subtly mediated by Jo.

Rosie's performance during the group game is markedly different from that when she is playing in a pair with Bella. I account for this in at least two ways. One, she takes up different positions as a player and observer, more feminised when playing, and in the group she is always a player. Two, she is friends with Jo and she seems to take up a more exaggerated feminine position around Jo's performance of authority. Rosie giggles more, sucks her thumb and generally works harder to assert her fear and failure: 'I'm innocent,' 'My enemy's myself,' 'I'm dead, see what you do when you hurt people? They cry [giggles],' 'Don't hurt me please,' 'I'm an idiot.' Completely absent from this episode is the type of power play that could be seen between Rosie and Bella in other exchanges. Jo positions herself as winner and Rosie is positioned by Bella as loser. However, careful scrutiny and insistence on Bella's part, reveals that Rosie is actually second and Gaby third, leaving Jo in fourth place and Bella in first. Jo is resistant to being fourth (last/loser) and Bella clearly establishes her position as first. Interestingly, whilst Bella positions herself as winner and cannot believe it when she has lost ('How can that be?,' 'I damn well came fourth'), Rosie positions herself as loser and cannot believe it when she is not ('Me? No I didn't . . . I never win'). Thus, the idea of fixity has to be challenged by the sense that these positions are fluid and changing – there is no fixed 'personality' but it is rather that relations are differently mobilised in different dynamic intersections across space and time [. . .].

What I've been trying to think about is the relationship between the positioning of players and how this is reflected in the way they play the game; their position in relation to fighting, killing, and winning; and the way they relate to other players, especially in terms of relations of power. I argue that the successful player/manager of the technology of the video game is a masculine subject and that this subject position is performed more often by some girls than others. I also argue that it requires complex, covert negotiations of power that position girls ambivalently in the sense that they seem to struggle for power whilst appearing not to. Girls are also positioned ambivalently in terms of the taking up of a masculine position in one context, game playing, and a feminine position in another, the interview, which I discussed briefly, where fighting and winning are disavowed and the cuteness (and other appropriately feminine inscriptions) of avatars emphasised.

This paper has explored the different constitution of shifting relations through which inscriptions of femininity and masculinity are performed. It might be thought from this analysis that Jo actually manages to maintain a position which is more comfortable with winning. However, from the interview material with Jo (together with her father), we understand that Jo is rather afraid of her abilities and ambitions. She says that she is scared of turning into 'someone mean' and violent through playing violent games (e.g. Duke Nukem) so she won't play them (she's heard the discourse of violent games turning children into playground killers on the news). Jo's father says she won't play Duke Nukem even though they have it at home – maybe she doesn't like it because of her fear of becoming someone she does not wish to become. This is also an interesting commentary on the 'real effects' of discourse. If you believe the discourse (e.g. games will turn you into a nasty person) you will regulate yourself accordingly, that is not play violent video games. However, we must wonder how Jo manages to cope with the difficult feelings her dominating play brings up for her. It is clearly not straightforward or unproblematic for her.

AND WHAT OF PLEASURE?

In relation to the complexity of self-management tasks for girls, I want to explore the equally contradictory site of pleasure. [. . .] Bella and Rosie gain considerable pleasure from winning (which in the games she is playing in this case, means killing) – in a way not unlike that of the boys. There is pleasure then for these girls in mastery. They can take up a masculine position, though not without having to almost simultaneously take up a feminine one as well for many. We saw that Rosie liked to display an exaggerated squeamishness of taking a vicarious pleasure in others doing the killing while saying she is afraid. As we know from horror movies, we can take great pleasure in squeamishness, watching the horror through our hands (Carol Clover 1992; Julia Kristeva 1982). What is the fascination? What is the vicarious pleasure? Is there any mileage in attempting to understand how Rosie manages to take pleasure (was it in winning or in killing or both?) while operating as though she had nothing to do with it? All those fluffy cuddly creatures – of course so well satirised in the boiling of the family bunny by the abandoned woman in *Fatal Attraction*. Just as the Glenn Close character seeks her revenge with a murderous fury, murdering too the sweet and acquiescing part of herself, so Rosie reveals that the violent must be kept in check to produce femininity while for boys its opposite is the case – as the exaggerated denials of any interest in the game of Barbie make clear. The work of performing masculinity and femininity is also psychic work, the work Freud talks of so clearly (Rose 1983). It is also about the complexities of positions of power. The power of the mother over the child/man, the power of the *femme fatale*, the power of the pleasure in mastery, of omnipotent control, of winning, killing. Performing femininity and masculinity requires social and psychic work to attempt to embody a position which is a necessary fiction in that it is the central constituent of the management and regulation of femininity and masculinity. So, what seems like power is, in Foucault's (1977) sense, deeply compromised, because it is the way in which we are managed and regulated as autonomous citizens in apparent control of ourselves and our lives.

PSYCHIC WORK

If we go on to think about the psychic work involved in both masculinity and femininity in the light of the arguments raised above, I want to think particularly about how we might think about the way the contradictions of femininity and masculinity are lived. In particular, I want to turn to the work of Sue Austin (2005), who makes an explicit link between some of my own earlier work and what she calls aggressive energies or fantasies. For Austin, aggressive fantasies, as for Lacan, can be understood as fantasies through which the discursive aspects of power are played out. In particular, she makes reference to a paper of mine (Walkerdine 1981), which analyses the way in which two 4-year-old boys in a nursery classroom bring a female teacher 'down to size' by treating her to a sexist chant involving body parts. She retorts by treating them as boys for whom such things are to be expected and which she must contain. Austin asks what it would take for the teacher to be able to experience anger at this positioning of her and to stand up to it. How might she be able to experience what she calls 'the thrill of a good fight?' I wonder if the game-playing girls I have discussed above are able to experience this thrill unreservedly? What would it take and what would it mean for them to do so? Let us examine Austin's case a bit further.

She argues against a view of object relations theory which looks at aggression as a product of development or problems as a result of a faulty inner life or psychic world. She attempts to engage both with Judith Butler's (1997) idea of an inner topography or landscape in melancholia and the idea of a metaphysics of absence, by inverting Derrida. She claims that self-hate is the most common form of female aggressive energy. She talks about the 'Not I' within. In this respect she is trying to link the ways in which violence towards femininity is taken in and cannot be pushed outward again by women. In her analysis of the incident in the nursery classroom I discussed above, she argues that the small boys aggressively make the teacher into a sex object but that her only response is feminine nurturance. Thus she does not and cannot marshal her aggression in return.

She gives the example of teachers in my work on girls and mathematics (Walkerdine et al. 1989, 1998) who simultaneously look for nice kind and helpful girls and then say how much they hate those girls and indeed those characteristics inside themselves. They are of course brought up to validate the qualities ascribed to boys. That is, reason, naughtiness, leaps of imagination, and to regard those things inside themselves and girls as crazy. While the Other is always validated they can never easily cross the divide and experience the joy of aggressive energy.

To discursive work therefore Austin adds the necessity to understand, following Butler, the *inner topology*. What it would mean to marshal that which has been denied. She argues that marshalling aggressive energies is central to the possibility of women's agency and their *jouissance*, which she opposes to *plaisir*, which can only be understood as the pleasure of being the object, of fitting the position accorded to woman. In relation to that inner topology, women's aggressive energies also get mobilised to create a containing space – so the space they themselves take up can only ever be 'diverted into creating and sustaining these categories of perception and experience which have become normalised as truths' (Austin 2005, p. 145). [. . .] The dangerous nature of femininity is thus reworked or tamed as the very basis of childhood, personhood. 'Space is not ours to take part in, since our substance has been used in the production of the concept of containment.' So women's aggressive energies have been dammed up and diverted.

Austin asks 'if the structure of femininity comprises solidified, disavowed aggressive energies, whose solidification and remanufacture is eroticised as being a "good thing" for the benefit of some imagined "Other," how might such energies be gathered together into something liveable, something which women can use in their inner and outer lives?' (2005, p. 173).

As we have seen, girls can play video games with relish. However, the constant subversion of this relish into a maintenance of a femininity which is its opposite, is, in Austin's sense, diverting. That it is at the very least not unproblematic for the girls in this research to display what Austin calls their aggressive energies because they must maintain the very internal space which renders them nurturant and caringly feminine, seems certainly to be the case here. More than that, aggression is sometimes displaced by some girls (e.g. Rosie) onto others to do their killing for them. However, as I have argued in the past in relation to girls and mathematics (Walkerdine 1989, 1998), it is not simply a question of allowing girls to behave in ways discursively sanctioned for boys because that behaviour is differently read and evaluated when displayed by girls. In one case in a secondary school mathematics classroom, one girl was called a 'madam' by her male teacher for displaying the kind of performance praised as brilliant in her male peers.

The discursive constitution and domestication of femininity has to be understood in relation to its other and opposite, the constitution of masculinity as unproblematically essentialising aggressive energies, precisely directed at that containing space which they both need and then disavow in the Cartesian rebirth, with respect to boys and with the help of their mothers (Walkerdine in press). If the fantasy of masculine aggressivity is the Other of feminine nurturance, it is that which takes up the space provided by the sucking out of the psychic space of the feminine. We might therefore ask why it is that the feminine is continually pathologised while the omnipotent fantasies of the boys, that they can indeed become the conquering action hero, is presented not only as unproblematic but is needed for the perpetuation of a technologically led mode of governance and multinational capital. Why is boys' competitiveness lauded? Why is the possibility of their emergent sensitivities to others suppressed and their anxiety about being able to win disavowed and projected onto women? Why is the fantasy of winning and beating not itself considered more of a problem than the problems for girls? Or more particularly, what kinds of fantasies and anxieties are displaced by the acting out of omnipotence? In particular, we might look to precisely the performance of help and nurturance by the mothers, which must be disavowed in order to produce the self-made man. Femininity may, as Austin suggests, create the psychic space which is taken to make masculinity possible, but it must equally be disavowed and denied as it produces dependency and infantilisation. It seems to me therefore that the lack of male anxiety could be worrying in itself. Of course the idea that woman is the container, the mother, the muse, the vagina, and man the subject, the phallus, is very far from new. The issue here is the place of games and new technologies more generally in creating places and possibilities for the subversion of the oppositions and a move to something new.

REFERENCES

Austin, Sue (2005) *Women's Aggressive Fantasies*, Routledge, London.
Butler, Judith (1997) *The Psychic Life of Power: Theories in Subjection*, Stanford University Press, Stanford.
Cassell, Justine & Jenkins, Henry (1998) *From Barbie to Mortal Kombat*, MIT Press, Cambridge Mass.
Clover, Carol (1992) *Men, Women and Chainsaws*, British Film Institute, London.
Deleuze, Gilles & Guattari, Felix (1987) *A Thousand Plateaus*, University of Minnesota Press, Minneapolis.
Foucault, Michel (1977) *Discipline and Punish*, Penguin, Harmondsworth.
Foucault, Michel (1986) *History of Sexuality, Vol 3, The Care of the Self*, Pantheon, New York.
Fromme, Johannes (2003) 'Computer games as part of children's culture', *Game Studies*, vol. 3, no. 1, [Online] Available at: http://gamestudies.org/0301/fromme/

Kennedy, Helen (2002) 'Lara Croft, feminist icon or cyberbimbo? On the limits of textual analysis', *Game Studies*, vol. 2, no. 2, [Online] Available at: www.gamestudies.org/0202/kennedy/

Kristeva, Julia (1982) *The Powers of Horror*, Columbia University Press, New York.

Riviere, Joan ([1929] (1986)) 'Womanliness as masquerade', in *Formations of Fantasy*, eds Victor Burgin, James Donald & Cora Kaplan, Methuen, London.

Rose, Jacqueline (1983) 'Femininity and its discontents', *Feminist Review*, vol. 14, pp. 78–91.

Walkerdine, Valerie (1981) 'Sex, power and Pedagogy', *Screen Education*, vol. 38, pp. 14–21.

Walkerdine, Valerie (1989) *Counting Girls Cut*, Virago, London.

Walkerdine, Valerie (1997) *Daddy's Girl: Young Girls and Popular Culture*, Palgrave, London.

Walkerdine, Valerie (1998) *Counting Girls Out* (2nd Edition), Falmer, London.

Walkerdine, Valerie (in press) *Playing the Game: Children, Relationality and Multimedia*, Palgrave, London.

FURTHER READING

Baehr, H. and Dyer, G. (eds), *Boxed In: Women and Television* (London: Pandora, 1987).

Baehr, H. and Gray, A. (eds), *Turning it On: A Reader in Women and Media* (London: Arnold, 1996).

Ballaster, R., Beetham, M., Frazer, E. and Hebron, S., *Women's Worlds: Ideology, Femininity and the Woman's Magazine* (London: Macmillan, 1991).

Betterton, R. (ed.), *Looking On: Images of Femininity in the Visual Arts and Media* (London: Pandora, 1987).

Brown, M. E. (ed.), *Television and Women's Culture* (London: Sage, 1990).

Brunsdon, C., *Screen Tastes* (London: Routledge, 1996).

Brunsdon, C., *The Feminist, The Housewife, and the Soap Opera* (Oxford: Oxford University Press, 2000).

Brunsdon, C., D'Acci, J. and Spigel, L. (eds), *Feminist Television Criticism: A Reader*, 2nd edn (London: Open University Press, 2007).

Butcher, H. et al., 'Images of Women in the Media'. CCCS Stencilled Paper, University of Birmingham (1974).

Byerly, C. M. and Ross, K. (eds), *Women and Media* (Oxford: Blackwell, 2006).

Creedon, P. (ed.), *Women in Mass Communication: Challenging Gender Values* (London: Sage, 1989).

Davies, K., Dickey, J. and Stratford, T. (eds), *Out of Focus: Writing on Women and the Media* (London: Women's Press, 1987).

Feuer, J., 'Melodrama, Serial Form and Television Today', *Screen*, 25:1 (1984) pp. 4–16.

Gamman, L. and Marshment, M. (eds), *The Female Gaze: Women as Viewers of Popular Culture* (London: Women's Press, 1988).

Gledhill, C., 'Pleasurable Negotiations', in E. D. Pribram (ed.), *Female Spectators* (London: Verso, 1988).

hooks, b., *Black Looks: Race and Representation* (London: Turnaround, 1992).

Kaplan, E. A. (ed.), *Regarding Television* (Los Angeles: American Film Institute, 1983).

Kaplan, E. A., 'Feminist Criticism and Television', in R. C. Allen (ed.), *Channels of Discourse, Reassembled* (London: Routledge, 1992).

Kirkham, P. and Skeggs, B., '*Absolutely Fabulous*: Absolutely Feminist?' in C. Geraghty and D. Lusted (eds), *The Television Studies Book* (London: Arnold, 1998) pp. 287–98.

Kuhn, A., 'Women's Genres', *Screen*, 25:1 (1984) pp. 18–28.

McCracken, E., *Decoding Women's Magazines* (London: Macmillan, 1993).

Macdonald, M., *Representing Women* (London: Arnold, 1995).

McRobbie, A., *Feminism and Youth Culture: From 'Jackie' to 'Just Seventeen'* (London: Macmillan, 1991).

McRobbie, A., *The Aftermath of Feminism* (London: Sage, 2009).

Mellencamp, P. (ed.), *Logics of Television* (Bloomington and London: Indiana University Press and BFI, 1990).

Modleski, T., *Loving with a Vengeance: Mass Produced Fantasies for Women* (London: Methuen, 1984).

Modleski, T. (ed.), *Studies in Entertainment: Critical Approaches to Mass Culture* (Bloomington: Indiana University Press, 1986).

Modleski, T., *Feminism Without Women* (London: Routledge, 1991).

Mulvey, L., 'Visual Pleasure and Narrative Cinema', *Screen* 16:3 (1975) pp. 6–18.

Negra, D., *What a Girl Wants?* (London: Routledge, 2009).

Pribram, E. D. (ed.), *Female Spectators: Looking at Film and Television* (London: Verso, 1988).

Steeves, L., 'Feminist Theories and Media Studies', *Critical Studies in Mass Communication* 4:2 (1987), pp. 95–135.

Tasker, Y. and Negra, D. (eds), *Interrogating Postfeminism* (Durham, NC and London: Duke University Press, 2007).

Thornham, S., *Women, Feminism and Media* (Edinburgh: Edinburgh University Press, 2007).

Tuchman, G. et al. (eds), *Hearth and Home: Images of Women in the Media* (New York: Oxford University Press, 1978).

van Zoonen, L., 'Feminist Perspectives on the Media', in J. Curran and M. Gurevitch (eds), *Mass Media and Society* (London: Edward Arnold, 1991).

van Zoonen, L., *Feminist Media Studies* (London: Sage, 1994).

Walkerdine, V., *Daddy's Girl: Young Girls and Popular Culture* (London: Palgrave Macmillan, 1997).

Winship, J., *Inside Women's Magazines* (London: Pandora Press, 1987).

Women's Studies Group, Centre for Contemporary Cultural Studies (eds), *Women Take Issue* (London: Hutchinson, 1978).

SECTION 4
AUDIENCES

4.1
'EFFECTS' DEBATES

INTRODUCTION: 'EFFECTS' DEBATES

The notion that media representations have direct behavioural and psychological effects on their audiences is one of the earliest forms of thinking about a developing mass media, but it remains in many ways a dominant tradition of thought – if no longer in academic research, then certainly in popular commentary. Graham Murdock has traced these arguments back to nineteenth-century fears about the vulnerability of the young and the poor to the influence of emergent popular media forms like the 'penny dreadfuls' – fears which actually concern the threat of social unrest from a new urban working class – but he points out that identical arguments have popular currency today. Here, for example, is Andrew Neil, writing in 1996 in the *Sunday Times*:

> [F]ar too much of what passes for popular entertainment pollutes our society and creates a new tolerance in which what was thought to be beyond the pale becomes acceptable. Young minds are particularly vulnerable. (Quoted in Murdock, 2001: 150)

When, therefore, early twentieth-century social sciences turned their attention to the question of media audiences, the dominant research tradition, in Murdock's words, 'adopted the definition of the "problem" already established in popular and political commentary' (2001: 152). American 'mass communication' research, in particular, adopted a 'scientific' methodology based either on a behaviourist, laboratory psychology or on the large-scale quantitative surveys produced by a functionalist sociology. The aim was to isolate direct links between media representations and behaviour by screening out all other cultural and social factors besides the 'pure' exposure to audiovisual material depicting violence. A British review of this research, *Sex, Violence and The Media*, published by Hans Eysenck and David Nias in 1978, for example, cites experiments which are noteworthy for their laboratory methods, for the immediate and imitative nature of the effects they expect to capture, and for the incorporation in several instances of a measurable *physiological* definition of media effects. The reported consequences of exposure to media portrayals of violence include a tendency for viewers to become 'disinhibited' about employing violence themselves, a tendency for some direct 'imitation' and a tendency to become 'desensitized' to 'violent materials'. Its publication was taken by many as implicit endorsement for the main lines of approach of the pro-censorship campaign being mounted by the Christian fundamentalist-led National Viewers' and Listeners' Association and the Festival of Light.

Other research, however, had suggested that media representations in fact had only very 'limited effects'. A widely read review of the American research, published in 1960, concluded that 'mass communication ordinarily does not serve as a necessary and sufficient cause of audience effects, but rather functions among and through a nexus of mediating factors' (Klapper, 1960: 8). This was the predominant drift of academic thinking by the 1960s when the pioneering social scientists of mass communication in Britain began their work – notably Denis McQuail, Jeremy Tunstall, Jay G. Blumler and James Halloran.[1] Chapter 32 comprises two extracts from *The Effects of Television* (1970), edited by James Halloran, head of the Centre for Mass Communication Research at the University of Leicester from 1966 to 1991. The first extract registers the view that 'attitude change has been over-used as the primary criterion of influence . . . Influence must not be equated with attitude change.' The second extract discusses studies of the reception of particular British television programmes (*Children of Revolution, Nature of Prejudice* and *Rainbow City*) that confirmed this view. The need for a more complex and comprehensive conception of the reception of broadcast transmissions had been demonstrated by these British studies. David Morley later remarked that 'The empirical work of the Leicester Centre at this time marked an important shift in research from forms of behavioural analysis to forms of cognitive analysis' (1980: 7).

Denis McQuail's work (Chapter 33) moved further than this, focusing on audience 'gratifications'.[2] This approach inverted the 'effects' approach, and set out 'to concentrate less on what the media do to people than on what people do *with* the media' (McQuail, 1969: 71). What are people's motives in reading a newspaper or listening to a particular radio programme? What are the uses for them of such activities? What needs are gratified, what satisfactions derived? The posing of these questions, and the pursuit of their answers, often within the framework of a functionalist sociology, had become known, from a phrase by Elihu Katz, as the 'uses and gratifications' approach (see Katz 1959). In the study reported in Chapter 33, McQuail and his colleagues Jay G. Blumler and J. R. Brown investigated what functions the television quiz shows *University Challenge, TV Brain of Britain* and *Ask the Family* served for a sample of viewers in Leeds. From the viewers' responses when questioned, they developed a four-part inventory of gratifications and uses, which they suggested might have a general applicability for media use. These four types of 'media–person interaction' are: surveillance (information gathering); personal identity; personal relationships (social integration and interaction); and diversion (entertainment). The attempt to correlate the expression of each of these kinds of satisfaction with social and demographic variables, however, proved rather inconclusive; the results 'were not without ambiguity and left many questions unanswered'. In relation to the various kinds of programmes, too, it seemed that 'people can look to quite different kinds of material for essentially the same gratification and, correlatively, find alternative satisfactions in the same televised material'.

In work that followed, notably the ethnographic studies that emerged from the British Cultural Studies approach (see Sections 4.2 and 5 of this volume), both 'effects' studies and the 'uses and gratifications' approach came under sustained attack. Both models, it was argued, failed to consider the *social* nature of audience formations and their readings of media representations. As David Morley argued, drawing on Stuart Hall's 'Encoding/Decoding' model (see Chapter 3), audiences should be considered 'not as an atomised mass of individuals, but as a number of sub-cultural formations or groupings of "members" who will, as members of those groups, share a cultural orientation towards decoding messages in particular ways' (1980: 15). To this argument Philip Elliott added a further criticism of uses and gratifications research: that it ignored issues of social *power*. Such research, he argued,

> can only point in one direction, towards a justification of the present situation ... If the media-output audience-satisfaction nexus were explored in uses and gratifications terms, the only possible conclusion would be that the audience was getting something out of it. But that is not in dispute. The issue in dispute is whose interests are being served in the process, and that is an issue which the approach itself is powerless to elucidate. (Elliott 1999: 461–2)

The issue of social power and its relationship to media 'effects' has returned in more recent debates within audience studies. David Miller and Greg Philo of the Glasgow Media Group, in particular, have attacked what they call 'anti-effects' arguments (1999: 22) which, they argue, in celebrating notions of the 'active audience' have removed questions of media power and influence from the agenda of audience researchers altogether. Researchers, they argue, have emphasised 'the ability of media audiences to interpret what they see and to bring their own experience and critical faculties to media texts', but this has been 'at the expense of questions of influence or effects, which have become objects of derision in some quarters' (ibid.: 24). In contrast, David Gauntlett's 'Ten Things Wrong with the "Effects Model"', published in 1998, argues that the 'effects model' has quite simply failed – its 'continued survival is indefensible and unfortunate' – and proceeds by subjecting 'effects' research to precisely the kind of derision to which Miller and Philo object.

Chapters 34 and 35 take up this debate. Chapter 34, by Jenny Kitzinger of the Glasgow Media Group, develops the view outlined by Miller and Philo. Arguing that 'it is vital to maintain concern with media "impact", besides being attentive to the ways in which people engage with, criticise, use and resist media messages', she draws on two audience reception studies by the Glasgow group to make her case: studies of audience reception of AIDS messages and of media coverage of child sexual abuse. Her conclusions, drawn from focus group discussions, are: that people draw on media representations to explain or justify certain points of view; that media provide an important conduit for basic information; that media can establish particular associations which are taken up by audiences; and that audiences may be influenced by broader cultural associations in media narratives. Thus, she argues, we may be able to deconstruct media messages but that does not mean that we are immune from their influence; our active engagement with media texts, and the sometimes diverse nature of our readings of those texts, can 'exist alongside media effects'.

Kitzinger's complex view of media effects, which acknowledges that 'audience reception is not an isolated encounter between an individual and a message' but nevertheless insists on the power of media influence, is clearly a far cry from the 'effects' research described above. The chapter by Martin Barker and Julian Petley which follows (Chapter 35) also describes recent qualitative audience research – specifically into audience responses to media portrayals of violence – but the direction of its argument is rather different. Such research, they argue, 'has moved far beyond the crudities of the "effects" paradigm'; its primary conclusion is that 'in order to understand the meaning of "violence" in the media, you have to understand the moral codes that different audiences bring to bear as they watch'. Viewing is a social activity, and people become experienced and knowledgeable in their understanding of media representations. Even very young children, the research suggests, 'are already making complex moral decisions about what they should watch, and for whom particular kinds of materials are appropriate'. To understand media audience readings we must understand, first, what meanings the text is itself making about the violence it depicts, and second, what frameworks of understanding diverse audience groups are bringing to bear on these depictions. Yet although Barker and Petley are concerned to refute the claims of 'effects' research, whereas Kitzinger is concerned to make claims *for* media effects, they too conclude that 'the media are *indeed* powerful'. To understand that power, however, we must find more complex and sophisticated research frameworks than any found in straightforward 'effects' research.

NOTES

1. William Belson, Hilde Himmelweit and Joseph Trenaman also carried out similar pioneering research in Britain.
2. Examples of 'gratification' studies from the classic period of American mass communication research include: Herta Herzog, 'Professor Quiz: A Gratification Study', in Paul F. Lazarsfeld (ed.), Radio and the Printed Page (New York: Duell, Sloane & Pearce, 1940); Bernard Berelson, 'What "Missing the Newspaper" Means', in Paul F. Lazarsfeld and Frank N. Stanton (eds), *Communication Research 1948–49* (New York: Harper & Bros, 1949); Katherine M. Wolfe and Marjorie Fiske, 'The Children Talk About Comics', in Paul F. Lazarsfeld and Frank N. Stanton (eds), *Communication Research 1948–49* (New York: Harper & Bros, 1949).

REFERENCES

Elliott, P., 'Uses and Gratifications Research: A Critique and Sociological Alternative', in P. Marris and S. Thornham (eds), *Media Studies: A Reader*, 2nd edn (Edinburgh: Edinburgh University Press, [1974] 1999) pp. 455–63.

Eysenck, H. and Nias, D., *Sex, Violence and the Media* (London: Maurice Temple Smith, 1978).

Gauntlett, D., 'Ten Things Wrong with the "Effects Model"', in R. Dickinson, R. Harindranath and O. Linné (eds), *Approaches to Audiences – A Reader* (London: Arnold, 1998) pp. 120–30.

Katz, E., 'Mass Communication Research and the Study of Culture', *Studies in Public Communication* 2 (1959) pp. 1–6.

Klapper, J. T., *The Effects of Mass Communication* (Glencoe, IL: Free Press 1960).

McQuail, D., *Towards a Sociology of Mass Communications* (London: Collier Macmillan, 1969).

Miller, D. and Philo, G., 'The Effective Media', in G. Philo (ed.), *Message Received: Glasgow Media Group Research 1993–1998* (Harlow: Addison Wesley Longman, 1999) pp. 21–32.

Morley, D., *The 'Nationwide' Audience* (London: British Film Institute, 1980).

Murdock, G., 'Reservoirs of Dogma: An Archaeology of Popular Anxieties', in M. Barker and J. Petley (eds), *Ill Effects: The Media/Violence Debate*, 2nd edn (London: Routledge, 2001) pp. 150–69.

32

ON THE SOCIAL EFFECTS OF TELEVISION

James D. Halloran

[. . .]

The early view of mass communication assumed that people could be persuaded by the media to adopt almost any point of view desired by the communicator. Manipulation, exploitation and vulnerability were the key words. In this crude sense this extreme view is no longer accepted, although some of the implications of this initial position are still with us. In one way or another it has provided a base from which so much of our thinking about mass communication (pessimistic as well as optimistic) has stemmed. Some people still write and talk about television as a powerful direct influence and of its tremendous potential for good or evil. In some quarters the myth of omnipotence dies hard.

Social science has undergone many changes since the days of instinct theory and the early ideas about mass society. Models of society, concepts of human nature and images of man, all change. Learning theory, work on motives and attitudes, the development of personality theory, the emphasis on selectivity in attention and perception, recognition of the importance of individual differences, the formulation of psychodynamic models of persuasion, the use of social categories in surveys and empirical work generally, the 'rediscovery' of the primary group, the acceptance of the influence of informal group ties, the development of such concepts as reference group and the work on diffusion of information and social interaction, have all played their part in producing

From James D. Halloran, 'Studying the Effects of Television' and James D. Halloran, 'The Social Effects of Television', in James D. Halloran (ed.), *The Effects of Television* (London: Panther Books, 1970) pp. 9–23 and 24–68.

more refined and elaborate approaches and more developed theories than the one referred to above.

It is sometimes said that one of the dangers today is that so much attention is given to the intervening or associated factors that we are in danger of neglecting what should always be central to our work, namely, the medium itself – television. In general the trend has been away from the idea of exploitation, away from an emphasis on the viewer as tabula rasa, as someone wide open just waiting to soak up all that is beamed at him. Now we think more in terms of interaction or exchange between medium and audience, and it is recognized that the viewer approaches every viewing situation with a complicated piece of filtering equipment. This filter is made up not only of his past and present, but includes his views of and hopes for the future. We should welcome this change in emphasis but there is always a possibility that in making the shift the baby might be thrown out with the bath water. Instead of having the false picture of the all-powerful influence of television presented to us we now run the risk of getting an equally false picture of no influence whatsoever.

Even today despite all the changes and developments the picture should not be regarded as final. Granted the state of our knowledge, we could not afford to let things stay as they are. One of the healthy signs about the current situation is that in research the established ways of doing things are being questioned and challenged. [. . .] There is, of course, plenty of room for change. For example, although we have seen that the viewer is no longer *thought of* as an isolated individual in front of a television set – the importance of his background, experiences and relationships are recognized – he is still frequently researched as though he were an isolated individual. In many research exercises the individual remains the main sampling unit, and *in practice* there would still appear to be a fairly widespread acceptance of the atomistic nature of the audience.[1]

Attitude has been one of the central concepts in both social psychology and mass communication research for a long time, but there is a growing body of opinion which holds that attitude change has been over-used as the primary criterion of influence. [. . .] [T]here is much more to television's influence than can be studied through direct changes in attitude and opinion as these have normally been defined and assessed. Television may provide models for identification, confer status on people and behaviour, spell out norms, define new situations, provide stereotypes, set frameworks of anticipation and indicate levels of acceptability, tolerance and approval. Influence must not be equated with attitude change.

It is neither necessary nor desirable to confine or even to concentrate our research on conventional approaches which seek to study viewer reactions before and after exposure to television programmes. Whilst accepting that quite often a concern with media content, to the exclusion of other factors, has led to misleading predictions about effects, we still cannot afford to ignore content. A *systematic* study of what television provides, whilst not telling us what happens to people, will tell us what is available, what there is for them to use. If we have also studied the patterns of use and the relevant relationships, predispositions and background experience of those who use television, then it is possible for predictions to be made about the consequence of that use.

[. . .]

A study[2] carried out at the Centre for Mass Communication Research at the University of Leicester on a programme which dealt with the lives of young people in Czechoslovakia, in addition to providing further support for the principle that different people get different things from the same programme, indicated that it could be misleading to think of the effects of television solely in terms of visual impact. The effects of this particular programme seemed to follow the commentary. Whilst accepting that any television programme is essentially a complex audio-visual message, it seemed that the clear and unambiguous statements about Czech life made in the programme had considerable impact. Several years ago the late Joe Trenaman also drew attention to the importance of the verbal element in what is sometimes regarded as a purely visual medium.[3]

This research also showed that it might be possible for a programme to produce short-term changes in attitude about certain topics covered by the programme (in this case favourable changes about specific aspects of Czech life) and yet produce no change at the more general or overall level (in this case, favourable change in attitude about Czechoslovakia as a political state).

The programme in question, *Children of Revolution*, was an Intertel programme, and Intertel aims to produce programmes which promote 'a wider knowledge of contemporary world affairs and a better mutual understanding of world problems'. We might ask if this is a realistic policy – can television hope to do this? It would be unwise to rely too much on the results from one small piece of research but this research did show that, after viewing the programme, people not only had more knowledge about life in Czechoslovakia but in general took a more favourable view of life in that country. In a sense then, the objectives of the programme were met. However, we have already seen that the favourable change in attitude did not extend to the government and the state. These were often more negatively evaluated after the programme. It is possible, as Roger Brown suggests, that people had their prior beliefs in the tensions supposedly inherent in a Communist society strengthened by the programme. The favourable shifts in attitude with regard to the parts of the programme (e.g. Czech youth) may have been bought at the price of a less favourable image of the Czech state. In this complex situation is it possible to assess whether or not the programme-makers really achieved their objectives?

What can one hope to achieve by presenting social and political issues on television? Unfortunately, good intentions are no guarantee of success, as the reactions to many a programme (drama, documentary and educational) clearly show. Research on the ATV seven-programme series *Nature of Prejudice*, presented in 1968, showed – like the findings from many other studies – that the same message can be used in different ways by different people. From this study it is possible to argue that audience members saw in the programme what was uppermost in their own minds, rather than what the programme itself stressed most. In general, viewers found a way of avoiding the anti-prejudice message. Different sorts of viewers did see different things in the programmes, and did respond in different ways. This comes out clearly both in the comparison between prejudiced and non-prejudiced respondents, and in that between adolescent and adult viewers. But this is only another way of saying that individuals brought to the viewing situation a range of differing interests, beliefs, concepts and levels of knowledge, and that these acted as filters through which the programmes were viewed. This latter description of the situation, in its turn, raises questions about the 'success' of the programme in penetrating the defences which all of us raise against alien ideas, and about the particular processes which take place between the time our eyes and ears receive a particular sort of stimulation and the time when we arrive at some vision of the original message which fits in as well as possible with our initial needs and predispositions.[4]

In a different genre, the BBC produced a six-episode serial, *Rainbow City*, in 1967. The avowed purpose of these programmes was to contribute to the reduction of inter-racial tensions and to promote a sympathetic understanding of coloured immigrants. The evidence available from a minor research project on these programmes indicates that sympathy was enlisted for particular characters, but that the attitudes of viewers to coloured people or immigrants in general were not modified. Identification or empathy with individual screen personalities belonging to an outgroup or minority group does not necessarily rub off on the group in general.

In view of the American experience over the years (e.g. with musicians, sporting personalities etc.) it might be argued that we do not require research to teach us this lesson. Nevertheless, it is worth emphasizing, with regard to prejudice as with other attitudes, that as far as this form of attitude change is concerned, television can only work within the existing climate.[5] If the general climate is hostile to the message, there is even the possibility of a boomerang effect, i.e. the hostility being increased. Although in this particular case we can say nothing about the overall quality of the series or about the form of presentation, it is possible that – with issues that produce strong reactions – these factors may not be particularly relevant. It seems reasonable to suggest that certain topics in television programmes will produce predictable reactions from given sections of the viewing audience independently of quality and mode of presentation.

In considering the presentation of social issues on television and the effects of such presentations, it is essential to make the distinction between a gain in knowledge or information, and a change in attitude. It is usually easier to convey knowledge than to change attitudes. Research carried out several years ago by the BBC Audience Research Department, on programmes dealing with such topics as crime and the death penalty,[6] showed that although in the latter case attitudes were modified (not changed), the former programme had very little effect on either knowledge or attitudes. Even where there was a considerable increase in knowledge about a particular topic or item covered in the programme, the majority of the viewing audience still remained ignorant on the same topic after viewing. It may be easier to impart knowledge than to change attitudes, but powerful restricting factors, external to the programme itself, would appear to operate in both cases.

Several points can be made about the apparent lack of effects of these programmes which dealt with social and political issues.[7] The first is that even within the limited terms of reference and possibilities of this type of research, it would be quite unreasonable to expect a single programme or even a series of programmes to bring about appreciable changes in attitudes. Change just doesn't take place so easily. The second is that it is a mistake to equate lack of change, in the sense of people not changing from a pro to a con position (or vice versa) after seeing a programme with the overall lack of influence of that programme. The programme may confirm or reinforce the existing attitudinal position or, on the other hand, as we have just seen, the attitude may be modified in intensity. Many researchers have confined their attention to the narrower interpretation of change (from a pro to a con position) and this has undoubtedly contributed to the idea, still widely held in some quarters, that the media have little influence.

There have, of course, been many occasions when the media have been credited with, or accused of having, too much influence. Perhaps television does not have the influence that some people would have us believe but it must be recognized that influence can take several forms. Influence should certainly not be equated with these relatively narrow definitions of change.

NOTES

1. Marten Brouwer. 'Prolegomena to a Theory of Mass Communication', in *Communication Concepts and Perspectives*, Ed. Lee Thayer, Spartan Books, 1967.
2. Roger L. Brown. *Some Effects of the Television Programme 'Children of Revolution'*. A Report prepared for the Television Research Committee, Centre for Mass Communication Research, University of Leicester. 1967. 160 p. & vi p.
3. Joseph Trenaman. 'The Effects of Television', in *Twentieth Century*. Nov. 1959. pp. 332–42.
4. Television Research Committee. *Second Progress Report and Recommendations*. Leicester University Press. 1969. p. 34.
5. The part played by television in creating the climate remains to be considered.
6. See B. P. Emmett. 'The Design of Investigations into the Effects of Radio and Television Programmes and other Mass Communications'. *Journal of the Royal Statistical Society*. Vol. 129. 1966.
7. Some studies have demonstrated that other programmes have been *slightly* more effective.

33

THE TELEVISION AUDIENCE: A REVISED PERSPECTIVE

Denis McQuail, Jay G. Blumler and J. R. Brown

The single concept which seems to have assumed most prominence in discussions of mass media experience has been that of 'escape'.

[. . .]

When all due allowance is made for distinctions and reservations, it must be admitted that the escapist hypothesis still occupies much of the central ground in discussion and study of the television audience.

Like several other notions that are deeply entrenched in the vocabulary of discourse about culture and society, the concept of escape is exceptionally potent because it inextricably intermingles what might otherwise be a merely descriptive assertion in the scientific spirit (hypothesizing that most viewers predominantly use television in order to forget stressful and disliked features of their environment) with a strongly held normative standpoint. Deployed in the latter sense, the escapist thesis has helped to precipitate and perpetuate certain derogatory assumptions about the typical relationship between television and the viewer, from which even the qualifications and reservations mentioned above are usually excluded.

Firstly there is the view that popularity is inconsistent with high quality, since the latter is assumed to connote educational attainment, critical standards, sensitivity of judgement, effort and creativity, all of which stand in contrast to the dominant meanings of the escape concept. Second, there is an assumption of homogeneity; the content of a mass medium like television

From Denis McQuail (ed.), *Sociology of Mass Communications* (Harmondsworth: Penguin, 1972).

is regarded virtually as a single commodity, in which one programme could stand in quite readily for any other. The audience is unselective because all or most programmes offer essentially the same satisfaction and are watched for broadly the same motive. A third and related point is that the experience of television is uninvolving and, by implication, unimportant according to a widely held scale of values. It is regarded as shallow, undemanding and trivial. Fourth, television is regarded as a residual category of leisure activity; it is a time-filler, a substitute for doing nothing or something more worthwhile, shaped more by variations in other demands on one's time than by any positive attractions or considered motivations. This view finds some support in the phenomenal *quantity* of time devoted to it. The general bearing of this set of views is to see the experience of watching television as largely lacking in meaning, hardly deserving of serious interest or respect, a chance outcome of a set of market circumstances. The explanatory formula is thus closed and virtually self-validating. So the evidence showing long hours of time spent watching television is not interpreted as pointing to the influence of powerful attraction or strong need, but as indicative instead of a vacancy of outlook, an emptiness of life and a uniformity of response. And when evidence shows that people do actually depend a good deal on television and are upset when it is not available, this is taken more as a sign of their stupidity than of the constructive role which the medium plays in their lives.

[. . .]

The danger is that an uncritical acceptance of the escapist thesis will go hand-in-hand with a simplistic view of the relations between audience and media content and an underestimation of the diversity and complexity of motives that may sustain the mass audience. It could also have undesirable consequences for the organization of television and the evolution of policies that determine its place in society – undesirable, that is, if television is not in fact so constrained as the escapist theory makes out from performing a wider range of social functions than is generally assigned to it in western societies today.

In this essay we aim, then, to advance, on the basis of empirical research evidence, a typology of viewer gratifications which can both enlarge our understanding of what escape implies and help to place it in a context of a number of other equally important orientations, motives and links between people and television. We strive to substantiate the claim that escape does not represent the only, or even the invariably most appropriate, formulation of the needs served by the mass communication process and to direct attention towards several other formulations of what this process may fundamentally involve and signify.

The evidence presented for illustration and support derives from a programme of investigation initiated in 1969 at the Centre for Television Research in the University of Leeds. It was designed to further in a systematic way the tradition of inquiry which has been concerned with audience 'uses and gratifications', and which seeks to explain, usually on the basis of the audience member's own subjective account of the media experience, just what functions a particular kind of content serves in particular circumstance.

[. . .]

Our work was guided by certain presuppositions, which should be briefly outlined. Most fundamentally, we adopted the view that an important part of television viewing is goal-directed. While this premise may seem question-begging, we could not proceed far with our investigation without it, and it does not imply in advance any single kind of motive. Second, we assumed that the goals of television viewing can only be discovered from viewers themselves and that people will be sufficiently self-aware to be able to report their interests and motives in particular cases or at least to recognize them when confronted with them in an intelligible and familiar verbal formulation. Third, we were prepared to find diverse and overlapping patterns of motive and satisfaction; if a viewer was moved by several different concerns to follow the same content, we want our instruments of investigation to disclose, not to ignore, this fact. Fourth, we were prepared to treat as a conceptually independent unit of analysis something which might variously be described as a satisfaction, a motive, a gratification, an interest or a function. These units could be distributed in varying ways amongst a given population of television viewers and also be associated with different programmes and programme types in varying degrees.

Because it stands on the same plane of generality as the assumptions specified above, a final orientation deserves to be mentioned here, even though it only emerged explicitly as evidence was collected and analysed. This is that media use is most suitably characterized as an interactive process, relating media content, individual needs, perceptions, roles and values and the social context in which a person is situated. Our model of this process is that of an open system in which social experience gives rise to certain needs, some of which are directed to the mass media of communication for satisfaction. It is also possible that media content may occasionally help to generate in the audience member an awareness of certain needs in relation to his social situation. The linkage is necessarily a complex one and may take diverse forms; it may involve a process of deprivation-compensation in which the media offer substitute satisfactions for something desired or valued, but relatively unavailable; or it may involve a process of value reinforcement in which salient values, beliefs or attitudes are sustained by attention to certain content forms; or materials taken from the media may contribute to certain processes of social interchange which go with the occupancy of certain roles. The essential point to be stressed is our belief that media use is interactive. That is, it does not conform to the typical lineaments of a subject-object relationship, and should not be treated merely as a one-way tension-reducing mechanism. Such a model would leave out of account the many ways in which, according to our evidence, audience members seem to bring back into their lives, their patterns of activity and their circles of familiar acquaintances some of the broadcast programmes to which they have become attached.

[. . .]

[An] account follows of one programme study, that which was concerned with television quiz programmes. This was the second study carried out and the first in which a group of programmes as a type, rather than a single programme, was examined. The choice was influenced by the fact that quiz programmes form a distinctive and popular category of television content with a seeming diversity of associations. In addition, there existed a link with early research in the form of an interesting study of a small sample of listeners to an American radio quiz programme, providing material for comparison and a source of some hypotheses (Herzog, 1940).

A series of tape-recorded discussions was first held with followers of television quiz programmes, and a questionnaire compiled in the light of the analysis of material thus obtained. This questionnaire was then administered to a quota sample of seventy-three Leeds residents (with controls for sex, age, housing type and social grade), all of whom had designated as among their favourite television programmes one of several quiz programmes from a wider list. The three quiz programmes were *University Challenge*, *TV Brain of Britain*, and *Ask the Family*, each of them involving genuine tests of knowledge rather than being merely parlour games with big prizes, gimmicks and a prominent element of chance.

The most relevant part of the questionnaire consisted of an inventory of forty-two statements about quiz programmes, divided into three sections, which were presented to respondents for endorsement on a four-point scale. The first section contained statements indicating expected satisfactions and accompanied by the wording: 'When I think of watching a quiz [the statement] applies very much, quite a lot, a little, not at all.' The second referred to experienced satisfactions in the following way: 'When watching quizzes [the experience] has happened very often, quite often, only now and then, never.' In the third section respondents were asked whether certain descriptive phrases applied 'very well', 'slightly', or 'not at all' to quiz programmes.

[. . .]

The pattern of the gratifications viewers seek from quiz programmes emerged from an analysis involving two stages. First, associations between endorsements of the scales were set out in a 42 × 42 matrix of intercorrelations. Second, the statements were re-arranged into sub-sets by means of a cluster analysis (McQuitty's elementary linkage analysis, 1957). This technique is designed to arrange intercorrelated items into clusters which maximize the average internal correlation of the clustered items and minimize the correlation between sub-sets. It is an approximate method, easy to apply, which provides an entirely empirical solution to the problem of ordering interrelated data.

Every item is assigned to one and only one cluster, although it may be the case that a particular statement could equally well fit in more than one cluster.

The results of the quiz programme cluster analysis are presented in Table [33.1]. We find four main clusters of items emerging, with several small groups in pairs also separated out.

[...]

[T]hey form a strikingly clear and interpretable pattern, or so we can conclude about the four relatively large clusters. The six later clusters add little to the results, partly because most of their meanings have already been covered and partly because two- or three-item groups are inevitably low in reliability.

According to this analysis, then, four main kinds of gratifications are involved in the viewing of quiz programmes. One stems from a *self-rating appeal*, whereby watching a quiz enables the viewer to find out something about himself. Inspection of the individual items in Cluster 1 suggests that it embraces several related elements. There is the possibility of assessing one's ability by comparing one's own responses to the questions with the performance of other contestants. There is the possibility of testing one's judgement by guessing which group of competitors will turn out to be the winners. There is the theme of projection, whereby the viewer can imagine how he would fare if he were on the programme himself. And there is the possibility of being reminded of what one was like as a schoolchild. In the last context it is interesting to note that Herzog also detected a self-rating appeal of quiz programmes and speculated that one of its ingredients was the attraction of 'being taken back to one's own school days' (1940).

The meaning of Cluster 2 seems equally definite. A second major appeal of quiz programmes is their provision of a *basis for social interaction* with other people. Each item in the cluster (with only one exception) bears this interpretation. A quiz programme offers shared family interest; there is the possibility of observing 'what the children get out of it'; the whole family can work together on the answers; alternatively, viewers can compete with each other in trying to answer the questions; and the occasion can form a topic of conversation afterwards. Clearly quiz programmes are well adapted to serving a 'coin of exchange' function.

A third main appeal of TV quizzes arises from the *excitement* they can engender. Many of the items in Cluster 3 convey this emphasis. Quiz programmes apparently offer the excitement of competition itself, guessing who might win and seeing how one's forecast turns out, and the prospect of a close finish. Herzog seemed to have this gratification in mind when referring to the so-called 'sporting appeal' of *Professor Quiz* (1940). Perhaps what is distinctive about the composition of Cluster 3 in this study is its injection of an 'escapist' note into the associated group of items ('I like to forget my worries for a while', and 'I completely forget my worries'). It is as if the various tensions of a quiz programme facilitate its 'escapist' function and help the viewer to shed his everyday cares for a while.

Finally, Cluster 4 picks out an *educational appeal* of quiz programmes. Here, too, several ingredients are involved. It is not just that quizzes can help to stimulate thought ('I think over some of the questions afterwards'). In addition, two of the items sound a note of 'self-improvement' ('I feel I have improved myself', and 'I find I know more than I thought'), in terms which suggest that people who feel insecure in their educational status may use quizzes to reassure themselves about their own knowledgeability. And this suggests yet another way of interpreting Cluster 4 – as expressive of the function of quiz programmes in projecting and reinforcing educational values.

Subsequent analysis involved the testing of relationships between the appeals represented by these main clusters and variables representative of social experience and attitudes. In effect we wished to know what kinds of people were most attracted to quiz programmes for reasons implied in these different clusters [. . .] [and] what kinds of social circumstances are associated with, and hence possibly causative of, liking the programme in question for a given type of reason. The results are of interest both as tests of certain hypotheses and as means of validating the distinctiveness of two separate clusters. The findings are complex, but for each of four quiz clusters we can report the sub-group or groups which are maximally involved.

Cluster 1 Self-rating appeal

The analysis separates out as relatively high scorers those members of the sample (thirty-six out of seventy-three) living in council housing. This suggests that the working-class fans of a programme type which in fact had a generally stronger appeal for middle-class people were more concerned to use it to 'learn things about themselves' than were other viewers.

Cluster 2 Basis for social interaction

Here the strongest associations were with social contact variables. The first high-scoring group to emerge from the analysis consisted of those respondents who reported having a very large number of acquaintances in their neighbourhoods. Among the other sample members, those with a large extended family were then distinguished as particularly high-scoring on this cluster. The use of quiz material as a 'coin of exchange' seemed, then, to be directly related to the number of opportunities for interaction available in the individual's immediate social environment.

Cluster 3 Excitement

The highest scoring group consisted of working-class viewers who had measured low on an index of acts of sociability and who were late-born children of large families. While the significance of the role of family background here is not clear, the predominant meaning of the link to low sociability seems to favour an escapist or compensatory explanation of this motive for watching quiz programmes.

Cluster 4 Educational appeal

The strongest and most clearcut association here was with educational background, since the analysis, after first distinguishing Leeds-born respondents from the 'immigrants' to the city, then split the former into a high-scoring group whose education had finished at the minimum school-leaving age. Thus the educational appeal of quiz programmes was strongest for those individuals with the most limited school experience.

These and other results which related to quiz programmes were not without ambiguity and left many questions unanswered, but they appeared to lend support to some of our basic working assumptions. They also foreshadowed some of the categories that figure in the typology of viewer gratifications which stemmed from our attempt to organize the results of several different studies, of which the quiz investigation was but one example.

The four most successful studies yielded a total of nineteen clusters to which substantive labels could be attached, and when these were regarded as a whole a relatively small number of recurrent categories were found to emerge. It was this striking, and only partly anticipated, degree of overlapping in the gratification clusters which makes it possible, without further detailed research, to prepare the outlines of the overall framework of appeals by which television may meet the needs of its audience. A major implication of this phenomenon of overlapping dispositions is that people can look to quite different kinds of material for essentially the same gratification and, correlatively, find alternative satisfactions in the same televised material. Thus an 'escape' motive seemed to feature in the structure of orientations to broadcast materials as diverse as *The Dales* radio serial, *The Saint*, television news and quiz programmes. It should be noted that these types of content are hardly comparable in terms of the degree to which they provide a faithful representation of reality; yet they still offer a recognizably similar kind of satisfaction to audience members. Other gratification types ranged with equal facility across a similarly diverse set of programme areas.

In fact, this repetition of a small number of themes was the starting point for the development of an overall framework of gratification types.

[. . .]

The conceptual status of the typology calls for a brief comment. What, exactly, it may be asked, *are* the sorts of things that we are classifying? However appropriate otherwise, the language of functionalism is so overworked, ambiguous and imprecise that we prefer to avoid it, and to attempt a new start. In keeping with our view of mass media use as being potentially

Table [33.1]   Results of cluster analysis of statements relating to television quiz programmes

	Coefficients of homogeneity	Reliability
Cluster 1 Self-rating appeal	0.24	0.69
I can compare myself with the experts		
I like to imagine that I am on the programme doing well		
I feel pleased that the side I favour has actually won		
I imagine that I was on the programme and doing well		
I am reminded of when I was in school		
I laugh at the contestant's mistakes		
Hard to follow		
Cluster 2 Basis for social interaction	0.31	0.79
I look forward to talking about it with others		
I like competing with other people watching with me		
I like working together with the family on the answers		
I hope the children get a lot out of it		
The children get a lot out of it		
It brings the family together sharing the same interest		
It is a topic of conversation afterwards		
Not really for people like myself		
Cluster 3 Excitement appeal	0.34	0.78
I like the excitement of a close finish		
I like to forget my worries for a while		
I like trying to guess the winner		
Having got the answer right I feel really good		
I completely forget my worries		
I get involved in the competition		
Exciting		
Cluster 4 Educational appeal	0.30	0.68
I find I know more than I thought		
I feel I have improved myself		
I feel respect for the people on the programme		
I think over some of the questions afterwards		
Educational		
Cluster 5		
It is nice to see the experts taken down a peg		
It is amusing to see the mistakes some of the contestants make		

Table [33.1]   (continued)

	Coefficients of homogeneity	Reliability

Cluster 6
I like to learn something as well as be entertained
I like finding out new things

Cluster 7
I like trying to guess the answers
I hope to find that I know some of the answers

Cluster 8
I find out the gaps in what I know
I learn something new
A waste of time

Cluster 9
Entertaining
Something for all the family

Cluster 10
I like the sound of voices in the house
I like seeing really intelligent contestants showing how
much they know

highly involving and also two-way, we propose to use the expression, 'media–person interaction', to refer to the orientations distinguished in the typology. Our clusters of items seem to reveal certain types of relationship between the user and the communicated content that depend on the perceptions of the audience member. A good deal of imprecision remains in the concept, but this stems from the variability inherent in the situation. What we wish to avoid is any specific inference about the presence of a discrete motive or the occurrence of a precise 'effect'. The audience member temporarily occupies a particular position in relation to what he is viewing, a position affected by a large number of factors, including those deriving from his personality, social background, experience, immediate social context, and, of course, from the content itself. He brings certain expectations and responds in line with these, and he derives certain affective, cognitive and instrumental satisfactions.

The typology of media–person interactions is intended to differentiate certain common constellations of disposition and response. It does so only very approximately and at present hypothetically. Its main strength as a heuristic device or source of hypotheses derives from its empirical base and its main weakness from the possibly limited character of this base.

The categories of our typology can first be presented in a summary form and then elaborated and illustrated more fully:

1. Diversion
   (a) Escape from the constraints of routine
   (b) Escape from the burdens of problems
   (c) Emotional release
2. Personal Relationships
   (a) Companionship
   (b) Social utility
3. Personal Identity
   (a) Personal reference
   (b) Reality exploration
   (c) Value reinforcement
4. Surveillance

Diversion

The meaning of the three sub-types listed under this heading can be illustrated from the results of the programme studies mentioned above. The first sub-type of the category labelled 'diversion' is instanced by the first main clustering of responses to *The Saint*. This cluster included the following set of empirically linked items:

'It helps you escape from the boredom of everyday life'
'It takes you out of yourself'
'The stories often have interesting backgrounds'
'It does you good to see somebody doing things you can't do yourself'
'*The Saint* keeps me in suspense'

What a programme of this kind offers is a fantasy world which is attractive in itself, and which the viewer can temporarily occupy.

A somewhat different relationship, justifying a second sub-type, is indicated by one of the clusters concerning quiz programmes where the item 'I completely forgot my worries' is closely linked with two others that refer to the mechanism involved: 'I like the excitement of a close finish', and 'I like trying to guess the winner'. Another expression of this kind of diversion seems implicit in one of the news-viewing clusters which linked the following items:

'It helps me to get away from my problems'
'It's like having a good gossip'
'I like the sound of voices in my house'

Third, the category of media function, which we have labelled 'emotional release' (familiar from Herzog's pioneering study (1944) of radio soap operas of thirty years ago) appeared in connection with *The Dales* radio serial. Only two linked items of response can bear this meaning – 'Sometimes I think "I wish that were me"', and 'Sometimes it makes me want to cry'– and probably it applies to only a minority of the audience for certain limited kinds of media material. Even so, the appropriate content may have been under-represented in the small sample of programmes studied, and additional evidence obtained in a follow-up study of the original sample of *The Dales* listeners seemed to confirm the presence of this kind of response. Thus, when fifty-five members of the sample were reinterviewed and asked directly if *The Dales* did provide an opportunity 'to relieve their feelings', sixteen answered affirmatively. The existence of this kind of reaction to books, films and plays is so familiar that it perhaps needs no further proof. More important is our wish to treat it as a form of 'diversion' and to distinguish it from an escape into a more desirable imaginary world or out of an oppressive reality.

Personal relationships

Two gratification types have been placed under this heading because they both refer to the viewer's relationships with other people – either real-life persons or media personalities. The 'companionship' category stands for a process whereby the audience member enters into a vicarious relationship with media personalities (fictional characters, entertainers, or presenters) as if he was on friendly terms with them, and as if they could stand in for real persons. Two perceptive observers have termed this tendency a 'para-social relationship' (Horton and Wohl, 1956). The clearest expression of the wish to use media in this way is represented in one of *The Dales* clusters, the most frequently endorsed item of which was 'It is good company when you're alone'. Some of the other related items were:

'The characters have become like close friends to me'
'It gives me something in common with other *Dales* listeners'
'I like the sound of the characters' voices in my house'

A familiar assumption about the mass media, and a phenomenon which will be within the experience of most people, is attested to by the occurrence of this set of attitudes in relation to a programme which attracted a large number of solitary listeners, *The Dales*. What our evidence about this programme suggested, however, was that the companionship element was even stronger than is often supposed: the characters may become virtually real, knowable and cherished individuals, and their voices are more than just a comforting background which breaks the silence of an empty house. This point can be illustrated by some further data, relating this time to the TV serial, *Coronation Street*. In the course of interviewing the sample of viewers, an opportunity arose of asking respondents how they felt about a road crash which had occurred in the programme. Amongst the many replies demonstrating the ease with which fictional events are integrated into real life were a number relevant to the idea of substitute companionship: 'I'm sorry. I like all of them. Minnie's just like Auntie; you feel you know them. You know you feel as if they had been in a real accident and you'd like to do something for them'; or 'Shattered. I'm very upset. I hope they'll be all right'; and 'My wife was very upset. So was I. I hope they'll be all right.'

The category we have called 'social utility' is a disparate one, but would cover those uses of the media which are instrumental for social interaction with real people in familiar surroundings. Social utility here may refer to media use as a source of conversational material, as a subject of conversation in itself, as a common activity for a family or other group engaging, say, in viewing together, or as something that helps an individual to discharge a definite social role or to meet the membership requirements of one or more of his peer groups. The research literature includes a number of examples describing a 'coin of exchange' function served by the media in conversational and other social situations (Riley and Riley, 1951). One of the clearest illustrations from our own work is provided by many of the items included in the second cluster of responses to television quiz programmes:

'I look forward to talking about it with others'
'I like competing with other people watching with me'
'I like working together with the family on the answers'
'It brings the family together sharing the same interest'
'It is a topic of conversation afterwards'

And a prominent cluster in the analysis of television newsviewing located a somewhat more specific information-relaying use of television, grouping the following items:

'I like to be the first with the news so that I can pass it on to other people'
'It satisfies my sense of curiosity'
'Keeping up with the news gives you plenty to talk about'
'Somehow I feel more secure when I know what is going on'

Perhaps this category of media use provides the best support for our contention that the relationship between medium and audience is not one-sided and that the role and social situation of the viewer may help to govern his selection and response. It also serves to make plausible the view that the specific content of the media can be relatively unhelpful in predicting the grounds of audience response; consequently, categorization of content based on overt meaning may have a limited value in mass communications research. The 'meaning' of an example of viewing behaviour is not self-evident from knowledge of content alone, or of the social-demographic parameters of the audience.

Personal Identity

The set of gratification types classified under this heading brings together ways of using programme materials to reflect upon or to give added salience to something important in the viewer's own life or situation. One such disposition – a use of television for what has been termed 'personal reference' – provided perhaps that most novel outcome of the exploratory research, for few previous uses and gratification studies have reported anything like it. This reflected a use of programme content to characterize or highlight for the viewer some feature of his own situation, character or life, past or present. For example, the dominant item of the first *Dales* cluster was worded 'The programme reminds me that I could be worse off than I am', while other items with which this was associated included:

> 'I can compare the people in the programme with other people I know'
> 'It reminds me of things that have happened in my own life'
> 'It sometimes brings back memories of certain people I used to know'

In addition, the first quiz cluster brought together a group of items which reflected the viewer's interest in rating his abilities by responding to the questions asked on the programmes and comparing his achievement with that of the performers. This orientation is reminiscent of the perspective of symbolic interactionism, according to which a central element in the world of every person is some notion of himself, and such a notion is formed in great part by looking at oneself through the eyes of others. Apparently, not only interpersonal exchanges but also mass communications can help some people to form or reassess impressions of their own 'selves'.

A second version of this concern of people to explore their own personal identity was distinguished from the first mainly by the kind of reflection that was evoked. In contrast to the more descriptive activities of classification and labelling subsumed under 'personal reference', the process of 'reality exploration' involved a use of programme content to stimulate ideas about certain problems which the viewer was experiencing, or might at some time experience, in his more immediate social environment. The *Dales* cluster which seemed to express this tendency included such items as: 'The people in *The Dales* sometimes have problems that are like my own', and 'It sometimes helps me to understand my own life'. The emergence of a similar cluster from the *Saint* analysis – centring on the dominant item 'It provides food for thought' – was more surprising, since this series would seem to many observers to provide no more than a succession of wish-fulfilling fantasies. The result suggests that keen 'fans' of almost any kind of fictional content may regard it as a stimulus relevant to their own real-life problems.

Less surprisingly, amongst the appeals of television news, we located a small group of items which together indicated an empathic response to news viewing. This cluster separated out the following: 'It helps me realize my life is not so bad after all'; 'It helps me to understand some of the problems other people have'; 'It sometimes makes me feel sad'. While the allocation of this type of response between the categories of 'personal reference' and 'reality exploration' is uncertain, there is little doubt that news enters into the process of establishing and maintaining identity and of relating the self to the wider society.

The third gratification category under 'personal identity' in the typology, termed 'value reinforcement', is more or less self-explanatory. It locates the appeal to a viewer of a programme which upholds certain values that he also believes in. This particular mode of media–person interaction is most clearly illustrated by one of the *Dales* clusters, the dominant item of which, worded, 'It's nice to know there are families like the Dales around today', was linked with two others: 'It reminds me of the importance of family ties', and 'It puts over a picture of what family life should be like'. Two other instances of a value-reinforcing relationship involving broadcast material may be noted. One of these emerged from the quiz study where a set of items expressive of a positive attitude to self-improvement and educational values generally was picked out by the analysis. The second was also found in *Dales* study and involved a valuation of the serial as a programme for women, including in this assessment an appreciation of its gentility and moral respectability in contrast to other media content deemed to emphasize sex and violence.

Surveillance

We have no empirical basis for subdividing this category which has been labelled in accordance with Lasswell's original classification of media functions (1948), although further research might make this necessary. As one would expect, our own work shows it to have an important place in news viewing dispositions. One large cluster included the following items:

> 'Television news provides food for thought'
> 'It tells me about the main events of the day'
> 'I like to see how big issues are finally sorted out'
> 'I follow the news so I won't be caught unawares by price increases and that sort of thing'
> 'Watching the news helps me to keep an eye on the mistakes people in authority make'
> 'Television news helps me to make my mind up about things'

Although the meaning of this cluster seems similar to that of the 'reality exploration' category, its main thrust is directed elsewhere – more towards having some information and opinions about events in the wider world of public affairs than towards stimuli for reflecting upon a set of more immediately experienced personal problems. In fact this very distinction was preserved in the analysis itself, since another cluster of attitudes to the news conveyed just such a more personal emphasis.

CONCLUSIONS

[. . .]

[I]t is unlikely that any universally valid structure of media–person interactions could ever be erected on an empirical basis, since the phenomena in question are to some extent variable according to changes in audience experience and perception and also to changes in communication content and differences of social context. But there is no reason why, with further research along the reported lines, a good deal more precision could not be attained. Moreover, we would be surprised if more extensive inquiry, using the same methods, were to necessitate a fundamental revision of the pattern we have located and described.

The main implications for the problems discussed at the outset of this essay are also fairly self-evident. If the typology is accepted as approximating to the true state of affairs, then the escapist formula, as it has often been applied to the television viewing experience, is clearly inadequate. For one thing the motives and satisfactions to which the term 'escape' has customarily been applied are far from exhaustive of audience orientations. Although we have grouped an important set of interactions under the heading of 'diversion' in our typology, it is clear that in many people these coexist with several other very important kinds of expectation and outlook.

[. . .]

Second, the relationship between content categories and audience needs is far less tidy and more complex than most commentators have appreciated. It is not just that most popular programmes are multi-dimensional in appeal. It is also the case that we have no single scale by which we can reliably attach a value to any given content category. Given the heterogeneity of materials transmitted over the broadcast media, not only is one man's meat another man's poison, but one man's source of escape from the real world is a point of anchorage for another man's place in it, defining or underlining certain features of his personality, of the problems he has encountered in daily living, and of the values he adheres to. There is neither a one-to-one correspondence between communication content and audience motivation, nor any such correspondence between the place on a presumed scale of cultural worth to which programme material may be assigned (according to prevailing standards of aesthetic judgement) and the depth of meanings that may be drawn from them by many of their most keen attenders.

And third, the supports of any sweepingly dismissive attitude to the popular viewing experience tend to crumble in so far as the predominantly escapist inter-pretation of its meaning is successfully challenged. Of course mass communica-tions research is still unable to shed much light on the lasting contributions made by time spent viewing television, but at least much of what they look for no longer seems quite so ignoble as depicted in the light of the escapist perspective.

But why should so many of the common assumptions about the television audience [. . .] have proven to be at odds with the evidence? Several explana-tions suggest themselves. An obvious one is the paucity in the past of the kind of data that might have better informed the views of critics and commentators. In addition, many vocal commentators are culturally disposed to adopt a supe-rior attitude towards a popular medium like television, perhaps supposing that people deprived of the richness and diversity of the communication materials made available by literature, the arts, the specialist press and personal asso-ciation with educated people, must simply go without altogether. In reality, people who, for whatever reason, lack access to multiple communication sources are much less functionally specific in their use of television; for them it is much more of an all-purpose medium than for the kinds of special popula-tion groups from which many critics and students of the mass media tend to be drawn. Finally, one must point to the dominance in television content of material which, on the face of it, is oriented to escape and diversion and which is often represented as such by its presenters because they believe that this will help to attract larger audiences. If one assumes a one-to-one relationship between the overt category of content and the kind of response it elicits, and if one also assumes a determining power in the media to shape audience response beyond what evidence and theory warrants, then the escapist interpretation becomes virtually inevitable. [. . .] The research we have described should pose a challenge to closed ways of thinking about mass communications. The typol-ogy which has emerged from it should provide a stimulus to further studies of the place of television in the lives of members of its audience.

References

Herzog, H. (1940), 'Professor Quiz: A gratification study', in P. F. Lazarsfeld (ed.) *Radio and the Printed Page*, Duell, Sloan & Pearce.

Herzog, H. (1944), 'What do we really know about daytime serial listeners?', in P. F. Lazarsfeld and F. N. Stanton (eds), *Radio Research, 1942–1943*, Duell, Sloan & Pearce.

Horton, D., and Wohl, R. (1956) 'Mass communication and para-social interaction', *Psychiat*, vol. 19, pp. 215–19.

Lasswell, H. D. (1948), 'The structure and function of communication in society', in L. Bryson (ed.), 1964, *The Communication of Ideas*, Institute for Religious and Social Studies, New York.

McQuitty, L. L. (1957), 'Elementary linkage analysis', *Educ. Psychol. Measurement*, vol. 17, pp. 207–29.

Riley, J., and Riley, M. W. (1951) 'A sociological approach to communications research', *Pub. Opinion Q.* vol. 15, pp. 445–60.

34

A SOCIOLOGY OF MEDIA POWER: KEY ISSUES IN AUDIENCE RECEPTION RESEARCH

Jenny Kitzinger

[. . .]

Within media theory it has become unfashionable to enquire into media effects. Concern about such issues is often characterised as old-fashioned and naïve, with 'ordinary people' assumed to be cast as 'cultural dopes'. Interrogations of media power have been replaced by celebrations of audience creativity. Challenges to media representations are being sidelined by faith in textual polysemy and semiotic democracy [. . .]. However, [. . .] media representations can be very influential under certain circumstances.

This chapter reviews some of the findings from research into media effects conducted at the Glasgow University Media Research Unit. I argue that many of the terms widely used in media/cultural studies obscure vital processes in the operation of media power. Concepts such as 'polysemy', 'resistance' and 'the active audience' are often used to by-pass or even negate enquiry into the effects of cinema, press or televisual representations. Our work shows that the complex processes of reception and consumption *mediate*, but do not necessarily *undermine*, media power. Acknowledging that audiences can be 'active' does not mean that the media are ineffectual. Recognising the role of interpretation does not invalidate the concept of influence.

From Greg Philo (ed.), *Message Received* (Harlow: Pearson, 1999).

Audience Studies: An Overview of Our Research Approach

During the 1990s, researchers at the Glasgow University Media Research Unit completed a series of studies into audience reception processes. This work covered a dozen different topic areas: from industrial disputes [. . .] and AIDS [. . .] to 'mad cow disease' [. . .], conflict in Northern Ireland [. . .], mental illness [. . .], and sexual abuse and domestic violence [. . .]. Most of these studies examined audience responses to general press and TV reporting, but additional work focused on specific genres such as soap opera [. . .], advertising campaigns [. . .] or a particular film [. . .]. All were accompanied by detailed content analysis of media texts, and most also included research into the production process (i.e. interviews with journalists and their sources).

Each of these research projects had specific insights, innovations, strengths and weaknesses. The projects varied in the depth of discussion and analysis. They also varied in the number of focus groups conducted, ranging from 5 to over 50. [. . .]

[. . .] However, each project did involve similar methods – employing group discussions and various group exercises. This means that researchers at the Glasgow University Media Research Unit have accumulated a substantial body of complementary experience and comparable empirical data, totalling over 250 focus groups involving over 1,500 people. In combination, these research projects not only offer compelling evidence of media influence, but also help to identify the ways in which media power actually operates, how it can be resisted and why some media messages 'succeed' while others fail.

Common Findings: Recall, References, Associations and Knowledge

One of the first common findings across all the projects is people's impressive ability to recall certain aspects of media reporting. For example, a key exercise used in most groups involved some kind of 'script-writing'. Research participants used stills taken from news coverage (or pictures from newspapers and advertisements) and attempted to reconstruct news bulletin texts (or picture captions and advertising slogans). We found that, when provided with a few photographs from a particular film or programme, people can reproduce dialogue which closely echoes the actual words used during that episode (even if it was viewed weeks, or even months, previously). This is true of children reproducing dialogue from *Pulp Fiction* or people recalling dramatic confrontations, with a 'mad' woman in *Coronation Street* (Philo, 1996) or a child abuser in *Brookside* (Henderson, 1996). When asked to complete a more general task, such as producing a 'typical' news broadcast about an industrial dispute, AIDS, or sexual abuse, great skill and recall is also demonstrated. People are fluent in the generic conventions of news and, although they may not be able to recall all the 'facts', they can often reconstruct particular phrases, images, impressions and narrative structures which recurred in the media coverage at the time. [. . .]

Of course, the ability to reconstruct dialogue or themes in reporting does not prove that the reporting has necessarily been 'effective' (or even that such reconstructions are necessarily based on memory, rather than on their understanding of the genre). People may reproduce reports while also criticising or rejecting them. The script-writing exercises were therefore used as springboards for further discussion. Research participants commented on their own scripts, explaining how they resembled or differed from actual media reporting while expanding on their views about the topic under discussion. Research participants usually had ample opportunity to talk 'around' an issue describing their personal experiences, displaying different narratives and discourses, exchanging jokes, anecdotes and opinions.

Such discussions revealed that, at the most basic level, the mass media (news reports, soap opera, films) are clearly used as common reference points to explain or justify certain points of view. Thus, explaining her distrust of people who are mentally ill, a woman referred to a film called *Fatal Attraction* and declared: 'They could be alright one minute and then just snap . . . that *Fatal Attraction*, she was as nice as ninepence and then . . .' (Philo, 1999). In another group, discussing sexual relationships, two young men referred to a popular film as evidence (and confirmation) that it was easy for women to 'act hysterical' and to lie about being assaulted. They described a false accusation of rape portrayed in *Disclosure* and talked about how they personally felt vulnerable to such accusations.

[. . .]

Over and above this, the media are an important conduit for basic information. The media introduce people to facts, phrases or images which are, sometimes, very effective conveyers of false information. The media focus on 'disorder' on picket lines may leave people with an exaggerated impression of violence (Philo, 1990), and highly publicised challenges to the validity of a particular medical opinion can leave people with the impression that it has been entirely discredited (Kitzinger, 1998). Indeed, media reporting of deliberate misinformation can be a very effective propaganda tool. [. . .]

On a more general level, the media can establish certain associations. For example, the persistent media association of paedophilia and homosexuality contributes to the mistaken belief that gay men pose a greater threat to children than their heterosexual counterparts (Kitzinger, 1996). Similarly, the way in which the media employ terms such as 'psycho' and 'schizophrenic', and focus on mental illness as a cause of violence, helps to create the impression that most people with mental illness are liable to unpredictable and dangerous behaviour (Philo, 1996). Such findings are not dependent on crude correlation; often research participants themselves are quite clear about the source of their views. Individuals interviewed for the study of mental illness, for example, made explicit comments such as:

> Yes, I would say that people that have a mental illness would be violent. I have this idea as I have seen films about people with mental illnesses being murderers or violent. In newspapers it is always referred to as a 'psycho' killing someone. (*See* Philo, 1996: 102)

More subtly, audiences may be influenced by broader cultural associations and the underlying logic of the reported narrative. Detailed analysis of group discussions allows us to begin to identify the impact of particular types of language, images, historical analogies and story trajectories. This can be illustrated with brief discussions of two of the most extensive audience reception projects, involving over 100 focus groups: the first on AIDS, the second looking at sexual abuse. [. . .]

Two Case Studies: Audience Reception of AIDS and Child Sexual Abuse Coverage

Audience understandings of AIDS

The AIDS project examined the production, content and reception of media AIDS messages (*see* Miller *et al.*, 1998). [. . .] In examining this issue we were not only concerned with abstract media theory; we also wanted to examine the ways in which the media might facilitate or inhibit the struggle against AIDS. In part we wanted to know how health education information might be conveyed more effectively.

The audience reception side of the research involved 52 focus group discussions. It will come as no surprise that these groups' discussions showed the media to be a vital source of information in the AIDS crisis. During the 1980s, television, the press and radio (complemented by health education leaflets) introduced basic awareness about the existence of the syndrome, its relationship to HIV, and knowledge about prevention strategies such as condom use.

However, the focus group's discussions also teased out ways in which particular language and imagery encouraged certain types of public perceptions, some of which undermined health education information. For example, there were frequent media references to body fluids containing HIV, with advice that 'mixing body fluids' or 'the exchange of body fluids' could transmit HIV infection. The focus group discussions revealed that this terminology had stuck in people's minds, leading some to believe that saliva was highly dangerous ('because it's a body fluid') in spite of this being contrary to orthodox scientific opinion at the time.

Visual representations proved equally important, with some of these images proving counter-productive for health promotion. One of the most powerful images was 'the face of AIDS': the portrait of a haggard, painfully thin person with jutting bones, sunken eyes and a listless expression of despair. This image had become fixed in people's minds. It was vividly recalled, and feared. The focus group discussions showed that such representations could undercut the health education information that people with HIV could look perfectly well for years. [. . .]

Ideas about 'body fluids' or the appearance of 'AIDS carriers' could be directly traced to the way in which AIDS was reported in the media. However, these ideas also interacted with broader media and cultural factors (ideas about saliva as polluting, pre-existing associations of homosexuality and death, etc.). Indeed, the AIDS work highlighted the way in which the power of any particular media message depends on how it taps into people's pre-existing perceptions. For example, the group discussions revealed the ways in which, when talking about Africa as the 'cradle' and 'hot-bed' of HIV infection, many white research participants drew on images of Africa as a disaster zone, a continent riddled with death and disease and a place of primitive and excessive sexuality (Kitzinger and Miller, 1992). The group work also helped to explain a common 'misconception' about AIDS: that lesbians are a 'high risk group'. When beliefs about lesbian risk status were explored in the focus groups, it became clear that such perceptions were not usually directly due to statements in the media (the press and TV reports were generally silent or vague on this topic). It was more to do with the underlying way in which AIDS came to be associated with 'perversity'. Lesbians, according to some research participants, must have a high rate of HIV infection because, as one person stated, 'they are leading the same life as what two men are' and this life is 'unnatural' or 'sinful'. Such associations could influence people even when they intellectually rejected the notion that lesbian sex was 'unnatural', and consciously criticised the idea that AIDS was associated with 'unnatural acts' (*see* Kitzinger, 1993).

Audience understandings of sexual abuse

The design of the research into sexual abuse echoed that for the AIDS project. The investigation of audience reception was complemented by examination of media content and production processes. This project was conducted by myself and my colleague Paula Skidmore, who conducted the interviews with journalists and their sources (*see* Kitzinger, 1998; Kitzinger and Skidmore, 1995; Skidmore, 1998).

The audience reception side of the project was concerned with how sexual abuse had emerged as a social problem, how people perceived the risks and how they envisaged 'solutions'. This work demonstrated the ways in which the media had, since the mid-1980s, conveyed new information (e.g. about the frequency of sexual abuse, and the likelihood of the perpetrator being known to the child). However, it also showed how the media subtly encouraged a contrary perspective emphasising danger from strangers (e.g. through the amount and style of coverage of child abductions). As already demonstrated in the AIDS project, some words and images from the media coverage were particularly significant. The ubiquitous photograph of Myra Hindley, taken on her arrest in the 1960s, has a key place in public consciousness, while images of suspicious strangers and dangerous wasteland proved more potent than images of dangerous uncles or threats from within the family home.

[. . .]

More broadly the focus group discussions showed that the issue of sexual abuse had become inextricably entwined with a series of high-profile 'social work scandals' which conveyed the impression that children suspected of being sexually abused would be immediately, and irresponsibly, taken from their homes. In particular, the study highlighted the power of association with historical analogies. Group discussions showed that the Orkney case had become associated with 'The Cleveland Scandal' – a case already seen as evidence of professional malpractice and unnecessary interference in family life. It appeared that both journalists and audiences were, by the early 1990s, working with conceptual frameworks whereby references to 'Cleveland' helped to shape their understandings of new cases such as 'Orkney'. The earlier 'Cleveland' crisis acted as a template for interpreting the meaning of subsequent events in other parts of the country (*see* Kitzinger, 1998).

This template proved to have a powerful impact on how people responded to suspicions or experiences of abuse. For example, while the media give the impression that children suspected of being abused will be immediately taken into care – this will only happen in 3 per cent of cases (Parton, 1995). But this information is not widely available to the public. On the contrary, people are often under the impression that children will automatically be taken into care if it is suspected that they have been abused. Several research participants told me about how this made them reluctant to seek help from social services. [. . .]

In another group, a young girl described how she had, for a long time, suffered sexual abuse in silence because, 'I used to think I'd get sent away if I told'. She added that journalists 'make social workers out to be big and bad . . . they sort of put a barrier up'.

THE SOCIAL AND CULTURAL CONTEXT OF AUDIENCE UNDERSTANDINGS

Both the AIDS study and the research into sexual abuse thus showed clear media effects and documented the impact of particular representations (at least on some of the people, some of the time). However, it would be wrong to suggest that public understandings are a result of simply viewing a particular set of news reports or a specific programme, as if this occurred in isolation. Every media message interacts, both with the universe of other media messages and with the material and social realities of people's lives. Thus a few (but only a minority) of the negative responses to social services were supported by negative personal experiences of social work (or the experiences of friends and acquaintances). Similarly, parental focus on the threat posed to children by strangers is not simply related to the quantitative and qualitative nature of media reporting of assaults by strangers, as opposed to assaults by friends and relatives. It also relates to broader expectations about abusers being obviously 'different' from 'ordinary people'. Although most research participants 'knew' intellectually that 'it's not just men in dirty macs', abusers were expected to be 'loners', 'dirty', 'obviously mentally unstable', or, very specifically, having 'staring eyes, like Myra Hindley . . . when you see a photo you think, oh, yeah, I can tell'.

Such images interact with, and are incorporated into, people's day-to-day reality and social setting. For example, a fear of strangers, rather than fathers, step-fathers and uncles, is in many ways easier to sustain (and communicate to children). [. . .] People also discussed how fear of child abduction, rather than incest, fitted into their own experiences of parenting (crosscut by variables such as class and access to supervised child-care or play areas). [. . .]

Analysing how people interact and communicate in the group discussions is an important part of the focus group method. Interaction between research participants is, after all, what distinguishes this data collection technique from interviews or questionnaires (Kitzinger, 1994a). Such analysis can take into account the fact that 'talk' is sometimes only a form of self-presentation and can never be assumed to provide unproblematic direct access to what people 'really believe'. Researchers needing to examine the meaning of talk, and analyse the context and nature of interactions, can invite research participants to comment on the status and meaning of their 'discourse' (for examples, see Kitzinger and Farquhar, 1998).

Alongside this, focus group transcripts can be analysed as (research-context generated) 'conversation'. This approach provides insights to what is 'routine' and 'everyday', and what is 'special' or unusual, about the discussion (Kitzinger and Farquhar, 1998). This is important because the power of any particular media message will partly depend on the way in which it is absorbed into, or challenged by, what people hear through other routes: discussions with friends, neighbours and colleagues. The influence of any particular message relates to its 'social currency', people's willingness to reiterate what they have read or seen, the value of a particular item of information or a specific story in a social context.

[. . .]

Where the sexual abuse project identified ways in which 'structured silences' reinforced an emphasis on 'stranger-danger', the AIDS study identified ways in which 'structured gossip' reinforced aspects of AIDS reporting. This was clearly illustrated in the lively exchange of particular phrases, stories and jokes in the group discussions about AIDS. For example, many of the groups spontaneously exchanged tales of the 'vengeful AIDS carrier' – the man or woman who deliberately infects their partner, perhaps leaving the message 'Welcome to the AIDS club' scrawled in lipstick on the mirror. The tale is attractive to audiences and has become an 'urban myth'. It was not just a tale read in a newspaper, it was said to have happened to a friend of a friend.

[. . .]

AUDIENCE DIVERSITY AND 'RESISTANCE'

The discussion so far has emphasised common patterns in audience perceptions and the way in which they 'meshed' with dominant media messages and cultural assumptions. However, identifying diversity and 'resistance' in audience responses can be equally informative.

It is important to note that cultural representations and media coverage of any issue are not homogenous. People may consume different messages, and they may also challenge one representation by drawing on another. For example, I have argued that coverage of the 'Orkney case' emphasised that Orkney was a rural idyll and that this image was largely accepted by research participants. However, some people drew on quite different cultural iconography to challenge this. Several research participants talked about island life as being backward, riddled with strange customs, and 'an ideal place for witchcraft'; they seemed predisposed to believe that the children on the island *had* been abused. These research participants explained this perspective by referring to films such as *The Wicker Man* (about devil worship in the Western Isles) and made comments such as, 'It's like *Lord of the Flies*, you develop your own rules.'

People could also 'resist' a message because it was seen as unrepresentative or because of the trajectory of a news story or contradictions between coverage in different media outlets. [. . .]

Diversity was not only related to differences in media consumption, conflicting information between different media outlets and reader 'selectivity'. It also related to people's social, political and personal positions and identifications. People used their identities, knowledge and politics around class, racism and gender relations to engage critically with media representations across all the topics we examined. Logic, distrust of the media and alternative sources of information were also used to reject media accounts or health education advice. Thus people challenged dominant representations around industrial disputes, Africa, BSE or sexual violence from a position informed by (for example) left-wing politics, anti-racism, national identity or feminism. [. . .] In the AIDS project, some questioned the notion of 'African AIDS' from an anti-racist perspective (Kitzinger and Miller, 1992). Others refused to accept the validity of certain slogans such as 'AIDS: you're as safe as you want to be' because of their experience, e.g. as prisoners without access to condoms or clean needles (Miller *et al.*, 1998: 200–10).

People are not dependent on the mass media for their information about everything. They may also 'know' about an issue in various ways from personal encounters, discussions with friends and their own experiences. Personal experience of the events reported (or related events) proved crucial in all the studies reported here. Thus those who had witnessed pickets resisted the idea that they were predominantly violent (Philo, 1990); knowingly meeting gay men or prostitutes challenged media-nurtured stereotypes (Kitzinger, 1993); people who had encountered convicted abusers had their images of abusers shattered: 'It was disturbing, he was so *ordinary*.' [. . .]

Such diversity and 'resistance' has been well documented. Indeed, some researchers have focused on this as their primary research topic. Evidence of diverse audience interpretations and responses has been used as the basis of theories about the polysemy of the text and the activity of the audience. However, I would argue that diversity and 'resistance' can exist alongside media effects. The research reported here certainly shows both together. In addition, there are limits to the ways in which people routinely use factors such as logic, political perspectives, personal experience, or scepticism in resisting media messages. Examples of how these limitations can operate are illustrated below:

The Limits of Scepticism, Logic and Political Consciousness

Research participants often declared that they did not trust the media. However, in practice, media messages were still accepted in at least some areas of their thinking. For example, a group of white Scottish men who declared their distrust of the media, rejected the idea that Edinburgh had a high rate of HIV infection. This was, they said, typical media hype and simply an attempt to stigmatise Edinburgh. However, the idea that *Africa* was an epicentre of HIV was accepted uncritically. Indeed, they had never thought to question this information (Kitzinger and Miller, 1992: 37–9). People may even rely on media-promoted 'facts' while distrusting the source. [. . .]

Over and above this, the focus group discussions revealed that people may accept assumptions which, on reflection, they would wish to reject. Thus while (as discussed earlier) many research participants believed that lesbians were a 'high-risk group', few could provide an explanation based on facts, rather than obvious value judgements along the lines of 'they're perverted'. [. . .]

The Limits of Personal Experience

I have already shown how personal experience can be a potent source of alternative information, allowing people to reject media representations. However, this is not always the case. The potential of 'personal experience' to challenge media representations may be curtailed in several ways. For a start, people may not bring their personal experience to bear on a subject, or only do so when asked to explain their point of view to a researcher. They may dismiss their own experience as highly unusual ('I must be the only person this happens to') or simply not apply it to their broader understandings. [. . .]

The second way in which the potential of 'personal experience' to challenge media representations may be curtailed is that, in some cases, media images clearly take precedence over what people know from other sources. Thus a person with direct experience of working in a 'mental hospital' may still feel that people with mental illnesses are very likely to be violent, even while recognising that this is not borne out by her own encounters [. . .].

Over and above this, the media image may shape perceptions of reality in a spiral of reinforcement. For example, in the AIDS project, a young male prostitute asserted that he 'knew' that people with HIV have obvious signs and symptoms of disease because he had seen a client covered in scabs, looking just like the images of 'AIDS carriers' on the television. His assumption that this person had HIV was then used to bolster his belief that people with HIV looked 'like that' (Kitzinger, 1994; Miller *et al.*, 1998: 209).

At a more fundamental level, the way in which personal experience is defined and evaluated is not a 'media-free zone'. Cultural representations inform how people understand events in their own lives. In discussions about acceptable and unacceptable sexual behaviour, for example, young men and women drew on cultural frameworks to evaluate what had happened to them (or what they did). For example, they might describe similar actions as 'abuse' or 'a bit of fun', 'harassment' or 'a laugh'. How people define their experiences is itself a culturally contested space in which different accounts may be employed: 'He's abusive/I provoked it.' 'That is offensive/I'm a prude.' 'This is a flattering affair/this is a teacher exploiting a pupil.'

[. . .]

Clearly, the ways in which experience is defined (evaluated and explained) and how it is brought to bear on one's understanding of the world is not a *fait accompli*, but is a process. Personal experience can be culturally validated or invalidated. Building theory on the basis of one's own experience in ways which challenge dominant cultural assumptions does not come 'naturally' but involves reflection and analysis, and often requires *collective* meaning-making (Kitzinger and Farquhar, 1998). Media representations (films, posters, soap operas and news reports) are part of this process. On the one hand, the above discussion illustrates the power of innovative media to contribute to revisioning experience. On the other hand, it demonstrates the power of media silence (or predominant mainstream categories) to invalidate aspects of experience, at least for a time. This is not to suggest that experience, representation and language form a closed circuit. Cultural representations may be challenged by the flow of experience and events, and direct experiences can be a powerful source from which to counter dominant representations. [. . .]

CONCLUSION

Engaging with questions about media effects is an important part of sociological inquiry. We cannot afford to dismiss inquiry into media influence as 'old-fashioned' or doomed to failure as it confronts the complexity of text–audience relations. Cultural representations and media power matter. It matters if boys are encouraged to frame their interactions with girls in one way rather than another when trying to make sense of developing sexual relationships. It matters if 'victims' are encouraged to blame themselves and to accept, rather than challenge, the abuse perpetrated against them. It matters that people know about AIDS and sexual violence, and have an idea how to protect themselves and each other. It is important that there are positive images of those who are isolated and stigmatised. Media representations can literally serve as a life-line in the face of suicidal despair, or constitute a powerful barrier to seeking help. Cultural debate and intervention must include engaging with the production, content and reception of such messages.

[. . .]

The research studies discussed in this chapter not only have direct practical significance, their findings also suggest some challenges to orthodox theory and concepts. I wish to highlight five concerns in relation to some key concepts within media/cultural studies.

First, it should be noted that the ability to deconstruct media messages and develop a critical reading in a research setting is not necessarily the same as being able to reject the message conveyed via the media on a day-to-day level. It was sometimes only when invited to do so, within the research setting, that people challenged attitudes or facts conveyed by the media which they had previously accepted without question. Evidence of critical readings from organised research sessions should not be unproblematically extrapolated to routine media–audience encounters.

Secondly, I think that the term 'reading' itself needs to be unpacked. This term is commonly used in a way which does not distinguish between interpretation and reaction; yet our research demonstrates that audiences frequently share a common interpretation of the intended meaning of a TV programme or news report, while differing in their reactions (see Miller *et al.*, 1998: 193–5). More fundamentally, sometimes people do not just 'read' a report 'differently' but simply refuse to believe the facts conveyed, or blatantly disagree with the media's interpretation. An intertwined issue is that the polysemy of texts has been exaggerated. Our research shows that diverse responses cannot be equated with diversity of 'meaning' and maps out some limits to any 'semiotic democracy' (see also Curran, 1990 and Philo and Miller, 1998).

Thirdly, it is important to recognise that 'deviant readings' may be as much influenced by other media messages as by some kind of counter-cultural reservoir of alternative perspectives. Observing that people 'resist', or read against the grain of any individual media product, does not mean that the media lack power. In any case, it is misleading to play-off textual power against reader 'freedom' as if the reader came to the text with an independent view. As Corner points out: 'Cultural power and ideological reproduction operate as much through the social factors bearing upon interpretive actions as they do through that "inscribed" in the text itself' (Corner, 1991).

This leads to the fourth point, which is that the 'active' audience is not immune from influence. Indeed, the way in which people use the media (and incorporate soap opera plots, media stories or slogans from advertisements into their everyday lives) can strengthen, rather than weaken, media effects. The way people re-read individual texts or take unexpected pleasures can actually *reinforce*, rather than undermine, broad media influence over public understandings.

The fifth and final point I wish to highlight is that 'resistance' becomes a problematic concept, once applied empirically to substantive topics. Certainly the work reported here warns against any rhetorical slippage in the way the term is employed. [. . .] Clearly, audiences do not always accept the dominant message, but I would argue that the normative implications of a word such as 'resistance' should be questioned. Audiences may quite simply misunderstand a 'progressive' or 'accurate' message in ways which preserve prejudice and endanger themselves or others. They may also resist the media in order to retain a reactionary stance in the face of the liberal medical orthodoxy. For all these reasons, evidence that audiences can criticise and deconstruct programmes in research sessions should not be used uncritically as positive evidence of audience 'freedom', 'power' and 'democracy'.

In conclusion, [. . .] I believe that it is vital to maintain concern with media 'impact', besides being attentive to the ways in which people engage with, criticise, use and resist media messages. Attention to the latter processes should not prevent us from acknowledging media power. It is clearly true that personal or collective experience, politics, logic and scepticism, as well as diversity of images within the media, allow for a more complex process than straightforward 'imprinting' of individual media messages on a tabula-rasa audience. However, it is still possible to chart media influences and to trace sources of inaccurate beliefs or particular frameworks of thinking. Acknowledging the complexity of audience reception processes does not necessitate deserting any attempt to theorise about media influence. Media power does not exist in a vacuum, and audience reception is not an isolated encounter between an individual and a message. In spite of this, or perhaps *because* of this, questions about the influence of the media remain a crucial area of inquiry.

REFERENCES

Corner, J. (1991) 'Meaning, Genre and Context: the problematics of "public knowledge" in the new audience studies', in Curran, J. and Gurevitch, M. (eds) *Mass Media and Society*, London: Edward Arnold.

Curran, J. (1990) 'The New Revisionism in Mass Communications Research: A Reappraisal', *European Journal of Communications*, 5 (2/3): 135–64.

Henderson, L. (1996) *Incest in Brookside: Audience Responses to the Jordache Story*, London: Channel Four.

Kitzinger, J. (1993) 'Understanding AIDS: Researching Audience Perceptions of

Acquired Immune Deficiency Syndrome', in Glasgow University Media Group (ed.) *Getting The Message: News, Truth and Power*, London: Routledge.

Kitzinger, J. (1994) 'The face of AIDS.' In I. Markova and R. Farr (eds), *Representations of Health and Illness*, pp. 49–66. Harwood Academic Publishers.

Kitzinger, J. (1994a) 'Focus group methodology: the importance of interaction between research participants', *Sociology of Health and Illness*, 16(1): 103–21.

Kitzinger, J. (1996) 'Media constructions of sexual abuse risks' in *Child Abuse Review*, 5(5): 319–33.

Kitzinger, J. (1998) 'Media templates: associations and the (re)construction of meaning over time', submitted to *Media, Culture and Society*.

Kitzinger, J. and Farquhar, C. (1998) 'The analytical potential of "sensitive moments" in focus groups' in Barbour, R. and Kitzinger, J. (eds), *Developing Focus Group Research*, London: Sage.

Kitzinger, J. and Miller, D. (1992) '"African AIDS": The Media and Audience Beliefs', in P. Aggleton, P. Davies and G. Hart, *AIDS: Rights, Risk and Reason*, London: Falmer Press.

Kitzinger, J. and Skidmore, P. (1995) *Child Sexual Abuse and the Media*, Summary report to ESRC – available from Glasgow University Media Research Unit, 61 Southpark Ave., Glasgow.

Miller, D., Beharrell, P., Kitzinger, J. and Williams, K. (1998) *The Circuit of Mass Communication: Media Strategies Representation and Audience Reception in the AIDS Crisis*, London: Sage.

Parton, N. (1995) 'Neglect as Child Protection: The Political Context and the Practical Outcomes', *Children and Society*, 9 (1): pp. 67–89.

Philo, G. (1990) *Seeing and Believing*, London: Routledge.

Philo, G. (1996) 'The Media and Public Belief' in Philo, G. (ed.) *Media and Mental Distress*, London: Longman.

Philo, G. (1999) 'Media and Mental Illness' in Philo, G. (ed.), *Message Received: Glasgow Media Group Research 1993–1998*, London: Longman.

Philo, G. and Miller, D. (1998) *Cultural Compliance*, Glasgow: Glasgow Media Group.

Skidmore, P. (1998) 'Gender and the agenda: the news reporting of child sexual abuse' in C. Carter, S. Allen, and G. Branston (eds) *News, Gender and Power*, London: Routledge.

35

FROM BAD RESEARCH TO GOOD – A GUIDE FOR THE PERPLEXED

Martin Barker and Julian Petley

[. . .]

Undoing the Category 'Violence'

We begin at the heart of the beast. A small but growing number of studies has begun to question the status of that central term 'violence', each in different ways showing that for real viewers, as against 'effects' researchers and moral campaigners, 'violence' is not some singular 'thing' which might grow cumulatively like poison inside people.

One of the earliest studies to explore the dimensions of 'violence' was Schlesinger *et al.*'s *Women Viewing Violence* (1992), which was undertaken for the Broadcasting Standards Council. The research focused on women's responses to four very different kinds of programme. One was *Crimewatch UK*, the BBC programme in which viewers are invited to call in with information to help solve current cases, focusing on an episode dealing with the rape and murder of a young hitchhiker. Second was *EastEnders*, the popular soap opera, and in particular a story-line about domestic violence. Third was a hard-hitting drama, *Closing Ranks*, also dealing directly with violence in the home, this time centred on a policeman's family. Finally, the 1989 feature film *The Accused*, which explored the difficulties of proving rape in a case in which men claimed that a woman had been behaving provocatively; the film ends by showing the rape. Schlesinger *et al.*'s research is particularly useful for the range of women interviewed, and its mix of research methods. They

From Martin Barker and Julian Petley (eds), *Ill Effects: The Media/Violence Debate*, 2nd edn (London: Routledge, 2001).

recruited women across a wide range of class, age and ethnic backgrounds, and distinguished those with and without personal experience of violence. Their research combined questionnaires giving a picture of the social positions of their respondents, and close interviewing of the women in order to gain access to the detailed patterns of their responses.

Their findings reveal many things. They show, for instance, that for many women there is an important distinction between finding something *disturbing* and nonetheless *wanting it to be shown*. The responses to *EastEnders* proved complicated, in that the violence involved a white man and a black woman, and the black women in the research tended to assess the events in terms of their *racial* significance rather than in terms of domestic violence. Again, in the responses to the *Crimewatch* hitchhiker story, wider cultural attitudes concerning women going out on their own cut across women's assessment of the programme. *The Accused* aroused strong feelings across almost all participants, with close identification with Jodie Foster's victim-character. But only in a few cases did these strong feelings result in demands for censorship. Rather, it brought forth discussion of 'men' as viewers, and of what might be done to control their ways of watching programmes containing violence against women. Here is perhaps their most important conclusion:

> The issue is not whether depictions of violence increase the likelihood of similar violence among potential perpetrators, but the feelings and reactions that it creates among those who are the actual or potential victims of violence. Are women likely to feel more vulnerable, less safe or less valued members of our society if, as a category, they are with some frequency depicted as those who are subjected to abuse? If so, the portrayal of violence against women may be seen as negative, even if women viewers have never experienced such violence and/or its likelihood is not increased. (Schlesinger *et al.*, 1992: 170)

These are not comfortable findings, and they challenge us all to a proper democratic debate about these issues. But comfortable or not, they change the terms in which that debate will need to take place. For it is not the sheer fact of the presence of violence that is the issue: it is its purpose and meanings, both within individual media items and the wider circuits and currents of feelings and ideas that accompany it, that have to be examined.

In 1998 Schlesinger *et al.* followed up this first investigation with a study of the ways in which groups of men perceived, understood and judged different kinds of media violence. They recognise that they are explicitly challenging the traditional 'effects' agenda: '[T]he present study, like its predecessor, is not a simplistic "effects" or "no effects" piece of research. Both studies represent attempts to move the research agenda away from this narrow debate onto more productive and relevant ground' (1998: 4).

The study used 88 men aged between 18 and 75, with a deliberate mix of class, ethnic memberships and sexual preferences, and showed them various combinations of: an episode of *EastEnders* featuring alcoholism leading to domestic violence; *Trip Trap*, a quality TV drama addressing issues of sexual violence; a documentary about street fighting; and two Hollywood box office successes, *Basic Instinct* and *Under Siege*. There was as much variety in the specific responses as there had been among their women interviewees, but even more strongly than the women, the men's perceptions and judgements of violent media were based on the *rules and standards of the groups and communities to which they belonged*. So, the street-fighting was judged 'ordinary' and in fact exciting by those men whose lives included the kinds of relationships and risks that fairly easily lead to such fights.

But even more strongly than in the case of the women, a line was drawn between 'realistic' violence – which could make you stop and think – and 'unrealistic' violence such as the two Hollywood films. These were assessed not against 'life' but against other movies – their meaning for men such as these was in terms of a world of entertainment.

Yet again, therefore, research that listens to the operative ideas of people, rather than encasing them in psychologistic language, finds people always responding to 'violent media' through their social and historical worlds, through shared understandings, and with (whether we like or approve of them or not) complicated moral codes.

Finally, in this section, we want to draw attention to *Defining Violence* (1999), by David Morrison. This research, which was commissioned by all the major broadcasters and carried out at Leeds University, set out to discover 'the subjective meaning of violence. How, in other words, did people classify acts as violent and other acts, although ostensibly violent, as not really violent? Did people, furthermore, have a common definition of violence, or were there many different definitions?' (1999: vii). To answer these questions, the researchers recruited a wide range of people who might be expected to have different experiences of and attitudes to violence both in real life and on screen: policemen; young men and women drawn from cultural groups familiar with violence; women who had a heightened fear, but no personal experience, of violence; women with small children; men with small children, and so on. The groups were shown a wide variety of visual material and, in a significant methodological move, were given the chance during discussions actually to re-edit the footage as a means of clarifying what they meant by 'violence'.

What the research showed was that it is not particular acts which make a programme seem violent, but the context in which they occur, a finding which clearly backs up the work of Schlesinger *et al.* (1992, 1998). The Leeds researchers were able to distinguish several different kinds of fictional screen violence:

> *Playful violence* is clearly acted violence, and is seen as unreal. The violence looks staged, and has little significance beyond its entertainment

value. It is invariably seen as violence with a little v. A lot of violent action may be involved, but it is not graphic and does not assault the sensibilities.

Depicted violence is violence that is characterised by 'realism'. It attempts to depict violence as it would appear in real life. It often includes close-up shots of injury, and is very graphic. This can indeed assault the sensibilities, and is invariably defined as violence with a big V.

Authentic violence is violence set in a world that the viewer can recognise. A classic case would be domestic violence. Violence in a pub or shopping precinct might be other examples. It is closer to the life of the viewer than other forms of violence. It might be seen as violence with a little v, depending on how the scene is played, although it does have the potential to be big V, and even massive V. In other words, it has the possibility of assaulting the senses very strongly indeed. (Morrison, 1999: 4–5)

These categories helped them to determine how their group members distinguished between violent scenes, but they still left a central question: what causes something to be perceived as violent? Group discussions revealed two determining factors: the *nature and quality* of the violence portrayed, which is a moral factor, and the *way in which* it was portrayed, which is an aesthetic one. The elements which make up the first factor the researchers called the *primary definers* of violence, those which contribute to the second factor the *secondary definers*. Together these determine the definition of violence. The primary definers are 'drawn from real life, and what is deemed violent on screen is the same as what is deemed violent in real life. An act is defined as violent in real life if it breaks a recognised and mutually agreed code of conduct' (ibid.: 6). Thus, for example, for some groups a punch thrown in a pub is not judged to be violent in any serious sense, whereas 'glassing' somebody in the same situation would universally be regarded as a violent act. The researchers also found that the most prevalent general rule seems to be that behaviour which is judged to be appropriate, fair and justified – even when overtly violent – is not usually seen to be seriously or 'really' violent.

Once the primary definers have come into play, the secondary ones establish and grade the *degree* of violence perceived by the viewer:

The secondary definers categorise a scene of violence if it looks 'real' – as the viewer imagines it would if witnessed in real life. Close-up shots of an injury, and splattering blood, both make violence look 'real'. So does the manner in which an injury is delivered, and how it is portrayed. Each of these elements helps to produce a greater sense of violence once the primary definers have established the scene to be violent in the first place. (ibid.: 7)

From their work with these groups, the researchers finally arrived at the following definition of violence:

> Screen violence is any act that is seen or unequivocally signalled which would be considered an act of violence in real life, because the violence was considered unjustified either in the degree or nature of the force used, or that the injured party was undeserving of the violence. The degree of violence is defined by how realistic the violence is considered to be, and made even stronger if the violence inflicted is considered unfair. (ibid.: 9)

This is valuable research with a great deal to teach, but here we simply draw attention to one of their central propositions, namely that in order to understand the meaning of 'violence' in the media, you have to understand the moral codes that different audiences bring to bear as they watch.

POSITIVE PLEASURES

[. . .]

One limitation of Schlesinger *et al.*'s first study was that many of its women respondents would not normally have watched, or certainly not watched with enjoyment, some of the materials about which they were asked to comment. In this, in fact, the research fits a little too comfortably with a stereotypical image that 'violent programming' is enjoyed only by men, not women. Annette Hill's (1997) research has begun to unpick this. Hill's study investigates in detail the kinds of pleasure that both men and women have taken in the crop of films that, post-Tarantino and *Pulp Fiction*, have generally been regarded by the media as upping the stakes in 'levels of violence'. Most interestingly, Hill found a great deal of overlap between the responses of male and female fans of these films. For both, the most important element in the films was not the violence *per se* but the ways in which they found them mentally challenging and boundary-testing. According to Hill, consumers of violent movies possess 'portfolios of interpretation', a concept which she uses to catch hold of the ways people become *experienced* and *knowledgeable* in their ways of understanding violent movies. These 'portfolios' include:

- a conscious awareness that violent movies test viewers in various ways.
- anticipation and preparation as an essential aspect of the enjoyment of viewing violent movies.
- building relationships and engaging with certain screen characters, whilst establishing a safe distance from others.
- bringing into play a variety of methods to self-censor violence.

- utilising violent images as a means of testing personal boundaries and as a safe way (within a clearly fictional setting) of interpreting and thinking about violence.
- actively differentiating between real-life violence and fictional violence.

Hill also draws attention to the fact that the process of viewing violent films is very much a social activity, arguing that 'part of the enjoyment of viewing violence is to monitor audience reactions, as the films themselves provoke reaction. Individual response is part of a much wider awareness of the variety of responses available to consumers of violent movies' (Hill, 1997: 105–6).

Understanding how its actual audiences respond to a film all too easily dismissed as simply 'violent' was part of a project into the reception of action-adventure movies by Martin Barker and Kate Brooks (1998). In particular, they were interested in the ways in which fans talked about how they used and enjoyed the film, which led them to analyse what they called the fans' 'vocabularies of involvement and pleasure'. These revealed a series of practices of pleasure which included: physical satisfaction; being part of a crowd; creating imaginative worlds; game-playing and role-playing; taking risks; rule-breaking and defying convention; confirming membership of communities of response; and critical appreciation. A key point about these practices of pleasure is that they all

> involve some kind of preparation, and therefore have a pattern of involvement which extends beyond the moments of pleasure, on which in significant ways the pleasures depend. Crudely, there are things we have to do, and to know, and to prepare for in advance if any of these pleasures are to be gained. (Barker and Brooks, 1998: 145)

[. . .]

One other piece of research acknowledges its small scale but still points up some important issues for us. John Fiske and Robert Dawson (1996) report on the way a group of homeless American men watch violent movies, in particular *Die Hard*. [. . .]

They observed, for instance, that the men shifted in who they favoured as the movie progressed. At the start, they cheered and commented on the terrorists who invade and seize a corporate building and kill its chief executive. But when the film's hero begins his lone action against the terrorists, the fact that he does it alone, outside the law and at some cost to himself made him also attractive to these viewers. But once he began to side overtly with the police, and to become in effect their agent, they not only lost interest in him, they went so far as to turn the video off. [. . .]

The men refused the 'lawful' positioning, and enjoyed their own refusal, Fiske and Dawson argue. What is interesting here is not just the demonstration of a political way of relating to the film, but that to make sense of it, Fiske and Dawson have to relate the men's behaviour to the detailed narrative workings of the film – something which moral campaigners simply don't understand how to do.

CHILDREN AND THE MEDIA

At the heart of the 'effects' tradition stands the figure of the 'child': innocent, vulnerable, corruptible. A small but growing group of researchers have undertaken the difficult task of learning how to investigate children's own views and understandings of the media. The results have been distinctly productive.

A good early example of such productive and challenging work is Robert Hodge and David Tripp's Australian study of children's responses to a television mock-horror cartoon *Fangface*. With an eye directly on the kinds of claim made about children and cartoons (too much violence, anti-educational because too undemanding, perhaps leading to confusions between fantasy and reality), Hodge and Tripp carried out a series of experiments with children aged 10 to 14. The experiments were aimed at opening up children's own understandings of such cartoons. [. . .]

[. . .] Their findings [. . .] show that a series of changes take place, as children are growing up, in the ways in which they learn to 'manage' the distinction between fantasy and reality, or how they learn how to make 'modality-judgements'. Children, they show, have a very complicated understanding, in which their judgements of 'reality' will for instance make distinctions between their parents (who is more 'real' can depend on who buys your clothes for you), and their friends and pets. So, 'reality' is not some simple category of 'true things versus fictional things'. But children learn over time to make sophisticated judgements – and one of the ways in which they learn this is precisely by engaging with story-forms. Cartoons and such equivalent materials are important to children *because* they simplify. They enable children to try out and develop complex conceptual connections, at the same time as they move from seeing stories as just composed of elements in a ('paratactic') series to perceiving and operating with the idea of a ('hypotactic') story-structure. [. . .]

Far from being 'harmful', Hodge and Tripp have shown ways in which these kinds of frequently damned materials are *necessary* to full human development.

Some of the most valuable work on children and television to have emerged in recent years has been carried out by David Buckingham, most notably in *Children Talking Television* (1993) and *Moving Images* (1996). Buckingham's work is concerned not with television's 'effects' in the conventional sense of the term, but rather with how children and young people actually perceive, define and understand television programmes. His [. . .] focus [. . .] is [. . .] upon the development of television literacy in children. His own qualitative researches lead him to this conclusion:

Children respond to and make sense of television in the light of what they know about its formal codes and conventions, about genre and narrative, and about the production process. In these respects, they are much more active and sophisticated users of the medium than they are often assumed to be. (1996: 7)

Buckingham's work is too wide to be adequately summarised here, but among his more specific conclusions are the following:

- most parents and children challenged the view that television on its own was a sufficient cause of violent behaviour. Parents were more likely to express concern about the possible 'effects' of television on other people's children than on their own, whilst the children themselves displaced such concerns onto younger children. Parents were more concerned that their children might be frightened or traumatised by violence on television than that they might try to imitate it.
- children had negative responses, such as fright, disgust, sadness or worry, not only to the more predictable genres such as horror, but also to a surprisingly wide and apparently innocuous range of programmes, including those specifically aimed at children. Negative responses are common amongst children, though they are rarely severe or long-lasting.
- children clearly distinguished between factual and fictional material on television, and found it easier to distance themselves from the latter than from the former. However, even where factual material, such as news coverage of wars and disasters, was described as upsetting it was also regarded by many as being important to watch, in that it provided necessary information about the real world.
- the main concern of children who watched horror films or true crime programmes was that they might become victims of violence. There was little sense of vicarious 'identification' with the monster or the perpetrator of violence.
- children had a wide range of strategies to protect themselves from or deal with negative responses. These ran the gamut from partial or total avoidance of potentially upsetting programmes to actively denying their reality status ('it's only a movie').
- children who watched fictional violence might become habituated to watching more fictional violence, but this did not 'desensitise' their perceptions of real-life violence, whether mediated by television or not.

Buckingham's work [. . .] challenges in detail many of the assumptions that underpin the 'figure' of the child which is so essential to media moral scares. [. . .] It shows the ways in which even young children are already making complex moral decisions about what they should watch, and for whom particular kinds of materials are appropriate. It also shows that children themselves know about, and indeed are influenced by, those scares – a point of greater weight than has so far been acknowledged.

SYMBOLIC POLITICS

[. . .] [T]here is a strong tendency for press, politicians and pundits to 'name' something as 'violence', to judge it in simplistic moral terms, and thus to warrant searches for simple 'causes' (such as 'violent media') of events which happen for a whole variety of complex social and political reasons. An important example of just this kind is explored in Darnell Hunt's (1997) study of responses to the television coverage of the 1992 Los Angeles 'riots', which followed the initial Not Guilty verdict for the police who had been filmed beating up black motorist Rodney King. An important study in much wider ways than concern this book, Hunt's work has much to say that is relevant to our argument. Hunt investigated the responses to the television coverage of white, Latino and black LA viewers, and shows the different ways in which these audiences understood the events, the key players, and the 'violent acts' committed according not simply to their 'colour' but to their sense of the communities to which they belong.

Hunt argues that people responded to the TV coverage in the light of their 'raced subjectivity', that is, their sense of who they are and what groups they belong to in the wider world. This strongly affected not only their responses to the particular coverage, but also their wider sense of which media and which spokespeople they will trust. But perhaps most interestingly for our purposes, Hunt uncovered the way people acknowledged or denied a 'racial' component:

> When one surveys intergroup patterns . . . evidence begins to mount for what I have referred to as 'raced ways of seeing'. Black-raced and Latino-raced study groups were quite animated during the screening of the KTTV text, while white-raced study groups watched quietly. For black-raced informants, in particular, raced subjectivity was clearly an important lens through which the events and the text were viewed . . . [W]hile white-raced and Latino-raced informants were *less* likely than their black-raced counterparts to talk about themselves in raced terms, they were *more* likely than black-raced informants to condemn the looting and fires and to support the arrests. (Hunt, 1997: 141)

Hunt is arguing that *everyone* responded via their sense of their 'racial' community, but that this was most clearly *acknowledged* in the case of black viewers. For white and Latino viewers, in ducking this, represented their responses through the seemingly 'neutral' categories of 'violence' and 'law and order'. The echoes for our own experiences of attitudes towards 'violence' are clear and audible.

[. . .]

'EFFECTS' AND BEYOND

It should by now be abundantly clear that a good deal of work on how audiences respond to media portrayals of violence of one kind or another has moved far beyond the crudities of the 'effects' paradigm. However, as David Buckingham points out:

> There are, of course, other effects which have been addressed within media research – effects which might broadly be termed 'ideological'. For example, the extensive debates about media representations of women or of ethnic minority groups are clearly premised on assumptions about their potential influence on public attitudes. (Buckingham, 1996: 310)

We agree. Anyone with half an eye on the recent *News of the World* campaign to 'name and shame' paedophiles couldn't help but see real 'effects' of media output. Vigilantism, attacks on innocent people, at times escalating to near-riots: all fed by the ways in which the media, and especially the tabloid press, covered the murder of Sarah Payne, 'informed' their readers and gave vent to the most brutish of feelings in their editorial columns. But the example is apposite. No one 'copied'. No direct 'message' was involved. There was no 'cumulative' influence. The issue of *how* the media can be influential must now move centre-stage. The trouble is, the word 'effects' has come to be burdened with such a mighty load of negative, judgmental and censorious connotations that we need virtually a new language in order to delineate the impacts which Buckingham rightly calls 'ideological'.

Some particularly useful work in this area has emerged from the Glasgow University Media Group, and we highlight two studies in particular. The first is *Seeing and Believing* (1990) by Greg Philo, which is based on a study of responses to television coverage of the 1984–5 coal dispute. Here, foreshadowing the study by Morrison (1999) described earlier, groups of people were asked not simply to comment on the news broadcasts which the researchers showed them, but also to write their own. [. . .] Philo was interested in the differences within the audience (including gender, regional location, class position, political culture and so on), and the consequences these might have for the way in which information from the media is received. Investigation of the complex interactions of media messages and their readers thus enabled the researchers to investigate 'long-term processes of belief, understanding and memory'.

[. . .]

What emerged [. . .] was that beliefs about how much violence occurred on picket lines, and about how accurately television reflected actual daily life on the lines, differed greatly according to how much specialist knowledge and direct experience of the strike group members possessed. In short, the more knowledge they possessed the less likely they were to believe that the picketing was mostly violent and that the television pictures of violence accurately represented the daily reality of the strike. But perhaps the most interesting finding came from a 'wild card' in the research. Respondents had been given a set of stills from news broadcasts which they were asked to put in order and then to write an accompanying news commentary. Among the stills was a shot of a gun (in fact, from a news item about a working miner threatening to defend himself). Such was the force of the news 'template' of picket line violence that even those who were most suspicious of the television coverage tended to associate the gun with the strikers or with 'militant outsiders'. Either way, even a year after the events, critics of the coverage and supporters of the striking miners still had to *defend themselves* against the perceived force of the news' claims.

Philo's work on television coverage of the coal dispute is particularly useful in that it clearly demonstrates that the interpretation of images is an extremely complex affair involving culture, logic and experience in a negotiation process that can lead to either acceptance or rejection of media messages, or even to a qualified mixture of both. [. . .]

This kind of subtle research can give no comfort to 'effects' theorising. Even though it works with the most direct form of media materials – news, and public information – it still recognises a complexity of symbolic forces which disallows crude discovery of 'messages' by moral campaigners. Like the rest of the research reviewed [here], it gives full force to the ways in which people have wider access to other sources of information and understanding. It understands the importance of the groups to which people belong, and of their political outlooks. The great strength of the recent rise of qualitative media audience research has been in the impetus which it has given to replacing figures of 'the audience' with detailed pictures of different kinds of audiences. This research, utilising increasingly sophisticated methodology, works from how those audiences themselves talk about or in other ways express their feelings about, responses to and relationships with different media.

This kind of research is not easy to conduct, but [. . .] [w]e badly need more [. . .] because now we are beginning to understand a number of important processes in the ways that the media can persuade particular groups of readers and viewers under particular circumstances.

[. . .]

REFERENCES

Barker, Martin and Kate Brooks (1998), *Knowing Audiences:* Judge Dredd, *Its Friends, Fans and Foes*, Luton: University of Luton Press.

Buckingham, David (1993), *Children Talking Television: the Making of Television Literacy*, London: Falmer Press.

Buckingham, David (1996), *Moving Images: Understanding Children's Emotional Responses to Television*, Manchester: Manchester University Press.

Fiske, John and Robert Dawson (1996), 'Audiencing violence: watching homeless men watch *Die Hard*', in Grossberg, Lawrence and Ellen Wartella, eds, *The Audience and its Landscape*, Boulder, Co.: Westview Press.

Hill, Annette (1997), *Shocking Entertainment: Viewer Response to Violent Movies*, Luton: University of Luton Press.

Hodge, Robert and David Tripp (1986), *Children and Television: A Semiotic Approach*, Cambridge: Polity Press.

Hunt, Darnell M. (1997), *Screening the Los Angeles 'Riots'*, New York: Cambridge University Press.

Morrison, David E. (1999), *Defining Violence: The Search for Understanding*, Luton: University of Luton Press.

Philo, Greg (1990), *Seeing and Believing: The Influence of Television*, London: Routledge.

Schlesinger, Philip, R. Emerson Dobash, Russell P. Dobash and Kay C. Weaver (1992), *Women Viewing Violence*, London: British Film Institute (in association with the Broadcasting Standards Council).

Schlesinger, Philip, Richard Haynes, Raymond Boyle, Brian McNair, R. Emerson Dobash and Russell P. Dobash (1998), *Men Viewing Violence*, London: Broadcasting Standards Council.

FURTHER READING

Barker, M. (ed.), *The Video Nasties: Freedom and Censorship in the Media* (London: Pluto, 1984).

Barker, M. and Petley, J. (eds), *Ill Effects: The Media/Violence Debate*, 2nd edn (London: Routledge, 2001).

Belson, W., *The Impact of Television* (London: Crosby Lockwood, 1967).

Blumler, J. G. and Katz, E., *The Uses of Mass Communications: Current Perspectives on Gratifications Research* (London: Sage, 1974).

Buckingham, D., *Moving Images: Understanding Children's Emotional Responses to Television* (Manchester: Manchester University Press, 1996).

Cumberbatch, G. and Howitt, D., *A Measure of Uncertainty: The Effects of the Mass Media* (London: John Libbey, 1989).

Dickinson, R., Harindranath, R. and Linné, O. (eds), *Approaches to Audiences – A Reader* (London: Arnold, 1998).

Eldridge, J. (Glasgow University Media Group) (ed.), *Getting the Message: News, Truth and Power* (London: Routledge, 1993).

Eysenck, H. J. and Nias, D. K. B., *Sex, Violence and the Media* (London: Maurice Temple Smith, 1978).

Gauntlett, D., *Moving Experiences: Understanding Television's Influences and Effects* (London: John Libbey, 1995).

Gunter, B., *The Effects of Video Games on Children: The Myth Unmasked* (Sheffield: Sheffield Academic Press, 1998).

Halloran, J. D. (ed.), *The Effects of Television* (London: Panther Books, 1970).

Halloran, J. D., Elliott, P. and Murdock, G., *Demonstrations and Communication Case Study* (Harmondsworth: Penguin, 1970).

Hodge, R. and Tripp, D., *Children and Television: A Semiotic Approach* (Cambridge: Polity Press, 1986).

Howitt, D. and Cumberbatch, G., Mass *Media, Violence and Society* (New York: John Wiley, 1975).

Klapper, J. T., *The Effects of Mass Communication* (New York: Free Press, 1960).

McQuail, D., *Towards a Sociology of Mass Communications* (London: Collier Macmillan, 1969).

McQuail, D. (ed.), *Sociology of Mass Communications* (Harmondsworth: Penguin, 1972).

McQuail, D., 'The Influence and Effects of Mass Media', in J. Curran, V. Gurevitch and J. Woollacott (eds), Mass *Communication and Society* (London: Edward Arnold, 1977).

McQuail, D., *McQuail's Mass Communication Theory*, 5th edn (London: Sage, 2005).

Philo, G., *Seeing and Believing: The Influence of Television* (London: Routledge, 1990).

Philo, G. (Glasgow University Media Group) (ed.), *Message Received* (Harlow: Addison Wesley Longman, 1999).

Schlesinger, P., Dobash, R. E., Dobash, R. R. and Weaver, K. C., *Women Viewing Violence* (London: BFI, 1992).

Schlesinger, P. et al., *Men Viewing Violence* (London: Broadcasting Standards Council, 1998).

4.2
THE POLITICS OF READING

INTRODUCTION: THE POLITICS OF READING

The early BBC was refused the rights to broadcast a royal wedding because a bishop felt that working men in pubs might watch it without taking their hats off (Wolfe, 1984: 79, cited in Scannell, 1989: 149). The question of respect (or disrespect) is at the heart of the politics of reading within mass culture. It informs a series of accounts asking *how* reading (viewing/using) a media text takes place within the frameworks offered by a political or ideological analysis of culture and society. It is also central to attempts to understand or develop an *activist* politics or an actively political way of reading. We might say that the politics of reading begins when audiences are accorded respect – when they are recognised as active and productive rather than passive or blankly receptive. Media studies has used a series of different methodologies to ask how this activity might be understood, how it might be understood in the contexts of social power, and/or to put this another way around, how social power is mediated through media texts and their reception.

The distance between the work of media scholars taking this general approach and the positivism of the effects scholars (see above) is marked. In this case the intention is not to ask why or how a form of media might be effective but to explore what different groups or individuals *do* with it within particular frameworks. Stuart Hall's work with the Birmingham School of Cultural Studies, which was highly influential in opening the way for new forms of audience studies (see Section 1, Chapter 3), is framed explicitly as a break with models of 'direct influence'. Hall, working with an ideological model of the media where the products of culture industry are seen to tend to reinforce dominant ideas, nonetheless rejects 'passive and undifferentiated conceptions of 'audience'. Instead he seeks a more active form of reception: audiences, he says, may *read* a text against the grain, in oppositional or resistant ways, as well as according to dominant codes. Here then, is (one version of) a politics of reading. Informing Hall's account is a more or less Gramscian modelling of the relationship between dominant and subordinate classes or groups, where culture is a battle of ideas, a struggle for hegemony or 'for moral, cultural, intellectual and thereby political leadership of society' (Bennett et al. 1986: 520) which takes place on uneven grounds.

What Hall and others such as David Morley began has been variously developed, transformed or in part rejected over time, in relation to developing media forms and cultural formations and in tension with other traditions. The five readings chosen here each make an intervention into the politics of reading, and while some come directly out of the Hall/British Cultural Studies tradition, others are part of a critique of its tenets. Thus Ien Ang attacks the methodology of effects and bids to keep critical approaches free from instrumentalism, Radway celebrates what readers can do, hooks and Doty differently consider social power and political projects of oppositional reading while Askoy and Robins argue against the structural semiotics of Hall in favour of a phenomenological approach designed to put individuals and their reflexive experience into the frame.

In Chapter 36, Janice Radway reports on a group of women reading romance novels and asks how the act of reading may be oppositional even in the face of a highly conservative text. Radway's research into the reading practices of a group of forty-two women romance readers took the form of questionnaires, interviews, focus groups and informal discussions and encounters, supplemented by textual analysis. As texts romance novels are conservative, 'simple recapitulation and recommendation of patriarchy and its social practices and ideologies'. The reading practices of her informants, however, revealed a different story: taking space and time for their reading pleasure, readers refuse, at least momentarily, their 'self-abnegating social role', a refusal that is viewed as significant even if ultimately it refreshes them for more household or caring work. Radway's project made an ethics of listening the central focus in a bid to gain a better understanding of a largely unvalued form of reading practice.

There is a nice irony in the fact that Radway's (literary) text has itself been appropriated – by media and cultural studies. It was she says 'hi-jacked by its own theory and subject and en route to its intended destination, gradually found itself directed to another'. This re-direction is understandable because there are clear parallels between Radway's project and others that worked with more conventional media forms. David Morley's *Nationwide* project, for instance, was finished around the same time and used broadly similar methodologies. It set out to investigate the 'potential disjuncture between the codes of those sending and receiving messages' through the mass media and finished with a call for new audience research to explore empirically the processes by which textual codes interact with those of an audience grouping to produce a range of 'social meanings' (Morley, 1980).

The qualitative, ethnographic methodologies, and semiological concepts (text and reader) of the new audience research seemed useful to other traditions – particularly those within uses and gratifications research (for instance Katz), for whom audience activity was already axiomatic (Ang, 1989). In *Wanted: Audiences* (Chapter 37), Ien Ang explores this engagement, defending the critical and methodological integrity of the Hall approach from what she views as the increasing problem of badly thought through incursions and boundary raids by the 'mainstream' of mass communications.

Ang says what is at issue is specifically the *politics* of reading; the founding distinction between the critical and mass communications research, which persists despite many overlaps, lies in the degree to which cultural studies views itself as producing a historicised insight into audience activity, one which embeds audience activity into networks of ongoing cultural practices and relationships. This is contrasted with the focus on (increasingly) fine-grained and 'scientific' mapping of audience activity and its variables. In the one, audiences are regarded as powerful, in the other as caught up in networks of power. For Ang at least, these two different positions also raise the question of the function of audience research. Why, she asks are we interested in knowing about audiences in the first place? That is, what is the difference between a critical project and one intended for commercial or political purposes? There is also the researcher's own position within the politics of interpretation. As Ang sees it 'what is at stake is *a politics of interpretation*: "to advance an interpretation is to insert it into a network of power relations"' (457).

bell hooks' essay *The Oppositional Gaze* might be said to conform to Ang's injunction. hooks explicitly explores the question of black female spectatorship as it has been historically experienced by black filmgoers – and does so through the optic of one of Hall's suggested modes of reception. For hooks the position of opposition is not negative but affirmative: 'by courageously looking, we defiantly declared: "not only will I stare. I want my look to change reality".' (hooks, 463). hooks work is biographical, referring to her own experience as well as that of her informants, and she eschews formal qualitative methods. Her work is at once an intervention into debates around reception/spectatorship and race, a form of cultural biography and a demand, made methodologically, to find new ways to bring forms of experience excluded from many supposedly objective, scientific studies into the ring.

Alexander Doty begins his discussion of queer by acknowledging (1) the sheer complexity of exploring the reception of what Radway called the 'dispersed, anonymous, unpredictable nature of the use of mass-produced, mass-mediated cultural forms' (cited in Doty), and (2) the danger of using conventional and pre-formed audience categories to explore this activity. The term queer and the (non-) categories it gathers under its 'inclusive' rather than 'instead of' banner might usefully work around this. Doty's argument is that it allows for a proper recognition of forms of readings and positions (queer readings, texts, discourses) that may emerge from (or in) basically heterosexist texts. This form of reading against the grain (contra-straight) is also a reading from the inside, an 'expression of queer perspective' (487), not an external description.

For Doty this is a critical project that operates on a theoretical vein but which may have resonances beyond the academic world. He suggests investigation of processes of complex, multiply articulated queer reception practices to look for instances of how queerness itself is constructed in dialogue with – perhaps at the intersection of – gender, class and race categories.

The sites discussed in the chapter are not those generally assumed to be queer. At issue is how moments within traditional narrative films may create spaces of 'sexual instability' that queer-positioned viewers may exploit. Where hooks is talking of a form of interrogation Doty is exploring forms of oppositional recognition, operating through different forms of identification and crossing between the star and the film. Narration, he argues, may be culturally conditioned but it may also resonate with the viewer's own experiences. Paradoxically, the reading explores the limits of polysemy as well as insisting on the potential of the text to be read in an oppositional way. Queer, Doty says, has 'been in popular culture texts and their audiences all along' (494). (Most) audiences just chose not to see it.

Chapter 40 marks something of a break. Abu Askoy and Kevin Robins set out to explore the self-conscious and reflexive processes through which their North London informants use Turkish television to negotiate an everyday landscape that is both Turkish and British. The concern is with the banal, everyday feelings and experiences of the informants and is based on a phenomenological rather than a narrowly political approach from which it is explicitly distinguished.

Askoy and Robins want to explore ordinary use, ordinary gratifications (rather than focusing only on those that might appear within a cultural politics founded on ethnic identity). They might therefore be said to be re-engaging with some of the approaches that Birmingham Cultural Studies (certainly that version espoused by Hall and discussed here by Ang) broke with. However, this is certainly not a simple reversion – and certainly does not take us back to an effects model with its pacification of the audience. The real target here in fact are forms of diasporic cultural studies which base themselves on the (national) identity founded in the imagined community of the migrant. The writers find this too restrictive: as they put it, people are not 'ciphers of "imagined communities" to which they are said to "belong"' (490). In other words, these audiences too are active and reflexively dispute or explore their own potential interpellation into the often frozen identity categories around which nostalgic forms of ethnic identity politics cohere.

Askoy and Robins' search for a way to consider 'the difference television makes' in transnational 'connection' rather than exploring it through concepts of 'imagined communities' and their members is thus based on a prioritisation of individuals' capacities to act and think reflexively not only about what is given to them as 'Turkish', but also about the forms and arrangements of distance and proximity, the ways and qualities of being in one place or two, that cheap transport and new media provide, that organise their own life experience beyond – although bound up with – their national identity. Askoy and Robins' critique of diasporic cultural studies is that it constrains the subject positions for those using media so that questions of globalisation and identity can only be understood 'ethnically'. Their contention is that a far larger and more complex formation emerges if this form of political interpellation is set aside and exchanged for a sustained focus on experience: both the experience of living and acting transnationally and the experience of media at a distance where the question might cohere around issues of address as much as content. 'Migrant' audiences – like other audiences – are not the terminal dupes of anybody's cultural industries. They think and act with varying degrees of autonomy rather than simply accepting their given interpellations (482).

REFERENCES

Bennett, T. 'Introduction: Popular Culture and 'the Turn to Gramsci'. In T. Bennett, C. Mercer and J. Woollacott (eds), *Popular Culture and Social Relations* (Milton Keynes: Open University Press, 1986) p. xiv.

Morley, D., *The 'Nationwide' Audience: Structure and Decoding* (London: BFI, 1980).

Scannell, P., 'Public Service Broadcasting and Modern Public Life', *Media, Culture & Society* 11:2 (1989) pp. 135–66.

36

READING THE ROMANCE

Janice Radway

If in concluding [these chapters], the reader remains unsure as to whether the romance should be considered fundamentally conservative on the one hand or incipiently oppositional on the other, that is not surprising. Until now, I have deliberately refrained from the formulation of a definitive conclusion. Indeed, the picture that emerges from this study of the romance-reading phenomenon is less distinct, though not less complete, than previous investigations of other mass-produced literary forms. Although the indistinctness is perhaps frustrating because it hinders the elaboration of a single conclusive statement about the meaning and effect of the romance, it is also an indistinctness born of ambiguity resulting from the planned superimposition or double exposure of multiple images. Those images are themselves produced by the several perspectives brought to bear upon the complicated, polysemic event known as romance reading. The indistinctness is not, then, simply the result of a faulty focus in a singular, comprehensive portrait of a fixed and unified object, the romantic text.

Had I looked solely at the act of reading as it is understood by the women themselves or, alternately, at the covert significance of the romance's narrative structure, I might have been able to provide one clear-cut, sharp-focus image. In the first case, the image would suggest that the act of romance reading is oppositional because it allows the women to refuse momentarily their self-abnegating social role. In the second, the image would imply that the romance's narrative structure embodies a simple recapitulation and recommendation of patriarchy and its constituent social practices and ideologies.

From Janice Radway, *Reading the Romance* (London: Verso, 1987) pp. 209–22.

However, by looking at the romance-reading behavior of real women through several lenses, each trained on a different component or moment of a process that achieves its meaning and effect over time, each also positioned differently in the sense that one attempts to see the women's experience from within while the other strives to view it from without, this study has consciously chosen to juxtapose multiple views of the complex social interaction between people and texts known as reading. Although I think each view accurately captures one aspect of the phenomenon of romance reading, none can account fully for the actual occurrence or significance of the event as such. In part, this is a function of the complexity inherent in any human action, but it is also the consequence of the fact that culture is both perceptible and hidden, both articulate and covert. Dot and the Smithton women know well both how and why they read romances. Yet at the same time, they also act on cultural assumptions and corollaries not consciously available to them precisely because those givens constitute the very foundation of their social selves, the very possibility of their social action. The multiple perspectives employed here have been adopted, therefore, in the hope that they might help us to comprehend what the women understand themselves to be gaining from the reading of romances while simultaneously revealing how that practice and self-understanding have tacit, unintended effects and implications.

Although it will be impossible, then, to use this conclusion to bring a single, large picture into focus simply because there is no context-free, unmarked position from which to view the activity of romance reading in its entirety, I can perhaps use it to remind the reader of each of the snapshots provided herein, to juxtapose them rapidly in condensed space and time. Such a review will help to underscore the semantic richness and ideological density of the actual process known as romance reading and thus highlight once and for all the complicated nature of the connection between the romance and the culture that has given rise to it.

If we remember that texts are read and that reading itself is an activity carried on by real peopl in a preconstituted social context, it becomes possible to distinguish *analytically* between the meaning of the act and the meaning of the text as read. This analytic distinction then empowers us to question whether the significance of the act of reading itself might, under some conditions contradict, undercut, or qualify the significance of producing a particular kind of story. When this methodological distinction is further complicated by an effort to render real readers' comprehension of each of the aspects of the activity as well as the covert significance and consequences underlying both, the possibilities for perceiving conflict and contradiction are increased even more. This is exactly what has resulted from this account of the reading preferences and behavior of Dorothy Evans and the Smithton women.

Ethnographic investigation, for instance, has led to the discovery that Dot and her customers see the act of reading as combative and compensatory. It is combative in the sense that it enables them to refuse the other-directed social role prescribed for them by their position within the institution of marriage. In picking up a book, as they have so eloquently told us, they refuse temporarily their family's otherwise constant demand that they attend to the wants of others even as they act deliberately to do something for their own private pleasure. Their activity is compensatory, then, in that it permits them to focus on themselves and to carve out a solitary space within an arena where their self-interest is usually identified with the interests of others and where they are defined as a public resource to be mined at will by the family. For them, romance reading addresses needs created in them but not met by patriarchal institutions and engendering practices.

It is striking to observe that this partial account of romance reading, which stresses its status as an oppositional or contestative act because the women use it to thwart common cultural expectations and to supply gratification ordinarily ruled out by the way the culture structures their lives, is not far removed from the account of folkloric practices elaborated recently by Luigi Lombardi-Satriani and José Limon.[1] Although both are concerned only with folkloric behavior and the way indigenous folk performances contest the hegemonic imposition of bourgeois culture on such subordinate groups as 'workers, . . . peasants, racial and cultural minorities, and women,'[2] their definitions of contestation do not rule out entirely the sort of behavioral activity involving mass culture that I have discovered among the Smithton readers.

[. . .]

When romance reading is examined, then, as an activity that takes place within a specific social context, it becomes evident that this form of behavior both supplements and counter-valuates in Limon's sense. Romance reading supplements the avenues traditionally open to women for emotional gratification by supplying them vicariously with the attention and nurturance they do not get enough of in the round of day-to-day existence. It counter-valuates because the story opposes the female values of love and personal interaction to the male values of competition and public achievement and, at least in ideal romances, demonstrates the triumph of the former over the latter. Romance reading and writing might be seen therefore as a collectively elaborated female ritual through which women explore the consequences of their common social condition as the appendages of men and attempt to imagine a more perfect state where all the needs they so intensely feel and accept as given would be adequately addressed.

I must stress here [. . .] that this is *not* the only view of romance reading that might be taken. Women's domestic role in patriarchal culture, which is simultaneously addressed and counter-valuated in the imagination through a woman's encounter with romantic fiction, is left virtually intact by her leisure-time withdrawal. Although in restoring a woman's depleted sense of self romance reading may constitute tacit recognition that the current arrangement of the sexes is not ideal for her emotional well-being, it does nothing to alter a woman's social situation, itself very likely characterized by those dissatisfying patterns. In fact, this activity may very well obviate the need or desire to demand satisfaction in the real world because it can be so successfully met in fantasy.

By the same token, it should also be pointed out that although romance writing and reading help to create a kind of female community, that community is nonetheless mediated by the distances that characterize mass production and the capitalist organization of storytelling. Because the oppositional act is carried out through the auspices of a book and thus involves the fundamentally private, isolating experience of reading, these women never get together to share either the experience of imaginative opposition, or, perhaps more important, the discontent that gave rise to their need for the romance in the first place. The women join forces only symbolically and in a mediated way in the privacy of their individual homes and in the culturally devalued sphere of leisure activity. They do nothing to challenge their separation from one another brought about by the patriarchal culture's insistence that they never work in the public world to maintain themselves but rather live symbiotically as the property and responsibility of men.

In summary, when the act of romance reading is viewed as it is by the readers themselves, from within a belief system that accepts as given the institutions of heterosexuality and monogamous marriage, it can be conceived as an activity of mild protest and longing for reform necessitated by those institutions' failure to satisfy the emotional needs of women. Reading therefore functions for them as an act of recognition and contestation whereby that failure is first admitted and then partially reversed. Hence, the Smithton readers' claim that romance reading is a 'declaration of independence' and a way to say to others, 'This is my time, my space. Now leave me alone.'

At the same time, however, when viewed from the vantage point of a feminism that would like to see the women's oppositional impulse lead to real social change, romance reading can also be seen as an activity that could potentially disarm that impulse. It might do so because it supplies vicariously those very needs and requirements that might otherwise be formulated as demands in the real world and lead to the potential restructuring of sexual relations. The question of whether the activity of romance reading does, in reality, deflect such change by successfully defusing or recontaining this protest must remain unanswered for the moment. Although it may appear on the surface that the leisure-time activity of reading an admittedly fantastic story could never provoke the women who recognize that they need such a 'crutch' to act to change their situation, the women themselves indicate otherwise. In fact, they claim to be transformed by their hobby. Because recent developments in the social practices of romance writing and reading and variations in the romantic plot structure suggest that some change *is* being generated as a consequence of the phenomenon, I will return to this question of the cumulative effect of romance reading shortly after reviewing the significance of the traditional narrative itself, both as it is consciously constructed by the Smithton women and as I think they experience it unconsciously.

If one begins, as I have here, with the premise that the construction of a narrative is an activity that takes place over time, it becomes clear that the significance of the whole process of assembling and understanding the romantic story itself is as ambiguous and conflicted as the simple act of reading the book that contains the tale. As with the act of reading, the women construct and understand the story in a positive manner that both underscores their capabilities as readers and interprets the heroine's actions in the most favorable of ways. Nonetheless, it can also be shown that those conscious processes have tacit and sometimes contradictory consequences. They do so because the activities of constructing the narrative world and of interpreting the heroine's role within it leave intact the very cultural categories, assumptions, and institutions that prompt the readers' desire to demonstrate repeatedly that they are capable and to be told again and again of the worth and power of a romantic heroine.

The narrative discourse of the romantic novel is structured in such a way that it yields easily to the reader's most familiar reading strategies. Thus the act of constructing the narrative line is reassuring because the romantic writer's typical discourse leads the reader to make deductions and inferences that are always immediately confirmed. As she assembles the plot, therefore, the reader learns, in addition to what happens next, that *she* knows how to make sense of texts and human action. Although this understanding of the process must be taken into account and attributed to a positive desire to assert the power and capability of the female self, it cannot be overlooked that the fictional world created as its consequence also reinforces traditional female limitations because it validates the dominance of domestic concerns and personal interaction in women's lives. The reader thus engages in an activity that shores up her own sense of her abilities, but she also creates a simulacrum of her limited social world within a more glamorous fiction. She therefore inadvertently justifies as natural the very conditions and their emotional consequences to which her reading activity is a response.

Similarly, in looking at the Smithton readers' conscious engagement with the manifest content of the ideal romance, it becomes evident that these women believe themselves to be participating in a story that is as much *about* the transformation of an inadequate suitor into the perfect lover-protector as it is about the concomitant triumph of a woman. Her triumph consists of her achievement of sexual and emotional maturity while simultaneously securing the complete attention and devotion of this man who, at least on the surface, admits her preeminent claim to his time and interest. The act of constructing the romantic tale thus provides the reader first with an opportunity to protest vicariously a man's initial inability to understand a woman and to treat her with sensitivity. Secondarily, the process enables a woman to achieve a kind of mastery over her fear of rape because the fantasy evokes her fear and subsequently convinces her that rape is either an illusion or something that she can control easily. Finally, by witnessing and approving of the ideal romantic conclusion, the reader expresses her opposition to the domination of commodity values in her society because she so heartily applauds the heroine's ability to draw the hero's attention away from the public world of money and status and to convince him of the primacy of her values and concerns.

It seems apparent, then, that an oppositional moment can be said to characterize even the production of the romantic story if that process is understood as the women themselves conceive it. I have elsewhere called this stage or aspect of the reading process a 'utopian' moment,[3] drawing on Fredric Jameson's important argument that every form of mass culture has a dimension 'which remains implicitly, and no matter how faintly, negative and critical of the social order from which, as a product and a commodity, it springs.'[4] In effect, the vision called into being at the end of the process of romance reading projects for the reader a utopian state where men are neither cruel nor indifferent, neither preoccupied with the external world nor wary of an intense emotional attachment to a woman. This fantasy also suggests that the safety and protection of traditional marriage will not compromise a woman's autonomy or self-confidence. In sum, the vision reforms those very conditions characterizing the real world that leave so many women and, most probably, the reader herself, longing for affective care, ongoing tenderness, and a strong sense of self-worth. This interpretation of the romance's meaning suggests, then, that the women who seek out ideal novels in order to construct such a vision again and again are reading not out of contentment but out of dissatisfaction, longing, and protest.

Of course, in standing back from this construction of the romance's meaning, once again to assess the implications of its symbolic negation and criticism of the social order, it becomes possible to see that despite the utopian force of the romance's projection, that projection actually leaves unchallenged the very system of social relations whose faults and imperfections gave rise to the romance and which the romance is trying to perfect. The romance manages to do so because its narrative organization prompts the reader to construct covert counter-messages that either undercut or negate the changes projected on an overt level. To begin with, although the narrative story provides the reader with an opportunity to indulge in anger at the initial, offensive behavior of the hero, we must not forget that that anger is later shown to be unwarranted because the hero's indifference or cruelty actually originated in feelings of love. Thus while the experience of reading the tale may be cathartic in the sense that it allows the reader to express in the imagination anger at men that she would otherwise censor or deny, it also suggests to her that such anger as the heroine's is, in reality, unjustified because the offensiveness of the behavior prompting it was simply a function of the heroine's inability to read a man properly. Because the reading process always confirms for the reader that she knows how to read male behavior correctly, it suggests that her anger is unnecessary because her spouse, like the hero, actually loves her deeply, though he may not express it as she might wish. In the end, the romance-reading process gives the reader a strategy for making her present situation more comfortable without substantive reordering of its structure rather than a comprehensive program for reorganizing her life in such a way that all needs might be met.

In this context, I should also call attention once again to the hole in the romance's explanatory logic with respect to the hero's transformation from the heroine's distant, insensitive, and cold superior into her tender, expressive intimate. Although this crucial transformation in the romance clearly derives from writers' and readers' desires to believe in the possibility of such an ideal partner, the manner in which it is effected implies once again that the transfiguration is accomplished largely by a shift in the heroine's perceptual gestalt. Of course, the ideal hero does become more expressive in the course of the story, but because the early descriptions of him emphasized that this tender side was always part of his true character even though it was suppressed, the narrative structure places ultimate responsibility for its nurturance and flowering on the heroine herself. In reassuring him about the purity of her motives, it is *she* who frees him to respond warmly to her. This structure covertly suggests, then, that male reticence and distance cannot be transmuted into something else entirely. All that is possible, really, is the cultivation and encouragement of tendencies already there in the personalities of particular men. If a woman wants to be treated tenderly and attentively, the story ultimately suggests, she must find a man who is already capable of such expression though perhaps fearful of indulging in it. By having it both ways to begin with, that is, by beginning with a hero who is traditionally masculine and somewhat expressive in a feminine way, the romance manages to sidestep the crucial issue of whether the traditional social construction of masculinity does not rule out the possibility of nurturant behavior in men.

Little need be said here about the way in which the romance's treatment of rape probably harms romance readers even as it provides them with a sense of power and control over their fear of it. Although their distaste for 'out-and-out' violation indicates that these women do not want to be punished or hurt as so many have assumed, their willingness to be convinced that the forced 'taking' of a woman by a man who 'really' loves her is testimony to her desirability and worth rather than to his power suggests once again that the romance is effectively dealing with some of the consequences of patriarchy without also challenging the hierarchy of control upon which it is based. By examining the whole issue of rape and its effect on the heroine, the romance may provide the reader with the opportunity to explore the consequences of related behavior in her own life. Nonetheless, by suggesting that rape is either a mistake or an expression of uncontrollable desire, it may also give her a false sense of security by showing her how to rationalize violent behavior and thus reconcile her to a set of events and relations that she would be better off changing.

Finally, it must also be noted here that even though the romance underlines the opposition between the values of love and those associated with the competitive pursuit of status and wealth, by perpetuating the exclusive division of the world into the familiar categories of the public and the private, the romance continues to justify the social placement of women that has led to the very discontent that is the source of their desire to read romances. It is true, certainly, that the romance accepts this dichotomy in order to assert subsequently that the commonly devalued personal sphere and the women who dominate it have higher status and the evangelical power to draw the keepers of the public realm away from their worldly interests. Yet despite this proclamation of female superiority, in continuing to relegate women to the arena of domestic, purely personal relations, the romance fails to pose other, more radical questions. In short, it refuses to ask whether female values might be used to 'feminize' the public realm or if control over that realm could be shared by women and by men. Because the romance finally leaves unchallenged the male right to the public spheres of work, politics, and power, because it refurbishes the institution of marriage by suggesting how it might be viewed continuously as a courtship, because it represents real female needs within the story and then depicts their satisfaction by traditional heterosexual relations, the romance avoids questioning the institutionalized basis of patriarchal control over women even as it serves as a locus of protest against some of its emotional consequences.

Given the apparent power of the romance's conservative counter-messages, then, it is tempting to suggest that romantic fiction must be an active agent in the maintenance of the ideological status quo because it ultimately reconciles women to patriarchal society and reintegrates them with its institutions. It appears that it might do so by deflecting and recontaining real protest and by supplying vicariously certain needs that, if presented as demands in the real world, might otherwise lead to the reordering of heterosexual relationships. If true, romances would do all of this within the already fenced-off realm of leisure and the imaginary and thereby protect the more important arenas of the culture from women's collective elaboration of their dissatisfaction with patriarchy's effects on their lives.

[. . .]

Other developments on the national romance scene suggest that the utopian current running through the experience of reading may move women in ways that conflict significantly with the more conservative push effected by the story's reaffirmation of marriage's ability to satisfy female needs completely. I am thinking here of the recent decision to organize among romance writers themselves. Founded by several Texas women in the spring of 1981, the Romance Writers of America has developed rapidly as a national organization that draws together writers and editors of romances and even some readers. Communicating through a monthly newsletter and at both regional and national conferences, these women are now sharing tips, techniques, and information about romance writing and reading. Indeed, the writers are, for the first time, disclosing facts and figures about their contracts with the express purpose of forcing better deals from publishers who the women now know are making enormous profits from the sales of their books.

[. . .]

Whether such developments will be widespread and general in the future is impossible to say since we have no way of knowing how many women will give up their safe, limited, and barely conscious contestation of patriarchy for the uncertainty of feminism's conscious assault on both its categorization of the world and its institutional structure. The developments bear watching, however, for they may indicate that the romance's long-present but covert challenge to the notion that traditional marriages satisfy all women's needs is about to take on a more combative, questioning tone. This could occur if romance writers and readers ever discover through the collective sharing of experiences that together they have strength, a voice, and important objections to make about current gender arrangements. However, because I suspect a demand for real change in power relations will occur only if women also come to understand that their need for romances is a function of their dependent status *as women* and of their acceptance of marriage as the only route to female fulfillment, I think we as feminists might help this change along by first learning to recognize that romance reading originates in very real dissatisfaction and embodies a valid, if limited, protest. Then by developing strategies for making that dissatisfaction and its causes consciously available to romance readers and by learning how to encourage that protest in such a way that it will be delivered in the arena of actual social relations rather than acted out in the imagination, we might join hands with women who are, after all, our sisters and together imagine a world whose subsequent creation would lead to the need for a new fantasy altogether.

Perhaps one final observation about the implications of this study for future investigation of mass-cultural forms is necessary before bringing the work to its conclusion. I do not think it would be claiming too much to suggest that the very fruitfulness of the methodology employed here indicates that we may not yet understand the complexity of mass culture's implication in social life as well as we might. Certainly, my study does not challenge absolutely the notion that mass-produced art forms like the romance are ideologically conservative in the sense that they restore at least temporarily the claims of presently existing institutions and practices to the loyalty of those who participate vicariously in these forms. After all, the romance does assert on one level that the perfect heterosexual lover is a possibility as is an ideal marriage in which a woman achieves independence, dependence, excitement, and nurturance all at the same time. Nonetheless, the study's investigation of reading as act suggests that real people can use the romance to address their unmet needs experienced precisely because that ideal relationship is made highly improbable by the institutional structure and engendering practices of contemporary society. Furthermore, the focus on reading as a process of construction reveals that the early stages of a reader's interpretation and response to the romantic form can be characterized by the expression of repressed emotions deriving from dissatisfaction with the status quo and a utopian longing for a better life. The methodology highlights, then, the complicated and contradictory ways in which the romance recognizes and thereby protests the weaknesses of patriarchy and the failure of traditional marriage even as it apparently acts to assert the perfection of each and to teach women how to *re*-view their own imperfect relationships in such a way that they seem unassailable.

All of this suggests that we must be careful not to reproduce the reifying tendencies of late capitalism and its supportive perceptual and analytical strategies in our methodologies and interpretive work. We must not, in short, look only at mass-produced objects themselves on the assumption that they bear all of their significances on their surface, as it were, and reveal them automatically to us. To do so would be to assume either that perceptible, tangible things alone are worth analyzing or that those commodified objects exert such pressure and influence on their consumers that they have no power as individuals to resist or alter the ways in which those objects mean or can be used.

Commodities like mass-produced literary texts are selected, purchased, constructed, and used by real people with previously existing needs, desires, intentions, and interpretive strategies. By reinstating those active individuals and their creative, constructive activities at the heart of our interpretive enterprise, we avoid blinding ourselves to the fact that the essentially human practice of making meaning goes on even in a world increasingly dominated by things and by consumption. In thus recalling the interactive character of operations like reading, we restore time, process, and action to our account of human endeavor and therefore increase the possibility of doing justice to its essential complexity and ambiguity as practice. We also increase our chances of sorting out or articulating the difference between the repressive imposition of ideology and oppositional practices that, though limited in their scope and effect, at least dispute or contest the control of ideological forms.

If we can learn, then, to look at the ways in which various groups appropriate and use the mass-produced art of our culture, I suspect we may well begin to understand that although the ideological power of contemporary cultural forms is enormous, indeed sometimes even frightening, that power is not yet all-pervasive, totally vigilant, or complete. Interstices still exist within the social fabric where opposition is carried on by people who are not satisfied by their place within it or by the restricted material and emotional rewards that accompany it. They therefore attempt to imagine a more perfect social state as a way of countering despair. I think it absolutely essential that we who are committed to social change learn not to overlook this minimal but nonetheless legitimate form of protest. We should seek it out not only to understand its origins and its utopian longing but also to learn how best to encourage it and bring it to fruition. If we do not, we have already conceded the fight and, in the case of the romance at least, admitted the impossibility of creating a world where the vicarious pleasure supplied by its reading would be unnecessary.

NOTES

1. Luigi Lombardi-Satriani, 'Folklore as Culture of Contestation', *Journal of the Folklore Institute* 11 (June–August 1974), 99–121. José Limon, 'Folklore and the Mexican in the United States: A Marxist Cultural Perspective' (unpublished paper), 1–21.
2. Ibid., 3.
3. Janice Radway, 'The Utopian Impulse in Popular Literature: Gothic Romances and "Feminist" Protest', *American Quarterly* 33 (summer 1981), 140–62.
4. Fredric Jameson, 'Reification and Utopia in Mass Culture', *Social Text* 1 (winter 1979), 144.

37

WANTED: AUDIENCES. ON THE POLITICS OF EMPIRICAL AUDIENCE STUDIES

Ien Ang

In his pioneering book *The 'Nationwide' Audience*, David Morley situates his research on which the book reports as follows: 'The relation of an audience to the ideological operations of television remains in principle an empirical question: the challenge is the attempt to develop appropriate methods of empirical investigation of that relation.'[1]

Although this sentence may initially be interpreted as a call for a technical discussion about empirical research methods, its wider meaning should be sought in the theoretical and political context of Morley's work. To me, the importance of *The 'Nationwide' Audience* does not so much reside in the fact that it offers an empirically validated, and thus 'scientific' account of 'the ideological operations of television,' or merely in its demonstration of some of the ways in which the television audience is 'active.' Other, more wide-ranging issues are at stake.

[. . .]

ACADEMIC CONVERGENCE?

The 'Nationwide' Audience has generally been received as an innovative departure within cultural studies, both theoretically and methodologically. If *Screen* theory can be diagnosed as one instance in which critical discourse on television suffered from the problem of the 'disappearing audience,'[2] Morley's project is an indication of a growing acknowledgment within cultural studies

From E. Seiter, H. Borchers, G. Kreutzner and E.-M. Warth (eds), *Remote Control: Television, Audiences and Cultural Power* (London: Routledge, 1989) pp. 96–115.

that television viewing is a practice that involves the active production of meanings by viewers.

But the book has also been welcomed by some adherents of the influential uses and gratifications approach, who see it as an important step on the part of 'critical' scholars in their direction, that is as an acceptance of, and possible contribution to, a refinement of their own basic axiomatic commitment to 'the active audience.' On the other hand, some uses and gratifications researchers, for their part, have begun to take over semiologically informed cultural studies concepts such as 'text' and 'reader,' thereby indicating an acknowledgment of the symbolic nature of negotiations between media texts and their readers which they, in their functionalist interest for the multiple relationships between audience gratifications and media 'uses,' had previously all but ignored.[3]

On top of this conceptual rapprochement, these social scientists have also expressed their delight in noticing a methodological 'concession' among 'critical' scholars: finally, so it is argued, some 'critical' scholars at least have dropped their suspicion of doing empirical research. In a benevolent, rather fatherly tone, three senior ambassadors of the uses and gratifications approach, Blumler, Gurevitch, and Katz, have thus proclaimed a gesture of 'reaching out' to the other 'camp,' calling for incorporating some of the insights developed within the 'critical' perspective into their own paradigm.[4] Evoked then is the prospect of merging the two approaches, to the point that they may ultimately fuse into a happy common project in which the perceived hostility between the two 'camps' will have been unmasked as academic 'pseudo-conflicts.' As one leading gratifications researcher, Rosengren, optimistically predicts: 'To the extent that the same problematics are empirically studied by members of various schools, the present sharp differences of opinion will gradually diminish and be replaced by a growing convergence of perspectives.'[5]

However, to interpret these recent developments in audience studies in terms of such a convergence is to simplify and even misconceive the issues at stake. For one thing, I would argue that the two perspectives only superficially share 'the same problematics,' and that what separates a 'critical' from a 'mainstream' perspective is more than merely some 'differences of opinion,' sharp or otherwise: it concerns fundamental differences not only in epistemological, but also in theoretical and political attitudes toward the aim and status of doing empirical research as such.

The academic idealization of joining forces in pursuit of a supposedly common goal as if it were a neutral, scientific project is a particularly depoliticizing strategy, because it tends to neutralize all difference and disagreement in favor of a forced consensus. If I am cautious about this euphoria around the prospect of academic convergence, it is not my intention to impose a rigid and absolute eternal dichotomy between 'critical' and 'mainstream' research. Nor would I want to assert that Morley's project is entirely 'critical' and the uses and gratifications approach completely 'mainstream.' As I have noted before, the relationship between 'critical' and 'mainstream' is not a fixed one; it does not concern two mutually exclusive, antagonistic sets of knowledge, as some observers would imply by talking in terms of 'schools' or 'paradigms.' In fact, many assumptions and ideas do not intrinsically belong to one or the other perspective. For example, the basic assumption that the television audience is 'active' (rather than passive) and that watching television is a social (rather than an individual) practice is currently accepted in both perspectives. There is nothing spectacular about that.[6] Also, I would suggest that the idea that texts can generate multiple meanings, and that the text/reader relationship takes the form of negotiations, is not in itself a sufficient condition for the declared convergence.[7]

In other words, in evaluating whether we can really speak of convergence, it is not enough to establish similar research questions, or to identify a common acknowledgment of the usefulness of certain methods of inquiry. Of course, such commonalities are interesting enough and it would be nonsense to discard them categorically. I do think it is important to get rid of any dogmatism or antagonism-for-the-sake-of-it, and to try to learn from others wherever that is possible. But at the same time we should not lose sight of the fact that any call for convergence itself is not an innocent gesture. It tends to be done from a certain point of view and therefore inevitably involves a selection process in which certain issues and themes are highlighted and others suppressed. And it is my contention that an all too hasty declaration of convergence could lead to neglecting some of the most important distinctive features of cultural studies as a critical intellectual enterprise.

A difference in conceptualizing the object of study is a first issue that needs to be discussed here. Thus, to take the common interest in 'audience activity' as an example in a cultural studies perspective, 'audience activity' cannot and should not be studied in isolation. Rather than dissecting 'audience activity' into variables and categories in order to be able to study them one by one, so that we could ultimately have a complete and generalizable formal 'map' of all dimensions of 'audience activity,' which seems to be the drive behind the uses and gratifications project,[8] the aim of cultural studies, as I see it, is to arrive at a more historicized insight into the ways in which 'audience activity' is related to social and political structures and processes. In other words, what is at stake is not the understanding of 'audience activity' as such as an isolated and isolable phenomenon and object of research, but the embeddness of 'audience activity' in a network of ongoing cultural practices and relationships.

As a result, an audience researcher working within a cultural studies sensibility cannot restrict herself or himself to 'just' studying audiences and their activities (and, for that matter, relating those activities with other variables such as gratifications sought or obtained, dependencies, effects, and so on). She or he will also engage with the structural and cultural processes through which the audiences she or he is studying are constituted and being constituted. Thus, one essential theoretical point of the cultural studies approach to the television audience is its foregrounding of the notion that the dynamics of watching television, no matter how heterogeneous and seemingly free it is, is always related to the operations of forms of social power. It is in this light that we should see Morley's decision to do research on viewers' decodings: it was first of all motivated by an interest in what he – in the quote at the beginning of this chapter – calls 'the ideological operations of television.'

It is important then to emphasize that the term 'active audience' does not occupy the same symbolic status in the two approaches. From a cultural studies point of view, evidence that audiences are 'active' cannot simply be equated with the rather triumphant, liberal-pluralist conclusion, often expressed by gratificationists, that media consumers are 'free' or even 'powerful' – a conclusion which allegedly undercuts the idea of 'media hegemony.' The question for cultural studies is not simply one of 'where the power lies in media systems' (i.e. with the audience or with the media producers),[9] but rather how relations of power are organized within the heterogeneous practices of media consumption. In other words, rather than constructing an opposition between 'the' media and 'the' audience, as if these were separate ontological entities, and, along with it, the application of a distributional theory of power (that is, power is a property that can be attributed to either side of the opposing entities), cultural studies scholars are interested in understanding media consumption as a site of cultural struggle, in which a variety of forms of power are exercised, with different sorts of effects.[10] Thus if, as Morley's study has shown, viewers can decode a text in different ways and sometimes even give oppositional meanings to it, this should not be conceived as an example of 'audience freedom,' but as a moment in that cultural struggle, an ongoing struggle over meaning and pleasure which is central to the fabric(ation) of everyday life.

I hope to have made clear by now that in evaluating the possibility or even desirability of convergence, it is important to look at how 'audience activity' is theorized or interpreted, and how research 'findings' are placed in a wider theoretical framework. So, if one type of 'audience activity' which has received much attention in both approaches recently has been the interpretative strategies used by audiences to read media texts (conceptualized in terms of decoding structures, interpretative communities, patterns of involvement, and so on), how are we to make sense of those interpretative strategies? The task of the cultural studies researcher, I would suggest, is to develop *strategic interpretations* of them, different not only in form and content, but also in scope and intent, from those offered in more 'mainstream'-oriented accounts.[11] I will return to this central issue of interpretation.

BEYOND METHODOLOGY

A troubling aspect about the idea of (and desire for) convergence, then, is that it tends to be conceptualized as an exclusively 'scientific' enterprise. Echoing the tenets of positivism, its aim seems to be the gradual accumulation of scientifically confirmed 'findings.' It is propelled by the hope that by seeking a shared agreement on what is relevant and by developing shared methodological skills the final scientific account of 'the audience' can eventually be achieved. In this framework, audience studies are defined as just another branch of an academic discipline (i.e. mass communication), in which it is unproblematically assumed that 'the audience' is a proper object of study whose characteristics can be ever more accurately observed, described, categorized, systematized, and explained, until the whole picture is 'filled in.' In principle (if not in practice), this scientific project implicitly claims to be able to produce total knowledge, to reveal the full and objective 'truth' about 'the audience.' Audience here is imagined as and turned into an object with researchable attributes and features (be it described in terms of arrays of preferences, decodings, uses, effects, or whatever) that could be definitively established – if only researchers of different breeding would stop quarreling with each other and unite to work harmoniously together to accomplish the task.[12]

From such an academic point of view, the question of methodology becomes a central issue. After all, rigor of method has traditionally been seen as the guarantee *par excellence* for the 'scientific' status of knowledge. In positivist social science, the hypothetico-deductive testing of theory through empirical research, quantitative in form, is cherished as the cornerstone of the production of 'scientific' knowledge. Theory that is not empirically tested, or that is too complex to be molded into empirically testable hypotheses, is dismissed as 'unscientific'. These assumptions, which are central to the dominant version of the uses and gratifications approach as it was established in the 1970s, are now contested by a growing number of researchers who claim that reality cannot be grasped and explained through quantitative methods alone. Furthermore, they forcefully assert that to capture the multidimensionality and complexity of audience activity the use of qualitative methods – and thus a move towards the 'ethnographic' – is desperately called for.[13]

From an academic point of view, it is this methodological challenge that forms the condition of possibility of the perceived convergence. However, although I think that the struggle for legitimization of qualitative research is a very important one, I do believe that it is not the central point for critical cultural studies. This is because the struggle is cast primarily in methodological terms, and therefore its relevance is confined to the development of audience research as an *academic* enterprise. Given the decade-long hegemony of positivism and the quantifying attitude in audience research, this development is a significant one indeed. Unfortunately, however, many discussions about the usefulness of qualitative methods still do not question the epistemological distinction between science and common sense that lies at the heart of positivism. The aim is still the isolation of a body of knowledge that can be recognized as 'scientific' (in its broadest meaning), the orientation is toward the advancement of an academic discipline, and concomitantly, the technical improvement of its instruments of analysis.

A cultural studies perspective on audience research cannot stop short at this level of debate. For a critical cultural studies, it is not questions of methodology or academic struggle as such that prevail. On the contrary, we should relativize the academic commitment to increasing knowledge for its own sake and resist the temptation to what Stuart Hall has called the 'codification' of cultural studies into a stable realm of established theories and canonized methodologies.[14] In this respect, the territorial conflict between 'mainstream' and 'critical,' quantitative and qualitative, humanistic and social scientific, and so on, should perhaps not bother us too much at all in the first place. As James Carey once remarked, 'perhaps all the talk about theory, method, and other such things prevents us from raising or permits us to avoid raising, deeper and disquieting questions about the purposes of our scholarship.'[15] And indeed: why are we so interested in knowing about audiences in the first place? In empirical audience research, especially, it is important to reflect upon the status of the knowledge produced. After all, scrutinizing media audiences is not an innocent practice. It does not take place in a social and political vacuum. Historically, the hidden agenda of audience research, even when it presents itself as pure and objective, has all too often been its commercial or political usefulness. In other words, what we should reflect upon is the *political* interventions we make when talking about audiences – political not only in the sense of some distant societal goal, but, more importantly, in that we cannot afford ignoring the political dimensions of the *process* and practice of knowledge production itself. What does it mean to subject audiences to the researcher's gaze? How can we develop insights that do not reproduce the kind of objectified knowledge served up by, say, market research or empiricist effects research? How is it possible to do audience research which is 'on the side' of the audience?[16] These are nagging political questions which cannot be smoothed out by the comforting canons of epistemology, methodology, and 'science.'

Of course, it is not easy to pin down what such considerations would imply in concrete terms. But it could at least be said that we should try to avoid a stance in which 'the audience' is relegated to the status of exotic 'other' – merely interesting in so far as 'we,' as researchers, can turn 'them' into 'objects' of study, and about whom 'we' have the privileged position to acquire 'objective' knowledge.[17] To begin with, I think, critical audience studies should not strive and pretend to tell 'the truth' about 'the audience.' Its ambitions should be much more modest. As Lawrence Grossberg has suggested, 'the goal of [critical research] is to offer not a polished representation of the truth, but simply a little help in our efforts to better understand the world.'[18] This modesty does not have so much to do with some sort of false humility as with the basic acknowledgment that every research practice unavoidably takes place in a particular historical situation, and is therefore principally of a partial nature. As Hammersley and Atkinson have provocatively put it, 'all social research takes the form of participant observation: it involves participating in the social world, in whatever role, and reflecting on the products of that participation.'[19]

The collection of data, either quantitative or qualitative in form, can never be separated from their interpretation; it is only through practices of interpretative theorizing that unruly social experiences and events related to media consumption become established as meaningful 'facts' about audiences. Understanding 'audience activity' is thus caught up in the discursive representation, not the transparent reflection, of realities having to do with audiences.

These considerations lead to another, more politicized conception of doing research. It is not the search for (objective, scientific) knowledge in which the researcher is engaged, but the construction of *interpretations*, of certain ways of understanding the world, always historically located, subjective, and relative. It is the decisive importance of this interpretative moment that I would like to highlight in exploring the possibilities of critical audience studies.[20]

In positivism, interpretation is assigned a marginal place: as a result of its emphasis on the empirical testing of theory, interpretation is assumed to follow rather automatically from the so-called 'findings.' Achieved then is an apparent innocence of interpretation, one that is seemingly grounded in 'objective social reality' itself. In fact, the term 'interpretation' itself would seem to have definite negative connotations for positivists because of its connection with 'subjectivism.' And even within those social science approaches in which the interpretative act of the researcher – not only at the moment of data analysis, but also at that of data collection – is taken more seriously, interpretation is more often than not problematized as a methodical rather than a political matter, defined in terms of careful inference making rather than in terms of discursive constructions of reality.

It should be recognized, however, that because interpretations always inevitably involve the construction of certain representations of reality (and not others), they can never be 'neutral' and merely 'descriptive.' After all, the 'empirical,' captured in either quantitative or qualitative form, does not yield self-evident meanings; it is only through the interpretative framework constructed by the researcher that understandings of the 'empirical' come about. The choice of empirical methods of investigation is only one part of a double venture: it is in the dialectic between the empirical and the theoretical, between experience and explanation, that forms of knowledge, that is interpretations, are constructed. Here then the thoroughly political nature of any research manifests itself. What is at stake is a *politics of interpretation*: 'to advance an interpretation is to insert it into a network of power relations.'[21]

This also implies a shift in the position of the researcher. She or he is no longer a bearer of truth, but occupies a 'partial' position in two senses of the word. On the one hand, she or he is no longer the neutral observer, but is someone whose job it is to produce historically and culturally specific knowledges that are the result of equally specific discursive encounters between researcher and informants, in which the subjectivity of the researcher is not separated from the 'object' s/he is studying. The interpretations that are produced in the process can never claim to be definitive: on the contrary, they are necessarily incomplete (for they always involve simplification, selection, and exclusion) and temporary. 'If neither history nor politics ever comes to an end, then theory (as well as research) is never completed and our accounts can never be closed or totalized.'[22] And on the other hand, and even more important, the position of the researcher is also more than that of the professional scholar: beyond a capable interpreter, she or he is also inherently a political and moral subject. She or he is an intellectual who is not only responsible to the Academy, but to the social world she or he lives in as well. It is at the interface of 'ethics' and 'scholarship' that the researcher's interpretations take on their distinctive political edge.[23]

Of course, all this entails a different status for empirical research. Material obtained by ethnographic fieldwork or depth-interviews with audience members cannot simply be treated as natural 'data.' Viewers' statements about their relation to television cannot be regarded as self-evident facts. Nor are they immediate, transparent reflections of those viewers' 'lived realities' that can speak for themselves. What is of critical importance, therefore, is the way in which those statements are made sense of, that is interpreted. Here lies the ultimate political responsibility of the researcher. The comfortable assumption that it is the reliability and accuracy of the methodologies being used that will ascertain the validity of the outcomes of research, thereby reducing the researcher's responsibility to a technical matter, is rejected. In short, to return to Morley's opening statement, audience ethnographies are undertaken because the relation between television and viewers is an empirical *question*. But the empirical is not the privileged domain of the *answers*, as the positivist would have it. Answers (temporary ones, to be sure) are to be constructed, in the form of interpretations.[24]

[. . .]

NOTES

1. David Morley, *The 'Nationwide' Audience: Structure and Decoding* (London: British Film Institute, 1980), p. 162.
2. See Fred Feyes, 'Critical Communications Research and Media Effects: The Problem of the Disappearing Audience,' *Media, Culture, and Society* 6 (1984): 219–32.
3. 'Gratifications researchers, in their paradigmatic personae, have lost sight of what the media are purveying, in part because of an overcommitment to the endless freedom of the audience to reinvent the text, in part because of a too rapid leap to mega-functions, such as surveillance or self-identity' (Jay G. Blumler, Michael Gurevitch, and Elihu Katz, 'Reaching Out: A Future for Gratifications Research,' in K. E. Rosengren, L. A. Wenner, and Ph. Palmgreen (eds) *Media Gratifications Research: Current Perspectives* (Beverly Hills, Calif.: Sage, 1985), p. 272).
4. Ibid.
5. Karl Erik Rosengren, 'Communication Research: One Paradigm, or Four?' *Journal of Communication* 33 (1983): 203; also Tamar Liebes, 'On the Convergence of Theories of Mass Communication and Literature Regarding the Role of the

Reader' (paper presented to the Conference on Culture and Communication, 1986); and Kim Christian Schroder, 'Convergence of Antagonistic Traditions? The Case of Audience Research,' *European Journal of Communication* 2 (1987): 7–31. Such an insistence upon convergence is not new among 'mainstream' communication researchers. For example, Jennifer Daryl Slack and Martin Allor have recalled how in the late 1930s Lazarsfeld hired Adorno in the expectation that the latter's critical theory could be used to 'revitalize' American empiricist research by supplying it with 'new research ideas.' The collaboration ended only one year later because it proved to be impossible to translate Adorno's critical analysis into the methods and goals of Lazarsfeld's project. Lazarsfeld has never given up the idea of a convergence, however. See Jennifer Daryl Slack and Martin Allor, 'The Political and Epistemological Constituents of Critical Communication Research,' *Journal of Communication* 33 (1983): 210.

6. Note, for instance, the striking similarities between the following two sentences, one from a uses and gratifications source, the other from a cultural studies one: 'There seems to be growing support for that branch of communications research which asserts that television viewing is an active and social process' (Katz and Liebes, 'Mutual Aid in the Decoding of *Dallas*: Preliminary Notes for a Cross-Cultural Study,' in Phillip Drummond and Richard Paterson (eds) *Television in Transition* (London: British Film Institute, 1985), p. 187); 'Television viewing, the choices which shape it and the many social uses to which we put it, now turn out to be irrevocably active and social processes' (Stuart Hall, 'Introduction,' in David Morley, *Family Television, Cultural Power and Domestic Leisure* (London: Co-media, 1986), p. 8).

7. Tamar Liebes suggests that 'the focus of the convergence is on the idea that the interaction between messages and receivers takes on the form of negotiation, and is not predetermined' ('On the Convergence,' p. 1). However, as I will try to show, what makes all the difference in the theoretical and political thrust of ethnographic audience studies is the way in which 'negotiation' is conceived. Furthermore, 'not predetermined' does not mean 'undertermined,' – and how (complex, structural, conjunctural) determinations should be conceived remains an important point of divergence between 'critical' and 'mainstream' studies. It is also noteworthy to point out that, while uses and gratifications researchers now seem to be 'rediscovering the text,' researchers working within a cultural studies perspective seem to be moving away from the text. This is very clear in Morley's second book, *Family Television*. In fact, it becomes more and more difficult to delineate what 'the television text' is.

8. See, for example, M. R. Levy and S. Windahl, 'Audience Activity and Gratifications: A Conceptual Clarification and Exploration,' in Rosengren et al., *Media Gratifications Research*, pp. 109–22.

9. Blumler et al., 'Reaching Out,' p. 260.

10. In stating this I do not want to suggest that cultural studies is a closed paradigm, or that all cultural studies scholars share one – say, Foucaultian – conception of power. Thus, the Birmingham version of cultural studies, with its distinctly Gramscian inflection, is critized by Lawrence Grossberg for its lack of a theory of pleasure. An alternative, postmodernist perspective on cultural studies is developed by Grossberg in his 'Cultural Studies Revisited and Revised,' in Mary S. Mander (ed.) *Communications in Transition* (New York: Praeger, 1983), pp. 39–70.

11. Strategic interpretations, that is interpretations that are 'political' in the sense that they are aware of the fact that interpretations are always concrete interventions into an already existing discursive field. They are therefore always partial in both senses of the word, and involved in making sense of the world in specific, power-laden ways. See Mary Louise Pratt, 'Interpretive Strategic Interpretations: On Anglo-American Reader-Response Criticism,' in Jonathan

Arac (ed.) *Postmodernism and Politics* (Minneapolis: University of Minnesota Press, 1986), pp. 26–54.

12. Rosengren expresses this view in very clear cut terms, when he reduces the existence of disagreements between 'critical' and 'mainstream' researchers to 'psychological reasons' ('Communication Research: One Paradigm, or Four?,' p. 191).

13. Cf. James Lull, 'The Naturalistic Study of Media Use and Youth Culture,' in Rosengren et al., *Media Gratifications Research*, pp. 209–24; Klaus Bruhn Jensen, 'Qualitative Audience Research: Towards an Integrative Approach to Reception,' *Critical Studies in Mass Communication* 4 (1987): 21–36; Thomas R. Lindlof and Timothy P. Meyer, 'Mediated Communications as Ways of Seeing, Acting and Constructing Culture: The Tools and Foundations of Qualitative Research,' in Lindlof, *Natural Audiences: Qualitative Research and Media Uses and Effects* (Norwood, NJ: Ablex Publishing Company, 1987), pp. 1–30.

14. Lawrence Grossberg (ed.) 'On Postmodernism and Articulation: An Interview with Stuart Hall,' *Journal of Communication Inquiry* 10, no. 2 (summer 1986): 59.

15. James Carey, 'Introduction,' in Mander, *Communications in Transition*, p. 5.

16. I borrowed this formulation from Virginia Nightingale, 'What's Happening to Audience Research?,' *Media Information Australia* 39 (February 1986): 21–2. Nightingale remarks that audience research has generally been 'on the side' of those with vested interests in influencing the organization of the mass media in society, and that it is important to develop a research perspective that is 'on the side' of the audience. However, it is far from simple to work out exactly what such a perspective would mean. The notion of the 'active audience,' for example, often put forward by uses and gratifications researchers to mark the distinctive identity of the 'paradigm,' is not in itself a guarantee for a stance 'on the side of the audience.' In fact, the whole passive/active dichotomy in accounts of audiences has now become so ideologized that it all too often serves as a mystification of the real commitments behind the research at stake.

17. Reflections on the predicaments and politics of research on and with living historical subjects have already played an important role in, for example, feminist studies and anthropology, particularly ethnography. At least two problems are highlighted in these reflections. First, there is the rather awkward but seldom discussed concrete relation between researcher and researched as human beings occupying certain positions invested with power; second, there is the problem of the discursive form in which the cultures of 'others' can be represented in non-objectifying (or better, less objectifying) ways. See, for example, Angela McRobbie, 'The Politics of Feminist Research,' *Feminist Review* 12 (October 1982): 46–57; James Clifford, 'On Ethnographic Authority,' *Representations* 1, no. 2 (1983): 118–46; James Clifford and George E. Marcus (eds) *Writing Culture. The Poetics and Politics of Ethonography* (Berkeley, Los Angeles, London: University of California Press, 1986). Researchers of media audiences have, as far as I know, generally been silent about these issues. However, for a perceptive and thought-provoking engagement with the problem, see Valerie Walkerdine, 'Video Replay: Families, Films and Fantasy,' in Victor Burgin, James Donald and Cora Kaplan (eds) *Formations of Fantasy* (London and New York: Methuen, 1986), pp. 167–99.

18. Lawrence Grossberg, 'Critical Theory and the Politics of Empirical Research,' in Michael Gurevitch and Mark R. Levy (eds) *Mass Communication Review Yearbook*, vol. 6 (Newbury Park, Calif.: Sage, 1986), p. 89.

19. Martyn Hammersley and Paul Atkinson, *Ethnography: Principles in Practice* (London and New York: Tavistock, 1983), p. 16.

20. For a general overview of the interpretative or hermeneutic turn in the social sciences, see Paul Rabinow and William M. Sullivan (eds) *Interpretive Social Science* (Berkeley, Los Angeles, London: University of California Press, 1979). A more radical conception of what they call 'interpretive analytics' is developed by Hubert

Dreyfuss and Paul Rabinow in their *Michel Foucault: Beyond Structuralism and Hermeneutics* (Chicago, Ill.: University of Chicago Press, 1982).

21. Pratt, 'Interpretative Strategies/Strategic Interpretations,' p. 52.
22. Grossberg, 'Critical Theory,' p. 89.
23. Cf. Paul Rabinow, 'Representations Are Social Facts: Modernity and Post-Modernity in Anthropology,' in Clifford and Marcus, *Writing Culture*, pp. 234–61.
24. A more general, lucid criticism of empiricist mass communications research is offered by Robert C. Allen in his *Speaking of Soap Operas* (Chapel Hill and London: University of North Carolina Press, 1985), chapter 2.

38

THE OPPOSITIONAL GAZE

Black Female Spectators

bell hooks

When thinking about black female spectators, I remember being punished as a child for staring, for those hard intense direct looks children would give grown-ups, looks that were seen as confrontational, as gestures of resistance, challenges to authority. The 'gaze' has always been political in my life. Imagine the terror felt by the child who has come to understand through repeated punishments that one's gaze can be dangerous. The child who has learned so well to look the other way when necessary. Yet, when punished, the child is told by parents, 'Look at me when I talk to you.' Only, the child is afraid to look. Afraid to look, but fascinated by the gaze. There is power in looking.

Amazed the first time I read in history classes that white slave-owners (men, women, and children) punished enslaved black people for looking, I wondered how this traumatic relationship to the gaze had informed black parenting and black spectatorship. The politics of slavery, of racialized power relations, were such that the slaves were denied their right to gaze. Connecting this strategy of domination to that used by grown folks in southern black rural communities where I grew up, I was pained to think that there was no absolute difference between whites who had oppressed black people and ourselves. Years later, reading Michel Foucault, I thought again about these connections, about the ways power as domination reproduces itself in different locations employing similar apparatuses, strategies, and mechanisms of control. Since I knew as a child that the dominating power adults exercised over me and over my gaze was never so absolute that I did not dare to look, to sneak a peep, to stare dangerously, I knew that the slaves had looked. That all attempts to repress

From bell hooks, *Black Looks* (Boston, MA: South End Press, 1992).

our/black peoples' right to gaze had produced in us an overwhelming longing to look, a rebellious desire, an oppositional gaze. By courageously looking, we defiantly declared: 'Not only will I stare. I want my look to change reality.' Even in the worse circumstances of domination, the ability to manipulate one's gaze in the face of structures of domination that would contain it, opens up the possibility of agency. In much of his work, Michel Foucault insists on describing domination in terms of 'relations of power' as part of an effort to challenge the assumption that 'power is a system of domination which controls everything and which leaves no room for freedom.' Emphatically stating that in all relations of power 'there is necessarily the possibility of resistance,' he invites the critical thinker to search those margins, gaps, and locations on and through the body where agency can be found.

[. . .]

Spaces of agency exist for black people, wherein we can both interrogate the gaze of the Other but also look back, and at one another, naming what we see. The 'gaze' has been and is a site of resistance for colonized black people globally. Subordinates in relations of power learn experientially that there is a critical gaze, one that 'looks' to document, one that is oppositional. In resistance struggle, the power of the dominated to assert agency by claiming and cultivating 'awareness' politicizes 'looking' relations – one learns to look a certain way in order to resist.

When most black people in the United States first had the opportunity to look at film and television, they did so fully aware that mass media was a system of knowledge and power reproducing and maintaining white supremacy. To stare at the television, or mainstream movies, to engage its images, was to engage its negation of black representation. It was the oppositional black gaze that responded to these looking relations by developing independent black cinema. Black viewers of mainstream cinema and television could chart the progress of political movements for racial equality *via* the construction of images, and did so. Within my family's southern black working-class home, located in a racially segregated neighborhood, watching television was one way to develop critical spectatorship. Unless you went to work in the white world, across the tracks, you learned to look at white people by staring at them on the screen. Black looks, as they were constituted in the context of social movements for racial uplift, were interrogating gazes. We laughed at television shows like *Our Gang* and *Amos 'n' Andy*, at these white representations of blackness, but we also looked at them critically. Before racial integration, black viewers of movies and television experienced visual pleasure in a context where looking was also about contestation and confrontation.

[. . .]

Critical, interrogating black looks were mainly concerned with issues of race and racism, the way racial domination of blacks by whites overdetermined representation. They were rarely concerned with gender. As spectators, black men could repudiate the reproduction of racism in cinema and television, the negation of black presence, even as they could feel as though they were rebelling against white supremacy by daring to look, by engaging phallocentric politics of spectatorship. Given the real life public circumstances wherein black men were murdered/lynched for looking at white womanhood, where the black male gaze was always subject to control and/or punishment by the powerful white Other, the private realm of television screens or dark theaters could unleash the repressed gaze. There they could 'look' at white womanhood without a structure of domination overseeing the gaze, interpreting, and punishing. That white supremacist structure that had murdered Emmet Till after interpreting his look as violation, as 'rape' of white womanhood, could not control black male responses to screen images. In their role as spectators, black men could enter an imaginative space of phallocentric power that mediated racial negation. This gendered relation to looking made the experience of the black male spectator radically different from that of the black female spectator. Major early black male independent filmmakers represented black women in their films as objects of male gaze. Whether looking through the camera or as spectators watching films, whether mainstream cinema or 'race' movies such as those made by Oscar Micheaux, the black male gaze had a different scope from that of the black female.

Black women have written little about black female spectatorship, about our moviegoing practices. A growing body of film theory and criticism by black women has only begun to emerge. The prolonged silence of black women as spectators and critics was a response to absence, to cinematic negation. In 'The Technology of Gender,' Teresa de Lauretis, drawing on the work of Monique Wittig, calls attention to 'the power of discourses to "do violence" to people, a violence which is material and physical, although produced by abstract and scientific discourses as well as the discourses of the mass media.' With the possible exception of early race movies, black female spectators have had to develop looking relations within a cinematic context that constructs our presence as absence, that denies the 'body' of the black female so as to perpetuate white supremacy and with it a phallocentric spectatorship where the woman to be looked at and desired is 'white.' [. . .]

Talking with black women of all ages and classes, in different areas of the United States, about their filmic looking relations, I hear again and again ambivalent responses to cinema. Only a few of the black women I talked with remembered the pleasure of race movies, and even those who did, felt that pleasure interrupted and usurped by Hollywood. Most of the black women I talked with were adamant that they never went to movies expecting to see compelling representations of black femaleness. They were all acutely aware of cinematic racism – its violent erasure of black womanhood. In Anne Friedberg's essay 'A Denial of Difference: Theories of Cinematic Identification' she stresses that 'identification can only be made through recognition, and all

recognition is itself an implicit confirmation of the ideology of the status quo.'
Even when representations of black women were present in film, our bodies
and being were there to serve – to enhance and maintain white womanhood as
object of the phallocentric gaze.

[. . .]

Remembering my past in relation to screen images of black womanhood,
I wrote a short essay, 'Do you remember Sapphire?' which explored both
the negation of black female representation in cinema and television and our
rejection of these images. Identifying the character of 'Sapphire' from *Amos 'n'*
Andy as that screen representation of black femaleness I first saw in childhood,
I wrote:

> She was even then backdrop, foil. She was bitch – nag. She was there to
> soften images of black men, to make them seem vulnerable, easygoing,
> funny, and unthreatening to a white audience. She was there as man
> in drag, as castrating bitch, as someone to be lied to, someone to be
> tricked, someone the white and black audience could hate. Scapegoated
> on all sides. *She was not us.* We laughed with the black men, with the
> white people. We laughed at this black woman who was not us. And
> we did not even long to be there on the screen. How could we long to
> be there when our image, visually constructed, was so ugly. We did not
> long to be there. We did not long for her. We did not want our con-
> struction to be this hated black female thing – foil, backdrop. Her black
> female image was not the body of desire. There was nothing to see. She
> was not us.

Grown black women had a different response to Sapphire; they identified with
her frustrations and her woes. They resented the way she was mocked. They
resented the way these screen images could assault black womanhood, could
name us bitches, nags. And in opposition they claimed Sapphire as their own,
as the symbol of that angry part of themselves white folks and black men could
not even begin to understand.

Conventional representations of black women have done violence to the
image. Responding to this assault, many black women spectators shut out the
image, looked the other way, accorded cinema no importance in their lives.
Then there were those spectators whose gaze was that of desire and complicity.
Assuming a posture of subordination, they submitted to cinema's capacity to
seduce and betray. They were cinematically 'gaslighted.' Every black woman
I spoke with who was/is an ardent moviegoer, a lover of the Hollywood film,
testified that to experience fully the pleasure of that cinema they had to close
down critique, analysis; they had to forget racism. And mostly they did not
think about sexism. What was the nature then of this adoring black female
gaze – this look that could bring pleasure in the midst of negation? In her first

novel, *The Bluest Eye*, Toni Morrison constructs a portrait of the black female spectator; her gaze is the masochistic look of victimization. Describing her looking relations, Miss Pauline Breedlove, a poor working woman, maid in the house of a prosperous white family, asserts:

> The onliest time I be happy seem like was when I was in the picture show. Every time I got, I went, I'd go early, before the show started. They's cut off the lights, and everything be black. Then the screen would light up, and I's move right on in them picture. White men taking such good care of they women, and they all dressed up in big clean houses with the bath tubs right in the same room with the toilet. Them pictures gave me a lot of pleasure.

To experience pleasure, Miss Pauline sitting in the dark must imagine herself transformed, turned into the white woman portrayed on the screen. After watching movies, feeling the pleasure, she says, 'But it made coming home hard.'

We come home to ourselves. Not all black women spectators submitted to that spectacle of regression through identification. Most of the women I talked with felt that they consciously resisted identification with films – that this tension made moviegoing less than pleasurable; at times it caused pain. As one black woman put it, 'I could always get pleasure from movies as long as I did not look too deep.' For black female spectators who have 'looked too deep' the encounter with the screen hurt. That some of us chose to stop looking was a gesture of resistance, turning away was one way to protest, to reject negation. My pleasure in the screen ended abruptly when I and my sisters first watched *Imitation of Life*. [. . .]

When I returned to films as a young woman, after a long period of silence, I had developed an oppositional gaze. Not only would I not be hurt by the absence of black female presence, or the insertion of violating representation, I interrogated the work, cultivated a way to look past race and gender for aspects of content, form, language. Foreign films and U.S. independent cinema were the primary locations of my filmic looking relations, even though I also watched Hollywood films.

From 'jump,' black female spectators have gone to films with awareness of the way in which race and racism determined the visual construction of gender. Whether it was *Birth of A Nation* or Shirley Temple shows, we knew that white womanhood was the racialized sexual difference occupying the place of stardom in mainstream narrative film. We assumed white women knew it to. Reading Laura Mulvey's provocative essay, 'Visual Pleasure and Narrative Cinema,' from a standpoint that acknowledges race, one sees clearly why black women spectators not duped by mainstream cinema would develop an oppositional gaze. Placing ourselves outside that pleasure in looking, Mulvey argues, was determined by a 'split between active/male and passive/female.'

Black female spectators actively chose not to identify with the film's imaginary subject because such identification was disenabling.

Looking at films with an oppositional gaze, black women were able to critically assess the cinema's construction of white womanhood as object of phallocentric gaze and choose not to identify with either the victim or the perpetrator. Black female spectators, who refused to identify with white womanhood, who would not take on the phallocentric gaze of desire and possession, created a critical space where the binary opposition Mulvey posits of 'woman as image, man as bearer of the look' was continually deconstructed. As critical spectators, black women looked from a location that disrupted, one akin to that described by Annette Kuhn in *The Power of The Image*:

> ... the acts of analysis, of deconstruction and of reading 'against the grain' offer an additional pleasure – the pleasure of resistance, of saying 'no': not to 'unsophisticated' enjoyment, by ourselves and others, of culturally dominant images, but to the structures of power which ask us to consume them uncritically and in highly circumscribed ways.

Mainstream feminist film criticism in no way acknowledges black female spectatorship. It does not even consider the possibility that women can construct an oppositional gaze via an understanding and awareness of the politics of race and racism. Feminist film theory rooted in an ahistorical psychoanalytic framework that privileges sexual difference actively suppresses recognition of race, reenacting and mirroring the erasure of black womanhood that occurs in films, silencing any discussion of racial difference – of racialized sexual difference. Despite feminist critical interventions aimed at deconstructing the category 'woman' which highlight the significance of race, many feminist film critics continue to structure their discourse as though it speaks about 'women' when in actuality it speaks only about white women. [. . .]

[. . .] For it is only as one imagines 'woman' in the abstract, when woman becomes fiction or fantasy, can race not be seen as significant. Are we really to imagine that feminist theorists writing only about images of white women, who subsume this specific historical subject under the totalizing category 'woman,' do not 'see' the whiteness of the image? It may very well be that they engage in a process of denial that eliminates the necessity of revisioning conventional ways of thinking about psychoanalysis as a paradigm of analysis and the need to rethink a body of feminist film theory that is firmly rooted in a denial of the reality that sex/sexuality may not be the primary and/or exclusive signifier of difference. [. . .]

Given the context of class exploitation, and racist and sexist domination, it has only been through resistance, struggle, reading, and looking 'against the grain,' that black women have been able to value our process of looking enough to publicly name it. Centrally, those black female spectators who attest to the oppositionality of their gaze deconstruct theories of female spectatorship that have relied heavily on the assumption that, as Doane suggests in her essay, 'Woman's Stake: Filming the Female Body,' 'woman can only mimic man's relation to language, that is assume a position defined by the penis-phallus as the supreme arbiter of lack.' Identifying with neither the phallocentric gaze nor the construction of white womanhood as lack, critical black female spectators construct a theory of looking relations where cinematic visual delight is the pleasure of interrogation. Every black woman spectator I talked to, with rare exception, spoke of being 'on guard' at the movies. Talking about the way being a critical spectator of Hollywood films influenced her, black woman filmmaker Julie Dash exclaims, 'I make films because I was such a spectator!' Looking at Hollywood cinema from a distance, from that critical politicized standpoint that did not want to be seduced by narratives reproducing her negation, Dash watched mainstream movies over and over again for the pleasure of deconstructing them. And of course there is that added delight if one happens, in the process of interrogation, to come across a narrative that invites the black female spectator to engage the text with no threat of violation.

[. . .]

Talking with black female spectators, looking at written discussions either in fiction or academic essays about black women, I noted the connection made between the realm of representation in mass media and the capacity of black women to construct ourselves as subjects in daily life. The extent to which black women feel devalued, objectified, dehumanized in this society determines the scope and texture of their looking relations. Those black women whose identities were constructed in resistance, by practices that oppose the dominant order, were most inclined to develop an oppositional gaze. Now that there is a growing interest in films produced by black women and those films have become more accessible to viewers, it is possible to talk about black female spectatorship in relation to that work. [. . .]

Critical black female spectatorship emerges as a site of resistance only when individual black women actively resist the imposition of dominant ways of knowing and looking. While every black woman I talked to was aware of racism, that awareness did not automatically correspond with politicization, the development of an oppositional gaze. When it did, individual black women consciously named the process. Manthia Diawara's 'resisting spectatorship' is a term that does not adequately describe the terrain of black female spectatorship. We do more than resist. We create alternative texts that are not solely reactions. As critical spectators, black women participate in a broad range of looking relations, contest, resist, revision, interrogate, and invent on multiple levels. Certainly when I watch the work of black women filmmakers Camille Billops, Kathleen Collins, Julie Dash, Ayoka Chenzira, Zeinabu Davis, I do not need to 'resist' the images even as I still choose to watch their work with a critical eye.

Black female critical thinkers concerned with creating space for the construction of radical black female subjectivity, and the way cultural production informs this possibility, fully acknowledge the importance of mass media, film in particular, as a powerful site for critical intervention. Certainly Julie Dash's film *Illusions* identifies the terrain of Hollywood cinema as a space of knowledge production that has enormous power. Yet, she also creates a filmic narrative wherein the black female protagonist subversively claims that space. Inverting the 'real-life' power structure, she offers the black female spectator representations that challenge stereotypical notions that place us outside the realm of filmic discursive practices. Within the film she uses the strategy of Hollywood suspense films to undermine those cinematic practices that deny black women a place in this structure. Problematizing the question of 'racial' identity by depicting passing, suddenly it is the white male's capacity to gaze, define, and know that is called into question.

[. . .]

Throughout *Illusions*, Mignon's power is affirmed by her contact with the younger black woman whom she nurtures and protects. It is this process of mirrored recognition that enables both black women to define their reality, apart from the reality imposed upon them by structures of domination. The shared gaze of the two women reinforces their solidarity. As the younger subject, Esther represents a potential audience for films that Mignon might produce, films wherein black females will be the narrative focus. Julie Dash's recent feature-length film *Daughters of the Dust* dares to place black females at the center of its narrative. This focus caused critics (especially white males) to critique the film negatively or to express many reservations. Clearly, the impact of racism and sexism so over-determine spectatorship – not only what we look at but who we identify with – that viewers who are not black females find it hard to empathize with the central characters in the movie. They are adrift without a white presence in the film.

Another representation of black females nurturing one another *via* recognition of their common struggle for subjectivity is depicted in Sankofa's collective work *Passion of Remembrance*. In the film, two black women friends, Louise and Maggie, are from the onset of the narrative struggling with the issue of subjectivity, of their place in progressive black liberation movements that have been sexist. They challenge old norms and want to replace them with new understandings of the complexity of black identity, and the need for liberation struggles that address that complexity. Dressing to go to a party, Louise and Maggie claim the 'gaze.' Looking at one another, staring in mirrors, they appear completely focused on their encounter with black femaleness. How they see themselves is most important, not how they will be stared at by others. Dancing to the tune 'Let's get Loose,' they display their bodies not for a voyeuristic colonizing gaze but for that look of recognition that affirms their subjectivity – that constitutes them as spectators. Mutually empowered they eagerly leave the privatized domain to confront the public. Disrupting conventional racist and sexist stereotypical representations of black female bodies, these scenes invite the audience to look differently. They act to critically intervene and transform conventional filmic practices, changing notions of spectatorship. *Illusions, Daughters of the Dust*, and *A Passion of Remembrance* employ a deconstructive filmic practice to undermine existing grand cinematic narratives even as they retheorize subjectivity in the realm of the visual. Without providing 'realistic' positive representations that emerge only as a response to the totalizing nature of existing narratives, they offer points of radical departure. Opening up a space for the assertion of a critical black female spectatorship, they do not simply offer diverse representations, they imagine new transgressive possibilities for the formulation of identity.

In this sense they make explicit a critical practice that provides us with different ways to think about black female subjectivity and black female spectatorship. Cinematically, they provide new points of recognition, embodying Stuart Hall's vision of a critical practice that acknowledges that identity is constituted 'not outside but within representation,' and invites us to see film 'not as a second-order mirror held up to reflect what already exists, but as that form of representation which is able to constitute us as new kinds of subjects, and thereby enable us to discover who we are.' It is this critical practice that enables production of feminist film theory that theorizes black female spectatorship. Looking and looking back, black women involve ourselves in a process whereby we see our history as counter-memory, using it as a way to know the present and invent the future.

REFERENCES

de Lauretis, Teresa. *Technologies of Gender: Essays on Theory, Film, and Fiction.* Bloomington, IN: Indiana University Press, 1987.

Diawara, Manthia. 'Black Spectatorship: Problems of Identification and Resistance.' *Screen*, Vol. 29, No. 4 (1988).

Doane, Mary Ann. 'Woman's Stake: Filming the Female Body.' In *Feminism and Film Theory*, edited by Constance Penley. New York: Routledge, 1988.

Foucault, Michel. *Power/Knowledge: Selected Interviews and Other Writings.* Edited by Colin Gordon, translated by Gordon et al. New York: Pantheon, 1980.

Friedberg, Anne. 'A Denial of Difference: Theories of Cinematic Identification.' In *Psychoanalysis & Cinema*, edited by E. Ann Kaplan. London: Routledge, 1990.

Hall, Stuart. 'Cultural Identity and Cinematic Representation.' In *Framework: The Journal of Cinema and Media*, No. 36 (1989).

Kuhn, Annette. *Power of the Image: Essays on Representation and Sexuality.* New York: Routledge, 1985.

Morrison, Toni. *The Bluest Eye.* New York: Holt, Rinehart and Winston, 1970.

Mulvey, Laura. *Visual and Other Pleasures.* Bloomington, IN: Indiana University Press, 1989.

39

THERE'S SOMETHING QUEER HERE

Alexander Doty

[. . .]

The most slippery and elusive terrain for mass culture studies continues to be negotiated within audience and reception theory. Perhaps this is because within cultural studies, 'audience' is now always already acknowledged to be fragmented, polymorphous, contradictory, and 'nomadic,' whether in the form of individual or group subjects. Given this, it seems an almost impossible task to conduct reception studies that capture the complexity of those moments in which audiences meet mass culture texts. As Janice Radway puts it:

> No wonder we find it so difficult to theorize the dispersed, anonymous, unpredictable nature of the use of mass-produced, mass-mediated cultural forms. If the receivers of such forms are never assembled fixedly on a site or even in an easily identifiable space, if they are frequently not uniformly or even attentively disposed to systems of cultural production or to the messages they issue, how can we theorize, not to mention examine, the ever-shifting kaleidoscope of cultural circulation and consumption?[1]

In confronting this complexity, Radway suggests that mass culture studies begin to analyze reception more ethnographically by focusing upon the dense patterns and practices 'of daily life and the way in which the media are integrated and implicated within it,' rather than starting with already established audience categories.[2] Clearly the danger of making essentializing statements

From Alexander Doty, *Making Things Perfectly Queer* (Minneapolis, MN and London: University of Minnesota Press, 1993).

about both audiences and their reception practices lurks behind any uncritical use of categories such as 'women,' 'teenagers,' 'lesbians,' 'housewives,' 'blue-collar workers,' 'blacks,' or 'gay men.' Further, conducting reception studies on the basis of conventional audience categories can also lead to critical blindness about how certain reception strategies are shared by otherwise disparate individuals and groups.

I would like to propose 'queerness' as a mass culture reception practice that is shared by all sorts of people in varying degrees of consistency and intensity.[3] Before proceeding, however, I will need to discuss – even defend – my use of 'queer' in such phrases as 'queer positions,' 'queer readers,' 'queer readings,' and 'queer discourses.' In working through my thoughts on gay and lesbian cultural history, I found that while I used 'gay' to describe particulars of men's culture, and 'lesbian' to describe particulars of women's culture, I was hard-pressed to find a term to describe a cultural common ground between lesbians and gays as well as other nonstraights – a term representing unity as well as suggesting diversity. For certain historical and political reasons, 'queer' suggested itself as such a term. As Adele Morrison said in an OUT/LOOK interview: 'Queer is not an "instead of," it's an "inclusive of." I'd never want to lose the terms that specifically identify me.'[4]

Currently, the word 'gay' doesn't consistently have the same gender-unifying quality it may once have possessed. And since I'm interested in discussing aspects of cultural identification as well as of sexual desire, 'homosexual' will not do either. I agree with those who do not find the word 'homosexual' an appropriate synonym for both 'gay' and 'lesbian,' as these latter terms are constructions that concern more than who you sleep with – although the objects of sexual desires are certainly central to expressions of lesbian and gay cultural identities. I also wanted to find a term with some ambiguity, a term that would describe a wide range of impulses and cultural expressions, including space for describing and expressing bisexual, transsexual, and straight queerness. While we acknowledge that homosexuals as well as heterosexuals can operate or mediate from within straight cultural spaces and positions – after all, most of us grew up learning the rules of straight culture – we have paid less attention to the proposition that basically heterocentrist texts can contain queer elements, and basically heterosexual, straight-identifying people can experience queer moments. And these people should be encouraged to examine and express these moments as queer, not as moments of 'homosexual panic,' or temporary confusion, or as unfortunate, shameful, or sinful lapses in judgment or taste to be ignored, repressed, condemned, or somehow explained away within and by straight cultural politics – or even within and by gay or lesbian discourses.

My uses of the terms 'queer readings,' 'queer discourses,' and 'queer positions,' then, are attempts to account for the existence and expression of a wide range of positions within culture that are 'queer' or non-, anti-, or contra-straight. I am using the term 'queer' to mark a flexible space for the expression of all aspects of non- (anti-, contra-) straight cultural production and reception.

As such, this cultural 'queer space' recognizes the possibility that various and fluctuating queer positions might be occupied whenever *anyone* produces or responds to culture. In this sense, the use of the term 'queer' to discuss reception takes up the standard binary opposition of 'queer' and 'nonqueer' (or 'straight') while questioning its viability, at least in cultural studies, because, as noted earlier, the queer often operates within the nonqueer, as the nonqueer does within the queer (whether in reception, texts, or producers). The queer readings of mass culture I am concerned with in this essay will be those readings articulating positions *within* queer discourses. That is, these readings seem to be expressions of queer perspectives on mass culture from the inside, rather than descriptions of how 'they' (gays and/or lesbians, usually) respond to, use, or are depicted in mass culture.

When a colleague heard I had begun using the word 'queer' in my cultural studies work, she asked if I did so in order to 'nostalgically' recapture and reassert the 'romance' of the culturally marginal in the face of trends within straight capitalist societies to co-opt or contain aspects of queer cultures. I had, in fact, intended something quite different. By using 'queer,' I want to recapture and reassert a militant sense of difference that views the erotically 'marginal' as both (in bell hooks's words) a consciously chosen 'site of resistance' and a 'location of radical openness and possibility.'[5] And I want to suggest that within cultural production and reception, queer erotics are already part of culture's erotic center, both as a necessary construct by which to define the heterosexual and the straight (as 'not queer'), and as a position that can be and is occupied in various ways by otherwise heterosexual and straight-identifying people.

But in another sense recapturing and reasserting a certain nostalgia and romance is part of my project here. For through playfully occupying various queer positions in relation to the fantasy/dream elements involved in cultural production and reception, we (whether straight-, gay-, lesbian-, or bi-identifying) are offered spaces to express a range of erotic desire frequently linked in Western cultures to nostalgic and romantic adult conceptions of childhood. Unfortunately, these moments of erotic complexity are usually explained away as part of the 'regressive' work of mass media, whereby we are tricked into certain 'unacceptable' and 'immature' responses as passive subjects. But when cultural texts encourage straight-identified audience members to express a less-censored range of queer desire and pleasure than is possible in daily life, this 'regression' has positive gender- and sexuality-destabilizing effects.

I am aware of the current political controversy surrounding the word 'queer.' Some gays, lesbians, and bisexuals have expressed their inability to also identify with 'queerness,' as they feel the term has too long and too painful a history as a weapon of oppression and self-hate. These nonqueer lesbians, gays, and bisexuals find the attempts of radical forces in gay and lesbian communities (such as Queer Nation) to recover and positively redefine the term 'queer' successful only within these communities – and unevenly successful at that. Preferring current or freshly created terms, non-queer-identifying lesbians, gays, and bisexuals often feel that any positive effects resulting from reappropriating 'queer' are more theoretical than real.

But the history of gay and lesbian cultures and politics has shown that there are many times and places where the theoretical can have real social impact. Enough lesbians, gays, bisexuals, and other queers taking and making enough of these moments can create a more consistent awareness within the general public of queer cultural and political spaces, as these theory-in-the-flesh moments are concerned with making what has been for the most part publicly invisible and silent visible and vocal. In terms of mass culture reception, there are frequent theory-in-the-flesh opportunities in the course of everyday life. For example, how many times do we get the chance to inform people about our particular queer perspectives on film, television, literature, or music during conversations (or to engage someone else's perhaps unacknowledged queer perspective)? And how often, even if we are openly lesbian, gay, or bisexual, have we kept silent, or edited our conversations, deciding that our queer opinions are really only interesting to other queers, or that these opinions would make people uncomfortable – even while we think family, friends, and strangers should, of course, feel free to articulate various heterosexual or straight opinions in detail at any time?

Of course, queer positions aren't the only ones from which queers read and produce mass culture. As with nonqueers, factors such as class, ethnicity, gender, occupation, education, and religious, national, and regional allegiances influence our identity construction, and therefore are important to the positions we take as cultural producers and reader-consumers. These other cultural factors can exert influences difficult to separate from the development of our identities as queers, and as a result, difficult to discuss apart from our engagement in culture as queers. For example, most people find it next to impossible to articulate their sexual identities (queer or nonqueer) without some reference to gender. Generally, lesbian- and gay-specific forms of queer identities involve some degree of same-gender identification and desire or a cross-gender identification linked to same-gender desire. The understanding of what 'gender' is in these cases can range from accepting conventional straight forms, which naturalize 'feminine' and 'masculine' by conflating them with essentializing, biology-based conceptions of 'woman' and 'man'; to imitating the outward forms and behaviors of one gender or the other while not fully subscribing to the straight ideological imperatives that define that gender; to combining or ignoring traditional gender codes in order to reflect attitudes that have little or nothing to do with straight ideas about femininity/women or masculinity/men. These last two positions are the places where queerly reconfigured gender identities begin to be worked out.

'Begin to be,' because most radically, as Sue-Ellen Case points out, 'queer theory, unlike lesbian theory or gay male theory, is not gender specific.'[6] Believing that 'both gay and lesbian theory reinscribe sexual difference, to some extent, in their gender-specific constructions,' Case calls for a queer theory that 'works not at the site of gender, but at the site of ontology.'[7] But while a nongendered notion of queerness makes sense, articulating this queer theory fully apart from gendered straight feminist, gay, and lesbian theorizing becomes difficult within languages and cultures that make gender and gender difference so crucial to their discursive practices. Through her discussions of vampire myths, Case works hard to establish a discourse that avoids gendered terms, yet she finds it necessary to resort to them every so often in order to suggest the queerness of certain things: placing 'she' in quotation marks at one point, or discussing R. W. Fassbinder's film character Petra von Kant as 'a truly queer creature who flickers somewhere between haute couture butch lesbian and male drag queen.'[8]

Since I'm working with a conception of queerness that includes gay- and lesbian-specific positions as well as Case's nonlesbian and nongay queerness, gender definitions and uses here remain important to examining the ways in which queerness influences mass culture production and reception. For example, gay men who identify with some conception of 'the feminine' through processes that could stem from conscious personal choice, or from internalizing longstanding straight imperatives that encourage gay men to think of themselves as 'not men' (and therefore, by implication or by direct attribution, as being like 'women'), or from some degree of negotiation between these two processes, are at the center of the gay culture cults built around the imposing, spectacular women stars of opera [. . .], theater [. . .], film [. . .], popular music [. . .], and television [. . .]. For the past two decades in the gay popular press, book chapters and articles on the connections between gay men and women stars have been a commonplace, but only occasionally do these works go beyond the monolithic audience label 'gay men' to suggest the potential for discussing reception in a manner attuned to more specific definitions of sexual identity, such as those constructed to some degree within the dynamics of gender and sexuality.

Given this situation, one strand of queer mass culture reception studies might be more precisely focused upon these networks of women performers who were, and are, meaningful at different times and places and for different reasons to feminine-identified gay men. [. . .]

Clearly we need more popular and academic mass culture work that carefully considers feminine gay and other gendered queer reception practices, as well as those of even less-analyzed queer readership positions formed around the nexus of race and sexuality, or class and sexuality, or ethnicity and sexuality, or some combination of gender/race/class/ethnicity and sexuality. These studies would offer valuable evidence of precisely how and where specific complex constructions of queerness can and do reveal themselves in the uses of mass culture, as well as revealing how and where that mass culture comes to influence and reinforce the process of queer identity formation.

[. . .]

[. . .] [T]raditional narrative films such as *Sylvia Scarlett, Gentlemen Prefer Blondes, Trapeze, To Live and Die in L.A., Internal Affairs,* and *Thelma and Louise,* which are ostensibly addressed to straight audiences, often have greater potential for encouraging a wider range of queer responses than such clearly lesbian- and gay-addressed films as *Scorpio Rising, Home Movies, Women I Love,* and *Loads.*[9] The intense tensions and pleasures generated by the woman-woman and man-man aspects within the narratives of the former group of films create a space of sexual instability that already queerly positioned viewers can connect with in various ways, and within which straights might be likely to recognize and express their queer impulses. For example, gays might find a form of queer pleasure in the alternately tender and boisterous rapport between Lorelei/Marilyn Monroe and Dorothy/Jane Russell in *Gentlemen Prefer Blondes,* or in the exhilarating woman-bonding of the title characters in *Thelma and Louise.* Or lesbians and straights could queerly respond to the erotic elements in the relationships between the major male characters in *Trapeze, To Live and Die in L.A.,* or *Internal Affairs.* And any viewer might feel a sexually ambiguous attraction – is it gay, lesbian, bisexual, or straight? – to the image of Katharine Hepburn dressed as a young man in *Sylvia Scarlett.*

Of course, these queer positions and readings can become modified or can change over time, as people, cultures, and politics change. In my own case, as a white gay male who internalized dominant culture's definitions of myself as 'like a woman' in a traditional 1950s and 1960s understanding of who 'a woman' and what 'femininity' was supposed to be, my pleasure in *Gentlemen Prefer Blondes* initially worked itself out through a classic gay process of identifying, alternately, with Monroe and Russell; thereby experiencing vicarious if temporary empowerment through their use of sexual allure to attract men – including the entire American Olympic team. Reassessing the feminine aspects of my gay sexual identity sometime in the 1970s (after Stonewall and my coming out), I returned to the film and discovered my response was now less rooted in the fantasy of being Monroe or Russell and gaining sexual access to men, than in the pleasure of Russell being the 'gentleman' who preferred blonde Monroe, who looked out for her best interests, who protected her against men, and who enjoyed performing with her. This queer pleasure in a lesbian text has been abetted by extratextual information I have read, or was told, about Russell's solicitous and supportive offscreen behavior toward Monroe while making the film. But along with these elements of queer reading that developed from the interaction of my feminine gay identity, my knowledge of extratextual behind-the-scenes gossip, and the text itself, I also take a great deal of direct gay erotic pleasure in the 'Is There Anyone Here for Love?' number, enjoying its blatantly homo-historic and erotic ancient Greek Olympics mise-en-scène (including Russell's large column earrings), while admiring Russell's panache and good humor as she sings, strides, and strokes her way through a sea of half-naked male dancer-athletes. I no longer feel the need to mediate my sexual desires through her.

[. . .]

Examining how and where these gay cults of women stars work in relation to what LaValley saw in the mid-1980s as the 'newer, more openly gay following for male stars' would also make for fascinating cultural history. Certainly there have been 'homosexual' followings for male personalities in mass culture since the late nineteenth century, with performers and actors – Sandow the muscleman, Edwin Booth – vying with gay enthusiasms for opera divas and actresses such as Jenny Lind and Lillian Russell. Along these lines, one could queerly combine star studies with genre studies in order to analyze the gay appreciation of women musical performers, and the musical's 'feminine' or 'effeminized' aesthetic, camp, and emotive genre characteristics (spectacularized decor and costuming, intricate choreography, and singing about romantic yearning and fulfillment), with reference to the more hidden cultural history of gay erotics centered around men in musicals.

[. . .]

I can't leave this discussion of gay erotics and musicals without a few [. . .] words about Gene Kelly's 'male trio' musicals, such as *On the Town, Take Me Out to the Ball Game,* and *It's Always Fair Weather.*[10] Clad in sailor uniforms, baseball uniforms, and Army uniforms, the male trios in these films are composed of two conventionally sexy men (Kelly and Frank Sinatra in the first two films, Kelly and Dan Dailey in the last) and a comic, less attractive 'buffer' (Jules Munshin in the first two, Michael Kidd in the last) who is meant to diffuse the sexual energy generated between the two male leads when they sing and dance together. Other Kelly films – *Singin' in the Rain, An American in Paris,* and *Anchors Aweigh* – resort to the more conventional heterosexual(izing) narrative device of using a woman to mediate and diffuse male-male erotics.[11] But whether in the form of a third man or an ingenue, these devices fail to fully heterosexualize the relationship between Kelly and his male costars. In *Singin' in the Rain,* for example, I can't help but read Donald O'Connor maniacally unleashing his physical energy to entertain Kelly during the 'Make 'Em Laugh' number as anything but a case of overwrought, displaced gay desire.

Kelly himself jokingly refers to the queer erotics of his image and his many buddy musicals in *That's Entertainment!*, when he reveals the answer to the often-asked question, 'Who was your favorite dancing partner . . . Cyd Charisse, Leslie Caron, Rita Hayworth, Vera-Ellen?,' by showing a clip of the dance he did with Fred Astaire ('The Babbit and the Bromide') in *Ziegfeld Follies*. 'It's the only time we danced together,' Kelly remarks over the clip, 'but I'd change my name to Ginger if we could do it again.' As it turned out, Kelly and Astaire did 'do it again' in *That's Entertainment 2*, and their reunion as a dancing couple became the focus of much of the film's publicity campaign, as had been the case when Astaire reunited with Ginger Rogers in *The Barkleys of Broadway*.[12]

While there has been at the very least a general, if often clichéd, cultural connection made between gays and musicals, lesbian work within the genre has been less acknowledged. However, the evidence of lesbian viewing practices – in articles such as 'Hollywood Transformed,' in videos such as *Dry Kisses Only* (1990, Jane Cottis and Kaucyila Brooke) and *Grapefruit* (1989, Cecilia Dougherty), and in informal discussions (mention *Calamity Jane* to a group of thirty- to forty-something American lesbians) – suggests that lesbian viewers have always negotiated their own culturally specific readings and pleasures within the genre.[13] [. . .]

Since this discussion of queer positions and queer readings seems to have worked itself out so far largely as a discussion of musical stars and the musical genre, I might add here that of the articles and books written about film musicals only the revised edition of Jane Feuer's *Hollywood Musicals* goes beyond a passing remark in considering the ways in which this genre has been the product of gay film workers, or how the ways in which musicals are viewed and later talked about have been influenced by gay and lesbian reception practices.[14] From most accounts of the musical, it is a genre whose celebration of heterosexual romance must always be read straight. The same seems to be the case with those other film genres typically linked to gays, lesbians, and bisexuals: the horror/fantasy film and the melodrama. While there has been a rich history of queers producing and reading these genres, surprisingly little has been done to formally express this cultural history. There has been more queer work done in and on the horror film: vampire pieces by Richard Dyer, Bonnie Zimmerman, and Sue-Ellen Case; Bruna Fionda, Polly Gladwin, Isiling Mack-Nataf's lesbian vampire film *The Mark of Lilith* (1986); Amy Goldstein's vampire musical film *Because the Dawn* (1988); a sequence in *Dry Kisses Only* that provides a lesbian take on vampire films; an article by Martin F. Norden on sexuality in *The Bride of Frankenstein*; and some pieces on *The Rocky Horror Picture Show* (although most are not written from a queer position), to cite a few examples.[15]

But there is still much left unexamined beyond the level of conversation. Carl Dreyer's lesbophobic 'classic' *Vampyr* could use a thorough queer reading, as could Tod Browning's *Dracula* – which opens with a coach ride through Transylvania in the company of a superstitious Christian straight couple, a suit-and-tie lesbian couple, and a feminine gay man, who will quickly become the bisexual Count Dracula's vampirized servant. Subsequent events in the film include a straight woman who becomes a child molester known as 'The Woman in White' after the count vampirizes her. It is also amazing that gay horror director James Whale has yet to receive full-scale queer auteurist consideration for films such as *Frankenstein* (the idea of men making the 'perfect' man), *The Bride of Frankenstein* (gay Dr. Praetorius; queer Henry Frankenstein; the erotics between the blind man, the monster, and Jesus on the cross; the overall campy atmosphere), *The Old Dark House* (a gay and lesbian brother and sister; a 103-year-old man in the attic who is actually a woman), and *The Invisible Man* (effete, mad genius Claude Rains spurns his fiancée, becomes invisible, tries to find a male partner in crime, and becomes *visible* only after he is killed by the police).[16] Beyond queer readings of specific films and directors, it would also be important to consider how the central conventions of horror and melodrama actually encourage queer positioning as they exploit the spectacle of heterosexual romance, straight domesticity, and traditional gender roles gone awry. In a sense, then, *everyone's* pleasure in these genres is 'perverse,' is queer, as much of it takes place within the space of the contra-heterosexual and the contra-straight.

Just how much everyone's pleasures in mass culture are part of this contra-straight, rather than strictly antistraight, space – just how *queer* our responses to cultural texts are so much of the time – is what I'd finally like this chapter to suggest. Queer positions, queer readings, and queer pleasures are part of a reception space that stands simultaneously beside and within that created by heterosexual and straight positions. These positions, readings, and pleasures also suggest that what happens in cultural reception goes beyond the traditional opposition of homo and hetero, as queer reception is often a place beyond the audience's conscious 'real-life' definition of their sexual identities and cultural positions – often, but not always, beyond such sexual identities and identity politics, that is. For in all my enthusiasm for breaking down rigid concepts of sexuality through the example of mass culture reception, I don't want to suggest that there is a queer utopia that unproblematically and apolitically unites straights and queers (or even all queers) in some mass culture reception area in the sky. Queer reception doesn't stand outside personal and cultural histories; it is part of the articulation of these histories. This is why, politically, queer reception (and production) practices can include everything from the reactionary to the radical to the indeterminate, as with the audience for (as well as the producers of) 'queercore' publications, who individually and collectively often seem to combine reactionary and radical attitudes.

What queer reception often does, however, is stand outside the relatively clear-cut and essentializing categories of sexual identity under which most people function. You might identify yourself as a lesbian or a straight woman yet queerly experience the gay erotics of male buddy films such as *Red River* and *Butch Cassidy and the Sundance Kid*; or maybe as a gay man your cult-like devotion to *Laverne and Shirley*, *Kate and Allie*, or *The Golden Girls* has less to do with straight-defined cross-gender identification than with your queer enjoyment in how these series are crucially concerned with articulating the loving relationships between women.[17] Queer readings aren't 'alternative' readings, wishful or willful misreadings, or 'reading too much into things' readings. They result from the recognition and articulation of the complex range of queerness that has been in popular culture texts and their audiences all along.

NOTES

1. Janice Radway, 'Reception Study: Ethnography and the Problems of Dispersed Audiences and Nomadic Subjects,' *Cultural Studies* 2, no. 3 (October 1988): 361.
2. Ibid., 366.
3. Stuart Hall's article 'Encoding/Decoding' informs much of my general approach to queer cultural readings of mass culture. [. . .]
4. Adele Morrison as quoted in 'Queer,' Steve Cosson, *OUT/LOOK* 11 (Winter 1991): 21.
5. bell hooks, 'Choosing the Margins as a Space of Radical Openness,' *Yearning: Race, Gender, and Cultural Politics* (Boston: South End Press, 1990), 153.
6. Sue-Ellen Case, 'Tracking the Vampire,' *differences* 3, no. 2 (Summer 1991): 2.
7. Ibid., 3.
8. Ibid., 8, 12.
9. Films mentioned in this section: *Sylvia Scarlett* (1936, RKO, George Cukor), *Gentlemen Prefer Blondes* (1953, Twentieth Century-Fox, Howard Hawks), *Trapeze* (1956, United Artists, Carol Reed), *To Live and Die in L.A.* (1985, New Century, William Friedkin), *Internal Affairs* (1990, Paramount, Mike Figgis), *Thelma and Louise* (1991, MGM, Ridley Scott), *Scorpio Rising* (1962–63, Kenneth Anger), *Home Movies* (1972, Jan Oxenberg), *Women I Love* (1976, Barbara Hammer), *Loads* (1980, Curt McDowell).
10. Films cited: *On the Town* (1950, MGM, Gene Kelly and Stanley Donen), *Take Me Out to the Ball Game* (1949, MGM, Busby Berkeley), *It's Always Fair Weather* (1955, MGM, Gene Kelly and Stanley Donen). [. . .]
11. Films cited: *Singin' in the Rain* (1952, MGM, Gene Kelly and Stanley Donen), *An American in Paris* (1951, MGM, Vincente Minnelli), *Anchors Aweigh* (1945, MGM, George Sidney).
12. Films cited: *That's Entertainment!* (1974, MGM, Jack Haley, Jr.), *Ziegfeld Follies* (1946, MGM, Vincente Minnelli), *That's Entertainment 2* (1976, MGM, Gene Kelly). *The Barkleys of Broadway* (1949, MGM, Charles Walters).
13. Film cited: *Calamity Jane* (1953, Warners, David Butler). [. . .]
14. Feuer's 'Gay Readings of Musicals' section in *The Hollywood Musical* (London: BFI/Macmillan, 199<??>) concentrates on gay male production and reception of musicals.
15. Articles mentioned in this section: Richard Dyer, 'Children of the Night: Vampirism as Homosexuality, Homosexuality as Vampirism,' *Sweet Dreams: Sexuality, Gender and Popular Fiction*, ed. Susannah Radstone (London: Lawrence and Wishart, 1988), 47–72; Bonnie Zimmerman, '*Daughters of Darkness*: Lesbian Vampires,' *Jump Cut* 24/25 (1981): 23–24; Sue-Ellen Case, 'Tracking the Vampire,' *differences* 3, no. 2 (Summer 1991): 1–20; Martin F. Norden, 'Sexual References in James Whale's *Bride of Frankenstein*,' *Eros in the Mind's Eye: Sexuality and the Fantastic in Art and Film*, ed. Donald Palumbo (New York: Greenwood Press, 1986), 141–50; Elizabeth Reba Weise, 'Bisexuality, *The Rocky Horror Picture Show*, and Me,' *Bi Any Other Name: Bisexual People Speak Out*, ed. Loraine Hutchins and Lani Kaahumanu (Boston: Alyson, 1991), 134–39.
16. Films mentioned in this section: *Vampyr* (1931, Gloria Film, Carl Theodore Dryer), *Dracula* (1931, Universal, Tod Browning), *Frankenstein* (1931, Universal, James Whale), *The Bride of Frankenstein* (1935, Universal, James Whale), *The Old Dark House* (1932, Universal, James Whale), *The Invisible Man* (1933, Universal, James Whale). [. . .]
17. Films and television series mentioned in this section: *Red River* (1948, United Artists, Howard Hawks), *Butch Cassidy and the Sundance Kid* (1969, Twentieth Century-Fox, George Roy Hill), *Laverne and Shirley* (1976–83, ABC), *Kate and Allie* (1984–90, CBS), *The Golden Girls* (1985–92, NBC).

40

BANAL TRANSNATIONALISM

The Difference that Television Makes

Asu Aksoy and Kevin Robins

[...]

THE DIFFERENCE THAT TELEVISION MAKES

There is a growing body of work on transnational communications within the framework of diasporic cultural studies. Here it is being argued that new media technologies are making it possible to transcend the distances that have separated 'diasporic communities' around the world from their 'communities of origin'. 'Diasporic media' are said to be providing new means to promote transnational bonding, and thereby sustain (ethnic, national or religious) identities and cultures at-a-distance. They are being thought about in terms of the possibilities they offer for dislocated belonging among migrant communities anxious to maintain their identification with the 'homeland' (and the basic premise is that this kind of belonging must be the primary aspiration of any and every such 'community').

Now, of course we can recognise a certain kind of truth in this argument. From our own work on Turkish migrants in London, it is clear that access to Turkish-language media can, indeed, be important for overcoming the migrant's experience of cultural separation. But if there is some kind of truth here, we would say that it is only a very meagre and partial truth. The problem with diasporic media studies is that its interests and concern generally come to an end at this point. The enquiry is brought to a premature halt, with the ready acceptance that transnational broadcasting does in fact, and

From Karim H. Karim (ed.), *The Media of Diaspora* (London: Routledge, 1993).

quite unproblematically, support the long-distance cohesion of transnational 'imagined communities' – and without ever confronting what it is that might be new and different about the experience of transnational broadcasting. Because it has been principally concerned with acts of bonding and belonging, the diasporic agenda has generally been blind to what else might be happening when migrants are, apparently, connecting in to the 'homeland' culture. The limits of diasporic media studies come from the readiness to believe and accept that migrant audiences are all behaving as the conventional and conforming members of 'diasporic communities'.

The problem is simply that the theoretical categories available to diasporic media and cultural studies make it difficult to see anything other than diasporic forms of behaviour. Individuals are derived from the social orders to which they 'belong'; they amount to little more than their membership of, and participation in, any particular 'imagined community'. This is clearly an example of the kind of social theory that is powerfully criticised by Anthony Cohen, an approach that treats society as an ontology 'which somehow becomes independent of its own members, and assumes that the self is required continuously to adjust to it' (1994: 21). In this kind of approach there is no place for self-awareness and self-consciousness – and, as Cohen argues, by neglecting self-consciousness, we inevitably perpetrate fictions in our descriptions of other people' (ibid.: 191). To see anything more than diasporic behaviour in migrant audiences, it is necessary to introduce the category of the self-conscious individual, who is 'someone who can reflect on her or his experience of and position in society, of "being oneself"' (ibid.: 65). As Cohen says, the imperative should be 'to elicit and describe the thoughts and sentiments of individuals which we otherwise gloss over in the generalisations we derive from collective social categories' (ibid.: 4). The crucial point is that individuals are endowed with the capacity for both emotion (feelings, moods) and thought (reflecting, comparing, interpreting, judging and so on). We should be concerned, then, with their minds and sensibilities, and not their cultures or identities – with how they think, rather than how they belong.

It is in such terms as these that we now want to think about the experiences of Turkish migrants living in London. What do they think and feel about Turkish channels and programming? What is the difference that transnational television has made for London Turks? We will start from the crucial question of distance – from the idea that the new media systems can now work to bridge global distances. And we will do so by reflecting on what this seemingly straightforward idea might actually mean. In the frame of diasporic cultural studies, we suggest, it is about the maintenance of at-a-distance ties; about the supposed capacity of transnational media to connect migrant communities back to the cultural space of their distant 'homeland'. On the basis of our own research, we would characterise what is happening somewhat differently: in terms of how – in the case of our informants – transnational media can now bring Turkish cultural products and services to them in London, and of how

'Turkey' is consequently brought closer to them. As one focus group participant puts it, '[I]t gives you more freedom, because you don't feel so far away,
because it's only six foot away from you, you don't feel so far away from it.
Cyprus is like one switch of a button away, or Turkey even, mainland Turkey,
you are there, aren't you?' (Focus group, Enfield, 21 April 2000). Even a
young woman who migrated when she was quite young, and who is therefore
not really familiar with the country, has this sense of greater proximity to the
actuality of Turkey. She thinks that it is very good to be able to watch satellite television 'because you too can see what's been going on in Turkey, the
news . . . I used to think that Turkey was a different kind of place [*başka bir
yer*]. It's bringing it [Turkey] closer [*yakınlaştırıyor*]' (Focus group, Islington,
London, 29 March 1999). Television makes a difference because it is in its
nature – in the nature of television as a medium – to bring things closer to its
viewers.

In one of our group discussions, two women tell us of how satellite television
now allows them to be synchronised with Turkish realities. 'Most certainly
[Turkish] television is useful for us,' says one. 'It's almost as if we're living
in Turkey, as if nothing has really changed for us.' The other confirmed this,
saying, 'When you're home, you feel as if you are in Turkey. Our homes are
already decorated Turkish style, everything about me is Turkish, and when I'm
watching television too' (Focus group, Hackney, London, 7 December 1999).
The key issue here is to do with the meaning of this feeling of 'as if nothing has
really changed for us'. In the context of the diasporic agenda, this feeling of
synchronisation would be thought of in terms of long-distance bonding with
the 'homeland', the maintenance of at-a-distance links with a faraway 'somewhere else'. For us, in contrast, it is simply about the availability in London
of imported things from Turkey – where we might regard the availability of
television programmes as being on a continuum with the (equally common)
availability of food, clothes or furnishings from Turkey. 'Nothing has really
changed' does not refer to ethno-cultural re-connection to some imagined
'homeland', but simply to the possibility of having access in London now to
Turkish consumer goods and the world of Turkish consumer culture. It is
'almost as if we're living in Turkey' in that sense, being Turkish in London,
that is to say, and not at all in the sense of 'being taken back home'.

Television brings the ordinary, banal reality of Turkish life to the migrants
living in London. The key to understanding transnational Turkish television
is its relation to banality. Jankélévitch notes how people who are in exile can
imagine they are living double lives, carrying around within them 'inner voices
. . . the voices of the past and of the distant city', while at the same time submitting to 'the banal and turbulent life of everyday action' (1974: 346). This
is precisely the mechanism of splitting – where the banality of the 'here and
now' provides the stimulus for nostalgic dreams and fantasies about the 'there
and then'. Now, what we regard as significant about transnational television
is that, as a consequence of bringing the mundane, everyday reality of Turkey

'closer', it is undermining this false polarising logic. The 'here and now' reality of Turkish media culture disturbs the imagination of a 'there and then' Turkey – thereby working against the romance of diaspora-as-exile, against the tendency to false idealisation of the 'homeland'. We might say, then, that transnational Turkish television is an agent of cultural de-mythologisation.

This process of de-mythologisation can work in different ways. Here we will give two examples of how television can be used as a kind of reality-testing device. The first comes from an interview with an active member of London's Turkish-Cypriot population, a man in his forties who has been settled in Britain for many years. We find ourselves discussing the question of young people, relationships and the family, and he expresses quite critical opinions about what he clearly regards as the out-of-date morality of the Turkish-Cypriot community. [. . .] What he is arguing is that television programmes and images that show how life and morals are in Turkey now can serve as a valuable corrective to migrant attitudes that, he believes, have become stuck in some ideal and timeless image of Turkish-Cypriotness.

Our second example comes from a young woman of eighteen, we shall call her Hülya, who migrated to Britain from eastern Turkey when she was seven years old. At one point, towards the end of our discussion, she tells us how much she likes watching old Turkish films on television, 'especially the love films', which she likes to watch 'to see the old Turkey . . . [] It gives you a very sweet sense'. But earlier she had spoken about a very different experience of watching Turkish television [. . .]. What is made apparent [. . .] is television's great capacity for conveying harsh and cruel aspects of the Turkish reality – Turkish news programmes are far more explicit than British ones in showing scenes of violence and bloodshed. For a great many Turkish viewers, news programmes are very disturbing – the often intense discomfort of watching the news was an issue that ran through practically all of our focus groups. In some parts of its schedules, then, television may nourish warm and nostalgic feelings. But at news time, especially, the principle of reality will always return, through images of Turkey that frequently provoke and shock. The news can be profoundly unsettling for migrant viewers. As Hülya says of her own experience, it 'creates a psychological disorder' [*psikolojik durum yaratıyor*].

What is important is the evidential nature of television (which may be constructive, as in our first example, but also disturbing, as our second example makes clear). What we want to emphasise here is the capacity of the reality dimension of television to undercut the abstract nostalgia of the diasporic imagination. Turkish viewers come to participate in the mundane and banal world of everyday television. It is this aspect of television culture that goes against the idea that the proliferation of Turkish transnational media is now associated with an ethnicisation of media cultures and markets in western Europe (for such an argument, see Becker 2001). In our own work, we have not found this to be the case. We are inclined to agree with Marisca Milikowski when she argues that it is, on the contrary, associated with a process of *de-ethnicisation*.

As she says, Turkish satellite television 'helps Turkish migrants, and in particular their children, to liberate themselves from certain outdated and culturally imprisoning notions of Turkishness, which had survived in the isolation of migration' (Milikowski 2000: 444). The world of Turkish television is an ordinary world, and its significance resides, we suggest, in its ordinary, banal and everyday qualities – which are qualities it has in common with countless other television worlds.

Turkish audiences look to the ordinariness of Turkish television. Like any other viewers of broadcast television, they want 'the familiar – familiar sights, familiar faces, familiar voices', as Thomas Elsaesser (1994: 7) puts it, 'television that respects and knows who they are, where they are, and what time it is'. And, to a large extent, we may say that they are able to find what they are looking for. And yet, at the same time, there is still something that is wrong, something that does not quite work properly with transnational Turkish television. At the same time as they can enjoy them, migrants can also find Turkish channels disturbing, unsettling, frustrating. This is apparent in a very dramatic fashion in Hülya's abrupt shift from feeling relaxed in front of the television to feeling worn out by what she saw on it. Many, many other people expressed these kinds of affronted and disgruntled feelings about the programmes they were watching. [. . .] There is something about Turkish television that presents itself as in some way inadequate, deficient, unacceptable. The experience of watching transnational television is ordinary, but never straightforwardly.

[. . .] We can perhaps get at what this something might be from a passing observation that was made by Hülya. We were talking about Muslim festivals, and about the sense that she and her friends had that the significance of religious holidays was diminishing in the London context. We asked whether Turkish television helped to remind people of the traditional holidays, and to create the festival atmosphere that seemed to have been lost. 'How could that help?', says one young woman sceptically. And Hülya says, 'It's coming from a distance . . . It's coming from too far. It loses its significance. I mean, it could have significance, but it's coming from too far.' Later, when asked whether the availability of satellite television had implications for her identity and her relation to Turkish culture, she picks up on the same idea. 'No', she says, 'it can't, because it's too distant. Imagine that you were talking to me from I don't know how many thousand miles away. How much would this affect me?' (Focus group, Hackney, London, 3 November 1999). Perhaps we can make sense of this by referring back to Thomas Elsaesser's observation that the audiences of broadcast television want television programmes that know who they are, where they are, and what time it is. Is it that television from Turkey does not seem to know its transnational audiences in this way? Is Hülya pointing to something that is new or different about the working of transnational television? Is she signalling something that might actually make transnational cultural interactions distinctive?

MIGRANT EXPERIENCE AND TELEVISION THEORY

Turkish migrants clearly have quite complex thoughts and sentiments about the television channels and programmes that they are watching. And what is also clear is that they have a *critical* engagement with the new transnational television culture.

What they say demonstrates considerable awareness and thoughtfulness about different aspects of this culture, from the aesthetic and production values of particular programmes, through to the overall impact of the new services on the quality of their lives in Britain. What we now want to do is to go on and reflect on these complex attitudes and relations of Turkish migrants towards transnational television. We want to try to make sense of what Turkish people are telling us in the context of more general ideas about the role and significance of broadcasting in modern life (which Turks are as much a part of as any other group).

For the most part, as we have suggested above, transnational media of the kind we are concerned with here have been considered in the special context of 'diasporic culture' and identity politics. Migrant audiences have been seen as, in some way, different; and the study of their supposedly different dispositions and preoccupations has seemed to belong to the specialised domain of ethnic and migration research. We ourselves believe that their media activities should be looked at with the very same media theories that have been applied to 'ordinary' (i.e. national, sedentary) audiences. Marisca Milikowski (2000: 460) is quite right to insist that we should look at migrant viewing from the point of view of 'ordinary uses and gratifications' – for, as she observes, 'non-ideological and non-political gratifications usually go a long way to explain a certain popular interest'. This we regard as an important principle of methodological democracy and justice. We should reflect on what is happening through transnationalisation of Turkish media culture in the light of media theory concerned with ordinary uses of, and gratifications from, everyday television.

Here, we think that the work of Paddy Scannell (1996, 2000) can serve as a particularly useful and productive point of reference. [. . .] Scannell's concern is with how, at a particular historical moment, broadcasting media came to develop communicative forms that functioned as arguably the primary mediation between the private domain of everyday life and the public life of the nation state.

It seems to us that these communicative and rhetorical aspects of programming and scheduling are absolutely crucial for our own exploration of transnational Turkish television and its audiences. Of course, the codes that have evolved in the Turkish context differ somewhat from those of Scannell's British case – the state broadcaster, TRT, has always had an 'official' tone, and it was only in the 1990s, through the development of private channels, that more informal modes of address came to be elaborated (Aksoy and Robins 1997).

But we may say that they have functioned in the integrative way, working to mediate the relation between private and public spheres of life in Turkey. And what seems to us to be a key issue, in the context of our own present concern with Turkish satellite broadcasting in the European space, is what happens to these communicative structures in the changed circumstances of transnationalisation. [. . .] What we would suggest is that there will be difficulties when communicative structures that have worked more or less well in a national context are then made to do service in new transnational contexts. We are concerned with the communicative limits of structures that have served to mediate between the private and public lives of the nation.

There are two (closely related) arguments that we want to make here. The first is straightforward, emerging directly from our previous discussion, and can be made quite briefly. Scannell is concerned with what he calls the 'care-structures' of radio and television, by which he means the practices that 'produce and deliver an all-day everyday service that is ready-to-hand and available always anytime at the turn of a switch or the press of a button' (1996: 145–6). What this means, he says, is 'making programmes so that they "work" every time', and in such a way that viewers or listeners come to regard them as 'a natural, ordinary, unremarkable, everyday entitlement' (ibid.: 145–6). In considering these care structures, Scannell has put particular emphasis on the temporality of broadcasting, on what he calls its 'dailiness'. 'This dailiness yields', he says, 'the sense we all have of the ordinariness, the familiarity and obviousness of radio and television. It establishes their taken for granted, "seen but unnoticed" character' (2000: 19). And what Scannell wants us to recognise and acknowledge is the immense pleasure that this mundane quality of broadcasting has for viewers – the pleasure that comes from the combination of familiarity, confirmation, entitlement and effortlessness.

And what we want to emphasise is that this particular pleasure principle is not exclusive to sedentary viewers. Turkish broadcasting culture also exists as an ordinary and mundane culture. And the appeal of Turkish television, as with other broadcasting cultures, is equally the appeal of its ordinariness. Through it, Turks living in Europe have access to, or can extend their access to, what Jostein Gripsrud (1999) calls the domain of 'common knowledge'. They can be part of the great domain of 'anonymous discourse' that broadcasting has brought into existence, the banal domain of 'inattentive attention' (Brune 1993: 37). What we are arguing, then, is that migrant viewers are looking to find what the national television culture has always provided. Like any other viewers, Turkish-speaking viewers in Europe are also in search of broadcast television that is meaningfully and effortlessly available. They are also wanting – and to a quite a large extent finding – the pleasures of familiarity and confirmation. And our point is that the desire for such an engagement with Turkish television is entirely social, and not at all ethno-cultural or 'diasporic', in its motivation. Migrant viewers are in search of ordinary social gratifications, precisely the kinds of gratification that Scannell is concerned with.

Our second argument is more complex, and takes us back to what Hülya said about Turkish television seeming to come from a distance and, consequently, losing its significance. What we want to get at is the particular feeling of ambivalence that very many Turkish people have about transnational television (which is more than the routine ambivalence that we all seem to have). They enjoy and appreciate the programmes they see yet, at the same time, watching them can frequently cause frustration and provoke resentment. Sometimes, it seems, transnational engagement with Turkish television culture does not 'work'. In Scannell's terms, we may say that the care structures of television break down. And what we want to suggest, as an explanation for this, is that, while considerable gratification may be got from everyday television, there are particular difficulties with its 'sociable dimension', which Scannell regards as 'the most fundamental characteristic of broadcasting's communicative ethos' (1996: 23). Put simply, Turkish television often seems to its transnational viewers to be failing or lacking in its sociable aspect.

Scannell draws our attention to the remarkable capacity of broadcasting to generate a sense of 'we-ness', through the creation of 'a public, shared and sociable world-in-common between human beings' (2000: 12). What Scannell means when he talks about the creation of a 'world in common' is, of course, a national world in common; what is at issue is the contribution of broadcasting to the institution of the 'imagined community'. [. . .] It is a world in which television and radio contribute to the shaping of our sense of days' (ibid.: 149). The dailiness of broadcast media gives rise to the sense of '*our* time – generational time – the time of *our* being with one another in the world' (ibid.: 174). The broadcasting calendar 'creates a horizon of expectations, a mood of anticipation, a directedness towards that which is to come, thereby giving substance and structure (a "texture of relevances") to everyday life' (ibid.: 155). According to this ideal-type scenario, broadcasting produces a 'common world – a shareable, accessible, available public world'; what it does is 'to create and to allow ways of being-in-public for absent listeners and viewers' (ibid.: 166, 168). It connects 'everyone's my-world' to the 'great world', which is 'a world in common, a world we share' (ibid.: 172, 174).

And what we are arguing here is that it is this sociable functioning of broadcasting that does not 'work' properly for migrants watching Turkish television in Europe. Transnational viewers are often disconcerted because, on very many occasions, they cannot relate to Turkish programmes as a natural, ordinary, unremarkable, everyday entitlement. In the case of news this is particularly apparent. If, as Scannell argues, 'the care structures of news are designed to routinise eventfulness' (ibid.: 160), then we may say that in our Turkish case, at least, these care structures do not function well across distance. In the transnational context, there is a problem with the mode of address. Broadcasting works on the basis of what Scannell calls a 'for-anyone-as-someone' structure of address: it is addressing a mass audience, and yet appears to be addressing the members of that audience personally, as individuals. 'The for-anyone-as-

someone structure expresses and embodies that which is between the impersonal third person and the personal first person, namely the second person (the
me-and-you)', says Scannell (2000: 9). 'The for-anyone-as-someone structure
expresses "we-ness". It articulates human social sociable life.' In the Turkish
case, it seems that viewers may often be made to feel like no one in particular.
The conditions no longer exist for feeling at home in the 'we-ness' of Turkish
broadcasting culture.

Why does the 'my world' of Turkish migrants no longer resonate properly
with a Turkish world in common? Why are there problems with the mode of
address in the case of transnational broadcasting? Why are the care structures
of broadcasting disrupted? The reasons are to do with the context of consumption. As we have said, transnational broadcasting is not about magically
transporting migrant viewers back to a distant homeland. It is about broadcasting services being delivered to them in their new locations – in the case of
the Turks we have been discussing, it is in London. What this means is that
the world of broadcasting is not seamlessly connected to the world of the
street outside, as it would be for viewers watching in Turkey. Migrant viewers
cannot move routinely between the media space and the 'outside' space of
everyday Turkish reality. And since so much of what broadcasting is about has
to do with connecting viewers to the life and rhythms of the real world of the
nation, there are bound to be difficulties with the dislocated kind of viewing
that migrancy enforces. [. . .] We may say that the decontextualisation of the
migrant viewing situation often results in a kind of interference in the reception
of cultural signals from Turkey.

A further consequence of the dislocated context of consumption is that
migrant viewers can never be in a position to watch Turkish television naively
or innocently. We must be aware that they actually operate in and across two
cultural spaces (at least) – Turkish and British. As well as watching Turkish
channels, most of them are very familiar with British television. And they will
often make comparisons between the two broadcasting cultures (concerning,
for example, programme quality, scheduling, bias, censorship). We may say
that there is a constant implicit comparison going on, and very often the comparisons are explicit – Turkish programmes are always watched and thought
about with an awareness of British television in mind. As one man put it to
us, 'We have the opportunity to compare things we see with what happens
here. Before, we didn't know what it was like here' (Focus group, Hackney,
London, 16 December 1999). When we say that Turkish migrants cannot
watch Turkish television innocently, we mean that they can no longer watch
it from the inside, as it were. They cannot recover the simple perspective of
monocultural (national) vision. They are compelled to think about Turkish
culture in the light of other cultural experiences and possibilities.

We have said that watching transnational Turkish television can be a frustrating and often disillusioning experience. What we want to add in conclusion
is that this disillusionment can also be a productive experience. Through their

engagement with Turkish (alongside British) media culture, Turkish migrants develop a comparative and critical attitude, and may become more reflexively aware of the arbitrariness and provisionality of cultural orders. In the present argument, we have been principally concerned with how the ordinary world of broadcast television can work to undermine the diasporic imagination. What should also have become apparent in the course of our argument, however, is the potential that exists, too, for working against the grain of the national imagination, against the confining mentality of imagined community.

CONCLUSION: THE MINDS OF MIGRANTS

> It all depends on the rifts and leaps in a person, on the distance from the one to the other *within himself*. (Elias Canetti 1991: 20)

In this chapter, we have been highly critical of diasporic cultural studies and the agenda centred on 'diasporic media'. Our objection has been to what we regard as a fundamental wrong assumption made by its exponents: that the people who watch transnational satellite television do so as mere ciphers of the 'imagined communities' to which they are said to 'belong'. What we think has to be called into question is the idea that migrants function principally in terms of the categories of collective attachment and identification. As Roger Rouse observes, 'the discourse of identity suggests that social collectivities are aggregates of atomised and autonomous elements, either individuals or subgroups, that are fundamentally equivalent by virtue of the common possession of a given social property' (1995: 358). Human individuals are reduced to the status of being the poor representatives of whatever imagined community they happen to have once been aggregated into. Rouse points to the socio-cultural efficacy of this logic of identity. We may consider it, he says, in terms of 'hegemonic efforts to make ideas about identity frame the ways in which people understand what it is to be a person, the kinds of collectivities in which they are involved, the nature of the problems that they face, and the means by which these problems can be tackled' (ibid.: 356). We have a fundamental problem with the project of diasporic cultural studies because it seems to us that it is, in the end, contributing to the extension and perpetuation of these hegemonic efforts in the context of contemporary global change. Everything, every possibility, remains predicated on the logic of identity.

In our discussion of transnational broadcasting from Turkey, we have been working actively against the diasporic imagination. We have tried to show how the rhetorical structures of Turkish television – the structures that have been mobilised to organise the experience of the national audience – are disrupted in the transnational context. In the migrant context, we think, where the ideal rhetorical situation of Turkish national television is significantly undermined, there may be possibilities for a more reflexive and critical engagement with television from the 'homeland'. What we have tried to suggest is that, in the Turkish case at least, transnational television might actually be working to subvert the diasporic imagination and its imperatives of identification and belonging. But our critique goes further than this. We have also argued that it is necessary to jettison the basic concepts of 'identity', 'imagined community' and 'diaspora'. Like Anthony Cohen, we have felt it necessary to go against the grain of the prevailing culturalism, and to take greater account of human consciousness and self-consciousness – to recognise that the minds of Turkish migrants may provide a more significant and interesting research focus than their identities. This means moving our agenda away from the 'problem' of migrant culture and identity, to consider how it is that migrants experience migration, and how they think and talk about and make sense of their experiences.

The point about identities is that they require simplicity. In the case of minds and consciousness, what is important is always their complexity. And it seems to us that transnational developments might open up new possibilities for the way we think about mental space – putting a new value on the rifts and leaps inside a person, and provoking those who are open to experience to travel the distance from the one to the other within themselves.

References

Aksoy, Asu and Robins, Kevin (1997), 'Peripheral Vision: Cultural Industries and Cultural Identities in Turkey', *Paragraph*, 20(1): 75–99.

Becker, Jörg (2001), 'Zwischen Abgrenzung und Integration: Anmerkungen zur Ethnisierung der türkischen Medienkultur', in Jörg Becker and Reinhard Behnisch (eds), *Zwischen Abgrenzung und Integration: Türkische Medienkultur in Deutschland*, Rehburg-Loccum: Evangelische Akademie, 9–25.

Brune, François (1993), '*Les Médias pensent comme moi!*': *Fragments du discours anonyme*, Paris: Harmattan.

Canetti, Elias (1991), *The Secret Heart of the Clock*, London: André Deutsch.

Cohen, Anthony P. (1994), *Self Consciousness: An Alternative Anthropology of Identity*, London, Routledge.

Elsaesser, Thomas (July 1994), 'European Television and National Identity, or "What's there to Touch when the Dust has Settled"', paper presented to the conference on Turbulent Europe: Conflict, Identity and Culture, London.

Gripsrud, Jostein (ed.) (1999), *Television and Common Knowledge*, London: Routledge.

Jankélévitch, Vladimir (1974), *L'Irréversible et la nostalgie*, Paris: Flammarion.

Milikowski, Marisca (2000), 'Exploring a Model of De-ethnicisation: The Case of Turkish Television in the Netherlands', *European Journal of Communication*, 15(4): 443–68.

Rouse, Roger (1995), 'Questions of Identity: Personhood and Collectivity in Transnational Migration to the United States', *Critique of Anthropology*, 15(4): 351–80.

Scannell, Paddy (1996), *Radio, Television and Modern Life*, Oxford, Blackwell.

Scannell, Paddy (2000), 'For-Anyone-As-Someone Structures', *Media, Culture and Society*, 22(1): 5–24.

FURTHER READING

Aldoory, L. and Parry-Giles, S. J., 'Women and Race in Feminist Media Research: Intersections, Ideology and Invisibility', in J. Curran and M. Gurevitch (eds), *Mass Media and Society*, 4th edn (London: Edward Arnold, 2005) pp. 336–55.

Bobo, J., 'The Colour Purple: Black Women as Cultural Readers', in J. Storey (ed.), *Cultural Theory and Popular Culture: A Reader*, 3rd edn (Edinburgh: Pearson, [1988] 2006) pp. 237–45.

Consalvo, M., 'Cyber-Slaying Media Fans: Code, Digital Poaching, and Corporate Control of the Internet', *Journal of Communication Inquiry* 27 (2003) pp. 67–86.

Ginsburg, F., Abu-Lughod, L. and Larkin, B., *Media Worlds: Anthropology on New Terrain* (Berkeley, CA: University of California Press, 2002).

Gray, J., Sandvoss, C. and Harrington, C. L., *Fandom: Identities and Communities in a Mediated World* (New York: NYU Press, 2007).

Grossberg, L., *We Gotta Get Out of This Place* (London: Routledge, 1992).

Guins, R. and Omayra, Z. C., *Popular Culture: A Reader* (London: Sage, 2005).

Hartley, J., 'From Republic of Letters to Television Republic? Citizen Readers in the Era of Broadcast Television', in L. Spigel and C. Brunsden (eds), *Television after TV* (London: Duke University Press, 2004) pp. 386–417.

Hills, M., *The Pleasures of Horror* (London: Continuum, 2005).

Hills, M., 'Not Just Another "Powerless Elite"? When Media Fans Become Subcultural Celebrities', in S. Holmes and S. Redmond (eds), *Framing Celebrity: New Directions in Celebrity Culture* (London: Routledge, 2006) pp. 101–18.

Liebes, T., 'Viewing and Reviewing the Audience: Fashions in Communication Research', in J. Curran and M. Gurevitch (eds), *Mass Media and Society*, 4th edn (London: Edward Arnold, 2005) pp. 356–74.

Littler, J., *Radical Consumption in Contemporary Culture* (Buckingham: Open University Press, 2008).

Medhurst, M., 'In Search of Nebulous Nancies: Looking for Queers in Pre-Gay British Film', in R. Griffith (ed.), *British Queer Cinema* (London: Routledge, 2006).

Miller, D., 'The Young and the Restless in Trinidad: A Case of the Local and Global in Mass Communication', in R. Silverstone and E. Hirsch (eds), *Consuming*

Technologies: Media and Information in Domestic Spaces (London: Routledge, 1992) pp. 163–82.

Mowlabocus, S., 'Life Outside the Latex: HIV, Sex and the Online Barebacking Community', in K. O'Riordan and D. J. Phillips (eds), *Queers Online: Media Technology and Sexuality* (New York: Peter Lang, 2007).

SECTION 5
MEDIA AND EVERYDAY LIFE

INTRODUCTION: MEDIA AND
EVERYDAY LIFE

We sleep through our lives in a dreamless slumber. But where is it, our life? Where are our bodies? Where is our space? (Georges Perec, cited in Clucas, 2000: 11)

The role of media systems within the constitution and practice of everyday life is one that media scholars are increasingly interested in exploring. What was once thought of as an offshoot of audience studies in the later decades of the twentieth century is now at the centre of a tradition of media anthropology that is being refreshed by the emergence of pervasive and locative media.

New media technologies are transforming the place of the media in home life and are contributing to the changing 'where' of the everyday. Increasingly, the pulse of the everyday, beating in streets, in workplaces, in transport hubs, in cars, trains, planes and buses as well as in homes, is multilayered and on the move, happening simultaneously here *and* there, or operating across thick global transport and communications connections. New work on the study of the role of the media in everyday life has set out to grapple with this shift, engaging with an established strand of largely ethnographic study that has explored the role of the media in the constitution of the everyday both through major theoretical works (e.g. Silverstone, 1984) and by way of media or site-specific historical studies.

There are many overlaps but a key distinction between reception studies and everyday life studies of the media is that the former tend to focus closely on audience responses to media *texts* (e.g. the Radway article in Chapter 36). Everyday life theorists expand the context of the text and they also attend to materiality, paying attention to ways in which the media artefact in its double or multiple articulation (Silverstone, 2006) is embedded materially as well as symbolically into the realm of the everyday. Studies of the media and everyday life thus expand and materialise the contexts of media use, and if they tend to decentre the media text somewhat, an exploration of the double articulation of the media (its medium and its message), which is an element of typical everyday life research, certainly does enable attention to be paid to the space-time shifting capabilities of the media and also provokes consideration of use or viewing as an *embodied* practice.

Henri Lefebvre, the sociologist of space, once said that everyday life had a certain obscurity. It is the site where our actions and practices, including those that are mediated, are revealed as largely routine, ritualised, habitual, embedded. What we do with the media on a daily basis is often insignificant. It is often gestural, inchoate and apparently having to do as much with our ontological security as with any desire to understand or be informed or even entertained. It is perhaps because so much of it is fleeting and unexplored that, even while it opens itself to us, something at the heart of everyday life – as a process we can fully understand or quantify – slides away. Blanchot, a French thinker in the same tradition as Lefebvre, described the contradictory nature of the everyday as 'platitude (what lags and falls behind, the residual life with which we fill our trash cans and cemeteries: scrap and refuse)', while also arguing that '. . . this banality is also what is most important if it brings us back to existence in its very spontaneity and as it is lived' (cited in Clucas, 2000: 10). The writing on the walls in Paris 1968 turned this into a politics of protest and a demand for transformation: 'Change Life'.

Media studies in this area are informed (directly and indirectly) by two distinct traditions. Already mentioned are Lefebvre and Blanchot, both associated with a body of French writing engaged in a critique of everyday life, often producing writings with a distinctive poetical style. Another important thinker here is De Certeau, whose *Practice of Everyday Life* explores the possibilities for tactical appropriation centred on stealing time in spaces that are largely owned and controlled by others (see Section 1).

There are parallels but also tensions between writings on the everyday in this tradition and approaches based on interpretive sociology and ethnomethodology. The latter include social action theorists such as Harold Garfinkel who set out to explore 'practical . . . reasoning in ordinary situations of action . . . how people realise and account for what they are and do' (Garfinkel, cited in Mattelart and Mattelart, 1995: 108–9) and also Alfred Schutz who studies everyday knowledge. One key difference between the French and US approaches concerns the degrees of self-reflexivity and agency accorded to social actors or social subjects within the structural constraints of an overarching system.

Joke Hermes (in Chapter 43) engages with both these traditions. In her study of magazine reading, Hermes takes up the question of the fragment, the scrap, the banal moment, and, like the French theorists of everyday life, finds it worthy of attention. However, she objects to the abstraction of the poetics of everyday life developed by French writers in this tradition – particularly that of De Certeau – which she says celebrates as resistance what is often drudgery, boredom and tedium. In their place she draws upon symbolic interactionist approaches of American interpretive sociology. Considering woman's magazines, which are often unread and which mostly go unremarked upon, Hermes explores 'salience' in the context of everyday media use, asking what happens 'when . . . use becomes meaningful' and what happens when it doesn't: when it remains 'virtually meaningless'. The centre of attention here is shifted from a question of the media text (content) and its signification, to the quotidian, which is to say to the matters and rhythms of daily life. The attempt is to open up the significance *users* accord to the experience of reading, glancing, flicking, of using media without stopping to think. The research upon which this article is based was conducted by exploring the interpretive frameworks (repertoires) readers use to legitimate their activities. This was done while also conducting a parallel – and more ethnographic – exploration of the use of magazines in routines, work days and 'living one's life the way one does' (520). Hermes' account thus looks at the capacity of different media to enable particular kinds of time-shifting, to reorganise the flow of events from the outside space into the lifeworld of the home. A focus on medium-specific features is matched by a rethinking of the user: now viewed less as a reader/non-reader than an embodied practitioner, an actor, thinking, feeling experiencing and producing an everyday life.

Writing exploring media technology and innovation has often focused on the everyday – and particularly the domestic – as a key site for debate on the social shaping of media technologies (the contrast is with the home as the site for textual reception). This tradition draws substantially on the work of feminist studies (for instance, work on domestic technology by Cynthia Coburn and others). It recognises that grasping the life cycle or the cultural biography of media systems requires a detour through embodied use even if the technology, at that point becoming invisible because scarcely noticed, is often no longer seen as technological at all (Bassett, 2007). Ann Gray's work on the use of video recorders in the home (Chapter 41) provides a classic case study of how pre-existing gender relations help shape the way a technology is incorporated and finds an identity in the home. The family – the site for 'constant social negotiation' – articulates this through the VCR which, while it may offer increased time flexibility and control for some members of the family, closes it down for others. Gray also makes a return to symbolic text, binding up the social context of reception, the time-shifting capacities of the technology which transform the rhythm of family life, with the gendered reception of content.

David Morley (Chapter 43) gathers up and expands upon work exploring domesticity and the home in relation to the dislocations and relocations performed by global media networks. In many ways a piece that speaks to the Askoy and Robins extract in the previous section (Chapter 40), it is concerned with the various 'modalities' of belonging. The optic is the home and the goal is to get at the central role which the media play in forming a particular kind of domesticity. The premise of the *Royale Family*, highly popular at the time of Morley's writing, is that family life and watching TV are indistinguishable. People have a 'habit of living with television' and it is this mutual imbrication Morley seeks to open up. As he views it a certain return to the home, a stress on the local form of life and the space of 'first-hand emotions' is complemented by a deterritorialisation of home space, a 'domestication of elsewhere': the same pervasive media networks enable both articulations (although their intensity may well be very different) and also to some extent connect them. The domestication of (media) technology thus has to do with how we understand and practice 'home'.

Part of what is at issue here is how the way of life characterised as mobile privatisation and associated by Raymond Williams with twentieth-century television, the car and the suburban home is being reforged. The key terms operating here are nostalgia (to be expected given the status of the home as a focus for family history and memory) and futurology. The material incorporation and embedding in the uses and practices and rhythms of the household of a new media artefact draws on both of these symbolic repositories, says Morley. Through these technologies the domestic space and domestic time is re-imagined, both within the framing context of 'home' with its connotations of stability and fixity and as the hub for new forms of technologised life: smart living perhaps, through the context of discourses of technology as future promise.

Clearly recourse to functional explanations does not explain these processes; Morley notes a more anthropological view is required – one that can recognise the influence of symbolic meanings on where and how a piece of technology is domesticated – and also one that draws on and understands the influence of taste cultures. His conclusion essentially is firstly that technology is now constitutive of what a home is, as well as supplemental to a sense of the domestic that stands external to it – and secondly that with the mobile we perhaps see a dispersal of the domestic so that, as he puts it, the mobile phone fills public spaces with the chatter of the hearth allowing us to take our home with us, as a tortoise stays in its shell as it travels. (Morley: 533).

Michael Bull, considering the iPod (Chapter 44), retains a focus on everyday life but does not begin with the shared domestic space at all, staying with the intimate, personal world of the traveller, often the city commuter. There is a certain romanticism in this account, which might be said to resonate with the poetic style of the French theorists – but it is also true that the informants involved in this article are given considerable voice through extended quotes. What is clear is that music has a particular power for Bull, who claims that it enables 'iPod users to construct meaningful and pleasurable narratives out of the routine linear and cyclical practices of their everyday movement through the city' (540). Most of Bull's participants are also enamoured – there are people who love their pods enough to want to talk about their experience – people who wish for 'no dead air'. Bull's point, however, is that the obviously compensatory nature of these forms of experience do not detract from 'the fact that the experiences might still be understood as oppositional, creative and pleasurable'. An interesting tension in this work is that degree to which these reflexive and conscious forms of management of experience are set in train in order precisely to release the listener into the power of music – which remains 'a largely utopian place' in consumer desire even while it also fills the streets (Bull: 540).

Bull's focus on the urban emerges in fact out of this sense of competing soundscapes: the pre-packaged (lift music, café music), the incidental (urban noise) and the chosen queue of iPod tunes. He also asks how the private sound-worlds into which users retreat functions to assist users in managing their presence in and experience of the fragmented but 'eversame' (Bull: 549) life of cities – by privatising them.

REFERENCES

Bassett, C., *The Arc and the Machine* (Manchester: Manchester University Press, 2007).

Clucas, S., 'Cultural Phenomenology and the Everyday', *Critical Quarterly* 42:1 (2000) pp. 8–34.

Cockburn, C., 'The Circuit of Technology: Gender Identity and Power', in R. Silverstone and E. Hirsch (eds), *Consuming Technologies* (London, Routledge, 1992) pp. 33–42.

Mattelart, A. and Mattelart, M., *Theories of Communication* (London: Sage, 1998).

Silverstone, R., *Television and Everyday Life* (London: Routledge, 1984).

Silverstone, R., 'Domesticating Domestication: Reflections on the Life of a Concept', in T. Berker, M. Hartmann, Y. Punie and K. J. Ward (eds), *Domestication of Media and Technology* (London: McGraw-Hill, 2006) pp. 229–48.

41

BEHIND CLOSED DOORS: VIDEO RECORDERS IN THE HOME

Ann Gray

The video cassette recorder is arguably the major innovation in home entertainment in Britain since television. When we address questions of how women watch television and video we inevitably raise a complex set of issues which relate to women and their everyday lives. In talking to women about home video cassette recorders (VCR) and television use, I have identified some of the determining factors surrounding these activities which take place within the domestic environment.[1] With the development of VCRs and other products such as home computers and cable services, the 1980s is seeing an ever increasing trend towards home-centred leisure and entertainment. New technology in the home has to be understood within a context of structures of power and authority relationships between household members, with gender emerging as one of the most significant differentiations. This far from neutral environment influences the ways in which women use popular texts in general and television and video in particular, and the pleasures and meanings which these have for them.

[. . .]

Video and Family Life

Although there are many aspects of the video phenomenon which are worthy of study, my research initially focuses on the potential choice which the VCR offers for viewing within the domestic and family context. The major reason for this is that, until recently, attention to the context of viewing seems to have

From H. Baehr and G. Dyer (eds), *Boxed In: Women and Television* (London: Pandora Press, 1987) pp. 38–54.

been largely neglected in media and cultural studies.[2] The relationship between the viewer and television, the reader and text, is often a relationship which has to be negotiated, struggled for, won or lost, in the dynamic and often chaotic processes of family life. As video recorders offer, above all, extended choice of content and time management for viewing within the home, research into its use has to be focused within that very context. The context of 'the family' is, for my purposes, conceived of as a site of constant social negotiation within a highly routinised framework of material dependency and normative constraint,[3] and all these elements enter into the negotiations which surround viewing decisions. This family setting, with its power relationships and authority structures across gender, is an extremely import.nt factor in thinking more generally of 'leisure' and, specifically, home-based leisure. The home has increasingly become the site for entertainment, and we can see VCRs as yet one more commodity which reduces the necessity for household members to seek entertainment outside the home, a situation reinforced by the present economic climate in Britain:

> JS: Well, we can't really afford to go out to the pictures, not any more. If we all go and have ice-creams, you're talking about eight or nine pounds. It's a lot of money.

What is especially important for women is that the domestic sphere is increasingly becoming defined as their only leisure space. Many married women are in paid work outside the home, but women are still largely responsible for the domestic labour in the home. Childcare, food provision, laundry, shopping and cleaning the living space, are ultimately women's responsibility even if their male partners help. While men in paid employment come home to a non-work environment, women who either work in the home all day or go out to paid employment still have to work at home in the evenings and at weekends:

> AS: Him? Oh, he sits on his backside all night, from coming in from work to going to bed.

Indeed, many women do not consider themselves as having any leisure at all. (Deem, 1984). And many certainly would not allow themselves the luxury of sitting down to watch television until the children are fed and put to bed and the household chores have been completed:

> JK: I'd feel guilty, I'd feel I was cheating. It's my job and if I'm sat, I'm not doing my job.

This is a context which, at the most basic and practical level, positions women in relation to the whole area of leisure, but particularly in relation to television and video viewing:

AS: Like, if he comes in and he's rented a video, straight after tea he wants to put it on. I say 'well let me finish the washing-up first'. I mean, I just wouldn't enjoy it if I knew it was all to do.

VIDEO AS TECHNOLOGY

Women and men have differential access to technology in general and to domestic technology in particular. The relations between domestic technology and gender are relatively unexplored,[4] though there is more work on gender and technology in the workplace where, as Jan Zimmerman notes, new technology is entering existing and traditional sets of relations. Old values in this way become encoded in new technologies (Zimmerman, 1981; Cockburn, 1983, 1985). It is interesting to note that American researchers discovered that in the early 1970s the full-time housewife was spending as much time on housework as her grandmother had done fifty years earlier. Domestic technology may be labour-saving, replacing the drudgery of household work, but it is time-consuming in that each piece of equipment requires work if it is to fulfil its advertised potential. Rothschild argues that far from liberating women from housework, new technology, embedded as it is in ideological assumptions about the sexual division of labour, has further entrenched women in the home and in the role of housewife (Rothschild, 1983).

When a new piece of technology is purchased or rented, it is often already inscribed with gender expectations. The gender specificity of pieces of domestic technology is deeply implanted in the 'commonsense' of households, operating almost at an unconscious level. As such it is difficult for the researcher to unearth. One strategy I have employed which throws the gender of domestic technology into high relief is to ask the women to image pieces of equipment as coloured either pink or blue.[5] This produces almost uniformly pink irons and blue electric drills, with many interesting mixtures along the spectrum. The washing machine, for example, is most usually pink on the outside, but the motor is almost always blue. VCRs and, indeed, all home entertainment technology would seem to be a potentially lilac area, but my research has shown that we must break down the VCR into its different modes in our colour-coding. The 'record', 'rewind' and 'play' modes are usually lilac, but the timer switch is nearly always blue, with women having to depend on their male partners or their children to set the timer for them. The blueness of the timer is exceeded only by the deep indigo of the remote control switch which in all cases is held by the man:

SW: Oh, yes, that's definitely blue in our house. He flicks from channel to channel, I never know what I'm watching – it drives me mad.

It does appear that the male of the household is generally assumed to have knowledge of this kind of technology when it enters the household, or at least he will quickly gain the knowledge. And certain knowledges can, of course, be withheld and used to maintain authority and control:

> AS: Well, at first he was the only one who knew how to record things, but then me and my young son sat down one day and worked it out. That meant we didn't have to keep asking him to record something for us.

Although women routinely operate extremely sophisticated pieces of domestic technology, often requiring, in the first instance, the study and application of a manual of instructions, they often feel alienated from operating the VCR. The reasons for this are manifold and have been brought about by positioning within the family, the education system and the institutionalised sexism with regard to the division of appropriate activities and knowledges in terms of gender. Or there may be, as I discovered, 'calculated ignorance':

> CH: If I learnt how to do the video it would become my job just like everything else.

If women do not feel confident or easy in approaching and operating the recorders, let alone in setting the timer for advance recording, they are at an immediate and real disadvantage in terms of exercising the apparent choices which the VCR offers. This, combined with constraints in the hiring of video tapes, either financial or simply normative, means that for women the idea of increased freedom and choice of viewing may well be spurious.

Genre and Gender

If women are 'positioned' within the context of consumption, it seems that they are also positioned, or even structured in absence, by the video industry itself in terms of the kind of audience it seems to be addressing. To enter a video library is to be visually bombarded by 'covers' depicting scenes of horror, action adventure, war, westerns and 'soft' pornography, traditionally considered to be 'male' genres.[6] Is it therefore mainly men who are hiring video tapes, and if so, what do women feel about the kinds of tapes they are watching at home? Do women ever hire tapes themselves, or do they feel alienated from both the outlets and what they have to offer? In other words, what are the circumstances surrounding the use of video libraries and what is the sexual division of labour associated with the hiring and viewing of tapes? I have already made reference to the so-called 'male' genres which imply that certain kinds of films address themselves to and are enjoyed by a male audience and the same, of course, could be said for 'female' genres. But why do certain kinds of texts or genres appeal to women and not to men and *vice versa* and how should we conceive of the audience for these texts made up of women and men?

The 'gendered audience' has a theoretical history which, as Annette Kuhn usefully points out, has developed within two different perspectives, one emerging from media studies and the other from film theory (Kuhn, 1984). This has resulted in two quite different notions of the gendered audience. The sociological emphasis of media studies has tended to conceive of a 'social audience', that is, an audience made up of already constituted male and female persons who bring (among other things) maleness or femaleness to a text, and who decode the text within that particular frame of reference. Film theory on the other hand, has conceived of a 'psychological audience', a collection of individual spectators who do not read the text, but rather the text 'reads' them. In other words, the film offers a masculine or feminine subject position and the spectator occupies that position. Of course, this is not automatic and there is nothing to prevent, for example, a female spectator taking up a masculine subject position. However, the construction of masculinity and femininity across the institutions within society is so powerfully aligned to the social categories 'male' and 'female' that the two usually coincide apparently seamlessly. But, as Kuhn points out, what is suggested by these two perspectives is a distinction between femaleness as a social gender and femininity as a subject position. The problem here is that neither of these two perspectives is sufficient in themselves to gain a full understanding of what happens when men and women watch films. In the former case, context is emphasised over text and in the latter text over context. The spectator–text relationship suggested by the psychoanalytic models used in film theory tend to disregard those important factors of social context involved in film and TV watching. Also, they find it difficult to allow for the subject constituted outside the text, across other discourses, such as class, race, age and general social environment. The social audience approach, conversely, sees the response to texts as a socially predetermined one, and in this way does not allow for consideration of how the texts themselves work on the viewers/readers.

There have been some attempts to link text with context by examining the particular features of 'women's genres'. Soap operas, for example, have been looked at in terms of their distinctive narrative pattern, which is open-ended and continuous; their concern with so-called 'female' skills; their scheduling on television which fits into the rhythm of women's work at home, all of which can be seen as specifically addressing a social audience of women (Brunsdon, 1981; Modleski, 1982). However, this would still seem to stress context over text and in this area the film theory perspective has certainly been limited by its implicit assumption of an intense and concentrated relationship between spectator and text in a darkened cinema. For television this relationship is more likely to be characterised by distinction and diversion. As Kuhn points out:

> This would suggest that each medium constructs sexual difference through spectatorship in rather different ways: cinema through the look and spectacle, and TV – perhaps less evidently – through a capacity to insert its flow, its characteristic modes of address and the textual

operations of different kinds of programmes into the rhythms and routines of domestic activities and sexual divisions of labour in the household at various times of day. (Kuhn, 1984, p. 25)

This distinction is important and useful, but when thinking about the use of VCRs the two media are viewed in the same context. Movies have long been a part of television's nightly 'flow' as well as part of daytime viewing. But in video recording movies off television for watching at a later date, and in hiring movies, we have a discrete 'event' which disrupts the flow of television and its insertive scheduling:

> AC: Oh yes, we all sit down and watch – 'we've got a video, let's sit down' – TV's different, that's just on.

Concepts of the psychological audience and the social audience are not sufficient in themselves to explore the whole complexity of text, subject and context and the ways in which they intersect. But both are necessary, representing as they do different instances within the process of consumption of popular texts. While the psychological model posits an unacceptably homogeneous and 'universal' audience, it does allow us to consider the importance of how texts work, not only in terms of subject positioning and interpellation, but also in terms of pleasure and desire. The social model demands that the audience is heterogeneous and requires us to explore those other differences and contexts which, to a greater or lesser extent, determine the ways in which women and men read those texts. It seems clear that the problem of the relationship between text and gendered audience cannot be resolved at the theoretical level, but rather must be kept in play and, if possible, problematised throughout the research enterprise.

Viewing Contexts

It would seem that women do have certain preconceptions about what constitutes a 'film for men' as against a 'film for women', and furthermore, a typology of viewing contexts is beginning to emerge, along with appropriate associated texts (see Table [41.1]).

I wish to focus mainly on Context (Female alone), but before I do it is worth mentioning the difference between the negotiations around Contexts (Male alone) and (Female alone). For the latter to exist, the male partner must normally be out of the house, either at work or at leisure, whereas Context (Male alone) would be likely to exist when both male and female were in the house together. The women simply wouldn't watch:

> BA: If he's watching something I'm not enjoying, I'll either knit or read.
> JS: Well, I can read when the telly's on if it's something I don't like.

DS: I usually go to bed with a book, or sometimes I'll watch the portable in the kitchen, but it's damned uncomfortable in there.

CH: Well, when he's in, Father has priority over what's on. Yes, he does, but I can go in the other room if I don't want to watch it.

WOMEN ONLY

For women who are at home all day, either with very small children or children of school age, and whose husbands are out at work, there are obvious opportunities for them to view alone. However, most of the women I have talked to are constrained by guilt, often referring to daytime viewing as some kind of drug:

SW: No, I've got too many things to do during the daytime, I couldn't do it to myself, I'd be a total addict.

JK: Well, I watch *Falcon Crest* – it's a treat, when I've done my work, then I sit down and it's my treat. But I'm not one to get videos during the day because I think you can get really addicted, then everything else suffers.

The second woman quoted indicates what is a fairly common strategy – that of using daytime television programmes to establish some time for herself as a reward to which completion of household tasks will lead. This assuages the guilt to a certain extent and the pleasure afforded by this particular viewing context seems to go far beyond the pleasures of the text itself. What it represents is a breathing space when the busy mother can resist the demands of her children and domestic labour for a brief period of time. One of the most popular daytime programmes cited was *Sons & Daughters*, an Australian imported soap opera, transmitted three afternoons a week in the Yorkshire region. Most of the women preferred to watch this alone, some taking the telephone off the hook to ensure uninterrupted concentration, but they would watch it with a friend if they happened to be in each other's houses at the time. Janice Radway in her study of women and romantic fiction talks with regret of the isolated context within which popular romances are consumed by women (Radway, 1984). The next viewing context I wish to discuss reveals a more optimistic state of affairs for women.

This context is again female only, but is one in which several women get together to watch a video which they have hired jointly. This would normally happen during the day when their children are at school. Far from being instrumental in isolating women, it would seem that there is a tendency to communal use of hired videos, mainly on economic grounds, but also on the grounds that the women can watch what they want together without the guilt or the distraction of children:

BS: There are three of us, and we hire two or three films a week and watch them together, usually at Joyce's house when the kids are at school. We can choose what we want then.

Table [41.1]   *Typology of viewing contexts*[7]

Context	Film	TV
1 Family together	*Superman*	Children's TV
	Walt Disney	Quiz shows
	Jaws	Comedy
2 Male and female partners together	*An Officer and a Gentleman*	Aufwiedersehen Pet
	Kramer v. Kramer	*Minder*
	The Rockys	Shows
	Any Clint Eastwood	*Coronation Street*
		EastEnders
3 Male alone	War	Sport
	Action adventure*	News
	Horror*	Documentaries
	Adults*	
4 Female alone	*Who Will Love My Children?*	*Coronation Street*
	Evergreen	*Crossroads*
	Romance	*Dallas*
		Dynasty
		A Woman of Substance
		Princess Daisy

* These are the category headings used by many video libraries

> JK: Yes, if there's something we want to see we wait 'til the kids have gone back to school so's we can sit and watch it without them coming in saying 'can I have . . . can I have . . .' it makes it difficult.

The idea of viewing toegether during the day for this particular network of women living on the same street came when one of them found herself continually returning the video tapes which her husband had hired the night before. She discovered that there were films which she would like to watch but which her husband never hired. A good relationship was established with the woman who worked in the video library who would look out for good films:

> BS: She comes into the shop where I work and I go 'have any new videos come out?' She tells me. She knows what we like.

One favoured form for this viewing network is that of the long family saga, often running to two or three tapes:

> JK: We like something in two or three parts; something with a really good story to it so's you can get involved.

> BS: Mm ... the other week we had a Clint Eastwood and Burt Reynolds film because she [MD] likes Clint Eastwood but we talked all the way through that, didn't we?

When the group views sagas which extend over two or three tapes there is obvious pleasure in anticipating both the outcome of the narrative and the viewing of the following tape. A considerable amount of discussion and speculation ensues and a day for the next viewing is fixed:

> MD: We like to spread them out – every other day, it helps to break the week up. Sometimes we have them on an evening, if our husbands are away or out. We'll have a bottle of wine then, then we don't even have to get up to make a cup of tea.

These women are also devotees of the American soap operas and operate a 'failsafe' network of video recording for each other, refusing to discuss each episode until they have all seen it. These popular texts form an important part of their friendship and association in their everyday lives and give a focus to an almost separate female culture which they can share together within the constraints of their positions as wives and mothers. Furthermore, they are able to take up the feminine subject positions offered by these texts comfortably and pleasurably. In contrast, the films which their husbands hire for viewing Context (Male and female partners together) mainly offer a masculine subject position which the women seem to take up through their male partners, who in turn give their approval to such texts.

The major impetus for a viewing group like this is that films which women enjoy watching are rarely, if ever, hired by their male partners for viewing together because they consider such films to be 'trivial' and 'silly' and women are laughed at for enjoying them:

> BA: I sit there with tears running down my face and he comes in and says 'you daft thing.'

This derision also applies to soap operas, and is reproduced in male children:

> JK: Oh, my son thinks I'm stupid because I won't miss Dallas – perhaps I am.

It is the most powerful member within the household who defines this hierarchy of 'serious' and 'silly', 'important' and 'trivial'. This leaves women and their pleasures in films downgraded, objects and subjects of fun and derision, having to consume them almost in secret. But the kinds of films and television soap operas which women enjoy watching alone deal with things of importance to them, highlighting so-called 'female' concerns – care of children, concern for members of one's own family, consideration for one's own sexual partner, selflessness in characters – all of which are the skills of competence, the thought and caring which husbands and children expect of women and assume as a matter of natural course.[8] This is a deeply contradictory position for women, lying between the realities of their day-to-day lives and the pleasures and gratifications that they seek to find in texts that their partners and very often their children, look upon as so much rubbish:

> JS: think a lot of storylines in soap operas are very weak and I think a man needs something to keep his interest more than a woman. That makes a man sound more intelligent, but that's not what I mean. It's got to be something worth watching before he'll sit down and actually watch it, but I'd watch anything. I think he thinks its unmanly to watch them.
>
> SW: All the soap operas are rubbish for men, fantasy for women.
>
> AG: *Do you think men need fantasy?*
>
> SW: They need fantasy in a different way, detectives and wars, that's their fantasy world, and science fiction, a tough, strong world. Not sloppy, who's fallen in love with who, who's shot JR – it's rubbish. Men know it's rubbish, that's the difference.

Here are two women talking about a genre they love in relation to their male partners, giving us a sense of the 'power of definition' within the partnerships, but also the ways in which the women themselves think of their own pleasures.

CONCLUSION

Theories of the gendered audience as they have been developed are useful, but when women and men watch movies and television they become that hybrid, the *social spectator* (Kuhn, ibid.) and, in understanding the subject–text–context relationship, the social and the psychological have to be kept in play to a proportionately greater or lesser degree. This allows us to consider how texts and contexts (both the specific and the wider social context) combine together in producing the gendered reading subject. Charlotte Brunsdon, writing on *Crossroads*, has attempted to resolve this dualism and suggests that, 'The relation of the audience to the text will not be determined solely by that text, but also by positionalities in relation to a whole range of other discourses – discourses of motherhood, romance and sexuality for example' (Brunsdon, 1981, p. 32).

This enables us to think of the subject in the social context occupying different positions in relation to different discourses which change across time. As particular discourses become central issues, they will affect the ways in which the social subject occupies, or resists, the subject position constructed by a text.

The viewing and reading of texts takes place, for the majority of people, within the domestic context. However, this is a context which is not singular and unchanging, but plural and open to different permutations, dependent upon the negotiations between members of the household and the particular texts involved. The VCR offers the potential for extended choice of viewing in terms of text and context. But in order to explore how this potential is being used the particular conditions of its consumption must be addressed. The viewing contexts and their associated texts which I have outlined here have emerged from my discussions with women who occupy different social positions and there are remarkable similarities in the ways in which all the women have spoken about their domestic viewing practices. However, it is simply not sufficient to have identified these similarities, and my analysis of the interview 'texts' continues in an attempt to make visible the important differences between the women's accounts of these practices. These differences must be seen in relation to their particular social positioning and the various specific discourses which they inhabit. The interview material I have gathered demands a framework of analysis which uses theories and concepts developed within different disciplines and will, I am sure, test their relative strengths and weaknesses in revealing the complexity of how women relate to television and video in their everyday lives.

NOTES

1. This research was initially funded by the Economic and Social Research Council and has taken the form of long, open-ended discussions with women whose age, social position, employment and family circumstances differ (race is a variable which has not been introduced). Part of my strategy has been to encourage open discussion and allow the women themselves to introduce topics which are of importance to them. By keeping the discussions open they can take pleasure in having the opportunity to explore and express their own ideas and feelings on these matters. For discussions on feminist research methods see Roberts (ed.), 1981; Stanley and Wise, 1983; Bell and Roberts, 1984.
2. There are notable exceptions (Hobson, 1981 and 1982; Morley, 1986; Collett, 1986).
3. I am grateful to Elizabeth Shove and Andrew Tudor for this working definition.
4. However, a recent publication by W. Faulkner and E. Arnold (eds), *Smothered by Invention Technology in Women's Lives*, Pluto Press, 1985, does address issues of domestic technology and gender.
5. These were ideas discussed at a seminar given by Cynthia Cockburn at York University, June 1985. See also Cockburn, 1985.
6. It is interesting to note that video tapes are now being distributed which are specifically aimed at a female audience; IPC and Videospace combined magazine and video to market their *Woman's Own Selection*, along with their more recent label *Image of Love*, while Polygram Video are offering a label, *Women's Choice*. However, in the North of England certainly, these have a very limited distribution.
7. These are the names which the women themselves gave to the different texts and genres.
8. Charlotte Brunsdon has made this point in relation to *Crossroads*, but we can see that it can apply to other 'women's genres' (Brunsdon, 1981).

REFERENCES

Barker, M. (ed.) (1984), *The Video Nasties*, London, Pluto Press.

Bell, C. and Roberts, H. (eds) (1984), *Social Researching*, London, Routledge & Kegan Paul.

Brunsdon, C. (1981), 'Crossroads: Notes on a soap opera', *Screen*, vol. 22, no. 4, pp. 32–7.

Cockburn, C. (1983), *Brothers*, London, Pluto Press.

Cockburn, C. (1985), *Machinery of Dominance*, London, Pluto Press.

Collett, P. (1986), 'Watching the TV audience', paper presented to International Television Studies Conference 1986.

Deem, R. (1984), 'Paid work, leisure and non-employment: shifting boundaries and gender differences', paper presented to British Sociological Association Conference 1984.

Hobson, D. (1981), 'Housewives and the mass media', in Hall, S. *et al.* (eds), *Culture, Media, Language*, London, Hutchinson.

Hobson, D. (1982), *'Crossroads': The Drama of a Soap Opera*, London, Methuen.

Kuhn, A. (1984), 'Women's genres', *Screen*, vol. 25, no. 1, Jan/Feb, pp. 18–28.

Modleski, T. (1982), *Loving With a Vengeance*, Hamden, Connecticut, Shoe String Press.

Morley, D. (1986), *Family Television: Cultural Power and Domestic Leisure*, London, Comedia.

Radway, J. A. (1984), *Reading the Romance*, Chapel Hill, University of North Carolina Press.

Roberts, H. (ed.) (1981), *Doing Feminist Research*, London, Routledge & Kegan Paul.

Rothschild, J. (1983), *Machina ex Dea*, New York, Pergamon Press.

Stanley, L. and Wise, S. (1983), *Breaking Out*, London, Routledge & Kegan Paul.

Zimmerman, J. (1981), 'Technology and the future of women: haven't we met somewhere before?', *Women's Studies International Quarterly*, vol. 4, no. 3, p. 355.

42

MEDIA, MEANING AND EVERYDAY LIFE

Joke Hermes

Stuart Hall's 'We are all in our heads different audiences at once', for me marks the definitive move away from a paradigm that was organized around texts producing subjectivies. Even though Hall related the different audiences we are to the text, he also said: 'We have the capacity to deploy different levels and modes of attention, to mobilise different competences in our viewing. At different times of the day, for different family members, different patterns of viewing have different "saliences"' (1986: 10). The departing point for this paper exactly is the question of salience. Or, more to the point, given the shift in media studies towards the audience and contexts of viewing, how and when everyday media use becomes meaningful needs to be carefully thought through. One of David Morley's respondents in *Family Television*, who has a habit of putting the television on in the early morning, says: 'Sometimes I intend to look at it ... but ... at the end of it I've seen everything but I've heard nothing. You know what I mean?' (1986: 56). Do we know what she means?

I suggest that from time to time, all of us (some perhaps more often than others), engage in virtually meaningless media use. In this paper I will argue that the consequences of such a point of departure, of radically decentring the media text in favour of an understanding of the specific routines of the everyday that media use is part of, are a challenge epistemologically and will constitute more space politically than a number of recent audience studies have done. I will draw upon my own research on women's magazines, based on seventy-five lengthy interviews with readers; upon David Morley's work on

From *Cultural Studies* 7:3 (1993) pp. 493–506.

families watching television and a small number of texts addressing the issues involved in studying media use and/or everyday life.

[. . .]

My respondents described their everyday lives as singularly stable and set routines. Routine easily associated with daily drag. But built into the routines was potential pleasure, too. It ranged, indeed, from sitting down with a cup of tea and a magazine that has just been bought, or in the summer going to a trailer that has been rented year after year with a shopping bag, passed on by a sister or a neighbour, crammed full with romances. There also was potential boredom: watching television is more rewarding if one is prepared for the occasional uninteresting items. And, only occasionally acknowledged, there is danger of the routines and pleasures breaking up . . . Everyday life is something of an enigma. Bausinger stresses its stability. Schutz (1973) defines everyday life by its taken-for-grantedness. Birte Bech Jørgensen, in her research on female youth employment, found that such a perspective didn't fit her interview material, nor does it fit mine.

> Modern everyday life is created as doubleness on the one hand of continuity, of trust and certainty, made possible by the norms, rules and routines of everyday life. And, on the other hand, change and a more or less frightening and joyful urge for autonomy. (Bech Jørgensen, 1990: 22)

Bech Jørgensen feels that the ways of handling the conditions of everyday life are basically repetitive, intuitive *and* inventive (1990: 22). Lodged deep within the everyday there is also transformative power, perceptible especially in the case of ruptures and dramas when the taken-for-grantedness is broken (1990: 23). Routines may fall short of their reassuring function, because of tensions in a relationship, unemployment or chance happenings. The point is to recognize that the everyday, on the one hand, is the site of the utterly superficial and repetitive that we need to respect for the sense of security it gives and, on the other hand, potentially is the site of major personal and societal change. (The women's movement is a case in point. In the early seventies women were mobilized on their feelings of dissatisfaction regarding their everyday routines.) Both sides to the everyday need to be part of media research.[1] Before I turn to the question of how to recognize routines, the boredom, the pleasures and the faultlines, the account needs to be settled regarding the issue of superficiality and everyday taken-for-grantedness.

The superficiality of accounts of media use partly is real, in the sense that it reflects taken-for-grantedness and pleasure derived from things being the way they are. Repetitiveness, knowing where to find what in a magazine or being familiar with the routines of a quiz show, or the formula of a popular genre can be reassuring, a guarantee one's viewing or reading pleasures will not be interfered with or uprooted. As one women's magazine reader put it: 'Reading those tips, you are reminded of all sorts of things that you knew already but kind of had forgotten.' In a sense then, media use may quite often be relatively meaningless.

The superficiality of interview transcripts also needs to be understood as an academic artefact, however. Media texts have been invested with so much meaning, anyone would be hard put to come up with an interesting reading. The audiences that have been researched, have, more often than not, been fans. Knowledgeable, ardent readers and television viewers have come to be confused with 'average' viewers and readers.[2] In other cases researchers switch from a reader perspective to a text-based perspective which saves them from engaging with questions regarding how media ordinarily become meaningful in everyday life.

[. . .]

Since we have some knowledge of how fans experience their favourite texts as meaningful and pleasurable[3] and also of how choice, use and pleasure are caught up in specific arrangements of the domestic[4] the issue is: how to deal with media use as a secondary, relatively meaningless activity; how to understand people's descriptions of such media use? How are all those texts one is not a 'fan' of, but that are used regularly, made sense of? In my own research project I have tried to foreground that a major part of media use is routine triggered behaviour that isn't meaningful in itself but as part of how (everyday) life is organized. Not *all* media use is meaningless. Meaninglessness, I believe, is part of media use in the sense that one simply cannot stop and think about every single thing one does during a normal day's work and leisure, in and outside of the home. Life is largely organized around routines that do not allow for elaborate self-reflection.

To use the word 'meaninglessness' is to dive headlong into a sea full of mines. The least one can do is defuse a number of them. No, I am not writing up yet another way of putting down not just everyday media use but also the quintessential everyday media consumer: someone supposedly lacking in cultural capital, or lacking in ambition to make her surroundings meaningful. This is not about different types of readers but about different ways of reading that all of us engage in. And no, I don't think that in this case the relative 'meaninglessness' of media use must be understood to mean that it is unresearchable. To clarify the position I take here, I will briefly turn to the work of Michel de Certeau, widely read expert on everyday life and how/whether it becomes meaningful.

De Certeau in *The Practice of Everyday Life* (1984) suggests we need to differentiate between tactics, (ways of making-do, *arts de faire*) and strategies. Strategies are used by such total institutions as armies, cities or supermarket chains to create and delimit their own place. Tactics, calculated actions determined by the absence of a proper locus, tend to insert themselves in these spaces that are created for the maintenance of power (de Certeau, 1984: 36–7).

Reading, in the framework sketched by de Certeau, like poaching, strolling, cooking or dwelling is 'to wander through an imposed system (that of the text, analogous to the constructed order of a city or a supermarket)' (1984: 169). Wanderers don't acquire status or build their memories and pleasures into recollectable structures, monuments so to speak.

> Writing accumulates, stocks up, resists time by the establishment of a place and multiplies its production through the expansionism of reproduction. Reading takes no measures against the erosion of time (one forgets oneself and also forgets), it does not keep what it acquires, or it does so poorly, and each of the places through which it passes is a repetition of the lost paradise. (1984: 174)

Theoretically, I couldn't agree more with the point put forward. Texts cannot impose upon readers how they are to be read. But, the nomadic imagery de Certeau offers is in fact a description (or so I believe) of having to serve your family meals seven days per week; or go to work every day; of going to the shops to find bargains in order to stretch a limited budget. Not only does de Certeau romanticize everyday life to an unacceptable extent; he also closes off all possibilities of change using a polar model of domination that is strengthened rather than changed by the tactics 'ordinary' people use and, thirdly, theorizing everyday life along these lines amounts to saying that the meanings and doings (one hesitates to say 'pleasures') of ordinary people can only be understood by actually doing it. As Frow points out:

> In the absence of realized texts which can be subject to determinate analysis – in the absence of a definite and graspable object – the analyst will inevitably reconstruct such an object. . . . [The result of which] . . . is a politically fraught substitution of the voice of a middle-class intellectual for that of the users of popular culture; and it is characteristically in the space of this substitution that the category of the popular is constructed. (1991: 60)

De Certeau's polar model of domination has high romantic quality. But it totally discounts that viewers will try to explain and legitimize their media use. It might well be the case that we have to do without academic understanding of the transient and fleeting qualities of media use, and that using 'meaninglessness' as a descriptive label is an act of power that delimits a proper space for academic knowledge. But for a researcher there is more to be found in interview transcripts, be it fragmented and in bits and pieces here and there, than either de Certeau or Frow would give one reason to believe. The issue is to understand the relative importance of the media text and media use. Relative, that is, to other practices people engage in at the same time. These other practices, in the case of such media use as reading women's magazines or viewing television, will quite often be routines that can be described; for the practices themselves there exists widely spread legitimatory discourse. The two together, descriptions of routines and legitimatory discourse, add up to a strong description of how media are used, that put 'meaninglessness' in perspective and make it researchable by default as it were, as a residue. The superficiality of interview transcripts that deal with the most ordinary of media use is a warning sign but not an impregnable barrier.

It is my point of view that people are rational, social actors who within the limited space and means available to them will have good reasons for doing the things they do, even if these 'good reasons' cannot always be clearly stated or articulated. Going back to the interview transcripts, there seem to be two sources of knowledge that one may draw on to come to an understanding of everyday media use. In the accounts people gave me they explained about their daily routines (which is one source), superimposed on these routines, specific legitimatory discourse, schemata that explain and justify media use, can be recognized. These schemata I will call interpretive repertoires. To analyze how media texts are made sense of, I propose that one has to make these repertoires explicit. Secondly, one has to map the sedimented, everyday routines readers give accounts of, on to how they have come to understand themselves as readers and viewers over the years, bearing in mind that for most this is accepted knowledge, not something to question or reflect upon.

During the course of my peregrinations I taped interviews with about sixty women, fifteen men and the occasional child . . .

I asked these readers to tell me about their 'reading histories', their everyday lives, their ambitions and their use of women's magazines and other mass media. The interviews were modelled on everyday lengthy conversation, as between friends. Most of the interview usually wasn't taken up with women's magazines but with my respondents describing themselves, their lives and their specific vantage points on life. While trying to explain how they read and chose particular magazines, apart from wandering off to tell me about themselves (encouraged, usually, by me – as these stories provided me with much needed background information that made other things that were said more comprehensible), readers would in a pragmatic and functionalist way use different interpretive repertoires. Interpretive repertoires are defined by Jonathan Potter and Margaret Wetherell as common interpretations or 'recurrently used systems of terms, used for characterizing and evaluating actions, events and other phenomena' (1987: 149).

[. . .]

Reconstructing the repertoires readers use resembles simultaneously doing a series of jigsaw puzzles. In the interviews one will find bits and pieces of different repertoires. Combined, the interviews will allow a number of repertoires, or regularities really, to emerge. The repertoires are an explanatory and justificatory discursive system. As Western culture is a class-based culture, justificatory systems come in hierarchies. (See Bourdieu, 1980.) Some ways of describing why and how one views, television or reads women's magazines are more legitimate than others.

[. . .]

As regards women's magazines, repertoires that underline the practical use of women's magazines and that one can learn from them (about human nature, relationships, oneself) are clearly the most legitimate. . . . Reading women's magazines, these repertoires say, is not wasting your time on drivel, or, taking time for yourself. One is keeping up with the trade journals to do the best possible job caring and providing for one's family. Again, a repertoire running counter to this one is mentioned as well, although it is much less clear or articulate. It mainly describes reading as a very pleasurable and relaxing activity; what is actually read may vary. Some respondents had a clear order in which they'd read what was available. One of the men I interviewed would read the free broadsheets with local news that are financed by advertising revenue after he had finished the newspaper and then read *Viva*, a magazine his wife buys occasionally, when he comes home from work and makes himself a cup of tea.

Another much used and legitimate repertoire to talk about magazines ranging from feminist magazines and glossies to traditional and gossip magazines was the therapeutical repertoire: a way to stress how one may learn about oneself by reading about the experiences of others. . . . Remarkably, the only repertoire that counters outright 'legitimate' reasons for reading, is a repertoire voiced usually by men. It is rooted in camp readings of popular culture. It presents the reader as one who has set out to 'rise below the vulgar'.[5] This is a repertoire strongly tied to gay subculture which bespeaks a totally different relation *vis-à-vis* the cultural spectrum. . . . To reconstruct these repertoires from the interview transcripts involved a considerable *tour de force* that would make any self-respecting researcher slightly suspicious of the value of such a reconstruction. To understand these repertoires as what reading women's magazines is about, is to grossly misread the interview transcripts. The repertoires are available cultural sources to explain and justify reading women's magazines and a range of other cultural practices. More important to understanding how women's magazines become meaningful are the everyday routines that over the years constitute specific reading histories, the historical counterpart to the contemporary repertoires.

Reading histories offer a different kind of understanding of how women's magazines become meaningful than do simple accounts of where, when and how magazines are read or than mapping available interpretative repertoires does. Reading histories evaluate routines and reading magazines or watching television in their own way, closely related to personal histories, to periods of uncomplicated making-do as well as to rupture and change, encompassing a series of understandings of the self. Going back and forth between everyday routines and understandings of the self, one is given a picture of how life for people is structured by having to go out to work, taking care of children, or pursuing education. Thus, a link can be forged between reading women's magazines, living one's life the way one does and how society is structured. Obviously, most of the stories one is told are safe stories to tell. Only occasionally and usually by chance one gets an inkling of the unfinished business people have to find ways to deal with: feeling unhappy in a marriage, having post-natal depression. Such things will be of some importance in what one will read and how. A historical perspective on daily life and routines, I expect, is the closest social research will come to understanding how everyday life is a mixture of being much the same from year to year and sudden, radical changes.

Everyday talk is not self-reflective. It is pragmatic, it is used to explain and to justify and therefore is no easy way to come to understand how women's magazines (or other media) are made sense of. Solely understanding how people come to love texts that offer spellbinding escape, a learning experience, suspense, moral outrage or good melodrama that carries one off, is equivalent to understanding the media landscape to be Nepal: nothing but peaks. Such a view easily confuses the ordinary viewer with a media critic: someone who has built up a specific knowledge of a particular kind of text. Media use is also a fleeting, transient experience that doesn't leave much trace except in how everyday practices are structured. There seems to be a gradual slope along which media use will slowly change from an intense, well-defined experience into an inextricable part of everyday life, in which the media text as such has no meaning of its own. I can see no other way to understand such media use, than by reconstructing how routines have led to specific ways of understanding the self and how this informs how a reader will feel about the magazines she reads, the television programmes she watches and by making explicit the repertoires that are used to describe and legitimate media use.

An analysis that, on the one hand, starts from everyday routines and, on the other, from repertoires, politically and epistemologically enriches our understanding of media use. Politically, by recognizing the double-edgedness of everyday life, i.e., by recognizing the repetitiveness and the legitimatory force of everyday life as well as its being a site of personal and social change, the image of ordinary viewers as being cultural dupes is undermined. The repertoires, politically, can be used to criticise dominant interpretations; despite their hierarchical organization repertoires will change over time.

Epistemologically, recognizing the importance of routines for media use, means that text and context cannot always be distinguished from one another, consequently the media text as such never becomes fully meaningful. Furthermore, the two sides to routines entails recognizing their internal dynamic which underlines that there is no essential meaning that can be actualized nor is there an essential viewing mode or practice of media use. A repertoire approach, last but not least, has the invaluable advantage of not imposing academic standards on everyday discourse; it doesn't require closure or consistency. It works with rather than against the contradictions no one in an everyday context feels are necessary to sort out.

NOTES

1. They may be less represented in Morley's interviews because he interviewed a group of families who for all of their lives had been living in the same area (1986: 53). The point is that he did not choose to read them that way.
2. Examples are Livingstone (1990) on soap opera viewers; Ang (1985) on watching *Dallas*; Walkerdine (1986) on a family's use of a Rocky video; Radway (1984) on romance reading.
3. E.g., Livingstone (1990); Schrøder (1988); Ang (1985); Radway (1984).
4. Gray (1992 and 1987); Morley (1986).
5. As Mel Brooks put it, quoted in Ross (1989: 153).

REFERENCES

Ang, Ien (1985) *Watching Dallas. Soap Opera and the Melodramatic Imagination*, London and New York: Methuen.

Ang, Ien and Joke Hermes (1991) 'Gender and/in media consumption', in James Curran and Michael Gurevitch (1991) editors, *Mass Communication and Society*, London: Edward Arnold: 307–28.

Bausinger, Herman (1984) 'Media, technology and daily life', *Media, Culture and Society* 6 (1984) 343–51.

Bech Jørgensen, Birte (1990) 'The impossibility of everyday life', in *Every Cloud has a Silver Liming. Lectures on Everyday Life, Cultural Production and Race*, Flemming Røgilds (1990) editor, Studies in Cultural Sociology, No. 28, Copenhagen: Akademisk Forlag: 20–8.

Bourdieu, Pierre (1980) 'The aristocracy of culture', *Media, Culture and Society* 2(3) 225–54.

Certeau, Michel de (1984) *The Practice of Everyday Life*, trans. Steven Randall, Berkeley, Los Angeles: University of California Press.

Frow, John (1991) 'Michel de Certeau and the practice of representation', *Cultural Studies* 5(1) 52–60.

Gray, Ann (1987) 'Behind closed doors: video recorders in the home', in Helen Baehr and Gillian Dyer (1987) editors, *Boxed In: Women and Television*, New York and London: Pandora: 38–54.

—— (1992) *Video Playtime: The Gendering of a Leisure Technology*, London: Comedia/Routledge.

Hall, Stuart (1986) 'Introduction', in Morley (1986) 7–10.

Livingstone, Sonia (1990) *Making Sense of Television*, Oxford: Pergamon.

Morley, David (1986) *Family Television, Cultural Power and Domestic Leisure*, London: Comedia.

Potter, Jonathan and Margaret Wetherell (1987) *Discourse and Social Psychology*, London: Sage.

Radway, Janice (1984) *Reading the Romance, Women, Patriarchy and Popular Literature*, Chapel Hill and London: The University of North Carolina Press.

Ross, Andrew (1989) *No Respect. Intellectuals and Popular Culture*, New York and London: Routledge.

Schrøder, Kim Christian (1988) 'The pleasure of Dynasty: the weekly reconstruction of self-confidence', in Philip Drummond and Richard Paterson (1988) editors, *Television and its Audience*. London: BFI: 61–82.

Schutz, Alfred (1973) 'On multiple realities', in *Collected Papers I*, The Hague: Martinus Nijhoff: 207–59.

Walkerdine, Valerie (1986) 'Video Replay: families, films and fantasy', in Victor Burgin, James Donald and Cora Kaplan (1986) editors, *Formations of Fantasy*, London and New York: Methuen: 167–99.

43

WHAT'S 'HOME' GOT TO DO WITH IT?

*Contradictory Dynamics in the Domestication of Technology
and the Dislocation of Domesticity*

David Morley

[. . .]

THEORIZING PLACE(LESSNESS)

[. . .] I want to consider how attention to questions of geography can best inform our work in media and cultural studies. I shall be specifically concerned with the ways in which different geographies systematically produce different types of events and, conversely, with how certain types of events tend to happen in particular types of places. Returning, as I have elsewhere (Morley, 2000), to Foucault's (1980) insistence that our analyses must be sensitive both to the 'grand strategies of geopolitics' and the 'little tactics of the habitat', my analysis of the interlinked processes of globalization and domestication will attempt to bring together micro and macro issues. I want here to address questions of identity from the point of view of how we understand the idea of home and to address questions of technology from the point of view of how we can understand the process of its domestication.

[. . .]

In this context, I also want to develop a perspective that tries to articulate the symbolic with the material dimensions of analysis. Lynn Spigel puts this point another way when she argues that the 'simultaneous rise of the mass produced suburb and a ubiquitous place called "Television-land" raises a set of questions that scholars have only recently begun to ask' (Spigel, 2001b: 15).

From *European Journal of Cultural Studies* 6:4 (2003) pp. 435–58.

In pursuing these questions, I return, following Spigel, to Raymond Williams's old formulation of 'mobile privatization' to describe the lifestyles of mediated suburbia. For Williams, mobile privatization offers the dual satisfactions of allowing people to simultaneously 'stay home' – safe within the realm of their familiar ontological security – and to travel (imaginatively or 'virtually') to 'places that previous generations could never imagine visiting' (Williams, 1974: 26).

Spigel argues that, in the North American context at least, we can usefully understand the genealogy of ideas about domesticity in a media-saturated world as developing through three main phases in the postwar period. The first phase involved the model of the 'home theatre' (based on ideas of accessibility) bringing 'an imaginary night out on the town' into the sedentary domestic culture of the passive viewers, safe at home in the 'family circle' in their living rooms, allowing imaginary visits to the delights of the city and an ersatz sense of participation in public life for family members who, in fact, remained safe in the suburbs. It is this first phase, in Spigel's view, that Williams's model of mobile privatization really encapsulated. With the advent of portable TV sets in the USA in the 1960s, designed to symbolize the aspirations of what the industry now figured as a more active and mobile audience of 'people on the go', this model, Spigel claims, was superseded by the (still dominant) model of the 'mobile home', characterized not so much by mobile privatization as by what she calls 'privatized mobility'.

In the latest stage of these developments, Spigel argues, we see the model of the digitalized 'smart house' (of which, more later) which offers not so much an image of mobility, but of a 'sentient space', which, we are often told, so thoroughly transcends the divisions of inside/outside and work/home as to make it unnecessary to actually go anywhere anymore (Spigel, 2001a: 386, 398). In its digitalized form, the home itself can then be seen as having become, in Virilio's (1991) terms, the 'last vehicle' (cited in Spigel, 2001a: 400), where comfort, safety and stability can happily coexist with the possibility of an instantaneous digitalized 'flight' to elsewhere or the instantaneous importation of desired elements of 'elsewhere' into the home. Nonetheless, as both Allon (2000) and Spigel argue, all this 'hi-tech' discourse is often carefully framed and domesticated by a rather nostalgic vision of 'family values'.

[. . .]

DREAMS OF THE FUTURE

Let me now turn to questions of 'futurology'. There is a long history of visions of how it has been imagined that technical advances in communications – from the telegraph, to the telephone, to the internet – will somehow lead to 'better understanding' (see Carey, 1989; Marvin, 1990). It should be remembered that the telegraph – or the 'Victorian internet', as it has recently been redescribed (Standage, 1999) – was heralded as ushering in an era of world peace for this very reason. Armand Mattelart (1996), among others, has already critiqued this ideological vision, which mistakes technical improvements in modes of communication for the growth of understanding in human affairs (see de Saint-Simon, 1976). As Robins and Webster (2000) argue, such utopian – seemingly futuristic – visions can also, paradoxically, often be seen to actually represent backward-looking forms of nostalgia for technological fixes to the supposed problem of the loss of the idealized communities of some lamented golden age.

Moreover, while the contemporary vision of virtual space is usually presented as one of openness and exploration, one can also readily see that virtual space often, in practice, actually functions as a space of withdrawal into closed communities of the 'like-minded', of those who subscribe to the same email list or bulletin board or chatroom. We might also think of the personalized computer news services, about which there has been so much excitement in some quarters, as providing the same 'cocooning' effect.

Mediated Histories

Surrounded, as we are, by future-orientated debates about the impact of new communications technologies, it may well be that the first thing we need, if we are to avoid the twin dangers of utopianism and nostalgia – and to avoid the historically egocentric error of treating the dilemmas of our own age as if they were unique – is some way of placing these futurological debates in historical perspective.

This concern, of course, leads us to one of the central issues in historical work: the question of periodization and the issue of how to distinguish between the developing forms of media access and provision as they are transformed by processes of institutional, economic, political, technological and cultural change. We have some guidelines to work with here. John Ellis (2000) rightly points to the necessity to distinguish, in the realm of TV broadcasting, between what he calls the 'age of scarcity' (when there were few channels), the 'age of availability' (as the number of channels on offer to the viewer gradually increased) and the current 'age of plenty and uncertainty' (as we move into a multichannel broadcast environment, replete with remote controls, time shift videos and audience fragmentation). The key issue is what exactly is being transformed here and how, in response to these changes, we need to adjust our analytical paradigms. Here, alongside Spigel's helpful genealogy of models of domesticity and media consumption, we might usefully also consult Robert Allen's (1999) work on the current transformation of the film industry. Allen's analysis focuses on the way in which, in the USA, not only has domestic video now become the main mode of film consumption, but film-on-video itself now functions, crucially, as a form of marketing for sales of the ancillary products that today constitute the industry's main source of profit. What Allen's and Spigel's analyses offer us is a way of tracing the interconnections between demographic changes in household structure, cultural definitions of domesticity, modes of media consumption and their retroactive effects on modes of industrial production.

[. . .]

THE DOMESTICATION OF TV

The development of historical work on the communications media has been one of the key developments of the recent period: notably that of Paddy Scannell (1996) in the UK; Spigel (1992) and Sconce (2000) in the USA; and, from a longer-term perspective, that of Siegfried Zielinski (1999) in Germany. However, despite these honourable exceptions, when media history is addressed, it is still too often conceived either in institutional or technological terms.

My own primary concern in this respect is with what Maud Lavin (1990) calls the 'intimate histories' of living with a medium such as broadcast TV. This Lavin describes as involving 'a collection of personal memories of growing up with TV . . . [of] how the TV set [has been] gradually incorporated into the home, family and leisure time . . . and [the] history of how we design our spaces, habits and even emotions around the TV' (1990: 85). This is a question of how our personal memories – especially of childhood – are formulated around media experiences such as emblematic programmes and TV characters. In this respect, we might usefully draw a parallel with Gaston Bachelard's (1994) analysis of how the material structure of the house provides the 'trellis' around which childhood memory is entwined – but perhaps we now need to extend the analogy so as to think also of how that trellis now has a mediated, as much as a material, structure.

From this perspective, we perhaps also need to treat TV not so much as a visual medium, but as a visible object (Morley, 1995) because, as Matthew Geller (1990: 7) puts it, too often we simply 'look through' the object of TV to the images it provides, while the set itself remains, as it were, 'invisible' to us and we ignore its role as a totemic object of enormous symbolic importance in the household. It is in this context that we must also address the long history of TV's domestication, as we trace its journey from its initial position as a singular 'stranger', allowed only into the most public/formal space of the house (in the living room), through the development of the multiset household and TV's gradual penetration of the more intimate spaces of our kitchens and bedrooms, to the point where the new individualized/personal media delivery systems, in their latest portable and miniaturized forms, might more properly be conceptualized as 'body parts'.

The domestic history of TV is by no means singular in this respect. Eliseo Veron in France details the similar pathway traced by the 'journey of the phone' in the household, as it gradually multiplied and moved from the public space of the hallway into the other rooms of the house (Veron, 1991). To jump forward for a moment, when we come to the era of the mobile phone, not only is it entirely personalized – and very much understood by many of its users as just as much a 'body part' as their wristwatch – but it becomes, in effect, the person's virtual address, while their land line becomes a merely secondary communication facility (and one of seeming irrelevance to many young people).

Earlier, Simon Frith (1983) rightly pointed to the historical role of broadcasting technologies in enhancing what he called the 'pleasures of the hearth', leading, as a consequence, to what he described as the 'rediscovery of the home' as a site for domestic leisure activities that had previously taken more public forms. The contemporary issue, in this connection, is what the emergence of public forms of TV and of the new personalized communications technologies now do to correspondingly destabilize the centrality of the domestic home.

Clearly, in the present context, we do have to move beyond media studies' historically rather exclusive focus on TV so as to also address the contemporary significance of a broader range of communications technologies. However, I also want to argue that we need to transcend the unfortunate media-centrism of much work in this area by decentring the media in our analytical framework, so as to better understand the ways in which media processes and everyday life are so closely interwoven with each other. That problem will not be solved by contemporary proposals to 'modernize' media studies by reconceptualizing it as 'web studies' or the like, for this would simply be to put the internet at the centre of the equation, where TV used to stand. Such a move would merely replicate a very old technologically determinist problematic in a new guise. The issue is both to understand how new and old media accommodate each other and coexist in symbiotic forms and also to better grasp the ways in which we live with them.

ANTHROPOLOGICAL PERSPECTIVES: FETISHISM AND TOTEMISM

In trying to understand how we live and work with technologies, the last thing we should do is to make the mistake of imagining that media and communications technologies are desired, consumed and used simply for their functional purposes – increasingly marvellous as these may appear. Everything that the anthropology of material consumption tells us indicates that, beyond their practical uses, communications technologies often have symbolic meanings that make them also function as powerful totems and fetishes for their owners. This might be to speak of the TV set as the symbolic centrepiece of the 'family hearth' in the discourse of the 1950s; or, in the terms of 1990s discourse, to speak of the computer as a signifier that modernity has entered the house, thus saving its children from the wrath of the god of unemployability (even if all they actually do is play games on it, rather than learning any more complex computer skills).

This, then, is to insist on the importance of the symbolic meanings, as much as the practical functions, of technology. Here we might do well to remember Ondina Leal's (1990) important work on the symbolic meaning of the TV set as a signifier of modernity in the Brazilian favelas or Alfred Gell's (1986) study of the Sri Lankan fishermen who buy TV sets that they cannot operate (for lack of electricity) to display as 'wealth signifiers' to their fellow villagers. From a different angle, we might recall the firm grasp of this point displayed by the Taliban government in Afghanistan when they hung TVs from the trees as a potent symbol of the unwanted westernization of their country.

This is by no means only a matter of strange cultural practices in 'exotic' places. In their studies of western owners of video collections, both Uma Dinsmore (1998) and Barbara Klinger (1998) demonstrate that these collections often have little to do with the opportunities they might be thought to provide for the rewatching of the tapes and rather more to do with the making of a domestic statement about their owner's self-image. Similarly, as I argue elsewhere (Morley, 1995), the purchase in the UK of one of the 'high definition' TV sets, advertised under the slogan 'the less you watch, the higher your standards', signifies to all who see it, whether or not it is ever switched on, key things about its owner as a person of discriminating tastes.

In the same way, the mobile phone's particular style [. . .] already communicates the particular cultural identity that the owner has chosen for themself and by means of which they wish to distinguish themselves from others. This is well illustrated in the work of the photographer Martin Parr (2002) on how the mobile phone is used in different global contexts and also, graphically, in that of Larissa Hjorth (2003) in her study of the 'customized' decoration of mobile phones in Japan. Here we might also begin to open up a set of other themes, to which I will return later, concerning the mobile phone's symbolic role as a means of signifying its owner's degree of social 'connectedness'.

There may also be more general statements that we can make about the specific type of technological objects that best symbolize the values of a particular time. Zygmunt Bauman argues that, in the current period of what he calls 'liquid modernity', we see a quite particular symbolic logic at play, in which portable or miniaturized technologies play a crucial role. As he puts it, 'fluidity is (now) the principal source of strength and invincibility . . . it is now the smaller, the lighter, the more portable that signifies improvement and "progress"' (Bauman, 2000: 13–14, cited in Lull, 2002). [. . .]

New Times and New Formats

Even if we need to avoid the dangers of any overly generalized nomadology of postmodern life, mobilities, of one sort or another, are clearly central to our analysis. In this context, the extended family has now sometimes to be seen as stretched out across the long distance phone wires, especially for migrants who often spend a high proportion of their wages on phone calls home. This, as Richard Rouse (1991: 13) puts it, allows them 'not just to "keep in touch", but to contribute to decision-making and participate in familial events from a distance'.

[. . .]

However, new technologies are not only relevant to the lives of migrant families. Brockes's (2000) report on research by Jan English-Lueck and James Freeman (of San Jose State University in California) reveals a picture of a situation where the new modes of electronic communication have themselves become the very infrastructure of family life. [. . .]

Clearly, family life is changing around us, as people adapt to new technologies and find ways to deal with new structures of work and mobility, and, for all its continuing ideological centrality, the nuclear family household is declining rapidly in the West. It may not be possible (or even, ultimately, important) to work out which is the chicken and which is the egg in this respect, but we have to develop a mode of analysis that can articulate these changes in household demographics with the rapid growth of individual 'personalized media delivery systems'. [. . .]

DOMESTICATING THE FUTURE

Questions of the future and of technology are, of course, inextricably intertwined with each other, not least because the future (and increasingly the present) is now defined so much in technological terms. If the future represents, for many people, a troublesome realm of constant change, much of this trouble comes to be symbolized by (and in) technological forms. The question, therefore, is how this problematic technological realm comes to be naturalized and domesticated so as to make it less threatening and more manageable for its inhabitants.

Many years ago, Bausinger (1984) argued that the everyday was coming to be characterized in the affluent West by what he called the 'inconspicuous omnipresence of the technical'. In the research on the domestic uses of information and communications technologies in which I have been involved (Silverstone and Hirsch, 1992), one of the most striking findings was how, in many households, people went to a great deal of trouble to disguise the presence of communications technologies in their homes, often hiding TV sets, computers and wiring in wooden cabinets or behind soft furnishings. The point is that, if an increasing array of technologies has now become naturalized to the point of literal (or psychological) invisibility in the domestic sphere, we need to understand the process of how that has come about.

The other reason why a historical perspective on new media should be central to our approach to these issues is because the dynamic of making technologies consumer-friendly in practice often means inserting them into recognizable forms from previous eras. To this extent, technological innovation often goes along with a continuing drive to make the techno-future safe by incorporating it into familiar formats, icons and symbols.

To take but one example, an advert for one of the latest multi-functional home entertainment systems takes the form of an image of family life which shows the new system installed in just the kind of traditional wooden cabinet into which, as Spigel's (1992) research shows, early TVs themselves were incorporated, when they were introduced into the household in an earlier period. Moreover, the advert's imagery, in which everyone in the family group is shown smiling under the benign gaze of the father, could almost be derived directly from a Norman Rockwell portrait of suburban family life in the USA in the 1950s. The potentially problematic nature of the new technology is thus neutralized by being shown as happily incorporated into the reassuring symbolism of this most conventional of homes.

[. . .]

[. . .] With the advent of the electronic 'dreamhouse' – whether in the earlier versions that Spigel (2001b) describes in the 1950s and 1960s or nowadays in Bill Gates's own 'fully-wired' domestic paradise, as analysed by Allon (2000) – we arrive at a new situation. Here, rather than electronic technologies being domesticated, as in the case of the 'smart house', the domestic realm itself is mediated and made fully electronic. In this vision of the household, the technologies are no longer merely supplementary to, but constitutive of, what the home itself now is.

All this leads us back to a new version of Raymond Williams's vision of 'mobile privatization' in so far as the technologies that can be used to engage in the new 'virtual' forms of in-home 'travel' are now far more powerful than Williams ever imagined. However, it is necessary to remember that the houses that were built in 'Levittown' in the postwar USA also had, as one of the key defining characteristics of their desirability, TVs built into their sitting room walls. The electronic home itself has a history, which we would do well to remember, as we puzzle over its future (Hayden, 2002). Moreover, to return to the issue of the domestication of 'futuristic' forms of technology, as Allon (2000) points out, even Bill Gates represents the form of family life that he envisages conducting in his fully-wired 'dreamhouse' in the most conventional suburban terms possible – which just goes to show the extent to which futurology is almost always as much 'backward' as it is 'forward looking'.

AND NOW? DE-DOMESTICATED/ING MEDIA?

Thus far, in my narrative, I have traced the long story of the gradual domestication of a range of media, most particularly TV, and have taken the 'smart house' as the culmination or 'end point' of this story, where the home itself becomes a fully technologized/wired place and comes to be defined by the technologies that constitute it. However, it could be argued that we now face the beginning of a quite different story, where the narrative drive runs in the opposite direction, towards the de-domestication of the media and the radical dislocation of domesticity itself. In many countries, TV began as a public medium, watched collectively in public places, and only gradually moved into the home and then into its further interstices [. . .]. However, it is evident that, having thoroughly colonized the home, TV has now re-escaped from its confines. Nowadays, we find TV everywhere, in the public spaces of bars, in restaurants, laundrettes, shops and airports, as Anna McCarthy (2001) documents in her study of what she calls 'ambient TV' in the USA.

These developments also need to be understood in the broader theoretical context of debates about the ongoing transformation of the relationships between the public and private spheres. In this regard, Mattelart (1995) rightly argues that, for many years now, public space has been gradually transformed by the increasing presence of advertising. Public space is now replete with commercial messages, visually – whether on large-scale billboards in the street or on the back of bus tickets – or aurally – as in the message on the UK telephone service that tells you that time itself is now 'sponsored by Accurist'. Thus, Abercrombie and Longhurst (1999) argue that, given the ubiquity of media of all forms in the contemporary world, the old distinction between those who are part of the media audience and those who are not is now quite outmoded for the simple reason that we are all now, in effect, audiences to some kind of media almost everywhere and all of the time.

But there is yet another dimension to this problem, which was first identified in studies of the cultural significance of the Walkman, as a technology that transformed the relations of the public and private, allowing its users to privatize public space by retreating into their own protective aural bubble of sound, setting their experience of public places to their own privatized soundtrack (Bull, 2000; Chambers, 1990; du Gay et al., 1997). If the Walkman is, in this sense, a privatizing technology, then, [. . .] the mobile phone is perhaps the privatizing (or individualizing) technology of our age, par excellence.

Evidently, one of the things that the mobile phone does is to dislocate the idea of home, enabling its user, in the words of the Orange advertising campaign in the UK, to 'take your network with you, wherever you go'. Like the Walkman, it also insulates its users from the geographical place that they are actually in. Often the user is paying no attention to those who are physically close to them, while speaking to others who are far away. To that extent, it might also be argued not only that the mobile phone often functions as a psychic cocoon for its user, but even as a kind of mobile 'gated community' (Luke, forthcoming).

It is usually taken for granted that the mobile phone is principally a device for transcending spatial distance. But just as we know that a large percentage of the world's email is sent between people working in the same building, the mobile phone seems also often to be used in counter-intuitive ways.

It is often used not so much to transcend distance as to establish parallel communications networks in the same space (i.e. text messaging by pupils in school) and, indeed, it turns out often to be used collectively, especially among groups of young people when they are together (Weilenmann and Larsson, 2002).

As we know, the mobile phone call also radically disrupts the physical space of the public sphere in a variety of ways, annoying others with its insistent demand for attention or imposing 'private' conversation on those near its user. It is also interesting to see the ways in which these developments have also given rise to a whole new set of debates, focused on this technology, about the etiquette of communications. However, there is evidently more than a question of etiquette at stake here, fascinating as it is to see the speed at which new modes of regulation of the device have been developing, such as 'quiet carriages' on trains, notices in restaurants and ads in cinemas banning their use (Harris, 2003).

The mobile phone is often understood (and promoted) as a device for connecting us to those who are far away, thus overcoming distance – and perhaps geography itself. It has been described as enabling the emergence of an even more mobile descendent of the *flaneur*: the '*phoneur*' (Luke, forthcoming). However, [. . .] the first question in many mobile phone conversations, as we all know, is often 'where are you?' (answer: 'I'm on the train/stuck in traffic/I'll be a bit late . . .'). It seems that geography is not, in fact, dead at all and that what the mobile phone allows is endless anxious commentary on our geographical locations and trajectories. Perhaps one might even say that the mobile phone is, among other things, a device for dealing with our anxieties about the problems of distance created by our newly mobile lifestyles and with the emotional 'disconnectedness' that this geographical distance symbolizes for us (Tomlinson, 2001).

George Myerson argues that 'the mobile is the object which most closely embodies the spirit of the changing environment. If you want to assure yourself that you belong to the new century, this is the object to have in your hand' (2001: 1). Linking back to my earlier comments on the symbolic significance of new technologies, Timo Kopomaa pushes the point further, arguing that the mobile phone has now acquired a particularly important symbolic role for many of its users – to the extent that it should be understood, he argues, as 'a portable magic charm', as the 'device that makes everything OK' (Kopomaa, 2001: 38).

[. . .] [T]he geographer Yi Fu Tuan (1996) distinguishes between 'conversation' (substantive talk about events and issues: a discourse of the public realm) and 'chatter' (the exchange of gossip principally designed to maintain solidarity between those involved in the exchange: what Tuan calls a 'discourse of the hearth'). Drawing on Tuan's distinction, John Tomlinson (2001) rightly argues that the discourse of most mobile phone use can be characterized as a form of phatic or gestural communication. In these terms, what the mobile phone does is to fill the space of the public sphere with the chatter of the hearth, allowing us to take our homes with us, just as a tortoise stays in its shell wherever it travels. To this extent, Tomlinson argues, we would be mistaken to see these new technologies simply as tools for the extension of cultural horizons; rather, he claims, we should see them as 'imperfect instruments, by which people try . . . to maintain some sense of security and location' amidst a culture of flow and deterritorialization (2001: 17).

If one of the key historical roles of broadcasting technologies has been their transformation of the relations of the public and private spheres, then the questions that face us now concern what these new technologies do to those relations and how they, in turn, may be regulated and domesticated. We now find ourselves in a world where we are all audiences to one or another medium, almost all of the time, and where, after its long process of domestication, TV and other media have now escaped the home – to (re)colonize the public sphere. While the domestic home itself might now be said to have become a fully technological artefact, it also seems that domesticity itself has now been dislocated.

As we wander the public realm, protected by the carapaces of our Walkmans and mobile phones, it may be a good moment to repose Heidegger's (1971) question about what it means to live in a culture of 'distancelessness', where things are neither near nor far, but, as it were, 'without distance'. But as soon as we make this connection to these earlier debates, we have to recognize that the questions we face today, while undoubtedly urgent, are not in themselves new. Moreover, we have to recognize, with Spigel (2001a, b), that, if we are ever to get any critical perspective on the discourses of futurology that now surround us, we shall certainly need to put them into a fuller historical perspective than that which they recognize for themselves.

REFERENCES

Abercrombie, Nicholas and Brian Longhurst (1999) *Audiences: Sociological Theory and Audience Research*. London: Sage.

Allen, Robert (1999) 'Home Alone Together: Hollywood and the Family Film', in M. Stokes and R. Maltby (eds) *Identifying Hollywood's Audiences*. London: British Film Institute.

Allon, Fiona (2000) 'Nostalgia Unbound', *Continuum* 14(3).

Bachelard, Gaston (1994) *The Poetics of Space*. Boston, MA: Beacon Press.

Bauman, Zygmunt (2000) *Liquid Modernity*, Cambridge: Polity Press.

Bausinger, Herman (1984) 'Media, Technology and Everyday Life', *Media, Culture & Society* 6(4).

Brockes, Emma (2000) 'Doing Family in Silicon Valley', *Guardian* (G2) (17 May): 8–9.

Bull, Michael (2000) *Sounding Out the City*. Oxford: Berg.

Carey, James (1989) *Communication as Culture*. London: Unwin Hyman.

Chambers, Iain (1990) 'A Miniature History of the Walkman', *New Formations* 11.

de Saint-Simon, Claude (1976) *The Political Thought of Saint-Simon* (ed. G. Ionescu). Oxford: Oxford University Press.

Dinsmore, Uma (1998) 'The Domestication of Film: Video, Cinephilia and the

Collecting and Viewing of Videotapes in the Home', PhD thesis, Department of Media and Communications, Goldsmiths College, University of London.

du Gay, Paul et al. (1997) *Doing Cultural Studies: The Story of the Sony Walkman*. London: Sage.

Ellis, John (2000) *Seeing Things: Television in an Age of Uncertainty*. London: I. B. Tauris.

Foucault, Michel (1980) 'Questions of Geography', in C. Gordon (ed.) *Michel Foucault: Power/Knowledge*. New York: Pantheon.

Frith, Simon (1983) 'The Pleasures of the Hearth', in J. Donald (ed.) *Formations of Pleasure*. London: Routledge.

Gell, Alfred (1986) 'Newcomers to the World of Goods: Consumption among the Muria Gonds', in A. Appadurai (ed.) *The Social Life of Things*. Cambridge: Cambridge University Press.

Geller, Matthew (ed.) (1990) *From Receiver to Remote Control: The TV Set*. New York: New Museum of Contemporary Art.

Harris, Kevin (2003) 'Keep Your Distance: Remote Communications, Face-to-face and the Nature of Community', *Journal of Community Work and Development* 4.

Hayden, Dolores (2002) *Redesigning the American Dream: Gender, Housing and Family Life*. New York: W. W. Norton.

Heidegger, Martin (1971) 'The Thing', in *Poetry, Language, Thought*. New York: Harper & Row.

Hjorth, Larissa (2003) '"Pop" and "Ma": The Landscape of Japanese Commodity Characters and Subjectivity', in C. Berry et al. (eds) *New Media in Queer Asia*. Durham, NC: Duke University Press.

Klinger, Barbara (1998) 'The Contemporary Cinephile: Film Collecting in the Post-video Era', paper presented to the 'Hollywood and Its Spectators' conference, University College, London, November.

Kopomaa, Timo (2001) *The City in Your Pocket: The Birth of the Mobile Information Society*. Helsinki: Gaudeamus.

Lavin, Maud (1990) 'TV Design', in Matthew Geller (ed.) *From Receiver to Remote Control: The TV Set*. New York: New Museum of Contemporary Art.

Leal, Ondina (1990) 'Popular Taste and Erudite Repertoire: The Place and Space of TV in Brazil', *Cultural Studies* 4(1).

Luke, Robert (forthcoming) 'The Phoneur: Mobile Commerce and the Digital Pedagogies of the Wireless Web', in P. Trifonas (ed.) *Pedagogies of Difference*. London: Routledge.

Lull, James (2002) 'Review of Bauman's *Liquid Modernity*', *International Journal of Cultural Studies* 5(1): 105–11.

McCarthy, Anna (2001) *Ambient Television*. Durham, NC: Duke University Press.

Marvin, Carolyn (1990) *When Old Technologies Were New*. Oxford: Oxford University Press.

Mattelart, Armand (1995) *Advertising International*. London: Routledge.

Morley, David (1995) 'Television: Not So Much a Visual Medium, More a Visible Object', in C. Jenks (ed.) *Visual Communication*. London: Routledge.

Morley, David (2000) *Home Territories: Media, Mobility and Identity*. London: Routledge.

Myerson, George (2001) *Heidegger, Habermas and the Mobile Phone*. London: Icon Books.

Parr, Martin (2002) *The Phone Book 1998–2002*. London: Rocket Books.

Robins, Kevin and Frank Webster (2000) *Times of the TechnoCulture*. London: Routledge.

Rouse, Roger (1991) 'Mexican Migration and the Social Space of Postmodernism', *Diaspora* 1(1).

Scannell, Paddy (1996) *Radio, Television and Modern Life*. Oxford: Blackwell.

Sconce, Jeff (2000) *Haunted Media*. Durham, NC: Duke University Press.

Silverstone, Roger and Eric Hirsch (eds) (1992) *Consuming Technologies*. London: Routledge.

Spigel, Lynn (1992) *Make Room for TV*. Chicago, IL: University of Chicago Press.

Spigel, Lynn (2001a) 'Media Homes: Then and Now', *International Journal of Cultural Studies* 4(4).

Spigel, Lynn (2001b) *Welcome to the Dreamhouse*. Durham, NC: Duke University Press.

Standage, Tom (1999) *The Victorian Internet*. Boston, MA: Phoenix Books.

Tomlinson, John (2001) *Instant Access: Some Cultural Implications of 'Globalising' Technologies*. University of Copenhagen, Global Media Cultures Working Paper No. 13.

Tuan, Yi Fu (1996) *Cosmos and Hearth*. Minneapolis: University of Minnesota Press.

Veron, Eliseo (1991) *Analyses pour Centre d'Etudes des Telecommunications*. Paris: Causa Rerum.

Virilio, Paul (1991) *Lost Dimension*. New York: Semiotext(e).

Weilenmann, Alexandra and Catherine Larsson (2002) 'Local Use and the Sharing of Mobile Phones', in B. Brown et al. (eds) *Wireless World*. London: Springer.

Williams, Raymond (1974) *Television: Technology and Cultural Form*. London: Fontana.

Zielinski, Siegfried (1999) *AudioVisions: Cinema and Television as Entr'actes in History*. Amsterdam: University of Amsterdam Press.

44

NO DEAD AIR! THE IPOD AND THE CULTURE OF MOBILE LISTENING

MICHAEL BULL

INTRODUCTION

When I was a child, I used to watch a kids show called 'The Music Machine' and I always dreamed of having something like that. A device that plays any song there is. The iPod comes pretty close to the fulfilment of this childhood fantasy. (Sarah 2) [1]

> I can't overestimate the importance of having all my music available all the time. It gives me an unprecedented level of emotional control over my life. (Terry 3)

The solitary movement of people through the city each day represents a significant yet under-researched aspect of contemporary urban experience. This solitariness is often imposed in the daily movement of people to and from their places of work, yet is equally often a preferable option for many as they either walk or drive to and from work (Bull, 2000; Putnam, 2000; Brodsky 2002). Yet this desire for solitude is often joined to a need for social proximity and contact in daily life (Katz & Aakhus, 2002; Bauman, 2003). For many this solitude is an accompanied solitude in which people walk to the personalised sounds of their personal stereos and MP3 players.

With the introduction of MP3 technology the user is given unparalleled access to their music collection whilst on the move. Previous generations of personal stereos, whilst providing for portability, limited the consumer to a

From *Leisure Studies* 24:4 (2005) pp. 343–55.

few choices of music due to their format, whereas machines like the Apple iPod enable users to store up to 10,000 songs. These entries can be arranged through 'play-lists' in any configuration the user desires. Technologies like the Apple iPod produce for their users an intoxicating mixture of music, proximity and privacy whilst on the move (Putnam, 2000; Brodsky, 2002).[2]

The use of these mobile sound technologies informs us about how users attempt to 'inhabit' the spaces within which they move. The use of these technologies appears to bind the disparate threads of much urban movement together, both 'filling' the spaces 'in-between' communication or meetings and structuring the spaces thus occupied. In the often-repressive 'realm of the eversame' (Adorno, 1976) or the 'ever-always-the-same' (Benjamin, 1973), the iPod user struggles to achieve a level of autonomy over time and place through the creation of a privatised auditory bubble. iPod users often refer to the magical nature of carrying their entire music collection with them wherever they go, thus giving them an unprecedented amount of choice of music to listen to. In this de-routinisation of time lies both the unalloyed pleasure of listening but also the management or control of the user's thoughts, feelings and observations as they manage both space and time.

It is to the notion of seamless auditory experience that the phrase 'no dead air' refers – this evocative phrase was used by Jean, a 35-year-old bank executive who was describing her morning commute to work in New York. She would scroll though her song titles looking for a particular song to listen to that would suit her mood at that particular moment and, whilst listening to that song, would scroll through her list for her next choice – her musical choices would merge seamlessly into one another during her journey time. Of course, this is merely one strategy for creating a seamless and aurally privatised listening experience for iPod users. More typically users will have a selection of play-lists that suit a variety of moods, times of the day or perhaps weather conditions or indeed times of the year. iPod users are often planners, spending hours creating play-lists for themselves in preparation for their routine journeys to and from work. Others, not so inclined, might just place their trust in the 'shuffle' mode of the iPod, which plays their music at random; in effect, giving themselves over to their music collection and the technology of the iPod. The ability to continually adjust music, whilst on the move, to moods with such sophistication and precision is relatively new if, indeed, the desire to do is not.

In my previous study of personal stereo use (Bull, 2000), I described the problematic strategies enacted by users in their attempt to judge what music to take with them on their daily commute. For some this was not a problem as they would play the same tape each day for months on end – forcing their environment to mimic the straightjacket of their own mindset. For others, however, a hastily bundled selection of tapes or CDs would go into their bag in the hope that it would serve the purpose. What united personal stereo users at the time was the claim that no music was better than the 'wrong' music, by which they meant music that did not correspond to their current mood. The development of MP3 players has now provided a technological fix to the management of the contingency of aural desire (most iPod users have a history of using other mobile listening technologies such as the personal stereo). Users now take their whole music collection with them in a machine that is not much larger than a small mobile phone. As one male user aptly describes, 'It gives me the ability to carry my entire music collection in my pocket instead of a steamer trunk' (Mark 4). Equally, the personal stereo was commonly used as an 'in-between device' – from door to door – whereas the iPod expands the possibilities of use, from the playing of music through the user's home hi-fi device, to plugging it into the automobile radio, to connecting it to the computer at work – giving the user unprecedented ability to weave the disparate threads of the day into one uniform soundtrack.

From home to street, from private setting to public arena, the media have helped link these two areas of daily life together in unexpected ways for many people. Whilst there has been much discussion on the nature of space/time compression involved in the use of communication technologies from the telegraph to the internet, and of the privatising potential of television (Harvey, 1996; Winston, 1998), most empirical research involving the use of these technologies has focused solely upon domestic consumption in fixed locales, as if media effects and influences stop at the front door. Yet the sense of proximity created through modes of domestic use of the media acts as a ground to mobile use:

> The early history of broadcast talk consisted largely in the attempt to create a world in which audiences would feel like participants. Today both the programming and reception of most commercial media, in the United States at least, actively cultivate a sense of intimate relations between persona and audience. Media culture is a lush jungle of fictional worlds where 'everyone knows your name', celebrities and politicians address audiences by first names, and conversational formats proliferate. (Peters, 1999: p. 217.)

Raymond Williams understood these phenomena in terms of 'mobile privatisation'. Not the street, but our living rooms – and increasingly our bedrooms – become emporiums of visual and auditory delight. Recently, Sonia Livingstone has charted the consumption of the media amongst teenagers within the home. She found that they increasingly liked to consume the media privately:

> The home increasingly becomes the site for individualised media consumption with children spending the majority of their home media use alone in their bedrooms. (Livingstone, 2002.)

Sole consumption is both pleasurable and controllable. Moreover, domestic consumption appears to fuel feelings of omnipotence (Morley, 2002). Equally, domestic use teaches consumers how to 'fill in' the spaces and times between activities. Consumers increasingly become used to the mediated presence of the media in our own privatised settings.

The desire for company or 'occupancy' whilst moving through the city is thus contextualised through the daily or habitual use of a variety of media. The array of mobile sound media increasingly enables users to successfully maintain a sense of intimacy whilst moving through the city. Theodor Adorno probably would not have been surprised by the success of personal stereos and iPods technologies – he recognised that sound technologies, in particular, transform our understanding of connection and proximity. Adorno described the nature of this aural proximity in terms of states of 'we-ness', the substitution or transformation of 'direct' experience by a mediated, technological, form of aural experience. For Adorno, music creates a form of sociability in a world that is increasingly bereft of it. As such, music performs an ideological function of integrating the user into the world:

> People dread time, and so they invent a compensatory metaphysics of time because they blame time for the fact that in a reified world they no longer feel alive. This is what music talks them out of. It confirms the society it entertains. The colour of the inner sense, the bright detailed imagery of the flow of time, assures a man that within the monotony of universal comparability there is still something particular. (Adorno, 1976: p. 48.)

For Adorno, the warmth of mediated music is contrasted to the chill of the immediate, and the inability of structured forms of the social to satisfy the desire for proximity:

> By circling them, by enveloping them as inherent in the musical phe-nomena – and turning them as listeners into participants, it [music] contributes ideologically to the integration which modern society never tires of achieving in reality. . . It creates an illusion of immediacy in a totally mediated world, of proximity between strangers, the warmth of those who come to feel a chill of unmitigated struggle of all against all. (Horkheimer & Adorno, 1973: p. 46.)

Adorno perceives the urban subject as increasingly and actively seeking out forms of mediated company within which to live. [. . .] Lefebvre, coming from a similar dialectical position as Adorno, points to a 'spontaneity' in the every-day. Resistance, for Lefebvre, is located in the very nature of experience – there can be no identity between the 'subject' and 'object'; the iPod user and the world he or she lives in:

> Moreover, the worker craves a sharp break with his work, compensa-tion. He looks for this in leisure seen as entertainment or distraction. In

this way leisure appears as the non-everyday in the everyday. We cannot step beyond the everyday. The marvellous can only continue to exist in fiction and the illusions that people share. There is no escape. And yet we wish to have the illusion of escape as near to hand as possible. An illusion not entirely illusory, but constituting a 'world' both apparent and real (the reality of appearances and the apparently real) quite different from the everyday world yet as open ended and as closely dovetailed into the everyday as possible. (Lefebvre, 1991b: p. 40.)

For Lefebvre, the partly illusory nature or compensatory factor in the above experiences does not detract from the fact that the experiences still might be understood as oppositional, creative and pleasurable. From this perspective, iPod users might be understood as creating spaces of freedom for themselves through the very use of technologies that tie them into consumer culture – yet, nevertheless, are not reducible to those technologies. The following iPod user points to the paradoxical nature of using a music technology to carve out her own sense of space in an effort to gain control of her daily experience:

Well, I think I've come to the conclusion that overall I feel pretty out of control in my life. Stores play music to get me to buy more. Work tells me what to do and when. Traffic decides how quickly I get from here to there. Even being in public places forces me to endure other people and their habits (the guy slurping his soup, the brat crying for a piece of candy.) I didn't realize how much I yearn for control and probably peace and quiet. Strange since I'm blasting music in my ears. I think I'm really tired of living on someone else's schedule. The MP3 digital music revolution has given me some control back. (Tracy 1)

In this article I demonstrate the power of music in enabling iPod users to construct meaningful and pleasurable narratives out of the routine linear and cyclical practices of their everyday movement through the city. In doing so I revisit and develop some of the themes first developed in my previous work on the nature and use of personal stereos. These issues concern the management of experience and the power of sound to direct experience.

A SOUND-CONSUMING CULTURE

Contemporary consumer culture is a sound-consuming culture in which daily life is increasingly mediated by a multitude of mechanically reproduced sounds (De Nora, 2000). We wake up to radio sounds, walk to music (Bull, 2000), drive to sound (Bull, 2003) and often relax and go to sleep accompanied by reproduced sound. Music follows us to work and is there when we shop, when we visit pubs, clubs and theme parks. Yet despite this routinisation of sound in consumer culture, it retains a largely 'utopian' place in consumer desire (Bull, 2004).

The ability of 'sound' to deliver what consumers want is increasingly wedded to the ability of consumers to create their own soundworlds. Privatised and mediated sound reproduction enables consumers to create intimate, manageable and aestheticised spaces in which they are increasingly able, and desire, to live. With the creation of Walkmans and now iPods we have seen a post-Fordist habitation of urban space. The packaged aural environment of the supermarket, departmental store or health club no longer necessarily fit the desires of the user. This despite the contemporary prevalence of niche marketing with health clubs and clothes stores creating an aural environment supposedly fashioned to their preferred consumers. iPod use demonstrates that, for many users, the uniqueness of their musical narrative and management of mood is no longer fulfillable even by the 'focused' production of auditory environments. iPod users often refer to the sense of power and wonderment achieved precisely through the individualising of 'representational space':

> Since I was 8 years old I have acquired a CD/LP collection of more than 5000 items over the years. The biggest issue to me has always been what music to take along (on vacation, driving in a car, going out jogging or walking etc.). I made hundreds of compilation tapes (and later CDs), but what I was missing was the flexibility to listen to exactly the right song at the right time. With the 40 GB iPod, I can take most of the music with me that I own, and I can choose at any time, what song to listen to. (Daniel 5)

> It was a revelation-having the ability to carry around several thousand songs (I think I've got about 3100 songs on my Pod now) and the ability to switch between them at will. It's a great deal of power to have over your environment. I love not being tied to the number of discs or tapes I can carry. (Kerry 6)

The personalised narratives of users' music choice is often incompatible with the 'muzak' found in an increasing number of public spaces. MP3 technology thus suits the progressively individualised aural taste of many consumers.

SONIC BRIDGES AND STREET AESTHETICS

Each morning millions of urban inhabitants place a pair of headphones over their heads, or place ear-pieces directly into their ears, turn the music on as they leave home and tend to keep listening until they reach their destination. The focusing upon mood and the directing of intention often begins for the user at the start of the day:

> I first put on my iPod either right before I leave my apartment in the morning, or right after. Most usually right before I step out the door, after

my coat and bag is on. I set it playing once I've gotten outside on most days, though. There are mornings when I'll have a song stuck in my head when I wake up, and if that's the case it's usually the first song I put on when I turn on the iPod. If I don't have something specific in mind, I usually continue whatever had been playing when I turned it off the previous day. If it's not in the middle of something already, I'll just browse by artist until I find something that strikes my fancy. If I'm feeling indecisive I'll pick one of my big playlists set to random. The iPod generally comes off right before I get to the door to my office. If an album ends before I get there I'll take it off then. If a song is playing that I'm particularly fond of I'll take it off when the song is over. This means that some mornings I will take off my bag and coat and sit down with the headphones on, just so I can hear the rest of a really good song. If nobody's around I'll dance around a bit, too. (Kerry 6)

When I leave my apartment in the morning I grab my iPod and shove it in my pocket. By the time I get to the subway platform I am listening to my morning mix. This mix is 80s music ranging from Eurythmics to Blondie and The Smiths. It's an upbeat and a subtle mix that wakes me up and gets me motivated for my day. I will admit that some days I am not into the mood to go to work so I will put on something more sombre like Cat Power. I always plan what I will listen to and it reflects what I want to hear or feel at that time. Once I get in the elevator at my job I shut down the iPod so I can say 'Good morning' to my co-workers. (Joey 7)

Many users rarely mention the spaces that they daily pass through on their way to work; this may well be because they are so habitual as to not merit mention. However, users are often more attentive to their own mood and orientation which is facilitated by the sound pumped through the iPod in harmony with their desired mood, orientation or surroundings. iPod use re-orientates and re-spatialises experience which users often describe in solipsistic and aesthetic terms. Users frequently mention feelings of calm gained through listening to their iPod, in which the street is often represented as a mere backcloth, having minimal significance to the user. iPod use functions to simplify the user's environment thus enabling them to focus more clearly on their own state of being precisely by minimising the contingency of the street:

I feel as though life is a movie and is playing especially for me. If I listen to sad music, which I only listen to when I'm down (boyfriend break up, bad grade, just bad news) then everything sort of has a grey shadow over it, even when its sunny outside. Music is like a drug to me, and not just one drug that does one thing, but many different drugs that magnetise your existing mood, or even sometimes the music is so powerful that it changes the mood your in. Music can make you feel happy, horny, sad, wanting, etc . . . It can do wonders. (Betty 8)

> Frequently the iPod is more of a contemplative device than the actual thought of 'let's listen to music now'. Music is such a huge part of my life that it's almost imperative that I have something happening all the time. I have music stuck in my head almost nonstop for the same reason. So, yes . . . in certain moods, the iPod serves to extend and accentuate the mood rather than being a source of something to listen to. In fact, unless I'm listening to something specific (like a new artist), it's usually just there to have something playing in the background . . . helps my thoughts along. (Brian 9)

Listening to chosen music enables these iPod users to focus in on themselves. In these situations the music enables users to clear a space for thought, imagination and mood maintenance. The random nature of the sounds of the street does not produce the correct configuration or force to successfully produce or create the focusing of thoughts in the desired direction. Users may also personalise the time of the journey through using music as a form of 'auditory mnemonic' through which they attempt to construct a sense of narrative within urban spaces. The construction of a narrative becomes an attempt to maintain a sense of pleasurable coherence through their journey. iPod use, in these situations, represents a form of biographical travelling. The narrative quality that users attach to music permits them to reconstruct these narrative memories at will in places where they would otherwise have difficulty in summoning them up. These memories provide the user with a feeling of being warmly wrapped up in their own personalised space – a re-inscribing of their spatial present:

> There are certain playlists that I have put specifically together to fit certain moods (e.g. childhood, melancholy, road trips, party, dinner etc.). A song can transport me to any time and place in my life in a matter of seconds. It plays 'Wake Me Up, Before You Go Go' by Wham! and I am immediately walking down Oxford Street in my mind. It plays 'For a Few Dollars More' by Smokie, and I am back in my room at my parent's home, looking out of my window over the city of Zurich. It plays 'Unbelievable' by EMF, and I am back with my best friends in 'Serfaus' on our annual ski vacation that we used to have during the 90s. It plays 'Happy When it Rains' by Jesus and Mary Chain, and I am immediately back in the 'Swiss army', the time that I hated the most, but also brings back some of my most treasured memories, because my girlfriend was waiting for me at the train station, every time I got back home for the weekend. (Daniel 5)

For users who are habitually accompanied by music there arises a need for accompaniment as a constituent part of their experience. The world and their biography is recollected and accompanied by sound. This continuation of mood from home to street is achieved by bridging these spaces with music. Use can be described as creating a 'space' within which users unwind and unravel their emotions, thus providing a base for thinking more clearly or lucidly. If attended to the street becomes a function of either their mood and/or the music listened to:

> I like to crank angry, loud music at night; the city seems so much more dark and brutal in the dark if I do that. Walking home, I sometimes listen to more soaring, passionate melodies and they make me see things differently (sorten Muld, in particular, has a lot of ancient-sounding hymns which are sort of trance-like, and they make everything seem to be reduced to more elemental things, just metal, wind, clouds and sunlight.) I listen to rhythmic and pulsating music sometimes, which makes me feel confident and secure . . . I don't have to be anything but 'following the beat', so to speak. Sometimes I listen to piano music, and because most of my piano music is kind of depressing/saddening (in a good way), it makes the world seem more fragile and on the verge of collapse. Delerium's music always strikes me in this emotional, soul-searching way, and elevates even the smallest details to some greater significance; every movement of the people in the streets seems spiritual and sacred. Every once in a while I find songs that do this, and they really change everything. Massive Attack's 'Angel' is another one that does that-makes me swell up with this euphoric feeling! (Brian 9)

iPods tend to be non-interactive in the sense that users construct fantasies and maintain feelings of security precisely by not interacting with others or the environment. Aesthetic colonisation plays an important role in the daily use of iPod users. iPods are used both as a mundane accompaniment to the everyday and as a way of aestheticising and controlling that very experience. In doing so the iPod reorganises the user's relation to space and place. Sound colonises the listener but is also used to actively recreate and reconfigure the spaces of experience. Through the power of sound the world becomes intimate, known, and possessed. In consumer culture the imagination appears to work better with an accompaniment – iPod users find it difficult to aestheticise the street without their own individual soundtrack playing as a spur to the imagination.

Traditionally, street aesthetics have been understood through the notion of flanerie. Yet iPod users are no flaneurs; flaneurs traditionally imagined themselves in the shoes of those they observed – an alienated urban presence that wished to belong. iPod users rather make the urban street conform to their own aesthetic desire:

> Just having my own personal soundtrack to life makes things more focused. When I have the music going I guess its best described as tunnel vision. Without it, everything going on is just sort of unordered and noisy and a mix of sounds and sights. There's 10 different conversations going

on about 10 different things; people looking at you or doing their own thing. But when you have the soundtrack going it's like there's more a purpose. You're not just doing the motions that get me from my house to my classroom, but I'm making the trip between there. There's a definite purpose and sense of self. By sense of self, I mean that I can concentrate more on what I'm doing and less on what's going on around me with everyone else. (Matt 10)

[. . .]

The world beyond the music being played through the iPod becomes a function of the desire of the user and is maintained through time through the act of listening. The world is thus brought into line through acts of privatised, yet mediated, cognition. The user's sense of space is one in which the distinction between private mood or orientation and their surroundings is often abolished. The world becomes one with the experience of the iPod user. This re-working of urban space and time further points to a post-Fordist urban stance enacted by iPod users through their individualising of space and time. This process is at odds with recent accounts of urban habitation centred on Auge's notion of 'non-space'. For Auge:

> The word 'non-place' designates two complementary but distinct realities: spaces formed in relation to certain ends (transport, transit, commerce, leisure), and the relations that individuals have with these spaces. (Auge, 1995: p. 94.)

Yet my analysis of iPod use demonstrates that any space might be subjectively experienced by iPod users as a 'non-space'. Whilst motorways, for example, might be conceived of as non-spaces in the sense Auge means, the spaces experienced by iPod users are not structurally determined in the way that Auge assumes. The above analysis suggests that the meaning of space and time is also the result of a cognitive orientation to space. Auge also significantly locates sound as the defining feature of the experiencing of time in non-space:

> What reigns there is actuality, the urgency of the present moment. Since non-places are there to be passed through, they are measured in units of time. Itineraries do not work without timetables, lists of departures and arrival times. . .Most cars are fitted with radios; the radio plays continuously in service stations and supermarkets . . . everything proceeds as if space had been trapped by time, as if there were no history. (Auge, 1995: p. 104.)

This structurally determined image of space and time is at odds with iPod users' accounts of urban experience. iPod use provides users with their own 'unique' regulated soundscape that mediates the experience of whatever space is passed through and regulates the flow of time as they wish. The meaning of these spaces, often received as 'non-spaces' by users, is overlain by the mediated space of their very own sonic envelope from which meaning emanates. iPod users choose the manner in which they attend to these spaces, transforming space and time into their own personalised narrative.

CROWDED STREETS

People do not flock to these temples in order to talk or socialise. Whatever company they may wish to enjoy they carry with them, like snails carry their homes (Bauman, 2003: p. 98).

Simmel was perhaps the first sociologist to attempt to explain the significance and desire of urban citizens to maintain a sense of privacy, to create a mobile bubble, whilst on the move. Simmel's concerns were with sensory overload, crowds, strangers, and the noisy maelstrom of the city from which citizens retreat. Simmel charted the changing nature of bourgeois civility within the increasingly technologised urban geography of the early 20th century, addressing the relational nature and problems associated with people continually on the move in the city (Simmel, 1997). Whilst the street was perceived as invariably unpleasant, travel often posed an equally impossible burden with occupants of railway carriages having to sit and stare at strangers in close proximity for hours on end (Schivelbusch, 1986). The alien nature of the city street thus became inscribed into mainstream urban studies. Richard Sennett describes a passivised urban space in which the urban subject falls silent:

> Individual bodies moving through urban space gradually became detached from the space in which they moved, and from the people the space contained. As space became devalued through motion, individuals gradually lost a sense of sharing a fate with others. . .individuals create something like ghettos in their own bodily experience. (Sennett, 1994: p. 366.)

Sennett perceives the geography of the city to be both neutral and repelling in the cognitive orientation of the Western city dweller. Historically, it was the ears that were thought of as the most defenceless sense: the ears through which all sounds pass; unlike vision: you could always shut your eyes on the crowded train for example. The use of iPods empower the ears of the city dweller: the user can now re-organise the sounds of the city to his or her liking. This is both a continuation from the use of earlier 'privatising' technologies such as the personal stereo and a 'qualitative' transformation in as much as the user can now manage the interface between themselves and their environment through a multiplicity of music options. iPods empower the ears; auditory defencelessness is historicised. This empowerment also affects the other senses, as this paper has pointed out: the city becomes a personalised audio visual environment, yet even the sense of touch and the concomitant relational experience of the street is transformed, invariably making the iPod user happier as they move, empowered through the street:

> It is usually a mood elevator or, at least, a mood intensifier. For example, if I'm wearing it on a crowded city street, the crush of people seems like an obstacle course and a fun challenge to wend my way through. Without it, I would be annoyed and frustrated at my lack of progress through the crowd, but with it, it's almost as if I'm dancing. If I'm frustrated or angry, intense, driving music makes me feel like I have company in my mood. Pleasant weather seems that much more pleasant with music to accompany me. I am aware that, even when I'm not singing along, the way I walk and move and my facial expressions are affected by what music is playing. (Malcolm 16)

> When listening I find the rhythm of my path through people changes. . .I can ignore people better – the crowd dynamic in France is often difficult to handle (a lot of shoving), so the iPod reduces the impact of this. I also catch myself evaluating or thinking about people around me more when listening to music. (Patrick 17)

> I must weave through a sea of people. I am usually in a big hurry and the music helps me do this weaving. I feel like I can slide in and out of peoples' pathways and not even brush up against them like the continuous beat of a song. Meanwhile sirens are going off, car horns honking, and people talking on their cell phones and so much urban chaos. I will have my iPod and be listening to music, staying focused on all the things I need to do. The iPod drowns out all this noise and chaos . . . The subway is noisy with scratchy announcements and squeaking wheels. The noises make me irritated and nauseous, but if I have my headphones on it blocks the noises and makes me less irritable and impatient. If I wait on the subway platform for a half-hour I do not mind if I have my iPod to listen to. (Joey 7)

iPods can also be used as a form of conversational preserve, delimiting who the user wishes to converse with. On an everyday level, the use of an iPod is a method of not attending to interactional possibilities:

> I treasure my commuting time as a much-needed private space. Having my iPod on decreases the chance that this will be invaded so makes me feel calmer. You see: the risk of a work colleague 'bumping into me', especially on the way home, and wanting to TALK(!) is reasonably high. The iPod helps. In fact, this evening, I was on the station platform and aware, out of the corner of my eye, that there was a colleague on the

station platform. Having my iPod on made it possible for me to focus on the space in front of me (and so ignore him) without feeling that I looked disturbed! He's a nice bloke, of course; it's just that that commute time is the only real private time I get. (Adam 12)

Other users maintain their sense of autonomy as they move through the city. The following user describes walking through the streets of New York unfazed by both the attention of men and the blandness of her surroundings. She does not have to attend to the sounds of others or be captured in the glimpse of the eye as she moves to her own soundworld:

If I forget my iPod, it pretty much ruins my day. I crave it – need it – in order to tune out guys 'hey baby'-ing me, other people's conversations on the bus or subway, and colleague's phone conversations (work-related or otherwise). It also helps me feel less bored and soul-drained in malls, and less claustrophobic in crowds, which is very important to me. (Joey 7)

Users rather construct a range of interpersonal strategies that are inherently asymmetrical. Ways of auditized looking are developed which are inherently non-reciprocal, functioning to bolster the user's sense of power and control in urban space.

CONCLUSION

The creation of a personalised soundworld through iPod use creates a form of accompanied solitude for its users in which they feel empowered, in control and self-sufficient as they travel through the spaces of the city. The disjunction between the interior world of control and the external one of contingency and conflict becomes suspended as the user develops strategies for managing their movement mediated by music. The mobile and contingent nature of the journey is experienced precisely as its opposite precisely by creating and managing their own soundworld. The iPod, in effect, warms up the spaces of mobile habitation for users.

The increasing ability and desire of users to make the 'public' spaces of the city mimic their desire for accompanied solitude also has other potentially ambiguous results. It appears that as users become immersed in their mobile media sound bubbles, so those spaces they habitually pass through in their daily lives may increasingly lose significance for them and progressively turn into the 'non-spaces' of daily lives which they try, through those self same technologies, to transcend. The use of iPods demonstrates a clear auditory re-conceptualisation of the spaces of habitation embodied in users' strategies of placing themselves 'elsewhere' in urban environments. Users tend to negate public spaces through their prioritisation of their own technologically mediated private realm. The uses of these technologies enable users to transform the site of their experience into a form of 'sanctuary' (Sennett, 1994). The attempted exclusion of all forms of unwanted intrusion constitutes a successful strategy for urban and personal management; a re-inscribing of personal space through the consumption of personalised music. In doing so, iPod users both re-claim representational space (Lefebvre, 1991a) and the daily 'realm of the eversame' precisely by privatising it.

NOTES

1. The following empirical material derives from an ongoing qualitative research project on the use of iPods internationally. The 426 respondents are mainly from the UK, USA, Switzerland and Denmark. Respondents responded to interview requests posted on a variety of internet sites including Wired News, Macworld, BBC News Online and the Guardian Unlimited. Respondents completed a qualitative questionnaire of 35 questions. Individual respondents were then contacted again in relation to their specific responses. I have listed those used in this article below. The research is investigating the structural possibilities of iPod use and as such issues of local differences are not addressed in this paper. 1, Tracy is a 32-year-old publisher who works in the USA. 2, Sarah is a 23-year-old systems analyst living in Boston, USA. 3, Terry is a 23-year-old manager living in Calgary, Canada. 4, Mark is a 41-year-old network administrator living in the USA. 5, Daniel is a 37-year-old manager living in the USA. 6, Kerry is a 25-year-old medical technician living in Chicago, USA. 7, Joey is a 28-year-old researcher living in New York, USA. 8, Betty is a 21-year-old student from the USA. 9, Brian is a 17-year-old student from New York, USA. 10, Matt is a 21-year-old student from Washington, USA. 11, June is a 27-year-old insurance underwriter from Boston, USA. 12, Adam in a 35-year-old bank manager from New York, USA. 13, Sean is a 17-year-old student from Manchester, UK. 14, Andy is a 32-year-old journalist from Cardiff, UK. 15, Karen is a 25-year-old social worker from Washington, USA. 16, Malcolm is a 32-year-old salesman from Chicago, USA. 17, Patrick is a 31-year-old IT specialist living in Grenoble, Switzerland. 19, June is a 29-year-old student living in Los Angeles, USA.
2. The present article focuses on iPod users rather than MP3 users in particular. At present the iPod is by far the most popular MP3 player on the market, taking 70% of all sales worldwide.

REFERENCES

Adorno, T. (1976) *Introduction to the Sociology of Music* (New York: Continuum Press).

Auge, M. (1995) *Non-Places: Introduction to the Anthropology of Supermodernity* (London: Verso).

Bauman, Z. (2003) *Liquid Love* (Cambridge: Polity Press).

Benjamin, W. (1973) *Illuminations* (London: Penguin).

Brodsky, W. (2002) The effects of music tempo on simulated driving performance and vehicular control, *Transportational Research*, Part F, pp. 219–241.

Bull, M. (2000) *Sounding Out the City: Personal Stereos and the Management of Everyday Life* (Oxford: Berg).

Bull, M. (2003) Soundscapes of the car: a critical ethnography of automobile, in M. Bull & L. Back (Eds). *The Auditory Culture Reader*, pp. 357–380 (Oxford: Berg).

Bull, M. (2004) Sound connections: an aural epistemology of proximity and distance in urban culture. *Society and Space*, 22(1), pp. 103–116.

DeNora, T. (2000) *Music and Everyday Life* (Cambridge: Cambridge University Press).

Harvey, D. (1996) *Justice, Nature and the Geography of Difference* (Oxford: Blackwell).

Horkheimer, M. & Adorno, T. (1973) *The Dialectic of Enlightenment* (London: Penguin).

Katz, J. & Aakhus, M. (Eds) (2002) *Perpetual Contact: Mobile Communication. Private Talk, Public Performance* (Cambridge: Cambridge University Press).

Lefebvre, H. (1991) *A Critique of Everyday Life* (London: Verso).

Lefebvre, H. (1991b) *The Production of Space* (Oxford: Blackwell).

Livingstone, S. (2002) *Young People and the Media* (London: Sage).

Morley, D. (2002) *Home Spaces* (London: Routledge).

Peters, J. (1999) *Speaking into the Air. A History of the Idea of Communication* (Chicago: Chicago University Press).

Putnam, R. (2000) *Bowling Alone. The Collapse and Revival of American Community* (New York: Simon and Schuster).

Schivelbusch, W. (1986) *The Railway Journey. The Industrialisation of Time and Space in the 19th Century* (Berkeley: University of California Press).

Sennett, R. (1994) *Flesh and Stone. The Body and the City in Western Civilisation* (New York: Norton).

Simmel, G. (1997) The metropolis and mental life, in D. Frisby & M. Featherstone (Eds), *Simmel on Culture* (London: Sage).

Winston, B. (1998) *Media, Technology and Society, a History: from the Telegraph to the Internet* (London: Routledge).

FURTHER READING

Clucas, S., 'Cultural Phenomenology and the Everyday', *Critical Quarterly* 42:1 (2000) pp. 8–34.

Cockburn, C., 'The Circuit of Technology: Gender Identity and Power', in R. Silverstone and E. Hirsch (eds), *Consuming Technologies* (London: Routledge, 1992) pp. 33–42.

Couldry, N., 'Everyday Life in Cultural Theory', *European Journal of Communication* 18:2 (2003) pp. 265–70.

Couldry, N., 'Passing Ethnographies: Rethinking the Sites of Agency and Reflexivity in a Mediated World', in P. Murphy and M. Kraidy (eds), *Global Media Studies: Ethnographic Perspectives* (London: Routledge, 2003) pp. 40–56.

Gorman-Murray, A., 'Queering Home or Domesticating Deviance?', *International Journal of Cultural Studies* 9:2 (2006) pp. 227–47.

Highmore, B., *The Everyday Life Reader* (London: Routledge, 2005).

Latour, B., 'When Things Strike Back – A Possible Contribution to Science Studies', *British Journal of Sociology*, Millennium Issue (2000) pp. 1–13. Online at: http://www.ensmp.tr/~latour/articles/78-sciencestudies.htm.

Merrifield, A., 'Henri Lefebvre: A Socialist in Space', in M. Crang and N. Thrift (eds), *Thinking Space* (London: Routledge, 2000) pp. 167–82.

Perec, G., *Species of Spaces and Other Pieces* (London: Penguin, 1997).

Pink, S., *Doing Visual Ethnography* (London: Sage, 2001).

Silverstone, R., *Television and Everyday Life* (London: Routledge, 1984).

Silverstone, R., 'Domesticating Domestication: Reflections on the Life of a Concept', in T. Berker, M. Hartmann, Y. Punie and K. J. Ward (eds), *Domestication of Media and Technology* (London: Open University Press, 2006) pp. 229–48.

PART TWO
CASE STUDIES

SECTION 6
'REALITY' TELEVISION

INTRODUCTION: 'REALITY' TELEVISION

'Reality TV', or 'popular factual television', has exploded over the past ten years, both as a programming category and as an object of academic research. A quick web search, for example, reveals over fifteen academic books containing this title published within the past five years. While critics are agreed that it has become all-pervasive on our television screens, in the process 'remaking television culture and our understandings of it' (Ouellette and Murray 2004: 1), defining this 'mutant' form and assessing its cultural significance are rather more difficult. Initially used as a descriptor for popular 'law and order' programmes using 'live' footage of police chases – the definition Bill Nichols employs in Chapter 45 – 'reality TV' has expanded to include a wide range of programme formats which combine popular entertainment with claims to access 'the real'. It is, as Annette Hill writes (2005: 2), 'located in border territories': between information and entertainment, drama and documentary, the public and the private. If one line of antecedents lies in the documentary form of *cinema vérité*, with its 'fly-on-the-wall' techniques, another can be found in the soap opera, game show and daytime talk show. While the 'truth' claims of documentary lie in notions of public responsibility – the provision of knowledge and understanding of, and arguments about, historical reality – the 'real people' who are the subjects of reality TV are presented for our entertainment.

On the one hand, then, it can be argued that reality TV is a democratising force. Ib Bondebjerg, for example, argues that it could be seen as an outcome of 'the democratic impact of visual media on public discourse through a new *integration* of forms of public and private interaction which used to be clearly separated'. What we may be witnessing, therefore, is 'the democratization of an old public service discourse . . . and the creation of a new mixed public sphere, where common knowledge and everyday experience play a much larger role' (1996: 29). Reality TV, argues Laura Grindstaff, challenges 'conventional boundaries separating public from private, reason from emotion, news from entertainment, fact from fiction, and expert knowledge from common opinion' (1997: 165). Yet the presentation of 'ordinary people' as objects of visual spectacle rather than political understanding, the constructed and packaged format of the shows and the element of performance which characterises the behaviour of participants all suggest the opposite: that reality TV commodifies and exploits its participants, leaving the hierarchy of television discourses intact.

For Bill Nichols (Chapter 45), writing in 1994, reality TV's blurring of boundaries between fact and fiction, reality and representation, signals the death of the documentary form, with its claims to authenticity and sense of a historical world beyond representation. Reality TV, in contrast, absorbs reality into spectacle, offering talk as distraction and news as non-history, a perpetual 'now'. Here, for Nichols, is Baudrillard's universe of tele-visual simulation (Chapter 6), and the viewer response invited, he argues, is one of detached consumption, distracted viewing and episodic amazement. Unlike documentary, reality TV does not address us as citizens who might act in the real world in response to the argument it makes. Instead, it absorbs us into its screen-world, substituting sensation for argument and the random and unforeseen for order and cohesion. It is a symptom, argues Nichols, of a collapse in the authority of the powerful: their explanations (or 'master narratives') are no longer believed. But it is not a *critical* response: its focus on localised events may produce a politics of sorts, but it will be a decontextualised and reactive politics, mobilised around emotion not explanation.

Chapter 46, by Annette Hill, traces 'the rise of reality TV' from its roots in tabloid journalism, documentary and popular entertainment. Beginning with the crime and emergency services programmes discussed by Nichols, Hill traces the development of this shifting and hybrid genre through the 'docu-soap', lifestyle programmes whose roots were in daytime programming, the reality gameshow with its use of convergent media technologies, reality gameshow-variety show hybrids like *Pop Idol* and finally 'life experiment programmes' such as *Wife Swap*. Reality formats, she argues, provide 'a never-ending supply of non-professional actors in new series of existing formats', but their performative character can lead to self-parody. The rise of reality TV was a product of the rising costs of existing programme formats, together with the deregulation and marketisation of media industries in the 1990s. Its success, however, has been at the expense of the traditional documentary form, news and current affairs – the heart of public service broadcasting.

Issues of gender and class in reality TV are raised by Chapters 47 and 48. In Chapter 47 Sue Thornham discusses the daytime talk show and makeover programme in terms of the claims that have been made that they represent a transformation or feminisation of the Habermasian public sphere (see Chapter 5).

Drawing on the work of Susan Bordo (Chapter 28), she argues that although notions of 'the real' and 'authenticity' are as central to such programmes as they are to news and documentary programming, the concept of 'the real' on which they draw is one centred on the body, and in particular the excessive bodies of (largely working-class) women. While these shows might have offered women a new public visibility, therefore, blurring the boundaries between public and private domains, their structures repeatedly enact a narrative structure in which 'a staged display of bodily and emotional excess' is contained and transformed. Finally, Thornham suggests three reasons why these programmes are problematic in terms of claims that they represent a 'democratisation' of the public sphere. First, participants are presented not as social and political actors but as 'mythical' figures who enact 'exemplary or cautionary' narratives. Second, the model of resolution which is employed is individual and therapeutic rather than social or political. Finally, these programmes are 'low culture', operating in the devalued domain of 'the feminine'. Despite their focus on women, therefore, 'real women' within them fulfil the same function as they do in news programming: their roles are as victims, 'ordinary people', embodiments of personal experience or the voice of popular opinion.

In Chapter 48 Anita Biressi and Heather Nunn discuss the narratives of class mobility and success which underpin reality TV shows like *Big Brother* or *Pop Idol*. In many reality shows, they argue, 'there is a submerged narrative about escape across classed boundaries' and participants are clearly presented as 'classed subjects'. Where once such mobility was a product of social and economic achievement, however, these new narratives are dependent on notions of celebrity, consumption and performance. They are thus 'media-driven' but also dependent on complex judgements by the 'ordinary people' who constitute their audiences. What Biressi and Nunn call 'classed cross-dressing' dominates participants' performances. The ability to 'pass' as a celebrity – to be 'distinctive' or 'outrageous' – is crucial for success, yet at the same time participants' behaviour must not move too far from their class origins lest they be seen as betraying the 'authentic' ordinariness which links them with their audiences. In the final section of the chapter, Biressi and Nunn turn to recent reality series in which the already permeable boundaries between audience and performers, media and social realm, are further eroded. In these series, in which celebrities perform labour within a space open to public participation, they argue, audiences are free to incorporate such mediated performances into their everyday lives, at the same time as they are themselves being recorded and packaged as objects for (their own) consumption.

The final chapter in this section (Chapter 49) by Nick Couldry develops further arguments about the social implications of what Couldry calls 'game-docs' like *Big Brother*. Such programmes, he argues, do not merely constitute a sub-genre of television programming: they are also social processes whose characteristics, structures and ideological functions are important for the understanding of the relationship of media to social space and social power.

His analysis draws on the work of Roland Barthes (see the Introduction to Section 3.1 'Textual Structures') and Michel Foucault (see Chapter 7), to argue that the gamedoc's (mythical) claims to represent social reality can be understood in terms of Foucault's concept of social power, in which power is enacted not simply through forms of regulation but also through forms of 'expression and self-definition'. The gamedoc like other media forms, he argues, operates through ritual action and processes of 'ritualisation' to reproduce particular forms of power relations through its claim to represent 'human reality'. This claim takes a number of forms: the claim that the controlled space of the gamedoc operates like the laboratory to reveal truths about 'human nature'; the claim that processes of surveillance *reveal* the social world; the claim that mediated reality is more significant – *tells us more* – than non-mediated reality. The rituals on which the gamedoc depends – the weekly vote, the Diary Room, the ceremonial crossing of space between the inside space of the gamedoc and the outside, the explicitly mediated space of the final interview – are not simply generic characteristics; they also enact specific social values. The 'celebrification process' enacted in *Big Brother*, for example, is based on the concept of a fundamental boundary between (unvalued) 'ordinary person' and (valued) 'media person' at the same time as it enacts the possibilities of transformation. Finally, Couldry calls for an 'ethical critique' of reality TV in order to address the ways in which media are transforming, and being transformed by, the social space in which we all live.

REFERENCES

Bondebjerg, I., 'Public Discourse/Private Fascination: Hybridization in "True-life-story" Genres', *Media, Culture & Society* 18:1 (1996) pp. 27–45.

Grindstaff, L., 'Producing Trash, Class and the Money Shot: A Behind-the-Scenes Account of Daytime TV Talk', in J. Lull and S. Hinerman (eds), *Media Scandals* (Cambridge: Polity, 1997) pp. 164–202.

Hill, A., *Reality TV: Audiences and Popular Factual Television* (London: Routledge, 2005).

Ouellette, L. and Murray, S., 'Introduction', in S. Murray and L. Ouellette (eds), *Reality TV: Remaking Television Culture* (New York: New York University Press, 2004) pp. 1–15.

45

REALITY TV AND SOCIAL PERVERSION

Bill Nichols

> Isn't it time you felt that way again?
> – Saturn car ad

> It protects you like a man, treats you like a woman.
> – Lady Speed Stick ad

> Kill the germs. Keep the kids.
> – Liquid Dial ad

Reality TV is to the documentary tradition as sexual 'perversion' was to 'normal' sexuality for Freud. The biological purpose of sexuality – reproduction – is no longer served by perversions that have purposes of their own. Similarly, representations whose purpose is to absorb and neutralize all questions of magnitude no longer serve the ostensible purpose of news: to facilitate collective action based on fresh information. (Perverse purposes need not necessarily be condemned; perversity's willingness to disregard social and moral codes lends it great potential for subversions of all kinds. Each case requires separate assessment. Sexual perversities can have great value for what they reveal, and refuse, of our culture's prohibitions and constraints; the value of the perversity of reality TV may lie in the gleeful abandon with which it mocks, or rejects, civic-mindedness and the positivist social engineering behind it.)

Reality TV extends into the zones that threaten to erupt within network

From Bill Nichols, *Blurred Boundaries: Questions of Meaning in Contemporary Culture* (Bloomington: Indiana University Press, 1994) pp. 51–60.

news itself but normally remain repressed. Reality TV anneals the felt gap opened by historical consciousness between representation and referent. Dan Rather's strangely hallucinatory tour of an Iraqi bunker reveals the symptomatic return of this repressed. Believing himself surrounded by booby traps, in constant bodily peril, Rather acts out a tableau of vicarious concern for American lives that might have been lost. News becomes dramatic spectacle, a simulacrum of eventfulness for which there is no original (this *is* the moment of discovery, and danger, such as it is, for Rather).[1]

> It's sorta like havin' a seat in the front row of life.
>> – Patrol car officer, speaking of his job, *Top Cops*

> While most of the outrageous events the realities and tabs are concerned with actually happen, they fortunately happen somewhere else, to someone else. And that allows us to be discrete voyeurs, occupying front-row seats for these displays of human folly.
>> – Van Gordon Sauter, 'Rating the Reality Shows,' *TV Guide*

Reality TV's perverse kinship with traditional documentary film, network newscasting, and ethnographic film lies in its ability to absorb the referent. The digestive enzymes of reality TV (its distracting quality and spectacle, its dramatic story lines and self-perpetuation) break the referent down into palatable confections that do not represent an absent referent so much as cannibalize and assimilate it into a different type of substance. The historical world becomes reduced to a set of simulations and idle talk (Heidegger's *gerede*). The webs of signification we build and in which we act pass into fields of simulation that absorb us but exclude our action. Referentiality dissolves in the nonbeing and nothingness of TV.

What characterizes reality TV most broadly is the production of a feeling tone in the viewer similar to that produced by an exceptional acrobatic feat, superb magic tricks, or the sudden appearance of a full-scale helicopter thirty feet above the stage in *Miss Saigon*: 'Isn't that amazing!'

> Now, how are they going to get the wife over here, because she can't swim.
>> – Elderly husband of a woman still trapped in her car by a torrential flood in the Arizona desert, *Code 3*

A reality TV special, *Miracles and Other Wonders* (June 5, 1992), reported the story of Barney, a black truck driver, who played good samaritan by deviating from his route to answer a distress call from a driver suffering a heart attack. Voice-over comments by the host accompany a reconstruction of the events, like the traditional *benshi* presenter of Japanese silent films. Barney finds the man and radios for paramedics who are able to stabilize the man and get him to a hospital where he recovers. The oddest part of the story, though, is that when they examine the man's car, they see no trace of the CB radio he would have needed in order to contact truck driver Barney.

This apparent act of telepathy would have been amazing enough, but several years later Barney succumbs to a heart attack of his own while trekking through remote country on a fishing trip. Friends manage to get him to a nearby Indian village but despair that the nurse who only visits once a month will not be there. Miraculously, she is. Even more miraculously, she is not alone. Her father, a cardiologist, happens to accompany her. The man steps into the room where Barney rests and, lo and behold, it is the very man Barney saved all those years before! His quick action spares Barney from certain death.

Isn't that amazing!

> When we return a woman needs your help to find her long-lost twin brother.

> – *Unsolved Mysteries*

This ebb and flow of detached consumption, distracted viewing, and episodic amazement exists in a time and space outside history, outside the realm in which physical, bodily engagement marks our existential commitment to a project and its realization. 'Project' refers to Sartre's idea of an engaged, committed life in the world, and in the body, where every 'experience' remains charged with importance in this larger context – exactly what reality TV denies or perverts. Here we have disembodied but visceral experience, a freewheeling zone in which the same set of emotional responses recycle with gradually diminishing force until the next raise of the ante in the production of spectacle.

These responses are keyed to a conventional story format. It is something like a perversely exhibitionistic version of the melodramatic imagination: provide a 'hook' by underlining an important aspect of the case – its scale, severity, uniqueness, or consequences; offer a dab of location realism; sketch in characters quickly; dramatize sensational aspects of the case – usually aspects of intense threat to human life and bodily integrity; move swiftly to an emotional climax; and urge a specific response – grief, alarm, fear, consolation, shock. Conclude the episode with a resonant moment and perhaps a pause for affective response to the marvelous and terrifying, the challenging and remarkable, the extraordinary and co upt.

In a phrase, 'Isn't that .nazing!'[2]

A chronicle of contingent, futureless moments strung together in a protracted morality play produces an entire telescape that does not so much screen us off from reality, or refer us back to it, as beam us aboard a tele-visual simulation. Our subjectivity streams toward the videoscreen that welcomes us to its cyborg circuits of information, noise, feedback, and homeostatic redundancy.

Instead of a charge up San Juan Hill (filmed by Vitagraph employees J. Stuart Blackton and Albert E. Smith in 1898), we see a charge into a suspected amphetamine lab (on *Cops* in 1992). The first charge was represented as news, as a report on the finality of the already done (with clear awareness of how public opinion might be shaped by such reports).[3] The second charge, even if news in some sense that is not examined, hangs in suspended animation: every moment, every action, takes shape around the sensation of contingency. We *are* at the moment of filming: 'Nothing has been changed, except, You are there.' Desperate criminals or terrified children may pop into the frame. Shots may be fired or profuse apologies offered. Suspects may submit immediately, in resigned silence or sullen anger, or they may resist, shouting, twisting, flailing at their captors. The stress on a sense that 'You never know what might happen next,' and the parallel admonition to 'Do your part to help bring criminals to justice,' makes this richly constructed sense of contingency a vital element in the pervasive 'now' of tele-reality. Social responsibility dissolves into tele-participation.

Our subjectivity is less that of citizens, social actors or 'people,' than of cyborg collaborators in the construction of a screen-world whose survival hinges on a support system designed to jack us into the surrounding commodity stream, around which an entire aesthetic of simulated pleasure exists. We cannot read these shows as built upon a prefigurative ground that would entail a particular moral or political stance toward the surrounding world.[4] Documentary film had a vested interest in our behavior and disposition beyond the theater. Reality TV has a vested interest in subsuming everything beyond itself into its own support system of circulating exchange values. This circulatory system incorporates the only behavior that really matters: consuming. Careful explication of episodes or shows serves little point at all, at least in the conventional terms of textual analysis and narrative structure. Their meaning comes from elsewhere, from the tele-world to which they belong and in which 'we' are constituted as messages-in-the-circuit of contingency, participation, consumption.

Reality TV, then, plays a complex game. It keeps reality at bay. It succeeds in activating a sense of the historical referent beyond its bounds but also works, constantly, to absorb this referent within a tele-scape of its own devising. Reference to the real no longer has the ring of sobriety that separates it from fiction. Such reference now *is* a fiction. Participation is fully absorptive. The gap is sealed, the referent assimilated. We enter the twilight border zone of virtual reality.

THE TELE-SACRAMENTAL

An odd characteristic of this ebb and flow of sensation and banality is its simulation of a spiritual dimension, well beyond the televangelism that exhorts us to participate by phoning in our donations as the crime shows urge us to call in our tips. Reality TV offers a continuous confessional for the sins of the world. It promises the absolution of sins when we participate in the redemption of everyday life. (Phone in, stay tuned, consume.)

Reality TV tenders charity for 'those poor people' it parades before us as victims of violence and disaster. It urges faith – in the ceaseless baptism in the tele-real for those wishing never to be bored again. It offers hope for a future constantly collapsing into an ever-expanding present.

> Now, when her daughter's killer escaped the death sentence, police say she showed up with a loaded gun. More in a moment.
>
> *– Hard Copy*

Reality TV may not be 'intimately bound up with women's work,' as Tania Modleski argued on behalf of daytime soap operas, but it is bound up with everyday experience.[5] Reality TV shares many of the characteristics Modleski assigns to fictional soap operas such as a participatory quality (connection to versus separation from); a sense that characters or social actors are 'like me' – unlike stars who are of decidedly different status; an emphasis on knowledge of what others might do or think (troubled characters, potential dates, criminals at large) rather than strictly factual 'know how';[6] acceptance and acknowledgment that viewers are subject to 'interruption, distraction, and spasmodic toil';[7] multiple plot lines; and casts of characters who may not know each other. As Modleski argues, soaps have a special meaningfulness for their target audience; they are more than filler, audiovisual wallpaper or escape. So is reality TV.

> All suspects are innocent until proven guilty in a court of law.
>
> *– Voice-over introduction, Cops*

> We asked for your help last week and you provided some good leads. If you see Peter Fisher, call 1–800-CRIME-92.

> If you see James Ashley, call us right now.

> If you think you know who kidnapped little Terry Molini, call our hot line tonight. . . . Please have the courage to call.
>
> *– John Walsh, host, America's Most Wanted*

> 'Shrift': the confession of one's sins, especially to a priest in the sacrament of penance (*Websters*).
>
> 'Short shrift' originally meant the abbreviated sacrament offered to criminals condemned to die and thence took on the meaning of summary treatment. The tele-confessional offers only short shrift. Now, see this. Act now. Tomorrow is too late.

If you know anything that can help solve this case, call us at
1–800–876–5353.

– Robert Stack, *Unsolved Mysteries*

Thanks for a nation of finks.

– William S. Burroughs

Reality TV patrols borders and affirms the law. It also offers a therapeutic
ritual for encounter with what lies beyond the law. Reality TV substitutes the
confessional dynamics of viewers who phone in their response for the confession that cannot be: the criminal's penance. Neither we nor the tele-confessional
itself can grant forgiveness for those whose guilt is not the point. But we can
obtain it for ourselves. What Foucault says of confession as a strategy for the
regulation of sexuality seems to apply vividly, but not to the suspects whom we
encounter as much as to our own vicariously participatory dynamic:

> [The confession] is a ritual that unfolds within a power relationship,
> for one does not confess without the presence (*or virtual presence*) of a
> partner who is not simply the interlocutor but the authority who requires
> the confession, prescribes and appreciates it and intervenes in order to
> judge, punish, forgive, console, and reconcile; . . . and finally, *a ritual in*
> *which the expression alone, independently of its external consequences*,
> produces intrinsic modifications in the person who articulates it: it
> exonerates, redeems, and purifies him; it unburdens him of his wrongs,
> liberates him, and promises him salvation.[8] (italics mine)

But the redemptive virtue of our calling, as it were, is not stressed as
much as the purgation of fear through the sensation/pleasure of vicariously
participating – a simulation of the form of the confessional without its content.
Our engagement is less in terms of a civic duty than in terms of the perpetuation of a moment, here and now, when confessional engagement is always possible. We have the pleasure of situating ourselves within a cybernetic feedback
loop, absolved, over and over, of all necessity to step beyond it.

The spiritual quality of this appeal permeates a dimensionless surface of
sensation. The phatic bond – the open channel, the phone operators 'standing
by,' the pleas of 'Don't go away,' the possibility that you may have something
to contribute at any moment – offer the sensation of connectedness, of tele-
communion. Here is a connectedness that affirms the work patterns and social
hierarchies from which we allegedly escape. Vicarious participation as (virtual)
confession constructs spirals of power and pleasure:

> The power that lets itself be invaded by the pleasure it is pursuing; and
> opposite it, power asserting itself in the pleasure of showing off, scandal-
> izing, or resisting. . . . These attractions, these evasions, these circular

incitements have traced around bodies and sexes, not boundaries not to be crossed, but *perpetual spirals of power and pleasure.*[9]

Reality TV offers communion drawn from atomized, dissociated figures who remain so; a sense of engagement, empathy, charity, and hope built on a disengaged, detached simulation of face-to-face encounter; and a sense of coherence and continuity, if not suspended animation, at a time when ideas and values *feel* worn, ineffective, abused, and bandied about. Here is another form of televisual perversion: the (virtual) conversion of spiritual ritual to social, institutional, hierarchical purposes of its own.

Spectacle: Grounded Sensation

Tele-spectacle treats sensations the way an electrical circuit treats shorts: it runs them to ground. The very intensity of feeling, emotion, sensation, and involvement that reality TV produces is also discharged harmlessly within its dramatic envelope of banality. The historical referent, the magnitudes that exceed the text, the narratives that speak of conduct in the world of face-to-face encounter, bodily risk, and ethical engagement ground themselves harmlessly in circuits devoted to an endless flux of the very sensations they run to ground, a perfect balancing act of homeostatic regulation.

Transitions from one attraction to the next are moments of risk. Alternatives to 'Isn't it amazing' threaten to intrude. 'Stay tuned,' 'Don't go away,' 'More in a minute.' These endless pleas to maintain the phatic connection between show and viewer while our hosts mysteriously 'go away' underscore the urgency of self-promotion. The pleas implore us to grant these denizens in a box the right to persist, as though it were in our power to annihilate them. And perhaps for a fleeting moment we believe they are at our mercy as we decide whether or not to grant them a continuing presence in the telescape they hope to share with us.

An orchestrated sense of distraction saves the day.

> After an extensive profile of ex-baseball pitcher Denny McLain which touched on his jail term for drug use, his rehabilitation as a radio talk-show host, and the death of his daughter at the hands of a drunk driver, the male co-host intones, speaking to the camera (us), 'No family should endure that much tragedy.'
>
> His female co-host looks toward her partner, pauses, then, looking back toward the camera, responds, 'Now, if you need to try pulling a few rabbits out of the boudoir, try the *magic* of making love.'
>
> A set of ads follow, then a story on Dr. Miriam Stoppard's new book, *The Magic of Sex*. At its conclusion the co-host says, 'Now, when her daughter's killer escaped the death sentence, police say she showed up with a loaded gun. More in a moment' (another set of ads follow).
>
> *– Hard Copy*

The melodramatic novel arose at a time when contending classes, the aristocracy and bourgeoisie, could see their own precarious class situation played out in fiction (for example, the sentimental novels and romantic dramas of the eighteenth century that surround the French revolution, such as *Clarissa* and *Nouvelle Héloise, Emilia Galiotti* and *Kabale und Liebe*).[10] Reality TV offers another version of this effort to represent anxieties of social stability and mobility at a time when economic solvency, let alone prosperity, hangs in doubt. The fate of middle-class 'in-betweeners' is uncertain, split as it is between a richer and more insulated upper class and a despondent and more isolated 'underclass.' White-collar, mid-level managers in Ohio may suddenly find their work delegated to a monitoring system and computer network based in Osaka in these days of transnational globalization. Paranoia may be one form of response to a system without a center; in this case, responsibility diffuses into an amorphous, unrepresentable 'they.'[11]

Reality TV, though, stems anxiety less with paranoia than with a schizoid-like detachment from and reconstruction of the 'reality' it re-presents. Beset by dreams of rising and nightmares of falling, plagued by the terror of pillage, plunder, and rape, the 'target' audience for reality TV (white, middle-class consumers with 'disposable' income) attends to a precarious world of random violence and moment-to-moment contingency (as inexplicable to viewers as it was to Tom Brokaw).

> The decimation of the men within the population is quite nearly total. Four of five births in East St. Louis are to single mothers. Where do the men go? Some to prison. Some to the military. Many to an early death. Dozens of men are living in the streets or sleeping in small, isolated camps behind the burnt-out buildings. There are several of these camps out in the muddy stretch there to the left.
> – Safir Ahmed, *St. Louis Post-Dispatch* reporter, quoted in Jonathan Kozol, *Savage Inequalities*

> In 1991, 21,859 white students earned Ph.D. degrees. In the same year, 933 black students earned Ph.D.s, the first year the percentage of black students earning doctorates had increased in thirteen years.
> – *S.F. Chronicle*, May 4, 1992

The aesthetics of immediacy, conjured in a timeless, spaceless telescape of mediated reality, drowns out the descriptions, like Ahmed's, that urge us to further action beyond exclamation or dismay. An aesthetics of sensation underlies reality TV: Its claims of authenticity, its construction of an endless 'now,' its preference for the chronicle, the random and the unforeseen over the order and cohesion of historiography and the problem-solving discourses of a technocratic order all come at a time when master narratives are a target of disparagement.

Under what conditions does the need to represent contingency and to reject order prevail? One answer is: Contingency looms when an elite, or ruling class, can no longer convince others or itself of its rightful primacy (when hegemony fails). Unpredictability, uncertainty, contingency: they loom as symptoms of incomprehension masquerading behind an aesthetics of sensation when those for whom hegemony has failed demand alternative visions and different futures. These demands cannot be understood in the form they are spoken. 'A riot is the language of the unheard,' asserted Martin Luther King, Jr. Instead these demands register as noise, confusion, chaos. Their negation of what is and their transformative call for what ought to be cannot be contained. They lie beyond the law. Those who speak no longer convince us that they can speak for others; a dumb silence haunts the endless talk. 'We' may be 'the people,' but 'we' are also many, and among that many are diverse cultures and subcultures, affinity groupings and collectivities that lie beyond the pale of reality TV.

An insistence on *differences that make a difference* confounds a sense of hierarchy, undermines standard reference points, and questions received notions of quality or excellence. This diffusion of power and control may seem closely akin to the form of reality TV. But there is a major difference that makes a difference. Reality TV may be as sensational as it wishes, it may be as seemingly decentered, ahistorical, and futureless as it chooses, but, in its present manifestations, it is never critical of the hierarchy perpetuated by its own form or of the power rooted in its dynamic of vicarious (or virtual) participation. Reality TV can be as heterogenous, dispersive, self-conscious, and reflexive as all get out, but it never calls our own position as virtual participant and actual consumer into question. It can tolerate our talking back and mocking its own self-mocking forms but not our refusal to listen to its (empty) talk at all.[12]

We presume immunity from this perversion or dis-ease at some peril, however. There is a risk that the *form* of political struggle may take on qualities akin to those of reality TV. The simple dramatic envelopes placed around localized events that rapidly play themselves out, passing our attention on to their successor, are a dangerous model for political struggle. Such dramatic protest rituals allow for sharply focused moral outrage but often channel it into partial or token victories that leave basic structural conditions unchanged. Celebrating the conviction of two LAPD officers for beating Rodney King 'ends' the story, on the episodic level, but does nothing to address the social conditions that underpin it structurally.

The danger exists that actual struggles will take their cue from the rhythms of reality TV: specific issues and events will become a target of concern or outrage; emotions will wax and wane in keeping with the dramatic curve of televised coverage (Three Mile Island, the Gulf War, Anita Hill and Clarence Thomas, the Panama invasion, 'ethnic cleansing,' Rodney King). Coalitions, support groups, ad hoc committees and rallies will spring up. Collective identities take shape and a common agenda will emerge. But the specific event will eventually reach a point of resolution. The forces once mobilized with fervor and outrage will disperse, potentially available for the next contingency. Such a pattern constructs a reactive politics that may mirror, in disturbing ways, the very forms of absorption and distraction that should be among its primary targets.

Reality TV seeks to reimagine as broad a collectivity or target audience for its sponsors as possible. Hence the tendency to represent experience as spectacle framed only by the banalities of a crude morality play. This form of orchestrated spectacle stands in an antithetical relationship to the project of an existential phenomenology.

Reality TV and Political Consciousness

What reality TV (a phrase that shows no embarrassment at its oxymoronic ring) eliminates is any coming to historical consciousness. By historical consciousness I mean something akin to consciousness raising: an awareness of the present in relation to a past active within it and a future constantly being made in the thick of the present, together with a heightened consciousness of one's relation to others in the common project of the social construction of reality. Such a consciousness holds production and consumption, past and future, in a dialectical relationship. It is what films like *Who Killed Vincent Chin?* and *JFK* may bring into being, and what reality TV perverts. We can turn off the tube to go shopping with no alteration in the distracted state of consciousness a perpetual 'now' encourages.

The founding principle of surrealism – the juxtaposition of incommensurate realities as a jarring act that forces the beholder to see things anew, casting off old habits and assumptions, seeing the strange quality of the familiar in ways that propose alternative values and action – this collage principle becomes absorbed by a telescape from which it cannot escape. There is no 'Aha!' on reality TV. A subsuming 'logic' absorbs all incommensurate juxtapositions. It denies contradiction by refusing to propose any frame from which more local gaps, disturbances, or incompatibilities could be rearranged coherently. Reality TV is one significant piece of a postmodern aesthetic in which what was once incompatible, incommensurate, and contradictory – experiences that compelled us to search for resolution, if not revolution – coexist inside a boundless envelope of presence that banishes historical consciousness from its bounds.

Notes

1. The appeal of reality TV approximates that of snuff movies, but tailored to the codes of taste required by prime-time broadcasting. The sober-minded trappings of respectable hosts and corporate sponsors, of documentary details and eyewitness reports, successfully deflect anger away from this perverse mode of production itself, allowing reality TV shows to prompt a discharge of anger and amazement at people who can be so extraordinary. 'How could this happen?' we ask of what we see rather than of what produces what we see.

2. This format has a ring of the familiar to it not only as a primal recipe for spectacle or for its own banality. It also cannibalizes many of the melodramatic elements of the morality plays of early films such as Edwin S. Porter's *The Life of an American Fireman* (1902) and *The Great Train Robbery* (1903); Cecil Hepworth's *Rescued by Rover* (1905); or D. W. Griffith's *A Corner in Wheat* (1909), *The Lonely Villa* (1909), *The Lonedale Operator* (1911), and *The Musketeers of Pig Alley* (1912). Characters are quickly sketched out in stereotypic fashion, playing roles that frequently recapitulate those of the nuclear family: strong and benevolent patriarchs, earnest sons and respectful suitors, devious rivals and underhanded villains, honorable but vulnerable women, corrupted women of the night, innocent children, and devoted mothers. Conflict centers around the struggle between good and evil, between virtuous Abels and immoral Cains, in domestic wars on drugs, robbery, theft, kidnapping, murder, gambling, and cruel confidence games.

   Reality TV, however, absorbs melodrama, like documentary, perversely. Its purposes may still allow us to think of these forms in terms of class (they both speak to the precariousness of a world order when perceived from a middle-class point of view), but seldom in terms of domestic drama, the affective domain of women's experience, the maternal dilemma imposed on women of choosing either self-fulfillment or sacrifice, or in terms of the use of stylistic excess to draw our attention to the very force of repression itself.

3. See Raymond Fielding, *The American Newsreel: 1911–1967* (Norman: University of Oklahoma Press, 1972), for a useful account of the blurred boundaries and social purposes of early news reporting. During the Spanish-American War, the Battle of Santiago Bay, for example, was reenacted on movie lots more than once, in one case using cutout photographs of the actual warships.

4. The reference here is to Hayden White's *Metahistory*, in which he argues that historiographic writing undergoes prefiguration as its authors opt for various modes of narrative representation. These choices then establish the moral tone of historical accounts that use reference to 'what happened' in a sort of *trompe d'oeil* move in which it now seems that the historical world itself has authorized this particular tone, this particular understanding of history. Reality TV, since it does not offer narratives on the level of historiography, also does not choose among prefigurative options. Its function and effect rely on its implosive quality: it does not so much account for the historical world as subsume it into a world of its own.

5. Tania Modleski, 'The Rhythms of Reception: Daytime Television and Women's Work', in E. Ann Kaplan, ed., *Regarding Television* (Frederick, MD: University Publications of America, 1983), 74.

6. 'How to' shows are another genre, testing another boundary. They, too, substitute vicarious participation for face-to-face encounter but also allow for viewers to 'follow along,' as they learn how to imitate what their mentors do. Cooking, home renovation, and gardening shows also activate a sense of the referent beyond and promise of easy passage to it. This *ease* of passage (no budget or bills, no issues of ownership or privacy, no questions of crime or poverty intrude) allows for everyday experience to effortlessly transform nature into culture, the raw into the cooked. The patrol-car duties performed elsewhere provide the guarantee for this ease.

7. Modleski, 'The Rhythms of Deception', 71.

8. Michel Foucault, *The History of Sexuality*, vol. 1 (New York: Vintage Books, 1980), 61–62.

9. Foucault, *The History of Sexuality*, 45.

10. For a superb sketch of the backdrop to Hollywood melodrama of the 1940s and '50s in the eighteenth and nineteenth-century novel, see Thomas Elsaesser, 'Tales of Sound and Fury', *Monogram*, no. 4 (1972): 2–15, reprinted in Bill Nichols, ed., *Movies and Methods*, vol. II (Berkeley: University of California Press, 1985).

11. See Fredric Jameson's *The Geopolitical Aesthetic: Cinema and Space in the World System* (Bloomington: Indiana University Press, 1992) for an extended discussion of representations of paranoia, particularly in Western cinema.

12. The variable, historically contingent linkage between subversion and form is made quite succinctly by Judith Butler in an interview: 'There is no easy way to know whether something is subversive. Subversiveness is not something that can be gauged or calculated. In fact, what I mean by subversion are those effects that are incalculable. I do think that for a copy to be subversive of heterosexual hegemony it has to both mime and displace its conventions. And not all miming is displacing.' Interview with Liz Kotz, 'The Body You Want', *Artforum* (November 1992): 84.

46

THE RISE OF REALITY TV

Annette Hill

Successful reality TV series such as *Survivor* or *Big Brother* are marketed as 'all new' – new concepts, new formats, new experiences. Few television shows are 'all new'. But it is certainly the case that reality programmes draw from existing television genres and formats to create novel hybrid programmes. 'Factual entertainment' is a category commonly used within the television industry for popular factual television, and the category indicates the marriage of factual programming, such as news or documentary, with fictional programming, such as gameshows or soap opera. Indeed, almost any entertainment programme about real people comes under the umbrella of popular factual television. Reality TV is a catch-all category, and popular examples of reality programming, such as *Changing Rooms* (BBC, 1996–), *Cops* (Fox, 1988–), *Animal Hospital* (BBC, 1993–), *Airport* (BBC, 1996–), *Popstars* (ITV, 2001–), or *The Osbournes* (MTV, 2002–), draw on a variety of genres to create ratings winners. It is no wonder that media owner Rupert Murdoch has launched a reality TV channel – there is something for everyone in the reality genre. [1]

The historical development of popular factual television is multifaceted. There is a growing body of literature that provides excellent analysis of crime reporting (e.g. Fishman and Cavender 1998; Palmer 2003), tabloid journalism (e.g. Langer 1998), documentary (e.g. Nichols 1994, Winston 1995, Corner 1995, Bruzzi 2000, Kilborn 2003, amongst others), docu-drama/drama-doc (e.g. Paget 1998), and mock documentary (e.g. Roscoe and Hight 2001), all of which have a role to play in the development of reality programming. In this chapter, I can only touch

From Annette Hill, *Reality TV* (London: Routledge, 2005).

on historical, cultural and industrial contexts, as my main intention is to provide an overview of the rise of reality TV throughout the 1990s and 2000s.

The Origins of Reality TV

Where did reality TV come from? There is no easy answer to this question. The genealogy of popular factual television is convoluted, as the type of hybrid programming we have come to associate with reality TV is difficult to categorise, and has developed within historically and culturally specific media environments. There are three main strands to the development of popular factual television, and these relate to three areas of distinct, and yet overlapping, areas of media production: tabloid journalism, documentary television, and popular entertainment. Production of tabloid journalism and popular entertainment increased during the 1980s. This growth was partly a result of the deregulation and marketisation of media industries in advanced industrial states, such as America, Western Europe and Australasia, and partly a result of an increasingly commercial media environment, where convergence between telecommunications, computers and media ensured competition amongst network, cable and satellite channels for revenue (Hesmondhalgh 2002). This media environment was one within which documentary television struggled to survive. In this chapter, I briefly outline these three main areas of media production, providing nationally specific examples in order to highlight the rise of reality TV within different countries and media industries.

Tabloid journalism

There are particular elements of reality programming which draw on the staple ingredients of tabloid journalism, such as the interplay between ordinary people and celebrities, or information and entertainment. John Fiske describes tabloid news as follows: 'its subject matter is that produced at the intersection between public and private life; its style is sensational . . . its tone is populist; its modality fluidly denies any stylistic difference between fiction and documentary' (1992: 48). The intersections between the public and the private, fact and fiction, highlight how tabloid journalism relies on personal and sensational stories to create informative and entertaining news.

Elizabeth Bird points out: 'journalism's emphasis on the personal, the sensational, and the dramatic is nothing new. Street literature, ballads, and oral gossip and rumor all contribute to the development of news' (2000: 216). For example, true crime stories were distributed through broadsheets, pamphlets and popular ballads during the early modern period in the UK. Trial pamphlets sensationalised the criminal, such as one of 1606 that told of a female robber who 'ripped open the belly of a pregnant woman with a knife and severed her child's tongue' (Biressi 2001: 45–6). *The Newgate Calendar*, first published in

1773, collected such pamphlets into bound volumes, and became so popular it outsold authors such as Charles Dickens. [. . .]

The tabloid style of storytelling has come to dominate much popular news. Although news reporting varies from country to country, the success of super-market tabloids in the USA, or tabloid papers such as the *Sun* in the UK, is an example of how the human-interest story has become a central part of popular journalism. Bird (2000: 213) argues that the 'tabloid audience' has moved on from tabloid papers to tabloid TV shows. The popularity of personal storytell-ing in both television news and print media has contributed to the prolifera-tion of reality programming. As John Langer points out, the impulse towards tabloidism' resides in the recirculation of traditional story forms, such as ordinary people doing extraordinary things (1998: 161). [. . .]

Tabloid TV did not develop in a vacuum. In America, early network tel-evision gave little consideration to popular news. It was after the quiz show scandals during the 1950s that network newscasts attempted to reach a wider audience, by increasing news and current affairs output and focusing on visual and narrative interest in news stories. During the 1960s 'network news held a privileged and profitable position', but during the 1970s 'local news emerged as a potentially profitable product, evolving into a popular hybrid of traditional hard news and gossipy chat that was often preferred by viewers' (Bird 2000: 214). Developments in technology, such as satellites and Minicams, ensured that local news bulletins could '"transport" their audiences to the scenes of crimes in progress, unfolding hostage situations, urban shooting sprees, raging fires, and the like' (Glynn 2000: 23). This reliance on raw footage would become a staple ingredient of reality programming. When Rupert Murdoch took advantage of deregulation policies during the Reagan administration and launched the Fox Television Network in the late 1980s, the channel featured programmes, such as *America's Most Wanted* or *Cops*, which took advantage of the growth of popular journalism, especially in local news. Indeed, Fox 'redefined US network practices' (Glynn 2000: 28) by producing cheap reality programming, which could compete in a competitive environment of network, cable and independent broadcasting. By the early 1990s, reality programming was an established part of peaktime network schedules, and other countries were beginning to take note.

Documentary television

In the UK, the rise of reality TV was connected with the success of American tabloid TV and the demise of documentary television. In the 1960s and 1970s, early magazine-style series, such as *Tonight* (BBC, 1957–1965) or *Nationwide* (BBC, 1969–1984), provided a mixture of news and humorous or eccentric stories. These magazine-style programmes were forerunners for much contem-porary popular factual television (Brunsdon *et al.* 2001: 51). But it was the introduction of British versions of American reality programming in the early

1990s that began a trend in what was commonly referred to at the time as 'infotainment'. For example, *999* (BBC, 1992–) was modelled on *Rescue 911* (CBS). The difference between *999* and its American cousin is significant in that *999* is made by the BBC, a public service channel that promotes itself as a platform for serious factual programming. As Kilborn points out:

> Given their major preoccupation with the human interest aspect and with their overriding concern with action-packed entertainment, reality programmes such as *999* run the risk of being seen as tabloid television. At a time when the BBC has publicly committed itself to high-quality, less populist forms of programming, the tabloid label is one which they will wish to avoid. (1994: 433)

The BBC's interest in popular factual programming in the early 1990s was a response to political pressure from the Conservative government in the 1980s and early 1990s to be a public, i.e. popular, service. This move from public to popular represented a major threat to the traditional relationship between documentary and public service broadcasting:

> Public service broadcasting (PSB) traditionally assumed that a responsibility to the audience was of more importance than, say, a commercial duty to shareholders. In this context, documentary, as a quality 'duty genre', flourished even though (or perhaps exactly because) it did not achieve mass appeal anywhere until the later 1990s. The relaxation and reformulation of PSB allowed broadcasters, however funded, to become more like other businesses. It became clear, as the ratings became more paramount, that documentary presence in the schedules was a real mark of public service commitment. (Winston 2000: 40)

The 1992 Broadcasting Act opened up competition from independent producers and placed pressure on the BBC to deliver cheaper programming to the general public. The emergence of reality programming in the early 1990s came at a time when documentary, along with news and current affairs, was already under-performing in the ratings. Popular factual programming became a key weapon in the BBC's successful ratings and scheduling war with its commercial rival ITV. Reality TV filled a gap in the schedules, but at the expense of more traditional documentary and current affairs. Indeed, as Kilborn points out, the BBC's use of its digital channel BBC4 as a space for documentary suggests that the success of popular factual television on mainstream channels such as BBC1 is at the expense of 'more challenging types of documentary work' which have been relocated to digital channels (2003: 48). [. . .]

The relationship between documentary television and reality TV is cause for concern amongst documentary practitioners and scholars, as the form and content of programmes such as *999* are somewhat removed from traditional documentary values. The primary aim of much reality programming is 'that of diversion rather than enlightenment'; and although some makers of reality programmes argue that certain formats can provide social value, it is the case that the reality genre as a whole is designed for entertainment value (Kilborn 2003: 11). And yet it is also the case that popular factual television owes a great deal to documentary television. Even the category of 'documentary' can be related to the category of 'reality TV' as both categories defy simple definitions. Just as reality TV is a broad category that is difficult to define, the category of documentary also 'escapes any tight generic specification', and 'what we understand by "documentary" is always dependent on the broader context of the kinds of audiovisual documentation currently in circulation' (Corner 2002a: 125).

The types of documentary television directly relevant to reality programming include documentary journalism, documentary realism, and, in particular, observational documentary. Documentary journalism addresses topical subjects in a series format, using journalistic conventions, and usually involving the '"quest" of a presenter/reporter . . . "delving behind the headlines"' (Corner 1995: 84). This type of documentary was popular with broadcasters in the 1960s and 1970s because it performed a public service, and programmes could become flagship productions for particular channels, for example *Sixty Minutes* (CBS) in America, or *World in Action* (ITV) in the UK. There are links between tabloid journalism and documentary journalism, as the latter too suffered from the popularity of magazine-style news bulletins and infotainment.

[. . .]

Other types of documentary have influenced reality programming, such as reflexive/performative documentaries, docu-drama and mock documentaries. Reflexive documentaries contain a self-conscious reference to generic conventions; performative documentaries blur boundaries between fact and fiction (Nichols 1991, 1994). Both types of documentary rely on dramatic techniques, including parody and irony, to question the genre. Docu-drama and mock documentary take this questioning of the documentary genre one stage further. Docu-drama uses a fictional setting in order to present a sequence of events as truthful, by drawing on generic conventions within documentary (Paget 1998). Mock documentary takes 'a fictive stance towards the social world, while utilising documentary aesthetics to "mock" the underlying discourses of documentary' (Roscoe and Hight 2001: 44). Reflexivity, performance, and boundaries between fact and fiction are all hallmarks of reality programming, and are discussed in more detail in later chapters.

Popular entertainment

As with tabloid journalism and documentary television, popular entertainment defies categorisation. It is an umbrella term that includes a collection of programmes that come from different industrial contexts, and which are primarily entertaining. For my purposes, popular entertainment refers to programmes such as talkshows, gameshows, sports and leisure programming, all of which are part of the development of popular factual television. These popular entertainment programmes include interaction between non-professional actors and celebrities, although increasingly non-professional actors are often treated as celebrities in their own right in such programmes. Many of these programmes also contain interactive elements, drawing a studio audience, and viewers at home, directly into a programme, usually as respondents or judges to the activities of the non-professional actors/ celebrities. In addition, talk shows, gameshows, sports and leisure programming often perform well within the international broadcasting market, with successful formats sold worldwide, and locally produced to nationally specific requirements. Perhaps one of the best-known examples of a popular entertainment series about ordinary people is *Candid Camera* (CBS, 1948–), which began on radio, and transferred to TV to become one of the top ten US network shows during the 1960s, spawning imitators around the world. *Candid Camera* was also a format familiar to UK audiences in the 1950s, presented by Jonathan Routh in the early years of ITV, the first commercial channel in the UK.

[. . .]

To summarise, popular factual television has developed during a period of cross fertilisation with tabloid journalism, documentary television and popular entertainment. The late 1980s and 1990s were a period of increased commercialisation and deregulation within the media industries. As audiences have shopped around, channel surfing between terrestrial, satellite/cable and digital channels, broadcasters (and narrowcasters) have looked to produce cheap, often locally made, factual programming which is attractive to general (and niche) viewers. The development of reality programming is an example of how television cannibalises itself in order to survive, drawing on existing genres to create successful hybrid programmes, which in turn generate a 'new' television genre.

REALITY TV ARRIVES

Although examples of reality TV can be found throughout the history of television, reality programmes arrived *en masse* in peaktime television schedules during the 1990s. The first wave of reality programming was based upon the success of crime and emergency services reality TV, or 'infotainment', and travelled from America to Europe and beyond in the late 1980s to early 1990s. The second wave of reality programming was based upon the success of popular observational documentaries, or 'docu-soaps', and lifestyle programming involving house and garden makeovers, and travelled from Britain to Europe and beyond in the mid-to late 1990s. The third wave was based upon the success of social experiments that placed ordinary people in controlled environments over an extended period of time, or 'reality gameshows', and travelled from Northern Europe to Britain, America and the rest of the world during the early 2000s. The current wave of reality programming is a free-for-all, with America leading the way with crime and relationship reality programming, Britain and Australia forging ahead with lifestyle and social experiment reality programming, and Northern Europe developing variations of the reality gameshow.

Infotainment

To begin at the beginning, infotainment, also called 'tabloid TV', began life as one-off programmes in various countries, but became popular on American network television after NBC aired the 'on-scene' reality series *Unsolved Mysteries* in 1987. Raphael (1997: 107) notes 'the international spread of Reali-TV cannot be explained as the outcome of US product innovation, since many European and Japanese programs pre-dated their US counterparts'. For example, *Crimewatch UK* (BBC) was first aired in 1984, and was in turn modelled on the German programme *AktenzeichenXY . . . Ungelöst* (ZDF, 1967–). Although *Crimewatch UK* was successful (in 1984 it commanded audiences of over 9 million) and inspired imitators, it did not create a landslide in reality programming. In America, on the other hand, producers of reality programming quickly grasped the potential of infotainment to boost ratings at home, and increase foreign export revenues (Raphael 1997). After the success of *Unsolved Mysteries*, other networks followed suit. By 1991, *Variety* estimated there were over thirty reality programmes on air:

> At any time of the day or night, a viewer can tune in to emergency rescues, sex scandals, re-enactments of grisly crimes, unwary bystanders stumbling into practical jokes recorded by hidden cameras, and salacious pseudo-gameshows centred on none-too-subtle sexual voyeurism . . . the broadcast networks are scheduling more of them than at any other time in TV history, mainly because an hour-long reality series typically costs about $500,000 an episode, only half of what the networks pay in license fees for a 60 minute dramatic series. (Dempsey 1991: 32)

The downsides to reality TV – low profits in off-network syndication markets and cautious advertisers (Raphael 1997) – were more than compensated for by economic and ratings success. In the 1991–1992 US season, viewers could tune into *America's Most Wanted* and *Cops* on Fox, *Rescue 911* and *Top Cops* on CBS, *Unsolved Mysteries* and *Expose* on NBC, and *FBI: the Untold Stories* on ABC (Raphael 1997: 109). The majority of these reality series were not deficit-financed which represented a major turnaround from the deficit-financed drama productions of the mid-1980s, when producers lost up to $100,000 per episode for half-hour shows (1997: 103). The economic success of reality TV ensured that producers developed new variations on existing formats. For example, the format for emergency services reality programming was popular in the mid-1990s, with reality series such as *Coastguard*, about adventures on US waterways, or *Extreme*, about a mountain rescue team in Utah, competing alongside familiar series such as *Rescue 911*.[2] [. . .]

European broadcasters were quick to pick up on the success of infotainment in America. Some American programmes were acquired by European broadcasters, such as *Rescue 911* which was aired in Germany and Denmark. More often formats were sold, or copied, in order to make locally produced versions of American reality TV. Kilborn (1994: 430) notes that local resistance to 'American-style reality' TV ensured 'styles and forms . . . evolved which are more in tune with national or cultural priorities'. The success of European versions of American reality formats illustrates reality TV's strong performance within the global television market.

[. . .]

DOCU-SOAP AND LIFESTYLE

The docu-soap emerged as an alternative, in some ways complementary, popular factual slot to infotainment in the UK. Docu-soaps, also called 'fly-on-the-wall' documentaries, 'soap-docs', or 'reality-soaps', became the 'motor of peaktime' during the mid- to late 1990s (Phillips 1999a: 23). There were as many as sixty-five docu-soaps broadcast on the main channels between 1995 and 1999, attracting audiences of up to 12 million. Docu-soaps were so popular that the term even made it into the *Oxford Dictionary* (1999a: 22). The docu-soap is a combination of observational documentary, and character-driven drama. One TV producer explained: 'We'd seen that flashing bluelight documentaries could work, but many of the latest ones are factual soaps, very character-led . . . nothing seems to be too mundane. It's the technique of a soap opera brought into documentaries' (Biddiscomb 1998: 16). Although there had been predecessors to the docu-soap, namely Paul Watson's *The Family* (BBC, 1974) or Craig Gilbert's *An American Family* (PBS, 1973) it was its 'prioritisation of entertainment over social commentary' that made the docu-soap so different from observational documentary, and perforce popular with general viewers (Bruzzi 2001: 132).

It was the BBC who, once again, became the driving force in the production of docu-soaps. A year after the arrival of *999*, the BBC aired *Children's Hospital*, a fly-on-the-wall documentary which had all the hallmarks of a docu-soap (see Hill 2000c for further discussion). Its personal, melodramatic stories appealed to viewers, with more than 8 million tuning in to the first series, despite widespread criticism from the press (Hill 2000c). In 1995, the BBC aired *HMS Brilliant* which attracted a 40 per cent share during midweek, and proceeded to swamp the peaktime schedules with half-hour docu-soaps, which usually aired between 8pm and 9pm. Docu-soaps filled the hole left behind by the decline in comedy and light entertainment during this period, and, once commercial channels entered the field, became ammunition in a ratings war, where even television drama – the 'dreadnoughts and destroyers' of peak time – took direct hits from the docu-soap. At their peak, docu-soaps fought each other head on for the coveted '8–9 slot'. Dovey, in a brief analysis of the schedules during 1998, counted 36 per cent of peaktime factual programming during one week, and concluded that 'right across the peaktime schedule the pattern is the same: light entertainment, sitcom and drama have been replaced by popular factual entertainment programmes' (2000: 19).

[. . .]

As the docu-soap reached its peak, the general audience began to switch off: 'in 1997, nine of 11 soap-doc runs beat their network's nightly [market share] averages; in 1998 it was 13 out of 22; and between January to May 1999 . . . 4 out of 21' (Phillips 1999b: 23). In addition, the docu-soap did not fare well abroad. [. . .]

Another strand of reality programming that dominated the peaktime schedules in the UK during the latter half of the 1990s is that of lifestyle programming, in particular makeover shows. [. . .]

Lifestyle programming, exemplified by *Changing Rooms* (BBC, 1996–), took its place alongside infotainment and docu-soaps, as popular factual for general audiences. The essence of lifestyle programming is the involvement of ordinary people and their ordinary leisure interests (gardening, cookery, fashion, home improvement) with experts who transform the ordinary into the extraordinary. Usually, the transformation of people or homes is linked to a competition, but it isn't the winning that counts, but rather the moment of surprise, or 'the reveal', when ordinary people respond to the end results. *Changing Rooms, Ground Force* (BBC, 1997–), and *Carol Vorderman's Better Homes* (ITV, 1999–) all draw on the makeover, along with elements from the gameshow, to heighten drama Brunsdon *et al.* comment:

> Contemporary lifestyle programmes in many cases introduce the possibility of humiliation and embarrassment for participants, through devices such as having neighbours decorate each other's room, or partners buy each other outfits. While the programmes do show what has been done to the room or the new outfit, it is the expression flitting across the participant's face in the attempt to organise their response in the public place of a close-up that is significant. It is the reaction, not the action that matters. (2001: 56)

Most lifestyle programming in the 1990s adopted this format, subsuming an informative address (the instructional part of the programme) within the spectacle of 'the reveal' (the makeover part of the programme). The producer of

Changing Rooms, Peter Bazalgette, summed up the success of the series: 'the key is the resolution, whether they like it or hate it . . . the show is really about watching other people in the raw' (cited in Moseley 2000: 312).

The success of lifestyle programming has ensured many variations of the makeover format. [. . .] The ability to makeover itself means lifestyle programming continues to perform well in the ratings.

Reality gameshows

The reality gameshow has become an international bestseller since its arrival in 2000. The birth of the reality gameshow format can be traced to British producer Charlie Parsons, who developed the idea for *Survivor* in the early 1990s, and sold an option on the rights to Endemol, before a Swedish company bought the format and renamed it *Expedition Robinson*. In the meantime, Endemol had been working on a similar idea, *Big Brother*, the brainchild of Dutch TV producer John de Mol, who described the format as

> the voluntary locking up of nine people during a hundred days in a house, watched continuously by 24 television cameras, to which the viewers, at the intercession of the inmates, once in two weeks vote against one of the inmates who has to leave the house, until the last person to stay in can be called a winner. (Costera Meijer and Reesink 2000: 10)[3]

Surprisingly, *Big Brother* was a hit. More than 3 million people watched the finale in the Netherlands (RTL, 1999) and voted by telephone for the winner. The fact that the format worked well with converging media, such as websites and telephones, only added to its strong economic performance in the television marketplace.

[. . .]

A more detailed breakdown for *Big Brother* in the UK (Channel 4) reveals the extent of the success of *Big Brother* across converging media. Channel 4 had the best Friday night ratings in its history, with 9 million viewers (46 per cent share) tuning in to watch the first series finale of *Big Brother*. Sixty-seven per cent of the UK population watched *Big Brother* at least once. Over 7 million viewers telephoned Channel 4's hotline to vote for the winner, which broke the record for viewer participation in a UK TV programme. As for the website, it received 3 million page impressions each day, which made it Europe's top website during the summer of 2000. The second series averaged more than 4 million viewers, giving Channel 4 more than a 70 per cent increase on their average broadcast share. Channel 4's digital youth channel, E4, screened *Big Brother 2* continuously during the second series, and at peak moments in the house (e.g. Paul and Helen's candlelit tryst) attracted record figures, propelling the digital channel ahead of terrestrial minority channels.[4]

More than 15 million viewers voted to evict contestants, either using interactive TV handsets, or phonelines. The website received a total of 159 million page impressions and 16.4 million video streams were requested.[5] The third series of *Big Brother* averaged 4 million viewers, with the live final attracting 10 million in the summer of 2002. The fourth series of *Big Brother* underperformed from the previous year, but was still in fifth place in the top ten programmes for viewers aged 16–25.[6] Table [46.1] illustrates the ratings for all series of *Big Brother* at the time of writing.

[. . .]

Another successful international format was *Popstars*, a combination of reality gameshow and variety show that originated in New Zealand. Contestants auditioned for a place in a pop band, or in the case of *Soapstars* (ITV, 2001), a soap opera. The format usually involved a series of open auditions for thousands of 'wannabes', followed by a knockout competition where the final contestants performed in front of a panel of judges, who, along with the viewers, voted for the winners. [. . .]

Another popular reality gameshow format is that of *I'm a Celebrity . . . Get Me Out of Here!* The first series of *I'm a Celebrity . . .* attracted 7.7 million viewers (34 per cent share). The format is similar to *Survivor*, but it is also different in that it places celebrities under pressure, rather than ordinary people. Castaway TV threatened court proceedings, which were later withdrawn in 2003, precisely because the company that owned the rights to *Survivor* felt that Granada (the makers of *I'm a Celebrity . . .*) had copied the *Survivor* format. CBS (the makers of the American version of *Survivor*) also issued court proceedings against Granada. The CBS courtcase against Granada was unsuccessful, and Castaway TV withdrew its allegations. In the case of CBS, the judge said that *I'm a Celebrity . . .* did not borrow more substantially from *Survivor* than other types of US reality gameshows. One of the reasons why the case was unsuccessful was because the judge thought that programme making was a 'continual evolutionary process involving borrowing frequently from what has gone before'.[7] The *I'm a Celebrity . . .* and *Survivor* copycat case, along with the *Survivor* and *Big Brother* copycat case, illustrate how reality gameshows freely borrow elements from existing formats in the television marketplace.

Table [46.1]   Ratings for *Big Brother*

Series	Average (weekdays)	First show	Final show
BB1	4.6 m (25%)	3.3 m (17%)	9 m (46.5%)
BB2	4.5 m (25%)	3.3 m (16.5%)	7.5 m (46%)
BB3	5.9 m (28%)	5.9 m (25.9%)	10 m (50.6%)
BB4	4.9 m (24%)	6.9 m (29.3%)	6.6 m (34%)

Source: *Broadcast*. 1 August 2003

The successful export of reality gameshows from Europe to the USA occurred at the same time as gameshows experienced a resurgence in international trade – *Who Wants to be a Millionaire?* was described by the *New York Times*, as 'England's most successful cultural export in the last 30 years' (cited in Boddy 2001: 81). *Survivor* rated number one in network peaktime (27 million viewers) and earned CBS during the final three episodes an estimated $50 million in advertising revenue. After the 'smash hit' of *Survivor*, the networks scrambled to glut the market with a winning formula of gameshow, observational documentary and high drama. *Temptation Island*, Fox's answer to *Survivor*, involved four unmarried couples on a 'paradise island'. The couples were separated from their partners, and forced to fraternise with eligible singles on 'dream dates', before being reunited in a final showdown. The heady mixture of passion and betrayal, island location, attractive contestants, staged flirtations and surveillance footage all made for a fascinating, morally dubious reality gameshow – as one contestant explained, 'it's like being able to go down and take part in the Pepsi Challenge but have the ladies be the actual soft drink'. *Temptation Island* attracted more than 16 million viewers, mainly in the 18–49 demographic, and gave NBC drama *The West Wing* a run for its money. However, after two series it was axed, although ABC's anti-*Temptation Island, The Last Resort* (2001–), where couples in distress tried to patch things up in Hawaii, suggests the series might be due for a revival. Other reality shows include Japanese-style extreme gameshow *Fear Factor* (Fox, 2001–), dating reality gameshow *Joe Millionaire* (Fox, 2002–), and the US version of *Pop Idol, American Idol* (Fox, 2002–).

Big Brother was not a hit in its first season on NBC (the finale ranked 18 in the network primetime top 20). The reasons for its lack of success were partly because *Big Brother* ran alongside *Survivor*, and partly because the mundanity of the *Big Brother* house, which European audiences found so enthralling, failed to enliven American viewers. According to Ellis (2001), the failure of *Big Brother* was related to poor casting, and the fact that it was live and hastily edited for nightly review, whereas *Survivor* was well cast, edited after filming had finished, and carefully put together to maximise drama. Conversely, *Survivor* (ITV, 2000–) did not fare well in the UK, with ratings lower than 5 million, precisely because it did not involve interaction with viewers, and was pre-packaged for them, rather than filmed live (Ellis 2001). Although Neilson ratings for the first series of *Big Brother* suggest it was the live eviction shows that attracted most viewers (just as in Europe), later series sought to minimise the risks of live TV by introducing a longer time delay between actual events and the nightly reviews of the *Big Brother* house.[8]

As with docu-soaps, reality gameshows are reliant on peaktime scheduling for their success. Most reality gameshows are scheduled between 7pm and 10pm on American network and cable TV. And, like docu-soaps, reality gameshows go head-to-head in the schedules. [. . .] The fierce competition between reality gameshows in peak time is partly to do with increased costs in the production of reality shows like *American Idol* (approximately $800,000 per hour), which places pressure on producers and schedulers to recoup revenue during high-profile first-runs.

The scheduling of reality gameshows in the UK is not quite as competitive, primarily because British schedulers have continued to position docu-soaps, lifestyle programming and infotainment at peak time, and so reality game-shows are part of the mix of popular factual television on offer from 7pm to 11pm. [. . .]

Life experiment programmes are a recent development in the reality genre. Part social experiment, part makeover, and part gameshow, life experiment programmes usually involve ordinary people experimenting with their lives in various different ways. [. . .]

And what of the future of reality TV? Television's ability to endlessly rein-vent itself means that hybrid reality formats continue to be a popular choice for producers and executives (Kilborn 2003). The formats for reality TV – infotainment, docu-soaps, lifestyle programming, reality gameshows, and others – do not lend themselves to repeat viewing. Indeed, they quickly become yesterday's news. Reality formats provide a never-ending fresh supply of non-professional actors in new series of existing formats. *Big Brother, Survivor* and *Popstars* are cases in point, as minor changes to the formats, such as a new house/island/panel of judges, allow television producers to create new series out of essentially the same shows. [. . .] [O]ne development within the reality gameshow is to include media celebrities as contestants. *Celebrity Big Brother* (Channel 4) takes celebrities and turns them into 'ordinary people', before releasing them back into the world of the media. Another example of a reality programme that uses celebrities rather than ordinary people is *I'm a Celebrity . . . Get Me Out of Here!* The trend in America for celebrity docu-soaps, such as *The Osbournes* (MTV, 2001–) or *The Anna Nicole Show* (El, 2002–), rely on just this premise. [. . .] Finally, let us not forget the significance of surveillance footage; as reality gameshows move into the realm of popular entertainment and performance becomes even more central to the success of contestants, raw footage of people going about their business with no knowledge they are being filmed will inevitably reappear on our television screens. The success of *The Secret Policeman*, an undercover investigative documentary about racism in the British police force, indicates audience attraction to surveillance footage, as 5 million people watched the one-off documentary. It won a Royal Television Society award, and the BBC have commissioned a series of similar undercover investigations into public sector institutions.[9]

CONCLUSION

The rise of reality TV came at a time when networks were looking for a quick fix solution to economic problems within the cultural industries. Increased costs in the production of drama, sitcom and comedy ensured unscripted, popular factual programming became a viable economic option during the 1990s. The deregulation and marketisation of media industries, especially in America and Western Europe, also contributed to the rise of reality TV, as it performed well in a competitive, multichannel environment. Reality TV has its roots in tabloid journalism and popular entertainment, but it owes its greatest debt to documentary television, which has almost disappeared from television screens in the wake of popular factual programming. Documentary television, a 'duty genre', has withered on the vine during a decade of the commercialisation of public service channels. Although the popularity of reality TV comes at a cost, there is hope that its very success in peak time is the 'price of survival' for documentary (Winston 2000).

[. . .]

NOTES

1. Byrne, C. (2002) 'News Corp Plans Reality TV Channel'. Online. Available at http://media.guardian.co.uk/broadcast/story/0,7493,769885,00.html (accessed 10 August 2002).
2. *Variety*, 9–15 January 1995: 55.
3. This quotation was cited in translation in de Leeuw, Sonja (2001) '*Big Brother*: How a Dutch Format Reinvented Living and Other Stories', unpublished paper.
4. The BARB ratings for Wednesday 11 July 2001 show that 626,000 viewers tuned in to watch E4, compared to 300,000 viewers for Channel 5 and 400,000 viewers for Channel 4 at the same time, 11pm.
5. See *Broadcast*, 31 July 2001.
6. See *Broadcast*, 1 August 2003.
7. Plunkett, John. (2003) 'I'm a Celebrity Copycat Claim Withdrawn', *Media Guardian*, 25 April. Online. Available at http://mediaguardian.co.uk/broadcast/story/0,7493,943008,00.html (accessed 24 February 2004).
8. I am grateful to Pam Wilson for providing me with ratings for *Big Brother 1* in America.
9. *Broadcast*, 5 March 2004: 1.

REFERENCES

Biddiscomb, Ross (1998) 'Real Life: Real Ratings', *Broadcasting and Cable's Television International*, January: 14, 16.

Bird, Elizabeth (2000) 'Audience Demands in a Murderous Market: Tabloidization in U.S. Television News', in C. Sparks and J. Tulloch (eds) *Tabloid Tales: Global Debate over Media Scandal*, London: Rowman and Littlefield, pp. 213–28.

Biressi, Anita (2001) *Crime, Fear and the Law in True Crime Stories*, Hampshire: Palgrave.

Boddy, William (2001) 'The Quiz Show', in G. Creeber (ed.) *The Television Genre Book*, London: BFI, pp.79–81.

Brunsdon, C., Johnson, C., Moseley, R. and Wheatley, H. (2001) 'Factual Entertainment on British Television: The Midlands TV Research Group's "8–9 Project"', *European Journal of Cultural Studies*, 4, 1:29–62.

Bruzzi, Stella (2000) *New Documentary: A Critical Introduction*, London: Routledge.

Bruzzi, Stella (2001) 'Observational ("Fly-on-the-Wall") Documentary', in G. Creeber (ed.) *The Television Genre Book*, London: BFI, pp. 129–32.

Corner, John (1995) *Television Form and Public Address*, London: Edward Arnold.

Corner, John (2002a) 'Documentary Values', in A. Jerslev (ed.) *Realism and 'Reality' in Film and Media*, Copenhagen: Museum Tusculanum Press, pp. 139–58.

Costera Meijer, I. and Reesink, M. (eds) *Reality Soap! Big Brother en de Opkomst van het Multimediaconcept*. Amsterdam: Boom.

Dempsey, J. (1991) 'Hot Genre Gluts TV Market', *Variety*, 3 June: 32.

Dovey, Jon (2000) *Freakshow: First Person Media and Factual Television*, London: Pluto.

Ellis, John (2001) '*Survivor* and *Big Brother*', *Sight and Sound*, February: 56.

Fishman, Mark and Cavender, Gray (1998) *Entertaining Crime: Television Reality Programmes*, New York: Aldine De Gruyter.

Fiske, John (1992) 'Popularity and the Politics of Information', in P. Dahlgren and C. Sparks (eds) *Journalism and Popular Culture*, London: Sage, pp.45–63.

Glynn, Kevin (2000) *Tabloid Culture: Trash Taste, Popular Power, and the Transformation of American Television*, Durham, NC, and London: Duke University Press.

Hesmondhalgh, David (2002) *The Cultural Industries*, London: Sage.

Hill, Annette (2000c) 'Fearful and Safe: Audience Response to British Reality Programming', *Television and New Media*, 2, May: 193–214.

Kilborn, John (1994) 'How Real Can You Get?: Recent Developments in "Reality" Television', *European Journal of Communication*, 9: 421–39.

Kilborn, John (2003) *Staging the Real: Factual TV Programming in the Age of Big Brother*, Manchester: Manchester University Press.

Langer, John (1998) *Tabloid Television: Popular Journalism and the 'Other News'*, London: Routledge.

Moseley, Rachael (2000) 'Makeover Takeover on British Television', *Screen*, 41, 3: 299–327.

Nichols, Bill (1991) *Representing Reality: Issues and Concepts in Documentary*, Bloomington and Indianapolis: Indiana University Press.

Nichols, Bill (1994) *Blurred Boundaries: Questions of Meaning in Contemporary Culture*, Bloomington and Indianapolis: Indiana University Press.

Paget, Derek (1998) *No Other Way to Tell it*, Manchester: Manchester University Press.

Palmer, Gareth (2003) *Discipline and Liberty*, Manchester: Manchester University Press.

Phillips, William (1999a) 'All Washed Out', *Broadcast*, 2 July: 22–3.

Phillips, William (1999b) 'Summertime Blues', *Broadcast*, 1 October: 22.

Raphael, Chad (1997) 'Political Economy of Reali-TV' in *Jump Cut*, 41: 102–9.

Roscoe, Jane and Hight, Craig (2001) *Faking It: Mock-Documentary and the Subversion of Factuality*, Manchester: Manchester University Press.

Winston, Brian (1995) *Claiming the Real: The Documentary Film Revisited*, London: BFI.

Winston, Brian (2000) *Lies, Damn Lies and Documentaries*, London: BFI.

47

PUBLIC AND PRIVATE BODIES

Sue Thornham

[. . .]

BODY POLITICS

[. . .] [W]hat separated much feminist analysis of the 1970s and 1980s from male-centred work in media and cultural studies was its 'body politics'. Arguing that in the discourses of modernity, corporeality has been, in Elizabeth Grosz's phrase, 'coded feminine', so that '[p]atriarchal oppression . . . justifies itself, at least in part, by connecting women much more closely than men to the body and, through this identification, restricting women's social and economic roles' (Grosz 1994: 14), feminists have analysed the ways in which cultural structures have functioned both to confine women *to* their objectified and passive bodies and to estrange them *from* their bodies. In later studies, the work of Michel Foucault has been used to argue that women's bodies are subject to very specific disciplinary controls through cultural images and norms. What these studies of the 'disciplining' of women's bodies have in common is a focus on the ways in which discursive practices intersect with social, economic, medical, legal and political structures to produce meanings about the female body which are embodied both in representations and in cultural practices. Thus Susan Bordo, for example, writes that 'the body that we experience and conceptualize is always *mediated* by constructs, associations, images of a cultural nature' (1993: 35). This construction of femininity functions as a homogenizing and normalizing discipline, 'erasing

Sue Thornham, *Women, Feminism and Media* (Edinburgh: Edinburgh University Press, 2007).

racial, class, and other differences and insisting that all women aspire to a coercive, standardized ideal' (Bordo 1989: 16). But it is through 'the practices and bodily habits of everyday life' that these bodily disciplines are enacted: for women, 'culture's grip on the body is a constant, intimate fact of everyday life' (Bordo 1993: 17).

Extending this analysis, Hilary Radner (1995) argues that what characterises manifestations of these disciplinary practices in the 1980s onwards is the way in which this 'feminine body' has become a 'public body'. As women have moved increasingly from their position within the private domestic realm and into the public sphere of work, she argues, so the disciplinary practices which have regulated and produced their bodies have become correspondingly organised as a form of 'public discipline'. Radner's focus in this essay is on the 'aerobics craze' in the US of the 1980s, and specifically on the *Jane Fonda's Workout* books and exercise videos, which promise women self-empowerment through submission to a regime of public visibility. But in the Fonda emphasis on self-empowerment through self-mastery, in her confession to a struggle with anorexia but commitment to achieving a 'healthy body', in her emphasis on a self-transformation to be accomplished by work (and plastic surgery) but manifested in appearance, and in the centrality of public visibility to these processes, we can see the paradigm which is currently played out in a multitude of talk shows and makeover programmes. The politics of this new public visibility, writes Radner, are at best ambiguous.

A New Public Sphere?

For some critics, the blurring of public-private boundaries which characterises these new hybrid genres signals a positive transformation of the public sphere. Ib Bondebjerg, for example, argues that it could be seen as 'a result of the democratic impact of visual media on public discourse through a new *integration* of forms of public and private interaction which used to be clearly separated'. What we may be witnessing, therefore, is the 'democratization of an old public service discourse . . . and the creation of a new mixed public sphere, where common knowledge and everyday experience play a much larger role' (1996: 29). In a similar way, Sonia Livingstone and Peter Lunt argue that 'in the audience discussion programme, experts and lay people are put together, setting an agenda of social issues and offering both established elites and ordinary people the opportunity at least to discuss the lived experience of current-affairs issues in relation to expert solutions'. In this process, both the Habermasian 'life-world' and his 'system world' experience the collapse of public-private distinctions (1994: 132, 180). Talk shows, argues Laura Grindstaff, challenge 'conventional boundaries separating public from private, reason from emotion, news from entertainment, fact from fiction, and expert knowledge from common opinion' (1997: 165). Other critics have pointed to the potential feminist implications of this boundary-blurring. Jane Shattuc, asking whether the audience of daytime talk shows might be 'the newest incarnation of the public sphere' (1997: 87), emphasises the debt which they owe to the 'feminist movement':

> Their principal aim has been to build up women's self-esteem, confidence, and identity ... The shows take place in an arena of collective feminine experience. The form of their practice results from the women's movement and feminist therapy – specifically, the consciousness-raising group as a democratic forum – a place where women create community in the absence of authority by drawing on their social experiences and morality. (Shattuc 1997: 122)

It is an argument which some of the shows' hosts, most notably Oprah Winfrey, have echoed, claiming to 'empower women' (quoted in Squire 1997: 98). 'It is not too far-fetched', comments Patricia Mellencamp, 'to imagine daytime talk as the electronic, syndicated version of consciousness-raising groups of the women's movement' (1992: 218).

Yet on the whole, critics have been ambivalent about these claims. Shattuc concludes that '[e]ssentially daytime talk shows are not feminist', although they 'do represent popular TV at its most feminist' (1997: 136). Mellencamp argues that if talk shows validate women's experiences and emotions, they also produce them as 'abnormalities or scandals', adding that in 'the divisions between daytime and primetime, entertainment and news, the aberrant and the normal (and homosexuality and heterosexuality), taxonomies emblematic of private/public spaces, TV enacts institutional containment – reminiscent of Foucault's definition of the disciplinary society' (1992: 265). So how can we best understand both the shows themselves and the ambivalence of their critics?

First, this is a genre in which notions of 'the real' and 'authenticity' are as central as they are for news. As Grindstaff argues, '"real" stories told by "ordinary" people are the bedrock of the genre' (1997: 189), and the processes by which stories are sourced, selected and authenticated are very similar to those employed in newsgathering. Yet despite their title, 'talk' in these programmes is on the whole restricted to the host, the 'expert', and occasional interjections by audience members; participants are inarticulate, tearful or aggressive – though in US shows they may on occasion also echo, tentatively, the therapeutic discourse of the 'expert'. This is a 'real' identified with women and the working class: the *body* is the domain in which it operates. As Elspeth Probyn puts it, the talk show 'is ruled by bodies' (1992: 93), and 'the real' of the bodies which it displays is one of emotion and excess. In an essay on 'body genres' in film, Linda Williams argues that what characterises these genres – horror, melodrama and pornography – is a form of bodily excess: 'the body "beside itself" with sexual pleasure, fear and terror'. It is an excess which is rendered not through language but through 'inarticulate cries' and tears, and it is one which invites the spectator into a lack of 'proper' distance, 'a sense of over-involvement in sensation and emotion'. Above all, it is on the bodies of *women* that these excesses have been written: women 'have functioned traditionally as the primary *embodiments* of pleasure, fear and pain'. Williams concludes that the function of these 'low' genres is 'cultural problem solving'; they address 'persistent problems in our culture, in our sexualities, in our very identities'. Their 'solutions' – excessive and performative – do not of course resolve the problems they address, but they do, repetitively, display them in what Williams elsewhere calls a 'frenzy of the visible' (Williams 1991: 2–12; 1990). Within the domain of the televised 'real', we can argue, talk shows offer a similar form of 'problem solving', presenting, as Grindstaff argues, narratives of 'explicit revelation where people . . . "bare it all" for the pleasure, fascination, or repulsion of viewers' (1997: 169).

The comparison of talk shows to other 'low' genres, particularly 'women's genres' has proved attractive to critics. Jane Shattuc describes the talk show as offering a 'melodramatic narrative', in which participants are cast in the role of victim (usually female) or perpetrator (male), and the ideal of 'home' and the fear or pathos of its loss are the strongest themes (1997: 80–1). Livingstone and Lunt prefer the parallel of romance, in which the victim is rescued by the hero (the host, especially when male) with the aid of helpers in the form of both bystanders (the studio audience) and those with knowledge (the 'experts') (1994: 60). Yet a further comparison can be made with the 'grotesque' or 'unruly' female body of comedy, particularly when it is the fat body. Fatness in women, as Kathleen Rowe argues, is a form of 'making a spectacle' of oneself. Both she and Mary Russo argue that this out-of-control body – the 'open, protruding, extended, secreting body', in Russo's words (1988: 219) – can be a figure of transgression, with 'oppositional potential' (Rowe 1997: 82). Yet, as Rowe admits, for working class women, this body is 'more likely to be a source of embarrassment, timidity, and alienation, because the norms of the "legitimate" body – beauty, fitness, and so on – are accepted across class boundaries while the ability to achieve them is not' (1997: 80).

An episode of *Trisha Goddard* (C5, 23 March 2006) shows these narratives at work. The episode features four stories of dysfunctional mother-child relationships, separated by advertising breaks, with a final coda which returns us to the first of the stories. The programme operates conventions common to many talk shows. The participants are brought onstage in turn to sit facing a studio audience, without the protection of the table or desk which would shield a panel of 'experts'. The host, Trisha, moves between stage and audience, often touching the onstage participants and crouching down to speak to them. Another camera takes us backstage, for reaction shots from those yet to be presented, and allows us to see glimpses of the therapeutic process which follows the onstage interactions. In the first story we meet a mother, Ann, whose teenage son, Trisha tells us, 'spends seven hours a day surfing the net to meet strangers for sex'. *His* story is of the isolation felt by a gay teenager who is, he says, searching for 'comfort . . . someone who I can talk to, tell all my troubles to'. But it is *Ann's* situation, that of a mother fearful of losing her child, her emotions manifested in tears and physical symptoms, on which we focus. The 'solution' to this problem of maternal suffering is to forbid him the internet, mend their relationship, and restore her self-esteem through a makeover in which the son will assist. At the end of the programme the pair re-appear, to applause; a newly glamorised Ann feels 'lovely' and, says her son, 'looks beautiful'. They plan to hold a party together.

In the second story the protagonist is a daughter, Sheena, whose mother, she feels, has rejected her. As a child, we learn, she constantly ran away from home. Again, there is a reunion with tears, but, with the help of audience questions, Trisha hints at a history of childhood abuse which led to Sheena's feeling of rejection and history of self-harm. 'A lot of women have been through what you have and come out the other side,' says Trisha. A counsellor takes Sheena by the hand and leads her offstage.

In the third story, a mother is again the protagonist, her daughter the object of concern. Cheryl has spent over £10,000 on cosmetic surgery and halved her body weight. She is now attractive and well dressed; the audience greets the details of her self-transformation with applause. Her daughter, Samantha, is grossly overweight, poorly dressed and dirty: an out-of-control body. 'What do you think of what your mum's achieved?' Trisha asks, without response. Samantha, suggests Trisha, is 'going through a cycle of depression' and probably needs 'some sort of help'. Samantha is enrolled at a gym and given a mood diary. She will return when her weight loss is sufficient to transform her from victim to 'expert'.

Finally, we are presented with a mother who is afraid of her daughter's violent temper. It will, she fears, cause her daughter, Sian, to harm, and lose, her own small children. Here, again, is a body out of control. The cause is revealed to be low self-esteem: 'As a child I wasn't liked', Sian confesses, and in answer to Trisha, reveals that she does not feel that she is a good person. A counsellor is called in and leads the pair offstage. 'Everybody needs their mum with them,' comments Trisha.

As in many of these shows, 'the real' is manifested here not in words (the childhood abuse suggested in the second story is never made explicit; none of the participants is able to articulate their feelings) but through emotional and bodily display (the marks of self-harming which Trisha uncovers on Sheena's arms, the suffocating and tearful embraces). It is presented by a host who combines the status of 'survivor' ('I'm thinking of when *I* was in my most depressed state,' she says to Samantha) and therapist, and displayed for a studio audience composed almost entirely of women. In the show's accompanying booklet, Trisha describes this audience as fulfilling the traditional role of 'extended families and friends [who] were just around the corner and always there to supply advice and support'. But sympathetic though they (and we) may be, it is the staged display of bodily and emotional excess which produces the show as media entertainment ('shocking revelations' are promised by its trailer), and it is the transformation and containment of this excess which provides its narrative structure. The normative values of the show combine the traditional (the family, conventional gender roles, a female community centred on the domestic) with post-feminist ideas of self empowerment through disciplinary bodily practices (the makeover, exercise, cosmetic surgery). But neither the personal nor the everyday is *politicised*.

STRATEGIES OF CONTAINMENT

In some shows these personal narratives *are* opened out to become more general statements: Sally Jesse Raphael provides statistics of marital abuse to accompany the personal stories of abuse we see; Oprah Winfrey includes figures on addiction to crystal meth as background to individual narratives of addiction and recovery. But it is rare to find *testimony*, as Macdonald [(1998)] defines it, in which the voice of individual experience can break through its framing, to challenge the structures of meaning which seek to contain it. More usually, framing discourses are imposed and accepted, from injunctions to self-empowerment and family support, to more authoritative therapeutic discourses and overt disciplinary control. From Trisha's 'You probably need some sort of help' and the injunction of Oprah's expert to 'make a commitment' to recovery, it is a short step to the advice of *Dr Phil* (himself an expert) that 'You've got to take your power back' by 'know[ing] your authentic self', and thence to the shouted instruction of Sally Jesse Raphael's expert, 'You're going to listen to what I have to say', followed by military-style exercises during which the victim of domestic abuse chants, 'We're not taking it no more, we're not living with lies no more . . .' Even more overtly disciplinary, courtroom programmes like *Judge Judy*, in Laurie Ouellette's words, fuse 'an image of democracy . . . with a privatized approach to conflict management and an intensified government of the self', seeking to 'shape and guide the conduct and choices of lower-income women in particular' (2004: 232). Here the set is courtroom rather than stage, the audience respectful and silent, host has become judge, and the discourse demanded of the participants is evidential. Stories of emotional and bodily excess are recounted and sometimes displayed, but they are used, in Ouellette's words, to train participants and viewers to become 'self-disciplining, self-sufficient, responsible, and risk-averting individuals' (2004: 232).

We can see the same structures at work in makeover programmes. C4's *Ten Years Younger* offers to reverse the passage of time for participants (or at least to turn back their 'poll age') through a series of expert interventions: dental and plastic surgery; hair, makeup and fashion training. As a result they will improve both their 'personal life' and, even more important, their careers. [. . .] [A]s women age, they become invisible in the public sphere. The *solution* is to change their clothes, their faces and their bodies, the *problem* not one of social structures but of inadequate self-management leading to poor self-esteem. Shirley, then, who is forty-one but, according to an audience of passers by, 'looks fifty-two', has 'sagging skin, Deputy Dawg eyebags and tombstone teeth'. Unlike her exact contemporaries Michelle Pfeiffer, Elle Macpherson and Courtney Cox, she has failed to 'work hard to look good'. She will be restored to an imaginary earlier self, the shameful traces of her present inadequacy erased, and so avoid the horrific future predicted in a series of computer-generated images of her ageing face. But first she must have her grotesque body exposed; her teeth are shown filed to stumps, her skin is peeled back and the fatty lumps on her face are removed one by one and displayed to camera. Finally she is reconstructed, ready for public display: passers by now judge her to be thirty-eight; she is 'a new woman' and, asked to comment, says she is 'speechless'. Her job serving gourmet food is safe.

Like other reality TV programmes, *Ten Years Younger* is constructed as a competition, a race against time to complete a successful transformation. But its material is 'the female body in disarray' (Mellencamp 1992: 274); the time to be beaten that of the ageing process as visible deterioration; the process of transformation a survival guide which is also a training exercise in normalisation. A re-made Shirley is restored to public visibility, but the gendered structures that insist that her visibility (and employment) depends on the appearance of youth have not been challenged. Nor, despite the process of 'mediated visibility' in which the private body has been subjected to a public gaze, have the boundaries between public and private been eroded. As private body, Shirley is fragmented into body parts, each subjected to the disciplinary gaze of the camera; once re-made as public self, the camera retreats, observing her at work with colleagues and clients, not powerful but surviving.

CONCLUSION: REAL WOMEN AND 'MEDIATED VISIBILITY'

It may be, then, that we should think of these genres not as a broadening, or indeed a degeneration, of the Habermasian public sphere, but rather as inheritors of the scandal sheets and other forms of scurrilous press popular from the eighteenth century onwards. Jane Shattuc (1997) traces the continuities between these early news-sheets, the penny press of the nineteenth century, the journalistic traditions of the 'sob sisters' of the early American tabloids, and the women's magazine's advice column. In all of these, 'sex, violence, crime and tragedy' dominate, as she demonstrates with a comparison of the contents of an 1884 issue of *The New York World* and those of one week's talk shows during 1994 (1997: 18). Like their predecessors, talk shows are agents of scandal and as such, as James Lull and Stephen Hinerman argue, they *can* become 'a popular forum for public awareness and debate of moral questions' in ways that may cross over into the 'public sphere' function of the media, as watchdog on the politically and economically powerful (1997: 28). But this crossover function is limited, in a number of ways.

First, within these narratives the real people who inhabit them are most likely to be presented, not within what Bill Nichols calls the 'indexical domain of historical time', in which individuals are presented as social and political actors, but rather within the domain of 'the mythical', in which cultural concerns are played out through stories of exemplary or cautionary figures (1991: 243). 'Love rats', addicts, abusers, neglected wives or estranged parents are displayed for us so that we, and the studio audience, can police the boundaries of the normal. 'Why do [these people] have to shout and scream and weep and threaten? Why are they so eager for confrontation that they often walk onstage already bellowing?' asks Lynn Barber of the participants on *Trisha Goddard* (*The Observer*, 23 March 2003), but they must, if they are to serve this 'mythic' function.

Second, the model of resolution these programmes employ is, as we have seen, therapeutic not political. The shame which is so persistently invoked is that of personal failure to live up to gendered or familial norms ('Be a man!' exhorts Jeremy Kyle; 'Why the heck did you get married?' asks Sally Jesse Raphael; 'Do you have a shower or a bath every single day?' demands Trisha). Thus the boundaries between a shared (masculine) political realm of rational discourse and a privatised (feminine) sphere of personal responsibility, guilt and shame are reinforced, not dismantled. The goal is to produce a 'whole' self, but the method, the display of bodily symptoms 'onstage' to a responsive audience, is more reminiscent of the performances of hysteria staged by Freud's precursor as scientist of female neurosis, Jean-Martin Charcot, than it is of feminist 'consciousness-raising'. Extending outwards, these personal problems may indeed become visible as *social* problems, but, as Denise Riley reminds us, this is not necessarily to politicise them. With the development of the 'human sciences' in the nineteenth century, she writes, the categories 'women' and 'society' were seen to form a continuum. Women were seen to be immersed in the social, as both agents and objects of reform, so that 'society' (as opposed to politics, or the rational individual) was seen as always 'already permeated by the feminine' (1988: 15). 'Social issues' thus line up with 'women's issues', as distinct from 'political issues'.

Finally, these programmes are 'low culture'. Andreas Huyssen has drawn attention to the way in which, from the nineteenth century onwards, 'mass culture is somehow associated with woman, while real, authentic culture remains the prerogative of men' (1986: 47). 'Low' or 'mass' culture, like the social, was seen to be permeated with the feminine; 'high culture', the realm of Habermas's 'literary public sphere', remained masculine. We have seen in the study of news how too much 'feminisation' can lead to its devaluation as an 'objective' form. Within both TV schedules and within the programmes themselves these boundaries are maintained. Thus on one weekday, BBC2's *Working Lunch*, 'a daily taste of the latest developments in business and personal finance', features only one female presenter, the consumer affairs reporter, and only one female 'expert', who speaks on behalf of the British Chamber of Commerce against a change in law which will benefit mainly low-paid women. Following it on ITV1, a women's discussion programme is called *Loose Women*; its participants discuss wedding-night sex, the value of opera, weight loss, and the issues raised by a current *Coronation Street* storyline. It is the *professional* expertise of the male experts that is referenced in makeover programmes; women are usually given no such introduction. Within BBC2's *The Apprentice*, a ruthlessly competitive context ('It's a dog-eat-dog situation') sees women 'fired' because they are too 'nice', too 'overpowering', or too emotional: 'she jumps up and down, she squawks, she claps her hands, she falls out with people, she stamps, she sulks and she cries' comments *The Guardian* (30 March 2006) on one contestant. *Men* are 'fired' because they are not aggressive enough. Indeed, we can argue that across the very different genres of news and talk shows, real women fulfil essentially the same function: they are, as Margaret Gallagher [(2006)] writes of news, victims, 'ordinary people', embodiments of personal experience, or the voice of popular opinion.

These boundaries, of course, are permeable: personal trauma, as Anita Biressi and Heather Nunn (2005) argue, is worked through in the realm of the public in talk shows and reality television; elsewhere, women *do* appear as 'experts'. Today's public space of 'mediated visibility' is indeed, as John B. Thompson argues, a more open-ended discursive space than the restricted Habermasian public sphere, one in which 'the consequences of becoming visible cannot be fully anticipated and controlled' (1995: 247). But the 'frenzy of the visible' which is so often the result reminds us that, as Mellencamp argues, 'TV both traverses *and* maintains Habermas's and Foucault's divide' between the public and the private (1992: 264), and that for the real women who are displayed there, the visibility which it confers can be far from liberatory.

REFERENCES

Biressi, Anita and Nunn, Heather (2005), *Reality TV: Realism and Revelation*, London: Wallflower Press.

Bondebjerg, Ib (1996), 'Public Discourse/Private Fascination: Hybridization in "True-life-story" Genres', *Media, Culture & Society* 18: 1, pp. 27–45.

Bordo, Susan (1989), 'The Body and the Reproduction of Femininity', in Bordo, Susan and Jaggar, Alison M. (eds), *Gender/Body/Knowledge: Feminist Reconstructions of Being and Knowing*, New Brunswick and London: Rutgers University Press, pp. 13–33.

Bordo, Susan (1993), *Unbearable Weight: Feminism, Western Culture, and the Body*, London: University of California Press.

Gallagher, Margaret (2006), *Who Makes the News? Global Media Monitoring Project 2005*, www.whomakesthenews.org.

Grindstaff, Laura (1997), 'Producing Trash, Class and the Money Shot: A Behind-the-scenes Account of Daytime TV Talk', in Lull, James and Hinerman, Stephen (eds), *Media Scandals*, Cambridge: Polity, pp. 164–202.

Grosz, Elizabeth (1994), *Volatile Bodies: Towards a Corporeal Feminism*, Bloomington and Indianapolis: Indiana University Press.

Huyssen, Andreas (1986), 'Mass Culture as Woman: Modernism's Other', in Huyssen, Andreas, *After the Great Divide: Modernism, Mass Culture and Postmodernism*, Basingstoke and London: Macmillan, pp. 44–62.

Livingstone, Sonia and Lunt, Peter (1994), *Talk on Television*, London: Routledge.

Lull, James and Hinerman, Stephen (1997), 'The Search for Scandal', in Lull, James and Hinerman, Stephen (eds), *Media Scandals*, Cambridge: Polity, pp. 1–33.

Macdonald, Myra (1998), 'Publicizing the Personal: Women's Voices in British Television Documentaries', in Carter, Cynthia, Branston, Gill and Allan, Stuart (eds), *News, Gender and Power*, London: Routledge, pp. 105–20.

Mellencamp, Patricia (1992), *High Anxiety: Catastrophe, Scandal, Age, and Comedy*, Bloomington and Indianapolis: Indiana University Press.

Nichols, Bill (1991), *Representing Reality*, Bloomington and Indianapolis: Indiana University Press.

Ouellette, Laurie (2004), '"Take Responsibility for Yourself": *Judge Judy* and the Neoliberal Citizen', in Murray, Susan and Ouellette, Laurie (eds), *Reality TV: Remaking Television Culture*, New York: New York University Press, pp. 231–50.

Probyn, Elspeth (1992), 'Theorizing Through the Body', in Rakow, Lana F. (ed.), *Women Making Meaning: New Feminist Directions in Communication*, New York: Routledge, pp. 83–99.

Radner, Hilary (1995), *Shopping Around: Feminine Culture and the Pursuit of Pleasure*, New York and London: Routledge.

Riley, Denise (1988), *'Am I that Name?' Feminism and the Category of 'Women' in History*, Basingstoke: Macmillan.

Rowe, Kathleen K. (1997), 'Roseanne: Unruly Woman as Domestic Goddess', in Brunsdon, Charlotte, D'Acci, Julie and Spigel, Lynn (eds), *Feminist Television Criticism: A Reader*, Oxford: Clarendon Press, pp. 74–83.

Russo, Mary (1988), 'Female Grotesques: Carnival and Theory', in de Lauretis, Teresa (ed.), *Feminist Studies/Critical Studies*, Basingstoke: Macmillan, pp. 213–29.

Shattuc, Jane (1997), *The Talking Cure: TV, Talk Shows and Women*, New York: Routledge.

Squire, Corinne (1997), 'Empowering Women? The *Oprah Winfrey* Show', in Brunsdon, Charlotte, D'Acci, Julie and Spigel, Lynn (eds), *Feminist Television Criticism: A Reader*, Oxford: Clarendon Press, pp. 98–113.

Thompson, John B. (1995), *The Media and Modernity*, Cambridge: Polity.

Williams, Linda (1991), 'Film Bodies: Gender, Genre and Excess', *Film Quarterly* vol. 44, no. 4, pp. 2–13.

48

CELEBRITY, SOCIAL MOBILITY AND THE FUTURE OF REALITY TV

Anita Biressi and Heather Nunn

[. . .]

[D]ISGUST DEMOCRATISATION AND DESIRE

Reality TV is not the end of civilisation as we know it: it is civilisation as we know it. It is popular culture at its most popular, soap opera come to life. (Greer 2001)

[. . .] [C]urrent responses to reality TV coalesce around several themes. One common strand is that of derision. This response is encapsulated in Germaine Greer's much cited quotation above. In her article on reality TV, Greer jeers at the mass audience of these shows and predictably situates them within a 'dumbed down' tabloid television arena in which, she claims, a mixture of banality, exhibitionism and character-play guarantee audience ratings and therefore their domination of the schedules.

In keeping with broader attacks on tabloid culture and of the 'feminisation' of factual programming, a number of cultural critics (often championing a lost cause which is implicitly 'high culture') decry those who produce, watch and perform for the cameras. The ethics of what is acceptable in mass media representation is linked to broader debates about the decline of more privileged objective factual reportage and programming. In Britain, this debate is specifically linked to the role of television in an arena in which the public service ethos has been diminished. Objectivity, fact and debate are

From Anita Biressi and Heather Nunn, *Reality TV: Realism and Revelation* (London: Wallflower Press, 2005).

bandied about as lost values of a formerly intellectually curious journalistic age.

The Reithian theme of self-improvement and a broadcasting service that strove to use television to take viewers outside their realm of immediate existence, to educate and inform, is lamented as a lost educative ideal in an increasingly commercially-pressured media environment. [. . .] [R]eality TV, it is claimed, replaces this intellectual adventure with the limited exhibitionist challenges of the game show or the emotional outpourings of confessional culture in which the biggest challenge is to get on with a small bunch of housemates/ prisoners/competitors for a limited period. With reality TV the aim is not to take viewers outside of their own experience but to present them with a fully recognisable and familiar realm of the ordinary and the everyday. The ethic of self-improvement seems, for media sceptics, to be parodied; as those without the traditional markers of media role models are seen to succeed – if not in Reithian terms, then at least within the terms of the populist media.

The disdain for the entertainment-led audience is matched by distress about changes to televisual form and genre. Frequently, the documentary becomes the marker of quality filming based on rational investigation of historical or socio-cultural fact. The detached but committed observational gaze of the documentary maker of the past has, it is claimed, been replaced by a slow slide through the docu-soap of the 1990s to the current reality TV show. An anxiety about the decline of documentary proper is often articulated to an anxiety about reality TV's dependence on spectacle linked to a manipulative misuse of the camera. Here, for example, the prominence of the 'close-up' is highlighted. This fear of the seductive image is captured in language that stresses the distraction of the viewer from rational viewing: 'we *cannot think straight* . . . if our *emotions* are being *jerked up and down* by . . . zoom lenses'(Broder in Glynn 2000: 22). Underlying this anxiety about 'easy' pleasure is recognition of the destabilisation of the status of the distant and powerful documentary camera and the move towards televisual intimacy.

[. . .] [I]n contrast to the above criticism, others have celebrated this cultural phenomenon as part of the contemporary expansion and democratisation of public culture. It is argued that reality TV's popular expression of social concerns and everyday events, conflicts and traumas within a highly managed environment signal the opening up of the public sphere to ordinary concerns and ordinary people who, if they are popular enough and lucky enough, can become famous. Where celebrities are already a prerequisite of the show – for example in the recent adaptations of survival shows for celebrity participants – the authenticity of the show is marked by the supposed provision of insights into the hidden 'real' aspect of celebrity personality. Phil Edgar-Jones, the executive producer of *Big Brother*, described the second *Celebrity Big Brother* as a stripping away of celebrity personas: 'With normal *Big Brother* we're making ordinary people extraordinary. With this, we're making famous people very, very ordinary' (in Day 2002). In short, reality TV is celebrated as a democratisation of public culture and the deconstruction of the components of fame that partially constitute the celebrity media subject and the construction of social identity more broadly. [. . .]

The process of constructing celebrity and stripping it away can be captured in John Langer's notion of 'the especially remarkable' (1998: 45–73). In his analysis of tabloid culture, he highlights the prominence in current media culture of the 'other news': a form of cultural discourse intimately connected with gossip, storytelling and the scrutiny of the newly famous as well as those with a longer-held celebrity persona. Langer situates the celebrity within a co-dependent media context in which celebrity status is both ratified by media presence but also operates as a privileged authority in media culture. Celebrities increasingly have taken on the role as 'primary definers' of news. The very force of representation of the celebrity gives their actions and statements a kind of privileged authority in a world increasingly characterised as divided by those who have access to image making and the rest (1998: 50–1). This other news does not represent elite persons within the context of their institutional backdrop and does not primarily consider their role as power brokers or decision makers – but rather values their informal activities, public rituals of display and consumption and their private lives.

This 'calculus of celebrity' then is flexible and focuses not only on celebrities but upon those who have achieved possibly fleeting public attention through specific personal achievement. For example, the 'ordinary' stars of reality shows suddenly acquire massive media visibility but possess very little in the way of institutional power or control and, unless they obtain excellent PR management, can find it hard to deal with media spin. Reality TV both proves and extends the mythic belief that traditional versions of mobility and success, once closely associated with economic or social achievement, are increasingly implicated in and beholden to the mass media processes of publicity. Langer suggests:

> On the one hand ordinary people are constructed as especially remarkable for what they do. How they breach expectations, their remarkableness is lodged in the extraordinary acts they perform. This separates them from us, makes them different and transcendent; they start where we are but move beyond. On the other hand . . . The implication is that, although these people are assigned especially remarkable qualities based on what they do, such qualities and performances could just as easily be within our grasp. If those seemingly mundane occupations and enthusiasms . . . can become the springboard from which those ordinary people ascend into the realms of the especially remarkable it could just as easily happen to us as well. (1998: 72)

The appeal of reality programming lies partly in how seemingly ordinary people are suddenly 'especially remarkable' and how that celebrity status is endorsed by the spectacle of their widespread public presence. For example, *Pop Idol UK* (2002) screened countless auditions of would-be pop celebrities. The show attracted over 30 million viewers who watched and voted for those singers who would remain until the final contest between Gareth Gates and the ultimate winner Will Young. These two contestants have both become chart-topping pop singers with massive media coverage.

The 2002 spin-off *American Idol* warned potential contestants that their appearance on television may be 'disparaging, defamatory, embarrassing or of an otherwise unfavourable nature which may expose you to public ridicule, humiliation or condemnation'.[1] Nonetheless its popularity with would-be idols and audiences alike ensured a second series in 2003. *American Idol 2* appeared on Fox TV and concurrently in the UK on ITV2 in March 2003. It followed the structure of the UK predecessor and the final twelve contestants were intro-duced to their audience through pre-recorded video cameos that emphasised their 'ordinariness', their smalltown American homes and the support of their local schools, military barracks, church or family. These to-camera testimonies by family and friends and shots of the contestants feeding the ducks, visiting their old workplace at a hair salon or supermarket, or training with ordi-nary soldiers located them as 'no-one particularly special', as 'regular' or 'all American' young men and women. But, at the same time, the 'folks' that spoke of them and their singing skills, as a child amateur performer, in the church choir, in a local bar, served to elevate their status. These subsidiary characters, like the live audience for whom the contestants then perform, function textu-ally as a sign of public acclamation: 'the especially remarkable are seen (by us) to be seen by others in the public domain' (Langer 1998: 63).

These short video narratives of personal triumph over ordinary obstacles and *over obscurity itself* anticipated their live stage performances held before music industry judges and the television audience. The appearance in front of cameras before a voting audience was constructed consequently as the tangible reward for their accomplishments *per se* despite the more obvious rewards and lure of winning the competition. In such competitions, the ordinary masses of viewers who follow the course of the contestant's path to fame are crucial. They serve a similar role to the subsidiary characters present at the edges of the frame in television camera or paparazzi shots of the star persona, for their presence 'watching, waiting, attending or serving' the ordinary celebrity endorses his or her status (Langer 1998: 72). Furthermore, this identifica-tion with the 'especially remarkable' individual allows for the possibility of a sense of activity for the television spectator, of a hand in the elevation of the ordinary person to celebrity status.

Correspondingly, Peter Balzagette (2001) argued that reality TV is 'diverse programming, and access to the airwaves for a more diverse spread of people'. He declared that this democratisation, also signalled by the audience's ability to contribute to the elevation or elimination of the stars, goes hand in hand with a change in social attitudes about television and identification. As signalled earlier, he characterises this as a desire for 'emotional investment' latched onto the appeal of interactivity and audience participation. For Balzagette, audience figures clarify this desire to participate in and determine a programme's conclusion; a motivation which ensured that over the first two series of *Big Brother* around 34 million phone votes were cast for who should stay and who should go in the *Big Brother* house.

[. . .]

But the issues we have raised throughout about the seemingly unremarkable subject of reality TV and their entry into the celebrity matrix are best exemplified by Jade Goody. Goody, a 21-year-old dental nurse from South London, fourth from last to be expelled from the house, received wildly fluctuating media coverage from the press whilst in the house and was the subject, halfway through the series, of vitriolic attacks from the tabloids. Goody was undoubtedly 'marked' negatively as working-class by her body, her voice and her supposed intellectual ignorance. She was loud, apparently uneducated, bibulous, excessive, overweight and getting fatter as the series progressed. The press revelled in quoting 'Jade-isms', the stupid things said by Goody in the course of the series. She displayed the bodily excesses that marked Roseanne Barr as a blatantly working-class woman but without the wisecracking wit that shielded Barr from the worst misogynistic criticisms (see Rowe 1995). Dominic Mohon, editor of the *Sun*'s showbiz column 'Bizarre' urged readers to evict Jade with the deeply misogynistic and class-based slogan, 'Vote out the pig.' He informed readers that 'Jade is one of the most hated women on British TV and life will be hard for her when she leaves the house.' She seemed to exemplify Annette Kuhn's observation that:

> Class is something beneath your clothes, under your skin, in your psyche, at the very core of your being. In the all-encompassing English class system, if you know you are in the 'wrong' class, you know that therefore you are a valueless person. (1995: 98)

However, tabloid attacks were upturned by positive viewer support for Goody resulting in tabloid battles for exclusive rights to her story when she emerged from the house. Ironically, Rupert Murdoch's *Sun* and *News of the World* outbid rival tabloids and paid £500,000 for exclusive interviews with her. Since then Goody has been re-branded as a 'national treasure'.

Goody's success fits the pattern highlighted for the 'especially remarkable' in that when the ordinary celebrity is prone to setbacks, these setbacks are played out before the public gaze. She won through only after a dialectic of ill-fortune and effort had been played out. And crucially her success was attributed to powers beyond her grasp: she was subject to the inexplicable hand of fate, the power of the television audience and the manipulations of the television production crew. When she exited from the house she appeared dressed in a glamorous evening gown three sizes too small and was soon confronted by *Big Brother* host Davina McCall with a montage of clips revealing her excessive behaviour and her apparent stupidity. Talk show comedian Graham Norton, who reclaimed her as a camp icon, was also there to meet her and went on to depict her in his shows as the plump, giggly and dense dental nurse reminiscent of a 1950s *Carry On* film.

Subsequent media coverage focused on the re-education of Miss Goody. The television programme *What Jade Did Next* (Channel 4, October 2002) followed her as she worked with a personal trainer, learned how to deal with the media, learned how to drive and was schooled in the very demanding work of public appearances. Her background with her single mother on a working-class social housing estate was contrasted with the opportunities on offer to her since her appearance on the reality show. She was a stark signifier of the possibility of self-transformation and social mobility in spite of class origins and limited social skills. Jade's narrative of desired transformation also revealed how class plays a central role in the production of femininity and the regulation of it. The escape which Jade articulates in *What Jade Did Next* reveals a knowledge on her part about the attainment of not just economic wealth but the cultural artefacts of taste and knowledge, of cultural capital. The possession of the 'right' car, of literacy, of designer clothes and private property are signifiers of social mobility hedged with the dangers of the disreputable: the trashy dress, the uninformed opinion, the too-loud laugh. In keeping with earlier fictional fantasies of achievement, reality TV offered Jade Goody a way to exhibit incipient talent for performance, 'rough at the edges but with the potential for learning' (McRobbie 1991: 215).

Celebrity Hybridity and Packaged Demotic Culture

The address to the reality audience varies depending on the format of the show. But across the board there is a shared assumption that the audience possesses the media literate capabilities to assess the contestants/participants of the reality TV show – even though the criteria of judgement are often unformulated and unspoken. These criteria are grounded in vague notions of identification, appreciation and also crucially of dislike and disdain. Participants of *Big Brother* or *Pop Idol* or *The Club* (ITV2, 2003) knowingly present themselves to a judgemental audience. Their task is one of interaction and the overt immersion in the competitive structure of the show. [. . .] [P]articipants are selected on the basis of contradictory criteria and are often stereotypes of the diverse identities that populate contemporary media culture – lesbian or gay, black, heterosexual bachelor, twenty-thirty something white 'Essex' girl or boy, stud, tart, shy loner. These types share (are presented as sharing) two features: an everyday commonality and a hunger for celebrity status. The winning group formula for a reality TV show appears to be a combination of the typecast, the banal and the exceptional.

Frequently, the participants are presented as classed subjects. Whilst the boundary between working class and lower-middle class is now often blurred in contemporary British culture and the very formations of classed hierarchies have radically altered, the participants generally are presented as residing some-where in this region: they are clerical workers, mechanics, bar keepers, service industry workers and so on. Where, as in the UK *Big Brother 5*, they include university graduates and entrepreneurs this aspect of their cultural context is heavily muted in the edited broadcasts of the show. They are also frequently aspirant media celebrities. In many reality shows there is a submerged narra-tive about escape across classed boundaries. Also the production and editing of the show reveals a level of unacknowledged cultural capital at play. The taste and disposition of the contestants is under scrutiny; their clothes, banal conversation, interactions with other contestants, ambitions, everyday activi-ties as related to the audience are markers of their position within the class hierarchy. As noted in our earlier discussions of the group dynamics of the UK version of *Survivor* and *Big Brother 1* it is important not to appear too wealthy, *too* cultured or *too* tasteful. Yet, as with Jade Goody, appearing too trashy, too sexual, too uncultured can also provoke media opprobrium and infamy. Contestants need to be distinctive but not too distinctive.

A strategy of 'violence' then is encouraged in the reality TV community. The judgement on which contestants should stay and which should go is struc-tured as a demotic decision but it is a decision formed through division and exclusion. This is a system of judgement and classification. A vote determines who is unworthy of respect or esteem – for the contestant the outcome of the vote makes overt the fact that one's performance on the show is readable for others: the people watch you, observe you and decide upon your fate. Here, we would argue the seemingly more fluid opportunities of celebrity identity fuse with the traces of a class-based system. There is both a celebration of aspiration (and the desire for escape from the limitations of ordinary life) and a judgemental scrutiny of the participants' behaviour – to appear too ambitious, too outrageous, too performative is to invite audience disdain. Yet to appear too dull, too isolated, too introverted is to also invite banishment. Of course, the conventional markers of class identity alone are inadequate to predict who will survive and thrive in this media environment. Yet the reality competition often takes place around two axes rooted in economic and social capital – that of material goods (prize money, media contracts) and that of less tangible phenomena such as popularity.

Crucial to the possession of the celebrity status that comes with popularity is a particular form of distinction in which the contestant, as he or she appears before the media audience, can be outrageous, bold, greedy, bitchy or ruth-less but they cannot appear pretentious. Pretentiousness is primarily a classed charge which calls aspirant working- or lower-middle-class identities to order: 'who does she think she is kidding?' or 'we can see right through him'. As Steph Lawler notes, 'pretentiousness is a charge levelled at people in whom what they *seem to be* is not (considered to be) what they are: in whom there is a gap between *being* and *seeming*' (2000: 121). One of the pleasures of reality TV for the audience then is trying to spot the gap, to see through the contestants' inauthenticity. Yet inauthenticity, the ability to put on a show, is at the same time part of the skill of the celebrity persona.

In this context 'classed cross-dressing' carries with it pleasures for both the aspirant celebrity subject and the media audience but also dangers. Arrogance, outrageous or overtly ruthless behaviour can be construed as part of older established narratives of transformation in which the working-class boy or girl who wants it badly enough eventually has it all. Consequently, such behaviour signifies a desire to escape limits, to 'be someone', to grab a status and power normally denied. Attendant on this performance is an inevitable lack of nuance or sophistication *within the terms of class by which the contestants are constrained*. To successfully adopt markers of 'cultured' identity *in their entirety* would be to underline too clearly that class and power can be vestments or trappings rather than some integral part of one's essential identity. Classed cross-dressing then involves always the danger of discovery, of passing as one of a 'higher order' and the attendant pleasure for the audience of unmasking someone's hubris.

REALITY TV – THE FUTURE?

The institutionalised cultural management that is at the core of celebrity culture was wedded to a new development of the reality show in the form of new series such as *The Club* and *The Salon*. In these, the distinction between the authentic celebrity and the would-be celebrity and between the reality of the game and of the game as a packaged show have been further muddied. In the 'fly-on-the-wall' series *The Salon* (C4) workers from a real salon are re-located with new recruits to run a salon undertaking hair and beauty treatments for both the ordinary public and for celebrities. Viewers can win the chance for an appointment. In a postmodern turn, both amusing and bizarre, the first series witnessed a visit from disgraced family variety-show presenter Michael Barrymore for a hair cut and the new series saw staff welcoming Brendan, a spectacularly bad candidate from *Pop Idol*, for a pedicure. In both cases the reality TV workers of *The Salon* were overheard indulging in celebrity gossip about their clients. The show pointed towards future forms that create a new social/media space in which 'real' people and celebrities co-exist side-by-side.

In early 2003 Carlton broadcast a new show called *The Club* which also provided this new social/media space. The show was staged in a real location, a retro-themed, two-floored bar called *Nylon*, in London's square mile. Each week for the duration of the six-week show, three celebrities took control of one of the bars at *Nylon* and their team of bartenders would battle it out to make theirs the coolest one. Each week the celebrity nominated a member of his or her team to get the sack; viewers were witnesses to the nomination and to the celebrity's frank appraisal of their staff. Television viewers were also asked to vote for the team member that they wanted to lose their job and the sacking took place live on TV. Open auditions were then held and those who voted *or who attended* the club could, if they chose, ask to be nominated to replace the sacked employee.

Chrysalis-owned Galaxy radio network teamed up with Carlton to promote the show and when it started, its presenters, celebrity bar managers and team members were featured on dance music stations; Galaxy DJ's even managed the decks at Nylon. The club had the capacity to pack in over 500 revellers (Day 2003). It was promoted using the now-common media practice of 'emotional branding' (Lull 2000: 170). In this case, the commodity was associated with the subjectivities of everyday working-class life. The three celebrities selected to run the bar were emblems of working-class culture made good. Samantha Fox, the former *Sun* 'page three girl' of the 1980s, who, as the official website profile stresses, started work on the *Sun* at sixteen years of age and has gone on to make a wide-ranging showbusiness career for herself. Fox had accrued an iconic status as a former tabloid star and still signifies a brash hedonism and visual excitement combined with a determined desire for celebrity success. She was presented throughout the programme as a tough achiever who combined glamour with tabloid's populist appeal. Her climb to success is marked by a significant gender and class realignment in which working-class women resist 'discourses of sobriety' through the unashamed use of their sexuality in the accrual of celebrity status; a positioning which sits easily with the personas and self-professed ambitions of reality TV's contestants.

The second bar manager was Dean Gaffney, who started work on the long running British TV soap opera *Eastenders*, again at the early age of fifteen. Gaffney is presented as a working-class success story, which melds real-life with his soap persona. The website states that he is 'no stranger to hard and unglamorous work, and he vividly remembers pounding the pavements on his paper round as a boy'. This is immediately juxtaposed with tales of his current penchant for fast cars and drinking sessions at *Stringfellows* nightclub: 'the trials of celebrity lifestyle!' Gaffney's bar eventually won the £15,000 prize money. The third bar manager was Richard Blackwood, a former MTV presenter turned Channel 4 presenter then pop star. The web profile again presents Blackwood as a person who wants to be remembered as 'a real personality that came from nothing'. All three managers work extremely hard and there is a strange juxtaposition of discourses as 'celebrities' labour intensively in the maintenance of the celebrity status. The best thing about the series is that it reveals the 'hard work' behind the superficially effortless image of entertainers.

But of course, in this context the revelation of the real work of stardom is also part and parcel of the unique selling point of the show. All three bar managers reveal the use of celebrity to represent the emotion of the cultural product: they signify the importance of ambition, exceptional personality and a drive to achieve success even with a poor start in life. What is interesting is the elision between their celebrity personas and their real-life status. All three are presented as working-class without specific reference to these terms. Gaffney's soap persona is melded with his personal media achievement whilst Fox exemplifies how being a working celebrity means interpreting economics in sexual as well as financial terms.

There are a number of points to be made about the innovation and self-referential and often hybrid status of *The Club*. The contestants too are mainly from fairly mundane jobs as clerical workers, bar men or women, supermarket workers and so on. They share the common desire to succeed in media terms. *The Club* breaks down the division between would-be and successful celebrity that had heretofore been maintained in, for example, the *Big Brother* and *Survivor* shows. Celebrities work alongside ordinary contestants in the bar and are overtly constructed as cultural workers with shared ambitions. Whilst the division in power is maintained – through the hierarchy of the bar managed by the established celebrity – there are moments when this breaks down. At one point, Fox's crew chastises her in the appraisal session for drinking too much and jeopardising their chances – a scene in which Sam walks off camera twice and later apologises to her team. The contestants and celebrities challenge any easy notion of classed identity. Both groups in a sense occupy ersatz class positions – drawing too easily on narratives of gritty success that, in the case of the celebrities, obliterate the distinctions between their public and private personas. Both perform for camera whilst also baring their more 'authentic' anxieties about other team members in by-now well rehearsed confessional to-camera moments that supposedly characterise reality TV's glimpse of the authentic person.

But finally then, both *The Salon* and *The Club* are worthy of attention because their formats erode the divisions and distinctions between the audience and the performers in ways which point towards the future development of factual entertainment programming. Shows such as the USA-based *Survivor* have operated a no-fly zone over their island-competition space to exclude the danger/chaos of outsiders breaking into the reality of the mediated event. *Big Brother* shuts contestants away from the physical presence of ordinary others and opens them up only to the televisual/computer gaze. In contrast, *The Salon* allowed anyone to make an appointment and *The Club* was open to the public who could visit every night of the week including the televised nights. For a minimal fee they could join in the media event, buying drinks at the bar, talking with and assessing the contestants and celebrities and, if they were lucky, appear on the small screen itself. *The Club* especially was a provocative re-inscription of the local and particular experience of the neighbourhood bar into the global distanced voyeurism of television land. If you were young enough, had disposable income, dressed smartly and lived in London you too could inhabit a reality TV space. This constituted a marked extension of the viewers' exercise of their discrimination in voting and offered a fleeting few-seconds of media fame as the camera caught them at the bar or nearby amidst *Nylon*'s customers. Even Blaine's 'Above the Below' took place in a public space and many visitors noted that it was the experience of seeing him in the flesh and the sensation of being part of the crowd on the ground – that is, being part of the event – that won them round as fans. These new hybrid forms are reality TV writ large, allowing people to routinely select and weave mediated, publicly available symbolic representations and discourses into their everyday lives and starkly revealing how their participation can be packaged, commodified and sold back to them as audiences.

CONCLUDING COMMENTS

[. . .] [W]e have returned to [. . .] a discussion of reality TV as a changing vehicle for the representation of ordinary (that is, non-elite) people and a platform for the projection of ordinary voices. We have charted quite extensively the ways in which realist genres, especially documentaries, broke new ground in the representation of ordinary people and everyday life and how they increasingly sought to provide a forum for the articulation of working-class experience. [W]e also noted how ordinary people and the 'working classes' in particular have been deployed by filmmakers and read by audiences as being *in themselves* signs of the real and of the authentic. The presence of ordinary people and the provision of access for demotic voices are often taken to be markers of the realist credentials of factual and fact-based programming. And many films and programmes that preceded popular observational documentary and reality TV (and some of those that continue to be made today) were also motivated by explicitly radical political agendas rooted in a celebration of the contribution of ordinary people to the life of the nation and in demands for political action, social justice or a change in social attitudes.

As has been demonstrated, the 'politics' of the more popular factual programming and reality TV in particular is quite differently articulated. It can be overwhelmingly conservative, producing knowledges ('revelations') disguised as truths ('reality') about the criminal subject, the sexualised subject, the confessing subject, the consuming subject, the traumatised subject and so on that close down any collective impetus to effect change or to challenge the status quo. Although reality TV frequently dwells on issues of social difference and hierarchies of classed or cultural distinction and it is predicated on the importance of depicting ordinary people's experience (and arguably practising cultural politics in doing so) its trajectory is nonetheless quite different from its more overtly politicised generic antecedents. It is attentive to individual aspiration and competitive individualism within frequently fake or highly proscribed micro-communities and attends to social mobility within an increasingly mediated social/public realm. This emphasis on the individual, their ambitions, fears and interpersonal relations with fellow contestants, neighbours, family or workmates brings pressure to bear on the filmic subject to reveal all on television. The increasingly destabilised and permeable borders between the media and the social realm facilitates this and, in doing so, radically alters the cultural landscape within which we all have to abide. Moreover, as noted throughout, the increasing presence of cameras in our lives, their incursion into public spaces and their apparent widespread acceptability is in itself altering the ground of our self-presentation and self-fashioning. To borrow an observation from Jon Dovey, 'We are all learning to live in the freakshow, it is our new public space' (2000: 4). The question which should perhaps preoccupy us now is how we choose to navigate this space and make it our own.

NOTE

1. Elstree Studio website, http://www.elstree.co.uk/, accessed 3 October 2002.

REFERENCES

Balzalgette, Peter, The Hun Weldon Lecture 2001, 'Big Brother and Beyond'.

Day, Julia (2002), 'Channel 4 Thinks Big for Celebrity Reality Show', *Guardian*, 4 November 2002.

Day, Julia (2003), 'New Reality Show Joins the Club', *Guardian*, 22 January 2003.

Dovey, Jon (2000) *Freakshow: First Person Media and Factual Television*. London: Pluto.

Glynn, Kevin (2000) *Tabloid Culture: Trash Taste, Popular Power and the Transformation of American Television*. Durham: Duke University Press.

Greer, Germaine (2001) 'Watch With Brother', *The Observer: Review*, 24 June.

Kuhn, Annette (1995) *Family Secrets: Acts of Memory and Imagination*. London: Verso.

Langer, John (1998) *Tabloid Television: Popular Journalism and the 'Other' News*. London: Routledge.

Lawler, Steph (2000) 'Escape and escapism: Representing Working-Class Women', in Sally R. Munt (ed.), *Cultural Studies and the Working Class: Subject to Change*. London: Cassell, 113–28.

Lull, James (2000) *Media, Communication, Culture: A Global Approach*. Cambridge: Polity.

Lumby, C. (2001) 'Sylvania Waters', available at: http://www.mbcnet.org/ETV/S/htmlS/sylvaniawate/sylvaniawate.htm.

Lyotard, Jean-Francois (1984) *The Postmodern Condition*. Minneapolis: University of Minnesota Press.

Macdonald, Kevin and Mark Cousins (eds) (1996) *Imagining Reality*. London: Faber and Faber.

MacDonald, Myra (1998) 'Politicising the personal: women's voices in British television documentaries', in Cynthia Carter, Gill Branston and Stuart Allan (eds) *News, Gender and Power*. London: Routledge, 105–20.

McRobbie, Angela (1991) 'Dance Narratives and Fantasies of Achievement', in *Feminism and Youth Culture: From Jackie to Just Seventeen*. Basingstoke: Macmillan Education, 189–219.

Rowe, Kathleen (1995) *The Unruly Woman: Gender and Genres of Laughter*. Austin: University of Texas Press.

49

TEACHING US TO FAKE IT

The Ritualized Norms of Television's 'Reality' Games

Nick Couldry

Whatever its contribution to the overblown claims of semiotics as a general 'science' of language, Roland Barthes's analysis of 'myth' and its connection to ideology remains useful as a specific tool to understand particular types of media language such as advertising and also that most striking of recent phenomena, reality TV.[1] Myth itself, Ernesto Laclau has argued, is increasingly a requirement of contemporary societies whose divisions and dislocations multiply.[2] If so, reality TV's mythical claim to represent an increasingly complex social space – for example, in the largely entertainment mode of the gamedoc or reality game show – may have significance far beyond the analysis of the television genre. I will make this assertion more precise by considering reality TV's ritual dimensions and their link to certain media-centric norms of social behavior.

The idea underlying reality TV is hardly new. Here is the television anchor who commented on the 1969 Apollo moon touchdown speaking three decades ago: '[Television's] real value is to make people participants in ongoing experiences. Real life is vastly more exciting than synthetic life, and this is real-life drama with audience participation.'[3] This notion – and the associated claim of television to present real life – does not disappear in the era of television 'plenty,' but rather comes under increasing pressure to take new forms.[4] The subgenre of gamedocs on which I will concentrate is a later adaptation to those pressures, succeeding an early wave of docusoaps and television verité in the mid-1990s, and a subsequent crisis of many docusoaps' documentary

From Susan Murray and Laurie Ouellette (eds), *Reality TV: Remaking Television Culture* (New York: New York University Press, 2004).

authority because of scandals about fake productions – for example, over Carlton TV's documentary. *The Connection* (1999), which supposedly uncovered an operation for smuggling drugs from Colombia, but was alleged by the *London Guardian* to have faked various scenes.[5] But if the gamedoc signifies a shift to a 'postdocumentary' television culture, the result is not an abandonment of reality claims but their transformation.[6] As John Corner puts it in regard to the first British series of *Big Brother*, '*Big Brother* operates its claims to the real within a fully managed artificiality, in which almost everything that might be deemed to be true about what people do and say is necessarily and obviously predicated on the larger contrivance of them being there in front of the camera in the first place.'[7]

My interest here is less in the gamedoc as generic form (excellently discussed by Corner), but in the wider social process that gamedocs constitute. At stake in these often much-hyped programs is a whole way of reformulating the media's (not just television's) deep-seated claim to present social reality, to be the 'frame' through which we access the reality that matters to us as social beings.[8] In the gamedoc, this involves the promotion of specific norms of behavior to which those who court popularity by living in these shows' constructed spaces must conform.

To get analytic purchase on this complex process, the term 'myth' by itself is too blunt. Instead, we need the more precise notions of 'ritual' and 'ritualization' that can link the television form to the wider issues of authority and governmentality.[9] Most contemporary self-performance can, as Gareth Palmer notes, be interpreted in light of Michel Foucault's theory of governmentality, whereby power is reproduced through norms not just of control but also of expression and self-definition. I want, however, to push further than Palmer does the implications of the fact that in gamedocs, 'What develop[s is] not so much a self [as] a *media self*.'[10]

What is this media self? What is its social status, and what are its social consequences? To link gamedocs to governmentality is not enough since all contemporary social space is in this sense governed by norms that regulate what is acceptable, meaningful, and pleasurable, and what is not. We need also to ask: Are gamedocs such as *Big Brother* spaces for reflecting on governmentality shared by performers and audiences alike, or spaces for audiences to reflect on governmentality by watching others (the performers) being governed, or finally, a process whereby both performers and audiences are in effect governed through the unreflexive naturalization of particular behavioral norms?[11]

THE RITUAL SPACE OF THE REALITY GAME SHOW

What might we mean by the ritual properties of television forms such as the gamedoc?[12]

Ritual action and media form

First, it is important to emphasize that by ritual, I mean more than habitual actions. While much of gamedocs *does* consist of rituals in this common-sense use of the term (as people get up, eat, wash up, chat, and sleep for the cameras), this use adds nothing to the idea of habit. Instead, I am interested in the two more substantive anthropological senses of ritual: as formalized action; and as action (often but not necessarily formalized) associated with certain transcendent values.

The first sense captures how certain action-patterns are not only repeated but organized in a form or shape that has a meaning over and above any meaning of the actions taken by themselves. So putting a ring on a finger in the context of a wedding signifies the act of marriage, and putting a wafer in a mouth, again in a specific context and not elsewhere, signifies the act of Holy Communion. The leading theorist of ritual, the late Roy Rappaport, defined ritual as 'the performance of more or less invariant sequences of formal acts and utterances *not entirely encoded* by the performers' – ritual action, in other words, is always more than it seems.[13] In the second sense of the term, less emphasis is placed on the formality of actions and more on the kinds of values with which those actions are associated. In a line of argument that goes back to the great French sociologist Émile Durkheim's *Elementary Forms of Religious Life*, many have seen in ritual action an affirmation of the values underlying the social bond itself that's more important than its exact formal properties.[14]

When I talk of media rituals, I want to combine aspects of these two senses. From the formal analysis of ritual, I want to take the idea that rituals can reproduce the building blocks of belief without involving any explicit content that is believed. Far from every ritual expressing a hidden essence in which the performers explicitly believe, rituals by their repetitive form reproduce categories and patterns of thought in a way that *bypasses* explicit belief. On the contrary, if made explicit, many of the ideas apparently expressed by ritual might be rejected, or at least called into question; it is their *ritualized* form that enables them to be successfully reproduced without being exposed to questions about their 'content.' This is useful in understanding how ritual works in relation to media, where quite clearly, there is no explicit credo of shared beliefs about media to which everyone signs up. From the transcendent account of ritual, I want to take the idea that there is an essential link between ritual and certain social values, or at least certain large *claims* about the social. As I have argued elsewhere, there is a striking similarity between the socially oriented values (our sense of what binds us as members of a society) that underlie Durkheim's sociology of religion and the types of claims that media, even now, implicitly make about their power to represent 'the social.'[15]

Media rituals are actions that reproduce the myth that the media are our privileged access point to social reality, yet they work not through articulated beliefs but the boundaries and category distinctions around which media rituals are organized. Let us adopt the following working definition: media rituals are formalized actions organized around key media-related categories and boundaries whose performances suggest a connection with wider media-related values.[16]

What aspects of the gamedoc process would count as media rituals under this definition? One example would be the 'ceremony' developed in the British version of *Big Brother* on each night when a housemate is evicted. Once the result of the week's popular vote has been announced to the inmates by live link from the *Big Brother* studio, the evictee is given one hour exactly to get their baggage ready. With one minute to go, the lead presenter, Davina McColl, walks live from the studio across the barrier to the house. The door to the house is opened and the evictee emerges, clutching belongings, usually to the cheers of supporters in the crowd outside. From the house door, McColl leads the evictee, as they take in the adulation of the crowd, back to the studio for a live interview, where the evictee is asked to reflect on their time in the house.

This weekly pattern has been repeated in each British *Big Brother* series until the series' final week, when the last inmate leaves the house as the winner. In its regularity, we have a clever simulation of other forms of television ceremonial. But it is not the formalization that I have most in mind in calling this a media ritual; rather, it is the way the whole sequence is based around a fundamental boundary between 'ordinary person' and 'media person' – in other words, around the media-value celebrity.[17] A basic point of *Big Brother* is to enact a transition for each housemate from ordinary person to media person; the eviction ceremony is designed to make that transition seem natural (natural as television event, that is). The 'celebrification process' in *Big Brother* is obvious to everyone, both performers and viewers, even though far from transparent in its details and exclusions.[18] But its significance is greater, since underlying the idea that the housemates become celebrities is another more basic media value: that being in the *Big Brother* house is somehow more significant than being outside the house. In short, mediated reality is somehow 'higher' or more significant than nonmediated reality – which as I have maintained elsewhere, is the value that underlies the legitimation of media institutions' general concentration of symbolic power.[19] Kate Lawler, the winner of the third series of *Big Brother* (hereafter BB3), in her reactions to her final hour in the house, vividly enacted the boundary and hierarchy between media and nonmedia 'worlds.' She cried and seemed overawed by the transition from the apparently private, though of course intensely mediated world of the *Big Brother* house to the explicitly mediated world outside with its cheering crowds and press flashbulbs. When McColl came to interview her *inside* the house (on the series' final night, the winner gets to be interviewed inside the house, where only they have earned the right to stay), Lawler had difficulty speaking. She acted starstruck in front of McColl (who in Britain, is a minor celebrity in her own right because of *Big Brother*). McColl gave Lawler the standard phrase used by fans on meeting their idol: 'No, it's me who can't believe I'm sitting here with *you*' (BB3, 26 July 2002).

At this point, I want to shift the focus to the related concept of ritualization. For it is in the dynamic relationship between the ritual high points of, say, *Big Brother* and the wider process of ritualizing the often banal actions in the *Big Brother* house that we find the best entry-point to the social, not merely textual, process that gamedocs constitute.

Acting 'up' for the cameras

Media rituals cannot, any more than rituals in general, be studied in isolation from the larger hinterland of ritualization: that is, the whole gamut of patterns of action, thought, and speech that generate the categories and boundaries on which media rituals are based. It is this hinterland of everyday action that makes the special case of media rituals possible.

As the anthropologist Catherine Bell contends in her study of religious ritual, ritualization organizes our movements around space, helps us to experience constructed features of the environment as real, and thereby reproduces the symbolic authority at stake in the categorizations on which ritual draws.[20] The background ritualizations that underlie media rituals work in a similar way, through the organization of all sorts of actions around key media-related categories ('media person/thing/place/world,' 'liveness,' 'reality').[21]

The term ritualization is our way of tracing how rituals connect to power; for media rituals, the link in question is to the increasing organization of social life around media centers. Drawing again on Bell, we must study how

> the orchestrated construction of power and authority in ritual ... engage[s] the social body in the objectification of oppositions and the deployment of schemes that effectively reproduce the divisions of the social order. In this objectification lie the resonance of ritual and the consequences of compliance.[22]

In principle this could lead us from the celebrification rituals of *Big Brother* to the mass of actions whereby all of us contribute to celebrity culture (buying celebrity magazines, for example). But with gamedocs, there is also a tighter link between ritual and ritualization: What are the nine weeks in the *Big Brother* house if not a space of ritualization, where inmates' banal, everyday routines are tested for their appropriateness to a mediated space?

If rituals are naturalized, stable forms for reproducing power relations, ritualization is the much wider process through which the categories underlying those power relations *become* naturalized in action, thought, and words. The raw material of ritualization is much more liable to be destabilized by doubt, reflexivity, and correction. The action in the BB3 house reflected similar instabilities, as various inmates thought about leaving the house voluntarily (see below). A particular focus in BB3 was inmates' mutual accusations of performing to the cameras and the anxious denials that resulted. It could be argued, of course, that all this was part of BB3's developing plot and entertainment value, but we see below how, on the contrary, this issue opened up conflicts among inmates, and between inmates and the show's producers, about the norms of behavior in the house – conflicts that could not be contained within BB3 as a 'game.'

Gamedocs and real 'experience'

One of the words most frequently used by BB3 contestants was 'experience': they wanted to make the most of the *Big Brother* experience, they were asked how their experience in the house had gone when they left, and so on. Although hardly a simple word to disentangle, experience connotes something both significant and real, and usually something *more* significant and real than the everyday run of things. But since the conditions of the *Big Brother* house made it exceptional from the start, there was always a tension: Was the *Big Brother* experience significant because it was exceptional, or was it significant because however exceptional it seemed, it showed something important about the underlying continuities of human nature? Such ambiguities are the very stuff of myth in Barthes's sense.[23]

Yet however ambiguous the claims of *Big Brother* and other gamedocs to represent reality, without *some* such claim their status – as shows that make celebrities out of real ordinary people – collapses. Every gamedoc has a specific myth about how it represents the social world. A number of British shows rely on the myth that in the face of extreme physical challenges, especially those requiring team collaboration (however artificially constructed), an important aspect of human reality is shown. This is the myth underpinning *Survivor* (Carlton TV, 2000), an international format less successful in Britain than *Big Brother*, perhaps because it is less obviously aimed at a stereotypical, 'young' audience (having some middle-aged contestants, and much less emphasis on celebrity and sex), although arguably the almost comic exoticism of *Survivor*'s British version (with its tribal gatherings and the like) undermines its wider reality claim in any case.[24]

In *Castaway 2000*, a failed variant on the *Survivor* theme produced for the millennial year (BBC1, 2000), thirty-five people were put onto Taransay, a deserted island just off the coast of the Hebridean island of Harris, for one year to see how they would survive. Taransay is, in fact, in full view of one of the most beautiful beaches in Scotland (I know because I holiday on Harris myself), so its claim to present a controlled experiment in genuine isolation was strained from the outset. Still, the program's mythical intent was clear from its opening voice-over:

> *Castaway 2000* is a unique experiment to discover what happens when a group representative of British society today is stranded away from modern life. On the deserted Scottish island of Taransay, they'll have

a year to decide how to run the community, devise new ways of living together, and reflect on what aspects of life are really important in the 21st century.[25]

Other recent experiments have sought to mine the old myth of 'human nature' even further. *The Experiment* (BBC2, 2002, with a subsequent U.S. version) offered a reworking by two psychologists of the well-known U.S. 1970s 'Prisoner' experiment, which had pitted two selected groups against each other, one in the role of 'guards' and the other in the role of 'prisoners,' in order to test how far the former exploited their artificial authority over the latter. The television program relied both on the myth of objectivity built into psychological experimentation and the additional myth that cameras changed nothing significant about the so-called experiment.

[. . .]

The particular success in Britain of *Big Brother* may derive, in part, from its clever mix of mythical authorities: the suggestion of scientific experiment is there (with 'top psychologists' even being given their own show on each Sunday night of BB3), but also the validating myths of celebrity and popular 'interactivity.' Popular participation is itself, of course, a useful myth; viewers of *Big Brother*, after all, have no control over its format, the initial choice of participants, the instructions or rules given to participants, the principles of editing, or indeed how the 'popular vote' is interpreted to contestants and audience.

None of these contradictions should surprise us. For it is precisely in the oscillation between contingent detail and some broader, mythical value that for the anthropologist Maurice Bloch, echoing Barthes, the power of ritual lies.[26] In Bloch's analysis of Madagascan rituals, the broader value is that of 'ancient history' lost in the mists of time; in contemporary societies, no one believes in history in that sense, but the myths of human nature, science, and what Marc Augé has called 'the ideology of the present' are powerful substitutes.[27]

THE NORMS OF REALITY PERFORMANCE

There is another myth reproduced through the gamedoc form and its apparently innocent rituals of television celebrity. I say myth, but it is more like a half statement that works largely by *not* being articulated – hence its affinity to ritual. This is the idea that surveillance is a natural mode through which to observe the social world. Few, perhaps, would subscribe explicitly to the will to 'omniperception' (as the leading sociologist of surveillance puts it) implied here.[28] Yet by constant media repetition, this notion risks rigidifying into a myth that is fully integrated into our everyday expectations of the social.

The pleasures of surveillance

What are we to make of the idea that to find out about an aspect of social reality, it is natural to set up an 'experimental situation' (with or without the endorsement of qualified psychologists), watch what happens when people are either not yet aware of the presence of cameras or are presumed to have forgotten it, and treat the result as 'reality'? You might think it hypocritical for a sociologist like myself, who regularly interviews and observes others, to protest so much. But there is an obvious difference between the gamedoc and the normal context for sociological or indeed psychological research: confidentiality. Remember that *The Experiment* was in part designed by two psychologists as a hybrid of the entertainment form and an experimental situation.[29] Never in the recent history of the social and psychological sciences have studies been conducted for a simultaneous *public* audience, unless we return to Jean-Martin Charcot's public demonstrations in the 1870s with hysterics at the Paris Salpêtrière, and also recall the long history of public operations on the living and dead that preceded Charcot. Yet even in that early modern history of public experiment, there is no parallel for experimental subjects being watched in permanently retrievable form by an audience of millions.

The emerging model of surveillance and governance, and the rejuvenated 'experimental science' that is parasitic on them, is disturbing. Its implications are greater than the popular legitimation of everyday surveillance, important as that is.[30] For surveillance-entertainment (a cumbersome, but equally accurate name for the gamedoc) has implications for everyday social relations that surveillance focused on criminal activity does not. While the saturation of public space with closed-circuit television is, of course, a matter of concern, the issue is more its effects on the quality of everyone's experience of public space, rather than the effects on how people might perform in front of the visible and invisible cameras – which is precisely why the New York art campaigners the Surveillance Camera Players' *performances* in front of surveillance cameras are striking, as ways of denaturalizing a dimension of public life that we screen out of our consciousness entirely. But in surveillance-entertainment, the impacts on 'performance' are surely the *key* issue since its underlying premise is that we can expect *any* everyday activity legitimately to be put under surveillance and monitored for a huge, unknown audience.

What is remarkable is how easy it is to hide this disturbing idea beneath the cloak of ritual. In a six-part series introduced by Britain's Channel Four in 2002 called *Make My Day*, the *Big Brother* format was turned adeptly into a pure entertainment package. The idea of the program was a simple, if alarming extension of the *Candid Camera* format: friends or family nominate someone to the producers to be put under secret surveillance for a day to test their reactions to five challenges; if all are passed, the unwitting contestant wins £5,000 and retrospectively the 'benefit' of having 'starred' for national television 'in her very own game show' (as one episode put it). The 'challenges' are simple tests of the subject's ability to act as a person with a 'normal' sexual appetite and a 'natural' interest in celebrity. Will this young woman let into her house a half-naked man (recruited to match her tastes in men) needing to make an urgent phone call? Yes! – move to stage two. Will the same young woman allow herself to be distracted from getting to work when a member of her favorite pop band approaches her in the street, pretending to be lost and needing help to find his way? Yes! – move to stage three, and so on.

This series attracted little attention, and the predictability of its challenges was surely a weakness. What is interesting, however, is how the unwitting contestants reacted at the end of that day, when its strange events were explained to them by the well-known British celebrity and show narrator Sara Cox.[31] What we saw on the program – and of course, we have no way of knowing how far this was rehearsed or edited – is the contestant delighted, even awestruck, at the revelation, clutching her face, crying out 'oh, my God!' and the like. Any later reflections by the contestant on having in effect consented to being submitted to twelve hours of secret filming for national television (including an opening scene in their bedroom) were left to our speculation.

My point is not to moralize about this particular series but to offer it as an example of how easily consent to the process of surveillance before a national audience (even if quite counterintuitive) can be made to seem natural, given the right ritual context. Here are Cox's explanatory words to one contestant:

> Hello, it's Sara Cox here. You must be thinking you have had the strangest day of your life. Well it's all because of Channel 4's *Make My Day*. We have been secretly filming you using hidden cameras all day long and we reckon it's about time you got out from under your mother's feet so as a big thank you we would love to give you a deposit on your first flat. . . . I really hope we've made your day.

The program is useful because it is so artless. Here we see quite directly how two positive behavioral norms (one automatically positive – obtaining your own, independent place to live – and the other increasingly constructed as positive in contemporary British culture – showing an interest in celebrity) are combined to make the program's whole sequence of events seem natural and legitimate. [. . .]

THE REAL (MEDIATED) ME

BB3 differed from previous British series of *Big Brother* in its emerging divide between those inmates who were clearly unhappy with the expected norms for behavior in the house and those who broadly accepted them. Even among the latter were a number who were unhappy at times, including the eventual finalists ('[*Big Brother* voice:] How are you feeling, Alex? [Alex:] Um . . . institutionalized').[32] Of the former, two left voluntarily, and another (Sandy, who happened to be the only housemate without fashionable, young looks) remained quiet and isolated for a few weeks before being voted out (as the *Big Brother* voice-over noted on one occasion: 'Sandy was the first to go to bed' (cut to Sandy reading a book in bed).[33]

An interesting case was Tim, the only obviously upper-class inmate, a later replacement in the house who never settled. He was not so much withdrawn, like Sandy, as openly complaining at the tasks given to the inmates and the way others played up to the cameras. His complaints (in the program's famous Diary Room) were portrayed by the producers through editing and commentary as those of a moaner, who conveniently, was also discovered to be physically vain when his black hair dye started to show and he was caught on camera shaving his chest in the apparent privacy of his bed.

There was no particular drama to his eviction (on 19 July 2002) since he had made it clear on camera that he was 'desperate' to leave the house. [. . .] His live interview was more dramatic; criticized by McColl for 'whinging' and his unwillingness to play the *Big Brother* game, Tim responded that he had thought the set tasks 'could have been a bit more mature.' He was challenged to defend his charge that other inmates were playing up to the cameras:

> *McColl:*   On a number of occasions, you talked about performing, other people performing. What did you mean by that?
> *Tim:*   The whole time I was in there I was very much myself. I don't think my whole personality came out because there wasn't much to stimulate a lot of it . . . but there were a lot of people in there who I'm convinced are not like that in their normal life . . .
> *McColl:*   [*interrupting*] Like who?
> *Tim:*   [*continuing over McColl*]: and when I spoke to them one-to-one and you found out more about them as a person, that's the side I really liked; but they never showed enough of that. As soon as a camera came in or they felt they were being watched, they were up and [mimes clapping to music] singing and dancing and sure the public obviously like it because they get really into it, but . . .
> *McColl:*   [*interrupting again*] But it's not that it's that. I think that generally some of them are quite up, positive people. [*cheering in background from crowd to whom the conversation is being relayed outside on large screens*] If you can't perform, physically you can't do it, not for seven or eight weeks, you can't do it.
> *Tim:*   No, there were times when they didn't and they dipped, and that's the times you saw them when they weren't acting.
> *McColl:*   OK, Tim . . . let's move onto something a bit more positive.[34]

There is an unresolvable conflict here between two norms of how to behave in the house: first, to give the public what they are assumed to want ('singing and dancing' [Tim], or being 'up positive people' [McColl]), and second, the unobjectionable, but also vague norm of 'being yourself.' If as an inmate you find the second norm is incompatible with the first, what are you to do? Many inmates betrayed anxiety about whether they had been themselves – for example, Jonny (the eventual runner-up), who asked Jade why his housemates had put him up for eviction more than once and was told it was because 'you've studied it, you know what the people on the outside would like.'[35] He vehemently denied this, but in his eviction interview on the series' final night (26 July 2002), he failed to resolve the contradiction. When asked by McColl, 'Who's the real you?' the melancholy loner smoking by the pool or the comic performer, he responded immediately:

> *Jonny*:   The real me's the stupid, idiotic clown, but it takes a lot to get us down to the serious, quiet Jonny, but it worked in there.
> *McColl*:   It stripped you down, did it?
> *Jonny*:   Yes.

Yet he admitted at another point: 'I don't care what anybody says, you're always aware of the cameras, and on the other end of them cameras is your family and your friends who you love.' [. . .] Here, contemporary media's wide-ranging myth that cameras tell us more about underlying reality because they magnify feelings that are presumed already to exist is directly contradicted. These contradictions matter because they cannot, in principle, be resolved. They are contradictions within the myth that *Big Brother* produces to legitimate itself: on the one hand, it claims to show us the human reality that must come out when ordinary people live for a long time under the cameras; on the other hand, it polices any differences of interpretation about what that reality should be, ruling out any behavior excluded by the production choices it makes and ruling in the so-called positive selves that it presumes the public wants to see and contestants want to display. Once contestants start to doubt the latter reality, as in BB3, there is nowhere for the producers to turn but ritual: rituals of vilification turned on Tim, who posed the most direct threat to the show's norms, or rituals of incorporation, affirming the show's status by including successful inmates in the club of celebrity. Here are McColl's final words on the last night:

> Kate entered the house unknown and now she's taking her first innocent steps into a world of unseen wealth and privilege, . . . offers of casual sex, fame beyond her dreams, and general admiration. . . . I hope you've enjoyed this as much as I have. This has been *Big Brother* 2002. Thank you for watching. Good-bye.

The producers could afford some irony here, of course, in the show's final moments, but not, as we have seen, when the show's myth was directly challenged.[36]

Toward an Ethics of Reality TV

Where has this brief, skeptical tour of the British gamedoc brought us? Clearly, the gamedoc is a generic adaptation of considerable robustness (after all, it no longer carries the docusoap's hostage to fortune, the residual claim to documentary authority), and in the case of the British version of *Big Brother*, great resourcefulness and commercial promise: BB3 was widely reported as having 'rescued' Channel Four in the 2002 season.[37]

This chapter's argument, however, has been that our analysis cannot rest with observations on the adaptability of television genres. For *Big Brother* and all gamedocs are *social* processes that take real individuals and submit them to surveillance, analysis, and selective display as means to entertainment and enhanced audience participation. It is this social process, not the program's textual properties, that should be our main focus, and I offered some concepts (myth, ritual, and ritualization) to help us grasp its real and ideological dimensions.

There is, of course, one further step to which the argument needs to be taken, and that is ethics. What are the ethics of surveillance-entertainment? Or perhaps as the first question, where should we stand to get an adequate perspective on the possible ethical dimensions of the social process that gamedocs constitute, both by themselves and in their interface with the rest of social life? Finding that perspective is not easy. Part of the fascination of that oxymoron 'reality TV' is its ambiguity, which in the case of *Big Brother* rests on another: between the expressive, almost obsessively self-reflexive individualization that it displays for us ('saturated individualism,' as Michel Maffesoli has called it) and the barely accountable 'exemplary center' that underwrites (or seeks to underwrite) the plausibility and legitimacy of that display.[38] By exemplary center, I mean the mythical 'social center' that media institutions, even as they face unprecedented pressures from the dispersal of media production and consumption, attempt to project: the apparently naturally existing social 'world' to which television likes to claim it gives us access.[39] The point is not that we can do without media or that media are exactly the same as other unaccountable forms of governmental or corporate power but rather that we cannot avoid at some point turning to an ethical critique if we are to address how media are transforming, and being transformed by, the social space in which, like it or not, we have to live. This chapter, I hope, has provided some useful starting points for that wider debate.

Notes

1. Roland Barthes, *Mythologies* (London: Paladin, 1972).
2. Ernesto Laclau, *New Reflections on the Revolution of Our Time* (London: Verso, 1990), 67.
3. Cited in Carolyn Marvin, *Blood Sacrifice and the Nation* (Cambridge: Cambridge University Press, 1999), 159.

4. On television 'plenty,' see John Ellis, *Seeing Things* (London: IB Tauris, 2000).
5. On the early wave of the mid-1900s, see Ib Bondebjerg, 'Public Discourse/Private Fascination,' *Media Culture and Society* 18 (1996): 27–45; Richard Kilborn, '"How Real Can You Get?" Recent Developments in "Reality" Television,' *European Journal of Communication* 13, no. 2 (1994): 201–18. On the subsequent crisis of many docusoaps, see Caroline Dover, 'British Documentary Television Production: Tradition, Change, and "Crisis" within a Practitioner Community' (Ph.D. diss., University of London, 2001).
6. See John Corner, 'Performing the Real: Documentary Diversions,' *Television and New Media* 3, no. 3 (August 2002): 255–69.
7. Ibid., 256.
8. Nick Couldry, *The Place of Media Power: Pilgrims and Witnesses of the Media Age* (London: Routledge, 2000); see also Roger Silverstone, 'Television, Myth and Culture,' in *Media, Myths and Narratives*, ed. James Carey (Newbury Park, Calif.: Sage, 1988).
9. See Nick Couldry, *Media Rituals: A Critical Approach* (London: Routledge, 2002); and Gareth Palmer, '*Big Brother*: An Experiment in Governance,' *Television and New Media* 3, no. 3 (2002): 311–22.
10. Palmer, '*Big Brother*,' 305–6, emphasis added.
11. *Big Brother*, third series (May–July 2002), is my main example.
12. The term 'ritual' is a difficult one, and there is no space here to explain in detail its history or my specific use of the term 'media rituals' (but see Couldry, *Media Rituals*).
13. Roy Rappaport, *Ritual and Religion in the Making of Humanity* (Cambridge: Cambridge University Press, 1999), 24, emphasis added.
14. Émile Durkheim, *The Elementary Forms of Religious Life*, trans. Karen Fields (1912; reprint, Glencoe, Ill.: Free Press, 1995).
15. Couldry, *Media Rituals*.
16. For further background, see ibid., chapters 1–3.
17. See Nick Couldry, 'Playing for Celebrity: *Big Brother* as Ritual Event,' *Television and New Media* 3, no. 3 (2002): 289.
18. See ibid. For 'celebrification process,' see Chris Rojek, *Celebrity* (London: Reaktion Books, 2001), 186–87.
19. See Couldry, *The Place of Media Power*, chapter 3.
20. Catherine Bell, *Ritual Theory, Ritual Practice* (New York: Oxford University Press, 1992).
21. On these categories, see Couldry, *Media Rituals*.
22. Bell, *Ritual Theory*, 215.
23. Barthes, *Mythologies*.
24. Interestingly, the *Survivor* prize money is £1 million, compared to *Big Brother*'s £70,000 – surprising until you realize that the more successful *Big Brother* contestants have in the past picked up promotional deals, hosted television shows, or issued pop singles.
25. *Castaway 2000*, 25 Jauary 2000.
26. Maurice Bloch, *Ritual, History, and Power* (London: Athlone Press, 1989), 130.
27. Marc Augé, 'Le Stade de l'écran,' *Le Monde Diplomatique*, June 2001, 24.
28. David Lyon, *Surveillance Society: Monitoring Everyday Life* (Milton Keynes, Buckingham [England]: Open University Press, 2001), 124–25.
29. Steve Reicher and Alex Haslam, cited in *Guardian*, 3 May 2002, 7.
30. See Mark Andrejevic, 'Little Brother Is Watching: The Webcam Subculture and the Digital Enclosure,' in *Media/Space*, ed. Nick Couldry and Anna McCarthy (London: Routledge, forthcoming); Couldry, *Media Rituals*, chapter 6; and Palmer, '*Big Brother*.'
31. Cox is host DJ of Radio 1's high-profile early morning show.

32. BB3, 17 July 2002.
33. Ibid., 29 May 2002.
34. This and later passages are the author's transcription.
35. BB3, 28 June 2002.
36. Such irony is often misinterpreted as skepticism or distance, when in fact its effect is just the opposite (Slavoj Žižek, *The Sublime Object of Ideology* [London: Verso, 1989], 32–33; see also Couldry, *The Place of Media Power*, 45).
37. See, for example, *Guardian*, 27 July 2002, 7.
38. Michel Maffesoli, *The Time of the Tribes* (London: Sage, 1996), 64. The phrase 'exemplary center' is from Clifford Geertz, *Negara: The Theatre State in Nineteenth-Century Bali* (Princeton, N.J.: Princeton University Press, 1980), 13.
39. See Couldry, *Media Rituals*, chapter 3.

FURTHER READING

Bignell, J., *Big Brother: Reality TV in the Twenty-First Century* (London: Palgrave Macmillan, 2005).

Biressi, A. and Nunn, H., *Reality TV: Realism and Revelation* (London: Wallflower Press, 2005).

Corner, J., 'Performing the Real: Documentary Diversions', *Television and New Media* 3:3 (2002) pp. 255–70.

Couldry, N., *Media Rituals: A Critical Approach* (London: Routledge, 2003).

Creeber, G. (ed.), *The Television Genre Book* (London: BFI, 2001).

Hartley, J., *Popular Reality: Journalism, Modernity, Popular Culture* (London: Arnold, 1996).

Hay, J. and Ouellette, L., *Better Living Through Reality TV: Television and Post-welfare Citizenship* (Oxford: Blackwell, 2008).

Heller, D. (ed.), *Makeover Television* (London: I. B. Taurus, 2007).

Hill, A., *Reality TV: Audiences and Popular Factual Television* (London: Routledge, 2005).

Hill, A., *Restyling Factual TV: Audiences and News, Documentary and Reality Genres* (London: Routledge, 2007).

Holmes, S. and Jermyn, D. (eds), *Understanding Reality Television* (London: Routledge, 2003).

Kilborn, R., *Staging the Real: Factual TV Programming in the Age of 'Big Brother'* (Manchester: Manchester University Press, 2003).

King, G., *The Spectacle of the Real: From Hollywood to Reality TV and Beyond* (Bristol: Intellect, 2005).

Livingstone, S. and Lunt, P., *Talk on Television: Audience Participation and Public Debate* (London: Routledge, 1994).

Lull, J. and Hinerman, S. (eds), *Media Scandals* (Cambridge: Polity Press, 1997).

Murray, S. and Ouellette, L. (eds), *Reality TV: Remaking Television Culture* (New York: New York University Press, 2004).

Nichols, B., *Blurred Boundaries: Questions of Meaning in Contemporary Culture* (Bloomington: Indiana University Press, 1994).

Rosenthal, A. and Corner, J. (eds), *New Challenges for Documentary*, 2nd edn (Manchester: University of Manchester Press, 2005).

Shattuc, J. M., *The Talking Cure: TV Talk Shows and Women* (London: Routledge, 1997).

Stratton, J. and Ang, I., '*Sylvania Waters* and the Spectacular Exploding Family', *Screen* 35:1 (1994) pp. 1–21.

SECTION 7
NEWS AND DOCUMENTARY

INTRODUCTION: NEWS AND DOCUMENTARY

News is the central component of media claims to the status of a fourth estate, independent of the working of government and governmental institutions and constituting a key element within the public sphere. For this reason news analysis has historically been at the heart of what John Corner has called the 'public knowledge project' within media studies (Corner, 1991). This project is centrally concerned with the investigation of the media as an 'agency of public knowledge, and 'definitional power' and with exploring the 'the politics of information and the viewer as citizen'. This project continues as the readings selected here will show. However, its nature is changing, not least because the line dividing news and current affairs from other formats is blurring while conceptions of citizenship are tending to place more focus on the broadly cultural at the expensive of the strictly political (Couldry, 2004). A consequence of this is that a shared sense of what 'public knowledge' is, is also eroding.

The news is distinctive but of course it shares much with other media forms. First, news is a commodity. Second, like any other kind of media, it comes to its viewers or users across a selected medium or technology. Third, the genres, conventions and formats of the news are not completely distinct from other forms of media. As John Ellis pointed out 'the first true use of the open-ended series format would seem to be the news bulletin, endlessly updating events and never synthesizing them' (Ellis, 1991) – the contrast being made is with soaps. More recently media commentators have noted that TV news is becoming softer and more sensationalised, while reality television in particular is blurring the line between documentary and fictional entertainment in all kinds of ways. Finally, consider the porous economy of the net, where news is not only a part of what Raymond Williams described as (television's) flow (Williams, 1990), but is interlaced with many other forms and formats, and may be explored on a screen simultaneously running other forms of professional media content, user generated content, music and personal communications. In these contexts some scholars have considered that the news is and can only be explored as entertainment. Others, however, have maintained a sense of the significance of news as the key means through which citizens receive their knowledge and information about the world around them and have set out to explore the changing politics of information. A key part of this inquiry concerns the tension between the claims made for news' neutrality, impartiality or lack of bias and its constructed nature: news media, like all media, *mediate*. Thus the process of news distribution, at once conditioning our access to the world and offering a way to see it, is powerful.

These readings look firstly at some of the key issues surrounding 'the news we get' and how it is produced as the product of institutional pressures and structures and of processes of selection, omission, formal construction and circulation. Next considered are questions of realism, this time not in relation to news but that other key form of non-fiction media: documentary. Finally, two articles explore these issues specifically in relation to new formations, the first looking at emerging global news networks, the second multimedia documentary.

'News Values and News Production' consists of extracts from Peter Golding and Philip Elliott's 1979 study of the operations of news organisations in three different countries, *Making the News*. It begins with a study of news values, defined as 'qualities of events or their journalistic construction, whose relative absence or presence recommends them for inclusion in the news product' – in other words, what makes a story appear newsworthy to journalists and editors and therefore likely to be published or otherwise distributed. Media institutions tend to claim that news values act to ensure journalistic integrity and impartiality. Elliott and Golding show that these values tend in fact to be invoked as justificatory or explanatory factors after publication. They are 'working rules' and constitute organisational responses to two key priorities of news-making: audience response and availability of material. The second extract explores the ideological aspects of these forms of news selection and justification. Golding and Elliott argue that news *is* ideology – at least in the sense that it offers an 'integrated picture of reality' which legitimates the interests of the powerful in society. It does this by making invisible processes of change, rendering the world as a succession of events rather than exploring the historical horizons of what it reports. The second 'absent dimension' is social power: the news offers us politics in the form of 'ritual office' and omits consideration of economic power. The result, once again, arising from a lack of historical consciousness, is the picture of a world that is, despite the 'news', unchanging and changeable.

The extract from *Policing the Crisis* (Chapter 51) builds on the discussion of ideology and its construction developed in the Golding and Elliot piece, taking a closer look at the ways in which news sets out to assign meaning to disorderly events by placing them within maps of meaning which the world already understands. The allocation of events into these frames provides a means through which the news not only defines for us 'what significant events are taking place' but also positions these events within an interpretive framework that both 'assumes and helps to construct society as a consensus'. Other theorists pursuing related lines of inquiry have considered the ways in which chaotic, disruptive or catastrophic events, natural or geopolitical, which threaten to overwhelm sense, are brought to order, as simple repetition of the event is replaced with increasingly elaborate forms of explanation and particularly with forms of narrative framing that take the event back out of the temporality of the unknown and into the familiar televisual time of the news (see Doanne, 1990).

A second key aspect of the Hall et al. article is its exploration of access to the media. The argument made is that 'working rules' supposedly guaranteed to ensure impartiality and balance themselves operate in the interests of the powerful in society. Over-access to the media by specific groups means they tend to be the primary definers of an event. Oppositional voices are more limited – often being confined to the Official Opposition – thereby producing a narrow range of responses. The argument is that in this way the definitions of the powerful thus become – in general – the accepted definitions of social reality and so consent to an existing social order is secured.

Stig Hjarvard's article, 'News Media and the Globalization of the Public Sphere' (Chapter 53), asks how adequate the concept of a global public sphere is for exploring developments in news media, but also turns the question around. The argument he makes is that changes in the news media environment arising out of the (digitally fuelled) internationalisation of the news industry undermine and produce tensions in the spheres of public life because they induce both fragmentation and interconnectedness. Changes in the social geography of public communication mean it has become in part disembedded from national public spheres. However, this has not tended to suggest the development of new global public sphere(s) or zones for global debate commensurate with the scale of events. In making this case Hjarvard takes cognisance of specific events that *have* mobilised global public opinion to produce forms of protest and dissent that governments have found hard to ignore (for instance the Tiananmen Square protests). The counterweight to this is the failure of transnational dialogue to engage with – or largely even notice – the many political, economic, trade, military and other decisions *routinely* taking place at the global level. What intervention or notice there is from minority or oppositional groups comes from NGOs and others who are, in some ways, a part of this political elite.

The global media – and in particular the global media conglomerates – are tending to confirm rather than undermine this process – and hence are not instrumental in the development of workable global public spheres.

Globalisation may indeed be regarded not as entailing the opening of public space at all. On the contrary, says Hjarvard, it is about 'privatisation'. Against this is set the increased connectedness and permeability of existing national public spheres, which as they become increasingly dependent on others, tend to deterritorialise. This then becomes the key to Hjarvard's suggestion that the concept of deterritorialisation can be used to interpret (global) public interaction as a process that may operate at a series of scales rather than as a single entity. Developments in the international news industry are integral to this process. In the 1980s and 1990s, these might be explored in terms of transnational actors, vertical integration, horizontal integration, commercialisation, diversification, regionalisation and abundance, while by the late 1990s and on into the first decade of the twenty-first century, the internet adds a new dimension, diversifying sources of information, but also producing new forms of connection.

'The work of the Glasgow University Media Group constitutes the most sustained analysis of television content to have come out of British media studies.' This quote comes from an earlier edition of this reader which included Greg Philo's discussion of *Seeing and Believing*, the group's first move into audience research, which explored the UK miners' strike of 1984–5. The intention was to 'examine how the structuring of news messages relate[s] to processes of understanding and belief within television audiences'. At the time Philo concluded that while there were negotiated readings (depending on beliefs and experiences brought to the strike coverage), the influence of the media was central. In this new edition the Glasgow group's work is again excerpted. 'Bad News from Israel' studies UK TV coverage of the Israel–Palestinian conflict and asks how this relates to the understanding, beliefs and attitudes of the television audience. The study, conducted by Greg Philo and Mike Berry, finds that television news coverage of the conflict features Israeli government views – both in terms of coverage (Israelis are quoted twice as much as Palestinians) and language (the two sides are described very differently). In addition UK news fails to describe the history or origins of the conflict and also leaves viewers confused about specific terms (for instance 'occupied territories'). The section excerpted here provides a glimpse into the multi-faced methodology the researchers adopted to elicit material from their interviewees. Through this a glimpse is offered of what users do with the coverage they are given, how they understand it and how it frames their views of the conflict and its actors, both emotionally and in terms of their understanding of events. Philo and Berry show that viewers' understandings (and mis-understandings) are shaped by their television experience in substantial ways. Demanding recognition that the news is the crucial means through which public opinion is formed they seek forms of inquiry into ways in which news coverage of such complex issues as this conflict might be improved.

Documentary is another 'informational genre' although its relation to news is complex and ambiguous. Myra Macdonald's account of women's voices in

British documentaries considers how a particular mode of address – the personal voice – operates in documentary situations, despite the evident tensions between the dispassionate voice of authority which often frames documentary's claim to authenticity and the intimate mode. Written at the moment when increasing intimatisation as a mainstream mode of informational television production was emerging as a popular new format, the article considers how feminist theories of experience can be brought into play with documentary aesthetics. It is framed in part as a commentary on the degree to which the feminist injunction to make the personal political, which was always an injunction to reorganise the division rather than abolish it, and which was not an acceptance of a rational/emotional masculine/feminine gender economy, might be taken up in documentary film-making. Three modes of presenting are considered, the confessional, the case study and testimony. Each, says Macdonald, provides a particular form of access to experience. However, only the last, the testimony, succeeds in 'challenging journalistic wariness . . . about . . . subjectivity as a form of knowledge'. Through an exploration of testimony considering voice, juxtaposition, memory work, reflexivity and questions of magnitude, Macdonald concludes that this is because testimony can reconcile a particular set of evidentiary demands made by documentary (observation, verifiable experience, dispassionate reportage) with those valuing experience. This becomes a feminist project not because one form, experience, triumphs over the other, knowledge, but because the reconciliation of these qualities across the grounds of documentary might question the ascription of gendered qualities to one side or the other.

Finally, in 'Picturizing Science' (Chapter 55), José van Dijck considers the flip side of intimatisation, exploring the rise of spectacle in multimedia science documentary. The tension between documentary's management of (particular forms of) realism, and the forms and ways in which scientific knowledge is accredited, is explored here in relation to two science documentary series – *Walking with Dinosaurs* and the *Elegant Universe* – both of which caused controversy among science commentators. At issue was the charge that the *Dinosaurs* series in particular negated content (meaning and the representation of information) for style (spectacle and form).

At the heart of this piece is a discussion of the 'pictorial effect' (spectacularisation), which is understood not as a demise of realism but as representing a new form of it. A form much used in the series was that of highly realistic (naturalised) effects employed in 'speculative mode'. This mode is explicitly linked to scientific speculations through an explanation of the work done to develop the models – which involved 'scientific' forms of visualisation. The display of pictures, sounds and graphics involved in these documentaries, it is argued, at the very least show how science itself is constructed. The larger claim is that through this mode of documentary the programme did not only illustrate science claims, but enable them. As science does, it visualised knowledge while substantiating hypotheses.

References

Corner, J., 'Meaning, Genre and Context: The Problematics of "Public Knowledge" in the New Audience Studies', in J. Curran and M. Gurevitch (eds), *Mass Media and Society* (London: Edward Arnold, 1991) pp. 267–84.

Couldry, N., 'The Productive "Consumer" and the Dispersed "Citizen"', *International Journal of Cultural Studies* 7:1 (2004) pp. 21–32.

Doane, M. A., 'Information, Crisis, Catastrophe', in P. Mellencamp (ed.), *Logics of Television: Essays in Cultural Criticism* (Bloomington: Indiana University Press, 1990).

Ellis, John, *Visible Fictions: Cinema, Television, Video* (London: Routledge, 1982).

Peters, J. D., 'Witnessing', *Media, Culture and Society* 23:Special Issue on Media Events (2001) pp. 707–23.

Philo, Greg, *Seeing and Believing: The Influence of Television* (London: Routledge, 1990).

Williams, R., *Television, Technology and Cultural Form* (London: Routledge, 1990).

50

NEWS VALUES AND NEWS PRODUCTION

Peter Golding and Philip Elliott

Discussions of news values usually suggest they are surrounded by a mystique, an impenetrable cloud of verbal imprecision and conceptual obscurity. Many academic reports concentrate on this nebulous aspect of news values and imbue them with far greater importance and allure than they merit. We have stressed that news production is rarely the active application of decisions of rejection or promotion to highly varied and extensive material. On the contrary, it is for the most part the passive exercise of routine and highly regulated procedures in the task of selecting from already limited supplies of information. News values exist and are, of course, significant. But they are as much the resultant explanation or justification of necessary procedures as their source.

News values are used in two ways. They are criteria of selection from material available to the newsroom of those items worthy of inclusion in the final product. Second, they are guidelines for the presentation of items, suggesting what to emphasise, what to omit, and where to give priority in the preparation of the items for presentation to the audience. News values are thus working rules, comprising a corpus of occupational lore which implicitly and often expressly explains and guides newsroom practice. It is not as true as often suggested that they are beyond the ken of the newsman, himself unable and unwilling to articulate them. Indeed, they pepper the daily exchanges between journalists in collaborative production procedures. Far more they are terse shorthand references to shared understandings about the nature and purpose of news which can be used to ease the rapid and difficult manufacture of bulletins and news programmes. News values are qualities of events or of their

From P. Golding and P. Elliott, *Making the News* (London: Longman, 1979) pp. 114–23.

journalistic construction, whose relative absence or presence recommends them for inclusion in the news product. The more of such qualities a story exhibits, the greater its chances of inclusion. Alternatively, the more different news values a story contains, the greater its chances of inclusion (see Galtung and Ruge, 1965). News values derive from unstated or implicit assumptions or judgements about three things:

1. The audience. Is this important to the audience or will it hold their attention? Is it of known interest, will it be understood, enjoyed, registered, perceived as relevant?
2. Accessibility – in two senses, prominence and ease of capture. Prominence: to what extent is the event known to the news organisation, how obvious is it, has it made itself apparent? Ease of capture: how available to journalists is the event, is it physically accessible, manageable technically, in a form amenable to journalism, is it ready-prepared for easy coverage, will it require great resources to obtain?
3. Fit. Is the item consonant with the pragmatics of production routines, is it commensurate with technical and organisational possibilities, is it homologous with the exigencies and constraints in programme making and the limitations of the medium? Does it make sense in terms of what is already known about the subject?

In other words, news values themselves derive from the two immediate determinants of news making, perceptions of the audience and the availability of material. Historically news values come to imbue the necessities of journalism with the lustre of good practice. They represent a classic case of making a virtue of necessity. This particularly applies to the broader values we have subsumed under the title of the occupational ideology – impartiality, objectivity, accuracy and so on. [. . .] News values are attached to the practice of the job, they are story values. Some of the more important are as follows. The first four derive from considerations of the audience, the remainder from a mixture of the three factors described above.

DRAMA

News stories are, as the term suggests, stories as well as news. Good ones exhibit a narrative structure akin to the root elements in human drama. To recall Reuven Frank, former President of NBC news in America, 'joy, sorrow, shock, fear, these are the stuff of news'. The good news story tells its tale with a beginning, a middle and an end, in that order.

[. . .]

Dramatic structure is often achieved by the presentation of conflict, most commonly by the matching of opposed viewpoints drawn from spokesmen of 'both sides of the question'. The audience is here felt to be served by being given the full picture as well as an interesting confrontation (cf. Epstein, 1973, pp. 168–9). [. . .]

Visual Attractiveness

Television is a visual medium and the special power of television news is its ability to exploit this advantage. Television journalists are not obsessed by notions of 'good television' or 'good film'. They can't be, given the limited number of stories for which film is available. But the temptation to screen visually arresting material and to reject stories unadorned with good film is ever present and sometimes irresistible. In turn judgements about newsworthiness will be shaped by aesthetic judgements about film. A former editor-in-chief of the British Independent Television News has written that 'the key to putting more hard news on to the air effectively lies, I am sure, in putting more pictures and less talk into news programmes'. [. . .]

Just as audiences often justify their trust in the veracity of television news by reference to its use of film: 'you can actually see it happening', so newsmen refer to this quality in their favourite stories. 'Another good one was a building disaster. Three people died when it collapsed. We were the first station there and you could actually see people being rescued on camera.' (Head of News, WNBC.)

A story may be included simply because film is available or because of the dramatic qualities of the film. A story narrated several days previously will be resurrected as film arrives simply to show the film. Film can also provide concrete evidence of the global surveillance of electronic journalism by demonstrating visually the journalist's presence at an event.

Entertainment

News programmes seek, and usually find, large audiences. To do so they must take account of entertainment values in the literal sense of providing captivating, humorous, titillating, amusing or generally diverting material. The 'human interest' story was invented for just this purpose. Broadcast news is generally sober and serious, taking its social responsibility and constitutional position as demanding less frivolity than might be licensed in the popular press. Helen Hughes, who over 30 years ago wrote a book on the human interest story, considered that human interest was a dimension added to other types of story. '. . . the news signalises [sic] a deviation from the expected, the normal and the traditional, which, when told with human interest is made human and comprehensible' (Hughes, 1942; see also Hughes, 1940). Although she was writing of the press this is especially true of broadcast news. The whimsical or bizarre events that are the currency of human interest stories, or the celebrities, children and animals that are their stars, are frequently too frivolous for broadcast news. But the human interest angle is an important way of making events palatable or comprehensible to audiences of broadcast news.

For some broadcast journalists there is a tension between the desire to ensure audience attentiveness and interest by following entertainment values, and a concern to maintain standards of seriousness and the plain honest narration of facts; between information and entertainment. This debate was alive in most newsrooms and linked back to arguments about how 'hard' or 'soft' news should be. It stems again from the dilemma of the journalist as producer of a marketable commodity, whose presentation and dressing up for the audience may cut across some of the professional ideals of the journalist *qua* journalist. The solution is normally the co-option of one ideal by the other, in the argument that to inform an audience you must first have its attention, and that there's no point preparing serious, well-intentioned, high-minded journalism if the audience registers its boredom by switching off. Thus entertainment is high on the list of news values both as an end in itself and as a means to other journalistic ideals.

IMPORTANCE

The most frequently cited reason for including a particular item in news bulletins is its importance. This is usually taken to mean that the reported event has considerable significance for large numbers of people in the audience. Most often importance is cited to explain the inclusion of items which might be omitted on the criteria of other audience-based news values. That is, items which may be boring, repetitive or non-visual must still be included despite audience disinterest. The item refers to something the audience needs to know. This news value is rooted in theories of the social role of journalism as tribune of the people. In broadcasting it has the further support that state-authorised corporations are expected to behave responsibly, informatively and educatively. Importance is often applied to political and foreign news. Both are assumed to be of greater interest to journalists than to their audience. Both are included however because of their unquestioned importance.

[. . .]

SIZE

The bigger the story the greater the likelihood of its inclusion, and the greater the prominence with which it will be presented. This simple rule of course begs the question of just how events are measured and which dimensions are relevant. The most common considerations are the numbers or type of people involved, or the scale of the event as an instance of a type. Thus the more people involved in a disaster or the presence of 'big names' at a formal occasion enhance the initial visibility of such events and hence their consequent news value. Size as a news value normally qualifies other news values. That is, subsequent to the selection of events in the world as news, the criterion of size is applied to decide which are the most important news events. Less commonly events not normally registered as news become eligible by the sheer scale on which they occur.

PROXIMITY

Like size, the criterion of proximity derives partly from considerations of the audience, partly from problems of accessibility. Proximity has two senses, cultural and geographical. Stories are culturally proximate if they refer to events within the normal experience of journalists and their audience. They are the kinds of events which require a wide range of common language and shared cultural assumptions. For this reason they are normally, but not necessarily, domestic stories. Thus in Ireland the importance of the Church in secular life provides a background for stories on church or religion in other countries which might be ignored in more secularised nations. Cultural proximity can be applied to stories by, for example, putting foreign news into a domestic context to explain its importance or significance.

Geographical proximity refers to the simple rules of thumb that suggest the primacy of domestic news and the allocation of news from the rest of the world according to their nearness to the audience (see Schlesinger, 1978, p. 117). Here geography is distorted by the mechanics of news collection. As we have seen, the distribution of news gatherers is far from random, and in journalistic terms Lagos is far closer to London than to, say, Accra. Nonetheless the criterion is applied, and several Nigerian sub-editors adopted a three-tier news geography: Nigeria, Africa, the world. In the other countries, too, there was a sense of concentric spheres of influence. This design was of course totally disrupted by the availability of material. The geographical criterion thus moderates to two rules. Either, the further away an event the bigger it has to be, or, nearby events take precedence over similar events at a distance.

BREVITY

A story which is closely packed with facts and little padding is preferred to loose 'soft' news. Partly this relates to the journalistic role of informing rather than explaining, partly to concerns for what are seen as audience requirements and limitations. Audiences want just the facts and nothing but the facts. Since they also require comprehensiveness clearly no single item can be allowed to drag on too long. [. . .] News bulletins are normally between 15 and 30 minutes, and contain less than a couple of dozen items. Limiting news stories to their apparently more obvious elements is essential if there is to be room for even a minimal selection of the day's events. This limit seems to emphasise the necessary objectivity of broadcast news while in fact merely disguising the vast edifice of assumptions and cultural packaging which allow such brief items to make sense at all.

NEGATIVITY

Bad news is good news. As is often observed there is little mileage in reporting the safe arrival of aircraft, the continued health of a film star, or the smooth untroubled negotiations of a wage settlement. News is about disruptions in the normal current of events. In the literal sense it is not concerned with the uneventful. The concentration on negative events, that is events perceived or presented as damaging to social institutions, is not the result of a mischievous obsession with misery or discontent among journalists, but the outcome of the history of their occupation. News began as a service to groups directly concerned for the uninterrupted flow of commercial life. Interruptions included loss of merchandise at sea, financial upheavals in mercantile centres or, of course, war. These events remain paradigm instances of bad news, and as a result of news per se.

It is for this reason that news is described as a social surveillance, registering threats to the normal fabric of society and explaining their significance. The news value of negativity is therefore an important contributor to the social values in news, defining by default both the status quo and the sources and nature of threats to it. [. . .] It is worth noting that negativity is not a universal primary news value. What western journalists often see as the tediousness and irrelevance of broadcast news in eastern Europe has much to do with the conventions in many of these countries of presenting positive news (industrial production achievements, the award of honours, etc.) while excluding accidents, violence, crime and other negative categories prominent in news elsewhere (Varis, 1974; Lansipuro, 1975).

Some categories of negative news are disliked in broadcasting for their lack of other values. Crime was deliberately under-reported [. . .] in deference to the view that its presentation was pandering to the sensational news values more appropriate to the popular press. [. . .] Many broadcast journalists regretted this tendency to play down crime, and it was more often an executive than a 'shopfloor' view. Many journalists also subscribed to the view that showing too much violence was irresponsible. However, this view was frequently swamped by the power of news values such as drama and visual attractiveness. Again this is defined by reference to the audience. The point is made by Brucker (1973, p. 175):

> It is, of course, a basic principle of journalism that the bigger, the more off-beat, or the more bloody the spectacle, the greater the news value. This is not because newspapermen are more ghoulish or less sensitive to the finer things of life than their fellow men. It merely reflects the ineluctable fact that readers will flock to a story that has shock value but ignore one that is routine.

Or, as a journalist once pointed out, given a choice of two calamities news editors choose both, in the belief that the audience will be held by the dramatic power of tragic narrative.

RECENCY

The next three news values are derived more from production requirements than the perceived demands of the audience. Recency, the requirement that news be up to date and refer to events as close to transmission time as possible, derives from two factors. First, traditional journalistic competition puts a premium on the supply of 'earliest intelligencies' ahead of rivals. At its most successful this aim produces the 'scoop', an exclusive capture of a news event ahead of all competition. Second, the periodicity of news production itself sets the frame within which events in the world will be perceived. Thus daily production sets a daily frame, and news events must have occurred in the twenty-four hours between bulletins to merit inclusion. Although this is often impossible, especially for newsrooms dependent on air-freighted news film, the dictum that 'it's news when the audience first sees it' was only offered rather sheepishly, in the certain knowledge that it was an unhappy transgression of a root news value. The main point, however, is that processes which do not fit this daily cycle do not register as news by producing news events. Since daily reports are required the necessity of filling a daily quota becomes a laudable goal, and recency emerges as a journalistic virtue. Speed in collection and processing becomes paramount and is often cited as the particular merit of individual journalists or newsrooms. Conversely it is one of the main complaints against non-journalist broadcasters that they do not understand the need for speed and that technical and other facilities are inadequate for journalistic demands. The favourite accolade for Eurovision was that it permitted same-day film of European events. One of the most frequently cited problems was late arrival of unprocessed film and the inadequacy of film processing facilities.

The broadcasting equivalent of newspaper editions is the sequence of bulletins through the day, or evening on television. Journalists were acutely aware of the need to 'keep the picture changing'. [. . .] Journalists were fond of the fast-breaking story where the rapid movement of events pre-empted any need for the artificial injection of pace or change. Recency emphasises the task of news in topping up information on those events and institutions already defined as the substance of news.

ELITES

As a value within 'bigness' news values emphasise that big names are better news than nobodies, major personalities of more interest than ordinary folk. There is an obvious circularity in this in that well-known personalities become so by their exposure in news media. It is this that leads us to root this news value in production rather than in audience interests. Clearly audiences are interested in major rather than minor figures, people they all know about rather than the acquaintances of a few. But [...] elites are only partially exposed, and concentration on powerful or ruling groups is neither uniform nor comprehensive.

PERSONALITIES

News is about people, and mostly about individuals. This news value emphasises the need to make stories comprehensible by reducing complex processes and institutions to the actions of individuals. This aim is, like many news values, a virtue born of necessity. Brief, and especially visual, journalism cannot deal with abstractions and has to narrate in the concrete. Thus it becomes a news value to 'seek the personal angle' or to 'personalise' the news. The effect of this is to treat institutional and international relations either as the interaction of individuals, or as being analogous to inter-personal relations. For example, international political news deals almost entirely with the diplomatic globe-trotting of major politicians, and international relations are seen to depend on how well political leaders get on. The analogies appear in the terminology of the emotions which characterises institutional or national relations. Governments become 'angry', unions are 'hot-headed', nations are 'anxious' or 'eager'. This is most easily portrayed by personalising such acts in the presentation of individuals.

This list may not exhaust all news values but it includes the main ones. Their obviousness can be illustrated by compiling a list of antonyms. It is hard to imagine broadcast journalists anywhere seeking news which dealt with small events, the long term, dull, distant, visually boring, unimportant people, and so on. Yet many of these labels describe events and processes which may well have significance for news audiences, but which are not news. The application of news values is part of the process by which this labelling occurs.

BIAS, OBJECTIVITY AND IDEOLOGY

[...]

It is possible to see broadcast news as simply the result of the bias of individual journalists, committed either to professional notions of how news should be structured, or to social views of the ideas it should convey. For David Brinkley, the authoritative American newscaster, 'News is what I say it is. It's something worth knowing by my standards' (Brinkley, 1964). Whether this is unguarded arrogance, or hyperbole to make a point about the essential indefinability of news, it represents to many people the most likely explanation of news output. The newscaster is the visible tip of the news production plant, a visual or aural reminder that it is a process handled by people; fallible, biased and opinionated, like the rest of us. The obvious weakness of this explanation is that the news changes very little when the individuals who produce it are changed. An occasional shift in partisanship may be detected in the reporting of particular issues, but the events covered, and the nature of their coverage, remain the same. [. . .] [E]ven in highly varied cultural and organisational settings broadcast news emerges with surprisingly similar forms and contents. In addition the division of labour required for production limits the impacts of individuals on news. [. . .] Epstein (1973, p. 28) describes how 'News executives decide on the development of correspondents and camera crews; assignment editors select what stories will be covered and by whom; field producers, in constant phone contact with the producers in New York, usually supervise the preparation of filming of stories . . . editors . . . reconstruct the story on film . . .' and so on.

Yet the notion of group, if not individual, bias persists. [. . .] The notion of bias is often contrasted with objectivity, and for clarity's sake two distinctions should be made. First impartiality and objectivity are distinct. Impartiality implies a disinterested approach to news, lacking in motivation to shape or select material according to a particular view or opinion. Objectivity, however defined, is clearly a broader demand than this. A journalist may well be impartial towards the material on which he works, yet fail to achieve objectivity – a complete and unrefracted capture of the world – due to the inherent limitations in news gathering and processing. Second, the bias of an individual reporter dealing with a single event may be reduced or even eliminated by, for example, the deliberate application of self-discipline and professional standards of process. In other words we should distinguish bias as the deliberate aim of journalism, which is rare, from bias as the inevitable but unintended consequence of organisation.

There are, then, three possible views of journalistic objectivity and impartiality. First, there is the professional view that it is possible to be both, based on the idea that objectivity and impartiality are attitudes of mind. Second is the view that objectivity may well be a nebulous and unattainable goal, but that impartiality is still desirable and possible.

[. . .]

The third view, that neither objectivity or impartiality are in any serious sense possible in journalism, comes from a change of analytical perspective, from the short-term and deliberate production of news stories to the long-term and routine, unreflective practices of journalism as we have analysed them in this study. Objectivity and impartiality remain the aims of most day-to-day journalism. But we should understand these terms as labels applied by journalists to the rules which govern their working routines. Objectivity is achieved by subscribing to and observing these sets of rules, which are themselves the object of our analysis. We have seen how these rules, both the explicit regulations of organisational charters and newsroom manuals, and the implicit understandings of news values, are derived from the currents of supply and demand which eddy round the newsroom.

The assumed needs and interests of audiences on the one hand, and the truncated supply of information into the newsroom on the other, both exert pressures to which the organisation of news production responds. What are the consequences of these pressures?

When we come to assess news as a coherent view of the world, that is to step up from news values to social values, we enter an altogether more complex and tangled argument. News is ideology to the extent that it provides an integrated picture of reality. But an ideology is more than this; it is also the world view of particular social groups, and especially of social classes. The claim that news is ideology implies that it provides a world view both consistent in itself, and supportive of the interests of powerful social groupings. This can come about in two ways.

First, news is structured by the exigencies of organised production which are the main concern of this study. These allow only a partial view of the reported world which may or may not coincide with a ruling ideology. The historical process by which this coincidence occurs is more than accidental, and is rooted in the development of news as a service to elite groups. [. . .] Thus most of the basic goals and values which surround journalism refer to the needs and interests of these groups. Second, in attempting to reach widespread, anonymous audiences news draws on the most broadly held common social values and assumptions, in other words the prevailing consensus, in establishing common ground for communication with its audiences. In the case of broadcast journalism the complex relationship with the state exaggerates this need to cling to the central and least challenged social values which provide implicit definitions of actions and events as acceptable or unacceptable, usual or unusual, legitimate or illegitimate.

[. . .]

There are two key elements to the world of broadcast news: the invisibility of social process, and the invisibility of power in society. We can discuss these two lacunae separately. First, the loss of a sense of social process. News is about the present, or the immediate past. It is an account of today's events. The world of broadcast news is a display of single events, making history indeed 'one damn thing after another'. Yet in this whirl of innumerable events the lingering impression is of stasis. Events are interchangeable, a succession rather than an unfolding. What is provided is a topping up of the limited range of regularly observed events in the world with more of the same. A reassuring sameness assimilates each succession of events to ready-made patterns in a timeless mosaic.

This fragmentation of social process, evacuating history, has been described as 'a kind of consecration to collective amnesia' (Gabel, 1967, p. 113). In a real sense reason disappears as actors flit **across** the journalistic stage, perform and hurriedly disappear. [. . .] Thus industrial relations appears not as an evolving conflict of interest but as a sporadic eruption of inexplicable anger and revolt (Hartmann, 1976; Glasgow University Media Group, 1976). Similarly the political affairs of foreign lands appear as spasmodic convulsions of a more or less violent turn, while international relations appear to result from the occasional urge for travel and conversation indulged in by the diplomatic jet-set.

The second absent dimension in broadcast news is that of power. News is about the actions of individuals, not corporate entities, thus individual authority rather than the exertion of entrenched power is seen to be the mover of events. News, and broadcast news in particular, is the last refuge of the great man theory of history. Yet faces change, power holders are replaced, and such changes take pride of place in the circumspection of the news. The continuing and consistent power of the position is masked by concentration on the recurrent changes of office-holder.

In domestic news the focus is on central political elites and their daily gamesmanship in the arenas of conflict resolution. Groups which may exert power but which do not make news disappear, by definition, from view, and with them the visibility of power itself. Prominent among the absentees are the owners of property and their corporate representatives. Of all the institutions which contribute to social process none is so invisible to broadcast news as the world of the company boardroom. In international news the world revolves round the news capitals in Europe and North America. For audiences in the Third World their fellows in three continents are invisible, a communality of interest cannot emerge and problems appear particular and separate to each watching nation. Thus it is not the *effect* of the rich and powerful nations on the Third World that is seen, but their attractiveness as models, benevolence as aid-givers and convenors of conferences, or wisdom as disinterested umpires in local disputes.

Power disappears in the institutional definitions the news provides, an agenda of issues and arenas to which attention is directed. In particular politics is separated from power. Power is seen only in the public display of formality, gesture and speech by major political actors. It is defined by reference to government and the central institutions of political negotiation. Rositi has similarly drawn attention in his analysis of European television news to 'the primacy of formal politics' in the television news world (Rositi, 1975, pp. 25–30), and remarks on the absence of financial and business elites. Thus power is reduced to areas of negotiated compromise, and politics to a recurrent series of decisions, debates and personalities. It is removed from the institutions of production. Thus news bears witness to the institutional separation of economics and politics, a precondition for the evacuation of power from its account of the world. Power is absent from news by virtue of this severance of politics from economics; power is located in authority not in control, in the office-holder not the property owner. News thus provides a particular and truncated view of power, and in this sense power is a dimension that is effectively missing from news.

With these two missing dimensions – social process or history, and power – news indeed provides a world view. The question remains to what extent this is a coherent ideology. Analyses which see news as necessarily a product of powerful groups, in society, designed to provide a view of the world consonant with the interests of those groups simplify the situation too far to be helpful. The occupational routines and beliefs of journalists do not allow a simple conduit between the ruling ideas of the powerful and their distribution via the airwaves. Yet the absence of power and process clearly precludes the development of views which might question the prevailing distribution of power, or its roots in the evolution of economic distribution and control. A world which appears fundamentally unchanging, subject to the genius or caprice of myriad powerful individuals, is not a world which appears susceptible to radical change or challenge.

There are three ways, then, in which broadcast news is ideological. First it focuses our attention on those institutions and events in which social conflict is managed and resolved. It is precisely the arenas of consensus formation which provide both access and appropriate material for making the news. Second, broadcast news, in studiously following statutory demands to eschew partiality or controversy, and professional demands for objectivity and neutrality, is left to draw on the values and beliefs of the broadest social consensus. It is this process which Stuart Hall (1970, p. 1056) describes as 'the steady and unexamined play of attitudes which, via the mediating structure of professionally defined news values, inclines all the media toward the status quo'. The prevailing beliefs in any society will rarely be those which question existing social organisation or values. News will itself merely reinforce scepticism about such divergent, dissident or deviant beliefs. Third, as we have seen, broadcast news is, for historical and organisational reasons, inherently incapable of providing a portrayal of social change or of displaying the operation of power in and between societies. It thus portrays a world which is unchanging and unchangeable.

The key elements of any ruling ideology are the undesirability of change, and its impossibility; all is for the best and change would do more harm than good, even if it were possible. Broadcast news substantiates this philosophy because of the interplay of the three processes we have just described.

REFERENCES

Brinkley, D. (1964) Interview, in *TV Guide*, 11 April.

Brucker, H. (1973) *Communication is Power: Unchanging Values in a Changing Journalism*, New York, Oxford University Press.

Epstein, E. J. (1973) *News from Nowhere – Television and the News*, New York, Random House.

Gabel, J. (1967) *La Falsa Conscienza*, Dedalo, Bari, quoted in Rositi (1975).

Galtung, J. and Ruge, M. (1965) The structure of foreign news, *Journal of Peace Research*, vol. 1, pp. 64–90.

Glasgow University Media Group (1976) *Bad News*, London, Routledge & Kegan Paul.

Hall, S. (1970) A world at one with itself, *New Society*, 18 June, pp. 1056–8.

Hartmann, P. (1976) *The Media and Industrial Relations*, unpublished, Leicester Centre for Mass Communication Research.

Hughes, H. M. (1940) *News and the Human Interest Story*, Chicago, University of Chicago Press.

Hughes, H. M. (1942) The social interpretation of news, *Annals of the American Academy of Political and Social Science*, vol. 219, pp. 11–17.

Lansipuro, Y. (1975) Joint Eurovision/Intervision news study, *EBU Review*, vol. XXVI, no. 3, May, pp. 37–40.

Rositi, F. (1975) The television news programme: fragmentation and recomposition of our image of society. Report presented to Prix Italia, Florence.

Schlesinger, P. (1978) *Putting 'Reality' Together: BBC News*, London, Constable.

Varis, T. (1974) *Television News in Eurovision and Intervision*, Report to EBU Working Party on Television News, Lisbon.

51

THE SOCIAL PRODUCTION OF NEWS

Stuart Hall, Chas Critcher, Tony Jefferson, John Clarke and Brian Roberts

The media do not simply and transparently report events which are 'naturally' newsworthy *in themselves*. 'News' is the end-product of a complex process which begins with a systematic sorting and selecting of events and topics according to a socially constructed set of categories. As MacDougall puts it:

> At any given moment billions of simultaneous events occur throughout the world. . . . All of these occurences are potentially news. They do not become so until some purveyor of news gives an account of them. The news, in other words, is the account of the event, not something intrinsic in the event itself.[1]

One aspect of the structure of selection can be seen in the routine organisation of newspapers with respect to regular types or areas of news. Since newspapers are committed to the regular production of news, these organisational factors will, in turn, affect what is selected. For example, newspapers become pre-directed to certain types of event and topic in terms of the organisation of their own work-force (e.g. specialist correspondents and departments, the fostering of institutional contacts, etc.) and the structure of the papers themselves (e.g. home news, foreign, political, sport, etc.).[2]

Given that the organisation and staffing of a paper regularly direct it to certain categories of items, there is still the problem of selecting, from the many contending items within any one category, those that are felt will be of interest

From S. Hall et al., *Policing the Crisis: Mugging, the State, and Law and Order* (Basingstoke: Macmillan Education, 1978) pp. 53–60.

to the reader. This is where the *professional ideology* of what constitutes 'good news' – the newsman's sense of *news values* – begins to structure the process.

[. . .]

These two aspects of the social production of news – the bureaucratic organisation of the media which produces the news in specific types or categories and the structure of news values which orders the selection and ranking of particular stories within these categories – are only part of the process. The third aspect – the moment of the *construction* of the news story itself – is equally important, if less obvious. This involves the presentation of the item to its *assumed* audience, in terms which, as far as the presenters of the item can judge, will make it comprehensible to that audience. If the world is not to be represented as a jumble of random and chaotic events, then they must be identified (i.e. named, defined, related to other events known to the audience), and assigned to a social context (i.e. placed within a frame of meanings familiar to the audience). This process – identification and contextualisation – is one of the most important through which events are 'made to mean' by the media. An event only 'makes sense' if it can be located within a range of known social and cultural identifications. If newsmen did not have available – in however routine a way – such cultural 'maps' of the social world, they could not 'make sense' for their audiences of the unusual, unexpected and unpredicted events which form the basic content of what is 'newsworthy'. Things are newsworthy because they represent the changefulness, the unpredictability and the conflictful nature of the world. But such events cannot be allowed to remain in the limbo of the 'random' – they must be brought within the horizon of the 'meaningful'. This bringing of events within the realm of meanings means, in essence, referring unusual and unexpected events to the 'maps of meaning' which already form the basis of our cultural knowledge, into which the social world is *already* 'mapped'. The social identification, classification and contextualisation of news events in terms of these background frames of reference is the fundamental process by which the media make the world they report on intelligible to readers and viewers. This process of 'making an event intelligible' is a social process – constituted by a number of specific journalistic practices, which embody (often only implicitly) crucial assumptions about what society is and how it works.

One such background assumption is the *consensual* nature of society: the process of *signification* – giving social meanings to events – *both assumes and helps to construct society as a 'consensus'*. We exist as members of one society *because* – it is assumed – we share a common stock of cultural knowledge with our fellow men: we have access to the same 'maps of meanings'. Not only are we all able to manipulate these 'maps of meaning' to understand events, but we have fundamental interests, values and concerns in common, which these maps embody or reflect. We all want to, or do, maintain basically the same perspective *on* events. In this view, what unites us, as a society and a culture – its consensual side – far outweighs what divides and distinguishes us as groups or classes from other groups. Now, at one level, the existence of a cultural consensus is an obvious truth; it is the basis of all social communication.[3] If we were not members of the same language community we literally could not communicate with one another. On a broader level, if we did not inhabit, to some degree, the same classifications of social reality we could not 'make sense of the world together'. In recent years, however, this basic cultural fact about society has been raised to an extreme ideological level. Because we occupy the same society and belong to roughly the same 'culture', it is assumed that there is, basically, only *one* perspective on events: that provided by what is sometimes called *the* culture, or (by some social scientists) *the* 'central value system'. This view denies any major structural discrepancies between different groups, or between the very different maps of meaning in a society. This 'consensual' viewpoint has important political consequences, when used as the taken-for-granted basis of communication. It carries the assumption that we also all have roughly the same *interest* in the society, and that we all roughly have an equal share of power in the society. This is the essence of the idea of the political consensus. 'Consensual' views of society represent society as if there are no major cultural or economic breaks, no major conflicts of interests between classes and groups. Whatever disagreements exist, it is said, there are legitimate and institutionalised means for expressing and reconciling them. The 'free market' in opinions and in the media is supposed to guarantee the reconciliation of cultural discontinuities between one group and another. The political institutions – parliament, the two-party system, political representation, etc. – are supposed to guarantee equal access for all groups to the decision-making process. The growth of a 'consumer' economy is supposed to have created the economic conditions for everyone to have a stake in the making and distribution of wealth. The rule of law protects us all equally. This consensus view of society is particularly strong in modern, democratic, organised capitalist societies; and the media are among the institutions whose practices are most widely and consistently predicated upon the assumption of a 'national consensus'. So that, when events are 'mapped' by the media into frameworks of meaning and interpretation, it is assumed that we all equally possess and know how to use these frameworks, that they are drawn from fundamentally the same structures of understanding for all social groups and audiences. Of course, in the formation of opinion, as in politics and economic life, it is conceded that there will be differences of outlook, disagreement, argument and opposition; but these are understood as taking place within a broader basic framework of agreement – 'the consensus' – to which everyone subscribes, and within which every dispute, disagreement or conflict of interest can be reconciled by discussion, without recourse to confrontation or violence.

[. . .]

Events, as news, then, are regularly interpreted within frameworks which derive, in part, from this notion of *the consensus* as a basic feature of everyday life. They are elaborated through a variety of 'explanations', images and discourses which articulate what the audience is assumed to think and know about the society.

[. . .]

What, then, is the underlying significance of the framing and interpretive function of news presentation? We suggest that it lies in the fact that the media are often presenting information about events which occur outside the direct experience of the majority of the society. The media thus represent the primary, and often the only, source of information about many important events and topics. Further, because news is recurrently concerned with events which are 'new' or 'unexpected', the media are involved in the task of making comprehensible what we would term 'problematic reality'. Problematic events breach our commonly held expectations and are therefore threatening to a society based around the expectation of consensus, order and routine. Thus the media's mapping of problematic events within the conventional understandings of the society is crucial in two ways. The media define for the majority of the population *what* significant events are taking place, but, also, they offer powerful interpretations of *how* to understand these events. Implicit in those interpretations are orientations towards the events and the people or groups involved in them.

PRIMARY AND SECONDARY DEFINERS

In this section we want to begin to account for the 'fit' between dominant ideas and professional media ideologies and practices. This cannot be simply attributed – as it sometimes is in simple conspiracy theories – to the fact that the media are in large part capitalist-owned (though that structure of ownership is widespread), since this would be to ignore the day-to-day 'relative autonomy' of the journalist and news producers from direct economic control. Instead we want to draw attention to the more routine *structures* of news production to see how the media come in fact, in the 'last instance', to *reproduce the definitions of the powerful*, without being, in a simple sense, in their pay. Here we must insist on a crucial distinction between *primary* and *secondary definers* of social events.

The media do not themselves autonomously create news items; rather they are 'cued in' to specific new topics by regular and reliable institutional sources. As Paul Rock notes:

> In the main journalists position themselves so that they have access to institutions which generate a useful volume of reportable activity at regular intervals. Some of these institutions do, of course, make themselves visible by means of dramatization, or through press releases and press agents. Others are known to regularly produce consequential events.

> The courts, sports grounds and parliament mechanically manufacture news which is . . . assimilated by the press.[4]

One reason for this has to do with the internal pressures of news production – as Murdock notes:

> The incessant pressures of time and the consequent problems of resource allocation and work scheduling in news organisations can be reduced or alleviated by covering 'pre-scheduled events'; that is, events that have been announced in advance by their convenors. However, one of the consequences of adopting this solution to scheduling problems is to increase the newsmen's dependence on news sources willing and able to preschedule their activities.[5]

The second has to do with the fact that media reporting is underwritten by notions of 'impartiality', 'balance' and 'objectivity'. This is formally enforced in television (a near-monopoly situation, where the state is directly involved in a regulatory sense) but there are also similar professional ideological 'rules' in journalism.[6] One product of these rules is the carefully structured distinction between 'fact' and 'opinion'. [. . .] For our present purposes, the important point is that these professional rules give rise to the practice of ensuring that media statements are, wherever possible, grounded in 'objective' and 'authoritative' statements from 'accredited' sources. This means constantly turning to accredited representatives of major social institutions – MPs for political topics, employers and trade-union leaders for industrial matters, and so on. Such institutional representatives are 'accredited' because of their institutional power and position, but also because of their 'representative' status: either they represent 'the people' (MPs, Ministers, etc.) or organised interest groups (which is how the TUC and the CBI are now regarded). One final 'accredited source' is 'the expert': his calling – the 'disinterested' pursuit of knowledge – not his position or his representativeness, confers on his statements 'objectivity' and 'authority'. Ironically, the very rules which aim to preserve the impartiality of the media, and which grew out of desires for greater professional neutrality, also serve powerfully to orientate the media in the 'definitions of social reality' which their 'accredited sources' – the institutional spokesmen – provide.

These two aspects of news production – the practical pressures of constantly working against the clock and the professional demands of impartiality and objectivity – combine to produce a systematically structured *over-accessing* to the media of those in powerful and privileged institutional positions. The media thus tend, faithfully and impartially, to reproduce symbolically the existing structure of power in society's institutional order. This is what Becker has called the 'hierarchy of credibility' – the likelihood that those in powerful or high-status positions in society who offer opinions about controversial topics will have their definitions accepted, because such spokesmen are understood to have access to more accurate or more specialised information on particular topics than the majority of the population.[7] The result of this structured preference given in the media to the opinions of the powerful is that these 'spokesmen' become what we call the *primary definers* of topics.

What is the significance of this? It could rightly be argued that through the requirement of 'balance' [. . .] alternative definitions do get a hearing: each 'side' *is* allowed to present its case. In point of fact [. . .] the setting up of a topic in terms of a debate within which there are oppositions and conflicts is also one way of *dramatising* an event so as to enhance its newsworthiness. The important point about the structured relationship between the media and the primary institutional definers is that it permits the institutional definers to establish the initial definition or *primary interpretation* of the topic in question. This interpretation then 'commands the field' in all subsequent treatment and sets the terms of reference within which all further coverage or debate takes place. Arguments *against* a primary interpretation are forced to insert themselves into *its* definition of 'what is at issue' – they must begin from this framework of interpretation as their starting-point. This initial interpretative framework – what Lang and Lang have called an 'inferential structure'[8] – is extremely difficult to alter fundamentally, once established. For example, once race relations in Britain have been defined as a 'problem of numbers' (i.e. how many blacks there are in the country), then even liberal spokesmen, in proving that the figures for black immigrants have been exaggerated, are nevertheless obliged to subscribe, implicitly, to the view that the debate is 'essentially' *about numbers*.

[. . .]

Effectively, then, the primary definition *sets the limit* for all subsequent discussion by *framing what the problem is*. This initial framework then provides the criteria by which all subsequent contributions are labelled as 'relevant' to the debate, or 'irrelevant' – beside the point. Contributions which stray from this framework are exposed to the charge that they are 'not addressing the problem'.[9]

The media, then, do not simply 'create' the news; nor do they simply transmit the ideology of the 'ruling class' in a conspiratorial fashion. Indeed, we have suggested that, in a critical sense, the media are frequently not the 'primary definers' of news events at all; but their structured relationship to power has the effect of making them play a crucial but secondary role in *reproducing* the definitions of those who have privileged access, as of right, to the media as 'accredited sources'. From this point of view, in the moment of news production, the media stand in a position of structured subordination to the primary definers.

It is this structured relationship – between the media and its 'powerful' sources – which begins to open up the neglected question of the *ideological role* of the media. It is this which begins to give substance and specificity to

Marx's basic proposition that 'the ruling ideas of any age are the ideas of its ruling class'. Marx's contention is that this dominance of 'ruling ideas' operates primarily because, in addition to its ownership and control of the means of material production, this class also owns and controls the means of 'mental production'. In producing their definition of social reality, and the place of 'ordinary people' within it, they construct a particular image of society which represents particular class interests as the interests of all members of society. Because of their control over material and mental resources, and their domination of the major institutions of society, this class's definitions of the social world provide the basic rationale for those institutions which protect and reproduce their 'way of life'. This control of mental resources ensures that theirs are the most powerful and 'universal' of the available definitions of the social world. Their universality ensures that they are shared to some degree by the subordinate classes of the society. Those who govern, govern also through ideas; thus they govern with the consent of the subordinate classes, and not principally through their overt coercion. Parkin makes a similar point: 'the social and political definitions of those in dominant positions tend to become objectified in the major institutional orders, so providing the moral framework for the entire social system.'[10]

In the major social, political and legal institutions of society, coercion and constraint are never wholly absent. This is as true for the media as elsewhere. For example, reporters and reporting *are* subject to economic and legal constraints, as well as to more overt forms of censorship (e.g. over the coverage of events in Northern Ireland). But the transmission of 'dominant ideas' depends *more* on non-coercive mechanisms for their reproduction. Hierarchical structures of command and review, informal socialisation into institutional roles, the sedimenting of dominant ideas into the 'professional ideology' – all help to ensure, within the media, their continued reproduction in the dominant form. What we have been pointing to in this section is *precisely how one particular professional practice ensures that the media, effectively but 'objectively', play a key role in reproducing the dominant field of the ruling ideologies.*

[. . .]

NOTES

1. C. MacDougall, *Interpretative Reporting* (New York: Macmillan, 1968) p. 12.
2. For a fuller account of the impact of these 'bureaucratic' factors in news production, see P. Rock, 'News as Eternal Recurrence', in *The Manufacture of News: Social Problems, Deviance and the Mass Media*, ed. S. Cohen and J. Young (London: Constable, 1973).
3. L. Wirth, 'Consensus and Mass Communications', *American Sociological Review*, vol. 13, 1948.
4. Rock, 'News as Eternal Recurrence', p. 77.
5. G. Murdock, 'Mass Communication and the Construction of Meaning', in *Rethinking Social Psychology*, ed. N. Armistead (Harmondsworth: Penguin, 1974) p. 210.

6. For a historical account of the evolution of those rules, see J. W. Carey, 'The Communications Revolution and the Professional Communicator', *Sociological Review Monograph*, vol. 13, 1969.

7. H. Becker, 'Whose Side are We on?', in *The Relevance of Sociology*, ed. J. D. Douglas (New York: Appleton-Century-Crofts, 1972).

8. K. Lang and G. Lang, 'The Inferential Structure of Political Communications', *Public Opinion Quarterly*, vol. 19, Summer 1955.

9. See S. M. Hall, 'The "Structured Communication" of Events', paper for the Obstacles to Communication Symposium, UNESCO/Division of Philosophy (available from Centre for Contemporary Cultural Studies, University of Birmingham); Clarke et al., 'The Selection of Evidence and the Avoidance of Racialism: a Critique of the Parliamentary Select Committee on Race Relations and Immigration', *New Community*, vol. III, no. 3, Summer 1974.

10. F. Parkin, *Class Inequality and Political Order* (London: MacGibbon & Kee, 1971) p. 83.

52

POLITICIZING THE PERSONAL

Women's Voices in British Television Documentaries

Myra Macdonald

Not every personal event is political, but all personal events certainly
have the potential to be political.

(Trinh T. Minh-ha)

INTRODUCTION

Informational genres on British television are coming under increasing pressure in the 1990s to locate the popular pulse. News bulletins have responded
in part with an added injection of 'human interest'; documentaries, longer
habituated to giving issues a human face, are defining this as an emphasis on
the intimate or the quirky to catch the scheduler's eye. For feminist critics,
greater 'intimization' (van Zoonen 1991: 217) and personalization in informational television have produced a curious ambivalence. Suggestive, on the one
hand, of a corrective move beyond a masculinized agenda and discourse, these
trends can also be seen as reinforcing old gendered hierarchies, with rational
debate of public issues still valued (as 'masculine') over affective explorations
of personal or social relationships (deemed 'feminine', and consequently trivi-
alized). Van Zoonen (1991) traces the roots of this quandary to the masculi-
nization of the public sphere in the eighteenth century and the corresponding
feminization of the private sphere. The slogan 'the personal is political', successful in epitomizing the feminist project to dismantle this ideological opposition, nevertheless over-simplifies the issues. As the epigraph from Trinh T.
Minh-ha indicates, the personal is not universally political. Neither can every

From Cynthia Carter et al. (eds), *News, Gender and Power* (London: Routledge, 1998).

inclusion of the personal in the public space of television be thought to mark a feminist advance.

By focusing on the incorporation of women's stories and women's voices within mainstream television documentary,[1] this chapter aims to examine the conditions in which the personal can become political, moving the audience beyond a fleeting fix of voyeurism to fresh perceptions about the workings of the contemporary or historical world. While feminist critiques of the Habermasian public sphere confirm that successful politicizing of the personal is not automatically achieved by airing the private in a public space, reworkings of the concept of 'experience' within feminist and cultural theory provide more positive help in identifying how conceptual boundaries between the personal and the political might be eroded. The applicability of these theories to television documentary will be considered in relation to three modes of presenting women's accounts of their own lives, which I classify as the confessional, the case study, and testimony. While each category allows public access to women's personal experiences, I will argue that it is only the last of these that succeeds in challenging journalistic wariness about subjectivity as a form of knowledge. Any undermining of binary oppositions between objectivity and subjectivity, or between evidence and experience, also breaks the habitual temptation to overlay these with sharply gendered values.

Limits of Access

Feminist critiques of the Habermasian public sphere and feminist linguistics both pinpoint the limitations of widening access to an informational genre without changing itsoperational rules. Feminist linguists argue that merely allowing women speaking rights in situations where the modes of speech and interaction have been established according to male priorities marks little progress for women. Equally, feminist critics of Habermas' idealization of the public sphere as an arena, free from commercial pressures, where citizens can openly and freely engage in rational-critical debate, describe this as 'a masculinist ideological notion', dependent for its very formation on the exclusion of women (Fraser 1992: 116). The feminist historian Mary Ryan (1992) has demonstrated that women, far from being absent from public life during the relevant period of the eighteenth and nineteenth centuries, played a major role in political activity and in developing women's rights. If this had been acknowledged, the rules of participation would have had to be rewritten. Rethinking the concept of the public sphere in 1992, Habermas accepts part of this feminist criticism: 'unlike the exclusion of underprivileged men, the exclusion of women had structuring significance' (1992: 428). Habermas differs from his feminist critics, however, in arguing that the challenge posed by feminism has been met by the public sphere's capacity for self-transformation from within (1992: 429–30).

Whether documentary should strictly be included within the Habermasian conceptualization of the public sphere is debatable. Purists who adhere to the Habermasian chronology would dispute its entitlement to be defined in these terms. Documentary belongs, after all, to the period that Habermas (1974, 1989) described as 're-feudalizing' the methods of public communication when 'critical publicity is supplanted by manipulative publicity' (1989: 178). Even when he moderated his earlier dismissal of the possibility of open rational-critical debate in the twentieth-century mass media, his model remained one where 'groups of concerned citizens' could come together to compete with commercially-driven media power to effect changes in social values (1992: 453–5). Documentary rarely allows citizens to exchange views directly with each other, preferring instead a form of serial monoglossia, linked through an intermediary. Yet, as several critics imply (Scannell 1986; Corner 1995), the access to 'ordinary' voices in documentary and its evolving challenge to the *status quo* support its alignment with a Habermasian public sphere, conceived as a normative ideal.

The Habermasian privileging of rational-critical discourse has in any case dominated thought about desired forms of informational television, and has helped to blind critics and producers alike to the partiality of the concept of citizenship that underpins it. If, as Ursula Vogel suggests, women or other marginalized groups are to emerge from their positioning as 'indirect citizens' (1991: 58), 'citizenship, as politics in general, should no longer be located in particular sites, or in relation to spaces occupied by particular institutions' (1991: 79). A dismantling of both the public/private divide and current practices of gendering the political and the personal is necessary to achieve this aim. Methods of including women's stories in the public space of the documentary that leave these boundaries untouched perpetuate the problem.

RETHINKING EXPERIENCE

Critical and production discourses on documentary have historically been wary of subjectivity and experience, concepts located on the wrong side of a binary divide that privileges observation, verifiable evidence, and dispassionate reportage. As Bill Nichols observes, 'the prevalence of a criterion of objectivity in documentary has left the exploration of subjectivity underdeveloped' (1991: 120). While welcoming subjectivity's ability 'to convey something of the specificity and uniqueness of a historical moment' (1991: 283, note 25), Nichols adds a cautionary reminder that the concept of experience was vehemently attacked in 1970s' film theory by semiology, psychoanalysis, feminism and poststructuralism (1991: 294, note 25). More recently, feminist theory has been actively reclaiming experience from the poststructuralist wilderness, without reinserting it into an Enlightenment paradigm as an ontological state of being or as a guarantor of authenticity. The terms of this rethinking provide the basis for my analysis of documentary's capacity to politicize the personal.

Despite differences in their formulations, feminist theorists unite in rejecting the Enlightenment model of experience as a fixed point of knowledge, conceptualizing it instead as provisional, situated and constantly subject to contestation. As early as 1984, Teresa de Lauretis depicts subjectivity and experience as permanently in formation:

> For each person . . . subjectivity is an ongoing construction, not a fixed point of departure or arrival from which one then interacts with the world. On the contrary, it is the effect of that interaction – which I call experience; and thus it is produced not by external ideas, values, or material causes, but by one's personal, subjective, engagement in the practices, discourses, and institutions that lend significance (value, meaning, and effect) to the events of the world. (De Lauretis 1984: 159)

In the 1990s, this view of experience as a process is echoed in the writings of Elspeth Probyn and Joan Scott. Scott describes experience as fluctuating perpetually between offering an interpretation '*and*' being itself 'in need of interpretation' (1992: 37). Elspeth Probyn argues that even in a poststructuralist age we need to recognize that experience has an ontological feel to it, but for feeling to become knowledge we need to shift gear: 'the ontological must be met with an epistemological analysis . . . I want to stretch my experience beyond the merely personal. . . . In other words, I want to put forward a mode of theorizing that encourages lines of analysis that move from her experience to mine, and mine to hers' (Probyn 1993: 4). Advocating 'a speaking position that entails a defamiliarization of the taken-for-granted', Probyn asserts that this depends on undermining 'any assurance of ontological importance' (1993: 80). Experience sharpens into 'a critical tool to analyse and cut into the specificity of the social formation' (1993: 29) precisely when it recognizes its own ontological limits. Probyn's political objectives are clear: 'to figure ways in which we can use our selves critically in order to trouble the material conditions that literally give rise to "us"' (1993: 168).

Feminist theory argues that political awareness emerges more productively out of intellectual and emotional discomfort and unease than out of the presumption of an already assured position of certainty. The stimulus of the jarring moment of disturbance recalls Raymond Williams' earlier formulation, acknowledged (if very differently) by both Probyn and Scott:

> I have found that areas which I would call structures of feeling as often as not initially form as a certain kind of disturbance or unease, a particular type of tension. . . . To put it another way, the peculiar location of a structure of feeling is the endless comparison that must occur in the process of consciousness between the articulated and the lived. (Williams 1981: 167–8)

Williams, typically agonizing over the precision and appropriateness of his terminology, admits that 'blockbuster words like experience' can produce problems in 'mak[ing] a god out of an unexamined subjectivity' (1981: 168), but he argues strongly none the less that we need to avert the possibility, posed by post-structuralist thinking, that the epistemological will 'wholly absorb the ontological' (1981: 167).

None of these theorists considers what happens when experience is mediated through television, but their observations have several implications for that process. For the movement between ontological and epistemological to be textually visible and evident to audiences, a sense of disjuncture or unease between these levels needs to become manifest. Equally, sufficient space needs to be provided for the process of 'speaking the self' (Probyn 1993) to enable this moment to arise. Packaging experience as either a commodity or as a colouring-in of what is already known merely prompts a reversion to earlier Enlightenment formulations. While my discussion focuses on textual manifestations rather than audience responses, feminist theories of experience also prompt work beyond the text. The notion of experience as situated, provisional and open to contestation has already strongly influenced models and methods of media audience research.

[...]

THE CONFESSIONAL

The 'confessional' mode of presenting women's stories refers to the expression of experience (in verbal, paralinguistic or bodily codes) where that experience is configured individualistically and ontologically, and where the viewer is positioned on the outside, looking in. To borrow terms used in a slightly different context by the documentarist and critic Trinh T. Minh-ha, the women doing the confessing are reduced to appearing as 'Someone's private zoo' (1989: 82). The viewer, refused a point of contact with the specimen in the confession box, is forced into a position of voyeurism where the pleasure comes from a position of detachment from the experiences offered to us as spectacle. Whereas individual confessions on a talk show may be contextualized into political significance by the host, the confessional documentary presents a series of instances of an onto-logical phenomenon (recent examples from British television include what it feels like to be in a marital breakdown; to have recurrent problems with nannies; to be jilted, or betrayed) without a metadiscursive commentary. The confessions are most often presented straight to camera with minimal obtrusion from an invisible interviewer.

As authenticity in the world of public affairs appears increasingly chimera-like, the expression of personal emotion on television provides a substitute fix for those who still want to believe that the screen offers a window on the world. Making its first televisual appearance in US talk shows, the public confessional has a longer heritage in popular print, from the nineteenth-century fabricated 'last-dying confessions' of convicted criminals to the first-person narration of personal dilemmas in women's weekly magazines. Michel Foucault sees the confession as a pervasive mode of truth-seeking in Western societies: 'Western man [sic] has become a confessing animal' (1979: 59). Confessionals now extend far beyond the penitence rituals of the Roman Catholic church to include secular interviews, autobiographies and consultations, but, in Foucault's view, they share with the religious practice in granting more power to the hearer than to the speaker. The listener or reader becomes an 'authority who requires the confession, prescribes and appreciates it, and intervenes in order to judge, punish, forgive, console, and reconcile' (Foucault 1979: 62).

In documentary, television's mediation of the confessional prevents the viewer from intervening directly or even from identifying with the speaker. The detached video-box style and avoidance of close-ups present emotion as spectacle. Far from removing the imbalance of power that Foucault notes, this intensifies the confessional's construction of the participants as ethnographically-observed 'others'. In addition, the focus on individuated reactions dissipates any possibility of developing the fleeting glimpses of political connectedness that these documentaries occasionally offer. A *Cutting Edge* documentary, 'Jilted', (Channel 4, 17 March 1997) presents five confessions from people who failed to go through with their wedding plans. Underlying the stories of several of the women is the unrealistic but seductive fantasy they or their mothers entertain about the romance of the wedding day, but this eludes attention as the documentary concentrates on following each jilted lover through a purely emotional journey from disbelief to devastation.

[. . .]

THE CASE STUDY

While the confessional is still a relatively rare phenomenon within British television documentaries, the case study is a staple ingredient of the expository form of the genre. By 'case study' I refer to the use of the experiences of 'ordinary' people to support and exemplify the documentary's central thesis. Although documentary increasingly avoids a strong central commentary, aiming instead for at least the illusion of letting the evidence speak for itself, few television documentaries favour dissonance between competing voices. A dominant discourse is established, with interviewees' stories subordinated to this. Women in this situation are allowed in one sense to speak in their own voices, but these voices are continually interrupted by the authoritative discourse of others (whether commentator, narrator, or experts). The epistemological work of the documentary is not carried forward by the women themselves. At worst, this leads to the women's experiences being translated into an alien rhetoric; at best it prevents experience from breaking out of its illustrative confines to create the unease and tension that might propel fresh insights into relations between the personal and the political.

Suspicions run high in the critical literature about the dangers of allowing interviewees free rein to set their own agenda and determine their own contributions. John Corner, for example, comments that 'it would clearly be a mistake to suppose that the public project of documentary is best served by privileging accessees over any sense of the independent integrity of the topic or of responsibilities to the viewer', although he also recognizes the political merit of 'access documentaries' which grant contributors more extensive speaking rights and 'in which the expression of ordinary and often marginalised experience becomes the primary directorial goal' (Corner 1995: 91). This distinction between documentaries that enable access to the marginalized, and documentaries that have an expository purpose, maintains a dichotomy between subjectivity and objectivity, between empathy and knowledge, that diminishes the political potential of the personal. The possibility of access *as* exposition needs to be explored, and will be pursued in my category of 'testimony' below.[2] The strategy favoured by both critics and documentary-makers has been to set the interviewees' voices within a clear discursive framework. While John Corner recommends that this be of sufficiently light a touch to avoid 'simply "appropriating" the speech of the interviewee for a project grounded elsewhere', he also accepts that 'subordination of interviewees to programme logics is a continuing requirement in documentaries' (Corner 1995: 90, 91). This may require documentary-makers to engage in not merely a tricky but an impossible balancing act.

The problems of appropriation are particularly acute in medical documentaries. Their frequently didactic purpose and their subservience to a symptom-based discourse of medicine mean that human case studies tend to be co-opted for expository purposes, reinforcing a familiar hierarchy of professional knowledge over lay experience. A Channel 4 documentary on schizophrenia, 'Edge of Madness' (23 July 1996), interweaves the experiences of four sufferers, two men and two women. The women outstrip the men in articulateness and self-awareness, and in their co-operativeness in performing for the camera. Yet both women become subordinated to the informational point they exemplify. After we are first introduced to Miranda Ryder as a lively and perceptive woman who paints in her spare time, and observe, *vérité* style, her humorous exchanges with her own psychiatrist about her condition, she next appears in a cut-away shot, sitting reading in a garden, while a male psychiatric expert delivers an authoritative account of schizophrenic delusions direct to camera. From being a personality in her own right, Miranda is reduced to being an exemplar or instance. As the documentary proceeds, the voice of this male psychiatrist, objectively discussing 'the patient' and impersonally explaining symptoms of schizophrenia, is established as the dominant point of reference. He is consistently filmed facing the camera, usually in medium close-up, whereas the women sufferers, despite their evident vitality and determination, are filmed periodically in poses or from angles that remind the audience of their lack of control over their own lives.

When Miranda speaks of her delusions following the expert's intervention, the camera looks down on her from a high angle, literally diminishing her stature. Later excerpts from Miranda's story suggest a complicated narrative of familial conflict and struggle for personal identity, but her positioning as a victim, and the fragmentary delivery of her own analysis, ensure this remains of secondary importance.

In some documentaries, the echoes established between the narrated experiences of the case-study participants are so strong as to forge their own lines of connection. Cumulatively acquiring the status of a quasi-authorial voice, they assert their authority beyond their illustrative role in the exposition. In 'Love child' (part of the *Witness* series on Channel 4, 24 September 1996), three women who were forced to give up their babies for adoption in the 1960s recount remarkably similar narratives of social prejudice and bigotry, despite being sharply individuated in terms of personality and temperament. Unveiling the flip side of the decade more typically associated with Woodstock and sexual liberation, this documentary combines archive film footage, reminiscences from church figures involved in running mother-and-baby homes, and the recollections of the women themselves, to communicate the contradictoriness of a decade that appeared to encourage sexual self-expression, while simultaneously denying contraceptive advice to many single women and surrounding births to unmarried mothers with intense shame and secrecy. The women's experiences, individually and separately presented, acquire the authority of testimony by establishing 'lines of analysis that move from her experience to mine and mine to hers' (Probyn 1993: 4). Strikingly identical in their accounts of how they were treated by their families, by the mother-and-baby homes, and by midwives, their individual expressions of identical feelings of emotional paralysis as they handed their babies over to strangers rebound powerfully off each other and also trigger fresh epistemological insights into the hypocritical social morality of the period. The achievement of resonance across differing case studies comes close in this instance to forming what Trinh T. Minh-ha applauds as a new form of subjectivity potentially emerging out of autobiography: 'the subjectivity of a non-I/plural I, which is different from the subjectivity of the sovereign I (subjectivism) or the non-subjectivity of the all-knowing I (objectivism)' (1991: 192).

Tensions between the documentary's expository line and the performances of its 'social actors' (Nichols 1991: 42, 120) also threaten at times to disrupt the authority of the dominant discourse. The vitality, openness and articulateness of people, selected on the basis of their credibility as performers as well as exemplars, is often at odds with their construction as victims of the problem being explored.[3] John Corner notes how evolving production practices, such as the elimination of the interviewer from the documentary frame, paradoxically 're-subjectivise' speakers by giving them apparent control over their own discourse (1996b: 169). More significantly for this discussion, the position of these interviewees on society's cutting edge makes them intensely acute witnesses to the interrelatedness of personal experience, social realities and political and economic forces. The ease with which their experience can bubble up to disturb the confines of the documentary's line of argument is illustrated in 'Marie's story' in 'Broken Promises', a Channel 4 documentary (9 June 1996) that formed part of a series of programmes on poverty in contemporary Britain.

Carefully framed in a manner that constructs her as a victim of an inadequate welfare system, Marie is chosen to illustrate the problems encountered by women who find themselves, after a lifetime of caring for others, thrown on the welfare scrap-heap, and dependent on charity for survival. Evocative mise-en-scène, inter-title quotations from 'expert' commentators, and voice-over text construct Marie as demeaned by a transition from welfare entitlement to charity dependency. Her own voice tells a different story. Robustly lacking self-pity, and incisive in her perceptions of the interrelations between benefit changes, loss of social cohesiveness and a personal experience that is plural rather than singular ('there must be thousands in the world like me'), her reaction to being burgled for the sixth time in a short period quickly moves beyond predictable expressions of shock and dismay to a trenchant comment on the decline of neighbourliness and community that allows burglars to work undisturbed. By cutting into the complex layers of a wider range of Thatcherite values than the documentary can hope to cover, Marie momentarily achieves Elspeth Probyn's aim of finding ways 'in which we can use our selves critically in order to trouble the material conditions that literally give rise to "us"' (1993: 168). Case studies, in such conditions, can occasionally acquire the authority of testimony.

TESTIMONY

'Testimony' has been used in critical writing on documentary to include any evidence given by speakers in their own words. In the distinctions drawn here between different forms of incorporating women's voices, I reserve 'testimony' for situations in which the movement between the woman's subjectivity and social or political circumstances is made textually visible. As feminist theory suggests, experience, under these circumstances, prompts fresh epistemological understanding, distinguishing it clearly from its role as spectacle in the confessional, or as an exemplary instance of someone else's narrative in the case study. Television, in a variety of ways, can make manifest the disturbance or shift between the ontological and epistemological that feminist theorists see as quintessential to a politics of experience. The remainder of this chapter explores four ways in which a demonstration of the interlinking between the personal and political comes to life. In outline, these consist of ironic juxtaposition; memory work; reflexivity; and, the most difficult to epitomize, a disruption of the habitual televisual rhetorics deployed to communicate historical magnitude.

Ironic juxtaposition

The juxtaposing of personal recollection and political evidence is common-place in documentaries, but often these merely co-exist on different planes. By bringing them into critical collision with each other, documentaries expose the limitations of any official or habitual discourse that postures as a singular version of 'the truth'. In 'Love child', as I described above, the power of the women's voices is largely achieved through an accumulating resonance, but the redefining authority of their story is also underlined by its ironic relation to populist images of the 1960s as the era of the permissive society, free love and self-indulgence. The programme's final commentary, defining the era as one intent on suppressing female sexuality, is spoken over images of the Woodstock festival, placing an ironic distance between this version of 1960s 'structures of feeling' and the lived reality of the period.

The twenty-six part series on twentieth-century history, *People's Century*, broadcast by BBC television between 1995 and 1997, also deploys ironic jux-taposition to allow personal recollections to interrogate authorized records. '1957 – Skin Deep' (BBC1, 20 October 1996) explores racial issues in the southern states of the USA and in South Africa. Official film commentary on the clearance of Sophiatown, a 1950s black settlement in Johannesburg, as part of the intensification of apartheid, ricochets off the testimony of one of the residents. Christine Hadebe's recollections are intercut with scenes from the archive film of the event, open to varying interpretations when deprived of the 'anchorage' of its own commentary. Hadebe relates how 'they [the authorities] forced us into the trucks at gun-point. There was no choice', as the documentary cuts to film of the events, now relocated by its own sound-track within an assured colonial discourse. A white male voice tells us that the 'rejoicing Bantu' are 'on their way to a new home – Meadowland – where one can breathe freely'.

Memory work

Memory work has been increasingly recognized within feminist cultural and historical studies as a means of making visible 'the web of interconnections' between 'outer and inner, social and personal, historical and psychical' (Kuhn 1995: 4). Most of the published accounts (for example, Kuhn 1995; Steedman 1986) are of individual recollections built around personal and familial auto-biography. Collective memory work might be yet more productive. The artifi-ciality of separating out witnesses seems particularly acute when the witnesses are women. Writers on gender and discourse have commented extensively on women's preference for interactive, co-operative modes of communication, and the relative neglect of this approach in many high-status forms of exchange.[4] Television practices are no exception, with interaction predominantly con-sisting of confrontation and contestation. Historians are now beginning to explore the benefits of bringing people who participated in past events or processes together to discuss their recollections in 'witness seminars'. These recognize that reminiscing collectively can trigger long-buried memories, and can also tease out the validity of some of the claims that individual memories offer. Documentary rarely provides such opportunities, but when it does, the movement from the personal to the political becomes palpable as we witness the moment of revelation on the screen.

'Playing to Survive' (BBC2, 30 October 1996) focuses on the experiences of cellist Anita Lasker-Wallfisch, who survived the concentration camps by becoming a member of the women's orchestra at Auschwitz. She shares rec-ollections with two friends, Violette and Hélène, who were also members of that orchestra and who later accompanied her to Belsen. From this collective remembering, acutely personalized perceptions emerge that add fresh horror to a historical period in danger of being drained of its power to shock through the clichéd familiarity of its imagery. Violette recalls how the women were asked to play an impromptu concert for Joseph Kramer, the notorious com-mandant at Belsen, and, after the recital, were invited back to his house, given a large bowl of rice pudding and left to enjoy it to the strains of a Bach suite on his gramophone. Suddenly Anita, whose recollection of this event has been uncharacteristically hazy, interjects that they were required to eat 'without spoons – I remember we ate like pigs that night'. Whether this is an actual rec-ollection (Violette does not remember this detail) or a projection of the feelings generated by the incident is immaterial to its impact on the viewer, vivifying as it does the sharp contradictoriness of the situation. The freshness and intensity of this memory takes us, like the women themselves, by surprise.

This example illustrates the dramatic and informational potential of col-lective witnessing on television. If documentary has failed to exploit this pos-sibility, it has also missed opportunities to allow witnesses to comment on archive film of the events or times they lived through. Annette Kuhn (1995) has demonstrated the productivity of this approach in relation to the family pho-tograph album, but the documentarist's conventional separation of historical evidence and personal memory bypasses opportunities of re-interpreting both by allowing them to spark off each other.

Suggestions of what this might achieve are indicated in a documentary on the Dionne quintuplets, born in a remote part of Canada in the 1930s, and brought up as a tourist attraction and virtual freak show ('Miracle babies', part of the *Inside Story* series, BBC1, 24 July 1996). Now suing the Ontario government for compensation for their past exploitation, the three surviving quins are reluctant witnesses to the suffering they endured, inhibited partly by awkwardness with English and partly by an unwillingness to blame individu-als. But while watching film footage of themselves, aged eight, wheeled out at a massive public rally in Toronto to raise money for the war effort, their feelings suddenly erupt. The movement from measured responses to spontaneous reac-tion, and from the ontological to the epistemological, triggered by this piece of film, suddenly tears away the veil of civility and rationality that has obscured the interconnectedness between these women's experiences and the public circumstances that helped to construct them. A technique that produces such powerful television in this specific instance holds wider promise as a means of producing new readings of archive film whose familiarity borders often on visual cliché.

Reflexivity

Postmodern celebrations of reflexivity find only tentative echo among documentary critics. Scepticism centres on its potential pretentiousness, although critics also recognize that at its most penetrating it 'emphasizes epistemological doubt' and can even recreate the processes of feminist consciousness-raising by instigating an interrogation of 'the ground of experience itself' (Nichols 1991: 61, 65). Trinh T. Minh-ha condemns reflexivity when it serves merely to enhance the status of the authorial voice, but her belief that 'meaning can . . . be political only when it does not let itself be easily stabilized' (1991: 41) demands a documentary aesthetic that refuses certainty without abdicating responsibility for analysis.

By drawing attention to the provisionality and locatedness of experience, and the contingent link between investigator and subject, reflexivity shifts the distant ethnographic gaze into the uncomfortable proximity of political contact. A documentary on the Rwandan genocide of 1994 for the *Witness* series on Channel 4 indicates how this can be achieved. Living in that country before and during the genocide, journalist Lindsey Hilsum, the presenter of the programme ('Rwanda: The Betrayal', 16 May 1996), becomes a self-reflexive participant in the moral dilemmas that confronted Rwanda's inhabitants at that time. As a result, the initial 'shock' she expresses at evidence of the Catholic church's involvement – however indirectly – in the massacres, many of which took place in churches where the Tutsis were taking refuge, is complicated by her own experiences. By exposing her own positioning in the intensely difficult battle between conscience, will, and political reality, easy moral judgements are undermined.

Shifting between commentator, interviewer and interviewee in the course of the documentary, Hilsum also denies her own voice interpretative authority. Asked, as interviewee, whether she herself had to refuse anyone help during the period of the genocide, she replies:

> In the first few days of the genocide my phone worked and a lot of Tutsis I knew rang me and asked me to come and save them, and I failed to do that because I didn't have any petrol in my car, and because I wasn't sure where they lived, and I didn't think that I could reach them. Now that means that I'm like a lot of Rwandans who might have wanted to save people or protect them but I didn't have the means, or maybe I wasn't

brave enough, or I wasn't strong enough, or I wasn't good enough, and I didn't do it.

By putting her own situation into play, Hilsum prevents the viewer from occupying a position of detachment. She also destabilizes the conventional aloofness of the presenter towards her interviewees. Janvière Uwizeye, a Tutsi whose relatives were killed in the church in Kaduha where one of the worst massacres took place in April 1994, is one of these. She was saved by a priest who was simultaneously exploiting his position by selling rice, donated by a Catholic relief agency, to the people who were about to be slaughtered. Chillingly, Hilsum reports that he had allegedly raised the price each day until the eve of the massacre, reducing it then to get rid of his stock. When Hilsum asks her how she now feels about this man, Janvière replies that, although she cannot forgive him, she cannot condemn him either, because he was caught in an impossible situation and could not save everyone. Resonating with Hilsum's diagnosis of her own experience, the ambivalence of Janvière's reaction, which in different circumstances might produce a sense of ethnographic distancing, is transformed into a moment of profound disturbance and unsettling of our security of knowledge about the genocide. Experience in this documentary is truly not a fixed point of departure for knowing and evaluating, but a disconcerting prompt to re-evaluation and involvement. More effectively than the schematic movement of irony, reflexivity is capable of producing intense moments of 'radical defamiliarization' when, as here, 'the "This is so, isn't it?" of hegemonic ideology hesitates and wavers' (Nichols 1991: 266, 263).

Reworking magnitude

Capturing the magnitude of historical experience is problematic on a small screen. Even in *film* documentary, Bill Nichols claims: 'narrative and exposition are always forms of miniaturization that seek to encapsulate a "world" that bears some meaning for us' whereas 'history is what hurts. . . . A magnitude of excess remains' (Nichols 1991: 230, 231). Informational television develops its own rhetorics for communicating scale. When celebration of democratizing processes is called for, such as during the free elections in South Africa or the collapse of the Berlin Wall, scale is painted large in mass scenes of public rapture. In situations of extreme public horror, on the other hand, barbarity and disaster are briefly glimpsed in their mass form, their extensiveness documented statistically, but it is to the personal dimension that the medium turns to manage its embodiment of magnitude. The experiences of witnesses and survivors are deployed to bring the events within the miniaturizing scale that makes them affectively intelligible to viewers. The broad canvas of the public arena has to be abandoned, when codes of taste and decency, or the limits of imagination, dictate a shift into personalized mode. When the habitual expectations of these differently constituted conventions for evoking magnitude are disturbed, relations between personal and political are once more thrown into relief.

Survivors of horror 'vivify' the 'incommensurateness between representation and historical referent, the refusal of containment and closure' (Nichols 1991: 240–1) when personal experience cannot carry the load of political or public trauma. In two of the documentaries already discussed, 'Playing to Survive' and 'Rwanda: the betrayal', there are moments of stasis when the expressivity of verbal and non-verbal language falters. Anita Lasker-Wallfisch, revisiting the site of the music block at Auschwitz, is asked by her daughter whether there were ever moments when the women in the orchestra forgot the situation they were in. Anita pauses before replying that it is impossible to say what she was thinking all that time ago. The camera at the same time draws back to position the two women in long shot at the edge of the frame. More of the magnitude of both experience and historical reality is communicated in the visual and verbal terseness of this static shot than could be achieved by any emotional excess. The impossibility of accurately recollecting or representing the unrepresentable leaves the contradictions of the experience lying rawly open, and prevents any comforting closure for the viewer.

In 'Rwanda: the betrayal', there is a similar sequence towards the end of the programme. Lindsey Hilsum is filmed in a wide-angled shot walking towards the church at Kaduha with Bernadette Uwamariya, whose relatives, like those of Janvière Uwizeye, were massacred there. Bernadette, Hilsum tells us in a voice-over, was previously thinking of becoming a nun, but now she is less sure. Between cut-away shots to the church, already firmly associated with unspeakable bloodshed, presenter and interviewee are filmed standing silently together, side by side, in two static shots, one at medium, the other at long range. Spatially composed to invoke a sense of solidarity between the two women, these shots last over ten seconds each, and are filmed without dialogue. Their temporal awkwardness, in a medium that normally edits out such *longueurs*, powerfully signifies the limits of communicability about a period in Rwandan history that has been slipping out from under the documentary's ability to contain or describe it. The chasm between the expressible.

[. . .]

CONCLUSION

Documentary-makers' concerns about the validity of subjectivity and experience as evidence have centred on issues of reliability and typicality. As one of the producers of the *People's Century* series put it, 'we had to make sure that our interviewees, while giving a highly personal account of a particular event, were in line with the consensus of what most people in their situations were feeling at the time . . . One oddball account could knock the whole narrative out of "true" ' (cited in *Radio Times*, 9–15 September 1995: 24). The discursive framing of this dilemma explains why documentary-makers so often choose to incorporate experience merely as an illustration of an argument developed from other sources. Subjectivity as spectacle produces no such anxieties, since its attention-arresting credentials increase in line with the idiosyncrasy of the confessor's experience.

This chapter has argued that bringing feminist theories of experience into play with documentary aesthetics opens up possibilities both for democratizing human interest and for preventing a stultifying repetition of gendered assumptions about the agenda and discourses of informational television. The personal and the political, access and exposition, do not inevitably exist on separate planes, or possess inherently different claims to legitimation. Documentary-makers, searching for novelty and besieged by the need to increase ratings, may find commodification of experience a tempting option in a medium that already gives prime space on confessional talk shows and self-immolating game shows to those whose experiences are least represented in the informational media. The creative opportunities and rewards of exploring how personal experience might activate the 'radical defamiliarization' (Nichols 1991: 266) that stimulates new forms of political insight could, however, be more exhilarating. As the examples in this chapter demonstrate, forms of testimony that collapse familiar boundaries between the personal and political often provide arresting and inspiring moments within television documentary. They also help to uncover a rich seam of witnesses who are still largely hidden from news and current affairs programming. Hearing more of the testimony of women, and of other groups under-represented in the televisual news agenda, might reconfigure the relation of centre to periphery as well as of the personal to the political. It might even help to reconstitute the public sphere as a democratic space.

NOTES

1. Although the video-diary format would repay analysis in the terms of this chapter, it has not been included here.
2. Interestingly, Corner implicitly suggests this himself by citing Connie Field's film *The Life and Times of Rosie the Riveter* (1980), both as an example of 'access' filming (1995: 183, note 11) and as enabling the women's contributions to emerge as 'testimony' (1995: 99; 1996a: 125), producing 'a *process* of reflection-as-self-awareness' that becomes 'the means by which the "personal is made political"' (1996a: 136).
3. See Winston (1988, 1995) for further discussion of the construction of people as 'victims' in the realist documentary tradition, and Nichols (1991) for a fuller discussion of the 'virtual performance' of 'social actors'.
4. See, for example, Cameron (1990), Coates (1986), Spender (1980) and Swann (1992).

53

NEWS MEDIA AND THE GLOBALIZATION OF THE PUBLIC SPHERE

Stig Hjarvard

The aim of this article is to provide a critical discussion of the concept of a global public sphere and the ways in which this concept has been used in recent media studies. It puts forward the argument, that a global public sphere should not be conceptualized as a larger, extended version of the national public sphere as has often been the case. Instead, it is suggested that the concept of deterritorialization may be used for reinterpreting a globalized public sphere as a process rather than a single entity. The globalization of the public sphere must be understood as a process through which public communication becomes restructured and partly disembedded from national political and cultural institutions. In order to discuss how changes in media systems influence a restructuration of public space, recent changes in the international news industry are examined. Changes in the news media environment create a series of tensions in the public sphere, because they induce both fragmentation and interconnectedness.

Icons of Globalization

In both scholarly work and public debate on globalization, the influence of media and particularly electronic media on social change is considered to be of prime importance. In sociological and cultural analyses of globalization (e.g., Giddens, 1999; Tomlinson, 1999), media such as satellite television, the Internet, computers, mobile phones etc. are often thought to be among the primary forces behind current restructurations of social and cultural

From Stig Hjarvard (ed.), *News in a Globalized Society* (Göteborg: Nordicom, 2001).

geography. Electronic media facilitate an increased interconnectedness across vast distances and a temporal flexibility in social interaction. Furthermore, a handful of media enterprises and media moguls such as Time-Warner-AOL, Disney, Rupert Murdoch, and Bill Gates have become icons of globalization. These media companies and actors both have ambitions of global market domination and serve as the messengers of a new global era. Particularly the transnational news services with a global or regional reach, such as CNN, BBC World, Euronews, Sky News, and Star News, have come to be regarded as the town criers of the global village. Their continuous, on-line, and live distribution of news to all corners of the world has become emblematic of a world in which place and time mean less and less.

Parallel to the emergence of this globalized media environment, a gradual change in the social geography of public and political communication has taken place. The national embeddedness of the public sphere and public opinion no longer goes unquestioned. Increasingly, the formation of public opinion also takes place across national boundaries. The 'opinion of the international community' no longer refers unambiguously to the opinions of assemblies of state leaders or the cosmopolitan elite, but increasingly to a less tangible, phantomlike, and much more volatile phenomenon emerging from extensive media coverage of world events. At least on certain special occasions, a transnational, if not global public sphere has emerged as a forum for political discussion and opinion formation. A series of international events during the last decade bear witness to the transnationalization of the public sphere and public opinion formation: Shell's plan to dump the Brent Spar oil platform in the North Sea, French nuclear testing in the Pacific Ocean, the suppression of student demonstrations in China, UN conferences on the environment, women, social development etc., the death of Lady Diana, Jörg Haider's Freedom Party's participation in Austria's government etc., etc.

During events like these, a series of interactions in different countries are activated and connected to each other partly as a result of intense media coverage. Actions by governments, corporate business interests, NGOs, and the civil society in general (demonstrations, appeals, strikes etc.) feed into a transnational public sphere and incite reactions and discursive responses in different regions and countries. The aggregation of public opinion during this process takes place both nationally and transnationally, and the media representation of this transnational public opinion acquires its own momentum. Although political leaders are still most sensitive to public opinion articulated within their own national boundaries, they cannot afford to ignore the public opinion articulated through the global media. This transnational public opinion represents a political force in its own right, and it has the ability to influence national opinions and, thus, to change the national political basis of power.

Under special circumstances, the power of such globalized public opinion poses a severe problem for even the mightiest nations, because public opinion demands political action that either contradicts national policies or outstrips the diplomatic, economic or military power of the nations involved. The intensive coverage by CNN and other global news media of the student demonstrations in China in 1989 created an urgent call for action by the international community, but the reality was that the major powers' political will and ability to act were quite limited. As a senior official from the US State Department said in reaction to the intensive media coverage of the Chinese authorities' violent suppression of protesters in Tiananmen Square: 'It demanded a solution we couldn't provide. We were powerless to make it stop'[1]. In some cases, the rise of an internationally mediated public opinion does make a difference, even in terms of subsequent political action. The killing of Brazilian street children became an international media story, and this had a profound impact on national politics in Brazil (Serra, 2000).

It is important to stress, however, that although transnational public opinion can be very forceful during events with intensive media coverage, it is most often the case that political, economic or military decisions and actions concerning transnational or global matters take place without intense public attention. The routine, day-to-day decisions and actions related to international politics may often receive news coverage, but rarely do they induce a transnational dialogue involving people other than cosmopolitan elites such as diplomats, government officials, NGO experts, transnational business executives and information officers etc. On most occasions, a broader public debate about international issues rarely extends beyond this political elite, and if it does, it is confined to the framework of the national public sphere.

Although news media increasingly transcend national borders, this does not in itself create a public sphere at a transnational or global level. In fact, it can be argued that the development of the public sphere has increasingly become out of sync with the globalization of economy, governance, and culture. As regards industrial production and financial transactions, the world is becoming more and more interconnected and interdependent, and the flows of cultural products and symbols across borders have intensified. Similarly, political governance increasingly transcends the nation-state, as in the case of the EU. This does not imply, however, that the nation-state is necessarily losing power, but rather that it is acquiring a new role as the mediator of political governance between local, national and supranational levels. The globalization of economy, governance, and culture has not been accompanied by a similar globalization of the public sphere. Opinion formation is still very much tied to the level of national political institutions.

As a starting point, the following paradox can be observed regarding the relationship between the development of the news media and the public sphere: Due to the growth in transnational and global news media, public opinion formation occasionally transcends national borders and acquires a political momentum of its own at a global level. However, compared to the globalization of politics, economy and culture, the public sphere and the formation of public opinion are still very much tied to a national level and oriented toward national political institutions. This seemingly contradictory development has provided support for very different interpretations of current media changes. The idea that the rise of global media has instituted a global public sphere has both been proclaimed and denounced by media scholars, and both sides have actually been able to provide some empirical support for their interpretations. However, the apparent inextricability of these opposing viewpoints may – at least to some extent – be due to a lack of theoretical consideration of how current transformations in the social geography of media may be conceptualized.

A Global Public Sphere?

In an overview of current globalization theories, Held et al. (1999) distinguish between the hyperglobalizers, on the one hand, and the sceptics, on the other, and this rough categorization can also be applied to the different interpretations of public sphere globalization and of the media's role in this process.

The *hyperglobalizers* state that a global public sphere has already emerged, and subsequently that the national public sphere has either disappeared or that its borders have become permeable or fuzzy, open to influences from both local and global media. This argument is clearly supported by the marketing activities of the global media conglomerates themselves and frequently given anecdotal support by statements from American presidents. Consider the words of George Bush, 'I learn more from the CNN than I do from the CIA,' and Jimmy Carter, 'CNN has done more to close gaps of misunderstanding between the world's people than any enterprise in recent memory'[2]. But certain academic studies of the CNN phenomenon also tend to take this position. In particular, CNN programs like 'World Report' – with its mix of contributions from broadcasters all over the world – have been taken as evidence of the emergence of a truly global media system (Flourney, 1992; Flourney & Stewart, 1997).

The hyperglobalization position has also been put forward from a more theoretically reflected position. Thus, Volkmer (1999) interprets current developments not only as a geographical expansion of the public sphere, but also in terms of a changing relationship between the public, the media and the state:

> It can be argued that because of global communication, the public and its opinion is no longer a substantial element of the political system of a society but has turned into a more or less autonomous global public sphere which can only be considered not as a space between the 'public' and the state but between the state and an extra-societal, global community. (Volkmer, 1999: 119).

[. . .]

Among the globalization *sceptics*, it is possible to discern two different lines of criticism. First, a critique of media globalization based on the political economy tradition (e.g., Schiller, 1993; Sparks, 1998), and second, a critique based on cultural and institutional analyses of current transnationalization processes in Europe (e.g., Collins, 1994, 1996 & 1998; Schlesinger, 1993 & 1999). Both lines of criticism have as a mutual starting point a fundamental reservation about the actual global impact of so-called global media. According to their views, most transnational media have only a regional reach and even within their primary region, they do not have universal penetration. Global media like CNN and BBC World may technically have a near global reach, but the actual audience figures tell quite a different story. Compared to the consumption of nationally based media, that of CNN and BBC World is very limited. In most countries, these channels are only used as a supplement to the national news media diet, and usage is generally restricted to the well-educated social strata and the political and business elite. During major world events, these channels may enjoy a rapid rise in viewing figures, but this is only short-lived. As audience studies have shown, CNN – even during the Gulf War, its biggest television success – was not able to keep high audience figures for more than a very limited period (Gutstadt, 1993). Thus, according to this line of criticism, the very label 'global media' and its regional counterparts such as 'European media' are in fact misleading. Audiences do not attend to the same global media at the same time, and consequently the media do not give rise to the formation of a global or European public sphere.

Criticism in the political economy tradition, however, holds that global media conglomerates do play an increasingly important role in that they actually dominate media industries all over the world. Transnational and particularly American media industries dominate the worldwide production and distribution of motion pictures, video, computer games, news channels, newspapers, magazines etc. The impetus for this development is primarily commercial and industrial, and the result is an increased commodification of both culture and public, political communication. As Schiller (1993) argues:

> I do not believe that globalization of the media industries sector has resulted in the formation of an international civil society as such. Rather, this process has resulted in an international order organized by transnational economic interests that are largely unaccountable to the nation-states in which they operate. (Schiller, 1993: 47).

Seen from the point of view of political economy, the globalization of media industries is of no benefit to civil society or to public deliberation in a public sphere. On the contrary, it represents the empowerment of large commercial interests at the expense of civil society and democracy. Citizens' ability to influence public debate and opinion formation diminishes when large media industries are no longer accountable to national political regulation. The political economy tradition holds that globalization is taking place, but it is typically not thought of as a new phenomenon. Rather it is understood as a new stage in a well-known process characteristic of capitalist society: imperialism. Globalization does not entail an opening of public space, on the contrary, it is all about privatization:

> If we need to abandon the term 'global public sphere' as manifestly inadequate to designate what we have been analyzing, then a better one is needed. The one that fits the evidence best is 'imperialist, private sphere'. If this is unfashionable, so be it. At least it is accurate. (Sparks, 1998: 122)

The criticism emerging from studies of cultural and political aspects of transnational media in Europe tends to stress the conservative nature of local and national culture and political institutions. The attempts to build a European public through European media (e.g., the satellite TV channel Euronews or the newspaper The European) have either completely failed or only survived as special interest media for a business or political elite. The attempts by the EU to support the creation of such Pan-European media have rested on the untenable political idea that a political community can be built upon a common European culture. As Collins (1996) argues, there is really no evidence that such a common European culture exists or provides a common ground for identification. On the contrary, Europe exhibits a wide and diverse pattern of languages, cultures, political practices etc. Even patterns of media usage in European countries are so divergent that Pan-European media have difficulties surviving. European cooperation may certainly be both desirable and necessary, but a common culture will not play a significant role as a basis for such cooperation. On the contrary, both language and culture are factors working against Europeanization and toward greater localization. A public political agenda of European issues may gradually develop, but this will not result from the formation of a European political public sphere. This agenda will, according to Schlesinger (1999: 21), be domesticated through national and local media: 'In reality, any common European public agenda is likely, in the process of media reception, to be diversely "domesticated" within each distinctive national or language context'. The process of domestication of foreign news is further enhanced at the level of audience reception. Empirical research demonstrates, for instance, that audiences' interpretation of foreign news is influenced by how they view the position of their own nation in the world (Jensen, 1998).

Both of these skeptical positions question the rise of a global public sphere on the grounds of empirical evidence: the audience for global or regional media is too small and too unevenly distributed among social groups to constitute a public sphere that can in any way be compared to the national public sphere. However, they emphasize different reasons for this phenomenon. The political economy position considers the commodification of public communication by global media companies to be the key factor explaining why a public sphere has not benefited from the rise of global media and has not extended itself into the global realm. According to the other position, this lack of success is due to the continuous strength of national and local political institutions, media, and culture. [. . .]

The Global: Entity or Process?

The argument put forward in this article tries to bridge the gap between some of these opposing viewpoints, while also criticizing the underlying notion of a global public sphere – a notion shared by these viewpoints in spite of their obvious differences. Both hyperglobalizers and sceptics tend to simplify the argument to a choice between a fundamentally new global situation, on the one hand, and a 'nothing new under the sun' position, on the other. Instead, it seems reasonable to argue that the advent of global media – particularly news media – has actually brought about some changes in, e.g., the structure of public communication, the formation of public opinion etc. Recognizing this, however, does not necessarily entail a view that the national public sphere is disappearing, nor does it mean that we should ignore the power and influence transnational commercial interests have over how public communication is structured.

The formation of public communicative spaces at a transnational level does not necessarily pose a threat to national public spheres; instead their very precondition might be the existence of national public spheres. In fact, it can be argued that the nation-state itself encourages the development of transnational public fora. As Köhler (1998) suggests, 'it is the state itself which, as a result of the need to adapt to processes of globalization and by the increasing involvement in intergovernmental cooperation, provides the impetus for the cosmopolitan enlargement of its own public sphere' (Köhler, 1998: 233–34). The national public sphere may potentially benefit from the growth of public communication across national borders, while it may also be gradually subjected to change itself due to this transnationalization. Thus, if we are to understand current developments, it seems unproductive to address them in an 'either-or' manner. The complex of ongoing transformations would better conceptualized as a 'both-and' development. A transnational public communicative space may be a sort of supplement or addition to a national public sphere that eventually – during a long evolutionary process – becomes transformed itself.

The most important theoretical problem in current discussions of the public sphere in relation to globalization arises from the fact that the public sphere has been conceptually and historically linked to the nation-state. Thus, the national framework – particularly the national entity – completely informs our perceptions of what a public sphere is – and should be – even when it transcends the national borders. Thus, most discussions of a global public sphere depict it as an extended, geographically expanded version of the national model. It is not different, simply bigger. Thus, a global public sphere is also portrayed as confined to a well-defined geographical territory and located at a specific institutional level. Typically, it is considered as a public forum for deliberation located somewhere between global or regional political institutions like the UN, EU etc., on the one hand, and the global civil society, on the other. Furthermore, it is thought to display the same characteristics as the national public sphere. It is considered to be universal, both in the sense that access to the public sphere is evenly distributed among all citizens, and in the sense that it is open for debate on all matters of public interest; as such it is conceived as a non-specialized and non-professionalized forum for public debate.

Considering the national embeddedness of the social and political sciences in general, this tendency to take the nation as the natural unit of analysis and project the national model of the public sphere to a global level is not at all surprising. Nevertheless, this theoretical heritage poses severe problems for identifying new spaces of publicity and for a discussion of the ways in which these new spaces actually connect to existing national public spheres and how they expand, limit or transform chances for public deliberation. In particular, the limitation lies in the idea that globalization means the creation of a new global *entity* with the same structural features as its national counterpart. Instead of considering the global as a new geographical unit or container of publicity, power and institutions, it may be better to think of it as a *process*: Globalization induces changes in the structure of the public sphere, but it does not necessarily create a new and larger public sphere entity.

An important aspect of this globalization process is an increased *connectedness* across distance. Thus, globalization may not result in an expansion of the public sphere from a national to a global level, but rather in an increased openness and dependency between different national public spheres and between the general public sphere of any national society and different specialized and professionalized public fora that have transnational connections. The boundaries between different public fora become permeable and each forum becomes increasingly influenced by and dependent upon the activities in other fora. As such, the process could be described as a gradual *deterritorialization* (Tomlinson, 1999) of the public sphere: The flow of information, the representation of interests, and the deliberation on arguments may still be primarily concerned with and addressed to a national community and its political institutions, but due to the public sphere's increased openness and connectedness to a world beyond national borders, including other public spheres, a *global reflexivity* gradually gains foothold. Fewer and fewer political topics can be dealt with in the absence of influential information and arguments originating from outside the national realm. Even the most urgent calls for strictly local or national political solutions can be thought of as a reaction to the increased presence of global problems inside the national public sphere. As such, the globalization of the public sphere can be reconceptualized: It should not be understood as the expansion of the national public sphere model to a global level, but as *the process through which the national public sphere gradually becomes deterritorialized*. Through this process it becomes open to and dependent upon other public fora at various geographical and institutional levels and with different degrees of universality and specialization. Thus, globalization of the public sphere is not about the creation of *the* global public sphere, but rather about the increased presence of global connections within the national framework. This introduces a global reflexivity in the public sphere that, in the long run, will influence and alter the structure of the national public sphere and its relation to both political institutions and civil society.

It is important to avoid a media-centric interpretation of current developments. The globalization of the public sphere is not only a product of increased media flows across borders. The presence and impact of global or regional problems within national political spheres may not even primarily be a media-driven process. In the case of Europe, the development of European political institutions and adjacent bureaucratic machinery and, subsequently, the creation of a general publicity around EU issues in member countries – as well as the rise of specialized and professionalized fora for more or less public debate about EU – have largely been driven by political and economic forces. The EU has tried to use media to foster the Europeanization of the public sphere. The reverse has not been the case: The EU has not been called for by a mediated transnational publicity.

In order to evaluate the influence of media upon the globalization of the public sphere, we must consider that current media developments take place more or less autonomously from the development of political institutions. This is very different from the history of the rise of the national public sphere. Here, the formation of the press, radio and later television was intertwined with the development of political parties, national cultural policies etc. The press, radio and television began as political or cultural institutions within the nation-state, whereas global media such as satellite television or the Internet are not political or cultural institutions in the same sense. Commercial media should rather be considered as media institutions, i.e., their activities are governed qua their status as commercial media enterprises and not by national political or cultural obligations. Global media may certainly influence national public spheres, but they are not from the outset part of political institutions. They may, through their function as mediators of publicity, become political institutions in their own right (Cook, 1998), but the activity and geographical expansion of global media firms are not closely connected to or determined by other political institutions. Thus, in order to understand the impact of news media on globalization of the public sphere, it is particularly important to consider the news media from the perspective of *news as an international industry and business*. The globalizing impact of news media stems from the transformations that are taking place within the international news industry.

CHANGES IN THE INTERNATIONAL NEWS INDUSTRY

For most of the 19th and 20th centuries, news media were confined to the nation-state. Newspapers, radio and television addressed a national audience, and only during wars and the Cold War were special news services originating in one country specifically aimed at other countries and regions. Propaganda channels like Radio Free Europe, Radio Liberty etc. were exceptions to the general rule of news media as a national service. News items about international and foreign affairs were either provided by national media correspondents or by international news agencies. The major news agencies such as Reuters, Associated Press, UPI, AFP and Tass acted on a global scale, but they were not global media in the same sense as some of the big media enterprises are today. They were *international* agencies, each originating in a specific country (The major powers Britain, USA, France, and Soviet Union), and their sole task was to provide news to be disseminated through national news media. Thus, the international agencies were attuned to the needs of national media. They were not news media with an audience of their own.

News media were embedded in a rather stable and simple two-level social geography: wholesale news agencies at an international level and news media at a national level. Due to the deregulation of media industries and the proliferation of new media distribution technologies such as satellite television and the Internet during the 1980s and 1990s, this stable structure gradually altered. Both wholesale news providers and national media began to cross the national borders in new ways, and news services operating at another geographical level began to emerge. Not only did the geographical levels begin to shift, but the types of services and customers also began to diversify and alter through this process. These developments reflected changes in the structure of the international news industry that can be summarized under the headings: The rise of transnational actors, vertical and horizontal integration, commercialization, diversification of output, regionalization, and abundance of supply.

The rise of transnational actors. News media have always operated across national borders in order to distribute news about the world. However, what is new about current developments is the spread of actors that do not operate on the basis of the national unit, but address a region (e.g., Euronews), a language community across several countries (German, Spanish etc.), a religious, ethnic or national community dispersed over a wide territory (e.g., Turks in Europe), or – potentially – the entire globe (BBC World, CNN International etc.).

Vertical integration. The boundaries between the wholesale news providers, the news agencies, the retail level, and the news services have become fuzzy. International news services like CNN and BBC World are aimed at a general audience, but some broadcasters also use them as news agencies. Wholesale news agencies like Reuters can similarly be reached directly by the general audience through the Internet, and some Internet portals use agencies as news services for a general audience almost without any re-editing (Paterson, 2001). Some wholesale news providers also offer complete packages with special news and current affairs that can be used directly by newspapers and broadcasters. Such prepackaged material is frequently used by commercial broadcasters with little money – or few ambitions – to spend on journalism.

Horizontal integration. Transnational media firms merge or develop strategic financial, technical and editorial cooperation with other media firms in order to provide a diverse media platform for whole regions. News and current affairs are important components in a varied media platform; without them a regional media package would appear incomplete. Thus, the broadcast news component CNN is to the Time-Warner-AOL conglomerate, as Sky News is to the Murdoch empire.

Commercialization. In the past, international news services were (apart from the wholesale news agencies) almost entirely an activity of public or government agencies. They served a nation's geopolitical strategies (e.g., keeping the British Empire together, US propaganda against Soviet Union etc.) and were not supposed to be financially viable. The transnational news services of today are predominantly commercial in nature. Some may have public service obligations or serve similar public 'duties', but increasingly they must be able to produce a profit in the market place. The same process is taking place at a national level, due to deregulation of national media industries. News is generally being subject to a process of commodification, in which the linkage between news and journalism, on the one hand, and political institutions, on the other, is being weakened.

Diversification of output. In the past, both wholesale news agencies and news services produced and distributed general news for a general audience. There were different journalistic formats such as short news and background stories, and other journalistic genres such as current affairs programs. But across these formats, the journalistic ambition was to present information of general interest to the general public. Today's transnational news services have diversified the output, providing special news themes for special audiences: sports news, entertainment news, business news, crime news, medical/health news, technology news, youth news etc. The wholesale news agencies have adjusted their services accordingly, providing a wide variety of news packages and feeds that make such diversification possible for even small broadcasters. General news is still important, but it has become one news genre among many others.

Regionalization. In the first years of satellite television, many channels tried to reach as broad an audience as possible: CNN tried to be as global as possible, several channels in Europe tried to reach the whole of Europe etc. This globalizing strategy – offering the same menu to more and more people – soon turned out to be a failure. The strategy for the last decade has been to regionalize programming, i.e., adjust it to 'local' interests and needs. Often – not least due to financial limitations – what really takes place is a kind of quasi-regionalization, in which some of the content is produced specifically for the region and some of it is recycled from the mother-company's global services. [. . .]

Abundance of supply. During the last two decades, the availability of news about events in the world has increased considerably. Not least the global distribution of pictures and video has grown enormously. Prior to this, foreign news, and particularly foreign news footage, was a scarce resource. Thus, editorial choices were limited to a much narrower scope than today. The Eurovision News Exchange, which has supplied the public service broadcasters in Europe with raw video footage since the late 1950s, only distributed 3-4 news items a day in the first half of the 1960s. Today, there is an almost continuous feed of news video 24 hours a day from both Eurovision and private agencies into the newsrooms of European broadcasters (Hjarvard, 1995). Previously, the editorial problem was to obtain foreign video news. Today, the problem is to choose among thousands of possible stories. Today there is at least the potential for much more diverse, individualized, and extended coverage of foreign news.

THE INTERNET CHALLENGE

Most of the above-mentioned changes in the news industry may be considered as responses to the overall deregulation of media markets during the 1980s and 1990s. However, current changes in the news industry are also spurred by the rise of a new media platform: the Internet. During its short existence the Internet has already had an enormous impact – until now perhaps more on the news industry itself than on the actual consumption of news. The Internet incites a globalization of both news media and public spaces.

Almost all actors in the news industry have developed Internet services. They began by putting more or less the same content on the net as was distributed through their traditional services (press or broadcasting). However, Internet news services have already bypassed this initial stage of development, and Internet news sites are no longer simple reproductions of the newspaper or the television newscast. Increasingly, news sites make use of properties of the Internet and integrate text, audio, and video by combining mass communication (one way distribution from one to many) with interactive, individualized communication (two-way distribution: chat, e-mail responses, opinion polls among readers etc.). The Internet medium challenges the traditional news services in many ways, one of which concerns the distinction between geographical entities. The Internet will gradually make the boundaries between national, foreign, and international news media less clear and obvious.

With the advent of the Internet, the problem of global reach is no longer a technical one as seen from the point of view of the news service providers. For television and radio stations, access to satellite distribution platforms has been – and still is – a crucial problem, and in order to have a global reach, TV and radio stations must purchase access to a series of satellite platforms around the world. In the case of the Internet, global reach is instantaneous once you have published your news on the net. Global reach is, of course, hampered by uneven (social and geographical) distribution of access to the Internet. From the point of view of the receiver, Internet news media may be inaccessible (due to economic, legal or other restrictions) or only accessible at certain places (work, school etc.). However, once the consumer has access to the Internet as such, *all* news services in the world are potentially available. This is very different from the printed press and broadcasting; they are only available individually or in packages, typically on a subscription basis. The abundance of available material on the Internet makes the question of consumer choice less a matter of technical limitations or distribution costs and more a matter of consumer knowledge about available services. Thus, branding of news and media services has acquired new importance, and we are currently witnessing a veritable 'battle of brands' on the Internet, in which transnational media firms try to consolidate themselves as 'the places' – places the consumer knows and regularly visits in the new media landscape (Hjarvard, 2000b).

With the Internet, the problem of global reach becomes a question of *language and content*. News broadcasters have had to expand their distribution network in order to technically reach a bigger audience, whereas Internet news providers can enlarge their audience through a differentiation of language (multi-language editions) and content (special editions for different segments of the audience). Differentiation through language has also been a possibility for international news broadcasters, but in practice it has been impeded by practical and financial problems. In Internet news, you can translate text and edit video segments with voice-over in another language, but the television news format is so dominated by the 'talking heads' of anchors and journalists that it is difficult to make multi-language editions without considerable extra expense. Euronews is one of the few examples of such an attempt to produce multi-language broadcast news, but not necessarily a successful one.

The experience of global Internet news services like BBC On-line has been that the audience wants to engage directly with the publisher, i.e., the journalists and editors (Burden, 1999). Practice has already demonstrated that audiences actually respond (through e-mail, chat etc.) to the news. Furthermore, the audience wants their active responses to be taken seriously, responded to, and represented as a part of the news service. In many ways, these responses resemble letters to newspaper editors or phone-ins to radio programs. However, in the case of Internet news, the responses can arrive from any corner of the world. This is not just a hypothetical possibility. Experience from, for instance, the BBC On-line service demonstrates that audiences from many parts of the world respond and become represented on the net. This is in contrast to the older news media. Newspaper readers may write letters to their national newspapers, but extremely few would write letters to the editor of an international newspaper. Similarly, viewers and listeners may write or phone their national broadcaster, but very few would phone international broadcasters like CNN or Euronews. On the Internet – due to the medium's interactive and more spontaneous character – users have fewer reasons to hesitate sending an e-mail to an organization in another part of the world. Internet news services have actively tried to make use of this phenomenon and developed special web-pages with thematic discussions about certain news topics (e.g., BBC On-line's

'Talking Point', CNN's 'Chat' section). The contributors to these discussions are not equally distributed throughout the world. On BBC's 'Talking Point', a majority of contributors come from Great Britain, former British colonies and English-speaking countries, which in part is a reflection of the 'British bias' in the editorial selection of themes for discussion. However, contributors are not only from countries with Anglo-American connections, but from many other countries with a different cultural heritage and colonial background. The public discussions on the Internet news sites are, thus, not global in the sense that they encompass all parts of the world to the same extent, but they are globalized fora of discussion because the boundaries between nationalities have become less important for the conduct of political discussion.

The Internet allows for an integration of formerly distinct news media and journalistic genres. Within the same news service, you get both video and audio reports, written news and background stories, on-line discussion etc. Internet news can have both speed and breadth, and as such, it combines qualities of broadcasting and the press. The international news broadcasters have primarily earned their reputation on their speediness. They can provide a news update and overview at short notice to a global audience, but they are rarely of much use for those seeking background information or in-depth analysis. Internet news services have an advantage compared to the TV news broadcasters, because they also provide background, documentation and analysis accessible where and when the user needs it. The Internet stimulates a transnationalization of the newspaper in the same way as broadcast news has been transnationalized via satellite broadcasting. With the Internet, the journalistic content and formats of the newspaper can be transnationalized. The Internet provides an opportunity for newspapers to develop a transnational audience, but it also poses a threat to newspapers because other actors (from broadcasting, publishing industries etc.) may develop transnational news services that in the long run could limit the national newspaper audience. The multimedia character of the new media environment also stimulates a transnationalization of media industries. Increasingly, it becomes necessary for news media to have industrial capacity and expertice within several media. In order to develop diverse news services in television, radio, newspaper and the Internet – and with few possibilities to finance the new services on the Internet directly and fully through advertising or subscription – many media firms are forced to merge or cooperate with other media firms, often forming transnational and regional alliances.

OUTWARD AND INWARD

Changes in the media sector influence the ways in which public spaces come to be organized and represented, and, subsequently, how social actors may interact with each other in these spaces. Globalization implies a deterritorialization of public spaces, but – as should be clear by now – this gradual de-linkage of social interaction from extant social spaces is not characterized by one singular logic and does not move the public sphere in any single direction. The different logics and directions as well as the tensions between them constitute the topic of the last part of this article.

New media technology has not only allowed transnational media firms to penetrate the national public sphere, but also made it possible for national media institutions to expand their presence on a worldwide scale. Emigrants have long been able to maintain some contact with their country of origin through the short-wave radio services of the national broadcaster or subscription to a newspaper in their mother tongue. With satellite radio and television as well as the Internet, this possibility has expanded both in volume and quality. Through satellite radio and television, they can receive a service that often addresses them as a majority and not as a special enclave living abroad, as has often been the case for short-wave radio. Furthermore, satellite television and Internet provide this long-distance contact with a more sensuous and interactive quality than that of short-wave radio and newspapers. It has become possible not only to hear and read, but also to see people, places, and current events and to some extent interact with them directly on an on-line basis.

The cultural repertoire has also been extended. Satellite television and Internet provide a mixture of music, drama, news, talk shows, information, current affairs etc., whereas the short-wave radio services typically provided a more narrow repertoire of (official) news, current affairs and high culture. It has become possible to maintain or revive a sense of belonging to a culture and society that in geographical terms is far away, but that due to electronic media has achieved a new presence and immediacy in everyday life. This belonging may not necessarily be related to the official national culture or society, but just as likely to a particular linguistic community or culture within a nation, which through transnational media connections is both invigorated and altered.

Current developments not only stimulate an outward distribution of national media, but also an inward orientation in the media content. This is at least the case for broadcasting, including broadcast news. The last decade has not only demonstrated an increase in transnational distribution of television programs but also a growth in nationally produced television programs. Thus, in many EC countries a domestication of prime time television is taking place (Moran, 1998). Due to increased competition and commercial pressures in television news, the proportion of news dealing with foreign or international events has tended to decline. In order to keep high ratings for the news, broadcasters often give priority to coverage of events that audiences can identify with. In story selection, *proximity* to the audience often becomes a more important criterion than societal importance (Hjarvard, 1999 and 2000a). As a result, foreign and international topics, and particularly stories dealing with complex international phenomena, receive less coverage than before. As competition and commercialization increase, this tendency becomes more profound. Thus, commercial broadcasters typically carry less (and shorter) news stories and current affairs programs about international problems than do public service broadcasters (Hjarvard, 1999; Krüger, 1997; Stone, 2000).

Although there is an abundance of stories available about international issues through different transnational media, deregulation of broadcasting has in some areas increased the focus on domestic issues. In terms of news content, national broadcast news media often become more national and domestic than previously. This domestic orientation is, however, somewhat countered by another tendency that potentially alters the notion of 'foreign news'. Previously, foreign news denoted news about international politics and events in other nations. Today, many other news topics have acquired a foreign or international dimension (e.g., the environment, technology, fashion, culture), making the borders between foreign and domestic news less clear and obvious (Holm et al., 2000).

[. . .]

DIFFERENTIATION AND INTERCONNECTIONS

In the beginning of this article, a paradox concerning globalization, media and the public sphere was observed: During major international events, the formation of public opinion occasionally expands to a global level, acquiring its own political momentum and influencing both governments and international organizations to act in specific ways. However, most questions concerning day-to-day international and foreign politics are primarily discussed at a national level, through the media and political institutions of the national public sphere. Special and professional public fora have developed at a transnational level, but not a general public sphere. As a result, public discussion in the media about international and foreign affairs is generally framed by national political interests. In this sense, political discussion in the public sphere is less globalized compared to transformations in industry, finance, governance, culture etc.

This apparently contradictory development may be reconsidered in light of the present interpretation of globalization of the public sphere. Globalization of media does not entail the creation of a singular global public sphere, but rather the development of a *multi-layered* structure of publicity, in which new transnational fora for public discussion and information dissemination develop, but also in which national and local public spheres continue to play a very important role. Globalization implies a gradual *differentiation* of the public sphere. This is due both to a general increase in the social complexity of modern societies requiring specialist knowledge even for public deliberation and to transformations in the media industry. News media not only transcend national borders, but are also specialized as regards content, audience, formats, geographical region etc. Differentiation implies a certain degree of separation of public fora, and this, to some extent, challenges the generalist model of the public sphere: general news media for a general public.

[...]

MUTUAL ACCOUNTABILITY

The globalization of industry, finance and culture has been seen by many as a potential threat to democracy. Because political institutions and the public sphere remain largely tied to a national level, it becomes difficult to exercise governance in global affairs through democratic processes. Neither industrial nor political actors at a transnational level tend to be accountable to the political deliberations of the national public sphere. Potentially, political action could be decoupled from public political deliberation: 'Globalization means that those who can be kept accountable have little control over the factors affecting peoples lives, and those who have the decisive power are beyond democratic reach' (Eriksen, 1999: 43). As a political response to globalization, there has been a call for the extension of both political accountability and the public sphere from a national to a global level (Garnham, 1990; Held, 1995). In light of the argument put forward in this article, current developments in (news) media industries do not suggest that a transnational or global public sphere is likely to emerge in the future, if such publicity is understood as a singular entity based on the national public sphere model. The public sphere is not unaffected by globalization, but the impact of globalization is best described as a gradual deterritorialization of the public sphere. However, this objection does not render the question of global publicity and democratic accountability superfluous.

Current developments carry both promises and dangers for democracy in relation to public discussion of governance in global affairs. Differentiation of news media services carries the danger of a fragmentation of the public sphere, in which transnational and specialist news media increasingly serve a well-educated elite, and national and local media increasingly cater to the taste of disempowered social groups for whom globalization only poses a threat. From this point of view, the biggest problem may not necessarily be the unaccountability of transnational media industries to nation-states – as the political economy tradition would suggest – but the tendency of national and local media to develop very domestic, in some cases even aggressive nationalistic perspectives on global affairs.

Globalization of media also provides some opportunities for democratic discussion of global public affairs. The multi-layered structure of publicity is open to a high level of interconnectivity, allowing for the creation of public debate across national borders and the formation of a transnational public opinion that can potentially make international actors (industries, governments etc.) accountable on specific issues. So far, the formation of public opinion on a transnational or global scale has been a very volatile phenomenon, not least because the interconnections between various levels of publicity do not exhibit predictable patterns. When or why an event or problem might develop into a global issue is very hard to foretell.

In order to improve both public debate on questions of a global nature and the accountability of political agency to this publicity, the connectivity between various levels must be strengthened. Globalization of the public sphere is not about creating a world citizenship, but about creating connections of mutual public accountability across various socio-geographical levels. Thus, as regards mediated publicity, the challenge is to make transnational news media more orientated toward and accountable to national and local public spheres, while keeping national and local media orientated toward and responsible to the agenda of the outside world.

NOTES

1. Quoted from Taylor (1997: 90).
2. Quoted from Taylor (1997: 92) and Flourney & Stewart (1997: vii), respectively.

REFERENCES

Burden, Peter (1999) Interactivity and Online News at the BBC. Leicester: University of Leicester (unpublished MA thesis).

Collins, Richard (1994) *Broadcasting and Audio-Visual Policy in the European Single Market.* London: John Libbey.

Collins, Richard (1996) 'Europæisk Kultur – et Fantasifoster?' [European Culture – a Chimera?], *MedieKultur* no. 25, September 1996.

Collins, Richard (1998) *From Satellite to Single Market.* London: Routledge.

Cook, Timothy E. (1998) *Governing with the News. The News Media as a Political Institution.* Chicago: University of Chicago Press.

Eriksen, Erik Oddvar (1999) *Is Democracy Possible Today?* Aarhus: Magtudredningen.

Flourney, Don M. (1992) *CNN World Report. Ted Turner's International News Group.* London: John Libbey (Acamedia Research Monograph 9).

Flourney, Don M. & Stewart, Robert K. (1997) *CNN. Making News in the Global Market.* Luton: University of Luton Press.

Garnham, Nicholas (1990) *Capitalism and Communication. Global Culture and the Economics of Information.* London: Sage.

Giddens, Anthony (1999) *Runaway World. How Globalisation is Reshaping Our Lives.* London: Profile Books.

Gutstadt, L.E. (1993) 'Taking the Pulse of the CNN Audience: A Case Study of the Gulf War', *Political Communication,* vol. 10.

Held, David (1995) *Democracy and the Global Order. From the Modern State to Cosmopolitan Governance,* Cambridge: Polity Press.

Held, David; McGrew, Anthony; Goldblatt, David & Perraton, Jonathan (1999) *Global Transformations. Politics, Economics and Culture.* Cambridge: Polity.

Hjarvard, Stig (1993) 'Pan European Television News. Towards a European Political Public Sphere?', in Drummond, Phillip; Paterson, Richard & Willis, Janet: *National Identity and Europe.* London: British Film Institute.

Hjarvard, Stig (1995) *Internationale tv-nyheder.* [International Television News.] København: Akademisk Forlag.

Hjarvard, Stig (1999) *Tv-nyheder in konkurrence.* [Television News in Competition.] København: Samfundslitteratur.

Hjarvard, Stig (2000a) 'Proximity. The Name of the Ratings Game', *Nordicom Review,* vol.21, no.2, Special Issue, Göteborg: Nordicom.

Hjarvard, Stig (2000b) *Mediated Encounters*. København: Global Media Cultures/ University of Copenhagen (Working Paper no. 2).

Holm, Hans-Henrik; Kabel, Lars; Kitaj, Torben; Møller, Lars & Ytzen, Flemming (2000) *Verden på Tilbud*. [The World on Offer.] Aarhus: CFJE/Ajour.

Jensen, Klaus Bruhn (1998) (ed.) *News of the World. World Cultures Look at Television News*. London: Routledge.

Krüger, Udo Michael (1997) 'Polltikberichterstattung in den Fernsehnachrichten', *Media Perspektiven*, no.5.

Köhler, Martin (1998) 'From the National to the Cosmopolitan Public Sphere', in Archibugi, Daniele; Held, David & Köhler, Martin (eds) *Re-imagining Political Community. Studies in Cosmopolitan Democracy*. Cambridge: Polity Press.

Moran, Albert (1998) *Copycat Television. Globalisation, Program Formats and Cultural Identity*. Luton: University of Luton Press.

Paterson, Chris (2001) 'Media Imperialism Revisited', in Hjarvard, Stig (ed.) *News in a Globalized Society*. Göteborg: Nordicom.

Schiller, Herbert I. (1993) 'Transnational Media: Creating Consumers Worldwide', *International Affairs*, vol.47, no.1.

Schlesinger, Philip (1993) 'Wishful Thinking: Cultural Politics, Media, and Collective Identities in Europe', *Journal of Communication*, vol.43, no.2, New York: Oxford University Press.

Schlesinger, Philip (1999) *Media and Belonging: Changing Communicative Spaces and the European Union*. The conference 'Reimagining Belonging', Aalborg University, 6-8 May 1999 (paper).

Serra, Sonia (2000) 'The Killing of Brazilian Street Children and the Rise of the International Public Sphere', in Curran, James (ed.) *Media Organisations in Society*. London: Arnold.

Sparks, Colin (1998) 'Is there a Global Public Sphere?', in Thussu, Daya K. (ed.) *Electronic Empires. Global Media and Local Resistance*. London: Arnold.

Stone, Jennie (2000) *Losing Perspective: Global Affairs on British Terrestrial Television 1989–1999*, Third World and Environment Broadcasting Project (3WE), United Kingdom.

Taylor, Philip M. (1997) *Global Communications, International Affairs and the Media Since 1945*. London: Routledge.

Tomlinson, John (1999) *Globalization and Culture*. Cambridge: Polity Press.

54

BAD NEWS FROM ISRAEL

Greg Philo and Mike Berry

INTRODUCTION

The Israeli-Palestinian conflict is deep and long-standing. In all such conflicts the origins and history of particular events are contested by the different parties involved. Participants tell the story from their own point of view and often to legitimise their own actions. In the course of this study we interviewed a large number of journalists who had worked in this area. [. . .]

[. . .]

Television news remains the main source of information on world events for a large majority of the population. A recent study by the Independent Television Commission of viewing habits found that in 2002, 79 per cent of the population regarded television news as their main source of world news (ITC, 2003). We have shown above the patterns of explanation which exist in news coverage and the manner in which some perspectives on the conflict are dominant. We will now explore the possible links between these structures in news content and the nature of audience belief. This will cover issues such as the role of visual imagery and how the inclusion or exclusion of different types of explanation may influence audience understanding. We will also examine the manner in which the structuring of reports may influence belief, for example, that one side in the conflict is often presented as initiating action while the other 'responds'. We also analyse links between audience understanding of stories and the effect of this on levels of interest – if people do not understand,

From Greg Philo and Mike Berry, *Bad News from Israel* (London: Pluto Press, 2004).

do they simply switch off? Another key area is to examine how it might be possible to increase audience comprehension in this very complex area of news output.

Samples and Method

For this work we used both questionnaire and focus group techniques. The focus groups consisted of seven to eight people on average, who engaged in activities and discussion with a single moderator. They were selected on the basis of income, age and gender. Thus they included ten groups of middle-class and low-income men and women (aged around 25–50), plus one group of elderly people (aged over 65) and three further groups of young people aged 17–23, who were students. This was a total of 100 people. A list of the groups is given below. As far as is possible we selected 'normally occurring' groups, that is, people who would meet and speak with each other in the normal course of their lives. Thus some groups were drawn from parents at a school in London, and were local residents; others met for social activities, such as a group of women who went to dance classes together; others worked together, such as groups of teachers, cleaners and office workers, and some groups included family members.

Participants in focus groups

1. Low income male and female cleaners/janitors, Glasgow (six people).
2. Low-income females, residents, Hammersmith, London (five people).
3. Low-income males, residents, Hammersmith, London (ten people).
4. Middle-class males, residents, St Albans (four people).
5. Middle-class females, office workers, Glasgow (four people).
6. Middle-class females, dance class, Paisley (eleven people).
7. Middle-class males, residents, Glasgow (four people).
8. Middle-class male and female teachers, Paisley (six people).
9. Middle-class females, residents, Hammersmith, London (six people).
10. Middle-class males, residents, Hammersmith, London (eight people).
11. Young male and female students, Glasgow (ten people).
12. Young male and female students, Glasgow (eleven people).
13. Young male and female students, Glasgow (five people).
14. Elderly/retired males and females, Glasgow (ten people).

This project was designed with the help of journalists and broadcasting professionals. One of its key features was that we invited journalists to sit in on focus groups, to take part in the discussions and to raise issues as they wished. [. . .]

We also had a specific interest in the responses of young people since there is a considerable contemporary debate on their usage of news and on whether this relates to how well they are informed on politics and world affairs and to their level of interest in these. Part of the work for the focus groups involved the detailed discussion of a series of questions about the Israeli-Palestinian conflict. We developed an abbreviated version of these and asked them in questionnaire form to two separate groups of British students (one of 300, the other 280) aged between 17 and 23. These two groups were asked the same questions one year apart, in October 2001 and October 2002. For purposes of comparison we also asked the same questions to two groups of students from Germany and the United States (114 from Germany who were High School students aged 16–18, and 49 from the US who were Journalism/Communications students aged 20–21). Thus our total sample was 100 in focus groups and 743 who answered the questionnaire.

Focus Group Methods and Questions Asked

A key feature of this work was to identify the nature and sources of audience belief. The media are a key source of information, so one dimension of the study was to analyse how people respond to messages and to examine the conditions under which they accepted or rejected what they heard or saw. At the beginning of each focus group, the moderator explained to those present that they would be asked questions about the conflict, but it was also stressed that this was not a 'quiz'. The group were told that we were only interested in what each person knows and understands and that it did not matter to us if their answers were 'right' or 'wrong'. We are studying the judgements they have made about the information they have received and the processes by which beliefs are formed. It is an important part of this method to explain very carefully what we are doing and to establish a level of trust with the participants so that they are not afraid to say what they are actually thinking.

The method and sequence of activities in the focus groups were as follows. First, we asked nine questions about the conflict and sources of information which had been used. Each member of the groups gave written answers to these questions:

1. What comes into your mind when you hear the words 'Israeli-Palestinian conflict?' It might be a picture, it might be something someone has said, it might be something you have read or seen, or even somewhere you went on holiday – but what comes into your head?

2a). What is the source of what came into you head when you heard 'Israeli-Palestinian conflict'?

2b). Are there any other sources which you have ever used to find out information about that particular conflict?

For questions 3 and 4 the groups were read a phrase from television news which used the words 'occupied' and 'settlers'. The phrase was 'the settlers who have made their homes in occupied territory' (BBC1 early evening News, 9 February 2001). They were then asked:

3. Who is occupying the occupied territories?
4. What nationality are the settlers?
5. In the period since the intifada began (September 2000), which side would you say has had the most casualties? Is it a lot more Israelis, a few more Israelis, about the same for each side, a few more Palestinians or a lot more Palestinians?
6. Why are they fighting? What is the conflict about?
7. There have been a number of wars in that region since the Second World War which involved Israel. Can you name any of them and give dates?
8. What land or countries were occupied in these conflicts?
9. Do you know of any United Nations resolutions or any criticisms that have been made by the UN about the actions of anyone in the conflict?

Following this, we then gave each group member a set of 16 photographs that were taken from TV news coverage. The photographs showed the main areas of reporting as revealed in our content analysis, They included images of fighting, stone-throwing, the aftermath of a suicide-bombing and pictures of past peace talks and negotiations (for example, of Yasser Arafat meeting President Clinton and Ehud Barak). The group members were then asked to imagine that they were journalists and to write a brief news story using the pictures as a stimulus. The purpose of this was to examine whether they were able to reproduce news language and the explanations of the conflict which were prominent in news accounts. This was then followed by a discussion about the pictures they had used and their understanding of them. For example, one picture featured a group of Palestinians burning an American flag. We asked the group members what they understood from this and what the motive for this action might be. An important element of this procedure was to establish what information group members were taking from news accounts and whether they believed what they were told. Some people who were well informed about the conflict could write very good versions of the news but were also quite critical of it, so the ability to reproduce a news programme is not the same as actually believing the news. However, the news writing exercise and the questions provided an excellent starting point for extended discussions about what the group members did understand and believe about the reasons for the conflict and the manner in which they were informed.

After the news writing exercise, the moderator initiated a further discussion by going through each of the questions and asking in detail about how the group members had arrived at their answers. In practice the participants often joined in spontaneously to offer their own personal histories and accounts of how they had come to understand the conflict. This then led to a more extended discussion on the origins and causes of the conflict. The moderator then raised other specific issues such as whether the group had heard of the Palestinian refugees or knew their history. They were also asked about how they 'saw' the conflict, for example, as 'religious' or 'economic' or simply as a dispute between bad neighbours. How did they see the 'trouble' as starting, and had they heard of other issues such as disputes over water and how it was controlled?

Finally we discussed the general issue of how understanding related to levels of interest. In the group sessions, many questions were addressed to the moderator and to the journalist present by group members who simply wanted to know more and to increase their own understanding. We will discuss this further in our results section, but it was clear that a major reason for viewers 'turning off' from the news was simply that they had little understanding of what they were watching.

QUALITATIVE AND QUANTITATIVE APPROACHES

'Qualitative' methods imply a concentration on processes of meaning and understanding. There are several advantages in using the qualitative techniques of focus group work (so called because they offer a higher qualitative integrity of data). The first is that they enable the investigator to check that the respondents have really understood the questions and that the answers given do reflect what is actually believed. A second advantage is that the detailed discussion often throws up other related issues which can be pursued. For example, when we asked questions about the reasons for the conflict, a frequent response was that it was over 'land'. But we did not realise until the discussions that some people understood this to mean that it was a form of border dispute in which two countries fought over a piece of land which separated them. Another advantage of such discussions is that, as people hear more arguments and information with which they are unfamiliar, it is possible to see how beliefs are modified and develop. A further very important element of the focus group approach is that it enables a rapport or level of trust to develop between those taking part and the moderator, so that people become less guarded and more prepared to say what they really believe. It takes time for people to think carefully about the origins of their own understanding and to be clear about what they are being asked to do. We can see this if we consider an actual exchange of views in a focus group. In this example, the moderator asks about the issue of who is seen to be 'starting' the violence and how this is shown on the news. The difficulty with this for the group was that some of them were sympathetic to the Palestinians. As it turned out they did think that the news presented the Israelis as responding to Palestinian 'action'. But they were reluctant to acknowledge this because they themselves rejected this way of seeing the conflict. It took some time to separate their beliefs about what was 'really' happening from what they were 'seeing' on the news. The moderator began by asking if the news gave the impression of one side starting the fighting while the other 'retaliates':

> *First speaker*: It depends what you call fighting because they are depriving them of the things they are depriving them of and that's an aggressive act in itself.
>
> *Moderator*: But do you get the sense that one side is starting the actual . . .
>
> *First speaker*: Yeah, the Israelis.
>
> *Moderator*: You get the sense that the Israelis are firing the guns first . . .
>
> *First speaker*: Not firing the guns but they're doing things that are leaving the Palestinians thinking they have no choice.
>
> *Moderator*: I just wonder if from the news you get the sense that one side is starting it and the other side retaliates . . .
>
> *First speaker*: Usually what we see on the news is the Palestinians doing something and the Israelis overreacting.
>
> *Moderator*: How many people think it comes across as the Palestinians doing something like a suicide-bomb and the Israelis retaliate? [*No response*]
>
> Nobody sees this thing about retaliation? Because a minute ago you were saying you did see it as the Palestinians starting it and the Israelis retaliating.
>
> *First speaker*: But you're assuming that I trust what I see on the news.
>
> *Moderator*: No, I'm not saying do you believe it, that's separate. I'm saying do you think it comes across as that?
>
> *First speaker*: Maybe to other people, yeah.
>
> *Moderator*: Let me make that point again, I'm asking you does it come across as that – whether you believe it or not is another matter – does it come across as one side doing something and then the other side retaliating? How many people think that? I'm not talking about whether you believe it or not. Before, you said it did come across as that.
>
> *First speaker*: Well that's obviously what we are led to believe and what most people believe.
>
> *Moderator*: I'm not sure that it is.
>
> *Second speaker*: In reality, you could have half a brain like me, but you wouldn't believe it – you could see the falsehoods in it.
>
> *Moderator*: That's a separate question – whether you believe it or not, I'm only interested in what you think the news is saying.
>
> *First speaker*: It does seem the way they report it on the news.
>
> *Second speaker*: It's being portrayed that way, yes.
>
> *First speaker*: It does seem that the Israelis are retaliating to something the Palestinians did.
>
> *Third speaker*: Yes.

> *Moderator*:   How many people think that? [*General nods*] How many, one, two, three, four . . . eight. (Low-income group, London)

Establishing what people do actually believe can take time. As the first speaker commented after this exchange: 'I just think we're a lot of paranoid people.'

Another advantage of the focus group discussion is that participants can reproduce the everyday speech and interaction with each other in which they might 'normally' discuss TV or what they have seen or read about current events. This can show how the assumptions of cause and the relationships presented in the media become part of everyday speech. For example, in the following exchange one participant explains why he thinks most casualties are Israeli, and then a second person spontaneously introduces the 'retaliation' theme which he expresses with the words 'getting their own back':

> *First speaker*:   Because of the indiscriminate attacks. It seems like there's been more Palestinian attacks.
> *Second speaker*:   But if you watch the news you know that they always get their own back. (Middle-class male group, St Albans)

The focus group can also be combined with other qualitative techniques such as the personal interview, in which participants may be spoken with individually after the main session, to clarify specific points and to enable people to say anything which they were reluctant to comment on in the context of a group. This is important in areas of great personal sensitivity, for example, where we have investigated issues such as media coverage of child abuse or mental distress. The disadvantage of focus groups is the amount of time and resources they consume to establish such a high level of qualitative integrity of data. The corresponding advantage of questionnaire methods is that they enable very large numbers of people to give replies relatively quickly. Such quantitative techniques can give a snapshot of what people know or believe at any one time. But to examine in detail the processes by which such beliefs are formed really requires qualitative approaches such as the focus group.

THE QUESTIONNAIRES

We gave an abbreviated version of the questions which we used with the focus groups to our two groups of British students. The questions were:

1. When you hear the words 'Israeli-Palestinian conflict', what comes into your mind? What do you see in your head?
2a. What is the source of what you have just thought of, where did it come from?
2b. Are there any other sources which you have used to find out information about this conflict?

The same phrase from TV news ('the settlers who have made their homes in occupied territory') was read to them as with the focus groups. They were then asked:

3. Who is occupying the occupied territories?
4. What nationality are the settlers?
5. Since the beginning of the intifada, which side has had the most casualties? Is it a lot more Israelis, a few more Israelis, about the same for each, a few more Palestinians or a lot more Palestinians?
6. Where did the Palestinian refugees come from? How did they become refugees?
7. TV news has shown pictures of Palestinians burning the US flag, why would Palestinians do this?

We also took two groups of seven to eight students from this main sample and met them separately to discuss their answers, in a similar way to a normal focus group. The intention was to identify any problems which might have existed in answering the questions.

We also gave the same questionnaire to groups of American and German students, since we had a specific interst in the knowledge which young people had of world and political events. For the same reason we asked a series of additional questions which were not about the Israeli-Palestinian conflict. These questions related to a range of historical and contemporary events. The British, American and German students all gave answers to these. Some related to wars such as the Second World War and Vietnam, others to the history of the Soviet Union and the slave labour camps about which Solzhenitsyn wrote. We also asked about US interventions in Latin America: Nicaragua, where a private army was financed by the Reagan administration, and Guatemala, where the US was involved in the so-called 'dirty war'. The questions were as follows:

8. What were the Gulags in the Soviet Union?
9. In the Vietnam War how many casualties were there on each side, was it a lot more Americans, a few more Americans, about the same, a few more Vietnamese or a lot more Vietnamese?
10. Who were the Contras in Nicaragua?
11. In 1999 President Clinton made a public apology in Guatemala – why?
12. In the Second World War, which country of the Allies defeated the most German divisions?

These questions also offered an interesting point of comparison with the Israeli-Palestinian conflict, since many of the subjects to which they related were not covered at all in recent news reporting. Others such as the Second

World War and the Vietnam War have been featured in fictional accounts such as Hollywood films and made-for-TV dramas. It was therefore interesting to examine any differences in knowledge or understanding which might emerge from these variations in media output. [. . .]

RESULTS

The replies to the questionnaires and the responses and discussion in the focus groups fell into seven categories. These were:

1. Memories, images and associations that group members had of the conflict.
2. The sources of information used.
3. The origins, history and causes of the conflict.
4. The news writing exercise.
5. Beliefs about casualties.
6. Cultural identification and empathy.
7. Understanding and interest in news.

We will discuss each of these in turn.

MEMORIES, IMAGES AND ASSOCIATIONS

The first question was on what came into people's minds when they heard the words 'Israeli-Palestinian conflict'. The responses overwhelmingly referred to images of war, conflict and violence, such as 'war, death, children dying'; 'bombings, people dying'; 'gunmen, suicide-bombers' and 'children throwing stones at Israeli soldiers'. In our two large samples of British students 71 per cent and 79 per cent of them gave such answers (for the German students 82 per cent and US students 74 per cent) and for the focus groups it was 75 per cent. Others named general issues such as 'religious conflict' or political figures, and a few cited personal experiences. [. . .] There was one very noticeable difference between the British students interviewed in 2001 and the second group a year later in 2002. In 2001, 2 per cent of the first group named suicide-bombings, but this rose to 24 per cent in the second group a year later, which may be a result of the increased emphasis on Israeli casualties which we noted in our content analysis.

[. . .]

ORIGINS, HISTORY AND CAUSES OF THE CONFLICT

Most of the participants in this research had little idea of the history or origins of the conflict. In the large sample groups of British students in 2001, 4 per cent wrote that the Palestinians had been forced from their homes on the formation of Israel. In 2002 the figure was 8 per cent (for the German and American students the figure was 26 per cent and 19 per cent respectively [. . .]). For the British students there were an additional 14 per cent in 2001 and 22 per cent in 2002 who suggested that the Palestinians had in some way lost their homes because of Israel, or who mentioned the occupation as a factor – they used words such as 'kicked out', 'deported', 'evicted' or 'excluded'. The majority simply did not know or made general references to the problems of refugees, such as 'driven out by fear of war and hunger' or 'through armed conflict, bombing'. It was also clear from the focus groups that most people had very little detailed knowledge. The British students were studying social sciences, arts and history at university and the focus groups contained a strong representation of middle-class males/professionals who are high consumers of news. Even so, in the focus groups as a whole just 19 per cent mentioned the formation of Israel in relation to the Palestinian refugees and most could not name any wars in the region. The level of public knowledge as a whole is probably even lower than this.

[. . .]

There were some other reservations expressed in this and other groups as to how much historical detail could be included in news and whether longer historical accounts should be shown in dedicated current affairs programmes. A small number of people indicated that they were not interested in the subject or were just too busy – 'it goes in one ear and out the other', as one participant said. Another questioned whether audiences would want more in-depth accounts (middle-class males, London), but overall there was a strong feeling in the groups that it was difficult to understand the present without some knowledge of the past. [. . .]

THE NEWS WRITING EXERCISE

For the news writing exercise, each member of the focus groups was given a set of 16 photographs which were taken from TV news footage of the conflict. They were then asked to write a short news item using the pictures as a stimulus. They were not constrained to focusing on these pictures but in practice could write anything they wished. As a method this was designed to show what audiences have retained from news programmes. The pictures they were given included the aftermath of a suicide-bombing, an image of a dead Israeli soldier being pushed from a window, groups of Israelis rioting, a Palestinian boy being sheltered by his father as he was shot, and other images of stone-throwing, Palestinians in masks with guns and Israeli tanks. There were also pictures of prominent leaders and of peace negotiations showing Ehud Barak, Yasser Arafat and Bill Clinton, and a picture of Palestinians burning the American flag.

We found in this, as with other research using the same method, that many participants had a remarkable ability to reproduce both the content and structure of news bulletins. These are examples of 'news items' written by participants:

> In response to yesterday's attack on the settlers' camp at Yashmin, Israeli tanks again battered [Palestinian] refugee camps. The Israeli tanks destroyed seven buildings. Palestinian sources reported 14 casualties including four children. The Israeli commander denied that any Palestinian civilians had been involved. Palestinian crowds stoned Israeli soldiers through the night. During the day a suicide-bomber blew himself up. This was the first such attack outside the occupied territories for some months. The Israeli Premier said that the Israeli army would continue to take a hard and aggressive line while attacks on Israeli citizens continued. (Middle-class male, London)

[...]

Not all showed such high levels of ability in writing the news. Some were vague over who was doing what and why it was significant:

> The conflict between Israel and Palestine has been very violent, lots of guns and tanks. It has been caused by one of the parties invading land owned by the others. This land is currently unused but still does not belong to them. Leaders have tried deals to bring the fighting to an end but they have been futile. The fighting continues; it is the people themselves that are involved not just armies. (Young female student, Glasgow)

[...]

One of the reasons for the 'vagueness' amongst viewers is perhaps that the news itself is unspecific. We noted above in our content analysis that in reports of the onset of the intifada, Ariel Sharon was not named in many news bulletins and the significance of him as a figure to the Palestinians was not explained. Another participant in a Glasgow focus group made an important point about the nature of news reporting. She argued that the news effectively conveyed a series of emotional sequences (such as violence and its innocent victims) which characterised war reporting. As she comments, although the news had not conveyed 'the facts' to her she could still write the 'emotional' story:

> When I wrote about the pictures, I could have been writing about any war because obviously the facts have not been communicated to me there on the news, but the emotion of it all has, so I wrote about it in an emotional way. So it's like emotional reportage rather than factual reportage. (Female office worker, Glasgow)

[. . .]

BELIEFS ABOUT CASUALTIES

We asked the participants: 'Which side has had the most casulties? Is it a lot more Israelis, a few more Israelis, about the same for each, a few more Palestinians or a lot more Palestinians?' In the period of our analysis the Palestinians had a casualty rate which was in fact much higher than that of the Israelis (with a ratio of 2–3:1 in terms of deaths). Yet, if we look at the sample of British students from 2002, just 35 per cent knew that the Palestinians had significantly more casualties, while 43 per cent stated that there were more Israeli casulties or that the figures were the same for each side (for the Geerman students the figures were respectively 24 per cent and 51 per cent, and for the US students, 18 per cent and 47 per cent).

In the focus groups we found that 42 per cent of the participants believed either that Israel had the most casualties or that the numbers were about equal. The key factor in the first of these beliefs appeared to be the extensive coverage of attacks on Israelis and in particular of suicide-bombings:

> I couldn't remember any figures, but then I thought it was the one, I remembered it was the suicide-bombers. They are the ones who go in and take maybe a whole busload and I thought it would be more Israelis. I don't remember anything showing me the amount of Palestinians who have been killed – I don't remember that, but when it's something about Israelis being killed that has more effect on me – maybe there's more publicity about that. (Middle-class female, Paisley)
> Because of the indiscriminate attacks – it seems like there's been more Palestinian attacks. (Middle-class male, St Albans)
> The view of Israeli casualties was also linked to the perception about the Palestinians as being 'more hostile'.

[. . .]

Some people stated simply that they had seen more coverage of Israeli casualties: 'I thought I'd heard more about Israeli casualties on the news' (female student, Glasgow). One speaker believed the casualties were about equal, but commented that 'Usually the images you see are wounded Israelis. They show Palestinians but not as often or as powerfully' (male student, Glasgow). Another student commented on how she had 'picked up' her view that most casualties were Israeli: 'It must have been something I picked up from watching the news – you are surrounded by the media and you're not consciously taking it in but you do take it in and get a perspective' (female student, Glasgow).

There was another key factor in the formation of belief which related to the manner in which news accounts were structured. The presentation of violence as a constant sequence of attacks by each side had led some people to believe that casualties would be about equal. A participant from a group of elderly people commented that he thought the casualties were the same because 'first of all it would be some of the Israelis being killed then it would be the Arabs being killed'. A student also noted that 'you hear stories about Israel bombing camps and stories about suicide-bombers in Israel' and this had led him to believe that the casualties were 'roughly the same'. The phrase 'tit for tat' which had been used on the news was used by some participants in explaining their beliefs:

> *Moderator*:   Why did you see [casualties] as even?
> *Female speaker*:   Because usually it is a case of you go in and shoot somebody and then the next thing somebody else is dead on the other side – it is usually a tit for tat. (Low-income group, Glasgow)
> *Male speaker*:   It's always portrayed as tit for tat – I believed that the numbers are about level. (Male student, Glasgow)

[. . .]

There were some people in the groups who had connections with Israel either through friends or through having stayed there. Two of these stated that most casualties were Palestinian but at the same time said that there was more 'fuss' made about these casualties on the TV news or that Palestinian deaths were treated with more sympathy. It may be that they simply watched different bulletins from those in our samples, but their view is not supported by the material which we analysed. An alternative explanation might be that they were sympathetic to Israel and that coverage of Palestinian casualties in some way upset or contradicted their preferred view. They were comparatively well informed about events in the conflict and any sympathies which they had did not affect their judgement about the number of casualties. Interestingly, as we have seen above, viewers who were informed by the TV news and had apparently no great interest in the area were more likely to believe that the casualties were about equal or that most had been sustained by Israel.

Cultural Identification and Empathy

Identification can be conditional on personal relationships – for example, contacts with friends – or on cultural or family history. One student told us how she had attended an Arab school and how this had affected her understanding of the conflict. Such cultural histories can also affect the 'facts' and versions of causes of disputes which are heard by the individual. It was also made clear to us that for some members of the Jewish community, memories of the Holocaust had a powerful influence on how the Israeli-Palestinian conflict was seen. In a one-to-one discussion outside the groups, a Jewish woman described her experience of visiting Auschwitz and the appalling sight of piles of children's shoes. She then said that 'Sharon is a thug', but commented that there are times when someone like that is needed. The conflict was seen through the prism of the Holocaust – as she said, 'We cannot go quietly into the gas chambers again.'

Another woman in a focus group expressed her view that the history of the Jewish people had affected how the Israeli-Palestinian conflict was understood. She saw Israeli actions as being motivated by fear and thought that public perceptions were influenced by feelings of guilt:

> I felt that [the Israelis] had tried to enlarge their area, but I could understand because there is a lot of fear from the Israeli point of view. They feel very frightened where they are, and also, because of the past history of the Jewish people, we feel quite guilty as well. (Middle-class female group, Paisley)

It is also possible for audiences to identify at a more general cultural level – for example, to see one side of the conflict as being 'people like us' with manners, customs and lifestyles which are readily understood and recognised. As one participant from London put it:

> It's much easier for those of us in the West to imagine that a car bomb in the middle of a city is a tremendously terrifying thing . . . when you see a car bomb go off in the middle of a sophisticated city, the experience is much closer to one we can 'imagine'. (Middle-class male group, London)

An additional factor to which this speaker pointed was that London had experienced being attacked during the IRA campaigns and he and another participant described being close to bombs when they went off. The issue of cultural identification was raised by other participants – Israel was referred to as 'an island of democracy' in the Middle East (middle-class male, London). At the same time, some aspects of Muslim culture were seen as strange and difficult to identify with. A female participant, who was actually quite sympathetic to the Palestinians, gave her own rather mixed feelings on this:

> I feel there are lots of images I have of Muslim women that I find it very hard to see them beyond my own sort of white Western perspective because they're all covered up. And when you hear them mourning – because I know that my voice goes 'What's that noise?' and I know that that must be my Western culture that makes me think [that], but it does come across as alien to me, and I'm aware that it is my perspective, but that doesn't make me get any closer, if you know what I mean. (Low-income female group, London)

[. . .]

There was a strong feeling in the groups that the news should explain origins and causes and that journalists should speak more directly to viewers about was happening and why. The participants in the groups did not want news that was in any way biased or inaccurate, but the desire for clear, straightforward accounts was very apparent. It was also the case that when viewers did understand the significance and relevance of what they were watching, then this could strongly affect their level of interest in the news.

UNDERSTANDING AND INTEREST IN NEWS

We asked the participants in the focus groups whether, when watching the news, they felt that journalists assumed a level of knowledge or understanding which they did not have. A clear majority assented to this. Not all agreed – the middle-class males were more likely to say they understood the news very well. But for many there was a problem and examples were given of how the lack of understanding impacted on the interest which viewers had on the news:

> Every time it comes on [the Israeli-Palestinian conflict] it never actually explains it so I don't see the point in watching it – I just turn it off and go and make a cup of tea or something. I don't like watching it when I don't really understand what's going on. (Female student, Glasgow)
> It's like the Kosovo conflict, I don't want to watch it, I don't understand it – I switch it off. (Middle-class female group, Paisley)

[. . .]

Another problem which some participants identified was that explanations may have been given at the beginning of a story, on the first day of being reported. But since they frequently came into stories 'halfway through' a cycle of events, they could not understand what was happening:

> *Moderator*: Do you ever have the feeling that the journalist expects you to have a background knowledge that you don't actually have?
> *Female speaker*: Yes definitely, there's loads of times when like, there's just the background stuff that I don't really know anything about.
> *Male speaker*: I think it's more of a case that they assume, kind of, it's part of an ongoing story. They assume that you've been there from the start and that you've constantly watched. (Student group, Glasgow)

[. . .]

A clear majority in the groups as a whole stated that their interest increased when they understood more. This was very marked in the responses of group members to discussions in which they took part. Some became extremely interested and stayed behind to ask extensive questions. In two groups it was suggested that they might meet again as informal discussion groups. Other participants told us subsequently that they had spoken for long periods with friends about the issues that were raised, and others told us that they would now watch the news with more interest. This was not true of everyone. A minority said that they understood the news or that they preferred it as it was or that they thought the subject matter of news was intrinsically boring and it would not make any difference if they understood it more. But for the bulk of the people in this study the relationship between understanding and interest in news was very marked. This did suggest the need for change in the current structure and content of news programmes to address the problem that so many people are apparently not well informed by the news services which they see as their primary source of information.

55

PICTURIZING SCIENCE

The Science Documentary as Multimedia Spectacle

José van Dijck

Introduction

After its initial launch in 1999, the BBC's *Walking with Dinosaurs* became an immediate hit with television audiences around the world, even if this reinvigorated genre of the natural history documentary drew profound criticism from renowned science commentators. At the heart of this criticism was the complaint that digital animation overwhelmed documentary intentions and that the series, despite its technical novelty, failed to offer a 'new and improved' approach to disseminating scientific knowledge. Others resented the BBC's claim to present an accurate vision of paleontology, while favouring spectacle and edutainment at the expense of factual representation and realism. *Walking with Dinosaurs* gave rise to a number of academic inquiries, some of which called the series a 'turning point' in the history of science documentaries (Darley, 2003; Jeffries, 2003; Scott and White, 2003). British media theorist Andrew Darley (2003) disparaged the documentary's postmodern style and techniques, rhetorical approach, and overall aesthetic orientation. Its most noted feature – the use of special effects and computer animation – allegedly drives science producers' affinity for spectacle and edutainment further towards contemporary filmmakers' preference for simulation, pastiche, and hyper-realism. According to Darley (2003: 229) *Walking with Dinosaurs* exemplifies the so-called postmodern science documentary, which falls prey 'to contemporary aesthetic strategies that tend to negate representation and

From *International Journal of Cultural Studies* 9:1 (2006) pp. 5–24.

meaning (content), promoting instead the fascinations of spectacle and form (style)'.

Indeed, recent science documentaries show a particular penchant for the abundant use of animated visuals, obviously facilitated by new digital television techniques such as videographic animation and computer animatronics. Computer engineers can create moving pictures out of pixels without the necessity of an analogue referent – a technique that lends itself well to illustrating abstract theories or speculative scientific hypotheses. However, I disagree with Darley's and others' critique that

a) there is a sharp division or turning point between the so-called modernist or realist paradigm in science documentaries and the postmodernist or 'fictionalist' paradigm, and

b) that visual spectacle ('form') in this series overrules scientific claims to knowledge ('content').

For one thing, science documentaries have never been objective popularizations of science, but have always relied on realist (e.g. visual and narrative) *effects* to convey the suggestion of trustworthiness and validity. Series like *Walking with Dinosaurs* do not negate realism; on the contrary, one of the series' most remarkable features is its adherence to the dominant realist paradigm, despite its abundant use of visual spectacle. Besides, the constitutive role of visualizing technologies in contemporary science is nothing new or disturbing; media technologies have never just served as tools for dissemination or popularization, but have always actively shaped scientific knowledge.

The current tendency to embellish science documentary with digital 'pictorial' techniques neither signals a break with the conventional genre, nor does it imply a victory of form over content or aesthetics over science. To support my claim, this article proposes a framework for analysing science documentaries and natural history documentaries in terms of visual and narrative rhetoric.[1] The model typifies the science documentary as a mixture of *narrative modes* and *(tele)visual styles*, the various combinations of which help construct and sustain a particular claim to knowledge – propositions of how things are, were, or could be. After applying this model to *Walking with Dinosaurs*, a series intended to present a reconstruction of prehistory, we will turn to another recent documentary series, *The Elegant Universe*, and extend the analytical model to the representation of an abstract and speculative branch of science: theoretical physics. It will be argued that these documentaries' truly remarkable feature is less their heavy use of visual aesthetics and animatronics than their prolonged reliance on conventional realist effects. Moreover, these analyses aim at disclosing how visual styles and narrative modes are constitutive, rather than illustrative, elements in the production of scientific claims to knowledge.

Narrative Modes and Visual Styles in Science Documentaries

Science documentaries made for television have a longstanding tradition of realism, a tradition cemented in the narrative modes of explanation and exposition, and displayed in the visual styles of realist footage, in some cases complemented by symbolic images. They are historically characterized as linear, expository, and didactic tales – features that were always regarded as the benchmarks of quality science programmes such as the British series *Horizon* (BBC) and its American counterpart *Nova* (PBS) (Gardner and Young, 1981: 177). Since the beginning of science programming, the big challenge for television producers and scientists alike has been to reconcile the inherent unruliness of science with the laws of visualization enforced by a medium primarily valued for its ability to entertain a large audience with moving images. Much of science seemed to be unsuitable for television: its disciplinary content was either too abstract (physics) or too theoretical (mathematics), its subject matter too remote in time (prehistory) or place (cosmology), its research object too infinitesimal (molecular biology) or inaccessible (genetic therapy) for cameras to convey 'realistic' images. In past decades, technologies for scientific imaging and televisual recording have yielded impressive new views, including, for instance, the endoscopic camera that can film inside our bodies and the satellite transmission enabling real time images from other planets (van Dijck, 2005). Yet despite television's grateful incorporation of every new imaging instrument for the purpose of popularization, there will always remain scientific areas that resist 'realistic' visualization. In order to show the imperceptible and to render the invisible imaginable, television producers, from the very onset, have wielded an array of visual and rhetorical strategies to visualize and narrate what science can never show and tell.

Arguably still the dominant storytelling strategy in science documentaries today is the coupling of expository and explanatory modes of narrative with realistic and metaphorical visual styles.[2] In this hierarchical constellation, visual modes are subjugated to the authority of the narrative mode – words reign over visuals. The expository mode in its most prototypical form consists of a voice (or voice-over) explaining what a scientific idea, paradigm, or discovery entails. Frequently, this voice is embodied by a scientist, who may also serve as the host of the programme. An invisible, anonymous voice-over can be alternated by on-camera expositions of scientists, whose authority is an indispensable asset to this narrative mode. Viewers are more likely to trust claims made by the very persons who researched them and whose authority is institutionally legitimate. Closely related to the expository mode is the method of explanation: someone clarifying how science works. Not all brilliant scientists are also good teachers; it is therefore quite common for television producers to rely on voice-overs for this specific task. Elucidation commonly involves the use of rhetorical strategies to enhance public understanding of scientific processes. Metaphors or analogies are universal tools for explanation, but they are also directive instruments, attaching quotidian, ideological, or political meanings to scientific subjects (Bucchi, 1998; Nash, 1990; van Dijck, 1998). The explanatory mode encompasses many rhetorical strategies: from metaphors to personal stories by scientists, from detailed instructions by technicians to historical excursions. Obviously, the more 'visualizable' the explanation, the better.

Within the realist paradigm of science documentary, expository or explanatory modes are often stitched onto video footage showing actual or symbolic events to produce a realistic or metaphorical effect. Much of science can be captured on film: if you want to show at what temperature ice melts, or if you want to demonstrate what threat forest fires pose to the animal population, you go film where the action is. Film or video footage of 'science in action' or 'scientists at work' is often used in connection to shots of scientists talking on-camera, enhancing the expository mode. When the subject matter prohibits realistic filming, producers often resort to metaphoric visualization; shots of common objects, processes, or events are linked to scientific ideas by means of analogy. For instance, in order to visualize geneticist David Suzuki's explanation of genetic mutation in his eight-part documentary series *The Secret of Life* (1993), directors used the extended metaphor of the 'language of life,' filming Suzuki sitting amidst stacks of printed pages, archives, and endless rows of books in libraries. Visual metaphors, like textual ones, are never neutral conduits for science, but are attempts to attach concrete, everyday meanings to theoretical ideas or scientific assumptions. Symbolic images are quite compatible with video footage of 'real' science and scientists and they hardly compromise the reality effect; particularly if coupled onto an explanatory narrative mode, the metaphorical effect enhances rather than interferes with the illusion of reality.

The two narrative modes (expository and explanatory) and televisual styles (realistic and metaphorical) together inform what I will call the 'realist paradigm' in science documentary – the most important markers of quality science programming produced by institutions like the BBC and PBS in the past 50 years. Western media still celebrate science's foundation in empiricism and positivism – the notion that all knowledge derives from observational experience – and grounds this foundation in the conventions of electronic-realistic representation. The scientific claim of film and video to observational truth, according to Brian Winston (1995: 137), is built into the media apparatus as well as inscribed in the documentary genre: 'The documentary becomes scientific inscription – evidence.' Science documentary's reality effect is rooted in technology and cultural form – a contract between makers and viewers pertaining to visual recording devices that inscribe 'what science is' or 'how it works'. Even though this contract is knowingly compromised by scripts, post-production editing, camera angles, and a host of technical-rhetorical devices, they do not infringe on the agreement between image and viewer. As Roger Silverstone (1985: 178) sums up cogently: 'The plausibility of a documentary film lies in its naturalization, in its internal coherence and in its matching of its own reality to a reality which "everyone knows".' Quite a few cultural theorists and social constructivists have pointed to suggestive, symbolic images that help construct scientific claims in documentaries as 'truth' rather than as hypotheses or claims to knowledge (Gardner and Young, 1981; Hornig, 1990). These criticisms particularly pertain to the natural history documentary, a (sub)genre which set the standard for the presentation of science on television both in terms of content and style (Jeffries, 2003). Detractors contend it is precisely the misleading combination of narrative authority and symbolic or metaphoric images that renders these documentaries' claims to veracity and accuracy controversial (Crowther, 1997; Haraway, 1989).

In the past 25 years, however, the realist paradigm in science documentary has been compromised each time innovative (tele)visual styles and expansive narrative modes were pushed to the fore, forcing documentary-makers to adjust their means of storytelling if they wanted to appeal to an audience increasingly acculturated by Hollywood productions. The perennial unattractiveness of the documentary form was that it could not tell past stories, and neither could it speculate about consequences or implications, due to a lack of 'real' footage that might serve as evidence to a voice-over or interviewee. In science documentary, particularly, the need for reconstruction and speculation was poignant because scientific discoveries were never captured in real time, and the relevance of many scientific discoveries and claims lay in the future – applications that had yet to emerge. Showing historical triumphs of science on television was inherently difficult if one could not resort to the techniques of fiction: the only suitable form in the realist mode was the talking head of a reminiscing scientist, looking back on 'what happened' at this memorable moment. By the same token, only legitimate spokespersons were authorized to speculate on the future of particular developments in science. Yet none of these modes was even remotely attractive without accompanying moving images. Whereas photographic stills of historical events and symbolic shots of potential implications could fill some of that void, the visual styles of fiction film substantially increased the narrative potential of television documentary.

Documentary television producers, when first using reconstructive and speculative modes, came under fire when they started to use these modes in conjunction with a new visual style that allegedly breached the contract between image and viewer. After the American evening news had included a reenactment in one of its news features – a scene played out by actors in an actual environment – critics and scholars lamented the beginning of a downward spiral of trustworthiness.[3] As more film-makers followed suit and incorporated the 'fiction effect' into the documentary genre, science documentary makers adopted this style to enhance the reconstructive mode (Winston, 1995: 254–5). [. . .] After 1980, BBC and PBS science documentaries increasingly included re-enactments and staged scenes, visual styles that greatly expanded the creative possibilities of producers and directors. Series like *Horizon* and *Nova* even embraced popular hybridizations like docu-drama to enliven historical episodes of science, such as a reconstruction of the double helix discovery by Watson and Crick (Franklin, 1988). Re-enactments, however, were almost invariably paired off with the authoritative expository mode, often voiced through a reminiscing scientist. As a result, the fiction effect was made subordinate to the reality effect.

Besides re-enactments becoming an accepted visual style in science documentaries, we can more recently witness an increasing use of digital animations to embellish this genre, causing what has also been called the 'pictorial effect' (Mitchell, 1992). Naturally, pictures and animation have always been used in science documentaries to visualize abstract projections, yet drawings, diagrams, flow charts, or cartoon-like illustrations always explicitly signalled their artificiality and accentuated their animated quality. With the emergence of digital video, we are witnessing a new type of 'picturizing': videographic animation and computer animatronics allow computer engineers to create moving images out of pixels that look like analogue video footage. In other words, digital videographics takes analogue video footage as its benchmark for reality, whereas the truth-claim for video footage was rooted in its verisimilitude. For producers of science documentaries, the use of digital video animations appears to be particularly fruitful in areas that conventionally resist visualization, such as the very abstract, remote, or inaccessible. In combination with the speculative mode, picturization allows visual substantiation of conditional, hypothetical, or even speculative scientific claims stating 'this could have happened in the past' or 'this is what could happen, if . . .'. This new visual style, in connection to the speculative mode, again expands the potential of rhetorical strategies for science documentary producers.

The pictorial effect, though, should be viewed in the context of its ubiquitous implementation in visual culture; its smooth incorporation into the science documentary cannot be seen apart from the abundant use of videographics and digital animation in all sorts of audiovisual genres. The immense quantity of digitally generated images in Hollywood productions, from *Batman* to *Jurassic Park*, as well as in video games like *Lara Croft*, have undoubtedly whetted the appetite and facilitated the acceptance of videographic embalming in science documentaries. Images are becoming more artefactual objects and pictures, not replications of the real, and their accumulation in audio-visual productions has an overwhelming aesthetic connotation, rather than a truthful or illusionist one (Cubitt, 2004). As digitization enables near-perfect imitation of video footage, the pictorial effect's prominence is augmented in relation to the reality effect, the metaphorical effect, or the fiction effect.

[. . .]

The following will illustrate the intricate interweaving of visual styles and narrative modes when analyzing two examples of recent science documentaries. *Walking with Dinosaurs* takes the reconstructive mode as a point of departure as it re-animates extinct species from prehistory; *The Elegant Universe* assumes the speculative mode to explore the highly abstract and hypothetical subject matter of 'string theory'. This layered model is not aimed at identifying distinctive technical and aesthetic features of these documentaries as if they intrinsically defined the genre; instead, it offers a framework for analyzing how these documentaries' respective claims to knowledge are constructed through various combinations of narrative modes and visual styles, thereby using innovative fictional techniques while heavily relying upon realist conventions.

THE RECONSTRUCTIVE MODE: WALKING WITH DINOSAURS

There are scenes that really are very good science and there are those which are more speculative, like mating. How on earth will we ever know how dinosaurs mated? We're not always showing people stuff that we know is right, we're showing people our best guess. (Tim Haines, producer of *Walking with Dinosaurs*)

When *Walking with Dinosaurs* was first aired in 1999, the six-part series was advertised by the BBC as 'a window on the lost world' allowing viewers to 'believe they were watching living creatures in their natural habitat'. Digital animations of the Tyrannosaurus rex, the Optalmosaurus, Stegosaurus and a number of other prehistoric animals populating planet earth 65 million years ago, vivified paleontologists' research by visualizing their claims on our television screens. Like its sequel *Walking with Beasts* (2001), this series popularized a somewhat dusty academic discipline to an audience substantially younger than the average science documentary viewer (Scott and White, 2003). The success of *Walking with Dinosaurs* was primarily due to its technological production mode – the use of digital animations and animatronics – cleverly hooking into a new cinematic tradition established by Steven Spielberg's *Jurassic Park* (1993) and *The Lost World* (1997). While the BBC adopted some of the visual styles wielded in these Hollywood blockbusters, it strategically framed the series as a natural history documentary. The 'reality effect' of *Walking with Dinosaurs* lies in its ability to make a hypothetical reconstruction from the past, produced entirely in fictional and pictorial styles, subservient to the explanatory and expository narrative modes, anchoring animated fiction in the realist paradigm of science documentary.

[...]

Undoubtedly the most notable feature confirming *Walking with Dinosaurs'* genre label is its narrative mode of explanation. A neutral, invisible voice-over comments on every scene as if it is taking place in real time, explaining in the present tense how dinosaurs go about daily acts like eating, mating, surviving: 'A young male tries to attract the attention of a female by walking next to her, but mating can be a dangerous act for the female Diplodocus.' As Scott and White (2003: 321) have noticed, the voice-over impersonates 'an authoritative commentary by an omniscient narrator, combining the "objective" discourse of scientific knowledge (facts and figures) with touches of anthropomorphism'. The voice-over firmly anchors the series in the narrative mode of explanation, but more than that, it articulates the reconstructive mode ('this is what assumedly happened') in the typical linguistic features of real-time exposition ('this is what happens'). Reconstruction and speculation hide behind an expository sheen of realistic visuals authenticated by a mixture of voice-over, 'real-time' (fabricated) sounds of animals, and background music to accentuate tense or romantic moments. It is exactly this mixture of scientific reconstruction and speculative imagination that turns *Walking with Dinosaurs* into attractive television, but this very blend also subverts the contract between maker and viewer as to what the images actually show.

Part of the series' claim to authentication (or scientific reconstruction) is made not in the documentary itself, but in the accompanying *The Making of Walking with Dinosaurs* series. The meta-documentary recounts how 100 scientists were involved in this monster production. Indeed, the involvement of scientists in television documentaries is nothing new, as scientists' participation in Hollywood (science) fiction is now the rule rather than the exception (Frank, 2003). [. . .]

What makes this meta-documentary so important, in my view, is the observation that its prominent visual style (animation) is no longer used as an *illustration*, but that computer graphics are an integral part of *constructing* science – an observation made earlier by social constructivists and philosophers of science (Latour, 1990; Lynch and Woolgar, 1990). Models and representations visually melting into a seamless whole demonstrate how scientific claims are intrinsically dependent upon their visualizations. Computer animations are concurrently instruments of mediating and constructing science. The pictorial effect, serving to 'authenticate' the realistic effect, is part of the scientific process, which is at the same time and by the same means a creative process to turn science into television. Visualization and scientific argumentation are mutually contingent. As this series seems to sustain, digital 'picturization' is not just an *effect* but a constitutive *tool* of science. Meanwhile, the series *Walking with Dinosaurs* derives much, if not all, of its scientific trustworthiness from its unarticulated framing as a realist documentary, in which voice is supposed to reign over visual. The reconstructive mode seems merely 'illustrated' by digital effects and animation, assuming its subordination to the conventional narrative modes of exposition and explanation. However, my interpretative analysis reveals this to be an effective rhetorical tactic aimed at anchoring the documentary's truth-claims in accepted realist conventions.

The Speculative Mode: The Elegant Universe

The decision to use animation, to use a lot of it, was completely essential to the process, because when you're doing that project about string theory, when you're talking about things that really cannot be seen, that can only be imagined, I don't know any other way to do it than through metaphor and animation. (Paula S. Apseil, senior executive producer of *The Elegant Universe*)

A similar blend of realist claims to scientific truth and animated visual aesthetics can be traced in a science programme that is primarily informed by the speculative mode. *The Elegant Universe*, a three-part documentary series aired by PBS in 2003, manages to make a very difficult, highly abstract and hypothetical subject from the field of theoretical physics imaginable to laypersons. The world of string theory – 'a world stranger than science fiction' according to the PBS announcement – conjectures a reconciliation of Isaac Newton's laws of gravity, Albert Einstein's discoveries on relativity, Niels Bohr's findings in quantum mechanics, and James Maxwell's mathematical equations describing electro-magnetism into a unified 'theory of everything'. String physicists assume the existence of a subatomic level where 'strings', entities smaller than particles or quarks, generate a variety of shapes, from black holes to membranes. An important tenet of string theory is the existence of not 4, but 11 dimensions – dimensions that we cannot see or even make visible – and a possible infinite number of parallel universes. It claims to bring together the divergent sets of laws formulated by famous physicists, and also prophesies a coherent explanation for all manifestations of matter now and in the future. As Brian Greene, physicist at Columbia University and host of *The Elegant Universe* suggests, questions of philosophy or religion may soon become questions of physics. String theorists' hypotheses are, not surprisingly, fiercely disputed amongst scientists, but how does this television documentary render their claims plausible and even likely?

The overwhelming use of digital animation and videographics in this series is partly responsible for a persuasive presentation of a contentious theory, but its scientific claims are ultimately validated by the explanatory mode. In contrast to *Walking with Dinosaurs*, *The Elegant Universe* relies on the conventional narrative strategy of an expert commentator. Host Brian Greene is an authority in the field and an engaging storyteller who lucidly explains the most difficult concepts by means of metaphors and analogies. He uses a cello to explain string vibrations, an analogy between a cup of coffee and a donut to illustrate the significance of shapes, and sliced bread to exemplify the existence of parallel universes. But Greene's explanatory narrative is never simply *illustrated* by pictures of everyday objects; all images, even those of the host himself, are choreographed into fast-paced animated sequences, to such an extent that it is impossible to distinguish video footage from morphing animations, or material objects from pictorial metaphors. For instance, Brian Greene's talking head appears on a slice of bread that he himself is cutting; in the same visual style, a cup of coffee digitally morphs into a donut. Even textual inserts, such as mathematical formulas or letters (G for gravity, EM for electromagnetism) smoothly change into visuals, just as the sound of strings transforms into images. To enhance the explanatory mode, Greene's words are frequently alternated by single quotes from an impressive parade of top-notch physicists. Initially, their talking heads appear in straightforward on-camera interviews, their authority signalled by name, title, and institutional affiliation.[4] But in subsequent scenes, their images are retouched to appear for example on large screens over Broadway or, when a scientist explains the existence of more dimensions, the screen shows his multiple faces. Animations 'hijack' the explanatory mode, subjecting all video footage to the elasticity of digital graphics; the hypothesized universe of string theory seems already real in the world of multimedia, where text, sound, video footage, and animation all merge into a unified visual style.

[. . .]

The Elegant Universe presents a multimedia spectacle which magically turns hypothesis into feasibility, and speculation into proven claim. But does the science represented in this documentary still pertain to questions of truth and falsehood or, perhaps more relevant here, to representational criteria of fact or fiction? Several detractors interviewed for the programme point out the weakness of string theory: even if this theory will prove to be mathematically sound, it can never be put to a test. Indeed, the programme's host Brian Greene admits that 'testing' string theory is impossible; even the giant atom smashers, currently being built by Fermilab in Texas and by CERN in Switzerland, will at best deliver circumstantial evidence for the existence of strings, sparticles, or gravitons. And yet, throughout the program, Greene subjects the laws of physics, along with the assumptions of string theory, to 'experiments' in virtual reality, executed in digital architecture. For instance, when he wants to show how the laws of electromagnetism interfere with the laws of gravity, Greene is filmed jumping from a tall building but magically landing on his two feet. This animated scene is, of course, an imitation of a made-in-Hollywood Batman leap, constructed in such a style that even if you don't believe in the existence of flying human bats, you have to admire the reality-effect caused by its visual artifice.

In the two-dimensional world of film and multimedia, the 11 dimensions of string theory can at least be turned into a visual reality – a universe that is governed by the rules of animation but subjected to the laws of verisimilitude and realism. Ultimately, the answer to the million-dollar question, posed at the end of the series – 'Can string theory be wrong?' – is as simple as it is revealing. Brian Greene philosophizes that so much of string theory makes sense, 'it has got to be right', and his judgement is supported by Nobel-prize-winning physicist Steven Weinberg, saying: 'I find it hard to believe that that much elegance and mathematical beauty would simply be wasted.' Ordinary viewers, overwhelmed by three hours of digital videography, may find it hard to believe that the sophistication and elegance of this multimedia spectacle would be wasted. Qualifications of verification and trustworthiness are subtly replaced by qualifications of aesthetics and persuasiveness.

And yet, despite its visual fireworks and aesthetic overload, the documentary astonishingly relies on the authority of voice(-over) and words to establish the trustworthiness of its claims. Like *Walking with Dinosaurs*, *The Elegant Universe* includes reenactments and animations to 'picturize' scientific theory that is otherwise too abstract to be understood by non-physicists. In addition, the speculative mode accounts for playful visual tricks borrowed directly from fiction to enhance the documentary's metaphorical and pictorial effects. But it is the distinguished commentary and appearance of physicist Brian Greene (supported by a large number of authorities in the field) who, at all times, subjects the artificiality of images to the 'authenticity' of his words, much like the neutral voice-over in *Walking with Dinosaurs* takes command of the animated pictures of conjectured prehistoric beasts. Even if visual spectacle seems at times to overwhelm the rational content of the science presented, it is in fact the rhetorical choreography of carefully intertwined narrative modes and visual styles that ultimately grounds both documentaries in a conventional realist paradigm. The authority and trustworthiness of its proposed scientific claims are ultimately contingent upon the reality effect created by the documentary's producers.

In the previous section, I explained how *Walking with Dinosaurs*, rather than being a popularized version of paleontology, actually helped construct its scientific claims – an observation that becomes particularly manifest in *The Making of Walking with Dinosaurs* episode. Along similar lines, the makers of *The Elegant Universe*, in the bonus material added to the DVD version, comment on the crucial function of animatronics to the construction of string theory. Without the possibilities of computer animation there would have been no documentary, but there also would have been no theory: computer graphics enable scientists to imagine the possible shapes the 'materialist world' can assume. [. . .]

In the past, documentaries based in the realist paradigm seemingly displayed science within the logical order of empiricism, affirming the Platonic hierarchy between reality and representation, thus constituting the mastery of words over visual illustration, of explanation over speculation, and of reality over fiction. The linear order of history, the empiricist order of science, and the representational order of science documentary were all grounded in the same ontological claims: what likely happened in the past or potentially happens in the future cannot be 'authentically' filmed, it can only be illustrated by artificial means. Recent documentaries like *Walking with Dinosaurs* and *The Elegant Universe* apparently subvert the proclaimed ontological order between science and reality vis-à-vis representation and fiction. And yet, more than ever, the science documentary relies on the presence of realist features, such as an authoritative voice-over, a well-respected host, or the appearance of an impressive number of experts in the field, to anchor its claims to trustworthiness in the realist paradigm. The science documentary, while subverting its own ontological claims, paradoxically affirms the hierarchy of 'science' over 'fiction', of 'content' over 'spectacle', and of 'popularization' over 'construction'.

Conclusion

Many academics and commentators, like Andrew Darley (2003: 229), conclude that documentaries like *Walking with Dinosaurs*, and by extension *The Elegant Universe*, emanate from a cultural context that favours simulation and hyper-realism, and therefore negates realism. Darley and others observe a sharp turning point between the evidently modernist (or realist) and postmodernist (or fiction-alist) documentary genre, the latter of which is resented because its aesthetic strategies and high-tech visual spectacle tend to overwhelm scientific content. Indeed, the technological is a significant part of a larger cultural transformation that some have labelled the 'postmodern condition' (Harvey, 1990; Lyotard, 1984). However, as I have argued in this article, assuming an intrinsic divide between modernist and postmodernist documentary genres may be ahistorical and insufficient as a mode of criticism. Applying a model that distinguishes visual styles and narrative modes, it becomes clear that the realist paradigm of science documentary, even in its earlier stages, incorporated fictional and pictorial styles as well as speculative and reconstructive narrative modes. And vice versa, while the multimedia spectacles produced by the BBC and PBS thrive on the dominant modes of speculation and reconstruction, their status and authority as science documentaries is ultimately contingent upon their use of explanation and expo-sition. Every *a priori* distinction between modern and postmodern, as Bruno Latour (1993) has convincingly argued, is epistemologically flawed because it hinges on fallacious dichotomies between science and representation, between scientific object and active agent, and between science and culture. Latour's argu-ment that 'we have never been modern' also applies to the science documentary: there has never been a purely 'realist' paradigm in science programming.

Arguing from a somewhat different angle, John Corner (2002: 266) has launched the term 'postdocumentary', not to proclaim the end of documentary as a truthful cultural form, but to signal 'its relocation as a set of practices, forms, and functions.' He argues that the legacy of documentary is still at work in current styles of televisuality, reaffirming the realist contract between viewers and makers but concurrently subverting it in favour of innovative claims to knowledge. Since digital technologies are changing our ontologi-cal relationship with the image (Manovich, 2001), we need a more refined analytical armamentarium to discuss the intrinsically mediated construction of scientific knowledge. The model proposed in this article provides such ana-lytical tool, allowing viewers to recognize the constructedness of documentary texts. And yet, it is not enough to identify the construction of documentaries; it is even more important to understand how science and documentary are mutually contingent and interdependent constructions of scientific claims.

[. . .]

Rather than lament the current effacement of science documentary's realism, we need to develop analytic models and tools that help clarify how science and science documentaries shape our world *in tandem*. Computers and digitization are certainly not a radical break with previous scientific practices which were always also mediated practices: the success of scientific claims often depended on the success of their visualizations. Analysis of two recent science documentaries reveals how the constructions of science and media are closely aligned and intricately intertwined. [. . .]

Science documentaries offer a unique opportunity to bare scientists' and media producers' struggles with old and new epistemological and ontological paradigms. Replacing attenuated realist claims of what science is, how it works, how it happened, or what could happen, we should foreground the question of *how science (documentary) shapes our world*. Towards that end, *The Making Of* episodes accompanying these documentaries form an integral part of the viewing experience: they teach viewers how technology shapes both science *and* media, and demonstrate how programme makers and scientists decide what to show, how to show it, and why to show it that way. The science documentary is a meeting place for the didactic and the scientific, the truthful and the elegant; yet it is precisely the awe-inspiring presence of accredited scientists or the overwhelming elegance of multimedia spectacles that obligate viewers to acknowledge its contents' stratified texture.

ACKNOWLEDGEMENT

I would like to thank the anonymous referees of the *International Journal of Cultural Studies* for their comments; they have helped to substantially improve a previous version of this article.

NOTES

1. This article will refer to the natural history documentary as a special subgenre of the science documentary. Even though many relevant comments can be made about the distinctions between these two, these differences are beyond the scope of the main argument here.
2. I use the term 'narrative mode' to indicate that every science documentary – or every television programme for that matter – tells a story about science using a particular strategy, both in terms of rhetoric and in terms of aesthetics. By '(tele)visual styles' I mean the effects created by using a specific type of image or image processing in relation to the truth-claim implied by that choice. For instance, a realist effect is an effect that is implicitly ascribed to unedited, unaltered video footage. Naturally, moving images of whatever technological basis are always intrinsically contrived, but visual styles have gradually come to connote particular effects.
3. In 1988, the ABC Evening News, for instance, used a re-enactment to reconstruct how an American spy had probably managed to steal secret information from a government building. For a detailed analysis of news documentary, see Beattie (2004), chapter 9.
4. A large number of highly esteemed physicists appear in this programme. First there are the 'grand old men' of string theory: John Schwarz, Michael Greene, and Ed Witten. Secondly, a number of authorities in various subdisciplines of physics comment in this programme, including Walter G. Lewin (MIT), Steven Weinberg

(Universty of Texas), Peter Galison (Harvard University), Alan Guth (MIT), Joseph Polchinski (UC Santa Barbara), S. James Gates (University of Maryland), and Michael Dugg (University of Chicago).

REFERENCES

Beattie, K. (2004) *Documentary Screens: Nonfiction, Film and Television*. Houndmills: Palgrave.

Bucchi, M. (1998) *Science and the Media: Alternative Routes in Scientific Communication*. London: Routledge.

Corner, J. (2002) 'Performing the Real: Documentary Diversions', *Television and New Media* 3(1): 255–69.

Crowther, B. (1997) 'Viewing What Comes Naturally: A Feminist Approach to Television Natural History', *Women's Studies International Forum* 20: 289–300.

Cubitt, S. (2004) *The Cinema Effect*. Cambridge, MA: MIT Press.

Darley, A. (2003) 'Simulating Natural History: Walking with Dinosaurs as Hyper-real Edutainment', *Science as Culture* 12(2): 227–56.

Frank, S. (2003) 'Reel Reality: Science Consultants in Hollywood', *Science as Culture* 12(4): 427–69.

Franklin, S.B. (1988) 'Life Story: The Gene as Fetish Object on TV', *Science as Culture* 1(1): 92–100.

Gardner, C. and R. Young (1981) 'Science on TV: A Critique', in T. Bennett (ed.) *Popular Television and Film*, pp. 171–93. London: British Film Institute.

Haraway, D. (1989) *Primate Visions: Gender, Race and Nature in the World of Modern Science*. New York: Routledge.

Harvey, D. (1990) *The Condition of Postmodernity: An Enquiry into the Origins of Cultural Change*. Cambridge: Blackwell.

Hornig, S. (1990) 'Television's NOVA and the Construction of Scientific Truth', *Critical Studies in Mass Communication* 7(1): 11–23.

Jeffries, M. (2003) 'BBC Natural History versus Science Paradigms', *Science as Culture* 12(4): 527–45.

Latour, B. (1990) 'Drawing Things Together', in M. Lynch and S. Woolgar (eds) *Representation in Scientific Practice*, pp. 19–67. Cambridge, MA: MIT Press.

Latour, B. (1993) *We Have Never Been Modern*. Cambridge, MA: Harvard University Press.

Lynch, M. and S. Woolgar, eds (1988) *Representation in Scientific Practice*. Cambridge, MA: MIT Press.

Lyotard, J.-F. (1984) *The Postmodern Condition: A Report on Knowledge*. Minneapolis, MN: University of Minnesota Press.

Manovich, L. (2001) *The Language of New Media*. Cambridge, MA: MIT Press.

Mitchell, W.J.T. (1992) *The Reconfigured Eye: Visual Truth in the Post-Photographic Era*. Cambridge, MA: MIT Press.

Nash, C., ed. (1990) *Narrative in Culture: The Uses of Story-telling in the Sciences, Philosophy, and Literature*. London: Routledge.

Scott, K.D. and A.M. White (2003) 'Unnatural History? Deconstructing the Walking with Dinosaurs Phenomenon', *Media, Culture and Society* 25: 315–32.

Silverstone, R. (1985) *Framing Science: The Making of a BBC Documentary*. London: British Film Institute.

van Dijck, J. (1998) *ImagEnation: Popular Images of Genetics*. New York: New York University Press.

van Dijck, J. (2005) *The Transparent Body: A Cultural Analysis of Medical Imaging*. Seattle, WN: University of Washington Press.

Winston, B. (1995) *Claiming the Real: The Documentary Film Revisited*. London: British Film Institute.

AUDIO VISUAL REFERENCES

Jurassic Park (1993) Director: Steven Spielberg. Based on a novel by Michael Crichton.

The Lost World (1997) Director: Steven Spielberg. Based on a novel by Michael Crichton.

The Elegant Universe (2003) Producers: David Hickman, Joseph McMaster and Julia Cort. Host: Brian Greene. Part of the PBS series NOVA (WGBH Educational Foundation). Premiered in the US on December 27, 2003.

The Secret of Life (1993) Host: David Suzuki. Eight-part documentary PBS series (WGBH Educational Foundation).

Walking with Dinosaurs (1999) Producer: Tim Haines. BBC/Discovery/TV Asahi co-production in association with Pro Sieben and France 3. Premiered in Great Britain on 4 October, 1999.

The Making of Walking with Dinosaurs (1999) Producer: Tim Haines. BBC/Discovery/ TV Asahi. Aired October 11, 1999.

Walking with Beasts (2001) Producer: Tim Haines. Narrator: Kenneth Branagh. BBC/ Discovery. Aired October, 2001.

FURTHER READING

Allan, S., *Online News: Journalism and the Internet* (Buckingham: Open University Press: 2006).

Austin, T. and de Jong, W. (eds), *Rethinking Documentary: New Perspective, New Practices* (London: McGraw Hill, 2008).

Burston, J., 'War and the Entertainment Industries: New Research Priorities in an Era of Cyber-Patriotism', in D. Thussu and D. Freedman (eds), *War and the Media: Reporting Conflict 24/7* (London: Sage, 2003).

Chomsky, N. and Herman, E., 'A Propaganda Model', in M. G. Durham and D. Kellner (eds), *Media and Cultural Studies: KeyWorks* (Oxford: Blackwell, 2003) pp. 280–317.

Cottle, S., *Global Crisis Reporting* (Buckingham: Open University Press, 2000).

Curran, J., 'Globalization Theory: The Absent Debate', in *Media and Power* (London: Routledge, 2003) pp. 166–83.

Hables Gray, C., *Peace, War and Computers* (London: Routledge, 2005).

Higgins, L. A., 'Documentary in an Age of Terror', *South Central Review* 22:2 (2005) pp. 20–38.

Homes, D., *Communication Theory* (London: Sage, 2005).

Knightley, P., *The First Causalty: The War Correspondent as Hero and Myth-Maker from the Crimea to Iraq* (Cambridge, MA: MIT Press, 2004).

McChesney, R., 'Corporate Media, Global Capitalism', in S. Cottle (ed.), *Media Organization and Production* (London: Sage, 2003) pp. 27–40.

Mirzoeff, N., *Watching Babylon* (London: Routledge, 2005).

Negt, O. and Kluge, A., *Public Sphere and Experience* (Minneapolis, MN: University of Minnesota Press, 1993) pp. 96–129.

Peters, J. D., 'Witnessing', *Media, Culture and Society* 23:Special Issue on Media Events (2001) pp. 707–23.

Robins, K., 'The War, the Screen, the Crazy Dog and Poor Mankind', *Media, Culture and Society*, 15:2 (1993) pp. 321–7.

Silverstone, R., *Mediapolis* (London: Polity, 2007).

Spigel, L., 'Entertainment Wars: Television Culture after 9/11', *American Quarterly* 56:2 (2004) pp. 235–70.

Taylor, M. P., 'Journalism under Fire: The Reporting of War and International Crisis', in S. Cottle (ed.), *News, Public Relations and Power* (London: Sage, 2003), pp. 63–80.

Temple, M., *The British Press* (Buckingham: Open University Press, 2008).

Thussu, D. and Freedman, D., *War and the Media* (London: Sage, 2005).

Washbourne, N., *Mediating Politics: Newspaper, Radio, Television and the Internet* (Buckingham: Open University Press, 2008).

Zelizer, B. and Allen, S. (eds), *Journalism After September 11*, 2nd edn (London: Routledge, 2005).

SECTION 8
ADVERTISING AND PROMOTIONAL CULTURE

INTRODUCTION: ADVERTISING AND PROMOTIONAL CULTURE

The study of advertising takes us into wider and more contested areas than do the first two case studies in this *Reader* (Sections 6 and 7). In the first place, advertising is not merely a highly visible system of social imagery but is itself an *industry*, a major sector in the global economy which wields considerable power within an increasingly globalised and marketised world. It has a far more direct connection to capitalism's economic structures than other media forms, functioning as part of a chain of marketing practices which sustain the flow of goods on which this economic system depends, while at the same time enhancing the power of large-scale corporations within it. It also exerts economic force upon the media system as a whole, since it acts, as James Curran has argued (1981: 44), as a 'concealed subsidy system' to whose demands media must be responsive. Thus it influences both media content and the structures of ownership and control in media industries.

Second, advertising has often been used by cultural theorists as a metonymic symbol for a contemporary culture in which it has become increasingly all-pervasive. For F. R. Leavis, writing in 1930 in defence of what he termed 'minority culture', advertising epitomised the 'exploitation of the cheap response' which characterises contemporary 'mass civilisation' (1994: 12).

In 1947, Theodor Adorno and Max Horkheimer, writing from the very different, Marxist perspective of the Frankfurt School (see Chapter 1), argued similarly that advertising pervades what has now become the 'culture industry', subsidising the 'ideological media' and turning culture into an 'assembly-line' whose standardised products it furnishes with artificial differences (1977: 380, 381). For more recent theorists, too, advertising functions in this emblematic way. Jean Baudrillard, for example, argues that it 'invades everything'. Both public and private space disappear, as does the separation between them, to be replaced by 'great screens on which are reflected atoms, particles, molecules in motion', in the 'era of hyperreality' (1985: 129, 130).[1] For these theorists, advertising functions as symbol or symptom of the condition of contemporary culture.

Third, advertising contests with academic media studies the space of audience research. As part of a marketing industry advertising conducts its own audience research, and at times this has been difficult to distinguish from certain strands of academic research, particularly within the American 'mass communication' tradition. Todd Gitlin, for example, in a 1978 critique of what he termed the 'dominant paradigm' of American media sociology, makes this attack on the American tradition:

> It is no secret that mass communications research descends directly from the development of sophisticated marketing techniques. The theory of 'effects' was first developed for the direct, explicit use of broadcasters and advertisers, and continues to be used mostly in those circles . . . (Gitlin, 1978: 232)

His conclusion – that by its complicity with the advertising industry, American media sociology has functioned to 'legitimize . . . mid-century capitalism' (Gitlin, 1978: 245) – is one echoed elsewhere within academic media studies. Ien Ang, for example, contrasts critical ethnographic studies, which 'foreground [. . .] the diverse, the particular and the unpredictable in everyday life' with the kind of large-scale 'audience measurement' that characterises those techniques linked to marketing, and which can produce only 'sweeping generalizations and meaningless abstractions' (Ang, 1991: x). Thus advertising becomes a ground on which opposing traditions of audience research – and the political and ideological perspectives on which they are based – may be fought out.

Finally, its links with both forms of persuasion and processes of consumption mean that advertising is caught up in wider arguments about the power of consumers to resist the meanings and pleasures produced by powerful media and create their own identities out of the cultural material supplied by popular forms like advertising. For John Fiske, for example, there exists a semi-autonomous 'cultural economy', in which consumers rather than producers are empowered. In this view, consumption can become 'an oppositional . . . act', whose 'guerrillas' – particularly women – cause the persuasive techniques of advertising always to fail. 'There is so much advertising', writes Fiske, not because it is all-powerful, as other theorists argue, but because 'it can never finally succeed in its tasks'.[2]

Chapter 56 by Raymond Williams which opens this section, written in 1960, takes up several of the issues outlined above. Advertising, he argues, is both crucial to the economic functioning of capitalism and a form of 'social communication', offering us new ways of understanding ourselves. Advertising, then, categorises us as 'consumers' rather than 'users', offering in response to real human needs (the 'problems of death, loneliness, frustration, the need for identity and respect') the illusory satisfaction provided by the consumption of material goods. In advertising's 'magic system' these goods are identified with human values and desires in order to obscure the 'real sources' of satisfaction whose discovery would involve radical changes in our way of life. Williams, however, is far less pessimistic than, for example, Adorno and Horkheimer. Advertisers, he writes, are as confused as their consumers, and the confused society for which they speak still has a choice: between 'capitalism and socialism . . . man as consumer and man as user'.

Chapter 57 comes from Sean Nixon's study of the construction of 'new masculinities' within advertising, retailing and men's 'style magazines' in the 1980s: *Hard Looks*. In this extract, he gives an account of the shifts within advertising practices which facilitated the influence of the 1980s 'style press' and general-interest men's magazines in establishing a distinctive imagery for the 'new man'. He also analyses the nature of that imagery and the changes in the codings of masculinity which it represented. Nixon argues that in order to understand the cultural significance of this 'new man' imagery, it is not enough simply to examine the imagery itself, nor can it be explained solely by reference to the economic shifts in the advertising and magazine industries which led to its appearance. Instead, we must explore the interdependence of economic and cultural practices. The two do not function as discrete, autonomous realms. Representations – in this case of the 'new man' – do not simply result from economic processes of production; they are a part of these processes and the discursive ground on which producers, advertisers and consumers meet.

The chapter by Anne McClintock which follows (Chapter 58) examines the relations of power and desire in the imperial discourses of nineteenth-century Britain. McClintock's focus is the soap advertisements which, she argues, legitimised racist conceptions of Britain's colonial others through a fetishising of 'whiteness' as cleanliness. In these advertisements, imperialism is 'domesticated', and soap comes to mediate 'the Victorian poetics of racial hygiene and imperial progress'. Its advertisements present the colonies as conquered by domestic commodities and offer imperial progress as commodity spectacle. If these advertisements mask the realities of imperial power, however, they also obscure the realities of the domestic sphere as the space of unpaid women's work. Working women are absent, the value of their work is displaced onto the commodity itself, and the advertisements' 'feminised' Africans are figured 'not as historic agents, but as frames for the commodity, for their exhibition value alone'. The fetishistic images which these advertisements present, argues McClintock, are a crucial part of the Victorian 'mass marketing of empire as a series of images', its 'civilising mission' embodied in the spectacular effects of the domestic commodity, soap.

Chapter 59, by Andrew Wernick expands the study of advertising to the analysis of what Wernick calls 'promotional culture'. While advertising, he argues, is simply one aspect of the process of cultural commodification, *promotion* now characterises the whole of our symbolic or cultural world. Thus all products are constructed as advertisements for themselves; all media forms are designed both to attract audiences and to promote themselves; all informational communication is suffused with promotional techniques; individuals, as celebrities, have become promotional resources; and finally, we ourselves are engaged in a constant process of self-promotion. This dominance has altered social communication so that the boundaries between culture and the economy have become blurred and all social discourses are caught up in promotional processes. It has also altered our sense of self, as we are caught up in a constant process of 'self-staging' and must build our identities from unstable cultural materials. Finally, it has produced a culture of profound distrust in which 'cynical privatism and mass apathy' become our only defences.

The final chapter in this section (Chapter 60) by William Leiss et al. returns to the issue of advertising's dual status as both representational system and economic power to ask what questions this raises for social policy. Advertising has attracted public policy debate, they write, both for its limited and stereotypical representations and because of the economic influence it wields. In response, advertisers argue that they both abide by regulatory standards and are subject to regulation not applied to other forms of media content. For Leiss et al., however, this defence misrepresents the huge importance of advertising within contemporary culture. It has become 'the economic fulcrum of the commercial media system', so that its exclusion of certain groups from marketing targets and overemphasis on others affects the representational range of commercial media as a whole. At the same time, advertising's own highly compressed and visible 'system of social imagery' is itself both powerful and intrusive. If, therefore, we are to both understand the controversies raised by advertising and respond to them effectively, we must address the full scale of the advertising industry's reach and influence which now extends well beyond its origins as 'salesmanship in print'.

NOTES

1. See also Chapter 6 in this volume.
2. See Fiske, 'Shopping for Pleasure', in *Reading the Popular* (London: Unwin Hyman, 1989) pp. 13–42 and 'Commodities and Culture', in *Understanding Popular Culture* (London: Unwin Hyman, 1989) p. 30.

REFERENCES

Adorno, T. and Horkheimer, M., 'The Culture Industry: Enlightenment as Mass Deception', in J. Curran, M. Gurevitch and J. Woollacott (eds), *Mass Communication and Society* (London: Edward Arnold, 1977) pp. 349–83.
Ang, I., *Desperately Seeking the Audience* (London: Routledge, 1991).

Baudrillard, J., 'The Ecstasy of Communication', in H. Foster (ed.), *Postmodern Culture* (London: Pluto Press, 1985) pp. 126–34.

Curran, J., 'The Impact of Advertising on the British Mass Media', *Media, Culture & Society* 3:1 (1981) pp. 43–69.

Gitlin, T., 'Media Sociology: The Dominant Paradigm', *Theory and Society* 6 (1978) pp. 205–53.

Leavis, F. R., 'Mass Civilisation and Minority Culture', in J. Storey (ed.), *Cultural Theory and Popular Culture: A Reader* (Hemel Hempstead: Harvester Wheatsheaf, 1994) pp. 12–20.

56

ADVERTISING: THE MAGIC SYSTEM

Raymond Williams

[. . .]

In the last hundred years [. . .] advertising has developed from the simple announcements of shopkeepers and the persuasive arts of a few marginal dealers into a major part of capitalist business organization. This is important enough, but the place of advertising in society goes far beyond this commercial context. It is increasingly the source of finance for a whole range of general communication, to the extent that in 1960 our majority television service and almost all our newspapers and periodicals could not exist without it. Further, in the last forty years and now at an increasing rate, it has passed the frontier of the selling of goods and services and has become involved with the teaching of social and personal values; it is also rapidly entering the world of politics. Advertising is also, in a sense, the official art of modern capitalist society: it is what 'we' put up in 'our' streets and use to fill up to half of 'our' newspapers and magazines: and it commands the services of perhaps the largest organized body of writers and artists, with their attendant managers and advisers, in the whole society. Since this is the actual social status of advertising, we shall only understand it with any adequacy if we can develop a kind of total analysis in which the economic, social and cultural facts are visibly related. We may then also find, taking advertising as a major form of modern social communication, that we can understand our society itself in new ways.

It is often said that our society is too materialist, and that advertising reflects this. We are in the phase of a relatively rapid distribution of what are called

From R. Williams, *Problems in Materialism and Culture* (London: Verso, 1980) pp. 184–91.

'consumer goods', and advertising, with its emphasis on 'bringing the good things of life', is taken as central for this reason. But it seems to me that in this respect our society is quite evidently not materialist enough, and that this, paradoxically, is the result of a failure in social meanings, values and ideals.

It is impossible to look at modern advertising without realising that the material object being sold is never enough: this indeed is the crucial cultural quality of its modern forms. If we were sensibly materialist, in that part of our living in which we use things, we should find most advertising to be of an insane irrelevance. Beer would be enough for us, without the additional promise that in drinking it we show ourselves to be manly, young in heart, or neighbourly. A washing-machine would be a useful machine to wash clothes, rather than an indication that we are forward-looking or an object of envy to our neighbours. But if these associations sell beer and washing-machines, as some of the evidence suggests, it is clear that we have a cultural pattern in which the objects are not enough but must be validated, if only in fantasy, by association with social and personal meanings which in a different cultural pattern might be more directly available. The short description of the pattern we have is *magic*: a highly organized and professional system of magical inducements and satisfactions, functionally very similar to magical systems in simpler societies, but rather strangely coexistent with a highly developed scientific technology.

This contradiction is of the greatest importance in any analysis of modern capitalist society. The coming of large-scale industrial production necessarily raised critical problems of social organization, which in many fields we are still only struggling to solve. In the production of goods for personal use, the critical problem posed by the factory of advanced machines was that of the organization of the market. The modern factory requires not only smooth and steady distributive channels (without which it would suffocate under its own product) but also definite indications of demand without which the expensive processes of capitalization and equipment would be too great a risk. The historical choice posed by the development of industrial production is between different forms of organization and planning in the society to which it is central. In our own century, the choice has been and remains between some form of socialism and a new form of capitalism. In Britain, since the 1890s and with rapidly continuing emphasis, we have had the new capitalism, based on a series of devices for organizing and ensuring the market. Modern advertising, taking on its distinctive features in just this economic phase, is one of the most important of these devices, and it is perfectly true to say that modern capitalism could not function without it.

Yet the essence of capitalism is that the basic means of production are not socially but privately owned, and that decisions about production are therefore in the hands of a group occupying a minority position in the society and in no direct way responsible to it. Obviously, since the capitalist wishes to be successful, he is influenced in his decisions about production by what other members of the society need. But he is influenced also by considerations of industrial convenience and likely profit, and his decisions tend to be a balance of these varying factors. The challenge of socialism, still very powerful elsewhere but in Britain deeply confused by political immaturities and errors, is essentially that decisions about production should be in the hands of the society as a whole, in the sense that control of the means of production is made part of the general system of decision which the society as a whole creates. The conflict between capitalism and socialism is now commonly seen in terms of a competition in productive efficiency, and we need not doubt that much of our future history, on a world scale, will be determined by the results of our competition. Yet the conflict is really much deeper than this, and is also a conflict between different approaches to and forms of socialism. The fundamental choice that emerges, in the problems set to us by modern industrial production, is between man as consumer and man as user. The system of organized magic which is modern advertising is primarily important as a functional obscuring of this choice.

'CONSUMERS'

The popularity of 'consumer', as a way of describing the ordinary member of modern capitalist society in a main part of his economic capacity, is very significant. The description is spreading very rapidly, and is now habitually used by people to whom it ought, logically, to be repugnant. It is not only that, at a simple level, 'consumption' is a very strange description of our ordinary use of goods and services. This metaphor drawn from the stomach or the furnace is only partially relevant even to our use of things. Yet we say 'consumer', rather than 'user', because in the form of society we now have, and in the forms of thinking which it almost imperceptibly fosters, it is as consumers that the majority of people are seen. We are the market, which the system of industrial production has organized. We are the channels along which the product flows and disappears. In every aspect of social communication, and in every version of what we are as a community, the pressure of a system of industrial production is towards these impersonal forms.

Yet it is by no means necessary that these versions should prevail, just because we use advanced productive techniques. It is simply that once these have entered a society, new questions of structure and purpose in social organization are inevitably posed. One set of answers is the development of genuine democracy, in which the human needs of all the people in the society are taken as the central purpose of all social activity, so that politics is not a system of government but of self-government, and the systems of production and communication are rooted in the satisfaction of human needs and the development of human capacities. Another set of answers, of which we have had more experience, retains, often in very subtle forms, a more limited social purpose. In the first phase, loyal subjects, as they were previously seen, became the labour market of industrial 'hands'. Later, as the 'hands' reject this version of themselves, and claim a higher human status, the emphasis is changed.

Any real concession of higher status would mean the end of class-society and the coming of socialist democracy. But intermediate concessions are possible, including material concessions. The 'subjects' become the 'electorate', and 'the mob' becomes 'public opinion'.

Decision is still a function of the minority, but a new system of decision, in which the majority can be organized to this end, has to be devised. The majority are seen as 'the masses', whose opinion, *as masses* but not as real individuals or groups, is a factor in the business of governing. In practical terms, this version can succeed for a long time, but it then becomes increasingly difficult to state the nature of the society, since there is a real gap between profession and fact. Moreover, as the governing minority changes in character, and increasingly rests for real power on a modern economic system, older social purposes become vestigial, and whether expressed or implied, the maintenance of the economic system becomes the main factual purpose of all social activity. Politics and culture become deeply affected by this dominant pattern, and ways of thinking derived from the economic market – political parties considering how to sell themselves to the electorate, to create a favourable brand image; education being primarily organized in terms of a graded supply of labour; culture being organized and even evaluated in terms of commercial profit – become increasingly evident.

Still, however, the purposes of the society have to be declared in terms that will command the effort of a majority of its people. It is here that the idea of the 'consumer' has proved so useful. Since consumption is within its limits a satisfactory activity, it can be plausibly offered as a commanding social purpose. At the same time, its ambiguity is such that it ratifies the subjection of society to the operations of the existing economic system. An irresponsible economic system can supply the 'consumption' market, whereas it could only meet the criterion of human use by becoming genuinely responsible: that is to say, shaped in its use of human labour and resources by general social decisions. The consumer asks for an adequate supply of personal 'consumer goods' at a tolerable price: over the last ten years, this has been the primary aim of British government. But users ask for more than this, necessarily. They ask for the satisfaction of human needs which consumption, as such can never really supply. Since many of these needs are social – roads, hospitals, schools, quiet – they are not only not covered by the consumer ideal: they are even denied by it, because consumption tends always to materialize as an individual activity. And to satisfy this range of needs would involve questioning the autonomy of the economic system, in its actual setting of priorities. This is where the consumption ideal is not only misleading, as a form of defence of the system, but ultimately destructive to the broad general purposes of the society.

Advertising, in its modern forms, then operates to preserve the consumption ideal from the criticism inexorably made of it by experience. If the consumption of individual goods leaves that whole area of human need unsatisfied, the attempt is made, by magic, to associate this consumption with human desires to which it has no real reference. You do not only buy an object: you buy social respect, discrimination, health, beauty, success, power to control your environment. The magic obscures the real sources of general satisfaction because their discovery would involve radical change in the whole common way of life.

Of course, when a magical pattern has become established in a society, it is capable of some real if limited success. Many people will indeed look twice at you, upgrade you, upmarket you, respond to your displayed signals, if you have made the right purchases within a system of meanings to which you are all trained. Thus the fantasy seems to be validated, at a personal level, but only at the cost of preserving the general unreality which it obscures: the real failures of the society which however are not easily traced to this pattern.

It must not be assumed that magicians – in this case, advertising agents – disbelieve their own magic. They may have a limited professional cynicism about it, from knowing how some of the tricks are done. But fundamentally they are involved, with the rest of the society, in the confusion to which the magical gestures are a response. Magic is always an unsuccessful attempt to provide meanings and values, but it is often very difficult to distinguish magic from genuine knowledge and from art. The belief that high consumption is a high standard of living is a general belief of the society. The conversion of numerous objects into sources of sexual or pre-sexual satisfaction is evidently not only a process in the minds of advertisers, but also a deep and general confusion in which much energy is locked.

At one level, the advertisers are people using certain skills and knowledge, created by real art and science, against the public for commercial advantage. This hostile stance is rarely confessed in general propaganda for advertising, where the normal emphasis is the blind consumption ethic ('Advertising brings you the good things of life'), but it is common in advertisers' propaganda to their clients. 'Hunt with the mind of the hunter', one recent announcement begins, and another, under the heading 'Getting any honey from the hive industry?', is rich in the language of attack:

> One of the most important weapons used in successful marketing is advertising. Commando Sales Limited, steeped to the nerve ends in the skills of unarmed combat, are ready to move into battle on any sales front at the crack of an accepted estimate. These are the front line troops to call in when your own sales force is hopelessly outnumbered by the forces of sales resistance . . .

This is the structure of feeling in which 'impact' has become the normal description of the effect of successful communication, and 'impact' like 'consumer' is now habitually used by people to whom it ought to be repugnant. What sort of person really wants to 'make an impact' or create a 'smash hit', and what state is a society in when this can be its normal cultural language?

It is indeed monstrous that human advances in psychology, sociology and communication should be used or thought of as powerful techniques *against* people, just as it is rotten to try to reduce the faculty of human choice to 'sales resistance'. In these respects, the claim of advertising to be a service is not particularly plausible. But equally, much of this talk of weapons and impact is the jejune bravado of deeply confused men. It is in the end the language of frustration rather than of power. Most advertising is not the cool creation of skilled professionals, but the confused creation of bad thinkers and artists. If we look at the petrol with the huge clenched fist, the cigarette against loneliness in the deserted street, the puppet facing death with a life-insurance policy (the modern protection, unlike the magical symbols painstakingly listed from earlier societies), or the man in the cradle which is an aeroplane, we are looking at attempts to express and resolve real human tensions which may be crude but which also involve deep feelings of a personal and social kind.

The structural similarity between much advertising and much modern art is not simply copying by the advertisers. It is the result of comparable responses to the contemporary human condition, and the only distinction that matters is between the clarification achieved by some art and the displacement normal in bad art and most advertising. The skilled magicians, the masters of the masses, must be seen as ultimately involved in the general weakness which they not only exploit but are exploited by. If the meanings and values generally operative in the society give no answers to, no means of negotiating, problems of death, loneliness, frustration, the need for identity and respect, then the magical system must come, mixing its charms and expedients with reality in easily available forms, and binding the weakness to the condition which has created it. Advertising is then no longer merely a way of selling goods, it is a true part of the culture of a confused society.

57

ADVERTISING, MAGAZINE CULTURE, AND THE 'NEW MAN'

Sean Nixon

[Agencies] know that the fashionable young man is out there, but they don't know how to address him. You can't address all men; there's been no one image specific to all men. (Lucy Purdy, Research Bureau Limited, *Arena*, Summer 1988: 24)

Lucy Purdy's comments captured the dilemma faced by advertising practitioners in the early to mid-1980s in advertising to men. Consumer research was producing a picture of shifts in the values and lifestyles of groups of male consumers. These shifts were represented in consumer types like the 'avant guardian', the 'self exploiter' or the 'innovator'. Advertising practitioners were confronted with the problem of making decisions about the significance of these findings and with assessing whether they were appropriate for the specific male markets they were producing adverts for.

Two practices within the process of making adverts shaped the way certain groups of practitioners responded to the evidence from consumer research. They were account planning and media buying. Both practices were important because it was through them that research findings – like that about new groups of male consumers – were incorporated into the advertising process and ultimately impacted on the decisions made in the production of adverts by art directors and writers.

[. . .]

From S. Nixon, *Hard Looks: Masculinities, Spectatorship and Contemporary Consumption* (London: UCL Press, 1996) pp. 103, 116–22, 131–37, 143–44.

'CREATIVE ADVERTISING' AND THE 'NEW MAN'

It is my contention that changes in the advertising industry [. . .] underpin in institutional terms the formation of the 'new man' imagery within advertising. I want to [. . .] focus on two campaigns that exemplify these developments. They are Bartle Bogle Hegarty's work for Levi-Strauss's 'Levi's 501 jeans' and Grey advertising's work for Beechams Healthcare and Toiletries' 'Brylcreem'. Both campaigns are significant because they were key to establishing a successful style of advertising to new male markets in the mid-1980s. As such, they provided a positive answer to the question posed by Lucy Purdy at the beginning of this chapter. As we saw, she argued that agencies and their clients were uncertain about how to address the 'fashionable young man'. BBH and Grey found the appropriate imagery to successfully do just that.

Levi's 501s

I have already signalled the significance of BBH's two television adverts for Levi-Strauss which ran from the end of 1985 and through 1986. These adverts formed part of a campaign which aimed to turn around Levi-Strauss's fortunes. These had been declining since the end of the 1970s and most rapidly during the early 1980s. They had reached a particularly low point in 1984. That year saw the year on year sales of jeans in the UK market as a whole down by 13 per cent, and Levi-Strauss's sales were hit particularly badly. The company themselves identified part of the reason for this decline in the failure of a marketing strategy which had been introduced at the end of the 1970s with the first signs of shifts in the jeans market. Levi-Strauss had diversified from its core business of jeans into menswear, womenswear and youthwear. In particular, it had more intensively targeted the 25 to 35 year old mainstream male market with a range of leisurewear. These included Levi's sweatshirts and trousers like the Levi's 'Action Slacks'. This strategy undermined, however, Levi-Strauss's core product area (the jeans) and what the company saw as their essential values (quality, durability, Americanness, tradition). Research by Levi-Strauss showed, in particular, that the credibility for young consumers of the Levi's name had slipped amidst the proliferation of leisure wear for older markets. As Peter Skilland, Levi-Strauss's marketing services manager at the time acknowledged, 'Putting the Levi's name on polyester trousers meant nothing to the polyester trouser buyer and left the jeans buyer totally unimpressed' (*Campaign*, 23/6/86: 50).

The company initiated a major rethink of its strategy. It decided upon what it called a 'back to basics' policy. In other words, the product diversification was reversed, and Levi-Strauss refocused its manufacturing and marketing on the jean market. The aim was to re-establish the association of the Levi's name with tradition, Americanness, durability and quality. Three strands of this policy were significant. First, a decision was made to move away from an emphasis on volume sales and instead concentrate on profitability per unit. What this meant for the product range was the relaunch of the company's longest-standing line – the 501 jean – as a quality fashion trouser at a higher price. Secondly, Levi-Strauss was concerned to refocus its marketing upon what it saw as the crucial jeans market – the 15 to 19 year old youth market, and especially 15 to 19 year old males. Thirdly, the new marketing of the relaunched Levi's 501 was to be co-ordinated across Levi-Strauss's European markets and be – in this sense – genuinely pan-European.

BBH, who had won the UK account in 1982, satisfied Levi-Strauss that they could co-ordinate the new pan-European strategy. In researching the creative strategy for the campaign, BBH discovered a significant trend:

> We uncovered a fascination, almost a reverence, for a mythical America of the past – the America that had produced Dean and Presley, the 57 Chevrolet, Sam Cooke, the Misfits and a host of other heroes and 'cult objects'. Clothes and shoes featured strongly in this, and the 'fifties' look, suitably processed for the mid-1980s, was current ... 501s featured heavily in this trend, and were being adopted by opinion-leading 'cognescenti' in small but interesting numbers in London, Paris, Hamburg, Berlin, Rome and Milan. (Broadbent 1990: 184)

The appropriation of the 'fifties' look in 'street style' and the valorization of a particular repertoire of 'classic' objects (like Zippo lighters and Ray Ban sunglasses) offered a potentially neat fit with Levi-Strauss's 'back to basics' strategy. BBH's brief, however, was to establish the Levi's 501 jeans in the arena of mass fashion. That is, it had not only to address opinion-leaders (or what BBH elsewhere termed 'innovators'), but – in BBH's terms – 'early adopters'. As the agency themselves put it:

> We wanted to make 501s compulsory equipment for anyone who cared about the way they looked. We wished to persuade the 15–20 year old males who represent the core jeans market that 501 were the right look, and the only label: the right look because 'anti-fit' [the 501 cut] was the way jeans were being worn by those in the know; the only label, because only Levi's 501 had laid genuine claim to the heady jeans heritage that was rooted in the fifties. (ibid.: 185)

A more detailed formulation of the brief followed from this specification of the target consumers. Using group discussions with consumers in London and Frankfurt based around video screenings of film footage and collages of magazine photos, BBH confirmed that – in their terms – the 'evocation of a mythical America was a motivating route ... We also deepened our understanding of the role of great pop classics in underlying the status of the product and learned that casting was absolutely crucial' (ibid.: 185).

The final creative brief was produced from these findings and the adverts were art directed by John Hegarty and written by Barbara Noakes. 'Bath' and 'Launderette' went on the air in the UK on Boxing Day 1985 on both ITV and Channel 4, together with a cinema run of the adverts. In addition, the marketing strategy included a press campaign, the development of extensive point-of-sale materials (to support the new campaign within retail outlets), the design of a 501 logo, coordination with record companies of the release of the two soundtrack songs, and – in 1987 – a second phase of marketing. I [will] come back to the press campaign. Importantly, as we will see, it was aimed not at the mass market of early-adopters targeted through television, but at a segmented market of 'innovators'.

'Bath' and 'Launderette' were immediately successful. Sales of the 501s expanded rapidly; so rapidly in fact that in March and April of 1986 the adverts were withdrawn from television because Levi's factories were unable to keep up with demand. Importantly for Levi-Strauss, sales of the 501s markedly improved the profits per units of the company. The adverts also prompted extended press and television commentary, and picked up a number of industry awards.

It was the codings of masculinity put together in the adverts which really concerns us. [. . .] I want to underline here five characteristics of the masculinity signified in 'Bath' and 'Launderette'. First, the appropriation and glamorization of 1950s style was important. It set the terms for the signification of an assertive masculinity. Secondly, the surface of the models' bodies – and specifically developed muscles – were displayed. Thirdly, the assertive masculinity of both the 'fifties' style and the models' physiques, were signified together with the coding of softness and sensuality. Both Nick Kamen and James Mardle had smooth, clear skins, full pouting lips, shiny eyes and glossy, highly groomed hair. Fourthly, the display of these bodies was presented to the viewer in highly distinctive ways. Cuts to arms, chest, face, bottom and thighs, together with a focus on the unbuttoning of the jeans and (in the case of 'Bath') a cut of the water seeping over the model's jean-clad crotch, undermined more conventional significations of power and aggression associated with displayed masculine bodies. Fifthly, the male hero was represented as self-contained and on his own.

What these characteristics established was a coherent grammar for addressing new male consumers in the mid to late 1980s. Not all the codings necessarily appeared in every advert, but a combination of them was characteristically present in a series of adverts for clothing and accessories, grooming and toiletries, financial services and electrical goods. This repertoire of codings was central to Grey Advertising's work with Brylcreem.

Brylcreem

If Levi-Strauss was suffering from a decline in its fortunes prior to its strategic rethink and BBH's campaign for the Levi's 501s, then Beechams's Brylcreem was in near terminal decline. From a peak in the early 1960s when Brylcreem sold one hundred million pots in the UK, by 1984 sales were down to five million because of longer hair and styles requiring blow-drying among men. This dramatic decline was aggravated by the nature of Brylcreem's remaining customer base, which was an ageing group of long-term male users. Beechams saw little opportunity in expanding sales within this market, and no advertising of the brand had been run since the 'Brylcreem bounce' campaign of the early 1970s. A general re-appraisal by Beechams of its key brands, however, changed this. Suffering from what industry analysts termed 'lack of executive direction' in the early 1980s, Beechams set in motion initiatives to reposition and reestablish brands like Lucozade, Horlicks, Ribena and (what Beechams saw as the most difficult task) Brylcreem. Underpinning this strategy was new product development and marketing. Grey Advertising, which won the new account in 1985, set about researching the creative strategy. A key finding for Grey was that among a younger generation of men, shorter hair and traditionally smart hairstyles were being worn in preference for what Grey called the '"scruffy" styles of the last twenty years' (*Campaign*, 4/10/85: 15). These were, specifically, a highly fashion conscious group of male consumers whom Grey termed 'stylepreneurs' (ibid.). Formulating a creative strategy for these target consumers was a problem, however, for the creatives at Grey. Art director Su Sareem and writer Jan Heron described how they came up with the final version.

> Jan and I were despairing – we knew that there was a solution there somewhere but we just couldn't seem to find it. For inspiration, we went through the old Brylcreem commercials and were watching the sixties reel in my flat. Suddenly the phone rang. I put the video on 'hold' and the image started to shake. We both realised that with good music, it would be perfect. (*Campaign*, 4/10/85: 15)

Three new commercials were cut and re-edited from the old commercials using video-editing techniques and a contemporary soundtrack was added. Beechams was not fully convinced by this creative strategy, and initially allocated only £1 million to test the campaign. Grey used all this budget for a television campaign in London. Both the agency and client were happy with the initial consumer response, and so in February 1986 a second campaign – using similar footage – was launched, together with an extensive press and poster campaign. The press and poster work extended the pastiche of the 1960s advertising using contemporary models. These included Nick Kamen's brother, Barry. This was accompanied by the design of a new tub style. In 1987, further product development was initiated and a range of 13 products (including mousse, gel and aftershave) was launched in black packaging and with a new typeface for the brand name. In 1988, this product range was backed by a new television commercial which – still focusing on the appropriation of 1950s style short hair by young men – extended the repositioning of the brand as an essential purchase for stylish young men (*Campaign*, 11/11/88: 3). The creative team at Grey, like their counterparts at BBH, identified casting as crucial to establishing the credibility of the advert among its target audience. In casting the 26 year old Corsican, Jean-Ange Chiapinini, the team 'were looking for the definitive modern man. A cross between Mickey Rourke and Matt Dillon, more of a man on the street than a pretty-boy model type like Nick Kamen' (ibid.: 12).

The advert was set in a barber's shop, amid the traditional paraphernalia of masculine grooming. The narrative of the advert was based around the model being wet shaved by the barber. In dramatically lit gloom we see the shaving cream being applied, the razor being used and the barber massaging the model's temples and then pulling a hot flannel over his face to complete the grooming. Throughout this ritual, which is shot in rapid close-ups, the model is narcissistically absorbed in the care he is receiving. His self-absorption is highlighted by the fact that the process of shaving is shot in such quick edits to a thunderous soundtrack. We glimpse a flame, the razor against his face, a razor being sharpened on leather and the steaming flannel being pulled across his face. The model remains self-absorbed amid these movements around him. In all of this there was more than a hint at sado-masochism connoted through the ritual of grooming between the barber and the model.

The masculine imagery of the campaigns echoed many of the codings at work in the Levi's 501 adverts, despite the self-conscious attempt (through casting in particular) to encode a different masculinity. The appropriation of the iconography of the neat and smart style of respectable 1950s masculinity was key to the first television campaigns, the press and poster campaign and the 1988 television commercial (even if, in the early television campaigns, the imagery was in fact from the early 1960s). The glamorization and – most clearly in the re-cut and re-edited adverts – playful quality of this appropriation was again important. The casting of the models was also significant. Chiapinini's 'look', in the 1988 advert, was certainly harder than Kamen's. More important, though, were the continuities in both this advert and the press and poster adverts: the combination of an assertively masculine 'look', which also contained elements of softness or sensuality connoted through the gloss of the hair and skin and the fullness of the lips. The television advert of 1988 for Brylcreem also explicitly displayed, like the Levi's 501 adverts, the narcissistic pleasures of grooming and adornment.

These codings of masculinity are at the heart of my contentions about the distinctiveness of the 1980s 'new man' imagery. In order to develop my argument about the break they represented in popular representations of masculinity and the forms of spectatorship associated with them, I want to turn to another institutional site in the regime of 'new man' imagery. This was the new magazine culture of the 'style press' and men's general interest magazines. These magazines are particularly important because the codings of masculinity represented in the Levi's 501 and Brylcreem adverts drew upon codings established within the 'style' magazines in the mid-1980s.

[. . .]

THE STYLE PRESS

The 'style press' was a term applied to three magazines which launched almost simultaneously in 1980. These were *The Face, I-D*, and *Blitz*. The term was deployed as a form of trade and journalistic shorthand for the kind of journalism and editorial mix which characterized the magazines. The magazines themselves were all produced by independent publishers – Wagadon (*The Face*), Jigsaw (*Blitz*) and Levelprint Ltd (*I-D*) – and who, among the company of publishing giants like IPC, National Magazines, Condé Nast, and even a smaller publisher like EMAP, were marginal enterprises.

The Face was the most successful of the three magazines, reaching a circulation peak of around 92,000 between 1985 and 1987, as well as picking up a number of trade awards (*Benn's Media Directory*, 1983–8).

[. . .]

The Face's circulation expanded strongly in 1983 and 1984. In the second half of 1984 sales rose by 20 per cent from 66,500 to 80,000 (*Media Week*, 3/5/85: 22). As the magazine grew, [publisher and editor Nick] Logan's strong sense of the 'look' of the magazine led to a somewhat idiosyncratic approach to competing for advertising revenue. Initially, he had planned that *The Face* would be able to survive on cover sales alone, and although Logan had been forced from early on to take advertising, *The Face* did not have an advertising manager until 1984. Logan's antagonism to advertising derived from his sense that advertising spoiled the 'look' of the magazine. In particular, half-page or smaller adverts were anathema to Logan in his concern to develop the design of the magazine (*Direction*, 9/1988: 32).

Rod Sopp's arrival as advertising manager in 1984 marked a more engaged – if still disingenuous – view of advertising in relation to the magazine. Sopp skilfully crafted Logan's dislike of the way advertising broke up the aimed for layouts of the magazine, into a piece of media folklore about *The Face*'s preparedness to refuse adverts on aesthetic grounds. More significantly, Sopp produced for the first time a worked-up picture of the type of persons who read *The Face*. Sopp presented *The Face* to advertisers as the perfect media form through which to target the consumer groups we have already encountered: namely, 'innovators' or 'opinion formers'. These were groups of consumers who, for Sopp, were at the forefront of social trends; taste-shapers who – and he gave this example – were behind the classic mid-1980s style for young men of a plain white T-shirt, Levi's 501s, white socks and bass weejun loafers.

Sopp's representation of *The Face*'s readership of 'innovators' through the figure of the stylish young man was significant. Attention to menswear and male style was an important element of the magazine's editorial between 1983 and 1987. As Logan acknowledged, in what is a telling comment for my argument in this chapter,

One area where we are particularly strong is in men's fashions, which is pretty badly represented generally. I keep reading about the need for a men's magazine, but I think we're closer to that than anyone. Two thirds of our readers are men. At the moment I'm caught between trying to attract more women readers, or expanding the trend towards men. (*Media Week*, 16/3/84: 56)

Other commentators, like Jane Reed of IPC, saw *The Face* as shaping up a new market of young male readers. She argued that the magazine had established 'new territory for young men', particularly in terms of promoting style and consumption (*Campaign*, 26/7/85: 37). Even critics recognized the address *The Face* made to young men. Thus, publisher Peter Jackson castigated the magazine for being 'narrow, mannered and obsessed with males' (*Campaign*, 27/3/87: 20).

It was *The Face*'s association with this consumer subject, however – the stylish young male 'innovator' – that attracted advertising media buyers to the magazine. *Media Week* succinctly enunciated the thinking behind media buyers' interest in the magazine when it suggested that '*The Face*'s 63% NRS male readership is used by hapless media planners [or buyers] stuck with the perennial problem of reaching the young male through the colour press' (*Media Week*, 12/2/88: 4).

The placing of *The Face* high up the media buying lists of advertising media buyers and planners was itself dependent upon shifts in media buying practice. Thus, despite its relatively small circulation, *The Face* was identified by media buyers as an effective place in which to advertise both because the magazine was read by key groups of consumers ('innovators', 'the style-conscious male') and because it provided a sympathetic context in which to place adverts for, in particular, a range of lifestyle-orientated goods and services: clothing, financial services, records, alcohol and consumer electronics. Two high-profile advertising campaigns which ran in the magazine between 1985 and 1987 illustrated the way *The Face* was classified by advertising practitioners within this form of 'qualitative' media buying. These were the adverts produced for Way In and Levi's 501s.

[. . .]

Levi's 501s

BBH's press campaign for Levi's 501 jeans, which followed the broadcasting and screening of the 'Bath' and 'Launderette' television and cinema commercials in January 1986, was even more explicit than Lynne Franks PR's work for Way In in the way it selected *The Face* in terms of 'qualitative' media buying criteria. As we saw, the television and cinema adverts produced by BBH were aimed at a mass market of consumers ('early adopters', in BBH's terms) and motivated by the ambition to make the Levi's 501s a compulsory purchase for anyone within this segment interested in fashion. A major concern, however, surfaced for the agency with this strategy.

> The early indications of the potential success of the 501 programme, gave us one major concern. We feared that, as 501s went 'public', the opinion leaders who had discovered the product without the aid of advertising would abandon the brand. We had to reassure this small (but very important) group that 501s really were the great classic they had always believed them to be. (Broadbent 1990: 188)

The press campaign put together by BBH was designed to do precisely this. John Hegarty art directed five adverts which displayed the 501s laid out on a flat surface as part of a coordinated 'look'. Each advert was immaculately styled and accessorized by contemporary British fashion designers – Scott Crolla, Wendy Dagworthy, Jasper Conran, Joseph Ettedgui and Paul Smith. The adverts ran in *The Face* – directly targeted by BBH at 'innovators' (*Campaign*, 24/1/86: 12, *Media Week*, 29/4/88: 28).

The interlinking of these forms of advertising media buying practice and creative strategy on the pages of *The Face* – exemplified in both the Way In and Levi's 501 adverts – drew the magazine, then, very directly into the advertising arguments about targeting new male consumers through the colour press, arguments which – as I have suggested – were an important determinant of the formation of men's magazines. In classifying *The Face*, however, the media buyers at BBH or Lynne Franks PR did not hold all the cards. What was distinctive about the relationship between *The Face* and advertising practitioners at this time (1984–7) was the ability of the magazine to lay claim to this group of young male consumers. In other words, the magazine – and especially Rod Sopp – was extremely successful in persuading advertising media buyers that *The Face* was not only the perfect media vehicle through which to target new male consumers, but also that the magazine's staff had a developed sense of this group of consumers' tastes, values and sensibilities. This last point was particularly critical. In a period where advertising practitioners had evidence of shifts in the 'values and lifestyles' of groups of men and yet were uncertain about how to represent the new male consumer, *The Face* offered the precepts of the necessary cultural knowledge to target these 'new men'. Pivotal to this, as I hinted in my comments on the Levi's 501 and Brylcreem adverts, was the styling of menswear in the magazine and the codings of masculinities that this threw up. These exerted considerable influence over a wider range of representations targeted at new male consumers.

As well as being central to the way advertisers targeted this segment of male consumers through the colour press, *The Face* was also subject to close scrutiny from other consumer magazine publishers. For a number of publishing practitioners, the success of *The Face* between 1984 and 1986 really testified to a shift in the magazine reading habits of important groups of young men.

In particular, it was seen to have educated a generation of young men into reading a general interest magazine for men. In doing so, *The Face* also shifted the terms of what the format of a general interest magazine could be, namely one based upon a style-led journalism and editorial approach rather than on the format offered by women's magazines. These findings gave considerable impetus to the formulation of a general interest men's magazine aimed at the segment of men in the age group above *The Face*'s target readership. That is, men aged between 20 and 45.

[. . .]

CONCLUSION

What, then, can we draw out from this account of the advertising and publishing knowledges and practices that drove the formation of general interest men's magazines in the UK? What has my attention to the advertising/publishing nexus associated with the 'style press' and men's magazines delivered? First, it is important to emphasize that the account I have put together reveals the extent of the interest from groups of media practitioners (within magazine publishing and advertising) in a new type of magazine for men in the period between 1983 and 1989. Secondly, the concern specifically to target men through new magazines was dependent, as we saw, on a sense amongst these practitioners of shifts in young men's 'values and life-styles'. This was largely drawn from evidence from consumer research, but also from assessments of developments within magazine culture itself. Thirdly, the concern to target men through new magazines was also dependent upon the production of new products and services by advertisers and the refocusing of the marketing of existing products in relation to the new male market. Fourthly, the identification and servicing of new male readerships was led by independent publishers. Thus, the development of a sector of UK general interest men's magazines was marked in its formation by the success of the 'style press' and the publishing practices of the independent publishers, Wagadon. It was the style-based format that set the precepts for general interest men's magazines in their formation. Fifthly, the shifts within advertising media buying practice were critical to the advertising arguments and practice that shaped the formation of the new sector and provided its economic underpinning.

Putting together an account of these advertising and publishing knowledges and practices also has other pay-offs. It sheds light, in particular, on the way a central institutional determinant of the magazines functioned, that is the economic relations between advertisers and publishers. It is to repeat a well worn conceptualization to suggest that these economic relations regulated the production of the magazines. For publishers, securing and maintaining healthy levels of advertising revenue and achieving sufficiently large circulation figures formed the *sine qua non* of their operations as commercial enterprises. However, rather than take on trust the assumption from economic theory that

these economic relations and their associated commercial imperatives constituted a primary level of determination on the production of the magazines, the
account I have offered in this chapter prompts us to consider their operation in
different terms. First, it points us to the key relationships that constituted these
economic relations. From the account it is clear that we are talking about relations produced between some specific practitioners, namely advertising media
buyers and magazine advertising managers. It was this key relationship that
effectively constituted the economic relation between advertisers and publishers. Secondly, foregrounding these knowledges and practices revealed the way
in which representations of the imagined target readerships were central to the
operationalizing of these economic relations. In other words, it was through
these shared representations of the consumer that the relationship between
media buyers and advertising managers functioned. This suggests, then, that
the economic relations between advertisers and publishers themselves had
cultural conditions of existence, cultural conditions of existence made up of
the way the market of consumers was represented through specific cultural
practices. It is not to overplay the argument to suggest that this work of representation was as much a condition of existence of these economic relations as
the exchange of money between advertising agencies and publishers.

REFERENCE

Broadbent, S. (ed.) 1990. *Advertising Works 5.*

58

SOFT-SOAPING EMPIRE: COMMODITY RACISM AND IMPERIAL ADVERTISING

Anne McClintock

Doc: My, it's so clean.
Grumpy: There's dirty work afoot.

(Snow White and the Seven Dwarfs)

EMPIRE OF THE HOME

In 1899, the year the Anglo–Boer war erupted in South Africa, an advertisement for Pears' Soap in *McClure's Magazine* accounted:

> The first step towards LIGHTENING THE WHITE MAN'S BURDEN is through teaching the virtues of cleanliness. PEARS' SOAP is a potent factor in brightening the dark corners of the earth as civilization advances, while amongst the cultured of all nations it holds the highest place – it is the ideal toilet soap.

The advertisement (Figure [58.1]) figures an admiral decked in pure imperial white, washing his hands in his cabin as his steamship crosses the oceanic threshold into the realm of empire. In this image, private domesticity and the imperial market – the two spheres vaunted by middle-class Victorians to be naturally distinct – converge in a single commodity spectacle: the domestic sanctum of the white man's bathroom gives privileged vantage on to the global

From G. Robertson, M. Mash, L. Tickner, J. Bird, B. Curtis and T. Putnam (eds), *Travellers' Tales: Narratives of Home and Displacement* (London and New York: Routledge, 1994) pp. 131–54.

Figure [58.1]:   A white man sanitizing himself as he crosses the threshold of empire.

realm of imperial commerce. Imperial progress is consumed at a glance: time consumed as a commodity spectacle, as *panoptical time*.

On the wall, the porthole is both window and mirror. The window, icon of imperial surveillance and the Enlightenment idea of knowledge as penetration, is a porthole on to public scenes of economic conversion: one scene depicts a kneeling African gratefully receiving the Pears' Soap as he might genuflect before a religious fetish. The mirror, emblem of Enlightenment self-consciousness, reflects the sanitized image of white, male, imperial hygiene. Domestic hygiene, the ad implies, purifies and preserves the white male body from contamination as it crosses the dangerous threshold of empire; at the same time, the domestic commodity guarantees white male power, the genuflexion of Africans and rule of the world. On the wall, an electric light bulb signifies scientific rationality and spiritual advance. In this ad, the household commodity spells the lesson of imperial progress and capitalist civilization: civilization, for the white man, advances and brightens through his four beloved fetishes: soap, the mirror, light and white clothing – the four domestic fetishes that recur throughout imperial advertising and imperial popular culture of the time.

The first point about the Pears' advertisement is that it figures imperialism as coming into being through domesticity. At the same time, imperial domesticity is a domesticity without women. The commodity fetish, as the central form of the industrial enlightenment, reveals what liberalism would like to forget: the domestic is political, the political is gendered. What could not be admitted into male rationalist discourse (the economic value of women's domestic labour) is disavowed and projected on to the realm of the 'primitive' and the zone of empire. At the same time, the economic value of colonized cultures is domesticated and projected on to the realm of the 'prehistoric' fetish.

A characteristic feature of the Victorian middle class was its peculiarly intense preoccupation with boundaries. In imperial fiction and commodity kitsch, boundary objects and liminal scenes recur ritualistically. As colonials travelled back and forth across the threshold of their known world, crisis and boundary confusion were warded off and contained by fetishes, absolution rituals and liminal scenes. Soap and cleaning rituals became central to the ceremonial demarcation of body boundaries and the policing of social hierarchies. Cleansing and boundary rituals are integral to most cultures; what characterized Victorian cleaning rituals, however, was their peculiarly intense relation to money.

I begin with the Pears' Soap ad because it registers what I see as an epochal shift that took place in the culture of imperialism in the last decades of the nineteenth century. This was the shift from *'scientific' racism* – embodied as it was in anthropological, scientific and medical journals, travel writing and ethnographies – to what can be called *commodity racism*. Commodity racism – in the specifically Victorian forms of advertising and commodity spectacle, the imperial Expositions and the museum movement – converted the imperial progress narrative into mass-produced consumer spectacles. Commodity racism, I suggest, came to produce, market and distribute evolutionary racism and imperial power on a hitherto unimagined scale. In the process, the Victorian middle-class home became a space for the display of imperial spectacle and the reinvention of race, while the colonies – in particular Africa – became a theatre for exhibiting the Victorian cult of domesticity and the reinvention of gender.

The cult of domesticity became indispensable to the consolidation of British imperial identity – contradictory and conflictual as that was. At the same time, imperialism gave significant shape to the development of Victorian domesticity and the historic separation of the private and public. An intricate dialectic emerged: the Victorian invention of domesticity took shape around colonialism and the idea of race. At the same time, colonialism took shape around the Victorian invention of domesticity and the idea of the home.[1] Through the mediation of commodity spectacle, domestic space became racialized, while colonial space became domesticated.[2] The mass marketing of empire as a system of images became inextricably wedded to the reinvention of domesticity, so that the cultural history of imperialism cannot be understood without a theory of domestic space and gender power.

Commodity Racism and the Soap Cult

At the beginning of the nineteenth century, soap was a scarce and humdrum item and washing a cursory activity at best. A few decades later, the manufacture of soap had burgeoned into an imperial commerce. Victorian cleaning rituals were vaunted as the God-given sign of Britain's evolutionary superiority and soap had become invested with magic, fetish powers. The soap saga captured the hidden affinity between domesticity and empire and embodied a triangulated crisis in value: the undervaluation of women's work in the domestic realm; the overvaluation of the commodity in the industrial market; and the disavowal of colonized economies in the arena of empire. Soap entered the realm of Victorian fetishism with spectacular effect, notwithstanding the fact that male Victorians promoted soap as the very icon of non-fetishistic rationality.

Both the cult of domesticity and the new imperialism found in soap an exemplary mediating form. The emergent middle-class values – monogamy ('clean' sex which has value), industrial capital ('clean' money which has value), Christianity ('being washed in the blood of the lamb'), class control ('cleansing the great unwashed'), and the imperial civilizing mission ('washing and clothing the savage') – could all be marvellously embodied in a single household commodity. Soap advertising, in particular the Pears' Soap campaign, took its place at the vanguard of Britain's new commodity culture and its civilizing mission.

In the eighteenth century, the commodity was little more than a mundane object to be bought and used – in Marx's words, 'a trivial thing'.[3] By the late nineteenth century, however, the commodity had taken its privileged place, not only as the fundamental form of a new industrial economy, but also as the fundamental form of a new cultural system for representing social value.[4] Banks and stock exchanges rose up to manage the bonanzas of imperial capital. Professions emerged to administer the goods tumbling hectically from the manufactures. Middle-class domestic space became crammed, as never before, with furniture, clocks, mirrors, paintings, stuffed animals, ornaments, guns and a myriad gewgaws and knick-knacks. Victorian novelists bore witness to the strange spawning of commodities that seemed to have lives of their own. Meanwhile huge ships lumbered with trifles and trinkets, plied their trade between the colonial markets of Africa, the East, and the Americas.[5]

The new economy created an uproar, not only of things, but of signs. As Thomas Richards has argued, if all these new commodities were to be managed, a unified system of cultural representation had to be found. Richards shows how in 1851 the Great Exhibition of Things at the Crystal Palace served as a monument to a new form of consumption: 'What the first Exhibition heralded so intimately was the complete transformation of collective and private life into a space for the spectacular exhibition of commodities.'[6] As a 'semiotic laboratory for the labour theory of value', the Great Exhibition showed once and for all that the capitalist system not only had created a dominant form of exchange, but was also in the process of creating a dominant form of representation to go with it: the voyeuristic panorama of surplus as spectacle. By exhibiting commodities not only as goods, but also as an organized system of images, the Great Exhibition helped to fashion 'a new kind of being, the consumer, and a new kind of ideology, consumerism'. The mass consumption of the commodity spectacle was born.

Victorian advertising reveals a paradox, however. As the cultural form entrusted with upholding and marketing abroad the middle-class distinctions between private and public and between paid work and unpaid work, advertising also from the outset began to confound those distinctions. Advertising took the intimate signs of domesticity (children bathing, men shaving, women laced into corsets, maids delivering nightcaps) into the public realm, plastering scenes of domesticity on walls, buses, shopfronts and billboards. At the same time, advertising took scenes of empire into every corner of the home, stamping images of colonial conquest on soap boxes, match boxes, biscuit tins, whiskey bottles, tea tins and chocolate bars. By trafficking promiscuously across the threshold of private and public, advertising began to subvert some of the fundamental distinctions that commodity capital was bringing into being.

From the outset, moreover, Victorian advertising took explicit shape around the reinvention of racial difference. Commodity kitsch made possible, as never before, the mass marketing of empire as an organized system of images and attitudes. Soap flourished not only because it created and filled a spectacular gap in the domestic market, but also because, as a cheap and portable domestic commodity, it could persuasively mediate the Victorian poetics of racial hygiene and imperial progress.

Commodity racism became distinct from scientific racism in its capacity to expand beyond the literate propertied elite through the marketing of commodity spectacle. If, after the 1850s, scientific racism saturated anthropological, scientific and medical journals, travel writing and novels, these cultural forms were still relatively class-bound and inaccessible to most Victorians, who had neither the means nor the education to read such material. Imperial kitsch as consumer *spectacle*, by contrast, could package, market and distribute evolutionary racism on a hitherto unimagined scale. No pre-existing form of organized racism had ever before been able to reach so large and so differentiated a mass of the populace. Thus, as domestic commodities were mass-marketed through their appeal to imperial jingoism, commodity jingoism itself helped reinvent and maintain British national unity in the face of deepening imperial competition and colonial resistance. The cult of domesticity became indispensable to the consolidation of British national identity, and at the centre of the domestic cult stood the simple bar of soap.[7]

Yet soap has no social history. Since it purportedly belongs in the female realm of domesticity, soap is figured as beyond history and beyond politics proper.[8] To begin to write a social history of soap, then, is to refuse, in part, the erasure of women's domestic value under imperial capitalism. It cannot be forgotten, moreover, that the history of Victorian attempts to impose their commodity economy on African cultures was also the history of diverse African attempts either to refuse, appropriate, or negotiate European commodity fetishism to suit their own needs. The story of soap reveals that fetishism, far from being a quintessentially African propensity, as nineteenth-century anthropology maintained, was central to industrial modernity, inhabiting and mediating the uncertain threshold zones between domesticity and industry, metropolis and empire.

EMPIRE OF THE HOME: RACIALIZING DOMESTICITY

Before the late nineteenth century, washing was done in most households only once or twice a year in great, communal binges, usually in public at streams or rivers.[9] As for body washing, not much had changed since the days when Queen Elizabeth I was distinguished by the frequency with which she washed: 'regularly every month whether she needed it or not'.[10] By the 1890s, however, soap sales had soared, Victorians were consuming 260,000 tons of soap a year, and advertising had emerged as the central cultural form of commodity capitalism.[11]

The initial impetus for soap advertising came from the realm of empire. For Britain, economic competition with the United States and Germany created the need for a more aggressive promotion of products, and led to the first real innovations in advertising. In 1884, the year of the Berlin Conference, the first wrapped soap was sold under a brand name. This small event signified a major transformation in capital, as imperial competition gave rise to the creation of monopolies. Henceforth, items formerly indistinguishable from each other (soap sold simply as soap) would be marketed by their corporate signature (Pears', Monkey Brand, etc.). Soap became one of the first commodities to register the historic shift from a myriad small businesses to the great imperial monopolies. In the 1870s, hundreds of small soap companies plied the new trade in hygiene, but by the end of the century, the trade was monopolized by ten large companies.

In order to manage the great soap show, an aggressively entrepreneurial breed of advertisers emerged, dedicated to gracing their small, homely product with a radiant halo of imperial glamour and racial potency. The advertising agent, like the bureaucrat, played a vital role in the imperial expansion of foreign trade. Advertisers billed themselves as 'empire builders', and flattered themselves with 'the responsibility of the historic imperial mission'. Said one: 'Commerce even more than sentiment binds the ocean sundered portions of empire together. Anyone who increases these commercial interests strengthens the whole fabric of the empire.'[12] Soap was credited not only with bringing moral and economic salvation to the lives of Britain's 'great unwashed', but also with magically embodying the spiritual ingredient of the imperial mission itself.

In an ad for Pears', for example, a black and implicitly racialized coal-sweeper holds in his hands a glowing, occult object. Luminous with its own inner radiance, the simple soap-bar glows like a fetish, pulsating magically with spiritual enlightenment and imperial grandeur, promising to warm the hands and hearts of working people across the globe.[13] Pears', in particular, became intimately associated with a purified nature, magically cleansed of polluting industry (tumbling kittens, faithful dogs, children festooned with flowers), and a purified working-class, magically cleansed of polluting labour (smiling servants in crisp white aprons, rosy-cheeked match-girls and scrubbed scullions).[14]

None the less, the Victorian obsession with cotton and cleanliness was not simply a mechanical reflex of economic surplus. If imperialism garnered a bounty of cheap cotton and soap-oils from coerced colonial labour, the middle-class Victorian fascination with clean white bodies and clean white clothing stemmed not only from the rampant profiteering of the imperial economy, but also from the unbidden realms of ritual and fetish.

Soap did not flourish when imperial ebullience was at its peak. It emerged commercially during an era of impending crisis and social calamity, serving to preserve, through fetish ritual, the uncertain boundaries of class, gender and race identity in a world felt to be threatened by the fetid effluvia of the slums, the belching smoke of industry, social agitation, economic upheaval, imperial competition and anti-colonial resistance. Soap offered the promise of spiritual salvation and regeneration through commodity consumption, a regime of domestic hygiene that could restore the threatened potency of the imperial body politic and the race.

Four fetishes recur ritualistically in soap advertising: soap itself; white clothing (especially aprons); mirrors; and monkeys. A typical Pears' advertisement figures a black child and a white child together in a bathroom (see Figure [58.2]). The Victorian bathroom is the innermost sanctuary of domestic hygiene, and by extension the private temple of public regeneration. The sacrament of soap offers a reformation allegory, whereby the purification of the domestic body becomes a metaphor for the regeneration of the body politic. In this particular ad, a black boy sits in the bath, gazing wide-eyed into the water as if into a foreign element. A white boy, clothed in a white apron – the familiar fetish of domestic purity – bends benevolently over his 'lesser' brother, bestowing upon him the precious talisman of racial progress. The magical fetish of soap promises that the commodity can regenerate the Family of Man by washing from the skin the very stigma of racial and class degeneration.

Soap advertising offers an allegory of imperial 'progress' as spectacle. In this ad, the imperial topos of panoptical time (progress consumed as a spectacle from a privileged point of invisibility) enters the domain of the commodity. In the second frame of this ad, the black child is out of the bath, and the white boy shows him his startled visage in the mirror. The boy's body has become magically white, but his face – for Victorians the seat of rational individuality

Figure [58.2]:   The sacrament of soap: racializing domesticity.

and self-consciousness – remains stubbornly black. The white child is thereby figured as the agent of history and the male heir to progress, reflecting his lesser brother in the European mirror of self-consciousness. In the Victorian mirror, the black child witnesses his predetermined destiny of imperial metamorphosis, but himself remains a passive, racial hybrid: part black, part white, brought to the brink of civilization by the twin commodity fetishes of soap and mirror. The advertisement discloses a crucial element of late Victorian commodity culture: the metaphoric transformation of *imperial time* into *consumer space* – imperial progress consumed, at a glance, as domestic spectacle.

[. . .]

DOMESTICATING EMPIRE

By the end of the century, a stream of imperial bric-à-brac had invaded Victorian homes. Colonial heroes and colonial scenes emblazoned a host of domestic commodities, from milk cartons to sauce bottles, tobacco tins to whiskey bottles, assorted biscuits to toothpaste, toffee boxes to baking powder.[15] Traditional *national* fetishes, such as the Union Jack, Britannia, John Bull and the rampant lion, were marshalled into a revamped celebration of *imperial* spectacle. Empire was seen to be patriotically defended by Ironclad

Figure [58.3]:   The myth of the first contact with the conquering commodity.

Porpoise Bootlaces and Sons of the Empire Soap, while Stanley came to the rescue of the Emin of Pasha laden with outsize boxes of Huntley and Palmers Biscuits.

Late Victorian advertising presented a vista of the colonies as conquered by domestic commodities.[16] In the flickering magic lantern of imperial desire, teas, biscuits, tobaccos, Bovril, tins of cocoa and, above all, soaps beach themselves on far-flung shores, tramp through jungles, quell uprisings, restore order and write the inevitable legend of commercial progress across the colonial land-scape. In a Huntley and Palmers' Biscuits ad, a group of male colonials sit in the middle of a jungle on biscuit crates, sipping tea. Towards them, a stately and seemingly endless procession of elephants, laden with more biscuits and colonials, brings tea-time to the heart of the jungle. The serving attendant in this ad, as in most others, is male. Two things happen: women vanish from the *Boy's Own* affair of empire, while colonized men are feminized by their association with domestic servitude.

Liminal images of oceans, beaches and shorelines recur in cleaning ads of the time. An exemplary ad for Chlorinol Soda Bleach shows three boys in a soda-box sailing in a phantasmic ocean bathed by the radiance of the imperial dawn (Figure [58.4]). In a scene washed in the red, white and blue of the Union Jack, two black boys proudly hold aloft their boxes of Chlorinol. A third boy, the familiar racial hybrid of cleaning ads, has presumably already applied his

Figure [58.4]:   Panoptical time: imperial progress consumed at a glance.

bleach, for his skin is blanched an eerie white. On red sails that repeat the red of the bleach box, the legend of black people's purported commercial redemption in the arena of empire reads: 'We are Going to Use "Chlorinol" and be like De White Nigger'.

The ad vividly exemplifies Marx's lesson that the mystique of the commodity fetish lies not in its use value, but in its exchange value and its potency as a sign: 'So far as [the commodity] is a value in use, there is nothing mysterious about it'. For three naked children, clothing bleach is less than useful. Instead, the whitening agent of bleach promises an alchemy of racial upliftment through historic contact with commodity culture. The transforming power of the civilizing mission is stamped on the boat-box's sails as the objective character of the commodity itself. More than merely a *symbol* of imperial progress, the domestic commodity becomes the *agent of* history itself. The commodity, abstracted from social context and human labour, does the civilizing work of empire, while radical change is figured as magic, without process or social agency. In this way, cleaning ads such as Chlorinol's foreshadow the 'before and after' beauty ads of the twentieth century: a crucial genre directed largely at women, in which the conjuring power of the product to alchemize change is all that lies between the temporal 'before and after' of women's bodily transformation.

The Chlorinol ad displays a racial and gendered division of labour. Imperial progress from black child to 'white nigger' is consumed as commodity spectacle – panoptical time. The self-satisfied, hybrid 'white nigger' literally holds the rudder of history and directs social change, while the dawning of civilization bathes his enlightened brow with radiance. The black children simply have exhibition value as potential consumers of the commodity, there only to uphold the promise of capitalist commerce and to represent how far the white child has evolved – in the iconography of Victorian racism, the condition of 'savagery' is identical to the condition of infancy. Like white women, Africans (both women and men) are figured not as historic agents, but as frames for the commodity, for their *exhibition* value alone. The working-women, both black and white, who spend vast amounts of energy bleaching the white sheets, shirts, frills, aprons, cuffs and collars of imperial clothes are nowhere to be seen. It is important to note that in Victorian advertising, black women are very seldom rendered as consumers of commodities, for, in imperial lore, they lag too far behind men to be agents of history.

In the Chlorinol ad, women's creation of social value through household work is displaced on to the commodity as its own power, fetishistically inscribed on the children's bodies as a magical metamorphosis of the flesh. At the same time, military subjugation, cultural coercion and economic thuggery get refigured in such cleaning ads as a benign, domestic process as natural and healthy as washing. The stains of Africa's disobligingly complex and tenacious past and the inconvenience of alternative economic and cultural values are washed away like grime.

Incapable of themselves actually engendering change, African men are figured only as 'mimic men', to borrow V. S. Naipaul's dyspeptic phrase, destined simply to ape the epic white march of progress to self-knowledge. Bereft of the white raiments of imperial godliness, the Chlorinol children appear to take the fetish literally, content to bleach their skins to white. Yet these ads reveal that, far from being a quintessentially African propensity, the faith in fetishism was a faith fundamental to imperial capitalism itself.

By the turn of the century, soap ads vividly embodied the hope that the commodity alone, independent of its use value, could convert other cultures to civilization. Soap ads also embody what can be called *the myth of first contact*: the hope of capturing, as spectacle, the pristine moment of originary contact fixed forever in the timeless surface of the image. In another Pears' ad (Figure [58.3]), a black man stands alone on a beach, examining a bar of soap he has picked from a crate washed ashore from a shipwreck. The ad announces nothing less than the 'The Birth of Civilization'. Civilization is born, the image implies, at the moment of first contact with the Western commodity. Simply by touching the magical object, African man is inspired into history. An epic metamorphosis takes place, as Man the Hunter-gather (anachronistic man) evolves instantly into Man the Consumer. At the same time, the magical object effects a *gender* transformation, for the consumption of the domestic soap is racialized as a male birthing ritual with the egg-shaped commodity as the fertile talisman of change. Since women cannot be recognized as agents of history, it is necessary that a man, not a woman, be the historic beneficiary of the magical cargo, and that the male birthing occur on the beach, not in the home.[17]

In keeping with the racist iconography of the gender degeneration of colonized men, the man is subtly feminized by his role as historic specimen on display. His jaunty feather displays what Victorians liked to believe was colonized men's fetishistic, feminine and lower-class predilection for decorating their bodies. Thomas Carlyle, in his prolonged cogitation on clothes, *Sartor Resartus*, notes, for example: 'The first spiritual want of a barbarous man is Decoration, an instinct we still see amongst the barbarous classes in civilized nations.'[18] Feminists have explored how, in the iconography of modernity, women's bodies are exhibited for visual consumption, but very little has been said about how, in imperial iconography, black men were figured as spectacles for commodity exhibition. If, in scenes set in the Victorian home, female servants are *racialized* and portrayed as frames for the exhibition of the commodity, in advertising scenes set in the colonies, colonized men are *feminized* and portrayed as exhibition frames for commodity display. Black women, by contrast, are rendered virtually invisible. Essentialist assumptions about a universal 'male gaze' require a great deal more historical complication.

Marx notes how under capitalism 'the exchange value of a commodity assumes an independent existence'. Towards the end of the nineteenth century, in many ads, the commodity itself disappears, and the corporate signature, as the embodiment of pure exchange value in monopoly capital, finds its independent existence. Another ad for Pears' features a group of dishevelled Sudanese 'dervishes' awestruck by a white legend carved on the mountain face: PEARS' SOAP IS THE BEST (Figure [58.5]). The significance of the ad, as Richards notes, is its representation of the commodity as a magic medium capable of enforcing and enlarging British power in the colonial world without the rational understanding of the mesmerized Sudanese.[19] What the ad more properly reveals is the colonials' own fetishistic faith in the magic of brand-names to work the causal power of empire. In a similar ad, the letters BOVRIL march boldly over a colonial map of South Africa – imperial progress consumed as spectacle (Figure [58.6]). In an inspired promotional idea, the word BOVRIL was recognized as tracing the military advance of Lord Roberts across the country, yoking together, as if writ by nature, the simultaneous lessons of colonial domination and commodity progress. In this ad, the colonial map enters the realm of commodity spectacle.

The poetics of cleanliness is a poetics of social discipline. Purification rituals prepare the body as a terrain of meaning, organizing flows of value across the self and the community, and demarcating boundaries between one community and another. Purification rituals, however, can also be regimes of violence and constraint. People who have the power to invalidate the boundary rituals of

Figure [58.5]:   The commodity signature as colonial fetish.

another people demonstrate thereby their capacity to impose violently their culture on others. Colonial travel writers, traders, missionaries and bureaucrats carped constantly at the supposed absence in African culture of 'proper domestic life', in particular Africans' purported lack of 'hygiene'.[20] But the invention of Africans as 'dirty' and 'undomesticated', far from being an accurate depiction of African cultures, served to legitimize the imperialists' violent enforcement of their cultural and economic values, with the intent of purifying and thereby subjugating the 'unclean' African body, and imposing market and cultural values more useful to the mercantile and imperial economy. The myth of imperial commodities beaching on native shores, there to be welcomed by awestruck natives, wipes from memory the long and intricate history of European commercial trade with Africans and the long and intricate history of African resistance to Europe. Domestic ritual became a technology of discipline and dispossession.

What is crucial, however, is not simply the formal contradictions that structure fetishes, but also the more demanding historical question of how certain groups succeed, through coercion or hegemony, in containing the ambivalence that fetishism embodies, by successfully imposing their economic and cultural system on others.[21] This does not mean that the contradictions are permanently resolved, nor that they cannot be used against the colonials themselves. None

Figure [58.6]: 'As if writ by nature.'

the less, it seems crucial to recognize that what has been vaunted by some as the permanent 'undecidability' of cultural signs can also be rendered violently decisive by superior force or hegemonic dominion.

[. . .]

NOTES

I explore this complex dialectic of race, class and gender in more detail in *Imperial Leather. Race, Gender and Sexuality in the Colonial Contest*, New York and London, Routledge, 1994.

1. See Jean and John L. Comaroff, 'Home-made hegemony: modernity, domesticity and colonialism in South Africa', in Karen Tranberg Hansen (ed.), *African Encounters with Domesticity*. New Brunswick, Rutgers University Press, 1992, pp. 37–74.
2. Commodity spectacle, though hugely influential, was not the only cultural form for the meditation of this dialectic. Travel writing, novels, postcards, photographs, pornography and other cultural forms can be as fruitfully investigated for the relation between domesticity and empire. I focus on commodity spectacle since its extensive reach beyond the literate and propertied elite gave imperial domesticity particularly far-reaching clout.
3. Karl Marx, 'Commodity fetishism', *Capital*, vol 1. Quoted in Thomas Richards, *The Commodity Culture of Victorian Britain. Advertising and Spectacle 1851–1914*, London, Verso, 1990.
4. See Richards' excellent analysis, especially the Introduction and Chapter 1.
5. See David Simpson's analysis of novelistic fetishism in *Fetishism and Imagination. Dickens, Melville, Conrad*, Baltimore, Johns Hopkins University Press, 1982.
6. Richards, op. cit., p. 72.

7. In 1889, an ad for Sunlight Soap featured the feminized figure of British national-ism, Britannia, standing on a hill and showing P. T. Barnum, the famous circus manager and impresario of the commodity spectacle, a huge Sunlight Soap factory stretched out below them. Britannia proudly proclaims the manufacture of Sunlight Soap to be: 'The Greatest Show On Earth'. See Jennifer Wicke's excellent analysis of P. T. Barnum in *Advertising Fictions: Literature, Advertisement and Social Reading*, New York, Columbia University Press, 1988.

8. See Timothy Burke, 'Nyamarira that I loved: commoditization, consumption and the social history of soap in Zimbabwe', in *The Societies of Southern Africa in the 19th and 20th Centuries*, Collected Seminar Papers, no. 42, vol. 17, Institute of Commonwealth Studies, University of London, 1992, pp. 195–216.

9. Leonore Davidoff and Catherine Hall, *Family Fortunes, Men and Women of the English Middle Class*, London, Routledge, 1992.

10. David T. A. Lindsey and Geoffrey C. Bamber, *Soap-Making. Past and Present. 1876–1976*, Nottingham, Gerard Brothers Ltd.

11. Ibid., p. 38. Just how deeply the relation between soap and advertising became embedded in popular memory is expressed in words such as 'soft-soap' and 'soap-opera'.

12. Quoted in Diana and Geoffrey Hindley, *Advertising In Victorian England 1837–1901*, London, Wayland, 1972, p. 117.

13. Mike Dempsey (ed.), *Bubbles. Early Advertising Art from A. & F. Pears Ltd*, London, Fontana, 1978.

14. Laurel Bradley, 'From Eden to Empire. John Everett Millais' Cherry Ripe', *Victorian Studies*, Winter 1991, vol. 34, no. 2.

15. During the Anglo–Boer war, Britain's fighting forces were seen as valiantly forti-fied by Johnston's Corn Flour, Pattisons' Whiskey and Frye's Milk Chocolate. See Robert Opie, *Trading on the British Image*, Harmondsworth, Penguin Books, 1985, for a collection of advertising images.

16. In a brilliant chapter, Richards explores how the explorer and travel writer, Henry Morton Stanley's conviction that he had a mission to civilize Africans by teaching them the value of commodities, 'reveals the major role that imperialists ascribed to the commodity in propelling and justifying the scramble for Africa', in T. Richards, *The Commodity Culture of Victorian Britain*, London, Verso, 1990, p. 123.

17. As Richards notes: 'A hundred years earlier the ship offshore would have been preparing to enslave the African bodily as an object of exchange; here the object is rather to incorporate him into the orbit of exchange. In either case, this liminal moment posits that capitalism is dependent on a noncapitalist world, for only by sending commodities into liminal areas where, presumably, their value will not be appreciated at first can the endemic overproduction of the capitalist system con-tinue.' Ibid., p. 140.

18. Thomas Carlyle, *The Works of Thomas Carlyle*, The Centenary Edition, 30 vols, London, Chapman and Hall, 1896–99, p. 30.

19. Richards, op. cit., pp. 122–3.

20. But palm-oil soaps had been made and used for centuries in West and equatorial Africa. In *Travels in West Africa*, Mary Kingsley records the custom of digging deep baths in the earth, filling them with boiling water and fragrant herbs, and luxuriating under soothing packs of wet clay. In southern Africa, soap from oils was not much used, but clays, saps and barks were processed as cosmetics, and shrubs known as 'soap bushes' were used for cleansing. Male Tswana activities like hunting and war were elaborately prepared for and governed by taboo. 'In each case,' as Jean and John Comaroff write, 'the participants met beyond the boundaries of the village, dressed and armed for the fray, and were subjected to careful ritual washing (*go foka marumo*).' Jean and John Comaroff, *Of Revelation and Revolution. Christianity, Colonialism and Consciousness in South Africa*, vol.

1, Chicago, University of Chicago Press, 1991. In general, people creamed, glossed and sheened their bodies with a variety of oils, ruddy ochres, animal fats and fine coloured clays.

21. For an exploration of colonial hegemony in Southern Africa, see Jean and John Comaroff, op. cit.

59

THE PROMOTIONAL CONDITION OF CONTEMPORARY CULTURE

Andrew Wernick

'There must be some way out of here' said the Joker to the Thief.

Bob Dylan

THE CATEGORY OF PROMOTION

In the same breath that cultural theorists, from Adorno to Jameson, have acknowledged the pervasiveness of advertising in the culture of late capitalism, they have limited the force of that insight by assimilating it to a critique of commercialism in general, and by circumscribing what advertising refers to precisely by using that term.

Advertising is commonly taken to mean *advertisements*, paid for and recognizable as such, together with the process of their production and dissemination. In that restricted sense, however vast and ubiquitous a phenomenon, advertising is certainly only one aspect of a wider process of cultural commodification: institutionally, a subsector of the culture industry; textually, a delimited sub-field within the larger field of commercially produced signs. At the same time, the word has a more general meaning. Originally, to animadvert to something was just to draw attention to it; whence to advertise came to mean to publicize, especially in a favourable light. By extension, then, the word refers us not only to a type of message but to a type of speech and, beyond that, to a whole communicative function which is associated with a much broader range of signifying materials than just advertisements *stricto sensu*. Whether as senders, receivers, or analysts of cultural messages we all recognize that

From Andrew Wernick, *Promotional Culture* (London: Sage, 1991).

advertising in this second, generic, sense exceeds advertising in the first. But it is hard to grasp the full significance of advertising for contemporary culture unless these meanings are clearly separated. A starting-point for the present study, then, has been to give the functional or expanded sense of advertising a name of its own: *promotion*.

The term has two semantic advantages. The first, reflecting its colloquial usage, is its generality, which directs our attention to the way in which all manner of communicative acts have, as one of their dimensions, and often only tacitly, the function of advancing some kind of self-advantaging exchange. *Promotion* crosses the line between advertising, packaging, and design, and is applicable, as well, to activities beyond the immediately commercial. It can even (as in 'promoting public health') be used in a way which takes us beyond the domain of competitive exchange altogether. For current purposes, though, I have confined it to cases where something, though not necessarily for money, is being promoted for sale – while recognizing that the metaphorical diffusion of the word, wherein it has come to mean any kind of propagation (including that of ideas, causes, and programmes), reflects a real historical tendency for all such discourse to acquire an advertising character. The second advantage stems from the word's derivation. Promotion (as a noun) is a type of sign, and the promoted entity is its referent. From this angle, the triple meaning of the Latin prefix 'pro' usefully highlights the compound and dynamic character of the relationship between promotion and what it promotes. A promotional message is a complex of significations which at once represents (moves in place of), advocates (moves on behalf of), and anticipates (moves ahead of) the circulating entity or entities to which it refers.

Given that definition, the thesis I have been exploring can be simply stated: that the range of cultural phenomena which, at least as one of their functions, serve to communicate a promotional message has become, today, virtually co-extensive with our produced symbolic world.

This may seem hyperbolic, until we start to enumerate the sorts of promotional message, and, associated with them, the circuits of competitive exchange, which are actually swirling about. As we have seen, these include not only advertising in the specific and restricted sense, that of clearly posted 'promotional signs'. They also include the whole universe of commercially manufactured objects (and services), in so far as these are imaged to sell, and are thus constructed as advertisements for themselves. A special case of the latter (in my terminology: 'commodity-signs') is cultural goods. These, indeed, are typically cast in a doubly promotional role. For not only are cultural goods peculiarly freighted with the need and capacity to promote themselves. Wherever they are distributed by a commercial medium whose profitability depends on selling audiences to advertisers they are also designed to function as attractors of audiences towards the advertising material with which they are intercut. In the organs of print and broadcasting, information and entertainment are the flowers which attract the bee. In this sense, too, the non-advertising content of such media can be considered, even semiotically, as an extension of their ads.

But this is not all. The multiply promotional communicative organs constituted by the commercial mass media (and even, via sports sponsorships and the like, by the organs of 'public broadcasting') are also transmissive vehicles for public information and discussion in general. Through that common siting, non-promotional discourses, including those surrounding the political process, have become linked [. . .] to promotional ones. It is this complex of promotional media, too, which mediates the communicative activity of all secondary public institutions – aesthetic, intellectual, educational, religious, etc. – to what used to be called 'the general public'. Furthermore, even if not directly commercial themselves, these secondary institutions also generate their own forms of promotional discourse, whether, as in the case of university recruitment campaigns, because they have become indirectly commodified, or, as in the case of electoral politics, because they have a market form which is analogous to the one which operates in the money economy.

There are several respects, finally, in which competition at the level of individuals generates yet a further complex of promotional practices. In part this is an outgrowth of the commodification of labour power, and more particularly, in the professional and quasi-professional sectors of the labour market, of the way in which differentially qualified labour power commands a differential price. Hence the dramaturgical aspects of careers and careerism. In addition, however, as Veblen and many others have described, the promotionalization of the individual also extends into the sphere of consumption, both through fashion and more generally through the way in which status competition is conducted through the private theatre of projected style. At a quite different level of social practice [. . .], the entry, on increasingly symmetrical terms, of (unattached) women and men into free (or non-parentally supervised) socio-sexual circulation has also created a mate/companion/friendship market which generates its own forms of competitive self-presentation. Lastly, when any instance of individual self-promotion spills over from the private realm to become a topic of public communication, whether unintentionally, as a personal drama that makes the news, or deliberately, as the amplified staging of a career (sporting, political, artistic, intellectual, etc.), inter-individual competition gives rise to yet a further form of promotional practice: the construction of celebrityhood. This itself enters into the realm of public promotion not just as self-advertising, but as an exchangeable (and promotable) promotional resource both for the individual involved and for other advertisers.

It is tempting to summarize these developments by saying that in late capitalism promotion has become, as Frederic Jameson (appropriating the term from Raymond Williams) has argued of postmodernism (1984: 57), a 'cultural dominant'. Given the provenance of that term, however, and the peculiarity of promotion itself as a cultural category, such a formulation will only do if carefully qualified.

Raymond Williams (1982: 204–5) originally developed his distinction between 'dominant', 'residual', 'oppositional' and 'emergent' culture in the context of class-cultural analysis. For him, the interplay of these complexes was conditioned by (and in turn conditioned) that of the emergent, dominant, and oppositional classes whose positions and sensibilities were expressed in them. In taking over this terminology Jameson gave it a different sociological spin. His problematization of postmodernism focused not on class dynamics, but on the structuring effects of 'third stage' capital on social relations as a whole. This has evident parallels with the approach to the rise of promotion being taken here. Still, in Jameson's hands, as in Williams', the notion of 'cultural dominant' remains linked to a notion of culture as (collective) expression. It refers us to the impact of (ascendant) cultural values on the styles, themes, and inflections of artistic, pop cultural, architectural, etc., symbolic domains. In late capitalism, he writes (1984: 57), postmodernism has replaced modernism as 'a new systemic cultural norm'.

The problem is that promotion – unlike any cultural movement – is not only not a class phenomenon, it is not an expressive one either. To be sure, it is embodied in significations, and it is ramified by socialization practices, psychological strategies and habits, and cultural/aesthetic norms and values. But in the first instance, promotion is a mode of communication, a species of rhetoric. It is defined not by what it says but by what it does, with respect to which its stylistic and semantic contents are purely secondary, and derived.

I can put the matter more precisely, perhaps, by saying that promotion has become a key, structuring element of what Scott Lash (1990: 4–5 and passim) has termed contemporary society's 'regime of signification'. He defines this as a combinatory structure, parallel to the material economy (conceived of as a 'regime of accumulation'), which comprises two sub-formations. The first is the 'cultural economy', which itself consists of a combination of four elements: (a) the relations of symbolic production (its property regime), (b) conditions of reception, (c) a mediating institutional framework, and (d) the means of symbolic circulation. The second is the 'mode of signification', involving a determinate set of relations (for example the realist model of representation) between the signifier, signified, and referent of symbolic objects. In general, while allowing for a certain 'relative autonomy', the causal assumption is that the second complex of relations is shaped by the first.

The case of promotion fits the model well. In a promotional message the relation between sign and referent has been (re)arranged in such a way that, first, the former is an anticipatory advocate of the second, and second, within the construction of a promotional image, the boundary between sign and object is blurred. What the suffusion of promotion throughout all levels of social communication has amounted to, then, is a change in the prevalent mode of signification. Moreover, this transformation has itself been associated with changes in the mode of production and circulation of signs (commodification, the rise of the culture industry, and the commercial mass media), that is, with changes in the cultural economy. Indeed, while Lash's model [. . .] allows for a certain degree of autonomy of the mode of signification from the cultural economy, the causal relation in the case of the late capitalist rise of promotion is direct and virtually unmediated.

But here the notion of a 'regime of signification', a structure of structures, definable in itself, which can enter into interactive relations with the (capitalist) economy proper, reveals a limitation. For the rise of commercialized culture, in symbiotic relation with mass media advertising, has itself been intrinsic to a more general process of capitalist development. Not only has culture become a sector of consumer goods production just like any other produced object of human use. Industrialization and mass production have also, and again for purely economic reasons, led to an expansion of the sphere of commodity circulation, of which the culture industry, via advertising, has itself become a heavily subsidized adjunct. In addition, and further complicating the picture, the rise of inter-individual and non-commercial promotion has registered the effects of a parallel, and only indirectly related, socio-cultural process in which social life in every dimension has increasingly come to assume a commodity or quasi-commodity form.

In trying to locate the place of promotion on the sociological map, in other words, the very distinction between the symbolic and material economies, between the regime of accumulation and the regime of signification, cannot be clearly drawn. And for good reason. Promotional practice is generated exactly on the boundary, a locus which implies the dissolution of the boundary itself.

What the rise of promotion as a cultural force signals, in fact, is not simply a shift to a new mode of producing and circulating signs (cultural commodification), but an alteration in the very relation between culture and economy. Baudrillard (1981), following Debord (1977), has depicted this movement ('the union of sign and commodity') as a merger, although it might be more accurate to depict it as a takeover, since culture has lost its autonomy thereby, while the (market) economy has hypostatized into an all engulfing dynamic. The result is a mutation: still capitalism, but a capitalism transformed. In effect, during the course of advanced capitalist development the globalization and intensification of commodity production have led to a crucial economic modification in which (a) with mass production and mass marketing the moments of distribution, circulation, and exchange have become as strategic as technical improvements in production for profitability and growth and (b) through commodity imaging the circulation and production processes have come to overlap. In which context (with disturbing implications for even an updated Marxism) it has further come about that the ('superstructural') domain of expressive communication has been more and more absorbed, not just as an industry but as a direct aspect of the sale of everything, into the integral workings of the commodified economic 'base'.

This has been a complex transformation, and it evidently did not occur all at once. There have been many phases and stages: from industrialism and the first consumer-oriented urban centres to the radio/film age, coca-colonization and the electronic malls of commercial TV. Whence a further caveat. Besides eschewing an expressionist view of its object, any thesis about the changed weight of promotion within 'late' capitalist culture must also be careful to avoid too sharp a sense of periodization.

Promotion has culturally generalized as commodification has spread, as consumer goods production has industrialized, leading to the massive expansion of the sphere of circulation, and as competitive exchange relations have generally established themselves as an axial principle of social life. But there has been no catastrophe point, no single historical juncture (for example in the 1950s and 1960s) at which we can say that promotion, having previously been 'emergent', finally became a 'dominant' structuring principle of our culture. It is a question, rather, of a cumulative tendency; a tendency, indeed, of very long standing, since, as Bourdieu (1977: 177) has reminded us, the market as a principle of socio-cultural organization predates capitalism and, even in 'primitive' societies, the symbolic and material economies are to some degree 'interconvertible'. Nor can the process of promotionalization be said to be complete. As with commodification as a whole, the advance of promotion has been uneven, both internationally and also within leading capitalist countries themselves. Even in Baudrillard's America, the mirage runs out at the desert and there are low-intensity zones.

Both for the present and historically, then, all that can be safely asserted is that *pari passu* with the development of the market, promotion is a condition which has increasingly befallen discourses of all kinds; and the more it has done so, the more its modalities and relations have come to shape the formation of culture as a whole. [. . .]

PROMOTION AS A CULTURAL CONDITION

The guiding thesis of Horkheimer and Adorno's essay on the culture industry in *The Dialectic of Enlightenment* was that 'culture now impresses the same stamp on everything' (1972: 120). In support, they cited such tendencies as the monopolistic centralization of cultural production, the standardization of cultural produce (which reflects and transmits the rhythms of industrial mass production), the classification of goods and consumers ('Something is provided for all so that none may escape'), the sensate emphasis of style over work, and the promiscuous, mid-market, merging of serious art and distractive entertainment.

[. . .]

Now, implicit in Horkheimer and Adorno's account, though they do not consider it as an independent factor, is that one of the ways in which commodification has been a culturally homogenizing force is through the similar ways in which, whatever the medium and genre, the products of the culture industry present themselves to us as objects and sites of a promotional practice.

[. . .] Not only are the same forms – imaged commodities as advertisements for themselves – to be found throughout the whole world of commercially produced goods. From the clothes we wear, to the parties we vote for at election time, wherever in fact a market of some kind operates, everything mirrors back the same basic signifying mode.

However, the rise of promotion has entailed more than just the boundary-crossing spread of similar rhetorical forms. In a multitude of instances, promotion in one sector has come to dovetail with promotion in another. [. . .] In addition, promotional messages borrow their imaging ideas and techniques from one another, whether through direct quotes (in the cola wars), through the logic of positioning wherein a market is segmented into differentially imaged niches, or, more diffusely, by circulating the same stock of promotionally tried-and-tested motifs and social types.

Promotion in different spheres, then, multiply interconnects – both in terms of the common pool of myths, symbols, tropes, and values which it employs, and through the way in which each of the objects to which a promotional message is attached is itself a promotional sign, and so on in an endless chain of mutual reference and implication. [. . .] I have described the symbolic world which results as a giant vortex in which, for producers and receivers of culture alike, all signifying gestures are swallowed up. But having in mind the *promesse de bonheur* which the discourses of promotion continually proffer, and defer, that vortex can also be thought of as a maze. In fact, an infinite maze: in which there is no final destination, no final reward, and where the walls are pictures (and pictures of pictures) of ever-multiplying varieties of cheese.

[. . .]

[. . .] I would add only one further point. It concerns not the psychology or anthropology of consumption but the impact on individual consciousness of promotional culture as a whole. If we accept that the symbolic universe reconstituted by the rise of promotion has been de-referentialized – a quality which stems, on the one hand, from promotion's instrumentalization of values and symbols, and on the other from its perpetual deferral of the promoted object, together with any closure of the gap of desire which that object's final arrival might bring – then the promotionally addressed subject has been placed in a novel cultural predicament: how to build an identity and an orientation from the materials of a culture whose meanings are unstable and behind which, for all the personalized manner in which its multitudinous messages are delivered, no genuinely expressive intention can be read. Schizophrenic disintegration and the consumerized conformism of the Pepsi Generation are only the most extreme poles of a possible response. More common is a sensibility which oscillates between a playful willingness to be temporarily seduced and a hardened scepticism about every kind of communication in view of the selling job it is probably doing. In that light, cynical privatism and mass apathy – an index of which is the falling participation rate in American elections – can even be construed as a sign of resistance: for Baudrillard, (1983), the only form of resistance still open to the media-bombarded 'silent majority'.

But the envelopment of the individual by promotion must be grasped from both sides of the promotional sign. It is not enough to look at this question only from the side of reception, that is to look at subjects only as readers/listeners addressed by a certain kind of speech. We must also take account of the way in which the contemporary subject has become implicated in promotional culture as a writer/performer of its texts.

Of course, only a minority play a directly authorial role in the imaging and marketing of commercial produce. Fewer still are the named creators or performers of cultural goods, though these have an exemplary importance since media stars are our equivalent of mythic heroes, providing the most salient paradigms of how individual praxis contributes to the shaping of our world. But the list grows if we also include all those playing a more specialist or subordinate role in commercial promotion, as well as those engaged in non- or quasi-commercial forms of promotional practice like electoral politics, or the public relations side of hospitals, schools, and churches. In any case, from dating and clothes shopping to attending a job interview, virtually everyone is involved in the self-promotionalism which overlays such practices in the micro-sphere of everyday life.

At one level or another, then, and often at several levels at once, we are all promotional subjects. Nor can we practically choose not to be. The penalty of not playing the game is to play it badly; or even, inadvertently, to play it well. Sincerity has become a prized virtue in a society where phoniness is a universal condition. Hence the cult of the natural and unaffected – a cult which is catered to even in the transparently artificial world of show business [. . .].

[. . .] Individuals who self-advertise are doubly implicated in such practice. They are, that is, not only promotional authors but promotional products. The subject that promotes itself constructs itself for others in line with the competitive imaging needs of its market. Just like any other artificially imaged commodity, then, the resultant construct – a persona produced for public consumption – is marked by the transformative effects of the promotional supplement. The outcome is not just the socially adapted self of mainstream social-psychology, a panoply of self-identified roles attuned to the requirements of the social position(s) which a person has come to occupy. It is a self which continually produces itself for competitive circulation: an enacted projection, which includes not only dress, speech, gestures, and actions, but also, through health and beauty practices, the cultivated body of the actor; a projection which is itself, moreover, an inextricable mixture of what its author/ object actually has to offer, the signs by which this might be recognized, and the symbolic appeal this is given in order to enhance the advantages which can be obtained from its trade.

[. . .] The contemporary subject, and nowhere more than in the competitively mediated zones of work and play where our personal self-presentations directly affect our inter-individual rates of exchange, is faced with a profound problem of authenticity. If social survival, let alone competitive success, depends on continual, audience-oriented, self-staging, what are we behind the mask? If the answer points to a second identity (a puppeteer?) how are we to negotiate the split sense of self this implies?

Intersubjectivity, too, is infected by doubt. Knowing how our own promotional moves will be read, how can we make credible to others the imaged egos we want to project as truly our own? And conversely: how can we decipher aright the self-stagings which are similarly projected towards us? To be sure, the result need not be total moral chaos. An ironic distantiation is always possible, and signalling this, or just mutually acknowledging it to be the case, enables us, despite the promotional enactments normally dissimulated on the surface of our discourse, to preserve dialogical respect. Nonetheless, public acts of communication will always be distorted, and properly distrusted, in a social universe in which market forms, and the promotional dynamics to which they give rise, are universally operative. Inauthentic writers are constantly being counterposed to cynical readers: a relationship in which the latter always need to be convinced, while the former must find ways to obviate that resistance when crafting messages for release.

From top to bottom, in short, promotional culture is radically deficient in good faith. For those with sensitive moral digestions, this description will seem too weak. Considering the sugar coating which pastes a personal smile, and a patina of conformist values, over the pervasively self-interested motives which underlie virtually all publicly communicated words and images, the total impression it makes (against which, of course, we screen ourselves through wise inattention) is not merely vacuous, but emetic in its perpetual untruth.

[. . .]

REFERENCES

Baudrillard, J. (1981) *Towards a Critique of the Political Economy of the Sign*. Translated by C. Levin and A. Younger. St Louis: Telos.
Baudrillard, J. (1983) *In the Shadow of the Silent Majority*. New York: Semiotext(e).
Bourdieu, P. (1977) *Outline of a Theory of Practice*. Translated by R. Nice. Cambridge: Cambridge University Press.
Debord, G. (1977) *The Society of the Spectacle*. Detroit: Black and Red.
Horkheimer, M. and Adorno, T. (1972) *Dialectic of Enlightenment*. New York: Herder and Herder.
Jameson, F. (1984) 'Postmodernism, or the cultural logic of capital', *New Left Review*, No. 146: 55–92.
Lash, S. (1990) *The Sociology of Postmodernism*. London: Routledge.
Wiliams, R. (1982) *The Sociology of Culture*. New York: Schocken.

60

SOCIAL COMMUNICATION IN ADVERTISING

William Leiss, Stephen Kline, Sut Jhally, Jacqueline Botterill

Through our cultural-historical analysis, we have drawn attention to how the emergence of advertising forms within mediated communication radically changed the cultural discourse of modern industrial societies, and how these forms assumed a privileged place in that discourse. As such advertising impinges directly upon some very sensitive and important areas of life, and forces policy makers to think very carefully about its proper place within a democratic society. The uniqueness of advertising agencies, and the regulatory issues confronting them, is that they have emerged as the point of mediation between the industrial, cultural, and communications sectors of society. Accordingly, advertising has encountered three different sets of social policy considerations – those connected with business, the media, and social relations.

In North America and Europe throughout the 1960s and 1970s several regulatory initiatives were legislated and enacted to limit and or control advertising. However, during the 1980s we witnessed a reversal of this trend, bringing a broad drift toward the 'business perspective,' especially in the United States and the UK, including the deregulation of advertising and media industries and increasing commercialization of broadcasting systems in other Western countries such as France. To advance the global marketplace and to facilitate new technology, industry officials argued that the consumer was best suited to shape and monitor the marketplace. Consumers (including children) were recognized as being intelligent enough to select their own pleasures and to use

From William Leiss et al. (eds), *Social Communication in Advertising: Consumption in the Mediated Marketplace*, 3rd edn (London: Routledge, 2005).

their critical capacities to protect themselves against being manipulated. The active consumer view also came from academics in the arts, humanities, and social sciences who felt critics exaggerated the role of advertising and who were overly scornful toward the popular pleasures afforded by it (Nava and Nava 1992; Featherstone 1991; Twitchell 1997; Cronin 2004). Advertisers, these commentators believed, had reached an institutional maturity – and so too have audiences.

Yet advertising remains a point of friction among a number of controversial issues and social policy debates (Singer 1986). In the twenty-first century Western liberal democracies continue to grapple with these changes. For example, as the power and prevalence of advertising grew, many nations called for increased regulation to mitigate the potentially adverse effects of high-risk products on consumers, particularly on vulnerable constituencies such as the elderly (Nikoltchev, Prosser, and Scheuer 2000). In fact the regulatory system is in a state of constant revision. In this chapter we explore some of the changes and recurring themes of the post-1970s regulatory environment. We explore the implications of our rethinking of advertising's role for the broader questions of social policy that arise in market societies, and we consider how regulatory systems are responding to the intensive processes of globalization, new technology, and increased emphasis on cross media and integrated campaigns of the last twenty years.

A Narrow and Wide View of Regulation

The policy debates about advertising have evolved historically, both as the broader climate of opinion changed and in response to particular changes in the advertising industry. For example, advertising representations continue to agitate feminists and civil rights activists, parents, university students and the not for profit sector. Debate continued over advertising to children and the promotion of tobacco and alcohol, even as new concerns were raised about the promotion of pharmaceutical drugs, fast food, and financial services. There have been regular calls for advertising to take responsibility for some of its perceived social and cultural impacts. According to Anne Cronin (2004), advertising has become a lightening rod for our discontents about negative consumption habits. And yet, after more than a century of modern advertising the uncertainties about its social role and mandate continue, and we still have little understanding of how, within a free and democratic society, we may define reasonable limits to marketing's social communication. One way to analyze the varied advertising regulation debates is to consider the assumptions made about the role of advertising.

The history of regulation has been heavily shaped by assumptions about its role in the marketplace. Advertising, from this perspective, is seen as a means of distributing product information that supports consumer choice. So important is this contribution considered that many nation states protect the rights of commercial speech in the same manner as they do the speech rights of citizens and the press. This narrow role of advertising and the corresponding regulatory stance was recently reaffirmed by a current member of the U.S. Federal Trade Commission (FTC), Mary L. Azcuenaga (1997):

> Some might say that the very idea of regulation of advertising is incompatible with the concept of a free market. In fact, I believe, the opposite is true. One of the fundamentals of a market economy is the free flow of information about goods and services offered for sale. The underlying theory is that the more fully consumers are informed, the better equipped they will be to make purchase decisions appropriate to their own needs. The phrase 'appropriate to their own needs' expresses an important point. The appropriateness of a purchasing choice in a free-market economy depends on consumer preference, not governmental fiat. It is the exercise of informed choice by consumers that ensures that unwanted goods and services eventually will disappear from the market, and that prices that are too high to induce purchase ultimately will be lowered as selling firms seek to attract buyers.

The central argument of this book, on the other hand, is that advertising extends well beyond an economic function, for contemporary advertising provides much more than product information and utilitarian features. Studies confirm that consumers do not look to advertising solely in order to evaluate the performance, durability, and effectiveness of products. The narrow view also fails to appreciate the structural relationship between advertisers and the media, upon which democracy and culture has become overwritten, as well as the complex relationship between advertising and over consumption, cultural values, socialization, identity formation, environmental degradation, erosion of the public sphere, and distortion of social communication. The policy arena has had difficulty in addressing these problem issues.

Advertising is more than a mechanism for communicating product information to individuals: It is in truth an entire cultural system, a social discourse whose unifying theme is the meaning of consumption. The primary field of the content of modern advertising is contemporary culture itself, and advertising represents a contested discourse precisely for this reason. This we see as the 'broad perspective' of advertising as a form of social communication. We argue that the institutionalization of advertising and its vast role in modern life requires our conception of advertising to accommodate the unintended social consequences of marketing communication, as well as the broader cultural effects of our particular market communication system, which narrower regulatory approaches will continually fail to approach.

[. . .]

MEDIATED PRACTICES

Because advertising emerged at a time of great uncertainty about the cultural role of the media, special concerns about community standards and values have been raised and acknowledged by advertisers. As Canadian Advertising Foundation Chairman Frank Philcox has stated, 'Commercial free speech does not come without constraints. . . . Corporations must operate within the ethical standards of honesty and good taste our society demands [of public communications].' Thus, like all public expressions of opinion, advertising is also subject to legislated limits to public discourse, including sedition, libel, slander, and copyright restrictions (varying by country), and to other laws and regulatory frameworks that govern the media in general. There are very few instances worldwide in which advertisements have violated these general principles. In this context the controversy over advertising's communicative practices has centered around the industry's special obligations to respect community standards and values. In many cases, broadcasters use community standards to reject controversial advocacy advertising. It is not in any broadcaster's interest to deeply offend community standards or public taste, and most advertisers respect such provisions as ultimately working in their own interest – although they are sometimes chastened for adopting such a mainstream and bland view of life.

A closer review of social policy disputes reveals, however, that the social concerns expressed by the critics of advertising have gone well beyond the narrow issues of honesty and good taste that are readily acknowledged by industry spokespersons. For example, the industry has been accused of being insensitive to how its images degrade or objectify women or diminish particular racial and ethnic groups with unrealistic and limited images of their social life. Feminist accusations have been the most vociferous. [. . .] [C]ommentators have launched many criticisms against the representations of women and racial groups in advertising. Although these criticisms have been voiced since the 1970s, on the whole advertising has not changed a great deal in the intervening period. Advertising as a whole continues to be accused of reinforcing a biased and predominantly male view of life and male fantasies in its representation of women, and more generally of giving priority to white, middle-class community standards. The dynamics of 'addressing the market' also underscore [. . .] disputes of ethnic and racial stereotypes [. . .]. Advertisers limited attempts to address blacks and Hispanics in the United States, along with the industry's disinterest in supporting minority media, remain contentious issues. Despite the serious consideration given to this issue, new guidelines and self-regulation appear to have failed to change advertising practices; public policy seems to be at a loss as to how to deal with problems like gender imagery beyond monitoring and chastening advertisers (CRTC 1992).

Identifying stereotypical misrepresentation in advertisements is relatively easy to do, but attempting to remedy the situation is harder than would appear at first glance. Perhaps one could require matching representations to social statistics. Would advertisers be allocated proportional characterizations – say, one child-minding ethnic father, three yuppie lawyers, and two working businesswomen? Such a directive would not really solve the problems of stereotypical misrepresentation because, of course, it would only perpetuate whatever inequities still exist in society. The problem lies not so much in the relationship that advertising content bears to reality, as in the reasons that advertising uses condensed codes of characterization and in the strategies for targeting particular audiences. In other words, stereotyping in advertising cannot be solved by treating it as a matter of inaccurate representation. Advertising personnel are no more sexist or racist than people in other areas; their overriding concern is with forms of communication that will sell products. Operating in a cluttered environment with severe time restrictions and targeting to segmented audiences, advertisers draw upon generalized representations of social groupings to enhance communication. As Erving Goffman (1979, 84) has said of advertisers, 'their hype is hyper-ritualization.' However, ads are not only about selling, for they operate in a social context and have social effects. Thus, we must try to sift out the aspects of advertising practice that have potentially negative social effects and seek to address them as precisely as possible.

The questions of greatest societal import that advertising raises are best summed up in disputes about the industry's role in the socialization of children. The issues – which emerge in clear relief because this particular audience is still in a process of formation and occupies an uncertain position in the population of consumers – touch on all of the three domains to which we have called attention in this chapter. First, the stereotyped and unrealistic representations common in children's advertising can become templates that shape children's social attitudes and development, particularly in the way they interact with their peers and parents. Second, the commercialization of programming has profoundly influenced the quality and emphasis of children's television. Third, the industrial sectors (toys, snacks, and cereal manufacturers) with interests in children's marketing are very limited. In short, the fundamental issue at stake is the flow of culture to children.

[. . .]

Advertising as an enormously versatile and attractive genre of social communication, and with its overall relation to culture and society raises difficult policy questions. How does advertising itself affect the development of personal identity and the social aspects of consumption? We have traced the historical process in which the meaning of goods and the nature of the satisfactions to be derived through them have been systematically reformulated by economic institutions. These transformations were, in part, responses to changes in social composition such as the blurring of class distinctions, but more directly they were an internal response by the advertising industry to the problem of selling goods in the environment of mediated communication. Both factors gave rise to a great increase in the number of portrayals of human relationships in advertisements. The systematic emphases and obsessions in these portrayals show clearly that advertising is less at ease with depicting some types of human relationships or consumption patterns than others.

No matter what gave rise to the bias, however, there are calls to supplement current restrictions on misleading advertising content and inference (implied claims) with restrictions on 'irrational' advertising, lifestyle advertising (for beer and cigarettes especially), and stereotyping; matters of advertising's 'rhetorical forms' and appeal approaches may, as a result, become part of a regulatory policy agenda.

The case of stereotypic representation of people in advertising is especially instructive. We usually understand discrimination in this respect as involving the under-representation of a particular category of people or groups – for example, not enough working women or blacks in middle-class occupations. Two factors are responsible for the attention given to advertising stereotypes: (1) advertising is so visible that people have come to regard criticism of it as an effective way to address the broader social problem of inequality; and (2) advertising is such a compressed form of communication that its dramas, characterizations, and role structures are both clearer and more 'typical' than what is shown during programming time.

An Unfair Burden of Blame?

Advertisers maintain that many of the ads criticized by activists and watchdog groups do not, in fact, violate community standards but only the personal, somewhat prudish, and highly politicized taste of the critics. Advertisers also claim that the admittedly erotic or ambiguous images of women used in many campaigns are similar to arts and fashion photography and do not violate community standards. They claim that, according to their own research findings, many women like and respond positively to the images in these advertisements. Truly offensive ads, they contend, would receive complaints and be quickly withdrawn.

Advertisers also wonder why, among so many communication practices that treat life similarly, their industry is singled out. Advertising professionals often react to suggestions of a connection between 'larger' social issues and their own creative activities on behalf of their clients with a mixture of contempt, wariness, and surprise. As one of our interviewees said, 'I think advertising can play a role in helping to integrate people, though not a very substantial role. But I don't think advertising should be saddled with the various social problems.' And yet the number of people complaining to regulators about UK advertising, for example, is rising; in 2003 'the ITC received a record number of complaints about ads – nearly 10,000 compared with 8300 in 2002' (Independent Television Commission 2002). These changes might reflect new procedures that made it easier for people to lodge a complaint. In the UK, unlike the United States, regulatory bodies are required to undertake community outreach and promotion to inform the public of their rights to complain and the procedures for doing so.

[. . .]

There is a familiar ring to the industry arguments against regulation. [Bruce] Hains [President of the Institution of Advertising Practitioners] clearly articulates the long-held industry argument that advertisers are simply 'in business' and advocates that rights to commercial speak should override public offense – a position which nicely ignores advertising's broader cultural role. [Hamish] Pringle [Director-General of the IPA] also upholds the economic doctrine of fairness, equating cultural producers and advertisers, which leads him to conclude that lack of regulations on programming content represents an unfair competitive advantage. Statements such as these illustrate the point that advertisers no longer see other brands, but also the entire media system, as their competitive environment. [Raoul] Pinnell [of Shell] also subscribes to a narrow economic definition of advertising, focusing on its role as a media subsidy: because advertisers pick up the tab, they deserve to have their say, unencumbered by legal controls.

There are many limitations to these arguments. First, as our systemic analysis of the promotional system makes clear, it is wholly incorrect to assert that advertising pays for the media. Consumers pay for the media through the promotional costs that make up the price of goods. Agencies redirect or bridge this money to the media. Because consumers pay for advertising, their interests should be acknowledged. Even if we look at advertising from a strictly marketing position, many of the assertions above do not hold. One of the principles of the market is that consumer choice is paramount for market efficiency and individual satisfaction. Yet audience ad choice is limited, particularly in broadcasting media and public spaces. Studies have consistently shown that audiences find radio, television, and billboard advertising to be the most intrusive of all media (Cronin and Menelly 1992; Elliott and Speck 1999; Speck and Elliott 1997). Programming guides are provided for the television schedule, and audiences have the power to select what they want. But audiences have little ability to select advertising, particularly on broadcasting and public space advertising; their only good option is to avoid it, which they have done in increasing numbers with their zappers.

We have stated our reasons for concluding that the economic view is too narrow a framework to support useful debates about the role of advertising. The economic perspective fails to recognize that advertising is an accomplished and versatile form of social communication. Commercial messages have permeated the entire fabric of life during the course of the twentieth century, subtly blending their materials and techniques with those of the consumer culture as a whole, until they became virtually identical with it. As a result, the meaning and impact of advertisements considered in isolation is difficult to pin down. The significance of advertising is not confined to specific ads, to particular product categories or brands, or even to specific effects on a single medium. Advertising should be viewed as part of the institutionalization of marketing communication in our society, for its implications extend to the whole realm of mediated communication and popular culture. Whatever limitations we impose on marketing communication must, likewise, be grounded in a recognition of advertising as a robust form of social communication.

[. . .]

Our own research has confirmed that advertising is a form of communtion that adopts a very limited perspective on our society and the way people aspire, act, and interact in it. In reflecting an image of life governed by merchandising objectives, advertising has inherited all our cultural uncertainties about the consequences of consumerism, about cultural diversity, and about the role that social inequality plays in modern life. Although they are under no legal obligation to provide a view of life that authentically reflects the situations and conditions in society, advertisers should not be surprised by the number of people who find fault with a public discourse of social life solely determined by marketing criteria.

The above debates about representation serve to provide a clearer sense of both the unresolved issues in our system of advertising communication and our general discomfort with censorship when it borders on matters of depicting social life. Our society seems unable to attack the issue of social representation directly, precisely because it is both a highly controversial and deeply rooted social problem. Conceiving of communication as a marketplace, we are content to let consumers' preferences be the best judge of cultural preference. So why are the same criteria not extended to advertising representation?

This question reminds us that it is not simply the representation of a group in the advertisements, but the relationship of advertising to the media system as a whole that is truly at stake when a group is excluded from marketing's view. And this, perhaps, explains why advertising fails to provide any sense of social diversity and change. In the current commercial arrangements for media, targeted programming formats and alternative images survive only when that audience is of interest to a sufficient group of advertisers.

Because advertising is the economic fulcrum of the commercial media system, its influence on media markets has also been a matter of public policy debate. To the degree that commercialized media adopt a biased view in their productions, marketing dynamics appear to be one of the causes of this bias. A clear example of this systemically biased relationship occurred in 1999, when the FCC expressed concern over research that indicated advertisers spent less on minority media (Ofori 1996). The FCC reminded everyone that all audiences are created equal before the eyes of the law, and that the First Amendment supports diversity of speech. Wally Snyder, president and CEO of the American Advertising Federation, took a stand, arguing to his members, 'It is time to acknowledge the problem' (American Advertising Association 1999).

But this situation is very difficult to address, for it is structural in nature. Media in the United States operate as a marketplace in which audiences are bought and sold. Market principles are based on choice and price differentials. Through their purchases consumers support commodities that match their interests and needs and drive out those that do not. Despite their rhetoric advertisers certainly do not see all audiences as equal; whether this is a function of monopoly control, racism, stereotyping, or sound market data, pressures to turn profits for shareholders, scrutiny of promotional budgets, and target marketing force media buyers to be selective and strategic in their purchases. Thus, while it is unpalatable to face the biases of the marketplace, audiences are commodities, advertisers are shoppers, and the Hispanic audience commodity, at least as of 1999, was not considered to be as valuable as other audiences were. To force advertisers to pay the same price for all audiences would be to suppress the highly cherished market element in media.

Advertising throws back at us deep and unresolved tensions about the representation of social life in media. Attacking advertising for its biased view, and for its undoubted contribution to perpetuating regressive social practices, is one thing; but actually seeking to modify or eliminate practices enshrined in public attitudes, behavior, and institutional structures by reforming advertising representation alone is another. Actions directed at correcting social problems, in domains where advertising is only a bit player in a much more grand drama, will inevitably prove frustrating and inept. It seems far simpler for critics to focus on the representations of contested social relations as they appear in advertising than to confront the deeply rooted afflictions in our society that lie at their source. Advertising is particularly vulnerable as a system of social imagery because it is so prominent and intrusive, and because its condensed format implies greater simplification and typification in its representations, which leaves advertisers open to accusations of distorting real social conditions and denying the authentic experiences of ordinary people.

There may be good reasons for limiting certain sorts of persuasive techniques, for controlling stereotyped representations, or for regulating economic demand, but these are policy matters that cannot be addressed solely by controlling advertisements. Where social policy demands it, advertising policy should be seen rather as an integral part of more general economic, communications, and social initiatives. Questions about the economic function of advertising are not easily resolved, but one thing is clear: We cannot criticize advertising independently of the social context in which it performs. The focus should be, not on advertising practices, but on the specific set of institutional relationships through which advertising is tied to the social issues that concern us most.

WATCHING THE WATCHERS

[. . .]

The advertising industry has always responded emphatically, and often deftly, to issues of special concern that threaten its autonomy, by urging self-regulatory mechanisms as the best means of controlling the potential for abuses. But the industry's attempts at self-regulation, beyond the rather simple issues of 'truth in advertising' and 'fair business practice,' have not always been effective or long-lasting. In the 1980s the FCC and FTC in the United States, after many years of lobbying and submissions by the advertising industry, began the process of deregulating commercial television and advertising in the hope that market forces and industry self-regulation would eliminate the need for regulation, particularly in the controversial area of children's advertising. They did so without much appreciation of how the industry would react, and in the face of some clear warnings that self-regulation was not likely to be successful. Yet the deregulation did not bring about a reduction in the intensity of debates about advertising. As Armstrong and Brucks (1988, 111) noted in their review of children's advertising policy:

> Self-regulation alone cannot deal effectively with the complex problems of children's advertising. . . . Neither government regulation, consumer education for children and parents, advertiser and media efforts, nor self-regulation can work alone. But if all of the parties could work together – under a delicate blend of checks, balances and compromise – then these issues may finally be resolved.

Such cooperation rarely occurs. More often bitter critics, who accuse advertising of all manner of evil, are ranged against self-appointed advertising spokespersons set to defend unwaveringly their right to regulate themselves. [. . .]

Few Clear Answers

The fact that advertising does not fit within neat policy categories helps to explain why there is so little consensus on how to regulate it. Because it stands at the intersection of industry and culture, advertising can (and has) come under attack from diverse perspectives. At the same time, and perhaps as a result, comparatively little critical attention has been paid to the cultural and institutional nexus within which advertising works. It is easier, of course, simply to lay blame for everything that is going wrong with our market-driven society at the feet of advertising. But the result is a chaotic litany of unrelated complaints that fails to provide a framework in which to set policy.

The absence of guidelines has made it difficult for both supporters and opponents of advertising interests. Because so many different social issues are bound up with advertising one way or another, the rights or restrictions applicable in some cases do not appear to be relevant in others. This was evident when Canada's then Department of National Health and Welfare banned tobacco advertising from all media in 1989. In presenting its reasons for going to court over the legislated ban, Bob Foss of the Association of Canadian Advertisers

(ACA) asked, 'What will be next? We know there are many places people would like to see [an ad ban]. Numerous products have been targets, like tobacco and children's toys and alcoholic beverages. . . . We're afraid it could come about if a precedent is set.' The clear implication behind Foss's question is that there is a unitary principle for advertising's role and impacts that extends to all forms of advertising, in all media, and for all purposes. But should advertisements for hazardous products like cigarettes not be regulated differently from those for milk? Should television not be more restrictive in the way it advertises beer than it does cookies? Are not children less able than adults to understand the purposes and messages of advertising? To suggest that the protective mantle of free speech covers all cases equally is to overlook the very significant practical differences between the social issues involved in each of them.

Such differences arise precisely because [. . .] advertising is not just about the goods it displays; it also communicates much about the meaning and desirability of those particular goods, the social context in which consumption takes place, and the use and purposes of products and their production. In short, advertising orients people to goods, provides images of users, and conveys a mood, tempo, and stylistic that can be associated with various consumption patterns and images of well-being. The policy debates about advertising should now assimilate this understanding and recognize that the increasing sophistication of marketing communication demands a new way of thinking about the consequences of the unique combination of economic and cultural forces at work in our society.

Advertising is the apex of a cultural subsystem, a distinctive pattern of social communication that continues to alter our society in a number of important ways: It has transformed the institutional framework for market society, enhancing the power of large-scale corporate entities who undertake strategic marketing communications; it has created a highly concentrated and increasingly narrowly owned group of agencies that are experts in the new practices and forms of persuasive communications and the audience research upon which they are based; it has radically reordered the economics and audience bases of communications media; and it has changed many of the forms and practices of socialization in our society generally, including the television commercial itself, programming formats such as the rock video or children's television, as well as the entire spectrum of social, governmental, and political marketing. If we are to assess the controversies surrounding advertising, we can do so only by understanding the full scale and cultural significance of all this communications activity.

We have seen some efforts in this review of regulatory measures that have sought to address the new regulatory challenges posed by the mediated marketplace specifically globalization, new technologies, and promotional and cross marketing techniques that erode the line between commercial messages and media and cultural content. Recognizing the global spread of media, there have been efforts to extend regulatory measures across national borders.

Efforts have also been made to try to understand and regulate emergent forms of advertising channeled through new media technologies such as interactive advertising and mobile phone marketing. Cognizant of the erosion of the line between above the line advertising techniques and below the line promotion techniques many regulators today are aware that banning and regulating advertising alone is not effective unless promotional efforts (sponsorship, product placement, public relations) are also taken into account.

[. . .]

Media Controls

As we have seen, the media work within broad parameters established primarily to serve the needs of advertisers who wish to create and gain access to particular kinds of audiences. Has the commercialization of the media optimized the quality and potential uses of these media themselves? There is no doubt that advertising influences the performance of media, not only in the exercise of direct control over content, but also in the avoidance of controversial subjects, banal program formats, stereotyping of audience segments, and ownership concentration in media industries – broader issues that should draw more attention.

The question of how well the media function under largely commercialized conditions is related to a number of our most cherished beliefs about democracy. With media output controlled by the audience logic of advertising, there is no real marketplace for ideas – that is, no public forum where widely different types of social actors can buy and sell information, opinion, and images that express their interests. One serious consequence flowing from advertising's predominance in the media marketplace is that the combination of economic and audience logistics has led to a high degree of concentrated ownership and control in the media industries, prompting many commentators to ask whether diversity of views, quality of programming, and attention to minority interests or special audience needs have been sacrificed in the mad scramble for large or 'upscale' audiences (Curran 1977; Murdock 1982; [. . .] Urry and Lash 1994; Turow 1997). Certainly, the transition from small and politically committed audiences for newspapers to massive general-interest ones was a byproduct of commercialization. The light entertainment bias and other programming rigidities are all based on the competition for audiences within and among media; this affects public broadcasters, as well, because they must compete for audiences in order to justify receiving government funds.

Conclusion

Advertising professionals, throughout their history and into the twenty-first century, continue to react to suggestions of a connection between this type of 'larger' social issue and their own creative activities on behalf of their clients with a mixture of contempt, wariness, and surprise. As one of our interviewees said, 'I think advertising can play a role in helping to integrate people, though not a very substantial role. But I don't think advertising should be saddled with the various social problems.' And yet, we cannot continue to talk about advertising as if it were still nothing but 'salesmanship in print,' or as a form of persuasive communication that is exclusively concerned with merchandising concerns, for it now impinges upon many dimensions of politics, education, and society. To talk about advertising demands that we deal with a wide array of promotional communication activities that have been mobilized, by those who have access to the mass media, to extend various channels of influence over social life.

References

Azcuenaga, M. 1997. The role of advertising and advertising regulation in the free market: Speech by Federal Trade Commissioner Mary L. Azcuenaga before the Turkish Association of Advertising Agencies. Conference on Advertising for Economy and Democracy. Istanbul, Turkey.

Armstrong, G. M. and Brucks, M. 1988. 'Dealing with children's advertising: public policy issues and alternatives.' *Journal of Public Policy and Marketing*, 7(1), pp. 98–113.

Cronin, A. 2004. *Advertising myths: The strange half-lives of images and commodities*. London: Routledge.

Cronin, J. J. and Menelly, N. E. 1992. 'Discrimination vs. Avoidance: "zipping" of television commercials.' *Journal of Advertising*, vol. 21, no. 2: 1–7.

Curran, J. 1977. 'Capitalism and the control of the press, 1800–1975.' In *Mass communication and society*. eds. J. Curran, M., Gurevitch, & J. Woollacott. London: Arnold.

*Elliott, M. T. and Speck, P. S. 1998. 'Consumer perceptions of advertising clutter and its impact across various media.' *Journal of Advertising Research*, vol. 38, no. 1: 29–42.

Featherstone, M. 1991. *Consumer culture and postmodernism*. Thousand Oaks, CA: Sage Publications.

Goffman, E. 1979. *Gender advertisements*. New York: Harper and Row.

Independent Television Commission. 2002. Annual report and accounts for 2002, London.

Lash, S. and Urry, J. 1993/1994. *Economies of signs and space*. Thousand Oaks, CA: Sage.

Murdock, G. 1982. 'Large corporations and the control of the communications industries.' In *Culture, society and the media*, eds. M. Gurevitch, T., Bennett, J., Curran, and J. Woollacott. London, Methuen.

Nava, M. and Nava, O. 1992. Discriminating or duped? Young people as consumers of advertising and art. In *Changing cultures: Feminism, youth and consumerism*, ed. M Nava. London, Sage.

Nikoltchev, S., Prosser, T., and Scheuer, A. 2000. *Regulation on advertising aimed at children in EU-member states and some neighbouring states: The legal framework*. Strasbourg: European Audio Visual Observatory.

Ofori, K. A. 1996. *When being no. 1 is not enough: The impact of advertising practices on minority-owned and minority-formatted broadcast stations*. Tides Center Civil Rights Forum on Communications Policy. Washington D.C., Office of Communications Business Opportunities, Federal Trade Commission.

Singer, B. D. 1986. *Advertising and society*. Don Mills: Addison-Wesley.

*Speck, P. S. and Elliott, M. T. 1997. 'Predictors of advertising avoidance in print and broadcast media.' *Journal of Advertising*, vol. 26, no. 3: 61–76.

Turow, J. 1997/1998. *The breaking up of America: Advertisers and the new media world*. Chicago: University of Chicago Press.

Twitchell, J. 1997. *Adcult USA: The triumph of advertising in American culture*. New York: Columbia University Press.

FURTHER READING

Adorno, T. and Horkheimer, M., 'The Culture Industry: Enlightenment as Mass Deception', in J. Curran, M. Gurevitch and J. Woollacott (eds), *Mass Communication and Society* (London: Edward Arnold, 1977).

Ang, I., *Desperately Seeking the Audience* (London: Routledge, 1991).

Baehr, H., *Women and Media* (Oxford: Pergamon Press, 1980).

Barthes, R., *Mythologies* (London: Paladin, 1973).

Baudrillard, J., 'The Ecstasy of Communication', in H. Foster (ed.), *Postmodern Culture* (London: Pluto Press, 1985) pp. 126–34.

Berger, J., *Ways of Seeing* (Harmondsworth: Penguin, 1972).

Bonney, B. and Wilson, H., 'Advertising and the Manufacture of Difference', in M. Alvarado and J. O. Thompson (eds), *The Media Reader* (London: BFI, 1990).

Brierley, S., *The Advertising Handbook* (London and New York: Routledge, 1995).

Cook, G., *The Discourse of Advertising* (London: Routledge, 1992).

Corner, J., 'Adworlds', in J. Corner, *Television Form and Public Address* (London: Edward Arnold, 1995).

Coward, R., *Female Desire* (London: Paladin, 1984).

Cronin, A. M., *Advertising and Consumer Citizenship* (London and New York: Routledge, 2000).

Cronin, A. M., *Advertising Myths: The Strange Half-Lives of Images and Commodities* (London and New York: Routledge, 2004).

Curran, J., 'Advertising and the Press', in J. Curran (ed.), *The British Press . . . A Manifesto* (London: Macmillan, 1978).

Curran, J. and Seaton, J., *Power without Responsibility: The Press and Broadcasting in Britain*, 4th edn (London: Routledge, 1991).

Davis, H. and Walton, P. (eds), *Language, Image, Media* (Oxford: Blackwell, 1983).

Dickey, J. (1987), 'Women for Sale – the Construction of Advertising Images', in K. Davies, J. Dickey and T. Stratford (eds), *Out of Focus: Writings on Women and the Media* (London: Women's Press) pp. 74–7.

Dyer, G., *Advertising as Communication* (London: Methuen, 1982).

Earnshaw, S., 'Advertising and the Media: The Case of Women's Magazines', *Media, Culture and Society* 6:4 (1984) pp. 411–21.

Ewen, S., *Captains of Consciousness* (New York: McGraw-Hill, 1976).

Ewen, S. and Ewen, E., *Channels of Desire* (New York: McGraw-Hill, 1982).

Fiske, J., *Television Culture* (London: Methuen, 1987).

Fiske, J., *Reading the Popular* (London: Unwin Hyman, 1989).

Fiske, J., *Understanding Popular Culture* (London: Unwin Hyman, 1989).

Goffman, E., *Gender Advertisements* (London: Macmillan, 1978).

Goldman, R., *Reading Ads Socially* (London: Routledge, 1992).

Goldman, R. and Papson, S., 'Advertising in the Age of Hypersignification', *Theory, Culture and Society* 11:3 (1994) pp. 23–53.

Hebdige, D., *Subculture: The Meaning of Style* (London: Methuen, 1979).

Hebdige, D., *Hiding in the Light: On Images and Things* (London: Routledge, 1988).

Inglis, F., *The Imagery of Power* (London: Heinemann, 1972).

Jhally, S., *The Codes of Advertising: Fetishism and the Political Economy of Meaning in the Consumer Society* (London: Routledge, 1990).

Klein, N., *No Logo* (London: Flamingo, 2001).

Leiss, W., Kline, S., Jhally, S. and Botterill, J., *Social Communication in Advertising*, 3rd edn (London: Routledge, 2005).

Lury, C., *Consumer Culture* (Oxford: Polity, 1996).

Lury, C., *Brands: The Logos of the Global Economy* (London: Routledge, 2004).

Myers, K., *Understains: The Sense and Seduction of Advertising* (London: Comedia, 1986).

Nava, M., *Changing Cultures: Feminism, Youth and Consumerism* (London: Sage, 1992).

Nava, M., Blake, A., MacRury, I. and Richards, B., *Buy this Book: Studies in Advertising and Consumption* (London: Routledge, 1997).

Nixon, S., *Hard Looks: Masculinities, Spectatorship and Contemporary Consumption* (London: UCL Press, 1996)

Nixon, S., *Advertising Cultures* (London: Sage, 2003).

Packard, V., *The Hidden Persuaders* (Harmondsworth: Penguin, 1979).

Schudson, M., *Advertising: The Uneasy Persuasion* (London: Routledge, 1993).

Sinclair, J., *Images Incorporated: Advertising as Industry and Ideology* (London: Routledge, 1989).

Tomlinson, A. (ed.), *Consumption, Identity and Style: Marketing, Meanings, and the Packaging of Pleasure* (London: Routledge, 1990).

Tuchman, G., Kaplan Daniels, A. and Benet, J. (eds), *Hearth and Home: Images of Women in the Media* (New York: Oxford University Press, 1978).

van Zoonen, L., *Feminist Media Studies* (London: Sage, 1994).

Wernick, A., *Promotional Culture: Advertising, Ideology and Symbolic Expression* (London: Sage, 1991).

Williams, R., *Problems in Materialism and Culture* (London: Verso, 1980).

Williamson, J., *Decoding Advertisements* (London: Marion Boyars, 1978).

Willis, S., *A Primer for Daily Life* (London: Routledge, 1991).

Winship, J., 'Sexuality for Sale', in S. Hall, D. Hobson, A. Lowe and P. Willis (eds), *Culture, Media, Language* (London: Hutchinson, 1980).

Winship, J., 'Handling Sex', *Media, Culture and Society* 3:1 (1981) pp. 25–41.

SECTION 9
NEW TECHNOLOGIES, NEW MEDIA?

INTRODUCTION: NEW TECHNOLOGIES, NEW MEDIA?

What is the difference between new media and old media? One key distinction concerns *scale*: new media technologies are increasingly intimate and also link their users seamlessly into vast global webs.

A second distinction is *integration*. Narrowly defined, this refers to the integration of older media technologies into new digital systems, a concomitant reorganisation of previously relatively discrete industries, and the merging of previously discrete genres and formats. More generally integration concerns the development of a global media ecology that incorporates and thus displaces discrete media systems.

A third marker of difference is *open architecture and portability*. Portability was one of the technical promises of digital convergence and/or digital equivalence and although unevenly delivered and often under threat at the local or specific level (for instance the browser wars, backwards compatibility issues, demands to break the lower level protocols that have ensured the Internet remains one web), it has had visible effects. Limitations on content migration (across platforms) and content reuse become a matter of law and commerce rather than being based on technical limitations – as tussles around music and intellectual property rights suggest.

The fourth distinction is *interactivity*, a formal possibility of digital architectures. Interactivity is retooling the relationship between the audience/user and the content and system they use.

Fifth, digital media systems are *expanding the realm of what is commonly referred to as media*. Chief among these extensions are visual and data surveillance systems used by security services (CCTV but also Google Earth), large databases used for public welfare, health and other administrative services (for instance health and social security records), and various forms of portable positioning systems (e.g. GPS), which have added locative capabilities to media systems of all kinds. More radical expansions are linking conventional media technologies (e.g. digital cameras for everyday use or television production) with specialist systems (e.g. imaging systems for very small and very distant objects such as those being used in medical science and genomics and astronomy). Among the consequences of this may be a shift in the cultural sense of the relationship between the visual and the indexical.

A final distinction concerns *the pace and speed of change*. New media technologies (hardware devices, code standards, platforms) rise and fall very rapidly. Users migrate promiscuously from one mode of use to another (famously from MySpace to Facebook, but over a slightly longer period, from home pages to blogs, or from IRC to Twitter). They also migrate from one new device to the next. The speed of innovation has also impacted on the rate of convergence between old and new media – as evidenced by the rapid growth of multi-platform productions or in the converged content constellations of contemporary multimedia. The new media ecology is a genre machine, it devours and remixes old media, it innovates, it produces new forms of social interaction, new kinds of symbolic content and new public places.

It is also important to talk not about breaks and distinctions but continuity. This is because what is also striking about new media in general – and the web in particular – is the amount that, at any one moment, has become conventional, naturalised and reusable. 'Web 2.0', for instance, is often seen as 'all new' but in fact it rather collates a series of developments and tendencies and signals the relative *maturity* of a set of technologies, modes of production, forms of use and kinds of content management which begin to sketch out a new media environment.

The digital media environment that has emerged involves both new and old formations. New generations of digital technologies do not start a world or start the whole world or start the whole of media studies over again. New media has a history as well as a future. Indeed it might be suggested that it has many histories, since it emerges at the intersection of so many other technologies and draws into itself so many formats, genres, forms of social practice and indeed so much previously 'non-digital' content.

The writers in this section are aware of what could be termed the 'long history' of new media and refer to it in more or less explicit ways. One of its characteristics is recursivity. Familiar arguments emerge repeatedly in relation to new developments and phases in new media: the Internet explosion, for instance, revived discussions around technology and determination, embodiment and questions of computers, control and freedom, many of which arose in the founding decades of computerisation in the early twentieth century. One reason these debates come back is because they take up intractable questions that cannot be finally solved. Another, however, concerns technology's relationship to the future. It is because new technology, being innovative, points towards the future that it has so often operated as the bearer of many possible worlds – not all of them in sympathy with each other.

In Chapter 61, Kevin Robins takes up the question of virtual dreams, exploring the Internet explosion of the 1990s and the forms of cyber-hype and utopian projection that it provoked and locating the cyber-imaginary of the twentieth-century's end within a longer tradition of the technological sublime, gnostic flight from the flesh and Cartesian dualism. The article is striking for the clarity and force of its attack. Robins is outraged at the vapidity of forms of highly technologically deterministic cyber-dreaming he encounters, and although his target of attack is less the underpinning sense of technology as the new sole agent of change than the forms of dreams the web vision appeared to be supporting, he is clear that the former supports the latter. The characterisation of virtual space as new space to be colonised with no guilt, a space offering flight from the body, a space offering weightless ecstasy, and above all the presumption that a space 'beyond the body' can 'therefore' be free of the ideological conditioning of built space (a claim that forgets the basic sense in which any space humans build is essentially a social place), all are the subject of fierce critique. The strength of the article is its precision; rarely does the frustration of the author spill over – although the lobster-impersonating cyber enthusiasts are subject to the written equivalent of a roasting.

Helen Kennedy's account of the use practices of a group of London women (Chapter 64) also focuses on embodied practice. This piece tracks changing popular and academic readings of cyber-subjectivities, discerning a shift from cyber-feminist fantasies of disembodiment and anonymity (some along the lines described by Robins) towards a more sober assessment of how different groups of women with specific social backgrounds experience the net in their everyday practice. Kennedy's insistence on the value of considering embedded experience when exploring web practices catches a mood and parallels can found in areas of new media. In the field of games, for instance, Helen Thornham (2008) and Seth Giddens (2007) have both been concerned to explore the everyday life of gaming, as it gathers up texts, bodies and technologies, rather than focusing purely on the 'other-worldly' openings it offers.

Marc Andrejevic's 'The Work of Being Watched' (Chapter 62) explores the degree to which interactive media demands (more) work from its audiences turned users. The article traces out ways in which interactive media forms not only continue to make viewing a form of 'work' (which television also did), but now also turn 'being watched' (being surveilled) into a form of labour. Andrejevic then points out that this work is itself already being automated: the web cookie, for instance, which works to explain how we are watching, or what we are doing, can be seen as a 'labour-saver' or digital butler. This kind of relationship might be characterised as inter-passivity. Much speculative and industrial discussion of future web platforms – for instance Web 3.0 or the semantic web – is also dealing with these ideas, albeit often in a slightly different register.

Jonathan Sterne's article (Chapter 63) explores MP3 formats. Drawing on what he describes as the 'common sense' of technology studies, he launches an investigation of MP3 as a cultural artifact focusing on the specifically auditory aspects of the MP3, often largely ignored in accounts focusing on style and brand, and also sidelined in accounts taking up intellectual property/piracy issues. Setting aside law and market economics and bringing into view the cultural or political technologies that are bound up in a specific object, argues Sterne, both decentres the question of illegality and gives it a new source: the compression and other processing technologies that make up the MPEG standard were pulled together to solve issues of file transfer. In other words, MP3 formats were perfectly suited – and were suited by design – for the uses to which they was later put by (often unauthorised) users.

Sterne's analysis takes two forms. First he argues (following Lewis Mumford) that MP3 is a container technology – a form of technology that contains others and tends to efface itself – for instance in discussion MP3 is often used to refer to a particular kind of music – people have MP3 collections. Second, he stresses the need to understand the aesthetic dimensions of the MP3, particularly its auditory dimensions. The MP3 format (or the subsection of that wider format which has come to stand for 'MP3' in general use) is based on a psycho-acoustic model that exploits the limits of human auditory perception and our generally distracted listening habits. Working within these listening contexts allowed extreme forms of compression to be developed that still produce acceptable listening. These in turn allow the easy exchange of music files upon which the new music market and the new piracy are based. Thus the MP3 format, agreed upon for market reasons between the industry participants involved in forging it, 'wants music to be free' – and it is in this sense it operates against the logic of markets. Sterne acknowledges Richard Barbrook's work on the digital economy as a gift economy (see Barbrook, 2000) and there are clear parallels between the two approaches here. The force of Sterne's piece lies partly in the way that it grasps the ambiguous status of the MP3 which is at once a cultural artifact or a thing *and* something that dissolves into 'the music we play and/or into the social practices that coalesce around it'.

Finally, Caroline Bassett's account of digital media and cultural theory (Chapter 65) explores the dynamics of technological innovation as it has emerged across the history of new media and also looks at conflicts and failures to connect that have occurred between various schools of inquiry. Specifically, it asks if a more medium theory aware approach, drawing on later German medium theory, but also on the software politics of digital activism, can be used within media studies to redevelop critical frameworks for thinking through the cultural politics of digital media? In this article new media history has already been described as recursive: here it is suggested that the long-distance (archaeological) perspective of the German medium historians (e.g. Zielinksi, 2006) could reinvigorate an engagement between medium theorists and media studies that began with McLuhan and the Canadian school that was never broken but that has fallen into disuse.

Bassett argues that an awareness of the long history of new media, and of the dynamics of innovation, might be used to interrogate contemporary and developing relationships between technology, culture and society in order to understand recent developments and their framing. Viewed through this more extended perspective the questions about 'continuity' and 'transformation' can be more precisely understood to concern the relationship between material technological innovation, culture and social power. That is the relationship between the material forms of culture instantiated in new media systems, the embodied and embedded uses authors, producers, consumers, surfers, writers, viewers, listeners make of these systems, and the political economies within which they emerge.

Her article also suggests that a medium politics (in contrast to approaches focusing heavily on representation) might fruitfully be intersected with a politics of interpretation, and might constitute an effective form of critique for a new medium era. If a new era of semantic web technologies lets computers deal with human-produced 'meaning' as is claimed, then this kind of approach may find its time.

References

Barbrook, R., 'Cyber-Communism', *Science as Culture* 9:1 (2000) pp. 5–39.

Giddens, S. 'Playing with Nonhumans: Digital Games as Technocultural Form', in S. de Castells and J. Jenson (eds), *Worlds in Play: International Perspectives on Digital Games Research* (London: Peter Lang, 2007).

Mumford, L., *Technics and Civilization* (London: Routledge, 1946).

Thornham, H., 'Making Games? Towards a Theory of Domestic Videogaming', *FibreCulture Journal* 13 (2008). Online at: http://journal.fibreculture.org/issue13/issue13_thornham.html.

Zielinski, S., *Deep Time of the Media* (Boston: MIT, 2006).

61

CYBERSPACE AND THE WORLD
WE LIVE IN

Kevin Robins

The idea of an Earthly Paradise was composed of all the elements
incompatible with History, with the space in which the negative states
flourish.

E. M. Cioran

[. . .]

Cyberspace is, according to the guruesque William Gibson, a 'consensual
hallucination'. The contemporary debate on cyberspace and virtual reality is
something of a consensual hallucination, too. There is a common vision of a
future that will be different from the present, of a space or a reality that is more
desirable than the mundane one that presently surrounds and contains us. It is
a tunnel vision. It has turned a blind eye on the world we live in.

You might think of cyberspace as a utopian vision for postmodern times.
Utopia is nowhere (*outopia*) and, at the same time, it is also somewhere good
(*eutopia*). Cyberspace is projected as the same kind of 'nowhere-somewhere'.
Nicole Stenger tells us that 'cyberspace is like Oz – it is, we get there, but it has
no location'; it 'opens up a space for collective restoration, and for peace . . .
our future can only take on a luminous dimension!'[1] In their account of virtual
reality, Barrie Sherman and Phil Judkins describe it as 'truly the technology of
miracles and dreams'. Virtual reality allows us 'to play God':

From Mike Featherstone and Roger Burrows (eds), *Cyberspace, Cyberbodies, Cyberpunk*
(London: Sage, 1995).

We can make water solid, and solids fluid; we can imbue inanimate objects (chairs, lamps, engines) with an intelligent life of their own. We can invent animals, singing textures, clever colours or fairies.

With charmless wit (or perhaps banal gravity, I cannot tell which), they suggest that 'some of us may be tempted to hide in VR; after all, we cannot make of our real world whatever we wish to make of it. Virtual Reality may turn out to be a great deal more comfortable than our own imperfect reality.'[2] All this is driven by a feverish belief in transcendence; a faith that, this time round, a new technology will finally and truly deliver us from the limitations and the frustrations of this imperfect world. Sherman and Judkins are intoxicated by it all. Virtual reality, they say, 'is the hope for the next century. It may indeed afford glimpses of heaven.'[3] When I read this, I can hardly believe my eyes. We must consider what these spectacular flights of fantasy are all about.

But utopia is surely about more than a new pleasure domain? Krishan Kumar reminds us that it is also 'a story of what it is to encounter and experience the good society'.[4] In this respect, too, the self-proclaiming visionaries tell us they have good news and great expectations. The utopian space – the Net, the Matrix – will be a nowhere-somewhere in which we shall be able to recover the meaning and the experience of community. Recognising 'the need for rebuilding community in the face of America's loss of a sense of a social commons', wishful Howard Rheingold believes that we have 'access to a tool that could bring conviviality and understanding into our lives and might help revitalise the public sphere.'[5] We shall be able to rebuild the neighbourhood community and the small-town public sphere, and, in a world in which every citizen is networked to every other citizen, we can expand this ideal (or myth) to the scale of the global village. 'Virtual communities,' says Rheingold, 'are social aggregations that emerge from the Net when enough people carry on [electronically-mediated] public discussions long enough, with sufficient human feeling, to form webs of personal relationships in cyberspace.'[6] Communication translates directly into communion and community. It is a familiar dogma, and there is good reason to be sceptical about its technological realisation. But we should also consider the worth of this vision of electronic community as the 'good society'.

In the following discussion, I shall be concerned with these utopian aspirations and sentiments. But I shall not accept them on their own terms: my interest is in their discursive status and significance in the world we presently inhabit. The propagandists of the virtual technological revolution tend to speak as if there really were a new and alternative reality; they would have us believe that we could actually leave behind our present world and migrate for this better domain. It is as if we could simply transcend the frustrating and disappointing imperfection of the here and now. This is the utopian temptation:

Men can, in short, become gods (if not God). What need then for 'politics', understood as the power struggles of a materially straitened and socially divided world? The frequently noted contempt for politics in utopian theory is the logical complement of its belief in perfectibility.[7]

I think we should urgently set about disillusioning ourselves. There is no alternative and more perfect future world of cyberspace and virtual reality. We are living in a real world, and we must recognise that it is indeed the case that we cannot make of it whatever we wish. The institutions developing and promoting the new technologies exist solidly in this world. We should make sense of them in terms of its social and political realities, and it is in this context that we must assess their significance. Because it is a materially straitened and socially divided world, we should remember how much we remain in need of politics.

The prophets of cyberspace and virtual reality are immersed in the technological imaginary. What concern them are the big questions of ontology and metaphysics:

> What does it mean to be *human* in today's world? What has stayed the same and what has changed? How has technology changed the answers we supply to such questions? And what does all this suggest about the future we will inhabit?[8]

This opens up a whole domain of speculation on disembodied rationality, tele-existence, the pleasures of the interface, cyborg identity, and so on. Of course, these issues are not without interest. But, at the same time, there is the exclusion of a whole set of other issues that also pertain to what it is to be human now and what future humans can look forward to. It is as if the social and political turbulence of our time – ethnic conflict, resurgent nationalism, urban fragmentation – had nothing at all to do with virtual space. As if they were happening in a different world. I think it is time that this real world broke in on the virtual one. Consider the cyberspace vision in the context of the new world disorder and disruption. The technological imaginary is driven by the fantasy of rational mastery of humans over nature and their own nature. Let us consider these fantasies of mastery and control in the context of what Cornelius Castoriadis has called the 'dilapidation of the West', involving a crisis of the political and the erosion of the social fabric.[9] In looking at cyberspace and virtual reality from this different vertex, we can try to re-socialise and re-politicise what has been posed in an abstract, philosophical sense as the question of technology and what it means to be human in today's world.

CYBERSPACE AND SELF-IDENTITY

Let us first consider the question of self-identity, which has become a pervasive theme in all discourses on cyberspace and virtual reality. In this new techno-reality, it is suggested, identity will be a matter of freedom and choice:

In the ultimate artificial reality, physical appearance will be completely composable. You might choose on one occasion to be tall and beautiful; on another you might wish to be short and plain. It would be instructive to see how changed physical attributes altered your interactions with other people. Not only might people treat you differently, but you might find yourself treating them differently as well.[10]

Identities are composable in so far as the constraints of the real world and real-world body are overcome in the artificial domain. The exhilaration of virtual existence and experience comes from the sense of transcendence and liberation from the material and embodied world. Cultural conditions now 'make physicality seem a better state to be from than to inhabit':

In a world despoiled by overdevelopment, overpopulation, and time-release environmental poisons, it is comforting to think that physical forms can recover their pristine purity by being reconstituted as informational patterns in a multidimensional computer space. A cyberspace body, like a cyberspace landscape, is immune to blight and corruption.[11]

In cyberspace, 'subjectivity is dispersed throughout the cybernetic circuit . . . the boundaries of self are defined less by the skin than by the feedback loops connecting body and simulation in a techno-bio-integrated circuit.'[12] In this accommodating reality, the self is reconstituted as a fluid and polymorphous entity. Identities can be selected or discarded almost at will, as in a game or a fiction.

This question of technology and identity has been taken up in quite different ways, and we should take good care to distinguish them. At the banal end of the spectrum are invocations of a new world of fantasy and imagination. When they suggest that 'in VR we can choose to represent ourselves as anything we wish', Sherman and Judkins have in mind the idea that we might want to represent ourselves as 'a lobster or a book-end, a drumstick or Saturn'.[13] The guru of the Virtual Reality industry, Timothy Leary, has similar powers of imagination. In the electronic domain, he says, 'anything you can think of, dream of, hallucinate can be created. And communicated electronically. As Jimmy Hendrix sang, 'I'm a million miles away and I'm right here in your windowpane as Photon the Clown with a 95-foot-long triple penis made of marshmallows.'[14] In less grandiose fashion, Howard Rheingold describes how electronic networks 'dissolve boundaries of identity':

I know a person who spends hours of his day as a fantasy character who resembles 'a cross between Thorin Oakenshield and the Little Prince', and is an architect and educator and bit of a magician aboard an imaginary space colony. By day, David is an energy economist in Boulder, Colorado, father of three; at night he's Spark of Cyberion City – a place where I'm known only as Pollenator.[15]

New identities, mobile identities, exploratory identities – but, it seems, also banal identities. Only the technology is new: in the games and encounters in cyberspace, it seems, there is little that is new or surprising. [. . .]

The imagination is dead: only the technology is new. The visions are bereft (lobsters and drumsticks), but the point is that the technology will, supposedly, let us experience them *as if they were real*. Another self-styled seer, Jaron Lanier, reveals why the technology is the crucial element. [. . .] The new technology promises to deliver its user from the constraints and defeats of physical reality and the physical body. It provides the opportunity to go back and to explore what might have been, if we had been able to sustain the infantile experience of power and infinite possibility.[16] There are more radical and challenging encounters with cyberspace, however. These other discourses can no longer accept the ontological status of the subject, and take as their premise the fractured, plural, decentred condition of contemporary subjectivity. They take very seriously the argument that the postmodern condition is one of fragmentation and dissolution of the subject. Continuing belief, or faith, in the essential unity and coherence of the personal self is held to be ideological, illusionary and nostalgic. In the postmodern scheme of things, there is no longer any place for the Kantian (even less the Cartesian) anthropology. Virtual technology is welcomed as the nemesis of the transcendental ego and its imagination. In cyberspace, there are possibilities for exploring the complexities of self-identity, including the relation between mental space and the bodily other. We are provided with a virtual laboratory for analysing the postmodern – and perhaps post-human – condition.

Weaving together a blend of post-structuralist theory and cyberpunk fiction, this other discourse charts the emergence of cyborg identities. In the new world order, old and trusted boundaries – between human and machine, self and other, body and mind, hallucination and reality – are dissolved and deconstructed. With the erosion of clear distinctions, the emphasis is on interfaces, combinations and altered states. David Tomas writes of the 'technologising' of ethnic and individual identities: 'The continuous manipulation . . . of the body's ectodermic surface and the constant exchange of organic and synthetic body parts can produce rewritings of the body's social and cultural form that are directly related to the reconstitution of social identities.'[17] In an already hybrid world, it introduces 'another *technologically* creolised cultural laminate with a different set of ethnic-type rules of social bonding.' But, more than this, through the configurations of electronic and virtual space, 'it presents an all-encompassing sensorial ecology that presents opportunities for alternative dematerialised identity compositions.'[18] In its most sustained form – a kind of cyborg schizoanalysis – the collapse of boundary and order is linked to the deconstruction of ego and identity and the praise of bodily disorganisation, primary processes and libidinal sensation.[19]

This critical and oppositional discourse on cyberspace and virtual reality has been developed to great effect within a feminist perspective and agenda.

The imaginative project was initiated by Donna Haraway in her manifesto for cyborgs as 'an effort to contribute to a socialist-feminist culture and theory in a post-modernist, non-naturalist mode, and in the utopian tradition of imagining a world without gender.' Cyborg identity represented an 'imaginative resource' in developing an argument for *pleasure* in the confusion of boundaries and for *responsibility* in their construction.'[20] [...]

This political edge is not always sustained, however, and it is not all that there is to cyborg feminism. It is accompanied by other desires and sentiments, reminiscent of – though not entirely the same as – the phantasies of omnipotent gratification evoked by Jaron Lanier. Cyberspace is imagined as a zone of unlimited freedom, 'a grid reference for free experimentation, an atmosphere in which there are no barriers, no restrictions on how far it is possible to go'; it is a place that allows women's desire 'to flow in the dense tapestries and complex depth of the computer image.'[21] [...]

It is time that we let this reality intrude into the discussion again. We should consider these various, and conflicting, discourses on cyberspace and self-identity in the context of wider debates on identity and identity crisis in the real world.[22] It is, of course, in accounts of the 'postmodern condition' that the question of identity has been problematised, with the idea of a central and coherent self challenged and exposed as a fiction. The argument, as Stephen Frosh observes, is that 'if the reality of modernity is one of fragmentation and the dissolution of the self, then belief in the integrity of the personal self is ideological, imaginary, fantastic ... whatever illusions we may choose to employ to make ourselves feel better, they remain illusory, deceptive and false.'[23] No longer stable and continuous, identity becomes uncertain and problematical. Carlo Mongardini takes note of the inconsistency of the ego-image in the postmodern era, and of the disturbing consequences of that inconsistency.

> A capacity for resistance in the individual is what is lacking here and above all *a historical consciousness which would permit him to interpret and thus control reality*. The individual becomes a mere fraction of himself, and loses the sense of being an actor in the processes of change.[24]

The loss of coherence and continuity in identity is associated with the loss of control over reality.

This crisis of self-identity is, then, more than a personal (that is, psychological) crisis. As Christopher Lasch has argued, it registers a significant transformation in the relationship between the self and the social world outside. It is associated with 'the waning of the old sense of a life as a life-history or narrative – a way of understanding identity that depended on the belief in a durable public world, reassuring in its solidity, which outlasts an individual life and passes some sort of judgement on it.'[25] This important cultural shift involves a loss of social meaning, and a consequent retreat from moral engagement.

Mongardini observes a loss of the ethical dimension of life, which requires precisely continuity and stability of individual identity and social reality. There is now, he argues,

> a greater sense of alienation that makes it increasingly difficult to have relationships that demand more of the personality, such as love, friendship, generosity, forms of identification . . . The loss of ability to give meaning to reality is also the product of psychic protection, the desire of the individual not to put himself at risk by exposing himself to the stimulus of a reality he can no longer interpret.[26]

There is dissociation and disengagement, withdrawal and solipsism. 'Change acts like a drug', argues Mongardini. 'It leads individuals to give up the unity and coherence of their own identity, both on the psychological and social level.'[27]

In the discourses on cyberspace and identity, however, things do not appear so problematical or bad. This is because the technological realm offers precisely a form of psychic protection against the defeating stimulus of reality. Techno-reality is where identity crisis can be denied or disavowed, and coherence sustained through the fiction of protean imagination; or it is where the stressful and distressing consequences of fragmentation can be neutralised, and the condition experienced in terms of perverse pleasure and play. Cyberspace and Virtual Reality are not new in this respect. Mary Ann Doane describes the psychic uses of early cinematographic technologies in a way that is strikingly similar: 'One could isolate two impulses in tension at the turn of the century – the impulse to rectify the discontinuity of modernity, its traumatic disruption, through the provision of an illusion of continuity (to resist modernity), and the impulse to embody (literally give body to) discontinuity as a fundamental human condition (to embrace modernity). The cinema, in effect, does both.'[28] The new virtual technologies now provide a space in which to resist or embrace postmodernity. It is a space in which the imperatives and impositions of the real world may be effaced or transcended. In the postmodern context, it might be seen in terms of the turn to an aesthetic justification for life: 'Morality is thus replaced by multiple games and possibilities of aesthetic attitudes.'[29] Lost in the funhouse. Through the constitution of a kind of magical reality and realism, in which normal human limits may be overcome and usual boundaries transgressed, the new technological medium promotes, and gratifies, (magical) phantasies of omnipotence and creative mastery.

The technological domain readily becomes a world of its own, dissociated from the complexity and gravity of the real world. Brenda Laurel thinks of it as a virtual theatre, in which we can satisfy 'the age-old desire to make our fantasies palpable'; it provides 'an experience where I can play make-believe, and where the world automagically pushes back.'[30] We might also see it in the context of what Joyce McDougall calls 'psychic theatre', involving the acting out of more basic and primitive instincts and desires.[31] The techno-environments of cyberspace and Virtual Reality are particularly receptive to the projection and acting out of unconscious phantasies. In certain cases, as I have already argued, this may involve receptiveness to narcissistic forms of regression. Narcissism may be seen as representing 'a retreat from reality into a phantasy world in which there are no boundaries; this can be symbolised by the early monad, in which the mother offers the new-born infant an extended period of self-absorption and limitless, omnipotent contentment'.[32] In this context, the virtual world may be seen as constituting a protective container within which all wishes are gratified (and ungratifying encounters with the frustrations of the real world 'auto-magically' deferred). In other cases, as I have again suggested, the created environment may respond to psychotic states of mind. Peter Weibel describes virtuality as 'psychotic space':

> This is the space of the psychotic that stage-manages reality in hal-lucinatory wish-fulfilment, uttering the battle-cry 'VR everywhere' . . . Cyberspace is the name for such a psychotic environment, where the boundaries between wish and reality are blurred.[33]

In this psychotic space, the reality of the real world is disavowed; the coherence of the self deconstructed into fragments; and the quality of experience reduced to sensation and intoxication. It is what is evoked in the fiction of cyberpunk, where 'the speed of thrill substitutes for affection, reflection and care,' and where, as 'hallucinations and reality collapse into each other, there is no space from which to reflect.'[34]

Marike Finlay argues that such narcissistic and psychotic defences are characteristic of postmodern subjectivity, representing strategies 'to overcome the ontological doubt about one's own status as a self by retreating to the original omnipotence of the child who creates the breast by hallucinating it.'[35] Virtual subjectivity – one crucial form through which the postmodern subject exists – may be understood in this light. The new technological environments of virtual reality and cyberspace confuse the boundaries between internal and external worlds, creating the illusion that internal and external realities are one and the same. Artificial reality is designed and ordered in conformity with the dictates of pleasure and desire. To interact with it entails suspension of the real and physical self, or its substitution by a disembodied, virtual surrogate or clone. Under these conditions of existence, it appears as if there are no limits to what can be imagined and acted out. Moreover, there are no others (no other bodies) to impose restrictions and inhibitions on what is imagined or done. The substantive presence of (external) others cannot be differentiated from the objects created by the projection of (internal) phantasies. Virtual empowerment is a solipsistic affair, encouraging a sense of self-containment and self-sufficiency, and involving denial of the need for external objects.

Such empowerment entails a refusal to recognise the substantive and independent reality of others and to be involved in relations of mutual dependency and responsibility. [. . .]

It is not my intention to deny the imaginative possibilities inherent in the new technologies, but rather to consider what is the nature of the imagination that is being sustained. From this perspective, it is useful to look at experiences in and of cyberspace and virtual reality in the light of Winnicott's notion of potential space: the 'third area of human living', neither inside the individual nor outside in the world of shared reality, the space of creative playing and cultural experience.[36] In elaborating his ideas, Winnicott drew attention to the continuity between the potential space that supports infantile illusions of magical creative power, and that which is associated with mature aesthetic or spiritual creativity. In virtual environments, this link between infantile and imaginative illusion becomes particularly apparent, as I have already indicated, and it seems appropriate to think of them in terms of the technological institution of potential or intermediate space. This magical-aesthetic aspect of the technologies is clearly that which has gathered most interest.

But we cannot be concerned with creative illusion alone (which is precisely what the new romancers of cyberspace do). In his discussion of potential space, Winnicott also put great emphasis on the moment of disillusionment, which involves 'acknowledging a limitation of magical control and acknowledging dependence on the goodwill of people in the external world.'[37] As Thomas Ogden points out, the infant then 'develops the capacity to see beyond the world he has created through the projection of internal objects.' The individual thereby becomes

> capable of entering into relationships with actual objects in a manner that involves more than a simple transference projection of his internal object world . . . mental representations acquire increasing autonomy from [their] origins and from the omnipotent thinking associated with relations between internal objects.[38]

Potential space is a transitional space. It is in this intermediate space, through the interaction of both internal and external realities, that moral sense is evolved. Transitional experience involves the differentiation of internal and external worlds – it is on this basis that aesthetic transgression becomes possible – and the acknowledgement of 'a world of utilisable objects, i.e. people with whom [one] can enter into a realm of shared experience-in-the-world outside of [oneself].'[39] This enables the development of capacities for concern, empathy and moral encounter. Potential space is, in this sense, transitive. We should hold on to this point in our discussions of the cultural aspects of cyberspace and virtual reality technologies. When it seems as if the new technologies are responding to regressive and solipsistic desires, we should consider the consequences and implications for moral-political life in the real world.

VIRTUAL COMMUNITY AND COLLECTIVE IDENTITY

This takes us to the question of collective identity and community in virtual space. Many of those who have considered these issues have made the (perverse) assumption that they are dealing with a self-contained and autonomous domain of technology. I shall argue, again, that the new technological developments must be situated in the broader context of social and political change and upheaval. The world is transforming itself. The maps are being broken apart and re-arranged. Through these turbulent and often conflictual processes of transformation, we are seeing the dislocation and re-location of senses of belonging and community. The experience of cultural encounter and confrontation is something that is increasingly characteristic of life in our cities. Virtual communities do not exist in a different world. They must be situated in the context of these new cultural and political geographies. How, then, are we to understand the significance of virtual communities and communitarianism in the contemporary world? What are their possibilities and what are their limitations?

Virtual Reality and cyberspace are commonly imagined in terms of reaction against, or opposition to, the real world. They are readily associated with a set of ideas about new and innovative forms of society and sociality. In certain cases, these are presented in terms of some kind of utopian project. [. . .]

Not all Virtual Realists are quite so unrealistic, however. There are others with a more pragmatic and political disposition who have more to contribute to our understanding of the relation between cyberspace and the real world. There is still the sense of Virtual Reality as an alternative reality in a world gone wrong. Techno-sociality is seen as the basis for developing new and compensatory forms of community and conviviality. Networks are understood to be 'social nodes for fostering those fluid and multiple elective affinities that everyday urban life seldom, in fact, supports.'[40] Virtual communities represent:

> flexible, lively, and practical adaptations to the real circumstances that confront persons seeking community . . . They are part of a range of innovative solutions to the drive for sociality – a drive that can be frequently thwarted by the geographical and cultural realities of cities . . . In this context, electronic virtual communities are complex and ingenious strategies for *survival*.[41]

But this involves a clear recognition that such communities exist in, and in relation to, everyday life in the real world: 'virtual communities of cyberspace live in the borderlands of both physical and virtual culture.'[42] Virtual interaction is about adjustment and adaptation to the increasingly difficult circumstances of the contemporary world. We may then ask how adequate or meaningful it is as a response to those circumstances.

The most sustained attempt to develop this approach and agenda is that of Howard Rheingold in his book, *The Virtual Community*. While there is something of the utopian in Rheingold (West-Coast style), there is also a clear concern with the social order. If we look at his arguments in a little detail, we can perhaps see some of the appeal of the pragmatic approach to virtual community, but also identify its limitations and weaknesses. Like other virtual communitarians, Rheingold starts out from what he sees as the damaged or decayed state of modern democratic and community life. The use of computer-mediated communications, he argues, is driven by 'the hunger for community that grows in the breasts of people around the world as more and more informal public spaces disappear from our real lives.'[43] Rheingold emphasises the social importance of the places in which we gather together for conviviality, 'the unacknowledged agorae of modern life'. 'When the automobile centric, suburban, fast-food, shopping mall way of life eliminated many of these "third places" from traditional towns and cities around the world, the social fabric of existing communities started shredding.' His hope is that virtual technologies may be used to staunch such developments. Rheingold's belief is that cyberspace can become 'one of the informal public places where people can rebuild the aspects of community that were lost when the malt shop became the mall.'[44] In cyberspace, he maintains, we shall be able to recapture the sense of a 'social commons'.

The virtual community of the network is the focus for a grand project of social revitalisation and renewal. Under conditions of virtual existence, it seems possible to recover the values and ideals that have been lost to the real world. Through this new medium, it is claimed, we shall be able to construct new sorts of community, linked by commonality of interest and affinity rather than by accidents of location. Rheingold believes that we now have 'access to a tool that could bring conviviality and understanding into our lives and might help revitalise the public sphere': that, through the construction of an 'electronic agora', we shall be in a position to 'revitalise citizen-based democracy.'[45] It is envisaged that on-line communities will develop in ways that transcend national frontiers. Rheingold thinks of local networks as 'gateways to a wider realm, the worldwide Net-at-large.'[46] In the context of this 'integrated entity', he maintains, we will be in a position to build a 'global civil society' and a new kind of international culture.

Like many other advocates of virtual existence, Rheingold is a self-styled visionary. His ideas are projected as exercises in radical imagination. It is this preachy posture that seems to give cyberspace ideology its popular appeal. There is another aspect to Rheingold's discourse, however, and I think that this has been an even more significant factor in gaining approval for the project of virtual sociality. For all its futuristic pretensions, Rheingold's imagination is fundamentally conservative and nostalgic. He is essentially concerned with the restoration of a lost object: community:

> The fact that we need computer networks to recapture the sense of co-operative spirit that so many people seemed to lose when we gained all

this technology is a painful irony. I'm not so sure myself anymore that tapping away on a keyboard and staring at a screen all day by necessity is 'progress' compared to chopping logs and raising beans all day by necessity. While we've been gaining new technologies, we've been losing our sense of community, in many places in the world, and in most cases the technologies have precipitated that loss. But this does not make an effective argument against the premise that people can use computers to cooperate in new ways.[47]

The Net is seen as re-kindling the sense of family – 'a family of invisible friends'. It recreates the ethos of the village pump and the town square. Rheingold can envisage 'not only community but true spiritual communion' in what he describes as 'communitarian places online.'[48] The electronic community is characterised by commonality of interests, by the sense of 'shared consciousness' and the experience of 'groupmind'.[49] The images are of maternal-familial containment. The ideas are of unity, unanimity and mutualism. [. . .]

Because virtual experiences and encounters are becoming increasingly prevalent in the contemporary world, I believe we must, indeed, take very seriously their significance and implications for society and sociality. What I would question, however, is the relevance of techno-communitarianism as a response to these developments. Let us consider what is at issue. That which is generally presented in terms of technological futures is much more a matter of social relations and representations of social life in the present. In a period of turbulent change, in part a consequence of technological innovations, the nature of our relation to others and to collectivities has become more difficult and uncertain. 'The old forms of solidarity were internalised within the extended family and the village community,' argues Edgar Morin, 'but now these internalised social bonds are disappearing.'[50] We must search for new senses and experiences of solidarity, he maintains, though these must now be at more expansive scales than in the past. And, of course, this is what virtual community seems to be all about. Solidarity in cyberspace seems to be a matter of extending the security of small-town *Gemeinschaft* to the transnational scale of the global village. There is, however, something deceptive in this sense of continuity and fulfilment. In considering another postmodern space, Disneyland, Michael Sorkin suggests that it 'invokes an urbanism without producing a city . . . it produces a kind of aura-stripped hypercity, a city with billions of citizens . . . but no residents.'[51] Jean Baudrillard says that it is 'an entire synthetic world which springs up, a maquette of our entire history in cryogenised form.'[52] We might see virtual and network association in the same light. There is the invocation of community, but not the production of a society. There is 'groupmind', but not social encounter. There is on-line communion, but there are no residents of hyperspace. This is another synthetic world, and here, too, history is frozen. What we have is the preservation through simulation of the old forms of solidarity and community. In the end, not an alternative society, but an alternative to society.

[. . .]

The new technologies seem responsive to the dream of a transparent society. Communitarianism promotes the ideal of the immediate co-presence of subjects:

> Immediacy is better than mediation because immediate relations have the purity and security longed for in the Rousseauist dream: we are transparent to one another, purely copresent in the same time and space, close enough to touch, and nothing comes between us to obstruct our vision of one another.[53]

It is precisely this experience of immediacy that is central to the advocacy of virtual reality and relationships. According to Barrie Sherman and Phil Judkins, Virtual Reality 'can transmit a universal "language" . . . It is a perfect medium through which to communicate in what will be difficult times . . . Common symbols will emphasise common humanity, expose common difficulties and help with common solutions.'[54] Jaron Lanier puts particular emphasis on this quality of virtual encounter. He likes to talk of 'post-symbolic communication' and a 'post-symbolic world'. He believes that it will be possible 'to make up the world instead of talking about it', with people 'using virtual reality a lot and really getting good at making worlds to communicate with each other.' The frustrations of mediated communication will be transcended in an order where 'you can just synthesise experience.'[55] These virtual ideologies are perpetuating the age-old ideal of a communications utopia. Immediacy of communication is associated with the achievement of shared consciousness and mutual understanding. The illusion of transparency and consensus sustains the communitarian myth, now imagined at the scale of global electronic *Gemeinschaft*. It is an Edenic myth.

Techno-community is fundamentally an anti-political ideal. Serge Moscovici speaks of the dialectic of order and disorder in human societies. Order, he maintains, has no basis in reality; it is a 'regressive phantasy'. A social system is only viable if it can 'create a certain disorder, if it can admit a certain level of uncertainty, if it can tolerate a certain level of fear.'[56] Richard Sennett has put great emphasis on this need to provoke disorder in his discussion of urban environments. In arguing that 'disorder and painful dislocation are the central elements in civilising social life', Sennett makes the 'uses of disorder' the basis of an ethical approach to designing and living in cities.[57] He is in opposition to those planners – 'experts in *Gemeinschaft*' – who 'in the face of larger differences in the city . . . tend to withdraw to the local, intimate, communal scale.'[58] Sennett believes that this denial of difference reflects 'a great fear which our civilisation has refused to admit, much less to reckon':

> The way cities look reflects a great, unreckoned fear of exposure . . . What is characteristic of our city-building is to wall off the differences

between people, assuming that these differences are more likely to be mutually threatening than mutually stimulating. What we have made in the urban realm are therefore bland, neutralising spaces, spaces which remove the threat of social contact . . .'[59]

What is created is the blandness of the 'neutralised city'. Disneyland is no more than the parodic extension of this principle. [. . .]

Cyberspace and virtual reality have generally been considered as a technological matter. They have seemed to offer some kind of technological fix for a world gone wrong, promising the restoration of a sense of community and communitarian order. It is all too easy to think of them as alternatives to the real world and its disorder. Containing spaces. I am arguing that we should approach these new technologies in a very different way. We must begin from the real world, which is the world in which virtual communities are now being imagined. And we must recognise that difference, asymmetry and conflict are constitutive features of that world. Not community. As Chantal Mouffe argues, the ideal of common substantive interests, of consensus and unanimity, is an illusion. We must recognise the constitutive role of antagonism in social life and acknowledge that 'a healthy democratic process calls for a vibrant clash of political positions and an open conflict of interests.'[60] For that is the key issue: a political framework that can accommodate difference and antagonism to sustain what Mouffe calls an 'agonistic pluralism'. This is so even in the matter of virtual association and collectivity.

[. . .]

NOTES

1. Nicole Stenger, 'Mind is a leaking rainbow', in Michael Benedikt (ed), *Cyberspace: First Steps*, MIT Press, Cambridge, Massachusetts 1991, pp53, 58.
2. Barrie Sherman and Phil Judkins, *Glimpses of Heaven, Visions of Hell: Virtual Reality and Its Implications*, Hodder and Stoughton, London 1992, pp126–127.
3. *Ibid.*, p134.
4. Krishan Kumar, *Utopianism*, Open University Press, Milton Keynes 1991, p28.
5. Howard Rheingold, *The Virtual Community: Finding Connection in a Computerised World*, Secker and Warburg, London 1994, pp12, 14.
6. *Ibid.*, p5.
7. Krishan Kumar, *op.cit.*, p29.
8. Larry McCaffery, 'Introduction: The Desert of the Real', in Larry McCaffery (ed), *Storming the Reality Studio*, Duke University Press, Durham 1991, p8.
9. Cornelius Castoriadis, 'Le délabrement de l'occident', *Esprit*, December 1991.
10. Myron W. Krueger, *Artificial Reality 11*, Addison-Wesley, Reading, Massachusetts 1991, p256.
11. N. Katherine Hayles, 'Virtual bodies and flickering signifies', *October*, 66, Fall 1993, p81.
12. *Ibid.*, p72.
13. Sherman and Judkins, *op.cit.*, p126.
14. David Sheff, 'The Virtual Realities of Timothy Leary' (interview), in Gottfried

Hattinger *et al* (eds), *Arts Electronica 1990, vol.2, Virtuelle Welten*, Linz, Veritas-Verlag, 1990, p250.

15. Rheingold, *op.cit.*, p147.
16. Jaron Lanier, 'Riding the Giant Worm to Saturn: Post-Symbolic Communication in Virtual Reality', in Goffried Hattinger, *op.cit.*, pp186–187.
17. David Tomas, 'The Technophilic Body: on Technicity in William Gibson's Cyborg Culture', *New Formations*, 8, Summer 1989, pp114–115.
18. *Ibid.*, pp124–125.
19. Nick Land, 'Machinic Desire', *Textual Practice*, 7(3), Winter 1993.
20. Donna Haraway, 'A Manifesto for Cyborgs: Science, Technology, and Socialist Feminism in the 1980s', *Socialist Review*, 80, 1985, pp66–67.
21. Sadie Plant, 'Beyond the Screens: Film, Cyberpunk and Cyberfeminism', *Variant*, 14, 1993, p. 14.
22. See, *inter alia*, Stephen Frosh, *Identity Crisis: Modernity, Psychoanalysis and the Self*, Macmillan, London 1991; Anthony Giddens, *Modernity and Self-Identity: Self and Society in the Late Modern Age*, Polity Press, Cambridge 1991; Barry Richards (ed), *Crises of the Self*, Free Association Books, London 1989.
23. Frosh, *op.cit.*, pp57–58.
24. Carlo Mongardini, 'The Ideology of Postmodernity', *Theory, Culture and Society*, 9(2), May 1992, p62.
25. Christopher Lasch, *The Minimal Self: Psychic Survival in Troubled Times*, Pan, London 1985, p32.
26. Mongardini, *op.cit.*, p62.
27. *Ibid.*, pp56–57.
28. Mary Ann Doane, 'Technology's Body: Cinematic Vision in Modernity', *Differences: A Journal of Feminist Cultural Studies*, 5(2), 1993 pp13–14.
29. Mongardini, *op.cit.*, p61.
30. Brenda Laurel, 'On dramatic interaction', in G. Hattinger *et al* (eds), *op.cit.*, pp262–263.
31. Joyce McDougall, *Theatres of the Mind: Illusion and Truth on the Psychoanalytic Stage*, Free Association Books, London 1986.
32. Frosh, *op.cit.*, p93.
33. Peter Weibel, 'Virtual worlds: the emperor's new bodies', in G. Hattinger *et al* (eds), *op.cit.*, p29.
34. Istvan Csicsery-Ronay, Jr., 'Cyberpunk and Neuromanticism', in L. McCaffery (ed), *op.cit.*, pp192, 190.
35. Marike Finlay, 'Post-Modernising Psychoanalysis, Psychoanalysing Post-Modernity', *Free Associations*, 16, 1989, p59.
36. D.W. Winnicott, *Playing and Reality*, Tavistock, London 1971.
37. D.W. Winnicott, *Human Nature*, Free Association Books, London 1988, p107.
38. Ogden, *op.cit.*, pp193–194.
39. *Ibid.*, p196.
40. Heim, *op.cit.*, p73.
41. Allucquere Rosanne Stone, 'Will the Real Body Please Stand Up? Boundary Stories About Virtual Cultures', in Michael Benedikt (ed), *op.cit.*, p111.
42. *Ibid.*, p112.
43. Rheingold, *op.cit.*, p6.
44. *Ibid.*, pp25–26.
45. *Ibid.*, p14.
46. *Ibid.*, p10.
47. *Ibid.*, p110.
48. *Ibid.*, pp115, 56.
49. *Ibid.*, pp245, 110.
50. Edgar Morin, 'Les anti-peurs', *Communications*, 57, 1993, p138.

51. Michael Sorkin, 'See You in Disneyland', in Michael Sorkin (ed), *Variations on a Theme Park*, Farrar, Straus and Giroux, New York 1992, p231.
52. Jean Baudrillard, 'Hyperreal America', *Economy and Society*, 22(2), May 1993, p246.
53. Young, *op.cit.*, p233.
54. Sherman and Judkins, *op.cit.*, p134.
55. Timothy Druckrey, 'Revenge of the Nerds: An Interview with Jaron Lanier', *Afterimage*, May 1991, pp6–7.
56. Serge Moscovici, 'La crainte du contact', *Communications*, 57, 1993, p41.
57. Richard Sennett, *The Uses of Disorder: Personal Identity and City Life*, Penguin, Harmondsworth 1973, p109.
58. Richard Sennett, *The Conscience of the Eye: The Design and Social Life of Cities*, Alfred A. Knopf, New York, 1990, p97.
59. *Ibid.*, pxii.
60. Chantal Mouffe, *The Return of the Political*, Verso, London 1993, p6.

62

THE WORK OF BEING WATCHED: INTERACTIVE MEDIA AND THE EXPLOITATION OF SELF-DISCLOSURE

Mark Andrejevic

During the halcyon days of the high-tech economy – at the dawn of the new millennium – an entrepreneurial-minded former employee of the AirTouch corporation decided to change his name to DotComGuy and live his life online. For the former Mitch Maddox (a.k.a. DotComGuy) the decision was more than just a lifestyle decision; it was a business decision. By living his life in front of 25 cameras installed in his house and yard, DotComGuy hoped to demonstrate the benefits of e-commerce, ordering everything he needed online so that he wouldn't have to leave his home for a year. As an on-line advertisement for e-commerce – an entrepreneurial Truman Burbank – DotComGuy hoped to turn his Website into a for-profit corporation that would generate enough money to support his handlers and earn him a $98,000 paycheck for his year-long stint in the DotCompound.

The plan started swimmingly – DotComGuy's stunt resulted in media coverage that drew sponsors and captured the attention of viewers, who generated more than a million hits a day for his Website during its first few months (personal interview with Mitch Maddox, Sept. 16, 2000). By the end of the year, the euphoria over the online economy had been replaced by a healthy dose of skepticism, and as the NASDAQ headed south, so did DotComGuy's fortunes. On New Year's Day 2001, DotComGuy left the compound behind and forfeited his $98,000 payday, keeping as payment only those products that the company had purchased or received for promotional purposes (Copeland, 2001). DotComGuy's venture may have failed as a business enterprise, but it

From *Critical Studies in Media Communication* 19:2 (2002) pp. 230–48.

succeeded in drawing attention to an important aspect of the emerging online economy: the productivity of comprehensive surveillance.

DotComGuy understood that while he was in the DotCompound, he was *working* 24-hours-a-day. Even when he was sleeping, the image of Maddox tucked into bed in his Dallas home was surrounded with banner ads and the names of sponsors, some of which were posted on the walls of his house. [. . .] [T]he emerging online economy increasingly seeks to exploit the work of being watched. DotComGuy may have failed to capitalize on this labor as an entrepreneur, but major corporations continue to attempt to exploit the economic potential of this labor on a much larger scale.

Some 15 years ago, Jhally and Livant (1986), inspired by the work of Dallas Smythe (1977; 1981), argued that communication theory needed to take seriously the notion that audiences were working when they were watching television. This paper seeks to develop their argument a bit further – to update it, as it were, for an era of new-media interactivity – by highlighting the emerging significance of the work not just of watching, but of *being* watched. The two complement each other, insofar as the development of interactive media allows for the rationalization of viewing and consumption in general, thanks to devices like interactive television that watch us while we watch. In the era of 'reality' TV, wherein networks are winning ratings battles by enlisting people to submit their lives to comprehensive scrutiny, the claim that being watched is a form of value-generating labor ought not to be a particularly surprising one. We are not just facing a world in which a few select members of the audience are entering the celebrity ranks and cashing in on their 15 minutes of fame, but one in which non-celebrities – the remaining viewers – are being recruited to participate in the labor of being watched to an unprecedented degree by subjecting the details of their daily lives to increasingly pervasive and comprehensive forms of high-tech monitoring. [. . .]

The drawback of much of the discussion about privacy, as authors including Lyon (1994) and Gandy (1993) have suggested, is that the attempt to defend privacy rights has a disconcerting tendency to work as much in the interest of the corporations doing the monitoring as in that of the individuals being monitored. The development of demographic databases relies heavily on the protection accorded to private property, since these databases are profitable in large part because the information they contain is proprietary. As Lyon (1994) puts it, 'Privacy grows from the same modern soil as surveillance, which is another reason for doubting its efficacy as a tool of counter-surveillance' (p. 21).

As an alternative to the popular portrayal of the proliferation of corporate surveillance in terms of the incredible shrinking private sphere, this essay suggests an approach influenced by the concerns of political economy and the analysis of disciplinary panopticism. Conceived as a form of labor, the work of being watched can be critiqued in terms of power and differential access to both the means of surveillance and the benefits derived from their deployment. The operative question is not whether a particular conception of privacy has been violated but, rather: what are the relations that underwrite entry into a relationship of surveillance, and who profits from the work of being watched? Such an analysis draws its inspiration from Robins and Webster's (1999) assessment of the Information Revolution as 'a matter of differential (and unequal) access to, and control over, information resources' (p. 91). Gandy (1993), quoting Klaus Lenk, cuts to the heart of the matter:

> The real issue at stake is not personal privacy, which is an ill-defined concept, greatly varying according to the cultural context. It is power gains of bureaucracies, both private and public, at the expense of individuals and the non-organized sectors of society. (p. 52)

Foucault's (1975/1977) discussion of disciplinary surveillance offers an approach to the question of power that seems particularly relevant to the development of the online economy since it focuses not so much on the repressive force of panopticism, but its productive deployment. The potential of the online economy that has recently attracted so much speculation – both financial and cultural – is predicated in large part on the anticipated productivity of generalized network surveillance. The power in question is not the static domination of a sovereign Big Brother, but that of a self-stimulating incitement to productivity: the multiplication of desiring subjects and subjects' desires in accordance with the rationalization of consumption. [. . .]

[. . .] The following sections attempt to trace the outlines of the process whereby the work of being watched comes to serve as a means of rationalizing not just what Jhally and Livant (1986) call the work of watching, but the process of online consumption in general. The goal is to offer an alternative approach to the debate over online privacy in the era of new-media interactivity. Not only is the privacy defense aligned with the process it ostensibly contests, but, practically speaking, it has failed to provide effective resistance to encroaching surveillance. Indeed, opponents of corporate surveillance seem unable to provide a compelling rationale for privacy protection in an era when consumers remain surprisingly willing to surrender increasingly comprehensive forms of personal information in response to offers of convenience and customization.

Perhaps some awareness of the way in which the new 'transparency' exacerbates informational asymmetries and power imbalances, serving as a form of marketplace discipline, might provide stronger grounds for a critique of the proliferation of corporate surveillance. Such a critique might also help challenge the promotion of interactive technologies (and the forms of consumption and production they facilitate) as inherently democratic and empowering. This essay seeks to provide one starting point for such a challenge by exploring how the promise of interactivity functions as an invitation to engage in the work of being watched. [. . .]

Productive Surveillance

The productivity of surveillance, for the purposes of this article, can be understood as being always parasitic upon another form of labor. For example, Braverman's (1974) discussion of the pioneering work of Frederick Taylor in developing a system of workplace rationalization in the late 19th and early 20th centuries highlights the reliance of what Taylor called 'scientific management' upon comprehensive forms of workplace monitoring. Taylor's description of how he succeeded in dramatically increasing the productivity of steel workers starts off with a description of the role of surveillance in deciding which workers would be targeted. Managers observed the entire workforce for four days before choosing several workers upon whom to focus their efforts [. . .]. The selected worker's training consisted in his being supervised by a manager who observed his every action, timing him with a stopwatch, and dictating the laborer's actions down to the most specific detail. The result of all this monitoring and managing was that the productivity of the day laborer, whom Taylor refers to in his case study as 'Schmidt,' almost quadrupled. The activity of being watched wasn't productive on its own, but coupled with another form of labor, it helped multiply the latter's productivity. Over time, the recognition of the productivity of surveillance helped to institutionalize the rationalization of production based on ever more detailed forms of workplace monitoring, including Gilbreth's famous time and motion studies.

Among those who write about surveillance, Foucault (1975/1977; 1976/1978) has powerfully thematized its productive aspect, which all too often gets short shrift in the critical literature on surveillance [. . .] [where the] emphasis is upon the ways in which disciplinary surveillance creates 'docile bodies' and not upon the more suggestive aspect of Foucault's analysis: the spiraling cycle of productivity incited by disciplinary regimes: the fact that docile bodies are not rendered inert, but stimulated. As Foucault puts it in *Discipline and Punish* (1975/1977): 'Let us say that discipline is the unitary technique by which the body is reduced as a "political" force at the least cost and maximized as a useful force' (p. 221). Docility and pacification are certainly among the goals of discipline, but the real power of surveillance is a relentlessly productive and stimulating one:

> The Panopticon . . . has a role of amplification; although it arranges power, although it is intended to make it more economic and effective, it does so not for power itself . . . its aim is to strengthen the social forces – to increase production, to develop the economy . . . to increase and multiply. (1977, p. 208)

This power – and not the sterile juridical 'repressive' gaze of Big Brother – is what attracts the interest and the capital of the online economy.

[. . .] Recording and measuring, specifying and naming, these are the current watchwords of the marketing industry, which doesn't 'set boundaries' for consumption, but extends its various forms, 'pursuing them to lines of indefinite penetration' (Foucault 1976/1978, p. 47). For example, the proponents of mass customization (Negroponte, 1995; Pine, 1993; Gates 1996) imagine the possibilities of specifying desire ever more narrowly based not just on consumers' past preferences and socio-economic backgrounds, but on the details of the moment: location, the time of day, the weather. As in the case of sexuality, the elaboration and proliferation of desire is achieved through subjection to a discursive regime of self-disclosure whose contemporary cultural manifestations include not just the mania for interactivity, but the confessional culture of a talk show nation, and, most recently, the ethos of willing submission to comprehensive surveillance associated with the booming reality TV trend.

The power of Foucault's approach is that it extends its consideration of the productive role of panoptic surveillance beyond the realm of the workplace. The accumulation of bodies – their organization and deployment not just within the factory walls, but in the 'privacy' of homes and bedrooms – is a necessary corollary to the accumulation of capital (and vice versa). As Foucault puts it, capitalism 'would not be possible without the controlled insertion of bodies into the machinery of production and the adjustment of the phenomena of population to economic processes' (1975/1977, p. 141). Disciplinary surveillance does not just underwrite subjection to the proliferation of desire, it also – and not incidentally – enhances economic productivity.

[. . .]

RATIONALIZING THE WORK OF WATCHING

Jhally and Livant (1986) describe another form of labor for which consumers are 'paid': the work of watching. Building on their approach, this section takes the argument a step further by exploring the way in which the work of *being watched* contributes to the rationalization of the work of watching. Jhally and Livant's analysis is straightforward: audiences perform work by viewing advertising in exchange for 'payment' in the form of programming content. The viewing of advertising is productive because it helps 'speed up the selling of commodities, their circulation from production to consumption. . . . Through advertising, the rapid consumption of commodities cuts down on circulation and storage costs for industrial capital' (p. 125). In these terms, watching advertising might be understood as an activity in which, as Harvey (1999) puts it, the process of consumption completes itself in the process of production.

For the purposes of a consideration of the labor of *being* watched, the crucial point made by Jhally and Livant (1986) is that the goal of media management is to rationalize the work of watching – to 'make the audience watch harder' (p. 133), just as Taylor made Schmidt quadruple his daily productivity. [. . .]

Within the context of the mass media, the labor of being watched faced certain limitations, both structural and cultural. Watching advertising may be a form of work, according to Jhally and Livant, but it does not take place within a centralized space that would allow broadcasters to stand over viewers with a stopwatch, as in the case of the scientific management of the factory labor force. Indeed, a certain expectation of privacy outside the workplace is one of the hurdles that those who would rationalize the work of being watched need to overcome. The fact that we accept surveillance more readily in the workplace is a function of the characteristic spatio-temporal differentiation associated with wage labor in modernity, according to Giddens (1981): 'Two opposed modes of time-consciousness, "working time" and "one's own" or "free time", become basic divisions within the phenomenal experience of the day' (p. 137). Surveillance, within this schema, is associated with time that is not free, but which is subject to the asymmetrical power relations of the workplace, underwritten by the workers' subordination to those who control the space of production.

The productive potential of the labor of being watched is further limited by the structure of the mass media, which are only capable of exploiting the logic of market fractionation up to a point. It is desirable to isolate an affluent demographic, but to continue to subdivide the audience beyond a certain point would be counter-productive, not least because the existing technology is not well-suited to individualized programming. At the same time, detailed monitoring has tended to be relatively costly and has relied to a large extent on the consent of the monitored. Thus, the television industry has, until recently, contented itself with the relatively small sample offered by the Nielsen ratings, rather than attempting more detailed and comprehensive approaches to managing the work of watching. However, the advent of interactive, networked forms of content delivery promises to overcome these limitations and to develop the potential of the work of being watched to its fullest.

INTERACTIVE SURVEILLANCE IN THE DIGITAL ENCLOSURE

The emerging model of the online economy is explicitly based on the strategy for rationalizing and disciplining the labor of viewing – and of consumption in general – so as to make it more productive. The goal is to replace mass marketing and production with customized programming, products, and marketing. In the business literature (Mougayar, 1998; Pine, 1993), this paradigm is described as 'mass customization': the ability to produce mass quantities of products that are, at the same time, custom-tailored to niche markets and, at the extreme, to specific individuals. [. . .]

In the media market, as well as in other segments of the economy, the promise of interactive communication technologies is to surpass the structural limitations that prevented the exploitation of increasingly compact market niches. If the advent of cable television allowed for market segmentation up to a point, the development of digital delivery allows for its extension down to the level of the individual viewer. Bill Gates (1996), for example, anticipates a world in which not just the timing and choice of programs will be customized, but in which the content and the advertising can be adapted to viewer preferences, allowing individuals to choose the type of ending they want, the setting of the movie, and even the stars (who can be 'customized' thanks to digitization). Similarly, customized advertising would ensure that every ad is tailored to the demographics of its recipient. A similar logic could be extended to products other than media programming. [. . .]

The attempt to develop increasingly customized programming and products foregrounds the economic importance of what might be described as the 21st century digital confessional: an incitement to self-disclosure as a form of self-expression and individuation. Interactive (cybernetic) media promote this self-disclosure insofar as they offer the potential to integrate the labor of watching with that of *being* watched. The cybernetic economy thus anticipates the productivity of a digital form of disciplinary panopticism, predicated not just on the monitoring gaze, but on the vast array of digital data made available by interactive and convergent communication technologies.

The accumulation of detailed demographic information allows not only for the customization of products and programming, but also for customized pricing. Whereas mass production was reliant on the aggregation of individual demand curves, customization allows for the disaggregation of demand curves, and thus for the possibility that producers can extract some of the 'surplus' previously realized by consumers. Amazon.Com's recent experiments in 'variable pricing' anticipated this disaggregation by attempting to charge customers different prices for the same product, based on demographic information gleaned online from purchasers' 'cookies' (Grossman, 2000).

DIGITAL ENCLOSURE

The current deployment of the Internet for e-commerce may be viewed as an attempt to achieve in the realm of consumption what the enclosure movement achieved in the realm of production: an inducement to enter into a relationship of surveillance-based rationalization. The process of digital enclosure can be defined, in these terms, as the process whereby activities formerly carried out beyond the monitoring capacity of the Internet are enfolded into its virtual space. The process is still very much in its early stages, but is heavily underwritten by investments in new media technologies (Schiller, 1999) and by the enthusiastic and breathless predictions of cyber-futurists that continue to make their way into the mass media. Lester (2001) notes that entrance into what I call the digital enclosure is often voluntary (at least for the moment), but he coins an interesting term to suggest that consumers are compelled to go online for an increasing array of transactions by 'the tyranny of convenience' (p. 28). The current trend suggests that over time, alternatives to this 'tyranny' may be increasingly foreclosed. The result is that consumption and leisure behaviors will increasingly migrate into virtual spaces where they can double as a form of commodity-generating labor. If the latest work of a popular author or musical group is available *only* online, consumers are compelled to enter a virtual space within which very detailed forms of surveillance can take place. Electronic databases can keep track not only of who is reading or listening to what, but when and where.

The exploitation of the labor of being watched is thus crucially reliant upon public acceptance of the penetration of digital surveillance into the realm of 'free' time. That this acceptance may not be immediately forthcoming is reflected in surveys like the 1999 *Wall Street Journal*-NBC poll cited by Lester (2001) for its finding that 'privacy is the issue that concerns Americans most about the twenty-first century, ahead of overpopulation, racial tensions, and global warming' (p. 27). Lawmakers have recognized the importance to the digital economy of assuaging these concerns and are attempting to pass legislation to ensure consumers a certain degree of 'privacy protection' (Labaton, 2000, p. A1). [. . .]

The more promising approach, from a corporate perspective, has been to attempt to reposition surveillance as a form of consumer control. The popular reception of the Internet as a means of democratizing mediated interaction and surpassing the one-way, top-down mass media certainly works in favor of this attempt. Thus, the claims of the cyber-celebrants, such as George Gilder's (1994) oft-cited prediction that 'The force of microelectronics will blow apart all the monopolies, hierarchies, pyramids, and power grids of established industrial society' (p. 180) line up neatly with the corporate promise that the interactive digital market is 'a customer's paradise,' presumably because the 'customer is in control' (Mougayar, 1998, p. 176). [. . .]

In short, the promise of the 'revolutionary' potential of new media bears a marked similarly to the deployment of the supposedly subversive potential of sex that Foucault (1976/1978) outlines in his discussion of the 'repressive hypothesis.' When, for example, the *New York Times* informs its readers that the advent of interactive digital television is 'the beginning of the end of another socialistic force in American life: the mass market' (Lewis, 2000), it contributes to the deployment of what might be called 'the mass society repressive hypothesis.' The latter underwrites the ostensibly subversive potential of interactivity even as it stimulates the productivity of consumer labor. The most familiar version of this hypothesis suggests that mass production worked to stifle the forms of individuation and self-expression that will be fostered in the upcoming digital revolution: that the incitement to divulge our consumption-related behavior (and what else is there, from a marketing perspective?) paradoxically represents a subversion of the totalitarian, homogenizing forces of the mass market. As in the case of the deployment of the repressive hypothesis, the promised subversion turns out to be an incitement to multiply the very forms of self-disclosure that serve the disciplinary regime they purportedly subvert. As Marchand (1985) suggests, the promise of individuation – of the self-overcoming of mass homogeneity – was a strategy of the regime of mass society *from its inception*. Mass society's ostensible self-overcoming becomes a ruse for the incitement to self-disclosure crucial to the rationalization of what undoubtedly remains a form of mass consumption.

THE EXAMPLE OF TIVO

Recent developments in television technology can perhaps provide a more concrete example of how the work of being watched is deployed to rationalize the work of watching. The emergence of digital VCR technology, including TiVo, ReplayTV, and Microsoft's Ultimate TV, anticipates the way in which the digital enclosure overcomes the limitations of the mass media while enhancing their productivity.

[. . .]

Whether or not TiVo and its competitors are ultimately successful, they are helping to forge the commercial paradigm of interactive media as a means of inducing viewers to watch more efficiently. [. . .]

The model of interactive television is generalizable to an increasing variety of activities that take place within the digital enclosure – and, to the extent that monitoring is involved, more and more activities seem to fall under the umbrella of consumption. The work of being watched can, in other words, help to rationalize the entire spectrum of consumption-related activities that have traditionally taken place beyond the monitoring gaze of the workplace. The general outlines of a commercial model for interactive media can thus be gleaned from the example of TiVo. Its main components are: customization (the disaggregation of demand curves, the direct linkage between a specific act of production and a targeted act of consumption), interactivity (the ability to monitor consumers in the act of consumption), offloading labor to consumers (who perform the work of generating their own demographic information), and the development of an ongoing relationship with consumers (that allows for the exploitation of demographic information gathered over time).

Perhaps not surprisingly, several elements of this business model can be discerned in the development of a recent, supposedly subversive media technology: that of the music file-sharing utility Napster. As *Wired* magazine recently noted in a short aside to its celebratory coverage of the revolutionary potential of 'peer-to-peer' networking, Napster represents a forward-looking business model for the online economy: 'the system keeps customer relationships in-house, but outsources the lion's share of infrastructure back to a captive audience [. . .]' (Kuptz, 2000). [. . .]

Like TiVo, Napster-style technology allows for the comprehensive documentation of online consumption: it enables not only the monitoring of music selections downloaded by users, but potentially, the retrieval of their entire online music inventory. [. . .] Napster technology makes possible the future envisioned by Gates (1996), wherein subscribers will be able to download music to portable digital devices and to pay according to how often they plan to listen to an individual track. In this respect the future of online music and television delivery envisioned by the industry represents the application of mediated interactivity to the emerging paradigm of surveillance-based customization. The result is the promise that consumers will be able to perform the work of being watched with even greater efficiency.

CONCLUSION

Rumors of the death of privacy in the 21st century have been greatly exaggerated. The increasingly important role of online surveillance in the digital economy should be construed not as the disappearance of privacy per se, but as a shift in control over personal information from individuals to *private* corporations. The information in question – behavioral habits, consumption preferences, and so on – is emphatically not being publicized. It is, rather, being aggregated into proprietary commodities, whose economic value is dependent, at least in part, upon the fact that they are privately owned. Such commodities are integral to the exploitation of customized markets and the administration of the 'flexible' mode of production associated with mass customization. Making markets more efficient, according to this model, means surpassing the paradigm of the mass market and its associated inefficiencies, including the cost of gathering demographic information, of storing inventory, and of attempting to sell a mass-produced product at a standardized price. Interactive media combined with the development of computer memory and processing speed allow for the comprehensive forms of surveillance crucial to the scientific management of consumption within the digital enclosure.

Like the factory workers of the early 20th century, the consumers of the early 21st century will be subjected to more sophisticated monitoring techniques and their attendant forms of productive discipline. The intended result is the stimulation of the forces of consumption – the indirect complement of the enhanced productivity associated with network technology. If the effort expended in shopping feels more and more like labor, if we find ourselves negotiating ever more complex sets of choices that require more sophisticated forms of technological literacy, the digital economy is poised to harness the productive power of that labor through the potential of interactivity.

At the same time, it is worth pointing out the potentially productive contradiction at the heart of the promise of the digital 'revolution.' If indeed its promise is predicated on the subversion of the very forms of market control it serves, this promise invokes a moment of critique. [. . .] From this perspective, it is telling that in the celebratory discourse of the digital revolution, centralized forms of market control are re-presented as homologous with their former opponent: totalitarian, centralized planning. Intriguing avenues for resistance open up in an era when the *New York Times* can liken the television network system to Stalinism. [. . .]

Of central interest from a critical perspective, therefore, is the extent to which the marketers of the digital revolution continue to base its appeal upon the interpellation of an 'active,' empowered consumer. As consumers start to realize that their activity feels more like labor (filling out online surveys, taking the time to 'design' customized products and services) and less like empowerment, it is likely that the explicit appeal to shared control will be replaced by the emerging trend toward automated, autonomous forms of 'convenient' monitoring. This is the direction anticipated by futurists like Negroponte (1995) and the planners behind the MIT 'Project Oxygen,' whose goal is to make computers as invisible and ubiquitous as air. Their approach represents a retreat from the version of the 'active' consumer associated with explicitly participatory forms of data gathering that characterized some of the early experiments in interactivity (the 'design your own sneaker' or 'write a review of this book' approach). Instead, the goal is the proliferation of an increasingly invisible, automated, and autonomous network. The agency of the active consumer is displaced onto what Negroponte (1995) calls 'the digital butler.' Interactivity will likely be increasingly reformulated as inter-*passivity* insofar as the goal is to make the monitoring process as unobtrusive as possible. The call to 'action' will be displaced onto the ubiquitous technology, whose autonomy is designed to replace that of the consumer/viewer. [. . .]

In the face of the emergence of increasingly ubiquitous and invisible forms of monitoring, the appeal to privacy is often enlisted as a form of resistance. This type of resistance is rendered problematic by the fact that what is taking place – despite the recurring claim that the end of privacy is upon us – is the extensive *appropriation* of personal information. More information than ever before is being privatized as it is collected and aggregated so that it can be re-sold as a commodity or incorporated into the development of customized commodities. The enclosure and monopolization of this information reinforces power asymmetries in two ways: by concentrating control over the resources available for the production of subjects' desires and desiring subjects, and by the imposition of a comprehensive panoptic regime. The digital enclosure has the potential to become what Giddens (1981), following Goffman, terms a 'total institution.' The good news, perhaps, is that once the red-herring of the 'death' of privacy is debunked, the enclosure of personal information can be properly addressed as a form of exploitation predicated on unequal access to the means of data collection, storage, and manipulation. A discussion of surveillance might then be couched in terms of conditions of power that compel entry into the digital enclosure and submission to comprehensive monitoring as a means of stimulating and rationalizing consumption. [. . .] For too long, the discussion of mediated interactivity has tended to assume that as long as the Internet allowed unfettered interactivity, questions of network control and ownership were rendered moot by the revolutionary potential of the technology itself. Perhaps it is not too much to hope that an understanding of the relation of interactivity to disciplinary surveillance and, thus, to the labor of being watched might work to counter the unwonted euphoria of the utopian cyber-determinists and to refocus the question of the fate of collective control over personal information. Otherwise, we may all find ourselves toiling productively away in the DotCom-pound, narrowcasting the rhythms of our daily lives to an ever smaller and more exclusive audience of private corporations.

REFERENCES

Bedell, D. (2000, March 2). FTC to survey e-commerce sites on how they use customers' data. *The Dallas Morning News*, p. 1F.

Bryan, C. (1998). Electronic democracy and the civic networking movement. In R. Tsagarou-sianou, D. Tambini, & C. Bryan (Eds.), *Cyberdemocracy: Technology, cities, and civic networks* (pp. 1–17). London: Routledge.

Choney, S. (2001, March 27). Juno may not charge, but it's no free lunch. *The San Diego Union-Tribune*, p. 2.

Copeland, L. (2001, Jan. 3). For DotComGuy, the end of the online line. *The Washington Post*, p. C2.

Foucault, M. (1976/1977). *Discipline and punish: The birth of the prison* (A. Sheridan, Trans.). New York: Vintage Books.

Foucault, M. (1976/1978). *The history of sexuality: An introduction* (Vol. I) (R. Hurley, Trans.). New York: Vintage Books.

Foucault, M. (1980). *The Foucault reader* (P. Rabinow, Ed.). New York: Pantheon Books.

Gandy, O. (1993). *The panoptic sort: A political economy of personal information.* Boulder, CO: Westview.

Gates, B. (1996). *The road ahead.* New York: Penguin.

Giddens, A. (1981). *A contemporary critique of historical materialism.* Berkeley: University of California Press.

Gilder, G. (1994). *Life after television: The coming transformation of media and American life.* New York: Norton.

Grossman, W. (2000, Oct. 26). Shock of the new for Amazon customers. *The Daily Telegraph* (London), p. 70.

Harvey, D. (1999). *The limits to capital.* London: Verso.

Harvey, D. (1990). *The condition of postmodernity.* Cambridge: Blackwell.

Jhally, S., & Livant, B. (1986). Watching as working: The valorization of audience consciousness. *Journal of Communication, 36*, 124–143.

Kellner, D. (1999). Globalisation from below? Toward a radical democratic technopolitics. *Angelaki, 4*, 101–111.

Labaton, S. (2000, May 20). U.S. is said to seek new law to bolster privacy on Internet. *New York Times*, p. A1.

Lester, T. (2001, March). The reinvention of privacy. *The Atlantic Monthly*, 27–39.

Lyon, D. (1994). *The electronic eye: The rise of surveillance society.* Minneapolis: University of Minneapolis Press.

Marchand, R. (1985). *Advertising the American dream: Making way for modernity, 1920–1940.* Berkeley: University of California Press.

Mougayar, W. (1998). *Opening digital markets.* New York: McGraw-Hill.

Negroponte, N. (1995). *Being digital.* New York: Alfred A. Knopf.

Norris, C., and Armstrong, G. (1999). *The maximum surveillance society: The rise of CCTV.* Oxford: Berg.

Papa, M. J., Auwal, M.A., & Singhal, A. (1997, September). Organizing for social change within concertive control systems: Member identification, empowerment, and the masking of discipline. *Communication Monographs, 64*, 219–249.

Pine, J. (1993). *Mass customization: The new frontier in business competition.* Cambridge, MA: Harvard University Press.

Rheingold, H. (1993). *Virtual community.* Reading, MA: Addison-Wesley.

Robins, K., & Webster, F. (1999). *Times of the technoculture: From the information society to the virtual life.* London: Routledge.

Rosen, J. (2000). *The unwanted gaze: The destruction of privacy in America.* New York: Random House.

Schiller, D. (1999). *Digital capitalism.* Cambridge, MA: The MIT Press.

Schiller, D. (1988). How to think about information. In V. Mosco & J. Wasko (Eds.), *The Political Economy of Information* (pp. 27–43). Madison: University of Wisconsin Press.

Shapiro, A. (1999). *The control revolution: How the Internet is putting individuals in charge and changing the world we know.* New York: PublicAffairs.

Smythe, D. (1981). *Dependency road: Communications, capitalism, consciousness, and Canada.* Toronto: Ablex.

Smythe, D. (1977). Communications: Blindspot of western Marxism. *Canadian Journal of Political and Social Theory, 1*, 1–27.

Whitaker, R. (1999). *The end of privacy: How total surveillance is becoming a reality.* New York: New Press.

63

THE MP3 AS CULTURAL ARTIFACT

Jonathan Sterne

For the last seven years or so, the mp3 has occupied center stage in the world of digital audio formats. It has been the subject of academic papers, court cases, congressional and parliamentary hearings and countless magazine and newspaper articles. Mp3 trading has been the case in point in a major international controversy over the status of intellectual property, copyright and the economics of entertainment. A whole series of authors have argued that the debate over intellectual property is incredibly important for intellectuals, academics, artists and anyone else who works with ideas (see e.g. Bettig, 1997; Burkart and McCourt, 2004; Jones, 2000; Lessig, 2000, 2002; McCourt and Burkart, 2003; McLeod, 2001, 2005). Writings on mp3s and file-sharing almost uniformly sound a note of crisis, as if the battle over mp3s and intellectual property is the most important cultural conflict of our time.

Therefore, it is surprising how little of the common sense of technology studies has been applied to mp3s. Scholars in a range of fields – philosophy of technology, science and technology studies and the cultural study of technology – have all advocated the study of technologies as artifacts. Philosopher Langdon Winner writes that technological artifacts 'embody specific forms of power and authority' (1986: 19). He groups the politics of technologies into two main categories: 'instances in which the invention, design, or arrangement of a specific technical device or system becomes a way of settling an issue in the affairs of a political community', and '"inherently political technologies", man-made systems that appear to require or be strongly compatible with particular kinds of political relationships' (1986: 22). In Winner's heuristic,

From *New Media and Society* 8:5 (2006) pp. 825–42.

the mp3 partakes of both categories: it originated as an attempt to solve the problem of exchangeable formats across segments of the media industry and it may require particular social and cultural systems of both intellectual property and listening.

The mp3 is an artifact in another sense. The mp3 is a crystallized set of social and material relations. It is an item that 'works for' and is 'worked on' by a host of people, ideologies, technologies and other social and material elements. Writers in the social construction of technology and actor–network theory traditions (e.g. Bijker, 1995; Latour, 1996; Pinch and Bijker, 1984) have focused on the relation of human and non-human actors in the construction of technologies, showing how technologies come together from what one might consider otherwise as disparate elements. Cultural studies of technology have been more concerned with broader accounts of social context and stratified social power as they shape technologies and as technologies are implicated in these contexts (see e.g. Slack, 1984; Stabile, 1994; Wise, 1997). But all these approaches point to the artifactual nature of technologies such as the mp3. They urge us to consider it as a result of social and technical processes, rather than as outside them somehow. Uncovering that process is not simply a matter of showing the artificiality or 'constructedness' of the mp3, although that is part of the project. This article will use the mp3 as a tour guide for social, physical, psychological and ideological phenomena of which otherwise we might not have been fully aware. It will consider the mp3 as an artifact shaped by several electronics industries, the recoding industry and actual and idealized practices of listening.

Of course, this is not the first cultural study of mp3s. Kembrew McLeod (2005) notes that because the mp3 format is software, its uses are somewhat less determined than hardware and, even there, uses can change. Steve Jones (2002) has argued cleverly that the mp3 is an occasion to bring questions of distribution to the forefront of cultural studies. Yet in most accounts, writers still represent the mp3 itself as a mute, inert object that 'impacts' an industry, a social environment or a legal system. The writing on the subject most often takes the form of the mp3 as either 'given' or obvious, with little further thought on the matter required for addressing real legal and economic issues. At the same time, surprisingly little discussion has occurred around the aesthetic dimensions of mp3s, whether by that one means the experience of mp3 listening, the sound of mp3s themselves or the meanings that the form of the mp3 might take. Discussions of the sound of mp3s have been limited largely to audio engineers and audiophiles, who range from dismissals on the basis that mp3s sound 'bad' (e.g. Atkinson, 1999) to analyses of the sonic limitations of mp3s as a 'problem' (e.g. Eide, 2001). In the academic world, one could read for a long time before confronting the fact that mp3s are sound files. [. . .]

This article advances an alternate position. A robust understanding of the technological and aesthetic dimensions of the mp3 provides an important context for discussions of the legal, political economic and broader cultural dimensions of file-sharing. By examining the mp3 as an auditory technology, it reveals some important dimensions of the relationship between the so-called 'new' media[1] and the human body that have been neglected largely by scholars who privilege the visual dimensions of new media. In short, it will show that a gestural, tactile form of embodiment is the requirement and result of digital audio. This contrasts greatly with the mentalist and self-conscious disembodiment that some scholars still describe as a central feature of virtual space.

To borrow a term from Lewis Mumford, the mp3 is a 'container technology'. Mumford wrote that technology scholars' emphasis on tools over containers 'overlooks' their equally vital role (see Mumford, 1959, 1966). [. . .] [Zoë Sofia argues that] to keep utensils, apparatus and utilities[2] in mind is difficult because these kinds of technological objects are designed to be unobtrusive and . . . make their presence felt, but not noticed' (2000: 188). Indeed, this is the mode in which mp3s work: they are important precisely because they are useful but do not call attention to themselves in practice. They take up less space than other kinds of digital recordings and when they are listened to, they are experienced as music, not as file formats. Thus, we should not be surprised to find media among Sofia's many examples of container technologies.

The rest of this article explores the mp3 as a container technology for sound recordings. Mumford and Sofia both use the term 'apparatus' to describe a container that transforms as it holds (Sofia, 2000). The mp3 clearly belongs to this category, but it differs in one important way: it is a container for containers. Like an oven that holds a casserole and transforms its contents, the mp3 is a holder for sound recordings. It is a media technology designed to make use of other media technologies. As we will see below, the transformations effected by mp3 encoding are themselves heavily-directed cultural practices. Mp3s contain within them a whole philosophy of audition and a praxeology of listening. As a philosophy of audition, the mp3 makes use of the limitations of healthy human hearing. One might even say that the mp3 is a celebration of the limits of auditory perception. The anticipated praxeology of listening encoded in each mp3 emphasizes distraction over attention and exchange over use. If that were not enough, the technology itself is perfectly and lovingly shaped for the very purposes to which it is not supposed to be put: the mp3 is perfectly designed for illegal file-sharing. Thus, the next section explains the form of the mp3 and what makes it different from other kinds of recording technologies and then offers an analysis of the mp3 as a cultural artifact.

THE SUPPLY OF MP3S

The point of mp3s is to make audio files smaller through data compression[3] so that they are easier to exchange in a limited bandwidth environment such as the internet, and easier to store in a limited dataspace environment, such as a hard drive. This section discusses the reasons why a consortium of communication industries built the mp3 to be so portable. Then it explains the psychoacoustic dimensions of mp3s, which are the crucial technical and cultural components of their portability. In short, the mp3 was designed by an electronics industry interested in maximum compatibility across platforms, which would allow for easy exchange of files. At the same time, the mp3 uses a specific form of data compression based on a model of how the human ear works. Therefore it is a machine designed to anticipate how its listeners perceive music and to perceive for them. Both explanations are a bit 'gear-headed', but like the 'detour through theory' so central to good cultural studies writing (Hall, 1992: 283), this 'detour through technology' will help us to reconstitute our object of study and thereby gain new insights into hitherto hidden auditory dimensions of digital media culture.

MP3 stands for MPEG-1, Layer-3. MPEG (Motion Picture Experts Group) is a consortium of engineers and others formed with the support of the International Standards Organization (ISO) and the International Electrotechnical Commission.[4] MPEG started out in 1988 as an ad hoc group that aimed to standardize data compression schemes in the broadcast, telecommunications and consumer electronics industries. In collaboration with academics, all of the big corporate players had a role and an interest, even as internal divisions within corporations sometimes led them to create proprietary standards while supporting research on standardized compression. For those who believed in standardization, one format was needed that could cut across digital technologies as diverse as compact discs, digital video, high-definition television, teleconferencing and satellite communications, to name just a few of the disparate industries interested in a shared standard (Mitchell et al., 1997).[5] [. . .]

To borrow another phrase from Zoë Sofia, the MPEG standard carried with it a certain 'logic of resourcing and supply' (2000: 195–6). The logic was this: once standardized, data could be moved with ease and grace across many different kinds of systems and over great distances frequently and with little effort. This was the dream of the Motion Picture Experts Group and its many benefactors. If one is looking for the cultural origins of the promiscuity among illegal file-sharers, one need look no further than this founding moment. The possibility for quick and easy transfers, anonymous relations between provider and receiver, cross-platform compatibility, stockpiling and easy storage and access – all were built into the MPEG form itself long before the age of Napster, Gnutella, Hotline, iTunes and Rio.

Attempts to commercialize the mp3 and its likely successor, Advanced Audio Coding (AAC), make use of various digital rights management algorithms that make it more difficult to share files. For instance, Apple's iTunes Music Store and RealNetworks use incompatible technologies to prevent sharing. These recent innovations do mark a recognition on the part of the industry that the compatibility of the mp3 is part of the reason why it is so widely shared. But the net result of such practices is to require users who legally purchase mp3s from iTunes and RealNetworks to use two separate programs for playback. As Patrick Burkart and Tom McCourt (2004) argue, digital rights management is hampered by vast incompatibilities across software and hardware and an industry climate hostile to a shared standard. In other words, it is probably easier to install a Gnutella client and acquire illegal files than it is to manage two separate mp3 collections and two separate playback programs.

Through its design as a portable container technology, the mp3 has been ascribed the status of a thing in everyday practice, even though it is nothing more than a format for encoding digital data. Both listeners and companies that sell mp3s (or the equipment to play them) readily talk of mp3 collections analogously to record collections or book collections. Articles on the original incarnation of Napster, for example, tended to describe it as a 'program for searching other people's mp3 collections' (e.g. McCollum, 2000; Wood and Jenish, 2000). More recently, magazine advertisements for Apple's iPod and iPod Mini extol their virtues by listing the number of 'songs' that each device can hold (Apple, 2004). Further, mp3s have been objectified as articles of intellectual property in the US legal system, Canadian legislature and in several other countries as well (Evangelista, 2003; Krim, 2003; Lazin, 2003).

This raises the problem of use-value and exchange-value. Use-value, first identified by John Locke (1692) and elaborated by Karl Marx and others, is a perspective on value which treats commodities in terms of their actual utility. Exchange-value, meanwhile, is the market value of a commodity. While this would appear to be an arbitrary relationship, Marx argues – following Adam Smith – that exchange-value is actually based on the labor required to make the commodity, once that labor is exchanged for money which in turn can be traded for the commodity (Marx, 1967[1867]; Smith, 1993[1776]). Thus, we have a bifurcation of value: use-value, which is about the work of expenditure; and exchange-value, which is about the work of creation. Most interesting for our purposes is the relationship of exchange-value to music. In his romantic and polemical book on music, Jacques Attali argues that sound recording occasions a shift from use-value to exchange-value in music:

> We must not forget that music remains a very unique commodity; to take on meaning, it requires an incompressible lapse of time, that of its own duration. Thus the gramophone, conceived as a recorder to stockpile time, became instead its principle user. Conceived as a word preserver, it became a sound diffuser. The major contradiction of repetition is evident here: *people must devote their time to producing the means to buy recordings of other people's time*, losing in the process not only the use of their time, but also the time required to use other people's time. Stockpiling thus becomes a substitute, not a preliminary condition, for use. *People buy more records than they can listen to. They stockpile what they want to find the time to hear.* Use-time and exchange-time destroy one another. (Attali, 1985: 101; emphasis in original)

One can see the problem immediately with mp3s in Attali's formulation: usually, people do not buy them. Attali argues that recording substitutes exchange-value for use-value because people do not have the time to listen to all of the recordings that they may buy. Yet compared to the number of mp3s freely given and received through file-sharing, few meet the basic definition of exchange-value: they are not paid for and therefore do not require as much labor (in exchange for a wage or salary) to procure. Further, the exchange itself does not deprive the original owner of the file's use. The peculiar status of the mp3 as a valued cultural object which can circulate outside the channels of the value economy is one of the fundamental, enabling conditions for the intellectual property debates that surround it. [. . .]

In use, mp3s can seem a bit like mollusks without their shells – recorded music without the commodity form – since generally they are not exchanged for money. One response to this condition would be to consider the internet as a gift economy, as Richard Barbrook (1998) has done so elegantly and provocatively. But if the mp3s are mollusks free of their shells, they still need air and water: listeners must still pay for the descendents of the gramophone and the record dealer: computers, speakers, internet connections (or membership in institutions such as universities that provide access to such things) and possibly other playback devices such as Rios or iPods. Further, most of the recordings now available in mp3 form once lived in a money economy, paid for by record companies (or less often, independent musicians) who in turn put them up for sale in the hope of realizing a profit. Thus, whatever side we take in the debates over intellectual property and digital rights management, the question of value persists. If for no other reason, we know this because users continue to desire, collect, stockpile – and yes, use – mp3s.

'For a collector,' wrote Walter Benjamin, 'ownership is the most intimate relationship that one can have to objects' (1968[1936]: 67). That one can collect mp3s suggests that they appear to users as cultural objects, even if they are not, in any conventional sense, physical objects that can be held in a person's hand. In a review of Traktor, a software DJ program, Philip Sherburne pauses to note that digital audio formats and their manipulation on computers reflect

> the ongoing dematerialization of music (or perhaps a better term would be 'micromaterialization' since even mp3s live in silicon, invisible as they may seem). More and more, our collections exist not on our record shelves, but in our iPods and hard drives. (2003: 46)

This is key: although mp3s exist as software, people tend to treat them like objects (and indeed, the argument here is that we should analyze them as artifacts) perhaps because they are used to handling recordings as physical things. But because of their micromaterialization, users can handle mp3s quite differently from the recordings they possess in a more obviously 'physical' form such as a record or compact disc (CD), even though they may talk about mp3s as if they are physical objects. Consider this review of the iPod and iTunes Music Store:

> [Y]ou'll even find that you listen to music in new ways. Recently the Talking Heads' sublime 'Heaven' popped up on my jukebox in random play mode; I'd owned the CD for years but hadn't played it much and never noticed this amazing song. That kind of discovery happens all the time now that my music collection has been liberated from shiny plastic disks. (Regnier, 2003: 113)

There are really two kinds of object indicated in the quote: there are objects that can be collected, which include mp3s, and there are objects that can be touched (in some conventional sense), such as CDs but unlike mp3s. All this is to say that if we accept the language of the materialization and dematerialization of music,[6] mp3s present us with an interesting bifurcation. Users refer to the dematerialization of music in discussing their practices of use, but they insist on treating music as a cultural object when they discuss their possession of the music.

Inside the MP3

Because it is so small, the mp3 format makes collecting all that much easier: an entire collection can fit in a relatively small space. An mp3 takes an existing CD-quality digital audio file and removes as much data content as possible, relying on listeners' bodies and brains to make up the difference. [. . .] The patents for the audio section of the MPEG standard continue to be held mostly by a German company named Fraunhofer IIS. A traditional zip utility gets rid of redundant data to make a file a little smaller. However, if you were to zip a CD track, it would not get much smaller. Fraunhofer's basic innovation was to use a mathematical model of human auditory perception to allow for greater data compression in mp3 files. In essence, the file is designed to figure out what you will not hear anyway and to get rid of the data for that portion of the sound.

Although it is a data file, it has been suggested already here that users treat mp3s as cultural objects. Mp3s are like other technologies in another important way: they are assembled by other technologies. The name for a program that assembles mp3s is an encoder. For the purposes of this argument, an encoder will be treated like any other container technology that transforms its contents. The encoder takes an existing digital recording and processes it through six related steps ([see] Hacker, 2000).

[. . .]

As a form of data compression, the most compelling part of the mp3 is the psychoacoustic model encoded within it. To personify the technology, it presumes that the sense of hearing discards most of the sound that it encounters, attempting to imitate the process by which the human body discards soundwaves in the process of perception. It preemptively discards data in the soundfile that it anticipates the body will discard later, resulting in a smaller file.

That the ear (or any sense) acts as a filter is an old idea. From Aristotle on the senses to Aldous Huxley on psychedelic drugs, it is well established that the senses do not mimetically reproduce the world they encounter – they shape it (Aristotle, 1976 [350BC]; Huxley, 1954). Today, the explanation is a bit more clinical. Put simply, the auditory nerve fires with less frequency than the frequencies of sound. The nerve in the inner ear cannot keep up with sound as it actually happens. Yet somehow, between the cochlea, the auditory nerve and the auditory center in the brain, people get a sense of the detailed rise and fall of sounds. Scholars of psychoacoustics have proposed a number of analyses as to why the ear works in the way that it does, but no one theory is dominant (Mathews, 2001a). The key point is that while traditionally, sound reproduction technologies have been theorized in terms of their relation of absolute fidelity to a sound source, the human ear is not capable of such fine distinctions. In fact, people can lose most of the vibrations in a recorded sound and still hear it as roughly the same sound as the version with no data compression. This is the principle upon which the mp3 rests.

This discussion of psychoacoustics is not meant to be 'psychological' as humanities scholars generally understand the term. Psychoacoustics is a crucial component of the embodiment of sound. Psychoacoustic response is not localized in a single place: the ear concentrates, focuses and stratifies vibrations into sounds, which the auditory nerve translates into signals for the brain to perceive. But the ear canal is not the only place that conducts vibrations to the auditory nerve: the whole head can and does conduct vibration, as does the chest cavity. [. . .] So what we have here is a psychacoustic body, a body that 'does stuff' to vibration in order to turn it into sound. Sound is a product of perception, not a thing 'out there' – the only thing 'out there' is vibration, which the body organizes and stratifies into what we call sound (Sterne, 2003). The body shapes vibrations before they enter the ear and become sound. This is obvious in cases of tinnitus (ringing of the ears) and frequency-dependent hearing loss. But it is also true of people who have undamaged hearing. Psychoacoustic effects are based on the fact that the body creates sound by organizing vibrations.

Mp3s use psychoacoustic principles to get rid of the sounds that we supposedly would not hear anyway. There are three specific psychoacoustic tricks that mp3 encoders use to reduce the size of data files: simultaneous or auditory masking, temporal masking and spatialization. Auditory masking is the elimination of similar frequencies, based on the principle that when two sounds of similar frequency are played together and one is significantly quieter, people will hear only the louder sound. Temporal masking is a similar principle across time: if there are two sounds very close together in time (less than about five milliseconds apart, depending on the material) and one is significantly louder than the other, listeners can only hear the louder sound. The third principle is spatialization. While it is very easy to locate the direction of sounds in the middle of the audible range when they are played back in stereo, it is close to impossible for people to locate very low or very high sounds. To save more dataspace, the mp3 encoder saves sounds at either end of the frequency spectrum only once for both channels, rather than twice and plays them back as mono files. [. . .] Psychoacoustically, the mp3 is designed to throw away sonic material that listeners supposedly would not hear otherwise.

This process requires a good deal of compromise. Mp3s of songs do not sound the same as the CD recordings; a professional audio engineer could certainly tell the difference. But the amazing thing is that as we move from ideal listening environments into the situations in which people usually hear mp3s, it becomes increasingly difficult to distinguish. Mp3s are designed to be heard via headphones while outdoors, in a noisy dorm room, in an office with a loud computer fan, in the background as other activities are taking place and through low-fi or mid-fi computer speakers. They are meant for casual listening, moments when listeners may or may not attend directly to the music – and are therefore even *less* likely to attend to the sound of the music. In other words, the mp3 is a medium which, in most practical contexts, gives the full experience of listening to a recording while only offering a fraction of the information and allowing listeners' bodies to do the rest of the work. The mp3 plays its listener. Built into every mp3 is an attempt to mimic and, to some degree preempt, the embodied and unconscious dimensions of human perception in the noisy, mixed-media environments of everyday life.

It has been suggested already here that the portability of mp3s was built into their form by an industry which believed that exchange and compatibility were in their objective interests. Some of the innovations were technical, but a whole other set of innovations dealt with how people hear things. Since the 1910s, AT&T's Bell Laboratories has researched ways to cram more sound into limited bandwidth telephone lines because it would allow a massive increase in signal exchange with no expansion of infrastructure.[7] For example, although you may think that you hear my booming voice on the other end of the telephone line, you actually only hear what Hermann Helmholtz (1954[1863]) called the 'upper partials' of the signal. Helmholtz showed that when certain higher frequencies are played together, they effectively synthesize a sound an octave lower. The phone system does not have to transmit any low-frequency signal – your ears and brain will simply fill it in.

The audio media that we encounter every day use a whole set of techniques such as this to shape our sonic environments. But the portability also exists in the psychoacoustic dimensions. The mp3 fetishizes and makes use of the imperfections of healthy hearing while presuming a so-called normal listening situation. The ideal listener implied by the mp3's psychoacoustic coding is Theodor Adorno's nightmare: the 'distracted' consumer of mass culture (2002[1938], 1993[1945]). In a media-saturated environment, portability and ease of acquisition trumps monomaniacal attention. Of course, actual listening practices and environments vary widely, and as Michael Bull (2000) has shown with portable stereos, the meanings attributed to a sound technology by its users are quite variable depending on its actual use. But the point to take here is simple: at the psychoacoustic level as well as the industrial level, the mp3 is designed for promiscuity. This has been a long-term goal in the design of sound reproduction technologies.

AROUND THE MP3

Although it stands in a long line of technologies that have made use of acoustic and psychoacoustic principles, the mp3 has applied psychoacoustics to a much greater degree than any major sound reproduction technology that preceded it. The embodied mp3 stands in stark contrast to the concept of 'the virtual', which has received so much play in cultural analyses of digital media. [. . .] The mp3 suggests an even more radical challenge to the concept of virtuality because of its direct and sensuous interaction with an embodied, sensing, unthinking subject. If sound is not 'out there' but rather created by the process of perception, then the mp3 is not a simulation of sound or a virtual sound. It is simply another mode through which the effect of sound is produced and embodiment is the defining characteristic of the experience. The subject of the mp3 is almost the opposite of the supposed intending, self-knowing, consciously self-constructing subject of virtual reality.

[. . .]

Mp3 technology also has an interesting relationship with other bodily technologies of communication. The mp3 works automatically on the body. Mp3 listening might involve 'practical knowledge' (Bourdieu, 1990), where the body goes through routines that do not enter the conscious mind. Certainly, mp3 listening requires a whole set of bodily techniques, dispositions and attitudes. But the mp3 goes even further than this. The encoded mathematical table inside the mp3 that represents psychoacoustic response suggests less a 'technique of the body' [. . .] than a concordance of signals among computers, electrical components and auditory nerves.

Scale matters here: quantitatively speaking, the coordinated movements of mp3 sonics are so much smaller than the movements produced by a socialized body, that we may be talking about a *qualitative* difference between listening practice as a technique of the body and the mp3 as a concordance of signals. In the techniques of the body, bodily movement is conditioned as part of the socialization process. People learn how to walk, sit, gesture, etc. Certainly, there is a whole set of techniques of listening that are assumed or enabled by mp3 technology. But mp3s also *anticipate* the tiny movements of the inner ear, which are not so much organized and disciplined in the mathematical table as they are modeled and anticipated. Thus, the mp3 uses a construct of the body to modify data, electrical signals and eventually sounds before they get to listeners' ears. This is to say that mp3s require body techniques, but are not themselves body techniques in the same sense – they model perception in order to affect it.

The mp3 carries with it a sonic logic of resourcing and supply. At the risk of overextending a metaphor, the logic could be cast in economic terms: the mp3 encoding process puts the body on a sonic austerity program. It decides for its listeners what they need to hear and gives them only that. Listeners' bodies, brains and ears then contribute a kind of surplus activity (if not quite labor) to make the system run. Of course, commentators from *Wired Magazine* to Courtney Love have touted the mp3 as some kind of sonic liberation. But it represents a liberation of just-in-time sound production, where systems give listeners less and ask their bodies to do more of the work.

Despite the attractiveness of the economic metaphor, it does not quite work when it comes to assessing the mp3 as a cultural artifact. The mp3 is not nearly as nefarious as neoliberal economic policies. One could rightly argue that rather than being a cruel exploitation of the limits of auditory perception, the mp3 encoder instrumentalizes and even celebrates the limits of the human ear. It suggests how little 'input' people need in order to have powerful and significant aesthetic experiences. [. . .] At the very least, the success of the mp3 adds a new twist to the critique of correspondence theories of representation and their corresponding aesthetics. To use a term from Ivan Illich (1973), the mp3 is a comparably 'convivial' technology for listening to mediated music in noisy, multimedia or otherwise distracting (or 'distracted') contexts. It is all the more remarkable because it grew up amid such unconvivial technical systems as the recording industry, recording studios, CD plants and computer networks.

The mp3 is a form designed for massive exchange, casual listening and massive accumulation. As a container technology designed to execute a process on its contents, it does what it was made to do. The primary, illegal uses of the mp3 are not aberrant uses or an error in the technology; they are its highest moral calling: 'Eliminate redundancies! Reduce bandwidth use! Travel great distances frequently and with little effort! Accumulate on the hard drives of the middle class! Address a distracted listening subject!' These are the instructions encoded into the very form of the mp3. This is the mission that an mp3 carries out as it travels down network lines onto my hard drive; as it instructs my computer to construct a datastream that will become electricity, that in turn will vibrate the speakers on my desk and the membranes in my ears as I type this sentence. The mp3 has a job to do, and it does it very well.

ACKNOWLEDGEMENTS

Many thanks to Carrie Rentschler, Emily Raine, Jeremy Morris, Will Straw, Jenny Burman, Louise Meintjes, Larry Grossberg, Ken Hillis, Ken Wissoker,

Lisa Nakamura, Christian Sandvig, Alex Mawyer, Brian Horne, two anonymous reviewers and audiences in Montreal, Durham, Madison, Pittsburgh and Chicago for their comments on earlier versions of this article.

NOTES

1. *Pace* Lev Manovich (2001), who has argued that 'new media' is a more robust phrase than 'digital media' or some other name, most so-called 'new' media are not that new anymore. The term 'new' is incredibly value-laden in our heavily commercialized culture, but I use it here and throughout the article with the recognition that 'new media' signifies a fairly coherent set of objects of study and a number of emergent intellectual traditions.
2. These three categories indicate three different kinds of container technology for Sofia. Parsing them out is not necessary for the current argument, but interested readers should refer to her article.
3. I use the term 'data compression' to signal the difference between the processes that remove data from audio files (traditionally called 'compression', which only can be accomplished digitally) and the process of reducing the distance between the loudest and quietest points in an audio signal. This is also called 'compression', but it can be accomplished through either analog or digital signal processing.
4. The ISO is a network of national standards institutes from 148 countries which collaborate with international organizations, governments, industry, business and consumer representatives. The International Electrotechnical Commission focuses on standards for electronic and magnetic devices and is now affiliated with the World Trade Organization.
5. A full academic history of the mp3 has yet to be written. The only thorough journalistic history currently available is Bruce Haring's *Beyond the Charts* (2000). Taking his cues from intellectual property debates, he presents the mp3 as part of a longer story about digital audio, online distribution and the music industry.
6. Forthcoming work will explore this question in greater detail.
7. The line of psychoacoustic research first developed at Bell Laboratories in the 1910s is the genealogical point of origin for digital audio as we know it today. It is also an important origin point for cybernetic models of communication.

REFERENCES

Adorno, T. (1993[1945]) 'A Social Critique of Radio Music', in N. Strauss (ed.) *Radiotext(e)*, pp. 272–9. New York: Semiotext(e).

Adorno, T. (2002[1938]) 'On the Fetish Character of Music and the Regression of Listening', in R. Leppert (ed.) *Adorno: Essays on Music*, pp. 288–317. Berkeley, CA: University of California Press.

Apple (2004) 'iPod Mini', *Wired* 12(March), back cover.

Aristotle (1976[350BC]) *De Anima* (trans R.D. Hicks). New York: Arno Press.

Atkinson, J. (1999) 'Mp3 and the Marginalization of High End Audio', *Stereophile* (February): 22.

Attali, J. (1985) *Noise: the Political Economy of Music* (trans B. Massumi). Minneapolis, MN: University of Minnesota Press.

Barbrook, R. (1998) 'The Hi-Tech Gift Economy', *First Monday* 3(12) (available at: http://www.firstmonday.org/issues/issue3_12/barbrook/index.html).

Benjamin, W. (1968[1936]) *Illuminations* (trans. H. Zohn). New York: Schocken.

Bettig, R. (1997) 'The Enclosure of Cyberspace', *Critical Studies in Mass Communication* 14(2): 138–58.

Bijker, W. (1995) *Of Bicycles, Bakelites and Bulbs: Toward a Thoery of Sociotechnical Change*. Cambridge, MA: MIT Press.

Bourdieu, P. (1990) *The Logic of Practice* (trans. R. Nice). Stanford, CA: Stanford University Press.

Bull, M. (2000) *Sounding Out the City: Personal Stereos and Everyday Life*. New York: New York University Press.

Burkart, P. and T. McCourt (2004) 'Infrastructure for the Celestial Jukebox', *Popular Music* 23(3): 349–62.

Corbett, J. (1994) *Extended Play: Sounding Off from John Cage to Dr. Funkenstein*. Durham, NC: Duke University Press.

Eide, O. (2001) 'Bob Ludwig', *Mix*, 1 December (available at: http://mixonline.com/mag/audio_bob_ludwig/index.html).

Evangelista, B. (2003) '4 Students Sued Over Music Trading Software; Record Industry Goes After Campus File-Sharing Programs', *San Francisco Chronicle*, 4 April: 2.

Hacker, S. (2000) *Mp3: The Definitive Guide*. Cambridge, MA: O'Reilly.

Hall, S. (1992) 'Cultural Studies and Its Theoretical Legacies', in L. Grossberg, C. Nelson and P. Treichler (eds) *Cultural Studies*, pp. 277–94. New York: Routledge.

Haring, B. (2000) *Beyond the Charts: Mp3 and the Digital Music Revolution*. Los Angeles, CA: OTC Books.

Helmholtz, H. (1954[1863]) *On the Sensations of Tone as a Physiological Basis for the Theory of Music* (2nd edn, trans. A.J. Ellis). New York: Dover.

Hillis, K. (1999) *Digital Sensations: Space, Identity and Embodiment in Virtual Reality*. Minneapolis, MN: University of Minnesota Press.

Huxley, A. (1954) *The Doors of Perception*. New York: Harper.

Illich, I. (1973) *Tools for Conviviality*. New York: Harper & Row.

Jones, S. (2000) 'Music and the Internet', *Popular Music* 19(2): 217–30.

Jones, S. (2002) 'Music that Moves: Popular Music, Distribution and Network Technologies', *Cultural Studies* 16(2): 213–32.

Krim, J. (2003) 'File Sharing Forfeits Right to Privacy: Judge Tells Verizon to Identify Customer', *Washington Post*, 25 April: 1.

Latour, B. (1996) *Aramis, Or the Love of Technology*. Cambridge, MA: Harvard University Press.

Lazin, D. (2003) 'New Levy Boosts Price of Mp3 Players', *Edmonton Journal*, 13 December: 1.

Lessig, L. (2000) *Code and Other Laws of Cyberspace*. New York: Basic Books.

Lessig, L. (2002) *The Future of Ideas: The Fate of the Commons in a Connected World*. New York: Vintage Books.

Locke, J. (1692) *Some Considerations on the Consequences of the Lowering of Interest and Raising the Value of Money*. London: A. & J. Churchill.

McCollum, K. (2000) 'Students Jam College Networks with Use of Napster to Find Audio Files', *Chronicle of Higher Education* 25, 25 February: A50.

McCourt, T. and P. Burkart (2003) 'When Creators, Corporations and Consumers Collide: Napster and the Development of On-Line Music Distribution', *Media, Culture & Society* 25(3): 333–50.

McLeod, K. (2001) *Owning Culture*. New York: Peter Lang.

McLeod, K. (2005) *Freedom of Expression: Tales from the Dark Side of Intellectual Property Law*. New York: Doubleday.

Manovich, L. (2001) *The Language of New Media*. Cambridge, MA: MIT Press.

Marx, K. (1967[1867]) *Capital: A Critical Analysis of Capitalist Production*, Vol. 1 (trans. S.M.A.E. Aveling). New York: International Publishers.

Mathews, M. (2001) 'The Auditory Brain', in P.R. Cook (ed.) *Music, Cognition and Computerized Sound: An Introduction to Psychoacoustics*, pp. 11–20. Cambridge, MA: MIT Press.

Mitchell, J.L., W.B. Pennebaker, C.E. Fogg and D.J. LeGall (eds) (1997) *MPEG Video Compression Standard*. New York: Chapman & Hall.

Mowitt, J. (1987) 'The Sound of Music in the Era of its Electronic Reproducibility', in R. Leppert and S. McClary (eds) *Music and Society: the Politics of Composition, Performance and Reception*, pp. 173–97. New York: Cambridge University Press.

Mumford, L. (1959) 'An Appraisal of Lewis Mumford's Technics and Civilization', *Daedalus* 88: 527–36.

Mumford, L. (1966) *The Myth of the Machine: Technics and Human Development*, Vol. 1. New York: Harcourt, Brace and World.

Pinch, T. and W. Bijker (1984) 'The Social Construction of Facts and Artefacts: Or How the Sociology of Science and the Sociology of Technology Might Benefit Each Other', *Social Studies of Science* 14(3): 399–441.

Regnier, P. (2003) 'Digital Music for Grown-Ups', *Money*, July: 113.

Rothenbuhler, E. and J.D. Peters (1997) 'Defining Phonography: An Experiment in Theory', *Musical Quarterly* 81(2): 242–64.

Sherburne, P. (2003) 'Digital DJing App that Pulls You In', *Grooves* 10: 46–7.

Slack, J.D. (1984) *Communication Technologies and Society: Conceptions of Causality and the Politics of Technological Intervention*. Norwood, NJ: Ablex.

Smith, A. (1993[1776]) *An Inquiry into the Nature and Causes of the Wealth of Nations*. New York: Oxford University Press.

Sofia, Z. (2000) 'Container Technologies', *Hypatia* 15(2): 181–219.

Stabile, C. (1994) *Feminism and the Technological Fix*. New York: Manchester University Press.

Sterne, J. (2003) *The Audible Past: Cultural Origins of Sound Reproduction*. Durham, NC: Duke University Press.

Winner, L. (1986) *The Whale and the Reactor: A Search for Limits in the Age of High Technology*. Chicago, IL: University of Chicago Press.

Wise, J.M. (1997) *Exploring Technology and Social Space*. Thousand Oaks, CA: Sage.

Wood, C. and D.A. Jenish (2000) 'Free Music!', *Maclean's*, 20 March: 42.

64

BEYOND ANONYMITY, OR FUTURE DIRECTIONS FOR INTERNET IDENTITY RESEARCH

Helen Kennedy

Introduction: The Internet, Identity and Anonymity

In his overview of the short history of the field that he defines as cyberculture studies (which has many overlaps with new media studies), Silver (2000) suggests that the area has moved through three key phases. The first phase he defines as 'popular cyberculture', consisting of descriptive journalism, often in the columns of magazines. The second phase builds on this and is defined as 'cyberculture studies': while more academic and less journalistic, it was marked by equally celebratory literature such as Rheingold's *The Virtual Community* (1993) and Turkle's *Life on the Screen* (1996). These texts also reflect the focus on virtual communities and online identities that marked this historical phase. Writing in 2000, Silver claims that we are now in a phase of 'critical cybercultural studies', characterized by a concern with contextualizing cyber-experiences and the emergence of a broader range of empirical studies of cyberworlds. Consequently, cyberculture studies are now more theoretically nuanced and more empirically based than they were in the past.

Although the neat chronology of events implied in Silver's account is somewhat oversimplified, he makes a number of important claims – that, today, cyberculture studies is increasingly populated by empirical research and focused on a broader range of concerns than identity and community, resulting in more diverse and richer theorizations than existed 15 years ago. Nevertheless, a number of writers continue to argue that there has been too much focus on identity in cultural studies of the internet. For example, Hine

From *New Media and Society* 8:6 (2006) pp. 859–76.

(2001) proposes that conceiving of webpages as performances of identity fails to acknowledge the social and cultural meaning of webpage production, and McPherson (2000) argues that instead of focusing on identity play online, we should consider politics and participation in order to understand cyberworlds. Furthermore, within some sectors of cultural studies, for some time there has been debate about the usefulness of the very concept of identity – from Hall's essay 'Who Needs Identity?' (1996), which criticizes the essentialist model of human subjectivity embodied in this concept, to more recent literature influenced by the work of Deleuze, which proposes alternatives to identity as more effective starting points for carrying out sociocultural research (for example, Parisi and Terranova, 2001).

Despite these critical interventions, the tropes of identity and community endure, and it is within this context of debates about whether identity remains a useful focus for studies of the internet and other new media that this article is located.[1] The aim of the article is to map the field of internet identity research, point to some of its limitations and suggest some future directions. The article problematizes the specific claim in internet identity research that virtual identities are anonymous (Turkle, 1996); some of them might be, but there are problems with this generalized, enduring claim. I argue that online identities are often continuous with offline selves, not reconfigured versions of subjectivities in real life; for this reason it is necessary to go *beyond* internet identities, to look at offline contexts of online selves, in order to comprehend virtual life fully. More importantly, the concept of anonymity is problematic because it fixes the relationship between being and feeling in a way that limits the exploration of the significant differences between these two conditions – concepts other than anonymity, therefore, might be more helpful in conceptualizing internet identities. If internet identity research is to reposition itself conceptually, as is proposed here, then it needs to engage with and learn from ongoing debates within cultural studies which call into question the usefulness of the concept of identity. To date, such an engagement has been surprisingly absent from considerations of identity within new media studies, despite the close relationship between these two fields. This engagement may lead internet identity researchers to start with a different set of conceptual tools than those mobilized to date which, in turn, might lead to some new conceptual developments within the broader field of new media studies, within which internet identity research is located.

This article draws on empirical research into internet use by a group of minority ethnic women in the UK on Project Her@, which took place in the late 1990s.[2] Project Her@ was an experiment in computer-mediated distance learning which aimed to enhance access to university education for women from disadvantaged backgrounds. Fourteen mature,[3] minority ethnic, working-class women took part in the project, whose purpose was to respond to a range of inequalities in a region of the UK which is characterized by economic disadvantage, limited engagement in university education and subsequent high unemployment. The extent of the digital divide at the time meant that many inhabitants of the region were unlikely to have access to digital networks. It is within this social and economic context that Project Her@ was developed.[4]

Project Her@ developed a foundation course, delivered partly by computer-mediated distance learning, which offered women who had been out of education for some time the opportunity to improve study and communication skills, and which guaranteed its students places on degree courses upon successful completion. Both the foundation course and the degree courses to which successful students could progress aimed to develop students' technical skills in media, multimedia or information technology, as well as their critical understanding of the range of complex relationships between technologies and societies. It was felt that distance and e-learning approaches might attract a group of women otherwise unable to commit to full-time study, by providing a flexible learning environment in which communication could take place asynchronously. The project funded the purchase of personal computers, which were loaned to students and installed in their own homes for the duration of the course. It subsidized students' online time for several hours a week, and their phone calls to their tutors, each other and the project's technical support team.

A condition of acceptance onto Project Her@ was that students consented to our use of their distance-learning assessed work as research data and to participating in interviews with us – indeed, the students chose their own pseudonyms for research purposes. The assessed work included written reflections about students' techno-experiences and individual homepages, the latter of which are the central focus of this article. Individual interviews were carried out in students' own homes about halfway through the course. Later, when the majority of the students had entered the first year of their degree programmes, a second round of interviews was completed, this time in small groups on the university campus. [. . .]

IDENTITY IN THE AGE OF THE INTERNET: MAPPING THE FIELD

A history of internet identity research has no better starting point than Turkle's *Life on the Screen: Identity in the Age of the Internet*, first published in the USA in 1995 and the UK in 1996. In *Life on the Screen* (Turkle, 1996), a classic study of the relationship between identity construction and networked technologies, Turkle argued that online, identity changes, becoming fluid and fragmented. Most of what Turkle claimed about the relationship between the internet and fragmented identity was based on the experiences of her research subjects, largely college students, in multi-user domains (MUDs). The comment of one MUD participant, who said that 'part of me, a very important part of me, only exists inside PernMUD'[5] (Turkle, 1996: 12), was symptomatic of her respondents' experiences, which suggested that in such anonymous environments, identity can be broken into fragments, deconstructed and reconstructed. Turkle also argued that homepages reflect fragmented identities, as 'home pages on the web are one recent and dramatic illustration of new notions of identity as multiple yet coherent' (Turkle, 1996: 259). In these words Turkle indicated that, despite her attraction to the postmodern notion of decentred identity and the experiences of fragmentation that her research subjects reported, ultimately she had difficulty with these concepts. Other writers have demonstrated a greater commitment to the notion of digitally-fragmented identity, such as Plant (1997) and Haraway (1998). Haraway has argued that it is politically important to split identity because acknowledging identity as always partial, never complete, allows the subject to join with and understand other partial beings, therefore facilitating political alliances and coalitions across difference: 'the split and contradictory self is the one who can interrogate positionings and be accountable; the one who can construct and join rational conversations and fantastic imaginings that change history' (Haraway, 1998: 195).

In contrast, Turkle demonstrated a commitment to the centred and unified self when she concluded her study with the following words:

> Virtual environments are valuable as places where we can acknowledge our inner diversity. But we still want an authentic experience of self. One's fear is, of course, that in the culture of simulation, a word like authenticity can no longer apply. (Turkle, 1996: 254)

Despite this conclusion, Turkle's work is not known for its ultimate loyalty to authentic, coherent identity, but rather for its celebration of fragmented and multiple identity experimentation. Indeed, for some time, this latter reading of Turkle informed much writing on digital, virtual identity (for example, Cheung, 2000; Poster, 1999; Shields, 1996). More recently, however, as detailed empirical, ethnographic and biographical studies have been carried out, different conceptualizations of internet identity have begun to populate the theoretical landscape. For example, as a result of her ethnographic study of the online forum BlueSky, Kendall concludes that, despite prevailing claims about multiple and fluid identities in such environments, BlueSky participants 'continually work to reincorporate their experiences of themselves and of others' selves into integrated, consistent wholes' (Kendall, 1999: 62). In other words, in some cases, virtual identity is not fragmented but stable; in some forums, relatively unified cyber-identities are presented.

Furthermore, it is now evident that it is necessary to differentiate between the types of identity presented in distinct internet environments. Tetzlaff (2000), for example, makes a distinction between digital identities in homepages and other more text-based forums, arguing that while in the latter, identity may be fluid, in the former it is more fixed because of the types of 'data' located there – photographs, contact details and so on (see also Miller and Mather, 1998).

Clearly, new digital forms may result in new digital identities and, as Wakeford argues, it is necessary to specify which aspects of new media are under examination in order to avoid the kind of 'conceptual leakage' (Wakeford, 1997: 54) that occurs when ideas about identity in one virtual context are applied to others. At the same time, the empirical research reported in this article suggests that it is not helpful to polarize virtual identity types as Tetzlaff does (as is argued later).

Perhaps the most enduring concern about internet identity to emerge from Turkle's work addresses the relationship between virtuality and anonymity. Turkle argued that in anonymous MOOs and MUDs, people can disguise aspects of identity which might lead to discrimination, such as race or gender, and so can perform a range of identity positions, hiding marginal identities and becoming part of the mainstream. Implicit in Turkle's claim is the assumption that anonymity in cyberspace is potentially empowering: because we cannot see each other, we cannot judge each other; consequently, virtual worlds are equalizing. What is more, anonymous online settings are empowering because they facilitate identity exploration, or occupying identity positions which may be difficult to occupy in real life (see Shaw, 1997, for an example of this argument). Not surprisingly, however, a number of scholars have pointed out that online anonymity is more problematic than this. For example, discussing the increased incivility in the electronic exchanges he witnessed in the site of his research, Santa Monica's Public Electronic Network, Schmitz (1997) has disputed the claim that such environments are necessarily democratic because of the absence of visual clues to identity. Instead, he argued that although some 'markers of difference' are difficult to detect in online communication, others are easy to identify, so that judgement and discrimination still exist. He wrote that:

> although physical appearance, dress, and other status cues recede, educational competencies and linguistic skills increase in importance. Computer-communication media are not neutral with regard to culture, education, and socio-economic class. And electronic persons are not more 'equal' than proximate individuals, we just use different criteria to rate them. (Schmitz, 1997: 85)

Further, other more recent studies have indicated that not all online communities are created for anonymous identity performance and not all participants engage in virtual environments anonymously. As a result of their research, Roberts and Parks (2001) have concluded that the performance of alternative genders is practised by a small minority and viewed by many as dishonest. Similarly, Kendall (1999) has argued that anonymity is not a factor in the MUD she studied and that many MUDders would object to the trivializing of all MUDs as forums for playing identity games. Baym summed up the issues at stake in 1998 when she wrote that:

Judging from the scholarly attention paid to anonymous CMC interaction and its uses in identity play, one would think most on-line interaction is anonymous and few people ever interact as themselves. The reality seems to be that many, probably most, social users of CMC create on-line selves consistent with their off-line identities. (1998: 55)

Of course, the fluidity and fragmentation that Turkle claims for internet identities can be found also in a broader range of literature concerned with postmodern identity more generally – digital, virtual environments are commonly seen as arenas in which fragmented, fluid postmodern identities can be realised. Therefore, debates about internet identities within new media studies need to be located in the context of wider debates about identity. Despite the origins of much new media studies in the more established discipline of cultural studies, fewer discussions of internet identities locate themselves within the rich debate about identity than can be found within cultural studies (Bell's chapter 'Identities in Cyberculture' in *An Introduction to Cybercultures* [2001] is one exception to this). This absence is problematic, because it means that studies of internet identities in particular, and new media studies more generally, fail to engage with debates that might help to develop new media theory. What is needed is an identification of, and engagement with, important debates about identity that can inform future new media studies.

For example, in his seminal essay 'Who Needs Identity?', Hall (1996) traces a move in cultural studies towards an understanding of identity as decentred and multiple, along similar lines to those outlined by Turkle. Despite increasing acknowledgement of identity as hybrid, Hall claims that the term 'identity' itself is too bound up with essentialist approaches to human subjectivity, which leads him to reject this concept in favour of his preferred notion of identification. He favours identification because:

it accepts that identities are never unified and, in late modern times, increasingly fragmented and fractured; never singular but multiply constructed across different, often intersecting and antagonistic, discourses, practices and positions. They are subject to a radical historicization, and are constantly in the process of change and transformation. (Hall, 1996: 4)

For Hall, identification means 'points of temporary attachment to the subject positions which discursive practices construct for us' (1996: 19); it is less fixed than identity, more fluid and contingent. Like Hall, Braidotti (1994) seeks a more useful term than 'identity' with which to theorize contemporary subjectivity; she settles upon the concept of 'nomadic subjects'. For Braidotti, this term also captures the positionality that characterizes postmodern identity; the nomad is thoroughly postmodern because s/he 'ha[s] relinquished all idea, desire, or nostalgia for fixity' (Braidotti, 1994: 22). Identity is a matter of constant becomings, which Braidotti refers to as the practice of 'as-if', 'the affirmation of fluid boundaries, a practice of the intervals, of the interfaces, and the interstices' (1994: 7).

Braidotti takes her concept of becoming from Deleuze (1973), who has influenced a number of contemporary cultural theorists to reject the concept of identity and start the project of cultural theorization with a different set of conceptual tools. As with Hall, the problem with identity for Deleuze is that it implies stability and stasis, whereas what really offers creative and theoretical potential is difference – not being (as implied in the term 'identity'), but becoming. Building on the work of Deleuze and others, a number of alternatives to identity are proposed – for example, some writers have argued that the concept of affect is a useful starting point for cultural theory (such as Parisi and Terranova, 2001). Affects in cultural objects result in affections, or emotional and bodily reactions, in experiencing subjects, but affects themselves are free from 'the particular observers or bodies who experience them' (Colebrook, 2002: 22), so that the concept of affect moves beyond identity or the experiencing subject. The concept of affect also shifts the focus of analysis away from what cultural objects *mean*, which has been the central concern in cultural studies to date, by encouraging consideration of what such objects *are* and *do*, how they *feel* and their bodily impacts, intensities and intimacies.

When I first analysed the homepages of Project Her@ students (Kennedy, 1999), I wanted to explore the extent to which some of the generalized claims that took hold as a result of Turkle's study could be applied to the homepage form, particularly those regarding online anonymity. The conclusions drawn as a result of the analysis changed over time, as I moved from a focus on the homepage text to consider the contexts of their production and the meanings of the texts for their producers. This process led me to rethink my original conclusions about the apparent absence of anonymity in the homepages. It led me to identify the limitations not only of focusing on the homepage texts, but also of common uses of the concept of anonymity in internet identity research, which assume a fixed, continuous relationship between *being* and *feeling*. In contrast, my empirical material pointed to a distinction between being and feeling, between being anonymous and feeling anonymous in the internet identities of the research subjects. Recognizing the limits of anonymity for making sense of internet identities and the subsequent need to seek a different set of conceptual tools, I suggest that there is much to be learned from the cultural studies debates about identity outlined previously, in which the problems associated with markedly fixed concepts are also addressed and alternative theoretical tools are also sought. The next section discusses this analytical process in detail.

Anonymity in Her@ Students' Homepages

The Her@ students' personal homepages were produced at the end of their year-long studies after they had carried out a range of preparatory activities, including thinking about the uses, advantages, disadvantages and potential risks of having a homepage, and participating in the production of a collective, group homepage in order to learn about the process of webpage creation. The students did not receive any guidance about the specific content that they should include in their homepages. Instead, the criteria for assessing their efforts focused on the extent to which they had considered technical and design issues such as quantity of text, size of images, download time, balance and use of hyperlinks. Clearly, the Her@ students' familiarity with the homepage genre, the themes of the course that they were undertaking and the fact that they were submitting their homepages for assessment will have influenced, to some extent, their production of this 'research data'. Reflecting on the research data that interviews generate, Day Sclater has written that 'the interview is an intersubjective process, and the narrative account is jointly produced' (1998: 90); a claim which, arguably, applies to all research data. The general educational context and specific assessment conditions set by the Her@ research team contributed to the joint production of the students' homepages, but other research data is also produced in conditions controlled by the researcher, like interviews. Therefore, the Her@ students' homepages can be read as expressions of their identity in conditions which were not of their making.

In the initial analysis of the Her@ students' homepages (Kennedy, 1999), the claim was questioned that online, people hide aspects of their identity which might otherwise lead to discrimination (such as 'race' or gender), and that this is empowering for a number of reasons. First, homepages generate different types of online identities and experiences than textual forums such as MUDs and Turkle's (1996) findings in relation to these text-based spaces did not apply to the more visual and multimedia form of the world wide web homepages of the Her@ students. More importantly, it was found that the students showed no sign of wanting to hide their gender and ethnicity and so 'benefit' from the possibility of anonymity that cyberspace offered them. Rather, they made explicit and implicit references to their gender and ethnicity in their homepages. Many of the Her@ students made their ethnicity central to their homepages, just as it is central to their identity, through the inclusion of images such as: an image of an African mother and child on Askari's site, a painting of a group of black graduates on Teti's, Sasha's link to Flavortown, a black entertainment site, and Tessa's inclusion of a flag of Trinidad.

In addition to images, another way in which identity is constructed in homepages is through links – as Miller (1995) claims, 'Show me what your links are, and I'll tell you what kind of person you are'. In this case, the sites to which Her@ students linked are also statements of their ethnicity. Lorraine linked to a black cultural bookshop, Sasha to BlackNetUK, Roni to a site about beauty products for black women, with the words 'Black women need cosmetics that are specific to *our* skin types' (emphasis added). In one version of her site, Teti included a link to 'World of Black Studies' and Noori linked to a site by and about Asian women. Once students were familiar with surfing the web it became clear that, as Askari put it, 'being part of the Black Internet community' was important to many students. Furthermore, their identities and experiences as minority ethnic women led them to make their gender, like their ethnicity, central to their homepages, particularly through references to their roles as mothers. Askari's image of an African mother and child could be read as a representation of her own motherhood; Teti and Lorraine stated that the most important role in their lives was being a mother; Sha and Tessa mentioned that they were mothers; Roni chose to share her site with her daughter; Lorraine's links to educational sites could be read as evidence of her motherly concerns; and Noori and Chimwe wrote about their difficulties combining their responsibilities as mothers with their studies. Noori's homepage reflected on the difficulties she experienced in fulfilling the conventional expectations of a Muslim wife and mother. At one point she wrote that:

> During Ramadan I used to wake up to cook at 3 or 4 a.m. and not go back to sleep again because I would not be able to wake up to take the children to school or go to class. I used the time wisely, though I managed to get the revision done for the exam, sometimes I would almost miss the *Fajar* [dawn prayer] because I was on the computer.

Like links, guestbooks could be conceived as spaces in which the identity of the self is constructed through identifications with and recognition from others. The people who signed Sasha's guestbook constitute the community of which she was a part and the language that they used, like Sasha's, identified them as young and black. For example, 'Mr Lover' made the following entry in Sasha's guestbook:

> Say Wha happen Miss Sasha how come mi never did see you from time and you kyant call Mr Lover But still mi have nuff love fi you, Anyway mi come fi say BIG up your Sexy and Fine self and mi go talk to you soon coz mi have someting fi say to you (I bet you worried now don't be) seen.
>
> one love Girl!!
>
> The one and only MR LOVER XXXX[6]

While Mr Lover's message needs to be paraphrased in a footnote so that it can be understood by the geographically dispersed and ethnically diverse readership of this journal, it would be more easily recognized and understood by young African-Caribbeans in the UK as locating both Mr Lover and Sasha as part of a young, black, internet community. [. . .]

Consideration of the students' comments in their written reflections about their homepages suggests that, while their internet identities could not be defined as anonymous, neither are they 'fixed', as Tetzlaff (2000) and Miller and Mather (1998) have argued. Consequently, these polarized understandings of internet identities – fragmented and anonymous *or* fixed and archived – are not helpful. After all, a webpage is a media form which is never entirely finished, just as identity composition is a continuous process – both are constantly 'under construction'. Sasha's homepage, which has changed several times since she first built it, suggests that she wanted the representation of herself on the web to change, not to be fixed. The numerous versions of her website that Teti produced indicate that she constructed slightly altered representations of her identity in each new version, none of which was more or less her. The final version was chosen not because it was a 'better' or 'truer' representation of herself, but rather because time was up and the latest version had to do. As Askari wrote of her website, 'I felt it was difficult to incorporate the "right" image of myself, an image I wanted the rest of the world to see and like.' [. . .]

Nevertheless, despite the initial conclusion that Her@ students showed no signs of anonymous identity experimentation in their homepages, the intimate, confessional style of some of their homepage content suggested that, in fact, they appeared to *feel* anonymous online. A number of students demonstrated a tendency to be 'extraordinarily frank and revealing', to use Chandler's description of the authors of the homepages he studied (Chandler, 1998). One student, Noori, wrote at length about the lack of support offered to her by her husband, who insisted that she continued her domestic duties while studying full-time, even though he was out of work at the time. In her first draft of her homepage, she was very critical of her husband, writing:

> It hasn't been easy with a husband who won't lift a finger or offer any kind of support. Sometimes I am in the middle of typing an assignment and he will ask for a cup of tea, if I don't get it for him right away he will start complaining.

After some discussion with her tutors about homepages as public documents, she decided to remove these comments from her final draft. Although some students demonstrated caution over the inclusion of personal information on their homepages (one student, Sasha, included photographs of herself; only one other, Roni, included her email address) and some, like Oyen and Lorraine, reflected on the need to be careful about the inclusion of personal data in homepages, there is a lot of personal detail on the Her@ students' homepages: for example, all of them include their first names and the majority of them include their surnames.

As a result of these apparently contradictory tendencies, on the one hand confessional and intimate (in other words, *feeling* anonymous) and, on the other, including detailed personal data (in other words, not *being* anonymous), three years after the homepages had been produced, some of the former Her@

students were interviewed about the issue of anonymity in internet identities. They were asked whether anonymity had been an issue for them – for example, had they wanted to preserve their anonymity, or remove it by stating openly who they were? Their responses problematized the earlier reading of the homepages (which had depended heavily on a textual analysis of the students' online selves), in which it was felt that their references to their gender and race, as well as their inclusion of names and surnames, meant that their virtual identities were not anonymous. As these interviews revealed, the concept of anonymity is more complex than this.

For example, one student, Tessa, questioned the reading of her inclusion on her homepage of an image of a Trinidadian flag and her reference to Caribbean foods such as plantain and avocado as an indication of her black identity. She suggested that this aspect of her identity was less visible than the researcher thought; she pointed out that there are white Trinidadians and that white people like Caribbean food, so her ethnicity was more hidden than the reading suggested. Noori, the student who wrote critically about her husband, said that she still felt a degree of anonymity in her homepage, despite including her name and surname – she might identify herself as Noori Begum, but which Noori Begum? These interview responses suggested that, for some homepage producers, there is a distinction between *being* anonymous and *feeling* anonymous, which arguably derives from the dual role of the world wide web as both public (publishing thoughts, feelings and identities to a potentially large audience) and private (located in the home, a medium used to construct thoughts, feelings and identities) (Chandler, 1998). Some Her@ students may have given their names and surnames, but they still appeared to feel a degree of anonymity in their homepages. Anonymity, therefore, was not as absent from the Her@ students' homepages as was first thought.

These findings indicate the need for internet identity research to move beyond a simple acceptance of the claim that whereas people experiment with anonymous identities in virtual contexts such as MUDs, the inclusion of photographs and other autobiographical detail in homepages reveals the 'true' identities of their authors and so erases the possibility of anonymity (Tetzlaff, 2000). Such understandings need to take account of the importance of going beyond online lives and selves to consider the offline context of their production and consumption. This means not just acknowledging who the producers of online selves are offline, but also considering how they feel about their online selves. To use Hine's phrase, it is necessary to think about the ways in which online selves are socially meaningful to their offline counterparts: 'In order to understand the form of WWW pages it is crucial to understand their significance for their authors' (Hine, 2001: 183). Studying online texts in offline contexts makes this possible, argues Hine, and such an approach enhances understanding of the context of production of the online text, as well as the text itself. That many of the Her@ students identify as black women in their homepages and, arguably, empower themselves and other black women in this process, indicates the importance of who the Her@ students are *offline* in shaping who they are *online*, demonstrating that online lives are lived and produced in the context of life offline – as Kendall points out: 'Nobody lives only in cyberspace' (1999: 70).

[. . .]

In contrast to refining the concept of anonymity, I suggest that it may be more productive to turn to some new conceptual tools. The problem with the concept of anonymity is that it is too fixed and stable to allow for recognition of the differences between being anonymous and feeling anonymous – internet identities either are, or are not, anonymous. Consequently, the being/feeling relationship is fixed: being and feeling are locked together in a way that limits exploration of the significant differences between them and what these differences might reveal about the simultaneously public and private character of the internet. It is here that internet identity research could learn fruitfully from cultural studies debates about identities. The parallels between the problem with identity, which has been identified in cultural studies, and the problem with anonymity, which has been identified here – that both are too fixed to recognize the fragmentation, temporality and contingency of the experiencing subject – suggest that, like cultural studies, internet identity research could benefit from considering whether there are other conceptual tools which could be effectively mobilized more, which acknowledge, for example, the distinction between being and feeling in internet identities, concepts like identification, affect, 'as-if' and becoming. The argument here is not that internet identity researchers should abandon all existing conceptual tools, but rather that a more rudimentary step needs to be taken – to engage with such cultural studies debates about identity. This is the next conceptual step for internet identity research in particular, and new media studies in general.

CONCLUSION: FUTURE DIRECTIONS FOR INTERNET

[. . .] The empirical research from Project Her@ discussed in this article also does these two things. It has demonstrated how moving beyond the Project Her@ student homepages to discuss their meanings for their producers with the producers themselves led to a richer reading of the online texts. One of the conclusions drawn as a result of this process is that the concept of anonymity is more complex than it seems at first glance – there is a distinction between feeling and being anonymous, and there are degrees of anonymity which are varied and situated. Like others, I too have found the terms of internet identity research limited and problematic.

While some academics have identified that terms such as 'anonymity' are too simplistic for understanding internet identities (for example, Åkesson, 2001; Baym, 1998) and others have stressed the importance of looking at contexts (for example, Hine, 2001; Kendall, 1999), very few internet identity researchers have engaged with contemporary cultural studies debates about identity. Even fewer have brought all three together, and I propose that this is what is needed now – for future research to move beyond anonymity, look at contexts and engage with and learn from the theoretical work that is taking place within cultural studies. In particular, researchers of virtual identities need to consider whether the concepts which are taking ground in cultural studies, such as affect, identification, nomadic practice, 'as-if' and becoming, might open up new insights and allow for new conceptual developments within internet identity research in particular, and new media research in general. For empirical researchers, this means two things. The first is to reflect on how research is conceived and whether identity remains a useful and illuminating starting point for new media research. The second is to reflect on the way that empirical material is analysed and consider whether the alternative notions identified here provide new methodological and analytical tools, as well as conceptual ones.

The argument of this article raises the question of whether identity still matters, in theory, in internet and new media research, and in practice, 'as a contested fact of contemporary political life' (Gilroy, 1997: 301). It has been argued here that, theoretically, it is time for internet identity research to reposition itself conceptually and that reflection is needed on the appropriateness of the concepts mobilized in this field for future research, concepts such as anonymity or, indeed, if we are to follow cultural studies' lead, identity itself. However, while academics may have a duty to contemplate whether identity retains validity conceptually and theoretically, those involved in identity politics on the ground – those experiencing hostility because of their 'different' identities, for example – may not feel that they share this duty (or indeed luxury). Therefore, what is important is to take these conceptual steps without losing sight of identity as embodied experience, of the real struggles of real people whose identities are fiercely contested or defended – in other words, without losing sight of identity-as-practice. This is the real challenge for internet identity research.

NOTES

1. Although there is no simple definition of identity which is suitable for my purposes, some brief introductory comments are useful in framing the discussion that follows. Even a somewhat clichéd source such as a dictionary gives useful pointers to some of the characteristics of identity. The *Collins English Dictionary*, for example, defines identity simultaneously as 'the state of having unique identifying characteristics held by no other person or thing', 'the individual characteristics by which a person or thing is identifiable' and 'the state of being the same in nature, quality, etc.' (Collins, 1979: 728). In these definitions, identity is characterized both by uniqueness and sameness. Woodward (2000) argues that the construction of identity, the process of actively taking up identity positions and presenting the resulting constructions to others, is what distinguishes identity from other, similar terms such as subjectivity. The concept of subjectivity also embodies some of the tensions, contradictions and characteristics of identity – subjectivity, the state of being a subject, implies agency,

yet to be a subject also can mean to be subjected, as well as to be the grammatical subject of a sentence, constructed through language, ideology and processes of representation. However, while subjectivity is necessarily subjective, identity works to connect the subjective, or the internal, with the external; identity construction makes connections between who we are, how we imagine ourselves and how we want others to see us.

2. Project Her@ is a pseudonym, taken from the Greek goddess Hera, worshipped by women at every stage of their lives. It was funded by a British Telecommunications PLC University Development Award and was staffed by Linda Leung, Nod Miller and myself.

3. In the British higher education system, a mature student is defined as someone who is more than 21 years of age.

4. For further discussion of the context of Project Her@, see Miller et al. (2000).

5. PernMUD is one of the text-based, online spaces in which Turkle's research subjects participated.

6. To paraphrase: Mr Lover asks why he has not seen Sasha around, and tells her that he likes her and wants to meet up with her because he has something to say to her.

REFERENCES

Åkesson, M. (2001) 'Gay Identities On-line and Off-line', master's thesis, University of Amsterdam.

Baym, N.K. (1998) 'The Emergence of On-line Community', in S.G. Jones (ed.) *Cybersociety 2.0: Revisiting Computer-mediated Communication and Community*, pp. 35–68. Thousand Oaks, CA: Sage.

Bell, D. (2001) 'Identities in Cyberculture', in *An Introduction to Cybercultures*, pp. 113–36. London: Routledge.

Braidotti, R. (1994) *Nomadic Subjects: Embodiment and Sexual Difference in Contemporary Feminist Theory*. New York: Columbia University Press.

Chandler, D. (1998) 'Personal Home Pages and the Construction of Identities on the Web', URL (consulted November 2001): http://www.aber.ac.uk/media/Documents/short/webident.html

Cheung, C. (2000) 'A Home on the Web: Presentations of Self in Personal Homepages', in D. Gauntlett (ed.) *Web.Studies: Rewiring Media Studies for the Digital Age*, pp. 43–51. London: Arnold.

Colebrook, C. (2002) *Gilles Deleuze*. London and New York: Routledge.

Collins (1979) *Collins Dictionary of the English Language*. London: Collins.

Day Sclater, S. (1998) 'Creating the Self: Stories as Transitional Phenomena', *Auto/biography* 6(1–2): 85–92.

Deleuze, G. (1973) *Proust and Signs* (trans. R. Howard). London: Allen Lane/Penguin.

Gilroy, P. (1997) 'Diaspora and the Detours of Identity', in K. Woodward (ed.) *Identity and Difference*, pp. 299–346. London: Sage/Open University Press.

Hall, S. (1996) 'Who Needs Identity?', in S. Hall and P. du Gay (eds) *Questions of Cultural Identity*, pp. 1–17. London: Sage.

Haraway, D. (1998) 'The Persistence of Vision', in N. Mirzoeff (ed.) *The Visual Culture Reader*, pp. 191–8. London: Routledge.

Hine, C. (2001) 'Web Pages, Authors and Audiences: the Meaning of a Mouse Click', *Information, Communication and Society* 4(2): 182–98.

Kendall, L. (1999) 'Recontextualising "Cyberspace": Methodological Considerations for Online Research', in S. Jones (ed.) *Doing Internet Research: Critical Issues and Methods for Examining the Net*, pp. 57–74. London: Sage.

Kennedy, H. (1999) 'Identity Construction in a Virtual World: the Homepage as Auto/biographical Practice', *Auto/biography* 7(1–2): 91–8.

McPherson, T. (2000) 'I'll Take My Stand in Dixie-Net: White Guys, the South and Cyberspace', in B.E. Kolko, L. Nakamura and G.B. Rodman (eds) *Race in Cyberspace*, pp. 117–32. New York: Routledge.

Miller, H. (1995) 'The Presentation of Self in Electronic Life: Goffman on the Internet', paper presented at the Embodied Knowledge and Virtual Space Conference, Goldsmiths' College, University of London, June, URL (consulted October 2001): http://www.ntu.ac.uk/soc/psych/miller/goffman.htm

Miller, H. and R. Mather (1998) 'The Presentation of Self in WWW Home Pages', URL (consulted October 2001): http://www.sosig.ac.uk/iriss/articles/article21.htm

Miller, N., H. Kennedy and L. Leung (2000) 'Tending the Tamagotchi: Rhetoric and Reality in the Use of New Technologies for Distance Learning', in S. Wyatt, F. Henwood, N. Miller and P. Senker (eds) *Technology and In/equality: Questioning the Information Society*, pp. 129–46. London: Routledge.

Parisi, L. and T. Terranova (2001) 'A Matter of Affect: Digital Images and the Cybernetic Re-wiring of Vision', *Parallax* 7(4): 122–7.

Plant, S. (1997) *Zeros + Ones: Digital Women and the New Technoculture*. London: Fourth Estate.

Poster, M. (1999) 'Underdetermination', *New Media & Society* 1(1): 12–17.

Rheingold, H. (1993) *The Virtual Community: Homesteading on the Electronic Frontier*. Reading, MA: Addison-Wesley.

Roberts, L.D. and M.R. Parks (2001) 'The Social Geography of Gender-switching in Virtual Environments on the Internet', in E. Green and A. Adam (eds) *Virtual Gender: Technology, Consumption and Identity*, pp. 265–85. London: Routledge.

Schmitz, J. (1997) 'Structural Relations, Electronic Media, and Social Change: the Public Electronic Network and the Homeless', in S.G. Jones (ed.) *Virtual Culture: Identity and Communication in Cyberspace*, pp. 80–101. London: Sage.

Shaw, D.F. (1997) 'Gay Men and Computer Communication: A Discourse of Sex and Identity in Cyberspace', in S.G. Jones (ed.) *Virtual Culture: Identity and Communication in Cyberspace*, pp. 133–45. London: Sage.

Shields, R. (1996) 'Introduction: Virtual Spaces, Real Histories and Living Bodies', in R. Shields (ed.) *Cultures of Internet: Virtual Spaces, Real Histories, Living Bodies*, pp. 1–10. London: Sage.

Silver, D. (2000) 'Looking Backwards, Looking Forwards: Cyberculture Studies 1990–2000', in D. Gauntlett (ed.) *Web.Studies: Rewiring Media Studies for the Digital Age*, pp. 19–30. London: Arnold.

Tetzlaff, D. (2000) 'Yo-Ho-Ho and a Server of Warez: Internet Software Piracy and the New Global Information Economy', in A. Herman and T. Swiss (eds) *The World Wide Web and Contemporary Cultural Theory*, pp. 99–126. London: Routledge.

Turkle, S. (1996) *Life on the Screen: Identity in the Age of the Internet*. London: Weidenfeld & Nicolson.

Wakeford, N. (1997) 'Networking Women and Grrrls with Information/Communication Technology', in J. Terry and M. Calvert (eds) *Processed Lives: Gender and Technology in Everyday Life*, pp. 51–66. London: Routledge.

Woodward, K. (2000) *Questioning Identity*. London: Routledge/Open University Press.

65

CULTURAL STUDIES AND NEW MEDIA

Caroline Bassett

ON BEING LESS FORGETFUL

Digital codes currently direct themselves against letters, to overtake them
. . . a new form of thinking based on digital codes directs itself against
procedural 'progressive' ideologies, to replace them with structural,
systems-based, cybernetic moments of thought . . . a sudden almost
incomprehensible leap from one level to another. (Flusser, *Die Schrift:
Hat Schreiben Zukunft?*, cited in Strohl 2002: xxxiii)

Although 'New media theory' does open the way for the decline or end
of mass communication, it has not really introduced any fundamentally
new issues of communication theory. (McQuail 2002: 19)

A FLASHBACK

Two summers ago, in Washington, DC, I encountered what was popularly
supposed to be the city's first flashmob. A sudden flock of cell phone users
descended on Books A Million in Dupont Circle and read magazines together.
Old media became the content of a new media action. As DC militarised and
the concrete barriers around the administrative centre of America at war multiplied, this 'happening', faintly redolent of situationism but utterly lacking
its political heart, made the pages of the *Washington Post*, which subtitled its

From Gary Hall and Clare Birchall (eds), *New Cultural Studies: Adventures in Theory* (Edinburgh:
Edinburgh University Press, 2006).

story '"Flashmobs" Gather Just Because'. Perhaps Terry Eagleton had a point when he said that sometimes some culture is not the most important thing (Eagleton 2002: 51).

Despite its apparent emptiness, or because of it, this event poses some interesting questions for the theorisation of new media, one of which is how media actions can be understood not only in relation to the historical and geo-political contexts within which they take place, but also in relation to questions of technology and medium. The flashmob event might be understood within critical horizons that locate technology in a dominant relation to culture (or vice versa), or within less dichotomous frameworks, for instance those that place technology and culture on an immanent plane.

Flashmobs, of course, are part of a larger new media ecology predicated on media technologies/media systems arising through processes of digital convergence. Convergence began in the 1980s, with the rise of popular personal computing and the rapid expansion of global computer networks, and continues today. It describes a process through which previously discrete media forms, media industries and media contents are drawn together, so that many old media forms are re-mediated, and many new forms are produced, although distinctions between new, old and recombinant media are rarely absolute. The mobile phone, a highly converged object within a highly converged system, is thus typical in that it contains old media forms alongside new ones and recombines them in new ways. The extent and reach of convergence, and in particular the degree to which digitalisation has redrawn or dissolved distinctions between media systems and other forms of material culture, are fiercely debated within the academy (by political economists, sociologists and media theorists in particular), and beyond it (by those who play the markets, by those who are players in the media industry, and by those who legislate, for instance). Fuelling the arguments is a series of different assessments of the scope and power of these new media forms/new media systems and of the degree to which they impose new modes of significance or instantiate new cultural logics.

The place of cultural studies within all this is interesting. Its interdisciplinary constitution, its history of engagement with the new, the unsanctified and the marginal, and its commitment, at least in some versions, to the study of questions of power mean it ought to be a useful or even a 'natural' site for the analysis of the converging, boundary-breaking, heterogeneous forms that constitute the new media landscape. This has not been the case. Instead, a different formation has emerged. Most strikingly, within writing that explores techno-culture (defined here as 'techno-cultural theory'), an increasingly influential body of work that finds its roots in medium theory and media philosophy has rejected cultural studies more or less entirely. This work finds inspiration in the German tradition of medium theory exemplified by Kittler and by Luhmanite systems theory (see, for instance, Hayles 2002, as well as Winthrop-Young in this volume) and has also relied heavily on the monist philosophy of Deleuze and Guattari (see Rossiter 2003; Rodowick 2001). A number of these theorists, while acknowledging work on cybernetics and information theory by intradisciplinary pioneers such as Kittler (1997) and Flusser (2002), also tend to draw directly on first- and second-wave cybernetics and information theory, reconsidering the work of Shannon and Wiener (see Terranova 2004, and below). The aim has been to build new models for the study of new media, based not only on cybernetics' modelling of complex feedback loops, and on information theory as a system for message transmission and control, but also on the logics of probability on which these sciences draw.

This development has been balanced by the burgeoning of fine-grained empirical work on new media and new media use emanating from a 'sociological turn' within media studies (Mansell 2004: 96), evidence of which can frequently be found in journals such as *New Media & Society*. This work stands in stark contrast to the often highly speculative critical-theoretical accounts described above, but is different again from the 'mainstream' cultural studies accounts that do exist, not least because the latter are marked by their tight focus on the discursive construction both of techno-cultures and of techno-logical artefacts/systems 'themselves' (see Penley and Ross 1991 for an early example; or Sterne 2003 for an excellent later one).

Finally, the *focus* of study within techno-cultural writing is also changing. Many scholars who were active in the field of new media in the 1990s are now fixing their gaze on new 'new horizons' (biotechnology, nanotechnology, genomics) and moving away from the 'media sector' as it is narrowly defined – I recognise that this last term begs a question.

The splits and divisions now developing within the field of technocultural writing need to be understood in relation to the popular and critical techno-cultural hysteria that accompanied the explosive growth of networked technologies in the 1990s. This period was marked by a series of accounts of techno-culture which were highly celebratory and which often, despite their theoretical abstraction, simply tail-ended corporate boosterism, *processing* the industry's tales of the networking revolution that would render us all free rather than critiquing their fundamental assumptions – one of which might be what constitutes freedom in the first place. (As Barbrook and Cameron (1995) pointed out, this 'Californian' ideology only found its mirror image in the 'European dystopianism' that was also in vogue at the time.) Taking the techno-cultural narratives offered by the marketing wings of the new media corporations for real was bound to fail. The software industry has been famous for vapourware of all kinds; accurate prediction was never really the point, which was rather to gain support for a particular version of the future – to be guaranteed by one or other software standard. It is because they are essentially all the same that corporate visions of new media worlds were and are revealed to be ideologically loaded. As Kittler put it, in one of his lighter moments, cyberspace ideology is the 'foam packaging' of the products of the software industry 'turned to the outside' (Kittler, cited in Johnston 1997: 3).

I am interested here in why techno-cultural theory so often cleaved to the info-corporate line, and in whether it is likely to do so again, perhaps when faced with *new* new media technologies. Do the theoretical approaches currently being undertaken look likely to avoid such a reversion in the future? These are the questions addressed in this chapter, which is also an appeal for a form of cultural studies that is less forgetful, less susceptible to the scouring power of the new. This form of cultural studies needs to relate to, but not collapse into, other recent approaches to the study of new media, including some of those adumbrated above. One of my questions, indeed, is whether the turn to media philosophy and medium theory could mark a rewriting/rewiring of cultural studies, rather than registering as a hostile response to it.

The chapter comes in two parts. The first half looks at early encounters between cultural studies and computer science, exploring technology and forgetfulness. The second half considers Jameson's account of cyberpunk and dirty realism, in the context of Terranova's conception of informational culture, reading both in relation to speculative software, here understood as a critical art practice, as a form of tactical media, and possibly as a way of 'doing' cultural studies.

UNDER THE SIGN OF LANGUAGE

> Traditionally, mass communications research has conceptualized the process of communication in terms of a circuit or loop. (Hall 1992a: 128)

Contemporary medium theory is marked by a series of returns to the early cybernetics and information theory of Shannon and Wiener, which was developed alongside computers themselves, in the nascent Cold War contexts of the 1940s and on. These returns come as hard science attempts to wrest ownership of 'theory' from cultural studies and from the humanities, demanding that science is understood in its 'own' terms (see Žižek 2002: 19); that its own response to the 'systematic, totalizing claims of philosophy' (Weber 2000) produces a valid and complete understanding of a totality that encompasses the social and the physical world, perhaps.

There are some parallels here. Cybernetics in particular was formulated as a '*general* concept' model, one 'capable of modelling command and control systems '*in man and machine*' (Wiener 1961; Johnson 1997: 7; my italics), and the potential for this new 'computer science' to cross over from the hard sciences to the social and human sciences was recognised – and championed – early on. Studies of formally organised cross-over events such as the Macy conferences have begun to document this activity (see Gere 2002: 52) but only brush the surface of a process of diffusion that was largely informal and no less pervasive for that. Indeed, in the decades following its inception, the direct and indirect influence of cybernetics and information theory within the humanities was profound. Briefly, this influence is evident in structuralism/

poststructuralism (e.g. Barthes 1982), psychoanalysis (e.g. Lacan 1988), apparatus and screen theory (e.g. Metz 1974) and mass communications theory (Carey 2002). In the post-Cold War years, however, cybernetics was consigned to relative obscurity, certainly falling out of favour as a model equally capable of describing the social world and the human psyche and of defining the dynamics of (information) machines. Information theory too became understood as operating in a more restricted field.

Cultural studies itself was not developed in ignorance of first-wave cybernetics/information theory or of systems theory. In fact it might be said to be an indirect response to the extension of various scientific and functionalist models of analysis in the humanities, and was certainly, at least in its Birmingham years, a very *direct* response to dissatisfaction with the dominance of mass culture/mass communication theories (the latter being itself directly influenced by information theory). Stuart Hall points out that any search for the origins of cultural studies is largely an illusory process (Hall 1992b: 16), but 'Encoding/Decoding' *is* an extremely important and influential text within a particular era and tradition of cultural studies and in it Hall broke with cybernetics and information theory's models and principles, rejecting the more or less absolute division between communication and meaning posited by these theories, and with it the view that interference in the system amounted to 'noise' and should be set aside (Hall 1992c: 118).

In the place of cybernetics' and information theory's transmission models and feedback loops Hall set a circuit of culture. This encompasses production and reception, but prioritises the semiotic moment, ensuring that 'the symbolic form of the message has a privileged position in the communicative exchange' (Hall 2002: 303). Cultural studies thus works 'under the sign of language'. Indeed, there is nothing in this model that is *outside* of language since, as D'Acci notes, despite the inclusion of moments of production and reception, the circulant in the encoding/decoding model is semiotic/discursive (D'Acci 2004: 425). This linguistic model produces particular lacunae, one of which concerns media technology. As Joshua Meyrowitz, a long-standing medium theorist, comments: 'most studies of the impact of media ignore the study of the media themselves . . . [since] the medium itself is viewed as a neutral delivery system' (Meyrowitz 2002: 101). While the turn to language in cultural studies certainly enabled some encounters to be staged (arguably it allowed the encounter between Marxism and psychoanalysis begun in *Screen* theory to be continued on new grounds), it ruled out others. In particular, this turn meant that technology was either rendered into discourse or set aside (set *outside*), irrelevant to questions of signification or significance.

This is inevitably schematic, but now, having pointed to a break, I want to flag the degree to which Hall's encoding/decoding model *retains* traces of these earlier histories, in the sense that it clearly remains a *communicational* model. As such, it tends to reduce the complexity and breadth of culture to communication (or even transmission), thus ignoring its more expansive and/

or ritual aspect. This is a point Lawrence Grossberg has made from within cultural studies (Grossberg 1997; see also D'Acci 2004: 430), drawing on James Carey's early exploration of ritual aspects of culture and communication to do so (see, for instance, Carey 2002: 43). In sum, Hall's model for cultural studies, apparently resolutely linguistic, is haunted by the technological, which comes in the form of an informing structural model or, to put it another way, *in the form of an abstraction*. What's more, if models employed by communication studies, themselves influenced by cybernetics/information theory, still influence cultural studies in particular ways, *biasing* the latter towards communication, this certainly isn't often acknowledged in relation to new media – and although Steve Jones' consideration of the 1990s rhetoric of the information superhighway takes up some of these points in suggestive ways (Jones 2001: 57), what is not acknowledged is the technological redoubling involved here.

Theorisations of contemporary forms of networked new media have been conditioned by this early and often forgotten encounter between information technology (in its first-wave cybernetic moment) and cultural theory. The widespread adoption of strong theories of social construction within media studies' explorations of media technology and everyday life might be understood within this trajectory (marking a move to remain within the media studies/ cultural studies tradition whilst grappling with the technological); however, it also begins to suggest why many contemporary techno-cultural scholars have tended to move away from the (attenuated) communications model Hall et al. offer (where what is attenuated is precisely the materiality of media technology; the medium), instead either returning to forms of medium theory *avowedly* influenced by cybernetic models and by information theory, or turning to empirical social science, but in both cases rejecting cultural studies.

The first cybernetics/information theory moment is thus key to thinking through some of the distinctions between contemporary cultural studies models and medium theory/medium philosophy's treatments of new media. Consideration of the dynamics of innovation and diffusion of media technologies – of the question of the new – can add to this account in useful ways. This is provided in the next section in relation to amnesia.

Technology and Forgetfulness

[A] technical invention as such has comparatively little significance. It is only when it is selected for investment towards production, and when it is consciously developed for particular social uses – that is, when it moves from being a technical invention to what can properly be called available technology – that the general significance begins. (Williams 1989: 120)

The continuous process of innovation influences popular and critical understandings of media technologies and the cultures in which they arise. New media technologies tend to be understood (given to us) as determinant and it is only later, *when they are no longer new, when the next new media technology has come along*, that they are reassessed and explored in terms of their social shaping. This process operates in the critical sphere as well as the popular and produces a form of oscillatory amnesia, an incapacity to hold technology and culture in view simultaneously. As Stallabrass notes, such amnesia often extends from the object under consideration to become a general condition (Stallabrass 1999: 108–10), so that within these amnesiac circuits each significant new media technology in turn appears to hold the promise of revealing information's nature, *as if for the very first time*. This 'nature' is later forgotten as the moment of innovation is exhausted. That is, a previously new media technology (if it survives) becomes an accepted part of everyday life, and is largely forgotten *as a technology* (in this case as an information technology). Put yet another way, the popular invisibility that comes with consumption is paralleled by *dematerialisation* in the theoretical register. Raymond Williams' claim that technologies gain their significance and meaning as they are used and deployed as 'available technology' (Williams 1989: 120) suggests how this might operate. Examples can also be found in the cases of electricity (Marvin 1988), television (Silverstone and Hirsch 1992) and cinema (in much reception theory). In all of these cases the passage of the media technology in question into everyday use has been marked in large part by its dissolution as an object. Slotted into a worldview characterised by a strong sense of social construction, the material specificity of these technologies is forgotten and technological objects become cultural placeholders or fetishes, as Latour notes (2000). In sum, not only the status of particular new media technologies, but the status of technology per se, thus *oscillates* within these circuits.

Reviewing the recent history of techno-cultural theory in relation to these circuits is interesting. The early technophobia described above occurred at a moment of innovation, a moment in which specific new technologies (notably the Internet) appeared to be extraordinarily powerful *as technologies*, and in which the relationship between technology and culture was reassessed and the power of the former to rewrite the latter affirmed. Today we have reached a different point in the circuit, and the cyber-theoretical works of the early cyberspace years – futurological, speculative, snake-oily, revolutionary, celebratory – have been largely taken over by the micro-sociological, by the media-philosophical, or by medium theory of a more considered kind, as I've noted above. In addition, the trend towards the reterritorialisation of new media into old disciplines (particularly noticeable in film studies) suggests that others agree with Denis McQuail's robust claim that not much fundamental has changed in the media/communications scene and that therefore no new models are needed. Finally, some of the early attempts to produce a political response to the expected transformations of information appear to be exhausted. Donna Haraway, patron saint of all forms of boundary-breaking within cyberculture, has abandoned her cyborg in favour of another other(ed) species, this time canine rather than robotic (Haraway 2003). Man's best friend has become a cyborg surrogate for cultural studies' most famous cyber-feminist. Truly, we live in slightly odd times.

The kinds of amnesiac circuits outlined here are not to be read mechanically, and certainly operate simultaneously, in overlapping ways, and at various scales. They do, I believe, produce particular recursions and lacunae and have resulted in a history of thinking about innovation that is marked by abrupt shifts and turns, ruptures, breaks and (absolutely) new starts.

These circuits offer a new perspective on the haunted history of cultural studies, described above. As I read it, a certain form of cultural studies, marked both by its first encounter with cybernetics and systems theory in general, and by its retreat from that encounter, has switched into an absolutely cultural mode, operating either within semiotic/discursive channels typical of cultural studies or within fairly strong versions of social construction (to this extent poststructural and phenomenological or everyday-life theorisations mesh). This form of cultural studies has therefore been rendered problematic as a discipline able to handle new forms of science and/or new forms of technology. In other words, in relation to technology, cultural studies has been more *oscillatory* than it has been genuinely *interdisciplinary*.

Sadie Plant has argued that cultural studies exhibits a form of interdisciplinarity that confirms rather than breaks boundaries. As a consequence it sets out to legitimate what is already known rather than exploring 'how and to what extent it is possible to think differently' (Plant 1996: 216). This argument is revealed here to operate with some force. Plant's response is to reject cultural studies entirely, in favour of new forms of connectionism, based on a second-wave cybernetics (Plant 1996: 213). My sense is that, despite these problems, cultural studies remains a site for productive forms of thinking. Which raises the question: would it be possible to break the amnesiac circuit? Would it be possible to read and use the past differently, to deploy it in order to reconnect with some of the impulses that produced cultural studies as a critical discourse in the first place, whilst not losing the impulse to insist on the materiality of the object that continues to power medium theory?

Taking this up, the second half of the chapter seeks forms of cultural theory and practice that have been less forgetful in their attempts to think through connections between information and cultural form. It begins with Tiziana Terranova's bid to combine new left cultural studies and medium theory through a return to, and updating of, cybernetics and information theory.

'INFORMATIONAL CULTURE?'

Network culture is inseparable from a kind of network physics and a network politics. (Terranova 2004: 3)

Tiziana Terranova claims that 'cultural processes are increasingly grasped and conceived in terms of their informational dynamics' and that, as a consequence, there is 'no meaning outside of an informational milieu' (Terranova 2004: 7–9). Her project is at once a commentary on these developments and part of them, since the concept of 'informational culture' as she develops it is not understood purely as a form of cybernetics. Rather, it rethinks the *connections* between new and old forms of cybernetics and the contemporary cultural horizons that are developing as a result of the rise of informational dynamics. Terranova's premise (like Plant's in fact) is that while old forms of information science are problematic models for culture, newer systems based on second-order cybernetics, Artificial Life (AL) and chaotic systems, all of which allow for generation or emergence, are much more hopeful prospects. As she puts it:

> We are no longer mostly dealing with information that is transmitted from a source to a receiver, but increasingly also with an informational dynamics – that is with the relation of noise to signal, including fluctuations and micro-variations, entropic emergencies and negentropic emergences, positive feedback and chaotic processes. (Terranova 2004: 7)

Terranova herself defines the *terms* of the connections she explores through the (Deleuzian) concept of the correlative. Different models of computer science are explored not as they are instantiated in culture, but as they correlate. This marks a break with the ways in which earlier generations understood cybernetics to be operational. However, the claims to general applicability at the heart of the cybernetics project, which are the basis for the proposed epistemological break information produces, remain and continue to produce particular consequences for reading the relation between theory and real-world effects, so that, as Saul Ostrow puts it, digital media systems 'dissolve our ability to differentiate, on the level of the natural and the artificial, between such [digital media effects] and those of the theoretical import of information theory and cybernetics' (Ostrow 1997: xii). The argument that new forms of information theory avoid the reductive modernism (see Plant 1996) of early cybernetics, enabling less totalising ways of thinking about informational culture that might also avoid the paradeictic privileging of science 'itself', cannot therefore be entirely justified. 'Informational culture' switches between science and culture (correlatively), but also makes arguments based on the assertion that these are the same, or indeed, that they always already operate on the same plane.

The wriggle room here is that Terranova's account does not operate through a simple delete-and-insert process (i.e. the deletion of one cybernetically determined worldview and the insertion of the next). Instead, a more-or-less simultaneous consideration of different *generations* of information science exposes distinctions between contemporary cultural (now informational) forms. Thus, while the medium theory of Kittler tends to erase medial difference even while expanding the terrain of media into a general information-scape (Kittler 1997: 31), Terranova's approach exposes the new forms such differences might take. In particular, distinctions made between communication and information, or discourse and dialogue, are here put into play and considered not in terms of representation, but in terms of medium specificity. The paradox of re-mediation is that these 'medium-specific' qualities may migrate onto older or newer platforms: being informational they become general, although they flourish in some environments and not others (Innis's sense of media bias might pertain here) (Innis 1991). Informed by this paradoxical specificity, Terranova develops an account of an informational regime in which the active, conscious practices of activists or tactical media operators are distinguished from a new form of mass audience, while both are integral to a new media ecology (Terranova 2004: 136). This 'other mass', the 'television public held hostage by powerful media monopolies in a topsy-turvy world of propaganda and simulation' (Terranova 2004: 135), is as integral to the informational landscape as the net activists, and in that sense is (also) made by new media.

Of course, throughout its history cultural studies has looked at the supposedly inert mass and found within it active movements of various kinds. The difference is that the mass described here arises *after* the end of an era in which *encoding/decoding*-style theorisations of reception might pertain, *after* the epistemic break information produced (which is to say within 'informational culture'). In this sense it arises *after* cultural studies, at least of the kind that cleaves to Hall. This mass is read as a terminal 'for the receptive power of images' existing where 'meaning no longer takes hold' and where 'all mediations have collapsed', 'where images are not encoded but absorbed' (Terranova 2004: 138–40). The prospects for new forms of network politics arise when this terminal mass changes state. For Terranova this is when it becomes *virtual*.

Dirty Realism

A precursor to Terranova's concept of 'informational culture' can be found in Fredric Jameson's exploration of 'dirty realism', a term he uses to interrogate the informing process of information on (global) culture in 'The Constraints of Postmodernism' (in Jameson 1994). In Jameson's hands, dirty realism, a figure for the cultural logic of informed capital, implies 'the ultimate rejoining and re-identification of the organic with the mechanical that Deleuze and Haraway . . . theorize and celebrate; but within a category – that of *totality* – alien to either of them' (Jameson 1994: 138). This totality is described partly through an exploration of a Rem Koolhaas cube, a design for the Library of France. Within this vast cube are various organs – stairs, rooms, pipes – bounded by but also floating freely within their container, which certainly cannot be grasped from the inside. Jameson argues that an archetypal form of dirty realism is also to be found in the cyberpunk-inspired environment of Ridley Scott's film *Blade Runner*, both in the forms of everyday life that the vertiginous blocks of the city (which produce a different version of an enclosure that cannot be grasped) and the crowded streets enable, and in the erasure of a certain viewing distance.

If cyberpunk 'realism' (resolving impossible geographies) is here held up in opposition to forms of naturalism, what is 'dirty' is 'the collective as such . . . the traces of mass, anonymous living and using' (Jameson 1994: 158) that are found in and illuminate *Blade Runner*'s dark (*noir*) streets. For Jameson, *Blade Runner* is a prefiguration of the end of traditional forms of community, an ushering in of 'a form of society beyond the end of the civil society' that will produce new forms of action and interaction (Jameson 1994: 160). These include new possibilities for 'corporate comebacks' as capital finds *its* uses for street uses of technology. Jameson's account of these new forms of collective life forcibly brings to mind Hardt and Negri's (later) account of the biopolitical multitude in *Empire*, and this latter is a work Terranova explicitly draws on. Whereas Terranova's multitude operates in an immanent plane *beyond* the degree-zero of the political, however, some form of historical horizon remains in Jameson's account of connections made on the street, even if this horizon is beyond reach. Having said that, Terranova's sense of the vitality of the multitude that springs to life after meaning clearly resonates with Jameson's account of the libidinal connotations of dirty realism, and above all with that vitality (the life that burns brightly and too fast) found in *Blade Runner*'s androids themselves. In both cases there is a utopian gesture, a hope for new kinds of cultural politics that might be founded on forms of human interaction with the machine – although of course Jameson's utopian moment, in contrast to Terranova's, is configured in fiction, and also in the text.

TACTICAL MEDIA: 'HOW LOW CAN YOU GO?'[1]

> With the exception of the telephone we dialogue with each other in the same way as those who lived during the Roman age. At the same time discourses raining down on us avail themselves of the most recent scientific advances. However, if there is hope in preventing the totalitarian danger of massification through programming discourses, it lies in the possibility of opening up the technological media to dialogue. (Flusser, cited in Strohl 2002: xix)

Operating in a very different sphere from Jameson's cultural semiotics but sharing his sense of the importance of what the street can do, and resonating also with Terranova's concern to explore the phase change that switches the mass to the multitude, are new forms of medium activism. These trade in software itself. They seek to get low (for real), rather than getting dirty within the text or remaining purely within the grounds of theory, and use media technology to provoke various kinds of disturbance.

One approach to tactical media is found in speculative software. This is defined by Matt Fuller as a form of art production and a form of cultural critique that 'plays with the form not the content [of new media] or rather refuses the distinction while staying on the right side of it' (Fuller 2003: 14). Tactical media/speculative software thus begins with a focus on the medium itself. It certainly involves playing tricks in code (Rtmark's notorious web redirects, or the recent Google hacks linking 'Bush' and 'Blair' with various search terms, might be understood as speculative software), and also exposes tricks in the code of others. Clearly these tactical interventions do not confine themselves to the medium. They rather refuse – and therefore expose – naturalised distinctions between form and content. These distinctions include those that are conventionally drawn between higher- or lower-level layers in complex software architectures, governed by various protocols, which are assumed to be more or less 'transparent' or 'neutral'. Playing with this, one of Fuller's works, for instance, explores the ways in which Microsoft Word shapes user productions through its menu-driven interface 'options'.

In refusing form/content distinctions at all levels, speculative software breaks with traditional hacker values, which are predicated on a modernist kind of cybernetics and which therefore also valorise form over content. The desire to 'get close to the metal', a paradoxical way of expressing that wish to find 'the truth in code', is recognised as characteristic of a particular era of hacking (see Taylor 1999). It amounts in the end to a *romance* of information and is a form of media sublime (Rossiter 2003). Kittler's modernist approach to information shares this characteristic since for Kittler, too, the only honest way to approach information technology and the only possibility for democracy in information society is through the granting of full or unmediated access to the machine-level code. The interface is *intrinsically* dishonest, denying access to the system, the latter being understood only *as* code. In refusing this romance of code, speculative software is thus also rejecting an essentially structural view of information technology in favour of an exploration of the *processual* characteristics and possibilities of a medium that is only understandable in use, and in terms that include the user. This exploration, both critical and political, interventionist and speculative, is a form of cultural politics. As Fuller puts it, speculative software is 'built to critically expose the mainstream model of the user – whilst at the same time creating *social* utopias in computer code' (Fuller 2003: 3, my italics).

Speculative software and tactical media thus try to harness the force of new media to oppositional ends. In doing so, they both create and draw on medium theory. However, while tactical media might find a new god in software, it most certainly refuses the injunction of all good cybernetic gods, which is to keep the *noise* down.[2] Its point indeed is to practise a form of pollution; precisely to open the system. Despite tactical media's supposed hostility to cultural studies, then, and despite its firm commitment to the medium, its refusal to dissolve technology into discourse, as Terranova once put it (2000), we are not so far from Stuart Hall here as it might at first appear.

Which raises the question: does tactical media offer a form of cultural politics that is amenable to cultural studies? And what might Terranova's and Jameson's accounts have to offer in this respect? It is important to be mindful of the very real differences in their respective approaches, whilst also considering the connections. One link between tactical media's bid to reconfigure and reimagine 'using', Terranova's vision of the mass turned multitude, and Jameson's reading of *Blade Runner*, is the shared concern to find a cultural politics within this new milieu, and to do so by rethinking the relationship between communication and culture. What I mean by this is that all of these accounts explore the possibilities for rethinking new media politics around forms of *communion* that might oppose or undermine what Deleuze aptly called communicational stupidity, and all to some extent do so by considering forms of communication *in process*.

There are of course *distinctions* to be made between tactical media as medium action, dirty realism as a cultural semiotics, and Terranova's systems-influenced account of informational culture. These are very evident in the form that the particular turn (or return) to the medium takes in each case, as I have shown. Jameson embarks on an exercise in cognitive mapping in a coming information milieu, described textually. Terranova does this by way of a return to cybernetic theory that is largely if not entirely immanent to the cultural forms she explores. Tactical media sets out to remap the possibilities for use and does so partly through an insistence on cultural politics as (also) practice.

FLASH FORWARD

I close the chapter with three doubts. My first is that tactical media, at least in its less theoretically engaged forms, is all too easily subsumed within cultural studies' discourses of resistance, so that despite the hostility of some of its practitioners, it comes to be viewed as (just) another form of subcultural activity. As such, it might lose its medium specificity, since this derives less from the potential of an information system in the abstract than from a sense of what the possibilities are for politics within a new sphere of engagement or interaction between humans and machines, when this interaction begins with the medium.

My second doubt is that this neglects what is most interesting about tactical media, which is its insistence on breaking the barrier between critical theory and critical practice. Many, like the unfortunate electronic Zapatistas, have had their moment in a cultural studies sun that, at its worst, does more to warm those who *study* forms of resistance than it does to contribute to a movement. This works the other way around too, since, in so far as contemporary medium theory and medium practice lionise the 'processual as political', it is in danger of repeating, albeit in the register of medium specificity rather than in relation to media 'content', both cultural studies' old fondness for the romance of resistance and its incapacity to register the limits of this resistance. This is to disparage neither theory nor tacticalism/hactivism. It is to question certain presumed connections between theory and (creative) practice, and more broadly to question the connections drawn between (system) theory and the world it models.

My third doubt concerns the degree to which a focus on tactical media obscures a strength of cultural studies, which is its capacity to consider forms of practice that do not register as explicitly political, and that do not require the kinds of active skills or expert knowledge that the free software movement valorises and that tactical media employs, but which none the less do not conform.

A return to forms of cultural studies sensitive to questions of material creativity, material creative practice, and the material use of material technologies within broader historical and economic contexts might avoid these obstacles. This amounts to a demand for the (re)incorporation of the political economy of the new media into cultural studies, here taking the notion of political economy at its broadest, and reading cultural studies in its most interdisciplinary and least *oscillatory* moment: which is to say in its least forgetful moment. To abjure oscillation is not to abandon the hope of political transformation, or of critique.

Terranova's insistence that the 'other' mass, a *many* rather than the expert few, can change state insists on the inherently political possibilities contained in all cultural forms and cultural practices. A flashmob that refused the injunction 'only connect' and in doing so refused the injunction to *disperse* might be significant in all kinds of new ways.

ACKNOWLEDGEMENT

This chapter stems from a research abroad period funded by the Leverhulme Trust and I would like to acknowledge their support. Thanks also to Clare Birchall and Gary Hall for their comments and suggestions.

NOTES

1. Slogan for 'The Next Five Minutes', Tactical Media conference, Amsterdam, 1999.
2. The demand of the gods of Gilgamesh.

REFERENCES

Barbrook, Richard and Cameron, Andy (1995), 'The Californian Ideology', *Mute*, 3, Autumn, pp. iv–v.
Barthes, Roland (1982), *Image, Music, Text*, London: Flamingo.
Carey, James (2002), 'A Cultural Approach to Communication', in Denis McQuail (ed.), *McQuail's Reader in Mass Communication*, London: Sage, pp. 36–45.
D'Acci, Julie (2004), 'Cultural Studies, Television Studies and the Crisis in the Humanities', in Lynn Spigal and Jan Olsson (eds), *Television After TV*, London: Routledge, pp. 418–46.
Eagleton, Terry (2002), *The Idea of Culture*, Oxford: Blackwell.
Eagleton, Terry (2003), *After Theory*, Harmondsworth: Penguin.
Flusser, Vilém (2002), *Vilém Flusser, Writings*, London: University of Minnesota Press.
Fuller, Matthew (2003), *Behind the Blip: Essays on the Culture of Software*, London: Autonomedia.

Gere, Charlie (2002), *Digital Culture*, London: Reaktion Books.

Grossberg, Lawrence (1997), *Bringing It All Back Home: Essays on Cultural Studies*, Durham, NC, and London: Duke University Press.

Hall, Stuart [1973] (1992a), 'Encoding/Decoding', *Culture, Media and Language*, London: Routledge, pp. 128–138.

Hall, Stuart (1992b), 'Cultural Studies and the Centre: Some Problematics and Problems', *Culture, Media and Language*, London: Routledge, pp. 15–47.

Hall, Stuart [1973] (1992c), 'Introduction to Media Studies at the Centre', in *Culture, Media and Language*, London: Routledge, pp. 117–21.

Hall, Stuart [1973] (2002), 'The Television Discourse; Encoding and Decoding', in Denis McQuail (ed.), *McQuail's Reader in Mass Communication*, London: Sage, pp. 302–9.

Haraway, Donna (2003), *The Companion Species Manifesto*, Chicago: Prickly Paradigm Press.

Hardt, Michael and Negri, Antonio (2000), *Empire*, London: Harvard University Press.

Hayles, Katherine (2002), *Writing Machines*, London: MIT Press.

Innis, Harold [1951] (1991), *The Bias of Communication*, Toronto: University Of Toronto Press.

Jameson, Fredric (1994), *The Seeds of Time*, New York: Columbia University Press.

Johnston, John (1997), 'Introduction: Friedrich Kittler: Media Theory after Post-Structuralism', in Friedrich Kittler, *Essays: Literature, Media, Information Systems*, ed. John Johnston, London: G&B Arts, pp. 2–26.

Jones, Steve (2001), 'Understanding Micropolis and Compunity', in Charles Ess and Fay Sudweeks (eds), *Culture, Technology, Communication*, New York: State University of New York Press, pp. 53–66.

Kittler, Friedrich (1997), *Essays: Literature, Media, Information Systems*, ed. John Johnston, London: G&B Arts.

Lacan, Jacques (1988), *The Seminars of Jaques Lacan. Vol. 1: The Ego in Freud's Theory and in the Technique of Psychoanalysis*, Cambridge: Cambridge University Press.

Latour, Bruno (2000), 'When Things Strike Back', *British Journal of Sociology*, millennium special issue, 51:1, pp. 107–24.

Lessig, Lawrence (2004), *Free Culture*, New York: Penguin, www.free-culture.cc/freeculture.pdf.

Libre Society (2004), *Libre Culture Manifesto*, www.libresociety.org/library/libre.pl/Libre_Manifesto.

Mansell, Robin (2004), 'Political Economy, Power and New Media', *New Media and Society*, 6:1, pp. 96–105.

Marvin, Carolyn (1998), *When Old Technologies Were New*, New York: Oxford University Press.

Mattelart, Armand and Mattelart, Michelle (1995), *Theories of Communication*, London: Sage.

McQuail, Denis (2002), 'Introduction', in Denis McQuail (ed.), *McQuail's Reader in Mass Communication*, London: Sage, pp. 1–20.

Metz, Christian (1974), *Film Language: A Semiotics of Cinema*, New York: Oxford University Press.

Meyrowitz, Joshua (2002), 'Media and Behaviour – A Missing Link', in Denis McQuail (ed.), *McQuail's Reader in Mass Communication*, London: Sage, pp. 99–109.

Ostrow, Saul (1997), 'Preface', in Friedrich Kittler, *Essays: Literature, Media, Information Systems*, ed. John Johnston, London: G&B Arts, pp. vii–viii.

Penley, Constance and Ross, Andrew (1991), *Technoculture*, Minneapolis: University of Minnesota Press.

Plant, Sadie (1996), 'The Virtual Complexity of Culture', in George Robertson, Melinda

Mash, Lisa Tickner, John Bird, Barry Curtis and Tim Putnam (eds), *Futurenatural: Nature, Science, Culture*, London: Routledge, pp. 203–17.

Rodowick, David (2001), *Reading the Figural Or, Philosophy after the New Media*, Durham, NC: Duke University Press

Rossiter, Ned (2003), 'Processual Media Theory', *Symploke*, 11:1–2, pp. 104–31.

Silverstone, Roger and Hirsch, Eric (1992), *Consuming Technologies: Media and Information in Domestic Spaces*, London: Routledge.

Sterne, Jonathan (2003), 'Bourdieu, Technique and Technology', *Cultural Studies*, 17:3–4, May–July, pp. 367–89.

Stallabrass, Julian (1999), 'The Ideal City and the Virtual Hive', in John Downey and Jim McGuigan (eds), *Technocities*, London: Sage, pp. 108–20.

Strohl, Andreas (2002), 'Introduction', in *Vilém Flusser, Writings*, Minneapolis: University of Minnesota Press.

Taylor, Paul A. (1999), *Hackers: Crime in the Digital Sublime*, London: Routledge.

Terranova, Tiziana (2000), 'Infallible Universal Happiness', in Angela Dimitrakaki, Pam Skelton and Mare Tralla (eds), *Private Views, Spaces and Gender: Contemporary Art from Britain and Estonia*, London: WAL, pp. 110–20.

Terranova, Tiziana (2004), *Network Culture: Politics for the Information Age*, London: Pluto Press.

Weber, Samuel (2000), 'The Future of the Humanities: Experimenting', *Culture Machine*, 2, www.culturemachine.tees.ac.uk.

Wiener, Norbert (1961), *Cybernetics, or Control and Communication in the Animal and the Machine*, Cambridge, MA: MIT Press.

Williams, Raymond (1989), *The Politics of Modernism: Against the New Conformists*, London: Verso.

Žižek, Slavoj (2002), 'Cultural Studies versus the "Third Culture"', *South Atlantic Quarterly*, 101:1, Winter, pp. 19–32.

FURTHER READING

Andrejevic, M., 'The Work of Being Watched: Interactive Media and the Exploitation of Self-Disclosure', *Critical Studies in Media Communication* 19:2 (2002) pp. 230–48.

Andrejevic, M., 'The Work of Watching One Another: Lateral Surveillance, Risk and Governance', *Surveillance and Society* 2:4 (2005) pp. 479–97.

Barbrook, R., 'Cyber-Communism', *Science as Culture* 9:1 (2000) pp. 5–39.

Bassett, C., 'How Many Movements?', in M. Bull and L. Beck (eds), *The Auditory Cultures Reader* (Oxford: Berg, 2003) pp. 343–56.

Bassett, C., *The Arc and the Machine: Narrative and New Media* (Manchester: Manchester University Press, 2007).

Berry, D., *Copy, Rip, Burn* (London: Pluto, 2008).

Cooley, H. R., 'It's All About the Fit: The Hand, the Mobile Screenic Device and Tactile Vision', *Journal of Visual Culture* 3:2 (2004) pp. 133–55.

Dyson, F., 'Wireless Affections: Embodiment and Emotions', *New Media/Theory and Art*, *Convergence* 11:4 (2005) pp. 85–105.

Ferguson, M., 'Electronic Media and the Redefining of Time and Space', in M. Ferguson (ed.), *Public Communication: The New Imperatives* (London: Sage, 1990) pp. 152–72.

Flew, T., *Understanding Global Media* (London: Palgrave Macmillan, 2007).

Galloway, A., *Protocol: How Control Exists After Decentralization* (Cambridge, MA: MIT, 2004).

Giddens, S., 'Playing with Nonhumans: Digital Games as Technocultural Form', in S. de Castells and J. Jenson (eds), *Worlds in Play: International Perspectives on Digital Games Research* (Oxford: Peter Laing, 2007).

Goggin, G., *Cell Phone Culture* (London and New York: Routledge, 2006).

Hables Gray, C., *Peace, War and Computers* (London: Routledge, 2005).

Hassan, R. and Thomas, J. (eds), *The New Media Theory Reader* (Maidenhead: Open University Press, 2006).

Jenkins, H., *Convergence Culture: Where Old and New Media Collide* (New York: New York University Press, 2006).

Kerr, A., *Digital Games* (London: Sage, 2005).

Kittler, F. A., *Friedrich A. Kittler Essays: Literature, Media, Information Systems* (London: Routledge, 1998).

Lessig, L., *The Future of Ideas: The Fate of the Commons in a Connected World* (New York: Vintage, 2001).

Lessig, L., *Code and Other Laws of Cyberspace* (New York: Basic Books, 2002).

Levy, P., *Becoming Virtual: Reality in the Digital Age* (New York: Plenum Press, 1998).

Lister, M. et al., *New Media: A Critical Introduction* (London: Routledge, 2003).

Livingstone, S. and Lievrouw, L., *Handbook of New Media, Social Shaping and Consequences of ICTs* (London: Sage, 2005).

Lovejoy, M., *Digital Currents, Arts in the Electronic Age* (London: Routledge, 2004).

Mackenzie, A., 'Untangling the un-wired: Wi-Fi and the cultural inversion of infrastructure', *Space and Culture* 8:3 (2005) pp. 269–85.

Marks, L., *Touch: Sensuous Theory and Multisensory Media* (Minneapolis, MN: Minnesota Press, 2002).

Marvin, C., *When Old Technologies Were New: Thinking about Electric Communication in the Late Nineteenth Century* (New York: Oxford University Press, 1988).

Mitchell, R. and Thurtle, P. (eds), *Data Made Flesh: Embodying Information* (New York: Routledge, 2004).

Munster, A., *Materialising New Media: Embodiment in Information Aesthetics* (Hanover, NH: Dartmouth College Press, 2006).

O'Riordan, K., 'Technologised Bodies: Virtual Women and Transformations in Understandings of the Body as Natural', in J. Hargreaves and P. Vertinsky (eds), *Physical Culture, Power and the Body* (London: Routledge, 2006).

Perron, B. and Wolf, M. J. P., *The Video Game Theory Reader II* (London: Routledge, 2008).

Pinch, T. J. and Bijker, W., 'The Social Construction of Facts and Artefacts, Or How the Sociology of Science and the Sociology of Technology Might Benefit Each Other', *Social Studies of Science* 14 (1984) pp. 399–441.

Pinch, T. and Kline, R., 'The Social Construction of Technology', in D. MacKenzie and J. Wacjman (eds), *The Social Shaping of Technology* (Buckingham: Open University Press, 1999) pp. 113–16.

Plant, S., *Zeroes and Ones* (London: Fourth Estate, 1997).

Reilly, T., *What Is Web 2.0: Design Patterns and Business Models for the Next Generation of Software* (2005). Online at: http://www.oreillynet.com/pub/a/oreilly/tim/news/2005/09/30/what-is-web-20.html.

Rheingold, H., *Smart Mobs: The Next Social Revolution* (Cambridge, MA and London: MIT Press, 2003).

Sterne, J., 'The Historiography of Cyberculture', in D. Silver and A. Massanari (eds), *Critical Cyberculture Studies* (New York: New York University Press, 2006).

Terranova, T., *Network Culture* (London: Pluto, 2004).

Williams, R., *Television, Technology and Cultural Form* (London: Routledge, 1990).

Winner, L., 'Do Artifacts Have Politics?', in D. MacKenzie and J. Wacjman (eds), *The Social Shaping of Technology* (Buckingham: Open University Press, 1999) pp. 28–41.

PUBLISHER'S ACKNOWLEDGEMENTS

Grateful acknowledgement is made to the following sources for permission to reproduce material in this book previously published elsewhere. Every effort has been made to trace copyright holders, but if any have been inadvertently overlooked the publisher will be pleased to make the necessary arrangements at the first opportunity.

Theodor Adorno, 'Culture Industry Reconsidered', translated by Anson G. Rabinbach, from *The Culture Industry: Selected Essays on Mass Culture* edited by J. M. Bernstein, © 1991, Routledge. Reproduced by permission of Taylor & Francis Books UK.

Marshall McLuhan, 'The Medium is the Message', from *Understanding Media* by Marshall McLuhan, © 1964, Routledge. Reproduced by permission of Taylor & Francis Books UK.

Stuart Hall, 'Encoding/Decoding', from *Culture, Media, Language* edited by Stuart Hall, Dorothy Hobson, Andrew Lowe and Paul Willis, © 1980, Routledge. Reproduced by permission of Taylor & Francis Books UK.

Annette Kuhn, 'The Power of the Image', from *The Power of the Image* by Annette Kuhn, © 1985, Routledge. Reproduced by permission of Taylor & Francis Books UK.

Jürgen Habermas, 'The Public Sphere', translated by Shierry Weber Nicholson, from *Jürgen Habermas on Society and Politics: A Reader* edited by Steven

Seidman, © 1989, Beacon Press. Originally printed as 'Öffentlichkeit' from *Kultur und Kritik*. © 1973, Suhrkamp Verlag, Frankfurt am Main.

Jean Baudrillard, 'The Masses: The Implosion of the Social in the Media'. *New Literary History*, 16:3 (Spring 1985), © 1985, New Literary History, University of Virginia. Reprinted by permission of the Johns Hopkins University Press.

Michel Foucault, extract from POWER/KNOWLEDGE, edited by Colin Gordon, copyright © 1972, 1975, 1976, 1977 by Michel Foucault. Preface and Afterword © 1980 by Colin Gordon. Bibliography © 1980 by Colin Gordon. This collection © 1980 by The Harvester Press. Used by permission of Pantheon Books, a division of Random House, Inc. © 1980, Harold Matson.

Michel de Certeau, 'General Introduction' from *The Practice of Everyday Life*, by Michel de Certeau, © 2002, The University of California Press.

Gilles Deleuze, 'Postscript on the Societies of Control', copyright © 1988 by *Les Editions de Minuit*. (From *October 59*, Winter 1992, MIT Press. Originally appeared in *L'Autre* journal, no. 1, May 1990.) Reprinted by permission of Georges Borchardt, Inc., for *Les Editions de Minuit*.

Pierre Bourdieu, 'Some Properties of Fields', reproduced by permission of Sage Publications, London, Los Angeles, New Delhi and Singapore, from Pierre Bourdieu, *Sociology in Question*, © Pierre Bourdieu, 1993.

Edward W. Said, extract from *Orientalism*, copyright © 1978 by Edward W. Said. Used by permission of Pantheon Books, a division of Random House, Inc.

Andreas Huyssen, extract from 'Mass Culture as Woman: Modernism's Other', from *After the Great Divide* by Andreas Huyssen, © 1986, Palgrave Macmillan. Reproduced with permission of Palgrave Macmillan.

John B. Thompson, extract from 'The Globalization of Communication', in *The Media and Modernity* by John B. Thompson, © 1994, Polity Press.

Manuel Castells, 'An Introduction to the Information Age', from *City: Analysis of Urban Trends, Culture, Theory, Policy, Action*, 2:7, © 1997, Taylor & Francis Ltd. Reprinted by permission of the publisher (Taylor & Francis Group, http://www.informaworld.com).

Annabelle Sreberny, 'Not Only, But Also: Mixedness and Media', in *Journal of Ethnic and Migration Studies* 31:3, © 2005, Taylor & Francis Ltd. Reprinted by permission of the publisher (Taylor & Francis Group, http://www.informaworld.com).

Raymond Williams, 'Programming as Sequence or Flow', from *Television, Technology and Cultural Form*, by Raymond Williams, © 1974, Routledge. Reproduced by permission of Taylor & Francis Books UK.

John Ellis, 'Broadcast TV Narration', from *Visible Fictions: Cinema, Television, Video* by John Ellis, © 1982, Routledge. Reproduced by permission of Taylor & Francis Books UK.

Richard Dyer, 'Stereotypes', from *The Matter of Images* by Richard Dyer, © 1993, Routledge. Reproduced by permission of Taylor & Francis Books UK.

Christine Gledhill, 'Genre, Representation and Soap Opera', reproduced by permission of Sage Publications, London, Los Angeles, New Delhi and Singapore, from *Representation* edited by Stuart Hall, © Christine Gledhill, 1997.

Roger Silverstone, 'Rhetoric, Play, Performance', from *Television and Common Knowledge* edited by Jostein Gripsrud, © 1999, Routledge. Reproduced by permission of Taylor & Francis Books UK.

Lev Manovich, 'Database as Symbolic Form', © Lev Manovich, 1998.

Janet Woollacott, 'Fictions and Ideologies: The Case of Situation Comedy', from *Popular Culture and Social Relations* edited by Tony Bennett, Colin Mercer and Janet Woollacott © 1986, Janet Woollacott.

Stuart Hall, 'New Ethnicities', reproduced by permission of Sage Publications, London, Los Angeles, New Delhi and Singapore, from *'Race', Culture and Difference* edited by James Donald and Ali Rattansi, © Stuart Hall, 1992.

Linda Williams, 'Skin Flicks on the Racial Border' in *Porn Studies* edited by Linda Williams, © 2004, Duke University Press. Used by permission of the publisher.

Paul Gilroy, 'Between the Blues and the Blues Dance', from *The Auditory Culture Reader* edited by Michael Bull and Les Back (Berg, 2003) © 1998, Paul Gilroy.

Andrew Gorman-Murray, 'Queering Home or Domesticating Deviance?', reproduced by permission of Sage Publications, London, Los Angeles, New Delhi and Singapore, from *International Journal of Cultural Studies* 9:2, © Andrew Gorman-Murray, 2006.

Janice Winship, 'Survival Skills and Daydreams', from *Inside Women's Magazines* by Janice Winship, © 1987, Pandora Press.

Susan Bordo, 'Reading the Slender Body.' Reproduced with permission of Taylor and Francis Group LLC – Books, from *Body/Politics* edited by Mary Jacobus et al., © 1990, Routledge; permission conveyed through Copyright Clearance Center, Inc.

Charlotte Brunsdon, 'The Role of Soap Opera in the Development of Feminist Television Scholarship', from *To be continued . . .: Soap Operas Around the World* edited by Robert C. Allen, © 1995, Routledge. Reproduced by permission of Taylor & Francis Books UK.

Angela McRobbie, 'Postfeminism and Popular Culture', from *Feminist Media Studies* 4:3, 2004, © 2004, Taylor & Francis. Reprinted by permission of the publisher (Taylor & Francis Group, http://www.informaworld.com).

Valerie Walkerdine, 'Playing the Game: Young Girls Performing Femininity in Video Game Play', from *Feminist Media Studies* 6:4, © 2006, Taylor & Francis. Reprinted by permission of the publisher (Taylor & Francis Group, http://www.informaworld.com).

James D. Halloran, 'Studying the Effects of Television' and 'The Social Effects of Television', from *The Effects of Television* edited by James Halloran, © 1970, Panther Books.

Denis McQuail, Jay G. Blumler and J. R. Brown, 'The Television Audience: A Revised Perspective', from *Sociology of Mass Communication* edited by Denis McQuail, © 1972, Penguin Books.

Jenny Kitzinger, 'A Sociology of Media Power: key issues in audience reception research', from *Message Received* edited by Greg Philo, © 1999, Pearson Education Limited.

Martin Barker and Julian Petley, extract from 'From Bad Research to Good – A Guide for the Perplexed', from *Ill Effects: The Media/Violence Debate* (second edition) edited by Martin Barker and Julian Petley, © 2001, Routledge. Reproduced by permission of Taylor & Francis Books UK.

Janice A. Radway, 'Conclusion', from *Reading the Romance: Women, Patriarchy, and Popular Literature* by Janice A. Radway, © 1987, Verso, © 1984, new introduction, © 1991 by the University of North Carolina Press. Used by permission of the publishers.

ACKNOWLEDGEMENTS

Ien Ang, 'Wanted: Audiences. On the Politics of Empirical Audience Studies', from *Remote Control: Television, Audiences and Cultural Power* edited by Ellen Seiter et al., © 1989, Routledge. Reproduced by permission of Taylor & Francis Books UK.

bell hooks, 'The Oppositional Gaze', from *Black Looks* by bell hooks, © 1992, South End Press.

Alexander Doty, 'There's Something Queer Here', from *Making Things Perfectly Queer* by Alexander Doty, © 1993, University of Minnesota Press.

Asu Aksoy and Kevin Robins, 'Banal Transnationalism: The Difference that Television Makes', from *The Media of Diaspora* edited by Karim H. Karim, © 1993, Routledge. Reproduced by permission of Taylor & Francis Books UK.

Ann Gray, 'Behind Closed Doors: Video Recorders in the Home', from *Boxed In: Women and Television* edited by Helen Baehr and G. Dyer, © 1987, Pandora Press.

Joke Hermes, 'Media, Meaning and Everyday Life', from *Cultural Studies* 7:3, © 1993, Taylor & Francis. Reprinted by permission of the publisher (Taylor & Francis Group, http://www.informaworld.com).

David Morley, 'What's "Home" Got to Do with It? Contradictory Dynamics in the Domestication of Technology and the Dislocation of Domesticity', reproduced by permission of Sage Publications, London, Los Angeles, New Delhi and Singapore, from *European Journal of Cultural Studies* 6:4, © David Morley, 2003.

Michael Bull, 'No Dead Air! The iPod and the Culture of Mobile Listening', from *Leisure Studies* 24:4, © 2005, Taylor & Francis Ltd. Reprinted by permission of the publisher (Taylor & Francis Group, http://www.informaworld.com).

Bill Nichols, 'Reality TV and Social Perversion', from *Blurred Boundaries: Questions of Meaning in Contemporary Culture* by Bill Nichols, © 1994, Indiana University Press. Reprinted with permission of Indiana University Press.

Annette Hill, 'The Rise of Reality TV', from *Reality TV* by Annette Hill, © 2005, Routledge. Reproduced by permission of Taylor & Francis Books UK.

Sue Thornham, 'Public and Private Bodies', from *Women, Feminism and Media* by Sue Thornham, © 2007, Edinburgh University Press.

Anita Biressi and Heather Nunn, 'Celebrity, Social Mobility and the Future of Reality TV', from *Reality TV: Realism and Revelation* by Anita Biressi and Heather Nunn, © 2005, Wallflower Press.

Nick Couldry, 'Teaching Us to Fake it: The Ritualized Norms of Television's "Reality" Games', from *Reality TV: Remaking Television Culture* edited by Susan Murray and Laurie Ouellette, © 2004, New York University Press.

Peter Golding and the late Philip Elliott, 'News Values and News Production', from *Making the News* by Peter Golding and Philip Elliott, © 1979, Longman. Reproduced by permission of the author.

Stuart Hall, Chas Critcher, Tony Jefferson, John Clarke and Brian Roberts, 'The Social Production of News', from *Policing the Crisis: Mugging, the State, Law and Order* by Stuart Hall et al., © 1979, Palgrave Macmillan. Reproduced with permission of Palgrave Macmillan.

Myra Macdonald, 'Politicizing the Personal: Women's Voices in British Television Documentaries', from *News, Gender and Power* edited by Cynthia Carter et al., © 1998, Routledge. Reproduced by permission of Taylor & Francis Books UK.

Stig Hjarvard, 'News Media and the Globalization of the Public Sphere', from *News in a Globalized Society* edited by Stig Hjarvard, © 2001, Nordicom.

Greg Philo and Mike Berry, extract from 'Audience Studies', from *Bad News from Israel* by Greg Philo and Mike Berry, © 2004, Pluto Press.

José van Dijck, 'Picturizing Science: The Science Documentary as Multimedia Spectacle', reproduced by permission of Sage Publications, London, Los Angeles, New Delhi and Singapore, from *International Journal of Cultural Studies* 9:1, © José van Dijck, 2006.

Raymond Williams, 'Advertising: The Magic System', from *Problems in Materialism and Culture* by Raymond Williams, © 1980, Verso.

Sean Nixon, 'Advertising, Magazine Culture and the "New Man"', from *Hard Looks: Masculinities, Spectatorship and Contemporary Consumption* by Sean Nixon, © 1996, Routledge. Reproduced by permission of Taylor & Francis Books UK.

Anne McClintock, 'Soft-Soaping Empire: Commodity Racism and Imperial Advertising', from *Travellers' Tales: Narratives of Home and Displacement* edited by G. Robertson, M. Mash, L. Tickner, J. Bird, B. Curtis and T.

Putnam, © 1994, Routledge. Reproduced by permission of Taylor & Francis Books UK.

Andrew Wernick, 'The Promotional Condition of Contemporary Culture', reproduced by permission of Sage Publications, London, Los Angeles, New Delhi and Singapore, from *Promotional Culture* by Andrew Wernick, © Andrew Wernick, 1991.

William Leiss, Stephen Kline, Sut Jhally and Jacqueline Botterill, 'Issues in Social Policy'. Republished with permission of Taylor & Francis Group LLC – Books, from *Social Communication in Advertising: Consumption in the Mediated Marketplace*, Third Edition edited by William Leiss et al., © 2005, Routledge; permission conveyed through Copyright Clearance Center, Inc.

Kevin Robins, 'Cyberspace and the World We Live In', reproduced by permission of Sage Publications, London, Los Angeles, New Delhi and Singapore, from *Cyberspace, Cyberbodies, Cyberpunk* edited by Mike Featherstone and Roger Burrows, © Kevin Robins, 1995.

Mark Andrejevic, 'The work of being watched: interactive media and the exploitation of self-disclosure', from *Critical Studies in Media Communication* 19:2, © 2002, Taylor & Francis Ltd. Reprinted by permission of the publisher (Taylor & Francis Ltd, http://www.tandf.co.uk/journals).

Jonathan Sterne, 'The MP3 as Cultural Artifact', reproduced by permission of Sage Publications, London, Los Angeles, New Delhi and Singapore, from *New Media and Society* 8:5, © Jonathan Sterne, 2006.

Helen Kennedy, 'Beyond Anonymity, or Future Directions for Internet Identity Research', reproduced by permission of Sage Publications, London, Los Angeles, New Delhi and Singapore, from *New Media and Society* 8:6, © Helen Kennedy, 2006.

Caroline Bassett, 'Cultural Studies and New Media', from *New Cultural Studies: Adventures in Theory* edited by Gary Hall and Clare Birchall, © 2006, Caroline Bassett.

NAME INDEX

SUBJECT INDEX

ABC, 579, 584, 718n
abuses
  of communications, 18
Actor-Network Theory, 826
advertising and advertisers (advertisements),
  772
  audience studies, 406, 726
  breaks in TV programmes, 591
  and children, 776, 781, 782
  consumption of, 726, 727, 733
  deregulation, 772, 781
  discourse of, 33, 610
  and domesticity, 751
  exploitation, 725
  feminist critique of, 354, 773, 775
  funding for commercial TV, 143, 144, 147,
    197
  funding for Internet services, 684
  and genre theory, 214
  industry, 725, 726, 728, 737, 773, 780
  intervals in films, 195
  language of, 327
  levelling down of culture, 187
  magazines, 208, 325, 727
  as the 'magic system', 727, 730–5
  medium of, 325
  mobile phone marketing, 783
  and 'new masculinities', 727, 736–46
  Orange campaign, 531
  political marketing through, 158
  promotional culture, 728
  regulation, 728, 772–4, 777, 783
  revenue, 222, 519, 584, 742, 745,
    778

soap advertisements in nineteenth-century
    Britain and commodity racism, 747–62
social communication, 774, 776, 778–9
spot advertising, 201
stereotyping, 776–7, 780
symbol/symptom of consumer/commodity
    culture, 726, 735, 725, 767, 774, 779
transformation of public space, 531
US model, 195
visual signs, 33, 84
watching adverts a form of work, 817
and women's liberation, 220
Africa(n), 110, 155, 253, 284, 298, 412, 639,
  727
  culture, 275, 293–4, 759
  and HIV, 409, 412, 413
  identity, 175
  pornography, 278, 282
  representations of, 727, 748–9, 757, 759,
    846
  stereotypes of animality, 285, 288
alcoholism, 207, 208, 209, 211, 420
Americanism, 135
American culture and media products, 142,
    144, 146, 149, 171, 285–6, 576, 579,
    585–6, 675, 710
American system of broadcasting, 143, 144,
    175, 195, 196–7, 575, 726
Anti-Nazi League, 263
archaic media (handwritten pamphlets, oral
    poems), 245, 575
art, 6; see also high art
artists, 17, 97, 117, 129, 135, 137n, 241, 245,
    246, 270, 275, 298, 730, 735, 825